W9-CDD-004

"THE MEMORABLE DOCUMENTS IN THE HISTORY OF OUR NATION. THEY REVEAL OUR TRIUMPHS AND OUR FAILURES . . . OUR FREEDOMS, OUR OBLIGATIONS, OUR IDEALS. THE EDITOR-IN-CHIEF HAS RENDERED A SUPERLATIVE SERVICE."—*Library Journal*

"When in the course of human events . . ." *"Four score and seven years ago . . ."* *"Ask not what your country can do for you . . ."* Reflected in the selections which comprise this memorable volume are the personalities, ideas, and events that help form the fascinating mosaic of our history. Enriched by the commentary of leading historians, this collection brings the past vividly alive— and in so doing sheds vital light on America and Americans today.

DANIEL J. BOORSTIN, editor of *An American Primer*, was Professor of American History at the University of Chicago, and editor of the Chicago History of American Civilization series. He is author of *America and the Image of Europe; Genius of American Politics; The Americans; The Colonial Experience; Image, or What Happened to the American Dream;* and *The Lost World of Thomas Jefferson.*

AN AMERICAN PRIMER

Edited by Daniel J. Boorstin

A MERIDIAN BOOK

MERIDIAN
Published by the Penguin Group
Penguin Books USA Inc., 375 Hudson Street,
New York, New York 10014, U.S.A.
Penguin Books Ltd, 27 Wrights Lane,
London W8 5TZ, England
Penguin Books Australia Ltd, Ringwood,
Victoria, Australia
Penguin Books Canada Ltd, 10 Alcorn Avenue,
Toronto, Ontario, Canada M4V 3B2
Penguin Books (N.Z.) Ltd, 182–190 Wairau Road,
Auckland 10, New Zealand

Penguin Books Ltd, Registered Offices:
Harmondsworth, Middlesex, England

Published by Meridian, an imprint of Dutton Signet,
a division of Penguin Books USA Inc.

Library of Congress Catalog Card Number: 84-62654

This is an authorized reprint of a hardcover edition published
by the University of Chicago Press.

 REGISTERED TRADEMARK—MARCA REGISTRADA

First Meridian Printing, February, 1995
First Meridian Classic Printing, January, 1985

17 16 15 14 13 12 11 10 9

PRINTED IN THE UNITED STATES OF AMERICA

To All Rediscoverers
of the
New World

... the Eies of all people are vppon vs; soe that if wee shall deale falsely with our god in this worke wee haue vndertaken and soe cause him to withdrawe his present help from vs, wee shall be made a story and a by-word through the world. ...

JOHN WINTHROP, 1630

I believe that man will not merely endure: he will prevail.

WILLIAM FAULKNER, 1950

Contents

CONTENTS

CONTENTS

Introduction

DANIEL J. BOORSTIN

We call this an American Primer because it is a book of beginnings. It is a book of elements and, we hope, is elementary in the most sophisticated sense of the word. Like the New England Primer, one of the most popular books in the first century of settlement, it is a kind of American catechism—a catechism not of orthodoxy but of hopes and institutions. It introduces us to ourselves.

This is a book of Citizen's History. Our American past always speaks to us with two voices: the voice of the past, and the voice of the present. We are always asking two quite different questions. Historians reading the words of John Winthrop usually ask, "What did they mean to him?" Citizens ask, "What do they mean to us?" Historians are trained to seek the original meaning; all of us want to know the present meaning. These are two quite different quests which often get in each other's way. This book aims to bring the historian to the aid of the citizen, to vivify our sense of our past and remind us how we keep our traditions alive.

The historian plays a waiting game. He must be willing to work twenty years to give us a little more knowledge of the precise circumstances under which Grant and Lee met at Appomattox. He commits himself to a wager that in the race between the destructive powers of time and the reminiscent, reconstructive powers of man, somehow man is always gaining a little. Historian's history is the patient, endless effort to resurrect the dead past.

But the citizen cannot wait. The world will not let him be patient. Today he must act on the meaning of all the words uttered by the Winthrops and Franklins and Washingtons and Jeffersons. He must draw the moral from what they said— long before the historian is ready with an unambiguous, professionally satisfying account of what they really meant. The citizen must vote today, even though he might know more about the subject after another decade. The good historian warns against a too-simple moral, a too-clear answer to any question. The citizen's duty is to think and feel and act promptly. The historian who refuses to draw conclusions— until more evidence is in, or because we can never know—is fulfilling his vocation. The citizen who postpones (until historians have agreed on the true original meaning of the Monroe Doctrine) taking a position on his government's policies in Cuba or in the Dominican Republic is evading his duty. Therefore he must draw the best conclusions he can from the incomplete story and the inchoate tradition, and hope that the fuller, truer story will not disprove him.

Citizen's History, then, is but another name for the living tradition. The materials of Citizen's History are not mere relics. Unlike the fossils of geology or the artifacts of archeology, they are valuable actually because they were *not* petrified and so have *not* survived in their original unaltered shape. On the contrary, they have come to us because they were capable of a life of their own. Organisms, not things, they have responded to their changing environment. They have actually changed their environment in ever-changing fashion, and are likely to continue to do so. If words were mere things—like an Indian tomahawk, a Revolutionary musket, or the bed that George Washington slept in—they would not have this uncanny organic quality which makes them immortal forces.

Historians may lament the perversity which leads every generation to hear not what dead men wanted to say, but what the living want to hear. They may be shocked at the ventriloquism of the citizen who forces the past to speak his illusions about the present and his hopes for the future. And it is a duty of the historian to help us distinguish the true voice of the past from the echoes of ourselves. In this volume, our historians have tried to help us witness the alchemy by which a vital tradition transforms its past. In a nation which aims at self-government, Historian's History must be brought to enlighten Citizen's History. For, reality or illusion, Citizen's History rules the world.

It has become ever more difficult for us to see the irony, the adventure, and the drama in the living documents of our national past, precisely because they have become documentary equivalents of the Statue of Liberty—dignified, important, and inspiring, but somehow rigid and impersonal. This and other reasons have led me to enlist eighty-three historians to make a book of unfamiliar plan which may have some novel advantages, and may help refresh our past.

This book will, I hope, be personal. Personal in the sense that it speaks to the reader today, and that it speaks from the writer and the editor of each document. Along with standard items—the Declaration of Independence, the Constitution, and the Gettysburg Address—we also include many which are less familiar—the petition of the accused witch Mary Easty, Thomas A. Edison on the industrial research laboratory, Louis H. Sullivan on the skyscraper, and others. All these are the choice of the editor, with the advice and collaboration of the contributing editors. No item is here simply because it has always been included in anthologies of Americana. These are all here because they seem to us significant for the American present. These are not mere historical documents, but also *living* documents.

We hope that each item actually merits its place here; we know that others might have been added. We hope this book will be judged by what it has included, not by what it has omitted. While this is a long book, to make it even longer would have been easier. Although we have been selective, seeking only vivid messengers of still-living attitudes, beliefs, institutions, hopes, and prayers, we have aimed not to be arbitrary. American life is far more than merely our political life (what statesmen and politicians say or do) or what is sometimes called the "life of the mind" (what academic persons and professional intellectuals write and say).

The reader will find here samples of the rich complexity and contrariness of American life. He will hear Herbert Hoover cautioning against and Franklin Delano Roosevelt urging the vigorous and extensive uses of government; Louis D. Brandeis warning of the curse of bigness and John Wanamaker explaining its blessings; John Winthrop hoping for a firmer faith and Oliver Wendell Holmes, Jr., worrying over a too-firm faith; Henry Cabot Lodge pleading for national independence and Woodrow Wilson expounding global interdependence; Andrew Jackson extolling and Henry David Thoreau mistrusting the will of the majority. Here, the reader

will find a hint of the American diapason, the concord of opposing notes which make our tradition. If this book were
twenty times its present size it could not comprehend the full
variety of our institutions. But even in these samples we can
sense the vast range.

Here we have a hint, too, of the changefulness of our tradition. We find that words live and help make a tradition, not
only by their vivid precision, but also by their iridescence,
their ability to reflect the shifting new lights and new colors
of each age. From the casual origins of many of these utterances we discover the ironic disproportion between the occasions which call words forth and the uses to which they are
destined: between the imprisoning of Thoreau for one night
for his failure to pay his poll-tax, and the political liberation
of millions of American Negroes and hundreds of millions of
Indian peasants; between the dispute of a single Boston shoemaker with his unionists, and the growth of a powerful
American labor movement; between Frederick W. Taylor's
personal preoccupation with how best to shovel coal and a
national obsession with efficiency; between Albert Einstein's
interest in theoretical physics, and the atomic Leviathan. We
see also how hard it is to draw the line between the "use" and
the "abuse" of the testaments of our history. Nearly everything reprinted here was called forth by unique personal, political, or social circumstances which can never be repeated.
The Monroe Doctrine could never again have the precise
meaning that it carried to President Monroe; George Washington's first inaugural address, Elizabeth Cady Stanton's
speech on divorce, Louis H. Sullivan's comments on the skyscraper, none could ever again convey the precise meanings
and ambiguities it once conveyed to its author's contemporaries.

A different editor has been selected for each item. He has
been selected because he has been long familiar with the document and its subject; he is therefore qualified to interpret his
subject with a rare intimacy. This has meant more than fourscore editors, and, inevitably, more than fourscore different
ways of interpreting.

Glib talk about broad currents of history leads us to imagine that the crucial documents of our past were somehow delivered on an American Sinai, direct from God to the American people. But in this book we have emphasized the personal and the accidental. We have asked each editor to begin his
chapter with a brief statement of when, where, how, and by
whom the document was written. Whatever grand themes
these momentous statements may illustrate—a "climate of

opinion," a principle of political thought, a trait of national character, a long historical movement—each one was actually the work of a real person or persons. Sometimes these remain persons unknown. But we have tried in this book, so far as the evidence permits, to identify the actual human authors and the peculiar places, times, and circumstances of their work.

The core of each chapter is the living document. The editor for each chapter has selected the form in which the document is printed here. He has provided an authentic text, and, in his source note at the foot of the page where the document begins, he has explained any variations from the indicated source. Footnotes are those of the author, not of the chapter-editor. The titles here given to the documents are not always those under which they were first published (eg., Thoreau's "Civil Disobedience" was originally titled "Resistance to Civil Government," Theodore Roosevelt's "New Nationalism" was originally simple "Speech at Osawatomie, Kansas"), but are chosen for ease and familiarity of identification.

Wherever feasible, the whole original document has been reprinted. In the few instances (e.g., Hamilton's "Report on Manufactures," Mann's "Twelfth Annual Report," Willkie's "One World," etc.) where the document is abridged, the abridgment has been made by the chapter-editor (all omissions are indicated), to provide us here with portions of the document which best serve the purposes of this volume.

The most interesting, most subtle, and most adventurous time in the life of a document is what I call its "Afterlife"— its life after the death of its author. Each contributor has concluded his chapter by a brief "Afterlife" essay, finally interpreting its significance for us today.

The afterlife of a document is vagrant, unpredictable, and often astonishing. The disproportion between the circumstances of the inspiration and the reach of the product is remarkable and sometimes bizarre. Words that have the inexplicable quality that makes them live on, become more and more transformed, enriched, and transmuted with the passage of time; they become more vital and more vivid the longer their authors have been dead. Some of this comes from the mere passage of time; the transmutation of the Declaration of Independence of 1776 (with its meaning to the men who fought the American Revolution) into the Declaration of Independence of 1876 (with its meaning to the men who had fought the Civil War) or the Declaration of Independence of 1966 (with its meaning to men who had fought two world wars) is as basic as the transmutation by which carbon-14 becomes carbon-12. Much of the history of our national testament consists in the ironies and the whimsies by which slogans cried up in one cause become shibboleths of quite other causes, causes which as often as not their original authors would have fought against. To read these remarkable "Afterlives" is to acquire a sobering humility about our power over our grandchildren, and to discover the extent and the limits of our ancestors' power over us. But it is also to realize our great power and our need, in every generation, to rediscover and to re-create our tradition.

The Mayflower Compact
1620

EDITED BY SAMUEL ELIOT MORISON

The Mayflower Compact, so called because it was drafted and signed on board the Mayflower *as that ship approached Cape Cod on November 11, 1620, is justly regarded as a key document in American history. It proves the determination of the small group of English emigrants to live under a rule of law, based on the consent of the people, and to set up their own civil government. Also, it is the first (so far as we know) of hundreds of similar compacts or agreements made not only by other English colonists but, after 1775, by American citizens when they sought to "pitch new States, ez Old-World men pitch tents" beyond the pale of established government.*

Special circumstances led to this compact. The Pilgrim Fathers, belonging to an English separatist congregation which had taken refuge in Leyden, decided to seek a new life in the English colonies. Owing to the liberal policy of the Virginia Company of London, they obtained from it a patent to a "particular plantation," giving them the right to locate where they chose within the vast domain of that Company, and to enjoy local self-government. They intended to locate near the northern boundary of the Company's territory, around the mouth of the Hudson River. Had they reached this objective they would have formed a civil compact after landing, as is proved by a farewell letter from their Leyden pastor, the Reverend John Robinson, who, assuming that they would form a "civil community," tells them they had better choose their officials with care.

But the Mayflower sailed so late in the year, and took so long on the voyage, that on November 10, 1620, when she encountered head winds and shoals south of Cape Cod, the leaders decided to double the Cape, anchor in what is now Provincetown Harbor, and thence "look out a place for habitation." This decision voided their patent, since they were now under the jurisdiction of the Northern Virginia Company, then being reorganized as the Council for New England. At the same time, some of the "strangers" who had been given passage on the Mayflower at the behest of the London merchants who were paying the expenses of this venture "let fall . . . that when they came ashore they would use their own liberty, for none had power to command them, the patent they had being for Virginia." William Bradford, the historian and for thirty-one years governor of Plymouth Colony, states that these threats of the "strangers" to do as they pleased ashore were one reason for the Compact's being hurriedly drafted and concluded before landing. The other reason he gives is even more significant: a "combination" (as he calls it) among themselves "might be as firm as any patent, and in some respects more sure." In other words, a compact freely entered into would be a stronger foundation than a company patent which might be revoked.

Church compacts, or covenants, as they were then called, were familiar to English Puritans and Scots Presbyterians. When a group of men and women decided to leave a church and set up a new one of their own, they drafted a covenant promising to live in love and charity with one another, to endeavor to lead the New Testament life, to support their church financially, and to obey the church elders whom they might elect. Every adult accepted as church member had to "own [accept or sign] the covenant." The Pilgrim Fathers, owing to their successive moves, had done this thrice. Thus it was natural for them to do likewise, for civil purposes, when locating outside any recognized jurisdiction. The forty-one signers of the Mayflower Compact included every head of a family, every adult bachelor—including those who had threatened trouble—and most of the hired menservants. The only males who did not sign were those under age, and two sailors who were obligated to stay but a year.

☆

IN THE NAME of God Amen. We whose names are under-writen, the loyall subjects of our dread soveraigne Lord King James by the grace of God, of great Britaine, Franc, & Ireland king, defender of the faith, &c.

Haveing undertaken, for the glorie of God, and advancements of the Christian faith and honour of our king & countrie, a voyage to plant the first colonie in the Northerne parts of Virginia, doe by these presents solemnly & mutualy in the presence of God, and one of another, covenant & combine our selves togeather into a civill body politick; for our better ordering, & preservation & furtherance of the ends aforesaid; and by vertue hearof to enacte, constitute, and frame shuch just & equall lawes, ordinances, Acts, constitutions, & offices, from time to time, as shall be thought most meete & convenient for the generall good of the Colonie: unto which we promise all due submission and obedience.

In witnes whereof we have hereunder subscribed our names at Cap-Codd the • 11 • of November, in the year the raigne of our soveraigne Lord King James of England, France, & Ireland the eighteenth and of Scotland the fiftie fourth. An°: Dom. 1620.

John Carver
William Bradford
Edward Winslow
William Brewster
Isaac Allerton
Myles Standish
John Alden
Samuel Fuller
Christopher Martin
William Mullins
William White
Richard Warren
John Howland
Stephen Hopkins
Edward Tilley
John Tilley
Francis Cooke
Thomas Rogers

John Turner
Francis Eaton
James Chilton
John Crakston
John Billington
Moses Fletcher
John Goodman
Degory Priest
Thomas Williams
Gilbert Winslow
Edmund Margeson
Peter Brown
Richard Britterige
George Soule
Richard Clarke
Richard Gardiner
John Allerton
Thomas English

Thomas Tinker   Edward Doty
John Rigdale   Edward Leister
Edward Fuller

After the signing, relates Bradford, "They chose . . . Mr. John Carver (a man godly and well approved amongst them) their Governor for that year."

The extent of the Mayflower Compact's influence is debatable. It was certainly no constitution, or declaration of independence (note the references to the king), yet it was something more than a temporary expedient to keep trouble-makers in line. The twenty signers who survived the first six months ashore acted as "freemen" (voters) and as the governing body of the colony. In May, 1621, Governor Carver having died, they elected William Bradford their governor, and re-elected him no fewer than thirty times. The freemen admitted to the franchise, individually and sparingly, boys as they grew up, newcomers who proved cooperative, and hired servants who wished to remain in the colony after their terms of service expired. The freemen elected annually, from among their number, a governor, a secretary, and a few assistants. They also met at least once a year in a general court or assembly, which passed laws, acted as a supreme judicial court, and, after the colony had begun to spread out, set up a representative system. In 1636 the general court adopted a body of laws called the "general fundamentals," which included a bill of rights. But the Compact seems to have been at the bottom of everything; we have evidence from the records that it used to be read aloud when the assembly met.

William Hubbard, an early New England historian who knew the Pilgrim Fathers, confirms our view of the Compact in his *Ecclesiastical History*, written prior to 1682. The Compact, or "combination," as he calls it, was adopted because of "missing of the place" (i.e., the destination) intended and was meant to be temporary, pending the procurement of a royal

---

The original paper or parchment on which the Compact was engrossed, and signed, has long since disappeared. The text was first printed in London in 1622 in a pamphlet generally known as *Mourt's Relation*, which contained extracts from Bradford's and Winslow's journals. Bradford copied the Compact into his history *Of Plymouth Plantation* at some time in the 1630's. It was next printed by the secretary of the colony, Nathaniel Morton, in *New Englands Memoriall* (1669), together with a list of the signers. Bradford's text is reprinted here, with the names of the signers from Morton's edition. The word "ye" of the original has been spelled out here as "the," since the "y" is really an abbreviated "th" and should be so read; and the interchangeable use of "u" and "v" has been modernized (in Bradford's day "v" was always used at the beginning of a word and "u" within).

charter. Hubbard adds, significantly, that the Plymouth people did not pretend to be governed exclusively by their own self-made laws, but also considered themselves bound by the common law of England. And it is evident from the Plymouth Colony records that they applied the common law in appropriate cases which were not covered by their own statutes.

The colony never did obtain a royal charter. The Warwick Patent, dated January 13, 1630, which it received from the Council for New England, besides defining the colony's boundaries, conferred the exclusive right to govern on William Bradford, "his heires associates & assignes." But Governor Bradford "surrendered" his rights to "the whole Court, consisting of the Freemen . . . of New Plymouth," and government went on as before, based on the Compact. Obviously, the governor, even if he had secret yearnings to become another Lord Baltimore, would not have dared accept this responsibility after the colony for almost a decade had enjoyed government by consent of the freemen.

Now comes the question of the Compact's influence outside Plymouth. Lois K. Matthews cites about twenty civil compacts formed by English colonists in America, or by Americans going west after 1775. The first three were formed by secessionist movements from Massachusetts Bay: William Pynchon's Springfield Agreement of May 14, 1636, Roger Williams' Providence Covenant of August 20, 1636, and John Wheelwright's Exeter (New Hampshire) Covenant of 1639. Williams, who had sojourned at Plymouth, may well have read the original Compact; the language of the Providence Covenant is similar to that of the earlier document. And the Exeter Covenant states explicitly that the signers will apply not only their own laws, but also "such godly & christian laws as are established in the realme of England to our best knowledge."

Although the Providence and Exeter agreements may have been conscious imitations of the Mayflower Compact, it would be farfetched to claim Plymouth influence on the many later compacts cited by Mrs. Matthews, down to and including that of the San Francisco Committee of Vigilance of 1851. Much more likely they are other results of the circumstance that produced the Mayflower Compact—the propensity of English Protestants already accustomed to church covenants to use the same method of free association to create a temporary civil government in the wilderness. This was certainly the case with early compacts in the "Old West": e.g., the constitution for the Colony of Transylvania drawn up by a convention at Boonesborough in 1775; the "Articles of Agreement, or Compact of Government," the Cumberland County Compact of 1780; and the informal organization of the State of Franklin in 1785. It is highly improbable that the covenanters in any of these cases had heard of the Mayflower Compact; but, faced with a situation similar to that of the Pilgrim Fathers in 1620, they took parallel action to ensure a rule of law in a region which had none.

John Adams may possibly have had the Mayflower Compact in mind when he wrote, in the preamble to the Massachusetts Constitution of 1780, "The Body-Politic . . . is a social compact, by which the whole people covenants with each Citizen, and each Citizen with the whole people, that all shall be governed by certain Laws for the Common good." But Adams' phraseology stems from John Locke's Second Treatise of Government (1690) and J. J. Rousseau's Contrat Social (1762), in which the theory is presented that all just government rests on a compact, implicit or explicit, between the people and their rulers. That idea was the basis of the Declaration of Independence: George III had broken the compact between himself and his American subjects, who consequently were justified in forming a new government of their own.

In any case, nobody applied the word "compact" to the Mayflower agreement until the works of Locke and Rousseau had become well known. Prior to 1793 the few writers who refer to the Mayflower document call it, variously, a "combination," an "association and agreement," or a "covenant." In 1764 appeared the first of many English translations of Rousseau, entitled The Social Compact; and the first American edition came out in 1784. The connection of the Mayflower document with Rousseau's theory was first noted by Alden Bradford, a young Harvard graduate who, writing in 1793 about his ancestor John Alden, said that he signed "the compact established immediately upon the arrival of the first settlers." Nobody since has called it anything else.

But it remained for John Quincy Adams to start the Mayflower Compact tradition. In an oration delivered at Plymouth in 1802 he declared that it was "perhaps the only instance, in human history, of that positive, original social compact, which speculative philosophers have imagined as the only legitimate source of government." This idea, that the Pilgrim Fathers had anticipated the compact theory 70 years before Locke and 140 years before Rousseau, was very flattering to Americans. Naturally it led to exaggeration. George Bancroft wrote, in his History of the United States (1837), "In the cabin of the Mayflower, humanity recovered its rights, and instituted government on the basis of 'equal laws' for 'the general good.'" And Winslow Warren, in a tercentennial address in 1920, asked the rhetorical question, "What other than a renewal of the spirit of earlier days sustained the men of the Revolution in their long contest and enabled them to embody in the Declaration of Independence and the Constitution of the United States the principles clearly shadowed forth in the Compact of 1620?"

Few today would subscribe to these fancies. But the fact remains that the Mayflower Compact is an early and very significant instance of the seventeenth-century Englishman's genius for self-government, and his determination to live under a rule of law, even "unto the uttermost part of the earth." It is the earliest known case in American history of people establishing a government for themselves by mutual agreement. Significant, also, is the opening invocation, indicating that these men believed Almighty God to be the author of all government. Moreover, their promise of "all due submission and obedience" to the laws they themselves would pass and the authorities they would elect indicates their belief that political liberty is fundamental to all liberty; that without it religion cannot flourish or social order be maintained.

John Winthrop

A Modell of Christian Charity

1630

EDITED BY LAWRENCE W. TOWNER

In the spring of 1630 eleven small cargo vessels, seven of them haphazardly converted for carrying passengers, worked their perilous and various ways three thousand miles across the Atlantic Ocean. On board were some seven hundred men, women, and children, who were risking their lives to establish a godly, Puritan community on Massachusetts' shores. This was the Winthrop fleet, so called by historians after the Moses of his people, Governor John Winthrop, Esq., lord of Groton Manor, justice of the peace, and attorney in the royal Court of Wards. Those he led were drawn from many ranks and stations of English life. Sir Richard Saltonstall and the Lady Arbella Johnson, daughter of the Earl of Lincoln, represented the upper classes. Lady Arbella's husband, Isaac, held the rank of esquire along with John Winthrop. Robert Feake, Josiah Plaistow, and William Pynchon were gentlemen; and nearly twenty others could call themselves "Mister," including the Reverend Mr. John Wilson, who was to become pastor of First Church, Boston. The bulk of the passengers were artisans, tradesmen, and yeomen, with their wives and children. Lowest in rank were a sprinkling of la-

borers and servants, men and maids, and a few boys and girls of tender age who belonged to the same class. The geographical origins of the emigrants were as varied as their classes. They came from nineteen English counties, from London, and from Holland. Not all were Puritans, even, and those who were, were likely to run off in different geographical and religious directions once land was reached. Strong people, capable of risking authority at home for conscience' sake and of daring the hazards of sea and a wild land for a new chance at life, they would not be easily shaped into a community or easily ruled. John Winthrop knew that great deeds would have to be done lest God's chosen people scatter widely and the holy experiment come to nothing.

As the Arbella, the flagship of the fleet, rose and fell on the Atlantic, John Winthrop composed his lay sermon "A Modell of Christian Charity," which he probably read to the assembled ship's company. It expresses his intention to unite his people behind a single purpose, the creation of a due form of government, ecclesiastical as well as civil, so that their community would be a model for the Christian world to emulate. Theirs was to be a "Citty vpon a Hill," as Winthrop called it in a paraphrase from Matthew 5:14.

The Governor had high hopes that the sacrifices to be demanded of those he led would be freely made in harmony with the precepts of Christian charity, or love. His sermon is a moving expression of that ideal. At the same time it is a recognition of the reality of the Puritans' situation. They were prepared to work with real people of all classes and with the human frailties common to us all. With pride, wrath, greed, sloth, and the other deadly sins of the medieval world, the Puritans were thoroughly familiar, and these they were ready to handle. If the spirit of Christ would not work from within, Winthrop was prepared to impose it from without. Otherwise the "Citty vpon a Hill" would become not a Modell for Christians everywhere, but a reproach to mankind. The alternatives to Life and Salvation were Death and Damnation, not just for the few who failed, but perhaps for all mankind.

The basis of the text here reproduced is that edited by Dr. Stewart Mitchell, late director of the Massachusetts Historical Society and editor of the *Winthrop Papers* (5 vols.; Boston, 1929———). His text (II, 282–95) has been compared with the contemporary manuscript in the possession of the New-York Historical Society, and minor alterations have been made accordingly. Dr. Mitchell's notes, especially his biblical references, have also been used freely.

A MODELL OF CHRISTIAN CHARITY.

Written
On Boarde the Arrabella,
On the Attlantick Ocean.
By the Honorable JOHN WINTHROP, Esq.

In His passage, (with the great Company of Religious people, of which Christian Tribes he was the Brave Leader and famous Governor;) from the Island of Great Brittaine, to New-England in the North America.
Anno 1630.

CHRISTIAN CHARITIES.

A Modell hereof

God Almightie in his most holy and wise providence hath soe disposed of the Condicion of mankinde, as in all times some must be rich some poore, some highe and eminent in power and dignitie; others meane and in subieccion.

The Reason hereof

1. REAS: First, to hold conformity with the rest of his workes, being delighted to shewe forthe the glory of his wisdome in the variety and differance of the Creatures and the glory of his power, in ordering all these differences for the preservacion and good of the whole, and the glory of his greatnes that as it is the glory of princes to haue many officers, soe this great King will haue many Stewards counting himselfe more honoured in dispenceing his guifts to man by man, then if hee did it by his owne immediate hand.

2. REAS: Secondly, That he might haue the more occasion to manifest the worke of his Spirit: first, vpon the wicked in moderateing and restraineing them: soe that the riche and mighty should not eate vpp the poore, nor the poore, and dispised rise vpp against theire superiours, and shake off theire yoake; 2ly in the regenerate in exerciseing his graces in them, as in the greate ones, theire loue mercy, gentlenes, temperance etc., in the poore and inferiour sorte, theire faithe patience, obedience etc:

3. REAS: Thirdly, That every man might haue need of other, and from hence they might be all knitt more nearly together in the Bond of brotherly affeccion; from hence it appeares plainely that noe man is made more honourable

than another or more wealthy etc., out of any perticuler and singuler respect to himselfe but for the glory of his Creator and the Common good of the Creature, Man; Therefore God still reserues the propperty of these guifts to himselfe as Ezek. 16:17. he there calls wealthe his gold and his silver etc. Prov. 3:9. he claimes theire seruice as his due[.] honour the Lord with thy riches etc. All men being thus (by divine providence) rancked into two sortes, riche and poore; vnder the first, are comprehended all such as are able to liue comfortably by theire owne meanes duely improued; and all others are poore according to the former distribution. There are two rules whereby wee are to walke one towards another: Justice and Mercy. These are allwayes distinguished in theire Act and in theire obiect, yet may they both concurre in the same Subiect in eache respect; as sometimes there may be an occasion of shewing mercy to a rich man, in some sudden danger of distresse, and allsoe doeing of meere Justice to a poor man in regard of some perticuler contract etc. There is likewise a double Lawe by which wee are regulated in our conversacion one towardes another: in both the former respects, the lawe of nature and the lawe of grace, or the morrall lawe or the lawe of the gospell, to omitt the rule of Justice as not propperly belonging to this purpose otherwise then it may fall into consideracion in some perticuler Cases; By the first of these lawes man as he was enabled soe withall [is] commaunded to loue his neighbour as himselfe[.] vpon this ground stands all the precepts of the morrall lawe, which concernes our dealings with men. To apply this to the works of mercy this lawe requires two things[,] first that every man afford his help to another in every want or distresse Secondly, That hee performe this out of the same affeccion, which makes him carefull of his owne good according to that of our Saviour Math. [7:12] Whatsoever ye would that men should doe to you. This was practised by Abraham and Lott in entertaineing the Angells and the old man of Gibea.

The Lawe of Grace or the Gospell hath some differance from the former as in these respectes first the lawe of nature was giuen to man in the estate of innocency; this of the gospell in the estate of regeneracy: 2ly, the former propounds one man to another, as the same fleshe and Image of god, this as a brother in Christ allsoe, and in the Communion of the same spirit and soe teacheth vs to put a difference betweene Christians and others. Doe good to all especially to the household of faith [Gal. 6:10]; vpon this ground the Israelites were to putt a difference betweene the brethren of such as were strangers though not of the Canaanites. 3ly. The

Lawe of nature could giue noe rules for dealeing with enemies for all to be considered as freinds in the estate of innocency, but the Gospell commaunds loue to an enemy. proofe.
If thine Enemie hunger feede him; Loue your Enemies doe
good to them that hate you Math. 5:44.

This Lawe of the Gospell propoundes likewise a difference
of seasons and occasions: there is a time when a christian
must sell all and giue to the poore as they did in the Apostles
times. There is a tyme allsoe when a christian (though they
giue not all yet) must giue beyond theire abillity. as they of
Macedonia Cor. 2:6. likewise community of perills calls for
extraordinary liberallity and soe doth Community in some
speciall seruice for the Churche. Lastly, when there is noe
other meanes whereby our Christian brother may be releiued
in this distresse wee must help him beyond our ability, rather
than tempt God, in putting him vpon help by miraculous or
extraordinary meanes.

This duty of mercy is exercised in the kindes, Giueing,
lending, and forgiueing.

Quest: What rule shall a man observe in giueing in respect
of the measure?

Ans: If the time and occasion be ordinary he is to giue out
of his aboundance—let him lay aside as god hath blessed
him. If the time and occasion be extraordinary he must be
ruled by them; takeing this withall, that then a man cannot
likely doe too much especially, if he may leaue himselfe and
his family vnder probable meanes of comfortable subsistance.

Obiect[ion]. A man must lay vpp for posterity, the fathers
lay vpp for posterity and children and he is worse then an
Infidell that prouideth not for his owne [I Tim. 5:8].

Ans: For the first, it is plaine, that it being spoken by way
of Comparison it must be meant of the ordinary and vsuall
course of fathers and cannot extend to times and occasions
extraordinary; for the other place the Apostle speakes against
such as walked inordinately, and it is without question, that
he is worse than an Infidell whoe throughe his owne Sloathe
and voluptuousnes shall neglect to prouide for his family.

Obiect. The wise mans Eies are in his head (saith Salomon) [Eccles. 2:14] and foreseeth the plague, therefore wee
must forecast and lay vpp against euill times when hee or his
may stand in need of all he can gather.

Ans: This very Argument Salomon vseth to perswade to
liberallity. Eccle. [11:1] cast thy bread vpon the waters etc.
for thou knowest not what euill may come vpon the land
Luke 16. make you freinds of the riches of Iniquity; you will
aske how this shall be; very well for first he that giues to the

poore lends to the lord. and he will repay him euen in this life an hundred fold to him or his. The righteous is ever mercifull and lendeth and his seed enioyeth the blessing; and besides wee know what advantage it will be to vs in the day of account when many such Witnesses shall stand forthe for vs to witnesse the improuement of our Tallent. And I would knowe of those whoe pleade soe much for layeing vp for time to come, whether they hold that to be Gospell Math. 16:19. Lay not vpp for yourselues Treasures vpon Earth etc. if they acknowledge it what extent will they allowe it; if onely to those primitiue times lett them consider the reason wherevpon our Saviour groundes it, the first is that they are subiect to the moathe, the rust the Theife. Secondly, They will steale away the hearte, where the treasure is there will the heart be allsoe. The reasons are of like force at all times therefore the exhortacion must be generall and perpetuall which [applies] allwayes in respect of the loue and affeccion to riches and in regard of the things themselues when any speciall seruice for the churche or perticuler distresse of our brother doe call for the vse of them; otherwise it is not onely lawfull but necessary to lay vpp as Joseph did to haue ready vppon such occasions, as the Lord (whose stewards wee are of them) shall call for them from vs: Christ giues vs an Instance of the first, when hee sent his disciples for the Asse, and bidds them answer the owner thus, the Lord hath need of him [Matt. 21:2–3]; soe when the Tabernacle was to be builte his [he?] sends to his people to call for their silver and gold etc.: and yeildes them noe other reason but that it was for his worke, when Elisha comes to the widowe of Sareptah and findes her prepareing to make ready her pittance for herselfe and family, he bids her first provide for him, he challengeth first gods parte which shee must first giue before shee must serue her owne family, all these teache vs that the lord lookes that when hee is pleased to call for his right in any thing wee haue, our owne Interest wee haue must stand aside, till his turne be serued, for the other wee need looke noe further than to that of John 1. he whoe hath this worlds goodes and seeth his brother to neede, and shutts vpp his Compassion from him, how dwelleth the loue of god in him, which comes punctually to this Conclusion; if thy brother be in want and thou canst help him, thou needst not make doubt, what thou shouldst doe; if thou louest god thou must help him.

Quest: What rule must wee obserue in lending?

Ans: Thou must obserue whether thy brother hath present or probable, or possible meanes of repayeing thee, if ther be none of these, thou must giue him according to his necessity, rather than lend him as hee requires: if he hath present meanes of repayeing thee, thou art to looke at him, not as an Act of mercy, but by way of Commerce; wherein thou arte to walke by the rule of Justice, but, if his meanes of repayeing thee be onely probable or possible then is hee an obiect of thy mercy thou must lend him, though there be danger of looseing it Deut. 15:7. If any of thy brethren be poore etc. thou shalt lend him sufficient that men might not shift off this duty by the apparent hazzard, he tells them that though the Yeare of Jubile were at hand (when he must remitt it, if hee were not able to repay it before) yet he must lend him and that chearefully; it may not greiue thee to giue him (saith hee) and because some might obiect, why soe I should soone impoverishe my selfe and my family, he adds with all thy Worke etc. for our Saviour Math. 5:42. From him that would borrow of thee turne not away.

Quest: What rule must wee obserue in forgiueing?

Ans: Whether thou didst lend by way of Commerce or in mercy, if he haue noething to pay thee [thou] must forgiue him (except in cause where thou hast a surety or a lawfull pleadge) Deut. 15:2. Every seauenth yeare the Creditor was to quitt that which hee lent to his brother if hee were poore as appeares ver: 8[4]: saue when there shall be noe poore with thee. In all these and like Cases Christ was a generall rule Math. 7:22. Whatsoever ye would that men should doe to you doe yee the same to them allsoe.

Quest: What rule must wee obserue and walke by in cause of Community of perill?

Ans: The same as before, but with more enlargement towardes others and lesse respect towards our selues, and our owne right hence it was that in the primitiue Churche they sold all [,] had all things in Common, neither did any man say that that which he possessed was his owne [Acts 2:44–45; 4:32–35] likewise in theire returne out of the Captiuity, because the worke was greate for the restoreing of the church and the danger of enemies was Common to all Nehemiah exhortes the Jewes to liberallity and readiness in remitting theire debtes to theire brethren, and disposeth liberally of his owne to such as wanted and stands not vpon his owne due, which hee might haue demaunded of them, thus did some of our forefathers in times of persecucion here in England, and soe did many of the faithfull in other Churches whereof wee keepe an honourable remembrance of them, and it is to be obserued that both in Scriptures and latter stories of the Churches that such as haue beene most bountifull to the poore Saintes especially in these extraordinary times and occasions god hath left them highly Commended to posterity, and Zacheus, Cornelius, Dorcas[,] Bishop Hooper, the Cuttler of Brussells and divers others[.] obserue againe that the scripture giues noe causion to restraine any from being over liberall this way; but all men to the liberall and cherefull practise hereof by the sweetest promises as to instance one for many[.] Isaiah 58:6: Is not this the fast that I haue chosen to loose the bonds of wickednes, to take off the heavy burdens to lett the oppressed goe free and to breake every Yoake, to deale thy bread to the hungry and to bring the poore that wander into thy house, when thou seest the naked to cover them etc. then shall thy light breake forthe as the morneing, and thy healthe shall growe speedily, thy righteousnes shall goe before thee, and the glory of the lord shall embrace thee, then thou shalt call and the lord shall Answer thee etc. 2:10 [Isa. 58:10]: If thou power out thy soule to the hungry, then shall thy light spring out in darknes, and the lord shall guide thee continually, and satisfie thy Soule in draught, and make fatt thy bones; thou shalt be like a watered Garden, and they shall be of thee that shall build the old wast places etc. on the contrary most heavy cursses are layd vpon such as are straightened towards the Lord and his people Judg. 5:[23] Cursse ye Meroshe because the[y] came not to help the Lord etc. Pro. [21:13] Hee whoe shutteth his eares from hearing the cry of the poore, he shall cry and shall not be heard: Math. 25:[41–42] Goe ye curssed into everlasting fire etc. I was hungry and ye fedd mee not. Cor. 2:9–16. [6.] he that soweth spareingly shall reape spareingly.

Haueing allready sett forth the practise of mercy according to the rule of gods lawe, it will be vsefull to lay open the groundes of it allsoe being the other parte of the Commaundement and that is the affeccion from which this exercise of mercy must arise, the Apostle tells vs that this loue is the fullfilling of the lawe, not that it is enough to loue our brother and soe noe further but in regard of the excellency of his partes giueing any motion to the other as the Soule to the body and the power it hath to sett all the faculties on worke in the outward exercise of this duty as when wee bid one make the clocke strike he doth not lay hand on the hammer which is the immediate instrument of the sound but setts on worke the first mouer or maine wheele, knoweing that will certainely produce the sound which hee intends; soe the way to drawe men to the workes of mercy is not by force of Argument from the goodnes or necessity of the worke, for though this course may enforce a rationall minde to some present Act of mercy as is frequent in experience, yet it cannot worke such a habit in a Soule as shall make it prompt vpon all occasions to produce the same effect but by frameing these affeccions of loue in the hearte which will as natiuely bring forthe the other, as any cause doth produce the effect.

The diffinition which the Scripture giues vs of loue is this Loue is the bond of perfection [Col. 3:14]. First, it is a bond, or ligament. 2ly, it makes the worke perfect. There is noe body but consistes of partes and that which knitts these partes together giues the body its perfeccion, because it makes each parte soe contiguous to other as thereby they doe mutually participate with eache other, both in strengthe and infirmity in pleasure and paine, to instance in the most perfect of all bodies, Christ and his church make one body: the severall partes of this body considered aparte before they were vnited were as disproportionate and as much disordering as soe many contrary quallities or elements but when christ comes and by his spirit and loue knitts all these partes to himselfe and each to other, it become the most perfect and best proportioned body in the world Eph. 4:16. Christ by whome all the body being knitt together by every ioynt for the furniture thereof according to the effectuall power which is in the measure of every perfeccion of partes a glorious body without spott or wrinckle the ligaments hereof being Christ or his loue for Christ is loue 1 John 4:8. Soe this definition is right Loue is the bond of perfeccion.

From hence wee may frame these Conclusions.

1. first all true Christians are of one body in Christ 1. Cor. 12:12–13. 17. [27.] Ye are the body of Christ and members of [your?] parte.

2ly. The ligamentes of this body which knitt together are loue.

3ly. Noe body can be perfect which wants its propper ligamentes.

4ly. All the partes of this body being thus vnited are made soe contiguous in a speciall relacion as they must needes partake of each others strength and infirmity, ioy, and sorrowe, weale and woe. 1. Cor. 12:26. If one member suffers all suffer with it, if one be in honour, all reioyce with it.

5ly. This sensiblenes and Sympahty of each others Condicions will necessarily infuse into each parte a natiue desire and endeavour, to strengthen defend preserue and comfort the other.

To insist a little on this Conclusion being the product of all the former the truthe hereof will appeare both by precept and patterne i. John 3:10. yee ought to lay downe your liues for the brethren Gal. 6:2. beare ye one anothers burthens and soe fulfill the lawe of Christ.

For patterns wee haue that first of our Saviour whoe out of his good will in obedience to his father, becomeing a parte of this body, and being knitt with it in the bond of loue, found such a natiue sensiblenes of our infirmities and sorrowes as hee willingly yeilded himselfe to deathe to ease the infirmities of the rest of his body and soe heale theire sorrowes: from the like Sympathy of partes did the Apostles and many thousands of the Saintes lay downe theire liues for Christ againe, the like wee may see in the members of this body among themselues. 1. Rom. 9. Paule could haue beene contented to haue beene seperated from Christ that the Jewes might not be cutt off from the body: It is very obseruable which hee professeth of his affectionate part[ak]eing with every member: whoe is weake (saith hee) and I am not weake? whoe is offended and I burne not; and againe. 2 Cor. 7:13. therefore wee are comforted because yee were comforted. of Epaphroditus he speaketh Phil. 2:30. that he regarded not his owne life to [do] him seruice soe Phebe and others are called the seruantes of the Churche, now it is apparant that they serued not for wages or by Constrainte but out of loue, the like wee shall finde in the histories of the churche in all ages the sweete Sympathie of affeccions which was in the members of this body one towardes another, theire chearfullnes in serueing and suffering together how liberall they were without repineing harbourers without grudgeing and helpfull without reproacheing and all from hence they had feruent loue amongst them which onely mak[s] the practise of mercy constant and easie.

The next consideracion is how this loue comes to be wrought; Adam in his first estate was a perfect modell of mankinde in all theire generacions, and in him this loue was perfected in regard of the habit, but Adam Rent in himselfe from his Creator, rent all his posterity allsoe one from another, whence it comes that every man is borne with this principle in him, to loue and seeke himselfe onely and thus a man continueth till Christ comes and takes possession of the soule, and infuseth another principle of loue to God and our brother, and this latter haueing continuall supply from Christ, as the head and roote by which hee is vnited get the predominency in the soule, soe by little and little expells the former 1 John 4:7. loue cometh of god and every one that loueth is borne of god, soe that this loue is the fruite of the new birthe, and none can haue it but the new Creature, now when this quallity is thus formed in the soules of men it workes like the Spirit vpon the drie bones Ezek. 37:[7] bone came to bone, it gathers together the scattered bones or perfect old man Adam and knitts them into one body againe in Christ whereby a man is become againe a liueing soule.

The third Consideracion is concerning the exercise of this loue, which is twofold, inward or outward, the outward hath beene handled in the former preface of this discourse, for vnfolding the other wee must take in our way that maxime of philosophy, Simile simili gaudet or like will to like; for as it is things which are carried with disafeccion to eache other, the ground of it is from a dissimilitude or [blank] ariseing from the contrary or different nature of the things them-selues, soe the ground of loue is an apprehension of some re-semblance in the things loued to that which affectes it, this is the cause why the Lord loues the Creature, soe farre as it hath any of his Image in it, he loues his elect because they are like himselfe, he beholds them in his beloued sonne; soe a mother loues her childe, because shee throughly conceiues a resemblance of herselfe in it. Thus it is betweene the members of Christ, each discernes by the worke of the spirit his owne Image and resemblance in another, and therefore cannot but loue him as he loues himselfe; Now when the soule which is of a sociable nature findes anything like to it selfe, it is like Adam when Eue was brought to him, shee must haue it one with herselfe this is fleshe of my fleshe (saith shee) and bone of my bone shee conceiues a greate delighte in it, therefore shee desires nearenes and familiarity with it; shee hath a greate propensity to doe it good and receiues such content in it as feareing the miscarriage of her beloued shee bestowes it in the inmost Closett of her heart, shee will not endure that it shall want any good which shee can giue it, if by occasion shee be withdrawne from the Company of it, shee is still lookeing towardes the place where shee left her beloued, if shee heare it groane shee is with it presently, if shee finde it sadd and disconsolate shee sighes and mournes with it, shee hath noe such ioy, as to see her beloued merry and thriueing, if shee see it wronged, shee cannot beare it without passion, shee setts noe boundes of her affeccions, nor hath any thought of re-ward, shee findes recompence enoughe in the exercise of her loue towardes it, wee may see this Acted to life in Jonathan and David.

Jonathan a valiant man endued with the spirit of Christ, soe soone as hee Discovers the same spirit in David had pres-ently his hearte knitt to him by this linement of loue, soe that it is said he loued him as his owne soule, he takes soe great pleasure in him that hee stripps himselfe to adorne his beloued, his fathers kingdome was not soe precious to him as his beloued David; Dauid shall haue it with all his hearte, himselfe desires noe more but that hee may be neare to him to reioyce in his good hee chooseth to converse with him in the wildernesse even to the hazzard of his owne life, rather then with the greate Courtiers in his fathers Pallace; when hee sees danger towards him, hee spares neither care paines, nor perill to divert it, when Iniury was offered his beloued David, hee could not beare it, though from his owne father, and when they must parte for a Season onely, they thought theire heartes would haue broake for sorrowe, had not theire affeccions found vent by aboundance of Teares: other instances might be brought to shewe the nature of this affeccion as of Ruthe and Naomi and many others, but this truthe is cleared enough.

If any shall obiect that it is not possible that loue should be bred or vpheld without hope of requitall, it is graunted but that is not our cause, for this loue is allwayes vnder reward it never giues, but it allwayes receiues with advantage: first, in regard that among the members of the same body, loue and affection are reciprocall in a most equall and sweete kinde of Commerce. 2ly, in regard of the pleasure and content that the exercise of loue carries with it as wee may see in the naturall body the mouth is at all the paines to receiue, and mince the foode which serues for the nourishment of all the other partes of the body, yet it hath noe cause to complaine; for first, the other partes send backe by secret passages a due proporcion of the same nourishment in a better forme for the strengthening and comforteing the mouthe. 2ly the labour of the mouthe is accompanied with such pleasure and content as farre exceedes the paines it takes: soe is it in all the labour of loue, among christians, the partie loueing, reapes loue againe as was shewed before, which the soule covetts more than all the wealthe in the world. 2ly [3ly]. noething yieldes more pleasure and content to the soule then when it findes that which it may loue fervently, for to loue and liue beloued is the soules paradice, both heare and in heaven; In the State of Wedlock there be many comfortes to beare out the troubles of that Condicion; but let such as haue tryed the most, say if there be any sweetnes in that Condicion comparable to the exercise of mutuall loue.

From the former Consideracions ariseth these Conclusions.

1 First. This loue among Christians is a reall thing not Imaginarie.

2ly. This loue is as absolutely necessary to the being of the body of Christ, as the sinewes and other ligaments of a naturall body are to the being of that body.

3ly. This loue is a divine Spirituall nature free, actiue strong Couragious permanent vnder valueing all things beneathe its propper obiect, and of all the graces this makes vs nearer to resemble the virtues of our heavenly father.

4ly, It restes in the loue and wellfare of its beloued, for the full and certaine knowledge of these truthes concerning the nature vse, [and] excellency of this grace, that which the holy ghost hath left recorded 1. Cor. 13. may giue full satisfaccion which is needfull for every true member of this louely body of the Lord Jesus, to worke vpon theire heartes, by prayer meditacion continuall exercise at least of the speciall [blank] of this grace till Christ be formed in them and they in him all in eache other knitt together by this bond of loue.

It rests now to make some applicacion of this discourse by the present designe which gaue the occasion of writeing of it. Herein are 4 things to be propounded: first the persons, 2ly, the worke, 3ly, the end, 4ly the meanes.

1. For the persons, wee are a Company professing our selues fellow members of Christ, In which respect onely though wee were absent from eache other many miles, and had our imploymentes as farre distant, yet wee ought to account our selues knitt together by this bond of loue, and liue in the exercise of it, if wee would haue comforte of our being in Christ, this was notorious in the practise of the Christians in former times, as is testified of the Waldenses from the mouth of one of the adversaries Æneas Syluius, mutuo [blank] penè antequam norint, they vse to loue any of theire owne religion even before they were acquainted with them.

2ly. for the Worke wee haue in hand, it is by a mutuall consent through a speciall overruleing providence, and a more then an ordinary approbation of the Churches of Christ to seeke out a place of Cohabitation and Consorteshipp vnder a due forme of Government both ciuill and ecclesiasticall. In such cases as this the care of the publique must oversway all private respects, by which not onely conscience, but meare Ciuill pollicy doth binde vs; for it is a true rule that perticuler Estates cannott subsist in the ruine of the publique.

3ly. The end is to improue our liues to doe more seruice to the Lord the comforte and encrease of the body of christe whereof wee are members that our selues and posterity may be the better preserued from the Common corrupcions of this euill world to serue the Lord and worke out our Salvacion vnder the power and purity of his holy Ordinances.

4ly for the meanes whereby this must bee effected, they are

2fold, a Conformity with the worke and end wee aime at, these wee see are extraordinary, therefore wee must not content our selues with vsuall ordinary meanes whatsoever wee did or ought to haue done when wee liued in England, the same must wee doe and more allsoe where wee goe; That which the most in theire Churches maineteine as a truthe in profession onely, wee must bring into familiar and constant practise, as in this duty of loue wee must loue brotherly without dissimulation, wee must loue one another with a pure hearte feruently wee must beare one anothers burtheens, wee must not looke onely on our owne things, but allsoe on the things of our brethren, neither must wee think that the lord will beare with such faileings at our hands as hee dothe from those among whome wee haue liued, and that for 3 Reasons.

1. In regard of the more neare bond of mariage, betweene him and vs, wherein he hath taken vs to be his after a most strickt and peculiar manner which will make him the more Jealous of our loue and obedience soe he tells the people of Israell, you onely haue I knowne of all the families of the Earthe therefore will I punishe you for your Transgressions.

2ly, because the lord will be sanctified in them that come neare him. Wee know that there were many that corrupted the seruice of the Lord some setting vpp Alters before his owne, others offering both strange fire and strange Sacrifices allsoe; yet there came noe fire from heaven, or other sudden Judgement vpon them as did vpon Nadab and Abihu [Lev. 10:1–2] whoe yet wee may thinke did not sinne presumptuously.

3ly When God giues a speciall Commission he lookes to haue it strictly obserued in every Article, when hee gaue Saule a Commission to destroy Amaleck hee indented with him vpon certaine Articles and because hee failed in one of the least, and that vpon a faire pretence, it lost him the kingdome, which should haue beene his reward, if hee had obserued his Commission [I Sam. 15; 28:16–18]; Thus stands the cause betweene God and vs, wee are entered into Covenant with him for this worke, wee haue taken out a Commission, the Lord hath giuen vs leaue to drawe our owne Articles wee haue professed to enterprise these Accions vpon these and these ends, wee haue herevpon besought him of fauour and blessing; Now if the Lord shall please to heare vs, and bring vs in peace to the place wee desire, then hath hee ratified this Covenant and sealed our Commission, [and] will expect a strickt performance of the Articles contained in it, but if wee shall neglect the observacion of these Articles which are the ends wee haue propounded, and dissembling with our God, shall fall to embrace this present world and prosecute our carnall intencions, seekeing greate things for our selues and our posterity, the Lord will surely breake out in wrathe against vs be revenged of such a periured people and make vs knowe the price of the breache of such a Covenant.

Now the onely way to avoyde this shipwracke and to provide for our posterity is to followe the Counsell of Micah, to doe Justly, to loue mercy, to walke humbly with our God, for this end wee must be knitt together in this worke as one man, wee must entertainee each other in brotherly Affeccion, wee must be willing to abridge our selues of our superfluities, for the supply of others necessities, wee must vphold a familiar Commerce together in all meekenes, gentlenes, patience and liberallity, wee must delight in eache other, make others Condicions our owne reioyce together, mourne together, labour, and suffer together, allwayes haueing before our eyes our Commission and Community in the worke, our Community as members of the same body, soe shall wee keepe the vnitie of the spirit in the bond of peace, the Lord will be our God and delight to dwell among vs, as his owne people and will commaund a blessing vpon vs in all our wayes, soe that wee shall see much more of his wisdome power goodnes and truthe then formerly wee haue beene acquainted with, wee shall finde that the God of Israell is among vs, when tenn of vs shall be able to resist a thousand of our enemies, when hee shall make vs a prayse and glory, that men shall say of succeeding plantacions: the lord make it like that of New England; for wee must Consider that wee shall be as a Citty vpon a Hill, the Eies of all people are vppon vs; soe that if wee shall deale falsely with our god in this worke wee haue vndertaken and soe cause him to withdrawe his present help from vs, wee shall be made a story and a by-word through the world[,] wee shall open the mouthes of enemies to speake euill of the wayes of god and all professours for Gods sake; wee shall shame the faces of many of gods worthy seruants, and cause theire prayers to be turned into Cursses vpon vs till wee be consumed out of the good land whether wee are goeing; And to shutt vpp this Discourse with that exhortacion of Moses that faithfull seruant of the Lord in his last farewell to Israell Deut. 30: [15–19]. Beloued there is now sett before vs life, and good, deathe and euill in that wee are Commaunded this day to loue the Lord our God, and to loue one another to walke in his wayes and to keepe his Commaundements and his Ordinance, and his lawes, and the Articles of our Covenant with him that wee may liue and be multiplyed, and that the Lord our God may blesse vs in the land whether wee goe to possesse it: But if our heartes shall turne away soe that wee will not obey, but shall be seduced and worshipp [serue *cancelled*] other Gods our pleasures, and proffitts, and serue them; it is propounded vnto vs this day, wee shall surely perishe out of the good Land whether wee passe over this vast Sea to possesse it;

> Therefore lett vs choose life,
> that wee, and our Seede,
> may liue; by obeying his
> voyce, and cleaueing to him,
> for hee is our life, and
> our prosperity.

The fate of the original manuscript of Winthrop's sermon is unknown. After the Arbella *dropped anchor at Salem on June 14, 1630, at the end of her voyage of two and one-half months, the sermon was probably circulated in manuscript form, perhaps in several copies. Not until the early nineteenth century did a copy—in a contemporary hand other than Winthrop's—reappear, when it was given to the New-York Historical Society by a descendant of the Governor. It has subsequently been published several times, the first edition being that of the Massachusetts Historical Society in its Collections in 1838. But long before that, back in the seventeenth century, there was at least one divine who argued that the sermon's vitality had already been largely dissipated.*

Massachusetts failed as a Modell of Christian Charity at the same time that it achieved worldly success: the generations which followed Winthrop's concerned themselves less and less with the perfection of souls and the achievement of salvation, and what had begun as a community dominated by religious purpose rapidly became a society with a secular orientation. Only thirty-four years after the Arbella *anchored and but fifteen after Winthrop's death, Roger Williams predicted in sorrow to John Winthrop, the younger: "Sir, when we that have been the eldest, and are rotting, (to-morrow or next day) a generation will act, I fear, far unlike the first Winthrops and their Models of Love: I fear that the common Trinity of the world, (Profit, Preferment, Pleasure) will here be the* Tria omnia, *as in all the world beside . . . that God Land will be (as now it is) as great a God with us English as God Gold was with the Spaniards. . . ."*

By Williams' standards, Winthrop's message had ceased to be relevant. In reality, however, the sermon written on board the Arbella is almost as relevant to an understanding of America today as it is to an understanding of the Puritans of 1630. Implicit in the Puritans' point of view, and certainly in the "Modell of Christian Charity," despite its opening argument, is the concept of change. Society was no longer considered fixed and immutable as it had been in the Middle Ages. Economic, social, religious, and political institutions had changed in the past for the worse and might be changed in the present for the better. Man need not be a hostage to his past; he could free himself from it and construct a new order based, in this case, on the revealed word of God. This idea of change, still revolutionary in the seventeenth century and still seen then within the context of the Christian interpretation of history, has become commonplace in America of the twentieth. Some may curse that change as too fast, others as too slow, but all know it to be a part of American life. From the time of the Puritans, and more particularly, of the Revolution, we have believed that change need not be blind and purposeless, but, instead, directed and purposeful. The vast improvement in the lot of the American Negro over the past twenty years, a consequence of conscious thought and deliberate action, is but the latest remarkable demonstration of this fact.

This change and others like it in the twentieth century have been brought about in part because of a reawakened sense of community, an idea and an ideal made very explicit in Winthrop's "Modell." The Puritans had a strong sense of community, not only because of their precarious position on the edge of the wilderness, but also because it was a part of their cultural heritage. The idea of an intimately related community in which all parts were joined organically to the whole and suffered or prospered together was as natural to their way of thinking as was the use of the word "body" as a metaphor for the community. We may not use the same metaphor today, and we do not formulate the idea in religious terms as the Puritans did, but much of the social legislation enacted in the twentieth century under the two Roosevelts, Wilson, and Truman, and ratified by the Republicans under Eisenhower, is a practical, undoctrinaire expression of the sense of community that Winthrop wrote about. The graduated income tax, social security, public housing, unemployment compensation, the regulation of rates for public utilities are all evidence that we indeed consider ourselves our brother's keeper.

Under ordinary circumstances, the kind of community Winthrop described would have been rooted in a particular soil and linked together by ties of family, church, government, and ancient custom. By these standards, the Puritan community established in Massachusetts in 1620 was quite heterogeneous. Most of the settlers were English, and many were Puritan, but they all had been uprooted and they lacked the ordinary and expected common ties. This was a new community on new land with a new church not yet established, with a government of questionable legal force and without the customary forms. What Winthrop counted on to hold this body together was an extraordinary outpouring of Christian love. And it was the idea that they were a chosen people with a mission to perform that would call forth such an outpouring. That which was true of John Winthrop's America is even more true of ours. With every race, nationality, and culture represented among us, we are a far more various people than Winthrop ever could have imagined. We lack the common cultural roots, the single ancient homeland, to make a people of us. What unites America is devotion to an idea as worked out in the institutions and practical affairs of men.

Like the Puritan, the modern American also has a strong sense of being a part of a chosen people with a mission to perform. Our successful revolution provided the Revolutionary generation and its heirs with a set of dual goals, the extension of liberty within the country, according to its grand statement in the Declaration of Independence, and to other peoples and lands outside the American union. Democracy was our idea, and our mission was to spread it everywhere. Jefferson's Empire of Freedom, the nineteenth century's Manifest Destiny, the concept of the Civil War as a war to "test whether that nation or any nation so conceived and so dedicated can long endure," and our twentieth-century role in world affairs are all expressions, on different levels of understanding, of the sense that America is the stronghold of democracy, a "Citty vpon a Hill," which, if it should fail, would carry mankind with it down into the darkness of despotism or to destruction.

Mary Easty

Petition of an Accused Witch

1692

EDITED BY EDMUND S. MORGAN

In the nineteenth century, when the human race was moving rapidly toward perfection, through manifest destiny, survival of the fittest, and the gospel of wealth, American historians found the Salem witch trials a difficult topic. Everyone was proud of the progress that had carried America away from the superstition and injustice exhibited at Salem, but it was a little embarrassing that there had been so much progress to make. A man of the early nineteenth century could actually (as a child) have touched hands with someone who had (as a child) witnessed the hanging of the Salem witches. Though one might grow accustomed to the existence of apes among one's ancestors, it was unpleasant to contemplate the presence of witch-hunters almost within the family.

The twentieth century has learned more familiarity with the outrageous—and less contempt. As the witch trials have receded to a more comfortable distance in time, we have found ourselves approaching closer to them in spirit, in our new progress through total war and genocide toward holocaust. Anyone who reads today the record of the Salem witch trials will discover in them the devices of judicial murder familiar to our own age: secret torture, irregular procedures, in-admissible evidence, and false confessions.

Historians of early New England now see these phe-nomena as signs of the times, signs of a people with more problems than they knew how to handle. In 1692 Massachu-setts was hard pressed. The charter that had given the colony virtual autonomy was gone; a new one subjected the holy Pu-ritan experiment to unsympathetic English control; an expedi-tion against Catholic Quebec had failed; bankruptcy was im-minent; and subversive agents were evidently attempting to enlist youth in a covenant with hell. The devil appeared as a real threat to the seventeenth century, and in 1692 the devil seemed to be getting the upper hand in Massachusetts. It was no time to stand on ceremony, no time to follow ordinary or orderly procedures when dealing with an enemy who knew no scruples. So a special court tried the cases, following procedures that would not have been acceptable in normal times.

The result was the hanging of nineteen men and women and the pressing to death of one man who refused to plead either guilty or not guilty. Thousands of Europeans had died for witchcraft in the seventeenth century, but these twenty Americans stand out more painfully, like an Anne Frank among millions of Jews. Among the twenty, Mary Easty (or Eastick) is memorable, because she left behind a testament of courage and honesty.

It was because of her courage and because of her honesty that Mary Easty died. One purpose of punishment in a Puri-tan court was to demonstrate the community's disapproval of crime. Unless the criminal was punished, the community shared his guilt and God would visit His judgment upon in-nocent and guilty alike, if not by fire and brimstone, then by drought, depression, and disease. But another purpose of pun-ishment was repentance. God welcomed the penitent sinner, and so must his viceregents on earth, the governors of the state. If a man repented, he had already averted God's wrath, and there was no longer so much need for the state to punish him. Puritan courts were accordingly merciful to those who repented. But it was impossible to repent without having something to repent about, and persons accused of crime learned that it might be easier to admit guilt and repent than to demonstrate innocence.

In the witch trials the possibility of proving innocence scarcely existed. It was taken as evidence of guilt if hysterical teen-age girls testified that a disembodied image of the ac-cused was pinching them. The only escape was to confess.

And those who did so often sought to establish the sincerity of their confessions and to take attention from themselves by naming others as their confederates in crime. Mary Easty was accused by the afflicted girls as one whose image was tormenting them. They later changed their minds and denied it, only to accuse her again two days later. The accusations were then confirmed by confessions of other accused witches, and Mary Easty was condemned to death.

She might easily have escaped the punishment by admitting guilt and throwing herself on the mercy of the court. To have done so would have been to belie her conscience and jeopardize her soul. Mary Easty did not share our enlightenment about the nonexistence of witchcraft. She knew that Satan was abroad in the world and that the court which condemned her was doing its best to combat him. She wished her judges well. But she knew she was not guilty, and she did not dare lie to save her life. In the hope, however, of saving others from a death they did not deserve, and in order to assist the court in its conflict with Satan, she wrote a petition to her judges, directing their attention to the imperfection of their procedures. Since they had convicted her, and since she knew herself to be innocent, she knew, as they could not, that they must be wrong.

THE HUMBL petition of Mary Eastick unto his Excellencyes Sir Wm Phipps and to the honourd Judge and Bench now s[i]tting In Judiacature in Salem and the Reverend ministers humbly sheweth

That wheras your poor and humble Petition[er] being condemned to die Doe humbly begg of you to take it into your Judicious and pious considerations that your poor and humble petitioner knowing my own Innocencye Blised be the Lord for it and seeing plainly the wiles and subtility of my accusers by my selfe can not but Judg charitably of Others that are going the same way of my selfe if the Lord stepps not mightily in i was confined a whole month upon the same account that I am condemned now for and then cleared by the afflicked persons as some of your honours know and in two dayes time I was cryed out upon by them and have been confined and now am condemned to die the Lord above knows my Inno-

---

The original of the petition, from which it is here reprinted, is in the Essex County Archives, Essex County Courthouse, Salem, Massachusetts, in a set of documents labeled "Withcraft, 1692," I, 126.

cencye then and likewise does now as att the great day will be known to men and Angells I petition your honours not for my own life for I know I must die and my appointed time is sett but the Lord he knowes it is that if be possible no more Innocent blood may be shed which undoubtidly cannot be Avoyd[e]d In the way and course you goe in I Question not but your honours does to the uttmost of your Powers in the discovery and detecting of witchcraft and witches and would not be gulty of Innocent blood for the world but by my own Innocencye I know you are in the wrong way the Lord in his infinite mercye direct you in this great work if it be his blessed will that no more innocent blood be shed. I would humbly begg of you that your honours would be plesed to examine theis Aflicted persons strictly and keepe them apart some time and likewise to try some of these confesing wichis I being confident there is severall of them has belyed themselves and others as will appeare if not in this world I am sure in the world to come whither I am now agoing and I question not but youll see an alteration of thes things they say my selfe and others having made a League with the Divel we cannot confesse I know and the Lord knowes as will thorlly appeare they belye me and so I Question not but they doe others the Lord above who is the searcher of all hearts knowes that as I shall answer it att the Tribunall Seat that I know not the least thinge of witchcraft therfore I cannot I dare not belye my own soule I beg your honers not to deny this my humble petition from a poor dying Innocent person and I Question not but the Lord will give a blesing to yor endevers

Five years after they killed Mary Easty, the people of Massa-chusetts recognized that she had been right and they had been wrong. It was time now for them to confess their sin before God and man. They had not ceased to believe in the power of Satan, and they did not suppose that all the witches had been innocent, but only "that such grounds were then laid down to proceed upon, which were too slender to evi-dence the crime they were brought to prove." Looking back, they remembered those days as a time when "we walked in the clouds, and could not see our way," a time when their own frantic zeal had trapped them into the very evil they strove to suppress.

The colony held a day of fasting on January 14, 1697, and in the churches men who had sat in judgment on the witches

*or testified against them examined their consciences. Samuel
Sewall, one of the judges, stood with bowed head while the
minister read aloud his wish to take "the Blame and shame" of
it upon himself, lest God visit the whole land with wrath.
"We ourselves," said some of the jurors, "were not capable to
understand, nor able to withstand the mysterious delusions of
the Powers of Darkness and Prince of the Air; but were for
want of Knowledge in our selves, and better Information
from others, prevailed with to take up with such Evidence
against the Accused, as on further consideration, and better
Information, we justly fear was insufficient for the
touching the Lives of any, Deut. 17.6. whereby we fear we
have been instrumental with others, tho Ignorantly and unwittingly, to bring upon ourselves and this People of the Lord,
the Guilt of Innocent Blood."*

*Though it did not help the dead, it was a good thing for
the living to do—as it would be a good thing for the state of
Massachusetts to admit today that it did wrong in 1927 to
two men who may or may not have been guilty but who received no more fair a trial than Mary Easty. It would also be
good for future guardians of the public safety to heed in
troublous times the words of Mary Easty and guard the rights
of those who risk all because they cannot confess to what
they did not do.*

Gabriel Thomas

An Account of Pennsylvania

1698

EDITED BY DAVID M. POTTER

In the autumn of 1681, William Penn sent out a ship, the
John and Sarah, *from London with the first company of emigrants who were to settle his colony of Pennsylvania. Among this company was a twenty-one-year-old Welshman named Gabriel Thomas, a Quaker from the little town of Pontemoil in Monmouthshire. Thomas' parents and sisters also migrated to Pennsylvania, but the record does not show whether all of them went together on the* John and Sarah, *or whether the rest of the family followed him on a later voyage.*

Thomas remained in Pennsylvania for about fifteen years. During these years, the colony flourished, and Philadelphia began the growth which was soon to make it the largest town in North America. Pennsylvania was the last of the colonial settlements except for Georgia, and the settlers knew how to avoid the mistakes of earlier colonists. Consequently, progress was steady and hardships were few. Penn advertised the attractions of his colony very widely and offered a measure of religious toleration that was not matched in the other colonies. As a result, immigrants, mostly of dissenting religions, poured in from Germany and Wales as well as from England,

*and the new colony became ethnically more diversified than
any of the older ones.*

*About 1697, Thomas went back to London, and there, in
1698, he published a little book entitled* An Historical and
Geographical Account of the Province and Country of Pensilvania; and of West-New-Jersey in America. . . . *This book
was designed to inform and to encourage potential migrants
to Penn's colonies.*

*After this brief appearance in history, Thomas again disap-
pears into obscurity. Apparently he returned to Pennsylvania,
and later quarreled with Penn, who had not given him the
kind of reward which he thought he deserved for writing a
book which had "proved to the province's great advancement
by causing great numbers of people to go over to those
parts." He died in Philadelphia, perhaps somewhat embittered, in 1714.*

THIS City [Philadelphia] is Situated between Schoolkill-River and the great River Delaware, which derives its Name
from Captain Delaware, who came there pretty early: Ships
of Two or Three Hundred Tuns may come up to this City,
by either of these two Rivers. Moreover, in this Province are
Four Great Market-Towns, *viz*, Chester, the German Town,
New-Castle, and Lewis-Town, which are mightily Enlarged in
this latter Improvement. Between these Towns, the Water-

The full title of Thomas' account was *An Historical and Geographical Account of the Province and Country of Pensilvania; and of West-
New-Jersey in America. The Richness of the Soil, the Sweetness of the
Situation, the Wholesomness of the Air, the Navigable Rivers, and others, the prodigious Encrease of Corn, the flourishing Condition of the
City of Philadelphia, with the stately Buildings, and other Improvements there. The strange Creatures, as Birds, Beasts, Fishes, and Fowls,
with the several sorts of Minerals, Purging Waters, and Stones, lately
discovered. The Natives, Aboroqmes, their Language, Religion, Laws,
and Customs; The first Planters, the Dutch, Sweeds, and English, with
the number of its Inhabitants; As also a Touch upon George Keith's
New Religion, in his second Change since he left the Quakers, with a
Map of both Countries. By Gabriel Thomas, who resided there about
Fifteen Years.* London, Printed for, and Sold by A. Baldwin, at the
Oxon Arms in Warwick-Lane, 1698.
  The text which is used here reproduces all of Thomas' tract except:
a dedication to Penn; a preface; a long account of the physical appearance of Philadelphia and the layout of its streets; an account of the
Indians; a criticism of some of the religious practices of a Quaker
named George Keith; and a long, separate treatment of the West-Jersey
province. The original text is followed exactly, with a few corrections
and explanatory comments inserted in brackets, but the marginal gloss-
es in the original are omitted.

Men constantly Ply their Wherries; likewise all those Towns have Fairs kept in them, besides there are several Country Villages, *viz.* Dublin, Harford [Haverford], Merioneth, and Radnor in Cumbry [Cambria, a tract occupied by the Welsh settlers]; all which Towns, Villages and Rivers, took their Names from the several Countries whence the present Inhabitants came.

The Air here is very delicate, pleasant, and wholesom; the Heavens serene, rarely overcast, bearing mighty resemblance to the better part of France; after Rain they have commonly a very clear Sky, the Climate is something Colder in the depth of Winter and Hotter in the height of Summer; (the cause of which is its being a Main Land or Continent; the Days also are two Hours longer in the shortest Day in Winter, and shorter by two Hours in the longest Day of Summer) than here in England, which makes the Fruit so good, and the Earth so fertil.

The Corn-Harvest is ended before the middle of July, and most Years they have commonly between Twenty and Thirty Bushels of Wheat for every one they Sow. Their Ground is harrowed with Wooden Tyned Harrows, twice over in a place is sufficient; twice mending of their Plow-Irons in a Years time will serve. Their Horses commonly go without being shod; two Men may clear between Twenty and Thirty Acres of Land in one Year, fit for the Plough, in which Oxen are chiefly us'd, though Horses are not wanting, and of them Good and well shap'd. A Cart or a Wain may go through the middle of the Woods, between the Trees without getting any damage, and of such Land in a convenient place, the Purchase will cost between Ten and Fifteen Pounds for a Hundred Acres. Here is much Meadow Ground. Poor People both Men and Women, will get near three times more Wages for their Labour in this Country, than they can earn either in England or Wales.

What is Inhabited of this Country, is divided into Six Counties, though there is not the Twentieth Part of it yet Peopled by the Christians: It hath in it several Navigable Rivers for Shipping to come in, besides the Capital Delaware, wherein a Ship of Two Hundred Tuns may Sail Two Hundred Miles up. There are also several other small Rivers, in number hardly Credible; these, as the Brooks, have for the most part gravelly and hard Bottoms; and it is suppos'd that there are many other further up in the Country, which are not yet discover'd; the Names of the aforesaid Rivers, are, Hoorkill-River, alias Lewis River, which runs up to Lewis Town, the chiefest in Sussex County; Cedar-River, Muskmellon-River, all taking their Names from the great plenty of these things growing thereabouts; Mother-kill alias Dover-River, St. Jones's alias Cranbrook-River, where one John Curtice lives, who hath Three Hundred Head of Neat Beasts, besides great Numbers of Hogs, Horses, and Sheep; Great Duck-River, Little Duck-River, Black-Bird-River, these also took their Original Names from the great Numbers of those Fowls which are found there in vast quantities; Apequinemy-River, where their Goods come to be Carted over to Mary-Land, St. George's-River, Christen-River, Brandy-Wine-River, Upland alias Chester-River, which runs by Chester-Town, being the Shire or County-Town; Schoolkill-River, Frankford-River, near which, Arthur Cook hath a most Stately Brick-House; and Nishamany-River, where Judge Growden hath a very Noble and Fine House, very pleasantly Situated, and likewise a Famous Orchard adjoyning to it, wherein are contain'd above a Thousand Apple Trees of various sorts; likewise there is the famous Derby-River, which comes down from the Cumbry by Derby-Town, wherein are several Mills, viz. Fulling-Mills, Corn-Mills, etc.

There is curious Building-Stone and Paving-Stone, also Tile-Stone, with which latter, Governor Penn covered his Great and Stately Pile, which he call'd Pennsbury-House, the Name it still retains. There is likewise Iron-Stone or Oar, (lately found) which far exceeds that in England, being Richer and less Drossy; some Preparations have been made to carry on an Iron-Work: There is also very good Lime-Stone in great plenty, and cheap, of great use in Buildings, and also in Manuring Land, (if there were occasion) but Nature has made that of it self sufficiently Fruitful; besides here are Load-Stones, Ising-Glass, and (that Wonder of Stones) the Salamander-Stone [asbestos], found near Brandy-Wine-River, having Cotton in Veins within it, which will not consume in the Fire; though held there a long time.

As to Minerals, or Metals, there is very good Copper, far exceeding ours in England, being much Finer, and of a more glorious Colour. Not two Mile from the Metropolis, are also Purging Mineral-Waters, that pass both by Siege and Urine, all out as good as Epsom; And I have reason to believe, there are good Coals also, for I observ'd, the Runs of Water have the same Colour as that which proceeds from the Coal-Mines in Wales.

Here is curious Diversion in Hunting, Fishing, and Fowling, especially upon that Great and Famous River Suskahanah, which runs down quite through the heart of the Country to Mary-Land, where it makes the Head of Chesepeck-Bay, in which place there are an Infinite Number of Sea and Land Fowl, of most sorts, *viz.* Swans, Ducks, Teal, (which two are the most Grateful and most Delicious in the World), Geese, Divers, Brands, Snipe, Curlew; as also Eagles, Turkies (of Forty or Fifty Pound Weight) Pheasants, Partridges, Pidgeons, Heath-Birds, Black-Birds; and that Strange and Remarkable Fowl, call'd (in these Parts) the Mocking-Bird, that Imitates all sorts of Birds in their various Notes. And for Fish, there are prodigious quantities of most sorts, *viz.* Shadds, Cats-Heads, Sheeps-Heads, Herrings, Smelts, Roach, Eels, Perch. As also the large sort of Fish, as Whales (of which a great deal of Oyl is made), Salmon, Trout, Sturgeon, Rock, Oysters (some six Inches long), Crabs, Cockles (some as big as Stewing Oysters of which are made a Choice Soupe or Broth), Canok and Mussels, with many other sorts of Fish, which would be too tedious to insert.

There are several sorts of wild Beasts of great Profit, and good Food; *viz.* Panthers, Woolves, Fither, Deer, Beaver, Otter, Hares, Musk-Rats, Minks, Wild-Cats, Foxes, Rackoons, Rabits, and that strange Creature, the Possam, she having a false Belly to swallow her Yonng ones, by which means she preserveth them from danger, when any thing comes to disturb them. There are also Bears some[;] Wolves, are pretty well destroy'd by the Indians, for the sake of the Reward given them by the Christians for that Service. Here is also that Remarkable Creature the Flying-Squirrel, having a kind of Skinny Wings, almost like those of the Batt, though it hath the like Hair and Colour of the Common Squirrel, but is much less in Bodily Substance; I have (my self) seen it fly from one Tree to another in the Woods, but how long it can maintain its Flight is not yet exactly known.

There are in the Woods abundance of Red Deer (vulgarly called Stags) for I have bought of the Indians a whole Buck (both Skin and Carcass), for two Gills of Gunpowder. Excellent Food, most delicious, far exceeding that in Europe, in the Opinion of most that are Nice and Curious People. There are vast Numbers of other Wild Creatures, as Elks, Bufalos, &c., all which as well Beasts, Fowl, and Fish, are free and common to any Person who can shoot or take them, without any lett, hinderance or Opposition whatsoever.

There are among other various sorts of Frogs, the Bull-Frog, which makes a roaring noise, hardly to be distinguished from that well known of the Beast, from whom it takes its Name: There is another sort of Frog that crawls up to the tops of Trees, there seeming to imitate the Notes of several

Birds, with many other strange and various Creatures, which
would take up too much room here to mention.

Next, I shall proceed to instance in the several sorts of
Wild Fruits, as excellent Grapes, Red, Black, White, Musca-
del, and Fox, which upon frequent Experience have produc'd
Choice Wine, being daily Cultivated by skilful Vinerons; they
will in a short space of time, have very good Liquor of their
own, and some to supply their Neighbours, to their great advantage; as these Wines are more pure, so much more whol-
som; the Brewing Trade of Sophisticating and Adulterating
of Wines, as in England, Holland (especially) and in some
other places not being known there yet, nor in all probability
will it in many Years, through a natural Probity so fixed and
implanted in the Inhabitants, and (I hope) like to continue.
Wallnuts, Chesnuts, Filberts, Heckery-Nuts, Hartleberries,
Mulberries, (white and black) Rasberries, Strawberries,
Cramberries, Plumbs of several sorts, and many other Wild
Fruits, in great plenty, which are common and free for any
to gather; to particularize the Names of them all, would take
up too much time; tire, not gratifie the Reader, and be inconsistent with the intended Brevity of this little Volume.

The common Planting Fruit-Trees, are Apples, which from
a Kernel (without Inoculating) will shoot up to be a large
Tree, and produce very delicious, large, and pleasant Fruit,
of which much excellent Cyder is made, in taste resembling
that in England press'd from Pippins and Pearmains, sold
commonly for between Ten and Fifteen Shillings per Barrel.
Pears, Peaches, &c. of which they distil a Liquor much like
the taste of Rumm, or Brandy, which they Yearly make in
great quantities: There are Quinces, Cherries, Goosberries,
Currants, Squashes, Pumpkins, Water-Mellons, Muskmellons,
and other Fruits in great Numbers, which seldom fail of
yielding great plenty. There are also many curious and excellent Physical Wild Herbs, Roots, and Drugs of great Vertue,
and very sanative, as the Sassafras, and Sarsaparilla, so much
us'd in Diet-Drinks for the Cure of the Veneral Disease,
which makes the Indians by a right application of them, as
able Doctors and Surgeons as any in Europe, performing celebrated Cures therewith, and by the use of some particular
Plants only, find Remedy in all Swellings, Burnings, Cuts &c.
There grows also in great plenty the Black Snake-Root,
(fam'd for its sometimes preserving, but often curing the
Plague, being infused only in Wine, Brandy or Rumm) Rat-
tle-Snake-Root, Poke-Root, called in England Jallop, with
several other beneficial Herbs, Plants and Roots, which Phy-

sicians have approved of, far exceeding in Nature and Vertue, those of other Countries.

The Names of the Counties are as followeth; First, Philadelphia County; Second, Bucks County; Third, Chester County; Fourth, New-Castle County; Fifth, Kent County; Sixth, Sussex County.

The chiefest and most commodious places for raising Tobacco, as also for Breeding and Improving all sorts of Cattle, are the Counties of Kent and New-Castle; the other[s] chiefly depend upon Raising and Improving English Grain, of which they have a prodigious Encrease, which I have particularly instanced in the beginning of this Book, both as to their Quality and Quantity: All those Counties also very much abound in all sorts of Cattle, both small and great, for the Use and Service of Man.

Their sorts of Grain are, Wheat, Rye, Pease, Oates, Barley, Buck-Wheat, Rice, Indian-Corn, Indian-Pease, and Beans, with great quantities of Hemp and Flax; as also several sorts of eating Roots, as Turnips, Potatoes, Carrats, Parsnips, &c., all which are produc'd Yearly in greater quantities than in England, those Roots being much larger, and altogether as sweet, if not more delicious; Cucumbers, Coshaws, Artichokes, with many others; most sorts of Saladings, besides what grows naturally Wild in the Country, and that in great plenty also, as Mustard, Rue, Sage, Mint, Tanzy, Wormwood, Penny-Royal and Purslain, and most of the Herbs and Roots found in the Gardens in England. There are several Husband-Men, who sow Yearly between Seventy and Eighty Acres of Wheat each, besides Barley, Oates, Rye, Pease, Beans, and other Grain.

They have commonly Two Harvests in the Year; First, of English Wheat, and next of Buck, (or French) Wheat. They have great Stocks both of Hogs and Horses, kept in the Woods, out of which, I saw a Hog kill'd, of about a Year old, which weigh'd Two Hundred weight; whose Flesh is much sweeter, and even more luscious than that in England, because they feed and fatten on the rich (though wild) Fruits, besides those fatned at home by Peaches, Cherries and Apples. Their Horses are very hardy, insomuch that being very hot with riding or otherwise, they are turn'd out into the Woods at the same Instant, and yet receive no harm; some Farmers have Forty, some Sixty, and from that Number to Two or Three Hundred Head of Cattle: Their Oxen usually weigh Two Hundred Pounds a Quarter. They are commonly fatter of Flesh, and yield more Tallow (by feeding only on Grass) than the Cattle in England. And for Sheep, they have considerable Numbers which are generally free from those infectious Diseases which are incident to those Creatures in England, as the Rot, Scab, or Maggots; They commonly bring forth two Lambs at once, some twise in one Year, and the Wooll is very fine, and thick, and also very white.

Bees thrive and multiply exceedingly in those Parts, the Sweeds often get great store of them in the Woods, where they are free for any Body. Honey (and choice too) is sold in the Capital City for Five Pence per Pound. Wax is also plentiful, cheap, and a considerable Commerce. Tame Fowls, as Chickens, Hens, Geese, Ducks, Turkeys, &c., are large, and very plentiful all over this Countrey.

And now for their Lots and Lands in City and Countrey, in their great Advancement since they were first laid out, which was within the compass of about Twelve Years, that which might have been bought for Fifteen or Eighteen Shillings, is now sold for Fourscore Pounds in ready Silver; and some other Lots, that might have been then Purchased for Three Pounds, within the space of Two Years, were sold for a Hundred Pounds a piece, and likewise some Land that lies near the City, that Sixteen Years ago might have been Purchas'd for Six or Eight Pounds the Hundred Acres, cannot now be bought under One Hundred and Fifty, or Two Hundred Pounds.

Now the true Reason why this Fruitful Countrey and Florishing City advance so considerably in the Purchase of Lands both in the one and the other, is their great and extended Traffique and Commerce both by Sea and Land, *viz.* to New-York, New-England, Virginia, Mary-Land, Carolina, Jamaica, Barbadoes, Nevis, Monserat, Antego, St. Cristophers, Barmudoes, New-Found-Land, Maderas, Saltetudeous, and Old-England; besides several other places. Their Merchandize chiefly consists in Horses, Pipe-Staves, Pork and Beef Salted and Barrelled up, Bread, and Flower, all sorts of Grain, Pease, Beans, Skins, Furs, Tobacco, or Pot-Ashes, Wax, &c. which are Barter'd for Rumm, Sugar, Molasses, Silver, Negroes, Salt, Wine, Linen, Houshold-Goods, &c.

However there still remain Lots of Land both in the aforesaid City and Country, that any may Purchase almost as cheap as they could at the first Laying out or Parcelling of either City or Country; which is (in the Judgment of most People) the likeliest to turn to account to those that lay their Money out upon it, and in a shorter time than the aforementioned Lots and Lands that are already improved, and for several Reasons. In the first place, the Countrey is now well inhabited by the Christians, who have great Stocks of all sorts of Cattle, that encrease extraordinarily, and upon that account they are oblig'd to go farther up into the Countrey, because there is the chiefest and best place for their Stocks, and for them that go back into the Countrey, they get the richest Land, for the best lies thereabouts.

Secondly, Farther into the Countrey is the Principal Place to Trade with the Indians for all sorts of Pelt, as Skins and Furs, and also Fat Venison, of whom People may Purchase cheaper by three Parts in four than they can at the City of Philadelphia.

Thirdly, Backwards in the Countrey lies the Mines where is Copper and Iron, besides other Metals, and Minerals, of which there is some Improvement made already in order to bring them, to greater Perfection; and that will be a means to erect more Inland Market-Towns, which exceedingly promote Traffick.

Fourthly, and lastly, Because the Countrey at the first laying out, was void of Inhabitants (except the Heathens, or very few Christians not worth naming) and not many People caring to abandon a quiet and easie (at least tolerable) Life in their Native Countrey (usually the most agreeable to all Mankind) to seek out a new hazardous, and careful one in a Foreign Wilderness or Desart Countrey, wholly destitute of Christian Inhabitants, and even to arrive at which, they must pass over a vast Ocean, expos'd to some Dangers, and not a few Inconveniencies: But now all those Cares, Fears and Hazards are vanished, for the Countrey is pretty well Peopled, and very much Improv'd, and will be more every Day, now the Dove is return'd with the Olive-branch of Peace in her Mouth.

I must needs say, even the present Encouragements are very great and inviting, for Poor People (both Men and Women) of all kinds, can here get three times the Wages for their Labour they can in England or Wales.

I shall instance in a few, which may serve; nay, and will hold in all the rest. The first was a Black-Smith (my next Neighbour), who himself and one Negro Man he had, got Fifty Shillings in one Day, by working up a Hundred Pound Weight of Iron, which at Six Pence per Pound (and that is the common Price in that Countrey) amounts to that Summ.

And for Carpenters, both House and Ship, Brick-layers, Masons, either of these Trades-Men, will get between Five and Six Shillings every Day constantly. As to Journey-Men Shooe-Makers, they have Two Shillings per Pair both for Men and Womens Shooes: And Journey-Men Taylors have Twelve Shillings per Week and their Diet. Sawyers get between Six and Seven Shillings the Hundred for Cutting of Pine-Boards. And for Weavers, they have Ten or Twelve Pence the Yard for Weaving of that which is little more than half a Yard in breadth. Wooll-Combers, have for combing Twelve Pence per Pound. Potters have Sixteen Pence for an Earthen Pot which may be bought in England for Four Pence. Tanners may buy their Hides green for Three Half Pence per Pound, and sell their Leather for Twelve Pence per Pound. And Curriers have Three Shillings and Four Pence per Hide for Dressing it; they buy their Oyl at Twenty Pence per Gallon. Brick-Makers have Twenty Shillings per Thousand for their Bricks at the Kiln. Felt-Makers will have for their Hats Seven Shillings a piece, such as may be bought in England for Two Shillings a piece; yet they buy their Wooll commonly for Twelve or Fifteen Pence per Pound. And as to the Glaziers, they will have Five Pence a Quarry [diamond-shaped pane] for their Glass. The Rule for the Coopers I have almost forgot; but this I can affirm of some who went from Bristol (as their Neighbours report), that could hardly get their Livelihoods there, are now reckon'd in Pensilvania, by a modest Computation to be worth some Hundreds (if not Thousands) of Pounds. The Bakers make as White Bread as any in London, and as for their Rule, it is the same in all Parts of the World that I have been in. The Butchers for killing a Beast, have Five Shillings and their Diet; and they may buy a good fat large Cow for Three Pounds, or thereabouts. The Brewers sell such Beer as is equal in Strength to that in London, half Ale and half Stout for Fifteen Shillings per Barrel; and their Beer hath a better Name, that is, is in more esteem than English Beer in Barbadoes, and is sold nor a higher Price there. And for Silver-Smiths, they have between Half a Crown and Three Shillings an Ounce for working their Silver, and for Gold equivalent. Plasterers have commonly Eighteen Pence per Yard for Plastering. Last-Makers have Sixteen Shillings per dozen for their Lasts. And Heel-Makers have Two Shillings a dozen for their Heels. Wheel and Mill-Wrights, Joyners, Brasiers, Pewterers, Dyers, Fullers, Comb-Makers, Wyer-Drawers, Cage-Makers, Card-Makers, Painters, Cutlers, Rope-Makers, Carvers, Block-Makers, Turners, Button-Makers, Hair and Wood Sieve-Makers, Bodies-Makers, Gun-Smiths, Lock-Smiths, Nailers, File-Cuters, Skinners, Furriers, Glovers, Pattern-Makers, Watch-Makers, Clock-Makers, Sadlers, Coller-Makers, Barbers, Printers, Book-Binders, and all others Trades-Men, their Gains and Wages are about the same proportion as the forementioned Trades in their Advancements, as to what they have in England.

Of Lawyers and Physicians I shall say nothing, because this Countrey is very Peaceable and Healthy; long may it so continue and never have occasion for the Tongue of the one, nor the Pen of the other, both equally destructive to Mens Estates and Lives; besides forsooth, they, Hang-Man like, have a License to Murder and make Mischief. Labouring-Men have commonly here, between 14 and 15 Pounds a Year, and their Meat, Drink, Washing and Lodging; and by the Day their Wages is generally between Eighteen Pence and Half a Crown, and Diet also; But in Harvest they have usually between Three and Four Shillings each Day, and Diet. The Maid Servants Wages is commonly betwixt Six and Ten Pounds per Annum, with very good Accommodation. And for the Women who get their Livelihood by their own Industry, their Labour is very dear, for I can buy in London a Cheese-Cake for Two Pence, bigger than theirs at that price, when at the same time their Milk is as cheap as we can buy it in London, and their Flour cheaper by one half.

Corn and Flesh, and what else serves Man for Drink, Food and Rayment, is much cheaper here than in England, or elsewhere; but the chief reason why Wages of Servants of all sorts is much higher here than there, arises from the great Fertility and Produce of the Place; besides, if these large Stipends were refused them, they would quickly set up for themselves, for they can have Provision very cheap, and Land for a very small matter, or next to nothing in comparison of the Purchace of Lands in England; and the Farmers there, can better afford to give that great Wages than the Farmers in England can, for several Reasons very obvious.

As First, their Land costs them (as I said but just now) little or nothing in comparison, of which the Farmers commonly will get twice the encrease of Corn for every Bushel they sow, that the Farmers in England can from the richest Land they have.

In the Second place, they have constantly good price for their Corn, by reason of the great and quick vent [market] into Barbadoes and other Islands; through which means Silver is become more plentiful than here in England, considering the Number of People, and that causes a quick Trade for both Corn and Cattle; and that is the reason that Corn [wheat] differs now from the Price formerly, else it would at at half the Price it was at then; for a Brother of mine (to my own particular knowledge) sold within the compass of one Week, about One

Hundred and Twenty fat Beasts, most of them good handsom large Oxen.

Thirdly, They pay no Tithes, and their Taxes are inconsiderable; the Place is free for all Persuasions, in a Sober and Civil way; for the Church of England and the Quakers bear equal Share in the Government. They live Friendly and Well together; there is no Persecution for Religion, nor ever like to be; 'tis this that knocks all Commerce on the Head, together with high Imposts, strict Laws, and cramping Orders. Before I end this Paragraph, I shall add another Reason why Womens Wages are so exorbitant; they are not yet very numerous, which makes them stand upon high Terms for their several Services, in Sempstering, Washing, Spinning, Knitting, Sewing, and in all the other parts of their Imployments; for they have for Spinning either Worsted or Linen, Two Shillings a Pound, and commonly for Knitting a very Course pair of Yarn Stockings, they have half a Crown a pair; moreover they are usually Marry'd before they are Twenty Years of Age, and when once in that Noose, are for the most part a little uneasie, and make their Husbands so too, till they procure them a Maid Servant to bear the burden of the Work, as also in some measure to wait on them too.

It is now time to return to the City of Brotherly-Love (for so much the Greek Word or Name Philadelphia imports) which though at present so obscure, that neither the Map-Makers, nor Geographers have taken the least notice of her, tho she far exceeds her Namesake of Lydia, (having above Two Thousand Noble Houses for her Five Hundred Ordinary) or Celisia, or Cælesyria; yet in a very short space of time she will, in all probability, make a fine Figure in the World, and be a most Celebrated Emporeum. Here is lately built a Noble Town-House or Guild-Hall, also a Handsom Market-House, and a convenient Prison. The Number of Christians both Old and Young Inhabiting in that Countrey, are by a Modest Computation, adjudged to amount to above Twenty Thousand.

The Laws of this Countrey, are the same with those in England; our Constitution being on the same Foot: Many Disputes and Differences are determined and composed by Arbitration; and all Causes are decided with great care and Expedition, being concluded (generally) at furthest at the Second Court, unless they happen to be very Nice and Difficult Cases; under Forty Shillings any one Justice of the Peace has Power to Try the Cause. Thieves of all sorts, are oblig'd to restore four fold after they have been Whipt and Imprison'd, according to the Nature of their Crime; and if they be not of Ability to restore four fold, they must be in Servitude till 'tis satisfied. They have Curious Wharfs, as also several large and fine Timber-Yards, both at Philadelphia, and New-Castle, especially at the Metropolis, before Robert Turner's Great and Famous House, where are built Ships of considerable Burthen; they Cart their Goods from that Wharf into the City of Philadelphia, under an Arch, over which part of the Street is built, which is called Chesnut-Street-Wharf, besides other Wharfs, as High-Street Wharf, Mulberry-Street Wharf, and Vine-S[t]reet Wharf, and all those are Common Wharfs; and likewise there are very pleasant Stairs, as Trus and Car-penter-Stairs, besides several others. There are above Thirty Carts belonging to that City, Four or Five Horses to each. There is likewise a very convenient Wharf called Carpenter's Wharf, which hath a fine necessary Crain belonging to it, with suitable Granaries, and Store-Houses. A Ship of Two Hundred Tun may load and unload by the side of it, and there are other Wharfs (with Magazines and Ware-Houses) which front the City all along the River, as also a Curious and Commodious Dock with a Draw Bridge to it, for the convenient Reception of Vessels; where have been built some Ships of Two or Three Hundred Tuns each: They have very Stately Oaks to build Ships with, some of which are between Fifty and Sixty Foot long, and clear from Knots, being very straight and well Grain'd. In this famous City of Philadelphia there are several Rope-Makers, who have large and curious Rope-Walks especially one Joseph Wilcox. Also Three or Four Spacious Malt-Houses, as many large Brew-Houses, and many handsom Bake-Houses for Publick Use.

In the said City are several good Schools of Learning for Youth, in order to the Attainment of Arts and Sciences, as also Reading, Writing, &c. Here is to be had on any Day in the Week, Tarts, Pies, Cakes, &c. We have also several Cooks-Shops, both Roasting and Boyling, as in the City of London; Bread, Beer, Beef, and Pork, are sold at any time much cheaper than in England (which arises from their Plen-ty) our Wheat is very white and clear from Tares, making as good and white Bread as any in Europe. Happy Blessings, for which we owe the highest Gratitude to our Plentiful Pro-vider, the great Creator of Heaven and Earth. The Water-Mills far exceed those in England, both for quickness and grinding good Meal, their being great choice of good Timber, and earlier Corn than in the aforesaid Place, they are made by one Peter Deal, a Famous and Ingenious Workman, espe-cially for inventing such like Machines.

All sorts of very good Paper are made in the German-

Town; as also very fine German Linen, such as no Person of Quality need be asham'd to wear; and in several places they make very good Druggets, Crapes, Camblets, and Serges, besides other Woollen Cloathes, the Manufacture of all which daily improves: And in most parts of the Countrey there are many Curious and Spacious Buildings, which several of the Gentry have erected for their Country-Houses. As for the Fruit-Trees they Plant, they arrive at such Perfection, that they bear in a little more than half the time that they commonly do in England.

The Christian Children born here are generally well-favoured, and Beautiful to behold; I never knew any come into the World with the least blemish on any part of its Body, being in the general, observ'd to be better Natur'd, Milder, and more tender Hearted than those born in England.

There are very fine and delightful Gardens and Orchards, in most parts of this Countrey; but Edward Shippey (who lives near the Capital City) has an Orchard and Gardens adjoyning to his Great House that equalizes (if not exceeds) any I have ever seen, having a very famous and pleasant Summer-House erected in the middle of his extraordinary fine and large Garden abounding with Tulips, Pinks, Carnations, Roses, (of several sorts) Lilies, not to mention those that grow wild in the Fields.

Reader, what I have here written, is not a Fiction, Flam, Whim, or any sinister Design, either to impose upon the Ignorant, or Credulous, or to curry Favour with the Rich and Mighty, but in meer Pity and pure Compassion to the Numbers of Poor Labouring Men, Women, and Children in England, half starv'd, visible in their meagre looks, that are continually wandering up and down looking for Employment without finding any, who here need not lie idle a moment, nor want due Encouragement or Reward for their Work, much less Vagabond or Drone it about. Here are no Beggars to be seen (it is a Shame and Disgrace to the State that there are so many in England) nor indeed have any here the least Occasion or Temptation to take up that Scandalous Lazy Life.

Jealousie among Men is here very rare, and Barrenness among Women hardly to be heard of, nor are old Maids to be met with; for all commonly Marry before they are Twenty Years of Age, and seldom any young Married Woman but hath a Child in her Belly, or one upon her Lap.

What I have deliver'd concerning this Province, is indisputably true, I was an Eye-Witness to it all, for I went in the first Ship that was bound from England for that Countrey,

since it received the name of Pensilvania, which was in the
Year 1681. The Ship's Name was the *John* and *Sarah* of London, Henry Smith Commander. I have declin'd giving any
Account of several things which I have only heard others
speak of, because I did not see them my self, for I never held
that way infallible, to make Reports from Hear-say. I saw the
first Cellar when it was digging for the use of our Governour
Will. Penn.

Gabriel Thomas' Account of Pennsylvania *has had no lasting
fame, and did not mark a change in the course of history.
But it represents a category of writings which played a
unique and important role in American history. These were
the tracts, broadsides, pamphlets, advertisements, letters, sermons, and other pieces which made up an immense body of
what is called "promotional literature." Much of it was
ephemeral, for it was prone to exaggerate the merits of particular places, to be unreliable in terms of fact, and to partake in general of the quality of advertising. But it is important because it reflected, as nothing else did, the motives and
the hopes which drew immigrants first from their homes in
Britain and Europe to the wilderness across the Atlantic, and
later from settled and civilized communities in the older parts
of America to the frontier regions which moved like a shifting battle line across North America during the eighteenth
and nineteenth centuries. Other, more official, documents explained why the government wanted colonies to be founded,
or why the financial backers of settlements believed that their
projects would pay off. But nothing else has shown so clearly
the aspirations of the American settlers. The authors of the
promotional literature sensed what these men and women
were seeking and hoping, what they would respond to, what
they visualized as the "good life." The literature promised
them a fulfillment of these dreams. It can be read today,
therefore, either as an idealized description of realistic conditions, or as a supremely realistic definition of ideals that were
never stated in philosophical or conceptual terms.*

*Thomas' is one of many thousands of items which testified,
unconsciously, to what men wanted America to be, why they
had faith in America, and what they wanted to make it. The
fact that this testimony was unconscious makes it all the
more reliable—it was a very direct expression of what people
wished, not too much complicated by any sense of obligation
to include also what they may have thought that they ought*

to wish. Thus, it is striking that Thomas said very little about abstract ideals. Although he was himself a Quaker (he left the Society of Friends before his death), he gave little emphasis to the religious freedom that existed in Pennsylvania. Although he was familiar with the diversity of peoples (Swedes, Finns, Dutch, Germans, English, Welsh) who made Pennsylvania America's first "melting pot," he did not comment on the toleration that the various ethnic groups showed toward each other. Instead, he bore down incessantly upon the economic abundance which Pennsylvania offered—the fertility of its soil, the easy availability of its land, the purity and navigability of its streams, the profusion of its game and water-fowl and fish, the high yield of its crops, the superiority of its wage-scales to those in England, the geniality of its climate. This emphasis in Thomas is thoroughly characteristic of the promotional writings in general, for as Howard Mumford Jones has observed after a broad survey, "Perhaps the commonest element in the promotion literature is the allure of economic plentitude."

The American emphasis on economic abundance has sometimes been denounced as materialism, and, no doubt, in some of the forms it takes, it has deserved this denunciation. But in the eighteenth-century world, where men were stunted and deprived by poverty, the goal of abundance for everyone seemed touched with real idealism. The perfect society would be one where the age-old striving to escape want would be mitigated, and where scarcity would not force men to fight with one another over an insufficient supply of the necessities of life. As the bitter struggle for existence was relaxed, the harsher, meaner qualities of human nature would disappear, and men would approach nearer to perfection. Even in their physiques they would be better. Women would bear more children, and Thomas found that there was "seldom any young Married Woman but hath a Child in her Belly or one upon her Lap." The children would reflect this tendency toward perfection, and Thomas had never known an infant born in Pennsylvania with "the least blemish on any part of its Body." Even the temperament of the people—what we may call their character—would be improved; the children born in Pennsylvania, Thomas noted, were "in the general, observ'd to be better Natur'd, Milder, and more tender Hearted than those born in England."

In a world where men could enjoy life in peace and amity, without having to fight one another for the means of subsistence, there seemed no great need for ideologies, since ideologies are weapons in social combat. In a world which was free of physical and social ills, there would be no need for such men as doctors and lawyers, whose business it is to deal with these ills: thus, Thomas hoped there would be no doctors and lawyers in Pennsylvania. His hope was doomed to frustration, and the term "Philadelphia lawyer" later became a byword for the most cunning and devious kind of legal practitioner.

The social ideal expressed in Gabriel Thomas' description of Pennsylvania has, like other ideals, failed of complete fulfillment. Even with the world's highest standard of living, Americans have not escaped the wounds and antagonisms of social conflict and ideological clash. American crime rates and social deviancy do not seem to bear out the hope that Americans would be better-natured or more tender-hearted than people with fewer blessings. American enterprise, in its recklessness, has done much to despoil nature of the riches which Thomas so lovingly described. If the dream has partially failed on the one side, it has also, to some extent, been perverted on the other—perverted into what we call boosterism. The optimism of the promotional literature, its tendency to look on the bright side, and to treat hopes for the future as if they were realities for the present—these qualities lent themselves to the impulse of every crossroads settlement to exaggerate its prospects, to inflate its claims, and to indulge in absurd pretensions. Thus there has been a touch of Gabriel Thomas in every Chamber of Commerce secretary who ever minimized the defects of some booming city or magnified the merits of some nondescript town.

But though the ideal represented by Thomas' Account may have been both frustrated and caricatured, it has historical significance simply because it has dominated the thought of several generations of Americans. The vision of social betterment through widespread economic abundance in a land of plenty has been one of the enduring concepts in the American mind. It has conditioned American attitudes and influenced American responses on many issues. For this reason and in this sense, Gabriel Thomas' little book of nearly three centuries ago, although poorly remembered, may still be entitled to a place among the living documents of American history.

Benjamin Franklin

Father Abraham's Speech,
or, The Way to Wealth

1757

EDITED BY LEONARD W. LABAREE

One of Benjamin Franklin's most successful ventures as a printer was the annual publication of an almanac he called Poor Richard. Beginning with the issue for 1733, he compiled twenty-six of the little pamphlets, ending with the one for 1758. Then, having gone to England as agent of the Pennsylvania Assembly, he turned over the responsibility for future issues to his partner David Hall. Poor Richard met heavy competition from other almanacs, especially in the early years, but it was so brightly entertaining that it soon became immensely popular; in time Franklin was selling about 10,000 copies every year in three editions, adapted respectively to the New England, middle, and southern colonies.

One of its most attractive features was the series of proverbs, maxims, and witty sayings with which Franklin "filled all the little Spaces that occur'd between the Remarkable Days in the Calendar." Very few of these aphorisms were wholly original; he took nearly all from well-known anthologies of proverbial expressions. But in many instances Franklin rewrote them, shortening them and giving them more snap and point, and adapting them to an American public.

They dealt with all sorts of matters: personal conduct, the foibles and weaknesses of human nature, the relations between the sexes, and man and society. Perhaps 10 or 15 per cent were aimed at encouraging industry, careful management, and thrift, as means toward financial success.

Before Franklin set sail for England in June, 1757, he apparently found time to prepare the calendar part of Poor Richard for 1758, including the space-filling proverbs, but he had not yet completed the preface that "Richard Saunders," mathematician and stargazer ("philo-math") and ostensible compiler of the almanac, always addressed to the "Courteous Reader," nor had he put together the other "literary" materials that ordinarily filled at least a third of the pamphlet. These jobs he reserved to occupy part of his time during the five-week voyage to England.

As it turned out, the "preface" he wrote while at sea served both purposes. It was long enough to occupy not just the usual second page of the almanac but most of fourteen pages spread through the whole. In it "a plain clean old Man, with white Locks," called Father Abraham, delivered a speech to a crowd waiting to attend a "vendue" or public sale. Great Britain and her colonies were then involved in an expensive war with France, and, in answer to questions on how people could meet the "heavy Taxes" then in force, the old man selected about a hundred proverbs from the previous twenty-five Poor Richard almanacs dealing with industry, prudence, good management, and thrift, and strung them together in a connected discourse.

Franklin completed and dated his "preface" on July 7, 1757; when he landed in England twenty days later he sent it back by the first available ship. Upon receiving the manuscipt David Hall set his printers to work and was able to advertise the new almanac as "just published" on October 6.

COURTEOUS READER,

I HAVE HEARD that nothing gives an Author so great Pleasure, as to find his Works respectfully quoted by other learned Authors. This Pleasure I have seldom enjoyed; for

The text here is that of the original pamphlet, the title page of which bore the following data: *"Poor Richard improved: Being an Almanack and Ephemeris . . . for the Year of our Lord 1758: . . . By Richard Saunders, Philom. Philadelphia: Printed and Sold by B. Franklin, and D. Hall."*

tho' I have been, if I may say it without Vanity, an *eminent Author* of Almanacks annually now a full Quarter of a Century, my Brother Authors in the same Way, for what Reason I know not, have ever been very sparing in their Applauses; and no other Author has taken the least Notice of me, so that did not my Writings produce me some solid *Pudding,* the great Deficiency of *Praise would have quite discouraged me.*

I concluded at length, that the People were the best Judges of my Merit; for they buy my Works; and besides, in my Rambles, where I am not personally known, I have frequently heard one or other of my Adages repeated, with, *as Poor Richard says,* at the End on't; this gave me some Satisfaction, as it showed not only that my Instructions were regarded, but discovered likewise some Respect for my Authority; and I own, that to encourage the Practice of remembering and repeating those wise Sentences, I have sometimes *quoted myself* with great Gravity.

Judge then how much I must have been gratified by an Incident I am going to relate to you. I stopt my Horse lately where a great Number of People were collected at a Vendue of Merchant Goods. The Hour of Sale not being come, they were conversing on the Badness of the Times, and one of the Company call'd to a plain clean old Man, with white locks, *Pray, Father Abraham, what think you of the Times? Won't these heavy Taxes quite ruin the Country? How shall we be ever able to pay them? What would you advise us to?*—Father Abraham stood up, and reply'd, If you'd have my Advice, I'll give it you in short, for a *Word to the Wise is enough,* and *many Words won't fill a Bushel,* as *Poor Richard says.* They join'd in desiring him to speak his Mind, and gathering round him, he proceeded as follows;

"Friends, says he, and Neighbours, the Taxes are indeed very heavy, and if those laid on by the Government were the only Ones we had to pay, we might more easily discharge them; but we have many others, and much more grievous to some of us. We are taxed twice as much by our *Idleness,* three times as much by our *Pride,* and four times as much by our *Folly,* and from these Taxes the Commissioners cannot ease or deliver us by allowing an Abatement. However let us hearken to good Advice, and something may be done for us; *God helps them that help themselves,* as Poor Richard says, in his Almanack of 1733.

It would be thought a hard Government that should tax its People one tenth Part of their *Time,* to be employed in its Service. But *Idleness* taxes many of us much more, if we reckon all that is spent in absolute *Sloth,* or doing of nothing, with that which is spent in idle Employments or Amusements, that amount to nothing. *Sloth,* by bringing on Diseases, absolutely shortens Life. *Sloth, like Rust, consumes faster than Labour wears, while the used Key is always bright,* as Poor Richard says. But *dost thou love Life, then do not squander Time, for that's the Stuff Life is made of,* as Poor Richard says. How much more than is necessary do we spend in Sleep! forgetting that *The sleeping Fox catches no Poultry,* and that *there will be sleeping enough in the Grave,* as Poor Richard says. How much more than is necessary do we spend in Sleep! *Time* must be, as Poor Richard says, *the greatest Prodigality,* since, as he elsewhere tells us, *Lost Time is never found again;* and what we call *Time-enough, always proves little enough.* Let us then be up and be doing, and doing to the Purpose; so by Diligence shall we do more with less Perplexity. *Sloth makes all Things difficult, but Industry all easy,* as Poor Richard says; and *He that riseth late, must trot all Day, and shall scarce overtake his Business at Night.* While *Laziness travels so slowly, that Poverty soon overtakes him,* as we read in Poor Richard, who adds, *Drive thy Business, let not that drive thee;* and *Early to Bed, and early to rise, makes a Man healthy, wealthy and wise.*

So what signifies *wishing* and *hoping* for better Times. We may make these Times better if we bestir ourselves. *Industry need not wish,* as Poor Richard says, and *He that lives upon Hope will die fasting. There are no Gains, without Pains;* then *Help Hands, for I have no Lands,* or if I have, they are smartly taxed. And, as Poor Richard likewise observes, *He that hath a Trade hath an Estate,* and *He that hath a Calling hath an Office of Profit and Honour;* but then the *Trade* must be worked at, and the *Calling* well followed, or neither the *Estate,* nor the *Office,* will enable us to pay our Taxes. If we are industrious we shall never starve; for, as Poor Richard says, *At the working Man's House Hunger looks in, but dares not enter.* Nor will the Bailiff nor the Constable enter, for *Industry pays Debts, while Despair encreaseth them,* says Poor Richard. What though you have found no Treasure, nor has any rich Relation left you a Legacy, *Diligence is the Mother of Good luck,* as Poor Richard says, and *God gives all Things to Industry.* Then *plough deep, while Sluggards sleep, and you shall have Corn to sell and to keep,* says Poor Dick. Work while it is called To-day, for you know not how much you may be hindered To-morrow, which makes Poor Richard say, *One To-day is worth two To-morrows;* and farther, *Have you somewhat to do To-morrow, do it To-day.* If you were a Servant, would you not be ashamed that a good Master should catch you idle? Are you then your own Master, *be ashamed to catch yourself idle*, as Poor Dick says. When there is so much to be done for yourself, your Family, your Country, and your gracious King, be up by Peep of Day; *Let not the Sun look down and say, Inglorious here he lies.* Handle your Tools without Mittens; remember that *the Cat in Gloves catches no Mice*, as Poor Richard says. 'Tis true there is much to be done, and perhaps you are weak handed, but stick to it steadily, and you will see great Effects, for *constant Dropping wears away Stones*, and by *Diligence and Patience the Mouse ate in two the Cable;* and *little Strokes fell great Oaks*, as Poor Richard says in his Almanack, the Year I cannot just now remember.

Methinks I hear some of you say, *Must a Man afford himself no Leisure?* I will tell thee, my Friend, what Poor Richard says, *Employ thy Time well if thou meanest to gain Leisure;* and, *since thou art not sure of a Minute, throw not away an Hour.* Leisure, is Time for doing something useful; this Leisure the diligent Man will obtain, but the lazy Man never; so that, as Poor Richard says, a *Life of Leisure and a Life of Laziness are two Things.* Do you imagine that Sloth will afford you more Comfort than Labour? No, for as Poor Richard says, *Trouble springs from Idleness, and grievous Toil from needless Ease. Many without Labour, would live by their* WITS *only, but they break for want of Stock.* Whereas Industry gives Comfort, and Plenty, and Respect: *Fly Pleasures, and they'll follow you. The diligent Spinner has a large Shift*, and *now I have a Sheep and a Cow, every Body bids me Good morrow;* all which is well said by Poor Richard.

But with our Industry, we must likewise be *steady, settled and careful*, and oversee our own Affairs *with our own Eyes*, and not trust too much to others; for, as Poor Richard says,

I never saw an oft removed Tree,
Nor yet an oft removed Family,
That throve so well as those that settled be.

And again, *Three Removes is as bad as a Fire*, and again, *Keep thy Shop, and thy Shop will keep thee;* and again, *If you would have your Business done, go; If not, send.* And again,

He that by the Plough would thrive,
Himself must either hold or drive.

And again, *The Eye of a Master will do more Work than both his Hands;* and again, *Want of Care does us more Damage than Want of Knowledge;* and again, *Not to oversee Workmen, is to leave them your Purse open.* Trusting too much to others Care is the Ruin of many; for, as the Almanack says, *In the Affairs of this World, Men are saved, not by Faith, but by the Want of it;* but a Man's own Care is profitable; for, saith Poor Dick, *Learning is to the Studious,* and *Riches to the Careful,* as well as *Power to the Bold,* and *Heaven to the Virtuous.* And farther, *If you would have a faithful Servant, and one that you like, serve yourself.* And again, he adviseth to Circumspection and Care, even in the smallest Matters, because sometimes *a little Neglect may breed great Mischief;* adding, *For want of a Nail the Shoe was lost; for want of a Shoe the Horse was lost; and for want of a Horse the Rider was lost,* being overtaken and slain by the Enemy, all for want of Care about a Horse-shoe Nail.

So much for Industry, my Friends, and Attention to one's own Business; but to these we must add *Frugality,* if we would make our *Industry* more certainly successful. A Man may, if he knows not how to save as he gets, *keep his Nose all his Life to the Grindstone,* and die not worth a *Groat* at last. *A fat Kitchen makes a lean Will,* as Poor Richard says; and,

> Many Estates are spent in the Getting,
> Since Women for Tea forsook Spinning and Knitting,
> And Men for Punch forsook Hewing and Splitting.

If you would be wealthy, says he, in another Almanack, think of Saving as well as of Getting: *The Indies have not made Spain rich, because her Outgoes are greater than her Incomes.* Away then with your expensive Follies, and you will not have so much Cause to complain of hard Times, heavy Taxes, and chargeable Families; for, as Poor Dick says,

> Women and Wine, Game and Deceit,
> Make the Wealth small, and the Wants great.

And farther, *What maintains one Vice, would bring up two Children.* You may think perhaps, That a *little* Tea, or a *little* Punch now and then, Diet a *little* more costly, Clothes a *little* finer, and a *little* Entertainment now and then, can be no *great* Matter; but remember what Poor Richard says, *Many* a Little *makes a Mickle;* and farther, *Beware of little Expences; a small Leak will sink a great Ship;* and again, *Who Dainties love, shall Beggars prove;* and moreover, *Fools make Feasts, and wise Men eat them.*

Here you are all got together at this Vendue of *Fineries* and *Knicknacks.* You call them *Goods,* but if you do not take Care, they will prove *Evils* to some of you. You expect they will be sold *cheap,* and perhaps they may for less than they cost; but if you have no Occasion for them, they must be *dear* to you. Remember what Poor Richard says, *Buy what thou hast no Need of, and ere long thou shalt sell thy Necessaries.* And again, *At a great Pennyworth pause a while:* He means, that perhaps the Cheapness is *apparent* only, and not *real;* or the Bargain, by straitning thee in thy Business, may do thee more Harm than Good. For in another Place he says, *Many have been ruined by buying good Pennyworths.* Again, Poor Richard says, *'Tis foolish to lay out Money in a Purchase of Repentance;* and yet this Folly is practised every Day at Vendues, for want of minding the Almanack. *Wise Men,* as Poor Dick says, *learn by others Harms, Fools scarcely by their own;* but, *Felix quem faciunt aliena Pericula cautum.* Many a one, for the Sake of Finery on the Back, have gone with a hungry Belly, and half starved their Families; *Silks and Sattins, Scarlet and Velvets,* as Poor Richard says, *put out the Kitchen Fire.* These are not the *Necessaries* of life; they can scarcely be called the *Conveniencies,* and yet only because they look pretty, how many *want* to *have* them. The *artificial* Wants of Mankind thus become more numerous than the *natural;* and, as Poor Dick says, *For one* poor *Person, there are an hundred* indigent. By these, and other Extravagancies, the Genteel are reduced to Poverty, and forced to borrow of those whom they formerly despised, but who through *Industry* and *Frugality* have maintained their Standing; in which Case it appears plainly, that a *Ploughman on his Legs is higher than a Gentleman on his Knees,* as Poor Richard says. Perhaps they have had a small Estate left them, which they knew not the Getting of; they think *'tis Day, and will never be Night;* that a little to be spent out of *so much,* is not worth minding; (*a Child and a Fool,* as Poor Richard says, *imagine Twenty Shillings and Twenty Years can never be spent*) but, *always taking out of the Meal-tub, and never putting in, soon comes to the Bottom;* then, as Poor Dick says, *When the Well's dry, they know the Worth of Water.* But this they might have known before, if they had taken his Advice; *If you would know the Value of Money, go and try to borrow some;* for, *he that goes a borrowing goes a sorrowing;* and indeed so does he that lends to such People, when he goes to *get it in again.* Poor Dick farther advises, and says,

> *Fond* Pride of Dress, *is sure a very Curse;*
> *E'er* Fancy *you consult, consult your Purse.*

And again, *Pride is as loud a Beggar as Want, and a great deal more saucy.* When you have bought one fine Thing you must buy ten more, that your Appearance may be all of a Piece; but Poor Dick says, *'Tis easier to* suppress *the first De-*

sire, than to satisfy *all that follow it*. And 'tis as truly Folly
for the Poor to ape the Rich, as for the Frog to swell, in
order to equal the Ox.

> *Great Estates may venture more,*
> *But little Boats should keep near Shore.*

'Tis however a Folly soon punished; for *Pride that dines on
Vanity sups on Contempt*, as Poor Richard says. And in another Place, *Pride breakfasted with Plenty, dined with Poverty, and supped with Infamy*. And after all, of what Use is
this *Pride of Appearance*, for which so much is risked, so
much is suffered? It cannot promote Health, or ease Pain; it
makes no Increase of Merit in the Person, it creates Envy, it
hastens Misfortune.

> *What is a Butterfly? At best*
> *He's but a Caterpillar drest.*
> *The gaudy Fop's his Picture just,*

as Poor Richard says.

But what Madness must it be to *run in Debt* for these Superfluities! We are offered, by the Terms of this Vendue, *Six
Months Credit;* and that perhaps has induced some of us to
attend it, because we cannot spare the ready Money, and
hope now to be fine without it. But, ah, think what you do
when you run in Debt; *You give to another Power over your
Liberty*. If you cannot pay at the Time, you will be ashamed
to see your Creditor; you will be in Fear when you speak to
him; you will make poor pitiful sneaking Excuses, and by
Degrees come to lose your Veracity, and sink into base
downright lying; for, as Poor Richard says, *The second Vice
is Lying, the first is running in Debt*. And again, to the same
Purpose, *Lying rides upon Debt's Back*. Whereas a freeborn
Englishman ought not to be ashamed or afraid to see or
speak to any Man living. But Poverty often deprives a Man
of all Spirit and Virtue: *'Tis hard for an empty Bag to stand
upright*, as Poor Richard truly says. What would you think of
that Prince, or that Government, who should issue an Edict
forbidding you to dress like a Gentleman or a Gentlewoman,
on Pain of Imprisonment or Servitude? Would you not say,
that you are free, have a Right to dress as you please, and
that such an Edict would be a Breach of your Privileges, and
such a Government tyrannical? And yet you are about to put
yourself under that Tyranny when you run in Debt for such
Dress! Your Creditor has Authority at his Pleasure to deprive
you of your Liberty, by confining you in Gaol for Life, or to
sell you for a Servant, if you should not be able to pay him!
When you have got your Bargain, you may, perhaps, think
little of Payment; but *Creditors*, Poor Richard tells us, *have*

better *Memories than Debtors;* and in another Place says, *Creditors are a superstitious Sect, great Observers of set Days and Times.* The Day comes round before you are aware, and the Demand is made before you are prepared to satisfy it. Or if you bear your Debt in Mind, the Term which at first seemed so long, will, as it lessens, appear extreamly short. *Time* will seem to have added Wings to his Heels as well as Shoulders. *Those have a short Lent,* saith Poor Richard, *who owe Money to be paid at Easter.* Then since, as he says, *The Borrower is a Slave to the Lender, and the Debtor to the Creditor,* disdain the Chain, preserve your Freedom; and maintain your Independency: Be *industrious* and *free;* be *frugal* and *free.* At present, perhaps, you may think yourself in thriving Circumstances, and that you can bear a little Extravagance without Injury; but,

> *For Age and Want, save while you may;*
> *No Morning Sun lasts a whole Day,*

as Poor Richard says. Gain may be temporary and uncertain, but ever while you live, Expence is constant and certain; and *'tis easier to build two Chimnies than to keep one in Fuel, as* Poor Richard says. So *rather go to Bed supperless than rise in Debt.*

> *Get what you can, and what you get hold;*
> *'Tis the Stone that will turn all your Lead into Gold,*

as Poor Richard says. And when you have got the Philosopher's Stone, sure you will no longer complain of bad Times, or the Difficulty of paying Taxes.

This Doctrine, my Friends, is *Reason* and *Wisdom;* but after all, do not depend too much upon your own *Industry,* and *Frugality,* and *Prudence,* though excellent Things, for they may all be blasted without the Blessing of Heaven; and therefore ask that Blessing humbly, and be not uncharitable to those that at present seem to want it, but comfort and help them. Remember Job suffered, and was afterwards prosperous.

And now to conclude, *Experience keeps a dear School, but Fools will learn in no other, and scarce in that;* for it is true, *we may give Advice, but we cannot give Conduct,* as Poor Richard says: However, remember this, *They that won't be counselled, can't be helped,* as Poor Richard says: And farther, That *if you will not hear Reason, she'll surely rap your Knuckles.*"

Thus the old Gentleman ended his Harangue. The People heard it, and approved the Doctrine, and immediately practised the contrary, just as if it had been a common Sermon; for the Vendue opened, and they began to buy extravagantly, notwithstanding all his Cautions, and their own Fear of Taxes. I found the good Man had thoroughly studied my Almanacks, and digested all I had dropt on those Topicks during the Course of Five-and-twenty Years. The frequent Mention he made of me must have tired any one else, but my Vanity was wonderfully delighted with it, though I was conscious that not a tenth Part of the Wisdom was my own which he ascribed tò me, but rather the *Gleanings* I had made of the Sense of all Ages and Nations. However, I resolved to be the better for the Echo of it; and though I had at first determined to buy Stuff for a new Coat, I went away resolved to wear my old One a little longer. *Reader,* if thou wilt do the same, thy Profit will be as great as mine. I am, as ever, Thine to serve thee, RICHARD SAUNDERS. July 7, 1757.

Franklin's nephew, Benjamin Mecom, who had just started a new printing office in Boston, reproduced this extended preface, together with seven shorter "curious Pieces of Writing," as a twenty-four-page pamphlet, March 30, 1758; he reissued the preface alone in the autumn of 1760. Other printings in New London and New Haven followed soon after. In England the March, 1758, issue of the Grand Magazine of Universal Intelligence, *which appeared a day or two after Mecom's first reprinting, also contained the piece, and it was reproduced almost at once in the* London Chronicle. *A Mrs. Ann Slack included it in 1770 in an anthology she called enticingly* The Pleasing Instructor or Entertaining Moralist, *and the next year the popular* Gentleman's Magazine *published it in the February issue, this time cut to about five-sixths of its original length. These earliest reprintings attached various titles to Franklin's preface, but in 1773 appeared the first of the hundreds of editions under the name by which it has been best known ever since: "The Way to Wealth." This happily chosen phrase was obviously taken from a passage in "Advice to a Young Tradesman," a Franklin composition of 1748: "In short, the Way to Wealth, if you desire it, is as plain as the Way to Market. It depends chiefly on two words,* INDUSTRY and FRUGALITY." *The new version was about the same length as that in* Gentleman's Magazine, *though not all the cuts and other changes were identical. From this time on printings in the British Isles and America rapidly increased in number, sometimes using the full original form, more often the new, shorter version, including the new title.*

*Translations also began to appear, the first in Paris in
1773. Before the end of the century Father Abraham's
speech was available also in Dutch, Gaelic, German, Italian,
and Swedish. A French edition of 1777 (soon after Franklin
had arrived in Paris on his diplomatic mission) gave the piece
a new title, one destined to become as familiar in France, and
in American naval history through the name of John Paul
Jones's famous ship, as "The Way to Wealth" was becoming
in England:* La Science du Bonhomme Richard, ou moyen
facile de payer les impôts. *By 1800, at least 36 English-lan-
guage reprints had been published in American towns and
cities and 64 in the British Isles, and there had been 45 issues
in other languages. It had appeared as a separate pamphlet, a
chapbook, or a broadside to be hung up on the wall of a
room, in anthologies, magazines, school readers, and other almanacs.*

*The popularity of the work continued. How many times it
has been reprinted since 1800 nobody knows. Certainly the
total runs into several hundred; perhaps it is as high as a
thousand. Translations into ten additional languages are definitely known, including Catalan, Chinese, Greek, Hungarian,
Japanese, Polish, and Russian. Perhaps many others would
turn up in a systematic search of distant libraries. All in all, it
seems probable that Father Abraham's speech has been reprinted more often than any other composition by an individual American, with the exception of that much shorter
speech a very different Abraham once delivered at Gettysburg.*

*It was mentioned earlier that few of Poor Richard's say-
ings were strictly original with Franklin, yet because of the
widespread and continued popularity of "The Way to
Wealth" many of them have become part of the folklore only
because Father Abraham repeated them. And, because
Franklin chose to use in the compilation only those of his
maxims which inculcated the somewhat materialistic
"virtues" of hard work, diligence, careful management of
one's affairs, and thrift, the public conception of his sense of
values has been greatly distorted. He did believe, and many
times he said so, that a young person wanting to get on in the
world ought to plan carefully, work hard, and avoid extravagance and waste; but, as he also taught and as he showed in
his own life, these practices ought not to be regarded as ends
in themselves, but merely as means to a larger end, freedom
and capacity to serve one's fellows. Witness the fact that after
accumulating a modest competence, as wealth was measured
in his day, he retired from active business as a printer at the*

age of forty-two to devote himself thereafter to science and public service at home and abroad. In a sense, too, in his compilation of sayings he was giving a highly secularized homily on the Puritan and Quaker "duty" of industriously pursuing one's calling.

It is not surprising, however, that he has been misunderstood, that he has been called the Apostle of Thrift, that, for example, the savings banks of the country have designated the week in January which includes his birthday as National Thrift Week. Nor is it surprising that various commentators have held views of "The Way to Wealth" which derive from their own attitudes toward the materialistic aspects of modern society. D. H. Lawrence complained that, having been brought up on "those Poor Richard tags," it had taken him "many years and countless smarts to get out of the barbed wire moral enclosure that Poor Richard rigged up." By contrast, a canny eithteenth-century Scot declared enthusiastically that Franklin's piece reflected "the quintessence of the wisdom accumulated in all the ages." However one may regard such opposing judgments as these, it is clear that "The Way to Wealth" has enriched the English language with many pithy sayings, and that the attitudes it reflects so entertainingly have played an important part, for better or for worse, in the development of the society in which we live.

Logan's Speech
1774

EDITED BY WILCOMB E. WASHBURN

In October of 1774, near the banks of the Scioto River in Ohio, the Mingo Indian leader Tachnechdorus, whom the whites called Logan, walked with General John Gibson, the Virginia emissary sent to arrange for peace with the Indians following their unsuccessful attempt to resist white settlement in the Ohio Valley. They approached a wooded spot close by the Indian camp, where Logan, "after shedding abundance of tears," spoke in his own language words that were to be projected far beyond that place and time. General Gibson, related by marriage to Logan, returned to the English camp and delivered the message, in translation, to Lord Dunmore, the royal governor of Virginia. Logan's speech was so striking and affecting that, according to Thomas Jefferson, "it became the theme of every conversation, in Williamsburgh particularly, and generally, indeed, wheresoever any of the officers resided or resorted." Jefferson learned it in Williamsburg at the time and recorded it in his pocket account book. The speech was published in the Virginia Gazette *and in other periodicals in America and abroad.*

In 1785 Jefferson privately printed in Paris several copies of his Notes on the State of Virginia, *which he had composed a few years earlier. In this book, he attempted to refute the*

78

assertions of several European philosophers that, as he put it, there was "something in the soil, climate and other circumstances of America, which occasion animal nature to degenerate, not excepting even the man, native or adoptive, physical or moral." In rejecting the theory, Jefferson adduced Logan's speech as evidence of the high talents of the aborigines of the country.

In 1787 a regularly published, enlarged, and corrected edition of the Notes was brought out with Jefferson's approval. In 1797 a Maryland political opponent of Jefferson, Luther Martin, attacked him in the public press for accepting Logan's charge that Michael Cresap, Martin's father-in-law, was responsible for the murder of Logan's family. At the same time, Martin ridiculed Logan's speech as a fabrication. Jefferson, though declining to answer the attack in the newspapers, immediately wrote to General Gibson and others who were familiar with the affair, and obtained sworn depositions concerning it, which he published, in 1800, in an Appendix to the Notes. From the evidence gathered, Jefferson concluded that his first account had been essentially correct, though Logan's family may not have been among Cresap's victims, as Logan himself believed and as reported in the accounts upon which Jefferson relied at the time. Jefferson also secured additional evidence to support the authenticity of Logan's speech. In the light of his researches into the affair he prepared a revised account for later editions of the Notes on Virginia.

IN THE SPRING of the year 1774, a robbery was committed by some Indians on certain land adventurers on the River Ohio. The whites in that quarter, according to their custom, undertook to punish this outrage in a summary way. Captain Michael Cresap, and a certain Daniel Greathouse, leading on these parties, surprized, at different times, travelling and hunting parties of the Indians, having their women and children with them, and murdered many. Among these were unfortunately the family of Logan, a chief celebrated in peace and war, and long distinguished as the friend of the whites. This unworthy return provoked his vengeance. He accordingly signalized himself in the war which ensued. In the autumn of the same year a decisive battle was fought at the mouth of

The account of Logan and his speech is reprinted here from Jefferson's *Notes on Virginia* (New York, 1801).

the Great Kanhaway, between the collected forces of the Shawanese, Mingoes and Delawares, and a detachment of the Virginia militia. The Indians were defeated and sued for peace. Logan, however, disdained to be seen among the suppliants. But lest the sincerity of a treaty should be distrusted, from which so distinguished a chief absented himself, he sent, by a messenger [General Gibson], the following speech, to be delivered to lord Dunmore.

I appeal to any white man to say, if ever he entered Logan's cabin hungry, and he gave him not meat: if ever he came cold and naked, and he cloathed him not. During the course of the last long and bloody war Logan remained idle in his cabin, an advocate for peace. Such was my love for the whites, that my countrymen pointed as they passed, and said, 'Logan is the friend of white man.' I had even thought to have lived with you, but for the injuries of one man. Colonel Cresap, the last spring, in cold blood, and unprovoked, murdered all the relations of Logan, not even sparing my women and children. There runs not a drop of my blood in the veins of any living creature. This called on me for revenge. I have sought it: I have killed many: I have fully glutted my vengeance: for my country I rejoice at the beams of peace. But do not harbour a thought that mine is the joy of fear. Logan never felt fear. He will not turn on his heel to save his life. Who is there to mourn for Logan?—Not one.

The impact of Logan's speech, as previously noted, was immediate in Williamsburg and elsewhere. Jefferson's retelling of the story gave it a further impetus. His account was widely reprinted in school readers throughout the last half of the eighteenth century and the first half of the nineteenth century. When Logan's story appeared in the early editions of Dr. William Holmes McGuffey's Eclectic Fourth Reader: containing elegant extracts in prose and poetry, from the best American and English writers *(Cincinnati, 1838), it started on a career that was to make it familiar to millions more American school children because of the incredible sales of the McGuffey Readers, estimated at more than 122,000,000 between 1836 and 1920. The story appeared also in the* Fifth Reader *prepared by Alexander H. McGuffey, a younger brother of Dr. McGuffey. Although the speech was published in various editions of the* Readers *throughout the nineteenth*

century and into the twentieth, its use was heaviest in the pre-Civil War period.

Logan and his speech were remembered in other ways. On July 28, 1841, at an assemblage of pioneers and citizens of the Scioto Valley, meeting at Westfall, in Pickaway County, the Logan Historical Society was formed to "perpetuate those principles for which Logan suffered the sneers of his red brethren, by the erection of a monument to his memory, and by the careful collection, safe keeping, and lasting preservation, for the use of posterity, [of] the many scattered but interesting fragments of the history of the early settlements of the western country, . . ." Logan's speech, as reported by Jefferson, was to be "fully engraved in gilt letters on said monument," and the hope was expressed of finding the remains of the Indian statesman. Other monuments were erected at his presumed birthplace in Auburn, New York, and under an elm near Circleville, Ohio, where local tradition assumed his speech to have been made.

Throughout the nineteenth century, friends of Cresap and enemies of Jefferson, following the lead of Luther Martin, sought to impeach the veracity of Jefferson and of his Indian subject. Typical of such critics was John J. Jacob, who, in A Biographical Sketch of the Life of the Late Captain Michael Cresap (Cumberland, Maryland, 1826, reprinted in Cincinnati, 1866), insisted that "your Logan speech, your fine specimen of Indian oratory, is a lie, a counterfeit, and never in fact had any existence as a real Indian speech!" In 1903, M. Louise Stevenson, in an uncritical filiopietistic defense of Cresap, concluded that "it is high time that this 'conversation' should be eliminated from the school books. . . ." And, in fact, it is rare to find, in the school books of the twentieth century, the celebrated speech of Logan. Indeed, such was the force of the attack on the speech that even the detail, implicit in the accounts of both Jefferson and General Gibson, the translator, that Logan delivered his message in his native tongue was forgotten or challenged.

The language of the translation, with its overtones of biblical power and directness, made a strong impression on a people whose principal literary inheritance was the Bible. It is only in the present age, in which biblical rhetoric is lost amidst the blaring of "commercials," the elephantine obscurity of "governmentese," and the saccharine hypocrisy of social chit-chat, that Logan's prose is beginning to seem archaic, if it is remembered at all.

But though the words may be forgotten, Logan's message remains imprinted in the minds of white Americans. Logan's *history is, in microcosm, the history of the Indian-white relationship. Its outline follows the conventional pattern: (1) initial befriending of whites by the Indians; (2) personal outrage against the Indians by frontier ruffians; (3) seeking of violent revenge by the Indians, since other avenues were closed to them; (4) a formal retaliatory military expedition from the interior to "put down" the "Indian uprising"; and (5) the defeat of the Indians followed by their loss of land and spirit.*

Logan's story is the story of the American Indian from Jamestown and Plymouth Rock forward. It symbolizes the death of one society as the Declaration of Independence marks the creation of a new one. It is a tragedy because, given human behavior, it was inevitable, though, given human ideals, it was unnecessary. The American may not have a material past of castles and monuments, but he has a psychological past of wrongs committed and not expiated. The recency of those wrongs gives our emotional past greater strength, as the lack of ruins gives our material past less significance. As mythos, *Logan's story has become part of the American experience—not as a fable, but as a poetic rendering of a historic process. That historic process has incorporated Logan's past into America's past and given a national answer to Logan's private plaint: "Who is there to mourn for Logan?"*

Thomas Jefferson
The Declaration of Independence
1776

EDITED BY HENRY STEELE COMMAGER

It was in March of 1775 that Patrick Henry made his famous appeal to the Virginia Convention to endorse those resolutions from Fairfax County "that the Colony be immediately put into a posture of defense." "Gentlemen may cry Peace, Peace"—so William Wirt later reported it—"but there is no peace. The war is actually begun. The next gale that sweeps from the north will bring to our ears the clash of resounding arms! Our brethren are already in the field! Why stand we here idle?"

The next gale did bring the news of Lexington and Concord, yet there was still to be Ticonderoga and the invasion of Canada, Bunker Hill and the siege of Boston, there was still to be the Declaration of the Causes and Necessity of Taking Up Arms, the Olive Branch petition, the Royal Proclamation of Rebellion, before Americans generally were ready to consider independence. Not until the winter and spring of 1776 did the intransigence of George III, the failure of peace overtures to materialize, the ever-increasing scope of military operations, and the influence of Thomas Paine's revolutionary pamphlet Common Sense *combine to bring about a swift change in American opinion.*

Finally, during May and June, the continuing deliberations and debates of the Continental Congress over the issue of independence for the American colonies reached a high point. On June 7, Richard Henry Lee, "the Cicero of America," introduced three resolutions calling for independence, foreign alliances, and confederation. After spirited debate, the Congress voted to postpone a decision for three weeks, and on June 11 appointed a committee to "prepare a declaration" of independence. The members of this committee were Thomas Jefferson, Dr. Franklin, John Adams, Roger Sherman—all strong advocates of independence—and Robert Livingston of New York, a moderate.

Thomas Jefferson had come up to the Continental Congress the previous year, bringing with him, as John Adams recalled, "a reputation for literature, science, and a happy talent of composition. "His writings," Adams added, were "remarkable for the peculiar felicity of expression." In the Congress he had contributed the answer to Lord North's proposal for reconciliation, and a substantial part of the Declaration of the Causes and Necessity of Taking Up Arms. Back to Virginia in late December, he had not returned to Philadelphia until May 14, 1776, just in time for the great debates on independence.

Then the committee appointed to draw up a declaration of independence asked him to draft the document. John Adams, to be sure, remembered it differently. There was a subcommittee of two—Jefferson and himself—and it was he who persuaded Jefferson to take on the task of providing the first draft, with the improbable argument that "you can write ten times better than I can." Jefferson himself recalled nothing of a subcommittee, but only that the committee "unanimously" asked him to prepare a draft. While there is no precisely contemporary account of the writing of the Declaration, we can reconstruct it with some accuracy, chiefly from Jefferson's recollections, written shortly after the event. We know that Jefferson wrote the Declaration in some two weeks, for it was worked over by the committee and submitted to the Congress on June 28. We know that he wrote it at a desk in a second-floor parlor of the house of a young German bricklayer named Graff. We have his word for it that in the writing he "turned neither to book nor pamphlet" but that "all its authority rests . . . on the harmonizing sentiments of the day, whether expressed in conversation, in letters, printed essays or in the elementary books of public right, as Aristotle, Cicero, Locke, Sidney, etc." We know too, though Jefferson himself fails to mention the matter, that the body of the Declara-

tion—the statement of that "long train of abuses and usurpations" which evinced "a design to reduce them under absolute despotism"—was taken over from the parallel list of grievances which he had written into his draft Constitution for Virginia only a few weeks earlier. And we may confidently accept Jefferson's statement made, to be sure, almost fifty years later, that the object of the Declaration was "an appeal to the tribunal of the world," that in the Declaration he undertook "to place before mankind the common sense of the subject, in terms so plain and firm as to command their assent," and that "neither aiming at originality of principle or sentiment . . . it was intended to be an expression of the American mind, and to give to that expression the proper tone and spirit called for by the occasion."

We have every reason to believe that the committee, or some of its members, met frequently to discuss what was to go into the proposed declaration, and we know that Jefferson submitted it, privately, to both Dr. Franklin and John Adams. Franklin, it appears, made five changes, and Adams two, largely verbal. Jefferson himself revised his first draft, doubtless in the light of criticisms and suggestions from Franklin and Adams, and made no less than sixteen changes. In addition he added three paragraphs to his original draft, one of which—that which referred to "calling legislative bodies at places unusual, etc."—was pretty clearly suggested by Adams. On June 28 Jefferson's draft was finished, and submitted to the Congress.

After herculean efforts by the radical delegates to intimidate the intransigents and convert the moderates, on July 2 the Congress, approving Lee's resolution, voted "unanimously" for independence, with the New York delegates abstaining. With Lee's resolution out of the way, the Congress turned at once to a consideration of Jefferson's draft of a declaration of independence, and discussed and debated it on the afternoon of July 2, on July 3, and, apparently, on much of July 4 as well. We have no record of these debates, except those by Jefferson himself, which are fragmentary and almost desultory. In the course of the discussion the Congress made fairly substantial changes in the document, mostly in striking out Jefferson's highly emotional denunciation of slavery and the slave trade, and some sharp animadversions on George III.

Writing some time later—we do not know precisely when —Jefferson asserted that "on the evening of [the fourth of July] . . . the declaration was reported by the commee., agreed to by the house, and signed by every member present *except Mr. Dickinson." Whether this was a lapse of memory, or whether there may have been two signings, we do not know with certainty. The evidence, however, is strongly against a signing on July 4. On that day the Congress ordered that the Declaration be "authenticated and printed." On July 19 it further resolved that the Declaration "be fairly engrossed on parchment" and that the same, "when engrossed, be signed by every member of Congress." Not until August 2 do we read that "the declaration of independence being engrossed and compared at the table was signed by the members." At least one additional name was added as late as November. And not for almost six months were the names of the signers published. On January 18, 1777, an authenticated copy of the Declaration, with the names of members of the Congress subscribing to the same, was sent to each of the United States.*

Wᴴᴱᴺ in the Course of human events, it becomes necessary for one people to dissolve the political bands which have connected them with another, and to assume among the powers of the earth, the separate and equal station to which the Laws of Nature and of Nature's God entitle them, a decent respect to the opinions of mankind requires that they should declare the causes which impel them to the separation. We hold these truths to be self-evident, that all men are created equal, that they are endowed by their Creator with certain unalienable Rights, that among these are Life, Liberty and the pursuit of Happiness. That to secure these rights, Governments are instituted among Men, deriving their just powers from the consent of the governed, That whenever any Form of Government becomes destructive of these ends it is the Right of the People to alter or to abolish it, and to institute new Government, laying its foundation on such principles and organizing its powers in such form, as to them shall seem most likely to effect their Safety and Happiness. Prudence, indeed, will dictate that Governments long established should not be changed for light and transient causes; and accordingly all experience hath shewn, that mankind are more disposed to suffer, while evils are sufferable,

---

The text is reprinted here from *The Papers of Thomas Jefferson*, edited by Julian P. Boyd (Princeton: Princeton University Press, 1950——). This is the text of the parchment copy of the Declaration (now in the National Archives) which was signed on August 2, 1776. It is generally accepted as the most authentic of various copies.

than to right themselves by abolishing the forms to which they are accustomed. But when a long train of abuses and usurpations, pursuing invariably the same Object evinces a design to reduce them under absolute Despotism, it is their right, it is their duty, to throw off such Government, and to provide new Guards for their future security. Such has been the patient sufferance of these Colonies; and such is now the necessity which constrains them to alter their former Systems of Government. The history of the present King of Great Britain is a history of repeated injuries and usurpations, all having in direct object the establishment of an absolute Tyranny over these States. To prove this, let Facts be submitted to a candid world. He has refused his Assent to Laws, the most wholesome and necessary for the public good. He has forbidden his Governors to pass Laws of immediate and pressing importance, unless suspended in their operation till his Assent should be obtained; and when so suspended, he has utterly neglected to attend to them. He has refused to pass other Laws for the accommodation of large districts of people, unless those people would relinquish the right of Representation in the Legislature, a right inestimable to them and formidable to tyrants only. He has called together legislative bodies at places unusual, uncomfortable, and distant from the depository of their public Records, for the sole purpose of fatiguing them into compliance with his measures. He has dissolved Representative Houses repeatedly, for opposing with manly firmness his invasions on the rights of the people. He has refused for a long time, after dissolutions, to cause others to be elected; whereby the Legislative powers, incapable of Annihilation, have returned to the People at large for their exercise; the State remaining in the mean time exposed to all the dangers of invasion from without, and convulsions within. He has endeavoured to prevent the population of these States; for that purpose obstructiong the Laws for Naturalization of Foreigners; refusing to pass others to encourage their migrations hither, and raising the conditions of new Appropriations of Lands. He has obstructed the Administration of Justice, by refusing his Assent to Laws for establishing Judiciary powers. He has made Judges dependent on his Will alone, for the tenure of their offices, and the amount and payment of their salaries. He has erected a multitude of New Offices, and sent hither swarms of Officers to harrass our people, and eat out their substance. He has kept among us, in times of peace, standing Armies without the Consent of our legislatures. He has affected to render the Military independent of and superior to the Civil power. He has combined with others to subject us to a jurisdiction foreign to our constitution, and un-acknowledged by our laws; giving his Assent to their Acts of pretended Legislation: For Quartering large bodies of armed troops among us: For protecting them, by a mock Trial, from punishment for any Murders which they should commit on the Inhabitants of these States: For cutting off our Trade with all parts of the world: For imposing Taxes on us without our Consent: For depriving us in many cases of the benefits of Trial by Jury: For transporting us beyond Seas to be tried for pretended offences: For abolishing the free System of English Laws in a neighbouring Province, establishing therein an Arbitrary government, and enlarging its Boundaries so as to render it at once an example and fit instrument for intro-ducing the same absolute rule into these Colonies: For taking away our Charters, abolishing our most valuable Laws, and altering fundamentally the Forms of our Governments: For suspending our own Legislatures, and declaring themselves invested with power to legislate for us in all cases whatsoever. He has abdicated Government here, by declaring us out of his Protection and waging War against us. He has plundered our seas, ravaged our Coasts, burnt our towns, and destroyed the Lives of our people. He is at this time transporting large Armies of foreign Mercenaries to compleat the works of death, desolation and tyranny, already begun with circum-stances of Cruelty & perfidy scarcely paralleled in the most barbarous ages, and totally unworthy the Head of a civilized nation. He has constrained our fellow Citizens taken Captive on the high Seas to bear Arms against their Country, to be-come the executioners of their friends and Brethren, or to fall themselves by their Hands. He has excited domestic insurrec-tions amongst us, and has endeavoured to bring on the inhab-itants of our frontiers, the merciless Indian Savages, whose known rule of warfare, is an undistinguished destruction of all ages, sexes and conditions. In every stage of these Oppres-sions We have Petitioned for Redress in the most humble terms: Our repeated Petitions have been answered only by re-peated injury. A Prince, whose character is thus marked by every act which may define a Tyrant, is unfit to be the ruler of a free people. Nor have We been wanting in attentions to our Brittish brethren. We have warned them from time to time of attempts by their legislature to extend an unwarrant-able jurisdiction over us. We have reminded them of the cir-cumstances of our emigration and settlement here. We have appealed to their native justice and magnanimity, and we have conjured them by the ties of our common kindred to disavow these usurpations, which, would inevitably interrupt our connections and correspondence. They too have been deaf to the voice of Justice and of consanguinity. We must, therefore, acquiesce in the necessity, which denounces our Separation, and hold them, as we hold the rest of mankind, Enemies in War, in Peace Friends.

We, therefore, the Representatives of the United States of America, in General Congress, Assembled, appealing to the Supreme Judge of the world for the rectitude of our intentions, do, in the Name, and by Authority of the good People of these Colonies, solemnly publish and declare, That these United Colonies are, and of Right ought to be Free and Independent States; that they are Absolved from all Allegiance to the British Crown, and that all political connection between them and the State of Great Britain, is and ought to be totally dissolved; and that as Free and Independent States, they have full Power to levy War, conclude Peace, contract Alliances, establish Commerce, and to do all other Acts and Things which Independent States may of right do. And for the support of this Declaration, with a firm reliance on the protection of divine Providence, we mutually pledge to each other our Lives, our Fortunes and our sacred Honor.

John Hancock

Button Gwinnett
Lyman Hall
Geo Walton.
Wm. Hooper
Joseph Hewes,
John Penn
Edward Rutledge.
Thos. Heyward Junr.
Thomas Lynch Junr.
Arthur Middleton
Samuel Chase
Wm. Paca
Thos. Stone
Charles Carroll of
    Carrollton
George Wythe
Richard Henry Lee
Th: Jefferson
Benja. Harrison
Thos. Nelson jr.
Francis Lightfoot Lee
Carter Braxton
Robt. Morris

Benjamin Rush
Benja. Franklin
John Morton
Geo Clymer
Jas. Smith.
Geo. Taylor
James Wilson
Geo. Ross
Cæsar Rodney
Geo Read
Tho M:Kean
Wm. Floyd
Phil. Livingston
Frans. Lewis
Lewis Morris
Richd. Stockton
Jno Witherspoon
Fras. Hopkinson
John Hart
Abra Clark
Josiah Bartlett
Wm: Whipple
Saml. Adams

John Adams	Roger Sherman
Robt. Treat Paine	Saml. Huntington
Elbridge Gerry	Wm. Williams
Step. Hopkins	Oliver Wolcott
William Ellery	Matthew Thornton

To members of the Continental Congress, and to most of their contemporaries, it was the "facts submitted to a candid world" that were important about the Declaration of Independence. Here, after all, was the argument on which the signers proposed to rest their case; here was the evidence that George III, and Parliament—though that body was not mentioned in the Declaration—did indeed propose "the establishment of an absolute Tyranny over these States." But with the passing of years these "facts," once so sensational and so persuasive, have lost their luster and their pride of place, and become dim and elusive. Interest has shifted to the preamble, to the statement of political philosophy with which Jefferson introduced his list of grievances. Nothing in the original Resolution of June 11 required Jefferson and his committee to formulate a statement of political principles as a preamble to the actual declaration of independence. It was because members of that committee—notably Jefferson and Franklin and Adams—were children of the Enlightenment and adopted naturally the vocabulary of political philosophy, that we have what has proved the most memorable and influential part of the Declaration.

What we have in the condensed, lucid, and eloquent preamble is nothing less than a comprehensive philosophy of politics. The principles of this philosophy are almost too familiar for repetition: And Jefferson does not undertake to prove the validity of these principles. The truths which he here announces are "self-evident," such as all men of good sense and good will would inevitably endorse. That is why it was quite safe to display a "decent respect to the opinions of mankind."

Here, in summary form, are the principles:

First, that all men are created equal.

Second, that they are endowed with "unalienable" rights.

Third, that these rights include "life, liberty, and the pursuit of happiness."

Fourth, that it was to "secure" these rights that governments were instituted among men.

Fifth, that such governments "derive" (perhaps the most

crucial word in the Declaration) their powers—their "just" powers—from the consent of the governed.

Sixth, that, when government becomes destructive of these ends men may "alter or abolish" it.

Seventh, that they have a right to "institute" new governments designed to "effect their safety and happiness."

We need not inquire here into the sources of this philosophy; that mine has been sufficiently quarried. Certainly it was not original with Jefferson, nor with the revolutionary generation, but was, as Jefferson himself admitted, deeply rooted in the past. Further, as Jefferson also observed, borrowing, perhaps unconsciously, from Tom Paine, the ideas of the Declaration were "the common sense" of the matter.

Americans did not originate or invent these principles, but they did something more: they institutionalized them. As John Adams wrote, "they realized the doctrines of the wisest writers." The concept of natural and inalienable rights was as old as philosophy itself and, in the hands of a James Otis or a Samuel Adams, had proved immensely useful in the debate with the Mother Country over the question whether the "original" rights of the colonists could be forfeited, or "alienated" by ignorance or neglect. Now Americans, for the first time in history, translated this concept of natural rights into constitutional guarantees. Philosophers had long asserted that all power is limited, that no government could exercise unlimited power—indeed, according to the Reverend Jonathan Mayhew, God himself was "limited by law . . . and the everlasting tables of right reason." The Americans, however, were the first to set up governments which were, in fact, limited—limited by written constitutions, bills of rights, separation of powers, checks and balances, and, in time, judicial review. Philosophers had said, or imagined, that men originally made government by compact, or contract. The Americans contrived the fundamental mechanism whereby men did, in fact, come together (even in a state of nature) and set up government by compact—the constitutional convention. This famous institution not only provided the mechanism whereby government could "derive" its powers from the "consent of the governed," but also, for the first time in history, it legalized revolution.

The implementation of other parts of the Preamble was more difficult, if for no other reason than that the words themselves elude definition. What did Jefferson, what did members of the Congress mean by such phrases as "created equal" and "pursuit of happiness"? This is not only a difficult question; it is an unfair question. "No language," as Madison was later to remark, "is so copious as to supply words and phrases for every complex idea, or so correct as not to include many equivocally denoting different ideas." He was speaking of the Constitution and it is relevant to keep in mind that Justices of the Supreme Court have differed for a century and a half on the meaning of such words as "due process of law," "interstate commerce," an "establishment of religion," and "the executive power." There is no reason to suppose that we can know, with certainty, what Jefferson and his colleagues meant by "happiness" or "equality."

"Pursuit of happiness"—a familiar enough phrase in that eighteenth century which was everywhere obsessed with happiness—probably embraced not only the right to, and the search for, but also the attainment of happiness. Many American state constitutions guarantee not only the pursuit of happiness but its attainment as well. "Created equal" is a more difficult phrase. It is absurd to suppose that Jefferson was not aware that Negro slaves and, for that matter, indentured servants, did not enjoy equality with their masters; absurd to suppose that he was insensitive to the palpable inequalities in natural talents and fortunes among individuals in his own society. What Jefferson probably meant was what he said—that men were created equal, created by Nature, created by God. Such inequalities as flourished were a product not of Nature or of God but of man, of society, of government, of good or bad fortune. It should be remembered that Jefferson's original draft of the Declaration read that "all men are created equal and independent, that from that equal creation they derive rights inherent and inalienable"; and that it contained, too, a violent attack upon Negro slavery. And it should not be forgotten that Jefferson's campaign to overthrow primogeniture and entail and the Established Church, his crusade for education, and his contributions to a more democratic order in the West were all designed to ameliorate the inequalities which had been created by the political and social order.

As with so much of the Declaration, the words "created equal" proved to have a life of their own. Indeed what "created equal" came to mean is a good deal more important than what it may have meant at the time it was so casually accepted by members of the Continental Congress: its significance is not descriptive but prophetic. That ultimate meaning was best stated by Lincoln in his Springfield speech of 1857. The Founding Fathers, said Lincoln,

> meant to set up a standard maxim for free society which should be familiar to all, and revered by all; constantly looked

to, constantly labored for, and even though never perfectly attained, constantly approximated, and thereby constantly spreading and deepening its influence and augmenting the happiness and value of life to all people of all colors everywhere. . . . Its authors meant it to be—as, thank God, it is now proving itself—a stumbling-block to all those who in after times might seek to turn a free people back into the hateful paths of despotism. They knew the proneness of prosperity to breed tyrants, and they meant when such should reappear in this fair land and commence their vocation, they should find left for them at least one hard nut to crack.

Certainly it is true that the concept of equality, first announced as a general principle in the Declaration, worked like a ferment in American society. Each successive generation, none more guiltily than our own, has felt called upon to square the reality with principle. The concept of equality was applied to the political processes, and helped to strike down limitations on suffrage and office-holding for men, and eventually for women, too. It was applied to social institutions and practices and challenged every manifestation of class and privilege; and if it did not prevent such manifestations it ameliorated them. It was applied to the economy and helped create an economic order where material well-being came to be assumed both as a foundation to equality, and as a right. It was applied to religion and made impossible not only a religious establishment, but the association of any one church with social or political power; violations of this principle, as in Congregational Connecticut or Mormon Utah, proved only temporary. It was applied to education, and eventually required an equal opportunity for education to all who were fortunate enough to be white, and in our time to all, white or black.

Nor was the influence of the Declaration confined to America. Along with such documents as the Virginia Bill of Rights, Common Sense, and the Virginia Statute of Religious Liberty, it inspired radicals in England and rebels in Ireland and excited the enthusiasm of the philosophes who were precursors to the French Revolution and of leaders of that Revolution like Mirabeau, Lafayette, Condorcet, and Brissot. It was translated into German, and Italian, and gave comfort to the liberals in some of the states of Germany and Italy, while Henrik Steffens recalled the enthusiasm with which it was greeted by his family in Denmark. It fired the spirit of the ardent Miranda, and of other leaders of the South American crusade for freedom and independence. It entered, eventually, into the mainstream of history—especially revolutionary history—on every continent.

Benjamin Franklin
Address to the Federal Convention
1787

EDITED BY RALPH L. KETCHAM

---

*Near the end of the troubled year 1786, George Washington
wrote that he hoped "the federal government, may be considered with calm and deliberate attention. . . . Let prejudices,
unreasonable jealousies, and local interests, yield. . . . Let us
look to our national character, and to things beyond the present moment. No morn ever dawned more favorably than ours
did; and no day was ever more clouded than the present.
Wisdom and good examples are necessary at this time to rescue the political machine from the impending storm." A few
months later, after it was certain that the Federal Convention, to meet in May, 1787, would have a large and distinguished membership, James Madison further cautioned that
". . . no very sanguine expectations can well be indulged.
The probable diversity of opinions and prejudices . . . renders the issue totally uncertain. The existing embarrassments
and mortal diseases of the Confederacy form the only ground
of hope, that a spirit of concession on all sides may be produced by the general chaos, or at least partitions of the
Union, which offers itself as the alternative." At the threshold
of its national organization, the leaders of the new United
States knew that brilliant theories of government, heartfelt
concern for the public welfare, and delegates of prestige and*

power would not be enough; a disposition to compromise was essential.

Fortunately, a world-famous conciliator had been elected to the Convention. Benjamin Franklin, already the patron saint of prudence and practicality, had agreed to head the Pennsylvania delegation. At eighty-two he was more than twenty years older than any other delegate. Over half the rest were under forty. He told his sister that he "attended the Business of [the Convention] 5 Hours in every Day from the Beginning, which is something more than four Months . . . my Health continues; some tell me I look better, and they suppose the daily Exercise of going and returning from the Statehouse has done me good." As President of Pennsylvania he entertained the delegates with tea and lively conversation under a large mulberry tree in the courtyard of his new house near Independence Hall.

Though the Convention quickly but respectfully rejected Franklin's pet ideas—a unicameral legislature, unsalaried officials, and a plural executive—the delegates were grateful for his presence and somehow expected he would make a crucial contribution. Since he was too infirm to remain long on his feet, his few formal speeches were read by James Wilson; otherwise he took only an occasional and often ineffectual part in the debates. Successfully, he opposed absolute executive veto, approved impeachment of officeholders, opposed federal property qualifications for voters, and urged liberal naturalization laws. Unsuccessfully, he disapproved any Senate voice in money bills, urged that the President be ineligible for re-election, and sought explicit power for federal canal-building. Twice during the hot summer (one delegate recorded thirty-three "hot" and three "warm" days, and only twenty-four "cool" and four "cold" days), however, he made important conciliatory moves.

On June 28, after a long harangue by Luther Martin, Franklin moved that "henceforth Prayers imploring the assistance of Heaven and its blessings on our Deliberations, be held in this assembly every morning," observing that without God's aid "we shall succeed in this Building no better than the Builders of Babel; we shall be divided by our little, partial Interests. . . ." Though rejected because the members were unlikely to agree on the mode of prayer, the motion lifted the attention of the members above the acrimonies of debate, emphasized the need for compassion and humility, and marked the beginning of the move toward "the Great Compromise." Shortly thereafter, Franklin made the key motion

*that the states be represented equally in the Senate, and the
people be represented equally in the House.*

*His legendary charm and readiness with an appropriate
story prepared the way for the acceptance of this motion. In
recommending some accommodation between the large and
small states, he remarked that "When a broad table is to be
made, and the edges of the plank do not fit, the artist takes a
little from both and makes a good joint." At another time,
during a hot, frustrating stretch in July when Washington reported that "the counsels . . . are now if possible in a worse
train than ever. . . . I almost despair of seeing a favorable
issue to the proceedings," Franklin dramatized the need for
compromise by showing to a group having tea in his garden a
phial containing a two-headed snake. The elder scientist-
statesman observed that the reptile, if its heads took opposite
sides of a stalk on the way to a stream, might die of thirst
unless the difference were accommodated. Franklin might
have added, from Poor Richard's Almanac, "the wise and the
brave dares own he was wrong." When the members approved a final draft of the Constitution, scarcely daring to believe the extent of their success, it was proposed that Franklin address the Convention asking all the delegates, despite
misgivings, to sign the document. At an evening meeting
Franklin presented a draft of his proposed remarks and final
strategy was settled. The next morning, September 17, 1787,
the day set for the final signing of the Constitution, Franklin
rose and asked the Convention's attention while Wilson read
Franklin's words.*

MR. PRESIDENT

I CONFESS that I do not entirely approve of this Constitution
at present, but Sir, I am not sure I shall never approve it:
For having lived long, I have experienced many Instances of
being oblig'd, by better Information or fuller Consideration,
to change Opinions even on important Subjects, which I once
thought right, but found to be otherwise. It is therefore that
the older I grow the more apt I am to doubt my own Judgment, and to pay more Respect to the Judgment of others.
Most Men indeed as well as most Sects in Religion, think
themselves in Possession of all Truth, and that wherever oth-

Franklin's address is transcribed here from the original, which is in
the Cornell University Library.

ers differ from them it is so far Error. Steele, a Protestant in a Dedication tells the Pope, that the only Difference between our two Churches in their Opinions of the Certainty of their Doctrine, is, the Romish Church is infallible, and the Church of England is never in the Wrong. But tho' many private Persons think almost as highly of their own Infallibility, as of that of their Sect, few express it so naturally as a certain French Lady, who in a little Dispute with her Sister, said, I don't know how it happens, Sister, but I meet with no body but myself that's *always* in the right. *Il n'y a que moi qui a toujours raison.*

In these Sentiments, Sir, I agree to this Constitution, with all its Faults, if they are such; because I think a General Government necessary for us, and there is no *Form* of Government but what may be a Blessing to the People if well administred; and I believe farther that this is likely to be well administred for a Course of Years, and can only end in Despotism as other Forms have done before it, when the People shall become so corrupted as to need Despotic Government, being incapable of any other. I doubt too whether any other Convention we can obtain, may be able to make a better Constitution: For when you assemble a Number of Men to have the Advantage of their joint Wisdom, you inevitably assemble with those Men all their Prejudices, their Passions, their Errors of Opinion, their local Interests, and their selfish Views. From such an Assembly can a perfect Production be expected? It therefore astonishes me, Sir, to find this System approaching so near to Perfection as it does; and I think it will astonish our Enemies, who are waiting with Confidence to hear that our Councils are confounded, like those of the Builders of Babel, and that our States are on the Point of Separation, only to meet hereafter for the Purpose of cutting one anothers Throats. Thus I consent, Sir, to this Constitution because I expect no better, and because I am not sure that it is not the best. The Opinions I have had of its Errors, I sacrifice to the Public Good. I have never whisper'd a Syllable of them abroad. Within these Walls they were born, and here they shall die. If every one of us in returning to our Constituents were to report the Objections he has had to it, and use his Influence to gain Partizans in support of them, we might prevent its being generally received, and thereby lose all the salutary Effects and great Advantages resulting naturally in our favour among foreign Nations, as well as among ourselves, from our real or apparent Unanimity. Much of the Strength and Efficiency of any Government, in procuring and securing Happiness to the People depends on Opinion, on the general Opinion of the Goodness of that Government as well as of the Wisdom and Integrity of its Governors. I hope therefore that for our own Sakes, as a Part of the People, and for the sake of our Posterity, we shall act heartily and unanimously in recommending this Constitution, wherever our Influence may extend, and turn our future Thoughts and Endeavours to the Means of having it well administred.

On the whole, Sir, I cannot help expressing a Wish, that every Member of the Convention, who may still have Objections to it, would with me on this Occasion doubt a little of his own Infallibility, and to make *manifest* our *Unanimity,* put his Name to this instrument.

After his address had been read Franklin moved, as Gouverneur Morris had planned, that the Convention vote to approve the Constitution by the "unanimous consent of the states present," a form adopted to allow delegates who refused a personal approval, to sign their names. After some debate, the Convention, voting by states, adopted Franklin's motion unanimously, but three delegates present nevertheless withheld their signatures.

Though the Convention proceedings were secret, the nature of Franklin's speech and the respect everywhere accorded him made the early disclosure of his remarks certain. On October 11, 1787, William Lewis, an ardent Philadelphia federalist, sent a paraphrase of the speech to Thomas Jefferson in Paris, probably intending that through him it would be shown to Franklin's friends there. Later that month Nathaniel Gorham, a Massachusetts delegate, asked for a copy to print in Boston newspapers since it was "exceedingly well calculated to correct positive attachment which men are apt to have for their own ideas. . . . [It] inculcates . . . a temper . . . which prevents war and bloodshed. You can have no idea of the weight and influence it would have in N England and I verily believe throughout America." Franklin readily sent "a Copy of that little Speech," observing that though he had "hitherto refused to permit its Publication, . . . your Judgment that it may do good weighs much more with me than my own Scruples." On December 3 the speech, minus some of the most candid remarks about disagreements within the Constitutional Convention, began appearing in newspapers in Boston, where it had "a wonderful effect" on the hotly contested election of delegates to the state convention. Gorham wrote that "it has been read and applauded by almost every-

body—it has been much in use in Town Meetings to incul-
cate moderation and a due respect to the opinions of others,
and is said . . . to contain those sentiments which only can
procure the establishment of a Government in Peace—some
of your old Friends in Boston say that by this Speech they
can see you . . . as the same Man you was forty years ago."

Antifederalists attacked "the puerile speech" and its
author: ". . . it is beneath the dignity of a statesman to consent to a constitution he confessedly dislikes. . . . The doubting Doctor, who has been remarkable for skepticism from
fourteen to four score, [should have doubts about the new
Constitution]. It is not surprising, that when the body is debil-
itated, and the mind worn out . . . the enfeebled sage should
wish to rid himself the trouble of thinking deeply on the fatal
consequences of the assumed powers and bold designs of the
system makers in Philadelphia . . . [his speech contains] confusion and doubt, inconsistencies and absurdities." A Franklin defender replied that the person "whose little mind poured
forth the unqualified torrent of abuse on the GREAT Franklin . . . is advised to attempt an enlargement (if possible) of
his little faculties, which, if effected, he may be able to discern the wisdom of the doctor's address."

New York newspapers reprinted the speech on December
10 and 11, and it appeared in Connecticut during the next
two days, helping to elect federalist delegates in both states.
Franklin approved publication of the full speech in The
American Museum (Philadelphia) in December, 1787. John
Armstrong of Carlisle, Pennsylvania, wrote Franklin on
Christmas Day that "Your last speech in the federal Convention will be in our paper tomorrow" In heavily antifederal
western Pennsylvania, Armstrong hoped it would have "some
good effect" in persuading the people to accept the new Constitution. To defend Franklin against Luther Martin's slan-
ders, Daniel Carroll read the speech before the Maryland
House of Delegates. Madison sent copies of it to George
Washington for his use and information. In South Carolina,
Charles Pinckney noted that had Franklin's final advice been
heeded, abusive charges about the Constitutional Convention
could have been avoided. In the critical months when the
Constitution was under review, Franklin's speech was reprinted at least fifty times, much more often than the Federalist
Papers, and probably was the most influential contribution to
the ratification debates.

In delivering his final speech, Franklin was the right man
saying the right thing at the right time. In 1787 he was
widely reckoned the wisest man in America. As Poor Richard

he had dispensed folklore for a generation. As the conqueror of lightning he seemed in league with the Heavens. As plain Ben Franklin at the Court of Versailles he had persuaded the proudest monarch in Europe to furnish vital help to a band of republican rebels. All through the summer of 1787 he had listened patiently and spoken calmly as the Constitution had been hammered into shape. That he discerned the key to the Convention's success and at the same time sensed the spirit necessary to vitalize the new Constitution surprised no one. James Madison was a more astute political theorist, James Wilson was more learned in the law, and Alexander Hamilton planned more brilliantly for national greatness, but Franklin taught them all the art of conciliation needed to make the Constitution work.

In placing the principle of compromise at the center of the new government, Franklin marked out a feature of American public life indispensable from that day to this. Without day-to-day compromises no nation would have survived for Jefferson, Jackson, Lincoln, and Wilson to inspire with redefined ideals and purposes. Faithful to the mood of Franklin's final speech, Henry Clay, the Great Compromiser, held the Union together on three notable occasions and in innumerable smaller ways as well. From the Supreme Court bench Oliver Wendell Holmes revived a spirit of toleration and humility in a nearly petrified Constitution. Speaker Sam Rayburn's peerless stature as a constructive congressional leader was due largely to his patient adherence to the art of accomplishing the possible by accepting generously and good-naturedly what he could of the dogmas and whims of his colleagues. Franklin's final speech is well known to students of American politics and it has had occasional direct use in pleas for later desperately needed accommodations; the New Republic, for example, printed it in 1919 as part of an appeal for the League of Nations. Pre-eminently, however, it is a landmark in the development of Anglo-American willingness to make a principled concession of principles to give full scope to what a modern philosopher of compromise, T. V. Smith, has called "the unearned increment created by human accord."

The Constitution of the
United States of America
1787

The Preamble

EDITED BY CLARENCE L. VER STEEG

The Preamble to the Constitution of the United States consists of two parts: the first part defines the source of authority from which the constitutional instrument is derived; the second defines the objects for which the Constitution and the government based upon it are formed. The theoretical constitutional relationship expressed by the Preamble remains unchanged today, but the meaning invested in the phrases employed has changed dramatically.

Although repetitive use has softened its revolutionary connotation, the assertion "We the people . . . do ordain and establish this Constitution" set a decidedly radical tone to the ordered blueprint of constitutional government. The Articles of Confederation, adopted in 1781, had been introduced by the explicit statement that the authority of that document was derived from the sovereign states. The Preamble to the Constitution makes clear from the outset that a wholly different constitutional framework, what we have since called the federal system, was being established, in which the people in their sovereign capacity delegated certain powers to the national government and other powers to the states.

Considered in its eighteenth-century context, "people"

101

meant the responsible electorate; thus the basis of authority for the Constitution in a literal sense was a selective group rather than all the people. More precisely, in fact, "people" implied the layer upon layer of oligarchical ruling groups rooted in town and county which rose like a pyramid to an apex of state and interstate connections. Only as democratization occurred did the theoretical and literal definition of "people" more closely correspond.

The second part of the Preamble, which designates the objectives of the Constitution—to form a more perfect union, to insure domestic tranquillity, to provide for the common defense, to promote the general welfare, and to secure the blessings of liberty—reflects, in its contemporary context, the anxieties of the 1780's. The Articles of Confederation, it was feared, had not measured up to the exigencies of the union; thus, "a more perfect union" was desirable. The specter of Shays' Rebellion, as well as other domestic disturbances, awakened latent fears that "domestic tranquillity" would end, that disorder would degenerate into chaos, that chaos would lead to tyranny, and that tyranny would bring a loss of liberty for all men. Historians recognize that these fears were greatly exaggerated and even unwarranted, as many men realized at the time, but the objectives outlined in the Preamble derived at least a part of their definition from these fears. Fortunately, the nobility of expression in the Preamble allowed its familiar phrases to be invested with new and more profound meaning as the American experiment in government unfolded. In this way the "objectives" as stated in the Preamble became principles.

In the Philadelphia convention on August 6, 1787, the first draft of the Constitution was reported by the Committee of Detail (also called the Committee of Five), Nathaniel Gorham, Oliver Ellsworth, Edmund Randolph, John Rutledge, and James Wilson. The Preamble in this draft embraced the intent of the final version, but lacked grace, felicity, and precision. "We, the people of the states of [the names of the various states] do ordain, declare, and establish, the following Constitution for the government of ourselves and our posterity." This draft of the Preamble was followed by Article I, "The style of this government shall be 'The United States of America.' " No change was made in this draft until the Federal Convention neared the end of its work. A five-member Committee of Revision was elected on September 8 "to revise the style." William Samuel Johnson, Alexander Hamilton, Gouverneur Morris, James Madison, and Rufus King were named, with Johnson designated as chairman. The committee entrusted the principal task of rewriting the document to Gouverneur Morris, and one of his specific contributions was the revision of the Preamble into its final form.

WE THE People of the United States, in Order to form a more perfect Union, establish Justice, insure domestic Tranquillity, provide for the common defence, promote the general Welfare, and secure the Blessings of Liberty to ourselves and our Posterity, do ordain and establish this Constitution for the United States of America.

The meaning of the Preamble was debated in the state ratifying conventions of Massachusetts, New York, Pennsylvania, and North Carolina, but the issues involved in the debate were best represented in the Virginia convention. The flaming patriot and founder, Patrick Henry, challenged the right of the delegates to the Federal Convention to introduce the Constitution on the basis of "We, the people." "What right had they to say, We, the people? . . ." he demanded. "Who authorized them to speak the language of, We the people, instead of, We the states? . . . The people gave them no power to use their name. That they exceeded their power is perfectly clear."

Governor Randolph and Edmund Pendleton answered Henry. "Who," Pendleton asked, "but the people can delegate powers? Who but the people have a right to form a government? . . . If the objection be, that the Union ought to be not of the people, but of the state governments, then I think the choice of the former very happy and proper. What have the state governments to do with it? Were they to determine, the people would not, in that case, be the judges upon what terms it was adopted."

This exchange skirted the essential issue, and it remained for Henry ("Light-Horse Harry") Lee, a veteran soldier of the Revolution, to pronounce the truth of the matter. "This expression [We the people] was introduced into that paper [the Constitution] with great propriety. This system is submitted to the people for their consideration, because on them it

The Preamble and the other parts of the Constitution are quoted in this volume from the "literal print" of the document, as reproduced in *The Constitution of the United States of America: Analysis and Interpretation* (Washington, D.C.: U.S. Government Printing Office, 1964). The original manuscript is in the National Archives, Washington, D.C.

is to operate, if adopted. It is not binding on the people until it becomes their act." *Judge Iredell in the North Carolina Convention agreed with this interpretation.* "We, the People, was not to be applied to the members [of the Federal Convention] themselves, but was to be the style of the Constitution, when it should be ratified in their respective states."

This construction became the touchstone for judicial decision, once the Constitution was ratified by the appropriate number of state conventions. In M'Culloch v. Maryland, *1819, Chief Justice Marshall declared:*

> *From these Conventions the constitution derives its whole authority. The government proceeds directly from the people; is "ordained and established" in the name of the people; and is declared to be ordained "in order to form a more perfect union, establish justice, insure domestic tranquillity, and secure the blessings of liberty to themselves and to their posterity." The assent of the States, in their sovereign capacity, is implied in calling a Convention, and thus submitting that instrument to the people. But the people were at perfect liberty to accept or reject it; and their act was final. . . . The government of the Union, then . . . is emphatically and truly a government of the people. In form and in substance it emanates from them, its powers are granted by them, and are to be exercised directly on them, and for their benefit.*

In effect, the Preamble serves as the artery which transmits life to the Constitution by infusing it with authority in somewhat the same fashion as Article VI, Section 2, specifies precisely how that authority is to operate.

The theme enunciated in the Preamble pervades almost every convolution of the national mind—from President Lincoln's Gettysburg Address to the shrill of the political hack, from Whittier's "The Poor Voter on Election Day" to the rote recitation of classroom exercises in government, from the Insular Cases (especially Downes v. Bidwell, *182 U.S. 244 [1901]) of judicial import to the oversimplified superpatriotism of the newspaper tabloids, from the serious education of the immigrant-citizen who wishes to learn his responsibilities, to the complaint of the deported mobster who believes his rights are being denied.*

In fact, after more than a century of experience with the Constitution, the theme of the Preamble was invoked so frequently as to become perfunctory. In An Economic Interpretation of the Constitution (1913), Charles A. Beard reminded his readers that the Constitution was not created by "the whole people." He painstakingly reviewed the contemporary economic interests which, in his judgment, challenged the "juristic" view of the origins and nature of the Constitution and the misleading use of "We the people . . . do ordain and establish this Constitution . . ." Beard's book was invaluable in rescuing the Preamble and, indeed, the Constitution as a whole, from the antiseptic milieu that had enveloped it. But Beard, while bringing a renewed sense of reality and earthiness back into the twentieth-century discussion, failed to recognize that the theoretical statement of the relationship to the people as the source of constitutional authority was life-giving rather than lifeless, simply because the framers had the perception to allow the definition of "people" to change.

Abandonment of property requirements for voting, emancipation of slaves, the Fourteenth Amendment, the enfranchisement of women, and civil-rights legislation of 1964–65 broadened the definition of "people" who do (present tense), not did, "ordain and establish this Constitution. . . ." In accordance with the Preamble, therefore, the people as currently conceived continually animate anew the Constitution and the objects of government it enunciates. This is true even though the theoretical equality implied by the source of authority is not fulfilled in its exercise, because of special interests which are reflected in the unequal financial power and social organization of those who live under the Constitution, a fact clearly recognized by the framers. Unfortunately, the source of constitutional authority is too frequently confused with the empirical operation of the government under that authority.

Article I

EDITED BY C. HERMAN PRITCHETT

Article I of the Constitution established the national legislature and defined the legislative powers of the new government. In creating the Congress of the United States, the framers of the Constitution had a model which it was their conscious purpose not to follow—the Congress then existing under the Articles of Confederation. That body had grudgingly authorized the Constitutional Convention to meet for the "sole and express purpose of revising the Articles of Confederation."

Congress under the Articles was a single house representing the thirteen states, each of which had one vote. A two-thirds vote was required for the adoption of important measures, and amendments to the Articles required unanimous consent. There was no separation of executive from legislative powers; Congress appointed such committees and civil officers as seemed necessary to carry on executive work. Congress could not levy taxes; it could only make requisitions on the states for its fiscal needs. Nor could Congress regulate interstate commerce, with the result that the states freely retaliated against each other's trade.

When the Convention met in Philadelphia in May, 1787, its members agreed that a stronger governmental structure was required. Two competing plans were presented. The Virginia Plan proposed to scrap the Articles and create a strong national government. The New Jersey Plan, supported by the smaller states, would have maintained a confederation while giving it more adequate powers. The New Jersey Plan was defeated within the first few weeks of the Convention, and from that point on the framers accepted the obligation to design a new national government with the power to collect its own taxes, control commerce among the states, make its own laws and enforce them in its own courts.

The legislature under the new Constitution, unlike Congress under the Articles, had to share governmental power with the executive and the judiciary. Montesquieu's work on the separation of powers was known in America at that time and was occasionally quoted at the Convention, but it was probably not very influential with the delegates. The allocation of powers to three separate branches, and the division of authority so that each could impose some limits on the actions of the other two, were adopted not to fit any theoretical models but to handle the very practical problems the Convention faced.

In determining that Congress would be composed of two houses, the Convention was following the example of England and almost all of the states. The delegates generally agreed from the beginning that the members of the House of Representatives would be elected directly by the people, and that the number allotted to each state would be proportionate to its population. Much more difficult was the composition and basis of selection of the Senate. The general sentiment was for election of senators by the state legislatures. The Virginia Plan called for Senate representation to be based on population, just as in the House.

This issue was the rock on which the Convention almost foundered. The small states, which under the Articles, and in the Convention itself, had equal voting strength with the large states, would not agree to any plan which did not guarantee their status in some way. The discussions and arguments were long and bitter. Compromises were proposed by the large states, such as that Senate representation be on the basis of state wealth, or that the states be divided into three population classes, with one, two, and three senators respectively. But on July 16 equal representation of the states in the Senate was adopted by a five-to-four vote, with Massachusetts divided and New York not voting. Madison records that the next morning the large states held an indignation meeting to discuss what could be done, but that "the time was wasted in vague conversation." And so the decision stood.

At first the Convention sought to avoid spelling out the powers of Congress, proposing instead that it have the right "to legislate in all cases to which the separate States are incompetent," or "in all cases for the general interests of the

Union." But several delegates objected, asking for a more
"exact enumeration" of powers. Ultimately the Convention
agreed, and spelled out in detail in Section 8 of Article I a
long list of powers, the absence of which in the Confederation had made the movement for a new Constitution necessary.

While the general emphasis of the Convention was on
assuring that Congress had sufficient authority, conflicting sectional interests led the delegates to insist on certain prohibitions on national power. The slave interest was
the one which most feared discriminatory action by the new
government. A majority of the Convention was opposed to
"this infernal trafic," as George Mason called it, but North
Carolina, South Carolina, and Georgia would have refused to
join the Union without some guarantee of the status of slavery. Consequently a compromise was adopted in Section 9,
guaranteeing no interference with the importation of slaves
until 1808. The prohibition placed on the power of Congress
to levy direct taxes, unless they were apportioned among the
states according to population, also represented the efforts of
slavery supporters to assure that internal taxes applying solely
to slaves could not be adopted.

The relation of congressional powers to those of the
states was considered in several contexts. The original Virginia Plan proposed that Congress have the power "to negative
all laws passed by the several States, contravening in the
opinion of the National Legislature the articles of Union."
This idea of congressional veto of state laws was not popular
and was dropped, being replaced by the supremacy clause of
Article VI. However, there were certain areas in which the
delegates so strongly opposed state action that, in Section 10,
they banned legislation in forthright language. The sharpest
antagonism was toward state paper money and debtor relief
laws, which were among the subjects specifically prohibited to
the states.

Article I is by far the longest of the seven articles composing the original Constitution. In fact, it amounts in length to
more than half of the entire document. It incorporates most
of the basic decisions made by the Convention, decisions
which primarily determined the nature and character of the
new government. In inventive genius it may not quite compare with Article II, which created the Presidency. But it established a representative, responsible, and workable legislature; it successfully blended the principles of a national and a
federal system; and it implemented the conclusion that

domestic tranquillity, the common defense, and the general welfare could not be achieved except through a government endowed with adequate powers.

☆

Section. 1. All legislative Powers herein granted shall be vested in a Congress of the United States, which shall consist of a Senate and House of Representatives.

Section. 2. The House of Representatives shall be composed of Members chosen every second Year by the People of the several States, and the Electors in each State shall have the Qualifications requisite for Electors of the most numerous Branch of the State Legislature.

No Person shall be a Representative who shall not have attained to the age of twenty five Years, and been seven Years a Citizen of the United States, and who shall not, when elected, be an Inhabitant of that State in which he shall be chosen.

Representatives and direct Taxes shall be apportioned among the several States which may be included within this Union, according to their respective Numbers, which shall be determined by adding to the whole Number of free Persons, including those bound to Service for a Term of Years, and excluding Indians not taxed, three fifths of all other Persons. The actual Enumeration shall be made within three Years after the first Meeting of the Congress of the United States, and within every subsequent Term of ten Years, in such Manner as they shall by Law direct. The Number of Representatives shall not exceed one for every thirty Thousand, but each State shall have at Least one Representative; and until such enumeration shall be made, the State of New Hampshire shall be entitled to chuse three, Massachusetts eight, Rhode-Island and Providence Plantations one, Connecticut five, New-York six, New Jersey four, Pennsylvania eight, Delaware one, Maryland six, Virginia ten, North Carolina five, South Carolina five, and Georgia three.

When vacancies happen in the Representation from any State, the Executive Authority thereof shall issue Writs of Election to fill such Vacancies.

The House of Representatives shall chuse their Speaker and other Officers; and shall have the sole Power of Impeachment.

Section. 3. The Senate of the United States shall be composed of two Senators from each State, chosen by the Legislature thereof, for six Years; and each Senator shall have one Vote.

Immediately after they shall be assembled in Consequence of the first Election, they shall be divided as equally as may be into three Classes. The Seats of the Senators of the first Class shall be vacated at the Expiration of the second Year, of the second Class at the Expiration of the fourth Year, and of the third Class at the Expiration of the sixth Year, so that one third may be chosen every second Year; and if Vacancies happen by Resignation, or otherwise, during the Recess of the Legislature of any State, the Executive thereof may make temporary Appointments until the next Meeting of the Legislature, which shall then fill such Vacancies.

No Person shall be a Senator who shall not have attained to the Age of thirty Years, and been nine Years a Citizen of the United States, and who shall not, when elected, be an Inhabitant of that State for which he shall be chosen.

The Vice President of the United States shall be President of the Senate, but shall have no Vote, unless they be equally divided.

The Senate shall chuse their other Officers, and also a President pro tempore, in the Absence of the Vice President, or when he shall exercise the Office of President of the United States.

The Senate shall have the sole Power to try all Impeachments. When sitting for that Purpose, they shall be on Oath or Affirmation. When the President of the United States is tried the Chief Justice shall preside: And no Person shall be convicted without the Concurrence of two thirds of the Members present.

Judgment in Cases of Impeachment shall not extend further than to removal from Office, and disqualification to hold and enjoy any Office of honor, Trust or Profit under the United States: but the Party convicted shall nevertheless be liable and subject to Indictment, Trial, Judgment and Punishment, according to Law.

Section. 4. The Times, Places and Manner of holding Elections for Senators and Representatives, shall be prescribed in each State by the Legislature thereof; but the Congress may at any time by Law make or alter such Regulations, except as to the Places of chusing Senators.

The Congress shall assemble at least once in every Year, and such Meeting shall be on the first Monday in December, unless they shall by Law appoint a different Day.

Section. 5. Each House shall be the Judge of the Elections, Returns and Qualifications of its own Members, and a Majority of each shall constitute a Quorum to do Business; but a smaller Number may adjourn from day to day, and may be authorized to compel the Attendance of absent Members, in such Manner, and under such Penalties as each House may provide.

Each House may determine the Rules of its Proceedings, punish its Members for disorderly Behaviour, and, with the Concurrence of two thirds, expel a Member.

Each House shall keep a Journal of its Proceedings, and from time to time publish the same, excepting such Parts as may in their Judgment require Secrecy; and the Yeas and Nays of the Members of either House on any question shall, at the Desire of one fifth of those Present, be entered on the Journal.

Neither House, during the Session of Congress, shall, without the Consent of the other, adjourn for more than three days, nor to any other Place than that in which the two Houses shall be sitting.

Section. 6. The Senators and Representatives shall receive a Compensation for their Services, to be ascertained by Law, and paid out of the Treasury of the United States. They shall in all Cases, except Treason, Felony and Breach of the Peace, be privileged from Arrest during their attendance at the Session of their respective Houses, and in going to and returning from the same; and for any Speech or Debate in either House, they shall not be questioned in any other Place.

No Senator or Representative shall, during the Time for which he was elected, be appointed to any civil Office under the Authority of the United States, which shall have been created, or the Emoluments whereof shall have been encreased during such time; and no Person holding any Office under the United States, shall be a Member of either House during his Continuance in Office.

Section. 7. All Bills for raising Revenue shall originate in the House of Representatives; but the Senate may propose or concur with amendments as on other Bills.

Every Bill which shall have passed the House of Representatives and the Senate, shall, before it become a Law, be presented to the President of the United States; If he approve he shall sign it, but if not he shall return it, with his Objections to that House in which it shall have originated, who shall enter the Objections at large on their Journal, and proceed to reconsider it. If after such Reconsideration two thirds of that House shall agree to pass the Bill, it shall be sent, together with the Objections, to the other House, by which it shall likewise be reconsidered, and if approved by two thirds of that House, it shall become a Law. But in all such Cases the Votes of both Houses shall be determined by yeas and Nays, and the Names of the Persons voting for and against the Bill shall be entered on the Journal of each House respectively. If any Bill shall not be returned by the President within ten Days (Sunday excepted) after it shall have been presented to him, the Same shall be a Law, in like Manner as if he had signed it, unless the Congress by their Adjournment prevent its Return, in which Case it shall not be a Law.

Every Order, Resolution, or Vote to which the Concurrence of the Senate and House of Representatives may be necessary (except on a question of Adjournment) shall be presented to the President of the United States; and before the Same shall take Effect, shall be approved by him, or being disapproved by him, shall be repassed by two thirds of the Senate and House of Representatives, according to the Rules and Limitations prescribed in the Case of a Bill.

Section. 8. The Congress shall have Power To lay and collect Taxes, Duties, Imposts and Excises, to pay the Debts and provide for the common Defence and general Welfare of the United States; but all Duties, Imposts and Excises shall be uniform throughout the United States;

To borrow Money on the credit of the United States;

To regulate Commerce with foreign Nations, and among the several States, and with the Indian Tribes;

To establish an uniform Rule of Naturalization, and uniform Laws on the subject of Bankruptcies throughout the United States;

To coin Money, regulate the Value thereof, and of foreign Coin, and fix the Standard of Weights and Measures;

To provide for the Punishment of counterfeiting the Securities and current Coin of the United States;

To establish Post Offices and post Roads;

To promote the Progress of Science and useful Arts, by securing for limited Times to Authors and Inventors the exclusive Right to their respective Writings and Discoveries;

To constitute Tribunals inferior to the supreme Court;

To define and punish Piracies and Felonies committed on the high Seas, and Offences against the Law of Nations;

To declare War, grant Letters of Marque and Reprisal, and make Rules concerning Captures on Land and Water;

To raise and support Armies, but no Appropriation of Money to that Use shall be for a longer Term than two Years;

To provide and maintain a Navy;

To make Rules for the Government and Regulation of the land and naval Forces;

To provide for calling forth the Militia to execute the Laws of the Union, suppress Insurrections and repel Invasions;

To provide for organizing, arming, and disciplining, the Militia, and for governing such Part of them as may be employed in the Service of the United States, reserving to the States respectively, the Appointment of the Officers, and the Authority of training the Militia according to the discipline prescribed by Congress;

To exercise exclusive Legislation in all Cases whatsoever, over such District (not exceeding ten Miles square) as may, by Cession of Particular States, and the Acceptance of Congress, become the Seat of the Government of the United States, and to exercise like Authority over all Places purchased by the Consent of the Legislature of the State in which the Same shall be, for the Erection of Forts, Magazines, Arsenals, dock-Yards, and other needful Buildings;—And

To make all Laws which shall be necessary and proper for carrying into Execution the foregoing Powers, and all other Powers vested by this Constitution in the Government of the United States, or in any Department or Officer thereof.

Section. 9. The Migration or Importation of such Persons as any of the States now existing shall think proper to admit, shall not be prohibited by the Congress prior to the Year one thousand eight hundred and eight, but a Tax or duty may be imposed on such Importation, not exceeding ten dollars for each Person.

The Privilege of the Writ of Habeas Corpus shall not be suspended, unless when in Cases of Rebellion or Invasion the Public Safety may require it.

No Bill of Attainder or ex post facto Law shall be passed.

No Capitation, or other direct, Tax shall be laid, unless in Proportion to the Census of Enumeration herein before directed to be taken.

No Tax or Duty shall be laid on Articles exported from any State.

No Preference shall be given by any Regulation of Commerce or Revenue to the Ports of one State over those of another; nor shall Vessels bound to, or from, one State, be obliged to enter, clear or pay Duties in another.

No Money shall be drawn from the Treasury, but in Consequence of Appropriations made by Law; and a regular Statement and Account of the Receipts and Expenditures of all public Money shall be published from time to time.

No Title of Nobility shall be granted by the United States: And no Person holding any Office of Profit or Trust under them, shall, without the Consent of the Congress, accept of any present, Emolument, Office, or Title, of any kind whatever, from any King, Prince or foreign State.

Section. 10. No State shall enter into any Treaty, Alliance, or Confederation; grant Letters of Marque and Reprisal; coin Money; emit Bills of Credit; make any Thing but gold and silver Coin a Tender in Payment of Debts; pass any Bill of Attainder, ex post facto Law, or Law impairing the Obligation of Contracts, or grant any Title of Nobility.

No State shall, without the Consent of the Congress, lay any Imposts or Duties on Imports or Exports, except what may be absolutely necessary for executing it's inspection Laws: and the net Produce of all Duties and Imposts, laid by any State on Imports or Exports, shall be for the Use of the Treasury of the United States; and all such Laws shall be subject to the Revision and Controul of the Congress.

No State shall, without the Consent of Congress, lay any Duty of Tonnage, keep Troops, or Ships of War in time of Peace, enter into any Agreement or Compact with another State, or with a foreign Power, or engage in War, unless actually invaded, or in such imminent Danger as will not admit of delay.

As far as the organization and structure of Congress is concerned Article 1 of the Constitution did its job well. Little has been required in the way of amendment. The principal change was that effected by the Seventeenth Amendment, adopted in 1913, which provided for the election of senators by popular vote instead of by the state legislatures.

A major issue in regard to the House of Representatives has been its size and the districting problem. The number of seats, originally 65, was increased by Congress after each decennial census until a figure of 435 was reached in 1911. That number was then fixed as the permanent size of the House, on the ground that any further increase would make the body unwieldy. These 435 seats are reapportioned among the states according to population after each census, with the aid of complicated mathematical formulas.

Having been informed of its quota of seats in the House, each state is then responsible for dividing its territory into the appropriate number of electoral districts. Fair principles of representation require that these districts be roughly equal in population, but in fact they have often been quite unequal, either because the state legislatures refused to redraw the boundaries when there had been population changes or because boundaries were redrawn with deliberate discriminatory intent. In Colegrove v. Green, *328 U.S. 549 (1946),* the Supreme Court refused to compel the remedying of gross inequalities in Illinois congressional districts, on the ground that this was a "political" question in which courts should not interfere. However, in Baker v. Carr, *369 U.S. 186 (1962),* the Court reversed itself to the extent of opening the way for judicial review of legislative apportionments. Then in Wesberry v. Sanders, *376 U.S. 1 (1964),* the Court held that the Constitution had the "plain objective of making equal representation for equal numbers of people the fundamental goal for the House of Representatives." Consequently congressional districts were required to be made roughly equal in population, and the long-standing overrepresentation of rural areas in the House was ended.

With respect to participation in elections, Article I, Section 2, provided that persons in each state having "the qualifications requisite for electors of the most numerous branch" of that state's legislature would be eligible to vote in federal elections. Under this arrangement the states determine which of their citizens have the privilege of the franchise. However, once a state has decided who is eligible to vote, then Section 2 steps in to guarantee their right to vote for federal officials.

The freedom of a state to determine its electorate has subsequently been limited by four of the Amendments to the Constitution. The "equal protection" clause of the Fourteenth Amendment has been interpreted to forbid discriminatory practices by state election officials. The Fifteenth Amendment forbids denial of the franchise because of race or color, and the Nineteenth guarantees the vote to women. The Twenty-fourth Amendment, adopted in 1964, forbids the states to use the poll tax as a voting requirement in federal elections. These constitutional standards are not self-enforcing, however, and federal action has been required to remedy the long-standing denial of the franchise to Negroes in southern states. The Civil Rights Acts of 1957 and 1960 marked the beginning of congressional interest in this problem, but it was not until the

Voting Rights Act of 1965 that Congress effectively inter-
vened to compel the grant of the franchise to Negroes in cer-
tain recalcitrant areas. The Act, which suspended voting qual-
ification laws such as literacy tests in states where these tests
had been used to bar Negroes from voting, and provided for
the appointment of federal voting registrars where local regis-
trars had refused to register Negroes, was upheld by the Su-
preme Court in South Carolina v. Katzenbach, 86 S. Ct. 803
(1966).

Although Article I vests "all legislative powers herein grant-
ed" in Congress, it also makes the President a necessary partic-
ipant in the lawmaking process. All legislation must be sub-
mitted to the President for his signature before it becomes
effective. Initially Presidents vetoed proposed legislation only
when they believed it to be unconstitutional. Andrew Jackson
was the first President to veto bills simply because he regarded
them as objectionable. Vetoes are seldom overridden by Con-
gress, since to do so requires a two-thirds majority in both
houses. Franklin Roosevelt vetoed 631 bills, and only 9 were
repassed over his veto.

The congressional power of impeachment has proved to be
too cumbersome to be of much importance. While the threat
to impeach the President is sometimes heard during periods of
political turmoil, the attempt was actually made only once. In
the aftermath of the Civil War, the Radical Republicans in
Congress, motivated by vindictive partisanship, sought to im-
peach Andrew Johnson, but the Senate failed by a margin of
one vote to convict him. The defeat of that effort has discour-
aged subsequent use of impeachment as a weapon for political
purposes. Apart from Andrew Johnson's case, impeachment
actions have been brought against nine federal judges, four of
whom were convicted, and one Cabinet member.

Problems of interpreting the powers granted to Congress by
Article I arose very early in American history. At the end of
the long list of powers granted in Section 8, Congress is au-
thorized "to make all laws which shall be necessary and prop-
er for carrying into execution the foregoing powers. . . ." The
relationship of this clause to the enumerated powers preceding
it became very quickly the subject of controversy between
Federalists and Jeffersonians, between broad and strict con-
structionists. The issue was joined over Hamilton's plan for a
national bank, as accepted by the First Congress. There was
no authorization in the Constitution for Congress to create a
bank, so President Washington invited Hamilton and Jefferson
to submit their respective views on whether he should sign the
bill.

Jefferson denied that Congress could create a bank. He emphasized the "necessary" in the necessary and proper clause. Since all the enumerated powers could be carried out without a bank, it was not necessary and consequently not authorized. Hamilton, on the other hand, argued that the powers granted to Congress included the right to employ "all the means requisite and fairly applicable to the attainment of the ends of such power," unless they were specifically forbidden or immoral or contrary to the "essential ends of political society." Washington signed the bill.

In 1819 Chief Justice John Marshall gave the definitive statement of the Hamiltonian theory in the great case of M'Culloch v. Maryland, 4 Wheat. 316. Again congressional authority to incorporate a bank—the Second Bank of the United States—was at issue. Marshall found implied congressional authority to establish a bank in the expressly granted powers to collect taxes, to borrow money, to regulate commerce, to declare and conduct a war; for "it may with great reason be contended, that a government, entrusted with such ample powers, on the due exercise of which the happiness and prosperity of the nation so vitally depends, must also be entrusted with ample means for their execution." The Jeffersonian interpretation, he said, would "almost annihilate" the right of Congress to select the means for carrying out its purposes.

Among the enumerated powers in Section 8, the authority "to regulate commerce with foreign nations and among the several states . . ." has been perhaps the most significant and certainly the most litigated. The language is in terms of a positive grant of power to Congress, but in fact its purpose was also to take away from the states this power which they had so seriously abused under the Articles of Confederation. As it turned out, Congress was slow to utilize its authority over commerce, and for the first century of national existence the primary problem in interpreting the commerce clause was to decide how much regulatory power remained with the states.

In the famous case of Gibbons v. Ogden, 9 Wheat. 1 (1824), John Marshall held that New York State could not grant a monopoly of steamboat transportation on waters within the state. In the course of his opinion Marshall laid down principles which have largely dominated all subsequent thinking about the commerce clause. One of his important pronouncements was that congressional power over commerce "may very well be restricted to that commerce which concerns more states than one." Eventually this suggestion was developed into the distinction between "interstate" and "intrastate" commerce.

Interstate commerce is typically defined as commerce which crosses a state line, and over such commerce Congress has complete control insofar as it wishes to exercise it—not only to protect and promote, but also to restrict or even to prohibit. Congress has thus been able to use the commerce power as a kind of national police power to proceed against such evils as lottery tickets, impure food and drugs, and the white-slave traffic.

Congressional power has never depended entirely on the test of crossing a state line, however. Marshall also recognized that commercial transactions taking place entirely within a state might have such an effect on commerce among the states as to justify or require their regulation. The Court has employed the "effect" doctrine in numerous decisions to justify congressional regulation, but in 1935 and 1936 it struck down certain New Deal recovery statutes which relied on this claim. This proved to be only a temporary aberration, however, for in NLRB v. Jones & Laughlin Corp., 301 U.S. 1 (1937), the Court returned to what it called a "practical conception" of interstate commerce and upheld the constitutionality of the Wagner Act. This decision stated such a broad basis for the commerce power that few serious questions about the constitutional scope of congressional authority over commerce have subsequently arisen. In the words of Justice Cardozo, the commerce power is "as broad as the need that evokes it."

The grant of taxing power to Congress in Section 8 has proved adequate for federal needs and has created few problems. The ban in Section 2 on direct taxes unless apportioned by population did cause trouble, however. A federal income tax adopted by Congress in 1894 was held by the Supreme Court to be a direct tax, and since it was not apportioned by population it was unconstitutional. This decision, for which there was little justification, delayed the inauguration of income taxation until 1913, when the Sixteenth Amendment was adopted.

Similarly the spending authority of Section 8 leaves Congress substantially free from limitations. The principal tests have occurred in connection with federal grant-in-aid legislation under which Congress makes federal funds available to the states for financing programs which Congress wishes to promote. An effort to attack the constitutionality of such federal spending under the Maternity Act of 1921 was frustrated by the Supreme Court in Massachusetts v. Mellon, 262 U.S. 347 (1923), on the ground that no federal taxpayer had

*legal standing to bring such a suit. The only exception to this
rule that the appropriating power is judicially unreview-
able occurred in* United States v. Butler, 297 U.S. 1
*(1936), where the joining of a taxing and spending program in
the same agricultural program made it possible for the Supreme Court to consider the purpose of the spending and to
hold it unconstitutional.*

*Congress has constitutionally unlimited power to borrow
money. There is no specific authority to issue paper money,
and the "greenbacks" by which the Civil War was financed
were at first held unconstitutional in 1870 by a four-to-three
vote of the Supreme Court. However, after two vacancies on
the Court had been filled by President Grant, the Court reconsidered and overruled the earlier decision by a vote of five to
four.*

*The power of Congress to conduct investigations is not
mentioned in Article I. It is an implied power, supplementary
to the specifically assigned functions to legislate, to appropriate, to pass on the elections and returns of members, and so
on. It is an extremely broad power, because the need of Congress for information is broad, but it is not entirely free from
constitutional limitations. In* McGrain v. Daugherty, 273 U.S.
135 *(1927), the Supreme Court, while upholding the inquiry
Congress had made into the Teapot Dome scandals, did point
out that Congress had no "general" power to inquire into private affairs and compel disclosures, and that a witness might
rightfully refuse to answer where the bounds of congressional
power were exceeded, or the questions were not pertinent to
the matter under inquiry. In* Watkins v. United States, 354
U.S. 178 *(1957), the Court said that investigatory power was
limited by the First Amendment and upheld the refusal of a
witness to testify before the House Un-American Activities
Committee, but this position was substantially abandoned in
1959, when the Court reverted to the policy earlier urged by
Justice Jackson: "I should . . . leave the responsibility for the
behavior of its committees squarely on the shoulders of Congress."*

*The American Congress has had its successes and its fail-
ures. The Senate, with its special responsibility in the ratifying
of treaties and the confirmation of executive and judicial appointments, has certainly been the most influential and distinguished second house in the history of representative institutions. For the most part the failures of Congress have not resulted from provisions of Article I, but from practices adopted
voluntarily by the two houses—the seniority rule on committees, archaic rules of procedure, abuse of unlimited debate in*

the Senate. Congress has performed least well when, either because of weakness in the executive or the ambition of its own leaders, it has sought to run the government. Congress is an institution adapted to discussion, not to action. Its task is appraisal and judgment, not leadership. Article I created a sound legislative structure, but each generation has to supply the wisdom and understanding to make it work.

Article II

EDITED BY ARTHUR SCHLESINGER, JR.

Article II of the Constitution—the article dealing with the executive power—emerged, like the rest of the document, from the debates at Philadelphia in 1787. Its initial source was the so-called Virginia Plan, drafted in large lart by James Madison and presented to the Federal Convention by Edmund Randolph. Randolph's seventh resolution proposed a "National Executive" to be "chosen by the National Legislature" for a fixed term and to be ineligible a second time. The executive, "besides a general authority to exeeute the National laws, . . . ought to enjoy the Executive rights vested in Congress by the Confederation."

This language immediately raised a number of questions: Should the executive consist of one person or of several persons? Who should be eligible for it? How long should its term be? Should it indeed be chosen by the national legislature? Should it indeed be ineligible for a second term? What were these "Executive rights"? Should it share these rights with some form of executive council? Should it, by itself or in association with the council, have the authority to negative acts of the national legislature? What should happen in case of death or disability? Should it be liable to impeachment?

On June 1, 1787, three days after Randolph submitted his plan, the Committee of the Whole began its consideration of these matters. It was evident from the start that a deeper question lay beneath the particular issues—the question whether the proposed executive should be, as Roger Sherman of Connecticut believed, "Nothing more than an institution for car-

121

rying the will of the Legislature into effect," or, as Gouverneur Morris of Pennsylvania argued, "the guardian of the people, even of the lower classes, agst Legislative tyranny." Those who wished to subordinate the executive to the legislature tended to favor a plural executive, chosen by the legislature, ineligible for reapportionment, hedged in by an executive council, endowed with specific and limited powers, and subject to impeachment. Those who wished to secure the independence and authority of the executive tended to favor a single executive, chosen by the people, indefinitely re-eligible, unhampered by an executive council, endowed with general power, and free from the threat of impeachment.

Thus, on the first day of debate over Randolph's seventh resolution, James Wilson of Pennsylvania advocated a single magistrate "as giving most energy, dispatch and responsibility to the office," while Randolph denounced "unity in the Executive magistracy" as "the foetus of monarchy" and called for an executive of three, to be drawn from different parts of the country. The Convention itself soon decided on a single executive. The question of who should choose this single executive gave more trouble. Roger Sherman, supporting the approach in the Virginia Plan, contended for his "appointment by the Legislature, and for making him absolutely dependent on that body, as it was the will of that which was to be executed." Gouverneur Morris responded that the executive "will be the mere creature of the Legisl: if appointed & impeachable by that body. He ought to be elected by the people at large." The Convention seemed to favor the thesis of the Virginia Plan and endorsed the idea of legislative choice at least five times in the course of the debates. In similar manner the argument between dependence and authority in the executive determined the reaction of the delegates to questions of length of term, re-eligibility, veto power, and the rest.

On July 24 the Convention appointed a Committee of Detail to embody the recommendations of the Committee of the Whole in a comprehensive draft of the new Constitution. The Committee of Detail reported back on August 6. Article X of its draft began: "The Executive Power of the United States shall be vested in a single person." The article went on to provide that this person should be chosen by the national legislature for one term of seven years; he could not serve a second time. He was to be charged with executing the laws. He could appoint officers in all cases not otherwise provided for by the Constitution (but Article IX gave the Senate power to appoint ambassadors and Supreme Court justices). He would be commander-in-chief of the armed forces. He had the power to receive foreign ambassadors (but Article IX gave the Senate power to make treaties). He could convene and adjourn the legislature. He was subject to impeachment; and, in case of removal, disability, or death, the President of the Senate was to exercise his powers and duties. In addition, Article VI gave the executive the power to veto acts of the legislature (and the legislature the power to override his veto by a two-thirds vote).

The advocates of a strong executive had made progress; but several provisions, notably those giving Congress authority to elect the executive, make treaties, and appoint high officials, still made for the clear subordination of the executive to the legislative. The Convention discussed these and other questions for another five weeks and then, on September 8, appointed a Committee on Style to write a final draft. Gouverneur Morris, chairman of this committee, was probably the main author of the text submitted to the Convention on September 12, and he undoubtedly took full advantage of the opportunity to strengthen the presidential prerogative.

Article II of the final draft began with an unequivocal affirmation of presidential autonomy and authority: "The executive power shall be vested in a president of the United States of America." This represented a notable expansion of the language in the earlier draft. In other respects too the new text differed from the proposals of the Committee of Detail. Most important of all, it took the election of the President away from the national legislature and assigned it to electors designated in whatever manner each state legislature might direct; the executive, said Madison, a little sweepingly, "is now to be elected by the people." The new draft also shortened the presidential term to four years and removed the ban to indefinite re-eligibility. It transferred to the President the authority to make treaties, though with the advice and consent of the Senate. It transferred to him authority to appoint all government officials, including ambassadors and Supreme Court justices, though again with the Senate's advice and consent. In case of removal, disability, or death, his powers and duties would now devolve on the Vice-President; Congress was authorized to make provision by law for succession beyond the Vice-President. And it added a definition of the conditions of presidential eligibility.

These changes provoked surprisingly little debate, partly because the delegates were eager to wrap the document up and go home, partly because, as Pierce Butler of South Carolina wrote a friend, "many of the members cast their eyes toward General Washington as President; and shaped their ideas of the Powers to be given a President, by their opinions of his Virtue." In any case the Convention adopted the Constitution, including Article II, on September 15, the document was ratified in another year, and the world's first modern experiment in democratic government began.

Section. 1. The executive Power shall be vested in a President of the United States of America. He shall hold his Office during the term of four Years, and, together with the Vice President, chosen for the same Term, be elected, as follows

Each State shall appoint, in such Manner as the Legislature thereof may direct, a number of Electors, equal to the whole Number of Senators and Representatives to which the State may be entitled in the Congress: but no Senator or Representative, or Person holding an Office of Trust or Profit under the United States, shall be appointed an Elector.

The Electors shall meet in their respective States, and vote by Ballot for two Persons, of whom one at least shall not be an Inhabitant of the same State with themselves. And they shall make a List of all the Persons voted for, and of the Number of Votes for each; which List they shall sign and certify, and transmit sealed to the Seat of the Government of the United States, directed to the President of the Senate. The President of the Senate shall, in the Presence of the Senate and House of Representatives, open all the Certificates, and the Votes shall then be counted. The Person having the greatest Number of Votes shall be the President, if such Number be a Majority of the whole Number of Electors appointed; and if there be more than one who have such Majority, and have an equal Number of Votes, then the House of Representatives shall immediately chuse by Ballot one of them for President; and if no Person have a Majority, then from the five highest on the List the said House shall in like Manner chuse the President. But in chusing the President, the Votes shall be taken by States, the Representation from each State having one Vote; a quorum for this Purpose shall consist of a Member or Members from two thirds of the States, and a Majority of all the States shall be necessary to a Choice. In every Case, after the Choice of the President, the Person having the greatest Number of Votes of the Electors shall be the Vice President. But if there should remain two or more who have equal Votes, the Senate shall chuse from them by Ballot the Vice President.

The Congress may determine the Time of chusing the Electors, and the Day on which they shall give their Votes; which Day shall be the same throughout the United States.

No Person except a natural born Citizen, or a Citizen of the United States, at the time of the Adoption of this Constitution, shall be eligible to the Office of President; neither shall any person be eligible to that Office who shall not have attained to the Age of thirty five Years, and been fourteen Years a Resident within the United States.

In Case of the Removal of the President from Office, or of his Death, Resignation, or Inability to discharge the Powers and Duties of the said Office, the Same shall devolve on the Vice President, and the Congress may by Law provide for the Case of Removal, Death, Resignation or Inability, both of the President and Vice President, declaring what Officer shall then act as President, and such Officer shall act accordingly, until the Disability be removed, or a President shall be elected.

The President shall, at stated Times, receive for his Services, a Compensation, which shall neither be encreased nor diminished during the Period for which he shall have been elected, and he shall not receive within that Period any other Emolument from the United States, or any of them.

Before he enter on the Execution of his Office, he shall take the following Oath or Affirmation:—"I do solemnly swear (or affirm) that I will faithfully execute the Office of President of the United States, and will to the best of my Ability, preserve, protect and defend the Constitution of the United States."

Section. 2. The President shall be Commander in Chief of the Army and Navy of the United States, and of the Militia of the several States, when called into the actual Service of the United States; he may require the Opinion, in writing, of the principal Officer in each of the executive Departments, upon any Subject relating to the Duties of their respective Offices, and he shall have Power to grant Reprieves and Pardons for Offenses against the United States, except in Cases of Impeachment.

He shall have Power, by and with the Advice and Consent of the Senate, to make Treaties, provided two thirds of the Senators present concur; and he shall nominate, and by and with the Advice and Consent of the Senate, shall appoint Ambassadors, other public Ministers and Consuls, Judges of the Supreme Court, and all other Officers of the United States, whose Appointments are not herein otherwise provided for, and which shall be established by Law: but the Congress may by Law vest the Appointment of such inferior Officers, as they think proper, in the President alone, in the Courts of Law, or in the Heads of Departments.

The President shall have Power to fill up all Vacancies that may happen during the Recess of the Senate, by granting Commissions which shall expire at the End of their next Session.

Section. 3. He shall from time to time give to the Congress Information of the State of the Union, and recommend to their Consideration such Measures as he shall judge necessary and expedient; he may, on extraordinary Occasions, convene both Houses, or either of them, and in Case of Disagreement between them, with Respect to the Time of Adjournment, he may adjourn them to such Time as he shall think proper; he shall receive Ambassadors and other public Ministers; he shall take Care that the Laws be faithfully executed, and shall Commission all the Officers of the United States.

Section. 4. The President, Vice President and all Civil Officers of the United States, shall be removed from Office on Impeachment for, and Conviction of, Treason, Bribery, or other high Crimes and Misdemeanors.

Though Article II established the basic framework within which the executive power would operate, it did not seek to solve all the problems of scope and application. The drafters knew they were writing a document not just for their own generation, but for many generations to come. With their masterly instinct for ambiguity, they bequeathed a series of vital questions to the future. Thus the language of the Constitution did not end the debate over whether the executive should be weak or strong. It only settled the context in which subsequent phases of that debate would take place.

From the start, Article II was subject to minimum and maximum interpretations. Thomas Paine and those who understood democracy as meaning the supremacy of the legislative power contended for a passive President serving as the executive officer of the Congress. They became advocates of a "strict" construction of the Constitution. Alexander Hamilton, on the other hand, wrote in The Federalist, *No. 79, "Energy in the executive is a leading character in the definition of good government." As Secretary of the Treasury under George Washington, he became the champion of executive initiative and a "broad" construction of the Constitution. The debate has gone on ever since—and history, as it has subjected the institution of the Presidency to strain and challenge, has had to speak where the Constitution was silent.*

It fell to George Washington, the first President under the Constitution, to begin the process of filling out the blank spaces in Article II. While not an activist President in the modern sense, Washington was a strong executive who effectively vindicated the dignity and independence of the presidential office. John Adams followed in his footsteps, if with less success. The next great test of the Presidency came with the election of the third President, Thomas Jefferson, who was nominally a strict constructionist. But Jefferson's decision to go ahead with the Louisiana Purchase—a decision for which he could find no warrant in the Constitution—showed how national need could enlarge the presidential authority, even when the President himself might be disposed against it.

The Jefferson Administration also saw the replacement of paragraph 3 of Article II, Section 1, by the Twelfth Amendment. The drafters of the Constitution had supposed that the members of the electoral college would make their own decisions about President and Vice-President; they had not anticipated the rise of political parties. By 1796 these assumptions were plainly wrong. The election of 1800, resulting in a tie between Jefferson and Aaron Burr in the electoral college, emphasized the urgency of reform. The Twelfth Amendment required electors to vote separately for President and Vice-President and thereby accommodated the method of choice to the party system.

The first man to realize the Hamiltonian conception of the Presidency was Andrew Jackson, who took his oath half a century after the ratification of the Constitution. Jackson revolutionized the presidential office and may be said to have invented the modern Presidency. He saw himself as the tribune of the people, defending the people's rights against whatever body might threaten them—the executive bureaucracy, the Congress, the judiciary, state governments which set themselves against the national authority. In this spirit, Jackson subdued the Cabinet and the executive branch; he expanded presidential powers of initiation and control in Congress (he vetoed more bills, for example, than all his predecessors put together and secured the presidential right to veto clearly constitutional measures); he set his own interpretation of the Constitution beside that of the Supreme Court; and he made it impossible for sovereign states to nullify federal legislation.

One effect of the Jacksonian revolution was to transform the conception of the strong President, which Gouverneur

Morris and Alexander Hamilton had seen as the instrument of the elite, into an instrument of the people. Another was to revive in full vigor the old debate about the powers of the President. Jackson's opponents, led by the great senators of the time, Henry Clay and Daniel Webster, denounced Jackson as a tyrant and strove to reassert the legislative prerogative. They formed the Whig Party, dedicated to the thesis of a strong Congress and a weak President. And, though James K. Polk a decade later sustained the Hamilton-Jackson view of the President, a succession of weak Presidents before the Civil War renewed hopes of congressional supremacy.

The next great expansion of presidential authority came during the Civil War, when Abraham Lincoln, claiming to act in response to "a popular demand and a public necessity," invoked the new idea of "the war power of the government" to justify acts undertaken by no previous President. But the years after the Civil War were another time of revulsion against executive activism. The Presidency was in decline; and Woodrow Wilson, writing about the American political system in this period, entitled his book Congressional Government. *During this period, too, Congress used the authority granted by Section II to pass the Presidential Succession Act of 1886, providing that, if both the President and Vice-President were eliminated, the Secretary of State would succeed to the Presidency, and so on down through the Cabinet.*

But new developments brought the reign of Congress to an end. For one thing, the emergence of a national economy created domestic problems requiring national policies and national solutions. For another, the emergence of the United States as a world power created foreign problems requiring national leadership to defend the national interest. These developments, seizing public attention at the turn of the century, imposed new demands on the national government and thus on the Presidency. With the accession of Theodore Roosevelt in 1901 came an exuberant rebirth of the Hamilton-Jackson (or, as Roosevelt called it, the Jackson-Lincoln) thesis of the Presidency. "I declined," Roosevelt wrote in his Autobiography, *"to adopt the view that what was imperatively necessary for the Nation could not be done by the President unless he could find some specific authorization to do it. My belief was that it was not only his right but his duty to do anything that the needs of the Nation demanded unless such action was forbidden by the Constitution or by the laws." This view was opposed by Roosevelt's successor, William Howard Taft, who advanced what Roosevelt called the Buchanan-Taft thesis in these words: "The true view of the Ex-*

ecutive function is, as I conceive it, that the President can exercise no power which cannot be fairly and reasonably traced to some specific grant of power or justly implied and included within such express grant as proper and necessary to its exercise. Such specific grant must be either in the Federal Constitution or in an act of Congress. . . . There is no undefined residuum of power which he can exercise because it seems to him to be in the public interest." The debate has continued throughout this century, with Wilson, Franklin Roosevelt, Truman, Kennedy, and Johnson supporting the Jackson-Lincoln thesis and Harding, Coolidge, Hoover, and Eisenhower in the Buchanan-Taft camp.

While the "strong" Presidents of the century, acting under the spur of war, depression, and social need, proceeded to unfold potentialities inherent in the Constitution—Congress, the Supreme Court, and the nation through the amending process have modified various aspects of Article II, some modifications strengthening, others limiting, the executive power. Thus not only did Congress, especially in the 1930's, multiply the functions of government; but the Government Reorganization Act of 1939 offered the Presidency new means of personal control through the establishment of the Executive Office of the President, in which are now gathered such powerful presidential agencies as the Bureau of the Budget, the National Security Council, and the Council of Economic Advisers. On the other hand, the Presidential Succession Act of 1947 revised the act of 1886 by having the succession devolve from the Vice-President to the Speaker of the House and the President pro tempore of the Senate rather than, at first instance, to the cabinet. The Supreme Court in the Curtiss-Wright case of 1936 (299 U.S. 304) confirmed the President's right to exercise very wide powers in foreign policy; in the Steel Seizure case of 1952 (343 U.S. 579), however, it struck a blow at the conception of the implied powers of the Presidency. The Twentieth Amendment (1933) provided for the speedier installation of a newly elected President and Congress, thereby reducing the "lame duck" presence in the government. Then the Twenty-second Amendment (1951) gave the two-term tradition constitutional status.

American history thus by no means records an uninterrupted enlargement of the powers granted the President under Article II. Nearly every strong President has provoked a reaction in favor of the limitation of executive powers, even if the reaction has never quite cut these powers back to their earlier level. Moreover, every branch of the government in *recent years has enlarged its own powers as against the Presidency. The Congress, as a result of the increasing dependence of foreign policy on appropriations, has more control over the conduct of foreign affairs than ever before in American history. The Supreme Court has shown a new and aggressive activism. Even the executive bureaucracy has developed an independence and obduracy which enable it on occasion to ignore or sabotage presidential policy. With all these qualifications, however, the course of American history and the tempo of world change appear to have created an increasing demand for vigorous presidential leadership if the system is not to bog down in a morass of checks-and-balances. Over the long haul, the role of the President has increased steadily in American history. As Woodrow Wilson wrote of the responsibilities of the President, "The Constitution bids him speak and times of stress and change more and more thrust upon him the attitude of originator of policies."*

Article III

EDITED BY DAVID FELLMAN

Those who drafted the American Constitution at the Philadelphia Convention of 1787 did not write upon a clean slate or act upon merely abstract excogitation. Their stock of knowledge was drawn from many sources, notably the precedents of English constitutional history and common-law principles, the colonial political and legal experience, the existing state constitutions, and the Articles of Confederation, the grave inadequacies of which had led to the convoking of the Convention in 1787. The over-all purpose of the authors of the Constitution was to lay the foundations for a federal union strong enough to promote and protect the national interests of the American people. The third article of the Constitution, which authorized the creation of national courts operating independently of state power, and endowed with ample jurisdiction, was an essential part of the plan to create a truly adequate national authority.

Under the Articles of Confederation, the central government had some judicial power, but not very much. Congress was authorized to appoint ad hoc courts which could make "final and conclusive" decisions in disputes between two or more states. It also was empowered to appoint courts for the trial of piracies and felonies on the high seas, but it simply designated the state courts for this purpose. In addition, Congress was authorized to establish an appeals court for prize cases, and this it promptly did. The three-judge Court of Appeals in Cases of Captures was, during the short life of the

Articles of Confederation, the only appellate tribunal with jurisdiction over the whole country. All other judicial power was exercised, during the Confederation period, by the state courts.

The delegates to the Constitutional Convention had serious disagreements which led to justly celebrated compromises, but with regard to the judicial branch of the proposed national government there was substantial agreement from the start. The delegates recognized that the lack of an effective judiciary had been a central weakness of the Confederation government. Thus, very early in its proceedings, on June 4, the Convention adopted, by unanimous vote, a resolution "that a national Judiciary be established," and then added a provision that it should consist of one "supreme tribunal" and a number of "inferior tribunals." During the course of the Convention's deliberations there was no controversy as to the jurisdiction of the federal courts. There was some disagreement over the method of selecting federal judges, but the main disagreement was concerned with the desirability of having inferior federal courts. Many delegates preferred to leave all judicial business in the hands of the state courts, subject to appeal to a federal supreme court where questions of federal law were concerned. Thus the New Jersey Plan, which reflected the localistic inclinations of some of the small states, provided only for a "supreme Tribunal" with appellate powers over state courts in cases involving legal issues of a federal character. The solution was a compromise, engineered by Madison and Wilson, which merely authorized, but did not require, Congress to create inferior courts. The very first Congress, in the seminal Judiciary Act of 1789, created the United States district courts to serve as the trial courts of the national government, and we have had inferior federal tribunals ever since. Finally, a proposal was made, repeatedly, to unite the Supreme Court with the executive in a council of revision which would exercise a veto power over legislation, but it was voted down four times on the ground of incompatibility with the principle of the separation of powers.

There was relatively little debate about Article III in the Convention. The Convention agreed with the general language of the Randolph or Virginia Plan, and the specifications were worked out partly on the floor, but largely by the Committee of Detail and later the Committee on Style. The five members of the Committee of Detail—especially James Wilson, who was probably its most effective member—favored a strong judiciary. Similarly, the five members of the Committee on Style were all in favor of a strong judiciary, and Gouverneur Morris, who was mainly responsible for the final language of the document, once said that in drafting Article III he had gone as far as he could go.

The ninth Randolph Resolution proposed that the federal judicial power should extend to "all piracies and felonies on the high seas; captures from an enemy; cases in which foreigners, or citizens of other States, applying to such jurisdictions, may be interested; or which respect the collection of the national revenue; impeachments of any national officers; and questions which may involve the national peace and harmony." With the exception of the clause relating to impeachments, the jurisdictional provisions of Article III followed the line taken by the Virginia Plan, a line which was also taken, with minor differences, by the New Jersey Plan.

The federal judicial power was structured to enable the new national government to enforce its own laws, which were to be binding directly upon the individual, in its own courts, and which were to be construed in a uniform way throughout the country. Thus national supremacy and uniformity were two of the main objectives of the jurisdictional clauses of Article III. In addition, the federal judiciary was given great responsibilities for umpiring the inevitable controversies between states and between citizens of different states. Accordingly, the Supreme Court was given original jurisdiction over suits between states, and the judicial power of the United States was made applicable to suits between citizens of different states. In order to protect the vital interests of the national government, and especially its fiscal needs, the judicial power was extended to all cases in which the United States is a party. Since a central purpose of the new Constitution was to give the national government full control over foreign affairs, to the exclusion of the states, the federal judicial power was extended to admiralty and maritime cases, piracies, and felonies on the high seas, and cases involving ambassadors, public ministers, treaties, foreign states, and foreign citizens.

Maritime commerce was much more important, relatively, in the eighteenth century than it is today, and the authors of the Constitution had no doubt that it would be most unwise to permit jurisdiction over such commerce to remain in the state courts. "The most bigotted idolizers of State authority," Hamilton wrote in No. 80 of The Federalist, "have not thus far shewn a disposition to deny the national judiciary the cognizance of maritime causes. These so generally depend on the law of nations, and so commonly affect the rights of foreigners, that they fall within the considerations which are relative to the public peace." Furthermore, the Convention delegates must have had fresh in their memories the famous circular letter which the Secretary of Foreign Affairs had drafted, and which the Confederation Congress had sent to the states on April 13, 1787, as a result of the protests of the British government against American violations of the peace treaty of 1783. The states were asked to take steps to abrogate all laws which were contrary to the treaty obligations of the Confederation. The letter pleaded that "the faith of treaties remain inviolate," and pointed out that when a treaty has been constitutionally entered into, "it immediately becomes binding on the whole nation, and superadded to the laws of the land, without the intervention of State legislatures." In addition, the Congress urged the state courts to declare all legislation in conflict with treaty provisions a nullity. This experience was clearly reflected in the jurisdictional clauses of Article III.

The federal judicial power extends, under Article III, to two types of cases. First, there are the cases where jurisdiction proceeds from the fact that they involve questions arising under the Constitution, or statutes or treaties made under its authority, or questions of admiralty or maritime law. These are known as the "federal question" cases. The other class of cases includes those which come within the jurisdiction of the federal courts because of the nature of the parties involved. These include cases in which the United States is itself a party, cases involving ambassadors and other public ministers, controversies between two or more states, or between a state and citizens of another state, or between citizens of different states.

The jurisdictional clauses of Article III were intended, first and foremost, to help establish an effective national government which could maintain the supremacy of federal law, protect the interests of the national government, and umpire the federal system. In addition, they were designed to give the central government effective control over international affairs. Finally, they extended federal protection to property and trade, and thus enlisted the support of the business and propertied community. The federal question and diversity of citizenship jurisdictions were designed to protect property and trade from unfriendly state legislation, and to give traders access to federal courts which would be independent of local political influence.

The last three paragraphs of Article III expressed a concern with the protection of basic civil liberties. The ancient right of trial by jury in the vicinage was guaranteed in criminal cases. The elements of the heinous crime of treason were

*spelled out precisely, as a protection against use of the charge
of treason for mere political ends. Finally, through the prohibition of bills of attainder, Congress was forbidden to try
men for crimes legislatively.*

Section. 1. The judicial Power of the United States, shall
be vested in one supreme Court, and in such inferior Courts
as the Congress may from time to time ordain and establish.
The Judges, both of the supreme and inferior Courts, shall
hold their Offices during good Behaviour, and shall, at stated
Times, receive for their Services, a Compensation, which
shall not be diminished during their Continuance in Office.

Section. 2. The judicial Power shall extend to all Cases, in
Law and Equity, arising under this Constitution, the Laws of
the United States, and Treaties made, or which shall be
made, under their Authority;—to all Cases affecting Ambassadors, other public Ministers and Consuls;—to all Cases of
admiralty and maritime Jurisdiction;—to Controversies to
which the United States shall be a Party;—to Controversies
between two or more States;—between a State and Citizens
of another State;—between Citizens of different States;—between Citizens of the same State claiming Lands under
Grants of different States, and between a State, or the Citizens thereof, and foreign States, Citizens or Subjects.

In all Cases affecting Ambassadors, other public Ministers
and Consuls, and those in which a State shall be Party, the
supreme Court shall have original Jurisdiction. In all the
other Cases before mentioned, the supreme Court shall have
appellate Jurisdiction, both as to Law and Fact, with such
Exceptions, and under such Regulations as the Congress shall
make.

The Trial of all Crimes, except in Cases of Impeachment,
shall be by Jury; and such Trial shall be held in the State
where the said Crimes shall have been committed; but when
not committed within any State, the Trial shall be at such
Place or Places as the Congress may by Law have directed.

Section. 3. Treason against the United States, shall consist
only in levying War against them, or in adhering to their Enemies, giving them Aid and Comfort. No Person shall be
convicted of Treason unless on the Testimony of two Witnesses to the same overt Act, or on Confession in open Court.

The Congress shall have Power to declare the Punishment of Treason, but no Attainder of Treason shall work Corruption of Blood, or Forfeiture except during the Life of the Person attainted.

While our national system of government is based on the principle of the separation of powers, there are in fact many important points of contact between the three great branches of government. All federal judges are appointed by the President, subject to confirmation by the Senate. The Senate, sitting as a court of impeachment, may remove federal judges from office, after trial on charges brought by the House of Representatives. All federal courts are created by acts of Congress, and Congress determines how many judges shall serve in these courts, and how much salary they shall be paid. In addition, Congress may abolish courts and judgeships, except that it cannot constitutionally abolish the Supreme Court. Finally, Congress defines by statute the jurisdiction of all federal courts, with the exception of the limited original jurisdiction of the Supreme Court, which is spelled out in Article III. At the same time, the federal judges enjoy a great deal of independence, since they hold office for "good behavior," and can be removed only by impeachment. They do not live in fear that political retribution may unseat them if their decisions prove unpopular.

The courts have much to do with Congress and the President because the judges are called upon to construe the meaning of statutes and of executive ordinances, and to help enforce them. Above all, the courts have the authority to declare acts of Congress or of the President to be unenforceable on the ground that they violate the Constitution. This is known as the power of judicial review. Of all the powers of the federal courts, it is the most distinctive, the most crucial, and the most controversial.

Since Article III does not say, in so many words, that the courts possess the power of judicial review, the legitimacy of the exercise of this authority has always been a subject of debate. That judicial review is a natural outgrowth of a written constitution has always been the position of the Supreme Court. In 1803, in the celebrated case of Marbury v. Madison, 1 Cranch 137, *Chief Justice John Marshall, speaking for the Court, held that since it is the province of a court to declare the law, and since the written Constitution is both law and the supreme law of the land, it follows that when a stat-*

ute is in conflict with a provision of the Constitution, the latter must prevail over the former. This assertion of the power of judicial review was consistent with practice in the state courts, and had been regarded by most of the authors of Article III to be a normal aspect of judicial power. Accordingly, Hamilton declared, in No. 78 of The Federalist:

> The interpretation of the laws is the proper and peculiar province of the courts. A Constitution is in fact, and must be, regarded as a fundamental law. It therefore belongs to them to ascertain its meaning as well as the meaning of any particular act proceeding from the legislative body. If there should happen to be an irreconcileable variance between the two, that which has the superior obligation and validity ought of course to be preferred; or in other words, the constitution ought to be preferred to the statute, the intention of the people to the intention of their agents.

The Supreme Court's power of judicial review also extends to state legislation. There were members of the Constitutional Convention who were strongly in favor of a congressional veto over state statutes. Thus on August 23, Charles Pinckney moved to give the Congress the power "to negative all laws passed by the several States interfering, in the opinion of the Legislature, with the general interests and harmony of the Union. . . ." A lively debate ensued, during which the motion was opposed on the ground that in any event, as Sherman argued, the laws of the federal government would be paramount and supreme. On the other hand, the Pinckney motion was supported with the contention that, as Wilson maintained, "the firmness of Judges is not of itself sufficient." The Pinckney motion was finally defeated by a vote of 5 to 6. Accordingly, the Convention settled for a federal judicial rather than a legislative veto of unconstitutional state legislation. In fact, this was one of the great compromises of the Convention.

As the agency which interprets the Constitution authoritatively and with finality, the Supreme Court has been, in the words of Lord Bryce, "the living voice of the Constitution," and indeed, "the conscience of the people, who have resolved to restrain themselves from hasty or unjust action by placing their representatives under the restriction of a permanent law." While judicial review is an important aspect of American government, and a source of great power, the Supreme Court has exercised this power over the years with considerable restraint. It should always be assumed, the Court maintains, that when a legislative body enacted a given statute, it did not intend to violate the Constitution; thus the burden of proof is on those who attack the validity of the statute, and all doubts should be resolved in favor of upholding the statute. Furthermore, if a statute can reasonably be read in more than one way, the Court prefers so to construe the statute as to lead to a conclusion which will sustain its validity. The Court has always taken the position that it will not exercise its great powers except in actual cases or controversies in which adverse parties are concerned with valuable legal rights; it will not give advisory opinions, therefore, and will not hear a suit unless the parties to it have proper standing to sue. The parties must have used up all other possible remedies, and must present substantial legal problems for decision. The Court regards some constitutional questions as political in character, and therefore nonjusticiable. The Court also declines to rule on the motives of legislators, or the wisdom of their legislation.

Whether the Supreme Court observes its own rules of self-restraint is often a matter of lively debate. There have been periods of great judicial activism, when the Court has used its judicial review powers rather freely, and then there have been other periods of relative quiescence. The Supreme Court was very active, for example, in the Reconstruction period, and invalidated a large body of federal legislation through a process of strict construction of the Civil War Amendments to the Constitution. There was another flurry of activity in the 1890's, which led, above all, to judicial nullification of the first modern federal income tax. In the 1920's and during the first four years of the New Deal in the 1930's, the Court was dominated by a majority which found ways of invalidating a great amount of reform legislation, especially in the field of economic regulation. More recently, during the 1950's and 1960's, the Court has been concerned primarily with questions regarding civil rights and civil liberties. The 1954 decision outlawing racial segregation in the public schools, and the 1962 decision which asserted jurisdiction over the problem of the reapportionment of legislative bodies, have in recent years stirred up immense interest and great controversy.

Throughout the course of American history, the Supreme Court has performed the vital functions of defining the limits of state and national power. The Court, however, is itself an agency of the national government, and while there have been some exceptions, as a general rule the tendency of the Court has been to take a national point of view. Thus, it has generally construed the commerce power of the federal government broadly, and has given its sanction to a growing body of national legislation in the field of interstate commerce. At the same time, the Court has tried to accommodate the local needs of the states in the commerce field by upholding a large body of police legislation enacted to protect the health, safety, and welfare of the public in areas where Congress has taken no action and where uniform national rules do not seem to be essential. In the past quarter of a century, however, the Court has been preoccupied with spelling out the meaning of civil rights and civil liberties, especially in regard to freedom of religion, liberty of speech, press, and association, the right to vote, the fair-procedure rights of defendants in criminal cases, and freedom from racial discrimination. So far as state action is concerned this has involved a broad and generous construction of the "due process" and "equal protection" clauses of the Fourteenth Amendment. The steady growth of the concept of due process of law may well be regarded as the central theme of modern constitutional law in the jurisprudence of the United States Supreme Court.

Article IV

EDITED BY J. A. C. GRANT

In the drafting of Article IV of the Constitution, Section 1 and the first two clauses of Section 2 of Article IV were copied from the similar provisions in the Articles of Confederation. Of these, only the second sentence of Section 1 was subjected to debate either in the Philadelphia Convention or in the state ratifying conventions. This sentence had been added on the motion of Gouverneur Morris, and although a committee recommended restricting congressional authority to the effect of judgments, the broader language ultimately adopted was restored by a vote of 6 to 3. The third clause of Section 2 was modeled after Article 6 of the Northwest Ordinance of July 13, 1787. The northern delegates first protested that there is "no more propriety in the public seizing and surrendering a slave or servant, than a horse," but in the end insisted only upon omitting such words as "slave" and "legally held."

Whereas the Articles of Confederation had required that (except in the case of Canada) nine states would have to agree to the admission of a new state, it was generally agreed at Philadelphia that this power should be given to the national legislature. However, Gouverneur Morris proposed that "the rule of representation ought to be so fixed us to secure to the Atlantic States a prevalence in the National Councils," and John Rutledge and Pierce Butler hoped that the same end could be accomplished through basing representation on taxes or property rather than population. Elbridge Gerry proposed that the total number of representatives in the lower

*house from the new states should never exceed the total from
the original states. Apparently only James Madison, George
Mason, Charles C. Pinckney, Edmund Randolph, Roger
Sherman, and James Wilson spoke in favor of admitting new
states on a plane of equality, but their views prevailed in the
Committee of Detail. It proposed, "If the admission be consented to, the new States shall be admitted on the same terms
with the original States." Following further debate this sentence was deleted by a vote of 9 to 2, a spokesman for the
majority explaining that it "did not wish to bind down the
Legislature to admit Western States on the terms here stated."*

*The Committee of Detail's draft also required the consent
of a state's legislature before the state could be divided. This
version prevailed, but only after strenuous opposition from
many delegates who felt that Congress should be free to
admit Maine, Vermont, and the western territories of Georgia, of North Carolina, and of Virginia to statehood without
consulting the states from which the new states would be
carved. This provision was one of those relied upon by Luther Martin for recommending that Maryland should not ratify the Constitution. He insisted that "republican government"
was suited only to a small and compact territory and could
not prevail unless the larger and less compact states were divided.*

*The passage of the Northwest Ordinance pointed up the
need for an express provision in the Constitution for the
power of Congress to govern and dispose of western and
other lands and property belonging to the nation. The first
phrase of clause 2 of Section 3 was thus accepted almost automatically. But the rest of the clause was hammered out in
the course of debate. The language finally adopted was that
proposed on August 30 by Gouverneur Morris, whose fine
hand is to be seen so often in this Article. It was assumed
that contested claims would be settled by negotiation or by
suit in the federal Supreme Court.*

*Item 11 in the plan submitted to the Convention on May
29, 1787, by Edmund Randolph provided that "a Republican
Government and the territory of each State . . . ought to be
guaranteed by the United States to each State." Six weeks
later Article 5 of the Northwest Ordinance provided that "the
constitution and government" of each of the new states to be
erected beyond the Ohio "shall be republican." James Madison expressed doubts as to the accuracy of "republican" to
describe a government where slavery existed, but the Convention accepted it for lack of a better word to distinguish popu-*

lar government from aristocracy and monarchy. Our records of the debates yield no other meaning of the word.

While everyone seemed anxious to guarantee to each state a republican form of government, that was as far as unanimity went. Gouverneur Morris was "very unwilling that such laws as exist in Rhode Island should be guaranteed." William Houston "was afraid of perpetuating the existing Constitution of the States," some of which—especially that of his own state, Georgia—he considered very defective. Consequently the additional guarantee of "its existing laws," although approved on June 11, was abandoned, making it clear that each state was to remain free to alter either its constitution or its laws by peaceful means.

Although all the Convention delegates readily agreed to a national guarantee against foreign invasion, the provision concerning the power of the United States government to protect against domestic violence was secured only after long debate. Luther Martin's motion to permit Congress to divide a state without the consent of its legislature was defeated by a 6 to 5 vote. That led many, including John Dickinson, to stress "the impropriety of requiring the small States to secure the large ones in their extensive claims of territory." Martin himself, in pleading with Maryland not to ratify the Constitution, could foresee his state "called upon to assist, with her wealth and her blood, in subduing the inhabitants of Franklin, Kentucky, Vermont, and the provinces of Maine and Sagadohock" when in all justice they should be independent states. Dickinson's disappointment was shorter lived. He actually led an unsuccessful effort to authorize national intervention to suppress domestic violence without any request from the state. He was successful in a less ambitious move, securing insertion of the phrase, "or of the Executive (when the Legislature cannot be convened)." But nothing that he or others said seems to justify the charge made later by the opponents of the Constitution, in the Virginia ratifying convention, that the language used in Section 4 gives exclusive jurisdiction to the nation to use the state's militia to put down domestic violence. This was left, and was intended to be left, as a primary obligation of the state itself.

Section. 1. Full Faith and Credit shall be given in each State to the public Acts, Records, and judicial Proceedings of every other State. And the Congress may by general Laws

prescribe the Manner in which such Acts, Records and Proceedings shall be proved, and the Effect thereof.

Section. 2. The Citizens of each State shall be entitled to all Privileges and Immunities of Citizens in the several States.

A Person charged in any State with Treason, Felony, or other Crime, who shall flee from Justice, and be found in another State, shall on Demand of the executive Authority of the State from which he fled, be delivered up, to be removed to the State having Jurisdiction of the Crime.

No Person held to Service or Labour in one State, under the Laws thereof, escaping into another, shall, in Consequence of any Law or Regulation therein, be discharged from such Service or Labour, but shall be delivered up on Claim of the Party to whom such Service or Labour may be due.

Section. 3. New States may be admitted by the Congress into this Union; but no new State shall be formed or erected within the Jurisdiction of any other State; nor any State be formed by the Junction of two or more States, or Parts of States, without the Consent of the Legislatures of the States concerned as well as of the Congress.

The Congress shall have Power to dispose of and make all needful Rules and Regulations respecting the Territory or other Property belonging to the United States; and nothing in this Constitution shall be so construed as to Prejudice any Claims of the United States, or of any particular State.

Section. 4. The United States shall guarantee to every State in this Union a Republican Form of Government, and shall protect each of them against Invasion; and on Application of the Legislature, or of the Executive (when the Legislature cannot be convened) against domestic Violence.

Congressional legislation under the "full faith and credit" clause has provided that properly authenticated legislative acts and judicial rulings "have the same full faith and credit in every court within the United States and its Territories and Possessions as they have by law in the courts of such State, Territory or Possession." It was logical of Congress to go beyond the sweep of Article IV and include all American jurisdictions under a single set of rules. The extension to legislative acts was not added until 1948, but the courts had applied the same doctrines under the accepted principles of private

international law. In fact, the only important effect of the clause and its implementing statute was to nationalize the basic principles of private international law.

Without such a clause we would be a league of states instead of a nation. Undoubtedly some states would have clung to the common-law doctrine that a money judgment is only presumptively valid, so that the merits of the original controversy could always be reopened when enforcement is sought in another state. The Supreme Court, in Mills v. Duryee, 7 Cranch 481 (1813), *rejected this rule for the sounder one that such a judgment is conclusive of the merits. Although many disagree with the rules the Supreme Court has adopted on such contentious subjects as migratory divorces or the exterritorial application of workmen's compensation acts, there can be little question that the benefit of a single set of rules interpreted by a single court of last resort is far superior to any result possible under a system of fifty-one courts of last resort.*

Congress has left the development of the "full faith and credit" clause largely to the courts. There is much that Congress could do that courts cannot do. It could, for example, provide more expeditious means for enforcing foreign judgments or the service of process. Doubtless it could provide standards to determine jurisdiction over divorce and the allied problems of alimony, child support, and the like. Indeed, even the legislative possibilities envisioned by the framers have scarcely been approached.

Section 2 opens with the "comity" clause. This is self-executing, and as construed by the Supreme Court merely forbids one state to discriminate against the citizens of other states in favor of its own. But it does not require that nonresidents be permitted to share the "public patrimony" of a state. Thus game fishing or hunting by outsiders may be restricted or even forbidden: but "commercial shrimping in the marginal sea, like other common callings, is within the purview" of the guarantee (Toomer v. Witsell, 334 U.S. 385, 403 [198]). *One does not carry his status as a doctor, as a dentist, or even as an insurance broker with him to another state, but must meet the standards set by the state concerned, including where appropriate a prescribed period of residence* (La Tourette v. McMaster, 248 U.S. 465 [1919]). *Nor does the clause protect corporations* (Paul v. Virginia, 8 Wall. 168 [1869]),*which must rely upon the commerce clause and the Fourteenth Amendment when they seek recognition beyond the confines of their state of incorporation.*

The second clause of Section 2 provides for interstate ren-

dition. *Although Congress long has required governors to cause fugitives to be arrested and delivered up upon demand, the Supreme Court has construed this to be merely declaratory, unenforceable by court action* (Kentucky v. Dennison, 24 How. 66 [1861]). *The recent reapportionment decisions and particularly statements in* Baker v. Carr, 396 U.S. 1864 210 (1962), *indicate that Congress can strengthen this act if it chooses. It also has made fleeing from one state to another to evade prosecution for felony a federal crime. Accepted principles of international law dictate that an offender may be tried only "for the offence with which he is charged in the proceedings for his extradition, until a reasonable time and opportunity have been given him, after his release or trial upon such charge, to return to the country from whose asylum he had been forcibly taken"* (United States v. Rauscher, 119 U.S. 407, 430 [1886]). *As no such limitation has been found in Article IV, a fugitive extradited from another state may be tried for an offense other than that for which he was surrendered* (Lascelles v. Georgia, 148 U.S. 537 [1893]).

The third clause of Section 2 was the basis for passage of the Fugitive Slave Acts of 1793; the Thirteenth Amendment, of course, rendered it obsolete in 1865.

The power of Congress to admit new states has now made us more than a mere continental union. Maine, Vermont, and the western territories of Georgia, of North Carolina, and of Virginia received the independent status so earnestly desired by many delegates to the Philadelphia Convention without the bloodshed or other difficulties envisaged by some. The first clause of Section 3 has proved to be one of the most successful provisions in the Constitution, in part because it has not been construed or applied as those who wrote it intended. Whereas Vermont (1791) and Kentucky (1792) were simply admitted as states, Tennessee (1796) was welcomed "on an equal footing with the original states in all respects whatsoever." Although such a statement is found either in the Enabling Act or the Act of Admission of every state subsequently admitted, Congress soon departed from it by imposing restrictions intended to be binding upon the new state forever. Examples are Louisiana (1812), forbidden to curb religious liberty, to deny jury trial in criminal cases, or to charge tolls for the use of its navigable waters; Nevada (1864), forbidden to authorize slavery or to curb religious freedom; Nebraska (1867), denied the right to use a racial test for voters; Utah (1896), required to grant religious toleration and to forbid polygamy. The Supreme Court held the restrictions against Louisiana unenforceable in Permoli v.

Municipality No 1, *3 How. 589 (1845)*, and has never departed from the views there expressed. *The most frequently quoted ruling sustained Oklahoma in its disregard of the attempt of Congress to prevent it from establishing a permanent state capital until the state was more developed* (Coyle v. Smith, *221 U.S. [1911]*). *Thus state equality, rather than congressional discretion, has become the command of the living Constitution.*

The second clause of Section 3 has been used by Congress to lease federally owned lands as well as to dispose of them by gift, sale, or under homestead acts. The decision of the Supreme Court in Ashwander v. T.V.A., *297 U.S. 288 (1936), relied on it, together with the war power and control over navigation, to sustain a vast electric power and area development program. It has been cited to justify both the establishment of territorial governments and direct congressional control over the territories, although the Supreme Court conceded that "the right to govern may be the inevitable consequence of the right to acquire territory"* (American Insurance Co. v. Canter, *1 Pet. 511, 543 [1828]*).

It is "the United States" that under Section 4 "shall guarantee to every State in this Union a republican form of government" and protect it against invasion or domestic violence. These are the only instances where the government by its corporate name is given a duty. Literally the obligation would seem to rest upon all departments of the government, but obviously the courts must have only a minor role so far as invasion or insurrection are concerned. Although the only meaning that can be gathered from the Convention debates is that a republican government is a popular rather than an aristocratic or monarchical one, the majority opinion in Calder v. Bull. *3 Dall. 386, 387–88 (1798), intimated that it is one in which the government respects "the purposes for which men enter into society." Thus construed, it could have become the equivalent of a full bill of rights binding upon all branches of the state governments, giving the courts authority to void even statutes considered by them to violate basic principles of right and justice. But this early promise failed to develop. Instead, the Supreme Court soon withdrew completely from the field, treating all questions of "republican government" as political ones where the decisions of Congress or the executive are final. The only exception is* Minor v. Happersett, *21 Wall. 162 (1875), holding (prior to the Nineteenth Amendment) that the suffrage may be denied to women.*

Congress used the clause to justify the Reconstruction Acts following the Civil War. At that time Charles Sumner referred to it as "a sleeping giant in the Constitution." It may yet become significant, although the expanded meaning given to the Fourteenth Amendment militates against this.

The final clause of Article IV requires a request from the legislature or the executive of a state before the nation may protect it from domestic violence. The vastly expanded scope of federal activity, coupled with the In Re Debs, 158 U.S. 564, 582 (1895), doctrine that "the entire strength of the nation" may be used "to enforce in any part of the land the full and free exercise of all national powers and the security of all rights entrusted by the Constitution to its care" have virtually removed this limitation. It is rare indeed that violence on a scale that is of interest to the nation can fail to meet this test. John Dickinson has finally had his way.

Article V and the Amending Process

EDITED BY PHILIP B. KURLAND

However natural it may now seem for the Constitution to provide for its own amendment, we should remember Holmes's warning against confusing the familiar with the necessary. There are other, more recent, national constitutions that make no such provision. The nature of the political compromises that resulted from the 1787 Convention was reason enough for those present not to tolerate a ready method of undoing what they had done. Article V, like most of the important provisions of the Constitution, must be attributed more to the prevailing spirit of compromise that dominated the Convention than to dedication to principle.

Although the original Virginia Plan provided for a method of amendment, the first essential question resolved by the Convention was whether any method of amendment should be provided. Despite strong opposition from men such as Charles Pinckney of South Carolina, the Convention soon agreed in principle to the desirability of specifying a mode for amendment, with Mason, Randolph, and Madison of Virginia, Gouverneur Morris of Pennsylvania, Elbridge Gerry of Massachusetts, and Hamilton of New York leading the Convention toward accepting the necessity of such a provision.

The Virginia Plan not only specified an amendment process but provided also that the national legislature be excluded from participation in that process. And it was on the question of the proper role of Congress that the second major *conflict was fought. When first reported by the Committee of Detail, the provision called for amendment by a convention to be called—apparently as a ministerial action—by the national legislature on application of the legislatures of two-thirds of the states. Although this plan was first approved, the issue was again raised on Gerry's motion for reconsideration, seconded by Hamilton, and supported by Madison. On reconsideration, Sherman of Connecticut sought to have the power given to the national legislature to propose amendments to the states for their approval. Wilson of Pennsylvania suggested that the approval of two-thirds of the states should be sufficient, and when this proposal was lost he was able to secure consent to a requirement of three-fourths of the states. At this point Madison offered what was in effect a substitute for the Committee of Detail's amended recommendation. It read, as the final draft was to read, in terms of alternative methods. Two-thirds of each house of Congress or two-thirds of the state legislatures could propose amendments. The amendments were to be ratified when approved either by three-fourths of the state legislatures or by conventions in three-fourths of the states. This compromise eventually overcame the second difficulty. By providing for alternative methods of procedure, the Madison proposal also made possible the compromise between those who would, from fear of the reticence of the national legislature to correct its own abuses, utilize the convention as the means of initiating change, and those who, like Mason, wanted the national legislature to be the sole sponsor of amendments.*

This compromise did not, however, end the disputes over the content of the amendment article. Rutledge of South Carolina insisted that approval could not be forthcoming if the provisions relating to slavery theretofore approved were to be subject to amendment. Again compromise carried the day and it was decided that these sections of the Constitution were not to be subject to amendment prior to 1808. Having learned that state interests could be protected against amendment, at least for some period of time, Sherman moved that the Constitution should not be subject to amendment to limit the internal authority of the states nor to deprive any of them of their equal representation in the Senate. A different form of compromise was the result of this effort. Sherman lost in his effort to secure the states against interference with the exercise of their police power, but he won a guaranty that the right of equal representation in the Senate should not be changed. The latter protection, it quickly became apparent, was absolutely necessary to assure approval by the small states that had backed the New Jersey Plan, and it was written into the Constitution without a single objection.

Article V, which resulted from these deliberations, must be attributed largely to Madison, with the obvious active participation of Hamilton.

The Congress, whenever two thirds of both Houses shall deem it necessary, shall propose Amendments to this Constitution, or, on the Application of the Legislatures of two thirds of the several States, shall call a Convention for proposing Amendments, which, in either Case, shall be valid to all Intents and Purposes, as Part of this Constitution, when ratified by the Legislatures of three fourths of the several States, or by Conventions in three fourths thereof, as the one or the other Mode of Ratification may be proposed by the Congress; Provided that no Amendment which may be made prior to the Year One thousand eight hundred and eight shall in any Manner affect the first and fourth Clauses in the Ninth Section of the first Article; and that no State, without its Consent, shall be deprived of its equal Suffrage in the Senate.

Although the Constitution has been the subject of twenty-four different amendments, resort has never once been made to a national convention to initiate the process. And only once, in the case of the Twenty-first Amendment, was the state-convention process utilized for purposes of ratifying an amendment.

For the most part, the amendments have been minor rather than major rearrangements of the constitutional plan. The first ten amendments, the Bill of Rights, came so hard on the heels of the original document that they must be treated, for almost all purposes, as part of it. The only truly basic changes came in the Civil War amendments, the Thirteenth, Fourteenth, and Fifteenth. Although intended primarily for the benefit of the Negroes, who ultimately were the beneficiaries, the amendments have proved to be the essential vehicles for the transfer of power from the states to the national government and, within the national government, to the Supreme Court, which has since exercised a veto power over the actions of the state legislatures, executives, and judiciaries. This evolution, together with the authority of judicial review, secured earlier by the Court, has made the amendment process all but superfluous. The Court has been aptly referred to as a continuing constitutional convention, updating the meaning of the Constitution as new times and new situations demand that new meanings be given to the words of the document itself. Whether for this reason or another, there can be little doubt of the truth of Felix Frankfurter's observation that there has been throughout our history an "absence of any widespread or sustained demand for a general revision of the Constitution."

On the other hand, it should be noted that some of the amendments have been attributable solely to the need to correct a Supreme Court construction of the Constitution. Thus, the Eleventh Amendment was promulgated to overrule the case of Chisholm v. Georgia, 2 Dall. 419 (1793), in which the Court held that sovereign immunity was not available as a defense to a suit by a citizen of one state against another state. The necessity for the Civil War amendments derived in no small measure from the awful case of Dred Scott v. Sanford, 19 How. 393 (1857). The Sixteenth Amendment, authorizing the income tax, was a direct consequence of the Court's highly dubious decisions in Pollock v. Farmers' Loan and Trust Co., 157 U.S. 429 (1895), 158 U.S. 601 (1895).

The other major category of amendments includes those relating to the mechanics of the national government itself. These are due, first, to the need to eliminate ambiguities that became apparent through experience and, second, to the tendency toward extension of the franchise, a movement notable in all democratic countries during the nineteenth and twentieth centuries. In the first group fall the Twelfth Amendment, made necessary by the tied vote for Jefferson and Burr in the 1800 election; the Twentieth Amendment, a response to the increased efficiency of communications and transportation that made it possible to provide for the succession of the newly elected government at a date much closer to the election, as well as to the need to eliminate the ambiguities about filling a presidential vacancy; the Twenty-second Amendment, which adopted George Washington's notion that two terms were enough for any man to occupy the Presidency, an unwritten constitutional tradition broken by Franklin Delano Roosevelt's election to the office for four successive terms. In the second category, the amendments that enhance popular sovereignty, fall the Seventeenth, providing for popular election of senators; the Nineteenth, providing for women's suffrage, the Twenty-third, giving a voice to citizens of the District of Columbia in the election of the Presi-

dent; and the Twenty-fourth, eliminating the poll tax as a requirement for voting in national elections.

The only two other amendments are concrete evidence of the undesirability of promulgating a minority's notions of morality as part of the nation's fundamental law. The Eighteenth Amendment, the Prohibition Amendment, was a ban on commerce in intoxicating liquors. The horrible results of the "noble experiment" that led an entire nation into a lawlessness from which it has never recovered caused the repeal of the Eighteenth Amendment by the Twenty-first Amendment.

Perhaps the primary importance of Article V may be found in the in terrorem effect of an ultimate appeal to the people for the correction of the abuses of their government. But it is not a weapon ready for use and its cumbersome method is both its virtue and its vice.

The first ten amendments and the Civil War amendments (XIII–XV) are reproduced in the following sections of this volume. The text of the others appears here.

Amendment [XI.]

The Judicial power of the United States shall not be construed to extend to any suit in law or equity, commenced or prosecuted against one of the United States by Citizens of another State, or by Citizens or Subjects of any Foreign State.

Amendment [XII.]

The Electors shall meet in their respective states and vote by ballot for President and Vice-President, one of whom, at least, shall not be an inhabitant of the same state with themselves; they shall name in their ballots the person voted for as President, and in distinct ballots the person voted for as Vice-President, and they shall make distinct lists of all persons voted for as President, and of all persons voted for as Vice-President, and of the number of votes for each, which lists they shall sign and certify, and transmit sealed to the seat of the government of the United States, directed to the President of the Senate;—The President of the Senate shall, in the presence of the Senate and House of Representatives, open all the certificates and the votes shall then be counted;—The person having the greatest number of votes for President, shall be the President, if such number be a majority of the whole number of Electors appointed; and if no person have such majority, then from the persons having the highest numbers not exceeding three on the list of those voted for as President, the House of Representatives shall choose immediately, by ballot, the President. But in choosing the President, the votes shall be taken by states, the representation from each state having one vote; a quorum for this purpose shall consist of a member or members from two-thirds of the states, and a majority of all the states shall be necessary to a choice. And if the House of Representatives shall not choose a President whenever the right of choice shall devolve upon them, before the fourth day of March next following, then the Vice-President shall act as President, as in the case of the death or other constitutional disability of the President—The person having the greatest number of votes as Vice-President, shall be the Vice-President, if such number be a majority of the whole number of Electors appointed, and if no person have a majority, then from the two highest numbers on the list, the Senate shall choose the Vice-President; a quorum for the purpose shall consist of two-thirds of the whole number of Senators, and a majority of the whole number shall be necessary to a choice. But no person constitutionally ineligible to the office of President shall be eligible to that of Vice-President of the United States.

AMENDMENT [XVI.]

The Congress shall have power to lay and collect taxes on incomes, from whatever source derived, without apportionment among the several States, and without regard to any census or enumeration.

AMENDMENT [XVII.]

The Senate of the United States shall be composed of two Senators from each State, elected by the people thereof, for six years; and each Senator shall have one vote. The electors in each State shall have the qualifications requisite for electors of the most numerous branch of the State legislatures.

When vacancies happen in the representation of any State in the Senate, the executive authority of such State shall issue writs of election to fill such vacancies: *Provided,* That the legislature of any State may empower the executive thereof to make temporary appointments until the people fill the vacancies by election as the legislature may direct.

This amendment shall not be so construed as to affect the

election or term of any Senator chosen before it becomes valid as part of the Constitution.

AMENDMENT [XVIII.]

SECTION 1. After one year from the ratification of this article the manufacture, sale, or transportation of intoxicating liquors within, the importation thereof into, or the exportation thereof from the United States and all territory subject to the jurisdiction thereof for beverage purposes is hereby prohibited.

SEC. 2. The Congress and the several States shall have concurrent power to enforce this article by appropriate legislation.

SEC. 3. This article shall be inoperative unless it shall have been ratified as an amendment to the Constitution by the legislatures of the several States, as provided in the Constitution, within seven years from the date of the submission hereof to the States by the Congress.

AMENDMENT [XIX.]

The right of citizens of the United States to vote shall not be denied or abridged by the United States or by any State on account of sex.

Congress shall have power to enforce this article by appropriate legislation.

AMENDMENT [XX.]

SECTION 1. The terms of the President and Vice President shall end at noon on the 20th day of January, and the terms of Senators and Representatives at noon on the 3d day of January, of the years in which such terms would have ended if this article had not been ratified; and the terms of their successors shall then begin.

SEC. 2. The Congress shall assemble at least once in every year, and such meeting shall begin at noon on the 3d day of January, unless they shall by law appoint a different day.

SEC. 3. If, at the time fixed for the beginning of the term of the President, the President elect shall have died, the Vice President elect shall become President. If a President shall not have been chosen before the time fixed for the beginning of his term, or if the President elect shall have failed to qualify, then the Vice President elect shall act as President until a

President shall have qualified; and the Congress may by law provide for the case wherein neither a President elect nor a Vice President elect shall have qualified, declaring who shall then act as President, or the manner in which one who is to act shall be selected, and such person shall act accordingly until a President or Vice President shall have qualified.

Sec. 4. The Congress may by law provide for the case of the death of any of the persons from whom the House of Representatives may choose a President whenever the right of choice shall have devolved upon them, and for the case of the death of any of the persons from whom the Senate may choose a Vice President whenever the right of choice shall have devolved upon them.

Sec. 5. Sections 1 and 2 shall take effect on the 15th day of October following the ratification of this article.

Sec. 6. This article shall be inoperative unless it shall have been ratified as an amendment to the Constitution by the legislatures of three-fourths of the several States within seven years from the date of its submission.

Amendment [XXI.]

Section 1. The eighteenth article of amendment to the Constitution of the United States is hereby repealed.

Sec. 2. The transportation or importation into any State, Territory or possession of the United States for delivery or use therein of intoxicating liquors, in violation of the laws thereof, is hereby prohibited.

Sec. 3. This article shall be inoperative unless it shall have been ratified as an amendment to the Constitution by conventions in the several States, as provided in the Constitution, within seven years from the date of the submission hereof to the States by the Congress.

Amendment [XXII.]

Section 1. No person shall be elected to the office of the President more than twice, and no person who has held the office of President, or acted as President, for more than two years of a term to which some other person was elected President shall be elected to the office of the President more than once. But this Article shall not apply to any person holding the office of President when this Article was proposed by the Congress, and shall not prevent any person who may be holding the office of President, or acting as President, during the term within which this Article becomes operative from holding the office of President or acting as President during the remainder of such term.

SEC. 2. This Article shall be inoperative unless it shall have been ratified as an amendment to the Constitution by the legislatures of three-fourths of the several States within seven years from the date of its submission to the States by the Congress.

AMENDMENT [XXIII.]

SECTION 1. The District constituting the seat of Government of the United States shall appoint in such manner as the Congress may direct:

A number of electors of President and Vice President equal to the whole number of Senators and Representatives in Congress to which the District would be entitled if it were a State, but in no event more than the least populous State; they shall be in addition to those appointed by the States, but they shall be considered, for the purposes of the election of President and Vice President, to be electors appointed by a State; and they shall meet in the District and perform such duties as provided by the twelfth article of amendment.

SEC. 2. The Congress shall have power to enforce this article by appropriate legislation.

AMENDMENT [XXIV.]

SECTION 1. The right of citizens of the United States to vote in any primary or other election for President or Vice President, for electors for President or Vice President, or for Senator or Representative in Congress, shall not be denied or abridged by the United States or any State by reason of failure to pay any poll or other tax.

SECTION 2. The Congress shall have power to enforce this article by appropriate legislation.

Articles VI and VII

EDITED BY ALFRED H. KELLY

*By far the most significant provision in Article IV of the
United States Constitution is the "supremacy" clause. This
guarantees the ascendancy of all three forms of federal law
(Constitution, treaties, and congressional enactments) over
state law, and charges the state courts with enforcing that
guarantee.*

*The supremacy clause had its origins in the failure of the
Articles of Confederation, the charter of union which the
United States put into effect in 1781, to solve the problem of
federal-state relations. The problem was that of establishing
some principle for dividing sovereignty effectively between
the national government and the states, and of establishing
some mechanism to assure the smooth and effective coordina-
tion of the two spheres in actual operation. The Articles of
Confederation had delegated to the Confederation Congress
certain specific sovereign functions—notably foreign relations, war, treaties, Indian affairs, coinage, and the post office
—while at the same time reserving the great residue of sovereign powers, those not specifically delegated to Congress, to
the several states. The principle involved in this division of
powers anticipated directly that resorted to in the Constitution of 1789.*

*Unfortunately, however, the Articles had failed almost
completely to make this system effective or workable. First,
they left Congress without the means to execute its own functions properly. There was neither any federal court system*

157

for implementing the enforcement of Confederation law nor any federal revenue system for taxing individuals directly. Instead, in both instances, Congress was obliged to use the states as its agents to implement its will. This system in actual practice worked very badly, mainly because the states almost invariably subordinated national policy and law to their own legal systems. Thus in most instances where Confederation law came into conflict with that of a state in cases before the state courts, state judges chose to enforce the pertinent provisions of their own constitutions and laws and to ignore appropriate provisions of national law. The system of state agency was ineffective for the collection of federal revenues. The states were chronically deficient in the payment of their respective levies, a situation which soon brought about a condition of national bankruptcy.

The obvious defects in this system of state-agency early led to demands for the reform of the Articles. In 1780, even before the Articles had taken final effect, Hamilton wrote that Congress ought at once to assert "complete sovereignty" over the states in its sphere of authority. A year later, James Madison, then a member of Congress from Virginia, proposed a constitutional amendment authorizing Congress to use force to compel the states to fulfill their obligations to the Union. This idea that Congress ought somehow be empowered to coerce derelict states recurred repeatedly during the Confederation era, a "Grand Committee" of Congress suggesting it once more in 1786. More significant, however, was another suggestion Madison made several times, that Congress be provided with a veto of all state laws contravening the federal constitutional system, an idea he obviously had borrowed from the right of review and possibly disallowance formerly exercised by the Crown with respect to colonial legislation.

The Constitutional Convention which met in Philadelphia between May and September, 1787 was for the most part firmly in the control of a group of vigorous young nationalists who were strongly resolved to establish a supreme national government effectively equipped to implement its own sovereignty. At the outset of proceedings, one of their leaders, Gouverneur Morris of Pennsylvania, introduced a resolution declaring that "no union of states merely federal" would suffice, but "that a national government ought to be established, consisting of supreme Legislative, Executive, and Judiciary." Here was terse expression of the nationalists' intent: to abandon state agency and to create in its place a "national government," i.e., one operating directly upon individuals through its own agents, and to guarantee the supremacy of its laws over the states through some effective mechanism.

This last problem, that of providing some device to implement national supremacy, gave the delegates great difficulty. The Virginia Plan, mainly the work of James Madison, which became the basis for the Convention's labors, provided for a national government operating directly upon individuals through its own courts and its own personnel. This was a large part of the solution of the problem. But there remained a serious difficulty: how to guarantee the effective supremacy of national over state law where the two systems of sovereignty came into conflict. The Virginia Plan offered three possible solutions to this problem: first, that Congress be empowered to coerce states acting in violation of the federal Constitution; second, that Congress be empowered to disallow state laws conflicting with the federal Constitution and laws; and, third, that state officers be required to take an oath of loyalty to the national government.

After some debate, however, the delegates abandoned both coercion and disallowance as involving "wrong principles." Madison himself pointed out that coercion assumed that the states would still function as agents of the national government, a system the delegates now proposed to abandon. The national government, in short, now would impose coercion upon individuals, not upon the states as such. The Convention's lawyers also objected to congressional disallowance, which they considered to involve a judicial rather than a legislative type of function. Over Madison's bitter protest, the delegates voted to give up the idea.

The Convention's final solution was found in a hitherto obscure clause in the New Jersey Plan, a proposal introduced by a states'-rights faction in late June in an effort to check the nationalists' demands. In itself, the New Jersey Plan was little more than a revision of the Articles of Confederation. However, it contained a highly significant "supremacy clause" declaring the Constitution, acts of Congress, and treaties to be the supreme law of the respective states and binding the judges in the state courts to their enforcement as such.

Following the abandonment of congressional disallowance in late July, Luther Martin of Maryland, himself a strong states'-rights advocate, moved to incorporate the New Jersey Plan's "supremacy clause" in the new Constitution. Without opposition or debate, the delegates accepted this proposal. Later the Convention made one small but extremely important change in language: it substituted the phrase "supreme law of the land" for "supreme law of the respective states."

The provision that state officers should subscribe to an oath to support the Constitution, now modified by the Convention to include federal officials as well, was carried over into the Constitution unchallenged from the Virginia Plan. However, at the suggestion of Charles Pinckney of South Carolina, a further clause was attached to ban the imposition of any religious qualifications in any such oath for federal officials. This prohibition, adopted virtually without debate, obviously reflected the prevailing rationalistic Enlightenment spirit to which most of the delegates adhered. The clause was spiritual cousin to the Virginia Statute on Religious Liberty of 1785 and to the prohibition on religious establishments presently to be written into the First Amendment.

The clause in Article VI guaranteeing the Confederation debt was a product of very late deliberation in the Convention. As originally proposed by a "Committee of Eleven" in late August, the provision would have obliged Congress not only to "fulfill the engagements which have been entered into by the United States" but also "to discharge the debts of the United States as well as the debts incurred by the States" in the late war. Several delegates, notably George Mason of Virginia and Elbridge Gerry of Massachusetts, attacked this provision as calculated to "compel payment" of federal and state funds to "blood-sucking speculators" who had bought up such securities cheaply against the possibility of redemption. As a result, Edmund Randolph of Virginia, on August 25, introduced a provision that "all debts contracted, and engagements entered into, by and under the authority of Congress, shall be valid against the United States under this Constitution, as under the Confederation." This clause, which eliminated any mention of state debts and which was regarded as considerably more ambiguous in its import generally, satisfied the opponents of "speculative stock-jobbers," and the Convention thereupon adopted it.

Article VII, with its provision for ratification of the Constitution by state conventions, was also a product of the prevailing nationalistic spirit among the delegates. The Morris resolution of May had very plainly implied the outright abandonment of the Articles rather than their amendment. As the Convention drew to a close, the delegates agreed quite generally that it would be "folly" to submit the work to the hazard of the Articles' requirement of unanimous ratification by the several state legislatures. Accordingly, the Convention in late August voted first to "recommend to Congress" that the proposed Constitution be submitted to conventions in the several states. At the last moment, however, the delegates dropped

*the idea of a mere "recommendation" and decided instead to
provide in the Constitution itself that their work be submitted
directly to state conventions, and that ratification by any nine
would be sufficient for adoption. This provision not only virtually bypassed the Confederation Congress; what was more
important, it also symbolized the Convention's entire abandonment of the Articles of Confederation and the Convention's insistence upon the idea that it was endowed with original organic powers.*

Article. VI.

All Debts contracted and Engagements entered into, before
the Adoption of this Constitution, shall be as valid against the
United States under this Constitution, as under the Confederation.

This Constitution, and the Laws of the United States which
shall be made in Pursuance thereof; and all Treaties made, or
which shall be made, under the Authority of the United
States, shall be the supreme Law of the Land; and the Judges
in every State shall be bound thereby, any Thing in the Constitution or Laws of any State to the Contrary notwithstanding.

The Senators and Representatives before mentioned, and
the Members of the several State Legislatures, and all executive and judicial Officers, both of the United States and of the
several States, shall be bound by Oath or affirmation, to support this Constitution; but no religious Test shall ever be required as a Qualification to any Office or public Trust under
the United States.

Article. VII.

The Ratification of the Conventions of nine States, shall be
sufficient for the Establishment of this Constitution between
the States so ratifying the Same.

done in Convention by the Unanimous Consent of the States
present the Seventeenth Day of September in the Year of our
Lord one thousand seven hundred and Eighty seven and of
the Independence of the United States of America the
Twelfth In witness whereof We have hereunto subscribed our
Names,

G.° Washington—Presid.ᵗ
and deputy from Virginia

| New Hampshire | { | JOHN LANGDON
NICHOLAS GILMAN |

New Hampshire { JOHN LANGDON
                  NICHOLAS GILMAN

Massachusetts { NATHANIEL GORHAM
                 RUFUS KING

Connecticut { W.ᵐ SAM.¹ JOHNSON
               ROGER SHERMAN

New York . . . ALEXANDER HAMILTON

New Jersey { WIL: LIVINGSTON
              DAVID BREARLEY.
              W.ᵐ PATERSON.
              JONA: DAYTON

Pennsylvania { B FRANKLIN
                THOMAS MIFFLIN
                ROBT MORRIS
                GEO. CLYMER
                THO.ˢ FITZSIMONS
                JARED INGERSOLL
                JAMES WILSON
                GOUV MORRIS

Delaware { GEO: READ
            GUNNING BEDFORD jun
            JOHN DICKINSON
            RICHARD BASSETT
            JACO: BROOM

Maryland { JAMES MCHENRY
            DAN OF Sᵗ THO.ˢ JENIFER
            DAN.¹ CARROLL

Virginia { JOHN BLAIR—
            JAMES MADISON JR.

North Carolina { W.ᵐ BLOUNT
                  RICH.ᵈ DOBBS SPRAIGHT
                  HU WILLIAMSON

South Carolina
{ J. RUTLEDGE
CHARLES COTESWORTH PINCKNEY
CHARLES PINCKNEY
PIERCE BUTLER

Georgia
{ WILLIAM FEW
ABR BALDWIN

In Convention Monday, September 17th 1787.
Present
The States of
New Hampshire, Massachusetts, Connecticut, Mr. Hamilton
from New York, New Jersey, Pennsylvania, Delaware, Mary-
land, Virginia, North Carolina, South Carolina and Georgia.

Resolved,

That the preceeding Constitution be laid before the United
States in Congress assembled, and that it is the Opinion of
this Convention, that it should afterwards be submitted to a
Convention of Delegates, chosen in each State by the People
thereof, under the Recommendation of its Legislature, for
their Assent and Ratification; and that each Convention assenting to, and ratifying the Same, should give Notice thereof
to the United States in Congress assembled. Resolved, That it
is the Opinion of this Convention, that as soon as the Conventions of nine States shall have ratified this Constitution,
the United States in Congress assembled should fix a Day on
which Electors should be appointed by the States which shall
have ratified the same, and a Day on which the Electors
should assemble to vote for the President, and the Time and
Place for commencing Proceedings under this Constitution.
That after such Publication the Electors should be appointed,
and the Senators and Representatives elected: That the Electors should meet on the Day fixed for the Election of the
President, and should transmit their Votes certified, signed,
sealed and directed, as the Constitution requires, to the Secretary of the United States in Congress assembled, that the Senators and Representatives should convene at the Time and
Place assigned; that the Senators should appoint a President
of the Senate, for the sole Purpose of receiving, opening and
counting the Votes for President; and, that after he shall be

chosen, the Congress, together with the President, should, without Delay, proceed to execute this Constitution.

By the Unanimous Order of the Convention

G.° WASHINGTON—Presid.ᵗ

W. JACKSON Secretary.

The supremacy clause in Article VI was destined ultimately to become the very foundation of the American constitutional system. On the surface, the clause appeared to be innocuous enough. It affirmed the supremacy of the Constitution and federal law over all state law. But it entrusted the guardianship of that system of supremacy to agents of the several states, the judges of the state courts. Superficially considered, therefore, as the disappointed young nationalists maintained, state-federal relations under the new Constitution might be considered even now to be at the mercy of the several states, as had been the case under the Articles of Confederation.

Hamilton, Madison, and other staunch nationalists, however, soon detected a possible means for converting the comparatively weak supremacy clause into an adequate guarantee of federal sovereignty. If decisions in the state courts in cases involving the Constitution and laws of the United States were made subject to appeal to the federal judiciary, the entire import of the clause would be altered. An agent of the national government, the Supreme Court of the United States, now ultimately would be charged with maintaining the Constitution's guarantee of national supremacy. The Court would accomplish this simply by enforcing the primacy of federal law over state law in the federal courts, and presumably by taking on appeal and reversing those cases arising in the state courts where the latter had failed to recognize federal supremacy. Thus the Supreme Court would possess a veto over state laws "contravening the Articles of Union"—essentially the solution Madison had advocated in the Philadelphia Convention, except that he had sought to lodge the "veto" with Congress.

The new Constitution did not specifically grant the right of appeal from state to federal courts on constitutional questions. But it was possible to construe that right reasonably enough by a very plausible legal argument. And the nationalists soon realized that the right of appeal had to be established beyond question, were the new government to have its sovereignty protected effectively.

The First Congress under the Constitution, an assemblage firmly in the control of Madison and other nationalists, pres-

ently incorporated the right of appeal in the statute since known as the Judiciary Act of 1789. This law set up the federal court system, pursuant to authority granted to Congress in Article III of the Constitution. In Section 25 of the Act, Congress in effect provided that, whenever federal and state law came into conflict in a case arising in a state court and the state court ruled in favor of the application of the state law, there would exist an automatic right of appeal to the appropriate federal court. Since the Supreme Court of the United States, both by the Constitution and by the Judiciary Act itself, was the final court of appeals in federal cases, Article 25 thus in effect lodged the ultimate power to decide conflicts between national and state sovereignty in that Court —an agency of the national government.

The system of national supremacy incorporated in Article VI and the Judiciary Act of 1789 soon found a powerful champion in Chief Justice John Marshall, who presided over the Supreme Court of the United States between 1801 and 1835. In a series of great decisions beginning in 1810, Marshall repeatedly invoked the supremacy clause and Section 25 of the Judiciary Act of 1789 to strike down state laws contravening the Constitution and the laws of the United States. Again and again he pointed out that the Constitution had established a national government whose sphere of sovereignty was admitedly limited but which, by the terms of Article VI, was supreme in its own sphere and that all state laws to the contrary must fail as unconstitutional.

Marshall's most dramatic defense of Article VI and Section 25 of the Judiciary Act came in Cohens v. Virginia, 6 Wheat. 264, a case decided in 1821 on appeal from the supreme court of Virginia. The Cohens, father and son, had been convicted in the Virginia courts of selling lottery tickets and so violating the state's laws against gambling. In their defense, the Cohens had relied heavily upon a congressional act, adopted during the War of 1812 as a desperate financial expedient, authorizing the sale of lottery tickets in the District of Columbia. But the Virginia supreme court, on appeal, had swept the federal statute aside to uphold the state law. And when the Cohens then appealed to the United States Supreme Court, attorneys for Virginia, pursuant to a doctrine then popular in that state, had attacked Section 25 as unconstitutional, denying outright that any constitutional right of appeal from state to federal courts existed at all.

Marshall's opinion in which the Court concurred unanimously, rested very heavily upon Article VI and the doctrine of national supremacy. The Constitution, he pointed out, declared itself the supreme law of the land and bound state judges to observe it as such. Further, the Constitution created a sovereign government which "though limited as to its objects is supreme with respect to its objects." As a supreme government, he continued, the United States could "legitimately control all individuals or governments within the American territory." It followed that state laws, "so far as they are repugnant to the Constitution and laws of the United States, are absolutely void." It was, he said, a mere "corollary" from the foregoing that the federal courts possessed "a power to revise the judgment rendered in them by state tribunals." (Ironically, Marshall found that Virginia's gambling statute, properly construed, did not conflict with the federal lottery law in question, the latter being confined in application to the District of Columbia.)

Many years were to pass, however, before the right of the Supreme Court to function as the ultimate interpreter of the Constitution and expositor of national supremacy won general acceptance. In the Virginia and Kentucky Resolutions adopted by the legislatures of those states in 1798, Thomas Jefferson and Madison himself (the latter temporarily converted to the states'-rights cause) challenged directly the right of the federal courts to exercise final authority over the constitutional system and insisted instead that the final power to judge constitutional questions was properly lodged in the legislatures of the several states. Further, they argued somewhat vaguely, the states properly could "interpose" their sovereignty against a "usurpation" of power by the federal courts or by Congress.

A generation later John C. Calhoun of South Carolina took over this vague doctrine of interposition and elaborated and refined it into a complete doctrine of state sovereignty, which, had it won acceptance, would have rendered meaningless the supremacy clause in Article VI. According to Calhoun, the states antedated the federal Union. Since their sovereignty, he insisted, could not properly be divided or abrogated, it followed that the states were completely sovereign. The federal government, by the same token, was a mere agent of the sovereign states without sovereignty of its own. The Constitution, Calhoun asserted, despite the language in Article VI, was neither law nor supreme; it was, instead, a mere treaty between sovereign states. Final power to interpret the federal constitutional system properly was lodged not in the federal courts but in "Organic Conventions" in the several states, and a state through such a convention lawfully could "nullify" any federal law contravening the Constitution.

Should the other states, by a three-fourths vote of their own like organic conventions, refuse to concur in the state's act of nullification, the nullifying state had one final remedy—as an absolutely sovereign entity, it could withdraw from the Union.

In the tariff crisis of 1832, South Carolina actually invoked Calhoun's scheme, only to have nullification break down when put to the test of actual practice. Yet the doctrine of state sovereignty, completely contradictory to Marshall's interpretation of the supremacy clause, became "orthodox" political doctrine with southern sectionalists in the next generation, and the basis upon which rested the southern doctrine of the right of secession, invoked by the South in the crisis of 1860–61.

In a constitutional sense, the Civil War was a great conflict between two constitutional doctrines, that of John Marshall and that of John Calhoun. By 1861, Lincoln and the great majority of northerners had adopted the Hamilton-Marshall doctrine of national sovereignty and national supremacy, based upon the supremacy clause, as the orthodox view of the Union. Union victory in 1865 effectively established the final efficacy of Article VI and national constitutional supremacy as prevailing American constitutional doctrine. The impact of the supremacy clause upon the American constitutional system has not been challenged effectively since that time.

Thus the "shadow-doctrine" of interposition, raised by certain southern lawyers and politicians after 1954 in an effort to obfuscate the Supreme Court's judicial veto of state segregation laws, is hardly to be taken as serious constitutional doctrine. In November, 1960, Federal Judge Skelly Wright, denouncing Louisiana's attempt to defy federal judicial authority by invoking the ghostly doctrine of Madison and Jefferson, ridiculed "interposition" as "a preposterous perversion, disavowed by the Constitution of the United States" and "an illegal defiance of federal authority." Significantly, Judge Wright's decision shortly was upheld by the Supreme Court itself.

The oath provision in Article VI has had an uneventful history, only occasionally rising to the surface of political or judicial controversy. In 1866, Congress made the oath the basis for the provision in Section 3 of the Fourteenth Amendment which barred from federal and state office all former officeholders, state and federal, who in that capacity had taken the required oath to support the Constitution of the United States, and who thereafter participated in rebellion against the United States. Congress later removed this disability, in a series of amnesty acts passed between 1872 and 1898 by two-thirds vote, as the Fourteenth Amendment empowered it to do.

In the twentieth century, the oath clause has only occasionally been the object of judicial attention. In Cooper v. Aaron, however, a case decided in 1958, the Supreme Court handed down a stern rebuke to state officials who in disregard of their oath had defied and evaded desegregation orders of the federal judiciary. No state official, the Court warned, "can war on the Constitution without violating his oath to support it, . . . else . . . the Constitution becomes a solemn mockery."

The provision in Article VI guaranteeing the Confederation debt soon became the center of considerable political controversy. In 1790, Alexander Hamilton, now Secretary of the Treasury in the Washington Administration, submitted a comprehensive financial plan to Congress for the new government. One part of the plan called for funding the Confederation debt by paying off the former government's securities at face value to present holders, in bonds of the new government.

This proposal at once reawakened the controversy over rewarding "blood-sucking speculators" which had broken out three years earlier on the floor of the Constitutional Convention. Madison, now a member of the House of Representatives, attacked Hamilton's plan, suggesting instead that Confederation bond-holders be paid merely their purchase price, the difference between that sum and face value to be awarded to original purchasers. Hamilton objected in turn that Madison's scheme not only was impractical but also that it would endanger the credit of the new government. This argument carried the day, and Congress by law provided for redemption at par, in new bonds, to present holders.

Article VII, which provided that the new Constitution was to take effect when nine states had ratified the document, set the stage for a struggle over adoption of the Constitution that lasted ten months, from September, 1787, to July, 1788. Technically, the provisions of Article VII were "unconstitutional," since they violated the clause in the Article of Confederation requiring that all amendments to the Articles be submitted to the states by Congress for ratification by legislative action, the unanimous concurrence of all the states being necessary for adoption.

Yet the Conventions "unconstitutional" mode of submitting its work aroused remarkably little controversy. The Confederation Congress itself in effect acceded to the provision ten days after the Philadelphia Convention adjourned, when it submitted the new Constitution to the states for consideration. The legislatures in every state except one presently issued a call for ratifying conventions. Rhode Island alone, which had refused to send delegates to the Philadelphia Convention, now refused to call a state convention to consider ratification.

The argument over ratification soon divided the country along intense if temporary partisan lines. The supporters of the new Constitution, known as Federalists, were for the most part drawn from the coastal region, from urban centers, and from the propertied, mercantile, and professional classes and the more prosperous commercial farmers, all of whom stood to gain substantially from a stable and effective national government. By contrast, the opponents of the Constitution, known as anti-Federalists, were drawn generally from the small farmers of the interior upland plain. Federalist argument stressed the necessity for establishing an adequate and financially sound national government, and warned of the chaos which would ensue were the Constitution rejected. Anti-Federalists attacked the Constitution's lack of a bill of rights, the threat it posed to the sovereignty of the states, the "dictatorial" powers of taxation the new government would possess, and its remoteness from the people.

The Constitution, with its provision for state equality in the Senate, was thought to be favorable to the less populous states, and several small states—Delaware, New Jersey, Georgia, Connecticut, and Maryland—ratified the Constitution between December and April, by large majorities. The Federalists, strong in Pennsylvania and South Carolina, also easily swept these states into the fold. In Massachusetts, Virginia, New York, and New Hampshire, however, there were bitter ratification struggles, and adoption came only by the narrowest of margins. New York's ratification in July, by a vote of 30 to 27, made eleven states for the Union. North Carolina and Rhode Island failed to ratify until 1789 and 1790, respectively, after the government under the Constitution was in actual operation.

The Federalists carried the day mainly because in widespread national debate they had much the better argument. The Federalist essays in New York, the work of Madison, Hamilton, and John Jay, and like arguments elsewhere, won over numerous doubtful supporters. Pro-Federalist political management was also excellent, much opposition being dispelled by the promise that a bill of rights would be adopted once the Constitution was ratified. In addition, several of the *state conventions, in all of which the delegates were chosen from the same districts as those in the corresponding legislatures, were somewhat "gerrymandered" in favor of pro-Federalist tidewater regions. Yet the fact remains that the Constitution was ratified by a process more democratic than that available anywhere else in the world at that time, while the new Constitution was itself flexible enough to become the charter for a modern constitutional democracy.*

The Bill of Rights: Amendments I—X

EDITED BY MILTON R. KONVITZ

The Constitution as it was approved by the Convention on September 17, 1787, contained provisions of some important liberties. There was a prohibition against suspension of the privilege of the writ of habeas corpus. There was a prohibition on the enactment of ex post facto laws and bills of attainder. There was a guarantee of trial by jury for criminal offenses. And there was a prohibition against a religious test as a qualification for public office.

These could by no means be thought of as petty liberties, but there were many persons who thought that the Constitution did not go far enough. A few delegates had left the Convention with the determination to oppose ratification by their states; and Thomas Jefferson wrote to James Madison, three months after the Convention had ended its work, that while there were many things about the proposed Constitution that pleased him, first among the things he did not like was "the omission of a bill of rights, providing clearly, and without the aid of sophism, for freedom of religion, freedom of the press, . . . and trials by jury in all matters of fact triable by the laws of the land. . . ."

At the Convention hardly a word was said in favor of a bill of rights. George Mason's proposal of such a bill came late and almost as an afterthought. This was not because the delegates were against fundamental rights and liberties, but because they agreed with James Wilson that since the federal government was to have only powers explicitly granted by the

171

Constitution, the new government could never misuse powers not given to it—powers reserved to the states or the people. On the level of political theory, Wilson was right; but Mason, Jefferson, and others had the political instinct not to let so important a matter rest on mere inference. A bill of rights, Jefferson told Madison, "is what the people are entitled to against every government on earth, . . . and what no just government should refuse. . . ."

In 1787 the only governments on earth that were limited by bills of rights were those of the six states that had adopted such bills following the precedent set by Virginia's Declaration of Rights (1776), drawn up by Mason. The states that did not adopt separate bills of rights incorporated fundamental guarantees into their state constitutions or relied on their colonial charters.

The colonists had insisted, against England, that they should enjoy all the fundamental rights of Englishmen. They claimed to be beneficiaries of Magna Carta (1215), and of the laws of England that made provision for the writ of habeas corpus; for trial by jury; for the right of an accused to have aid of counsel; for the right to avoid self-incrimination; for liberties that flowed out of the Petition of Right (1628) and the Bill of Rights (1689), including a prohibition on cruel and unusual punishments, the right to bear arms, the right of petition for relief of grievances, and a prohibition on excessive bail. They knew that the press-licensing acts had come to an end in 1695. They knew of the successful attacks on general warrants by John Wilkes. They were familiar with the commendable but unsuccessful struggle of the Levellers to get a written bill of rights.

They had behind them notable colonial charters, like that of Rhode Island (1663), which, in its broad statement of religious liberty, reflected the work of Roger Williams; the Massachusetts Body of Liberties (1641), mainly the work of Nathaniel Ward, which had been enacted by the General Court; the Maryland Toleration Act (1649); the West Jersey Concessions or Agreements (1676–77), in large part the work of William Penn. They had the Pennsylvania Charter of Privileges (1701), signed by Penn and accepted by the colony's assembly, which spoke of a people's "greatest Enjoyment of civil Liberties" and against abridgment "of the Freedom of their Consciences," and of God as "the only Lord of Conscience." They had the Declaration and Resolves of the Continental Congress (1774), which referred to certain acts of Parliament affecting the colonies as "impolitic, unjust, and cruel, as well as unconstitutional, and most dangerous

*and destructive of American rights," and of the right of colo-
nists to "life, liberty, and property," which "they have never
ceded to any sovereign power whatever. . . ." They also had
as a model Jefferson's Bill for Establishing Religious Freedom, adopted by Virginia in 1786, which provided for absolute religious liberty and equality; and the Northwest Ordinance of 1787, which promised religious liberty, trial by jury,
and other basic freedoms to those who would colonize the
Ohio country.*

*They knew, too, John Locke's Second Treatise of Civil
Government (1689), which was one of the foundations of the
Declaration of Independence (1776); and thus doctrine could
be added to legal precedents, and the latter could be translated into and elevated to natural rights. In their turn, natural
rights could be translated into civil liberties. And the main
point of the argument by Jefferson and Mason for a bill of
rights was that civil liberties should be made into constitutional rights.*

*When the Convention was over, Mason left with the deter-
mination to carry his fight for a bill of rights to his state, Virginia, where the proposed Constitution would come up for
ratification, and Elbridge Gerry decided to do the same in
Massachusetts. The latter was the first state to ratify, but the
Convention in that state adopted recommendations for amendments. Virginia ratified, but with a vote of only 89 to 79; and
a committee was chosen to report on amendments to be
brought to the first Congress. New York ratified, but with a
bill of rights attached. Rhode Island and North Carolina waited with their ratifications.*

*Thus, when the First Congress convened, it was clear to
Madison, who had been elected to the House of Representatives, that practicalities were to overrule theoretical considerations and that he must sponsor constitutional amendments.
His own preference was to amend the Constitution by putting
into it at various points where they would seem to fit eight
provisions, five of which concerned fundamental freedoms.
The debate started on June 8, 1789. On July 21 Madison's
amendments were referred to a Committee of Ten. On August 13 the committee reported, recommending fourteen
amendments. These underwent some changes and were approved by the House of Representatives on August 24; and
the House decided that the amendments were to be appended
as a supplement to the Constitution rather than distributed
throughout the document.*

*These amendments were then introduced in the Senate.
There were some differences between the Senate and the*

House of Representatives, which were adjusted by a joint committee. The House had adopted seventeen amendments; but when on September 25 the Senate acted approvingly on the final draft recommended by the House, the amendments had been reduced to twelve. The first two (relating to apportionment of Representatives and compensation of members of Congress) failed of ratification by the states; the other ten were ratified in the form in which they had been submitted, and they were added to the Constitution as our Bill of Rights when Virginia, on December 15, 1791, became the eleventh state to ratify.

The Bill of Rights had been before Congress for only three and a half months. Perhaps no more than a total of seven or eight session days had been spent by Congress considering and debating the proposed amendments. The brevity of this process was possible because the Bill of Rights was the culmination of human experience with despotic governments. One hears in its phrases—"establishment of religion," "freedom of speech, or of the press," "a redress of grievances," "twice put in jeopardy of life or limb," "a witness against himself," "cruel and unusual punishment"—Wordsworth's "still, sad music of humanity." There is plenty of doctrine in the Bill of Rights, but it is no doctrinaire document; for it is rooted in the experience, no less than in the faith, of the people who wanted it.

AMENDMENT [I.]

Congress shall make no law respecting an establishment of religion, or prohibiting the free exercise thereof; or abridging the freedom of speech, or of the press; or the right of the people peaceably to assemble, and to petition the Government for a redress of grievances.

AMENDMENT [II.]

A well regulated Militia, being necessary to the security of a free State, the right of the people to keep and bear Arms, shall not be infringed.

AMENDMENT [III.]

No Soldier shall, in time of peace be quartered in any house, without the consent of the Owner, nor in time of war, but in a manner to be prescribed by law.

AMENDMENT [IV.]

The right of the people to be secure in their persons, houses, papers, and effects, against unreasonable searches and seizures, shall not be violated, and no Warrants shall issue, but upon probable cause, supported by Oath or affirmation, and particularly describing the place to be searched, and the persons or things to be seized.

AMENDMENT [V.]

No person shall be held to answer for a capital or otherwise infamous crime, unless on a presentment or indictment of a Grand Jury, except in cases arising in the land or naval forces, or in the Militia, when in actual service in time of War or public danger; nor shall any person be subject for the same offence to be twice put in jeopardy of life or limb; nor shall be compelled in any criminal case to be a witness against himself, nor be deprived of life, liberty, or property, without due process of law; nor shall private property be taken for public use, without just compensation.

AMENDMENT [VI.]

In all criminal prosecutions, the accused shall enjoy the right to a speedy and public trial, by an impartial jury of the State and district wherein the crime shall have been committed, which district shall have been previously ascertained by law, and to be informed of the nature and cause of the accusation; to be confronted with the witnesses against him; to have compulsory process for obtaining witnesses in his favor, and to have the Assistance of Counsel for his defence.

AMENDMENT [VII.]

In Suits at common law, where the value in controversy shall exceed twenty dollars, the right of trial by jury shall be preserved, and no fact tried by a jury, shall be otherwise reexamined in any Court of the United States, than according to the rules of the common law.

AMENDMENT [VIII.]

Excessive bail shall not be required, nor excessive fines imposed, nor cruel and unusual punishments inflicted.

AMENDMENT [IX.]

The enumeration in the Constitution, of certain rights,

shall not be construed to deny or disparage others retained by the people.

Amendment [X.]

The powers not delegated to the United States by the Constitution, nor prohibited by it to the States, are reserved to the States respectively, or to the people.

As recently as 1943 it was possible for an authority on constitutional law to state that the record "discloses not a single case, in a century and a half, where the Supreme Court has protected freedom of speech, press, assembly, or petition against congressional attack." There are, he said, "very few instances where the Congress has threatened the integrity of the constitutional system or the guarantee of the Bill of Rights." These statements were substantially correct when made, but they soon thereafter became "dated."

As to the subjection of state acts to judgment under the Bill of Rights: In a case that came before the Supreme Court in 1833 it was contended that a state had violated the Fifth Amendment by taking private property for public use without just compensation. The Court, in an opinion by Chief Justice Marshall, held that the Bill of Rights imposes no restriction on the states. The adoption of the Fourteenth Amendment in 1868 gave rise to the argument that some or all of the guarantees of the Bill of Rights may now be enforced against the states under the provision that no state shall deprive any person of his liberty without due process of law. But in 1907 Justice Holmes stated for the Court: "We leave undecided the question whether there is to be found in the 14th Amendment a prohibition similar to that in the 1st." Only Justice Harlan, dissenting, contended that freedom of speech and the press, being an essential part of every man's liberty, was protected by the "due process" clause of the Fourteenth Amendment against abridgment by state action. In 1925, however, in Gitlow v. New York, 268 U.S. 652, the Court for the first time assumed that freedom of speech and the press "are among the fundamental personal rights and 'liberties' protected by the due process clause of the Fourteenth Amendment from impairment by the states." In 1940 the Court included religious freedom in the concept of "liberty" as the term is used in the "due process" clause.

Are all the guarantees of the Bill of Rights incorporated

into this concept of "liberty," and thus protected against infringement by the states? There are conflicting schools of thought in the Supreme Court with respect to this matter. In 1937 Justice Cardozo, in Palko v. Connecticut, 302 U.S. 319, *distinguished fundamental liberties from those of inferior significance, and said that the Bill of Rights includes both types. The former are "implicit in the concept of ordered liberty." Were they sacrificed, "neither liberty nor justice would exist." These include, he said, the freedoms of the First Amendment, and "the right of one accused of crime to the benefit of counsel." On the other hand, he said, the requirement of trial by jury and the provision that no person may be compelled in any criminal case to be a witness against himself are not of "the very essence of a scheme of ordered liberty." This "selective process" has been followed by the Court. But a minority, led by Justice Black, have contended that the original purpose of the Fourteenth Amendment was to extend the complete protection of the Bill of Rights against infringement by the states.*

The "selective process" has not, however, proved to be a substantial obstacle standing in the way of a broadening of the concept of "liberty." Thus the Court has held, for example, that the guarantee of the Eighth Amendment against cruel punishment is a limit on the states; that the substance of the procedural requirements of the Sixth Amendment applies to the states insofar as these requirements provide for "fundamental rights." Thus the Bill of Rights, on one theory or another, has served as a standard for the states with almost the same degree of constitutional compulsion as that felt by the federal government. The Court progressively has assumed the burden of supervision over the administration of criminal justice, testing procedures by the guarantees of the Bill of Rights as requiring fundamentals of justice, fairness, and equality.

There has also been a broadening in the reach of the First Amendment freedoms. For instance, in 1907 the Court, in an opinion written by Justice Holmes, held that the purpose of the guarantee of freedom of the press was only to prevent all restraints previous to publication but not to prevent subsequent punishment—which was freedom of the press as it was understood by Blackstone. The First Amendment, it was assumed, was no bar against prohibiting or punishing acts that "may be deemed contrary to public welfare." Freedom of the press is no longer defined in Blackstonian terms, nor are the First Amendment freedoms limited by the sweep of "public welfare."

But it must be acknowledged that the Court is searching continually for rational ways of formulating the reach and the limits of these freedoms. In Schenck v. United States, 249 U.S. 47 (1919) Justice Holmes, for the Court, said that it may be "that the prohibition of laws abridging the freedom of speech is not confined to previous restraints," and then went on to say that the question in every case is "whether the words used are used in such circumstances and are of such a nature as to create a clear and present danger that they will bring about the substantive evils that Congress has a right to prevent. It is a question of proximity and degree." This "clear and present danger" test competed with the common law test of "public welfare" and the "dangerous tendency" of speech to bring about evil results (such as a breach of the peace). It was not until 1940 that the Court clearly adopted the "clear and present danger" test and reversed convictions. But the subsequent career of the test or doctrine has been extremely checkered. In Dennis v. United States, 341 U.S. 494 (1951) a majority of the Court made it clear that not all speech is constitutionally protected; that there are other social values to which the value of speech must at times give way; that the clear and present danger test is not a rigid rule; that the test means: "In each case [courts] must ask whether the gravity of the 'evil,' discounted by its improbability, justifies such invasion of free speech as is necessary to avoid the danger."

The Court has often found itself moderating between the extreme claim of Justice Black that the guarantees of the Bill of Rights are "absolutes" which allow no opposing considerations, and the extreme claim of Justice Frankfurter that the Court must exercise judicial self-restraint and must not convert any one interest or value into a dogma, but must always weigh competing interests in the light of many and complex factors.

The tensions within the Court have come out most clearly in cases involving acts of Congress dealing with Communism and involving the investigations of congressional committees into Communist and "front" organizations. There has been much more agreement on the breadth and depth of the religion clauses of the First Amendment, which have been interpreted in well-nigh absolute terms; and the Court has tended to give maximum protection to the claims of freedom in literature and the arts.

Madison in 1788 argued that the political truths declared in a solemn manner in a bill of rights would acquire "the character of fundamental maxims of free Government, and *as they become incorporated with the national sentiment, counteract the impulses of interest and passion." It can scarcely be questioned that the guarantees of the Bill of Rights have become fundamental maxims of American government; nor can it be questioned that they have served as a check on interest and passion. Thus the Bill of Rights has helped mold the American nation as well as its political institutions. In any case, it has interacted with the people and its governments in an amazingly organic way, so that it has become inextricably intertwined with the American character and with the ideals of an open, free, pluralistic society.*

Other nations, all over the world, have copied its form and words, but have not always succeeded in giving it meaning in the lives, thoughts, and aspirations of their peoples. But even the enemies of freedom pay homage to the virtues of the Bill of Rights by copying its guarantees, even if only as "parchment barriers," as Madison would say, against the exercise of power.

The Civil War Amendments: XIII—XV

EDITED BY FRANCIS A. ALLEN

The American Civil War was, among other things, a struggle between competing ideas of constitutionalism and the rights of man. When the epic conflict ended with victory of the Union forces on the battlefield, it was inevitable that there would be efforts to consolidate the military victory by giving expression in our fundamental law to certain principles and propositions until then in dispute. Between 1865 and 1870 three amendments were added to the Constitution which have ever since profoundly influenced our public law and policy.

The first problem demanding attention was the abolition of Negro slavery. The institution of slavery in the border states, as well as in the states in rebellion, created serious dilemmas for President Lincoln and Congress in the conduct of the war. The final proclamation of emancipation, issued by President Lincoln on January 1, 1863, left many fundamental issues unresolved. Even before the final proclamation was issued, President Lincoln had asked Congress to approve a constitutional amendment providing compensation to every state that abolished slavery before the beginning of the twentieth century. "In giving freedom to the slaves," he wrote, "we assure freedom to the free—honorable alike in what we give and what we preserve. We shall nobly serve or meanly lose the last best hope of earth." In the months following the final proclamation, Congress was offered various proposals for constitutional amendment. What was to become the Thirteenth Amendment passed the Senate on April 8, 1864, but the proposal received less than the requisite two-thirds vote in

the House of Representatives. Only after the re-election of
President Lincoln in November, 1864, did the amendment
carry the House. The vote was 119 to 56—a margin so narrow that a shift of only three votes would have altered the
result. The Thirteenth Amendment was declared adopted by
Secretary of State Seward on December 6, 1865. Included
among the ratifying states were eight of the former
Confederacy.

At the end of the military hostilities, Congress and the nation were confronted by the myriad problems involved in restoring the southern states to the Union, giving protection to
the rights of the recently emancipated Negro population, and
establishing new patterns of political power. Issues so fundamental were thought by many to require further alterations in
the fundamental law; and a great variety of proposals for
constitutional amendment were advanced within a year of
Appomattox. The purposes and motivation of those active in
the drafting of the Fourteenth Amendment were many and
complex. Because of the importance of the Fourteenth
Amendment in our developing constitutional law, the adoption of the amendment has been closely studied by modern
scholars. Although the main outlines are clear, many important matters remain in doubt and controversy. One of the important factors leading to the adoption of the Fourteenth
Amendment was congressional reaction to the "black codes"
adopted by southern state legislatures at the close of the war
—laws severely restrictive of the civil rights of the emancipated slaves. As demonstrated by the Freedman's Bureau Act
and the Civil Rights Law of 1866, many members of Congress felt that, unless vigorously defended by federal law, the
rights of the Negro which the Thirteenth Amendment was intended to establish would prove illusory. The Civil Rights
Law is particularly important, for it sought both to protect
Negroes from discrimination in the enjoyment of certain
basic rights, such as the right to acquire property, and to
effect a legislative repeal of the famous Dred Scott decision
which had denied the capacity of the Negro to become a citizen of the United States. Although the Act was vital to the
program of the Radical group in Congress and was passed by
a two-thirds vote of both Houses to override President
Johnson's veto, many members, even among the Radicals,
doubted its constitutional validity. One of the purposes of the
first section of the Fourteenth Amendment was, accordingly,
to establish the constitutional validity of the Civil Rights Law
of 1866 and to guard against the consequences of its possible
repeal by some subsequent Congress.

The text of the Fourteenth Amendment evolved slowly in the congressional joint committee on Reconstruction. The third and fourth sections relate to issues of immediate concern growing out of the Civil War and possess little but historical interest today. The second section represents an effort to protect rights of Negro suffrage, an effort soon perceived to be inadequate. The first and the fifth sections, however, remain among the most vital provisions of our public law. The Fourteenth Amendment was approved by Congress on June 13, 1866. Formal pronouncement of its ratification was made by Secretary Seward on July 28, 1868. Among the states counted as ratifying were two, Ohio and New Jersey, that had first adopted resolutions of ratification but later sought to withdraw consent and six southern states that were required to ratify the Fourteenth Amendment as a condition of their restoration in the Union.

The draftsmen of the Fourteenth Amendment sought to protect Negro rights of suffrage in Section 2, which, in effect, requires curtailment of congressional representation of any state in proportion to the number of persons disenfranchised in the state on grounds of race. Representative Thaddeus Stevens of Pennsylvania, a Radical leader, expressed the view that these provisions were the most important in the Fourteenth Amendment. Section 2 failed to achieve its purpose, however; and very soon proposals were advanced for constitutional amendment to provide more direct and effective protection of the Negro's right to vote. Various considerations underlay these proposals. To some it appeared that the civil rights of the Negro could be achieved only when he was accorded the right of full participation in the political life of the community. The proposals were also consistent with a general movement for expanded suffrage, which constituted one important aspect of nineteenth-century liberalism. Finally, it appears clear that some northern congressional leaders feared the rise of white political power in the South as a threat to their own political dominance in Congress and to the interests they represented. The Fifteenth Amendment was approved by Congress on February 26, 1869. Formal announcement of its ratification was made on May 30, 1870.

Amendment XIII.

Section 1. Neither slavery nor involuntary servitude, except as a punishment for crime whereof the party shall have been duly convicted, shall exist within the United States, or any place subject to their jurisdiction.

SECTION 2. Congress shall have power to enforce this article by appropriate legislation.

AMENDMENT XIV.

SECTION 1. All persons born or naturalized in the United States and subject to the jurisdiction thereof, are citizens of the United States and of the State wherein they reside. No State shall make or enforce any law which shall abridge the privileges or immunities of citizens of the United States; or shall any State deprive any person of life, liberty, or property, without due process of law; nor deny to any person within its jurisdiction the equal protection of the laws.

SECTION 2. Representatives shall be apportioned among the several States according to their respective numbers, counting the whole number of persons in each State, excluding Indians not taxed. But when the right to vote at any election for the choice of electors for President and Vice President of the United States, Representatives in Congress, the Executive and Judicial officers of a State, or the members of the Legislature thereof, is denied to any of the male inhabitants of such State, being twenty-one years of age, and citizens of the United States, or in any way abridged, except for participation in rebellion, or other crime, the basis of representation therein shall be reduced in the proportion which the number of such male citizens shall bear to the whole number of male citizens twenty-one years of age in such State.

SECTION 3. No person shall be a Senator or Representative in Congress, or elector of President and Vice President, or hold any office, civil or military, under the United States, or under any State, who, having previously taken an oath, as a member of Congress, or as an officer of the United States, or as a member of Congress, or as an officer of the United States, or as a member of any State legislature, or as an executive or judicial officer of any State, to support the Constitution of the United States, shall have engaged in insurrection or rebellion against the same, or given aid or comfort to the enemies thereof. But Congress may by a vote of two-thirds of each House, remove such disability.

SECTION 4. The validity of the public debt of the United States, authorized by law, including debts incurred for payment of pensions and bounties for services in suppressing insurrection or rebellion, shall not be questioned. But neither the United States nor any State shall assume or pay any debt or obligation incurred in aid of insurrection or rebellion against the United States, or any claim for the loss or emancipation of any slave; but all such debts, obligations and claims shall be held illegal and void.

SECTION 5. The Congress shall have power to enforce, by appropriate legislation, the provisions of this article.

AMENDMENT XV.

SECTION 1. The right of citizens of the United States to vote shall not be denied or abridged by the United States or by any State on account of race, color, or previous condition of servitude.

SECTION 2. The Congress shall have power to enforce this article by appropriate legislation.

The Fourteenth Amendment is, without doubt, the most important addition made to the text of the Constitution since the adoption of the Bill of Rights in 1790. Of the five sections of the amendment, the first has proved to be of prime significance. Included in the language of Section 1 are the great protean phrases, "due process of law" and "equal protection of the laws." The draftsmen of the amendment provided no specific meanings for these grand generalizations. This is not to say that the language was wholly devoid of historical content. The powers of Congress are limited in the Fifth Amendment by a "due process" clause; and many state constitutions contained similar provisions that had frequently been interpreted by state courts. Moreover, "due process" suggests the traditions of Magna Carta and "the law of the land." "Equal protection," too, although less redolent of the past, invokes certain historical connotations.

Yet the great moral imperatives of due process and equal protection could not be confined to their historical understandings when applied to the emerging issues of modern American life. There is evidence that those who drafted Section 1 intended that the meanings of these phrases should evolve and expand with the passage of time and changes of circumstance. This, in any event, is what occurred. As a result, the history of Fourteenth Amendment interpretation reveals in sharp and accurate focus the principal public issues with which generations of Americans have been preoccupied in the past three-quarters of a century.

Two great issues, one political and the other primarily economic, dominate the first half-century of Fourteenth Amendment interpretation. Neither is directly or necessarily concerned with the rights of racial minorities. The first issue was: What changes did the Civil War and the postwar amendments effect in the fundamental structure of American federalism? At least some of the congressional proponents of constitutional change desired basic and far-reaching alterations and assumed that significant aggrandizement of federal power had been achieved by adoption of the postwar amendments. From the first, however, the Supreme Court made clear that the amendments had not replaced the essential features of the American system. The most important teaching of the Slaughter-House Cases, 16 Wall. 36, decided in 1873 when nationalist feeling was still high in Congress, is that the postwar amendments did not effect a revolution in the American form of government. Ten years later Justice Bradley maintained that the Fourteenth Amendment does not grant Congress power "to establish a code of municipal law." In the years that followed, a practical redistribution of authority between state and federal governments occurred, and the Fourteenth Amendment sometimes contributed to this development. Broader interpretations of the powers of Congress under Section 5 of the amendment may one day significantly accelerate these tendencies. For the most part, however, the new importance of federal power has evolved in response to conditions of the modern world that are largely independent of the Fourteenth Amendment and its interpretation.

The second great issue confronted by the nineteenth-century Court involved the scope of the regulatory powers of the states over the burgeoning economic activity of the nation. The response was at first tentative and restrained. Thus in the Slaughter-House Cases, Justice Miller, speaking of the "due process" clause, observes: "We doubt very much whether any action of a state not directed by way of discrimination against the Negroes . . . will ever be held to come within the purview of this provision." Only a short time later the Court's decision in Munn v. Illinois, 94 U.S. 113 (1876), recognized broad state legislative authority over the rates of public utilities. But beginning in the eighties a much more restrictive view of state authority was expressed, and in the four decades that followed much state legislation fell afoul of the Court's interpretation of the "due process" clause. Among the casualties were state laws seeking to regulate rates, prices, minimum wages of workers, maximum hours of labor, and other terms of employment. These decisions expressed the judicial view then dominant that the full promise of American life could be realized only through the release of creative energies in the economic sphere, largely unimpeded by government restraint, and that the attainment of civil and political liberty in all aspects depended upon the defenses of freedom of economic enterprise. At no time were these assumptions fully shared by all segments of American public opinion; and after the turn of the century criticism of the Court's role in these cases became more vocal and more organized.

It was not until the decade of the thirties that the Court fundamentally revised its views as to the permissible scope of state regulatory power. A majority of the Court has never wholly forsworn its authority to test the validity of state economic regulation against the requirements of due process, but today state legislation is not to be invalidated when supportable on any rational basis. The validity of state economic regulation is, therefore, no longer a central problem of Fourteenth Amendment interpretation.

The twentieth century brought to the nation new issues and new concerns, many of which found expression in judicial interpretations of "due process" and "equal protection." The years beginning with World War I may be regarded as a period of crisis for individual liberty, not only in the United States, but throughout the Western world. These concerns have been faithfully reflected in the work of the Supreme Court. Virtually all the constitutional law relating to the freedoms of expression, of association, and of religion, has been announced in the years since World War I. In 1925 the Court recognized that the imperatives of the First Amendment were part of the concept of "liberty" protected by the Fourteenth Amendment against invasion by the states, and many modern "due process" cases present such issues as the establishment of religion and freedom of speech. One of the most important questions of modern constitutional law has been whether the Fourteenth Amendment "incorporates" the provisions of the first nine amendments, traditionally understood to apply only to Congress and the federal government, and makes them applicable to the states. Efforts to interpret the "privileges and immunities" clause of the Fourteenth Amendment to achieve that end were frustrated by the Court in early cases arising under the amendment. No majority of the modern court has gone the entire distance of recognizing the full applicability of the Bill of Rights to the states. But a series of recent decisions dealing with particular rights has recognized that in most essential matters the states are subject to restraints comparable to those that limit the powers of the federal government.

Included in the modern judicial preoccupation with problems of civil liberty are the Fourteenth Amendment cases involving issues of fair procedure in state criminal proceedings. In the first half-century of the amendment's life, the Court had numerous occasions to consider the application of the "due process" clause to state criminal procedure. In virtually all these cases, the state procedures were upheld and a broad area of local self-determination was recognized. With the important decisions of Powell v. Alabama, 287 U.S. 45 (1932), however, a new era of "due process" interpretation began. The Powell case recognized that the appointment of counsel for the impoverished accused was, in the circumstances presented, an indispensable part of the fair hearing which the state court was required to provide. Since that time the Court has spoken on an impressive range of questions involving, not only the right to counsel, but coerced confessions, unreasonable search and arrest practices, and many other aspects of the criminal trial and police activity. The consequence has been the formulation of an extensive body of constitutional doctrine within the span of a single generation.

The rights and interests of the recently emancipated slaves were obviously matters of primary concern to the proponents of the Civil War amendments. This concern is manifest in the explicit language of the Thirteenth and Fifteenth Amendments. The Fourteenth Amendment undoubtedly encompassed other objectives; but here, too, the problems of race were central. In general, the judicial interpretation of "involuntary servitude" in the Thirteenth Amendment has been kept within rather narrow bounds. Efforts to find in that amendment legal protections for a broad range of civil rights, such as the right of access to public accommodations, were firmly rejected by a majority of the Court in cases arising in the early postwar period. The Fifteenth Amendment has received numerous applications, but social conditions and, until recently, the absence of valid and effective implementing legislation have frustrated full realization of the rights of Negro suffrage.

Despite the purposes of its framers and the circumstances out of which it evolved, the Fourteenth Amendment made surprisingly small contributions to the civil rights of the Negro population in the half-century following its adoption.

Judicial holdings that the amendment's protections applied only to "state action," and not to the action of private persons, required invalidation of much protective legislation enacted by Congress in the postwar period. By the end of the century the Court found legally enforceable segregation of the races consistent with the requirements of equal protection of the laws, so long as "separate but equal" accommodations were provided. Not until the fourth decade of the twentieth century did stirrings of conscience in the American public and a new determination of Negro groups force substantial judicial consideration of racial discrimination as a Fourteenth Amendment problem. A series of decisions of the highest importance was handed down. The institution of the "white primary" in southern states was held to be in violation of the Constitution. Criminal convictions infected by racial discrimination were reversed. In Shelley v. Kraemer, *334 U.S. 1 (1948), enforcement of restrictive covenants barring Negroes from ownership and occupancy of dwellings was found to offend the "equal protection" clause. Beginning in the 1930's the Court entertained a succession of cases involving racial segregation in public education, culminating in the landmark decision of* Brown v. Board of Education, *347 U.S. 483 (1954). There the Court confronted the "separate but equal" doctrine, established more than a half-century before, and laid it to rest. The* Brown *case represents only the beginning of the Fourteenth Amendment's serious involvement in the issue of admitting minority groups to full participation in American life. Once again the great generalizations of the Fourteenth Amendment—"due process" and "equal protection"—have identified and illuminated the central issues of the time.*

George Washington

First Inaugural Address

1789

EDITED BY CLINTON ROSSITER

The First Inaugural Address was delivered by George Washington in the Senate Chamber of Federal Hall in New York City on April 30, 1789. Despite the historic importance of the occasion, and also of the words that graced it, we have almost no reliable evidence about the genesis of this first of all inaugural addresses. It must have been written sometime around March 1, 1789, by which date Washington could doubt no longer that he had been elected unanimously to the Presidency, and could therefore not beg off this last momentous duty to his country; and the place of writing, or at least of polishing, must have been Mount Vernon, from which he did not set forth for New York until April 16. Knowing what we do of his writing habits both as warrior and as statesman, we may take it for granted that he turned to a trusted friend for help in drafting the address. Never a man from whom words flowed in easy abundance, always a man of genuine modesty about his own intellectual capacities, he had given the American art of "ghost-writing" its first major trial in the course of the Revolution. Well satisfied with the results, he continued to rely heavily on the literary skills of his colleagues until the end of his career.

This is not at all to say that Washington made himself the

189

prisoner of the clever pens of clever men, or that, to be specific, the First Inaugural should be credited to another man. To the contrary, so explicit were the written and oral directions, so clearly understood the principles and prejudices, so piercing the critical eye, and so commanding the presence of this "first character of the world" that not even his most persuasive friends could make him say things he had not wanted to say in the first place. Like Andrew Jackson and Franklin D. Roosevelt he sought the help of men who were better with words than he could ever be, yet also like them he saw to it that the words of his great state papers were, in the most meaningful sense, his very own.

The man to whom Washington most probably turned in this instance was James Madison, who in 1789 was every bit as close to him as Alexander Hamilton had been a few years before and was to be forever after. Armed with a lengthy rough draft of Washington's ideas and guided by several face-to-face talks before the fireplace at Mt. Vernon, Madison seems to have spent his last few days in Virginia—from which he set forth March 2 to take his seat in the First Congress—putting these ideas in a form that would dignify the first official utterance of the first President of the first republic to arise in the New World as a challenge to the Old. That Washington was well satisfied with Madison's labors is plain from a letter of May 5, 1789, in which he invited his friend "to finish . . . the good work" he had begun by drafting a brief reply to the response of the House of Representatives.

Washington's purposes are clear on the face of this noble address. To remind his fellow citizens that the event of his accession to power was not of his own choosing, to beg their representatives not to embarrass him with "pecuniary compensation" for doing his duty, to invoke the blessings of Heaven, to jab a quick punch or two at "local attachments" and "party animosities," to celebrate morality as the foundation of liberty, and to put this experiment in free government in full historical perspective—these were the messages he had wanted to deliver, and these, thanks to Madison's loyal assistance and his own awareness of the gravity of the occasion, were delivered with the best of all possible effects. While the caustic senator from Pennsylvania, William Maclay, complained that Washington was "agitated and embarrassed more than ever he was by the leveled cannon or pointed musket," one suspects that his bearing was attuned perfectly to the demands of a fateful moment. The sense of the gathering that listened to these words was perhaps more accurately ex-

pressed by Fisher Ames, the most eloquent member of the First Congress, who confessed frankly that he had "sat entranced" in the face of this "allegory in which virtue was personified."

FELLOW CITIZENS OF THE SENATE AND OF THE HOUSE OF REPRESENTATIVES:

A MONG the vicissitudes incident to life, no event could have filled me with greater anxieties than that of which the notification was transmitted by your order, and received on the fourteenth day of the present month:—On the one hand, I was summoned by my Country, whose voice I can never hear but with veneration and love, from a retreat which I had chosen with the fondest predilection, and, in my flattering hopes, with an immutable decision, as the asylum of my declining years: a retreat which was rendered every day more necessary as well as more dear to me, by the addition of habit to inclination, and of frequent interruptions in my health to the gradual waste committed on it by time.—On the other hand, the magnitude and difficulty of the trust to which the voice of my Country called me, being sufficient to awaken in the wisest and most experienced of her citizens, a distrustful scrutiny into his qualifications, could not but overwhelm with dispondence, one, who, inheriting inferior endowments from nature and unpractised in the duties of civil administration, ought to be peculiarly conscious of his own deficiencies.—In this conflict of emotions, all I dare aver, is, that it has been my faithful study to collect my duty from a just appreciation of every circumstance, by which it might be affected.—All I dare hope, is, that, if in executing this task I have been too much swayed by a grateful remembrance of former instances, or by an affectionate sensibility to this transcendent proof, of the confidence of my fellow-citizens; and have thence too little consulted my incapacity as well as disinclination for the weighty and untried cares before me; my *error* will be palliated by the motives which misled me, and

The reading copy of this address in Washington's handwriting is preserved in the files of the United States Senate in the National Archives; it has been reproduced as National Archives Facsimile No. 22 (Washington, 1952), under the title *Washington's Inaugural Address of 1789*. The document is reprinted here in its original form, including a few misspelled words.

its consequences be judged by my Country, with some share of the partiality in which they originated.—

Such being the impressions under which I have, in obedience to the public summons, repaired to the present station; it would be peculiarly improper to omit in this first official Act, my fervent supplications to that Almighty Being who rules over the Universe,—who presides in the Councils of Nations,—and whose providential aids can supply every human defect, that his benediction may consecrate to the liberties and happiness of the People of the United States, a Government instituted by themselves for these essential purposes: and may enable every instrument employed in its administration to execute with success, the functions allotted to his charge.—In tendering this homage to the Great Author of every public and private good, I assure myself that it expresses your sentiments not less than my own;—nor those of my fellow-citizens at large, less than either.—No People can be bound to acknowledge and adore the invisible hand, which conducts the affairs of men more than the People of the United States.—Every step, by which they have advanced to the character of an independent nation, seems to have been distinguished by some token of providential agency.—And in the important revolution just accomplished in the system of their United Government; the tranquil deliberations and voluntary consent of so many distinct communities, from which the event has resulted, cannot be compared with the means by which most Governments have been established, without some return of pious gratitude along with an humble anticipation of the future blessings which the past seem to presage.—These reflections, arising out of the present crisis, have forced themselves too strongly on my mind to be suppressed.—You will join with me I trust in thinking, that there are none under the influence of which, the proceedings of a new and free Government can more auspiciously commence.—

By the article establishing the Executive Department, it is made the duty of the president "to recommend to your consideration, such measures as he shall judge necessary and expedient."—The circumstances under which I now meet you, will acquit me from entering into that subject, farther than to refer to the Great Constitutional Charter under which you are assembled; and which, in defining your powers, designates the objects to which your attention is to be given.—It will be more consistent with those circumstances, and far more congenial with the feelings which actuate me, to substitute, in place of a recommendation of particular measures, the tribute that is due to the talents, the rectitude, and the patriotism which adorn the characters selected to devise and adopt them.—In these honorable qualifications, I behold the surest pledges, that as on one side, no local prejudices, or attachments; no separate views, nor party animosities, will misdirect the comprehensive and equal eye which ought to watch over this great assemblage of communities and interests: so, on another, that the foundations of our National policy will be laid in the pure and immutable principles of private morality; and the pre-eminence of free Government, be exemplified by all the attributes which can win the affections of its Citizens, and command the respect of the world.—I dwell on this prospect with every satisfaction which an ardent love for my Country can inspire: since there is no truth more thoroughly established, than that there exists in the economy and course of nature, an indissoluble union between virtue and happiness,—between duty and advantage,—between the genuine maxims of an honest and magnanimous policy, and the solid rewards of public prosperity and felicity:—Since we ought to be no less persuaded that the propitious smiles of Heaven, can never be expected on a nation that disregards the eternal rules of order and right, which Heaven itself has ordained:—And since the preservation of the sacred fire of liberty, and the destiny of the Republican model of Government, are justly considered as *deeply,* perhaps as *finally* staked, on the experiment entrusted to the hands of the American people.—

Besides the ordinary objects submitted to your care, it will remain with your judgement to decide, how far an exercise of the occasional power delegated by the Fifth article of the Constitution is rendered expedient at the present juncture by the nature of objections which have been urged against the system, or by the degree of inquietude which has given birth to them.—Instead of undertaking particular recommendations on this subject, in which I could be guided by no lights derived from official opportunities, I shall again give way to my entire confidence in your discernment and pursuit of the public good:—For I assure myself that whilst you carefully avoid every alteration which might endanger the benefits of an United and effective Government, or which ought to await the future lessons of experience; a reverence for the characteristic rights of freemen, and a regard for the public harmony, will sufficiently influence your deliberations on the question how far the former can be more impregnably fortified, or the latter be safely and advantageously promoted.—

To the preceeding observations I have one to add, which will be most properly addressed to the House of Representatives.—It concerns myself, and will therefore be as brief as possible.—When I was first honoured with a call into the service of my country, then on the eve of an arduous struggle for its liberties, the light in which I contemplated my duty required that I should renounce every pecuniary compensation.—From this resolution I have in no instance departed. —And being still under the impressions which produced it, I must decline as inapplicable to myself, any share in the personal emoluments, which may be indispensably included in a permanent provision for the Executive Department; and must accordingly pray that the pecuniary estimates for the Station in which I am placed, may, during my continuance in it, be limited to such actual expenditures as the public good may be thought to require.—

Having thus imparted to you my sentiments, as they have been awakened by the occasion which brings us together,—I shall take my present leave;—but not without resorting once more to the benign parent of the human race, in humble supplication that since he has been pleased to favour the American people, with opportunities for deliberating in perfect tranquility, and dispositions for deciding with unparelleled unanimity on a form of Government, for the security of their Union, and the advancement of their happiness, so this divine blessing may be equally *conspicuous* in the enlarged views, the temperate consultations—and the wise measures on which the success of this Government must depend.—

The afterlife of this touching little sermon on personal duty and national glory has been marked by none of the excitement that has attended the progress of the Farewell Address through the pages of history. Yet if Washington's First Inaugural is no match for Jefferson's as an exposition of a mighty political faith, for Lincoln's as an appeal to "the better angels of our nature," or for Franklin D. Roosevelt's as a summons to greatness in a time of hesitation, it has an importance for Americans that is bound to grow with the passage of the years of our never-ending experiment in constitutional democracy.

In the first place, it was an audible if disciplined cry from the heart of George Washington, and those who go in search of an understanding of the urges and aspirations of "this great man" (as even Maclay felt compelled to salute him) can do no better than to begin with the critical inventory of his own "endowments" in the opening sentences, the assertions of the existence of a force or standard called "the public good" sprinkled all through the address, and the stoutly rationalist insistence upon calling God anything except God—"Almighty Being," "Great Author," "invisible hand," "benign parent of the human race."

Second, the address set an example that has been converted by time and memory into one of our few great national rituals. Just what persons or what reading or what intuition put it in Washington's mind to deliver an inaugural address can never be known for certain, but that he must have pondered this step carefully cannot be doubted. Throughout his eight years in the Presidency Washington was conscious almost to the point of anxiety that, as he wrote to Madison in his note of May 5, 1789, "the first of every thing, in our situation will serve to establish a Precedent," indeed a precedent that might guide men for centuries to come. This is one instance in which history has vindicated his judgment without reservation.

Finally, in a time in which it has suddenly become important for America to have a "national purpose," that is to say, a destiny more exalted than our own freedom and well-being, it is useful to recall that the first clear public acknowledgment of the suspicion that we had been granted such a destiny is to be found in the words in which Washington accepted the fateful, formless burdens of the Presidency. As Lincoln's quiet remarks at Gettysburg were the most refined expression of the old and unspoiled idea of the American Mission, so Washington's quiet remarks in New York were the most challenging. It made the Mission a living presence in American politics; it gave dignity and legitimacy to even the most savage contests for power in the next three generations. Of all the words of inspiration that Washington spoke in his career as public man, none were more influential, because none were more expressive of the American character, than this awesome reminder that into our hands had been committed the decisive trial of strength with the age-old enemies of free government—ignorance, cruelty, pride, poverty, disorder, irrational behavior. If it had said nothing else, the First Inaugural Address would be a document to cherish because it asks us, as it asked the men of 1789, to remember that "the preservation of the sacred fire of liberty, and the destiny of the Republican model of Government, are justly considered as deeply, perhaps as finally staked, on the experiment entrusted to the hands of the American people."

Alexander Hamilton

Report on Manufactures

1791

EDITED BY THOMAS C. COCHRAN

Submitted by Alexander Hamilton, as Secretary of the Treasury, to the House of Representatives on December 5, 1791, the Report on Manufactures *was the last of his famous messages to Congress. Since the population of the country was then predominantly agricultural and economic theories condemning industry were popular, the problem of writing a convincing report in favor of stimulating manufactures was a delicate one. Hamilton had delayed presentation of this message for nearly two years, both for the collection of data and for the discussion of successive drafts with various experts. He was able to draw upon the ideas of several advocates of manufacturing. One of these was William Barton, secretary of the Pennsylvania Society for the Encouragement of Manufactures and the Useful Arts, who in 1786 had published a paper on the benefits of manufacturing to agriculture; another was President Washington, who, before coming to the government, had been developing a plan for making Alexandria, Virginia, a textile-manufacturing center. More immediately, Hamilton had the aid of Tenche Coxe, who became Assistant to the Secretary of the Treasury in May, 1790. Coxe was the foremost economic thinker of the Pennsylvania Society, a man conversant with both theoretical literature and American facts. Since one draft of the lengthy* Report *exists in Coxe's handwriting, he must have cooperated extensively in its preparation; in particular, he probably supplied many of the facts and figures. Thus, while the final* Report *represents Hamilton's mature and carefully reasoned ideas, it is also a comprehensive statement of an important school of American thought that placed a pragmatic policy for the development of the nation ahead of any abstract economic principles.*

THE SECRETARY of the Treasury, in obedience to the order of the House of Representatives, of the 15th day of January, 1790, has applied his attention at as early a period as his other duties would permit, to the subject of Manufactures, and particularly to the means of promoting such as will tend to render the United States independent on foreign nations, for military and other essential supplies; and he thereupon respectfully submits the following report. . . .

The expediency of encouraging manufactures in the United States, which was not long since deemed very questionable, appears at this time to be pretty generally admitted. . . .

There still are, nevertheless, respectable patrons of opinions unfriendly to the encouragement of manufactures. . . . It has been maintained, that agriculture is not only the most productive, but the only productive species of industry. The reality of this suggestion, in either respect, has, however, not been verified by any accurate detail of facts and calculations; and the general arguments which are adduced to prove it, are rather subtile and paradoxical, than solid or convincing. . . .

One of the arguments made use of in support of the idea, may be pronounced both quaint and superficial. It amounts to this: That, in the production of the soil, nature co-operates with man; and that the effect of their joint labor must be greater than that of the labor of man alone.

This, however, is far from being a necessary inference. It is very conceivable, that the labor of man alone, laid out upon a work requiring great skill and art to bring it to perfection,

The *Report* is reprinted here, in abridged form, from *The Works of Alexander Hamilton*, edited by John C. Hamilton (New York: Charles S. Francis & Company, 1850–51), Vol. III. There are three drafts of the *Report* in the Hamilton Papers in the Library of Congress. Another draft, in Tenche Coxe's handwriting, is in the Tenche Coxe Papers in the collection of the Historical Society of Pennsylvania, Philadelphia. The parts of the *Report* reproduced here make up somewhat less than a third of the total manuscript, in which many of the arguments are expanded in great detail.

may be more productive, in value, than the labor of nature and man combined, when directed towards more simple operations and objects; and when it is recollected to what an extent the agency of nature, in the application of the mechanical powers, is made auxiliary to the prosecution of manufactures, the suggestion which has been noticed loses even the appearance of plausibility. . . .

Another, and that which seems to be the principal argument offered for the superior productiveness of agricultural labor, turns upon the allegation, that labor employed on manufactures, yields nothing equivalent to the rent of land; or to that net surplus, as it is called, which accrues to the proprietor of the soil.

But this distinction, important as it has been deemed, appears rather verbal than substantial.

It is easily discernible, that what, in the first instance, is divided into two parts, under the denominations of the ordinary profit of the stock of the farmer and rent to the landlord, is, in the second instance, united under the general appellation of the ordinary profit on the stock of the undertaker; and that this formal or verbal distribution constitutes the whole difference in the two cases. . . .

To affirm that the labor of the manufacturer is unproductive, because he consumes as much of the produce of the land as he adds value to the raw material which he manufactures, is not better founded, than it would be to affirm that the labor of the farmer, which furnishes materials to the manufacturer, is unproductive, because he consumes an equal value of manufactured articles. Each furnishes a certain portion of the produce of his labor to the other, and each destroys a correspondent portion of the produce of the labor of the other. In the mean time, the maintenance of two citizens, instead of one, is going on; the State has two members instead of one; and they, together, consume twice the value of what is produced from the land. . . .

It is now proper to proceed a step further, and to enumerate the principal circumstances from which it may be inferred that manufacturing establishments not only occasion a positive augmentation of the produce and revenue of the society, but that they contribute essentially to rendering them greater than they could possibly be, without such establishments. These circumstances are:

1. The division of labor.
2. An extension of the use of machinery.

3. Additional employment to classes of the community not ordinarily engaged in business.
4. The promoting of emigration from foreign countries.
5. The furnishing greater scope for the diversity of talents and dispositions, which discriminate men from each other.
6. The affording a more ample and various field for enterprise.
7. The creating, in some instances, a new, and securing, in all, a more certain and steady demand for the surplus produce of the soil.

Each of these circumstances has a considerable influence upon the total mass of industrious effort in a community; together, they add to it a degree of energy and effect, which are not easily conceived. . . .

Though it should be true that, in settled countries, the diversification of industry is conducive to an increase in the productive powers of labor, and to an augmentation of revenue and capital; yet it is scarcely conceivable that there can be any thing of so solid and permanent advantage to an uncultivated and unpeopled country, as to convert its wastes into cultivated and inhabited districts. If the revenue, in the mean time, should be less, the capital, in the event, must be greater.

To these observations, the following appears to be a satisfactory answer:

If the system of perfect liberty to industry and commerce were the prevailing system of nations, the arguments which dissuade a country, in the predicament of the United States, from the zealous pursuit of manufactures, would doubtless have great force. It will not be affirmed that they might not be permitted, with few exceptions, to serve as a rule of national conduct. In such a state of things, each country would have the full benefit of its peculiar advantages to compensate for its deficiencies or disadvantages. If one nation were in a condition to supply manufactured articles, on better terms than another, that other might find an abundant indemnification in a superior capacity to furnish the produce of the soil. And a free exchange, mutually beneficial, of the commodities which each was able to supply, on the best terms, might be carried on between them, supporting, in full vigor, the industry of each. . . .

But the system which has been mentioned, is far from characterizing the general policy of nations. The prevalent one has been regulated by an opposite spirit. The consequence of it is, that the United States are, to a certain extent, in the situation of a country precluded from foreign commerce. They can, indeed, without difficulty, obtain from abroad the manufactured supplies of which they are in want; but they experience numerous and very injurious impediments to the emission and vent of their own commodities. . . .

In such a position of things, the United States cannot exchange with Europe on equal terms; and the want of reciprocity would render them the victim of a system which should induce them to confine their views to agriculture, and refrain from manufactures. A constant and increasing necessity, on their part, for the commodities of Europe, and only a partial and occasional demand for their own, in return, could not but expose them to a state of impoverishment, compared with the opulence to which their political and natural advantages authorize them to aspire. . . .

The remaining objections to a particular encouragement of manufactures in the United States, now require to be examined.

One of these turns on the proposition, that industry, if left to itself, will naturally find its way to the most useful and profitable employment. Whence it is inferred, that manufactures, without the aid of government, will grow up as soon and as fast as the natural state of things and the interest of the community may require. . . .

Experience teaches, that men are often so much governed by what they are accustomed to see and practise, that the simplest and most obvious improvements, in the most ordinary occupations, are adopted with hesitation, reluctance, and by slow gradations. The spontaneous transition to new pursuits, in a community long habituated to different ones, may be expected to be attended with proportionably greater difficulty. . . .

The apprehension of failing in new attempts, is, perhaps, a more serious impediment. There are dispositions apt to be attracted by the mere novelty of an undertaking; but these are not always those best calculated to give it success. To this it is of importance that the confidence of cautious, sagacious capitalists, both citizens and foreigners, should be excited. And to inspire this description of persons with confidence, it is essential that they should be made to see in any project which is new—and for that reason alone, if for no other, precarious—the prospect of such a degree of countenance and support from government, as may be capable of overcoming the obstacles inseparable from first experiments.

The superiority antecedently enjoyed by nations who have preoccupied and perfected a branch of industry, constitutes a more formidable obstacle than either of those which have been mentioned, to the introduction of the same branch into a country in which it did not before exist. . . .

But the greatest obstacle of all to the successful prosecution of a new branch of industry in a country in which it was before unknown, consists, as far as the instances apply, in the bounties, premiums, and other aids, which are granted in a variety of cases, by the nations in which the establishments to be imitated are previously introduced. . . . Hence the undertakers of a new manufacture have to contend, not only with the natural disadvantages of a new undertaking, but with the gratuities and remunerations which other governments bestow. To be enabled to contend with success, it is evident that the interference and aid of their own governments are indispensable. . . .

The objections to the pursuit of manufactures in the United States, which next present themselves to discussion, represent an impracticability of success, arising from three causes: scarcity of hands, dearness of labor, want of capital. . . .

With regard to scarcity of hands, the fact itself must be applied with no small qualification to certain parts of the United States. There are large districts which may be considered as pretty fully peopled; and which, notwithstanding a continual drain for distant settlements, are thickly interspersed with flourishing and increasing towns. . . .

But there are circumstances . . . that materially diminish, every where, the effect of a scarcity of hands. These circumstances are, the great use which can be made of women and children, on which point a very pregnant and instructive fact has been mentioned—the vast extension given by late improvements to the employment of machines—which, substituting the agency of fire and water, has prodigiously lessened the necessity for manual labor; the employment of persons ordinarily engaged in other occupations, during the seasons or hours of leisure, which, besides giving occasion to the exertion of a greater quantity of labor, by the same number of persons, and thereby increasing the general stock of labor, as has been elsewhere remarked, may also be taken into the calculation, as a resource for obviating the scarcity of hands; lastly, the attraction of foreign emigrants. . . . It is not unworthy of remark, that the objection to the success of manufactures, deduced from the scarcity of hands, is alike applicable to trade and navigation, and yet these are perceived to flourish, without any sensible impediment from that cause.

As to the dearness of labor (another of the obstacles alleged), this has relation principally to two circumstances: one, that which has just been discussed, or the scarcity of hands; the other, the greatness of profits. . . . It is also evident, that the effect of the degree of disparity, which does truly exist, is diminished in proportion to the use which can be made of machinery. . . .

To procure all such machines as are known in any part of Europe, can only require a proper provision and due pains. The knowledge of several of the most important of them is already possessed. The preparation of them here is, in most cases, practicable on nearly equal terms. As far as they depend on water, some superiority of advantages may be claimed, from the uncommon variety and greater cheapness of situations adapted to millseats, with which different parts of the United States abound. . . .

The supposed want of capital for the prosecution of manufactures in the United States, is the most indefinite of the objections. . . .

It is very difficult to pronounce any thing precise concerning the real extent of the moneyed capital of a country, and still more, concerning the proportion it bears to the objects that invite the employment of capital. It is not less difficult to pronounce, how far the effect of any given quantity of money, as capital, or in other words, as a medium for circulating the industry and property of a nation, may be increased by the very circumstance of the additional motion which is given to it, by new objects of employment. . . .

The introduction of banks, as has been shown on another occasion, has a powerful tendency to extend the active capital of a country. Experience of the utility of these institutions, is multiplying them in the United States. It is probable that they will be established wherever they can exist with advantage; and wherever they can be supported, if administered with prudence, they will add new energies to all pecuniary operations. . . .

It is a well known fact that there are parts of Europe which have more capital than profitable domestic objects of employment. Hence, among other proofs, the large loans continually furnished to foreign States. And it is equally certain, that the capital of other parts may find more profitable employment in the United States than at home. . . .

It is not impossible, that there may be persons disposed to look, with a jealous eye, on the introduction of foreign capital, as if it were an instrument to deprive our own citizens of the profits of our own industry; but, perhaps, there never could be a more unreasonable jealousy. Instead of being viewed as a rival, it ought to be considered as a most valuable auxiliary, conducing to put in motion a greater quantity of productive labor, and a greater portion of useful enterprise, than could exist without it. It is at least evident, that, in a country situated like the United States, with an infinite fund of resources yet to be unfolded, every farthing of foreign capital which is laid out in internal meliorations, and in industrious establishments, of a permanent nature, is a precious acquisition.

And, whatever be the objects which originally attract foreign capital, when once introduced, it may be directed towards any purpose of beneficial exertion which is desired. And to detain it among us, there can be no expedient so effectual, as to enlarge the sphere within which it may be usefully employed: though introduced merely with views to speculations in the funds, it may afterwards be rendered subservient to the interests of agriculture, commerce, and manufactures. . . .

But, while there are circumstances sufficiently strong to authorize a considerable degree of reliance on the aid of foreign capital, towards the attainment of the object in view, it is satisfactory to have good grounds of assurance, that there are domestic resources, of themselves adequate to it. It happens that there is a species of capital, actually existing in the United States, which relieves from all inquietude, on the score of want of capital. This is the funded debt. . . . Public funds answer the purpose of capital, from the estimation in which they are usually held by moneyed men; and, consequently, from the ease and dispatch with which they can be turned into money. . . . This operation of public funds as capital, is too obvious to be denied; but it is objected to the idea of their operating as an augmentation of the capital of the community, that they serve to occasion the destruction of some other capital, to an equal amount. . . .

Hitherto, the reasoning has proceeded on a concession of the position, that there is a destruction of some other capital, to the extent of the annuity appropriated to the payment of the interest, and the redemption of the principal of the debt; but in this too much has been conceded. There is, at most, a temporary transfer of some other capital, to the amount of the annuity, from those who pay, to the creditor, who receives; which he again restores to the circulation, to resume the offices of a capital. This he does either immediately, by employing the money in some branch of industry, or mediately, by lending it to some other person, who does so employ it, or by spending it on his own maintenance. . . . When the payments of interest are periodical and quick, and made by the instrumentality of banks, the diversion or suspension of capital may almost be denominated momentary. . . .

In the question under discussion, it is important to distinguish between an absolute increase of capital, or an accession of real wealth, and an artificial increase of capital, as an engine of business, or as an instrument of industry and commerce. In the first sense, a funded debt has no pretensions to being deemed an increase of capital; in the last, it has pretensions which are not easy to be controverted. Of a similar nature is bank credit; and in an inferior degree, every species of private credit.

But, though a funded debt is not, in the first instance, an absolute increase of capital, or an augmentation of real wealth; yet, by serving as a new power in the operations of industry, it has, within certain bounds, a tendency to increase the real wealth of a community, in like manner, as money, borrowed by a thrifty farmer, to be laid out in the improvement of his farm, may, in the end, add to his stock of real riches. . . .

There remains to be noticed an objection to the encouragement of manufactures, of a nature different from those which question the probability of success. This is derived from its supposed tendency to give a monopoly of advantages to particular classes, at the expense of the rest of the community, who, it is affirmed, would be able to procure the requisite supplies of manufactured articles on better terms from foreigners than from our own citizens; and who, it is alleged, are reduced to the necessity of paying an enhanced price for whatever they want, by every measure which obstructs the free competition of foreign commodities. . . .

But, though it were true that the immediate and certain effect of regulations controlling the competition of foreign with domestic fabrics, was an increase of price, it is universally true that the contrary is the ultimate effect with every successful manufacture. When a domestic manufacture has attained to perfection, has engaged in the prosecution of it a competent number of persons, it invariably becomes cheaper. Being free from the heavy charges which attend the importation of foreign commodities, it can be afforded, and accordingly seldom ever fails to be sold, cheaper, in process of time, than was the foreign article for which it is a substitute. The internal competition which takes place, soon does away every thing like monopoly, and by degrees reduces the price of the article to the minimum of a reasonable profit on the capital employed. This accords with the reason of the thing, and with experience. . . .

The objections which are commonly made to the expediency of encouraging, and to the probability of succeeding in manufacturing pursuits, in the United States, having now been discussed, the considerations, which have appeared in the course of the discussion, recommending that species of industry to the patronage of the Government, will be materially strengthened by a few general, and some particular topics, which have been naturally reserved for subsequent notice.

There seems to be a moral certainty that the trade of a country, which is both manufacturing and agricultural, will be more lucrative and prosperous than that of a country which is merely agricultural. . . . There is always a higher probability of a favorable balance of trade, in regard to countries in which manufactures, founded on the basis of a thriving agriculture, flourish, than in regard to those which are confined wholly, or almost wholly, to agriculture. . . .

Not only the wealth, but the independence and security of a country, appear to be materially connected with the prosperity of manufactures. Every nation, with a view to those great objects, ought to endeavor to possess within itself, all the essentials of a national supply. These comprise the means of subsistence, habitation, clothing, and defence. . . .

The want of a navy, to protect our external commerce, as long as it shall continue, must render it a peculiarly precarious reliance for the supply of essential articles, and must serve to strengthen prodigiously the arguments in favor of manufactures. . . .

Our distance from Europe, the great fountain of manufactured supply, subjects us, in the existing state of things, to inconvenience and loss in two ways.

The bulkiness of those commodities, which are the chief productions of the soil, necessarily imposes very heavy charges on their transportation to distant markets. . . . The charges on manufactured supplies, brought from Europe, are greatly enhanced by the same circumstances of distance. . . .

The equality and moderation of individual property, and the growing settlements of new districts, occasion, in this country, an unusual demand for coarse manufactures; the charges of which being greater in proportion to their bulk, augment the disadvantage which has just been described. . . .

These disadvantages press, with no small weight, on the landed interests of the country. In seasons of peace, they cause a serious deduction from the intrinsic value of the products of the soil. In the time of a war, which should either involve ourselves, or another nation possessing a considerable share of our carrying trade, the charges on the transportation of our commodities, bulky as most of them are, could hardly fail to prove a grievous burthen to the farmer, while obliged to depend, in so great a degree as he now does, upon foreign markets, for the vent of the surplus of his labor. . . .

Particular encouragements of particular manufactures may be of a nature to sacrifice the interest of landholders to those of manufacturers; but it is nevertheless a maxim, well established by experience, and generally acknowledged, where there has been sufficient experience, that the aggregate prosperity of manufactures and the aggregate prosperity of agriculture are intimately connected. . . .

If, then, it satisfactorily appears, that it is the interest of the United States, generally, to encourage manufactures, it merits particular attention, that there are circumstances which render the present a critical moment for entering, with zeal, upon the important business. The effort cannot fail to be materially seconded by a considerable and increasing influx of money, in consequence of foreign speculations in the funds, and by the disorders which exist in different parts of Europe. . . .

The disturbed state of Europe inclining its citizens to emigration, the requisite workmen will be more easily acquired than at another time; and the effect of multiplying the opportunities of employment to those who emigrate, may be an increase of the number and extent of valuable acqisitions to the population, arts, and industry, of the country. . . .

In order to [form] a better judgment of the means proper to be resorted to by the United States, it will be of use to advert to those which have been employed with success in other countries. The principal of these are:

Protecting duties—or duties on those foreign articles which are the rivals of the domestic ones intended to be encouraged. . . .

The propriety of this species of encouragement need not be dwelt upon, as it is not only a clear result from the numerous topics which have been suggested, but is sanctioned by the laws of the United States, in a variety of instances; it has the additional recommendation of being a source of revenue. . . .

Pecuniary bounties.

This has been found one of the most efficacious means of encouraging manufactures, and is, in some views, the best. . . .

It is a species of encouragement more positive and direct than any other, and, for that very reason, has a more immediate tendency to stimulate and uphold new enterprises, increasing the chances of profit, and diminishing the risks of loss, in the first attempts.

It avoids the inconvenience of a temporary augmentation of price, which is incident to some other modes; or it produces it to a less degree, either by making no addition to the charges on the rival foreign article, as in the case of protecting duties, or by making a smaller addition. . . . Bounties have not, like high protecting duties, a tendency to produce scarcity. . . . Bounties are, sometimes, not only the best, but the only proper expedient for uniting the encouragement of a new object of agriculture with that of a new object of manufacture. . . .

It cannot escape notice, that a duty upon the importation of an article can no otherwise aid the domestic production of it, than by giving the latter greater advantages in the home market. It can have no influence upon the advantageous sale of the article produced in foreign markets—no tendency, therefore, to promote its exportation.

The true way to conciliate these two interests is to lay a duty on foreign manufactures of the material, the growth of which is desired to be encouraged, and to apply the produce of that duty, by way of bounty, either upon the production of the material itself, or upon its manufacture at home, or upon both. . . .

Except the simple and ordinary kinds of household manufacture, or those for which there are very commanding local advantages, pecuniary bounties are, in most cases, indispensable to the introduction of a new branch. . . .

Premiums.

Premiums serve to reward some particular excellence or superiority, some extraordinary exertion or skill, and are dispensed only in a small number of cases. But their effect is to stimulate general effort; contrived so as to be both honorary and lucrative, they address themselves to different passions—touching the chords, as well of emulation as of interest. They are, accordingly, a very economical mean of exciting the enterprise of a whole community. . . .

The encouragement of new inventions and discoveries at home, and of the introduction into the United States of such as may have been made in other countries; particularly, those which relate to machinery.

This is among the most useful and unexceptionable of the aids which can be given to manufactures. The usual means of that encouragement are pecuniary rewards, and, for a time, exclusive privileges. The first must be employed, according to the occasion, and the utility of the invention or discovery. For the last, so far as respects "authors and inventors," provision has been made by law. . . .

Judicious regulations for the inspection of manufactured commodities.

This is not among the least important of the means by which the prosperity of manufactures may be promoted. It is, indeed, in many cases, one of the most essential. Contributing to prevent frauds upon consumers at home, and exporters to foreign countries; to improve the quality, and preserve the character of the national manufactures; it cannot fail to aid the expeditious and advantageous sale of them, and to serve as a guard against successful competition from other quarters. . . .

The facilitating of the transportation of commodities. . . .

There is, perhaps, scarcely any thing, which has been better calculated to assist the manufactures of Great Britain, than the melioration of the public roads of that kingdom, and the great progress which has been of late made in opening canals. Of the former, the United States stand much in need; for the latter, they present uncommon facilities. . . .

There is little room to hope, that the progress of manufacturers will so equally keep pace with the progress of population, as to prevent even a gradual augmentation of the product of the duties on imported articles. . . .

. . . This surplus will serve—

First. To constitute a fund for paying the bounties which shall have been decreed.

Second. To constitute a fund for the operations of a board to be established, for promoting arts, agriculture, manufactures, and commerce. Of this institution, different intimations have been given in the course of this report. An outline of a plan for it shall now be submitted.

Let a certain annual sum be set apart, and placed under the management of commissioners, not less than three, to consist of certain officers of the Government and their successors in office.

Let these commissioners be empowered to apply the fund confided to them, to defray the expenses of the emigration of artists, and manufacturers in particular branches of extraordinary importance; to induce the prosecution and introduction of useful discoveries, inventions, and improvements, by proportionate rewards, judiciously held out and applied; to encourage by premiums, both honorable and lucrative, the exertions of individuals and of classes, in relation to the several objects they are charged with promoting; and to afford such other aids to those objects as may be generally designated by law. . . .

There is reason to believe that the progress of particular manufactures has been much retarded by the want of skilful workmen. And it often happens, that the capitals employed are not equal to the purposes of bringing from abroad workmen of a superior kind. Here, in cases worthy of it, the auxiliary agency of the Government would, in all probability, be useful. There are also valuable workmen in every branch, who are prevented from emigrating, solely, by the want of means. Occasional aids to such persons, properly administered, might be a source of valuable acquisitions to the country. . . .

The great use which may be made of a fund of this nature, to procure and import foreign improvements, is particularly obvious. Among these, the articles of machines would form a most important item. . . .

In countries where there is great private wealth, much may be effected by the voluntary contributions of patriotic individuals; but in a community situated like that of the United States, the public purse must supply the deficiency of private resource. In what can it be so useful, as in promoting and improving the efforts of industry?

All which is humbly submitted.

ALEXANDER HAMILTON
Secretary of the Treasury.

The analyses in Hamilton's Report *were so thorough and the arguments on subjects such as the tariff so cogent that over*

the next century they were paraphrased in editorials and political speeches whenever these topics became public issues. Mathew Carey, for example, the great champion of protective tariff between the War of 1812 and the Civil War, added little to the basic arguments of the Report. The same could be said of post-Civil War protectionists such as William ("Pig-Iron") Kelley, William McKinley or Nelson Dingley. Mid-twentieth-century students of economic development find Hamilton's explanation of the factors that hamper the initiation of industrial enterprise enlightened and penetrating.

On the other hand, to remember that Hamilton represented the extreme political right, and that Jefferson on the liberal left fought these proposals under the banner of laissez faire, gives perspective on the ebb and flow of ideas in politics. The arguments of the Report were those currently thought suitable by many business leaders in a country where capital and labor were scarce and management weak and inexperienced. A century later, with labor and capital ample and management confident and powerful, business leaders were turning against Hamilton's view of the use of the national state. Only his ideas on protective tariff had a strong conservative following.

Early in the twentieth century the Report's advocacy of the paternalistic state was embraced by Theodore Roosevelt, Herbert Croly, George F. Perkins, and other moderate progressives. But, whereas Hamilton and his school would have used the state chiefly to advance economic development, these progressives would have used it also to bring about social justice.

Still later the approach inherent in the Report was mirrored in such laws as the National Industrial Recovery and the Full Employment Acts. New Deal economists also agreed with the Report that there was no immediate danger in an increasing debt owed to the citizens of the nation. Thus, by mid-twentieth century, Hamilton, as a political figure, was in an anomalous position. While the Democrats, as in President Johnson's Great Society, supported Hamilton's economic view of the use of the state, they shunned his name because of his conservative politics. The Republicans, on the other hand, revered him as a political ancestor but were tacitly in opposition to most of his economic ideas.

George Washington

Farewell Address

1796

EDITED BY RICHARD B. MORRIS

Long in formulation, President Washington's great state paper took the shape of a political testament. Promulgated at the end of his second term in the Presidency, it embodied his momentous decision not to stand for a third term, a decision which for long was accepted as an unwritten law of the Constitution. As a matter of fact Washington had considered retiring at the end of his first term. Back in February, 1792, he had asked James Madison to prepare a draft of an address concerning his contemplated retirement. Madison complied, sending him a "Form for an Address." Washington put it aside for the time being.

When he definitely decided to retire at the end of his second term, Washington made a draft of his own, embodying some material from Madison's earlier draft, but introducing numerous new elements. These included his concern with the divisiveness of the evolving party alignments, a defense of his own integrity, and some cautions about America's foreign policy. The last had been prompted by the bitterness of the debates in the Senate over Jay's Treaty, and by the attempt of the House of Representatives to assert a role in the making of treaties. After consulting Madison again, Washington sent on to Madison's chief antagonist, Alexander Hamilton, a brief introduction, Madison's draft, and the President's own lengthy addition. Hamilton prepared two new drafts, faithfully following Washington's scheme of organization and the President's main ideas, but rephrasing these in a masterly way. At Washington's request, Hamilton discussed his drafts with John Jay, but we have no documentation on the changes Hamilton may have incorporated as a result of Jay's suggestions.

Despite a considerable amount of collaboration, the final state paper was still very much Washington's own. The President even rephrased Hamilton's revision in some cases, often making the text less wordy. For example, Hamilton's "Original Draft" asks:

> Why should we forego the advantages of so felicitous a situation? Why quit our own ground to stand upon foreign ground?

Washington changed that to read:

> Why forego the advantages of so peculiar a situation? Why quit our own to stand upon foreign ground?

Hamilton:

> Permanent alliances, intimate connection with any part of the foreign world is to be avoided; so far, (I mean) as we are now at liberty to do it.

Washington:

> It is our true policy to steer clear of permanent alliances with any portion of the foreign world, so far, I mean, as we are now at liberty to do it.

Washington showed himself to be a more cautious, and perhaps less full-blown isolationist than Hamilton. Thus, Hamilton's "Original Draft":

> Taking care always to keep ourselves by suitable establishments in a respectably defensive position, we may safely trust to occasional alliances for extraordinary war emergencies.

Washington changed the sentence to read:

> Taking care always to keep ourselves by suitable establishments on a respectable defensive posture, we may safely trust to temporary alliances for extraordinary emergencies.

*By substituting "temporary" for "occasional" Washington in-
troduced a subtle but important change of concept.*

*Washington wrote John Jay early in May, 1796, disclosing
his definite intention to retire, but he yielded to Hamilton's
urging to hold off his public announcement. Hamilton advised him to time the announcement for two months before
the meeting of the presidential electors, but Washington did
not wait quite that long. Three months before the electors
convened he submitted his Farewell Address to the Cabinet,
and, four days later, on September 19, 1796, he gave it to the
people in the columns of the Philadelphia* Daily American
Advertiser. *It was never delivered orally.*

FRIENDS AND FELLOW-CITIZENS

THE PERIOD for a new election of a citizen to administer
the Executive Government of the United States being not
far distant, and the time actually arrived when your thoughts
must be employed in designating the person who is to be
clothed with that important trust, it appears to me proper,
especially as it may conduce to a more distinct expression of
the public voice, that I should now apprise you of the resolution I have formed to decline being considered among the
number of those out of whom a choice is to be made.

I beg you at the same time to do me the justice to be assured that this resolution has not been taken without a strict
regard to all the considerations appertaining to the relation
which binds a dutiful citizen to his country; and that in withdrawing the tender of service, which silence in my situation
might imply, I am influenced by no diminution of zeal for
your future interest, no deficiency of grateful respect for your
past kindness, but am supported by a full conviction that the
step is compatible with both.

The acceptance of and continuance hitherto in the office to
which your suffrages have twice called me have been a uniform sacrifice of inclination to the opinion of duty and to a
deference for what appeared to be your desire. I constantly
hoped that it would have been much earlier in my power,
consistently with motives which I was not at liberty to disregard, to return to that retirement from which I had been reluctantly drawn. The strength of my inclination to do this
previous to the last election had even led to the preparation

The address is reprinted here as it originally appeared in the Philadelphia *Daily American Advertiser* of September 19, 1796.

of an address to declare it to you; but mature reflection on the then perplexed and critical posture of our affairs with foreign nations and the unanimous advice of persons entitled to my confidence impelled me to abandon the idea. I rejoice that the state of your concerns, external as well as internal, no longer renders the pursuit of inclination incompatible with the sentiment of duty or propriety, and am persuaded, whatever partiality may be retained for my services, that in the present circumstances of our country you will not disapprove my determination to retire.

The impressions with which I first undertook the arduous trust were explained on the proper occasion. In the discharge of this trust I will only say that I have, with good intentions, contributed toward the organization and administration of the Government the best exertions of which a very fallible judgment was capable. Not unconscious in the outset of the inferiority of my qualifications, experience in my own eyes, perhaps still more in the eyes of others, has strengthened the motives to diffidence of myself; and every day the increasing weight of years admonishes me more and more that the shade of retirement is as necessary to me as it will be welcome. Satisfied that if any circumstances have given peculiar value to my services they were temporary, I have the consolation to believe that, while choice and prudence invite me to quit the political scene, patriotism does not forbid it.

In looking forward to the moment which is intended to terminate the career of my political life my feelings do not permit me to suspend the deep acknowledgment of that debt of gratitude which I owe to my beloved country for the many honors it has conferred upon me; still more for the steadfast confidence with which it has supported me, and for the opportunities I have thence enjoyed of manifesting my inviolable attachment by services faithful and persevering, though in usefulness unequal to my zeal. If benefits have resulted to our country from these services, let it always be remembered to your praise and as an instructive example in our annals that under circumstances in which the passions, agitated in every direction, were liable to mislead; amidst appearances sometimes dubious; vicissitudes of fortune often discouraging; in situations in which not unfrequently want of success has countenanced the spirit of criticism, the constancy of your support was the essential prop of the efforts and a guaranty of the plans by which they were effected. Profoundly penetrated with this idea, I shall carry it with me to my grave as a strong incitement to unceasing vows that Heaven may continue to you the choicest tokens of its beneficence; that your union and brotherly affection may be perpetual; that the free Constitution which is the work of your hands may be sacredly maintained; that its administration in every department may be stamped with wisdom and virtue; that, in fine, the happiness of the people of these States, under the auspices of liberty, may be made complete by so careful a preservation and so prudent a use of this blessing as will acquire to them the glory of recommending it to the applause, the affection, and adoption of every nation which is yet a stranger to it.

Here, perhaps, I ought to stop. But a solicitude for your welfare which can not end but with my life, and the apprehension of danger natural to that solicitude, urge me on an occasion like the present to offer to your solemn contemplation and to recommend to your frequent review some sentiments which are the result of much reflection, of no inconsiderable observation, and which appear to me all important to the permanency of your felicity as a people. These will be offered to you with the more freedom as you can only see in them the disinterested warnings of a parting friend, who can possibly have no personal motive to bias his counsel. Nor can I forget as an encouragement to it your indulgent reception of my sentiments on a former and not dissimilar occasion.

Interwoven as is the love of liberty with every ligament of your hearts, no recommendation of mine is necessary to fortify or confirm the attachment.

The unity of government which constitutes you one people is also now dear to you. It is justly so, for it is a main pillar in the edifice of your real independence, the support of your tranquillity at home, your peace abroad, of your safety, of your prosperity, of that very liberty which you so highly prize. But as it is easy to foresee that from different causes and from different quarters much pains will be taken, many artifices employed, to weaken in your minds the conviction of this truth, as this is the point in your political fortress against which the batteries of internal and external enemies will be most constantly and actively (though often covertly and insidiously) directed, it is of definite moment that you should properly estimate the immense value of your national union to your collective and individual happiness; that you should cherish a cordial, habitual, and immovable attachment to it; accustoming yourselves to think and speak of it as of the palladium of your political safety and prosperity; watching for its preservation with jealous anxiety; discountenancing whatever may suggest even a suspicion that it can in any event be abandoned, and indignantly frowning upon the first dawning of every attempt to alienate any portion of our country from the rest or to enfeeble the sacred ties which now link together the various parts.

For this you have every inducement of sympathy and interest. Citizens by birth or choice of a common country, that country has a right to concentrate your affections. The name of American, which belongs to you in your national capacity, must always exalt the just pride of patriotism more than any appellation derived from local discriminations. With slight shades of difference, you have the same religion, manners, habits, and political principles. You have in a common cause fought and triumphed together. The independence and liberty you possess are the work of joint councils and joint efforts, of common dangers, sufferings, and successes.

But these considerations, however powerfully they address themselves to your sensibility, are greatly outweighed by those which apply more immediately to your interest. Here every portion of our country finds the most commanding motives for carefully guarding and preserving the union of the whole.

The *North*, in an unrestrained intercourse with the *South*, protected by the equal laws of a common government, finds in the productions of the latter great additional resources of maritime and commercial enterprise and precious materials of manufacturing industry. The *South*, in the same intercourse, benefiting by the same agency of the *North*, sees its agriculture grow and its commerce expand. Turning partly into its own channels the seamen of the *North*, it finds its particular navigation invigorated; and while it contributes in different ways to nourish and increase the general mass of the national navigation, it looks forward to the protection of a maritime strength to which itself is unequally adapted. The *East*, in a like intercourse with the *West*, already finds, and in the progressive improvement of interior communications by land and water will more and more find, a valuable vent for the commodities which it brings from abroad or manufactures at home. The *West* derives from the *East* supplies requisite to its growth and comfort, and what is perhaps of still greater consequence, it must of necessity owe the *secure* enjoyment of indispensable *outlets* for its own productions to the weight, influence, and the future maritime strength of the Atlantic side of the Union, directed by an indissoluble community of interest as *one nation*. Any other tenure by which the *West* can hold this essential advantage, whether derived from its own separate strength or from an apostate and unnatural connection with any foreign power, must be intrinsically precarious.

While, then, every part of our country thus feels an immediate and particular interest in union, all the parts combined can not fail to find in the united mass of means and efforts greater strength, greater resource, proportionably greater security from external danger, a less frequent, interruption of their peace by foreign nations, and what is of inestimable value, they must derive from union an exemption from those broils and wars between themselves which so frequently afflict neighboring countries not tied together by the same governments, which their own rivalships alone would be sufficient to produce, but which opposite foreign alliances, attachments, and intrigues would stimulate and imbitter. Hence, likewise, they will avoid the necessity of those overgrown military establishments which, under any form of government, are inauspicious to liberty, and which are to be regarded as particularly hostile to republican liberty. In this sense it is that your union ought to be considered as a main prop of your liberty, and that the love of the one ought to endear to you the preservation of the other.

These considerations speak a persuasive language to every reflecting and virtuous mind, and exhibit the continuance of the union as a primary object of patriotic desire. Is there a doubt whether a common government can embrace so large a sphere? Let experience solve it. To listen to mere speculation in such a case were criminal. We are authorized to hope that a proper organization of the whole, with the auxiliary agency of governments for the respective subdivisions, will afford a happy issue to the experiment. It is well worth a fair and full experiment. With such powerful and obvious motives to union affecting all parts of our country, while experience shall not have demonstrated its impracticability, there will always be reason to distrust the patriotism of those who in any quarter may endeavor to weaken its bands.

In contemplating the causes which may disturb our union it occurs as matter of serious concern that any ground should have been furnished for characterizing parties by *geographical* discriminations—*Northern* and *Southern, Atlantic* and *Western*—whence designing men may endeavor to excite a belief that there is a real difference of local interests and views. One of the expedients of party to acquire influence within particular districts is to misrepresent the opinions and aims of other districts. You can not shield yourselves too much against the jealousies and heart-burnings which spring from these misrepresentations; they tend to render alien to each other those who ought to be bound together by fraternal affection. The inhabitants of our Western country have lately had a useful lesson on this head. They have seen in the negotiation by the Executive and in the unanimous ratification by the Senate of the treaty with Spain, and in the universal satisfaction at that event throughout the United States, a decisive proof how unfounded were the suspicions propagated among them of a policy in the General Government and in the Atlantic States unfriendly to their interests in regard to the Mississippi. They have been witnesses to the formation of two treaties—that with Great Britain and that with Spain—which secure to them everything they could desire in respect to our foreign relations toward confirming their prosperity. Will it not be their wisdom to rely for the preservation of these advantages on the union by which they were procured? Will they not henceforth be deaf to those advisers, if such there are, who would sever them from their brethren and connect them with aliens?

To the efficacy and permanency of your union a government for the whole is indispensable. No alliances, however strict, between the parts can be an adequate substitute. They must inevitably experience the infractions and interruptions which all alliances in all times have experienced. Sensible of this momentous truth, you have improved upon your first essay by the adoption of a Constitution of Government better calculated than your former for an intimate union and for the efficacious management of your common concerns. This Government, the offspring of your own choice, uninfluenced and unawed, adopted upon full investigation and mature deliberation, completely free in its principles, in the distribution of its powers, uniting security with energy, and containing within itself a provision for its own amendment, has a just claim to your confidence and your support. Respect for its authority, compliance with its laws, acquiescence in its measures, are duties enjoined by the fundamental maxims of true liberty. The basis of our political systems is the right of the people to make and to alter their constitutions of government. But the constitution which at any time exists till changed by an explicit and authentic act of the whole people is sacredly obligatory upon all. The very idea of the power and the right of the people to establish government presupposes the duty of every individual to obey the established government.

All obstructions to the execution of the laws, all combinations and associations, under whatever plausible character, with the real design to direct, control, counteract, or awe the regular deliberation and action of the constituted authorities, are destructive of this fundamental principle and of fatal tendency. They serve to organize faction; to give it an artificial and extraordinary force; to put in the place of the delegated will of the nation the will of a party, often a small but artful and enterprising minority of the community, and, according to the alternate triumphs of different parties, to make the public administration the mirror of the ill-concerted and incongruous projects of faction rather than the organ of consistent and wholesome plans, digested by common counsels and modified by mutual interests.

However combinations or associations of the above description may now and then answer popular ends, they are likely in the course of time and things to become potent engines by which cunning, ambitious, and unprincipled men will be enabled to subvert the power of the people, and to usurp for themselves the reins of government, destroying afterwards the very engines which have lifted them to unjust dominion.

Toward the preservation of your Government and the permanency of your present happy state, it is requisite not only that you steadily discountenance irregular oppositions to its acknowledged authority, but also that you resist with care the spirit of innovation upon its principles, however specious the pretexts. One method of assault may be to effect in the forms of the Constitution alterations which will impair the energy of the system, and thus to undermine what can not be directly overthrown. In all the changes to which you may be invited remember that time and habit are at least as necessary to fix the true character of governments as of other human institutions; that experience is the surest standard by which to test the real tendency of the existing constitution of a country that facility in changes upon the credit of mere hypothesis and opinion exposes to perpetual change, from the endless variety of hypothesis and opinion; and remember especially that for the efficient management of your common interests in a country so extensive as ours a government of as much vigor as is consistent with the perfect security of liberty is indispensable. Liberty itself will find in such a government, with powers properly distributed and adjusted, its surest guardian. It is, indeed, little else than a name where the government is too feeble to withstand the enterprises of faction, to confine each member of the society within the limits prescribed by the laws, and to maintain all in the secure and tranquil enjoyment of the rights of person and property.

I have already intimated to you the danger of parties in the

State, with particular reference to the founding of them on geographical discriminations. Let me now take a more comprehensive view, and warn you in the most solemn manner against the baneful effects of the spirit of party generally.

This spirit, unfortunately, is inseparable from our nature, having its root in the strongest passions of the human mind. It exists under different shapes in all governments, more or less stifled, controlled, or repressed; but in those of the popular form it is seen in its greatest rankness and is truly their worst enemy.

The alternate domination of one faction over another, sharpened by the spirit of revenge natural to party dissension, which in different ages and countries has perpetrated the most horrid enormities, is itself a frightful despotism. But this leads at length to a more formal and permanent despotism. The disorders and miseries which result gradually incline the minds of men to seek security and repose in the absolute power of an individual, and sooner or later the chief of some prevailing faction, more able or more fortunate than his competitors, turns this disposition to the purposes of his own elevation on the ruins of public liberty.

Without looking forward to an extremity of this kind (which nevertheless ought not to be entirely out of sight), the common and continual mischiefs of the spirit of party are sufficient to make it the interest and duty of a wise people to discourage and restrain it.

It serves always to distract the public councils and enfeeble the public administration. It agitates the community with ill-founded jealousies and false alarms; kindles the animosity of one part against another; foments occasionally riot and insurrection. It opens the door to foreign influence and corruption, which find a facilitated access to the government itself through the channels of party passion. Thus the policy and the will of one country are subjected to the policy and will of another.

There is an opinion that parties in free countries are useful checks upon the administration of the government, and serve to keep alive the spirit of liberty. This within certain limits is probably true; and in governments of a monarchical cast patriotism may look with indulgence, if not with favor, upon the spirit of party. But in those of the popular character, in governments purely elective, it is a spirit not to be encouraged. From their natural tendency it is certain there will always be enough of that spirit for every salutary purpose; and there being constant danger of excess, the effort ought to be by force of public opinion to mitigate and assuage it. A fire not to be quenched, it demands a uniform vigilance to prevent its bursting into a flame, lest, instead of warming, it should consume.

It is important, likewise, that the habits of thinking in a free country should inspire caution in those intrusted with its administration to confine themselves within their respective constitutional spheres, avoiding in the exercise of the powers of one department to encroach upon another. The spirit of encroachment tends to consolidate the powers of all the departments in one, and thus to create, whatever the form of government, a real despotism. A just estimate of that love of power and proneness to abuse it which predominates in the human heart is sufficient to satisfy us of the truth of this position. The necessity of reciprocal checks in the exercise of political power, by dividing and distributing it into different depositories, and constituting each the guardian of the public weal against invasions by the others, has been evinced by experiments ancient and modern, some of them in our country and under our own eyes. To preserve them must be as necessary as to institute them. If in the opinion of the people the distribution or modification of the constitutional powers be in any particular wrong, let it be corrected by an amendment in the way which the Constitution designates. But let there be no change by usurpation; for though this in one instance may be the instrument of good, it is the customary weapon by which free governments are destroyed. The precedent must always greatly overbalance in permanent evil any partial or transient benefit which the use can at any time yield.

Of all the dispositions and habits which lead to political prosperity, religion and morality are indispensable supports. In vain would that man claim the tribute of patriotism who should labor to subvert these great pillars of human happiness—these firmest props of the duties of men and citizens. The mere politician, equally with the pious man, ought to respect and to cherish them. A volume could not trace all their connections with private and public felicity. Let it simply be asked, Where is the security for property, for reputation, for life, if the sense of religious obligation *desert* the oaths which are the instruments of investigation in courts of justice? And let us with caution indulge the supposition that morality can be maintained without religion. Whatever may be conceded to the influence of refined education on minds of peculiar structure, reason and experience both forbid us to expect that national morality can prevail in exclusion of religious principle.

It is substantially true that virtue or morality is a necessary spring of popular government. The rule indeed extends with more or less force to every species of free government. Who that is a sincere friend to it can look with indifference upon attempts to shake the foundation of the fabric? Promote, then, as an object of primary importance, institutions for the general diffusion of knowledge. In proportion as the structure of a government gives force to public opinion, it is essential that public opinion should be enlightened.

As a very important source of strength and security, cherish public credit. One method of preserving it is to use it as sparingly as possible, avoiding occasions of expense by cultivating peace, but remembering also that timely disbursements to prepare for danger frequently prevent much greater disbursements to repel it; avoiding likewise the accumulation of debt, not only by shunning occasions of expense, but by vigorous exertions in time of peace to discharge the debts which unavoidable wars have occasioned, not ungenerously throwing upon posterity the burthen which we ourselves ought to bear. The execution of these maxims belongs to your representatives; but it is necessary that public opinion should cooperate. To facilitate to them the performance of their duty it is essential that you should practically bear in mind that toward the payment of debts there must be revenue; that to have revenue there must be taxes; that no taxes can be devised which are not more or less inconvenient and unpleasant; that the intrinsic embarrassment inseparable from the selection of the proper objects (which is always a choice of difficulties), ought to be a decisive motive for a candid construction of the conduct of the Government in making it, and for a spirit of acquiescence in the measures for obtaining revenue which the public exigencies may at any time dictate.

Observe good faith and justice toward all nations. Cultivate peace and harmony with all. Religion and morality enjoin this conduct. And can it be that good policy does not equally enjoin it? It will be worthy of a free, enlightened, and at no distant period a great nation to give to mankind the magnanimous and too novel example of a people always guided by an exalted justice and benevolence. Who can doubt that in the course of time and things the fruits of such a plan would richly repay any temporary advantages which might be lost by a steady adherence to it? Can it be that Providence has not connected the permanent felicity of a nation with its virtue? The experiment, at least, is recommended by every sentiment which ennobles human nature. Alas! is it rendered impossible by its vices?

In the execution of such a plan nothing is more essential

than that permanent, inveterate antipathies against particular nations and passionate attachments for others should be excluded, and that in place of them just and amicable feelings toward all should be cultivated. The nation which indulges toward another an habitual hatred or an habitual fondness is in some degree a slave. It is a slave to its animosity or to its affection, either of which is sufficient to lead it astray from its duty and its interest. Antipathy in one nation against another disposes each more readily to offer insult and injury, to lay hold of slight causes of umbrage, and to be haughty and intractable when accidental or trifling occasions of dispute occur.

Hence frequent collisions, obstinate, envenomed, and bloody contests. The nation prompted by ill will and resentment sometimes impels to war the government contrary to the best calculations of policy. The government sometimes participates in the national propensity, and adopts through passion what reason would reject. At other times it makes the animosity of the nation subservient to projects of hostility, instigated by pride, ambition, and other sinister and pernicious motives. The peace often, sometimes perhaps the liberty, of nations has been the victim.

So, likewise, a passionate attachment of one nation for another produces a variety of evils. Sympathy for the favorite nation, facilitating the illusion of an imaginary common interest in cases where no real common interest exists, and infusing into one the enmities of the other, betrays the former into a participation in the quarrels and wars of the latter without adequate inducement or justification. It leads also to concessions to the favorite nation of privileges denied to others, which is apt doubly to injure the nation making the concessions by unnecessarily parting with what ought to have been retained, and by exciting jealousy, ill-will, and a disposition to retaliate in the parties from whom equal privileges are withheld; and it gives to ambitious, corrupted, or deluded citizens (who devote themselves to the favorite nation) facility to betray or sacrifice the interests of their own country without odium, sometimes even with popularity, gilding with the appearances of a virtuous sense of obligation, a commendable deference for public opinion, or a laudable zeal for public good the base or foolish compliances of ambition, corruption, or infatuation.

As avenues to foreign influence in innumerable ways, such attachments are particularly alarming to the truly enlightened and independent patriot. How many opportunities do they afford to tamper with domestic factions, to practice the arts of seduction, to mislead public opinion, to influence or awe the public councils! Such an attachment of a small or weak toward a great and powerful nation dooms the former to be the satellite of the latter. Against the insidious wiles of foreign influence (I conjure you to believe me, fellow-citizens) the jealousy of a free people ought to be *constantly* awake, since history and experience prove that foreign influence is one of the most baneful foes of republican government. But that jealousy, to be useful, must be impartial, else it becomes the instrument of the very influence to be avoided, instead of a defense against it. Excessive partiality for one foreign nation and excessive dislike of another cause those whom they actuate to see danger only on one side, and serve to veil and even second the arts of influence on the other. Real patriots who may resist the intrigues of the favorite are liable to become suspected and odious, while its tools and dupes usurp the applause and confidence of the people to surrender their interests.

The great rule of conduct for us in regard to foreign nations is, in extending our commercial relations to have with them as little *political* connection as possible. So far as we have already formed engagements let them be fulfilled with perfect good faith. Here let us stop.

Europe has a set of primary interests which to us have none or a very remote relation. Hence she must be engaged in frequent controversies, the causes of which are essentially foreign to our concerns. Hence, therefore, it must be unwise in us to implicate ourselves by artificial ties in the ordinary vicissitudes of her politics or the ordinary combinations and collisions of her friendships or enmities.

Our detached and distant situation invites and enables us to pursue a different course. If we remain one people, under an efficient government, the period is not far off when we may defy material injury from external annoyance; when we may take such an attitude as will cause the neutrality we may at any time resolve upon to be scrupulously respected; when belligerent nations, under the impossibility of making acquisitions upon us, will not lightly hazard the giving us provocation; when we may choose peace or war, as our interest, guided by justice, shall counsel.

Why forego the advantages of so peculiar a situation? Why quit our own to stand upon foreign ground? Why, by interweaving our destiny with that of any part of Europe, entangle our peace and prosperity in the toils of European ambition, rivalship, interest, humor, or caprice?

It is our true policy to steer clear of permanent alliances

with any portion of the foreign world, so far, I mean, as we are now at liberty to do it; for let me not be understood as capable of patronizing infidelity to existing engagements. I hold the maxim no less applicable to public than to private affairs that honesty is always the best policy. I repeat, therefore, let those engagements be observed in their genuine sense. But in my opinion it is unnecessary and would be unwise to extend them.

Taking care always to keep ourselves by suitable establishments on a respectable defensive posture, we may safely trust to temporary alliances for extraordinary emergencies.

Harmony, liberal intercourse with all nations are recommended by policy, humanity, and interest. But even our commercial policy should hold an equal and impartial hand, neither seeking nor granting exclusive favors or preferences; consulting the natural course of things; diffusing and diversifying by gentle means the streams of commerce, but forcing nothing; establishing with powers so disposed, in order to give trade a stable course, to define the rights of our merchants, and to enable the Government to support them, conventional rules of intercourse, the best that present circumstances and mutual opinion will permit, but temporary and liable to be from time to time abandoned or varied as experience and circumstance shall dictate; constantly keeping in view that it is folly in one nation to look for disinterested favors from another; that it must pay with a portion of its independence for whatever it may accept under that character; that by such acceptance it may place itself in the condition of having given equivalents for nominal favors, and yet of being reproached with ingratitude for not giving more. There can be no greater error than to expect or calculate upon real favors from nation to nation. It is an illusion which experience must cure, which a just pride ought to discard.

In offering to you, my countrymen, these counsels of an old and affectionate friend I dare not hope they will make the strong and lasting impression I could wish—that they will control the usual current of the passions or prevent our nation from running the course which has hitherto marked the destiny of nations. But if I may even flatter myself that they may be productive of some partial benefit, some occasional good—that they may now and then recur to moderate the fury of party spirit, to warn against the mischiefs of foreign intrigue, to guard against the impostures of pretended patriotism—this hope will be a full recompense for the solicitude for your welfare by which they have been dictated.

How far in the discharge of my official duties I have been

guided by the principles which have been delineated the public records and other evidences of my conduct must witness to you and to the world. To myself, the assurance of my own conscience is that I have at least believed myself to be guided by them.

In relation to the still subsisting war in Europe my proclamation of the 22d of April, 1793, is the index to my plan. Sanctioned by your approving voice and by that of your representatives in both Houses of Congress, the spirit of that measure has continually governed me, uninfluenced by any attempts to deter or divert me from it.

After deliberate examination, with the aid of the best lights I could obtain, I was well satisfied that our country, under all the circumstances of the case, had a right to take, and was bound in duty and interest to take, a neutral position. Having taken it, I determined as far as should depend upon me to maintain it with moderation, perseverance, and firmness.

The considerations which respect the right to hold this conduct it is not necessary on this occasion to detail. I will only observe that, according to my understanding of the matter, that right, so far from being denied by any of the belligerent powers, has been virtually admitted by all.

The duty of holding a neutral conduct may be inferred, without anything more, from the obligation which justice and humanity impose on every nation, in cases in which it is free to act, to maintain inviolate the relations of peace and amity toward other nations.

The inducements of interest for observing that conduct will best be referred to your own reflections and experience. With me a predominant motive has been to endeavor to gain time to our country to settle and mature its yet recent institutions, and to progress without interruption to that degree of strength and consistency which is necessary to give it, humanly speaking, the command of its own fortunes.

Though in reviewing the incidents of my Administration I am unconscious of intentional error, I am nevertheless too sensible of my defects not to think it probable that I may have committed many errors. Whatever they may be, I fervently beseech the Almighty to avert or mitigate the evils to which they may tend. I shall also carry with me the hope that my country will never cease to view them with indulgence, and that, after forty-five years of my life dedicated to its service with an upright zeal, the faults of incompetent abilities will be consigned to oblivion, as myself must soon be to the mansions of rest.

Relying on its kindness in this as in other things, and actuated by that fervent love toward it which is so natural to a man who views in it the native soil of himself and his progenitors for several generations, I anticipate with pleasing expectation that retreat in which I promise myself to realize without alloy the sweet enjoyment of partaking in the midst of my fellow-citizens the benign influence of good laws under a free government—the ever-favorite object of my heart, and the happy reward, as I trust, of our mutual cares, labors, and dangers.

G.º WASHINGTON

Written after the style of eighteenth-century European statesmen, Washington's political testament had far more durability than that of Frederick the Great or other monarchs who fancied this form of address to their respective nations. Not all portions of Washington's address were equally durable, however. His injunction against political factionalism did not prevent the rise of a two-party system, nor did his prophetic warning of the dangers of sectionalism deter civil war between North and South. What did survive was his "Great Rule," his guidelines for American foreign policy. This did not in fact represent a change in policy, but rather it gave literary articulation to the big decisions which had already been made in his Administration to avoid entanglement in the European war which came in the wake of the French Revolution. These decisions had been embodied in Washington's Proclamation of Neutrality and in Jay's Treaty with Great Britain, which gave the young nation a necessary breathing spell.

The "Great Rule" foreshadowed the end of the French alliance, terminated in the Administration of Washington's successor, John Adams. It was Jefferson, not Washington, who gave the "Great Rule" a more distinctively isolationist tinge. In his First Inaugural Address President Jefferson counseled his fellow citizens to enjoy "peace, commerce, and honest friendship with all nations, entangling alliances with none." Washington had not included that phrase in his "Farewell Address," but in the nation's memory the injunctions of the two Presidents have become intermingled and indistinguishable.

Washington's "Great Rule" later took concrete form in the Monroe Doctrine, which expressed the notion of two separate spheres of political action. The United States would abstain from involvement in European politics; Europe was to ab-

stain from interfering in the political affairs of the independent states of the New World. President Jackson's Secretary of State, John Forsyth, epitomized America's foreign policy as a "national reserve," a deliberate abstention from the political relationships entered into by most states. Thus, when, in the mid-nineteenth century, interventionists sought to have America give aid to Europe's revolutionary movements and called for the abandonment of isolation, they were met with arguments from statesmen like John Quincy Adams, who insisted that America could save the world only if it remained free to save itself. This policy was broadly construed to involve the avoidance of any entangling alliances or commitments; the United States would refrain from intervening or participating in European politics and even from acting jointly with other powers. The Monroe Doctrine was a unilateral action.

In essence, Washington's "Great Rule" was adhered to until the Spanish-American War involved the United States at once in both European and Asiatic political questions. Although the conquest of the Philippines may have seemed a violent departure from the injunctions of the Farewell Address and the Monroe Doctrine, it did not forecast an abrupt reversal from traditional isolationism. Wilson's studied neutrality in the early years of World War I voiced the strength of that tradition, as did the refusal of the Senate to ratify a postwar military alliance with France, or to enter the League of Nations or the World Court. Indeed, by the 1920's isolationism, in addition to its other historic connotations, involved avoiding the placing of limits on what some deemed to be "essential" rights of national sovereignty. The isolationist mood fitted America's postwar disenchantment about the goals of European states, and found concrete expression in the neutrality legislation of the 1930's.

The perils which totalitarianism seemed to pose to the civilization of the West, combined with the rude shock of Pearl Harbor, uprooted isolationism. The foreign policy of the United States had to be drastically refashioned, as America assumed a vastly enlarged role in world affairs. America's active participation in the United Nations and her broad system of alliances may seem a far cry from the "Great Rule," until it is remembered that Washington's concern was to formulate a policy of prudence which would allow the new nation a twenty-year period to gain strength and power through the avoidance of war. Washington was too realistic a statesman to imagine that rules of behavior appropriate for an infant republic, separated by what was then a vast distance from Europe's power struggles, could apply with equal force as *that nation grew larger and more powerful. By mid-twentieth century the revolution of science and technology and a multitude of other interests had tied the United States to all the other peoples on the face of this planet.*

Thomas Jefferson

First Inaugural Address

1801

EDITED BY DUMAS MALONE

The inaugural address which Thomas Jefferson delivered on March 4, 1801, was the first ever made by a President in Washington, whither the federal government had transferred from Philadelphia a few months earlier, during the Presidency of John Adams. Jefferson made the address in the Senate Chamber of the original Capitol, the only part of that structure then completed. His inauguration was also notable in that it was the first to mark a change in the control of the government from one party to another. The election preceding it was one of the most heated in American history; and, while it left no doubt that the Federalists had been defeated by the Republicans, there was grave doubt until February 17 whether Jefferson or Aaron Burr would be President. Under the system then in operation, the electors voted for two men without designating either specifically for the first or second office; and in this case the accidental result was a tie which, according to the Constitution, had to be resolved by the House of Representatives. In that body the Federalists supported Burr, while the Republicans loyally stood by Jefferson, who was obviously the popular choice. For a time the possibility existed that there would be no legally elected President to inaugurate, and as things turned out Jefferson had only a little more than two weeks in which to write his speech.

He wrote it, without secretarial assistance, at Conrad and McMunn's boarding house, where he was staying. The most pressing need of which he was conscious at this point was that of restoring unity to the country. Since the intransigent Federalist congressmen already stood rebuked by the outcome which they had succeeded only in delaying, his immediate purpose was to reassure his countrymen, whom he believed to be predominantly moderate, patriotic, and freedom-loving. In this respect his address was notably successful. He also took this occasion to set forth the principles on which he would conduct the government and the general lines of policy he expected to follow. Since he had made no speeches and issued no public statements in the recent campaign, his views had often been distorted and misrepresented. In private he had made frequent reference to the "spirit of 1776," and what he really meant by republicanism, as he now made clear in public, was loyalty to the ideals of the American Revolution. At the same time he also strongly advocated federalism, which to him was support of the Constitution and the federal principle underlying it. He sought to unite and rally the country by emphasizing the compatibility of the two ideas.

FRIENDS AND FELLOW-CITIZENS

CALLED upon to undertake the duties of the first executive office of our country, I avail myself of the presence of that portion of my fellow citizens which is here assembled to express my grateful thanks for the favor with which they have been pleased to look toward me, to declare a sincere consciousness that the task is above my talents, and that I approach it with those anxious and awful presentiments which the greatness of the charge and the weakness of my powers so justly inspire. A rising nation, spread over a wide and

The text given here is that printed in the *National Intelligencer* at the time of the inauguration, from a copy provided the editor by Jefferson. This differs little from the texts printed in the journals of the legislative and executive proceedings of the United States Senate. Later editors made more changes, and one of these, in capitalization, was particularly unfortunate. In Jefferson's own draft a famous sentence reads as follows: "We are all republicans: we are all federalists." In the earliest printed versions the key words remain in lower case. By capitalizing them, later editors have caused the sentence to seem more paradoxical than it was.

fruitful land, traversing all the seas with the rich productions of their industry, engaged in commerce with nations who feel power and forget right, advancing rapidly to destinies beyond the reach of mortal eye—when I contemplate these transcendent objects, and see the honor, the happiness, and the hopes of this beloved country committed to the issue and the auspices of this day, I shrink from the contemplation, and humble myself before the magnitude of the undertaking. Utterly indeed should I despair did not the presence of many whom I here see remind me that in the other high authorities provided by our Constitution I shall find resources of wisdom, of virtue, and of zeal on which to rely under all difficulties. To you then, gentlemen, who are charged with the sovereign functions of legislation, and to those associated with you, I look with encouragement for that guidance and support which may enable us to steer with safety the vessel in which we are all embarked amidst the conflicting elements of a troubled world.

During the contest of opinion through which we have past the animation of discussions and of exertions has sometimes worn an aspect which might impose on strangers unused to think freely and to speak and to write what they think. But this being now decided by the voice of the nation, enounced according to the rules of the constitution, all will of course arrange themselves under the will of the law, and unite in common efforts for the common good. All too will bear in mind this sacred principle, that though the will of the majority is in all cases to prevail, that will, to be rightful, must be reasonable; that the minority possess their equal rights, which equal laws must protect, and to violate would be oppression. Let us then, fellow citizens, unite with one heart and one mind, let us restore to social intercourse that harmony and affection without which liberty and even life itself are but dreary things. And let us reflect that, having banished from our land that religious intolerance under which mankind so long bled and suffered, we have yet gained little if we countenance a political intolerance as despotic, as wicked, and capable of as bitter and bloody persecutions. During the throes and convulsions of the ancient world, during the agonizing spasms of infuriated man, seeking through blood and slaughter his long lost liberty, it was not wonderful that the agitation of the billows should reach even this distant and peaceful shore; that this should be more felt and feared by some and less by others, and should divide opinions as to measures of safety; but every difference of opinion is not a difference of principle. We have called by different names brethren of the same principle. We are all republicans: we are all federalists. If there be any among us who wish to dissolve this Union or to change its republican form, let them stand undisturbed, as monuments of the safety with which error of opinion may be tolerated where reason is left free to combat it. I know, indeed, that some honest men fear that a republican government cannot be strong, that this government is not strong enough. But would the honest patriot, in the full tide of successful experiment, abandon a government which has so far kept us free and firm on the theoretic and visionary fear that this government, the world's best hope, may, by possibility, want energy to preserve itself? I trust not. I believe this, on the contrary, the strongest government on earth. I believe it the only one where every man, at the call of the law, would fly to the standard of the law, and would meet invasions of the public order as his own personal concern. Sometimes it is said that man cannot be trusted with the government of himself. Can he, then, be trusted with the government of others? Or have we found angels in the form of kings to govern him? Let history answer this question.

Let us then pursue with courage and confidence our own federal and republican principles, our attachment to union and representative government. Kindly separated by nature, and a wide ocean, from the exterminating havoc of one quarter of the globe; too high-minded to endure the degradations of the others; possessing a chosen country, with room enough for our descendants to the thousandth and thousandth generation; entertaining a due sense of our equal right to the use of our own faculties, to the acquisitions of our own industry, to honor and confidence from our fellow citizens, resulting not from birth, but from our actions and their sense of them; enlightened by a benign religion, professed, indeed, and practiced in various forms, yet all of them inculcating honesty, truth, temperance, gratitude, and the love of man; acknowledging and adoring an overruling providence, which by all its dispensations proves that it delights in the happiness of man here and his greater happiness hereafter—with all these blessings, what more is necessary to make us a happy and a prosperous people? Still one thing more, fellow citizens—a wise and frugal government, which shall restrain men from injuring one another, shall leave them otherwise free to regulate their own pursuits of industry and improvement, and shall not take from the mouth of labor the bread it has earned. This is the sum of good government, and this is necessary to close the circle of our felicities.

About to enter, fellow citizens, on the exercise of duties

which comprehend everything dear and valuable to you, it is proper you should understand what I deem the essential principles of this government, and consequently those which ought to shape its administration. I will compress them in the narrowest compass they will bear, stating the general principle, but not all its limitations. Equal and exact justice to all men, of whatever state or persuasion, religious or political; peace, commerce, and honest friendship with all nations, entangling alliances with none; the support of the state governments in all their rights, as the most competent administrations for our domestic concerns and the surest bulwarks against anti-republican tendencies; the preservation of the general government in its whole constitutional vigor, as the sheet anchor of our peace at home and safety abroad; a jealous care of the right of election by the people, a mild and safe corrective of abuses which are lopped by the sword of revolution where peaceable remedies are unprovided; absolute acquiescence in the decisions of the majority, the vital principle of republics from which is no appeal but to force, the vital principle and immediate parent of despotism; a well disciplined militia, our best reliance in peace and for the first moments of war, till regulars may relieve them; the supremacy of the civil over the military authority; economy in the public expence, that labor may be lightly burthened; the honest payment of our debts and sacred preservation of the public faith; encouragement of agriculture, and of commerce as its handmaid; the diffusion of information and arraignment of all abuses at the bar of the public reason; freedom of religion; freedom of the press, and freedom of person under the protection of the habeas corpus, and trial by juries impartially selected. These principles form the bright constellation which has gone before us and guided our steps through an age of revolution and reformation. The wisdom of our sages and blood of our heroes have been devoted to their attainment. They should be the creed of our political faith, the text of civic instruction, the touchstone by which to try the services of those we trust; and should we wander from them in moments of error or of alarm, let us hasten to retrace our steps and to regain the road which alone leads to peace, liberty, and safety.

I repair, then, fellow-citizens, to the post you have assigned me. With experience enough in subordinate stations to know the difficulties of this the greatest of all, I have learnt to expect that it will rarely fall to the lot of imperfect man to retire from this station with the reputation and the favor which bring him into it. Without pretensions to that high confidence you reposed in our first and greatest revolutionary character, whose preeminent services had entitled him to the first place in his country's love and destined for him the fairest page in the volume of faithful history, I ask so much confidence only as may give firmness and effect to the legal administration of your affairs. I shall often go wrong through defect of judgment. When right, I shall often be thought wrong by those whose positions will not command a view of the whole ground. I ask your indulgence for my own errors, which will never be intentional, and your support against the errors of others, who may condemn what they would not if seen in all its parts. The approbation implied by your suffrage is a great consolation to me for the past, and my future solicitude will be to retain the good opinion of those who have bestowed it in advance, to conciliate that of others by doing them all the good in my power, and to be instrumental to the happiness and freedom of all.

Relying, then, on the patronage of your good will, I advance with obedience to the work, ready to retire from it whenever you become sensible how much better choices it is in your power to make. And may that infinite power which rules the destinies of the universe lead our councils to what is best, and give them a favorable issue for your peace and prosperity.

March 4, 1801.

It is partly because of the historical significance of Jefferson's accession to the Presidency, and the felicitous language of his address on taking office, that this document is memorable. But the chief reason for its continuing appeal is that much of it has seemed timeless. Since his day there has been no necessity, except in 1860 and perhaps in 1876, to point out that a defeated group must accept the result of a national election. No one now questions the right of an opposition party to exist, and, if it can command the votes, to replace an Administration. After the verdict at the polls, political conflict in the United States has generally been resolved in a mood of sportsmanship. Political triumph has never been followed by the liquidation of enemy chieftains, and rarely if ever on a national scale by sweeping and vindictive proscription. By word and deed Jefferson taught his countrymen an unforgettable lesson in the peaceful transfer of authority. In this address he did more: he set forth ideals which still challenge us. With the maxim that the will of the majority must pre-

vail, he coupled the "sacred principle" that this will "to be rightful, must be reasonable," that the minority must always be protected. He virtually recapitulated the provisions of the Bill of Rights, and in matchless phrase proclaimed the inviolability of the individual and of his opinions. Such words and thoughts will never be out of date so long as self-governing society persists on earth.

The same cannot be claimed for what he said in the first year of the nineteenth century about the policies he proposed to follow; and the chief abuses of his First Inaugural have resulted from a failure to distinguish between these dated policies and the abiding principles of self-government which he proclaimed. Within the memory of men now living, advocates of national isolation have sought to buttress their position by quoting things he said about foreign policy in a wholly different world situation. Jefferson was indubitably wise in disavowing "entangling alliances" in 1801, and actually the policy of noninvolvement in Old World affairs had validity for a century and more, but it has been necessarily repudiated in our day. The third President was charting a wise course for his country when it was young and weak and needed nothing so much as time to grow.

Another anachronism is the continued citation of Jefferson's views on the operations and limitations of government. He pronounced those views in an age which was not only prenuclear but which in America was virtually preindustrial. Common sense requires that allowance be made for changed circumstances; American society has been so transformed since Jefferson's inauguration that almost the only factors common to that time and this are those of topography, climate, and human nature. A good government, as he described it in 1801, should be "a wise and frugal government, which shall restrain men from injuring one another, shall leave them otherwise free to regulate their own pursuits of industry and improvement, and shall not take from the mouth of labor the bread it has earned." These terms are susceptible of amplification, but Jefferson undoubtedly wanted to keep the sum of government very small. His contemporaries Alexander Hamilton and John Marshall thought it dangerously small, but his basically negative domestic policy was well adapted to the conditions of the country at the time, and it was immensely popular. To follow that policy under the conditions of a much later time would be manifestly impossible. It is unimaginable that a man of Jefferson's intelligence would defend it now, and, in fairness to the memory of this great champion of freedom and apostle of enlightenment, we *must recognize that his views about the limits of governmental power, and also about the relations between the states and the nation, are now quite irrelevant. Indeed, they have long been so. The first person to concede this would be the Jefferson who said: "The earth belongs always to the living generation." In his day he distrusted power as a potential instrument of tyranny; circumstances had not yet taught him, as they have taught us, that it is an indispensable weapon in defense of freedom. We cannot now learn from him the "how" of government, but we can learn the "why."*

Jacob Henry

On Religion and Elective Office

1809

EDITED BY JOSEPH L. BLAU

Article 34 of the constitution of the state of North Carolina, adopted in 1776, forbade the establishment of "any one religious church or denomination . . . in preference to any other," and maintained that "all persons shall be at liberty to exercise their own mode of worship." The Declaration of Rights adopted by North Carolina in the same year included both the acknowledgment that freedom of worship is an inalienable right of man and, in its forty-fourth article, the assertion that the Declaration of Rights had authority superior to that of the constitution. In the event of contradiction between the Declaration of Rights and the constitution, the constitution had to give way. Yet, in Article 32 of the constitution, the following provision appeared:

> *That no person, who shall deny the being of God or the truth of the Protestant religion, or the divine authority either of the Old or New Testaments, or who shall hold religious principles incompatible with the freedom and safety of the State, shall be capable of holding any office or place of trust or profit in the civil department within this State.*

This contradiction set the stage for a most interesting and im-

portant defense of the principle that civil rights are independent of religious affiliation.

In 1809, Jacob Henry was elected to the lower house of the legislature of North Carolina as a representative of Carteret County. When Mr. Henry had first been given this honor by his fellow citizens, one year earlier, his right to sit in the House of Commons went unchallenged. On his re-election, however, the question of his eligibility was raised, on the ground that Jacob Henry was a Jew. As a Jew he did not subscribe to the "divine authority" of the New Testament, nor did he accept "the truth of the Protestant religion." For Jacob Henry to hold the seat to which he had been elected violated Article 32 of the state constitution. For him to be denied his seat violated Article 34 of the same document, as well as refusing him a civil right apparently granted by the Declaration of Rights. As a special privilege, Mr. Henry was permitted to take part in the ensuing debate over his right to his elective office. The speech he delivered was soon recognized as a masterpiece of American oratory. It was often reprinted in collections of American public speeches after 1814. Its immediate effect was to lead the House of Commons to vote to sustain Henry's right to the seat to which he had been elected.

Little biographical information about Jacob Henry has been found. At one time it was suggested that he was a member of the famous Gratz family that spread out from Philadelphia to other parts of the country, but this suggestion lacks supporting evidence. With so little knowledge it is difficult to appraise the report, presented by the author of a major history of North Carolina, that the speech was "ghosted" for Jacob Henry by Attorney-General John Louis Taylor, a Roman Catholic. Undoubtedly it was to the interest of the Roman Catholics of the state that the question of the right of non-Protestants to hold elective office should be decided. If the right of a Jew to such a position could be vindicated, then the Catholic right would be even more certainly established.

I CERTAINLY, Mr. Speaker, know not the design of the Declaration of Rights made by the people of this State in the

Henry's speech is reprinted from John H. Wheeler, *Historical Sketches of North Carolina from 1584 to 1851* (Philadelphia, 1851), II, 74–76. The earliest reprinting probably appeared in a collection of addresses, *The American Speaker* (Philadelphia, 1814).

year 1776, if it was not to consecrate certain great and fundamental rights and principles which even the Constitution cannot impair; for the 44th section of the latter instrument declares that the Declaration of Rights ought never to be violated, on any pretence whatever; if there is any apparent difference between the two instruments, they ought, if possible, to be reconciled; but if there is a final repugnance between them, the Declaration of Rights must be considered paramount; for I believe it is to the Constitution, as the Constitution is to law; it controls and directs it absolutely and conclusively. If, then, a belief in the Protestant religion is required by the Constitution, to qualify a man for a seat in this house, and such qualification is dispensed with by the Declaration of Rights, the provision of the Constitution must be altogether inoperative; as the language of the Bill of Rights is, "that all men have a natural and inalienable right to worship ALMIGHTY GOD according to the dictates of their own consciences." It is undoubtedly a natural right, and when it is declared to be an inalienable one by the people in their sovereign and original capacity, any attempt to alienate either by the Constitution or by law, must be vain and fruitless.

It is difficult to conceive how such a provision crept into the Constitution, unless it is from the difficulty the human mind feels in suddenly emancipating itself from fetters by which it has long been enchained: and how adverse it is to the feelings and manners of the people of the present day every gentleman may satisfy himself by glancing at the religious belief of the persons who fill the various offices in this State: there are Presbyterians, Lutherans, Calvinists, Mennonists, Baptists, Trinitarians, and Unitarians. But, as far as my observation extends, there are fewer Protestants, in the strict sense of the word, used by the Constitution, than of any other persuasion; for I suppose that they meant by it, the Protestant religion as established by the law in England. For other persuasions we see houses of worship in almost every part of the State, but very few of the Protestant; so few, that indeed I fear that the people of this State would for some time remain unrepresented in this House, if that clause of the Constitution is supposed to be in force. So far from believing in the Thirty-nine Articles, I will venture to assert that a majority of the people never have read them.

If a man should hold religious principles incompatible with the freedom and safety of the State, I do not hesitate to pronounce that he should be excluded from the public councils of the same; and I trust if I know myself, no one would be more ready to aid and assist than myself. But I should really be at a loss to specify any known religious principles which are thus dangerous. It is surely a question between a man and his Maker, and requires more than human attributes to pronounce which of the numerous sects prevailing in the world is most acceptable to the Deity. If a man fulfills the duties of that religion, which his education or his conscience has pointed to him as the true one, no person, I hold, in this our land of liberty, has a right to arraign him at the bar of any inquisition: and the day, I trust, has long passed, when principles merely speculative were propagated by force; when the sincere and pious were made victims, and the light-minded bribed into hypocrites.

The purest homage man could render to the Almighty was the sacrifice of his passions and the performance of his duties. That the ruler of the universe would receive with equal benignity the various offerings of man's adoration, if they proceeded from the heart. Governments only concern the actions and conduct of man, and not his speculative notions. Who among us feels himself so exalted above his fellows as to have a right to dictate to them any mode of belief? Will you bind the conscience in chains, and fasten conviction upon the mind in spite of the conclusions of reason and of those ties and habitudes which are blended with every pulsation of the heart? Are you prepared to plunge at once from the sublime heights of moral legislation into the dark and gloomy caverns of superstitious ignorance? Will you drive from your shores and from the shelter of your constitution, all who do not lay their oblations on the same altar, observe the same ritual, and subscribe to the same dogmas? If so, which, among the various sects into which we are divided, shall be the favored one?

I should insult the understanding of this House to suppose it possible that they could ever assent to such absurdities; for all know that persecution in all its shapes and modifications, is contrary to the genius of our government and the spirit of our laws, and that it can never produce any other effect than to render men hypocrites or martyrs.

When Charles V., Emperor of Germany, tired of the cares of government, resigned his crown to his son, he retired to a monastery, where he amused the evening of his life in regulating the movements of watches, endeavoring to make a number keep the same time; but, not being able to make any two go exactly alike, it led him to reflect upon the folly and crimes he had committed, in attempting the impossibility of making men think alike!

Nothing is more easily demonstrated than that the conduct

alone is the subject of human laws, and that man ought to suffer civil disqualification for what he does, and not for what he thinks. The mind can receive laws only from Him, of whose Divine essence it is a portion; He alone can punish disobedience; for who else can know its movements, or estimate their merits? The religion I profess, inculcates every duty which men owes to his fellow men; it enjoins upon its votaries the practice of every virtue, and the detestation of every vice; it teaches them to hope for the favor of heaven exactly in proportion as their lives have been directed by just, honorable, and beneficent maxims. This, then, gentlemen, is my creed, it was impressed upon my infant mind; it has been the director of my youth, the monitor of my manhood, and will, I trust, be the consolation of my old age. At any rate, Mr. Speaker, I am sure that you cannot see anything in this Religion, to deprive me of my seat in this house. So far as relates to my life and conduct, the examination of these I submit with cheerfulness to your candid and liberal construction. What may be the religion of him who made this objection against me, or whether he has any religion or not I am unable to say. I have never considered it my duty to pry into the belief of other members of this house. If their actions are upright and conduct just, the rest is for their own consideration, not for mine. I do not seek to make converts to my faith, whatever it may be esteemed in the eyes of my officious friend, nor do I exclude any one from my esteem or friendship, because he and I differ in that respect. The same charity, therefore, it is not unreasonable to expect, will be extended to myself, because in all things that relate to the State and to the duties of civil life, I am bound by the same obligations with my fellow-citizens, nor does any man subscribe more sincerely than myself to the maxim, "whatever ye would that men should do unto you do ye so even unto them, for such is the law and the prophets."

The government of the United States, from its beginnings, was based upon an organic law that outlawed civil discrimination because of religious differences. Some of the older states, however, retained in their constitutions disqualifications of Jews, Roman Catholics, and members of other minority groups. Many years of conflict and struggle were needed before the promise of a religiously open society, as set forth in the federal Constitution, was to be realized. Only gradually were the constitutions of the states modified or re-

written. Massachusetts, for example, did not disestablish the Congregational Church until 1833. In North Carolina years after Jacob Henry's magnificent defense of the right of a member of a religious minority to hold office a change was finally made. At the constitutional convention of 1835 Roman Catholics were fully enfranchised by the changing of the word "Protestant" in Article 34 to "Christian." The status of the Jews of North Carolina remained anomalous. This legal disability of the Jews was not eliminated until after the Civil War, in a Reconstruction revision of the state constitution in 1868.

In Maryland, where the same sort of contradiction between the constitution of the state and its Bill of Rights existed, the interpretation was so narrow that no Jew could even enter upon a career as a lawyer, because a lawyer is, by definition, an officer of the court and therefore an occupant of a state office. A campaign of almost thirty years' duration was necessary before the passage of a bill in 1826 specifically exempted Jews from the operation of a clause requiring a test oath. This exemption did not end all discrimination on religious grounds in Maryland, for its constitution still required that all persons who might be elected or appointed to any office within the state must subscribe to a special oath affirming their belief in God. As a result, the agnostic, the atheist, or the person whose conscience would not permit his subscribing to such an oath was debarred from office in Maryland. This requirement of the Maryland constitution was put to a legal test by Roy Torcaso, an applicant for certification as a notary public. Denied his certification on the sole ground that he would not sign the oath affirming his belief in God, Torcaso appealed, first, to the highest court of Maryland, and then, when this appeal was denied, to the Supreme Court of the United States. In June, 1961, the Supreme Court, in a forceful opinion written by Justice Hugo Black, unanimously declared that "this Maryland religious test for public office unconstitutionally invades the appellant's freedom of belief and religion and therefore cannot be enforced against him." The principle for which Jacob Henry had argued in 1809, that the civil rights of American citizens may not be abridged in any respect because of their religious affiliation or beliefs, was finally vindicated and definitively established just over a century and a half after Henry's defense of it.

Public attitudes are never altogether identical with legal principles. At times, the attitudes of the public are in advance of the formal requirements of the law. So it was, for example, among those neighbors of Jacob Henry in Carteret Coun-

ty who elected him in 1808 and re-elected him in 1809. Knowing that Henry was Jewish, they still chose him as their representative, because, presumably, they liked and trusted him. Even though the law of their state retained expressions of outdated ideas, Henry's constituents were prepared to consider him on his own personal merits, as a unique individual, rather than as a member of a stereotyped group. There have been many other instances in the history of the American states in which the people have been ahead of their legal systems and have elected members not only of the Jewish minority but also of other minorities as their representatives, whatever the law might say.

In other cases, however, the law has been in advance of public opinion. This was notoriously the case in the presidential election of 1928, in which a major factor entering into the defeat of Alfred E. Smith, the Democratic Party's nominee for the Presidency, was his membership in the Roman Catholic Church. Whatever weight may be granted to the special circumstances of the age—especially to the turning away from American ideals in the name of American ideals that followed the disappointments of American participation in World War I—it still remains clear that the election campaign of 1928 brought out the most backward and bigoted elements in American public opinion. That the 1928 offenses against human decency were unsuccessfully and ineffectively repeated in the 1960 election campaign, in which there was again a Roman Catholic candidate for the Presidency, does not mean that the forces which use such appeals have been finally defeated. But it does indicate that there has been a measure of progress in the development of American public opinion. The election of John F. Kennedy is convincing evidence that a large section of the American electorate is willing to consider nominees for even the highest of offices on the grounds of their personal qualifications and their programs.

In recent years a growing appreciation of the contributions of minority groups to the development of all aspects of American life and culture has begun to appear in the work of historians and educators. This is, certainly, a consequence of the increasingly urban character of American society. In the urban communities of our nation, there is much more opportunity for man to meet man across the barriers of race, color, class, ethnic derivation, and religion. In the actuality of these many meetings, it becomes more and more difficult to maintain the traditional stereotypes that are so easy to hold in the isolation of rural life, where one's contacts may be largely—

even exclusively—with other members of one's own group. Our cosmopolitan cities hold forth the hope that our citizens may become more cosmopolitan, not just in the externals of life, but at its core. When such a genuine and deep-seated cosmopolitanism has developed in America, Jacob Henry's battle will have been completely won, not for the Jews alone, but for all members of minorities within American culture.

John Adams

What Do We Mean by the American Revolution?

1818

EDITED BY L. H. BUTTERFIELD

John Adams spent much of his retirement at Quincy after his Presidency refighting old battles. First came his episodic Autobiography, written between 1802 and 1807 and broken off in order to put Mercy Warren straight on mistakes in her recently published History of the American Revolution. *Then followed, from 1809 to 1812, the extraordinary outpouring of his letters to the* Boston Patriot, *in effect a second autobiography, which overwhelmed both the printers and the readers of that paper with material drawn from his old letterbooks, hastily copied, uncorrected, and held together by a thin but coruscating thread of commentary. The reminiscences Adams sent to his friends Dr. Benjamin Rush and former President Jefferson are gentler in tone, but he was still fighting the Revolution and complaining that nothing resembling a true history of it had yet been written—indeed ever would or could be written.*

Meanwhile he did his best for those who applied to him for information by replying with impetuous and copious generosity. Among a number of inquirers who hit the jackpot was Hezekiah Niles of Baltimore. Publisher of the first American news magazine and a thorough-going, even sentimental, nationalist, Niles had long made his Weekly Register a repository for documents on current affairs. In 1816, with the close of the second war with England and with the approach of the fiftieth anniversaries of important Revolutionary events, he appealed to the survivors of America's heroic age for their recollections, for unpublished letters and papers, for inspirational matter of every sort to satisfy a public suddenly grown as proud of its short past as it was confident of its long future. Adams replied serially by sending Niles his own early pamphlet publications for reprinting, long letters of reminiscence, copies of letters he had received from Revolutionary celebrities, and finally, since he had no clerical help, a great bundle of original letters addressed to him during the earliest years of the conflict. He was to regret this last step, for Niles did not print them all and never returned the irreplaceable originals.

What touched off John Adams' final account of the beginnings of the American Revolution in Massachusetts—of which the present letter to Niles is only one installment among many—was the appearance in 1817 of a phenomenal book, William Wirt's Sketches of the Life and Character of Patrick Henry. With the meagerest of materials and in some respects the most intractable of subjects, Wirt had in a stroke converted the Virginia stump orator into an American folk hero, lazily stretching his limbs like the young nation itself and bidding defiance to Old World tyranny "in a voice of thunder, and with the look of a god." John Adams read the Sketches with the same delight with which he read the novels of Sir Walter Scott and Jane Porter. He wrote Wirt to tell him so, but he added that, although he envied Virginia none of its "well merited glories," he was at the same time "Jealous, very jealous, of the honour of Massachusetts." He wished he were young enough to undertake a volume of "Sketches of the Life and writings of James Otis of Boston," in which he would demonstrate that Otis' services in resisting "the British System for Subjugating the Colonies" had begun earlier and been substantially greater than Patrick Henry's. Warming to his work, he sent off to Niles on January 14, 1818, a sketch of Otis for publication, in which he declared "in the most solemn manner that Mr. Otis's Oration against Writts of Assistance" in 1761—antedating by four years Henry's speech against the Stamp Act—"breathed into the Nation the Breath of Life." Here indeed was a Massachusetts Roland for Virginia's Oliver!

Adams' next letter to Niles, that of February 13, 1818, furnished Otis with a band of intrepid colleagues and vividly described their exploits. But it is Adams' leading question— "What do We mean by the American Revolution?"—and his grand answering assertions that lift this letter above mere reminiscence or, for that matter, above the liveliest historical narrative.

Quincy, February 13th. 1818

MR. NILES

THE AMERICAN REVOLUTION was not a common Event. It's Effects and Consequences have already been Awful over a great Part of the Globe. And when and where are they to cease?

But what do We mean by the American Revolution? Do we mean the American War? The Revolution was effected before the War commenced. The Revolution was in the Minds and Hearts of the People. A Change in their Religious Sentiments of their Duties and Obligations. While the King, and all in Authority under him, were believed to govern, in Justice and Mercy according to the Laws and Constitutions derived to them from the God of Nature, and transmitted to them by their Ancestors: they thought themselves bound to pray for the King and Queen and all the Royal Family, and all the Authority under them, as Ministers ordained of God for their good. But when they saw those Powers renouncing all the Principles of Authority, and bent upon the destruction of all the Securities of their Lives, Liberties and Properties, they thought it their Duty to pray for the Continental Congress and all the thirteen State Congresses, &c.

Adams' letter is here for the first time printed faithfully from the manuscript. The original, owned by the Maryland Historical Society, runs to nine pages and is entirely in John Adams' hand. The hand is still firm, but the manuscript is marred by careless blots and other marks of haste. No letterbook copy was made for retention in Adams' files. At the head of the text, crossed out, is the name "Samuel Adams," as if this letter were to have been devoted to that subject; it was not, but see its final paragraph. Scattered words, phrases, and sentences in the manuscript are underscored or doubly underscored in different hands, one of them doubtless that of Niles, but only what are believed to be John Adams' marks of emphasis are followed in the present text. Someone, very likely Niles himself, inked out a passage of fifteen words concerning Oxenbridge Thacher that he thought in doubtful taste. To restore this passage it has been necessary to guess at two words.

There might be, and there were others, who thought less about Religion and Conscience, but had certain habitual Sentiments of Allegiance and Loyalty derived from their Education; but believing Allegiance and Protection to be reciprocal, when Protection was withdrawn, they thought Allegiance was dissolved.

Another Alteration was common to all. The People of America had been educated in an habitual Affection for England as their Mother-Country; and while they thought her a kind and tender Parent (erroneously enough, however, for she never was such a Mother,) no Affection could be more sincere. But when they found her a cruel Beldam, willing, like Lady Macbeth, to "dash their Brains out," it is no Wonder if their fillial Affections ceased and were changed into Indignation and horror.

This radi[c]al Change in the Principles, Opinions, Sentiments and Affections of the People, was the real American Revolution.

By what means, this great and important Alteration in the religious, moral, political and social Character of the People of thirteen Colonies, all distinct, unconnected and independent of each other, was begun, pursued and accomplished, it is surely interesting to Humanity to investigate, and perpetuate to Posterity.

To this End it is greatly to be desired that Young Gentlemen of Letters in all the States, especially in the thirteen Original States, would undertake the laborious, but certainly interesting and amusing Task, of searching and collecting all the Records, Pamphlets, Newspapers and even hand-Bills, which in any Way contributed to change the Temper and Views of The People and compose them into an independent Nation.

The Colonies had grown up under Constitutions of Government, so different, there was so great a Variety of Religions, they were composed of so many Nations, their customs, Manners and Habits had so little resemblance, and their Intercourse had been so rare and their Knowledge of each other so imperfect, that to unite them in the same Principles in Theory and the same System of Action was certainly a very difficult Enterprize. The compleat Accomplishment of it, in so short a time and by such simple means, was perhaps a singular Example in the History of Mankind. Thirteen Clocks were made to strike together; a perfection of Mechanism which no Artist had ever before effected.

In this Research, the Glorioroles of Individual Gentlemen and of separate States is of little Consequence. The MEANS

AND THE MEASURES are the proper Objects of Investigation. These may be of Use to Posterity, not only in this Nation, but in South America, and all other Countries. They may teach Mankind that Revolutions are no Trifles; that they ought never to be undertaken rashly; nor without deliberate Consideration and sober Reflection; nor without a solid, immutable, eternal foundation of Justice and Humanity; nor without a People possessed of Intelligence, Fortitude and Integrity sufficient to carry them with Steadiness, Patience, and Perseverance, through all the Vicissitudes of fortune, the fiery Tryals and melancholly Disasters they may have to encounter.

The Town of Boston early instituted an annual Oration on the fourth of July, in commemoration of the Principles and Feelings which contributed to produce the Revolution. Many of those Orations I have heard, and all that I could obtain I have read. Much Ingenuity and Eloquence appears upon every Subject, except those Principles and Feelings. That of my honest and amiable Neighbour, Josiah Quincy, appeared to me, the most directly to the purpose of the Institution. Those Principles and Feelings ought to be traced back for Two hundred Years, and sought in the history of the Country from the first Plantations in America. Nor should the Principles and Feelings of the English and Scotch towards the Colonies, through that whole Period ever be forgotten. The perpetual discordance between British Principles and Feelings and those of America, the next Year after the Suppression of the French Power in America, came to a Crisis, and produced an Explosion.

It was not till after the Annihilation of the French Dominion in America, that any British Ministry had dared to gratify their own Wishes, and the desire of the Nation, by projecting a formal Plan for raising a national Revenue from America by Parliamentary Taxation. The first great Manifestation of this design, was by the Order to carry into strict Execution those Acts of Parliament which were well known by the Appelation of the Acts of Trade, which had lain a dead Letter, unexecuted for half a Century, and some of them I believe for nearly a whole one.

This produced, in 1760 and 1761, AN AWAKENING and a REVIVAL of American Principles and Feelings, with an Enthusiasm which went on increasing till in 1775 it burst out in open Violence, Hostility and Fury.

The Characters, the most conspicuous, the most ardent and influential, in this Revival, from 1760 to 1766, were—First and Foremost, before all, and above all, JAMES OTIS; Next to

him was OXENBRIDGE THATCHER; next to him SAMUEL
ADAMS; next to him JOHN HANCOCK; then Dr. Mayhew, then
Dr. Cooper and his Brother. Of Mr. Hancock's Life, Character, generous Nature, great disinterested Sacrifices, and important Services, if I had forces, I should be glad to write a
Volume. But this I hope will be done by some younger and
abler hand. Mr. Thatcher, because his Name and Merits are
less known, must not be wholly omitted. This Gentleman was
an eminent Barrister at Law, in as large practice as any one
in Boston. There was not a Citizen of that Town more universally beloved for his Learning, Ingenuity, every domestic
& social Virtue, and conscientious Conduct in every Relation
of Life. His Patriotism was as ardent as his Progenitors had
been ancient and illustrious in this Country. Hutchinson often
said "Thatcher was not born a Plebeian, but he was determined to die one." In May 1763, I believe, he was chosen by
the Town of Boston one of their Representatives in the Legislature, a Colleague with Mr. Otis, who had been a Member
from May 1761, and he continued to be reelected annually
till his Death in 1765, when Mr. Samuel Adams was elected
to fill his place, in the Absence of Mr. Otis, then attending
the Congress at New York. Thatcher had long been jealous
of the unbounded Ambition of Mr. Hutchinson, but when he
found him not content with the Office of Lieutenant Governor, the Command of the Castle and its Emoluments, of
Judge of Probate for the County of Suffolk, a Seat in his Majesty's Council in the Legislature, his Brother-in-Law Secretary of State by the Kings Commission, a Brother of that
Secretary of State a Judge of the Superiour Court and a
Member of Council, now in 1760 and 1761, soliciting and
accepting the Office of the Chief Justice of the Superior
Court of Judicature, he concluded as Mr. Otis did, and as
every other enlightened Friend of his Country did, that he
sought that Office with the determined Purpose of determining all Causes in favour of the Ministry at Saint James's and
their servile Parliament.

His Indignation against him henceforward, to 1765, when
he died, knew no bounds but Truth. I speak from personal
Knowledge and with [one word effaced by an accidental
blot]. For, from 1758 to 1765, I attended every Superiour
and Inferiour Court in Boston, and recollect not one in which
he did not invite me home to spend Evenings with him, when
he made me converse with him as well as I could on all Subjects of Religion, Morals, Law, Politicks, History, Phyloso-
phy, Belle Letters, Theology, Mythology, Cosmogony, Meta-
physicks, Lock, Clark, Leibnits, Bolinbroke, Berckley, the

Preestablished Harmony of the Universe, the Nature of Matter and Spirit, and the eternal Establishment of Coincidences between their Operations; Fate, foreknowledge, absolute— and We reasoned on such unfathomable Subjects as high as Milton's Gentry in Pandemonium; and We understood them as well as they did, and no better. To such mighty Mysteries he added the News of the day, and the Tittle Tattle of the Town. But his favourite Subject was Politicks, and the impending threatening System of Parliamentary Taxation and Universal Government over the Colonies. On this Subject he was so anxious and agitated that I have no doubt it occasioned his premature death. From the time when he argued the question of Writts of Assistance to his death, he considered the King, Ministry, Parliament and Nation of Great Britain as determined to new model the Colonies from the Foundation; to annul all their Charters, to constitute them all Royal Governments; to raise a Revenue in America by Parliamentary Taxation; to apply that Revenue to pay the Salaries of Governors, Judges and all other Crown Officers; and, after all this, to raise as large a Revenue as they pleased to be applied to National Purposes at the Exchequer in England; and farther to establish Bishops and the whole System of the Church of England, Tythes and all, throughout all British America. This System, he said, if it was suffered to prevail would extinguish the Flame of Liberty all over the World; that America would be employed as an Engine to batter down all the miserable remains of Liberty in Great Britain and Ireland, where only any Semblance of it was left in the World. To this System he considered Hutchinson, the Olivers and all their Connections, dependants, adherents, Shoelickers —and another Epithet with which I will not [pollute?] my page nor [tarnish?] his memory, to be entirely devoted. He asserted that they were all engaged with all the Crown Officers in America and the Understrapers of the Ministry in England, in a deep and treasonable Conspiracy to betray the Liberties of their Country, for their own private personal and family Aggrandisement. His Philippicks against the unprincipled Ambition and Avarice of all of them, but especially of Hutchinson, were unbridled; not only in private, confidential Conversations, but in all Companies and on all Occasions. He gave Hutchinson the Sobriquet of "Summa Potestas," and rarely mentioned him but by the Name of "Summa." His Liberties of Speech were no Secrets to his Enemies. I have sometimes wondered that they did not throw him over the Barr, as they did soon afterwards Major Hawley. For they hated him worse than they did James Otis or Samuel Adams, and they feared him more,—because they had no Revenge for a Father's disappointment of a Seat on the Superiour Bench to impute to him as they did to Otis; and Thatcher's Character through Life had been so modest, decent, unassuming,—his Morals so pure, and his Religion so venerated, that they dared not attack him. In his Office were educated to the Barr two eminent Characters, the late Judge Lowell and Josiah Quincy, aptly called the Boston Cicero. Mr. Thatcher's frame was slender, his Constitution delicate; whether his Physicians overstrained his Vessels with Mercury, when he had the Small Pox by Inoculation at the Castle, or whether he was overplyed by publick Anxieties and Exertions, the Small Pox left him in a Decline from which he never recovered. Not long before his death he sent for me to commit to my care some of his Business at the Barr. I asked him whether he had seen the Virginia Resolves.—"Oh yes.—They are Men! They are noble Spirits! It kills me to think of the Leathargy and Stupidity that prevails here. I long to be out. I will go out. I will go out. I will go into Court, and make a Speech which shall be read after my death as my dying Testimony against this infernal Tyrany they are bringing upon us." Seeing the violent Agitation into which it threw him, I changed the Subject as soon as possible, and retired. He had been confined for some time. Had he been abroad among the People he would not have complained so pathetically of the "Lethargy and Stupidity that prevailed," for Town and Country were all Alive; and in August became active enough and some of the People proceeded to unwarrantable Excesses, which were more lamented by the Patriots than by their Enemies. Mr. Thatcher soon died, deeply lamented by all the Friends of their Country.

Another Gentleman who had great influence in the Commencement of the Revolution, was Doctor Jonathan Mayhew, a descendant of the ancient Governor of Martha's Vineyard. This Divine had raised a great Reputation both in Europe and America by the publication of a Volume of seven Sermons in the Reign of King George the Second, 1749, and by many other Writings, particularly a Sermon in 1750, on the thirtieth of January, on the Subject of Passive Obedience and Non Resistance; in which the Saintship and Martyrdom of King Charles the first are considered, seasoned with Witt and Satyre, superior to any in Swift or Franklin. It was read by every Body, celebrated by Friends, and abused by Enemies. During the Reigns of King George the first and King George the second, the Reigns of the Stewarts, the Two Jameses, and the two Charleses were in general disgrace in

England. In America they had always been held in Abhorrence. The Persecutions and Cruelties suffered by their Ancestors under those Reigns, had been transmitted by History and Tradition, and Mayhew seemed to be raised up to revive all their Animosity against Tyranny, in Church and State, and at the same time to destroy their Bigotry, Fanaticism and Inconsistency. David Hume's plausible, elegant, fascinating and fallacious Apology in which he varnished over the Crimes of the Stewarts had not then appeared. To draw the Character of Mayhew would be to transcribe a dozen Volumes. This transcendant Genius threw all the Weight of his great Fame into the Scale of his Country in 1761, and maintained it there with Zeal and Ardour till his death in 1766. In 1763 appeared the Controversy between him and Mr. Apthorp, Mr. Caner, Dr. Johnson and Archbishop Secker, on the Charter and Conduct of the Society for propagating the Gospel in foreign Parts. To form a Judgment of this debate I beg leave to refer to a Review of the whole, printed at the time, and written by Samuel Adams, though by some, very absurdly and erroneously, ascribed to Mr. Apthorp. If I am not mistaken, it will be found a Model of Candour, Sagacity, Impartiality and close correct reasoning.

If any Gentleman supposes this Controversy to be nothing to the present purpose, he is grossly mistaken. It spread an Universal Alarm against the Authority of Parliament. It excited a general and just Apprehension that Bishops and Dioceses and Churches, and Priests and Tythes, were to be imposed upon Us by Parliament. It was known that neither King nor Ministry nor Archbishops could appoint Bishops in America without an Act of Parliament; and if Parliament could Tax Us they could establish the Church of England with all its Creeds, Articles, Tests, Ceremonies and Tythes, and proscribe all other Churches as Conventicles and Schism Shops.

Nor must Mr. Cushing be forgotten. His good Sense and sound Judgment, the Urbanity of his Manners, his universal good Character, his numerous Friends and Connections and his continual intercourse with all Sorts of People, added to his constant Attachment to the Liberties of his Country, gave him a great and salutary influence from the beginning in 1760.

Let me recommend these hints to the Consideration of Mr. Wirt, whose Life of Mr. Henry I have read with great delight. I think, that after mature investigation, he will be convinced that Mr. Henry did not "give the first impulse to the Ball of Independence," and that Otis, Thatcher, Samuel

Adams, Mayhew, Hancock, Cushing and thousands of others were labouring for several Years at the Wheel before the Name of Mr. Henry was heard beyond the limits of Virginia.

If you print this, I will endeavour to send You some thing concerning Samuel Adams, who was destined to a longer Career, and to act a more conspicuous and, perhaps, a more important Part than any other Man. But his Life would require a Volume. If you decline printing this Letter I pray to return it as soon as possible to

Sir, your humble Servant
JOHN ADAMS

Mr. Niles.

Niles made prompt use of both of John Adams' letters on the great issue of writs of assistance in Massachusetts. That January 14, 1818, on Otis, he printed in his Weekly Register *for January 31, and the present letter, on Otis' collaborators, in the* Register *for March 7. But Adams was not content to let matters rest there. For the benefit of the "Young Gentlemen of Letters" who he hoped would investigate the origins of the American Revolution, he published in the following year a collected edition of Daniel Leonard's "Massachusettensis" papers and his own "Novanglus" papers in reply to Leonard. To this republication of newspaper pieces written in 1774–75 he appended the whole suite of his letters addressed in 1818 to Niles, Wirt, and William Tudor on this (to him, at least) inexhaustibly fascinating subject. By far the greatest number of the letters—about two dozen, some of them very long indeed—he addressed to Tudor, his old friend and former law clerk, for Tudor's son William planned to write the "Sketches of the Life and Writings of James Otis of Boston," which Adams had told Wirt that he himself was too old to write, and he was determined that young Tudor should neither lack materials nor fail to show Otis' primacy among the founders of independence. In one of the first and longest of these letters (April 5, 1818), Adams related an incident that occurred in the Massachusetts House of Representatives in 1762, when Otis was rebuked by a supporter of the Crown for including treasonable language toward the King of Great Britain in a remonstrance to the royal governor. "Why," Adams demanded, "has the sublime Compliment of 'Treason! Treason!' made to Mr. Henry in 1765 been so celebrated, when that to Mr. Otis in 1762, three Years before, has been totally forgotten?" As usual, he answered his own question:*

"Because the Virginia Patriot has had many Trumpetters and very loud ones; but the Massachusetts Patriot none"—or, as Adams had said elsewhere, with George Washington in mind, "Virginia Geese are all Swans."

But most of the cataract of letters to Tudor dealt with a single subject—Otis as "a flame of Fire" in the first hearing on the legality of writs of assistance, held before Chief Justice Hutchinson and the other judges of the Massachusetts Superior Court of Judicature in February, 1761. As an accurate reconstruction of Otis' four- or five-hour argument, these epistolary reminiscences, so charged with learning and emotion alike, have long since been discredited by legal and historical scholars. The verdict of Adams' grandson, Charles Francis Adams, is as good as any. In a note at the end of the series, this usually highly restrained editor observed (Works of John Adams, X, 362): "By comparison of this sketch of Mr. Otis's speech with that taken at the time, vol. ii. pp. 521–525, as well as with Mr. Otis's published writings, it is difficult to resist the belief that Mr. Adams insensibly infused into this work much of the learning and of the breadth of views belonging to himself. It looks a little as Raphael's labor might be supposed to look, if he had undertaken to show how Perugino painted."

But it was the tableaux painted by "Raphael" Adams that fired the popular imagination and became fixed in the American mind (scholarly opinion to the contrary notwithstanding) as the way the Revolution really began. Tudor's Life of Otis, published in 1823, drew heavily and uncritically on Adams' highly colored narrative. According to George Ticknor, whom one might suppose a discriminating judge, Tudor's book gave "the best representation possible, and, indeed what might be called a kind of dramatic exhibition, of the state of feeling in New England out of which the Revolution was produced. There is nothing like it in print, . . . nor could such a book be made twenty years from hence, for then all the traditions will have perished with the old men from whose graves he has just rescued them. It takes prodigiously here, and will, I think, do much good by promoting an inquiry into the most interesting and important period of our history." The immediate and long-range effects of both Adams' letters and Tudor's rendering of them may be seen in the subsequent Fourth of July orations that were a Boston municipal institution and were published collectively in 1852 as The Hundred Boston Orators—a volume distributed free by a Boston philanthropist to every school in the city, every academy in the state, and every college in the United States.

Through these and countless other channels, Adams' letters helped shape the nineteenth-century pantheon of Massachusetts heroes in the struggle for independence and contributed to the new secular religion of American nationalism. Of the things he remembered, some had never happened except in his own excited recollection of those brave days. His own earlier opinions of some of these heroes—notably Otis, Hancock, and Cushing—were utterly at variance with his tributes to them in 1818. But no matter. The way he remembered and felt about both the characters and events of the Revolution in his old age was the way his countrymen wanted to feel about and to celebrate them. According to his and their view, the American Revolution was a grand but wholly foreordained action, midway between two others equally grand. The earlier one, the full meaning of which the Revolution itself had made clear, was the peopling of America with men determined to govern themselves. The later action, now just beginning but bound to follow the Revolution as inevitably as the Revolution had followed the planting of North America, was awesome in its implications for world history. Study of the "MEANS AND THE MEASURES" applied in the winning of American independence would enable men "of Intelligence, Fortitude and Integrity" to throw off the chains of the regnant legitimacies and assume self-government over the whole surface of the globe.

All this was implicit in John Adams' appraisal of the collective role of Otis, Mayhew, Sam Adams, Thacher, Hancock, and the rest of the radical leaders in the Bay Colony on the eve of the Revolution. No wonder these men took on for him—and, before long, for others—more than human proportions. All this became explicit in nineteenth-century America's view of itself and its destiny. It was, and in the twentieth century still is, the core of America's continuing sense of mission, the most driving force in our national consciousness.

John Marshall

M'Culloch v. Maryland

1819

EDITED BY ROBERT G. MC CLOSKEY

John Marshall's opinion in M'Culloch v. Maryland *is by almost universal assent his paramount state paper and, as William D. Lewis has said, "perhaps the most celebrated Judicial utterance in the annals of the English speaking world." And the opinion is surely Marshall's own in a genuine and important sense, for it is stamped from first to last with his unique rhetorical gifts—the capacity to condense and elucidate an enormously complex issue, the instinct for a memorable phrase, the black-and-white approach to right and wrong that made many of his arguments so hard to answer. Yet in another sense any Supreme Court opinion is the work of many authors, and this one is no exception. The writer's colleagues who concur in his pronouncements may help to decide what he says, although their precise influence is seldom easy to discern because of the privacy of the judicial conference. In this case we can only guess that such strong-minded justices as Joseph Story and William Johnson may have played a part in shaping the composition even of "the Great Chief Justice." A second influence is less conjectural. The arguments of counsel before the Court have often provided the judges with ideas and phrases, and counsel for M'Culloch (i.e., for the Bank of the United States) consisted of three of the best courtroom lawyers who have ever adorned the American bar—William Pinckney, William Wirt, and Daniel Webster. Marshall's famous statement "the power to tax involves the power to destroy" was, for example, foreshadowed in Webster's oral argument, although Webster had said that an "unlimited" tax power involves the power to destroy and Marshall, characteristically, omitted the qualification. Thirdly, Marshall's prose here contains echoes of the famous opinion of Story in Martin v. Hunter's Lessee in 1816, a case involving a related question of national power. Fourthly and most important of all, Marshall was drawing on Alexander Hamilton's 1791 opinion on the constitutionality of the Bank, an opinion composed at President Washington's request when the bill establishing the first Bank was under consideration. Marshall's great rule for judging the extent of the implied powers ("Let the end be legitimate. . . .") is simply a restatement of language used by Hamilton; and the discussion of the meaning of the word "necessary" is also heavily dependent on Hamilton's paper. Finally it is worth noting that the general viewpoint expressed in M'Culloch had been anticipated as long ago as 1786 by James Wilson in his defense of the Bank of North America.*

Nevertheless, to say that Marshall must share his glory is not to detract from it; form and substance are often inseparable. His opinion surpasses its sources in the way that a successful poem surpasses a paraphrase. The thing is not only said; it is said with a rightness, a persuasiveness, a vividness that make it unforgettable.

For three decades America had been debating the momentous issue of national versus state power; but the issue was still gravely in doubt. Indeed there was reason to believe in 1819 that the states' rights tide, which had seemed to ebb a few years before, was flowing again more strongly than ever.

The M'Culloch case involved a heavy Maryland tax on the issuance of bank notes by any bank which Maryland herself had not chartered (the Bank of the United States had been chartered by Congress). M'Culloch was cashier of the Baltimore branch of the Bank; he issued notes without paying the tax; Maryland brought an action to recover penalties for nonpayment. The Baltimore County Court rendered judgment for the state, and the Maryland Court of Appeals affirmed. M'Culloch then urged the Supreme Court to pronounce the Maryland tax unconstitutional. Maryland, on the other hand, argued that the congressional act incorporating the Bank was

*itself invalid, that in passing it Congress had extended its
powers beyond those granted by the Constitution.*

*Marshall was a passionate defender of national preroga-
tives, and the revival of state challenges to those prerogatives
filled him with dread. He hoped that his argument in
M'Culloch would influence the contemporary debate. But he
also hoped that it would ring in the ears of posterity as the
classic justification for national sovereignty and as a lasting
barrier to state encroachments. To fulfill these hopes it was
necessary for him to muster, as never before, his splendid talents. When he actually composed the opinion is uncertain. It
is one of his longest, and he read it aloud before the Court
on March 6, 1819, only three days after the oral arguments
had ended. Perhaps, as has been suggested, he had written
most of it at his home in Richmond during the preceding
months, and the three-day interval was used to polish and
sharpen the draft. Yet this inference is not inevitable. The
opinion, like most of Marshall's, is unencumbered by citation;
it is an essay, not a pandect. To write this much prose in
three days is a formidable assignment. But it does not seem
an insuperable one when we reflect that the author had been,
with the help of his generation, preparing himself to write it
for almost thirty years.*

I N THE CASE now to be determined, the defendant, a sovereign State, denies the obligation of a law enacted by the
legislature of the Union, and the plaintiff, on his part, contests the validity of an act which has been passed by the legislature of that State. The constitution of our country, in its
most interesting and vital parts, is to be considered; the conflicting powers of the government of the Union and of its
members, as marked in that constitution, are to be discussed;
and an opinion given, which may essentially influence the
great operations of the government. No tribunal can approach such a question without a deep sense of its importance, and of the awful responsibility involved in its decision.
But it must be decided peacefully, or remain a source of hostile legislation, perhaps of hostility of a still more serious nature; and if it is to be so decided, by this tribunal alone can
the decision be made. On the Supreme Court of the United
States has the constitution of our country devolved this important duty.

The opinion is reprinted from 4 Wheaton 316 (1819).

The first question made in the cause is, has Congress power to incorporate a bank?

. . . In discussing this question, the counsel for the State of Maryland have deemed it of some importance, in the construction of the constitution, to consider that instrument not as emanating from the people, but as the act of sovereign and independent States. The powers of the general government, it has been said, are delegated by the States, who alone are truly sovereign; and must be exercised in subordination to the States, who alone possess supreme dominion.

It would be difficult to sustain this proposition. The Convention which framed the constitution was indeed elected by the State legislatures. But the instrument, when it came from their hands, was a mere proposal, without obligation, or pretensions to it. It was reported to the then existing Congress of the United States, with a request that it might "be submitted to a Convention of Delegates, chosen in each State by the people thereof, under the recommendation of its Legislature, for their assent and ratification." This mode of proceeding was adopted; and by the Convention, by Congress, and by the State Legislatures, the instrument was submitted to the people. They acted upon it in the only manner in which they can act safely, effectively, and wisely, on such a subject, by assembling in Convention. It is true, they assembled in their several States—and where else should they have assembled? No political dreamer was ever wild enough to think of breaking down the lines which separate the States, and of compounding the American people into one common mass. Of consequence, when they act, they act in their States. But the measures they adopt do not, on that account, cease to be the measures of the people themselves, or become the measures of the State governments.

From these Conventions the constitution derives its whole authority. The government proceeds directly from the people; is "ordained and established" in the name of the people; and is declared to be ordained, "in order to form a more perfect union, establish justice, ensure domestic tranquillity, and secure the blessings of liberty to themselves and to their posterity." The assent of the States, in their sovereign capacity, is implied in calling a Convention, and thus submitting that instrument to the people. But the people were at perfect liberty to accept or reject it; and their act was final. It required not the affirmance, and could not be negatived, by the State governments. The constitution, when thus adopted, was of complete obligation, and bound the State sovereignties.

It has been said, that the people had already surrendered

all their powers to the State sovereignties, and had nothing more to give. But, surely, the question whether they may resume and modify the powers granted to government does not remain to be settled in this country. Much more might the legitimacy of the general government be doubted, had it been created by the States. The powers delegated to the State sovereignties were to be exercised by themselves, not by a distinct and independent sovereignty, created by themselves. To the formation of a league, such as was the confederation, the State sovereignties were certainly competent. But when, "in order to form a more perfect union," it was deemed necessary to change this alliance into an effective government, possessing great and sovereign powers, and acting directly on the people, the necessity of referring it to the people, and of deriving its powers directly from them, was felt and acknowledged by all.

The government of the Union, then, (whatever may be the influence of this fact on the case,) is, emphatically, and truly, a government of the people. In form and in substance it emanates from them. Its powers are granted by them, and are to be exercised directly on them, and for their benefit.

This government is acknowledged by all to be one of enumerated powers. The principle, that it can exercise only the powers granted to it, would seem too apparent to have required to be enforced by all those arguments which its enlightened friends, while it was depending before the people, found it necessary to urge. That principle is now universally admitted. But the question respecting the extent of the powers actually granted, is perpetually arising, and will probably continue to arise, as long as our system shall exist.

In discussing these questions, the conflicting powers of the general and State governments must be brought into view, and the supremacy of their respective laws, when they are in opposition, must be settled.

If any one proposition could command the universal assent of mankind, we might expect it would be this—that the government of the Union, though limited in its powers, is supreme within its sphere of action. This would seem to result necessarily from its nature. It is the government of all; its powers are delegated by all; it represents all, and acts for all. Though any one State may be willing to control its operations, no State is willing to allow others to control them. The nation, on those subjects on which it can act, must necessarily bind its component parts. But this question is not left to mere reason: the people have, in express terms, decided it, by saying, "this constitution, and the laws of the United States, which shall be made in pursuance thereof," "shall be the supreme law of the land," and by requiring that the members of the State legislatures, and the officers of the executive and judicial departments of the States, shall take the oath of fidelity to it.

The government of the United States, then, though limited in its powers, is supreme; and its laws, when made in pursuance of the constitution, form the supreme law of the land, "any thing in the constitution or laws of any State to the contrary notwithstanding."

Among the enumerated powers, we do not find that of establishing a bank or creating a corporation. But there is no phrase in the instrument which, like the articles of confederation, excludes incidental or implied powers; and which requires that every thing granted shall be expressly and minutely described. Even the 10th amendment, which was framed for the purpose of quieting the excessive jealousies which had been excited, omits the word "expressly," and declares only that the powers "not delegated to the United States, nor prohibited to the States, are reserved to the States or to the people;" thus leaving the question, whether the particular power which may become the subject of contest has been delegated to the one government, or prohibited to the other, to depend on a fair construction of the whole instrument. The men who drew and adopted this amendment had experienced the embarrassments resulting from the insertion of this word in the articles of confederation, and probably omitted it to avoid those embarrassments. A constitution, to contain an accurate detail of all the subdivisions of which its great powers will admit, and of all the means by which they may be carried into execution, would partake of the prolixity of a legal code, and could scarcely be embraced by the human mind. It would probably never be understood by the public. Its nature, therefore, requires, that only its great outlines should be marked, its important objects designated, and the minor ingredients which compose those objects be deduced from the nature of the objects themselves. . . . In considering this question, then, we must never forget, that it is *a constitution* we are expounding.

Although, among the enumerated powers of government, we do not find the word "bank" or "incorporation," we find the great powers to lay and collect taxes; to borrow money; to regulate commerce; to declare and conduct a war; and to raise and support armies and navies. The sword and the purse, all the external relations, and no inconsiderable portion of the industry of the nation, are entrusted to its government.

It can never be pretended that these vast powers draw after them others of inferior importance, merely because they are inferior. Such an idea can never be advanced. But it may with great reason be contended, that a government, entrusted with such ample powers, on the due execution of which the happiness and prosperity of the nation so vitally depends, must also be entrusted with ample means for their execution. The power being given, it is the interest of the nation to facilitate its execution. It can never be their interest, and cannot be presumed to have been their intention, to clog and embarrass its execution by withholding the most appropriate means. Throughout this vast republic, from the St. Croix to the Gulph of Mexico, from the Atlantic to the Pacific, revenue is to be collected and expended, armies are to be marched and supported. The exigencies of the nation may require that the treasure raised in the north should be transported to the south, *that* raised in the east conveyed to the west, or that this order should be reversed. Is that construction of the constitution to be preferred which would render these operations difficult, hazardous, and expensive? Can we adopt that construction, (unless the words imperiously require it,) which would impute to the framers of that instrument, when granting these powers for the public good, the intention of impeding their exercise by withholding a choice of means? If, indeed, such be the mandate of the constitution, we have only to obey; but that instrument does not profess to enumerate the means by which the powers it confers may be executed; nor does it prohibit the creation of a corporation, if the existence of such a being be essential to the beneficial exercise of those powers. It is, then, the subject of fair inquiry, how far such means may be employed.

It is not denied, that the powers given to the government imply the ordinary means of execution. That, for example, of raising revenue, and applying it to national purposes, is admitted to imply the power of conveying money from place to place, as the exigencies of the nation may require, and of employing the usual means of conveyance. But it is denied that the government has its choice of means; or, that it may employ the most convenient means, if, to employ them, it be necessary to erect a corporation.

. . . The power of creating a corporation, though appertaining to sovereignty, is not, like the power of making war, or levying taxes, or of regulating commerce, a great substantive and independent power, which cannot be implied as incidental to other powers, or used as a means of executing them. It is never the end for which other powers are exercised, but a means by which other objects are accomplished. . . . The power of creating a corporation is never used for its own sake, but for the purpose of effecting something else. No sufficient reason is, therefore, perceived, why it may not pass as incidental to those powers which are expressly given, if it be a direct mode of executing them.

But the constitution of the United States has not left the right of Congress to employ the necessary means, for the execution of the powers conferred on the government, to general reasoning. To its enumeration of powers is added that of making "all laws which shall be necessary and proper, for carrying into execution the foregoing powers, and all other powers vested by this constitution, in the government of the United States, or in any department thereof."

The counsel for the State of Maryland have urged various arguments, to prove that this clause, though in terms a grant of power, is not so in effect; but is really restrictive of the general right, which might otherwise be implied, of selecting means for executing the enumerated powers.

In support of this proposition, they have found it necessary to contend, that this clause was inserted for the purpose of conferring on Congress the power of making laws. That, without it, doubts might be entertained, whether Congress could exercise its powers in the form of legislation.

But could this be the object for which it was inserted? . . . That a legislature, endowed with legislative powers, can legislate, is a proposition too self-evident to have been questioned.

But the argument on which most reliance is placed, is drawn from the peculiar language of this clause. Congress is not empowered by it to make all laws, which may have relation to the powers conferred on the government, but such only as may be *"necessary and proper"* for carrying them into execution. The word *"necessary,"* is considered as controlling the whole sentence, and as limiting the right to pass laws for the execution of the granted powers, to such as are indispensable, and without which the power would be nugatory. That it excludes the choice of means, and leaves to Congress, in each case, that only which is most direct and simple.

Is it true, that this is the sense in which the word "necessary" is always used? Does it always import an absolute physical necessity, so strong, that one thing, to which another may be termed necessary, cannot exist without that other? We think it does not. If reference be had to its use, in the common affairs of the world, or in approved authors, we find that it frequently imports no more than that one thing is convenient, or useful, or essential to another. To employ the means necessary to an end, is generally understood as employing any means calculated to produce the end, and not as being confined to those single means, without which the end would be entirely unattainable. Such is the character of human language, that no word conveys to the mind, in all situations, one single definite idea; and nothing is more common than to use words in a figurative sense. Almost all compositions contain words, which, taken in their rigorous sense, would convey a meaning different from that which is obviously intended. It is essential to just construction, that many words which import something excessive, should be understood in a more mitigated sense—in that sense which common usage justifies. The word "necessary" is of this description. It has not a fixed character peculiar to itself. It admits of all degrees of comparison; and is often connected with other words, which increase or diminish the impression the mind receives of the urgency it imports. A thing may be necessary, very necessary, absolutely or indispensably necessary. To no mind would the same idea be conveyed, by these several phrases. . . . This word, then, like others, is used in various senses; and, in its construction, the subject, the context, the intention of the person using them, are all to be taken into view.

Let this be done in the case under consideration. The subject is the execution of those great powers on which the welfare of a nation essentially depends. It must have been the intention of those who gave these powers, to insure, as far as human prudence could insure, their beneficial execution. This could not be done by confiding the choice of means to such narrow limits as not to leave it in the power of Congress to adopt any which might be appropriate, and which were conducive to the end. This provision is made in a constitution intended to endure for ages to come, and, consequently, to be adapted to the various *crises* of human affairs. To have prescribed the means by which government should, in all future time, execute its powers, would have been to change, entirely, the character of the instrument, and give it the properties of a legal code. It would have been an unwise attempt to provide, by immutable rules, for exigencies which, if foreseen at all, must have been seen dimly, and which can be best provided for as they occur. To have declared that the best means shall not be used, but those alone without which the power given would be nugatory, would have been to deprive the legislature of the capacity to avail itself of experience, to exercise its reason, and to accommodate its legislation to circumstances. . . .

But the argument which most conclusively demonstrates the error of the construction contended for by the counsel for the State of Maryland, is founded on the intention of the Convention, as manifested in the whole clause. To waste time and argument in proving that, without it, Congress might carry its powers into execution, would be not much less idle than to hold a lighted taper to the sun. As little can it be required to prove, that in the absence of this clause, Congress would have some choice of means. That it might employ those which, in its judgment, would most advantageously effect the object to be accomplished. That any means adapted to the end, any means which tended directly to the execution of the constitutional powers of the government, were in themselves constitutional. This clause, as construed by the State of Maryland, would abridge, and almost annihilate this useful and necessary right of the legislature to select its means. That this could not be intended, is, we should think, had it not been already controverted, too apparent for controversy. We think so for the following reasons:

1st. The clause is placed among the powers of Congress, not among the limitations on those powers.

2nd. Its terms purport to enlarge, not to diminish the powers vested in the government. It purports to be an additional power, not a restriction on those already granted. No reason has been, or can be assigned for thus concealing an intention to narrow the discretion of the national legislature under words which purport to enlarge it. The framers of the constitution wished its adoption, and well knew that it would be endangered by its strength, not by its weakness. Had they been capable of using language which would convey to the eye one idea, and, after deep reflection, impress on the mind another, they would rather have disguised the grant of power, than its limitation. . . .

The result of the most careful and attentive consideration bestowed upon this clause is, that if it does not enlarge, it cannot be construed to restrain the powers of Congress, or to impair the right of the legislature to exercise its best judgment in the selection of measures to carry into execution the constitutional powers of the government. If no other motive for its insertion can be suggested, a sufficient one is found in the desire to remove all doubts respecting the right to legislate on that vast mass of incidental powers which must be involved in the constitution, if that instrument be not a splendid bauble.

We admit, as all must admit, that the powers of the government are limited, and that its limits are not to be transcended. But we think the sound construction of the constitution must allow to the national legislature that discretion, with respect to the means by which the powers it confers are to be carried into execution, which will enable that body to perform the high duties assigned to it, in the manner most beneficial to the people. Let the end be legitimate, let it be within the scope of the constitution, and all means which are appropriate, which are plainly adapted to that end, which are not prohibited, but consist with the letter and spirit of the constitution, are constitutional.

. . . If a corporation may be employed indiscriminately with other means to carry into execution the powers of the government, no particular reason can be assigned for excluding the use of a bank, if required for its fiscal operations. To use one, must be within the discretion of Congress, if it be an appropriate mode of executing the powers of government. That it is a convenient, a useful, and essential instrument in the prosecution of its fiscal operations, is not now a subject of controversy. . . . The time has passed away when it can be necessary to enter into any discussion in order to prove the importance of this instrument, as a means to effect the legitimate objects of the government.

But, were its necessity less apparent, none can deny its being an appropriate measure; and if it is, the degree of its necessity, as has been very justly observed, is to be discussed in another place. Should Congress, in the execution of its powers, adopt measures which are prohibited by the constitution; or should Congress, under the pretext of executing its powers, pass laws for the accomplishment of objects not entrusted to the government; it would become the painful duty of this tribunal, should a case requiring such a decision come before it, to say that such an act was not the law of the land. But where the law is not prohibited, and is really calculated to effect any of the objects entrusted to the government, to undertake here to inquire into the degree of its necessity, would be to pass the line which circumscribes the judicial department, and to tread on legislative ground. This court disclaims all pretensions to such a power.

. . . After the most deliberate consideration, it is the unanimous and decided opinion of this Court, that the act to incorporate the Bank of the United States is a law made in pursuance of the constitution, and is a part of the supreme law of the land.

. . . It being the opinion of the Court, that the act incorporating the bank is constitutional; and that the power of establishing a branch in the State of Maryland might be properly exercised by the bank itself, we proceed to inquire—

. . . Whether the State of Maryland may, without violating the constitution, tax that branch?

That the power of taxation is one of vital importance; that it is retained by the States; that it is not abridged by the grant of a similar power to the government of the Union; that it is to be concurrently exercised by the two governments: are truths which have never been denied. But, such is the paramount character of the constitution, that its capacity to withdraw any subject from the action of even this power, is admitted. The States are expressly forbidden to lay any duties on imports or exports, except what may be absolutely necessary for executing their inspection laws. If the obligation of this prohibition must be conceded—if it may restrain a State from the exercise of its taxing power on imports and exports; the same paramount character would seem to restrain, as it certainly may restrain, a State from such other exercise of this power, as is in its nature incompatible with, and repugnant to, the constitutional laws of the Union. A law, absolutely repugnant to another, as entirely repeals that other as if express terms of repeal were used.

On this ground the counsel for the bank place its claim to be exempted from the power of a State to tax its operations. There is no express provision for the case, but the claim has been sustained on a principle which so entirely pervades the constitution, is so intermixed with the materials which compose it, so interwoven with its web, so blended with its texture, as to be incapable of being separated from it, without rending it into shreds.

This great principle is, that the constitution and the laws made in pursuance thereof are supreme; that they control the constitution and laws of the respective States, and cannot be controlled by them. From this, which may be almost termed an axiom, other propositions are deduced as corollaries, on the truth or error of which, and on their application to this case, the cause has been supposed to depend. These are, 1st. that a power to create implies a power to preserve. 2nd. That a power to destroy, if wielded by a different hand, is hostile to, and incompatible with these powers to create and to preserve. 3d. That where this repugnancy exists, that authority which is supreme must control, not yield to that over which it is supreme.

These propositions, as abstract truths, would, perhaps, never be controverted. Their application to this case, however, has been denied; and, both in maintaining the affirmative and the negative, a splendor of eloquence, and strength of argument, seldom, if ever, surpassed, have been displayed.

The power of Congress to create, and of course to continue, the bank, was the subject of the preceding part of this opinion; and is no longer to be considered as questionable.

That the power of taxing it by the States may be exercised so as to destroy it, is too obvious to be denied. But taxation is said to be an absolute power, which acknowledges no other limits than those expressly prescribed in the constitution, and like sovereign power of every other description, is trusted to the discretion of those who use it. . . .

The argument on the part of the State of Maryland, is, not that the States may directly resist a law of Congress, but that they may exercise their acknowledged powers upon it, and that the constitution leaves them this right in the confidence that they will not abuse it.

. . . That the power to tax involves the power to destroy; that the power to destroy may defeat and render useless the power to create; that there is a plain repugnance, in conferring on one government a power to control the constitutional measures of another, which other, with respect to those very measures, is declared to be supreme over that which exerts the control, are propositions not to be denied. But all inconsistencies are to be reconciled by the magic of the word CONFIDENCE. Taxation, it is said, does not necessarily and unavoidably destroy. To carry it to the excess of destruction would be an abuse, to presume which, would banish that confidence which is essential to all government.

But is this a case of confidence? Would the people of any one State trust those of another with a power to control the most insignificant operations of their State government? We know they would not. Why, then, should we suppose that the people of any one State should be willing to trust those of another with a power to control the operations of a government to which they have confided their most important and most valuable interests? In the legislature of the Union alone, are all represented. The legislature of the Union alone, therefore, can be trusted by the people with the power of controlling measures which concern all, in the confidence that it will not be abused. This, then, is not a case of confidence, and we must consider it as it really is.

If we apply the principle for which the State of Maryland contends, to the constitution generally, we shall find it capable of changing totally the character of that instrument. We shall find it capable of arresting all the measures of the government, and of prostrating it at the foot of the States. The American people have declared their constitution, and the laws made in pursuance thereof, to be supreme; but this principle would transfer the supremacy, in fact, to the States.

If the States may tax one instrument, employed by the government in the execution of its powers, they may tax any and every other instrument. They may tax the mail; they may tax the mint; they may tax patent rights; they may tax the papers of the custom-house; they may tax judicial process; they may tax all the means employed by the government, to an excess which would defeat all the ends of government. This was not intended by the American people. They did not design to make their government dependent on the States.

. . . It has also been insisted, that, as the power of taxation in the general and State governments is acknowledged to be concurrent, every argument which would sustain the right of the general government to tax banks chartered by the States, will equally sustain the right of the States to tax banks chartered by the general government.

But the two cases are not on the same reason. The people of all the States have created the general government, and have conferred upon it the general power of taxation. The people of all the States, and the States themselves, are represented in Congress, and, by their representatives, exercise this power. When they tax the chartered institutions of the States, they tax their constituents; and these taxes must be uniform. But, when a State taxes the operations of the government of the United States, it acts upon institutions created, not by their own constituents, but by people over whom they claim no control. It acts upon the measures of a government created by others as well as themselves, for the benefit of others in common with themselves. The difference is that which always exists, and always must exist, between the action of the whole on a part, and the action of a part on the whole— between the laws of a government declared to be supreme, and those of a government which, when in opposition to those laws, is not supreme.

. . . The Court has bestowed on this subject its most deliberate consideration. The result is a conviction that the States have no power, by taxation or otherwise, to retard, impede, burden, or in any manner control, the operations of the constitutional laws enacted by Congress to carry into execution the powers vested in the general government. This is, we think, the unavoidable consequence of that supremacy which the constitution has declared.

We are unanimously of opinion, that the law passed by the

legislature of Maryland, imposing a tax on the Bank of the United States, is unconstitutional and void.

Marshall's biographer, Albert Beveridge, once said that the M'Culloch opinion "has done more for the American Nation than any single utterance of any other one man, excepting only the Farewell Address of Washington." Beveridge was uncritically enamored of his great subject: perhaps he overstated the case. But there can be no doubt that Marshall's words have had a vital and continuing influence on the history of the Republic.

Their immediate result was, indeed, to excite a barrage of retaliatory tirades from the states' rights party. Spencer Roane and John Taylor of Virginia attacked the opinion bitterly and at length in the press; the legislatures of Virginia and Ohio passed resolutions damning it. Pennsylvania, Indiana, Illinois, and Tennessee joined in the assault. Marshall was chagrined and discouraged, and with some reason if he had hoped to slay the hydra of states' rights with a single stroke. This was too much to expect; no pen, not even Marshall's, was capable of that. Yet the very vehemence of the counterattack suggested that he had struck a telling blow, though not a mortal one. Insofar as logic and rhetoric could affect the contemporary debate, his opinion had done so, and his opponents found it easier to denounce the "crafty chief judge" (Jefferson's phrase) than to refute his reasoning.

The full greatness of the opinion, however, was to be revealed not in its own time but in the "ages to come" of which Marshall spoke. The marching logic, the infectious phrases reached out to a future in which changing historical circumstances were turning America toward the nationhood he had envisioned. Then the opinion, especially the first part with its classic defense of the national government's powers, could come into its own. The essential argument—that the people, not the states, created that government and endowed it with supremacy—was echoed by Webster in 1830 in the Reply to Hayne; it probably helped to form Lincoln's ideas about the nature of the Union; the outcome of the Civil War made it a dogma. The resulting principle—that the authority of the Union as construed by the Supreme Court overrides the authority of the states—did not in Marshall's day command the "universal assent of mankind" which he claimed for it, and it is still sometimes challenged in political rhetoric. But the Chief Justice's early assertion of the principle in decisions like M'Culloch *has helped in the long run to insure that those challenges would lack the support of the American people. "Let the end be legitimate . . . ," Marshall's expansive rule for judging the scope of the implied powers, is surely one of the most frequently cited sentences in constitutional annals. In 1819 and for some decades thereafter Congress was little disposed to exercise the vast range of power this rule bestows. But when it began, in the late nineteenth century, to pass national regulatory laws, the rule was ready as a justification for them, and it continues as the constitutional mainstay of national power to the present day. Even the terse statement "we must never forget, that it is a constitution we are expounding" is as pregnant today as in 1819, for it summarizes aphoristically what has come to be the dominant conception of the nature of the Constitution.*

The second part of the opinion, explaining why Maryland's tax on the Bank was unconstitutional, also has enjoyed an eventful, though very different, history. Marshall's words "the power to tax involves the power to destroy" were instrumental in promoting his nationalist purposes. Since the power to tax carries such a potential, we cannot concede a state's power to tax an agency of the national government; for that would mean that an inferior state could destroy its superior, that the part could frustrate the whole. But the phrase also had the epigrammatic, truistic ring that sometimes turns sentences into maxims and endows them with lives of their own. Its implications were seized by later judges to support the doctrine of "intergovernmental tax immunity"—that neither the states nor the nation could tax the instrumentalities of the other. For generations judges and lawyers elaborated this doctrine that had its origin in Marshall's special taste for sweeping language. It was only in the 1930's that the Supreme Court finally repudiated most of the inferences from his epigram by adopting in considerable degree the counter-epigram of Justice Holmes: "the power to tax is not the power to destroy while this court sits."

James Monroe

The Monroe Doctrine

1823

EDITED BY DEXTER PERKINS

The Monroe Doctrine, embodied in President James Monroe's message to Congress of December 2, 1823, had a dual origin.

On the one hand, it was related to the controversy between Russia and the United States over the northwest coast of America. The Russians claimed this coast from the Behring Straits south to an undetermined line on the Pacific Coast, and in February of 1821 the Russian government issued a ukase forbidding foreign ships to approach within one hundred miles of the shore. The American government contested this decree. In the course of discussions with the Russian minister in Washington, Secretary of State John Quincy Adams declared that "we should assume distinctly the principle that the American continents are no longer subjects for any new colonial establishments." Adams also suggested that a declaration to this effect be made in the presidential message of 1823, and his language was taken over by the President.

The second question that gave rise to the Monroe Doctrine was that of the Spanish-American colonies, most of which had revolted and attained independence by 1823, and some

274

of which the United States had recognized. At this time continental Europe was in the grip of reaction, and the continental powers, loosely known as the Holy Alliance (Russia, France, Austria, and Prussia), had intervened to put down revolution in Naples (1821) and Spain (1823). In the summer of 1823 conversations between the British Foreign Secretary, George Canning, and the American minister at London, Richard Rush, seemed to suggest the possibility of similar repressive action in Latin America. Only a little later the language of the Russian Tsar with regard to the colonies suggested that intervention to restore the colonies to Spain might be under consideration.

In lengthy Cabinet discussions in November Monroe and his advisers went over the whole question. Should the United States join with Great Britain, as Canning had suggested, in some common declaration of interest in the independence of the Spanish-American colonies? Or should it act unilaterally? Jefferson and Madison, whom Monroe had informed of the British overture, favored common action. But Monroe, on his own initiative, determined to deal with the problem in his message to Congress. His original draft, which included references to European repressive policies in Spain, and an expression of sympathy with the Greek rebels, was sharply criticized by Adams. The Secretary declared it necessary to "make an American cause and adhere inflexibly to that." He and Monroe accordingly revised the message, drawing a sharp line between the New World and the Old. Thus both the President and the Secretary deserve credit for the enunciation of the Monroe Doctrine.

. . . At the proposal of the Russian imperial government, made through the minister of the Emperor residing here, a full power and instructions have been transmitted to the Minister of the United States at St. Petersburgh, to arrange, by amicable negotiation, the respective rights and interests of the two nations on the northwest coast of this continent. A similar proposal has been made by his Imperial Majesty to the government of Great Britain, which has likewise been acceded to. The government of the United States has been de-

Monroe's draft of the message is in the National Archives. Senate and House versions of the text vary slightly. About one-sixth of the House version is reprinted here from *House Documents, Eighteenth Congress. First Session, 1823–1824*, Vol. I, No. 2 (Washington, D.C.: Gales and Seaton, 1823), December 2, 1823, pp. 3–15.

sirous, by this friendly proceeding, of manifesting the great value which they have invariably attached to the friendship of the emperor, and their solicitude to cultivate the best understanding with his government. In the discussions to which this interest has given rise, and in the arrangements by which they may terminate, the occasion has been judged proper for asserting, as a principle in which the rights and interests of the United States are involved, that the American continents, by the free and independent condition which they have assumed and maintain, are henceforth not to be considered as subjects for future colonization by any European powers.

. . . It was stated at the commencement of the last session, that a great effort was then making in Spain and Portugal, to improve the condition of the people of those countries; and that it appeared to be conducted with extraordinary moderation. It need scarcely be remarked, that the result has been, so far, very different from what was then anticipated. Of events in that quarter of the globe, with which we have so much intercourse, and from which we derive our origin, we have always been anxious and interested spectators. The citizens of the United States cherish sentiments the most friendly, in favor of the liberty and happiness of their fellow men on that side of the Atlantic. In the wars of the European powers, in matters relating to themselves, we have never taken any part, nor does it comport with our policy so to do. It is only when our rights are invaded, or seriously menaced, that we resent injuries, or make preparation for our defence. With the movements in this hemisphere, we are, of necessity, more immediately connected, and by causes which must be obvious to all enlightened and impartial observers. The political system of the allied powers is essentially different, in this respect, from that of America. This difference proceeds from that which exists in their respective governments. And to the defence of our own, which has been achieved by the loss of so much blood and treasure, and matured by the wisdom of their most enlightened citizens, and under which we have enjoyed unexampled felicity, this whole nation is devoted. We owe it, therefore, to candor, and to the amicable relations existing between the United States and those powers, to declare, that we should consider any attempt on their part to extend their system to any portion of this hemisphere, as dangerous to our peace and safety. With the existing colonies or dependencies of any European power, we have not interfered, and shall not interfere. But, with the governments who have declared their independence and maintained it, and whose independence we have, on great consideration, and on just prin-

ciples, acknowledged, we could not view any interposition for
the purpose of oppressing them, or controlling, in any other
manner, their destiny, by any European power, in any other
light than as the manifestation of an unfriendly disposition
towards the United States. In the war between these new governments and Spain, we declared our neutrality at the time of
their recognition, and to this we have adhered, and shall continue to adhere, provided no change shall occur, which, in
the judgment of the competent authorities of this government, shall make a corresponding change, on the part of the
United States, indispensable to their security.

The late events in Spain and Portugal, shew that Europe is
still unsettled. Of this important fact, no stronger proof can
be adduced than that the allied powers should have thought it
proper, on any principle satisfactory to themselves, to have
interposed, by force, in the internal concerns of Spain. To
what extent such interposition may be carried, on the same
principle, is a question, in which all independent powers,
whose governments differ from theirs, are interested; even
those most remote, and surely none more so than the United
States. Our policy, in regard to Europe, which was adopted at
an early stage of the wars which have so long agitated that
quarter of the globe, nevertheless remains the same, which is,
not to interfere in the internal concerns of any of its powers;
to consider the government *de facto* as the legitimate government for us; to cultivate friendly relations with it, and to preserve those relations by a frank, firm, and manly policy,
meeting, in all instances, the just claims of every power; submitting to injuries from none. But, in regard to those continents, circumstances are eminently and conspicuously different. It is impossible that the allied powers should extend
their political system to any portion of either continent, without endangering our peace and happiness; nor can any one
believe that our Southern Brethren, if left to themselves,
would adopt it of their own accord. It is equally impossible,
therefore, that we should behold such interposition, in any
form, with indifference. If we look to the comparative
strength and resources of Spain and those new governments,
and their distance from each other, it must be obvious that
she can never subdue them. It is still the true policy of the
United States, to leave the parties to themselves, in the hope
that other powers will pursue the same course. . . .

☆

The practical effects of the message of 1823 were not great.

It is now known that there was no danger whatsoever of the reconquest of the Spanish-American colonies by the Holy Alliance. As early as October, 1823, France, whose cooperation would have been essential to the enterprise, had assured the British government that no such project was contemplated. Without exception, the continental powers ignored Monroe's message in public, and condemned it in private. Metternich, the Austrian Chancellor, described it as an "indecent declaration"; and the Russian Foreign Minister declared that it merited the "most profound contempt." The physical power of the United States was quite inadequate to oppose a serious enterprise of reconquest.

Nor did the paragraph on the northwest coast have any impact. It was ignored by the Russian government; Russia and the United States later reached a compromise settlement on the northwest-coast controversy without any reference to Monroe's message.

Finally, the message was received with mixed emotions in Great Britain. British liberals applauded it, but Canning was chagrined that the American President had beaten him to the punch in issuing a public declaration in defense of the Latin-Americans, and was also displeased by the noncolonization principle.

The message did not, we now know, stave off European action against the colonies; no such action had been intended. It was not immediately accepted as a great declaration of principle—a "doctrine." And though discussed in 1824–26, it nearly faded from sight for almost twenty years thereafter. It was strikingly revived by President James K. Polk in his message of December 2, 1845, when he used Monroe's statement to support the American stand against British policy with regard to Texas and Oregon, and against suspected British designs on California, then a province of Mexico. It was frequently cited in the early 1850's in connection with Anglo-American rivalry in Central America.

By 1853 the phrase "Monroe Doctrine" appears, though more frequently among the Democrats than the Whigs. In the Civil War, and the years just after, the declaration was invoked in opposition to the French intervention in Mexico, which had as its object the establishment of the Austrian Archduke Maximilian as Emperor (though Secretary of State Seward never mentioned the Monroe Doctrine by name in his correspondence with the French). By the end of the sixties it had become a national dogma. It was broadened by President Grant to forbid the transfer of European territory in the New World from one power to another. President Hayes ex-

tended it still further, asserting the principle that any inter-oceanic canal should be under American control. Grover Cleveland, in one of the most extraordinary assertions of the Monroe principle, insisted upon the arbitration of a boundary dispute between Great Britain and Venezuela over the limits of British Guiana. By the end of the nineteenth century the Doctrine had become a deeply cherished principle of American foreign policy.

Down to this time the United States had never protested when European powers took punitive action against American states, so long as no question of territorial occupation was involved. In 1902 the British and German governments instituted a blockade against Venezuela, to force the Venezuelan government to give redress for damages suffered by their nationals. We know today that no more than this purpose was intended. But a vigorous movement of protest developed in the United States, and the Roosevelt Administration, though it had not originally objected to the British and German action, was influenced to extend the Monroe Doctrine. Fearing new interventions, Theodore Roosevelt enunciated in 1905 the principle that "chronic wrong-doing, or an impotence resulting in a general loosening of the ties of civilized society on the part of a country in the Western Hemisphere" might require the United States to exercise an international police power. This declaration has become known as the "Roosevelt Corollary."

The solicitude of the United States over its interests in the Caribbean was naturally increased by the construction of the Panama Canal. The Roosevelt Corollary seemed to fit this situation. Unsettled conditions in Nicaragua, in Haiti, and in the Dominican Republic also led to interventions on the part of the United States.

This extension of the Monroe Doctrine proved profoundly unpopular in Latin America. American troops withdrew from the Dominican Republic in 1924. By 1928 the United States was put very definitely on the defensive at the Havana meeting of the Pan-American Conference. In 1929, the Senate, in ratifying the Kellogg-Briand Pact for the renunciation of war, appended a gloss which dissociated the Corollary from the Doctrine. The pressure continued. By 1933, at the next Pan-American Conference, the United States put its name to a protocol which formally forbade intervention by any state in the domestic or foreign affairs of another. In 1936, at a special conference at Buenos Aires, the same principle was reasserted in still more binding form. These two protocols were overwhelmingly ratified by the Senate of the United States.

In the period since 1933, the Monroe Doctrine has been frequently invoked by American publicists, and by American politicians, as the need has arisen. But there has been a disposition on the part of the government itself to refer to the principle of Pan-American solidarity, rather than to use the language of Monroe. Thus the principles of 1823 have been sustained without giving offense to the sensitive pride of the Latin Americans, to whom the Doctrine has always seemed touched with a claim on the part of the United States to hegemony or domination.

During World War II, the United States made skillful use of the Grant doctrine without directly appealing to it. After the Germans conquered Holland and France, apprehension arose that they might seize Dutch or French colonies in the New World. At the Pan-American Conference in the summer of 1940, the principle was reasserted that no territory in the New World could be transferred from one power to another, and the United States was authorized, in an emergency, to act unilaterally to enforce this principle.

A further application of Monroe's principles is to be found in the agreements made by the United States and the Latin-American states against European aggression. The first of these agreements was made at Lima in 1938; more important and far-reaching compacts were made at Chapultepec in 1945 and at Rio de Janeiro in 1947. These agreements called for collective action in the event of direct attack from abroad. They do not touch the question of internal subversion, or of the establishment of Communist or proto-Communist regimes. Such a regime appeared in Guatemala in 1954. It was overthrown by Guatemalans themselves, but only after many references to the Doctrine in the press, and sub rosa assistance from the United States. At the time the other Latin-American states, devoted as they are to the principle of nonintervention, cannot be said to have been vigorous in support of the United States government.

A much more serious situation arose a few years later in Cuba. A Communist government was installed there in 1959. In 1962 that government, under Fidel Castro, accepted from the Russians missile weapons which threatened the southern United States and northern Latin America. President Kennedy instituted a blockade of Cuba, and demanded of the Kremlin the withdrawal of the weapons. After several days of crisis, the Russians yielded. In this confrontation the United States was supported by the Latin-American states. No mention was made of the Monroe Doctrine, but the principles of the Doctrine were brilliantly upheld.

In 1965 new difficulties in the Caribbean occurred. In the Dominican Republic a revolutionary movement, with certain Communist elements behind it, threatened the safety of the American residents. For the first time in a generation, the American government landed the Marines. But it sought to associate other Latin-American states with the occupation, and several such states accepted. As in the Cuban case, no mention was made of the Monroe Doctrine; the episode raises the question whether the nonintervention principle will be modified or abandoned when what is at stake is the Communization of a New World state.

The Monroe Doctrine has had a long existence, and it is still cherished by the American people. Its fundamental principle is sound: that is, the defense of the American continents against alien doctrine or conquest. But in the practice of diplomacy, it has been deemed more expedient to avoid reference to the Doctrine, which sometimes wounds Latin-American susceptibilities, and to rely, wherever possible, on the principle of self-defense and on the solidarity of the Americas.

Andrew Jackson

The Majority Is To Govern

1829

EDITED BY JOHN WILLIAM WARD

Because one of its premises was an implicit trust in the common sense of the common man, Jacksonian democracy lacks its philosopher. But a characteristic statement which asserts "the first principle" of Jacksonian democracy is Andrew Jackson's first message to Congress upon becoming President. Here he speaks for the principle which has kept his name alive in the historical memory of the American people: the will of the people is the fundamental source of all power. Power is responsible finally to the majority.

In 1824, Jackson had received a plurality of the popular and electoral vote in a four-cornered race for the Presidency, followed by John Quincy Adams, William Crawford, and Henry Clay. Since no candidate had a majority, selection devolved on the House of Representatives, where choice, according to the provision of the Constitution, lay among the three leading candidates. Clay, now excluded as a candidate, threw his political influence behind Adams, and after Adams became President he named Clay his Secretary of State, placing him in the office which to that time had been the conventional stepping stone to the Presidency. Immediately Jacksonian partisans raised the cry of a "corrupt bargain" between

*Adams and Clay and began the campaign which was to bring
Jackson to the White House in 1828.*

*James Parton, Jackson's contemporary and first and still
best biographer, tells how Jackson went about preparing his
messages. He used to begin, says Parton, some months before-
hand, gathering ideas and jotting down notes, and when the
time came all were turned over to his private secretary, Andrew Jackson Donelson, who then put them in order. Unlike
his predecessors in the office of President, Jackson did not
use his Cabinet as a council of state. He relied more on a
personal staff of advisers in the White House, the "Kitchen
Cabinet," and tended to treat Cabinet members as administrative officers. When Donelson had drafted a message, Jackson
would consult informally with his own intimate staff before
arriving at a final version. Characteristically, a Jackson message was a collective effort, but the ideas were always Jackson's.*

*Against the background of the "corrupt bargain" Jackson,
in his first presidential address to Congress, catechized the
legislative branch on the principles of democratic government. In the course of his message, delivered on December 8,
1829, he laid bare the major assumptions of his democratic
faith.*

FELLOW CITIZENS OF THE SENATE AND OF THE HOUSE OF REPRESENTATIVES:

I T AFFORDS me pleasure to tender my friendly greetings to
you on the occasion of your assembling at the Seat of
Government, to enter upon the important duties to which
you have been called by the voice of our countrymen. The
task devolves on me, under a provision of the Constitution, to
present to you, as the Federal Legislature of twenty-four sovereign States, and twelve millions of happy people, a view of
our affairs; and to propose such measures as, in the discharge
of my official functions, have suggested themselves as necessary to promote the objects of our Union.

In communicating with you for the first time, it is, to me, a

The text is reproduced here from *Message from the President of the
United States to the Two Houses of Congress at the Commencement
of the First Session of the Twenty-first Congress, December 8, 1829*
(Washington: Printed by Duff Green, 1829). Jackson's speech may
also be found in *Senate Documents* (1829–30), I, Document 1. Approximately two-fifths of the speech appears here.

source of unfeigned satisfaction, calling for mutual gratulation and devout thanks to a benign Providence, that we are at peace with all mankind; and that our country exhibits the most cheering evidence of general welfare and progressive improvement. Turning our eyes to other nations, our great desire is to see our brethren of the human race secured in the blessings enjoyed by ourselves, and advancing in knowledge, in freedom, and in social happiness.

Our foreign relations, although in their general character pacific and friendly, present subjects of difference between us and other Powers, of deep interest, as well to the country at large as to many of our citizens. To effect an adjustment of these shall continue to be the object of my earnest endeavors; and notwithstanding the difficulties of the task, I do not allow myself to apprehend unfavorable results. Blessed as our country is with every thing which constitutes national strength, she is fully adequate to the maintenance of all her interests. In discharging the responsible trust confided to the Executive in this respect, it is my settled purpose to ask nothing that is not clearly right, and to submit to nothing that is wrong; and I flatter myself, that, supported by the other branches of the Government, and by the intelligence and patriotism of the People, we shall be able, under the protection of Providence, to cause all our just rights to be respected. . . .

I consider it one of the most urgent of my duties to bring to your attention the propriety of amending that part of our Constitution which relates to the election of President and Vice President. Our system of government was, by its framers, deemed an experiment; and they, therefore, consistently provided a mode of remedying its defects.

To the People belongs the right of electing their Chief Magistrate: it was never designed that their choice should, in any case, be defeated, either by the intervention of electoral colleges, or by the agency confided, under certain contingencies, to the House of Representatives. Experience proves, that, in proportion as agents to execute the will of the People are multiplied, there is danger of their wishes being frustrated. Some may be unfaithful: all are liable to err. So far, therefore, as the People can, with convenience, speak, it is safer for them to express their own will.

The number of aspirants to the Presidency, and the diversity of the interests which may influence their claims, leave little reason to expect a choice in the first instance: and, in that event, the election must devolve on the House of Representatives, where, it is obvious, the will of the People may not be always ascertained; or, if ascertained, may not be regarded. From the mode of voting by States, the choice is to be made by twenty-four votes; and it may often occur, that one of these will be controlled by an individual representative. Honors and offices are at the disposal of the successful candidate. Repeated ballotings may make it apparent that a single individual holds the cast in his hand. May he not be tempted to name his reward? But even without corruption—supposing the probity of the Representative to be proof against the powerful motives by which it may be assailed—the will of the People is still constantly liable to be misrepresented. One may err from ignorance of the wishes of his constituents; another, from a conviction that it is his duty to be governed by his own judgment of the fitness of the candidates: finally, although all were inflexibly honest—all accurately informed of the wishes of their constituents—yet, under the present mode of election, a minority may often elect the President; and when this happens, it may reasonably be expected that efforts will be made on the part of the majority to rectify this injurious operation of their institutions. But although no evil of this character should result from such a perversion of the first principle of our system—*that the majority is to govern*—it must be very certain that a President elected by a minority cannot enjoy the confidence necessary to the successful discharge of his duties.

In this, as in all other matters of public concern, policy requires that as few impediments as possible should exist to the free operation of the public will. Let us, then, endeavor so to amend our system, that the office of Chief Magistrate may not be conferred upon any citizen but in pursuance of a fair expression of the will of the majority.

I would therefore recommend such an amendment of the Constitution as may remove all intermediate agency in the election of President and Vice President. The mode may be so regulated as to preserve to each State its present relative weight in the election; and a failure in the first attempt may be provided for, by confining the second to a choice between the two highest candidates. In connexion with such an amendment, it would seem advisable to limit the service of the Chief Magistrate to a single term, of either four or six years. If, however, it should not be adopted, it is worthy of consideration whether a provision disqualifying for office the Representatives in Congress on whom such an election may have devolved, would not be proper.

While members of Congress can be constitutionally appointed to offices of trust and profit, it will be the practice, even under the most conscientious adherence to duty, to select them for such stations as they are believed to be better qualified to fill than other citizens; but the purity of our Government would doubtless be promoted, by their exclusion from all appointments in the gift of the President in whose election they may have been officially concerned. The nature of the judicial office, and the necessity of securing in the Cabinet and in diplomatic stations of the highest rank, the best talents and political experience, should, perhaps, except these from the exclusion.

There are perhaps few men who can for any great length of time enjoy office and power, without being more or less under the influence of feelings unfavorable to the faithful discharge of their public duties. Their integrity may be proof against improper considerations immediately addressed to themselves; but they are apt to acquire a habit of looking with indifference upon the public interests, and of tolerating conduct from which an unpractised man would revolt. Office is considered as a species of property; and Government, rather as a means of promoting individual interests, than as an instrument created solely for the service of the People. Corruption in some, and, in others, a perversion of correct feelings and principles, divert Government from its legitimate ends, and make it an engine for the support of the few at the expense of the many. The duties of all public officers are, or, at least, admit of being made, so plain and simple, that men of intelligence may readily qualify themselves for their performance; and I cannot but believe that more is lost by the long continuance of men in office, than is generally to be gained by their experience. I submit therefore to your consideration, whether the efficiency of the Government would not be promoted, and official industry and integrity better secured, by a general extension of the law which limits appointments to four years.

In a country where offices are created solely for the benefit of the People, no one man has any more intrinsic right to official station than another. Offices were not established to give support to particular men, at the public expense. No individual wrong is therefore done by removal, since neither appointment to, nor continuance in, office, is matter of right. The incumbent became an officer with a view to public benefits; and when these require his removal, they are not to be sacrificed to private interests. It is the People, and they alone, who have a right to complain, when a bad officer is substituted for a good one. He who is removed has the same means of obtaining a living, that are enjoyed by the millions who never held office. The proposed limitation would destroy the idea of property, now so generally connected with official station; and although individual distress may be sometimes produced, it would, by promoting that rotation which constitutes a leading principle in the republican creed, give healthful action to the system.

No very considerable change has occurred, during the recess of Congress, in the condition of either our Agriculture, Commerce, or Manufactures. . . .

. . . To regulate its conduct, so as to promote equally the prosperity of these three cardinal interests, is one of the most difficult tasks of Government; and it may be regretted that the complicated restrictions which now embarrass the intercourse of nations, could not by common consent be abolished; and commerce allowed to flow in those channels to which individual enterprise—always its surest guide—might direct it. . . . Frequent legislation in regard to any branch of industry, affecting its value, and by which its capital may be transferred to new channels, must always be productive of hazardous speculation and loss.

In deliberating, therefore, on these interesting subjects, local feelings and prejudices should be merged in the patriotic determination to promote the great interests of the whole. All attempts to connect them with the party conflicts of the day are necessarily injurious, and should be discountenanced. Our action upon them should be under the control of higher and purer motives. Legislation, subjected to such influences, can never be just; and will not long retain the sanction of a People, whose active patriotism is not bounded by sectional limits, nor insensible to that spirit of concession and forbearance, which gave life to our political compact, and still sustains it. Discarding all calculations of political ascendancy, the North, the South, the East, and the West, should unite in diminishing any burthen, of which either may justly complain.

The agricultural interest of our country is so essentially connected with every other, and so superior in importance to them all, that it is scarcely necessary to invite to it your particular attention. It is principally as manufactures and commerce tend to increase the value of agricultural productions, and to extend their application to the wants and comforts of society, that they deserve the fostering care of Government. . . .

[The] state of the finances exhibits the resources of the nation in an aspect highly flattering to its industry; and auspicious of the ability of Government, in a very short time, to extinguish the public debt. When this shall be done, our population will be relieved from a considerable portion of its present burthens; and will find, not only new motives to patriotic affection, but additional means for the display of individual enterprise. The fiscal power of the States will also be increased; and may be more extensively exerted in favor of education and other public objects: while ample means will remain in the Federal Government to promote the general weal, in all the modes permitted to its authority.

After the extinction of the public debt, it is not probable that any adjustment of the tariff, upon principles satisfactory to the People of the Union, will, until a remote period, if ever, leave the Government without a considerable surplus in the Treasury, beyond what may be required for its current service. As then the period approaches when the application of the revenue to the payment of debt will cease, the disposition of the surplus will present a subject for the serious deliberation of Congress; and it may be fortunate for the country that it is yet to be decided. . . .

. . . It appears to me that the most safe, just, and federal disposition which could be made of the surplus revenue, would be its apportionment among the several States according to their ratio of representation; and should this measure not be found warranted by the Constitution, that it would be expedient to propose to the States an amendment authorizing it. I regard an appeal to the source of power, in cases of real doubt, and where its exercise is deemed indispensable to the general welfare, as among the most sacred of all our obligations. Upon this country, more than any other, has, in the providence of God, been cast the special guardianship of the great principle of adherence to written constitutions. If it fail here, all hope in regard to it will be extinguished. That this was intended to be a Government of limited and specific, and not general powers, must be admitted by all; and it is our duty to preserve for it the character intended by its framers. If experience points out the necessity for an enlargement of these powers, let us apply for it to those for whose benefit it is to be exercised; and not undermine the whole system by a resort to overstrained constructions. The scheme has worked well. It has exceeded the hopes of those who devised it, and become an object of admiration to the world. We are responsible to our country, and to the glorious cause of self-government, for the preservation of so great a good. The great mass of legislation relating to our internal affairs, was intended to be left where the Federal Convention found it—in the State Governments. Nothing is clearer, in my view, than that we are chiefly indebted for the success of the Constitution under

which we are now acting, to the watchful and auxiliary operation of the State authorities. This is not the reflection of a
day, but belongs to the most deeply rooted convictions of my
mind. I cannot, therefore, too strongly or too earnestly, for
my own sense of its importance, warn you against all encroachments upon the legitimate sphere of State sovereignty.
Sustained by its healthful and invigorating influence, the Federal system can never fall. . . .

   . . . I would suggest, also, an inquiry, whether the provisions of the act of Congress, authorizing the discharge of the
persons of debtors to the Government, from imprisonment,
may not, consistently with the public interest, be extended to
the release of the debt, where the conduct of the debtor is
wholly exempt from the imputation of fraud. Some more liberal policy than that which now prevails, in reference to this
unfortunate class of citizens, is certainly due to them, and
would prove beneficial to the country. The continuance of the
liability, after the means to discharge it have been exhausted,
can only serve to dispirit the debtor; or, where his resources
are but partial, the want of power in the Government to
compromise and release the demand, instigates to fraud, as
the only resource for securing a support to his family. He
thus sinks into a state of apathy, and becomes a useless drone
in society, or a vicious member of it, if not a feeling witness
of the rigor and inhumanity of his country. All experience
proves, that oppressive debt is the bane of enterprise; and it
should be the care of a Republic not to exert a grinding
power over misfortune and poverty. . . .

   The condition and ulterior destiny of the Indian Tribes
within the limits of some of our States, have become objects
of much interest and importance. It has long been the policy
of Government to introduce among them the arts of civilization, in the hope of gradually reclaiming them from a wandering life. This policy has, however, been coupled with
another, wholly incompatible with its success. Professing a
desire to civilize and settle them, we have, at the same time,
lost no opportunity to purchase their lands, and thrust them
further into the wilderness. By this means they have not only
been kept in a wandering state, but been led to look upon us
as unjust and indifferent to their fate. Thus, though lavish in
its expenditures upon the subject, Government has constantly
defeated its own policy; and the Indians, in general, receding
further and further to the West, have retained their savage
habits. A portion, however, of the Southern tribes, having mingled much with the whites, and made some progress in the
arts of civilized life, have lately attempted to erect an inde-

pendent government, within the limits of Georgia and Alabama. These States, claiming to be the only Sovereigns within their territories, extended their laws over the Indians; which induced the latter to call upon the United States for protection.

Under these circumstances, the question presented was, whether the General Government had a right to sustain those people in their pretensions? The Constitution declares, that "no new State shall be formed or erected within the jurisdiction of any other State," without the consent of its legislature. If the General Government is not permitted to tolerate the erection of a confederate State within the territory of one of the members of this Union, against her consent; much less could it allow a foreign and independent government to establish itself there. Georgia became a member of the Confederacy which eventuated in our Federal Union, as a sovereign State, always asserting her claim to certain limits; which having been originally defined in her colonial charter, and subsequently recognised in the treaty of peace, she has ever since continued to enjoy, except as they have been circumscribed by her own voluntary transfer of a portion of her territory to the United States, in the articles of cession of 1802. Alabama was admitted into the Union on the same footing with the original States, with boundaries which were prescribed by Congress. There is no constitutional, conventional, or legal provision, which allows them less power over the Indians within their borders, than is possessed by Maine or New York. Would the People of Maine permit the Penobscot tribe to erect an Independent Government within their State? and unless they did, would it not be the duty of the General Government to support them in resisting such a measure? Would the People of New York permit each remnant of the Six Nations within her borders, to declare itself an independent people under the protection of the United States? Could the Indians establish a separate republic on each of their reservations in Ohio? and if they were so disposed, would it be the duty of this Government to protect them in the attempt? If the principle involved in the obvious answer to these questions be abandoned, it will follow that the objects of this Government are reversed; and that it has become a part of its duty to aid in destroying the States which it was established to protect.

Actuated by this view of the subject, I informed the Indians inhabiting parts of Georgia and Alabama, that their attempt to establish an independent government would not be countenanced by the Executive of the United States; and ad-

vised them to emigrate beyond the Mississippi, or submit to
the laws of those States.

Our conduct towards these people is deeply interesting to
our national character. Their present condition, contrasted
with what they once were, makes a most powerful appeal to
our sympathies. Our ancestors found them the uncontrolled
possessors of these vast regions. By persuasion and force,
they have been made to retire from river to river, and from
mountain to mountain; until some of the tribes have become
extinct, and others have left but remnants, to preserve, for a
while, their once terrible names. Surrounded by the whites,
with their arts of civilization, which, by destroying the resources of the savage, doom him to weakness and decay; the
fate of the Mohegan, the Narragansett, and the Delaware, is
fast overtaking the Choctaw, the Cherokee, and the Creek.
That this fate surely awaits them, if they remain within the
limits of the States, does not admit of a doubt. Humanity and
national honor demand that every effort should be made to
avert so great a calamity. It is too late to inquire whether it
was just in the United States to include them and their territory within the bounds of new States whose limits they could
control. That step cannot be retraced. A State cannot be dis-
membered by Congress, or restricted in the exercise of her
constitutional power. But the people of those States, and of
every State, actuated by feelings of justice and a regard for
our national honor, submit to you the interesting question,
whether something cannot be done, consistently with the
rights of the States, to preserve this much injured race?

As a means of effecting this end, I suggest, for your consideration, the propriety of setting apart an ample district
West of the Mississippi, and without the limits of any State
or Territory, now formed, to be guarantied to the Indian
tribes, as long as they shall occupy it: each tribe having a distinct control over the portion designated for its use. There
they may be secured in the enjoyment of governments of
their own choice, subject to no other control from the United
States than such as may be necessary to preserve peace on
the frontier, and between the several tribes. There the benevolent may endeavor to teach them the arts of civilization;
and, by promoting union and harmony among them, to raise
up an interesting commonwealth, destined to perpetuate the
race, and to attest the humanity and justice of this Government.

This emigration should be voluntary: for it would be as
cruel as unjust to compel the aborigines to abandon the
graves of their fathers, and seek a home in a distant land. But

they should be distinctly informed that, if they remain within the limits of the States, they must be subject to their laws. In return for their obedience, as individuals, they will, without doubt, be protected in the enjoyment of those possessions which they have improved by their industry. But it seems to me visionary to suppose, that, in this state of things, claims can be allowed on tracts of country on which they have neither dwelt nor made improvements, merely because they have seen them from the mountain, or passed them in the chace. Submitting to the laws of the States, and receiving, like other citizens, protection in their persons and property, they will, ere long, become merged in the mass of our population. . . .

I now commend you, fellow-citizens, to the guidance of Almighty God, with a full reliance on his merciful providence for the maintenance of our free institutions; and with an earnest supplication, that, whatever errors it may be my lot to commit, in discharging the arduous duties which have devolved on me, will find a remedy in the harmony and wisdom of your counsels.

ANDREW JACKSON

The good society for which Jackson spoke embodied three themes: rule by the will of the people, the avoidance of corruption, and simplicity of government. When Jackson says "the first principle of our system" is "that the majority is to govern," he is himself on uncertain historical ground. The Constitution to which Jackson appeals is not a document devised to implement a thoroughgoing domination by the majority in politics. Jackson, in saying it is, seems to be verging toward the majoritarian position whose probable consequences so concerned Alexis de Tocqueville in his analysis of democracy in the America of Jackson's time. But as one watches the development of Jackson's argument, one sees him avoid in an astonishing way the tyranny of the majority which Tocqueville feared.

The premise of Jackson's message is a trust in the will of a virtuous and competent people. As far as they can, the "People" should act directly. But "experience proves," as for Jackson it clearly did in 1824, that agents trusted with the power of translating the will of the people into reality will, inevitably, be corrupted by that power: "Office is considered as a species of property; and Government, rather as a means of promoting individual interests, than as an instrument created solely for the service of the People." To avoid such corrup-

tion, Jackson spoke for limited tenure for the President and rotation in all appointive offices. Later generations would stigmatize the principle by remembering it only as the "spoils system." It is true that Jackson was enough of a politician to recognize the uses of patronage, but he embraced the system as a species of reform. His rejection of a trained and experienced class of civil servants, a gesture which made Jackson's memory a curse to reformers who came after him, was possible only on the assumption that the work of government was essentially so plain and simple that the average intelligent man could do the job. Jackson's solution to the paradox of politics, the corruption of the selfless will of the people by the power necessary to enact that will, was no less than to dismiss the need for power in politics at all. If power corrupts, then America was in the happy state of having no need for power.

Jackson's ideal in politics was the limited state of classical liberalism. The chief action of government was not to act, and the major issues of Jackson's Presidency bear witness to his ideal. His extensive use of the veto power, his removals from office, his attack on the Second Bank of the United States, and his denial of the propriety of federal participation in internal improvements were all designed to strip the central government of the accretions of power. Jackson's only positive assertion of federal power was his Proclamation against the doctrine of nullification in 1832 when South Carolina threatened the very existence of the Union. Paradoxically, Jackson's vigorous Presidency schooled subsequent Presidents in the power of the office, but his own intention ran in the opposite direction. It ran in the direction of a purely administrative state which beyond the minimal preservation of law and order left the business of society "to flow in those channels to which individual enterprise—always its surest guide—might direct it."

If the particular occasion of Jackson's address is important, the larger occasion, the general economic and social context in which he spoke, is even more so. Jackson assumed that the best way to serve the general interest of society was to have a simple and limited government which would leave each individual free to pursue his own self-interest. He could make this assumption only in the context of conditions of general equality in an agrarian society, unhampered by debt and untroubled by the threat of foreign enemies, supported by the seemingly limitless expanse of a virgin continent whose Indians posed the chief problem for the American conscience. Looked at from the vantage point of our own present, the *age of Jackson has a pastoral air about it. The consequence Jackson did not foresee, and which we see so clearly because we have experienced it, was that to dismiss power from the realm of politics left power unhampered and unchecked in other areas of society, especially the economic.*

"In elective government," wrote Frederick Grimké, a contemporary of Andrew Jackson, "public men may be said to be the representatives of the ideas of the age, as well as of the grosser interests with which they have to deal; and to give those ideas a visible form, is the most certain way of commanding public attention, and of stimulating inquiry." Because of Andrew Jackson's dramatic success in giving the ideas of his age a visible form, we remember that age by his very name. But the ideals he once acted out in politics seem still to speak to us, who live in a drastically different age.

"To most of us," said Franklin D. Roosevelt in a radio broadcast from Washington in 1936, "Andrew Jackson appropriately has become the symbol of certain great ideals." The ideal which Roosevelt saw embodied in Jackson's career bore upon the "real issue" still before the American people: "the right of the average man and woman to lead a finer, a better and a happier life." Yet long before Roosevelt discovered a use for the sanctions of the Jacksonian heritage, other Americans, also living in years of change and economic and social disorder, had looked to Jackson to find a meaning quite different from the one Roosevelt was to find. In 1883, the president of the Western Union Telegraph Company, arguing in behalf of the "laws of supply and demand" and against "legislative interference," said, "I am a believer in that old maxim of General Jackson: 'That people is governed best which is governed least.'" Intellectuals of the time agreed, just as intellectuals later were to agree with Roosevelt. William Graham Sumner argued that Jackson was, although by instinct rather than thought, a better political philosopher for America than Alexander Hamilton, because Jackson firmly opposed positive action by the state in the affairs of society. Intellectuals of the age of Roosevelt found Jackson to mean that government, acting on behalf of the common man, should intervene in the social and economic order and discipline the business community to make it conform to the interests of the majority.

William Lloyd Garrison
Prospectus for the "Liberator"
1831

EDITED BY KENNETH M. STAMPP

Emerson once asked: "What is man born for but to be a Reformer, a Remaker of what man has made; a renouncer of lies; a restorer of truth and good . . . ?" Many of Emerson's New England contemporaries agreed with him and devoted their lives to various movements for moral uplift or social reform, but none more fervently than William Lloyd Garrison.

Born in Newburyport, Massachusetts, in 1805, Garrison experienced both poverty and insecurity in his childhood. His father, a sailor, deserted the family when Garrison was an infant; his mother, an austere, pious Baptist, made her son aware of the prevalence of sin in the world but offered him neither warmth nor understanding. As a youth Garrison learned the printer's trade and developed a taste for polemical newspaper writing. He had considerable talent, and with it he combined a strong ambition to win public recognition —in order, as he once said, to have his name known "in a praiseworthy manner."

Reform journalism was Garrison's road to fame. In 1828 he went first to Boston to edit the National Philanthropist, *a temperance weekly, then to Bennington, Vermont, to edit the* Journal of the Times, *in whose columns he preached temper-*

ance, world peace, and the gradual abolition of slavery. The survival of slavery in the southern states, he told a Boston audience on July 4, 1829, was a "glaring contradiction" of the American creed of liberty and equality. The free states had a right to demand gradual emancipation, because as long as slavery existed "they participate in the guilt thereof." Soon after making this speech, Garrison abandoned gradualism and began to demand the immediate abolition of slavery. Since slaveholding was a sin, to advocate gradual emancipation was like asking a thief gradually to abandon a life of crime.

In August, 1829, Garrison moved to Baltimore to join the gentle Quaker Benjamin Lundy in editing an antislavery newspaper, the Genius of Universal Emancipation. Two months later, in one of his editorials, Garrison violently upbraided Francis Todd, a Newburyport shipowner, for transporting a cargo of slaves from Baltimore to New Orleans. Men such as Todd, he said, were "enemies of their own species—highway robbers and murderers," and they deserved to be punished with solitary confinement for life. For this editorial a Baltimore grand jury indicted Garrison for libel, and he was tried, convicted, and fined $50. Since he could pay neither the fine nor court costs, he was jailed from April 17 to June 5, 1830.

After his release from jail, Garrison returned to Boston determined to awaken the northern people to the evils of slavery. "A few white victims must be sacrificed to open the eyes of this nation," wrote the young martyr. "I expect and am willing to be persecuted, imprisoned and bound for advocating African rights." Thus, at the age of twenty-five, Garrison was prepared for his life's work. On January 1, 1831, in a dingy room on the third floor of Merchants' Hall in Boston, he began to publish a weekly abolitionist newspaper, the Liberator. The prospectus, printed below, appeared in the first issue.

IN THE MONTH of August, I issued proposals for publishing *The Liberator* in Washington city; but the enterprise, though hailed in different sections of the country, was palsied by public indifference. Since that time, the removal of the *Genius of Universal Emancipation* to the Seat of Government has rendered less imperious the establishment of a similar periodical in that quarter.

The text is reprinted here as it originally appeared in the *Liberator* of January 1, 1831.

During my recent tour for the purpose of exciting the minds of the people by a series of discourses on the subject of slavery, every place that I visited gave fresh evidence of the fact, that a greater revolution in public sentiment was to be effected in the free states—*and particularly in New-England*—than at the south. I found contempt more bitter, opposition more active, detraction more relentless, prejudice more stubborn, and apathy more frozen, than among the slave owners themselves. Of course, there were individual exceptions to the contrary. This state of things afflicted, but did not dishearten me. I determined, at every hazard, to lift up the standard of emancipation in the eyes of the nation, *within sight of Bunker Hill and in the birth place of liberty*. That standard is now unfurled; and long may it float, unhurt by the spoliations of time or the missiles of a desperate foe—yea, till every chain be broken, and every bondman set free! Let southern oppressors tremble—let their secret abettors tremble—let their northern apologists tremble—let all the enemies of the persecuted blacks tremble.

I deem the publication of my original Prospectus* unnecessary, as it has obtained a wide circulation. The principles therein inculcated will be steadily pursued in this paper, excepting that I shall not array myself as the political partisan of any man. In defending the great cause of human rights, I wish to derive the assistance of all religions and of all parties.

Assenting to the "self-evident truth" maintained in the American Declaration of Independence, "that all men are created equal and endowed by their Creator with certain inalienable rights—among which are life, liberty and the pursuit of happiness," I shall strenuously contend for the immediate enfranchisement of our slave population. In Park-street Church, on the Fourth of July, 1829, in an address on slavery, I unreflectingly assented to the popular but pernicious doctrine of *gradual* abolition. I seize this opportunity to make a full and unequivocal recantation, and thus publickly to ask pardon of my God, of my country, and of my brethren the poor slaves, for having uttered a sentiment so full of timidity, injustice and absurdity. A similar recantation, from my pen, was published in the *Genius of Universal Emancipation* at Baltimore, in September, 1829. My conscience is now satisfied.

I am aware that many object to the severity of my language; but is there not cause for severity? I *will be* as harsh

* I would here offer my grateful acknowledgments to those editors who so promptly and generously inserted my Proposals. They must give me an available opportunity to repay their liberality.

as truth, and as uncompromising as justice. On this subject, I do not wish to think, or speak, or write, with moderation. No! no! Tell a man whose house is on fire, to give a moderate alarm; tell him to moderately rescue his wife from the hands of the ravisher; tell the mother to gradually extricate her babe from the fire into which it has fallen;—but urge me not to use moderation in a cause like the present. I am in earnest—I will not equivocate—I will not excuse—I will not retreat a single inch—AND I WILL BE HEARD. The apathy of the people is enough to make every statue leap from its pedestal, and to hasten the resurrection of the dead.

It is pretended, that I am retarding the cause of emancipation, by the coarseness of my invective, and the precipitancy of my measures. *The charge is not true.* On this question my influence,—humble as it is,—is felt at this moment to a considerable extent, and shall be felt in coming years—not perniciously, but beneficially—not as a curse, but as a blessing; and posterity will bear testimony that I was right. I desire to thank God, that he enables me to disregard "the fear of man which bringeth a snare," and to speak his truth in its simplicity and power.

And here I close with this fresh dedication:

> "Oppression! I have seen thee, face to face,
>   And met thy cruel eye and cloudy brow;
>   But thy soul-withering glance I fear not now—
> For dread to prouder feelings doth give place
> Of deep abhorrence! Scorning the disgrace
> Of slavish knees that at thy footstool bow,
> I also kneel—but with far other bow
> Do hail thee and thy herd of hirelings base:—
> I swear, while life-blood warms my throbbing veins,
> Still to oppose and thwart, with heart and hand,
> Thy brutalizing sway—'till Afric's chains
> Are burst, and Freedom rules the rescued land,—
> Trampling Oppression and his iron rod:
> *Such is the vow I take*—SO HELP ME GOD!"

The crusade that Garrison thus helped to launch lasted until 1865, when the Thirteenth Amendment finally abolished slavery and the Liberator *was discontinued. In the intervening years many abolitionists proved to be better organizers, leaders, and strategists than Garrison, but none could match him as an agitator or polemicist. None ever penned a manifesto as stirring as the one that appeared in the first issue of*

the Liberator, *and no other abolitionist document is so well remembered.*

Garrison's severe indictment of slavery was hardly calculated to win converts among the slaveholders of the South. It was not meant to. Rather, the appearance of the Liberator and the organization of a northern abolitionist movement represented the abandonment of hope that slaveholders would voluntarily accept a program of gradual emancipation. With slavery flourishing in the South and spreading to the Southwest, few masters would tolerate criticism, however moderate, of the "peculiar institution." It can hardly be said that Garrison set back the cause of emancipation in the South, for there was no cause to set back.

Garrison's aim was to create massive moral indignation in the North, to isolate the slaveholders, to make the name slaveholder *itself a reproach.* But most Northerners were indifferent about slavery—"slumbering in the lap of moral death"—at the time the Liberator first appeared. In defense of Garrison, the Kentucky abolitionist James G. Birney expressed the belief that "nothing but a rude and almost ruffianlike shake could rouse . . . [the nation] to a contemplation of her danger."

Though Garrison's language was harsh, it was not his intention to achieve his goal by violence. Like most abolitionists he was a pacifist, and the New England Antislavery Society that he organized promised not to "operate on the existing relations of society by other than peaceful and lawful means." The violence was all in Garrison's words. He cried down slavery as the revivalist preachers of his day cried down other forms of sin. In the end, in spite of his pacifism, Garrison's chief contribution to the antislavery cause was to help give Northerners the moral strength to endure four years of civil war. That slavery died in the agony of this great conflict was in part due to the fact that Garrison had indeed been heard.

The prospectus for the Liberator is one among many protests against injustice that have from time to time been issued in the long and still unfinished struggle to achieve freedom and equality for American Negroes. This is a problem about which most white Americans have usually been apathetic, and whose solution they prefer to put off to a more convenient time. Each advance has usually been preceded by the shrill voice of a Garrison reminding us of the contradictions between American theory and practice. To this day it makes us uneasy to read Garrison, and few historians have shown much admiration for him. Garrison was a man of immense

conceit, of overbearing dogmatism, of irritating self-righteousness. But he was also a man who gave himself wholly to
the cause of the slave and who practiced the racial equality
that he preached. He was, no doubt, a "fanatic."

Garrison's message has been a constant reminder to us as
individuals of our moral responsibility in society. It was characteristic of the reformers of his age to feel directly involved
in social injustices and to feel a personal obligation to work
for their removal. What Garrison told his northern contemporaries was that there was no relief from guilt until slavery
was destroyed. Today, in our mass society, the individual
finds an escape from responsibility through a belief in his
powerlessness. What possible difference could his small voice
make? But Garrison tells us that as long as some men are
not free all are bound with them. Each man must speak out
for the sake of his own conscience, "till every chain be broken, and every bondman set free!"

Ralph Waldo Emerson

The American Scholar

1837

EDITED BY ROBERT E. SPILLER

It must have been a surprise to the young clergyman Ralph Waldo Emerson when, in the spring of 1837, he received an invitation, previously declined by the Reverend Jonathan Wainwright, to deliver the annual oration to the Harvard chapter of the national honorary fraternity Phi Beta Kappa, of which he was then not even a member. The occasion was a formal one which had commanded the best oratorical talent of the day, including Edward Everett, and the topic and the title "The American Scholar" were more or less assigned. When the officers and members of the Society and the faculty and students of the College filed into the white Meeting House in Harvard Square at noon on the last day of August, 1837, they were prepared to hear reaffirmed to one more group of picked young men their duty to the life of the mind and to the traditional culture of the race.

Emerson could not himself answer to any such definition of the scholar. As a student in both the College and the Divinity School, he had been rated by the faculty as no better than average, and he had, a few years previously, resigned his charge at the Second (Unitarian) Church in Boston because he found it too confining spiritually. Doubtless, his recent series of public lectures in the Masonic Temple in Boston on

"Human Culture" and related topics had brought him repute as an effective if unsensational speaker. Although a thoughtful man and a constant user of books, he was so far the author of only one slim volume, Nature *(1836), a poetical exhortation to the life of the spirit.*

What his audience probably did not realize on that day—at least before his hour-and-a-quarter address had been heard—was that here was a man who had had the courage, in the moment of his first maturity, to face illness, deaths in his family, and apparent professional defeat only to rebuild his life from its foundations. He was now ready to accept the challenge of the occasion, but to attack rather than to defend the system of values which it represented.

On July 29, when he began his preparation, he found his notebooks filled with ideas on self-reliance, on the misuse of history for escape into the past, on the duties of the free individual to rediscover life, and on the vital roles of nature and action, as well as books, in the shaping of character, both personal and national. "If the Allwise would give me light," *he noted (MS Journal "C," p. 100), "I should write for the Cambridge men a theory of the Scholar's office. . . . he must be able to read in all books . . . the one incorruptible text of truth." From that text he had faced the crisis in his own career, and he now made it a crisis in the history of American scholarship from which the American mind has fortunately never quite recovered.*

☆

MR. PRESIDENT, AND GENTLEMEN,

I GREET you on the re-commencement of our literary year. Our anniversary is one of hope, and, perhaps, not enough of labor. We do not meet for games of strength or skill, for the recitation of histories, tragedies and odes, like the ancient Greeks; for parliaments of love and poesy, like the Troubadours; nor for the advancement of science, like our contemporaries in the British and European capitals. Thus far, our holiday has been simply a friendly sign of the survival of the love of letters amongst a people too busy to give to letters any more. As such, it is precious as the sign of an indestructi-

The text is reproduced from the copy of the first edition in the library of Morton Perkins, now in the Harvard College Library. It was published in 1837 by James Monroe and Company, Boston, under the title *An Oration, Delivered Before the Phi Beta Kappa Society, at Cambridge, August 31, 1837.*

ble instinct. Perhaps the time is already come, when it ought to be, and will be something else; when the sluggard intellect of this continent will look from under its iron lids and fill the postponed expectation of the world with something better than the exertions of mechanical skill. Our day of dependence, our long apprenticeship to the learning of other lands, draws to a close. The millions that around us are rushing into life, cannot always be fed on the sere remains of foreign harvests. Events, actions arise, that must be sung, that will sing themselves. Who can doubt that poetry will revive and lead in a new age, as the star in the constellation Harp which now flames in our zenith, astronomers announce, shall one day be the pole-star for a thousand years.

In the light of this hope, I accept the topic which not only usage, but the nature of our association, seems to prescribe to this day,—the AMERICAN SCHOLAR. Year by year, we come up hither to read one more chapter of his biography. Let us inquire what new lights, new events and more days have thrown on his character, his duties and his hopes.

It is one of those fables, which out of an unknown antiquity, convey an unlooked for wisdom, that the gods, in the beginning, divided Man into men, that he might be more helpful to himself; just as the hand was divided into fingers, the better to answer its end.

The old fable covers a doctrine ever new and sublime; that there is One Man,—present to all particular men only partially, or through one faculty; and that you must take the whole society to find the whole man. Man is not a farmer, or a professor, or an engineer, but he is all. Man is priest, and scholar, and statesman, and producer, and soldier. In the *divided* or social state, these functions are parcelled out to individuals, each of whom aims to do his stint of the joint work, whilst each other performs his. The fable implies that the individual to possess himself, must sometimes return from his own labor to embrace all the other laborers. But unfortunately, this original unit, this fountain of power, has been so distributed to multitudes, has been so minutely subdivided and peddled out, that it is spilled into drops, and cannot be gathered. The state of society is one in which the members have suffered amputation from the trunk, and strut about so many walking monsters,—a good finger, a neck, a stomach, an elbow, but never a man.

Man is thus metamorphosed into a thing, into many things. The planter, who is Man sent out into the field to gather food, is seldom cheered by any idea of the true dignity of his ministry. He sees his bushel and his cart, and nothing beyond, and sinks into the farmer, instead of Man on the farm. The tradesman scarcely ever gives an ideal worth to his work, but is ridden by the routine of his craft, and the soul is subject to dollars. The priest becomes a form; the attorney, a statute-book; the mechanic, a machine; the sailor, a rope of a ship.

In this distribution of functions, the scholar is the delegated intellect. In the right state, he is, *Man Thinking*. In the degenerate state, when the victim of society, he tends to become a mere thinker, or, still worse, the parrot of other men's thinking.

In this view of him, as Man Thinking, the whole theory of his office is contained. Him nature solicits, with all her placid, all her monitory pictures. Him the past instructs. Him the future invites. Is not, indeed, every man a student, and do not all things exist for the student's behoof? And, finally, is not the true scholar the only true master? But, as the old oracle said, "All things have two handles. Beware of the wrong one." In life, too often, the scholar errs with mankind and forfeits his privilege. Let us see him in his school, and consider him in reference to the main influences he receives.

I. The first in time and the first in importance of the influences upon the mind is that of nature. Every day, the sun; and, after sunset, night and her stars. Ever the winds blow; ever the grass grows. Every day, men and women, conversing, beholding and beholden. The scholar must needs stand wistful and admiring before this great spectacle. He must settle its value in his mind. What is nature to him? There is never a beginning, there is never an end to the inexplicable continuity of this web of God, but always circular power returning into itself. Therein it resembles his own spirit, whose beginning, whose ending he never can find—so entire, so boundless. Far, too, as her splendors shine, system on system shooting like rays, upward, downward, without centre, without circumference,—in the mass and in the particle nature hastens to render account of herself to the mind. Classification begins. To the young mind, every thing is individual, stands by itself. By and by, it finds how to join two things, and see in them one nature; then three, then three thousand; and so, tyrannized over by its own unifying instinct, it goes on tying things together, diminishing anomalies, discovering roots running under ground, whereby contrary and remote things cohere, and flower out from one stem. It presently learns, that, since the dawn of history, there has been a constant accumulation and classifying of facts. But what is classification but the perceiving that these objects are not chaotic, and are not foreign, but have a law which is also a law of the human mind? The astronomer discovers that geometry, a pure abstraction of the human mind, is the measure of planetary motion. The chemist finds proportions and intelligible method throughout matter: and science is nothing but the finding of analogy, identity in the most remote parts. The ambitious soul sits down before each refractory fact; one after another, reduces all strange constitutions, all new powers, to their class and their law, and goes on forever to animate the last fibre of organization, the outskirts of nature, by insight.

Thus to him, to this school-boy under the bending dome of day, is suggested, that he and it proceed from one root; one is leaf and one is flower; relation, sympathy, stirring in every vein. And what is that Root? Is not that the soul of his soul? —A thought too bold—a dream too wild. Yet when this spiritual light shall have revealed the law of more earthly natures, —when he has learned to worship the soul, and to see that the natural philosophy that now is, is only the first gropings of its gigantic hand, he shall look forward to an ever expanding knowledge as to a becoming creator. He shall see that nature is the opposite of the soul, answering to it part for part. One is seal, and one is print. Its beauty is the beauty of his own mind. Its laws are the laws of his own mind. Nature then becomes to him the measure of his attainments. So much of nature as he is ignorant of, so much of his own mind does he not yet possess. And, in fine, the ancient precept, "Know thyself," and the modern precept, "Study nature," become at last one maxim.

II. The next great influence into the spirit of the scholar, is, the mind of the Past,—in whatever form, whether of literature, of art, of institutions, that mind is inscribed. Books are the best type of the influence of the past, and perhaps we shall get at the truth—learn the amount of this influence more conveniently—by considering their value alone.

The theory of books is noble. The scholar of the first age received into him the world around; brooded thereon; gave it the new arrangement of his own mind, and uttered it again. It came into him—life; it went out from him—truth. It came to him—short-lived actions; it went out from him—immortal thoughts. It came to him—business; it went from him—poetry. It was—dead fact; now, it is quick thought. It can stand, and it can go. It now endures, it now flies, it now inspires. Precisely in proportion to the depth of mind from which it issued, so high does it soar, so long does it sing.

Or, I might say, it depends on how far the process had

gone, of transmuting life into truth. In proportion to the completeness of the distillation, so will the purity and imperishableness of the product be. But none is quite perfect. As no air-pump can by any means make a perfect vacuum, so neither can any artist entirely exclude the conventional, the local, the perishable from his book, or write a book of pure thought that shall be as efficient, in all respects, to a remote posterity, as to contemporaries, or rather to the second age. Each age, it is found, must write its own books; or rather, each generation for the next succeeding. The books of an older period will not fit this.

Yet hence arises a grave mischief. The sacredness which attaches to the act of creation,—the act of thought,—is instantly transferred to the record. The poet chanting, was felt to be a divine man. Henceforth the chant is divine also. The writer was a just and wise spirit. Henceforward it is settled, the book is perfect; as love of the hero corrupts into worship of his statue. Instantly, the book becomes noxious. The guide is a tyrant. We sought a brother, and lo, a governor. The sluggish and perverted mind of the multitude, always slow to open to the incursions of Reason, having once so opened, having once received this book, stands upon it, and makes an outcry, if it is disparaged. Colleges are built on it. Books are written on it by thinkers, not by Man Thinking; by men of talent, that is, who start wrong, who set out from accepted dogmas, not from their own sight of principles. Meek young men grow up in libraries, believing it their duty to accept the views which Cicero, which Locke, which Bacon have given, forgetful that Cicero, Locke and Bacon were only young men in libraries when they wrote these books.

Hence, instead of Man Thinking, we have the bookworm. Hence, the book-learned class, who value books, as such; not as related to nature and the human constitution, but as making a sort of Third Estate with the world and the soul. Hence, the restorers of readings, the emendators, the bibliomaniacs of all degrees.

This is bad; this is worse than it seems. Books are the best of things, well used; abused, among the worst. What is the right use? What is the one end which all means go to effect? They are for nothing but to inspire. I had better never see a book than to be warped by its attraction clean out of my own orbit, and made a satellite instead of a system. The one thing in the world of value, is, the active soul,—the soul, free, sovereign, active. This every man is entitled to; this every man contains within him, although in almost all men, obstructed, and as yet unborn. The soul active sees absolute truth; and utters truth, or creates. In this action, it is genius; not the privilege of here and there a favorite, but the sound estate of every man. In its essence, it is progressive. The book, the college, the school of art, the institution of any kind, stop with some past utterance of genius. This is good, say they,—let us hold by this. They pin me down. They look backward and not forward. But genius always looks forward. The eyes of man are set in his forehead, not in his hindhead. Man hopes. Genius creates. To create,—to create,—is the proof of a divine presence. Whatever talents may be, if the man create not, the pure efflux of the Deity is not his:—cinders and smoke, there may be, but not yet flame. There are creative manners, there are creative actions, and creative words; manners, actions, words, that is, indicative of no custom or authority, but springing spontaneous from the mind's own sense of good and fair.

On the other part, instead of being its own seer, let it receive always from another mind its truth, though it were in torrents of light, without periods of solitude, inquest and self-recovery, and a fatal disservice is done. Genius is always sufficiently the enemy of genius by over-influence. The literature of every nation bear me witness. The English dramatic poets have Shakspearized now for two hundred years.

Undoubtedly there is a right way of reading,—so it be sternly subordinated. Man Thinking must not be subdued by his instruments. Books are for the scholar's idle times. When he can read God directly, the hour is too precious to be wasted in other mens' transcripts of their readings. But when the intervals of darkness come, as come they must,—when the soul seeth not, when the sun is hid, and the stars withdraw their shining,—we repair to the lamps which were kindled by their ray to guide our steps to the East again, where the dawn is. We hear that we may speak. The Arabian proverb says, "A fig tree looking on a fig tree, becometh fruitful."

It is remarkable, the character of the pleasure we derive from the best books. They impress us ever with the conviction that one nature wrote and the same reads. We read the verses of one of the great English poets, of Chaucer, of Marvell, of Dryden, with the most modern joy,—with a pleasure, I mean, which is in great part caused by the abstraction of all *time* from their verses. There is some awe mixed with the joy of our surprise, when this poet, who lived in some past world, two or three hundred years ago, says that which lies close to my own soul, that which I also had well nigh thought and said. But for the evidence thence afforded to the philosophical doctrine of the identity of all minds, we should suppose some pre-established harmony, some foresight of souls that were to be, and some preparation of stores for their future wants, like the fact observed in insects, who lay up food before death for the young grub they shall never see.

I would not be hurried by any love of system, by any exaggeration of instincts, to underrate the Book. We all know, that as the human body can be nourished on any food, though it were boiled grass and the broth of shoes, so the human mind can be fed by any knowledge. And great and heroic men have existed, who had almost no other information than by the printed page. I only would say, that it needs a strong head to bear that diet. One must be an inventor to read well. As the proverb says, "He that would bring home the wealth of the Indies, must carry out the wealth of the Indies." There is then creative reading, as well as creative writing. When the mind is braced by labor and invention, the page of whatever book we read becomes luminous with manifold allusion. Every sentence is doubly significant, and the sense of our author is as broad as the world. We then see, what is always true, that as the seer's hour of vision is short and rare among heavy days and months, so is its record, perchance, the least part of his volume. The discerning will read his Plato or Shakspeare, only that least part,—only the authentic utterances of the oracle,—and all the rest he rejects, were it never so many times Plato's and Shakspeare's.

Of course, there is a portion of reading quite indispensable to a wise man. History and exact science he must learn by laborious reading. Colleges, in like manner, have their indispensable office,—to teach elements. But they can only highly serve us, when they aim not to drill, but to create; when they gather from far every ray of various genius to their hospitable halls, and, by the concentrated fires, set the hearts of their youth on flame. Thought and knowledge are natures in which apparatus and pretension avail nothing. Gowns, and pecuniary foundations, though of towns of gold, can never countervail the least sentence or syllable of wit. Forget this, and our American colleges will recede in their public importance whilst they grow richer every year.

III. There goes in the world a notion that the scholar should be a recluse, a valetudinarian,—as unfit for any handiwork or public labor, as a penknife for an axe. The so called "practical men" sneer at speculative men, as if, because they speculate or *see,* they could do nothing. I have heard it said that the clergy,—who are always more universally than any other class, the scholars of their day,—are addressed as women: that the rough, spontaneous conversation of men they do not hear, but only a mincing and diluted speech. They are often virtually disfranchised; and, indeed, there are advocates for their celibacy. As far as this is true of the studious classes, it is not just and wise. Action is with the scholar subordinate, but it is essential. Without it, he is not yet man. Without it, thought can never ripen into truth. Whilst the world hangs before the eye as a cloud of beauty, we can not even see its beauty. Inaction is cowardice, but there can be no scholar without the heroic mind. The preamble of thought, the transition through which it passes from the unconscious to the conscious, is action. Only so much do I know, as I have lived. Instantly we know whose words are loaded with life, and whose not.

The world,—this shadow of the soul, or *other me*, lies wide around. Its attractions are the keys which unlock my thoughts and make me acquainted with myself. I launch eagerly into this resounding tumult. I grasp the hands of those next me, and take my place in the ring to suffer and to work, taught by an instinct that so shall the dumb abyss be vocal with speech. I pierce its order; I dissipate its fear; I dispose of it within the circuit of my expanding life. So much only of life as I know by experience, so much of the wilderness have I vanquished and planted, or so far have I extended my being, my dominion. I do not see how any man can afford, for the sake of his nerves and his nap, to spare any action in which he can partake. It is pearls and rubies to his discourse. Drudgery, calamity, exasperation, want, are instructers in eloquence and wisdom. The true scholar grudges every opportunity of action past by, as a loss of power.

It is the raw material out of which the intellect moulds her splendid products. A strange process too, this, by which experience is converted into thought, as a mulberry leaf is converted into satin. The manufacture goes forward at all hours.

The actions and events of our childhood and youth are now matters of calmest observation. They lie like fair pictures in the air. Not so with our recent actions,—with the business which we now have in hand. On this we are quite unable to speculate. Our affections as yet circulate through it. We no more feel or know it, than we feel the feet, or the hand, or the brain of our body. The new deed is yet a part of life,—remains for a time immersed in our unconscious life. In some contemplative hour, it detaches itself from the life like a ripe fruit, to become a thought of the mind. Instantly, it is raised, transfigured; the corruptible has put on incorruption. Always now it is an object of beauty, however base its origin and neighborhood. Observe, too, the impossibility of antedating this act. In its grub state, it cannot fly, it cannot shine,—it is a dull grub. But suddenly, without observation, the selfsame thing unfurls beautiful wings, and is an angel of wisdom. So is there no fact, no event, in our private history, which shall not, sooner or later, lose its adhesive inert form, and astonish us by soaring from our body into the empyrean. Cradle and infancy, school and playground, the fear of boys, and dogs, and ferules, the love of little maids and berries, and many another fact that once filled the whole sky, are gone already; friend and relative, profession and party, town and country, nation and world, must also soar and sing.

Of course, he who has put forth his total strength in fit actions, has the richest return of wisdom. I will not shut myself out of this globe of action and transplant an oak into a flower pot, there to hunger and pine; nor trust the revenue of some single faculty, and exhaust one vein of thought, much like those Savoyards, who, getting their livelihood by carving shepherds, shepherdesses, and smoking Dutchmen, for all Europe, went out one day to the mountain to find stock, and discovered that they had whittled up the last of their pine trees. Authors we have in numbers, who have written out their vein, and who, moved by a commendable prudence, sail for Greece or Palestine, follow the trapper into the prairie, or ramble round Algiers to replenish their merchantable stock.

If it were only for a vocabulary the scholar would be covetous of action. Life is our dictionary. Years are well spent in country labors; in town—in the insight into trades and manufactures; in frank intercourse with many men and women; in science; in art; to the one end of mastering in all their facts a language, by which to illustrate and embody our perceptions. I learn immediately from any speaker how much he has already lived, through the poverty or the splendor of his speech. Life lies behind us as the quarry from whence we get tiles and copestones for the masonry of to-day. This is the way to learn grammar. Colleges and books only copy the language which the field and the workyard made.

But the final value of action, like that of books, and better than books, is, that it is a resource. That great principle of Undulation in nature, that shows itself in the inspiring and expiring of the breath; in desire and satiety; in the ebb and flow of the sea, in day and night, in heat and cold, and as yet more deeply ingrained in every atom and every fluid, is known to us under the name of Polarity,—these "fits of easy transmission and reflection," as Newton called them, are the law of nature because they are the law of spirit.

The mind now thinks; now acts; and each fit reproduces

the other. When the artist has exhausted his materials, when the fancy no longer paints, when thoughts are no longer apprehended, and books are a weariness,—he has always the resource *to live*. Character is higher than intellect. Thinking is the function. Living is the functionary. The stream retreats to its source. A great soul will be strong to live, as well as strong to think. Does he lack organ or medium to impart his truths? He can still fall back on this elemental force of living them. This is a total act. Thinking is a partial act. Let the grandeur of justice shine in his affairs. Let the beauty of affection cheer his lowly roof. Those "far from fame" who dwell and act with him, will feel the force of his constitution in the doings and passages of the day better than it can be measured by any public and designed display. Time shall teach him that the scholar loses no hour which the man lives. Herein he unfolds the sacred germ of his instinct screened from influence. What is lost in seemliness is gained in strength. Not out of those on whom systems of education have exhausted their culture, comes the helpful giant to destroy the old or to build the new, but out of unhandselled savage nature, out of terrible Druids and Berserkirs, come at last Alfred and Shakspear.

I hear therefore with joy whatever is beginning to be said of the dignity and necessity of labor to every citizen. There is virtue yet in the hoe and the spade, for learned as well as for unlearned hands. And labor is every where welcome; always we are invited to work; only be this limitation observed, that a man shall not for the sake of wider activity sacrifice any opinion to the popular judgments and modes of action.

I have now spoken of the education of the scholar by nature, by books, and by action. It remains to say somewhat of his duties.

They are such as become Man Thinking. They may all be comprised in self-trust. The office of the scholar is to cheer, to raise, and to guide men by showing them facts amidst appearances. He plies the slow, unhonored, and unpaid task of observation. Flamsteed and Herschel, in their glazed observatory, may catalogue the stars with the praise of all men, and, the results being splendid and useful, honor is sure. But he, in his private observatory, cataloguing obscure and nebulous stars of the human mind, which as yet no man has thought of as such,—watching days and months, sometimes, for a few facts; correcting still his old records;—must relinquish display and immediate fame. In the long period of his preparation, he must betray often an ignorance and shiftlessness in popular arts, incurring the disdain of the able who shoulder him aside. Long he must stammer in his speech; often forego the living for the dead. Worse yet, he must accept—how often! poverty and solitude. For the ease and pleasure of treading the old road, accepting the fashions, the education, the religion of society, he takes the cross of making his own, and, of course, the self accusation, the faint heart, the frequent uncertainty and loss of time which are the nettles and tangling vines in the way of the self-relying and self-directed; and the state of virtual hostility in which he seems to stand to society, and especially to educated society. For all this loss and scorn, what offset? He is to find consolation in exercising the highest functions of human nature. He is one who raises himself from private considerations, and breathes and lives on public and illustrious thoughts. He is the world's eye. He is the world's heart. He is to resist the vulgar prosperity that retrogrades ever to barbarism, by preserving and communicating heroic sentiments, noble biographies, melodious verse, and the conclusions of history. Whatsoever oracles the human heart in all emergencies, in all solemn hours has uttered as its commentary on the world of actions,—these he shall receive and impart. And whatsoever new verdict Reason from her inviolable seat pronounces on the passing men and events of to-day,—this he shall hear and promulgate.

These being his functions, it becomes him to feel all confidence in himself, and to defer never to the popular cry. He and he only knows the world. The world of any moment is the merest appearance. Some great decorum, some fetish of a government, some ephemeral trade, or war, or man, is cried up by half mankind and cried down by the other half, as if all depended on this particular up or down. The odds are that the whole question is not worth the poorest thought which the scholar has lost in listening to the controversy. Let him not quit his belief that a popgun is a popgun, though the ancient and honorable of the earth affirm it to be the crack of doom. In silence, in steadiness, in severe abstraction, let him hold by himself; add observation to observation; patient of neglect, patient of reproach, and bide his own time,—happy enough if he can satisfy himself alone that this day he has seen something truly. Success treads on every right step. For the instinct is sure that prompts him to tell his brother what he thinks. He then learns that in going down into the secrets of his own mind, he has descended into the secrets of all minds. He learns that he who has mastered any law in his private thoughts, is master to that extent of all men whose language he speaks, and of all into whose language his own can be translated. The poet in utter solitude remembering his spontaneous thoughts and recording them, is found to have recorded that which men in "cities vast" find true for them also. The orator distrusts at first the fitness of his frank confessions,—his want of knowledge of the persons he addresses, —until he finds that he is the complement of his hearers;— that they drink his words because he fulfils for them their own nature; the deeper he dives into his privatest secretest presentiment,—to his wonder he finds, this is the most acceptable, most public, and universally true. The people delight in it; the better part of every man feels, This is my music: this is myself.

In self-trust, all the virtues are comprehended. Free should the scholar be,—free and brave. Free even to the definition of freedom, "without any hindrance that does not arise out of his own constitution." Brave; for fear is a thing which a scholar by his very function puts behind him. Fear always springs from ignorance. It is a shame to him if his tranquillity, amid dangerous times, arise from the presumption that like children and women, his is a protected class; or if he seek a temporary peace by the diversion of his thoughts from politics or vexed questions, hiding his head like an ostrich in the flowering bushes, peeping into microscopes, and turning rhymes, as a boy whistles to keep his courage up. So is the danger a danger still: so is the fear worse. Manlike let him turn and face it. Let him look into its eye and search its nature, inspect its origin—see the whelping of this lion,—which lies no great way back; he will then find in himself a perfect comprehension of its nature and extent; he will have made his hands meet on the other side, and can henceforth defy it, and pass on superior. The world is his who can see through its pretension. What deafness, what stone-blind custom, what overgrown error you behold, is there only by sufferance,—by your sufferance. See it to be a lie, and you have already dealt it its mortal blow.

Yes, we are the cowed,—we the trustless. It is a mischievous notion that we are come late into nature; that the world was finished a long time ago. As the world was plastic and fluid in the hands of God, so it is ever to so much of his attributes as we bring to it. To ignorance and sin, it is flint. They adapt themselves to it as they may; but in proportion as a man has anything in him divine, the firmament flows before him, and takes his signet and form. Not he is great who can alter matter, but he who can alter my state of mind. They are the kings of the world who give the color of their present thought to all nature and all art, and persuade men by the cheerful serenity of their carrying the matter, that this thing which they do, is the apple which the ages have desired to pluck, now at last ripe, and inviting nations to the harvest. The great man makes the great thing. Wherever Macdonald sits, there is the head of the table. Linnæus makes botany the most alluring of studies and wins it from the farmer and the herb-woman. Davy, chemistry: and Cuvier, fossils. The day is always his, who works in it with serenity and great aims. The unstable estimates of men crowd to him whose mind is filled with a truth, as the heaped waves of the Atlantic follow the moon.

For this self-trust, the reason is deeper than can be fathomed,—darker than can be enlightened. I might not carry with me the feeling of my audience in stating my own belief. But I have already shown the ground of my hope, in adverting to the doctrine that man is one. I believe man has been wronged: he has wronged himself. He has almost lost the light that can lead him back to his prerogatives. Men are become of no account. Men in history, men in the world of to-day are bugs, are spawn, and are called "the mass" and "the herd." In a century, in a millenium, one or two men; that is to say—one or two approximations to the right state of every man. All the rest behold in the hero or the poet their own green and crude being—ripened; yes, and are content to be less, so *that* may attain to its full stature. What a testimony —full of grandeur, full of pity, is borne to the demands of his own nature, by the poor clansman, the poor partisan, who rejoices in the glory of his chief. The poor and the low find some amends to their immense moral capacity, for their acquiescence in a political and social inferiority. They are content to be brushed like flies from the path of a great person, so that justice shall be done by him to that common nature which it is the dearest desire of all to see enlarged and glorified. They sun themselves in the great man's light, and feel it to be their own element. They cast the dignity of man from their downtrod selves upon the shoulders of a hero, and will perish to add one drop of blood to make that great heart beat, those giant sinews combat and conquer. He lives for us, and we live in him.

Men such as they are, very naturally seek money or power; and power because it is as good as money,—the "spoils," so called, "of office." And why not? for they aspire to the highest, and this, in their sleep-walking, they dream is highest. Wake them, and they shall quit the false good and leap to the true, and leave governments to clerks and desks. This revolution is to be wrought by the gradual domestication of the idea of Culture. The main enterprise of the world for splendor, for extent, is the upbuilding of a man. Here are the materials strown along the ground. The private life of one man shall be a more illustrious monarchy,—more formidable to its enemy, more sweet and serene in its influence to its friend, than any kingdom in history. For a man, rightly viewed, comprehendeth the particular natures of all men. Each philosopher, each bard, each actor, has only done for me, as by a delegate, what one day I can do for myself. The books which once we valued more than the apple of the eye, we have quite exhausted. What is that but saying that we have come up with the point of view which the universal mind took through the eyes of that one scribe; we have been that man, and have passed on. First, one; then, another; we drain all cisterns, and waxing greater by all these supplies, we crave a better and more abundant food. The man has never lived that can feed us ever. The human mind cannot be enshrined in a person who shall set a barrier on any one side to this unbounded, unboundable empire. It is one central fire which flaming now out of the lips of Etna, lightens the capes of Sicily; and now out of the throat of Vesuvius, illuminates the towers and vineyards of Naples. It is one light which beams out of a thousand stars. It is one soul which animates all men.

But I have dwelt perhaps tediously upon this abstraction of the Scholar. I ought not to delay longer to add what I have to say, of nearer reference to the time and to this country.

Historically, there is thought to be a difference in the ideas which predominate over successive epochs, and there are data for marking the genius of the Classic, of the Romantic, and now of the Reflective or Philosophical age. With the views I have intimated of the oneness or the identity of the mind through all individuals, I do not much dwell on these differences. In fact, I believe each individual passes through all three. The boy is a Greek; the youth, romantic; the adult, reflective. I deny not, however, that a revolution in the leading idea may be distinctly enough traced.

Our age is bewailed as the age of Introversion. Must that needs be evil? We, it seems, are critical. We are embarrassed with second thoughts. We cannot enjoy any thing for hankering to know whereof the pleasure consists. We are lined with eyes. We see with our feet. The time is infected with Hamlet's unhappiness,—

"Sicklied o'er with the pale cast of thought."

Is it so bad then? Sight is the last thing to be pitied. Would we be blind? Do we fear lest we should outsee nature and

God, and drink truth dry? I look upon the discontent of the literary class as a mere announcement of the fact that they find themselves not in the state of mind of their fathers, and regret the coming state as untried; as a boy dreads the water before he has learned that he can swim. If there is any period one would desire to be born in,—is it not the age of Revolution; when the old and the new stand side by side, and admit of being compared; when the energies of all men are searched by fear and by hope; when the historic glories of the old, can be compensated by the rich possibilities of the new era? This time, like all times, is a very good one, if we but know what to do with it.

I read with joy some of the auspicious signs of the coming days as they glimmer already through poetry and art, through philosophy and science, through church and state.

One of these signs is the fact that the same movement which effected the elevation of what was called the lowest class in the state, assumed in literature a very marked and as benign an aspect. Instead of the sublime and beautiful, the near, the low, the common, was explored and poetised. That which had been negligently trodden under foot by those who were harnessing and provisioning themselves for long journies into far countries, is suddenly found to be richer than all foreign parts. The literature of the poor, the feelings of the child, the philosophy of the street, the meaning of household life, are the topics of the time. It is a great stride. It is a sign —is it not? of new vigor, when the extremities are made active, when currents of warm life run into the hands and the feet. I ask not for the great, the remote, the romantic; what is doing in Italy or Arabia; what is Greek art, or Provencal Minstrelsy; I embrace the common, I explore and sit at the feet of the familiar, the low. Give me insight into to-day, and you may have the antique and future worlds. What would we really know the meaning of? The meal in the firkin; the milk in the pan; the ballad in the street; the news of the boat; the glance of the eye; the form and the gait of the body;—show me the ultimate reason of these matters;— show me the sublime presence of the highest spiritual cause lurking, as always it does lurk, in these suburbs and extremities of nature; let me see every trifle bristling with the polarity that ranges it instantly on an eternal law; and the shop, the plough, and the ledger, referred to the like cause by which light undulates and poets sing;—and the world lies no longer a dull miscellany and lumber room, but has form and order; there is no trifle; there is no puzzle; but one design unites and animates the farthest pinnacle and the lowest trench.

This idea has inspired the genius of Goldsmith, Burns, Cowper, and, in a newer time, of Goethe, Wordsworth, and Carlyle. This idea they have differently followed and with various success. In contrast with their writing, the style of Pope, of Johnson, of Gibbon, looks cold and pedantic. This writing is blood-warm. Man is surprised to find that things near are not less beautiful and wondrous than things remote. The near explains the far. The drop is a small ocean. A man is related to all nature. This perception of the worth of the vulgar, is fruitful in discoveries. Goethe, in this very thing the most modern of the moderns, has shown us, as none ever did, the genius of the ancients.

There is one man of genius who has done much for this philosophy of life, whose literary value has never yet been rightly estimated;—I mean Emanuel Swedenborg. The most imaginative of men, yet writing with the precision of a mathematician, he endeavored to engraft a purely philosophical Ethics on the popular Christianity of his time. Such an attempt, of course, must have difficulty which no genius could surmount. But he saw and showed the connexion between nature and the affections of the soul. He pierced the emblematic or spiritual character of the visible, audible, tangible world. Especially did his shade-loving muse hover over and interpret the lower parts of nature; he showed the mysterious bond that allies moral evil to the foul material forms, and has given in epical parables a theory of insanity, of beasts, of unclean and fearful things.

Another sign of our times, also marked by an analogous political movement is, the new importance given to the single person. Every thing that tends to insulate the individual,—to surround him with barriers of natural respect, so that each man shall feel the world is his, and man shall treat with man as a sovereign state with a sovereign state;—tends to true union as well as greatness. "I learned," said the melancholy Pestalozzi, "that no man in God's wide earth is either willing or able to help any other man." Help must come from the bosom alone. The scholar is that man who must take up into himself all the ability of the time, all the contributions of the past, all the hopes of the future. He must be an university of knowledges. If there be one lesson more than another which should pierce his ear, it is, The world is nothing, the man is all; in yourself is the law of all nature, and you know not yet how a globule of sap ascends; in yourself slumbers the whole of Reason; it is for you to know all, it is for you to dare all.

Mr. President and Gentlemen, this confidence in the unsearched might of man, belongs by all motives, by all prophecy, by all preparation, to the American Scholar. We have listened too long to the courtly muses of Europe. The spirit of the American freeman is already suspected to be timid, imitative, tame. Public and private avarice make the air we breathe thick and fat. The scholar is decent, indolent, complaisant. See already the tragic consequence. The mind of this country taught to aim at low objects, eats upon itself. There is no work for any but the decorous and the complaisant. Young men of the fairest promise, who begin life upon our shores, inflated by the mountain winds, shined upon by all the stars of God, find the earth below not in unison with these,—but are hindered from action by the disgust which the principles on which business is managed inspire, and turn drudges, or die of disgust,—some of them suicides. What is the remedy? They did not yet see, and thousands of young men as hopeful now crowding to the barriers for the career, do not yet see, that if the single man plant himself indomitably on his instincts, and there abide, the huge world will come round to him. Patience—patience;—with the shades of all the good and great for company; and for solace, the perspective of your own infinite life; and for work, the study and the communication of principles, the making those instincts prevalent, the conversion of the world. Is it not the chief disgrace in the world, not to be an unit;—not to be reckoned one character;—not to yield that peculiar fruit which each man was created to bear, but to be reckoned in the gross, in the hundred, or the thousand, of the party, the section, to which we belong; and our opinion predicted geographically, as the north, or the south. Not so, brothers and friends,—please God, ours shall not be so. We will walk on our own feet; we will work with our own hands; we will speak our own minds. Then shall man be no longer a name for pity, for doubt, and for sensual indulgence. The dread of man and the love of man shall be a wall of defence and a wreath of love around all. A nation of men will for the first time exist, because each believes himself inspired by the Divine Soul which also inspires all men.

The immediate reception of Emerson's academic heresies was somewhat mixed, but it was far more cordial than was that of his theological heresies in the Divinity School Address of the next year. The young men in his audience were enthusiastic,

and he was praised and toasted at the dinner after the ceremony. James Russell Lowell, then a student, recalled the event thirty years later as "without parallel in our literary annals." Carlyle wrote, "I could have wept to read that speech," and O. W. Holmes, Sr., later declared it "our intellectual Declaration of Independence." The pamphlet edition of five hundred copies was soon sold out and the collected edition of 1849 found its place as Volume I of the "complete" works thereafter. No anthology of American literature or thought could afford to omit it.

An intellectual Declaration of Independence it assuredly was—although not the first. Freneau, Bryant, Cooper, Irving, Channing, and many lesser men had begun to publish exhortations to literary nationalism almost before the ink was dry on the political document of 1776. But Emerson was cautious; he had already warned of nationalism as such. When he now proclaimed that "Our day of dependence, our long apprenticeship to the learning of other lands draws to a close," he was firing a double-barreled charge. Certainly the vigorous new nation must gain and assert its cultural independence; but only to give the world a new concept of freedom for the mind in any time or place. In the right state, he made it clear, "the scholar is the delegated intellect, . . . Man Thinking. In the degenerate state, when the victim of society he tends to become a mere thinker, or still worse, the parrot of other men's thinking."

"If the single man plant himself indomitably on his instincts, and there abide, the huge world will come round to him." From this focus on self-reliance, waves of influence moved out into all American life. To Emerson, scholarship was a dynamic force, a continuing process, a function of the whole personality, a way of life. Specialization for him became a function rather than a limitation of the activities of the mind. From this emphasis on the present, on experience, on the individual, it was easy to take the next steps with C. S. Peirce, William James, and John Dewey toward a wholly empirical approach to all knowledge. Learning springs from living and is tested by doing. A pragmatism based on idealistic premises became and remains the distinctive American philosophy.

To attribute to Emerson alone the freedom of inquiry that is characteristic of American science, the freedom of speech that inspires American journalism, and the freedom of learning that opens the schools to all young Americans would be going much too far. But we can say that his focus on the free individual as the beginning and end of wisdom was a princi-

pal agent in translating the political ideals of the American Revolution into the whole of American culture. Like most great documents, Emerson's oration created nothing; it condensed and focused the otherwise kaleidoscopic American faith in the possibilities of the human mind and spirit. "It is for you to know all; it is for you to dare all."

Lemuel Shaw

Commonwealth v. Hunt

1842

EDITED BY LEONARD W. LEVY

Judge Peter O. Thacher, charging the jury that tried the members of the Bootmakers' Society in Boston's Municipal Court in 1840, practically directed a verdict of guilty. The jury obliged, after deliberating twenty minutes. They were apparently persuaded by Thacher's frenetic forebodings: if unions became widespread, he had declared, free enterprise would be at an end, property insecure, the rich and poor pitted against each other in class warfare, and a "frightful despotism would soon be erected on the ruins of this free and happy commonwealth."

Technically the crime for which the union had been convicted was criminal conspiracy. The indictment luridly accused the little trade union of having conspired to maintain what a later age would call a "closed shop." Another count in the indictment charged a conspiracy to impoverish both employers and fellow employees who did not acquiesce in union regulations. The case had arisen when the union insisted on the firing of a shoemaker whom it had expelled for violating union rules; the employer, anxious to avoid a strike, complied: he knew the union's rule that its members would not work for anyone employing a nonmember whose discharge had been demanded. The prosecution, initiated on the complaint of the disgruntled worker, not of the employer,

321

*had depended upon a great many English and American prec-
edents which stigmatized as an unlawful conspiracy virtually
all union tactics and objectives—specifically, joining together
to obtain higher wages, shorter hours, or improved conditions
of employment. The conviction had been expected: convictions in such cases were routine.*

*But Robert Rantoul, Jr., the union's counsel, appealed the
case after objecting to points of law in Thacher's charge. In
the Supreme Judicial Court of the Commonwealth, Rantoul
argued that the "tyrannical" common law of conspiracies was
not in force in Massachusetts. In support of his radical position, he added that the indictment was defective because the
"combination" that it described was not per se a conspiracy.
The court that heard this argument was presided over by Lemuel Shaw, a man of formidable and majestic reputation who
gave the impression, it was said, of having "the absolute
power of a crag vitalized by a human spirit." During his thirty
years of service as Chief Justice of the Massachusetts court,
Shaw wrote a record number of opinions—over 2,200, only
one of which was a dissent—imbuing hoary doctrines with a
fresh spirit as, he once said, "the advancement of civilization
may require."*

*Commonwealth v. Hunt, despite the precedents, was the
first case of its kind in Massachusetts. Shaw's tendency, even
in a routine case, as a Senator who had once practiced before
him recalled, was "to unlimber the heavy artillery of his
mind, go down to the roots of the question, consider the matter in all possible relations, and deal with it as if he were be-
sieging a fortress." In this, his best-known opinion, handed
down in the March term of 1842, Shaw spoke, as usual, not
only for himself but also for all his associates—Samuel S.
Wilde, Charles A. Dewey, and Samuel Hubbard. They were
Whigs all, but jurists who saw, in this little case against the
shoemaker Hunt and his fellow unionists, momentous issues:
in a free, competitive society, are not combinations, whether
of workers or entrepreneurs, inevitable; and does not society
itself stand to gain from the competition between interest
groups?*

C ONSIDERABLE time has elapsed since the argument of this
case. It has been retained long under advisement, partly
because we were desirous of examining, with some attention,

Shaw's opinion is reprinted from 4 Metcalf 111 (1842).

the great number of cases cited at the argument, and others which have presented themselves in course, and partly because we considered it a question of great importance to the Commonwealth, and one which had been much examined and considered by the learned judge of the municipal court.

We have no doubt, that by the operation of the constitution of this Commonwealth, the general rules of the common law, making conspiracy an indictable offence, are in force here, and that this is included in the description of laws which had, before the adoption of the constitution, been used and approved in the Province, Colony, or State of Massachusetts Bay, and usually practised in the courts of law. . . . Still, it is proper in this connexion to remark, that although the common law in regard to conspiracy in this Commonwealth is in force, yet it will not necessarily follow that every indictment at common law for this offence is a precedent for a similar indictment in this State. The general rule of the common law is, that it is a criminal and indictable offence, for two or more to confederate and combine together, by concerted means, to do that which is unlawful or criminal, to the injury of the public, or portions or classes of the community, or even to the rights of an individual. This rule of law may be equally in force as a rule of the common law, in England and in this Commonwealth; and yet it must depend upon the local laws of each country to determine, whether the purpose to be accomplished by the combination, or the concerted means of accomplishing it, be unlawful or criminal in the respective countries. All those laws of the parent country, whether rules of the common law, or early English statutes, which were made for the purpose of regulating the wages of laborers, the settlement of paupers, and making it penal for any one to use a trade or handicraft to which he had not served a full apprenticeship—not being adapted to the circumstances of our colonial condition—were not adopted, used or approved, and therefore do not come within the description of the laws adopted and confirmed by the provision of the constitution already cited. This consideration will do something towards reconciling the English and American cases, and may indicate how far the principles of the English cases will apply in this Commonwealth, and show why a conviction in England, in many cases, would not be a precedent for a like conviction here. . . .

But the rule of law, that an illegal conspiracy, whatever may be the facts which constitute it, is an offence punishable by the laws of this Commonwealth, is established as well by legislative as by judicial authority. Like many other cases, that of murder, for instance, it leaves the definition or description of the offence to the common law, and provides modes for its prosecution and punishment. . . .

But the great difficulty is, in framing any definition or description, to be drawn from the decided cases, which shall specifically identify this offence—a description broad enough to include all cases punishable under this description, without including acts which are not punishable. Without attempting to review and reconcile all the cases, we are of opinion, that as a general description, though perhaps not a precise and accurate definition, a conspiracy must be a combination of two or more persons, by some concerted action, to accomplish some criminal or unlawful purpose, or to accomplish some purpose, not in itself criminal or unlawful, by criminal or unlawful means. We use the terms criminal or unlawful, because it is manifest that many acts are unlawful, which are not punishable by indictment or other public prosecution; and yet there is no doubt, we think, that a combination by numbers to do them would be an unlawful conspiracy, and punishable by indictment. . . .

Several rules upon the subject seem to be well established, —to wit, that the unlawful agreement constitutes the gist of the offence, and therefore that it is not necessary to charge the execution of the unlawful agreement. *Commonwealth v. Judd*, 2 Mass. 337. And when such execution is charged, it is to be regarded as proof of the intent, or as an aggravation of the criminality of the unlawful combination.

Another rule is a necessary consequence of the former, which is, that the crime is consummate and complete by the fact of unlawful combination, and, therefore, that if the execution of the unlawful purpose is averred, it is by way of aggravation, and proof of it is not necessary to conviction; and therefore the jury may find the conspiracy, and negative the execution, and it will be a good conviction.

And it follows, as another necessary legal consequence, from the same principle, that the indictment must—by averring the unlawful purpose of the conspiracy, or the unlawful means by which it is contemplated and agreed to accomplish a lawful purpose, or a purpose not of itself criminally punishable—set out an offence complete in itself, without the aid of any averment of illegal acts done in pursuance of such an agreement; and that an illegal combination, imperfectly and insufficiently set out in the indictment, will not be aided by averments of acts done in pursuance of it.

From this view of the law respecting conspiracy, we think it an offence which especially demands the application of that wise and humane rule of the common law, that an indictment shall state, with as much certainty as the nature of the case will admit, the facts which constitute the crime intended to be charged. This is required, to enable the defendant to meet the charge and prepare for his defence, and, in case of acquittal or conviction, to show by the record the identity of the charge, so that he may not be indicted a second time for the same offence. It is also necessary, in order that a person, charged by the grand jury for one offence, may not substantially be convicted, on his trial, of another. This fundamental rule is confirmed by the Declaration of Rights, which declares that no subject shall be held to answer for any crime or offence, until the same is fully and plainly, substantially and formally described to him.

From these views of the rules of criminal pleading, it appears to us to follow, as a necessary legal conclusion, that when the criminality of a conspiracy consists in an unlawful agreement of two or more persons to compass or promote some criminal or illegal purpose, that purpose must be fully and clearly stated in the indictment; and if the criminality of the offence, which is intended to be charged, consist in the agreement to compass or promote some purpose, not of itself criminal or unlawful, by the use of fraud, force, falsehood, or other criminal or unlawful means, such intended use of fraud, force, falsehood, or other criminal or unlawful means, must be set out in the indictment. Such, we think, is, on the whole, the result of the English authorities, although they are not quite uniform. . . .

With these general views of the law, it becomes necessary to consider the circumstances of the present case, as they appear from the indictment itself, and from the bill of exceptions filed and allowed.

One of the exceptions, though not the first in the order of time, yet by far the most important, was this:

The counsel for the defendants contended, and requested the court to instruct the jury, that the indictment did not set forth any agreement to do a criminal act, or to do any lawful act by any specified criminal means, and that the agreements therein set forth did not constitute a conspiracy indictable by any law of this Commonwealth. But the judge refused so to do, and instructed the jury, that the indictment did, in his opinion, describe a confederacy among the defendants to do an unlawful act, and to effect the same by unlawful means; that the society, organized and associated for the purposes described in the indictment, was an unlawful conspiracy, against the laws of this Commonwealth; and that if the jury believed, from the evidence in the case, that the defendants, or any of them, had engaged in such a confederacy, they were bound to find such of them guilty.

We are here carefully to distinguish between the confederacy set forth in the indictment, and the confederacy or association contained in the constitution of the Boston Journeymen Bootmakers' Society, as stated in the little printed book, which was admitted as evidence on the trial. Because, though it was thus admitted as evidence, it would not warrant a conviction for any thing not stated in the indictment. It was proof, as far as it went to support the averments in the indictment. If it contained any criminal matter not set forth in the indictment, it is of no avail. The question then presents itself in the same form as on a motion in arrest of judgment.

The first count set forth, that the defendants, with divers others unknown, on the day and at the place named, being workmen, and journeymen, in the art and occupation of bootmakers, unlawfully, perniciously and deceitfully designing and intending to continue, keep up, form, and unite themselves, into an unlawful club, society and combination, and make unlawful by-laws, rules and orders among themselves, and thereby govern themselves and other workmen, in the said art, and unlawfully and unjustly to exhort sums of money by means thereof, did unlawfully assemble and meet together, and being so assembled, did unjustly and corruptly conspire, combine, confederate and agree together, that none of them should thereafter, and that none of them would, work for any master or person whatsoever, in the said art, mystery and occupation, who should employ any workman or journeyman, or other person, in the said art, who was not a member of said club, society or combination, after notice given him to discharge such workman, from the employ of such master; to the great damage and oppression, &c.

Now it is to be considered, that the preamble and introductory matter in the indictment—such as unlawfully and deceitfully designing and intending unjustly to extort great sums, &c.—is mere recital, and not traversable, and therefore cannot aid an imperfect averment of the facts constituting the description of the offence. The same may be said of the concluding matter, which follows the averment, as to the great damage and oppression not only of their said masters, employing them in said art and occupation, but also of divers other workmen in the same art, mystery and occupation, to the evil example, &c. If the facts averred constitute the crime, these are properly stated as the legal inferences to be drawn from them. If they do not constitute the charge of such an offence, they cannot be aided by these alleged consequences.

Stripped then of these introductory recitals and alleged injurious consequences, and of the qualifying epithets attached to the facts, the averment is this; that the defendants and others formed themselves into a society, and agreed not to work for any person, who should employ any journeyman or other person, not a member of such society, after notice given him to discharge such workman.

The manifest intent of the association is, to induce all those engaged in the same occupation to become members of it. Such a purpose is not unlawful. It would give them a power which might be exerted for useful and honorable purposes, or for dangerous and pernicious ones. If the latter were the real and actual object, and susceptible of proof, it should have been specially charged. Such an association might be used to afford each other assistance in times of poverty, sickness and distress; or to raise their intellectual, moral and social condition; or to make improvement in their art; or for other proper purposes. Or the association might be designed for purposes of oppression and injustice. But in order to charge all those, who become members of an association, with the guilt of a criminal conspiracy, it must be averred and proved that the actual, if not the avowed object of the association, was criminal. An association may be formed, the declared objects of which are innocent and laudable, and yet they may have secret articles, or an agreement communicated only to the members, by which they are banded together for purposes injurious to the peace of society or the rights of its members. Such would undoubtedly be a criminal conspiracy, on proof of the fact, however meritorious and praiseworthy the declared objects might be. The law is not to be hoodwinked by colorable pretences. It looks at truth and reality, through whatever disguise it may assume. But to make such an association, ostensibly innocent, the subject of prosecution as a criminal conspiracy, the secret agreement, which makes it so, is to be averred and proved as the gist of the offence. But when an association is formed for purposes actually innocent, and afterwards its powers are abused, by those who have the control and management of it, to purposes of oppression and injustice, it will be criminal in those who thus misuse it, or give consent thereto, but not in the other members of the association. In this case, no such secret agreement, varying the objects of the association from those avowed, is set forth in this count of the indictment.

Nor can we perceive that the objects of this association,

whatever they may have been, were to be attained by criminal means. The means which they proposed to employ, as averred in this count, and which, as we are now to presume, were established by the proof, were, that they would not work for a person, who, after due notice, should employ a journeyman not a member of their society. Supposing the object of the association to be laudable and lawful, or at least not unlawful, are these means criminal? The case supposes that these persons are not bound by contract, but free to work for whom they please, or not to work, if they so prefer. In this state of things, we cannot perceive, that it is criminal for men to agree together to exercise their own acknowledged rights, in such a manner as best to subserve their own interests. One way to test this is, to consider the effect of such an agreement, where the object of the association is acknowledged on all hands to be a laudable one. Suppose a class of workmen, impressed with the manifold evils of intemperance, should agree with each other not to work in a shop in which ardent spirit was furnished, or not to work in a shop with any one who used it, or not to work for an employer, who should, after notice, employ a journeyman who habitually used it. The consequences might be the same. A workman, who should still persist in the use of ardent spirit, would find it more difficult to get employment; a master employing such an one might, at times, experience inconvenience in his work, in losing the services of a skilful but intemperate workman. Still it seems to us, that as the object would be lawful, and the means not unlawful, such an agreement could not be pronounced a criminal conspiracy.

From this count in the indictment, we do not understand that the agreement was, that the defendants would refuse to work for an employer, to whom they were bound by contract for a certain time, in violation of that contract; nor that they would insist that an employer should discharge a workman engaged by contract for a certain time, in violation of such contract. It is perfectly consistent with every thing stated in this count, that the effect of the agreement was, that when they were free to act, they would not engage with an employer, or continue in his employment, if such employer, when free to act, should engage with a workman, or continue a workman in his employment, not a member of the association. If a large number of men, engaged for a certain time, should combine together to violate their contract, and quit their employment together, it would present a very different question. Suppose a farmer, employing a large number of men, engaged for the year, at fair monthly wages, and suppose that just at the moment that his crops were ready to harvest, they should all combine to quit his service, unless he would advance their wages, at a time when other laborers could not be obtained. It would surely be a conspiracy to do an unlawful act, though of such a character, that if done by an individual, it would lay the foundation of a civil action only, and not of a criminal prosecution. It would be a case very different from that stated in this count.

The second count, omitting the recital of unlawful intent and evil disposition, and omitting the direct averment of an unlawful club or society, alleges that the defendants, with others unknown, did assemble, conspire, confederate and agree together, not to work for any master or person who should employ any workman not being a member of a certain club, society or combination, called the Boston Journeymen Bootmaker's Society, or who should break any of their by-laws, unless such workmen should pay to said club, such sum as should be agreed upon as a penalty for the breach of such unlawful rules, &c; and that by means of said conspiracy they did compel one Isaac B. Wait, a master cordwainer, to turn out of his employ one Jeremiah Horne, a journeyman boot-maker, &c. in evil example, &c. So far as the averment of a conspiracy is concerned, all the remarks made in reference to the first count are equally applicable to this. It is simply an averment of an agreement amongst themselves not to work for a person, who should employ any person not a member of a certain association. It sets forth no illegal or criminal purpose to be accomplished, nor any illegal or criminal means to be adopted for the accomplishment of any purpose. It was an agreement, as to the manner in which they would exercise an acknowledged right to contract with others for their labor. It does not aver a conspiracy or even an intention to raise their wages; and it appears by the bill of exceptions, that the case was not put upon the footing of a conspiracy to raise their wages. Such an agreement, as set forth in this count, would be perfectly justifiable under the recent English statute, by which this subject is regulated. *St.* 6 Geo. IV. *c.* 129. See Roscoe Crim. Ev. (2d Amer. ed.) 368, 369.

As to the latter part of this count, which avers that by means of said conspiracy, the defendants did compel one Wait to turn out of his employ one Jeremiah Horne, we remark, in the first place, that as the acts done in pursuance of a conspiracy, as we have before seen, are stated by way of aggravation, and not as a substantive charge; if no criminal or unlawful conspiracy is stated, it cannot be aided and made good by mere matter of aggravation. If the principal charge falls, the aggravation falls with it. *State* v. *Rickey*, 4 Halst. 293.

But further; if this is to be considered as a substantive charge, it would depend altogether upon the force of the word "compel," which may be used in the sense of coercion, or duress, by force or fraud. It would therefore depend upon the context and the connexion with other words, to determine the sense in which it was used in the indictment. If, for instance, the indictment had averred a conspiracy, by the defendants, to compel Wait to turn Horne out of his employment, and to accomplish that object by the use of force or fraud, it would have been a very different case; especially if it might be fairly construed, as perhaps in that case it might have been, that Wait was under obligation, by contract, for an unexpired term of time, to employ and pay Horne. As before remarked, it would have been a conspiracy to do an unlawful, though not a criminal act, to induce Wait to violate his engagement, to the actual injury of Horne. To mark the difference between the case of a journeyman or a servant and master, mutually bound by contract, and the same parties when free to engage anew, I should have before cited the case of the *Boston Glass Co.* v. *Binney*, 4 Pick. 425. In that case, it was held actionable to entice another person's hired servant to quit his employment, during the time for which he was engaged; but not actionable to treat with such hired servant, whilst actually hired and employed by another, to leave his service, and engage in the employment of the person making the proposal, when the term for which he is engaged shall expire. It acknowledges the established principle, that every free man, whether skilled laborer, mechanic, farmer or domestic servant, may work or not work, or work or refuse to work with any company or individual, at his own option, except so far as he is bound by contract. But whatever might be the force of the word "compel," unexplained by its connexion, it is disarmed and rendered harmless by the precise statement of the means, by which such compulsion was to be effected. It was the agreement not to work for him, by which they compelled Wait to decline employing Horne longer. On both of these grounds, we are of opinion that the statement made in this second count, that the unlawful agreement was carried into execution, makes no essential difference between this and the first count.

The third count, reciting a wicked and unlawful intent to impoverish one Jeremiah Horne, and hinder him from following his trade as a bootmaker, charges the defendants, with others unknown, with an unlawful conspiracy, by wrongful and indirect means, to impoverish said Horne and to deprive and hinder him, from his said art and trade and getting his support thereby, and that, in pursuance of said unlawful combination, they did unlawfully and indirectly hinder and prevent, &c. and greatly impoverish him.

If the fact of depriving Jeremiah Horne of the profits of his business, by whatever means it might be done, would be unlawful and criminal, a combination to compass that object would be an unlawful conspiracy, and it would be unnecessary to state the means. . . .

Suppose a baker in a small village had the exclusive custom of his neighborhood, and was making large profits by the sale of his bread. Supposing a number of those neighbors, believing the price of his bread too high, should propose to him to reduce his prices, or if he did not, that they would introduce another baker; and on his refusal, such other baker should, under their encouragement, set up a rival establishment, and sell his bread at lower prices; the effect would be to diminish the profit of the former baker, and to the same extent to impoverish him. And it might be said and proved, that the purpose of the associates was to diminish his profits, and thus impoverish him, though the ultimate and laudable object of the combination was to reduce the cost of bread to themselves and their neighbors. The same thing may be said of all competition in every branch of trade and industry; and yet it is through that competition, that the best interests of trade and industry are promoted. It is scarcely necessary to allude to the familiar instances of opposition lines of conveyance, rival hotels, and the thousand other instances, where each strives to gain custom to himself, by ingenious improvements, by increased industry, and by all the means by which he may lessen the price of commodities, and thereby diminish the profits of others.

We think, therefore, that associations may be entered into, the object of which is to adopt measures that may have a tendency to impoverish another, that is, to diminish his gains and profits, and yet so far from being criminal or unlawful, the object may be highly meritorious and public spirited. The legality of such an association will therefore depend upon the means to be used for its accomplishment. If it is to be carried into effect by fair or honorable and lawful means, it is, to say the least, innocent; if by falsehood or force, it may be stamped with the character of conspiracy. It follows as a necessary consequence, that if criminal and indictable, it is so by reason of the criminal means intended to be employed for its accomplishment; and as a further legal consequence, that as the criminality will depend on the means, those means must be stated in the indictment. If the same rule were to prevail in criminal, which holds in civil proceedings—that a case defectively stated may be aided by a verdict—then a court might presume, after verdict, that the indictment was supported by proof of criminal or unlawful means to effect the object. But it is an established rule in criminal cases, that the indictment must state a complete indictable offence, and cannot be aided by the proof offered at the trial. . . .

The fourth count avers a conspiracy to impoverish Jeremiah Horne, without stating any means; and the fifth alleges a conspiracy to impoverish employers, by preventing and hindering them from employing persons, not members of the Bootmakers' Society; and these require no remarks, which have not been already made in reference to the other counts. . . .

It appears by the bill of exceptions, that it was contended on the part of the defendants, that this indictment did not set forth any agreement to do a criminal act, or to do any lawful act by criminal means, and that the agreement therein set forth did not constitute a conspiracy indictable by the law of this State, and that the court was requested so to instruct the jury. This the court declined doing, but instructed the jury that the indictment did describe a confederacy among the defendants to do an unlawful act, and to effect the same by unlawful means—that the society, organized and associated for the purposes described in the indictment, was an unlawful conspiracy against the laws of this State, and that if the jury believed, from the evidence, that the defendants or any of them had engaged in such confederacy, they were bound to find such of them guilty.

In this opinion of the learned judge, this court, for the reasons stated, cannot concur. Whatever illegal purpose can be found in the constitution of the Bootmakers' Society, it not being clearly set forth in the indictment, cannot be relied upon to support this conviction. So if any facts were disclosed at the trial, which, if properly averred, would have given a different character to the indictment, they do not appear in the bill of exceptions, nor could they, after verdict, aid the indictment. But looking solely at the indictment, disregarding the qualifying epithets, recitals and immaterial allegations, and confining ourselves to facts so averred as to be capable of being traversed and put in issue, we cannot perceive that it charges a criminal conspiracy punishable by law. The exceptions must, therefore, be sustained, and the judgment arrested.

☆

Commonwealth v. Hunt, *by removing the stigma of criminality from labor organizations, became the Magna Carta of American trade unionism. Shaw was a tough and fair-minded realist who understood that the conspiracy doctrine, if not restricted, might throttle industrial development and professional organizations as well as unions. He was tolerant of unionism even beyond approving the right of workers to organize. It was the legality of the union's activities, its methods and purposes, not just the lawfulness of its existence, that constituted the issue in the case. The express holding was that a combination of workers to establish and maintain a closed shop by the employment of peaceable coercion is not an indictable conspiracy. Even after more than a century, this holding still implies a latitudinarian attitude toward unions. Shaw also indicated that a strike for the purpose of raising wages was not a crime. Because the dicta as well as the holding demonstrated his belief that the common law should not penalize normal union activities, Shaw made it legally possible for unions to operate and grow. This fact has given his opinion its enduring significance. Without repudiating the conspiracy doctrine, he narrowed its applicability though leaving it available for use in future labor cases. His means-ends formulation of the doctrine became the definitive one; it has been cited hundreds of times by American courts. For two generations* Commonwealth v. Hunt *dominated the American law of labor combinations. A New Jersey decision of 1867 is notable only as the exception that proved the rule, a case in which a court did not come to the same conclusion as Shaw did; yet in that case the judge contrived an explanation for his decision after he was forced to allege his complete concurrence in the principles of* Commonwealth v. Hunt.

Shaw's opinion was destined to survive as the leading statement of the law even in our own time. Yet it passed through a period of oblivion or, rather, judicial circumvention. The conspiracy doctrine, like the crime it described, remained inherently nebulous, so that courts could still discover criminality in some labor activity that was personally repugnant to the judges sitting. The letter of Shaw's opinion could be satisfied, if not its spirit, by the naming of ends or means as illegal. Picketing or boycotting, for example, were judicially regarded as acts of violence in many states, and often the purpose of a strike was deemed an unwarrantable interference with private property. In the late nineteenth century and well into the twentieth, when judges were acting on the presupposition that the Fourteenth Amendment protected only entrepreneurial liberty, Shaw's opinions in this and other cases seemed faintly socialistic. His name was respected, even revered, but Commonwealth v. Hunt *was politely evaded.*

American law, from the late nineteenth century to the ultimate victory of Holmesian jurisprudence, became a deathbed for general-welfare or public-interest doctrines. In the meanwhile, doctrines of vested rights dominated, the conspiracy doctrine enjoyed a revival, and only a few states responded to labor's protest by enacting statutes half-heartedly intended to nullify labor's common law crimes. After the passage of the Sherman Act of 1890, with its prohibitions on combinations and conspiracies in restraint of trade, courts found in this "antitrust" legislation an effective weapon against unions. Almost any union activity could be speedily enjoined as a conspiracy in restraint of trade. The issuance of an injunction, the law's new and streamlined antilabor instrument, was often rationalized on the basis of the old conspiracy doctrine. Few successors to Lemuel Shaw—dispassionate and beholden to no special interests; concerned for the integrity of the law and of the judicial process; towering in stature and influence —were on the scene to protest.

In 1896, for example, when Justice Oliver Wendell Holmes of the Massachusetts Supreme Judicial Court invoked Shaw's name and decried the use of an injunction against peaceful picketing, he spoke in dissent. Holmes made explicit an implication that he found in Shaw: conflict between employers and employed is a form of competition. "If," declared Holmes, "the policy on which our law is founded is too narrowly expressed in the term free competition, we may substitute free struggle for life. Certainly, the policy is not limited to struggles between persons of the same class, competing for the same end. It applies to all conflicts of temporal interests." That it was lawful for a union to benefit itself even at the expense of injuring its antagonists was "decided as long ago as 1842 by the good sense of Chief Justice Shaw, in Com. v. Hunt 4 Metc. (Mass.) 111." Holmes relied on Shaw's belief that benefits to the public would accrue from the contest between unions and employers. He explained his position by advancing the proposition that "free competition is worth much more to society than it costs, and that on this ground the infliction of the damage is privileged. Commonwealth v. Hunt, 4 Metc. 111, 134." A young Massachusetts attorney, Louis Dembitz Brandeis, subscribed to the same view of the matter, indeed, made it a commitment to which he passion-

ately dedicated himself. Together Holmes and Brandeis, most often in dissent from the Court's majority opinion, gave continued life to Shaw's vision of the law as a means of releasing the energies and range of choices for all Americans who utilized the right of association to advance their interests.

In the time of the New Deal, national law embodied protections to labor unions that had been foreshadowed in a tentative, groping way by Lemuel Shaw almost a century earlier. In the passage of the Wagner Labor Relations Act of 1936, Commonwealth v. Hunt received its greatest vindication. The first great victory for labor in the courts of this nation has today become so deeply accepted that it has been accorded the ultimate honor: it is taken for granted. Long a courageous, trail-blazing opinion, it is now a historical antique that bears the same relationship to modern labor law as the tin lizzie does to the new vehicles of space travel. The opinion continues, however, to bear witness to the estimate of Shaw by Justice Holmes, who remarked on his "accurate appreciation of the requirements of the community." Few have lived, thought Holmes, "who were his equals in their understanding of the grounds of public policy to which all laws must be ultimately referred. It was this which made him . . . the greatest magistrate which this country has produced."

Henry David Thoreau

Civil Disobedience

1846

EDITED BY FREDERICK B. TOLLES

A legend is not history. By definition it is a story that cannot be documented. Some legends nevertheless are too good not to be true. It is so with a conversation Ralph Waldo Emerson is said to have had with his friend Henry David Thoreau, whom, one evening in July, 1846, he was surprised to find locked up in the town jail at Concord, Massachusetts.

"Henry, why are you there?"

"Waldo, why are you not here?"

Now Emerson really didn't need to ask his question. He should have known why his friend was in jail. Thoreau was, like himself, a Transcendentalist, a philosophical individualist, yes, an anarchist, resistant on principle to civil government whenever it trenched upon his private life or made him support measures of which he morally disapproved. Resistant in practice, too, as on that very afternoon. He was living in his one-room hut on Walden Pond. He had gone there with a purpose: to live "deliberately, to front only the essential facts of life . . . to drive life into a corner," and find out what it really was. He had strolled into town, that afternoon, to pick up a repaired shoe at the cobbler's. Sam Staples, the town constable, had stopped him, reminded him that his poll tax was overdue. For three years Thoreau had declined to pay his poll tax. But now, in the summer of 1846, the United States was at war with Mexico. Like other abolitionists, he was convinced that the war was being fought to extend the area of slaveholding. To pay his tax would be to imply his approval. He had told Sam Staples that he would not pay his poll tax. So off to jail he went. If Emerson did come by and asked why he was there, how else could he have replied but by asking, "Why are you not here?"

Next morning, to his annoyance, he was set free. A veiled woman—probably his Aunt Maria—had gone to Staples' house after nightfall and paid the tax. The constable told her that, having taken off his boots for the evening, he would not go back to release his prisoner. So Thoreau spent one night in jail.

To explain his motives to his fellow townsmen, he wrote out and delivered at the Concord Lyceum a lecture entitled "The Relation of the Individual to the State." A few years later, in 1849, Elizabeth Peabody published it in the one issue of her periodical Aesthetic Papers *under the title "Resistance to Civil Government." Later reprints carried the title "On the Duty of Civil Disobedience." But it is best known simply as "Civil Disobedience."*

I HEARTILY accept the motto—"That government is best which governs least;" and I should like to see it acted up to more rapidly and systematically. Carried out, it finally amounts to this, which also I believe,—"That government is best which governs not at all;" and when men are prepared for it, that will be the kind of government which they will have. Government is at best but an expedient; but most governments are usually, and all governments are sometimes, inexpedient. The objections which have been brought against a standing army, and they are many and weighty, and deserve to prevail, may also at last be brought against a standing government. The standing army is only an arm of the standing government. The government itself, which is only the mode which the people have chosen to execute their will, is equally liable to be abused and perverted before the people can act through it. Witness the present Mexican war, the work of comparatively a few individuals using the standing

The essay is given here as it appeared in *Aesthetic Papers* (Boston, 1849).

government as their tool; for, in the outset, the people would not have consented to this measure.

This American government,—what is it but a tradition, though a recent one, endeavoring to transmit itself unimpaired to posterity, but each instant losing some of its integrity? It has not the vitality and force of a single living man; for a single man can bend it to his will. It is a sort of wooden gun to the people themselves; and, if ever they should use it in earnest as a real one against each other, it will surely split. But it is not the less necessary for this; for the people must have some complicated machinery or other, and hear its din, to satisfy that idea of government which they have. Governments show thus how successfully men can be imposed on, even impose on themselves, for their own advantage. It is excellent, we must all allow; yet this government never of itself furthered any enterprise, but by the alacrity with which it got out of its way. *It* does not keep the country free. *It* does not settle the West. *It* does not educate. The character inherent in the American people has done all that has been accomplished; and it would have done somewhat more, if the government had not sometimes got in its way. For government is an expedient by which men would fain succeed in letting one another alone; and, as has been said, when it is most expedient, the governed are most let alone by it. Trade and commerce, if they were not made of india rubber, would never manage to bounce over the obstacles which legislators are continually putting in their way; and, if one were to judge these men wholly by the effects of their actions, and not partly by their intentions, they would deserve to be classed and punished with those mischievous persons who put obstructions on the railroads.

But, to speak practically and as a citizen, unlike those who call themselves no-government men, I ask for, not at once no government, but *at once* a better government. Let every man make known what kind of government would command his respect, and that will be one step toward obtaining it.

After all, the practical reason why, when the power is once in the hands of the people, a majority are permitted, and for a long period continue, to rule, is not because they are most likely to be in the right, nor because this seems fairest to the minority, but because they are physically the strongest. But a government in which the majority rule in all cases cannot be based on justice, even as far as men understand it. Can there not be a government in which majorities do not virtually decide right and wrong, but conscience?—in which majorities decide only those questions to which the rule of expediency is applicable? Must the citizen ever for a moment, or in the least degree, resign his conscience to the legislator? Why has every man a conscience, then? I think that we should be men first, and subjects afterward. It is not desirable to cultivate a respect for the law, so much as for the right. The only obligation which I have a right to assume, is to do at any time what I think right. It is truly enough said, that a corporation has no conscience; but a corporation of conscientious men is a corporation *with* a conscience. Law never made men a whit more just; and, by means of their respect for it, even the well-disposed are daily made the agents of injustice. A common and natural result of an undue respect for law is, that you may see a file of soldiers, colonel, captain, corporal, privates, powder-monkeys and all, marching in admirable order over hill and dale to the wars, against their wills, aye, against their common sense and consciences, which makes it very steep marching indeed, and produces a palpitation of the heart. They have no doubt that it is a damnable business in which they are concerned; they are all peaceably inclined. Now, what are they? Men at all? or small moveable forts and magazines, at the service of some unscrupulous man in power? Visit the Navy Yard, and behold a marine, such a man as an American government can make, or such as it can make a man with its black arts, a mere shadow and reminiscence of humanity, a man laid out alive and standing, and already, as one may say, buried under arms with funeral accompaniments, though it may be

> "Not a drum was heard, nor a funeral note,
> As his corse to the ramparts we hurried;
> Not a soldier discharged his farewell shot
> O'er the grave where our hero we buried."

The mass of men serve the State thus, not as men mainly, but as machines, with their bodies. They are the standing army, and the militia, jailers, constables, *posse comitatus*, &c. In most cases there is no free exercise whatever of the judgment or of the moral sense; but they put themselves on a level with wood and earth and stones; and wooden men can perhaps be manufactured that will serve the purpose as well. Such command no more respect than men of straw, or a lump of dirt. They have the same sort of worth only as horses and dogs. Yet such as these even are commonly esteemed good citizens. Others, as most legislators, politicians, lawyers, ministers, and office-holders, serve the State chiefly with their heads; and, as they rarely make any moral distinctions, they are as likely to serve the devil, without intending it, as God. A very few, as heroes, patriots, martyrs, reformers in the great sense, and *men* serve the State with their consciences also, and so necessarily resist it for the most part; and they are commonly treated by it as enemies. A wise man will only be useful as a man, and will not submit to be "clay," and "stop a hole to keep the wind away," but leave that office to his dust at least:—

> "I am too high-born to be propertied,
> To be a secondary at control,
> Or useful serving-man and instrument
> To any sovereign state throughout the world."

He who gives himself entirely to his fellow-men appears to them useless and selfish; but he who gives himself partially to them is pronounced a benefactor and philanthropist.

How does it become a man to behave toward this American government to-day? I answer that he cannot without disgrace be associated with it. I cannot for an instant recognize that political organization as *my* government which is the *slave's* government also.

All men recognize the right of revolution; that is, the right to refuse allegiance to and to resist the government, when its tyranny or its inefficiency are great and unendurable. But almost all say that such is not the case now. But such was the case, they think, in the Revolution of '75. If one were to tell me that this was a bad government because it taxed certain foreign commodities brought to its ports, it is most probable that I should not make an ado about it, for I can do without them: all machines have their friction; and possibly this does enough good to counterbalance the evil. At any rate, it is a great evil to make a stir about it. But when the friction comes to have its machine, and oppression and robbery are organized, I say, let us not have such a machine any longer. In other words, when a sixth of the population of a nation which has undertaken to be the refuge of liberty are slaves, and a whole country is unjustly overrun and conquered by a foreign army, and subjected to military law, I think that it is not too soon for honest men to rebel and revolutionize. What makes this duty the more urgent is the fact, that the country so overrun is not our own, but ours is the invading army.

Paley, a common authority with many on moral questions, in his chapter on the "Duty of Submission to Civil Government," resolves all civil obligation into expediency; and he proceeds to say, "that so long as the interest of the whole society requires it, that is, so long as the established government cannot be resisted or changed without public inconveniency, it is the will of God that the established government be obeyed,—and no longer. This principle being admitted, the justice of every particular case of resistance is reduced to a computation of the quantity of the danger and grievance on the one side, and of the probability and expense of redressing it on the other." Of this, he says, every man shall judge for himself. But Paley appears never to have contemplated those cases to which the rule of expediency does not apply, in which a people, as well as an individual, must do justice, cost what it may. If I have unjustly wrested a plank from a drowning man, I must restore it to him though I drown myself. This, according to Paley, would be inconvenient. But he that would save his life, in such a case, shall lose it. This people must cease to hold slaves, and to make war on Mexico, though it cost them their existence as a people.

In their practice, nations agree with Paley; but does any one think that Massachusetts does exactly what is right at the present crisis?

> "A drab of state, a cloth-o'-silver slut,
>   To have her train borne up, and her soul trail in the dirt."

Practically speaking, the opponents to a reform in Massachusetts are not a hundred thousand politicians at the South, but a hundred thousand merchants and farmers here, who are more interested in commerce and agriculture than they are in humanity, and are not prepared to do justice to the slave and to Mexico, *cost what it may*. I quarrel not with far-off foes, but with those who, near at home, co-operate with, and do the bidding of those far away, and without whom the latter would be harmless. We are accustomed to say, that the mass of men are unprepared; but improvement is slow, because the few are not materially wiser or better than the many. It is not so important that many should be as good as you, as that there be some absolute goodness somewhere; for that will leaven the whole lump. There are thousands who are *in opinion* opposed to slavery and to the war, who yet in effect do nothing to put an end to them; who, esteeming themselves children of Washington and Franklin, sit down with their hands in their pockets, and say that they know not what to do, and do nothing; who even postpone the question of freedom to the question of free-trade, and quietly read the prices-current along with the latest advices from Mexico, after dinner, and, it may be, fall asleep over them both. What is the price-current of an honest man and patriot to-day? They hesitate, and they regret, and sometimes they petition; but they do nothing in earnest and with effect. They will wait, well disposed, for others to remedy the evil, that they may no longer have it to regret. At most, they give only a cheap vote, and a feeble countenance and God-speed, to the right, as it goes by them. There are nine hundred and ninety-nine patrons of virtue to one virtuous man; but it is easier to deal with the real possessor of a thing than with the temporary guardian of it.

All voting is a sort of gaming, like chequers or backgammon, with a slight moral tinge to it, a playing with right and wrong, with moral questions; and betting naturally accompanies it. The character of the voters is not staked. I cast my vote, perchance, as I think right; but I am not vitally concerned that that right should prevail. I am willing to leave it to the majority. Its obligation, therefore, never exceeds that of expediency. Even voting *for the right* is *doing* nothing for it. It is only expressing to men feebly your desire that it should prevail. A wise man will not leave the right to the mercy of chance, nor wish it to prevail through the power of the majority. There is but little virtue in the action of masses of men. When the majority shall at length vote for the abolition of slavery, it will be because they are indifferent to slavery, or because there is but little slavery left to be abolished by their vote. *They* will then be the only slaves. Only *his* vote can hasten the abolition of slavery who asserts his own freedom by his vote.

I hear of a convention to be held at Baltimore, or elsewhere, for the selection of a candidate for the Presidency, made up chiefly of editors, and men who are politicians by profession; but I think, what is it to any independent, intelligent, and respectable man what decision they may come to, shall we not have the advantage of his wisdom and honesty, nevertheless? Can we not count upon some independent votes? Are there not many individuals in the country who do not attend conventions? But no: I find that the respectable man, so called, has immediately drifted from his position, and despairs of his country, when his country has more reason to despair of him. He forthwith adopts one of the candidates thus selected as the only *available* one, thus proving that he is himself *available* for any purposes of the demagogue. His vote is of no more worth than that of any unprincipled foreigner or hireling native, who may have been bought. Oh for a man who is a *man*, and, as my neighbor says, has a bone in his back which you cannot pass your hand through! Our statistics are at fault: the population has been returned too large. How many *men* are there to a square thousand miles in this country? Hardly one. Does not America offer any inducement for men to settle here? The American has dwindled into an Odd Fellow,—one who may be known by the development of his organ of gregariousness, and a manifest lack of intellect and cheerful self-reliance; whose first and chief concern, on coming into the world, is to see that the alms-houses are in good repair; and, before yet he has lawfully donned the virile garb, to collect a fund for the support of the widows and orphans that may be; who, in short, ventures to live only by the aid of the mutual insurance company, which has promised to bury him decently.

It is not a man's duty, as a matter of course, to devote himself to the eradication of any, even the most enormous wrong; he may still properly have other concerns to engage him; but it is his duty, at least, to wash his hands of it, and, if he gives it no thought longer, not to give it practically his support. If I devote myself to other pursuits and contemplations, I must first see, at least, that I do not pursue them sitting upon another man's shoulders. I must get off him first, that he may pursue his contemplations too. See what gross inconsistency is tolerated. I have heard some of my townsmen say, "I should like to have them order me out to help put down an insurrection of the slaves, or to march to Mexico,—see if I would go;" and yet these very men have each, directly by their allegiance, and so indirectly, at least, by their money, furnished a substitute. The soldier is applauded who refuses to serve in an unjust war by those who do not refuse to sustain the unjust government which makes the war; is applauded by those whose own act and authority he disregards and sets at naught; as if the State were penitent to that degree that it hired one to scourge it while it sinned, but not to that degree that it left off sinning for a moment. Thus, under the name of order and civil government, we are all made at last to pay homage to and support our own meanness. After the first blush of sin, comes its indifference; and from immoral it becomes, as it were, unmoral, and not quite unnecessary to that life which we have made.

The broadest and most prevalent error requires the most disinterested virtue to sustain it. The slight reproach to which the virtue of patriotism is commonly liable, the noble are most likely to incur. Those who, while they disapprove of the character and measures of a government, yield to it their allegiance and support are undoubtedly its most conscientious supporters, and so frequently the most serious obstacles to reform. Some are petitioning the State to dissolve the Union, to disregard the requisitions of the President. Why do they not dissolve it themselves,—the union between themselves and the State,—and refuse to pay their quota into its treasury? Do not they stand in the same relation to the State that the State does to the Union? And have not the same reasons prevented the State from resisting the Union, which have prevented them from resisting the State?

How can a man be satisfied to entertain an opinion merely, and enjoy *it?* Is there any enjoyment in it, if his opinion is that he is aggrieved? If you are cheated out of a single dollar by your neighbor, you do not rest satisfied with knowing that you are cheated, or with saying that you are cheated, or even with petitioning him to pay you your due; but you take effectual steps at once to obtain the full amount, and see that you are never cheated again. Action from principle,—the perception and the performance of right,—changes things and relations; it is essentially revolutionary, and does not consist wholly with any thing which was. It not only divides states and churches, it divides families; aye, it divides the *individual,* separating the diabolical in him from the divine.

Unjust laws exist: shall we be content to obey them, or shall we endeavor to amend them, and obey them until we have succeeded, or shall we transgress them at once? Men generally, under such a government as this, think that they ought to wait until they have persuaded the majority to alter them. They think that, if they should resist, the remedy would be worse than the evil. But it is the fault of the government itself that the remedy *is* worse than the evil. *It* makes it worse. Why is it not more apt to anticipate and provide for reform? Why does it not cherish its wise minority? Why does it cry and resist before it is hurt? Why does it not encourage its citizens to be on the alert to point out its faults, and *do* better than it would have them? Why does it always crucify Christ, and excommunicate Copernicus and Luther, and pronounce Washington and Franklin rebels?

One would think, that a deliberate and practical denial of its authority was the only offence never contemplated by government; else, why has it not assigned its definite, its suitable and proportionate penalty? If a man who has no property refuses but once to earn nine shillings for the State, he is put in prison for a period unlimited by any law that I know, and determined only by the discretion of those who placed him there; but if he should steal ninety times nine shillings from the State, he is soon permitted to go at large again.

If the injustice is part of the necessary friction of the machine of government, let it go, let it go: perchance it will wear smooth,—certainly the machine will wear out. If the injustice has a spring, or a pulley, or a rope, or a crank, exclusively for itself, then perhaps you may consider whether the remedy will not be worse than the evil; but if it is of such a nature that it requires you to be the agent of injustice to another, then, I say, break the law. Let your life be a counter friction to stop the machine. What I have to do is to see, at any rate, that I do not lend myself to the wrong which I condemn.

As for adopting the ways which the State has provided for remedying the evil, I know not of such ways. They take too much time, and a man's life will be gone. I have other affairs to attend to. I came into this world, not chiefly to make this a good place to live in, but to live in it, be it good or bad. A man has not every thing to do, but something; and because he cannot do *every thing,* it is not necessary that he should do *something* wrong. It is not my business to be petitioning the governor or the legislature any more than it is theirs to petition me; and if they should not hear my petition, what should I do then? But in this case the State has provided no way: its very Constitution is the evil. This may seem to be harsh and stubborn and unconciliatory; but it is to treat with the utmost kindness and consideration the only spirit that can appreciate or deserves it. So is all change for the better, like birth and death which convulse the body.

I do not hesitate to say, that those who call themselves abolitionists should at once effectually withdraw their support, both in person and property, from the government of Massachusetts, and not wait till they constitute a majority of one, before they suffer the right to prevail through them. I think that it is enough if they have God on their side, without waiting for that other one. Moreover, any man more right than his neighbors constitutes a majority of one already.

I meet this American government, or its representative the State government, directly, and face to face, once a year, no more, in the person of its tax-gatherer; this is the only mode in which a man situated as I am necessarily meets it; and it then says distinctly, Recognize me; and the simplest, the most effectual, and, in the present posture of affairs, the indispensablest mode of treating with it on this head, of expressing your little satisfaction with and love for it, is to deny it then. My civil neighbor, the tax-gatherer, is the very man I have to deal with,—for it is, after all, with men and not with parchment that I quarrel,—and he has voluntarily chosen to be an agent of the government. How shall he ever know well what he is and does as an officer of the government, or as a man,

until he is obliged to consider whether he shall treat me, his
neighbor, for whom he has respect, as a neighbor and well-
disposed man, or as a maniac and disturber of the peace, and
see if he can get over this obstruction to his neighborliness
without a ruder and more impetuous thought or speech corresponding with his action? I know this well, that if one thousand, if one hundred, if ten men whom I could name,—if ten
honest men only,—aye, if *one* HONEST man, in this State of
Massachusetts, *ceasing to hold slaves,* were actually to withdraw from his copartnership, and be locked up in the county
jail therefor, it would be the abolition of slavery in America.
For it matters not how small the beginning may seem to be:
what is once well done is done for ever. But we love better to
talk about it: that we say is our mission. Reform keeps many
scores of newspapers in its service, but not one man. If my
esteemed neighbor, the State's ambassador, who will devote
his days to the settlement of the question of human rights in
the Council Chamber, instead of being threatened with the
prisons of Carolina, were to sit down the prisoner of Massachusetts, that State which is so anxious to foist the sin of
slavery upon her sister,—though at present she can discover
only an act of inhospitality to be the ground of a quarrel with
her,—the Legislature would not wholly waive the subject the
following winter.

Under a government which imprisons any unjustly, the
true place for a just man is also in prison. The proper place
to-day, the only place which Massachusetts has provided for
her freer and less desponding spirits, is in her prisons, to be
put out and locked out of the State by her own act, as they
have already put themselves out by their principles. It is there
that the fugitive slave, and the Mexican prisoner on parole,
and the Indian come to plead the wrongs of his race, should
find them; on that separate, but more free and honorable
ground, where the State places those who are not *with* her,
but *against* her,—the only house in a slave-state in which a
free man can abide with honor. If any think that their influence would be lost there, and their voices no longer afflict the
ear of the State, that they would not be as an enemy within
its walls, they do not know by how much truth is stronger
than error, nor how much more eloquently and effectively he
can combat injustice who has experienced a little in his own
person. Cast your whole vote, not a strip of paper merely,
but your whole influence. A minority is powerless while it
conforms to the majority; it is not even a minority then; but
it is irresistible when it clogs by its whole weight. If the alternative is to keep all just men in prison, or give up war and

slavery, the State will not hesitate which to choose. If a thousand men were not to pay their tax-bills this year, that would not be a violent and bloody measure, as it would be to pay them, and enable the State to commit violence and shed innocent blood. This is, in fact, the definition of a peaceable revolution, if any such is possible. If the tax-gatherer, or any other public officer, asks me, as one has done, "But what shall I do?" my answer is, "If you really wish to do any thing, resign our office." When the subject has refused allegiance, and the officer has resigned his office, then the revolution is accomplished. But even suppose blood should flow. Is there not a sort of blood shed when the conscience is wounded? Through this wound a man's real manhood and immortality flow out, and he bleeds to an everlasting death. I see this blood flowing now.

I have contemplated the imprisonment of the offender, rather than the seizure of his goods,—though both will serve the same purpose,—because they who assert the purest right, and consequently are most dangerous to a corrupt State, commonly have not spent much time in accumulating property. To such the State renders comparatively small service, and a slight tax is wont to appear exorbitant, particularly if they are obliged to earn it by special labor with their hands. If there were one who lived wholly without the use of money, the State itself would hesitate to demand it of him. But the rich man—not to make any invidious comparison—is always sold to the institution which makes him rich. Absolutely speaking, the more money, the less virtue; for money comes between a man and his objects, and obtains them for him; and it was certainly no great virtue to obtain it. It puts to rest many questions which he would otherwise be taxed to answer; while the only new question which it puts is the hard but superfluous one, how to spend it. Thus his moral ground is taken from under his feet. The opportunities of living are diminished in proportion as what are called the "means" are increased. The best thing a man can do for his culture when he is rich is to endeavour to carry out those schemes which he entertained when he was poor. Christ answered the Herodians according to their condition. "Show me the tribute-money," said he;—and one took a penny out of his pocket;—if you use money which has the image of Caesar on it, and which he has made current and valuable, that is, *if you are men of the State,* and gladly enjoy the advantages of Caesar's government, then pay him back some of his own when he demands it. "Render therefore to Caesar that which is Caesar's, and to God those things which are God's,"—leaving them no wiser than before as to which was which; for they did not wish to know.

When I converse with the freest of my neighbors, I perceive that, whatever they may say about the magnitude and seriousness of the question, and their regard for the public tranquillity, the long and the short of the matter is, that they cannot spare the protection of the existing government, and they dread the consequences of disobedience to it to their property and families. For my own part, I should not like to think that I ever rely on the protection of the State. But, if I deny the authority of the State when it presents its tax-bill, it will soon take and waste all my property, and so harass me and my children without end. This is hard. This makes it impossible for a man to live honestly, and at the same time comfortably in outward respects. It will not be worth the while to accumulate property; that would be sure to go again. You must hire or squat somewhere, and raise but a small crop, and eat that soon. You must live within yourself, and depend upon yourself, always tucked up and ready for a start, and not have many affairs. A man may grow rich in Turkey even, if he will be in all respects a good subject of the Turkish government. Confucius said,—"If a State is governed by the principles of reason, poverty and misery are subjects of shame; if a State is not governed by the principles of reason, riches and honors are the subjects of shame." No: until I want the protection of Massachusetts to be extended to me in some distant southern port, where my liberty is endangered, or until I am bent solely on building up an estate at home by peaceful enterprise, I can afford to refuse allegiance to Massachusetts, and her right to my property and life. It costs me less in every sense to incur the penalty of disobedience to the State than it would to obey. I should feel as if I were worth less in that case.

Some years ago, the State met me in behalf of the church, and commanded me to pay a certain sum toward the support of a clergyman whose preaching my father attended, but never I myself. "Pay it," it said, "or be locked up in the jail." I declined to pay. But, unfortunately, another man saw fit to pay it. I did not see why the schoolmaster should be taxed to support the priest, and not the priest the schoolmaster; for I was not the State's schoolmaster, but I supported myself by voluntary subscription. I did not see why the lyceum should not present its tax-bill, and have the State to back its demand, as well as the church. However, at the request of the selectmen, I condescended to make some such statement as this in writing:—"Know all men by these presents, that I, Henry

Thoreau, do not wish to be regarded as a member of any incorporated society which I have not joined." This I gave to the town-clerk; and he has it. The State, having thus learned that I did not wish to be regarded as a member of that church, has never made a like demand on me since; though it said that it must adhere to its original presumption that time. If I had known how to name them, I should then have signed off in detail from all the societies which I never signed on to; but I did not know where to find a complete list.

I have paid no poll-tax for six years. I was put into a jail once on this account, for one night; and, as I stood considering the walls of solid stone, two or three feet thick, the door of wood and iron, a foot thick, and the iron grating which strained the light, I could not help being struck with the foolishness of that institution which treated me as if I were mere flesh and blood and bones, to be locked up. I wondered that it should have concluded at length that this was the best use it could put me to, and had never thought to avail itself of my services in some way. I saw that, if there was a wall of stone between me and my townsmen, there was a still more difficult one to climb or break through, before they could get to be as free as I was. I did not for a moment feel confined, and the walls seemed a great waste of stone and mortar. I felt as if I alone of all my townsmen had paid my tax. They plainly did not know how to treat me, but behaved like persons who are underbred. In every threat and in every compliment there was a blunder; for they thought that my chief desire was to stand the other side of that stone wall. I could not but smile to see how industriously they locked the door on my meditations, which followed them out again without let or hinderance, and *they* were really all that was dangerous. As they could not reach me, they had resolved to punish my body; just as boys, if they cannot come at some person against whom they have a spite, will abuse his dog. I saw that the State was half-witted, that it was timid as a lone woman with her silver spoons, and that it did not know its friends from its foes, and I lost all my remaining respect for it, and pitied it.

Thus the State never intentionally confronts a man's sense, intellectual or moral, but only his body, his senses. It is not armed with superior wit or honesty, but with superior physical strength. I was not born to be forced. I will breathe after my own fashion. Let us see who is the strongest. What force has a multitude? They only can force me who obey a higher law than I. They force me to become like themselves. I do not hear of *men* being *forced* to live this way or that by masses of men. What sort of life were that to live? When I meet a government which says to me, "Your money or your life," why should I be in haste to give it my money? It may be in a great strait, and not know what to do: I cannot help that. It must help itself; do as I do. It is not worth the while to snivel about it. I am not responsible for the successful working of the machinery of society. I am not the son of the engineer. I perceive that, when an acorn and a chestnut fall side by side, the one does not remain inert to make way for the other, but both obey their own laws, and spring and grow and flourish as best they can, till one, perchance, over-shadows and destroys the other. If a plant cannot live according to its nature, it dies; and so a man.

The night in prison was novel and interesting enough. The prisoners in their shirt-sleeves were enjoying a chat and the evening air in the doorway, when I entered. But the jailer said, "Come, boys, it is time to lock up;" and so they dispersed, and I heard the sound of their steps returning into the hollow apartments. My room-mate was introduced to me by the jailer, as "a first-rate fellow and a clever man." When the door was locked, he showed me where to hang my hat, and how he managed matters there. The rooms were white-washed once a month; and this one, at least, was the whitest, most simply furnished, and probably the neatest apartment in the town. He naturally wanted to know where I came from, and what brought me there; and, when I had told him, I asked him in my turn how he came there, presuming him to be an honest man, of course; and, as the world goes, I believe he was. "Why," said he, "they accuse me of burning a barn; but I never did it." As near as I could discover, he had probably gone to bed in a barn when drunk, and smoked his pipe there; and so a barn was burnt. He had the reputation of being a clever man, had been there some three months waiting for his trial to come on, and would have to wait as much longer: but he was quite domesticated and contented, since he got his board for nothing, and thought that he was well treated.

He occupied one window, and I the other; and I saw, that, if one stayed there long, his principal business would be to look out the window. I had soon read all the tracts that were left there, and examined where former prisoners had broken out, and where a grate had been sawed off, and heard the history of the various occupants of that room; for I found that even here there was a history and gossip which never circulated beyond the walls of the jail. Probably this is the only house in the town where verses are composed, which are afterward printed in a circular form, but not published. I was shown quite a long list of verses which were composed by some young men who had been detected in an attempt to escape, who avenged themselves by singing them.

I pumped my fellow-prisoner as dry as I could, for fear I should never see him again; but at length he showed me which was my bed, and left me to blow out the lamp.

It was like travelling into a far country, such as I had never expected to behold, to lie there for one night. It seemed to me that I never had heard the town-clock strike before, nor the evening sounds of the village; for we slept with the windows open, which were inside the grating. It was to see my native village in the light of the middle ages, and our Concord was turned into a Rhine stream, and visions of knights and castles passed before me. They were the voices of old burghers that I heard in the streets. I was an involuntary spectator and auditor of whatever was done and said in the kitchen of the adjacent village-inn,—a wholly new and rare experience to me. It was a closer view of my native town. I was fairly inside of it. I never had seen its institutions before. This is one of its peculiar institutions; for it is a shire town. I began to comprehend what its inhabitants were about.

In the morning, our breakfasts were put through the hole in the door, in small oblong-square tin pans, made to fit, and holding a pint of chocolate, with brown bread, and an iron spoon. When they called for the vessels again, I was green enough to return what bread I had left; but my comrade seized it, and said that I should lay that up for lunch or dinner. Soon after, he was let out to work at haying in a neighboring field, whither he went every day, and would not be back till noon; so he bade me good-day, saying that he doubted if he should see me again.

When I came out of prison,—for some one interfered, and paid the tax,—I did not perceive that great changes had taken place on the common, such as he observed who went in a youth and emerged a tottering and gray-headed man; and yet a change had to my eyes come over the scene,—the town, and State and country,—greater than any that mere time could effect. I saw yet more distinctly the State in which I lived. I saw to what extent the people among whom I lived could be trusted as good neighbors and friends; that their friendship was for summer weather only; that they did not greatly purpose to do right; that they were a distinct race from me by their prejudices and superstititions, as the Chinamen and Malays are; that, in their sacrifices to humanity, they ran no risks, not even to their property; that, after all, they were not so noble but they treated the thief as he had treated them, and hoped, by a certain outward observance and a few prayers, and by walking in a particular straight though useless path from time to time, to save their souls. This may be to judge my neighbors harshly; for I believe that most of them are not aware that they have such an institution as the jail in their village.

It was formerly the custom in our village, when a poor debtor came out of jail, for his acquaintances to salute him, looking through their fingers, which were crossed to represent the grating of a jail window, "How do ye do?" My neighbors did not thus salute me, but first looked at me, and then at one another, as if I had returned from a long journey. I was put into jail as I was going to the shoemaker's to get a shoe which was mended. When I was let out the next morning, I proceeded to finish my errand, and, having put on my mended shoe, joined a huckleberry party, who were impatient to put themselves under my conduct; and in half an hour,—for the horse was soon tackled,—was in the midst of a huckleberry field, on one of our highest hills, two miles off; and then the State was nowhere to be seen.

This is the whole history of "My Prisons."

I have never declined paying the highway tax, because I am as desirous of being a good neighbor as I am of being a bad subject; and as for supporting schools, I am doing my part to educate my fellow-countrymen now. It is for no particular item in the tax-bill that I refuse to pay it. I simply wish to refuse allegiance to the State, to withdraw and stand aloof from it effectually. I do not care to trace the course of my dollar, if I could, till it buys a man, or a musket to shoot one with,—the dollar is innocent,—but I am concerned to trace the effects of my allegiance. In fact, I quietly declare war with the State, after my fashion, though I will still make what use and get what advantage of her I can, as is usual in such cases.

If others pay the tax which is demanded of me, from a sympathy with the State, they do but what they have already done in their own case, or rather they abet injustice to a greater extent than the State requires. If they pay the tax from a mistaken interest in the individual taxed, to save his property or prevent his going to jail, it is because they have not considered wisely how far they let their private feelings interfere with the public good.

This, then, is my position at present. But one cannot be too much on his guard in such a case, lest his action be biassed by obstinacy or an undue regard for the opinions of men. Let him see that he does only what belongs to himself and to the hour.

I think sometimes, Why, this people mean well; they are only ignorant; they would do better if they knew how: why give your neighbors this pain to treat you as they are not inclined to? But I think, again, this is no reason why I should do as they do, or permit others to suffer much greater pain of a different kind. Again, I sometimes say to myself, When many millions of men, without heat, without ill-will, without personal feeling of any kind, demand of you a few shillings only, without the possibility, such is their constitution, of retracting or altering their present demand, and without the possibility, on your side, of appeal to any other millions, why expose yourself to this overwhelming brute force? You do not resist cold and hunger, the winds and the waves, thus obstinately; you quietly submit to a thousand similar necessities. You do not put your head into the fire. But just in proportion as I regard this as not wholly a brute force, but partly a human force, and consider that I have relations to those millions as to so many millions of men, and not of mere brute or inanimate things, I see that appeal is possible, first and instantaneously, from them to the Maker of them, and, secondly, from them to themselves. But if I put my head deliberately into the fire, there is no appeal to fire or to the Maker of fire, and I have only myself to blame. If I could convince myself that I have any right to be satisfied with men as they are, and to treat them accordingly, and not according, in some respects, to my requisitions and expectations of what they and I ought to be, then, like a good Mussulman and fatalist, I should endeavor to be satisfied with things as they are, and say it is the will of God. And, above all, there is this difference between resisting this and a purely brute or natural force, that I can resist this with some effect; but I cannot expect, like Orpheus, to change the nature of the rocks and trees and beasts.

I do not wish to quarrel with any man or nation. I do not wish to split hairs, to make fine distinctions, or set myself up as better than my neighbors. I seek rather, I may say, even an excuse for conforming to the laws of the land. I am but too ready to conform to them. Indeed I have reason to suspect myself on this head; and each year, as the tax-gatherer comes round, I find myself disposed to review the acts and position of the general and state governments, and the spirit of the people, to discover a pretext for conformity. I believe that the State will soon be able to take all my work of this sort out of my hands, and then I shall be no better a patriot than my fellow-countrymen. Seen from a lower point of view, the Constitution, with all its faults, is very good; the law and the courts are very respectable; even this State and this American government are, in many respects, very admirable and rare things, to be thankful for, such as a great many have described them; but seen from a point of view a little higher, they are what I have described them; seen from a higher still, and the highest, who shall say what they are, or that they are worth looking at or thinking of at all?

However, the government does not concern me much, and I shall bestow the fewest possible thoughts on it. It is not many moments that I live under a government, even in this world. If a man is thought-free, fancy-free, imagination-free, that which *is not* never for a long time appearing *to be* to him, unwise rulers or reformers cannot fatally interrupt him.

I know that most men think differently from myself; but those whose lives are by profession devoted to the study of these or kindred subjects, content me as little as any. Statesmen and legislators, standing so completely within the institution, never distinctly and nakedly behold it. They speak of moving society, but have no resting-place without it. They may be men of a certain experience and discrimination, and have no doubt invented ingenious and even useful systems, for which we sincerely thank them; but all their wit and usefulness lie within certain not very wide limits. They are wont to forget that the world is not governed by policy and expediency. Webster never goes behind government, and so cannot speak with authority about it. His words are wisdom to those legislators who contemplate no essential reform in the existing government; but for thinkers, and those who legislate for all time, he never once glances at the subject. I know of those whose serene and wise speculations on this theme would soon reveal the limits of his mind's range and hospitality. Yet, compared with the cheap professions of most reformers, and the still cheaper wisdom and eloquence of politicians in general, his are almost the only sensible and valuable words, and we thank Heaven for him. Comparatively, he is always strong, original, and, above all, practical. Still his quality is not wisdom, but prudence. The lawyer's truth is not Truth, but consistency or a consistent expediency. Truth is always in harmony with herself, and is not concerned chiefly to reveal the justice that may consist with wrong-doing. He well deserves to be called, as he has been called, the Defender of the Constitution. There are really no blows to be given by him but defensive ones. He is not a leader, but a follower. His leaders are the men of '87. "I have never made an effort," he says, "and never propose to make an effort; I have never countenanced an effort, and never mean to countenance an effort, to disturb the arrangement as originally made, by which the various States came into the Union." Still thinking of the sanction which the Constitution gives to slavery, he says, "Because it was a part of the original compact,—let it stand." Notwithstanding his special acuteness and ability, he is unable to take a fact out of its merely political relations, and behold it as it lies absolutely to be disposed of by the intellect,—what, for instance, it behoves a man to do here in America to-day with regard to slavery, but ventures, or is driven, to make some such desperate answer as the following, while professing to speak absolutely, and as a private man,—from which what new and singular code of social duties might be inferred?—"The manner," says he, "in which the governments of those States where slavery exists are to regulate it, is for their own consideration, under their responsibility to their constituents, to the general laws of propriety, humanity, and justice, and to God. Associations formed elsewhere, springing from a feeling of humanity, or any other cause, have nothing whatever to do with it. They have never received any encouragement from me, and they never will." *

They who know of no purer sources of truth, who have traced up its stream no higher, stand, and wisely stand, by the Bible and the Constitution, and drink at it there with reverence and humility; but they who behold where it comes trickling into this lake or that pool, gird up their loins once more, and continue their pilgrimage toward its fountainhead.

No man with a genius for legislation has appeared in America. They are rare in the history of the world. There are orators, politicians, and eloquent men, by the thousand; but the speaker has not yet opened his mouth to speak, who is capable of settling the much-vexed questions of the day. We love eloquence for its own sake, and not for any truth which it may utter, or any heroism it may inspire. Our legislators have not yet learned the comparative value of free-trade and of freedom, of union, and of rectitude, to a nation. They have no genius or talent for comparatively humble questions of taxation and finance, commerce and manufactures and agriculture. If we were left solely to the wordy wit of legislators in Congress for our guidance, uncorrected by the seasonable experience and the effectual complaints of the people, America would not long retain her rank among the nations. For eighteen hundred years, though perchance I have no right to

* These extracts have been inserted since the Lecture was read.

say it, the New Testament has been written; yet where is the legislator who has wisdom and practical talent enough to avail himself of the light which it sheds on the science of legislation?

The authority of government, even such as I am willing to submit to,—for I will cheerfully obey those who know and can do better than I, and in many things even those who neither know nor can do so well,—is still an impure one: to be strictly just, it must have the sanction and consent of the governed. It can have no pure right over my person and property but what I concede to it. The progress from an absolute to a limited monarchy, from a limited monarchy to a democracy, is a progress toward a true respect for the individual. Is a democracy, such as we know it, the last improvement possible in government? Is it not possible to take a step further towards recognizing and organizing the rights of man? There will never be a really free and enlightened State, until the State comes to recognize the individual as a higher and independent power, from which all its own power and authority are derived, and treats him accordingly. I please myself with imagining a State at last which can afford to be just to all men, and to treat the individual with respect as a neighbor; which even would not think it inconsistent with its own repose, if a few were to live aloof from it, not meddling with it, nor embraced by it, who fulfilled all the duties of neighbors and fellowmen. A State which bore this kind of fruit, and suffered it to drop off as fast as it ripened, would prepare the way for a still more perfect and glorious State, which also I have imagined, but not yet anywhere seen.

His protest made, Thoreau went cheerily off to pick huckleberries. His essay in Aesthetic Papers *did not cause much comment. Perhaps it only confirmed the common belief that he was, after all, either a wild man who lived in the woods or a conceited fool who delighted, said James Russell Lowell, in perversity of thought. Even Emerson told Bronson Alcott that Thoreau's action had been "mean and skulking, and in bad taste." But privately to his journal Emerson confided that at least Thoreau was different from Daniel Webster. Webster had lately warned Congress that the war would be expensive, but had voted for it and sent his son off to it. "They calculated rightly on Mr. Webster." But, he went on, "My friend Mr. Thoreau has gone to jail rather than pay his tax. On him they could not calculate."*

Nor could one have calculated in 1849 that his essay would have blossomed into a long and splended life of world-wide usefulness, continuing long after his death. Around 1900, Leo Tolstoy, in Russia, happened to read it. Tolstoy was a man of intense moral convictions. For him, as for Thoreau, complex problems of state and society resolved themselves into simple, radical, moral imperatives. Having read it, he sat down and wrote a letter to the North American Review: *Why, he asked, did Americans listen to their big businessmen and military leaders? Why not to Thoreau? He had wisdom. His mind cut through conventions to the simple truth of things. What he believed, that he did.*

Down in South Africa, a few years later, a little-known Hindu lawyer happened to read Thoreau's essay. He was hard at work defending his fellow Indians who had violated the discriminatory Asiatic Registration Act. He found the essay "so convincing and truthful" that he became a lifelong admirer of Thoreau. In the end, by turning Thoreau's individual protest into a mass movement of civil disobedience, he set India free. His name was Mohandas K. Gandhi. On October 22, 1907, he reprinted part of Thoreau's essay in his newspaper, Indian Opinion. *Soon after, it appeared in pamphlet form. Readers of* Indian Opinion *were invited to submit essays in a contest on "The Ethics of Passive Resistance," using Thoreau's essay as one of their sources. When the entries were judged, Gandhi was himself in jail for refusing to register as an Indian. He had started his forty-year campaign of civil disobedience and nonviolent resistance.*

With Gandhi civil disobedience was a potent instrument of social action. It required the strictest self-discipline from his followers. Often they were beaten, clubbed, trampled upon; sometimes they died. But always unprotestingly. Always, when the first rank was beaten down, there came a second rank, and a third, and a fourth. And always in the end they won. In 1930, the British government having established a monopoly of salt manufacture, Gandhi led his followers to the seashore to produce salt by evaporating sea water. For this violation of law he was thrown into prison. But Indians by the hundreds, by the thousands, followed his example. They marched up to the stockades around the salt pans to be struck down by policemen with five-foot steel-tipped clubs. But, ultimately, the law was repealed. By similar campaigns Mahatma Gandhi and his faithful followers broke down the traditional restrictions which made the lives of the untouchables almost beyond endurance. By nonviolent civil disobedience, with much suffering but with stoic self-control, the

Gandhian movement of mass civil disobedience moved on to achieve in 1947 its ultimate goal—self-government for India.

Gandhi always carried a copy of Thoreau's essay with him, even to jail. So he told Roger Baldwin, the American libertarian. It contained, he said, "the essence of his political philosophy, not only as India's struggle related to the British, but as to his own views of the relation of citizens to government." One might almost say that Henry David Thoreau of Concord freed India, a century after his own night in prison.

All over the world strong-minded individuals have read Thoreau's essay, and it has made a difference to them. In 1898 Robert Blatchford, an English writer, published a book called Merrie England. Its pages were steeped in Thoreau. Its stimulation of a little group of men and women, some have said, led to the founding of the British Labour Party. Emma Goldman, the Russian-born anarchist whose radical activities shocked staid middle-class Americans before and after 1900, drew on Thoreau for some of her ideas. She and novelist Upton Sinclair and Socialist Norman Thomas, each acting independently, have read Thoreau's essay in public in times of tension—and have been arrested for it. When Denmark was occupied by the Nazis in World War II, the essay was widely circulated in the resistance movement. Even King Christian took part in some of the mass acts of civil disobedience. These Thoreau-inspired acts often baffled and frustrated the Nazi occupying forces.

In recent years in the United States, Thoreau's ideas have come to life most fruitfully, chiefly among the Negroes in the South. In Montgomery, Alabama, Negroes steadfastly refused to ride on segregated buses—and gained thereby the right to sit where they chose. In Nashville, Tennessee, and elsewhere they entered white churches in a "kneel-in"—and won the right there to worship God, who is no respecter of persons. And so on through a long list of courageous well-disciplined acts of nonviolent civil disobedience.

The leaders of these movements have left little doubt about the ultimate source of their philosophy. More than twenty years ago, the Reverend James Robinson noted that the abolitionists, a century before, had paid little attention to Thoreau's "Civil Disobedience." But "as one reads the essay," he went on, writing for a Negro audience, "it is impossible not to notice that almost every sentence is loaded with meaning for us today. . . . Substitute the economic, political, and social persecution of American Negroes today where Thoreau condemns Negro slavery—and you will scarcely find half a dozen sentences in the entire essay which you cannot apply to your own actions in the present crisis." Among the readers of Robinson's article were the founders of CORE (the Congress of Racial Equality), one of the organizations which have led the way toward civil rights for Negroes in the United States.

And the Reverend Martin Luther King in his autobiographical Stride toward Freedom *recalls that early in December, 1955, when he was planning the boycott of segregated buses in Montgomery, Alabama, he suddenly remembered Thoreau's essay, which he had read in college. What he and his fellow Negroes were about to do, he realized, was precisely what Thoreau had done in 1846. "We were simply saying to the white community, 'We can no longer lend our coöperation to an evil system.' . . . From this moment on I conceived of our movement as an act of massive non-coöperation."*

Thoreau would have been pleased. His own protest had been purely an individual act. Long after he was dead, it had become the inspiration for a mass movement.

Horace Mann

Report of the Massachusetts Board of Education

1848

EDITED BY RALPH H. GABRIEL

Horace Mann was born and reared in poverty on a farm in Franklin, Massachusetts. As a child he endured winter terms of school which were presided over by ignorant masters, much given to the use of the rod. The hellfire Sunday sermons of his minister caused the sensitive boy many nights of mental anguish. A fortunate contact with an itinerant schoolmaster enabled young Mann to prepare for Brown University, from which he graduated in 1819 with high honors. He completed his training for the law at Tapping Reeve's famous law school at Litchfield, Connecticut. A successful legal practice, first in Dedham and then in Boston, prepared the way for state politics. Mann served first in the Massachusetts House and then in the Senate, becoming president of the latter body. In this capacity he signed a revolutionary educational bill which became law on April 20, 1837. The law, passed for the purpose of improving the quality of public education in the state, created a Board of Education, and empowered it to appoint a secretary and to make annual reports to the legislature.

Moved by the low estate of the schools of the Common-

wealth, Mann surprised his friends by abandoning his lucra-
tive practice and his political career to become secretary of the
Board of Education at a considerable reduction in income.
Traveling over the state, he surveyed a discouraging situation.
In 1843 he went abroad to study the school systems of Prus-
sia and England. The state support of schools in Prussia espe-
cially impressed the American, who felt more and more
strongly that education should be made available to all citi-
zens. Mann presented his findings in his seventh annual re-
port before the Massachusetts legislature, extolling the virtues
not only of tax support but also of graded schools. At the
same time, pulling no punches, he discussed the shortcomings
of the existing Massachusetts system. The Boston schoolmas-
ters replied with a drumfire attack which finally, together
with overwork, impaired Mann's health. In 1848 he wrote his
valedictory, the twelfth annual report of the Massachusetts
Board of Education. Later that year he resigned, having been
elected to the United States House of Representatives to suc-
ceed John Quincy Adams.

GENTLEMEN,—

Massachusetts may be regarded either as a State by herself, or as a member of a mighty and yet increasing
confederacy of States. In the former capacity, she has great
and abiding interests, which are mainly dependent upon her
own domestic or internal policy. In the latter relation, her
fate depends upon the will of her partners in the
association. . . .

Now, it is the especial province and function of the statesman and the lawgiver—of all those, indeed, whose influence
moulds or modifies public opinion—to study out the eternal
principles which conduce to the strength, wisdom, and righteousness of a community; to search for these principles as for
hidden riches; to strive for them as one would strive for his
life; and then to form public institutions in accordance with
them. And he is not worthy to be called a statesman, he is
not worthy to be a lawgiver or leader among men, who, either through the weakness of his head or the selfishness of his
heart, is incapable of marshalling in his mind the great ideas
of knowledge, justice, temperance, and obedience to the laws

The text is quoted from Mary Mann, ed., *Life and Works of Horace
Mann* (Boston, 1868).

of God,—on which foundation alone the structure of human welfare can be erected; who is not capable of organizing these ideas into a system, and then of putting that system into operation, as a mechanic does a machine. This only is true statesmanship. . . .

Without undervaluing any other human agency, it may be safely affirmed that the common school, improved and energized as it can easily be, may become the most effective and benignant of all the forces of civilization. Two reasons sustain this position. In the first place, there is a universality in its operation, which can be affirmed of no other institution whatever. If administered in the spirit of justice and conciliation, all the rising generation may be brought within the circle of its reformatory and elevating influences. And, in the second place, the materials upon which it operates are so pliant and ductile as to be susceptible of assuming a greater variety of forms than any other earthly work of the Creator. The inflexibility and ruggedness of the oak, when compared with the lithe sapling or the tender germ, are but feeble emblems to typify the docility of childhood when contrasted with the obduracy and intractableness of man. It is these inherent advantages of the common school, which, in our own State, have produced results so striking, from a system so imperfect, and an administration so feeble. In teaching the blind and the deaf and dumb, in kindling the latent spark of intelligence that lurks in an idiot's mind, and in the more holy work of reforming abandoned and outcast children, education has proved what it can do by glorious experiments. These wonders it has done in its infancy, and with the lights of a limited experience; but when its faculties shall be fully developed, when it shall be trained to wield its mighty energies for the protection of society against the giant vices which now invade and torment it,—against intemperance, avarice, war, slavery, bigotry, the woes of want, and the wickedness of waste,—then there will not be a height to which these enemies of the race can escape which it will not scale, nor a Titan among them all whom it will not slay.

I proceed, then, in endeavoring to show how the true business of the schoolroom connects iteslf, and becomes identical, with the great interests of society. The former is the infant, immature state of those interests; the latter their developed, adult state. As "the child is father to the man," so may the training of the schoolroom expand into the institutions and fortunes of the State.

PHYSICAL EDUCATION.

In the worldly prosperity of mankind, health and strength are indispensable ingredients. . . .

Leaving out, then, for the present purpose, all consideration of the pains of sickness and the anguish of bereavement, the momentous truth still remains, that sickness and premature death are positive evils for the statesman and political economist to cope with. The earth, as a hospital for the diseased, would soon wear out the love of life; and, if but the half of mankind were sick, famine, from non-production, would speedily threaten the whole.

Now, modern science has made nothing more certain than that both good and ill health are the direct result of causes mainly within our own control. In other words, the health of the race is dependent upon the conduct of the race. The health of the individual is determined primarily by his parents, secondarily by himself. The vigorous growth of the body, its strength and its activity, its powers of endurance, and its length of life, on the one hand; and dwarfishness, sluggishness, infirmity, and premature death on the other,—are all the subjects of unchangeable laws. These laws are ordained of God; but the knowledge of them is left to our diligence, and the observance of them to our free agency. . . .

My general conclusion, then, under this head, is, that it is the duty of all the governing minds in society—whether in office or out of it—to diffuse a knowledge of these beautiful and beneficent laws of health and life throughout the length and breadth of the State; to popularize them; to make them, in the first place, the common acquisition of all, and, through education and custom, the common inheritance of all, so that the healthful habits naturally growing out of their observance shall be inbred in the people, exemplified in the personal regimen of each individual, incorporated into the economy of every household, observable in all private dwellings, and in all public edifices, especially in those buildings which are erected by capitalists for the residence of their work-people, or for renting to the poorer classes; obeyed, by supplying cities with pure water; by providing public baths, public walks, and public squares; by rural cemeteries; by the drainage and sewerage of populous towns, and by whatever else may promote the general salubrity of the atmosphere: in fine, by a religious observance of all those sanitary regulations with which modern science has blessed the world.

For this thorough diffusion of sanitary intelligence, the

common school is the only agency. It is, however, an adequate agency. . . .

INTELLECTUAL EDUCATION AS A MEANS OF REMOVING POVERTY, AND SECURING ABUNDANCE.

. . . According to the European theory, men are divided into classes,—some to toil and earn, others to seize and enjoy. According to the Massachusetts theory, all are to have an equal chance for earning, and equal security in the enjoyment of what they earn. The latter tends to equality of condition; the former, to the grossest inequalities. . . .

But is it not true that Massachusetts, in some respects, instead of adhering more and more closely to her own theory, is becoming emulous of the baneful examples of Europe? The distance between the two extremes of society is lengthening, instead of being abridged. With every generation, fortunes increase on the one hand, and some new privation is added to poverty on the other. We are verging towards those extremes of opulence and of penury, each of which unhumanizes the human mind. A perpetual struggle for the bare necessaries of life, without the ability to obtain them, makes men wolfish. Avarice, on the other hand, sees, in all the victims of misery around it, not objects for pity and succor, but only crude materials to be worked up into more money.

I suppose it to be the universal sentiment of all those who mingle any ingredient of benevolence with their notions on political economy, that vast and overshadowing private fortunes are among the greatest dangers to which the happiness of the people in a republic can be subjected. Such fortunes would create a feudalism of a new kind, but one more oppressive and unrelenting than that of the middle ages. The feudal lords in England and on the Continent never held their retainers in a more abject condition of servitude than the great majority of foreign manufacturers and capitalists hold their operatives and laborers at the present day. The means employed are different; but the similarity in results is striking. What force did then, money does now. The villein of the middle ages had no spot of earth on which he could live, unless one were granted to him by his lord. The operative or laborer of the present day has no employment, and therefore no bread, unless the capitalist will accept his services. The vassal had no shelter but such as his master provided for him. Not one in five thousand of English operatives or farm-laborers is able to build or own even a hovel; and therefore they must accept such shelter as capital offers them. The baron

prescribed his own terms to his retainers: those terms were
peremptory, and the serf must submit or perish. The British
manufacturer or farmer prescribes the rate of wages he will
give to his work-people; he reduces these wages under whatever pretext he pleases; and they, too, have no alternative but
submission or starvation. In some respects, indeed, the condition of the modern dependant is more forlorn than that of
the corresponding serf class in former times. Some attributes
of the patriarchal relation did spring up between the lord and
his lieges to soften the harsh relations subsisting between
them. Hence came some oversight of the condition of children, some relief in sickness, some protection and support in
the decrepitude of age. But only in instances comparatively
few have kindly offices smoothed the rugged relation between
British capital and British labor. The children of the work-
people are abandoned to their fate; and notwithstanding the
privations they suffer, and the dangers they threaten, no
power in the realm has yet been able to secure them an education; and when the adult laborer is prostrated by sickness,
or eventually worn out by toil and age, the poor-house, which
has all along been his destination, becomes his destiny. . . .

Now, surely nothing but universal education can counter-
work this tendency to the domination of capital and servility
of labor. If one class possesses all the wealth and the education, while the residue of society is ignorant and poor, it matters not by what name the relation between them may be
called: the latter, in fact and in truth, will be the servile dependants and subjects of the former. But, if education be equa-
bly diffused, it will draw property after it by the strongest
of all attractions, for such a thing never did happen, and
never can happen, as that an intelligent and practical body of
men should be permanently poor. Property and labor in different classes are essentially antagonistic; but property and
labor in the same class are essentially fraternal. The people of
Massachusetts have, in some degree, appreciated the truth,
that the unexampled prosperity of the State—its comfort, its
competence, its general intelligence and virtue—is attributable to the education, more or less perfect, which all its people
have received: but are they sensible of a fact equally important; namely, that it is to this same education that two-thirds
of the people are indebted for not being to-day the vassals of
as severe a tyranny, in the form of capital, as the lower classes of Europe are bound to in the form of brute force?

Education, then, beyond all other devices of human origin,
is the great equalizer of the conditions of men,—the bal-
ance-wheel of the social machinery. I do not here mean that

it so elevates the moral nature as to make men disdain and abhor the oppression of their fellow-men. This idea pertains to another of its attributes. But I mean that it gives each man the independence and the means by which he can resist the selfishness of other men. It does better than to disarm the poor of their hostility towards the rich: it prevents being poor. Agrarianism is the revenge of poverty against wealth. The wanton destruction of the property of others—the burning of hay-ricks and corn-ricks, the demolition of machinery because it supersedes hand-labor, the sprinkling of vitriol on rich dresses—is only agrarianism run mad. Education prevents both the revenge and the madness. On the other hand, a fellow-feeling for one's class or caste is the common instinct of hearts not wholly sunk in selfish regards for person or for family. The spread of education, by enlarging the cultivated class or caste, will open a wider area over which the social feelings will expand; and, if this education should be universal and complete, it would do more than all things else to obliterate factitious distinctions in society. . . .

In this fact, then, we find a solution of the problem that so long embarrassed inquirers. The reason why the mechanical and useful arts,—those arts which have done so much to civilize mankind, and which have given comforts and luxuries to the common laborer of the present day, such as kings and queens could not command three centuries ago,—the reason why these arts made no progress, and until recently, indeed, can hardly be said to have had any thing more than a beginning, is, that the labor of the world was performed by ignorant men. As soon as some degree of intelligence dawned upon the workman, then a corresponding degree of improvement in his work followed. At first, this intelligence was confined to a very small number, and therefore improvements were few; and they followed each other only after long intervals. They uniformly began in the nations and among the classes where there was most intelligence. The middle classes of England, and the people of Holland and Scotland, have done a hundred times more than all the Eastern hemisphere besides. What single improvement in art, or discovery in science, has ever originated in Spain, or throughout the vast empire of the Russias? But just in proportion as intelligence—that is, education—has quickened and stimulated a greater and a greater number of minds, just in the same proportion have inventions and discoveries increased in their wonderfulness, and in the rapidity of their succession. The progression has been rather geometrical than arithmetical. By the laws of Nature, it must be so. If, among ten well-educated children, the chance is that at least one of them will originate some new and useful process in the arts, or will discover some new scientific principle, or some new application of one, then, among a hundred such well-educated children, there is a moral certainty that there will be more than ten such originators or discoverers of new utilities; for the action of the mind is like the action of fire. One billet of wood will hardly burn alone, though dry as suns and north-west winds can make it, and though placed in the range of a current of air; ten such billets will burn well together; but a hundred will create a heat fifty times as intense as ten, will make a current of air to fan their own flame, and consume even greenness itself.

For the creation of wealth, then,—for the existence of a wealthy people and a wealthy nation,—intelligence is the grand condition. The number of improvers will increase as the intellectual constituency, if I may call it, increases. In former times, and in most parts of the world even at the present day, not one man in a million has ever had such a development of mind as made it possible for him to become a contributor to art or science. Let this development precede, and contributions, numberless, and of inestimable value, will be sure to follow. That political economy, therefore, which busies itself about capital and labor, supply and demand, interest and rents, favorable and unfavorable balances of trade, but leaves out of account the element of a widespread mental development, is nought but stupendous folly. The greatest of all the arts in political economy is to change a consumer into a producer; and the next greatest is to increase the producer's producing power,—an end to be directly attained by increasing his intelligence. For mere delving, an ignorant man is but little better than a swine, whom he so much resembles in his appetites, and surpasses in his powers of mischief. . . .

POLITICAL EDUCATION.

The necessity of general intelligence,—that is, of education (for I use the terms as substantially synonymous, because general intelligence can never exist without general education, and general education will be sure to produce general intelligence),—the necessity of general intelligence under a republican form of government, like most other very important truths, has become a very trite one. It is so trite, indeed, as to have lost much of its force by its familiarity. Almost all the champions of education seize upon this argument first of all, because it is so simple as to be understood by the ignorant, and so strong as to convince the sceptical. Nothing would be easier than to follow in the train of so many writers, and to demonstrate by logic, by history, and by the nature of the case, that a republican form of government, without intelligence in the people, must be, on a vast scale, what a madhouse, without superintendent or keepers, would be on a small one,—the despotism of a few succeeded by universal anarchy, and anarchy by despotism, with no change but from bad to worse. . . .

However elevated the moral character of a constituency may be, however well informed in matters of general science or history, yet they must, if citizens of a republic, understand something of the true nature and functions of the government under which they live. That any one, who is to participate in the government of a country when he becomes a man, should receive no instruction respecting the nature and functions of the government he is afterwards to administer, is a political solecism. In all nations, hardly excepting the most rude and barbarous, the future sovereign receives some training which is supposed to fit him for the exercise of the powers and duties of his anticipated station. Where, by force of law, the government devolves upon the heir while yet in a state of legal infancy, some regency, or other substitute, is appointed to act in his stead until his arrival at mature age; and, in the mean time, he is subjected to such a course of study and discipline as will tend to prepare him, according to the political theory of the time and the place, to assume the reins of authority at the appointed age. If in England, or in the most enlightened European monarchies, it would be a proof of restored barbarism to permit the future sovereign to grow up without any knowledge of his duties,—and who can doubt that it would be such a proof?—then, surely, it would be not less a proof of restored or of never-removed barbarism amongst us to empower any individual to use the elective franchise without preparing him for so momentous a trust. Hence the Constitution of the United States, and of our own State, should be made a study in our public schools. The partition of the powers of government into the three co-ordinate branches,—legislative, judicial, and executive,—with the duties appropriately devolving upon each; the mode of electing or of appointing all officers, with the reasons on which it was founded; and, especially, the duty of every citizen, in a government of laws, to appeal to the courts for redress in all cases of alleged wrong, instead of undertaking to vindicate his own rights by his own arm; and, in a government where the people are the acknowledged sources of power, the duty of changing laws and rulers by an appeal to the ballot, and not by rebellion,—should be taught to all the children until they are fully understood.

Had the obligations of the future citizen been sedulously inculcated upon all the children of this Republic, would the patriot have had to mourn over so many instances where the voter, not being able to accomplish his purpose by voting, has proceeded to accomplish it by violence; where, agreeing with his fellow-citizens to use the machinery of the ballot, he makes a tacit reservation, that, if that machinery does not move according to his pleasure, he will wrest or break it? If the responsibleness and value of the elective franchise were duly appreciated, the day of our state and national elections would be among the most solemn and religious days in the calendar. Men would approach them, not only with preparation and solicitude, but with the sobriety and solemnity with which discreet and religious-minded men meet the great crises of life. No man would throw away his vote through caprice or wantonness, any more than he would throw away his estate, or sell his family into bondage. No man would cast his vote through malice or revenge, any more than a good surgeon would amputate a limb, or a good navigator sail through perilous straits, under the same criminal passions.

But perhaps it will be objected, that the Constitution is subject to different readings, or that the policy of different administrations has become the subject of party strife; and, therefore, if any thing of constitutional or political law is introduced into our schools, there is danger that teachers will be chosen on account of their affinities to this or that political party, or that teachers will feign affinities which they do not feel in order that they may be chosen; and so each schoolroom will at length become a miniature political clubroom, exploding with political resolves, or flaming out with political addresses, prepared by beardless boys in scarcely legible hand-writing and in worse grammar.

With the most limited exercise of discretion, all apprehensions of this kind are wholly groundless. There are different readings of the Constitution, it is true; and there are partisan topics which agitate the country from side to side: but the controverted points, compared with those about which there is no dispute, do not bear the proportion of one to a hundred. And, what is more, no man is qualified, or can be qualified, to dicuss the disputable questions, unless previously and thoroughly versed in those questions about which there is no dispute. In the terms and principles common to all, and recognized by all, is to be found the only common medium of language and of idea by which the parties can become intelligible to each other; and there, too, is the only common ground whence the arguments of the disputants can be drawn. . . .

. . . Thus may all the children of the Commonwealth receive instruction in all the great essentials of political knowledge,—in those elementary ideas without which they will never be able to investigate more recondite and debatable questions; thus will the only practicable method be adopted for discovering new truths, and for discarding, instead of perpetuating, old errors; and thus, too, will that pernicious race of intolerant zealots, whose whole faith may be summed up in two articles,—that they themselves are always infallibly right, and that all dissenters are certainly wrong,—be extinguished,—extinguished, not by violence, nor by proscription, but by the more copious inflowing of the light of truth.

MORAL EDUCATION.

Moral education is a primal necessity of social existence. The unrestrained passions of men are not only homicidal, but suicidal; and a community without a conscience would soon extinguish itself. Even with a natural conscience, how often has evil triumphed over good! From the beginning of time, wrong has followed right, as the shadow the substance. . . .

But to all doubters, disbelievers, or despairers in human progress, it may still be said, there is one experiment which has never yet been tried. It is an experiment, which, even before its inception, offers the highest authority for its ultimate success. Its formula is intelligible to all; and it is as legible as though written in starry letters on an azure sky. It is expressed in these few and simple words: *"Train up a child in the way he should go; and, when he is old, he will not depart from it."* This declaration is positive. If the conditions are complied with, it makes no provision for a failure. Though pertaining to morals, yet, if the terms of the direction are observed, there is no more reason to doubt the result than there would be in an optical or a chemical experiment.

But this experiment has never yet been tried. Education has never yet been brought to bear with one-hundredth part of its potential force upon the natures of children, and, through them, upon the character of men and of the race. In all the attempts to reform mankind which have hitherto been made, whether by changing the frame of government, by aggravating or softening the severity of the penal code, or by substituting a government-created for a God-created religion, —in all these attempts, the infantile and youthful mind, its amenability to influences, and the enduring and self-operating character of the influences it receives, have been almost wholly unrecognized. Here, then, is a new agency, whose powers are but just beginning to be understood, and whose mighty energies hitherto have been but feebly invoked; and yet, from our experience, limited and imperfect as it is, we do know, that, far beyond any other earthly instrumentality, it is comprehensive and decisive. . . .

. . . So far as human instrumentalities are concerned, we have abundant means for surrounding every child in the State with preservative and moral influences as extensive and as efficient as those under which the present industrious, worthy, and virtuous members of the community were reared. And as to all those things in regard to which we are directly dependent upon the divine favor, have we not the promise, explicit and unconditional, that the men SHALL NOT depart from the way in which they should go, if the children are trained up in it? It has been overlooked that this promise is not restricted to parents, but seems to be addressed indiscriminately to all, whether parents, communities, states, or mankind. . . .

RELIGIOUS EDUCATION.

But it will be said that this grand result in practical morals is a consummation of blessedness that can never be attained without religion, and that no community will ever be religious without a religious education. Both these propositions I regard as eternal and immutable truths. Devoid of religious principles and religious affections, the race can never fall so low but that it may sink still lower; animated and sanctified by them, it can never rise so high but that it may ascend still higher. And is it not at least as presumptuous to expect that mankind will attain to the knowledge of truth, without being instructed in truth, and without that general expansion and development of faculty which will enable them to recognize and comprehend truth in any other department of human interest as in the department of religion? . . .

. . . That our public schools are not theological seminaries, is admitted. That they are debarred by law from inculcating the peculiar and distinctive doctrines of any one religious denomination amongst us, is claimed; and that they are also prohibited from ever teaching that what they do teach is the whole of religion, or all that is essential to religion or to salvation, is equally certain. But our system earnestly inculcates all Christian morals; it founds its morals on the basis of religion; it welcomes the religion of the Bible; and, in receiving the Bible, it allows it to do what it is allowed to do in no other system,—*to speak for itself*. But here it stops, not because it claims to have compassed all truth, but because it disclaims to act as an umpire between hostile religious opinions.

The very terms "public school" and "common school" bear upon their face that they are schools which the children of the entire community may attend. Every man not on the pauper-list is taxed for their support; but he is not taxed to support them as special religious institutions: if he were, it would satisfy at once the largest definition of a religious establishment. But he is taxed to support them as a *preventive* means against dishonesty, against fraud, and against violence, on the same principle that he is taxed to support criminal courts as a *punitive* means against the same offences. He is taxed to support schools, on the same principle that he is taxed to support paupers,—because a child without education is poorer and more wretched than a man without bread. He is taxed to support schools, on the same principle that he would be taxed to defend the nation against foreign invasion, or against rapine committed by a foreign foe,—because the general prevalence of ignorance, superstition, and vice, will breed Goth and Vandal at home more fatal to the public well-being than any Goth or Vandal from abroad. And, finally, he is taxed to support schools, because they are the most effective means of developing and training those powers and faculties in a child, by which, when he becomes a man, he may understand what his highest interests and his highest duties are, and may be in fact, and not in name only, a free agent. The elements of a political education are not bestowed upon any school child for the purpose of making him vote with this or that political party when he becomes of age, but for the purpose of enabling him to choose for himself with which party he will vote. So the religious education which a child receives at school is not imparted to him for the purpose of making him join this or that denomination when he arrives at years of discretion, but for the purpose of enabling him to judge for himself, according to the dictates of his own reason and conscience, what his religious obligations are, and whither they lead. . . .

I hold it, then, to be one of the excellences, one of the moral beauties, of the Massachusetts system, that there is one place in the land where the children of all the different denominations are brought together for instruction, where the Bible is allowed to speak for itself; one place where the children can kneel at a common altar, and feel that they have a common Father, and where the services of religion tend to create brothers, and not Ishmaelites. . . .

. . . In bidding an official farewell to a system with which I have been so long connected, to which I have devoted my means, my strength, my health, twelve years of time, and, doubtless, twice that number of years from what might otherwise have been my term of life, I have felt bound to submit these brief views in its defence. . . .

Such, then, in a religious point of view, is the Massachusetts system of common schools. Reverently it recognizes and affirms the sovereign rights of the Creator, sedulously and sacredly it guards the religious rights of the creature; while it seeks to remove all hinderances, and to supply all furtherances, to a filial and paternal communion between man and his Maker. In a social and political sense, it is a *free* school-system. It knows no distinction of rich and poor, of bond and free, or between those, who, in the imperfect light of this world, are seeking, through different avenues, to reach the gate of heaven. Without money and without price, it throws open its doors, and spreads the table of its bounty, for all the children of the State. Like the sun, it shines not only upon the good, but upon the evil, that they may become good; and, like the rain, its blessings descend not only upon the just, but upon the unjust, that their injustice may depart from them, and be known no more.

To the great founders of this system we look back with filial reverence and love. Amid the barrenness of the land, and in utter destitution of wealth, they coined the rude comforts, and even the necessaries, of life, into means for its generous support. Though, as laborers by day, they subdued the wilderness, and, as sentinels by night, they guarded the camp, yet they found time for the vigilant administration and oversight of the schools in the day of their infancy and weakness. But for this single institution, into which they transfused so much of their means and of their strength, and of which they have made us the inheritors, how different would our lot and our life have been! Upon us its accumulated blessings have descended. It has saved us from innumerable pains and perils that would otherwise have been our fate,—from the physical wretchedness that is impotent to work out its own relief, from the darkness of the intellect whose wanderings after light so often plunge it into deeper gloom, and from the moral debasement whose pleasures are vices and crimes. It has surrounded us with a profusion of comforts and blessings of which the most poetic imagination would never otherwise have conceived. It has found, not mythologic goddesses, but gigantic and tireless laborers, in every stream; not evil and vindictive spirits, but beneficent and helping ones, in all the elements; and, by a profounder alchemy than the schoolmen ever dreamed of, it transmutes quarries and ice-fields into gold. It has given cunning to the hand of the mechanic, keenness to the artisan's eye, and made a sterile soil grow grateful beneath the skill of the husbandman. Hence the absence of poverty among our native population; hence a competency for the whole people, the means for mental and moral improvement, and for giving embellishment and dignity to life, such as the world has never known before, and such as nowhere else can be found upon the face of the earth. . . .

Horace Mann launched the common school in the United States on a course which has brought public education to that extraordinary tax-supported system now extending from the kindergarten through the university. Laboring in an age when seminal ideas in educational theory and pedagogical practice came from Europe, Mann made no contribution to either. Instead, he worked to persuade the citizens of Massachusetts that the public interest required free schools for all children and that these schools should have the strength which only public funds could give. In carrying out this task he was supported by the lyceum movement inaugurated in 1826 and by the activities of the Western Literary Institute, which after its founding in Cincinnati, Ohio, in 1832 spread rapidly to most of the other states.

Mann's chief contribution to life in his own times lay in his formulation of a broad social philosophy which detailed the significance of universal education. He assumed the importance of the individual person as a unique center of value. He assumed that the institutions of society are instruments to further the welfare of men and women. He began with the problem of health in an age before the development of scientific medicine, when life expectancy was much less than half a century. His hopeful imagination enabled him to visualize an era protected and invigorated by an understanding of the requirements and the practices of public health. He felt the school to be an adequate instrument with which to bring in the new day. His confidence has proved justified; the historical record makes it clear that the role of the school, when the university is included, has been decisive on the issue of public health. The assumption of the importance of the individual person (child or adult) further led Mann to the conclusion that justice demands equality of opportunity for all citizens. He argued to his generation that "education . . . is the

great equalizer of the condition of men." The ideal of equality
of opportunity has become basic to American thought.

From the humanism and optimism of the eighteenth-
century Enlightenmeni Mann inherited the concept that man
is plastic and improvable. He saw universal education as an
instrument for bringing about more fully developed individuals and a more advanced society. Education furnishes the
mind of the individual and enables him to further his own
material well-being. When Sputnik I went into orbit in 1957,
complacent Americans were jolted into a new understanding
of Mann's remark in 1848: ". . . in proportion as intelligence
—that is education—has quickened and stimulated a greater
and greater number of minds, just in the same proportion
have inventions and discoveries increased in their wonderfulness, and in the rapidity of their successior." Anxious
Americans reacted appropriately.

Mann, working in a decade when universal manhood
suffrage represented a new democratic advance, carried on in
the tradition of Jefferson and Madison in his insistence that a
republican form of government requires a literate and informed electorate. He foresaw the dangers posed to public
schools by "the tempest of political strife." The developments
in history, social studies, and the social sciences in our
public educational establishment have validated his belief that
American democracy in essential things can rise above destructive partisanship. Mann believed in reason, in rational
analysis of the problems of society, and in rational efforts to
achieve their solution. This faith also is fundamental to twentieth-century American thought. Finally, the storm which
gathered in the 1960's about the question of religion in the
public school aemonstrated the importance which vast numbers of Americans attach to Mann's contention (made in
1848) that the Judeo-Christian tradition, which provides the
background of American civilization, must have a recognized
place in American schools.

The Seneca Falls Declaration of Sentiments and Resolutions

1848

EDITED BY BARBARA M. SOLOMON

At the obscure village of Seneca Falls, New York, in the summer of 1848, five women formulated a Declaration of Sentiments and Resolutions. The adoption of this document at the convention which followed marked the beginning of the organized movement for woman's rights in the United States.

For half a century before their meeting, there had been intellectual discussion of the proper sphere of woman in the new republic. The inherited doctrine of English law expounded in the influential Commentaries of Sir William Blackstone had made the married woman a legal nonentity; this was not consistent with the facts of her evolution. Since the 1600's, wives had been respected partners in American frontier communities. Moreover, religious freedom nurtured the individual conscience and spirit of woman, whether married or single. New opportunities through education and industrialization in the 1800's provided them with new outlets for independent activities.

At the same time, women were part of a nation in which the natural rights of man had been continuously invoked, first *to create and then to enlarge the meaning of democracy for its members. By the 1840's, improvement of the whole society was the common element in particular goals, whether reformers worked for temperance, peace, public schools, universal manhood suffrage, or the abolition of human slavery. For those who shared the vision of a perfectible society in America, steps to include women were logical. An important sign of the advancing times was the final passage, in April, 1848, by the New York state legislature of a law giving married women equal property rights. The radical demand for suffrage at Seneca Falls carried the social and political revolution for women into a new era.*

The particular impetus for this historic event came from Elizabeth Cady Stanton, a new resident in the remote community. Feeling for the first time the domestic isolation of most housewives, Mrs. Stanton shared her concern with her old colleague, Lucretia Mott, of Philadelphia, who was attending a Friends' Meeting nearby. Eight years earlier, the two had been among the delegates rejected from the Antislavery Convention in London because they were women. Now these feminists recalled their old resolve to hold a convention in America in behalf of their sex. Joined by Mrs. Mott's sister, Martha C. Wright, and two other Quaker friends, Jane Hunt and Mary Ann McClintock, they sent an unsigned notice to the Seneca Falls Courier *stating that "a Convention to discuss the social, civil, and religious conditions and rights of woman, will be held on Wednesday and Thursday, the 19th and 20th of July."*

Gathering the next day in the McClintocks' parlor to plan the meetings of the convention, the organizers used reports of antislavery and temperance conventions as guides. Still they were perplexed in their search for a convincing framework in which to present their cause to the public. Elizabeth Cady Stanton's reading of the Declaration of Independence to the group provided the solution. Responding to the enthusiasm of this legal-minded woman, daughter of a judge and wife of an abolitionist, the group paraphrased the familiar words of the nation's manifesto, substituting "man" for "King George" as the object of attack. Consulting even their husbands, they worked hard to find, in literal imitation of the great model, eighteen grievances reflecting the tyranny of man. The group then agreed that resolutions were needed to implement the "Declaration of Sentiments" they had composed.

When they dispersed to return for the convention five days later, it was left to Mrs. Stanton to complete the document, which was still in rough form. At home, she drafted the fa-

mous ninth resolution, asserting woman's sacred right to the vote. She had not discussed this resolution with the others. Henry Stanton, a journalist and reformer who was usually sympathetic with his wife's aspirations, urged her to abandon so revolutionary a statement. Despite his threat to leave town during the convention, Stanton could not dissuade her. Nor would she accept Lucretia Mott's counsel of moderation. Mrs. Stanton came to the convention determined to gain acceptance of the ninth resolution.

The convention attracted young and old women from outlying farms; and a surprising number of interested men, though uninvited, also appeared at the meeting in the Wesleyan Chapel. Since none of the leaders felt competent to conduct the assembly, James Mott, husband of Lucretia, was called to the chair. During the six sessions held in the two-day period, the audience discussed, amended, and voted upon each part of the "Declaration of Sentiments and Resolutions." Although the majority feared that the demand for suffrage would jeopardize the cause of woman's rights, Frederick Douglass, the emancipated Negro, eloquently defended Mrs. Stanton. After heated debate, the convention voted to acknowledge the right of American women to the elective franchise. When the document had been thoroughly reviewed and approved, Lucretia Mott offered a final resolution at the last session urging men and women to work for professional and vocational equality.

Having adopted the approaches of other reform groups, the feminists envisaged a succession of meetings in the near future. The final paragraph of the "Declaration" outlined their general plan of voluntary action, describing various means by which they hoped to engage wider support in the nation.

At the close of the convention, sixty-eight women and thirty-two men signed the new declaration for woman's rights, though some sources claim that when faced with the ridicule of the press many withdrew their names. One of the signers, Charlotte Woodward Pierce, lived to vote for President of the United States in 1920.

DECLARATION OF SENTIMENTS

WHEN, IN THE course of human events, it becomes necessary for one portion of the family of man to assume among the people of the earth a position different from that which they have hitherto occupied, but one to which the laws of nature and of nature's God entitle them, a decent respect to the opinions of mankind requires that they should declare the causes that impel them to such a course.

We hold these truths to be self-evident: that all men and women are created equal; that they are endowed by their Creator with certain inalienable rights; that among these are life, liberty, and the pursuit of happiness; that to secure these rights governments are instituted, deriving their just powers from the consent of the governed.—Whenever any form of Government becomes destructive of these ends, it is the right of those who suffer from it to refuse allegiance to it, and to insist upon the institution of a new government, laying its foundation on such principles, and organizing its powers in such form as to them shall seem most likely to effect their safety and happiness. Prudence, indeed, will dictate that governments long established should not be changed for light and transient causes; and accordingly, all experience hath shown that mankind are more disposed to suffer, while evils are sufferable, than to right themselves by abolishing the forms to which they are accustomed. But when a long train of abuses and usurpations, pursuing invariably the same object, evinces a design to reduce them under absolute despotism, it is their duty to throw off such government, and to provide new guards for their future security. Such has been the patient sufferance of the women under this government, and such is now the necessity which constrains them to demand the equal station to which they are entitled.

The history of mankind is a history of repeated injuries and usurpations on the part of man toward woman, having in direct object the establishment of an absolute tyranny over her. To prove this, let facts be submitted to a candid world.

The text used here is the earliest form of the "Declaration of Sentiments and Resolutions of the Seneca Falls Convention," included in the *Report of the Woman's Rights Convention, Held at Seneca Falls, N.Y., July 19th and 20th, 1848* (Rochester: North Star Office, 1848). The text differs in a few respects from a better-known version quoted in E. C. Stanton, S. B. Anthony, and M. J. Gage, *History of Woman Suffrage* (New York: Fowler and Wells, 1881), I, 70–73. According to the original *Report,* the resolutions were read the first day of the convention, discussed and approved the second afternoon; and finally at the evening session of the second day Lucretia Mott made the significant addition which was then incorporated permanently as the last resolution. A final statement ("Firmly relying upon the final triumph of the Right and the True, we do this day affix our signatures to this declaration") and an accompanying list of signers were omitted from the later version. Other differences between the 1848 and the 1881 texts, involving minor word changes and variations in punctuation, do not alter the basic meaning of the document.

He has never permitted her to exercise her inalienable right to the elective franchise.

He has compelled her to submit to laws, in the formation of which she had no voice.

He has withheld from her rights which are given to the most ignorant and degraded men—both natives and foreigners.

Having deprived her of this first right of a citizen, the elective franchise, thereby leaving her without representation in the halls of legislation, he has oppressed her on all sides.

He has made her, if married, in the eye of the law, civilly dead.

He has taken from her all right in property, even to the wages she earns.

He has made her, morally, an irresponsible being, as she can commit many crimes with impunity, provided they be done in the presence of her husband. In the convenant of marriage, she is compelled to promise obedience to her husband, he becoming, to all intents and purposes, her master—the law giving him power to deprive her of her liberty, and to administer chastisement.

He has so framed the laws of divorce, as to what shall be the proper causes of divorce; in case of separation, to whom the guardianship of the children shall be given; as to be wholly regardless of the happiness of women—the law, in all cases, going upon the false supposition of the supremacy of man, and giving all power into his hands.

After depriving her of all rights as a married woman, if single and the owner of property, he has taxed her to support a government which recognizes her only when her property can be made profitable to it.

He has monopolized nearly all the profitable employments, and from those she is permitted to follow, she receives but a scanty remuneration.

He closes against her all the avenues to wealth and distinction, which he considers most honorable to himself. As a teacher of theology, medicine, or law, she is not known.

He has denied her the facilities for obtaining a thorough education—all colleges being closed against her.

He allows her in Church as well as State, but a subordinate position, claiming Apostolic authority for her exclusion from the ministry, and, with some exceptions, from any public participation in the affairs of the Church.

He has created a false public sentiment, by giving to the world a different code of morals for men and women, by which moral delinquencies which exclude women from society, are not only tolerated but deemed of little account in man.

He has usurped the prerogative of Jehovah himself, claiming it as his right to assign for her a sphere of action, when that belongs to her conscience and her God.

He has endeavored, in every way that he could to destroy her confidence in her own powers, to lessen her self-respect, and to make her willing to lead a dependant and abject life.

Now, in view of this entire disfranchisement of one-half the people of this country, their social and religious degradation,—in view of the unjust laws above mentioned, and because women do feel themselves aggrieved, oppressed, and fraudulently deprived of their most sacred rights, we insist that they have immediate admission to all the rights and privileges which belong to them as citizens of these United States.

In entering upon the great work before us, we anticipate no small amount of misconception, misrepresentation, and ridicule; but we shall use every instrumentality within our power to effect our object. We shall employ agents, circulate tracts, petition the State and national Legislatures, and endeavor to enlist the pulpit and the press in our behalf. We hope this Convention will be followed by a series of Conventions, embracing every part of the country.

Firmly relying upon the final triumph of the Right and the True, we do this day affix our signatures to this declaration.

[The names of sixty-eight women and thirty-two men follow.]

RESOLUTIONS

Whereas, the great precept of nature is conceded to be, "that man shall pursue his own true and substantial happiness." Blackstone, in his Commentaries, remarks, that this law of Nature being coeval with mankind, and dictated by God himself, is of course superior in obligation to any other. It is binding over all the globe, in all countries, and at all times; no human laws are of any validity if contrary to this, and such of them as are valid, derive all their force, and all their validity, and all their authority, mediately and immediately, from this original; Therefore,

Resolved, That such laws as conflict, in any way, with the true and substantial happiness of woman, are contrary to the great precept of nature, and of no validity; for this is "superior in obligation to any other."

Resolved, That all laws which prevent woman from occupying such a station in society as her conscience shall dictate, or which place her in a position inferior to that of man, are contrary to the great precept of nature, and therefore of no force or authority.

Resolved, That woman is man's equal—was intended to be so by the Creator, and the highest good of the race demands that she should be recognized as such.

Resolved, That the women of this country ought to be enlightened in regard to the laws under which they live, that they may no longer publish their degradation, by declaring themselves satisfied with their present position, nor their ignorance, by asserting that they have all the rights they want.

Resolved, That inasmuch as man, while claiming for himself intellectual superiority, does accord to woman moral superiority, it is pre-eminently his duty to encourage her to speak, and teach, as she has an opportunity, in all religious assemblies.

Resolved, That the same amount of virtue, delicacy, and refinement of behavior, that is required of woman in the social state, should also be required of man, and the same transgressions should be visited with equal severity on both man and woman.

Resolved, That the objection of indelicacy and impropriety, which is so often brought against woman when she addresses a public audience, comes with a very ill grace from those who encourage, by their attendance, her appearance on the stage, in the concert, or in the feats of the circus.

Resolved, That woman has too long rested satisfied in the circumscribed limits which corrupt customs and a perverted application of the Scriptures have marked out for her, and that it is time she should move in the enlarged sphere which her great Creator has assigned her.

Resolved, That it is the duty of the women of this country to secure to themselves their sacred right to the elective franchise.

Resolved, That the equality of human rights results necessarily from the fact of the identity of the race in capabilities and responsibilities.

Resolved, therefore, That, being invested by the Creator with the same capabilities, and the same consciousness of responsibility for their exercise, it is demonstrably the right and duty of woman, equally with man, to promote every righteous cause, by every righteous means; and especially in regard to the great subjects of morals and religion, it is self-evidently her right to participate with her brother in teaching them, both in private and in public, by writing and by speaking, by any instrumentalities proper to be used, and in any assemblies proper to be held; and this being a self-evident truth, growing out of the divinely implanted principles of human nature, any custom or authority adverse to it, whether modern or wearing the hoary sanction of antiquity, is to be regarded as self-evident falsehood, and at war with the interests of mankind.

[At the last session Lucretia Mott offered and spoke to the following resolution:]

Resolved, That the speedy success of our cause depends upon the zealous and untiring efforts of both men and women, for the overthrow of the monopoly of the pulpit, and for the securing to woman an equal participation with men in the various trades, professions and commerce.

The authors of the Seneca Falls document succeeded in their immediate purposes. Through their endeavors a group of women and men had met and jointly endorsed a public statement of protest against the inequities experienced by American women in the law, in the economy, and in social and political relations.

Moreover, the convention attracted national attention, for newspapers throughout the country responded to its revolutionary theme with scorn, derision, or, less often, with praise. Retrospectively in 1881, the leaders felt impelled to record in the History of Woman Suffrage *that they themselves had been neither " 'sour old maids,' 'childless women,' nor 'divorced wives.' " Each stated that she had been married and, as a "proud, thinking woman," had begun the work for the rights of her sex. In fact, those initiating this movement could not fully interpret their own motives. They acted at Seneca Falls because the possibilities of self-realization for women were growing in the society of which they were a part. They were notable examples of the changing role of women in America.*

In 1848, the Seneca Falls "Declaration of Sentiments and Resolutions" went far beyond the expectations of most of the feminists present at the convention. In the perspective of history, however, the insistence upon the right to vote was an accurate forecast of things to come. During the next seventy-two years, the quest for suffrage proved the bond uniting three generations of women who believed with Elizabeth Cady Stanton that only through the exercise of the franchise would they eradicate the existing legal, economic, and social inequalities affecting their sex.

Although in subsequent conventions there were sporadic references to the Seneca Falls "Declaration" and even occasions at which the entire document was read, it never became an official manifesto of the movement. Yet it should be noted that no other document performed this function. Later advocates of woman's rights usually took for granted the philosophic rationale of the "Declaration of Sentiments" even when they tested new assumptions in their efforts to attain the original goals. Only after the passage of the Nineteenth Amendment in 1920 did the document acquire historic value and become a symbol of the pioneering feminist generations.

Even more basic to women's lives than the pursuit of suffrage was the long struggle to eliminate the economic and social grievances equally emphasized in the "Declaration of Sentiments and Resolutions." As the industrial society of democratic America matured during an era affected by three great wars, working women advanced in the professions, in the vocations, and in the labor force. Even though they enjoyed a good measure of achievement and an improved legal status in the 1960's, the psychological and social implications of the grievances of 1848 remained. From the Seneca Falls "Declaration" to the Report of the President's Commission on the Status of Women (October 11, 1963), there was a continuity of themes. The original concern for woman's rights and the attempt to resolve the diverse functions of women's lives still demanded consideration by those who shared, with the original group at Seneca Falls, a high standard of expectations for American women.

Elizabeth Cady Stanton

Address on the Divorce Bill

1861

EDITED BY NELSON M. BLAKE

In February, 1861, the New York legislature had under consideration a bill for liberalizing the state's divorce law. To the one ground—adultery—recognized since 1787, the proposed bill would add the grounds of willful desertion and cruel treatment. The proposal was by no means radical, since practically all the other states allowed divorce on a variety of grounds. Divorce law in America began to diverge from English law during colonial days. Although the mother country made no provision for absolute divorce until 1669 and then permitted it only by special act of Parliament, Puritan Massachusetts and Connecticut soon authorized their regular courts to dissolve marriages. After the Revolution most of the other states had made provision for granting divorce on several grounds. Between 1840 and 1861, reformers made persistent efforts to bring the New York law into line with that of the other states. On several occasions they came close to success, but they were never quite able to push their measures through against the opposition of powerful politicians like Horace Greeley and Thurlow Weed. The most able argument for the divorce bill of 1861 was delivered by Mrs. Elizabeth Cady Stanton at a special session attended not only by the

Senate Judiciary Committee but also by a large assemblage of curious politicians and guests.

Then near the midpoint of a remarkable life, Mrs. Stanton was one of the best-known public figures of the day. Born in 1815 in Johnstown, New York, Elizabeth Cady was strongly influenced by her early environment. Her father was Judge Daniel Cady, a shrewd country lawyer and politician; her mother was Margaret Livingston, daughter of a Revolutionary War colonel. Bantering debate with the young law clerks who studied in her father's office sharpened Elizabeth's wits, and two years at the famous Troy Female Seminary of Emma Willard rounded out her formal education. Most stimulating of all was the moral earnestness and passion for reform that Elizabeth encountered in frequent visits to the household of her cousin, the wealthy philanthropist Gerrit Smith. It was here, in the central New York village of Peterboro, that she met her future husband, Henry B. Stanton, ten years her senior and already a well-known abolitionist. Married at the age of twenty-four, she bore seven children. But the responsibilities of a large family did not prevent this strong-minded woman from playing an increasingly active role in the reform movements of the day. She helped organize the first woman's rights convention at Seneca Falls, New York, in 1848, and together with her close friend Susan B. Anthony she exercised leadership over the feminist movement throughout the succeeding years.

Although the right of suffrage was a major goal of the woman's rights movement, it was by no means the only one. Mrs. Stanton regarded contemporary marriage laws as hopelessly archaic, artfully contrived by male moralists and male legislators to bind women in a status not much better than slavery. The feminists won an important victory in 1860 when the New York legislature amended the laws to allow married women to retain their own property and earnings. Equally needed in Mrs. Stanton's eyes was a liberalized divorce law. Although happily married herself, she was filled with indignant compassion at the plight of many other wives deserted or cruelly treated, yet unable to gain their freedom under the harsh New York law.

GENTLEMEN OF THE JUDICIARY—In speaking to you, gentlemen, on such delicate subjects as marriage and divorce, in the revision of laws which are found in your statute books, I must use the language I find there.

May I not, without the charge of indelicacy, speak in a mixed assembly of Christian men and women, of wrongs which my daughter may to-morrow suffer in your courts, where there is no woman's heart to pity, and no woman's presence to protect?

I come not before you, gentlemen, at this time, to plead simply the importance of divorce in cases specified in your bill, but the justice of an entire revision of your whole code of laws on marriage and divorce. We claim that here, at least, woman's equality should be recognized. If civilly and politically man must stand supreme, let us at least be equals in our nearest and most sacred relations. . . .

When man suffers from false legislation, he has the remedy in his own hands; but an humble petition, protest or prayer, is all that woman can claim.

The contract of marriage, is by no means equal. From Coke down to Kent, who can cite one law under the marriage contract, where woman has the advantage? The law permits the girl to marry at twelve years of age, while it requires several years more of experience on the part of the boy. In entering this compact, the *man* gives up nothing that he before possessed; he is a *man* still: while the legal existence of the woman is suspended during marriage, and is known but in and through the husband. She is nameless, purseless, childless; though a woman, an heiress, and a mother.

Blackstone says, "the husband and wife are one, and that one is the husband." Kent says, "the legal effects of marriage are generally deducible from the principle of common law by which the husband and wife are regarded as one person, and her legal existence and authority lost or suspended during the continuance of the matrimonial union.". . .

The laws on divorce are quite as unequal as those on marriage; yes, far more so. The advantages seem to be all on one side, and the penalties on the other. In case of divorce, if the husband be the guilty party, he still retains a greater part of the property! If the wife be the guilty party, she goes out of the partnership penniless. . . . In New York, and some other states, the wife of the guilty husband can now sue for a divorce in her own name, and the costs come out of the husband's estate; but in a majority of the states she is still compelled to sue in the name of another, as she has no

The document is reprinted as it originally appeared, under the title *Address of Elizabeth Cady Stanton, on the Divorce Bill, Before the Judiciary Committee of the New York Senate, in the Assembly Chamber, Feb. 8, 1861* (Albany: Weed, Parsons and Company, Printers, 1861).

means of paying costs, even though she may have brought her thousands into the partnership. . . . "Many jurists," says Kent . . . , "are of opinion that the adultery of the husband ought not to be noticed or made subject to the same animadversions as that of the wife, because it is not evidence of such entire depravity, nor equally injurious in its effects upon the morals and good order, and happiness of domestic life." Montesquieu, Pothier, and Dr. Taylor, all insist, that the cases of husband and wife ought to be distinguished, and that the violation of the marriage vow, on the part of the wife, is the most mischievous, and the prosecution ought to be confined to the offense on her part." . . .

Say you, these are but the opinions of men? On what else, I ask, are the hundreds of women depending, who this hour demand in our courts a release from burdensome contracts? Are not these delicate matters left wholly to the discretion of the courts? Are not young women, from our first families, dragged into your public courts—into assemblies of men exclusively? The judges all men, the jurors all men! No true woman there to shield them, by her presence, from gross and impertinent questionings, to pity their misfortunes, or to protest against their wrongs! The administration of justice depends far more on the opinions of eminent jurists, than on law alone, for law is powerless, when at variance with public sentiment.

For years there has been before the legislature of this state, a variety of bills asking for divorce in cases of drunkenness, insanity, desertion, and cruel and brutal treatment, endangering life. My attention was called to this question very early in life, by the sufferings of a friend of my girlhood—a victim of one of those unfortunate unions, called marriage. What my great love for that young girl, and my holy intuitions, then decided to be right, has not been changed by years of experience, observation and reason. I have pondered well these things in my heart, and ever felt the deepest interest in all that has been written and said on this subject; and the most profound respect and loving sympathy for those heroic women, who, in the face of law and public sentiment, have dared to sunder the unholy ties of a joyless, loveless union.

If marriage is a human institution, about which man may legislate, it seems but just that he should treat this branch of his legislation with the same common sense that he applies to all others. If it is a mere legal contract, then should it be subject to the restraints and privileges of all other contracts. A contract, to be valid in law, must be formed between parties of mature age, with an honest intention in said parties to do what they agree. The least concealment, fraud, or intention to deceive, if proved, annuls the contract. A boy cannot contract for an acre of land, or a horse, until he is twenty-one, but he may contract for a wife at fourteen. If a man sell a horse, and the purchaser find in him "great incompatibility of temper"—a disposition to stand still, when the owner is in haste to go—the sale is null and void; the man and his horse part company. But in marriage, no matter how much fraud and deception are practised, nor how cruelly one or both parties have been misled; no matter how young or inexperienced or thoughtless the parties, nor how unequal their condition and position in life, the contract cannot be annulled. . . .

Marriage, as it now exists, must seem to all of you a mere human institution. Look through the universe of matter and mind—all God's arrangements are perfect, harmonious and complete; there is no discord, friction or failure in His eternal plans. Immutability, perfection, beauty, are stamped on all His laws. Love is the vital essence that pervades and permeates from center to circumference—the graduating circle of all thought and action; Love is the talisman of human weal and woe—the "open sesame" to every human soul. Where two human beings are drawn together by the natural laws of likeness and affinity, union and happiness are the result. Such marriages might be divine. But how is it now? You all know our marriage is, in many cases, a mere outward tie, impelled by custom, policy, interest, necessity; founded not even in friendship, to say nothing of love; with every possible inequality of condition and development. In these heterogeneous unions, we find youth and old age, beauty and deformity, refinement and vulgarity, virtue and vice, the educated and the ignorant, angels of grace and goodness with devils of malice and malignity; and the sum of all this is human wretchedness and despair—cold fathers, sad mothers and hapless children, who shiver at the hearthstone, where the fires of love have all gone out. The wide world and the stranger's unsympathizing gaze are not more to be dreaded for young hearts than homes like these. Now, who shall say that it is right to take two beings so unlike, and anchor them right side by side—fast bound—to stay all time, until God, in mercy shall summon one away?

Do wise Christian legislators need any arguments to convince them, that the sacredness of the family relation should be protected at all hazards? The family—that great conservator of national virtue and strength—how can you hope to build it up in the midst of violence, debauchery and excess. Can there be anything sacred, at that family altar, where the

chief priest who ministers, makes sacrifice of human beings
—of the weak and innocent? where the incense offered up is
not to a God of justice and mercy, but those heathen divini-
ties, who best may represent the lost man, in all his grossness
and deformity? Call that sacred, where woman, the mother
of the race—of a Jesus of Nazareth—unconscious of the true
dignity of her nature, of her high and holy destiny, consents
to live in legalized prostitution! her whole soul revolting at
such gross association! her flesh shivering at the cold contam-
ination of that embrace! held there by no tie but the iron
chain of the law, and a false and most unnatural public sentiment? Call that sacred, where innocent children, trembling
with fear, fly to the corners and dark places of the house, to
hide from the wrath of drunken, brutal fathers, but forgetting
their past sufferings, rush out again at their mother's frantic
screams, "Help! oh, help!" Behold the agonies of those
young hearts, as they see the only being on earth they love,
dragged about the room by the hair of her head, kicked and
pounded, and left half dead and bleeding on the floor! Call
that sacred, where fathers like these have the power and legal
right to hand down their natures to other beings, to curse
other generations with such moral deformity and death!

Men and brethren! look into your asylums for the blind,
the deaf and dumb, the idiot, the imbecile, the deformed, the
insane; go out into the by-lanes and dens of your cities, and
contemplate the reeking mass of depravity; pause before the
terrible revelations, made by statistics, of the rapid increase
of all this moral and physical impotency, and learn how fearful a thing it is, to violate the immutable laws of the beneficent Ruler of the Universe; and there behold the sorrowful
retributions of your violence on woman. Learn how false and
cruel are those institutions, which, with a coarse materialism,
set aside the holy instincts of the woman, to seek no union
but one of love.

Fathers! do you say, let your daughters pay a lifelong penalty for one unfortunate step? How could they, on the threshold of life, full of joy and hope, believing all things to be as
they seemed on the surface, judge of the dark windings of the
human soul? How could they foresee that the young man,
to-day, so noble, so generous, would, in a few short years, be
transformed into a cowardly, mean tyrant, or a foul-mouthed,
bloated drunkard? What father could rest at his home by
night, knowing that his lovely daughter was at the mercy of a
strong man, drunk with wine and passion, and that, do what
he might, he was backed up by law and public sentiment?
The best interests of the individual, the family, the state, the

nation, cry out against these legalized marriages of force and endurance.

There can be no heaven without love; and nothing is sacred in the family and home, but just so far, as it is built up and anchored in purity and peace. Our newspapers teem with startling accounts of husbands and wives having shot or poisoned each other, or committed suicide, choosing death rather than the indissoluble tie, and still worse, the living death of faithless men and women, from the first families in the land, dragged from the privacy of home into the public prints and courts, with all the painful details of sad, false lives.

Now, do you believe, honorable gentlemen, that all these wretched matches were made in heaven? that all these sad, miserable people are bound together by God? But, say you, does not separation cover all these difficulties? No one objects to separation, when the parties are so disposed. To separation, there are two serious objections: first, so long as you insist on marriage as a divine institution, as an indissoluble tie, so long as you maintain your present laws against divorce, you make separation, even, so odious, that the most noble, virtuous and sensitive men and women, choose a life of concealed misery, rather than a partial, disgraceful release. Secondly, those who, in their impetuosity and despair, do, in spite of public sentiment, separate, find themselves, in their new position, beset with many temptations to lead a false, unreal life. This isolation bears especially hard on woman. Marriage is not all of life to a man. His resources for amusement and occupation are boundless. He has the whole world for his home. His business, his politics, his club, his friendships, with either sex, can help to fill up the void, made by an unfortunate union, or separation. But to woman, as she is now educated, marriage is all and everything—her sole object in life —that for which she is taught to live—the all-engrossing subject of all her sleeping and her waking dreams. Now, if a noble girl of seventeen marries, and is unfortunate in her choice, because the cruelty of her husband compels separation, in her dreary isolation, would you drive her to a nunnery, and shall she be a nun indeed? She, innocent child, perchance the victim of a father's pride, or a mother's ambition, betrayed into a worldly union for wealth, or family, or fame, shall the penalty be all visited on the heart of the only guiltless one in the transaction? Henceforth, do you doom this fair young being, just on the threshold of womanhood, to a joyless, loveless solitude? By your present laws you say, though separated, she is married still; indissolubly bound to one she never loved; by whom she was never wooed or won; but by false guardians sold. And now, no matter though in the coming time her soul should, for the first time, wake to love, and one of God's own noblemen, should echo back her choice, the gushing fountains of her young affections must all be stayed. Because some man still lives, who once called her wife, no other man may give to her his love; and if she love not the tyrant to whom she is legally bound, she shall not love at all.

Think you that human law can set bounds to love? Alas! like faith, it comes upon us unawares. It is not by an act of will, we believe new doctrines, nor love what is true and noble in mankind. If you think it wise to legislate on human affections, pray make your laws with reference to what our natures are; let them harmonize in some measure with the immutable laws of God. A very wise father once remarked, that in the government of his children he forbid as few things as possible: a wise legislation would do the same. It is folly to make laws on subjects beyond human prerogative, knowing that in the very nature of things they must be set aside. To make laws that man cannot, and will not obey, serves to bring all law into contempt. It is all important in a republican government that the people should respect the laws: for if we throw law to the winds, what becomes of civil government?

What do our present divorce laws amount to? Those who wish to evade them have only to go into another state to accomplish what they desire. If any of our citizens cannot secure their inalienable rights in New York state, they may, in Connecticut and Indiana.

Why is it that all contracts, covenants, agreements and partnerships are left wholly at the discretion of the parties, except that which, of all others, is considered most holy and important, both for the individual and the race?

But, say you, what a condition we should soon have in social life, with no restrictive laws. I ask you, what have we now? Separation and divorce cases in all your courts; men disposing of their wives in every possible way; by neglect, cruelty, tyranny, excess, poison, and imprisonment in insane asylums. We would give the parties greater latitude, rather than drive either to extreme measures, or crime. If you would make laws for our protection, give us the power to release from legal conjugal obligations, all husbands who are unfit for that relation. Woman loses infinitely more than she gains, by the kind of protection you now impose; for, much as we love and honor true and noble men, life and liberty are dearer far to us, than even the legalized slavery of an indissoluble tie. In this state, are over forty thousand drunkards' wives, earnestly imploring you to grant them deliverance from their fearful bondage. Thousands of sad mothers, too, with helpless children, deserted by faithless husbands, some in California, some in insane asylums, and some in the gutter, all pleading to be released. They ask nothing, but a quit-claim deed to themselves.

Thus far, we have had the man-marriage, and nothing more. From the beginning, man has had the whole and sole regulation of the matter. He has spoken in Scripture, and he has spoken in law. As an individual, he has decided the time and cause for putting away a wife; and as a judge and legislator, he still holds the entire control. In all history, sacred and profane, woman is regarded and spoken of, simply, as the toy of man. She is taken or put away, given or received, bought or sold, just as the interests of the parties might dictate. But the woman has been no more recognized in all these transactions through all the different periods and conditions of the race, than if she had had no part or lot in the whole matter. The right of woman to put away a husband, be he ever so impure, is never hinted at in sacred history.

We cannot take our gauge of womanhood from the past, but from the solemn convictions of our own souls, in the higher development of the race. No parchments, however venerable with the mould of ages, no human institutions, can bound the immortal wants of the royal sons and daughters of the great I Am.

I place man above all governments, all institutions, ecclesiastical and civil, all constitutions and laws. It is a mistaken idea that the same law that oppresses the individual can promote the highest good of society. The best interests of a community never can require the sacrifice of one innocent being, of one sacred right.

In the settlement, then, of any question, we must simply consider the highest good of the individual. It is the inalienable right of all to be happy. It is the highest duty of all to seek those conditions in life, those surroundings, which may develop what is noblest and best, remembering that the lessons of these passing hours are not for time alone, but for the ages of eternity. They tell us, in that future home, the heavenly paradise, that the human family shall be sifted out, and the good and pure shall dwell together in peace. If that be the heavenly order, is it not our duty to render earth as near like heaven as we may? Inasmuch as the greater includes the less, let me repeat, that I come not before you to plead simply the importance of divorce in cases proposed in your bill, but the justice of an entire revision of your whole code of laws on marriage and divorce. In our common law, in our whole system of jurisprudence, we find man's highest idea of right. The object of law is to secure justice. But inasmuch as fallible man is the maker, administrator and adjudicator of law, we must look for many and gross blunders in the application of its general principles to individual cases. The science of theology, of civil, political, moral and social life, all teach the common idea that man ever has been, and ever must be, sacrificed to the highest good of society—the one to the many —the poor to the rich—the weak to the powerful—and all to the institutions of his own creation. Look, what thunderbolts of power man has forged in the ages for his own destruction! at the organizations to enslave himself! And through those times of darkness, those generations of superstition, behold, all along, the relics of his power and skill, that stand like milestones, here and there, to show how far back man was great and glorious. Who can stand in those vast cathedrals of the old world, as the deep-toned organ reverberates from arch to arch, and not feel the grandeur of immortality. Here is the incarnated thought of man, beneath whose stately dome, the man himself, now bows in fear and doubt—knows not himself—and knows not God, a mere slave to symbols— and with holy water signs the cross, while he who died thereon, declared man, God.

In closing, let me submit for your consideration the following propositions:

1st. In the language (slightly varied) of John Milton, "Those who marry intend as little to conspire their own ruin, as those who swear allegiance, and as a whole people is *to an ill government,* so is one man or woman to *an ill marriage.* If a whole people against any authority, covenant or statute, may, by the sovereign edict of charity, save not only their lives, but honest liberties, from unworthy bondage, as well may a married party, against any private covenant, which he or she never entered *to his or her mischief,* be redeemed from unsupportable disturbances to honest peace and just contentment."

2nd. Any constitution, compact or covenant between human beings, that failed to produce or promote human happiness, could not, in the nature of things, be of any force or authority; and it would be not only a right, but a duty to abolish it.

3rd. Though marriage be in itself divinely founded, and is fortified as an institution by innumerable analogies in the whole kingdom of universal nature, still, a true marriage is only known by its results; and like the fountain, if pure, will reveal only pure manifestations. Nor need it ever be said, "What God hath joined together, let not man put asunder," for man could not put it asunder; nor can he any more unite what God and nature have not joined together.

4th. Of all insulting mockeries of heavenly truth and holy law, none can be greater than that *physical impotency* is cause sufficient for divorce, while no amount of mental or moral or spiritual imbecility is ever to be pleaded in support of such a demand.

5th. Such a law was worthy those dark periods when marriage was held by the greatest doctors and priests of the Church to be a *work of the flesh only,* and almost, if not altogether, a defilement; denied wholly to the clergy, and a second time, forbidden to all.

6th. An unfortunate or ill-assorted marriage is ever a calamity, but not ever, perhaps never, a crime; and when society or government, by its laws or customs, compels its continuance, always to the grief of one of the parties, and the actual loss or damage of both, it usurps an authority never delegated to man, nor exercised by God himself.

7th. Observation and experience daily show how incompetent are men, as individuals, or as governments, to select partners in business, teachers for their children, ministers of their religion, or makers, adjudicators or administrators of their laws; and as the same weakness and blindness must attend in the selection of matrimonial partners, the dictates of humanity and common sense alike show that the latter and most important contract should no more be perpetual than either or all of the former.

8th. Children born in these unhappy and unhallowed connections, are in the most solemn sense of *unlawful birth*—the fruit of lust, but not of love; and so not of God, divinely descended, but from beneath, whence proceed all manner of evil and uncleanness.

9th. Next to the calamity of such a birth to the child, is the misfortune of being trained in the atmosphere of a household where love is not the law but where discord and bitterness abound; stamping their demoniac features on the moral nature, with all their odious peculiarities; thus continuing the race in a weakness and depravity that must be a sure precursor of its ruin, as a just penalty of a long violated law.

☆

Elizabeth Cady Stanton must be numbered among the com-

batants of history who have failed in their immediate objective but have been ultimately vindicated. Although the New York senate voted down the divorce bill of 1861, American attitudes toward divorce moved steadily in the direction of her humane point of view. No matter what the legal hurdles in any particular state, individuals unhappy in their marriages were usually able to find avenues of escape. And in the administration of the laws men and women were at last put upon an equal basis.

By no means daunted by her failure in 1861, Mrs. Stanton continued to agitate the marriage question. The arguments she had used in her address to the Judiciary Committee were repeated again and again in the post-Civil War years. From 1868 to 1870, Mrs. Stanton and Miss Susan B. Anthony published a weekly periodical called the Revolution, in which they advocated among other reforms the need for more rational divorce laws. When financial difficulties terminated this venture, the two women crisscrossed the country on arduous lecture tours. One of Mrs. Stanton's most popular addresses was that on "Marriage and Divorce"—an enlargement of her appeal to the New York legislature. "Women respond to this divorce speech," she declared, "as they never did to suffrage." Shortly before her death in 1902, she submitted to the newspapers her final plea for a more tolerant attitude toward divorce. "The States that have more liberal divorce laws," she wrote, "are for women today what Canada was for the fugitive in the old days of slavery."

By nailing the flag of liberal divorce laws to the staff of woman's rights, Mrs. Stanton provoked bitter controversy. Disagreement on this issue played a major part in splitting the feminist movement into radical and conservative factions for a period of twenty years. Indeed, Mrs. Stanton was waging her campaign in the face of a highly determined countermovement, led by the many religious leaders who were trying to make divorce more difficult.

Strong though the conservative movement appeared to be, changing economic and social conditions were favoring the more liberal attitude championed by Mrs. Stanton. As women acquired more education and more vocational opportunities, they demanded much more of marriage. Now confident of their ability to make an independent living, they would no longer endure unhappiness in their family affairs. In earlier days the woman who resorted to divorce had encountered a cruel form of social ostracism, but after World War I the harsher taboos were seldom imposed. Since the nation's divorce laws are not materially different today from those of a *hundred years ago, the increasing frequency of divorce in our own times is largely to be explained by changing popular attitudes. Resort to the divorce court now appears to be regarded as permissible conduct—except possibly for clergymen and presidential candidates.*

Before the nineteenth century divorce had been almost exclusively a masculine prerogative; indeed, the best argument for indissoluble marriage had been that it protected helpless wives against willful husbands who wanted to cast off their old mates and take on new ones. But Mrs. Stanton and likeminded women of the nineteenth century believed that wives were more injured than helped by rigid divorce laws. Husbands who tired of their partners had only to desert them and run away to other parts—often finding female companionship outside the law. But deserted or mistreated wives faced a life of misery unless they could be set free from their oppressors and allowed to marry again. In the late nineteenth and twentieth centuries many more women than men appeared as plaintiffs in divorce actions. The statistics were, to be sure, somewhat misleading, since in cases where husband and wife both wanted the divorce, gallantry usually demanded that the woman be allowed to make the formal accusations. But even when due allowance was made for this practice, it was clear that women more often than men were now the real initiators of divorce proceedings.

It is a measure of the slow response of legislation to changing mores that so much of Mrs. Stanton's criticism of the divorce laws of her day remains relevant a hundred years later. Not until 1966 did the New York legislature finally amend the law to permit divorce on grounds other than adultery. In the end, the logic of Mrs. Stanton's argument could not be denied. "What do our present divorce laws amount to? Those who wish to evade them have only to go into another state to accomplish what they desire."

But the larger implications of Mrs. Stanton's indictment reach much farther than New York State. She believed that marriage was a human institution—divine only to the degree that a particular union contributed to human happiness. When hatred displaced love, she was convinced that it was immoral to continue the relationship. Not only did it chain husband and wife to a life of misery, but it doomed children to be brought up amid discord and bitterness. Divorce, she believed, ought to be like surgery—not to be prescribed unless necessary, but to be performed as cleanly and expeditiously as possible when essential to the well-being of the parties. Even in states with supposedly liberal policies, today's divorce courts perform their function with deplorable inattention and cynicism. Mrs. Stanton would have highly approved the recommendations of contemporary divorce reformers who argue for special family courts. These would abandon the myth of adversary proceedings and make their inquiries with the aid of trained investigators. The filing of embittering charges and countercharges would be eliminated; the possibilities of reconciliation would be explored; the needs of the children would be studied; and a final settlement would be arranged that would protect the interests of all the parties. Thus, in words borrowed by Mrs. Stanton from the Puritan poet John Milton, another great advocate of rational divorce, married parties would be "redeemed from unsupportable disturbances to honest peace and just contentment."

Julia Ward Howe
The Battle Hymn of the Republic
1861

EDITED BY WILLIAM G. MC LOUGHLIN

---

*There is no mystery about the composition of the words of
"The Battle Hymn of the Republic," although there is about
its music. The words were written by Julia Ward Howe (wife
of the then more famous Samuel Gridley Howe) in Willard's
Hotel in Washington, D.C., on November 18, 1861, at about
five o'clock in the morning. Mrs. Howe, already well known
as an abolitionist, a poetess, and a humanitarian reformer,
had come to Washington with her husband in connection
with his appointment to the United States Sanitary Commission. With them was Governor John Andrew of Massachusetts and the Reverend James Freeman Clarke, noted pastor
of the Church of the Disciples (Unitarian) in Boston, which
Mrs. Howe attended. On November 17 their party had
watched some Army maneuvers south of the Potomac and
had sung with the soldiers the popular song "John Brown's
body lies a-mouldering in the grave,/ His soul is marching
on." The Reverend Mr. Clarke suggested, "Mrs. Howe, why
do you not write some good words for that stirring tune?"
She replied that she had often wished to do so, but "had not
yet found in my mind any leading toward it." She went to*

bed that night pondering the problem and awoke early in the morning to find the words springing spontaneously to her lips. In the gray dawn she wrote out six stanzas almost without hesitation or alteration of a word. Some weeks later she sent the poem to the editor of the Atlantic Monthly, James T. Field. (She omitted the sixth stanza as inferior; it was not printed until 1899, and is almost never sung.) He suggested the title and paid her four dollars for the poem. She never received any royalties from it. It appeared, without her name, on the first page of the magazine in February, 1862, in the form in which it has been used ever since.

The first sheet music bearing her words appeared a few months later in Boston; the publisher noted, under the title, that the song was "adapted to the favorite Melody of Glory Hallelujah." Three other sheet-music editions had appeared before the end of 1862. A large part of the song's immediate success lay in the rhythm and melody of the music to which it was written, but although two books have been written on the subject, no one has ever definitively identified the composer. Most authorities attribute the music to one William Steffe of South Carolina, who is said to have written it in 1856. But almost nothing is known about Steffe, and no versions of the melody with his name on it are extant. In later years a composer of popular songs named Thomas Brigham Bishop (among others) claimed the authorship, but there is no proof beyond his own word for this. The versions of the song which appeared prior to "The John Brown Song" (none of them is found before 1858) are contained in various Sunday school hymnbooks with no composer's name; the words usually given are "Say, Brothers, will you meet us, on Canaan's happy shore," and the chorus of "Glory, glory, Hallelujah" ends "For ever, ever more" instead of "His truth is marching on." But the melody of these early versions is essentially the same as that which accompanied Mrs. Howe's words.

Apparently this Sunday school song was known by those soldiers of the 12th Massachusetts Volunteers who were stationed at Fort Warren, Massachusetts, in 1861. A quartet of soldiers in Colonel Fletcher Webster's regiment is given credit for making up the words of "The John Brown Song" in the spring of 1861. The song was published in several sheet-music versions prior to the appearance of "The Battle Hymn of the Republic," and it too was described only as "Sung to the tune of Glory Hallelujah," with no author or composer mentioned.

"The Battle Hymn of the R   .c" was praised by Ralph Waldo Emerson, William Cullen Bryant, Henry W. Longfel-

low, and many of the other leading writers of the day. It is reported that Abraham Lincoln once wept at hearing it sung and told the singer that he had never heard a better song. Many stories have been told about its inspiriting effect upon the soldiers in the Civil War, and Chaplain Charles C. McCabe, later dubbed "The Singing Chaplain," raised thousands of dollars for the Christian Commission's war work by singing this song at rallies at which he gave his lecture on "The Bright Side of Life in Libby Prison."

Mine eyes have seen the glory of the coming of the Lord;
He is trampling out the vintage where the grapes of
wrath are stored;
He hath loosed the fateful lightning of His terrible swift
sword:

　　　　　His truth is marching on.

I have seen Him in the watch-fires of a hundred circling
camps;
They have builded Him an altar in the evening dews and
damps;
I can read His righteous sentence by the dim and flaring
lamps:

　　　　　His day is marching on.

I have read a fiery gospel writ in burnished rows of steel:
"As ye deal with my contemners, so with you my grace
shall deal;
Let the Hero, born of woman, crush the serpent with his
heel,

　　　　　Since God is marching on."

He has sounded forth the trumpet that shall never call
retreat;
He is sifting out the hearts of men before His judgment-
seat:
Oh, be swift, my soul, to answer Him! be jubilant, my
feet!

　　　　　Our God is marching on.

This is the text of the poem as it originally appeared in the *Atlantic Monthly*, IX (February, 1862), 10. The text in the original sheet-music edition published by Oliver, Ditson Co., Boston, 1862, contains these same words. Later editions often omitted the third verse. The original manuscript in Mrs. Howe's hand is in the Library of Congress.

In the beauty of the lilies Christ was born across the sea,
With a glory in his bosom that transfigures you and me:
As he died to make men holy, let us die to make men
   free,

While God is marching on.

*Born in and of the nation's greatest spiritual and social crisis,
"The Battle Hymn of the Republic" is the supreme example
of the elementary urge of Americans to equate their religious
and their patriotic ideals. Because it is more than a patriotic
anthem, it has had a far wider appeal and has been put to
more varied uses than such counterparts as "My Country,
'Tis of Thee," "America, the Beautiful," or "The Star-Spangled Banner." In addition to being a patriotic paean, it is also
a song of praise to the deity, a resurgent millennial hymn,
and a ringing ode to freedom. Appropriately enough, the origin of its music and chorus was a Sunday school song. In the
words she wrote to this music (and in her own career) Julia
Ward Howe perfectly embodied the whole crusading fervor
of the pre-Civil War generation's evangelical activism and
moral zeal.*

*"The Battle Hymn" fuses into a harmonious and eloquent
brevity the New World's conviction that here is the chosen
land, that Americans are God's chosen people, and that good
will eventually triumph over evil. It expresses also some of
that moralistic self-righteousness and Old Testament mili-
tancy which has been part of the American outlook since the
days when the Puritans under John Winthrop determined to
make New England a "Citty vpon a Hill." The song is saved
from being too self-righteous by the first two lines of its last
verse (which are often sung pianissimo in contrast to the
thumping martial spirit of the other verses and the chorus).
And it is significant that in one of her few revisions Mrs.
Howe altered the words "shines out in you and me" to
"transfigures you and me." By so doing she unconsciously
transcended her own minority (Unitarian) faith in the divinity
of man and spoke instead in the evangelical accents of the
majority of Americans.*

*For Mrs. Howe and the Union Army, "The Battle Hymn"
was assumed to be a sectional anthem, made so by its final
line, which meant to identify the war not (as Lincoln first saw
it) as a national effort to preserve the Union but as a Holy
War to free the slave. Yet by avoiding any specific mention
of slavery or the rebellious South the song transcended its or-*

igin. And not the least of many purposes it has since served, strange as it may seem, was the part it played in healing the division between the North and the South. Mrs. Howe was astonished to find when she visited the New Orleans Exposition in 1884 that a southern choir could serenade her with the music of "The Battle Hymn." And as Memorial Day services came to be celebrated in honor of the Blue and the Gray, "The Battle Hymn" itself became a tribute to the dead of both sides and a call for renewed loyalty to a more abstract ideal of freedom than abolition. Participating in a Memorial Day service in Boston in 1899, Mrs. Howe rode in the same carriage with former Confederate General Joseph Wheeler, who himself had risen above sectionalism by volunteering to serve in the United States Army in the Spanish-American War, then in progress. Few failed to see in this occasion a personification of national reunion, as the northern poetess and the southern general waved and sang "The Battle Hymn" along with the crowd. A Philadelphia newspaper reporter, carried away by the occasion, wrote, "If volunteers were really needed for the Philippines, McKinley could have had us all right there."

Because it is both a hymn and a patriotic song, and because its inspirational words lack specificity, "The Battle Hymn" is equally appropriate for church services and Fourth of July parades, for high school commencements and Kiwanis Club luncheons. It can be sung by any group which sees its cause in terms of freedom, of do-goodism, or of the millennial vision. It is suitable for times of national danger, mourning, and rejoicing. It was sung by American soldiers not only during the Civil War but in the Spanish-American War, World War I, and World War II. When a memorial tablet was unveiled in St. Paul's Cathedral in London for the first American soldier killed in World War II, the soldiers who were assembled to honor him sang this song. It has appeared in many of the standard hymnbooks of many denominations as well as in the gospel songbooks used in the revival crusades of D. L. Moody and Billy Sunday; Billy Graham used it as the theme song for his weekly broadcasts in the 1950's. The suffragettes (among whom Julia Ward Howe was a leader) sang it often in their meetings and marches, and so did the prohibitionists. During the Progressive Era it was frequently sung by reformers at political meetings (one notable occasion being at the election of Seth Low as reform mayor of New York in 1901 which overthrew Boss Richard Croker's long Tammany rule over the city). The Bull Moose Party made it virtually a campaign song in 1912 (alternating it with its closest religious counterpart, "Onward Christian Soldiers"). The novelist John Steinbeck took a phrase from the poem (a phrase, incidentally, which must be credited to Mrs. Howe and not to any text in the Bible) and used it to symbolize the plight and ultimate triumph of the common man over the evils of the Great Depression—"the grapes of wrath." A popular recording of "The Battle Hymn" in 1959 sold 200,000 copies within a few weeks. In recent years the song has played a prominent part in demonstrations, marches, and mass meetings on behalf of civil rights for Negroes. It was sadly intoned by an English choir at a memorial service for President John F. Kennedy held in Westminster Abbey on November 24, 1963. And on January 30, 1965, it was sung in St. Paul's Cathedral, London, at the funeral service of Sir Winston Churchill, in accordance with his express wishes.

Perhaps the clearest demonstration of the extent to which this song has come to embody the fundamental religious and patriotic attitudes of the general American public has been the frequently made suggestion, in some places carried into action, that the reading of the hymn be required in daily ceremonies in the public schools to replace recitation of the Lord's Prayer and Bible reading, exercises which the Supreme Court decision of 1963 declared unconstitutional.

Though it has been mercilessly parodied and burlesqued, "The Battle Hymn" has stood the test of time. Americans may no longer be so naively optimistic and buoyantly self-confident as they were fifty or one hundred years ago, but they still continue to believe that their faith in God and their patriotic commitment to American political ideals are and ought to be one and the same. Although, apart from its title, the hymn is not obviously nationalistic (any more than is the "Marseillaise"), nevertheless it has an indefinable quality which marks it as peculiarly American. As an anthem of American hope and faith, as an intonation of belief in the ultimate triumph of freedom and justice for all, and as an inspirational pledge to work for the coming of the millennium, "The Battle Hymn of the Republic" seems destined to live as long as the Republic itself. When it ceases to inspire Americans, something fundamental and elemental will have departed from the national spirit.

The Homestead Act
1862

EDITED BY PAUL W. GATES

The land policy of the United States was originally designed to produce revenue for the government. Its basic features were high minimum prices, competitive bids, and the sale of land only in large tracts. Gradually the representatives of the public-land states succeeded in breaking down this revenue policy and in reshaping the land legislation to make it easier for settlers to acquire ownership of small tracts. In 1820 the minimum price was reduced from $2.00 an acre to $1.25, and in 1854 to as little as 12½¢ for land that had been subject to sale for many years. The smallest tract one could acquire was 40 acres. After 1841 those who settled on public land not yet brought on the market could claim pre-emption rights on a location of 160 acres or less, and could safely begin improving it before they had title. Land newly surveyed continued, however, to be priced at a minimum of $1.25 when first offered for sale, and the West regarded this as excessively high.

The western view was that public land had no value until it was improved by the labor of settlers, by the expenditure of local tax money on roads and public buildings, and by the construction of railroads financed, to a considerable degree, out of public resources. These views became accentuated when settlers began moving into the treeless prairies, where they had to import their lumber for building, even for fuel, and had to expend much capital on fencing, on heavy steel plows and reapers, and on horses and oxen to draw them. Dangerously high farm mortgages and the growth of tenancy resulted, lending support to the view that the government should not compel the pioneer to buy the raw, unimproved land. Also, the West deplored the acquisition of much of the choice land on the frontier by speculators who did nothing to develop it and who withheld it from sale until near-by settlers had improved their tracts and had thereby added to the value of the speculators' holdings. In order to realize the Jeffersonian dream of molding public land policies to bring about a democratic society in which small landowners predominated, free land and curbs on land speculation were needed.

A combination of interests—workingmen's advocates who thought the salvation of the laborer was to migrate to the West and take up public land, sentimentalists who looked to the establishment of an Arcadia in the West, and agrarians —agitated for a free-land policy that would assure everyone who went West to settle and improve land the right to a free quarter-section of 160 acres. Horace Greeley's powerful New York Tribune was the principal spokesman for free land or homestead. The demand was taken up by the Free Soil Party in 1848, and in the 1850's the Republican Party stole the land-reform issue from the Democrats, who up to that time had worked for more liberal policies. In the administrations of Pierce and Buchanan the Democrats actually became hostile to the rapid growth of the West then being encouraged by the increasingly liberal land system. When the land reformers threatened to push through Congress a free-homestead policy, although one that had been shorn of most of the safeguards that Greeley favored, the southern-dominated Democrats made the measure as unpalatable to the reformers as possible before it was approved by Congress, and even then Buchanan vetoed it. This maneuvering wrecked the Democratic Party in the newly developing states and territories and contributed to the success of the Republicans under Lincoln in 1860.

With the South out of the Union in 1862, the Republicans wrote into law the Homestead Act. More than a third of a century of agitation and debate in which workingmen's groups, Greeley, Andrew Johnson of Tennessee, and Galusha Grow of Pennsylvania had played leading parts was finally successful.

☆

*Be it enacted by the Senate and House of Representatives of
the United States of America in Congress assembled,* That
any person who is the head of a family, or who has arrived at the age of twenty-one years, and is a citizen of the
United States, or who shall have filed his declaration of intention to become such, as required by the naturalization laws of
the United States, and who has never borne arms against the
United States Government or given aid and comfort to its enemies, shall, from and after the first January, eighteen hundred and sixty-three, be entitled to enter one quarter section
or a less quantity of unappropriated public lands, upon which
said person may have filed a preëmption claim, or which
may, at the time the application is made, be subject to
preëmption at one dollar and twenty-five cents, or less, per
acre; or eighty acres or less of such unappropriated lands, at
two dollars and fifty cents per acre, to be located in a body,
in conformity to the legal subdivisions of the public lands,
and after the same shall have been surveyed: *Provided,* That
any person owning and residing on land may, under the provisions of this act, enter other land lying contiguous to his or
her said land, which shall not, with the land so already
owned and occupied, exceed in the aggregate one hundred
and sixty acres.

Sec. 2. *And be it further enacted,* That the person applying
for the benefit of this act shall, upon application to the register of the land office in which he or she is about to make
such entry, make affidavit before the said register or receiver
that he or she is the head of a family, or is twenty-one years
or more of age, or shall have performed service in the army
or navy of the United States, and that he has never borne
arms against the Government of the United States or given
aid and comfort to its enemies, and that such application is
made for his or her exclusive use and benefit, and that said
entry is made for the purpose of actual settlement and cultivation, and not either directly or indirectly for the use or
benefit of any other person or persons whomsoever; and upon
filing the said affidavit with the register or receiver, and on
payment of ten dollars, he or she shall thereupon be permitted to enter the quantity of land specified: *Provided, however,* That no certificate shall be given or patent issued there-

The Homestead Act, which was approved May 20, 1862, is reprinted
from U.S. *Statutes at Large,* XII, 392–93. Its full title is *An Act to
secure Homesteads to actual Settlers on the Public Domain.*

fore until the expiration of five years from the date of such
entry; and if, at the expiration of such time, or at any time
within two years thereafter, the person making such entry;
or, if he be dead, his widow; or in case of her death, his heirs
or devisee; or in case of a widow making such entry, her
heirs or devisee, in case of her death; shall prove by two
credible witnesses that he, she, or they have resided upon or
cultivated the same for the term of five years immediately
succeeding the time of filing the affidavit aforesaid, and shall
make affidavit that no part of said land has been alienated,
and that he has borne true allegiance to the Government of
the United States; then, in such case, he, she, or they, if at
that time a citizen of the United States, shall be entitled to a
patent, as in other cases provided for by law; *And provided,
further,* That in case of the death of both father and mother,
leaving an infant child, or children, under twenty-one years
of age, the right and fee shall enure to the benefit of said infant child or children; and the executor, administrator, or
guardian may, at any time within two years after the death of
the surviving parent, and in accordance with the laws of the
State in which such children for the time being have their
domicil, sell said land for the benefit of said infants, but for
no other purpose; and the purchaser shall acquire the absolute title by the purchase, and be entitled to a patent from the
United States, on payment of the office fees and sum of
money herein specified.

Sec. 3. *And be it further enacted,* That the register of the
land office shall note all such applications on the tract books
and plats of his office, and keep a register of all such entries,
and make return thereof to the General Land Office, together
with the proof upon which they have been founded.

Sec. 4. *And be it further enacted,* That no lands acquired
under the provisions of this act shall in any event become liable to the satisfaction of any debt or debts contracted prior
to the issuing of the patent therefor.

Sec. 5. *And be it further enacted,* That if, at any time after
the filing of the affidavit, as required in the second section of
this act, and before the expiration of the five years aforesaid,
it shall be proven, after due notice to the settler, to the satisfaction of the register of the land office, that the person having filed such affidavit shall have actually changed his or her
residence or abandoned the said land for more than six
months at any time, then and in that event the land so entered shall revert to the government.

Sec. 6. *And be it further enacted,* That no individual shall
be permitted to acquire title to more than one quarter section

under the provisions of this act; and that the Commissioner of the General Land Office is hereby required to prepare and issue such rules and regulations, consistent with this act, as shall be necessary and proper to carry its provisions into effect; and that the registers and receivers of the several land offices shall be entitled to receive the same compensation for any lands entered under the provisions of this act that they are now entitled to receive when the same quantity of land is entered with money, one half to be paid by the person making the application at the time of so doing, and the other half on the issue of the certificate by the person to whom it may be issued; but this shall not be construed to enlarge the maximum of compensation now prescribed by law for any register or receiver: *Provided,* That nothing contained in this act shall be so construed as to impair or interfere in any manner whatever with existing preëmption rights. *And provided, further,* That all persons who may have filed their applications for a preëmption right prior to the passage of this act, shall be entitled to all privileges of this act: *Provided, further,* That no person who has served, or may hereafter serve, for a period of not less than fourteen days in the army or navy of the United States, either regular or volunteer, under the laws thereof, during the existence of an actual war, domestic or foreign, shall be deprived of the benefits of this act on account of not having attained the age of twenty-one years.

Sec. 7. *And be it further enacted,* That the fifth section of the act entitled "An act in addition to an act more effectually to provide for the punishment of certain crimes against the United States, and for other purposes," approved the third of March, in the year eighteen hundred and fifty-seven, shall extend to all oaths, affirmations, and affidavits, required or authorized by this act.

Sec. 8. *And be it further enacted,* That nothing in this act shall be so construed as to prevent any person who has availed him or herself of the benefits of the first section of this act, from paying the minimum price, or the price to which the same may have graduated, for the quantity of land so entered at any time before the expiration of the five years, and obtaining a patent therefor from the government, as in other cases provided by law, on making proof of settlement and cultivation as provided by existing laws granting preëmption rights.

Approved, May 20, 1862.

☆

The Homestead Act promised a grant of 160 acres to any citizen or intended citizen who settled upon a vacant unappropriated area of government land and made specified improvements upon it during the ensuing five years; technically the land itself was free, though the settlers were required to pay certain modest fees to the land officers for recording the applications. Land reformers were disappointed that the Act did not repeal the law permitting cash sale of public land in unlimited amounts and thus did not halt speculative purchasing. They were also left with a feeling of frustration because much of the best public land was being granted away to railroads and to states, and because the great Indian reservations, as they were cut into and eliminated, were to be sold, not opened to homestead.

Later critics were to maintain that the Act's 160-acre unit was wholly inadequate for farming in the drier portions of the Great Plains beyond the 98th or 100th meridian, and that homesteaders had to resort to fraud to build up holdings sufficient for practicable farming. In fact, Congress had been careful to retain and indeed to strengthen the Preëmption Law of 1841; homesteaders could therefore acquire an additional 160 acres for $200. In 1873, when settlement was moving still farther west into the less humid region of the high plains, Congress adopted the Timber Culture Act which enabled settlers in those areas to gain ownership of a third quarter-section by planting and maintaining trees on 40 acres of it for ten years. In 1877 the Desert Land Act made it possible for settlers to acquire a full section (640 acres) in addition to pre-emption and homestead quarters. Clearly the land system was not as inflexible as some critics maintained.

The rush to take advantage of the Homestead Act was immediate; before the Civil War was over, 26,552 entries had been made. Then came the expected postwar rush of hungry land seekers. The number of homestead filings rose from 15,355 in 1866 to 39,768 in 1871 and 61,638 in 1886. By 1890 a total of 957,902 people had filed entries for homestead land.

In that year the Superintendent of the Census expressed the opinion that the frontier was gone, but land seekers were not troubled by any such false notion. The scramble for the free lands continued unabated, reaching a high figure of 98,829 entries in 1902. Indeed, more than twice as many filings (2,038,558) were made on homesteads after 1890 as before.

By no means all homesteaders who filed original entries won title to their land. Many made poor selections and had to abandon their improvements; others lacked the capital to make necessary improvements and sold relinquishments of their claims to later comers; still others mortgaged their claims when money was abundant and let the mortgage company take over when prices fell and the land appeared to be worth less than the mortgage. Some made their entries without any intention of developing a farm for themselves, commuted their rights to cash purchases six months after filing, as the law allowed, and then sold, usually to a cattle, mining, or timber company. Fraud of this sort was extensive and tended to blacken the reputation of the Homestead Act. Approximately one-half of the original filings were never completed and a considerable portion of the 1,622,107 successful entries that were carried to patent were designed for other than the original entrymen. Notwithstanding this abuse of the Act and the evidence of concentrated ownership in certain areas, far more land went directly into the possession of farmers through the Homestead Act than through any other act of Congress.

In the twentieth century the homestead unit was increased to 320 acres and finally to 640 acres on the assumption that the remaining public lands were suitable for farming only in larger tracts. In 1934 homesteading on public land was practically halted by the adoption of the Taylor Grazing Act, which, with later amendments, withdrew remaining public lands of any value and placed them in organized grazing districts, currently being administered by the Bureau of Land Management.

The Homestead Act was the farmers' act. It contributed mightily to drawing population to the frontier, to making family farm ownership easier, and somewhat to reducing dependence on borrowed capital. This Act, together with the efforts of the states and of the land-grant railroads to promote colonization, greatly accelerated the development of the West. Out of that rapid growth came the agrarian issues of the 1870's. Later generations would look back and wonder that the government had had the wisdom and generosity to help so many people to acquire and develop farms from Florida to California, from Michigan to Washington.

Abraham Lincoln

Second Annual Message to Congress

1862

EDITED BY ROY F. NICHOLS

President Lincoln's means of communication with the public were decidedly limited, compared with those available a century later. He fully realized the value of such contact, however, and made the best use possible of the facilities at hand. He possessed to an unusual degree the capacity to clothe thought in simple and elegant language so that those who received his message could make it their own and cherish it. He could say things that people could not help remembering. The principal avenues available to him were his presidential messages, annual and special, which were printed in all newspapers and given the widest coverage.

As chief magistrate, Lincoln was conscious of the harassing responsibility of war leadership; he also conceived himself a tribune of the people, a statesman with the opportunity and, he came to believe, the responsibility of reordering the social structure of the nation. He was not at first aware of this great duty. At the time of his inauguration he had hoped to avoid war, and when the war came he had hoped to contain it within the lower South and to end it quickly. In order to confine secession and maintain the loyalty of the upper South, he carefully avoided any suggestion of possible interference with the southern social structure, particularly with slavery.

The chief issue at stake, he believed, was proof that a "government . . . conceived in liberty . . . could long endure." As he phrased it in his message to the Special Session of Congress on July 4, 1861, "This is essentially a Peoples' contest. On the side of the Union, it is a struggle for maintaining in the world, that form, and substance of government, whose leading object is, to elevate the condition of men—to lift artificial weights from all shoulders—to clear the paths of laudable pursuit for all—to afford all, an unfettered start, and a fair chance, in the race of life. Yielding to partial, and temporary departures, from necessity, this is the leading object of the government for whose existence we contend. I am most happy to believe that the plain people understand, and appreciate this."

Lincoln pursued this theme further in his First Annual Message, when he supplemented previous arguments in favor of popular institutions with one of greater depth. He referred to an effort which he perceived "to place capital on an equal footing with, if not above labor, in the structure of government."

He believed that there was "not, of necessity, any such thing as the free hired laborer being fixed to that condition for life. Many independent men everywhere in these States, a few years back in their lives, were hired laborers. The prudent, penniless beginner in the world, labors for wages awhile, saves a surplus with which to buy tools or land for himself; then labors on his own account another while, and at length hires another new beginner to help him. . . . No men living are more worthy to be trusted than those who toil up from poverty—none less inclined to take, or touch, aught which they have not honestly earned. Let them beware of surrendering a political power which they already possess, and which, if surrendered, will surely be used to close the door of advancement against such as they, and to fix new disabilities and burdens upon them, till all of liberty shall be lost."

Contrary to Lincoln's early hopes, soon after the war began the question of the future of slavery forced itself upon him. The slaves quite obviously were being used by the Confederacy as active agents in the conflict. Many of them fled to the Union lines or were captured. Congress repealed the Fugitive Slave Act of 1850, which required the return of escaping slaves, and in 1862, passed a Confiscation Act designed to free slaves who were able to reach northern lines or who lived in regions occupied by Union troops. Also, one of the Union commanders, General John C. Frémont, undertook to emancipate slaves in his area of command, the border slave state of Missouri, which was still loyal to the Union. This cumulation of events, together with the unsatisfactory progress of the war, brought Lincoln to a decision. He revoked Frémont's abolition proclamation, and in his First Annual Message he outlined rather sketchily a policy of his own. The slaves of seceding masters should be made free, with no compensation to be paid for them. He was willing to compensate loyal slave owners for their escaped property, but not to send these Negroes back to bondage. He would free them and would endeavor to colonize all the former slaves in the tropics of the Americas or Africa. He was also working on a plan, which he was talking over with loyal congressmen, to buy the slaves in the border states.

In the course of this consideration, during the winter of 1861–62, he called on the director of the census, Joseph C. G. Kennedy, for runs of statistics. In the midst of trying to get the newly appointed commander, General George B. McClellan, to fight, and of reorganizing the military campaigns, he came to a further decision. Slavery must go. He prescribed this objective first in outline to Congress in messages dated March 6 and July 14, 1862, submitting for the consideration of the lawmakers bills which provided for compensated emancipation. He also held conferences and wrote letters, but he made little progress. Therefore he made a third decision. He would issue a proclamation announcing that in December he would offer his plan in greater detail, with an extended argument in its favor, and if this was not accepted by Congress he would emancipate by his own fiat on January 1, 1863, all slaves within the Confederate lines. He believed that his own plan, which was more gradual, which involved the cooperation of the owners, and which would save them from drastic economic loss, would be much preferable. But if it was not accepted, emancipation by order of the Commander in Chief was the alternative.

In this spirit Lincoln prepared his Second Annual Message, which contains his most elaborate formulation of his economic and social thinking and marks one of the highest points in his statesmanship. He made the usual report on the state of the war and the work of the departments. Then he commented on the operation of two revolutionary laws, providing free homesteads and a subsidy to build a Pacific railroad, and announced the setting up of a Department of Agri-

culture. Next he introduced his main theme and detailed his argument for emancipation and social reorganization.

I ... RECALL your attention to what may be called "compensated emancipation."

A nation may be said to consist of its territory, its people, and its laws. The territory is the only part which is of certain durability. "One generation passeth away, and another generation cometh, but the earth abideth forever." It is of the first importance to duly consider, and estimate, this ever-enduring part. That portion of the earth's surface which is owned and inhabited by the people of the United States, is well adapted to be the home of one national family; and it is not well adapted for two, or more. Its vast extent, and its variety of climate and productions, are of advantage, in this age, for one people, whatever they might have been in former ages. Steam, telegraphs, and intelligence, have brought these, to be an advantageous combination, for one united people.

In the inaugural address I briefly pointed out the total inadequacy of disunion, as a remedy for the differences between the people of the two sections. I did so in language which I cannot improve, and which, therefore, I beg to repeat:

"One section of our country believes slavery is right, and ought to be extended, while the other believes it is wrong, and ought not to be extended. This is the only substantial dispute. The fugitive slave clause of the Constitution, and the law for the suppression of the foreign slave trade, are each as well enforced, perhaps, as any law can ever be in a community where the moral sense of the people imperfectly supports the law itself. The great body of the people abide by the dry legal obligation in both cases, and a few break over in each. This, I think, cannot be perfectly cured; and it would be worse in both cases after the separation of the sections, than before. The foreign slave trade, now imperfectly suppressed, would be ultimately revived without restriction in one section; while fugitive slaves, now only partially surrendered, would not be surrendered at all by the other.

The message is reprinted from *Collected Works of Abraham Lincoln*, edited by Roy P. Basler (New Brunswick, N.J.: Rutgers University Press, 1953), V, 527–37. The original is in the National Archives, RG 46, Senate 37A F1, except for the first two pages; for this missing portion Mr. Basler followed *House of Representatives Document No. 1*, 37th Cong., 3d sess.

"Physically speaking, we cannot separate. We cannot remove our respective sections from each other, nor build an impassable wall between them. A husband and wife may be divorced, and go out of the presence, and beyond the reach of each other; but the different parts of our country cannot do this. They cannot but remain face to face; and intercourse, either amicable or hostile, must continue between them. Is it possible, then, to make that intercourse more advantageous, or more satisfactory, *after* separation than *before?* Can aliens make treaties, easier than friends can make laws? Can treaties be more faithfully enforced between aliens, than laws can among friends? Suppose you go to war, you cannot fight always; and when, after much loss on both sides, and no gain on either, you cease fighting, the identical old questions, as to terms of intercourse, are again upon you."

There is no line, straight or crooked, suitable for a national boundary, upon which to divide. Trace through, from east to west, upon the line between the free and slave country, and we shall find a little more than one-third of its length are rivers, easy to be crossed, and populated, or soon to be populated, thickly upon both sides; while nearly all of its remaining length, are merely surveyor's lines, over which people may walk back and forth without any consciousness of their presence. No part of this line can be made any more difficult to pass, by writing it down on paper, or parchment, as a national boundary. The fact of separation, if it comes, gives up, on the part of the seceding section, the fugitive slave clause, along with all other constitutional obligations upon the section seceded from, while I should expect no treaty stipulation would ever be made to take its place.

But there is another difficulty. The great interior region, bounded east by the Alleghanies, north by the British dominions, west by the Rocky mountains, and south by the line along which the culture of corn and cotton meets, and which includes part of Virginia, part of Tennessee, all of Kentucky, Ohio, Indiana, Michigan, Wisconsin, Illinois, Missouri, Kansas, Iowa, Minnesota and the Territories of Dakota, Nebraska, and part of Colorado, already has above ten millions of people, and will have fifty millions within fifty years, if not prevented by any political folly or mistake. It contains more than one-third of the country owned by the United States—certainly more than one million of square miles. Once half as populous as Massachusetts already is, it would have more than seventy-five millions of people. A glance at the map shows that, territorially speaking, it is the great body of the republic. The other parts are but marginal borders to it, the magnificent region sloping west from the rocky mountains to the Pacific, being the deepest, and also the richest, in undeveloped resources. In the production of provisions, grains, grasses, and all which proceed from them, this great interior region is naturally one of the most important in the world. Ascertain from the statistics the small proportion of the region which has, as yet, been brought into cultivation, and also the large and rapidly increasing amount of its products, and we shall be overwhelmed with the magnitude of the prospect presented. An[d] yet this region has no sea-coast, touches no ocean anywhere. As part of one nation, its people now find, and may forever find, their way to Europe by New York, to South America and Africa by New Orleans, and to Asia by San Francisco. But separate our common country into two nations, as designed by the present rebellion, and every man of this great interior region is thereby cut off from some one or more of these outlets, not, perhaps, by a physical barrier, but by embarrassing and onerous trade regulations.

And this is true, *wherever* a dividing, or boundary line, may be fixed. Place it between the now free and slave country, or place it south of Kentucky, or north of Ohio, and still the truth remains, that none south of it, can trade to any port or place north of it, and none north of it, can trade to any port or place south of it, except upon terms dictated by a government foreign to them. These outlets, east, west, and south, are indispensable to the well-being of the people inhabiting, and to inhabit, this vast interior region. *Which* of the three may be the best, is no proper question. All, are better than either, and all, of right, belong to that people, and to their successors forever. True to themselves, they will not ask *where* a line of separation shall be, but will vow, rather, that there shall be no such line. Nor are the marginal regions less interested in these communications to, and through them, to the great outside world. They too, and each of them, must have access to this Egypt of the West, without paying toll at the crossing of any national boundary.

Our national strife springs not from our permanent part; not from the land we inhabit; not from our national homestead. There is no possible severing of this, but would multiply, and not mitigate, evils among us. In all its adaptations and aptitudes, it demands union, and abhors separation. In fact, it would, ere long, force reunion, however much of blood and treasure the separation might have cost.

Our strife pertains to ourselves—to the passing generations of men; and it can, without convulsion, be hushed forever with the passing of one generation.

In this view, I recommend the adoption of the following resolution and articles amendatory to the Constitution of the United States:

"*Resolved by the Senate and House of Representatives of the United States of America in Congress assembled,* (two thirds of both houses concurring,) That the following articles be proposed to the legislatures (or conventions) of the several States as amendments to the Constitution of the United States, all or any of which articles when ratified by three-fourths of the said legislatures (or conventions) to be valid as part or parts of the said Constitution, viz:

"Article ———.

"Every State, wherein slavery now exists, which shall abolish the same therein, at any time, or times, before the first day of January, in the year of our Lord one thousand and nine hundred, shall receive compensation from the United States as follows, to wit:

"The President of the United States shall deliver to every such State, bonds of the United States, bearing interest at the rate of ——— per cent, per annum, to an amount equal to the aggregate sum of   for each slave shown to have been therein, by the eig[h]th census of the United States, said bonds to be delivered to such State by instalments, or in one parcel, at the completion of the abolishment, accordingly as the same shall have been gradual, or at one time, within such State; and interest shall begin to run upon any such bond, only from the proper time of its delivery as aforesaid. Any State having received bonds as aforesaid, and afterwards reintroducing or tolerating slavery therein, shall refund to the United States the bonds so received, or the value thereof, and all interest paid thereon.

"Article ———.

"All slaves who shall have enjoyed actual freedom by the chances of the war, at any time before the end of the rebellion, shall be forever free; but all owners of such, who shall not have been disloyal, shall be compensated for them, at the same rates as is provided for States adopting abolishment of slavery, but in such way, that no slave shall be twice accounted for.

"Article ———.

"Congress may appropriate money, and otherwise provide, for colonizing free colored persons, with their own consent, at any place or places without the United States."

I beg indulgence to discuss these proposed articles at some length. Without slavery the rebellion could never have existed; without slavery it could not continue.

Among the friends of the Union there is great diversity, of sentiment, and of policy, in regard to slavery, and the African race amongst us. Some would perpetuate slavery; some would abolish it suddenly, and without compensation; some would abolish it gradually, and with compensation; some would remove the freed people from us, and some would retain them with us; and there are yet other minor diversities. Because of these diversities, we waste much strength in struggles among ourselves. By mutual concession we should harmonize, and act together. This would be compromise; but it would be compromise among the friends, and not with the enemies of the Union. These articles are intended to embody a plan of such mutual concessions. If the plan shall be adopted, it is assumed that emancipation will follow, at least, in several of the States.

As to the first article, the main points are: first, the emancipation; secondly, the length of time for consummating it—thirty-seven years; and thirdly, the compensation.

The emancipation will be unsatisfactory to the advocates of perpetual slavery; but the length of time should greatly mitigate their dissatisfaction. The time spares both races from the evils of sudden derangement—in fact, from the necessity of any derangement—while most of those whose habitual course of thought will be disturbed by the measure will have passed away before its consummation. They will never see it. Another class will hail the prospect of emancipation, but will deprecate the length of time. They will feel that it gives too little to the now living slaves. But it really gives them much. It saves them from the vagrant destitution which must largely attend immediate emancipation in localities where their numbers are very great; and it gives the inspiring assurance that their posterity shall be free forever. The plan leaves to each State, choosing to act under it, to abolish slavery now, or at the end of the century, or at any intermediate time, or by degrees, extending over the whole or any part of the period; and it obliges no two states to proceed alike. It also provides for compensation, and generally the mode of making it. This, it would seem, must further mitigate the dissatisfaction of those who favor perpetual slavery, and especially of those who are to receive the compensation. Doubtless some of those who are to pay, and not to receive will object. Yet the measure is both just and economical. In a certain sense the liberation of slaves is the destruction of property—property acquired by descent, or by purchase, the same as any other property. It is no less true for having been often said, that the people of the south are not more responsible for the original introduction of this property, than are the people of the north; and when it is remembered how unhesitatingly we all use cotton and sugar, and share the profits of dealing in them, it may not be quite safe to say, that the south has been more responsible than the north for its continuance. If then, for a common object, this property is to be sacrificed is it not just that it be done at a common charge?

And if, with less money, or money more easily paid, we can preserve the benefits of the Union by this means, than we can by the war alone, is it not also economical to do it? Let us consider it then. Let us ascertain the sum we have expended in the war since compensated emancipation was proposed last March, and consider whether, if that measure had been promptly accepted, by even some of the slave States, the same sum would not have done more to close the war, than has been otherwise done. If so the measure would save money, and, in that view, would be a prudent and economical measure. Certainly it is not so easy to pay *something* as it is to pay *nothing;* but it is easier to pay a *large* sum than it is to pay a larger one. And it is easier to pay any sum *when* we are able, than it is to pay it *before* we are able. The war requires large sums, and requires them at once. The aggregate sum necessary for compensated emancipation, of course, would be large. But it would require no ready cash; nor the bonds even, any faster than the emancipation progresses. This might not, and probably would not, close before the end of the thirty-seven years. At that time we shall probably have a hundred millions of people to share the burden, instead of thirty one millions, as now. And not only so, but the increase of our population may be expected to continue for a long time after that period, as rapidly as before; because our territory will not have become full. I do not state this inconsiderately. At the same ratio of increase which we have maintained, on an average, from our first national census, in 1790, until that of 1860, we should, in 1900, have a population of 103,-208,415. And why may we not continue that ratio far beyond that period? Our abundant room—our broad national homestead—is our ample resource. Were our territory as limited as are the British Isles, very certainly our population could not expand as stated. Instead of receiving the foreign born, as now, we should be compelled to send part of the native born away. But such is not our condition. We have two millions

nine hundred and sixty-three thousand square miles. Europe
has three millions and eight hundred thousand, with a population averaging seventy-three and one-third persons to the
square mile. Why may not our country, at some time, average as many? Is it less fertile? Has it more waste surface, by
mountains, rivers, lakes, deserts, or other causes? Is it inferior
to Europe in any natural advantage? If, then, we are, at some
time, to be as populous as Europe, how soon? As to when
this *may* be, we can judge by the past and the present; as to
when it *will* be, if ever, depends much on whether we maintain the Union. Several of our States are already above the
average of Europe—seventy three and a third to the square
mile. Massachusetts has 157; Rhode Island, 133; Connecticut,
99; New York and New Jersey, each, 80; also two other great
States, Pennsylvania and Ohio, are not far below, the former
having 63, and the latter 59. The States already above the
European average, except New York, have increased in as
rapid a ratio, since passing that point, as ever before; while
no one of them is equal to some other parts of our country,
in natural capacity for sustaining a dense population.

Taking the nation in aggregate, and we find its population
and ratio of increase, for the several decennial periods, to be
as follows:—

1790	3,929,827		
1800	5,305,937	35.02 per cent.	{ ratio of increase
1810	7,239,814	36.45	"
1820	9,638,131	33.13	"
1830	12,866,020	33.49	"
1840	17,069,453	32.67	"
1850	23,191,876	35.87	"
1860	31,443,790	35.58	"

This shows an average decennial increase of 34.60 per
cent. in population through the seventy years from our first,
to our last census yet taken. It is seen that the ratio of increase, at no one of these seven periods, is either two per
cent. below, or two per cent. above, the average; thus showing how inflexible, and, consequently, how reliable, the law of
increase, in our case, is. Assuming that it will continue, gives
the following results:—

1870	42,323,341	1910	138,918,526
1880	56,967,216	1920	186,984,335
1890	76,677,872	1930	251,680,914
1900	103,208,415		

These figures show that our country *may* be as populous as Europe now is, at some point between 1920 and 1930—say about 1925—our territory, at seventy-three and a third persons to the square mile, being of capacity to contain 217,-186,000.

And we *will* reach this, too, if we do not ourselves relinquish the chance, by the folly and evils of disunion, or by long and exhausting war springing from the only great element of national discord among us. While it cannot be foreseen exactly how much one huge example of secession, breeding lesser ones indefinitely, would retard population, civilization, and prosperity, no one can doubt that the extent of it would be very great and injurious.

The proposed emancipation would shorten the war, perpetuate peace, insure this increase of population, and proportionately the wealth of the country. With these, we should pay all the emancipation would cost, together with our other debt, easier than we should pay our other debt, without it. If we had allowed our old national debt to run at six per cent. per annum, simple interest, from the end of our revolutionary struggle until to day, without paying anything on either principal or interest, each man of us would owe less upon that debt now, than each man owed upon it then; and this because our increase of men, through the whole period, has been greater than six per cent.; has run faster than the interest upon the debt. Thus, time alone relieves a debtor nation, so long as its population increases faster than unpaid interest accumulates on its debt.

This fact would be no excuse for delaying payment of what is justly due; but it shows the great importance of time in this connexion—the great advantage of a policy by which we shall not have to pay until we number a hundred millions, what, by a different policy, we would have to pay now, when we number but thirty one millions. In a word, it shows that a dollar will be much harder to pay for the war, than will be a dollar for emancipation on the proposed plan. And then the latter will cost no blood, no precious life. It will be a saving of both.

As to the second article, I think it would be impracticable

to return to bondage the class of persons therein contemplated. Some of them, doubtless, in the property sense, belong to loyal owners; and hence, provision is made in this article for compensating such.

The third article relates to the future of the freed people. It does not oblige, but merely authorizes, Congress to aid in colonizing such as may consent. This ought not to be regarded as objectionable, on the one hand, or on the other, in so much as it comes to nothing, unless by the mutual consent of the people to be deported, and the American voters, through their representatives in Congress.

I cannot make it better known than it already is, that I strongly favor colonization. And yet I wish to say there is an objection urged against free colored persons remaining in the country, which is largely imaginary, if not sometimes malicious.

It is insisted that their presence would injure, and displace white labor and white laborers. If there ever could be a proper time for mere catch arguments, that time surely is not now. In times like the present, men should utter nothing for which they would not willingly be responsible through time and in eternity. Is it true, then, that colored people can displace any more white labor, by being free, than by remaining slaves? If they stay in their old places, they jostle no white laborers; if they leave their old places, they leave them open to white laborers. Logically, there is neither more nor less of it. Emancipation, even without deportation, would probably enhance the wages of white labor, and, very surely, would not reduce them. Thus, the customary amount of labor would still have to be performed; the freed people would surely not do more than their old proportion of it, and very probably, for a time, would do less, leaving an increased part to white laborers, bringing their labor into greater demand, and, consequently, enhancing the wages of it. With deportation, even to a limited extent, enhanced wages to white labor is mathematically certain. Labor is like any other commodity in the market—increase the demand for it, and you increase the price of it. Reduce the supply of black labor, by colonizing the black laborer out of the country, and, by precisely so much, you increase the demand for, and wages of, white labor.

But it is dreaded that the freed people will swarm forth, and cover the whole land? Are they not already in the land? Will liberation make them any more numerous? Equally distributed among the whites of the whole country, and there would be but one colored to seven whites. Could the one, in any way, greatly disturb the seven? There are many commu-

nities now, having more than one free colored person, to
seven whites; and this, without any apparent consciousness of
evil from it. The District of Columbia, and the States of Maryland and Delaware, are all in this condition. The District
has more than one free colored to six whites; and yet, in its
frequent petititons to Congress, I believe it has never presented the presence of free colored persons as one of its grievances. But why should emancipation south, send the free people north? People, of any color, seldom run, unless there be
something to run from. *Heretofore* colored people, to some
extent, have fled north from bondage; and *now*, perhaps,
from both bondage and destitution. But if gradual emancipation and deportation be adopted, they will have neither to flee
from. Their old masters will give them wages at least until
new laborers can be procured; and the freed men, in turn,
will gladly give their labor for the wages, till new homes can
be found for them, in congenial climes, and with people of
their own blood and race. This proposition can be trusted on
the mutual interests involved. And, in any event, cannot the
north decide for itself, whether to receive them?

Again, as practice proves more than theory, in any case,
has there been any irruption of colored people northward, because of the abolishment of slavery in this District last
spring?

What I have said of the proportion of free colored persons
to the whites, in the District, is from the census of 1860, having no reference to persons called contrabands, nor to those
made free by the act of Congress abolishing slavery here.

The plan consisting of these articles is recommended, not
but that a restoration of the national authority would be accepted without its adoption.

Nor will the war, nor proceedings under the proclamation
of September 22, 1862, be stayed because of the *recommendation* of this plan. Its timely *adoption,* I doubt not, would
bring restoration and thereby stay both.

And, notwithstanding this plan, the recommendation that
Congress provide by law for compensating any State which
may adopt emancipation, before this plan shall have been
acted upon, is hereby earnestly renewed. Such would be only
an advance part of the plan, and the same arguments apply to both.

This plan is recommended as a means, not in exclusion of,
but additional to, all others for restoring and preserving the
national authority throughout the Union. The subject is presented exclusively in its economical aspect. The plan would, I
am confident, secure peace more speedily, and maintain it

more permanently, than can be done by force alone; while all it would cost, considering amounts, and manner of payment, and times of payment, would be easier paid than will be the additional cost of the war, if we rely solely upon force. It is much—very much—that it would cost no blood at all.

The plan is proposed as permanent constitutional law. It cannot become such without the concurrence of, first, two-thirds of Congress, and, afterwards, three-fourths of the States. The requisite three-fourths of the States will necessarily include seven of the Slave states. Their concurrence, if obtained, will give assurance of their severally adopting emancipation, at no very distant day, upon the new constitutional terms. This assurance would end the struggle now, and save the Union forever.

I do not forget the gravity which should characterize a paper addressed to the Congress of the nation by the Chief Magistrate of the nation. Nor do I forget that some of you are my seniors, nor that many of you have more experience than I, in the conduct of public affairs. Yet I trust that in view of the great responsibility resting upon me, you will perceive no want of respect to yourselves, in any undue earnestness I may seem to display.

Is it doubted, then, that the plan I propose, if adopted, would shorten the war, and thus lessen its expenditure of money and of blood? Is it doubted that it would restore the national authority and national prosperity, and perpetuate both indefinitely? Is it doubted that we here—Congress and Executive—can secure its adoption? Will not the good people respond to a united, and earnest appeal from us? Can we, can they, by any other means, so certainly, or so speedily, assure these vital objects? We can succeed only by concert. It is not "can any of us imagine better?" but "can we all do better?" Object whatsoever is possible, still the question recurs "can we do better?" The dogmas of the quiet past, are inadequate to the stormy present. The occasion is piled high with difficulty, and we must rise with the occasion. As our case is new, so we must think anew, and act anew. We must disenthrall ourselves, and then we shall save our country.

Fellow-citizens, we cannot escape history. We of this Congress and this administration, will be remembered in spite of ourselves. No personal significance, or insignificance, can spare one or another of us. The fiery trial through which we pass, will light us down, in honor or dishonor, to the latest generation. We say we are for the Union. The world will not forget that we say this. We know how to save the Union. The world knows we do know how to save it. We—even we here

—hold the power, and bear the responsibility. In giving freedom to the slave, we assure freedom to the free—honorable alike in what we give, and what we preserve. We shall nobly save, or meanly lose, the last best, hope of earth. Other means may succeed; this could not fail. The way is plain, peaceful, generous, just—a way which, if followed, the world will forever applaud, and God must forever bless.

The end of slavery was not to be achieved gradually by the reasoned plan of cooperation which Lincoln elaborated. His argument brought no response from Congress; so on January 1, 1863, he issued the final Emancipation Proclamation. Time was to demonstrate that Lincoln's analysis of December, 1862, and its predictions were not wholly accurate. His statistical predictions have not been fulfilled. Nor did he reckon properly with the Negroes' tendency to migrate, or with society's resistance to the equalitarian implications of the change and to the reality of the liberty which emancipation was presumed to confer. Argument was to continue over Lincoln's basic premise that without slavery the conflict would not have occurred. Despite these questions, in view of the century of experience since, it can only be regretted that the President's wisdom was given such scant heed.

Because of the method chosen, namely, executive proclamation, quite another path was followed than that set forth in the Second Annual Message. The fiat itself did no more than attempt to destroy a Confederate military resource by freeing slaves within that part of the Confederacy not occupied by Union troops. It in effect advised the slaves to withdraw from the Confederate war effort. Morally the proclamation had tremendous impact. It informed the world and the slave that if the Union won the war that form of human bondage would come to an end. But it had no immediate legal effect, since it proclaimed freedom only in an area that was then outside the jurisdiction of the United States. Even after the South was brought back into the nation, the problem was still to find a means of giving the necessary legal force to Lincoln's proclamation.

Normally state law would define property in the United States, but the southern states could not be expected to emancipate their slaves; local interests and mores were too firmly established. Federal power must be invoked. Since no such federal power existed one must be created by constitutional amendment. The result was the Thirteenth Amendment, which was contrived amid formidable odds in the confused final months of the war and ratified under the dubious procedures characteristic of the early period of Reconstruction. But as events soon demonstrated, emancipation did not insure either civil rights or political privilege, and the Fourteenth and Fifteenth Amendments were inserted in the Constitution by means similar to those which ushered in the Thirteenth Amendment.

With the conclusion of this constitutional revision it became all too clear that the Emancipation Proclamation and the three Amendments had achieved only part of their purpose. Legal human bondage had, it is true, been destroyed, but the social barriers to the "unfettered start and the fair chance" had not been lifted. In fact, some parts of American society began immediately to create new social and legal obstacles to the equality prescribed by the Declaration of Independence and so eloquently reiterated by Lincoln at Gettysburg. The forces of custom, fear, and conscience emphasized a basic incapacity to understand the intricacies of racial difference. Political and legal instruments had been enacted without adequate study, analysis, or social engineering. Therefore, they produced more of the bitter fruits of the two centuries and a half of the "bond-man's . . . unrequited toil." With awful irony they grew ripe in the same vineyard where the nurture of human reason had produced the fine flowering of democracy.

Had Lincoln's suggestions in his Second Annual Message been accepted, the racial tensions of today might have been in some significant part avoided. As it was, there was so much malice and so little charity, that his and following generations have not been able effectively to bind up the nation's wounds. They still bleed.

Abraham Lincoln

The Emancipation Proclamation

1863

EDITED BY JOHN HOPE FRANKLIN

Once the Civil War had begun, there was never a time when the question of freedom for the slaves was not urgent. Abolitionists urged emancipation as a bold humanitarian step. Some military leaders favored it as a logical and necessary war measure. Many citizens, however, thought that the freeing of the slaves was not only inexpedient and impolitic but unconstitutional as well. For the first eighteen months of the war the debate was vigorous; and one delegation after another visited the President to advise him on what action to take.

President Lincoln had long been opposed to slavery, but he had grave doubts, even after the war began, that he possessed the necessary powers to abolish it. Even as he expressed these doubts he was seeking some opportunity and justification for taking action. By the late spring of 1862 he was convinced that he or Congress, perhaps both, should move against slavery. "Things had gone on from bad to worse," he said later, "until I felt that we had reached the end of our rope . . . and must change our tactics, or lose the game!" Action by Congress, in April and June, to abolish

428

*slavery in the District of Columbia and in the territories great-
ly encouraged him.*

In June, during his regular visits to the telegraph room of
the War Department, the President began to sketch out the
main features of the Emancipation Proclamation. By June 18
he had completed a draft; he read this to Vice-President Han-
nibal Hamlin, who seemed quite pleased. A few weeks later
he told Gideon Welles, Secretary of the Navy, and William
H. Seward, Secretary of State, of his decision to issue a proclamation to free the slaves. After Congress passed the Second
Confiscation Act of July 17, the President incorporated some
of its provisions into his draft.

Within a few days the President was ready to share his
plans with his entire Cabinet. On July 22, 1862, he told the
members of his decision, made it clear that it was firm, and
solicited their suggestions merely regarding language and tim-
ing. Some thought it unwise for Lincoln to make the Proclamation at all, while others thought that he should wait to issue
it when the military situation was more favorable. The President made no promises, but he waited. When the news came
of the limited victory of the Union forces at Antietam on September 17, he felt that the time had come. On that very evening he began reworking the draft and putting it into final
form in the quiet of Soldiers' Home near Washington. He returned to the White House on the twentieth, and on the following day he carefully rewrote the document that was the
culmination of months of work and worry.

On September 22, at a special meeting of the Cabinet, he
read the document and issued it the same day. This document, known as the Preliminary Emancipation Proclamation,
announced that on January 1, 1863, all slaves in states or
parts of states then in rebellion against the United States
would be "thenceforward, and forever free."

For the next hundred days there was discussion throughout
the country and in many other parts of the world regarding
the possible effect of emancipation by presidential proclamation. Critics were bitter in their strictures. Abolitionists were
not altogether happy, but were encouraged at Lincoln's action. There were some who doubted that the President would
fulfill his promise to free the slaves; but as the time approached, Lincoln was more determined than ever.

During the week following Christmas Day the Cabinet met
almost daily, and Lincoln had many opportunities to discuss
with the members the final wording of the Proclamation. At
the meeting on December 29 he read a draft of the Emancipation Proclamation on which he had been working, invited

criticism, and directed that copies be provided for each member of the Cabinet. During the meetings of December 30 and 31 the Proclamation was one of the main items on the agenda. Several members made suggestions for revision, largely of an editorial nature. During the evening the President began the final writing of the Proclamation. He completed it on the morning of January 1, 1863, and sent it over to the Department of State for the superscription and closing.

The New Year's Day reception at the White House had already begun when the Secretary of State and his son, Frederick Seward, the Assistant Secretary, returned with the Proclamation. After the reception the President went up to his study, where, in the presence of a few friends, he signed the Emancipation Proclamation. As he finished writing his signature, he said, "I never, in my life, felt more certain that I was doing right than I do in signing this paper."

January 1, 1863

BY THE PRESIDENT OF THE UNITED STATES OF AMERICA: A PROCLAMATION

WHEREAS, on the twenty-second day of September, in the year of our Lord one thousand eight hundred and sixty two, a proclamation was issued by the President of the United States, containing, among other things, the following, to wit:

> That on the first day of January, in the year of our Lord one thousand eight hundred and sixty-three, all persons held as slaves within any State or designated part of a State, the

There are several copies of the December 30 draft of the Emancipation Proclamation. The copies of some members of the Cabinet, Edward Bates, Salmon P. Chase, William H. Seward, and Montgomery Blair, are in the Library of Congress. The draft that the President worked with on December 31 and the morning of New Year's Day is considered the final manuscript draft. Later in the year Lincoln presented it to the women in charge of the Northwestern Fair in Chicago to be sold for the benefit of the Sanitary Commission. The President told the women that he had some desire to retain the paper, "but if it shall contribute to the relief or comfort of the soldiers that will be better." At the fair Thomas B. Bryan purchased it and presented it to the Soldiers' Home in Chicago, of which he was president. It was destroyed in the Great Fire of 1871. Fortunately, four photographic copies of the original had been made. The photograph from which the present copy is printed is in the National Archives.

people whereof shall then be in rebellion against the United States, shall be then, thenceforward, and forever free; and the Executive Government of the United States, including the military and naval authority thereof, will recognize and maintain the freedom of such persons, and will do no act or acts to repress such persons, or any of them, in any efforts they may make for their actual freedom.

That the Executive will, on the first day of January aforesaid, by proclamation, designate the States and parts of States, if any, in which the people thereof, shall on that day be, in good faith, represented in the Congress of the United States by members chosen thereto at elections wherein a majority of the qualified voters of such State shall have participated, shall in the absence of strong countervailing testimony, be deemed conclusive evidence that such State, and the people thereof, are not then in rebellion against the United States.

Now, therefore, I, Abraham Lincoln, President of the United States, by virtue of the power in me invested as Commander-in-Chief, of the Army and Navy of the United States in time of actual armed rebellion against authority and government of the United States, and as a fit and necessary war measure for suppressing said rebellion, do, on this first day of January, in the year of our Lord one thousand eight hundred and sixty three, and in accordance with my purpose so to do publicly proclaimed for the full period of one hundred days, from the day first above mentioned, order and designate as the States and parts of States wherein the people thereof respectively, are this day in rebellion against the United States the following towit:

Arkansas, Texas, Louisiana, (except the Parishes of St. Bernard, Plaquemines, Jefferson, St. Johns, St. Charles, St. James, Ascension, Assumption, Terrebone, Lafourche, St. Mary, St. Martin, and Orleans, including the City of New-Orleans) Mississippi, Alabama, Florida, Georgia, South-Carolina, North-Carolina, and Virginia (except the fortyeight counties designated as West Virginia, and also the counties of Berkley, Accomac, Northampton, Elizabeth-City, York, Princess Ann, and Norfolk, including the cities of Norfolk and Portsmouth, and which excepted parts are, for the present, left precisely as if this proclamation were not issued.

And by virtue of the power, and for the purpose aforesaid I do order and declare that all persons held as slaves within said designated States, and parts of States, are, and henceforward shall be free; and the Executive government of the United States, including the military and naval authorities thereof, will recognize and maintain the freedom of said persons.

And I hereby enjoin upon the people so declared to be free to abstain from all violence, unless in necessary self-defence; and I recommend to them that, in all cases when allowed, they labor faithfully for reasonable wages.

And I further declare and make known that such persons of suitable condition, will be received into the armed service of the United States to garrison forts, positions, stations, and other places, and to man vessels of all sorts in said service.

And upon this act, sincerely believed to be an act of justice, warranted by the Constitution, upon military necessity, I invoke the considerate judgment of mankind, and the gracious favor of Almighty God.

In witness whereof, I have hereunto set my hand and caused the seal of the United States to be affixed.

Done at the City of Washington, the first day of January, in the year of our Lord one thousand eight hundred and sixty three, and of the Independence of the United States of America the eighty-seventh.

By the President: ABRAHAM LINCOLN
WILLIAM H. SEWARD, Secretary of State.

Within a few hours, on the evening of January 1, 1863, the entire country knew that the President had signed the Emancipation Proclamation. Within a few days, the entire world knew that slavery in the United States was doomed. Emancipation celebrations, shared by Negroes and whites alike, were held from Boston to San Francisco. Bells were rung, poems written, hymns composed. One newspaper called the Proclamation "a great moral landmark, a shrine at which future visionaries shall renew their vows, a pillar of fire which shall yet guide other nations out of the night of their bondage. . . ." Almost overnight the war was transformed from a struggle to preserve the Union into one in which the crusade for human freedom became an equally important goal. The Proclamation sharpened the issues of the war. In Europe the opposition to the Union melted before the unequivocal position of the Proclamation. At home the Proclamation provided the moral and humanitarian ingredient that had been lacking in Union attempts to subdue the rebellious South.

In later years the Emancipation Proclamation was to become a significant rallying point for freedom and equality. In pleading for the enfranchisement of the Negro in 1866, Senator Charles Sumner said that in the Proclamation Lincoln had promised to maintain freedom for the Negro "not for any limited period, but for all time." But when real freedom and equality eluded Negroes, some came to believe that gratitude for the Emancipation Proclamation did not require them to remain loyal to a party that had not kept the faith. Nevertheless, if Negroes became disillusioned with the party of Lincoln, they continued to show their gratitude to the man who had issued the Emancipation Proclamation. Throughout the country New Year's Day became and remained a day of commemoration; and the reading of the Emancipation Proclamation became a regular part of scores of annual observances.

As the nation prepared to celebrate the fiftieth anniversary of the Proclamation, many Americans expressed their understanding of the Document's continuing importance. One editor of a magazine said, "The emancipation of the Negro race was the act of the American people. The greatness of Abraham Lincoln was the greatness of a statesman who could lead them to that act, who could understand their unexpressed will calling for that act, and who dared to do the act in their name and on their behalf."

The Proclamation has remained, through more than a century, a vital factor in the movement to broaden and deepen the meaning of democracy and equality in the United States. Negroes themselves have always regarded it as a significant beginning of their quest for full citizenship, while the larger community has recognized it as an important milestone in the nation's program to make its early promises of equality meaningful. On many occasions it has been invoked by those who are full of pride for what the nation has achieved, as well as by those who are critical of the nation for what it has not done.

On the occasion of the centennial of the Emancipation Proclamation, most of the nation was acutely conscious of how much was yet to be done in order for all citizens to enjoy equality. On September 22, 1962, the centennial of the Preliminary Emancipation Proclamation, more than 3,000 people gathered at the Lincoln Memorial in Washington. Governor Nelson Rockefeller of New York presented for public view the only known draft of the Preliminary Proclamation in President Lincoln's hand. In making the presentation he said, "May God give us the love, the courage, the understanding to see in perspective ourselves and the times in which we live—and to make the faith that lies behind this Proclamation truly live for all men in all places of our land." In a major address United Nations Ambassador Adlai Steven-

son called individual freedom the "great unfinished business of the world today." He observed that the defense of freedom by the United States "will be all the stronger for being based not on illusions but upon the truth about ourselves and our world."

President John F. Kennedy, who sent a special message to the centennial observance, had occasion to refer later to the Emancipation Proclamation when he asked Congress to enact a new civil rights bill in 1963. On that occasion, he said, "No one has been barred on account of his race from fighting for America—there are no 'white' and 'colored' signs on the foxholes and graveyards of battle. Surely, in 1963, one hundred years after emancipation, it should not be necessary for any American to demonstrate in the streets for opportunity to stop at a hotel, or to eat at a lunch counter." Statements like this one and a growing awareness of the unfulfilled promises of the Emancipation Proclamation had much to do with the groundswell for civil rights that reached a new high during the centennial year.

Once the centennial of the Emancipation Proclamation had passed, there remained a sense of urgency to complete the long delayed task of extending equality to Negro Americans. The Civil Rights Act of 1964, with its far-reaching provisions that guaranteed equal enjoyment of public accommodations and facilities and its machinery to accelerate school desegregation, was a result—at least in part—of this sense of urgency. When it became clear that existing legislation was inadequate to guarantee to Negroes their right to vote, President Lyndon B. Johnson urged Congress to enact new laws to eliminate barriers to the right to vote. He showed that he had the unfulfilled promises of the Emancipation Proclamation in mind when he said, "There must be no delay, no hesitation, no compromise with our purpose. We cannot wait another eight months. We have already waited 100 years and more. The time for waiting is gone." Congress agreed, and with the enactment of the voting-rights legislation in 1965 it moved one step closer toward the complete freedom for Negro Americans that the Emancipation Proclamation had begun.

Abraham Lincoln

The Gettysburg Address

1863

EDITED BY ALLAN NEVINS

At nightfall on November 18, 1863, a special train drew into the small station at Gettysburg, Pennsylvania, and President Abraham Lincoln and his party alighted. They were greeted by Judge David Wills, chairman of a committee supervising the dedication of a cemetery nearby, in which the bodies of most of the six thousand men killed in the Civil War battle fought there the preceding July might rest. Few could have dreamed that the President's brief address the following day would be remembered as long as the battle itself. Lincoln slept that night in Judge Wills's house. According to Wills's recollections, set down some years later, the President wrote all or part of his address in his room, then showed it to Secretary of State William H. Seward, who was housed next door, and read it to his audience the next afternoon from the very paper on which his host had seen him writing. But Lincoln's secretary, John G. Nicolay, had a different recollection. He believed that Lincoln had written part of the address in Washington on a sheet of Executive Mansion stationery, and that he took this in his pocket to Gettysburg. Later, in Wills's house, he composed the final part in pencil on a lined bluish sheet. When he read his immortal words it was from the two papers. Though controversy persists, Nicolay's hazy and ragged story appears the more correct, and the authoritative edition of Lincoln's Collected Works, *edited by Roy P. Basler, treats as the first draft the text found on the two sheets that Nicolay described.*

We have four other surviving holographs of the address, not differing vitally from the first in import or words. One is the so-called second draft, written on the same lined bluish paper that Lincoln used for the second sheet of the first draft, but containing emendations which indicate that its transcription followed the delivery of the speech. The President wrote a third draft for Edward Everett, who wished to bind it with his own long address—also delivered at the Gettysburg ceremonies—in a volume to be sold at the Sanitary Fair in New York in 1864. Lincoln made still another copy for George Bancroft, to be reproduced in facsimile in a book designed for the Baltimore Sanitary Fair, Autograph Letters of Our Country's Authors. *As this copy proved unsuitable for reproduction, for he had written on the back, Lincoln some time after March 4, 1864, made what is called the final text for facsimile engraving. This was long held by Alexander Bliss, another member of the Baltimore committee preparing the book of autograph documents. The copies made for Everett, Bancroft, and Bliss differ but slightly. All of them contain minor emendations which Lincoln made after he had consulted press reports of his address, the most important being the insertion of the phrase "under God," which he had uttered extempore, and which the newspapermen caught.*

FOURSCORE and seven years ago our fathers brought forth, on this continent, a new nation, conceived in Liberty, and dedicated to the proposition that all men are created equal.

Now we are engaged in a great civil war, testing whether that nation, or any nation so conceived, and so dedicated, can long endure. We are met on a great battlefield of that war. We have come to dedicate a portion of that field, as a final resting-place for those who here gave their lives, that that na-

The address is quoted here from the "final" or Bliss copy. This long remained in the hands of Alexander Bliss's family, and later was owned by Oscar B. Cintas of Havana, Cuba, former Ambassador to the United States. Mr. Cintas bequeathed the document to the United States, with the understanding that it should be placed in the White House; it is now kept there.

tion might live. It is altogether fitting and proper that we should do this.

But, in a larger sense, we can not dedicate—we can not consecreate—we can not hallow—this ground. The brave men, living and dead, who struggled here, have consecrated it far above our poor power to add or detract. The world will little note, nor long remember what we say here, but it can never forget what they did here. It is for us the living, rather, to be dedicated here to the unfinished work which they who fought here have thus far so nobly advanced. It is rather for us to be here dedicated to the great task remaining before us —that from these honored dead we take increased devotion to that cause for which they here gave the last full measure of devotion—that we here highly resolve that these dead shall not have died in vain—that this nation, under God, shall have a new birth of freedom—and that government of the people, by the people, for the people, shall not perish from the earth. November 19, 1863.   ABRAHAM LINCOLN.

The Associated Press report of Lincoln's address, published in the New York Times, Herald, *and* Tribune, *and in other newspapers throughout the country, was commendably accurate. It departed from the text here given only in minor respects, the most important variant, aside from an obvious typographical error, being that the AP version read "our power to add or detract" instead of "our poor power. . . ." The report in the* Chicago Tribune, *while defective in various other points, did use "poor." In spite of a few preposterously mangled newspaper records, one of the worst of which defaced the* Springfield (Illinois) State Journal, *the country thus had an opportunity to judge Lincoln's speech on its clear merits. Only a few papers, like the hostile* Springfield State Register, *neglected to print the President's address and fixed their attention on his awkward response to a band of serenaders on the evening before the dedication.*

It is true that many of the newspapers which printed Lincoln's words, including William Cullen Bryant's Evening Post, *Henry J. Raymond's* Times, *Horace Greeley's* Tribune, *and Manton Marble's* World (all in New York), *completely failed to discern the eloquence and force of the address, giving it no editorial notice. The* Chicago Tribune *placed Everett's oration, Lincoln's address, and a well-sung dirge all on the same level as "moving." The* Philadelphia Public Ledger *seemed to award the honors of the day to the opening prayer by the Reverend Mr. T. H. Stockton.*

On the other hand, the Boston Evening Transcript *termed the discourse an impressive illustration of Lincoln's power of reaching and holding every reader. It might seem rough (the paper had a defective report), "but the uncut fragment is full of jewels."* The Philadelphia Evening Bulletin *declared it a most happy effort. "It is warm, earnest, unaffected, and touching. Thousands . . . will read the President's few words, and not many will do it without a moistening of the eye and a swelling of the heart."* A strong eulogy in the Providence Journal *can probably be traced to the pen of James Burrill Angell, its editor, later president of the University of Michigan.* Harper's Weekly *also warmly praised the speech; the comments carried in that publication were probably written by George William Curtis, who was a cultivated literary critic, a polished orator, and a conscientious editor. "The few words of the President," ran the editorial note, "were from the heart to the heart. They cannot be read, even, without kindling emotion. . . . It was as simple and felicitous and earnest a word as was ever spoken."*

In short, *the frequent statement that Lincoln's masterly address received almost no praise at the time, but either criticism or a slighting inattention, is far from true. Edward Everett's speech, planned as the major oration at the dedication, had felicity and weight. He had given it arduous labor and might well have felt proud of it. Yet on November 20, with unquestioned sincerity, he wrote the President: "Permit me . . . to express my great admiration of the thoughts expressed by you, with such eloquent simplicity and appropriateness, at the consecration of the cemetery. I should be glad, if I could flatter myself, that I came as near to the central idea of the occasion in two hours, as you did in two minutes." Charles A. Dana quotes in his recollections the immediate comment of Edwin M. Stanton, Secretary of War. After lauding the eloquence of Edward Everett, Stanton added that a thousand people would read Lincoln's speech while one read that of the Bostonian, "and it will be remembered as long as anyone's speeches are remembered who speaks in the English language." Only a year or two were to pass before Charles Sumner, if we may believe Lincoln's friend Joshua Speed, characterized the speech as "the most finished piece of oratory he had ever seen." Longfellow in a private letter pronounced the address "admirable."*

Little by little, the values of the address sank into the minds not only of Americans but of all English-speaking peo-

ples. Inevitably, from the outset it was republished far and wide, for no thorough account either of Lincoln or of Gettysburg could omit it. Henry J. Raymond, for example, reproduced it in his popular History of the Administration of President Lincoln, *published in 1864. By the time that John G. Nicolay and John Hay planned their ten-volume* Abraham Lincoln; A History, *in the early 1880's, they found a whole chapter on the address necessary. Isaac N. Arnold, bringing out his biography in 1884, reprinted the speech with the comment that it "would be reaclled in all future ages, among all peoples; as often as men should be called upon to die for liberty and country." These earlier writers, while perceiving the greatness of the address, judged it primarily as a piece of oratory. Arnold, for example, compared it with the words of Demosthenes on the dead at Marathon, and with Daniel Webster's Bunker Hill oration. When Allen Thorndike Rice in 1885 collected a series of reminiscences of Lincoln by distinguished contemporaries, to be published first in the* North American Review *and then in book form, one contributor, Ben: Perley Poore, declared that the address had been compared with the Sermon on the Mount! Another, George S. Boutwell, asserted that it ranked with the noblest productions of antiquity, the works of Pericles, Demosthenes, and Cicero, and with the orations of such moderns as Grattan, Burke, and Webster. This was partial but by no means complete appreciation.*

In time men came to see that the address possessed religious, poetic, and philosophical implications which had at first eluded them. Lord Bryce grasped some of them, as an introduction he wrote for a brief selection from Lincoln's writings indicates. Lord Charnwood, in the first full attempt by an Englishman at a study of Lincoln's life, placed the address in a setting which made it a supreme expression of national courage and devotion. Never before had a war demanded such enormous sacrifices of wealth and life as did the Civil War; never before had a country been compelled to reorganize its energies so completely. As another and more titanic conflict ended, James G. Randall in 1945 carried the analysis a step further. To Linclon, he pointed out, Gettysburg meant the dominant values of human liberty, democracy, the aims of the Fathers, the essence of the Declaration, and the cause of free government in the world. His sense of these values he summed up in a speech which is "the stuff of literature," a speech completely Lincolnian, and completely American.

Carl Sandburg in 1946 hailed the address as one of the great American poems. One may delve deeply into its infolded meanings, he wrote, but its poetic significance carries it far beyond the limits of a state paper. "It curiously incarnates the claims, assurances, and pretences of republican institutions, of democratic procedure, of the rule of the people. It is a timeless psalm in the name of those who fight and do in behalf of great human causes rather than talk, in a belief that men can 'highly resolve' themselves, and can mutually 'dedicate' their lives to a cause."

Abraham Lincoln

Second Inaugural Address

1865

EDITED BY PAUL M. ANGLE

On March 4, 1865, Abraham Lincoln stood on the east porti-
co of the Capitol to take the presidential oath of office for
the second time. Four years earlier he had tried, with all the
persuasiveness at his command, to prevent a civil war. But
the war had come, and had lasted now for nearly four years.
It had taken 600,000 lives, and destroyed property valued at
somewhere between $5 billion and $10 billion. No one could
have computed statistically the heartbreaks of young wives
deprived of husbands, the sorrows of parents who had lost
sons, the hardships of children whose fathers had been swept
into enlistment by personal conviction or by the music of fife
and drum and had never come back, or the agonies of men
who dragged out their days with empty sleeves or hobbled on
stumps of legs.

Lincoln knew, as he approached his second inauguration, that
the war could not last much longer. To be sure, Lee with his
army was still entrenched at Richmond and Petersburg, but
Grant would soon strangle him. Sherman had devastated
Georgia and South Carolina, and was meeting only token re-
sistance as he moved into North Carolina. Two months ear-

441

lier, at Nashville, George H. Thomas, "the Rock of Chicka-
mauga," had smashed Hood's Army of Tennessee and thus
eliminated the last serious threat to the Union forces in the
West. Only Jefferson Davis could see a prolongation of the
conflict.

Throughout the war Lincoln had brooded over the essential nature of the conflict. He could not understand why some
men would offer their lives for the continued enslavement of
other men, but he took refuge in the biblical admonition,
"Judge not, that ye be not judged." Significantly, he spoke of
the Confederate forces as "adversaries" rather than as "enemies." He had faith in God, and wanted to do God's will, yet
he was never sure that he knew what God's will was.

All his life Lincoln had read the Bible—so assiduously that
its doctrines had come to permeate his approach to problems
and its cadences to color his literary style. So it was natural
that when he rose to speak on March 4, 1865, some of his
phrases might have been taken for passages from the King
James version of the Old Testament.

FELLOW COUNTRYMEN:

AT THIS second appearing to take the oath of the presidential office, there is less occasion for an extended address
than there was at the first. Then a statement, somewhat in detail, of a course to be pursued, seemed fitting and proper.
Now, at the expiration of four years, during which public
declarations have been constantly called forth on every point
and phase of the great contest which still absorbs the attention, and engrosses the energies of the nation, little that is
new could be presented. The progress of our arms, upon
which all else chiefly depends, is as well known to the public
as to myself; and it is, I trust, reasonably satisfactory and encouraging to all. With high hope for the future, no prediction
in regard to it is ventured.

On the occasion corresponding to this four years ago, all
thoughts were anxiously directed to an impending civil-war.
All dreaded it—all sought to avert it. While the inaugural address was being delivered from this place, devoted altogether

The address, the original copy of which is in the Library of Congress, is reprinted from *The Collected Works of Abraham Lincoln*, edited by Roy P. Basler (New Brunswick, N.J.: Rutgers University Press,
1953), VIII, 332–33. Three misspellings in the original document,
"enerergies," "inaugeral," and "dissole," have been corrected here.

to *saving* the Union without war, insurgent agents were in the city seeking to *destroy* it without war—seeking to dissolve the Union, and divide effects, by negotiation. Both parties deprecated war; but one of them would *make* war rather than let the nation survive; and the other would *accept* war rather than let it perish. And the war came.

One eighth of the whole population were colored slaves, not distributed generally over the Union, but localized in the Southern part of it. These slaves constituted a peculiar and powerful interest. All knew that this interest was, somehow, the cause of the war. To strengthen, perpetuate, and extend this interest was the object for which the insurgents would rend the Union, even by war; while the government claimed no right to do more than to restrict the territorial enlargement of it. Neither party expected for the war, the magnitude, or the duration, which it has already attained. Neither anticipated that the *cause* of the conflict might cease with, or even before, the conflict itself should cease. Each looked for an easier triumph, and a result less fundamental and astounding. Both read the same Bible, and pray to the same God; and each invokes His aid against the other. It may seem strange that any men should dare to ask a just God's assistance in wringing their bread from the sweat of other men's faces; but let us judge not that we be not judged. The prayers of both could not be answered; that of neither has been answered fully. The Almighty has His own purposes. "Woe unto the world because of offences! for it must needs be that offences come; but woe to that man by whom the offence cometh!" If we shall suppose that American Slavery is one of those offences which, in the providence of God, must needs come, but which, having continued through His appointed time, He now wills to remove, and that He gives to both North and South, this terrible war, as the woe due to those by whom the offence came, shall we discern therein any departure from those divine attributes which the believers in a Living God always ascribe to Him, Fondly do we hope—fervently do we pray—that this mighty scourge of war may speedily pass away. Yet, if God wills that it continue, until all the wealth piled by the bond-men's two hundred and fifty years of unrequited toil shall be sunk, and until every drop of blood drawn with the lash, shall be paid by another drawn with the sword, as was said three thousand years ago, so still it must be said "the judgments of the Lord, are true and righteous altogether."

With malice toward none; with charity for all; with firmness in the right, as God gives us to see the right, let us strive on to finish the work we are in; to bind up the nation's wounds; to care for him who shall have borne the battle, and for his widow, and his orphan—to do all which may achieve and cherish a just, and a lasting peace, among ourselves, and with all nations.

Shortly after the inauguration Thurlow Weed complimented Lincoln upon his address. The President replied: "I believe it is not immediately popular. Men are not flattered by being shown that there has been a difference of purpose between the Almighty and them. To deny it, however, in this case, is to deny that there is a God governing the world. It is a truth which I thought needed to be told; and as whatever of humiliation there is in it, falls most directly on myself, I thought others might afford for me to tell it."

Fewer today than in Lincoln's time would subscribe to his interpretation of the war as a punishment inflicted on the people of both sections by an almighty but inscrutable God for the share of both in the sin of human slavery. Nor would many acquiesce, as Lincoln was willing to acquiesce, in the indefinite prolongation of the agony if that were necessary for expiation. Faith today has narrower limits.

In little more than five weeks after Lincoln delivered the Second Inaugural he would be assassinated, and the clemency and effort toward rehabilitation for which he pleaded would be submerged, as far as the North was concerned, in a lust for punishment of the South. Reconstruction, with its excesses, would continue for a decade, and the aftereffects, in the form of suspicion, if not enmity, between the sections would persist much longer.

Yet Lincoln had spoken words that would live. One perceptive critic, Charles Francis Adams, Jr., recognized that fact immediately. Writing to his father, the American Minister to England, on March 7, 1865, Adams said: "What do you think of the inaugural? That rail-splitting lawyer is one of the wonders of the day. Once at Gettysburg and now again on a greater occasion he has shown a capacity for rising to the demands of the hour which we should not expect from orators or men of the schools. This inaugural strikes me in its grand simplicity and directness as being for all time the historical keynote of this war; in it a people seemed to speak in the sublimely simple utterance of ruder times. What will Europe think of this utterance of the rude ruler, of whom they have nourished so lofty a contempt? Not a prince or minister in all Europe could have risen to such an equality with the occasion."

The concluding sentence of the Second Inaugural, "With malice toward none . . . ," has been quoted over the years only less often than the last sentence of the Gettysburg Address. There is a difference, of course, between the parroting of words and the acceptance of what words stand for. No sensible person would contend that the United States has always moved in the spirit of charity for all, or that it has always striven for a just and lasting peace between its citizens and all other nations. Yet the fact remains that Lincoln gave expression to a strain of idealism that is part of the American character. The United States has kept its promise to the Philippines and has endowed that country with independence. Cuba could have been held as a dependency, and would have been held as such by most nations. After World War II what was the Marshall Plan, and much subsequent foreign aid, but a tangible expression of Lincoln's beneficent injunction? What is the whole network of American charity, supporting a maze of welfare societies unequaled in any other nation, but caring for the widow and the orphan? And what of the Peace Corps?

To contend that the attitude which results in these manifestations is universal among the American people would be foolish. To deny that it exists would be to do them less than justice. And is it far-fetched to believe that American benevolence, no matter how embodied, continues to draw nourishment from Lincoln's oft-repeated formulation of its goal?

Ulysses S. Grant

Terms of Surrender for the Army of Northern Virginia

1865

EDITED BY T. HARRY WILLIAMS

On the afternoon of April 9, 1865, General Ulysses S. Grant sat in a chair in the living room of the Wilmer McLean house in the little Virginia village of Appomattox Court House. Seated facing him with serious face and somewhat anxious eyes was General Robert E. Lee. It was for both the end of a bitter and bloody military road. It was also one of the great confrontations of American history—of two great generals and two great gentlemen. Only after some difficult and sometimes devious correspondence had they come together. Grant had proposed that Lee's retreating and dissolving army should surrender, and Lee, after much anguish, had brought himself to go to Grant to ask for terms. Lee went to the meeting formally and faultlessly attired and wearing his sword, in the old way of war. Grant came in from the lines after receiving Lee's last note. He wore his familiar nondescript uniform with only the shoulder straps to denote his rank and looked even more disheveled than usual. Even if he had had time to prepare, he would have still ap-

peared much the same—a technician of the age of modern and industrial war come to deal with a general of that dying warfare of knightly men and waving banners. Lee was accompanied only by his military secretary, Colonel Charles Marshall. Grant had with him his staff and some of his principal officers. They sat now to decide specifically the fate of the Army of Northern Virginia, but, as both must have known, to determine actually the outcome of the war. For if Lee's army surrendered, all other Confederate forces would follow suit. It was Palm Sunday, and peace, peace for the moment and peace for the long future, hung in the air between the two men in the room at the McLean house.

After some preliminary conversation about their having met in the Mexican War, Lee, for whom the interview was naturally painful, suggested that Grant state his terms of surrender and reduce them to writing. Grant called for his manifold order book, placed it on a small table, and wrote his conditions on two pages. He said later that when he put his pen to the paper he did not know the first word he would use, but that he knew what was in his mind and wanted to make it crystal clear. He also said that as he wrote his eye fell on Lee's sword and this led him to include the provision that the officers would retain their sidearms and horses. The paper was handed to Lee, who put on his spectacles to examine it. As the Confederate read, his facial expression showed that he was touched by the generosity of the terms. When he finished, he exclaimed: "This will have a very happy effect upon my army." Then, after a slight pause, Lee remarked that in the southern service the enlisted men owned their own horses and mules and wondered if they would be able to keep them. Grant replied that the terms regarding animals applied only to officers. But, he went on, as if talking partly to himself, most of the men were probably small farmers and would need their horses to put in a crop; he would pass down an oral order to let each man claiming to own an animal take it home with him. Lee, obviously moved, said this concession would have the best possible effect. With Colonel Marshall's help, he then composed a letter to Grant accepting the terms. Duplicate copies of the two letters were prepared, and shortly Lee departed. Appomattox had become one of the immortal American scenes.

☆

Appomattox C. H., Va.,
Apl 9th, 1865.

Gen. R. E. Lee,
    Comd'g C. S. A.

Gen: In accordance with the substance of my letter to you of the 8th inst., I propose to receive the surrender of the Army of N. Va. on the following terms, to wit: Rolls of all the officers and men to be made in duplicate. One copy to be given to an officer designated by me, the other to be retained by such officer or officers as you may designate. The officers to give their individual paroles not to take up arms against the Government of the United States until properly exchanged, and each company or regimental commander sign a like parole for the men of their commands. The arms, artillery and public property to be parked and stacked, and turned over to the officer appointed by me to receive them. This will not embrace the side-arms of the officers, nor their private horses or baggage. This done, each officer and man will be allowed to return to their homes, not to be disturbed by United States authority so long as they observe their paroles and the laws in force where they may reside.

Very respectfully,
U. S. GRANT,
Lt. Gen.

U. S. Grant was a soldier. He thought first and naturally in military terms, in terms of winning a battle or a war. When he went to Appomattox, his primary purpose was to get Lee and Lee's army out of the war. That general and that army constituted the chief resisting power of the Confederacy. If they were removed, all other resistance would shortly cease and the war would be ended. Throughout the negotiations Grant acted on the surface a purely military part. He told Lee in their exchange of notes before the meeting that he had no authority to discuss a general peace but only to conclude a military agreement for the surrender of one army. He did not make the mistake that his friend William T. Sherman made shortly afterward in treating with Joseph E. Johnston—of agreeing to an inclusive pact that contained political as well as military provisions. Sherman's document was referred to,

Grant's letter is transcribed from *Personal Memoirs of U. S. Grant* (New York: Charles L. Webster and Co., 1885–86), II, opposite p. 496.

with substantial accuracy, as a "treaty." Grant would never have concocted a treaty. He was too much the soldier to intervene in the political sphere, too aware that even if he had been so inclined his civil superior, Abraham Lincoln, would not have permitted him or any other general to dictate conditions of peace.

At the same time, Grant, as his actions showed and as his later utterances confirmed, was thinking about the ultimate peace beyond the immediate military ceremony. When he spoke so earnestly to Lee about the common soldiers needing their horses on their farms, he was looking a long way into the future. And on the day after the dramatic meeting he rode to Lee's camp to ask the Confederate leader, without success, to use his great influence to persuade other southern generals to quit the now hopeless struggle. Grant was the very model of a proper democratic soldier; he was always extremely careful not to obtrude his views on the civil authorities. But more than any other general of the time he had a sharp and realistic appreciation of the relation between policy and war. He knew that wars were not fought for their own sake or as an end in themselves but for political objectives. In this particular war the large objective was to restore the Union: to restore it, he hoped, with the least possible violence to the feelings of both sides but with all the vast changes and results wrought by the war affirmed and attested. If satisfactory military rituals could be concluded, without any big talk being indulged in or any specific conditions being required, then men of both sections could proceed to do many things —restore a spirit of national amity, build up the South's shattered economy, and work out a viable plan for the former slaves.

Grant's aproach to the problem of peace was startlingly similar to Lincoln's. The President proposed to get the mechanics of Reconstruction under way without discoursing too much about abstract principles. After the process was in motion, the plans and the principles could be fitted in. By somewhat different routes the professional politician and the professional soldier had arrived at the same strategy. Both were worthy representatives of the American pragmatic tradition. Of course, the peace did not develop as either Lincoln or Grant hoped. Perhaps it would have happened much as it did even if Lincoln had lived. Many forces dictated its failure, and Grant himself, as President during the period, has to bear some of the blame. After he left the Presidency he said sadly that neither the North nor the South had acted as he thought each should have. Perhaps, he concluded, it would *have been better for both sections and races if the South for a span had remained under military government.*

Grant's surrender document did not pass from men's minds with the end of the war. It undoubtedly had some influence on Lee, helping him determine to cast his influence for intersectional harmony. It was often quoted in the South, although generally with the bitter observation that its author had forgotten its spirit. And in the years after Reconstruction and the age of Grant it remained a part of the national consciousness. But there was a tendency to misunderstand the situation in which Grant wrote his terms and therefore to misinterpret his purpose. Men remembered that Grant at Appomattox had acted the part of a generous victor and had given the vanquished generous terms. That was the American way, people said. They said it especially in the disillusioned years after World War I and added that Grant's way was the proper mode to end a war—with terms that the defeated could live with. In World War II American leaders gave an opposite meaning to Grant's peace ideas. Franklin D. Roosevelt recalled that, at Fort Donelson, Grant had demanded of the Confederate garrison "unconditional surrender," and he proposed this formula as a condition to be imposed on the enemies of the Western alliance. Roosevelt forgot that at Donelson Grant was demanding the surrender of a single fort and not of a nation. The Americans of the post-World War I era forgot that at Appomattox Grant was lying down not a peace but a military convention that would make a workable peace possible. He would not punish the South heavily or with revenge, but neither would he give it a blank check to fill in as it pleased.

The war, the exercise in violence, had been brought to a close. But some at least of the political objectives of that exercise had to be attained and could best be attained with pragmatic experimentation in the peace that would follow. Grant was a great soldier, although an indifferent political leader. He had a good stock of common sense, and he was a thoroughly humane man. The terms he wrote at Appomattox have become a symbol of the essential humanity of the American character, and such they will always remain. They should stand too as a reminder of something Americans often forget—the vital and constant relation between war and national objectives.

The Oath of Office
1868

EDITED BY HAROLD M. HYMAN

Framers of the federal Constitution of 1787 and members of the first Congress held under its provisions decided that officeholders of the national government which they were laboring to create should be bound neither by religious tests nor by elaborate loyalty oaths. Instead, they believed that a simple oath of office was adequate.

This decision ran counter to the practice of almost every other government in the world at that time. It reflected the awareness of the men at Philadelphia of certain historical factors which from 1774 through 1783 had helped to initiate and to sustain the revolution against King George III. A century earlier (1640–60 and 1688–89) the ancestors of those men had mounted two successful revolutions, during which they executed one king and exiled another, because England's constitutional law bound inseparably together religious faith and secular allegiance. During the 1770's many colonists rebelled against Britain primarily because royal policy favored establishing the Anglican Church as the official church in America, as it was in England. This would have meant that general taxes would support the Anglican priests and that acquiescence in the Anglican creed would be required of all office-holders. America's religious diversity made dangerous any connection

451

between government and a particular religious organization.

Therefore, the "Federalists" who shaped the 1787 Constitution stated in one of the few presumably unamendable phrases of that document that "no religious Test shall ever be required as a Qualification to any Office or public Trust under the United States" (Article VI). Further to stress the American consensus on this point, the so-called "anti-Federalists" insisted on including, as part of the price of their agreement to the Constitution, the First Amendment's injunction that "Congress shall make no law respecting an establishment of religion, or prohibiting the free exercise thereof."

If religious tests were dangerous, loyalty tests were useless. After all, except for the relatively small number of diehard Tories, every single adult American had switched his allegiance at least once since 1774. Tens of thousands of "patriots" had shifted sides several times during the long course of the Revolution. Little wonder that a suggestion made at Philadelphia in 1787 for the inclusion in the Constitution of a uniform loyalty-oath test for federal and state officers, inquiring into past conduct, received little support. Instead, as Madison recorded it, Pennsylvania's James Wilson spoke for almost everyone at the meeting when he " . . . said that he was never fond of oaths, considering them as a left-handed security only. A good government did not need them and a bad government ought not to be supported."

The framers of the Constitution and the first congressmen agreed, however, that the new government was better off if its servants in national and state offices swore an oath to symbolize individual future commitment to the Constitution. The only office for which the form of the oath was specified in the Constitution was that of the President of the United States (Article II). But an oath requirement faced others in addition to the President; "the Senators and Representatives . . . and the Members of the several State Legislatures, and all executive and judicial officers, shall be bound by Oath or Affirmation, to support the Constitution" (Article VI). The first Congress that met under the ratified Constitution provided the oath form for officers lower than the President: "I, A.B., do solemnly swear or affirm (as the case may be) that I will support the Constitution of the United States" (U.S. Statutes at Large, I, 23).

This remained the standard text of the oath of office for all federal and state employees until 1861. Then the American experiment in political democracy structured in a federal system—unique in the world—split on the rock of *slavery. Clearly present danger in the North of homefront disloyalty inspired Congress and many state legislatures to apply loyalty tests widely. Naturally Congress paid special attention to the enlarging number of federal civil and military officers; and on August 6, 1861, it required these men, as a prerequisite to entering on their duties, to swear to their future loyalty "without any mental reservation or evasion whatsoever"* (U.S. Statutes at Large, XII, 326–27).

Then, on July 2, 1862, the low point in the war for the Union, Congress enacted the so-called "iron-clad test oath." Its lengthy provisions required all federal personnel to swear to their past as well as to their future loyalty (U.S. Statutes at Large, 502–8). *In its turn the standard text of the federal oath of office, the iron-clad oath expanded its coverage through subsequent congressional enactments. Congressmen themselves, pensioners, claimants, contractors, attorneys practicing in federal courts—in short, anyone having any business with or wanting favors from the national government—had to subscribe it. Although in 1867 the Supreme Court in* ex parte Garland (4 Wallace 333) *declared unconstitutional this oath requirement for attorneys, the remainder of the oath law's broad coverages remained as before.*

During Reconstruction, Republican framers and supporters of the iron-clad oath statute found themselves boxed in by their creation. Reconstruction statutes and the Fourteenth Amendment combined to send to Congress, from the South, delegates-elect who had been pardoned by Congress for past Confederate activity but who could not without perjury swear to the past-loyalty provision of the test oath. After much intra-Republican heartburning, Congress on July 11, 1868, specified a new oath of office for all federal officials caught in this manner between the pardoning provisions of the Fourteenth Amendment and the exclusion clauses of the 1862 oath law. Obviously it was not the purpose of the drafters of the new oath statute to create the text for a permanent oath of office. But, though designed for pardoned ex-rebels, the 1868 oath has served almost without alteration ever since for all government officials.

I A.B., do solemnly swear (or affirm) that I will support and defend the Constitution of the United States against all enemies, foreign and domestic; [that I will bear true faith and allegiance to the same;] that I take this obligation freely, without any mental reservation or purpose of evasion, and that I will well and truthfully discharge the duties of the office on which I am about to enter. So help me God.

Between the closing-off of the Reconstruction effort in 1877 and the choking-off of the Nazi-Fascist-Japanese empire in 1945, matters involving oaths of office and tests of loyalty constituted only a minor theme in America's history. But the onset after 1945 of the "cold war" against the Soviet Union pushed these questions into the forefront of public concern. They remain there still and are likely to keep a prominent place.

An astonishing number of government agencies, national, state, and local, have adopted special disclaimer oaths as standard requirements for office. Industries and other private associations also have plunged into the search for subversives. All this has immensely complicated the problems of national officers who are responsible for maintaining adequate security procedures while refraining from transgressing on the rights of individuals. Amateur efforts do not unearth Soviet agents or American subversives, nor are they likely to do so. The fuss they have raised, however, has permitted opportunistic individuals to exploit the public's concern over internal security. Other Americans, dedicated to protecting and advancing the cause of civil liberty, have carried into the highest courts appeals reminiscent of the Garland case a century past; they contend that oaths of office which also are non-Communist disclaimers offend the Bill of Rights and the constitutional prohibition against ex post facto laws and bills of attainder. On April 18, 1966, the Supreme Court struck down an Arizona law requiring a loyalty oath of all state employees (Elfbrandt v. Russell, 86 Sup. Ct. 1238). The Court, in a 5 to 4 decision, denounced the law as a threat to "the cherished freedom of association protected by the First Amendment."

Our jurists have not yet found a clear formula by which government may secure itself against disloyalty, through oaths or otherwise, while simultaneously holding to the uncertain but inspiring line set in the Bill of Rights. Scholars in political science, law, philosophy, theology, and history have been no more successful than the jurists. The oath of office will remain a matter of controversy as long as fears remain

This is the text of the 1868 statute, with the bracketed phrase indicating what the current code of federal laws has dropped from the older version (U.S. *Statutes at Large,* XV, 85 [1868]; U.S. *Code,* I, 99 [1959]).

that disloyalty exists in government offices. Perhaps the issue must boil down to the question whether the men legitimately entrusted with power to take action against disloyalty can employ that power with vigor, sensitivity, and restraint when —but only when—adequate danger exists. A hundred years ago an indignant and unquestionably loyal northerner challenged the legitimacy of Lincoln's employment of stern loyalty tests. The President asked, "Must I shoot a simple-minded soldier boy who deserts, while I must not touch a hair of a wily agitator who induces him to desert?" No, Lincoln replied to his own question: "I think that in such a case, to silence the agitator, and save the boy, is not only constitutional, but, withal, a great mercy."

The Ballad of John Henry

c. 1872

EDITED BY RICHARD M. DORSON

In 1870 workmen on the Chesapeake and Ohio Railroad began blasting through a hump of the Allegheny Mountains in West Virginia. Late in 1872 they completed the Big Bend Tunnel, at that time the longest in the United States, stretching a mile and a quarter under the wild and desolate terrain of Summers County in what was then a frontier wilderness. The tentacles of the transregional and transcontinental railroads were reaching out, in the aftermath of the Civil War, to embrace the nation. The railroad companies joined their trunk lines, standardized their track, patented safety devices like the automatic coupler and the air brake, and speeded up the building of bridges and tunnels. The steam drill made its appearance in these years, as a device to replace the old method of tunneling by hand drillers or "steel drivers." During the construction of the Big Bend Tunnel, reports say that a contest was staged between the newfangled steam drill and a Negro steel driver named John Henry, who defeated the machine, dying on the spot or soon after. From this event grew the most celebrated folk ballad composed on American soil, one whose popularity is still on the increase.

In the Big Bend Tunnel—named for a southerly dip of ten miles the engineers were avoiding along the Greenbrier River

—about a thousand laborers, mostly Negro ex-slaves, worked in small gangs driving steel and blasting rock. A steel driver struck a heavy hammer against a steel drill clenched between the legs of another workman, the "turner" or "shaker." The turner twisted the drill slightly every few strokes, to give the steel more cutting edge. When the hole had reached sufficient depth, the turner placed in it a charge of nitroglycerin or other explosive, and set the fuse. As they pounded, the drivers chanted verses, often ribald, or grunted choruses as idle turners sang. Danger and death lurked in the shadows, from falling rock, foul air, and jarring blasts. Most hazardous was the "heading" or upper cross section of the tunnel, which had to be opened before the lower part could be blasted with simple vertical drilling. Turners lay prone in the heading, and the driver drilled sideways. John Henry was supposed to have drilled in the east end of the heading at Big Bend.

A good many workmen, white and Negro, professed to remember John Henry and his contest with the steam drill when investigators interviewed them over half a century later. As with all enduring oral traditions of heroes and events, the details vary widely, even in first-hand reports. One mountaineer claimed John Henry was a black, rawboned man about thirty years old, who had come from North Carolina, was six feet tall, weighed nearly 200 pounds, and had a white—or nearly white—girl friend; he was killed not in the contest but some time after from a blast of rock in the heading, and was secretly buried at night. Another West Virginian remembered John Henry as "yaller-complected," stout, hailing from Virginia, only five feet eight inches tall, no more than 170 pounds in weight, and surviving the tunnel dangers.

And so the conflicting testimony goes, but with a core of agreement. One of the chief witnesses said over half a century after the tunnel was built that he remembered John Henry singing "Can't you drive 'er . . . huh?" A newspaper in nearby Hinton, West Virginia, the Mountain Herald, on January 1, 1874, printed the verse "Can't you drive her home, my boy?" as sung by the tunnel gangs.

In general, the accounts to be found in West Virginia newspapers and county histories point to savagery and violence and frank sexuality in the life of Big Bend tunnelmen. Later recollections likened Big Bend to an inferno, with half-naked men gasping and writhing in the yellow smoke that filled the cavern, while a din as of ten thousand hammers striking anvils beat on their ears. Men died from tunnel sickness, from falls of the crumbly red shale, from knife stabbings, and their bodies were summarily disposed of by the *railroad management. Relief was sought in whiskey-drinking, in talk of camp women, in singing. Sexual symbolism found a ready place in song phrases about "driving hard," "piece of steel," "wants my hammer, handle, too."*

From this background the ballad of John Henry arose. Its composer is not known, although several workmen at Big Bend possessed a talent for ballad-making. When the tunnel gangs dispersed, they carried with them the folk song about John Henry and distributed it throughout the nation.

John Henry was a very small boy
Setting on his mama's knee.
He picked up a hammer and a little piece of steel,
Said, "The hammer be the death of me,
The hammer be the death of me."

John Henry went upon the mountain,
Came down on the other side.
The mountain was so tall, John Henry was so small,
He laid down his hammer and he cried, "O Lord," etc.

John Henry on the right hand side,
The steam drill on the left,
"Before I'll let your steam drill beat me down,
I'm gonna hammer my fool self to death."

"Oh, look away over yonder, captain,
You can't see like me."
He hollered out in a lonesome cry,
"A hammer be the death of me."

John Henry told the captain,
"When you go to town,
Bring me back a twelve-pound hammer,
I will sho' beat your steam drill down."

The man that invented the steam drill
Thought he was mighty fine.
John Henry drove his fourteen feet
And the steam drill only made nine.

The ten-stanza version of the ballad is reprinted from Guy B. Johnson, *John Henry: Tracking down a Negro Legend* (Chapel Hill: University of North Carolina Press, 1929), pp. 115–16; the supplementary stanzas that follow come from Louis W. Chappell, *John Henry: A Folk-Lore Study* (Jena: W. Biedermann, 1933), pp. 104, and 120–21.

John Henry told his shaker,
"Shaker, you better pray,
For, if I miss the six-foot steel,
Tomorrow'll be your burying day."

John Henry had a pretty little wife,
Her name was Mary Ann.
He said, "Fix me a place to lay down, child,
I got a roaring in my head."

John Henry had a loving little wife,
The dress she wore was blue.
She walked down the track but never came back,
"John Henry, I've been true to you."

John Henry told the captain
Just before he died,
"Only one favor I ask of you:
Take care of my wife and child."

[One of the most popular "John Henry" stanzas, absent
from the above text, is the following:]

John Henry told the captain,
"A man ain't nothin' but a man,
And if I don't beat your steam drill down
I'll die with a hammer in my hand, Lawd, Lawd."

[And these three stanzas appear in yet another text:]

John Henry was a man just six feet in height,
Nearly two feet and a half across the breast.
He'd take a nine-pound hammer and hammer all day long
And never get tired and want to rest, O Lord,
And never get tired and want to rest.

John Henry was a steel-driving man, O Lord,
He drove all over the world.
He come to Big Bend Tunnel on the C. & O. Road
Where he beat the steam drill down, O Lord,
Where he beat the steam drill down.

The white folks all got scared,
Thought Big Bend was a-fallin' in;

John Henry hollered out with a very loud shout,
"It's my hammer a-fallin' in the wind, O Lord,
   It's my hammer a-fallin' in the wind."

For thirty-seven years after the completion of the Big Bend Tunnel, the tradition of John Henry escaped attention. Then in 1909 it received a short and cryptic note in the Journal of American Folklore. *A collector of folk songs from the North Carolina mountains, Louise Rand Bascom, coveted a ballad on "Johnie Henry," of which she possessed the first two lines.*

Johnie Henry was a hard-workin' man,
He died with his hammer in his hand.

Her informant declared the ballad to be sad, tearful, and sweet, and hoped to secure the rest "when Tobe sees Tom, an' gits him to larn him what he ain't forgot of hit from Muck's pickin'." Apparently Tobe never did see Tom, but the key stanza was enough to guide other collectors.

In the next decade half a dozen contributors to the Journal *expanded knowledge of the work song and the ballad carrying the name of John Henry, who at first was confused with John Hardy, a Negro desperado hanged in 1894 in West Virginia. By 1929 a sociologist at the University of North Carolina, Guy B. Johnson, had written a detailed, booklength study,* John Henry: Tracking Down a Negro Legend. *This was followed in 1933 by another, even more painstaking, inquiry,* John Henry: A Folklore Study, *by Louis W. Chappell, a professor of English at the University of West Virginia. While Chappell attacked Johnson's handling of evidence, both books persuasively argued for the existence of John Henry and the likelihood that a steam-drilling contest had actually been held at Big Bend Tunnel. Furthermore, they stimulated popular interest in the Negro hero.*

Already in his look into the John Henry tradition, Johnson had anticipated its potentialities for the creative arts. "I marvel," he wrote, "that some of the 'new' Negroes with an artistic bent do not exploit the wealth of John Henry lore. Here is material for an epic poem, for a play, for an opera, for a Negro symphony. What more tragic theme than the theme of John Henry's martyrdom?" A response was not long in coming. Within two years a fictionalized story, John Henry, *had been published and distributed by the Literary Guild. Its author, Roark Bradford, while not a "new Negro," had grown* up on a southern plantation near the Mississippi River, and had seen Negroes closely. (Bradford achieved his greatest success with Ol' Man Adam an' His Chillun [1928], a portrayal of Scripture seen through Negro eyes, which was rendered by Marc Connelly into the Broadway hit The Green Pastures [1930].) In Bradford's John Henry the contest with the machine occupies only 5 out of 223 pages, serving, however, as the dramatic climax for such structure as the book possesses. A cotton-rolling steam winch on the levee replaces the rock-boring steam drill, and New Orleans and the Mississippi River form the locale. John Henry is a cotton-loading roustabout, when he is working; much of the time he is loving and leaving his girl Julie Anne, who follows him to death after his fatal contest with the new machine. At other times he performs great feats of lifting, eating, and brawling. The whole narrative is written in a repetitious, rhythmic stage dialect, interspersed with plaintive little songs, and centering around Negro literary stereotypes. The sporting man, the hell-busting preacher, the woman of easy acquaintance, the old conjure mammy, are all present. John Henry, the frontier boaster, is a new stereotype for the Negro gallery, but a well-established one in other American lore, and he reiterates his tall-tale outcries on nearly every page.

In 1939 an adaptation of John Henry, billed as a play with music, appeared on the Broadway stage. Coauthor with Roark Bradford was Jacques Wolfe, who supplied the musical scores for the song numbers. The play followed closely the original story, which contained obvious elements for a musical drama. Paul Robeson starred as John Henry. The Broadway production closed after a short run.

The book and the play of Roark Bradford, with attendant newspaper reviews and magazine articles, popularized the name of John Henry, and fixed him in the public mind as a Negro Paul Bunyan. In many ways the growth of the John Henry legend and pseudo-legend parallels that of the tales of the giant logger, who was well established as a national property by the 1930's. Bradford's John Henry resembles James Stevens' Paul Bunyan of 1925, as a fictional portrayal of an American "folk" hero based on a slender thread of oral tradition, in one case a few northwoods anecdotes, in the other a single ballad. Bradford, like Stevens, created the picture of a giant strong man, although with a somber rather than a rollicking mien. In 1926 Odum and Johnson called John Henry the "black Paul Bunyan of the Negro workingman." Carl Sandburg made the comparison the following year in The American Songbag, saying both heroes were myths. Newspa-

pers referred to John Henry as the "Paul Bunyan of Negroes," "the Paul Bunyan of his race, a gigantic river roustabout whose Herculean feats of work and living are part of America's folk lore." In the later history of the two traditions, the parallelism persists. Writers, poets, and artists attempted to wrest some deeper meaning from the Paul Buyan and John Henry legends, and failed. But both figures lived on triumphantly in children's books of American folk heroes and in popular treasuries of American folklore.

The first presentation of John Henry as a folk hero came in 1930, in a chapter of Here's Audacity! American Legendary Heroes, *by Frank Shay. His account of "John Henry, the Steel Driving Man," followed Guy B. Johnson's preliminary essay of 1927, "John Henry: A Negro Legend." Shay's formula was repeated by a number of other writers for the juvenile market, all of whom inevitably included the story of John Henry and his contest with the steam drill in their pantheon of American comic demigods. Other authors of children's books found it rewarding to deal individually and serially with America's newfound folk heroes. One product of this trend was* John Henry: The Rambling Black Ulysses, *by James Cloyd Bowman (1942). Bowman's nearly three hundred pages went far beyond the ballad story to give a full-length improvisation of John Henry's career, from his life as a slave boy on the old plantation through the Civil War to freedom. In this version John Henry encourages unruly freedmen to mine coal, cut corn, pick cotton, and drive railroad ties. He outsmarts confidence men and gamblers, stokes the* Robert E. Lee *to victory over the* Natchez, *and at long last dies with his hammer in his hand at the Big Bend Tunnel. But a final chapter presents an alternate report, that John Henry recovered from overwork, and resumed his ramblin' around. In a much briefer story,* John Henry and the Double-Jointed Steam Drill, *by Irwin Shapiro (1945), John Henry never dies at all, but after beating the steam drill pines away to a ghost, until his old pal John Hardy convinces him that he should learn to use the machine he conquered, and the tale ends with John Henry drilling through the mountain, and the steam drill shivering to pieces in his hands! So for American children John Henry unites the Negroes in faithful service to their white employers, and accepts the machine. In these children's books the full-page illustrations of a sad-faced Negro giant swinging a hammer contributed as much as the printed words to fixing the image of John Henry.*

Folklore treasuries and collections of folk songs also continued to keep the story and song steadily before the public. In his best-selling A Treasury of American Folklore *(1944), currently in its twenty-third printing, B. A. Botkin reprinted accounts of John Henry in oral hearsay, balladry, and fiction. The lavishly illustrated* Life Treasury of American Folklore *(1961) offered a picture of John Henry spiking ties on a railroad track rather than driving steel in a tunnel. John A. and Alan Lomax, naturally sympathetic to the ballad hero first presented in a full text by the elder Lomax in 1915, always included John Henry ballads, some adapted and arranged, some recorded in the field, in their popular folksong compilations. "John Henry" was the opening song in their first book,* American Ballads and Folksongs *(1934), and in* Our Singing Country *(1941) they called it "probably America's greatest single piece of folklore." In the latest and most ornate garland, Alan Lomax (the sole author), having meanwhile shifted his emphasis from Marx to Freud, found John Henry equally receptive to his altered insights. The steel-driver shaking the mountains is a phallic image; singers know that John Henry died from love-making, not overwork:*

> *This old hammer—WHAM!*
> *Killed John Henry—WHAM!*
> *Can't kill me—WHAM!*
> *Can't kill me—WHAM!*

Thus the hammer song vaunted the sexual virility of the pounder. Lomax has returned full cycle to the psychoanalytic views of Chappell. The steel-driver also appealed to social reformers. In American Folk Songs of Protest *(1953, reprinted as a paperback in 1960), John Greenway called "John Henry" the "best-known (and best), Negro ballad, the best-known Negro work song, the best song of protest against imminent technological unemployment. . . ."*

The greatest impact of John Henry on American culture has come outside the printed page, through commercial recordings. In 1962 the most widely recorded folk song sold to the public was "John Henry." That year the Phonolog Record Index *listed some fifty current renditions of the ballad "John Henry" and fifteen of the work song "Nine Pound Hammer." As many popular singers have made recordings for the general public as have folk singers for collectors in the field. The* Library of Congress Copyright Catalogue *reveals the publication of over one hundred songs devoted to John Henry from 1916 on, embracing all kinds of musical arrangements from simple melodic line and text to full orchestral composition. Arrangers staking out claims include the well-known American composer Aaron Copland, the Negro song-compiler John W. Work, the musicologist Charles Seeger, the celebrated Negro ex-convict Huddie Ledbetter (Lead Belly), W. C. Handy (the "father of the blues"), concert arranger Elie Siegmeister, and popular singer Bob Gibson.*

Popular singers and recording artists have altered the formless sequence of independent stanzas, which comprised the folk ballad, into a swift-moving, tightly knit song story. John Henry has shifted from the sphere of Negro laborers and white mountaineers into the center of the entertainment world of jukebox and hootenanny, radio and television. The earlier texts from tradition show the usual variations characteristic of folklore. John Henry drives steel chiefly on the C & O, but once it is located in Brinton, New Jersey, and he also drives on the A C & L, the Air Line Road, the L & N, and the Georgia Southern Road. He comes from Tennessee most often, but also from eastern Virginia, from Louisiana, and from Mobile, Alabama. His hammer weighs nine, ten, twelve, sixteen, twenty, and thirty pounds; sometimes he carries a hammer in each hand. His girl is named Julie Ann, Polly Ann, Mary Ann, Martha Ann, Nellie Ann, Lizzie Ann, and Mary Magdalene. In one unique text, John Henry's partner kills him with the hammer. Among the visitors to his grave is, in one instance, Queen Elizabeth II.

Today the ballad of John Henry lives on in a form remarkably stable for an anonymous oral composition. It has been refashioned by the urban folk-song revival into a national property, shared by singers and composers, writers and artists, listeners and readers. The ballad commemorates an obscure event in which several lines of American history converged—the growth of the railroads, the rise of the Negro, the struggle of labor. Various interpreters have read in the shadowy figure of John Henry symbols of racial, national, and sexual strivings. The Negro and the white man, teen-ager and tot, professor and performer, have levied upon the John Henry tradition. The explanation for these multiple appeals lies in the dramatic intensity, tragic tension, and simple poetry combined in one unforgettable American folk ballad.

Mary Baker Eddy

Science and Health

1875

EDITED BY MARTIN E. MARTY

The presence of over 250 denominations in the United States is a sign of the religious inventiveness of the American people. But most of these religious groups are direct heirs of European church bodies. Many of them are closely related to each other. Few are original and authentically native products. In 1875 there appeared in Boston a book which ranks with The Book of Mormon *as one of the most influential original documents to give birth to an American church body. Entitled* Science *and* Health, *it was written by Mrs. Mary Baker Eddy. The book was occasioned by the author's experiences after a fall on ice in 1866. Claiming that she had been abandoned by medical science and that she was rescued by what then was called "faith healing," she reflected upon the spiritual implications of her recovery. The result of these reflections was the book which, through the careful custodianship of the denomination based on it, has formed the religious opinions of hundreds of thousands of Americans.*

Mary Baker Eddy was born near Bow, New Hampshire, in 1821. Her earlier years were marked by ill health, the death of a husband, and a later unhappy marital experience. Her generally unfulfilled literary aspirations seemed to predestine her for obscurity; she published nothing of consequence before Science and Health, *which appeared when she was well into the sixth decade of her life. During the years before the writing of* Science and Health *the author seems to have familiarized herself with terms and ideas employed by the New England Transcendentalists, who were experiencing some literary vogue. Later scholars have detected traces of Hegelianism and other European idealistic philosophies casually appropriated into her system of thought. Most important, she was apparently influenced by a faith healer named Phineas P. Quimby. The extent of all these influences upon her writings has been a subject of much controversy—as has almost anything associated with her career. Mrs. Eddy's followers take her word for it that the book was "hopelessly original," and, contending that it was divinely inspired as a revelation of ultimate truth, have withstood those critics who have suggested that some plagiarism was at work in* Science and Health.

In 1883 Mary Baker Eddy appended a Key to the Scriptures *to the book, which since then has appeared under the combined title. Two admirers of her thought provided funds for publication. Sales were disappointing at first, but increased greatly as the movement founded upon the book grew. Mrs. Eddy revised the book 89 times, and it had passed through 382 editions before her death in 1910. The representative and, indeed, authoritative text is therefore the last one to have been certified by her hand. This version, which bears the copyright date 1906, will remain the permanent source of doctrine and practice for the Church of Christ, Scientist, or "Christian Science," the religious movement founded on Mrs. Eddy's teachings. The rules of the church prevent tampering with the basic text. The book also contains, however, some testimonials by followers to the effects of spiritual healing, and a small number of these have been replaced through the years.*

Science and Health *was completed in 1875 in a small upstairs room at Lynn, Massachusetts, in austere surroundings which have been preserved by admirers. As Mrs. Eddy's career prospered, she revised the later editions in a more comfortable setting at Concord, New Hampshire, during the years of an energetic retirement. She was active until the end of her long life, spending the last three years near Boston, where she took a leading part in church affairs.*

The passage reprinted here from the 700-page work is one of the few which provide some comment on the American setting. The "metaphysical reflections" in the selection are representative of the character of the whole book.

[*Soul greater than body*]

MATTER does not express Spirit. God is infinite omnipresent Spirit. If Spirit is *all* and is everywhere, what and where is matter? Remember that truth is greater than error, and we cannot put the greater into the less. Soul is Spirit, and Spirit is greater than body. If Spirit were once within the body, Spirit would be finite, and therefore could not be Spirit.

[*The question of the ages*] The question, "What is Truth," convulses the world. Many are ready to meet this inquiry with the assurance which comes of understanding; but more are blinded by their old illusions, and try to "give it pause." "If the blind lead the blind, both shall fall into the ditch."

The efforts of error to answer this question by some *ology* are vain. Spiritual rationality and free thought accompany approaching Science, and cannot be put down. They will emancipate humanity, and supplant unscientific means and so-called laws.

[*Heralds of Science*] Peals that should startle the slumbering thought from its erroneous dream are partially unheeded; but the last trump has not sounded, or this would not be so. Marvels, calamities, and sin will much more abound as truth urges upon mortals its resisted claims; but the awful daring of sin destroys sin, and foreshadows the triumph of truth. God will overturn, until "He come whose right it is." Longevity is increasing and the power of sin diminishing, for the world feels the alterative effect of truth through every pore.

As the crude footprints of the past disappear from the dissolving paths of the present, we shall better understand the Science which governs these changes, and shall plant our feet on firmer ground. Every sensuous pleasure or pain is self-destroyed through suffering. There should be painless progress, attended by life and peace instead of discord and death.

[*Sectarianism and opposition*] In the record of nineteen centuries, there are sects many but not enough Christianity. Centuries ago religionists were ready to hail an anthropomorphic God, and array His vicegerent with pomp and splendor; but this was not the manner of truth's appearing. Of old the cross was truth's central sign, and it is to-day. The modern lash is less material than the Roman scourge, but it is equally as cutting. Cold disdain, stubborn resistance, opposition from church, state laws, and the press, are still the harbingers of truth's full-orbed appearing.

A higher and more practical Christianity, demonstrating justice and meeting the needs of mortals in sickness and in health, stands at the door of this age, knocking for admission. Will you open or close the door upon this angel visitant, who cometh in the quiet of meekness, as he came of old to the patriarch at noonday?

[*Mental emancipation*] Truth brings the elements of liberty. On its banner is the Soul-inspired motto, "Slavery is abolished." The power of God brings deliverance to the captive. No power can withstand divine Love. What is this supposed power, which opposes itself to God? Whence cometh it? What is it that binds man with iron shackles to sin, sickness, and death? Whatever enslaves man is opposed to the divine government. Truth makes man free.

[*Truth's ordeal*] You may know when first Truth leads by the fewness and faithfulness of its followers. Thus it is that the march of time bears onward freedom's banner. The powers of this world will fight, and will command their sentinels not to let truth pass the guard until it subscribes to their systems; but Science, heeding not the pointed bayonet, marches on. There is always some tumult, but there is a rallying to truth's standard.

[*Immortal sentences*] The history of our country, like all history, illustrates the might of Mind, and shows human power to be proportionate to its embodiment of right thinking. A few immortal sentences, breathing the omnipotence of divine justice, have been potent to break despotic fetters and abolish the whipping-post and slave market; but oppression neither went down in blood, nor did the breath of freedom come from the cannon's mouth. Love is the liberator.

[*Slavery abolished*] Legally to abolish unpaid servitude in the United States was hard; but the abolition of mental slavery is a more difficult task. The despotic tendencies, inherent in mortal mind and always germinating in new forms of tyranny, must be rooted out through the action of the divine Mind.

Men and women of all climes and races are still in bondage to material sense, ignorant how to obtain their freedom. The rights of man were vindicated in a single section and on the lowest plane of human life, when African slavery was abolished in our land. That was only prophetic of further steps towards the banishment of a world-wide slavery, found on higher planes of existence and under more subtle and depraving forms.

[*Liberty's crusade*] The voice of God in behalf of the African slave was still echoing in our land, when the voice of the herald of this new crusade sounded the keynote of universal freedom, asking a fuller acknowledgment of the rights of man as a Son of God, demanding that the fetters of sin, sickness, and death be stricken from the human mind and that its freedom be won, not through human warfare, not with bayonet and blood, but through Christ's divine Science.

[*Cramping systems*] God has built a higher platform of human rights, and He has built it on diviner claims. These claims are not made through code or creed, but in demonstration of "on earth peace, good-will toward men." Human codes, scholastic theology, material medicine and hygiene, fetter faith and spiritual understanding. Divine Science rends asunder these fetters, and man's birthright of sole allegiance to his Maker asserts itself.

I saw before me the sick, wearing out years of servitude to an unreal master in the belief that the body governed them, rather than Mind.

[*House of bondage*] The lame, the deaf, the dumb, the blind, the sick, the sensual, the sinner, I wished to save from the slavery of their own beliefs and from the educational systems of the Pharaohs, who to-day, as of yore, hold the children of Israel in bondage. I saw before me the awful conflict, the Red Sea and the wilderness; but I pressed on through faith in God, trusting Truth, the strong deliverer, to guide me into the land of Christian Science, where fetters fall and the rights of man are fully known and acknowledged.

[*Higher law ends bondage*] I saw that the law of mortal belief included all error, and that, even as oppressive laws are disputed and mortals are taught their right to freedom, so the claims of the enslaving senses must be denied and superseded. The law of the divine Mind must end human bondage, or mortals will continue unaware of man's inalienable rights and in subjection to hopeless slavery, because some public teachers permit an ignorance of divine power,—an ignorance that is the foundation of continued bondage and of human suffering.

[*Native freedom*] Discerning the rights of man, we cannot fail to foresee the doom of all oppression. Slavery is not the legitimate state of man. God made man free. Paul said, "I was free born." All men should be free. "Where the Spirit of the Lord is, there is liberty." Love and Truth make free, but evil and error lead into captivity.

[*Standard of liberty*] Christian Science raises the standard of liberty and cries: "Follow me! Escape from the bondage of sickness, sin, and death!" Jesus marked out the way. Citizens of the world, accept the "glorious liberty of the children of God," and be free! This is your divine right. The illusion of material sense, not divine law, has bound you, entangled your free limbs, crippled your capacities, enfeebled your body, and defaced the tablet of your being.

If God had instituted material laws to govern man, disobedience to which would have made man ill, Jesus would not have disregarded those laws by healing in direct opposition to them and in defiance of all material conditions.

[*No fleshly heredity*] The transmission of disease or of certain idiosyncrasies of mortal mind would be impossible if this great fact of being were learned,—namely, that nothing inharmonious can enter being, for Life *is* God. Heredity is a prolific subject for mortal belief to pin theories upon; but if we learn that nothing is real but the right, we shall have no dangerous inheritances, and fleshly ills will disappear.

[*God-given dominion*] The enslavement of man is not legitimate. It will cease when man enters into his heritage of freedom, his God-given dominion over the material senses. Mortals will some day assert their freedom in the name of Almighty God. Then they will control their own bodies through the understanding of divine Science. Dropping their present beliefs, they will recognize harmony as the spiritual reality and discord as the material unreality.

If we follow the command of our Master, "Take no thought for your life," we shall never depend on bodily conditions, structure, or economy, but we shall be masters of the body, dictate its terms, and form and control it with Truth.

[*Priestly pride humbled*] There is no power apart from God. Omnipotence has all-power, and to acknowledge any other power is to dishonor God. The humble Nazarene overthrew the supposition that sin, sickness, and death have power. He proved them powerless. It should have humbled the pride of the priests, when they saw the demonstration of Christianity excel the influence of their dead faith and ceremonies.

If Mind is not the master of sin, sickness, and death, they are immortal, for it is already proved that matter has not destroyed them, but is their basis and support.

[*No union of opposites*] We should hesitate to say that Jehovah sins or suffers; but if sin and suffering are realities of being, whence did they emanate? God made all that was made, and Mind signifies God,—infinity, not finity. Not far removed from infidelity is the belief which unites such opposites as sickness and health, holiness and unholiness, calls both the offspring of spirit, and at the same time admits that Spirit is God,—virtually declaring Him good in one instance and evil in another.

[*Self-constituted law*] By universal consent, mortal belief has constituted itself a law to bind mortals to sickness, sin, and death. This customary belief is misnamed material law, and the individual who upholds it is mistaken in theory and in practice. The so-called law of mortal mind, conjectural and speculative, is made void by the law of immortal Mind, and false law should be trampled under foot.

[*Sickness from mortal mind*] If God causes man to be sick, sickness must be good, and its opposite, health, must be evil, for all that He makes is good and will stand forever. If the transgression of God's law produces sickness, it is right to be sick; and we cannot if we would, and should not if we could, annul the decrees of wisdom. It is the transgression of belief of mortal mind, not of a law of matter nor of divine Mind, which causes the belief of sickness. The remedy is Truth, not matter,—the truth that disease is *unreal*.

If sickness is real, it belongs to immortality; if true, it is a part of Truth. Would you attempt with drugs, or without, to destroy a quality or condition of Truth? But if sickness and sin are illusions, the awakening from this mortal dream, or illusion, will bring us into health, holiness, and immortality. This awakening is the forever coming of Christ, the advanced appearing of Truth, which casts out error and heals the sick. This is the salvation which comes through God, the divine Principle, Love, as demonstrated by Jesus.

[*God never inconsistent*] It would be contrary to our highest ideas of God to suppose Him capable of first arranging law and causation so as to bring about certain evil results, and then punishing the helpless victims of His volition for doing what they could not avoid doing. Good is not, cannot be, the author of experimental sins. God, good, can no more produce sickness than goodness can cause evil and health occasion disease.

[*Mental narcotics*] Does wisdom make blunders which must afterwards be rectified by man? Does a law of God produce sickness, and can man put that law under his feet by healing sickness? According to Holy Writ, the sick are never really healed by drugs, hygiene, or any material method. These merely evade the question. They are soothing syrups to put children to sleep, satisfy mortal belief, and quiet fear.

[*The true healing*] We think that we are healed when a disease disappears, though it is liable to reappear; but we are never thoroughly healed until the liability to be ill is removed. So-called mortal mind or the mind of mortals being the remote, predisposing, and the exciting cause of all suffering, the cause of disease must be obliterated through Christ in divine Science, or the so-called physical senses will get the victory.

[*Destruction of all evil*] Unless an ill is rightly met and fairly overcome by Truth, the ill is never conquered. If God destroys not sin, sickness, and death, they are not destroyed in the mind of mortals, but seem to this so-called mind to be immortal. What God cannot do, man need not attempt. If God heals not the sick, they are not healed, for no lesser power equals the infinite All-power; but God, Truth, Life, Love, does heal the sick through the prayer of the righteous.

If God makes sin, if good produces evil, if truth results in error, then Science and Christianity are helpless; but there are no antagonistic powers nor laws, spiritual or material, creating and governing man through perpetual warfare. God is not the author of mortal discords. Therefore we accept the conclusion that discords have only a fabulous existence, are mortal beliefs which divine Truth and Love destroy.

[*Superiority to sickness and sin*] To hold yourself superior to sin, because God made you superior to it and governs man, is true wisdom. To fear sin is to misunderstand the power of Love and the divine Science of being in man's relation to God,—to doubt His government and distrust His omnipotent care. To hold yourself superior to sickness and death is equally wise, and is in accordance with divine Science. To fear them is impossible, when you fully apprehend God and know that they are no part of His creation.

Man, governed by his Maker, having no other Mind,—planted on the Evangelist's statement that "all things were made by Him [the Word of God]; and without Him was not anything made that was made,"—can triumph over sin, sickness, and death.

[*Denials of divine power*] Many theories relative to God and man neither make man harmonious nor God lovable. The beliefs we commonly entertain about happiness and life afford no scatheless and permanent evidence of either. Security for the claims of harmonious and eternal being is found only in divine Science.

Scripture informs us that "with God all things are possible,"—all good is possible to Spirit; but our prevalent theories practically deny this, and make healing possible only through matter. These theories must be untrue, for the Scripture is true. Christianity is not false, but religions which contradict its Principle are false.

In our age Christianity is again demonstrating the power of divine Principle, as it did over nineteen hundred years ago, by healing the sick and triumphing over death. Jesus never taught that drugs, food, air, and exercise could make a man healthy, or that they could destroy human life; nor did he illustrate these errors by his practice. He referred man's harmony to Mind, not to matter, and never tried to make of none effect the sentence of God, which sealed God's condemnation of sin, sickness, and death.

[*Signs following*] In the sacred sanctuary of Truth are voices of solemn import, but we heed them not. It is only when the so-called pleasures and pains of sense pass away in our lives, that we find unquestionable signs of the burial of error and the resurrection to spiritual life.

[*Profession and proof*] There is neither place nor opportunity in Science for error of any sort. Every day makes its demands upon us for higher proofs rather than professions of Christian power. These proofs consist solely in the destruction of sin, sickness, and death by the power of Spirit, as Jesus destroyed them. This is an element of progress, and progress is the law of God, whose law demands of us only what we can certainly fulfil.

[*Perfection gained slowly*] In the midst of imperfection, perfection is seen and acknowledged only by degrees. The ages must slowly work up to perfection. How long it must be before we arrive at the demonstration of scientific being, no man knoweth,—not even "the Son but the Father;" but the false claim of error continues its delusions until the goal of goodness is assiduously earned and won.

[*Christ's mission*] Already the shadow of His right hand rests upon the hour. Ye who can discern the face of the sky,—the sign material,—how much more should ye discern the sign mental, and compass the destruction of sin and sickness by overcoming the thoughts which produce them, and by understanding the spiritual idea which corrects and destroys them. To reveal this truth was our Master's mission to all mankind, including the hearts which rejected him.

[*Efficacy of truth*] When numbers have been divided according to a fixed rule, the quotient is not more unquestionable than the scientific tests I have made of the effects of truth upon the sick. The counter fact relative to any disease is required to cure it. The utterance of truth is designed to rebuke and destroy error. Why should truth not be efficient in sickness, which is solely the result of inharmony?

Spiritual draughts heal, while material lotions interfere with truth, even as ritualism and creed hamper spirituality. If we trust matter, we distrust Spirit.

[*Crumbs of comfort*] Whatever inspires with wisdom, Truth, or Love—be it song, sermon, or Science—blesses the human family with crumbs of comfort from Christ's table, feeding the hungry and giving living waters to the thirsty.

Mary Baker Eddy's own book and the Bible are the two authoritative texts of the Church of Christ, Scientist. This organization was chartered under Massachusetts law in 1879 and reorganized under a permanent, self-perpetuating board of directors in 1892. The denomination has grown to major size and influence and is efficiently organized, even though Mrs. Eddy at first seemed to be hesitant about forming a separate religious group at all.

The Mother Church, as the central organization in Boston is called (all local congregations are called branches), does not release statistics of membership. In order to qualify for eligibility as a religious group providing chaplaincies in World War II, Christian Scientists were forced to reveal their membership. They used the figures of a 1916 census which listed 268,915 people as affiliated with the denomination. At the founder's death in 1910 there had been 1,114 American branches; in 1965 there were approximately 3,300. The strength of the movement can be judged in part by the fact that millions of copies of Science and Health with Key to the Scriptures *have been sold—most of them in the United States, where perhaps 80 per cent of the world's Christian Scientists reside.*

To sociologists, Christian Science represents a typical "cult which became a church." Originally only a small following gathered around Mrs. Eddy. One of the first of the followers was Asa Gilbert Eddy, who became her third husband as well as the first "practitioner," as a professional healer within the denomination is called. After a period of slow growth the small band of admirers increased, gradually becoming the large, organized body just described. To the public, Christian Science is best known as a faith-healing movement because of its well-advertised belief that diseases of the body can be cured by a scientific application of the divine Principle which is the heart of the religion.

From a legal standpoint, Christian Scientists have frequently provided interesting test cases. From 1918 through 1921 in "The Great Litigation" in the Massachusetts courts, the Mother Church successfully fought off schisms and dissensions which would have broken the tight national organization. At other times Christian Scientists have opposed in the courts efforts to fluoridate public water supplies, or to enact or enforce compulsory measures for vaccination. Frequently Christian Science has come under legal attack and into public attention when it has been sued by those who were attracted from conventional medicine to religious healing which, they feel, failed them.

To church historians the Church of Christ, Scientist, and the book on which it is based represent "egocentricity" in religion. That is, it is not first of all preoccupied with social questions or the amelioration of society as such. It is directed to the felt needs of individuals, particularly to those who have experienced ill health. This is not to say that Christian Scientists have not been responsible as citizens or that the church body has never taken an interest in social problems. It distinguished itself after World War II with its record of war relief. But, characteristically it declines to involve itself and its members directly in social causes or, for that matter, in an understanding of religious faith as having its base and immediate consequence in men's social relations.

To literary experts Science and Health *has provided a text for continuing controversy. Most savage was Mark Twain's early satire: "When you read it you seem to be listening to lively and aggressive and oracular speech delivered in an unknown tongue." More moderate, but still repugnant to Christian Scientists, have been the numerous critical biographies and literary analyses. And there are balanced appraisals, sometimes written by members of the church, which find acceptance among both members and nonmembers.*

In the general consensus, Mrs. Eddy is seen to have captured in her writing and her movement the optimistic spirit of much of the nineteenth-century American experience. The promises of better health, of a serene outlook on life, of a meaningful religious experience, of the chance to escape poverty and enslaving habits have attracted many. Christian Scientists, whose attitudes and actions are presumably influenced strongly by this book, are known to be peace-loving, studious, and generally law-abiding.

In highly literate circles the denomination is best known for the Christian Science Monitor. *This daily newspaper was founded in 1908 by Mrs. Eddy, not only to perpetuate the* ideas of Science and Health *but also to combat the "yellow journalism" of the period. One of the most often quoted, most influential of the nation's newspapers, it fuses the emphases of Christian Science with calm and fair appraisals of world news. In particular, many of the attitudes toward freedom enunciated in* Science and Health *are reflected on the Monitor's pages.*

Except for its reintroduction of concern over faith healing into orthodox Christian circles and its influence on a number of imitative "new thought" religions, Christian Science has had little direct impact on the broad stream of national intellectual life. What Science and Health *and its author produced is a large, often-noticed, well-defined, and highly disciplined religious body. If any religion deserves to be represented by the documentary tradition associated with its founder, Christian Science is the one. The Board of Directors permits no adaptation of the text and no unofficial exegesis of it by members. It provides lectures which are read in all churches of the denomination and prepares lesson material for those under the age of twenty. There are no ordained ministers, and no missionaries, in the usual sense of those terms. Christian Scientists are uninterested in recreational and social activities in their churches. Instead, they propagate their beliefs "documentarily" through lectures, classes, reading rooms, and literary materials placed on public display. Every such literary evidence or teaching device is based on the Bible and, even more directly, on* Science and Health with Key to the Scriptures.

Emma Lazarus

The New Colossus

1883

EDITED BY JOHN HIGHAM

For nine frustrating years, from 1877 to 1886, a committee of New York business and society leaders collected funds to pay for a pedestal on which a gigantic Statue of Liberty might stand in New York Harbor. The statue itself, the inspiration and creation of a French sculptor, Frédéric Auguste Bartholdi, was under construction in Paris. It was to be a gift to America from the French people, a symbol and pledge of friendship between the two republics. Americans needed only to erect it properly; yet the task almost exceeded the limits of the sluggish public spirit of the day.

At one point, in 1883, when the statue was almost ready to ship and the pedestal only half-finished, the Pedestal Fund Committee organized a temporary art exhibition as a fundraising device. Prominent New Yorkers lent some of their treasures, and a number of artists and writers contributed original drawings and letters to a portfolio which was put up for auction. After some urging, Emma Lazarus produced a sonnet for the occasion. The entire portfolio, including the sonnet, sold for $1,500, a disappointing sum.

A finely bred, bookish young lady, Miss Lazarus rarely

wrote in a patriotic vein. But this occasion touched obliquely
a new and vital concern of hers. Until 1881 she had produced derivative, self-consciously literary verse, the tinkling
melodies then fashionable in the world of genteel culture. Belonging to one of the oldest and most secure of New York
Jewish families, she had abandoned the synagogue in her
youth and had largely lost a sense of Jewish identity. Then
the horrifying outbreak of anti-Jewish pogroms in Russia,
and the sight of the first bedraggled refugees arriving in New
York, gave her a theme and a mission. With a new passion,
she wrote henceforth mainly as a champion of the Jews. She
became the first modern American laureate of their history
and culture. To her the Statue of Liberty, facing seaward,
would hold out to all uprooted folk the same message of succor that she, Emma Lazarus, was expressing to and for her
fellow Jews.

Not like the brazen giant of Greek fame,
With conquering limbs astride from land to land;
Here at our sea-washed, sunset gates shall stand
A mighty woman with a torch, whose flame
Is the imprisoned lightning, and her name
Mother of Exiles. From her beacon-hand
Glows world-wide welcome; her mild eyes command
The air-bridged harbor that twin cities frame.

"Keep, ancient lands, your storied pomp!" cries she
With silent lips. "Give me your tired, your poor,
Your huddled masses yearning to breathe free,
The wretched refuse of your teeming shore.
Send these, the homeless, tempest-tost to me,
I lift my lamp beside the golden door!"

Absorbed in the cause of the Jews, Miss Lazarus seems to
have taken no further interest in the Statue of Liberty once
her poem was written. Nor did her contemporaries pay much
heed to "The New Colossus." When she died in 1887, four

The original manuscript of the poem, which is followed here, is in
the possession of the American Jewish Historical Society in New York
City. (The "brazen giant" referred to in the first line is the Colossus of
Rhodes, a statue of the sun god Helius which once stood at the harbor
of Rhodes; it was known in ancient and medieval times as one of the
Seven Wonders of the World.)

years after its composition, the obituaries failed to mention it. The reviewers of her collected works, which appeared in 1889, concentrated on her specifically Jewish poems. One critic conceded that "her noble sonnet" on the Bartholdi statue had given many their "first apprehension of the glory in even the more sordid elements in our American life." Others ignored the poem completely. After the turn of the century Miss Lazarus herself was largely forgotten outside a small Anglo-Jewish literary circle.

In 1903, on the twentieth anniversary of the writing of "The New Colossus," another shy, poetry-loving spinster who belonged to the old New York aristocracy, Georgina Schuyler, secured permission to put a bronze tablet containing the entire poem on an interior wall of the statue's pedestal. This she did primarily as a memorial to Miss Lazarus, whom she evidently had known and admired. The event passed without ceremony or public notice. In fact, the poem rested there for another thirty years without attracting any publicity at all.

This long neglect is remarkable; for the ideas that the poem expressed were deeply ingrained in American tradition. The concept of America as a refuge from European oppression supplied one of the original, fertilizing elements of our national consciousness. Jefferson, Emerson, Lowell, and many a lesser patriot had voiced its continuing appeal. In the late nineteenth century, however, pride in America's receptive mission dimmed. A gradual liberalization of political institutions throughout most of Europe blurred the once-sharp image of the immigrant as one who had been unfree in his native country. Meanwhile, the new problems of an urban, industrial age inspired a strong movement in America to restrict immigration. By 1886, when the New Colossus was finally unveiled upon her completed pedestal, there was already considerable alarm about the huddled masses streaming through the golden door. The lavish dedication ceremonies took place without a single reference to Miss Lazarus' sonnet and without serious attention to its theme.

Not only the uneasy mood of the time but also the statue itself resisted the generous construction Miss Lazarus placed upon it. The creators of the monument did not intend a symbol of welcome. Bartholdi and the French liberals who supported his work prized America not as an asylum but as an example of republican stability. They constructed a passive figure, austere and unresponsive, a model of frozen perfection, holding a torch high to illuminate the darker world beyond the sea. Its official name was "Liberty Enlightening the

World." The meaning of the physical object would have to change before the sonnet could become a living document.

The immigrants themselves wrought that transformation, as they arrived in this country in the years after the statue was erected. The vast majority debarked at New York, and to every exultant heart and straining eye this first American presence was a profoundly moving sight. The immigrants perceived the statue as waiting for them, big with promise. They saw it not as a beacon to other lands but as a redemptive salutation to themselves. The memory of that awesome moment and the unspoken greeting it contained was a thing to cherish, a thing to tell one's children about. In 1906 Edward A. Steiner, an immigrant intellectual who was unaware of Emma Lazarus' poem, predicted that a great poet would someday put into words the inspiring emotions that millions of immigrants felt on encountering "this new divinity into whose keeping they now entrust themselves."

Miss Lazarus' words were rediscovered only after the immigrants' response to the statue penetrated our fund of national myths, revitalizing the old eighteenth-century idea of America as an asylum. While a bitter controversy over immigration pitted older against newer American groups, the Statue of Liberty remained—in the dominant native culture —an aloof, impersonal symbol, conveying a warning rather than a welcome to the outside world. After the restrictive Immigration Act of 1924 was passed, however, fear and rancor subsided; the great influx from overseas was ended. Immigration as a mass movement receded into history. Meanwhile, the children of immigrants from southern and eastern Europe grew up into full participation in American life. To ease their Americanization, public school curricula devoted increasing attention to the immigrants' love for and contributions to America. By 1926 fourth-grade children in St. Louis, Missouri, were studying the Statue of Liberty with the object of understanding what it meant to immigrants. By then some of the school textbooks on American history included pictures of immigrant families gazing joyfully at Bartholdi's Colossus. That immobile figure gradually joined the covered wagon as a symbol of the migrations that had made America.

In the late 1930's, more than fifty years after its composition, Emma Lazarus' poem finally attracted public interest. The event that called it forth from obscurity was a recurrence of the very problem that had moved Miss Lazarus in the first place: the plight of Jewish refugees. Their efforts to escape Nazi barbarism coincided with a growing revulsion of American opinion against racism and with a steady movement of the United States toward war with Germany. In contrast to the situation in the 1880's, when Americans were turning away from a cosmopolitan, humane outlook, the circumstances of the late 1930's united a particular concern for the Jews with a broader movement to strengthen ethnic democracy. Immigration policy did not change significantly. But a nation striving to overcome its own ethnic hatreds, to dignify influential minority groups, and to gird for war against Hitler needed to define itself anew as a bastion against persecution.

Louis Adamic, a Yugoslav-American journalist, did more than anyone else to popularize "The New Colossus." About 1934 he launched a one-man crusade to elevate the status of immigrant groups and to propagate an eclectic sense of American nationality. After 1938 he adopted the Lazarus sonnet as the keynote of practically everything he wrote or said. He quoted it endlessly in books, pamphlets, and public lectures. During the 1930's the words of the poem became a familiar litany in mass-circulation magazines, children's stories, and high-school history texts. In 1945 Georgina Schuyler's commemorative tablet was moved from the second-story landing to the main entrance of the statue. Beginning in 1947, the World Almanac included the poem as a regular feature. Curiosity about its forgotten author awakened. Now she seemed less a Jewish than an American poet, a human statue of liberty. According to the title of one rapturous biography, she was Emma Lazarus, Woman with a Torch.

Although the Statue of Liberty was not intended to beckon the tired and the poor, they had come to it. Because it received them no longer in significant numbers, it could enshrine their experience as a transcendental national memory. Because few Americans now were immigrants, all Americans could think of themselves as having been immigrants. Like the myth of the frontier, the myth of the asylum acquired a remembered glory in an age that wished to preserve the spirit of a reality that was largely gone.

Yet the reality of refuge in America has never wholly disappeared, and the myth has not been merely compensatory. Its revival encouraged efforts to live up to the dictates of "The New Colossus." In 1965 Congress repealed the discriminatory features of the Immigration Law of 1924. President Lyndon B. Johnson, signing the new law at the base of the Statue of Liberty, alluded to the Lazarus poem and declared

*that the nation was returning "to the finest of its traditions."
In the same spirit the President used the occasion to an-
nounce a large-scale program for reception of refugees from
Cuba.*

Henry W. Grady
The New South
1886

EDITED BY THOMAS D. CLARK

The South of 1886 was a section struggling to forget the immediate past of Civil War and Reconstruction. It was trying to reckon with current economic and social realities, and to project itself into the future. Newspaper editors from Richmond to Dallas had published stories of centennial celebrations of the Declaration of Independence and the surrender at Yorktown, and they anticipated the centennial of the framing of the Constitution. Already Union veterans and even whole regiments were returning South to visit the scenes of their actions in battle, to cultivate friendship with former foes, and to engage in extravagant expressions of national unity.

On every hand there were challenges for a young and vigorous editor in the New South, such as Henry W. Grady of the Atlanta Constitution. The region was falling woefully behind in the development of industry. The earth contained minerals, but native sons often lacked the managerial experience and imagination to take advantage of this resource. The substance of the land was being drawn away by wasteful and primitive agricultural practices. And capital to finance prog-

ress in all these areas was scarce. *Travelers from the North wrote and published impressions of the land below the Potomac. Promotional departments of the various state governments published and distributed hundreds of pamphlets and reports at home and abroad. They sought to attract to the South capitalists and immigrants with ready purses and willing hands.*

There was, despite its surface stagnation, a distinguishable stirring in the South. At the same time there existed an uncertainty born of the confusion and excesses of Reconstruction, a reluctance to break ties with the traditions of the Old South, and a timidity and doubt as to the attitudes of the rest of the nation toward the region. This was the South of which Henry W. Grady wrote in the Constitution.

A native of Athens, Georgia, a graduate of the University of Georgia, and a former law student at the University of Virginia, Grady had come to maturity with the rise of the postwar South. In reporting the Florida election dispute in 1876, the young journalist gained national attention. He scooped his fellow reporters and wired reports of the election board's decisions to the Constitution *and the* New York Herald *well ahead of his competitors. The Charleston earthquake and tidal wave of 1886 gave Grady a second opportunity to attract widespread attention.*

In repeated editorials and stories, Henry W. Grady emphasized the South's promise, even though he was critical of its many failures. Frequently also he described the South's iron, marble, and coal deposits, its water and timber resources, and its reservoir of cheap labor. To him a New South was a-borning. The term "New South" was not original with Grady. No one knows when it was first used. Maybe southern soldiers turning back from Appomattox saw in their heartbreak and frustration some kind of new beginning for their section.

Grady's views were confirmed by John Hamilton Inman, who had gone north in 1865 from Dandridge, Tennessee, to make his fortune. Inman had helped organize the New York Cotton Exchange and the Tennessee Coal, Iron and Railroad Company. He had also played a part in expanding the Louisville and Nashville Railroad Company, and had organized several local railroads into the Southern Railway system. He, like Grady, sensed the new impulse in the Old Confederacy, and he was in a position to translate this optimism to men with capital in the North. He helped direct at least $100 million of northern investment capital to the South.

John H. Inman was a member of the New England Society in New York City. He suggested to his associates in that society that they invite a young southerner to speak at their annual banquet. In 1886 he believed, from his knowledge of the progressive editorials appearing in the Atlanta Constitution, that Henry W. Grady could convey a sense of the rising South to a New York audience, and at the same time cultivate a good will for the section. On November 6, 1886, an invitation arrived in Atlanta asking the young editor to address the New England Society at its meeting on December 22. Grady's editorial staff prevailed upon him to accept the challenge, and he chose the subject "The New South." Actually Grady made his speech in New York in response to a toast to "The New South."

In accepting an invitation to speak on such a subject, Grady was highly conscious of the fact that he risked uttering in New York some sentiment which would irritate members of his northern audience, or which would involve him in bitter controversy with sensitive and critical southerners. Though he gave most careful thought to the content of his speech, he did not prepare a text copy. Grady waited to judge first-hand the nature of his audience, and to allow the stimulus of the moment to buoy him up in his address. In this kind of speaking he was a genuis. Crowd psychology and excitement played an enormous part in his success as an orator.

Before the Georgia editor in the banquet hall of Delmonico's Restaurant in New York sat an illustrious audience of eastern business and professional men. At the head table Grady was flanked by Horace Russell, Dr. DeWitt Talmadge, General William T. Sherman, J. Pierpont Morgan, Lyman Abbott, Russell Sage, Seth Thomas, Elihu Root, George W. Lincoln, H. M Flagler, F. Hopkinson Smith, and John H. Inman. Many of these men were actively interested in the economic development of the South. Grady's address followed a speech by Dr. Talmadge and remarks by General Sherman. When he arose to speak the band played "Marching through Georgia." The young Georgian said later, of this moment, "Every nerve in my body was strung as tight as a fiddle string, and all tingling. I knew then that I had a message for that assemblage, and as soon as I opened my mouth it came rushing out."

"THERE was a South of slavery and secession—that South is dead. There is a South of union and freedom—that South, thank God, is living, breathing, growing every hour." These words, delivered from the immortal lips of Benjamin

H. Hill, at Tammany Hall in 1866, true then, and truer now, I shall make my text to-night.

Mr. President and Gentlemen: Let me express to you my appreciation of the kindness by which I am permitted to address you. I make this abrupt acknowledgment advisedly, for I feel that if, when I raise my provincial voice in this ancient and august presence, I could find courage for no more than the opening sentence, it would be well if, in that sentence, I had met in a rough sense my obligation as a guest, and had perished, so to speak, with courtesy on my lips and grace in my heart. (Laughter.) Permitted through your kindness to catch my second wind, let me say that I appreciate the significance of being the first Southerner to speak at this board, which bears the substance, if it surpasses the semblance, of original New England hospitality (applause), and honors a sentiment that in turn honors you, but in which my personality is lost, and the compliment to my people made plain. (Laughter.)

I bespeak the utmost stretch of your courtesy to-night. I am not troubled about those from whom I come. You remember the man whose wife sent him to a neighbor with a pitcher of milk, and who, tripping on the top step, fell, with such casual interruptions as the landings afforded, into the basement; and while picking himself up had the pleasure of hearing his wife call out: "John, did you break the pitcher?"

"No, I didn't" said John, "but I be dinged if I don't." (Loud laughter.)

So, while those who call to me from behind may inspire me with energy if not with courage, I ask an indulgent hearing from you. I beg that you bring your full faith in American fairness and frankness to judgment upon what I shall say. There was an old preacher once who told some boys of the Bible lesson he was going to read in the morning. The boys, finding the place, glued together the connecting pages. (Laughter.) The next morning he read on the bottom of one page: "When Noah was one hundred and twenty years old he took unto himself a wife, who was"—then turning the page— "140 cubits long (laughter), 40 cubits wide, built of gopher wood (laughter), and covered with pitch inside and out." (Loud and continued laughter.) He was naturally puzzled at this. He read it again, verified it, and then said: "My friends,

The speech is reprinted as it originally appeared in the *Anniversary Celebration of the New England Society in the City of New York* (December 22, 1886); it has been compared with the text published in *Joel Chandler Harris' Life of Henry W. Grady Including His Writings and Speeches* (New York, 1890), pp. 83–93.

this is the first time I ever met this in the Bible, but I accept it as an evidence of the assertion that we are fearfully and wonderfully made." (Immense laughter.) If I could get you to hold such faith to-night I could proceed cheerfully to the task I otherwise approach with a sense of consecration.

Pardon me one word, Mr. President, spoken for the sole purpose of getting into the volumes that go out annually freighted with the rich eloquence of your speakers—the fact that the Cavalier as well as the Puritan was on the Continent in its early days, and that he was "up and able to be about." (Laughter.) I have read your books carefully and I find no mention of that fact, which seems to me an important one for preserving a sort of historical equilibrium if for nothing else.

Let me remind you that the Virginia Cavalier first challenged France on this continent—that Cavalier John Smith gave New England its very name, and was so pleased with the job that while Miles Standish was cutting off men's ears for courting a girl without her parents' consent, and forbade men to kiss their wives on Sunday, the Cavalier was courting everything in sight, and that the Almighty had vouchsafed great increase to the Cavalier colonies, the huts in the wilderness being as full as the nests in the woods.

But having incorporated the Cavalier as a fact in your charming little books I shall let him work out his own salvation, as he has always done with engaging gallantry, and we will hold no controversy as to his merits. Why should we? Neither Puritan nor Cavalier long survived as such. The virtues and traditions of both happily still live for the inspiration of their sons and the saving of the old fashion. (Applause.) Both Puritan and Cavalier were lost in the storm of the first Revolution; and the American citizen, supplanting both and stronger than either, took possession of the Republic bought by their common blood and fashioned to wisdom, and charged himself with teaching men government and establishing the voice of the people as the voice of God. (Applause.)

My friends, Dr. Talmage has told you that the typical American has yet to come. Let me tell you that he has already come. (Applause.) Great types like valuable plants are slow to flower and fruit. But from the union of these colonist Puritans and Cavaliers, from the straightening of their purposes and the crossing of their blood, slow perfecting through a century, came he who stands as the first typical American, the first who comprehended within himself all the strength and gentleness, all the majesty and grace of this republic— Abraham Lincoln. (Loud and long continued applause.) He was the sum of Puritan and Cavalier, for in his ardent nature were fused the virtues of both, and in the depths of his great soul the faults of both were lost. (Renewed applause.) He was greater than Puritan, greater than Cavalier, in that he was American (renewed applause), and that in his homely form were first gathered the vast and thrilling forces of his ideal government—charging it with such tremendous meaning and so elevating it above human suffering that martyrdom, though infamously aimed, came as a fitting crown to a life consecrated from the cradle to human liberty. (Loud and prolonged cheering.) Let us, each cherishing the traditions and honoring his fathers, build with reverent hands to the type of this simple but sublime life, in which all types are honored; and in our common glory as Americans there will be plenty and to spare for your forefathers and for mine. (Renewed cheering.)

In speaking to the toast with which you have honored me, I accept the term, "The New South," as in no sense disparaging to the old. Dear to me, sir, is the home of my childhood and the traditions of my people. I would not, if I could, dim the glory they won in peace and war, or by word or deed take aught from the splendor and grace of their civilization —never equalled and, perhaps, never to be equalled in its chivalric strength and grace. There is a New South, not through protest against the old, but because of new conditions, new adjustments and, if you please, new ideas and aspirations. It is to this that I address myself, and to the consideration of which I hasten lest it become the Old South before I get to it. Age does not endow all things with strength and virtue, nor are all new things to be despised. The shoemaker who put over his door "John Smith's Shop. Founded in 1760," was more than matched by his young rival across the street who hung out this sign: "Bill Jones. Established 1886. No old stock kept in this shop."

Dr. Talmage has drawn for you, with a master's hand, the picture of your returning armies. He has told you how, in the pomp and circumstance of war, they came back to you, marching with proud and victorious tread, reading their glory in a nation's eyes! Will you bear with me while I tell you of another army that sought its home at the close of the late war—an army that marched home in defeat and not in victory—in pathos and not in splendor, but in glory that equalled yours, and to hearts as loving as ever welcomed heroes home. Let me picture to you the footsore Confederate soldier, as, buttoning up in his faded gray jacket the parole which was to bear testimony to his children of his fidelity and faith, he turned his face southward from Appomattox in April, 1865.

Think of him as ragged, half-starved, heavy hearted, enfeebled by want and wounds; having fought to exhaustion, he surrenders his gun, wrings the hands of his comrades in silence, and lifting his tear-stained and pallid face for the last time to the graves that dot the old Virginia hills, pulls his gray cap over his brow and begins the slow and painful journey. What does he find—let me ask you, who went to your homes eager to find in the welcome you had justly earned, full payment for four years' sacrifice—what does he find when, having followed the battlestained cross against overwhelming odds, dreading death not half so much as surrender, he reaches the home he left so prosperous and beautiful? He finds his house in ruins, his farm devastated, his slaves free, his stock killed, his barns empty, his trade destroyed, his money worthless; his social system, feudal in its magnificence, swept away; his people without law or legal status, his comrades slain, and the burdens of others heavy on his shoulders. Crushed by defeat, his very traditions are gone: without money, credit, employment, material or training; and beside all this, confronted with the gravest problem that ever met human intelligence—the establishing of a status for the vast body of his liberated slaves.

What does he do—this hero in gray with a heart of gold? Does he sit down in sullenness and despair? Not for a day. Surely God, who had stripped him of his prosperity, inspired him in his adversity. As ruin was never before so overwhelming, never was restoration swifter. The soldier stepped from the trenches into the furrow; horses that had charged Federal guns marched before the plow, and fields that ran red with human blood in April were green with the harvest in June; women reared in luxury cut up their dresses and made breeches for their husbands, and, with a patience and heroism that fit women always as a garment, gave their hands to work. There was little bitterness in all this. Cheerfulness and frankness prevailed. "Bill Arp" struck the keynote when he said: "Well, I killed as many of them as they did of me, and now I am going to work." (Laughter and applause.) Or the soldier returning home after defeat and roasting some corn on the roadside, who made the remark to his comrades: "You may leave the South if you want to, but I am going to Sandersville, kiss my wife and raise a crop, and if the Yankees fool with me any more I will whip em again." (Renewed applause.) I want to say to General Sherman—who is considered an able man in our parts, though some people think he is a kind of careless man about fire—that from the ashes he left us in 1864 we have raised a brave and beautiful city; that somehow or other we have caught the sunshine in the bricks and mortar of our homes, and have builded therein not one ignoble prejudice or memory. (Applause.)

But in all this what have we accomplished? What is the sum of our work? We have found out that in the general summary the free negro counts more than he did as a slave. We have planted the schoolhouse on the hilltop and made it free to white and black. We have sowed towns and cities in the place of theories and put business above politics. (Applause.) We have challenged your spinners in Massachusetts and your ironmakers in Pennsylvania. We have learned that the $400,000,000 annually received from our cotton crop will make us rich, when the supplies that make it are home-raised. We have reduced the commercial rate of interest from 24 to 6 per cent., and are floating 4 per cent. bonds. We have learned that one northern immigrant is worth fifty foreigners, and have smoothed the path to southward, wiped out the place where Mason and Dixon's line used to be, and hung our latchstring to you and yours. (Prolonged cheers.) We have reached the point that marks perfect harmony in every household, when the husband confesses that the pies which his wife cooks are as good as those his mother used to bake; and we admit that the sun shines as brightly and the moon as softly as it did "before the war." (Laughter.) We have established thrift in city and country. We have fallen in love with work. We have restored comfort to homes from which culture and elegance never departed. We have let economy take root and spread among us as rank as the crab grass which sprung from Sherman's cavalry camps, until we are ready to lay odds on the Georgia Yankee, as he manufactures relics of the battlefield in a one-story shanty and squeezes pure olive oil out of his cotton seed, against any Down-easter that ever swapped wooden nutmegs for flannel sausages in the valleys of Vermont. (Loud and continuous laughter.) Above all, we know that we have achieved in these "piping times of peace" a fuller independence for the South than that which our fathers sought to win in the forum by their eloquence or compel on the field by their swords. (Loud applause.)

It is a rare privilege, sir, to have had part, however humble, in this work. Never was nobler duty confided to human hands than the uplifting and upbuilding of the prostrate and bleeding South, misguided, perhaps, but beautiful in her suffering, and honest, brave and generous always. (Applause.) In the record of her social, industrial, and political illustration we wait with confidence the verdict of the world.

But what of the negro? Have we solved the problem he presents or progressed in honor and equity towards the solution? Let the record speak to the point. No section shows a more prosperous laboring population than the negroes of the South; none in fuller sympathy with the employing and land-owning class. He shares our school fund, has the fullest protection of our laws and the friendship of our people. Self-interest, as well as honor, demand that he should have this. Our future, our very existence depend upon our working out this problem in full and exact justice. We understand that when Lincoln signed the Emancipation Proclamation, your victory was assured; for he then committed you to the cause of human liberty, against which the arms of man cannot prevail (applause); while those of our statesmen who trusted to make slavery the corner-stone of the Confederacy doomed us to defeat as far as they could, committing us to a cause that reason could not defend or the sword maintain in the light of advancing civilization. (Renewed applause.) Had Mr. Toombs said, which he did not say, that he would call the roll of his slaves at the foot of Bunker Hill, he would have been foolish, for he might have known that whenever slavery became entangled in war it must perish, and that the chattel in human flesh ended forever in New England when your fathers—not to be blamed for parting with what didn't pay—sold their slaves to our fathers—not to be praised for knowing a paying thing when they saw it. (Laughter.) The relations of the southern people with the negro are close and cordial. We remember with what fidelity for four years he guarded our defenseless women and children, whose husbands and fathers were fighting against his freedom. To his eternal credit be it said that whenever he struck a blow for his own liberty he fought in open battle, and when at last he raised his black and humble hands that the shackles might be struck off, those hands were innocent of wrong against his helpless charges, and worthy to be taken in loving grasp by every man who honors loyalty and devotion. (Applause.) Ruffians have maltreated him, rascals have misled him, philanthropists established a bank for him, but the South, with the North, protests against injustice to this simple and sincere people. To liberty and enfranchisement is as far as law can carry the negro. The rest must be left to conscience and common sense. It should be left to those among whom his lot is cast, with whom he is indissolubly connected and whose prosperity depends upon their possessing his intelligent sympathy and confidence. Faith has been kept with him in spite of calumnious assertions to the contrary by those who assume to speak for us or by frank opponents. Faith will be kept with him in the future, if the South holds her reason and integrity. (Applause.)

But have we kept faith with you? In the fullest sense, yes. When Lee surrendered—I don't say when Johnston surrendered, because I understand he still alludes to the time when he met General Sherman last as the time when he "determined to abandon any further prosecution of the struggle"—when Lee surrendered, I say, and Johnston quit, the South became, and has since been, loyal to this union. We fought hard enough to know that we were whipped, and in perfect frankness accepted as final the arbitrament of the sword to which we had appealed. The South found her jewel in the toad's head of defeat. The shackles that had held her in narrow limitations fell forever when the shackles of the negro slave were broken. (Applause.) Under the old regime the negroes were slaves to the South, the South was a slave to the system. The old plantation, with its simple police regulation and its feudal habit, was the only type possible under slavery. Thus was gathered in the hands of a splendid and chivalric oligarchy the substance that should have been diffused among the people, as the rich blood, under certain artificial conditions, is gathered at the heart, filling that with affluent rapture, but leaving the body chill and colorless. (Applause.)

The old South rested everything on slavery and agriculture, unconscious that these could neither give nor maintain healthy growth. The new South presents a perfect Democracy, the oligarchs leading in the popular movement—a social system compact and closely knitted, less splendid on the surface but stronger at the core—a hundred farms for every plantation, fifty homes for every palace, and a diversified industry that meets the complex needs of this complex age.

The new South is enamored of her new work. Her soul is stirred with the breath of a new life. The light of a grander day is falling fair on her face. She is thrilling with the consciousness of growing power and prosperity. As she stands upright, full-statured and equal among the people of the earth, breathing the keen air and looking out upon the expanding horizon, she understands that her emancipation came because in the inscrutable wisdom of God her honest purpose was crossed and her brave armies were beaten. (Applause.)

This is said in no spirit of time-serving or apology. The South has nothing for which to apologize. She believes that the late struggle between the States was war and was not rebellion, revolution, and not conspiracy, and that her convictions were as honest as yours. I should be unjust to the dauntless spirit of the South and to my own convictions if I did not make this plain in this presence. The South has nothing to take back. In my native town of Athens is a monument that crowns its central hill—a plain, white shaft. Deep cut into its shining side is a name dear to me above the names of men, that of a brave and simple man who died in brave and simple faith. Not for all the glories of New England—from Plymouth Rock all the way—would I exchange the heritage he left me in his soldier's death. To the foot of that shaft I shall send my children's children to reverence him who ennobled their name with his heroic blood. But, sir, speaking from the shadow of that memory, which I honor as I do nothing else on earth, I say that the cause in which he suffered and for which he gave his life was adjudged by higher and fuller wisdom than his or mine, and I am glad that the omniscient God held the balance of battle in His Almighty hand, and that human slavery was swept forever from American soil—the American Union saved from the wreck of war. (Loud applause.)

This message, Mr. President, comes to you from consecrated ground. Every foot of the soil about the city in which I live is as sacred as a battle-ground of the republic. Every hill that invests it is hallowed to you by the blood of your brothers, who died for your victory, and doubly hallowed to us by the blow of those who died hopeless, but undaunted, in defeat—sacred soil to all of us, rich with memories that make us purer and stronger and better, silent but staunch witnesses in its red desolation of the matchless valor of American hearts and the deathless glory of American arms—speaking an eloquent witness in its white peace and prosperity to the indissoluble union of American States and the imperishable brotherhood of the American people. (Immense cheering.)

Now, what answer has New England to this message? Will she permit the prejudice of war to remain in the hearts of the conquerors, when it has died in the hearts of the conquered? (Cries of "No! No!") Will she transmit this prejudice to the next generation, that in their hearts, which never felt the generous ardor of conflict, it may perpetuate itself? ("No! No!") Will she withhold, save in strained courtesy, the hand which straight from his soldier's heart Grant offered to Lee at Appomattox? Will she make the vision of a restored and happy people, which gathered above the couch of your dying captain, filling his heart with grace, touching his lips with praise and glorifying his path to the grave; will she make this vision on which the last sigh of his expiring soul breathed a benediction, a cheat and a delusion? (Tumultuous cheering and shouts of "No! No!") If she does, the South, never abject in asking for comradeship, must accept with dignity its refusal; but if she does not; if she accepts in frankness and sincerity this message of good-will and friendship, then will the prophecy of Webster, delivered in this very Society forty years ago amid tremendous applause, be verified in its fullest and final sense, when he said: "Standing hand to hand and clasping hands, we should remain united as we have been for sixty years, citizens of the same country, members of the same government, united, all united now and united forever. There have been difficulties, contentions, and controversies, but I tell you that in my judgment

> Those opposed eyes,
> Which like the meteors of a troubled heaven,
> All of one nature, of one substance bred,
> Did lately meet in th'intestine shock,
> Shall now, in mutual well beseeming ranks,
> March all one way.

(Prolonged applause.)

☆

Although Grady was intoxicated by his visible audience at Delmonico's, he was even more eager to appeal to his vast unseen audience. He was conscious that his speech would have wide coverage in the national press. His words would be examined with the utmost editorial scrutiny. Friend and foe alike would respond to it. Sectional accord within the Union would be affected.

The oration was not really profound, nor did it have a meaty content. There were oratorical flourishes and conscious digressions into light after-dinner humor. In describing the Confederate soldier and his cause Grady resorted to pure southern melodrama. None of these things is important. The real importance of the speech lay in three areas: first, it fixed the term "New South" in the American mind; second, it assured men of capital of the stability of the South; and, finally, it made Henry W. Grady into an articulate leader of a New South which in his address he had to define much more clearly. He now had to think more specifically of the South's potentialities in terms of both human beings and natural resources. This he did a year later in speaking before a state-fair audience in Dallas, Texas. In the latter speech he enlarged upon many points which he had only hinted at in the

New York speech. In more precise detail he discussed the position of the Negro in the New South. He felt it would be wisest for southern whites not to separate the races politically. The white vote should be of such size and depth of integrity that it would automatically ensure white supremacy. Grady viewed a racially factionalized state as being worse than Reconstruction itself. Nevertheless he expressed a philosophy of race relations which was to fix in the southern mind the principle of "separate but equal" a decade before the Supreme Court handed down its decision of Plessy v. Ferguson.

Grady's utterances in New York and Dallas helped to change men's thinking both North and South. For the northern businessman, the South suddenly stood in a new perspective, social and economic. For the southerner, Grady spoke a new promise. The region after all was not irretrievably wedded to the traditions of the Old South, to a ruinous system of one-crop agriculture, or to technological or professional hopelessness. A fellow southerner had laid down the challenge of accepting change. Grady proposed replacing the old defeatism of war and Reconstruction with optimistic effort toward industrial and commercial progress. The South had struggled hard for a catch phrase, something that would help give it a sense of direction and an impetus to reunite itself spiritually and economically with the rest of the nation. The term "New South" as cast in Henry Grady's speech was just such a catch phrase.

Whether or not southern newspapers quoted the New South speech directly, its influence upon the region's editorial mind was evident. Scores of editorials discussed reunification of the nation, the need for industry in the South, threats of danger from staple-crop agriculture, and the Negro in southern society. Grady's speech also caught the imagination of northern editors. It appealed to them as an excellent piece of free-hand southern oratory which offered the North just enough gracious compliments to give assurance of the South's conciliatory attitude. Many believed that Grady revealed more clearly than anyone else the innermost emotions of the young postwar generation of southerners. He displayed his personal reactions without a trace of bitterness. He proved that northerner and southerner could communicate with each other in a spirit of good will.

On the other hand, the nation's press also carried adverse criticism of the Georgia orator. Some southern editors felt he had been too ready to admit failures of the old southern system. For some Grady had been too extravagant in praise of Lincoln, and not harsh enough with General Sherman. In the

North, the Chicago Tribune *felt the southern spokesman was insincere, and accused him of being a trimmer. Such criticism apparently had little influence. Grady overnight had become the spiritual embodiment of the New South. Seldom again would the term "New South" be used without invoking Grady's interpretation of it. The speech had the further effect, on the popular level, of stimulating interest in eloquent expression. It was widely praised as having set a new mark for American oratory; and in classrooms and on stages across the land, boy orators revived the excitement of Grady's message.*

Historians in the main have accepted Grady's thesis that in 1886 the Old South was a thing of memory, and the new was a current reality. Clearly the region would attract industry, revise its farming procedures, recognize the Negro as an important productive force, and heal the wounds of war and Reconstruction. The South's future lay in its unity with the rest of the nation, and in a more effective use of capital and resources. Sherman may have been a careless man with fire, but the sun of hope shone anew on the rising towers of the new urban and industrial South.

James Cardinal Gibbons

The Question of the "Knights of Labor"

1887

EDITED BY JOHN TRACY ELLIS

The most famous document in the history of the relationship of the Catholic Church in the United States to the American labor movement is known as "the memorial on the Knights of Labor." It was composed in February, 1887, at Rome and signed on February 20 by James Cardinal Gibbons, Archbishop of Baltimore, although in its composition the cardinal had the assistance of John Ireland, Bishop of St. Paul, John J. Keane, Bishop of Richmond, and Denis J. O'Connell, Rector of the American College at Rome. It was addressed to Giovanni Cardinal Simeoni, Prefect of the Congregational de Propaganda Fide, the department of ecclesiastical government which had jurisdiction over the Church in missionary lands, the category in which the United States was at the time placed by the Holy See.

The Knights of Labor, in which a very large number, if not a majority, of the members were Catholics, had recently passed through a series of severe trials. Among these were the railroad strikes of the late winter and early spring of 1886 and the Haymarket Massacre in Chicago in May of that year. For these disturbances of the public peace many

Americans held the Knights responsible. It was an attitude that was illustrated in Puck (March 23, 1887) in a cartoon drawn by Joseph Keppler concerning Gibbons' memorial. This showed a large group of union men attacking a single "scab," while a procession of Catholic bishops advanced to the scene. The latter were described as labor's "new ally," and the question was asked: "Does the Catholic Church sanction mob law?"

Although Cardinal Gibbons and his associates deplored the use of violence in any form in labor's attempts to gain its ends, they were convinced that the laboring men—in this case the Knights of Labor—had been the victims of grave abuses by their employers. To these prelates, labor's cause was worthy of support. And beyond the goal of support to a worthy cause, they were intent that the Catholic Church in the United States should not align itself with the enemies of labor when the overwhelming majority of the Church's members were working men and their families. Conscious as they were of the irreparable losses suffered by the Church in Europe because of alignments of the wrong kind, these churchmen were determined that the American people should not receive an image of the Catholic Church as the upholder of the rich and the powerful. They felt it imperative, therefore, to speak out. And a circumstance that gave a special urgency to their efforts related to their coreligionists in Canada. The American churchmen were aware that four years previously, Elzear-Alesandre Taschereau, Archbishop of Quebec, had sought a ruling on the Knights of Labor from Rome and that after a long delay the Holy Office had condemned them in September, 1884, as a forbidden society. They were further aware that the Archbishop of Quebec was then (1887) in Rome, like Gibbons, to get his red hat as a cardinal and that he was seeking confirmation from the Holy See of the decree of 1884 regarding the Knights. The American prelates also knew that there were some conservative bishops of their own country who would welcome a similar condemnation of the labor organization which would apply to the United States. To men of the mind of Gibbons, Ireland, Keane, and O'Connell, an action of that kind would have been an unmitigated calamity, and they determined, therefore, that the strongest possible protest should be lodged by the dean of the American hierarchy with the official of the Roman Curia who was most responsible for framing ecclesiastical policy relating to the Church in the United States.

☆

TO HIS EMINENCE CARDINAL SIMEONI, PREFECT OF THE SACRED CONGREGATION OF THE PROPAGANDA:

YOUR EMINENCE:

IN SUBMITTING to the Holy See the conclusions which after several months of attentive observation and reflection, seem to me to sum up the truth concerning the association of the Knights of Labor, I feel profoundly convinced of the vast importance of the consequences attaching to this question, which forms but a link in the great chain of the social problems of our day, and especially of our country.

In weighing this question I have been very careful to follow as my constant guide the spirit of the Encyclicals, in which our Holy Father, Leo XIII, has so admirably set forth the dangers of our time and their remedies, as well as the principles by which we are to recognize associations condemned by the Holy See. Such was also the guide of the Third Plenary Council of Baltimore in its teaching concerning the principles to be followed and the dangers to be shunned by the faithful either in the choice or in the establishment of those associations toward which the spirit of our popular institutions so strongly impels them. And considering the dire consequences that might result from a mistake by the thousands and hundreds of thousands, the council wisely ordained that when an association is spread over several dioceses, not even the bishop of one of these dioceses shall condemn it, but shall refer the case to a standing committee of all the archbishops of the United States; and even these are not authorized to condemn unless their sentence be unanimous; and in case they fail to agree unanimously, then only the supreme tribunal of the Holy See can impose a condemnation; all this in order to avoid error and confusion of discipline.

The committee of archbishops held a meeting, in fact, toward the end of last October, especially to consider the association of the Knights of Labor. We were not persuaded to hold this meeting because of any request on the part of our bishops, for none of them had asked for it; and it should also be said that, among all the bishops we know, only two or three desire the condemnation. But the importance of the

The document is taken from Henry J. Browne, *The Catholic Church and the Knights of Labor* (Washington, D.C.: The Catholic University of America Press, 1949), Appendix III, pp. 365–78.

question in itself, and in the estimation of the Holy See led us to examine it with greatest attention. After our discussion, the results of which have already been communicated to the Sacred Congregation of the Propaganda, only two out of the twelve archbishops voted for condemnation, and their reasons were powerless to convince the others of either the justice or the prudence of such a condemnation.

In the following considerations I wish to state in detail the reasons which determined the vote of the great majority of the committee—reasons whose truth and force seem to me all the more evident today: I shall try at the same time to do justice to the arguments advanced by the opposition.

1. In the first place, in the constitution, laws and official declarations of the Knights of Labor, there can clearly be found assertions and rules which we would not approve; but we have not found in them those elements so clearly pointed out by the Holy See, which places them among condemned associations.

(a) In their form of initiation there is no oath.

(b) The obligation to secrecy by which they keep the knowledge of their business from strangers or enemies, in no wise prevents Catholics from manifesting everything to competent ecclesiastical authority, even outside of confession. This has been positively declared to us by their president.

(c) They make no promise of blind obedience. The object and laws of the association are distinctly declared, and the obligation of obedience does not go beyond these limits.

(d) They not only profess no hostility against religion or the Church, but their declarations are quite to the contrary. The Third Plenary Council commands that we should not condemn an association without giving a hearing to its officers or representatives; "auditis ducibus, corypheis vel sociis praecipuis." Now, their president in sending me a copy of their constitution, says that he is a Catholic from the bottom of his heart; that he practices his religion faithfully and receives the sacraments regularly; that he belongs to no Masonic or other society condemned by the Church; that he knows of nothing in the association of the Knights of Labor contrary to the laws of the Church; that, with filial submission he begs the Pastors of the Church to examine all the details of their organization, and, if they find anything worthy of condemnation, they should indicate it, and he promises its correction. Assuredly one does not perceive in all this any hostility to the authority of the Church, but on the contrary a spirit in every way praiseworthy. After their convention last year at Richmond he and several of the officers and members, devout Catholics, made similar declarations concerning their feelings and the action of that convention, the documents of which we are expecting to receive.

(e) Nor do we find in this organization any hostility to the authority and laws of our country. Not only does nothing of the kind appear in their constitution and laws, but the heads of our civil government treat with the greatest respect the cause which they represent. The President of the United States told me personally, a month ago that he was then examining a law for the amelioration of certain social grievances and that he had just had a long conference on the subject with Mr. Powderly, president of the Knights of Labor. The Congress of the United States, following the advice of President Cleveland is busying itself at the present time with the amelioration of the working classes, in whose complaints they acknowledge openly there is a great deal of truth. And our political parties, far from regarding them as enemies of the country, vie with each other in championing the evident rights of the poor workmen, who seek not to resist the laws, but only to obtain just legislation by constitutional and legitimate means.

These considerations, which show that in this association those elements are not to be found which the Holy See condemns, lead us to study, in the second place, the evils which the associations contend against, and the nature of the conflict.

2. That there exists among us, as in the other countries of the world, grave and threatening social evils, public injustices, which call for strong resistance and legal remedy, is a fact which no one dares to deny, and the truth of which has been already acknowledged by the Congress and the President of the United States. Without entering into the sad details of these wrongs,—which does not seem necessary here,—it may suffice to mention only that monopolies on the part of both individuals and of corporations, have already called forth not only the complaints of our working classes but also the opposition of our public men and legislators; that the efforts of these monopolists, not always without success, to control legislation to their own profit, cause serious apprehension among the disinterested friends of liberty; that the heartless avarice which, through greed of gain, pitilessly grinds not only the men, but particularly the women and children in various employments, make it clear to all who love humanity and justice that it is not only the right of the laboring classes to protect themselves, but the duty of the whole people to aid them in finding a remedy against the dangers with which both civiliza-

tion and the social order are menaced by avarice, oppression and corruption.

It would be vain to deny either the existence of the evils, the right of legitimate resistance, or the necessity of a remedy. At most doubt might be raised about the legitimacy of the form of resistance and the remedy employed by the Knights of Labor. This then ought to be the next point of our examination.

3. It can hardly be doubted that for the attainment of any public end, association—the organization of all interested persons—is the most efficacious means, a means altogether natural and just. This is so evident, and besides so comfortable to the genius of our country, of our essentially popular social conditions, that it is unnecessary to insist upon it. It is almost the only means to invite public attention, to give force to the most legitimate resistance, to add weight to the most just demands.

Now there already exists an organization which presents a thousand attractions and advantages, but which our Catholic workingmen, with filial obedience to the Holy See, refuse to join; this is the *Masonic* organization, which exists everywhere in our country, and which, as Mr. Powderly has expressly pointed out to us, unites employer and worker in a brotherhood very advantageous for the latter, but which numbers in its ranks hardly a single Catholic. Freely renouncing the advantages which the Church and their consciences forbid, workingmen form associations, having nothing in common with the deadly designs of the enemies of religion and seeking only mutual protection and help, and the legitimate assertion of their rights. But here they also find themselves threatened with condemnation, and so deprived of their only means of defense. Is it surprising that they should be astonished at this and that they ask *Why?*

4. Let us now consider the objections made against this sort of organization.

(a) It is objected that in these organizations Catholics are mixed with Protestants, to the peril of their faith. Naturally, yes, they are mixed with Protestants in the workers' associations, precisely as they are at their work; for in a mixed people like ours, the separation of religions in social affairs is not possible. But to suppose that the faith of our Catholics suffers thereby is not to know the Catholic workers of America who are not like the workingmen of so many European countries —misguided and perverted children, looking on their Mother the Church as a hostile stepmother—but they are intelligent, well instructed and devoted children ready to give their blood, as they continually give their means (although small and hard-earned) for her support and protection. And in fact it is not in the present case that Catholics are mixed with Protestants, but rather that Protestants are admitted to the advantages of an association, two-thirds of whose members and the principal officers are Catholics; and in a country like ours their exclusion would be simply impossible.

(b) But it is said, could there not be substituted for such an organization confraternities which would unite the workingmen under the direction of the priests and the direct influence of religion? I answer frankly that I do not believe that either possible or necessary in our country. I sincerely admire the efforts of this sort which are made in countries where the workers are led astray by the enemies of religion; but thanks be to God, that is not our condition. We find that in our country the presence and explicit influence of the clergy would not be advisable where our citizens, without distinction of religious belief, come together in regard to their industrial interests alone. Without going so far, we have abundant means for making our working people faithful Catholics, and simple good sense advises us not to go to extremes.

(c) Again, it is objected that the liberty of such an organization exposes Catholics to the evil influences of the most dangerous associates, even of atheists, communists and anarchists. That is true; but it is one of the trials of faith which our brave American Catholics are accustomed to meet almost daily, and which they know how to disregard with good sense and firmness. The press of our country tells us and the president of the Knights of Labor has related to us, how these violent and aggressive elements have endeavored to seize authority in their councils, or to inject their poison into the principles of the association; but they also verify with what determination these evil spirits have been repulsed and defeated. The presence among our citizens of this destructive element, which has come for the most part from certain nations of Europe, is assuredly for us an occasion of lively regrets and careful precautions; it is an inevitable fact, however, but one which the union between the Church and her children in our country renders comparatively free from danger. In truth, the only grave danger would come from an alienation between the Church and her children, which nothing would more certainly occasion than imprudent condemnations.

(d) An especially weighty charge is drawn from the outbursts of violence, even to bloodshed, which have characterized several of the strikes inaugurated by labor organizations. Concerning this, three things are to be remarked: first, strikes are not an invention of the Knights of Labor, but a means almost everywhere and always resorted to by employees in our land and elsewhere to protest against what they consider unjust and to demand their rights; secondly in such a struggle of the poor and indignant multitudes against hard and obstinate monopoly, anger and violence are often as inevitable as they are regrettable; thirdly, the laws and chief authorities of the Knights of Labor, far from encouraging violence or the occasions of it, exercise a powerful influence to hinder it, and to keep strikes within the limits of good order and legitimate action. A careful examination of the acts of violence which have marked the struggle between capital and labor during the past year, leaves us convinced that it would be unjust to attribute them to the association of the Knights of Labor. This was but one of several associations of workers that took part in the strikes, and their chief officers, according to disinterested witnesses, used every possible effort to appease the anger of the crowds and to prevent the excesses which, in my judgment, could not justly be attributed to them. Doubtless among the Knights of Labor as among thousands of other workingmen, there are violent, or even wicked and criminal men, who have committed inexcusable deeds of violence, and have urged their associates to do the same; but to attribute this to the organization, it seems to me, would be as unreasonable as to attribute to the Church the follies and crimes of her children against which she protests. I repeat that in such a struggle of the great masses of the people against the mail-clad power, which, as it is acknowledged, often refuses them the simple rights of humanity and justice, it is vain to expect that every error and every act of violence can be avoided; and to dream that this struggle can be prevented, or that we can deter the multitudes from organizing, which is their only practical means of success, would be to ignore the nature and forces of human society in times like ours. The part of Christian prudence evidently is to try to hold the hearts of the multitude by the bonds of love, in order to control their actions by the principles of faith, justice and charity, to acknowledge frankly the truth and justice in their cause, in order to deter them from what would be false and criminal, and thus to turn into a legitimate, peaceable and beneficent contest what could easily become for the masses of our people a volcanic abyss, like that which society fears and the Church deplores in Europe.

Upon this point I insist strongly, because, from an intimate acquaintance with the social conditions of our country I am profoundly convinced that here we are touching upon a subject which not only concerns the rights of the working classes, who ought to be especially dear to the Church which our Divine Lord sent to evangelize the poor, but with which are bound up the fundamental interests of the Church and of human society for the future. This is a point which I desire, in a few additional words to develop more clearly.

5. Whoever meditates upon the ways in which divine Providence is guiding contemporary history cannot fail to remark how important is the part which the power of the people takes therein at present and must take in the future. We behold, with profound sadness, the efforts of the prince of darkness to make this power dangerous to the social weal by withdrawing the masses of the people from the influence of religion, and impelling them towards the ruinous paths of license and anarchy. Until now our country presents a picture of altogether different character—that of a popular power regulated by love of good order, by respect for religion, by obedience to the authority of the laws, not a democracy of license and violence, but that true democracy which aims at the general prosperity through the means of sound principles and good social order.

In order to preserve so desirable a state of things it is absolutely necessary that religion should continue to hold the affections, and thus rule the conduct of the multitudes. As Cardinal Manning has so well written, "In the future era the Church has no longer to deal with princes and parliaments, but with the masses, with the people. Whether we will or no this is our work; we need a new spirit, a new direction of our life and activity." To lose influence over the people would be to lose the future altogether; and it is by the heart, far more than by the understanding, that we must hold and guide this immense power, so mighty either for good or evil. Among all the glorious titles of the Church which her history has merited for her, there is not one which at present gives her so great influence as that of *Friend of the People*. Assuredly, in our democratic country, it is this title which wins for the Catholic Church not only the enthusiastic devotedness of the millions of her children, but also the respect and admiration of all our citizens, whatever be their religious belief. It is the power of precisely this title which renders persecution almost an impossibility, and which draws toward our holy Church the great heart of the American people.

And since it is acknowledged by all that the great questions of the future are not those of war, of commerce or finance, but the social questions, the questions which concern the improvement of the condition of the great masses of the people, and especially of the working people, it is evidently of supreme importance that the Church should always be found on the side of humanity, of justice toward the multitudes who compose the body of the human family. As the same Cardinal Manning very wisely wrote, "We must admit and accept calmly and with good will that industries and profits must be considered in second place; the moral state and domestic condition of the whole working population must be considered first. I will not venture to formulate the acts of parliament, but here is precisely their fundamental principle for the future. The conditions of the lower classes as found at present among our people, can not and must not continue. On such a basis no social edifice can stand." In our country, especially, this is the inevitable program of the future, and the position which the Church must hold toward the solution is sufficiently obvious. She must certainly not favor the extremes to which the poor multitudes are naturally inclined, but, I repeat, she must withhold them from these extremes by the bonds of affection, by the maternal desire which she will manifest for the concession of all that is just and reasonable in their demands, and by the maternal blessing which she will bestow upon every legitimate means for improving the condition of the people.

6. Now let us consider for a moment the consequences which would inevitably follow from a contrary course, from a lack of sympathy for the working class, from a suspicion of their aims, from a hasty condemnation of their methods.

(a) First, there is the evident danger of the Church's losing in popular estimation her right to be considered the friend of the people. The logic of men's hearts goes swiftly to its conclusions, and this conclusion would be a pernicious one for the people and for the Church. To lose the heart of the people would be a misfortune for which the friendship of the few rich and powerful would be no compensation.

(b) There is a great danger of rendering hostile to the Church the political power of our country, which openly takes sides with the millions who are demanding justice and the improvement of their condition. The accusation of being, "*un-American*," that is to say, alien to our national spirit, is the most powerful weapon which the enemies of the Church know how to employ against her. It was this cry which aroused the Know-Nothing persecution thirty years ago, and the same would be quickly used again if the opportunity offered itself. To appreciate the gravity of this danger it is well to remark that not only are the rights of the working classes loudly proclaimed by each of our two great political parties, but it is very probable that, in our approaching national elections there will be a candidate for the office of President of the United States as the special representative of these complaints and demands of the masses. Now, to seek to crush by an ecclesiastical condemnation an organization which represents nearly 500,000 votes, and which has already so respectable and so universally recognized a place in the political arena, would to speak frankly, be considered by the American people as not less ridiculous as it is rash. To alienate from ourselves the friendship of the people would be to run great risk of losing the respect which the Church has won in the estimation of the American nation, and of destroying the state of peace and prosperity which form so admirable a contrast with her condition in some so-called Catholic countries. Already in these months past, a murmur of popular anger and of threats against the Church has made itself heard, and it is necessary that we should move with much precaution.

(c) A third danger, and the one which touches our hearts the most, is the risk of losing the love of the children of the Church, and of pushing them into an attitude of resistance against their Mother. The whole world presents no more beautiful spectacle than that of their filial devotion and obedience. But it is necessary to recognize that, in our age and in our country, obedience cannot be blind. We would greatly deceive ourselves if we expected it. Our Catholic working men sincerely believe that they are only seeking justice, and seeking it by legitimate means. A condemnation would be considered both false and unjust, and would not be accepted. We might indeed preach to them submission and confidence in the Church, but these good dispositions could hardly go so far. They love the Church, and they wish to save their souls, but they must also earn their living, and labor is now so organized that without belonging to the organization there is little chance to earn one's living.

Behold, then, the consequences to be feared. Thousands of the most devoted children of the Church would believe themselves repulsed by their Mother and would live without practicing their religion. The revenues of the Church, which with us come entirely from the free offerings of the people, would suffer immensely, and it would be the same with Peter's pence. The ranks of the secret societies would be filled with Catholics, who had been up to now faithful. The Holy See, which has constantly received from the Catholics of America proofs of almost unparalleled devotedness, would be considered not as a paternal authority, but as a harsh and unjust power. Here are assuredly effects, the occasion of which wisdom and prudence must avoid.

In a word, we have seen quite recently the sad and threatening confusion caused by the condemnation inflicted by an Archbishop upon a single priest in vindication of discipline —a condemnation which the Archbishop believed to be just and necessary, but which fell upon a priest who was regarded as the friend of the people. Now, if the consequences have been so deplorable for the peace of the Church from the condemnation of only one priest, because he was considered to be the friend of the people, what will not be the consequences to be feared from a condemnation which would fall directly upon the people themselves in the exercise of what they consider their legitimate right?

7. But besides the danger which would result from such a condemnation and the impossibility of having it respected and observed one should note that the form of this organization is so little permanent, as the press indicates nearly every day, that in the estimation of practical men in our country, it cannot last very many years. Whence it follows that it is not necessary, even if it were just and prudent, to level the solemn condemnations of the Church against something which will vanish of itself. The social agitation will, indeed, last as long as there are social evils to be remedied; but the forms of organization and procedure meant for the attainment of this end are necessarily provisional and transient. They are also very numerous, for I have already remarked that the Knights of Labor is only one among several forms of labor organizations. To strike, then, at one of these forms would be to commence a war without system and without end; it would be to exhaust the forces of the Church in chasing a crowd of changing and uncertain phantasms. The American people behold with perfect composure and confidence the progress of our social contest, and have not the least fear of not being able to protect themselves against any excesses or dangers that may occasionally arise. And, to speak with the most profound respect, but also with the frankness which duty requires of me, it seems to me that prudence suggests, and that even the dignity of the Church demands that we should not offer to America an ecclesiastical protection for which she does not ask, and of which she believes she has no need.

8. In all this discussion I have not at all spoken of Canada, nor of the condemnation concerning the Knights of Labor in Canada. For we would consider it an impertinence to involve ourselves in the ecclesiastical affairs of another country which

has a hierarchy of its own, and with whose needs and social conditions we do not pretend to be acquainted. We believe, however, that the circumstances of a people almost entirely Catholic, as in lower Canada, must be very different from those of a mixed population like ours; moreover, that the documents submitted to the Holy Office are not the present constitution of the organization in our country, and that we, therefore, ask nothing involving an inconsistency on the part of the Holy See, which passed sentence *juxta exposita*. It is of the condition of things in the United States that we speak, and we trust that in these matters we are not presumptuous in believing that we are competent to judge. Now, as I have already indicated, out of the seventy-five archbishops and bishops of the United States, there are about five who would desire a condemnation of the Knights of Labor, such as we know them in our country; so that our hierarchy are almost unanimous in protesting against such a condemnation. Surely, such a fact ought to have great weight in deciding the question. If there are difficulties in the case, it seems to me that the prudence and experience of our bishops and the wise rules of the Third Plenary Council ought to suffice for their solution.

9. Finally, to sum it all up, it seems clear to me that the Holy See should not entertain the idea of condemning an association:

1. When the condemnation does not seem to be *justified* either by the letter or the spirit of its constitution, its law and the declaration of its leaders.

2. When the condemnation does not seem *necessary*, in view of the transient form of the organization and the social condition of the United States.

3. When it does not seem to be *prudent*, because of the reality of the grievances of the workers, and the admission of them made by the American people.

4. When it would be *dangerous* for the reputation of the Church in our democratic country, and possibly even arouse persecution.

5. When it would be *ineffectual* in compelling the obedience of our Catholic workers, who would regard it as false and unjust.

6. When it would be *destructive* instead of beneficial in its effects, impelling the children of the Church to disobey their Mother, and even to join condemned societies, which they have thus far shunned.

7. When it would be almost *ruinous* for the financial

maintenance of the Church in our country, and for the Peter's pence.

8. When it would turn into suspicion and hostility the outstanding devotedness of our Catholic people toward the Holy See.

9. When it would be regarded as a cruel blow to the authority of the bishops of the United States, who, it is well known, protest against such a condemnation.

Now, I hope the considerations here presented have shown with sufficient clearness that such would be the condemnation of the Knights of Labor in the United States.

Therefore, with complete confidence, I leave the case to the wisdom and prudence of your Eminence and the Holy See.

Rome, February 20, 1887.

> J. CARDINAL GIBBONS,
> Archbishop of Baltimore.

In March, 1925, Pope Pius XI told Monsignor Joseph Cardijn, Belgian crusader for social justice, that the principal scandal of the Catholic Church in Europe in the nineteenth century was its loss of the working classes. That a similar calamity did not overtake the Church in the United States was due largely to the energetic action of Cardinal Gibbons and his associates at Rome in February, 1887, in warning the Holy See of the dangers to the Church that would follow a condemnation of the Knights of Labor as a society forbidden to Catholic men. As Gibbons correctly foretold to Cardinal Simeoni, the Knights were even then entering a decline that would end in their extinction, and the American Federation of Labor, organized on another basis, was rapidly advancing to supplant them. Yet a blow dealt the Knights would have also been felt by the A.F.L., since so large a percentage of the latter's early membership was drawn from Catholic ranks.

It would be an exaggeration to say that the memorial on the Knights of Labor was responsible for winning over all Catholics of the United States, especially the well-to-do and highly placed, to a friendly attitude toward organized labor. But what was more important, it helped keep the vast majority of the Church's members, the workingmen and their families, loyal to their religious inheritance. In other words, the laboring classes here were given no excuses as they had been in Europe, to sever their affiliation with the Church because of its close alliance with the captains of industry. Strain and stress there certainly were from time to time between individual bishops and priests and their working-class flocks in the years after 1887. But the heightened tempo of industrialization in this country was never accompanied by any wholesale defection from the Catholic workmen's religious loyalties, as was true of so many of their European coreligionists. Less than half of the working classes of nominally Catholic countries in Western Europe—in France not more than 10 per cent of the males—attend Sunday Mass regularly, as compared to the 70 per cent or more of American Catholics who fulfill this weekly obligation.

It is frequently impossible for the historian to say precisely what factors account for the enduring importance and significance of a given event. The historian of American Catholicism is no exception in this regard, and yet he knows that the general influences flowing from an action taken by the leaders of an institution usually shape the behavior of those affiliated with that institution. Gibbons' memorial on the Knights of Labor served to fix the pattern of official Catholic policy toward labor, a pattern that in general has remained one of friendly interest and sympathy, even when many individual Catholics have declined to be guided by the reasoning underlying the statement of Gibbons and his coworkers. Without the strong stand taken in 1887 by these men, it is difficult to envision the advanced social consciousness displayed by their successors in signing the so-called Bishops' Program of Social Reconstruction of February, 1919. The latter document was, in fact, found so radical by some that Stephen C. Mason, President of the National Association of Manufacturers, predicted that it would lead to "a covert effort to disseminate partisan, pro-labor union, socialistic propaganda under the official insignia of the Roman Catholic Church in America." And John A. Ryan, the man who had written the offending document, as late as 1941 cited Cardinal Gibbons' action in the Knights of Labor case as one that had given him "great satisfaction, not only on account of my interest in organized labor but because it vindicated the vigilance and social vision of Cardinal Gibbons and the American Hierarchy." Here was proof of the enduring influence of the memorial of 1887 on the development and elaboration of Catholic thought in the field of labor relations.

Up to about 1820 the membership of the Catholic Church in the United States had been composed largely of native-born Americans. But a large-scale Catholic immigration began in that decade and grew until it was checked by the immigration-restriction acts of the 1920's. The most signifi-

cant fact in the Church's history in this country was that during the century from 1820 to 1920 an estimated total of over 9,300,000 immigrants were added to its fold, the overwhelming majority of whom were simple people of the farming and laboring classes. If, then, the minority of conservative prelates in the American Church led by Michael A. Corrigan, at the time Coadjutor Archbishop of New York, had prevailed in their desire to have the Knights of Labor condemned, there could not have been the remarkable progress that the Church has made in the free American society during the last three-quarters of a century, a progress that is reflected in its present membership of nearly 45,000,000 souls. The bond forged between the clergy and laity in the days of the immigrant's loneliness and bewilderment in a new environment has endured in spite of the enemies who have sought to break it down.

Thomas Alva Edison

On the Industrial Research Laboratory

1887

EDITED BY MATTHEW JOSEPHSON

In 1876 Thomas Alva Edison gave up his previous business of manufacturing telegraphic instruments and moved out to a quiet country retreat at Menlo Park, New Jersey. There he established himself in his own research laboratory devoted entirely to inventive work. Formerly it was only the cultivated devotees of pure science who possessed laboratories, and they used them for experiments touching the principles of natural science and aiming chiefly to add to the sum of human knowledge. Edison's was actually the world's first industrial research laboratory, intended for the uses of a freelance inventor; and, in many ways, it was his most important invention. By virtue of this achievement alone he became a central figure in the new age of technology.

The modest wooden-frame structure at Menlo Park resembled a country meeting house without a steeple. It had a drafting room, a scientific library, and a big workroom equipped with various instruments of precision and with quantities of chemicals, minerals, wire, batteries, and induction coils; in outbuildings were a steam engine, a furnace, a forge, and some of the new-fangled electric dynamos. At the time only a very few of America's leading universities boasted such laboratory equipment (Edison's had cost some $40,000). Certainly no engineering or industrial concern possessed such a laboratory, or such an unusual staff as Edison's "twenty earnest men" who resided with him in the "village of science" at Menlo Park.

Edison called his all-purpose research laboratory an "invention factory." Some thought he was a braggart when he vowed that he would turn out a minor invention every ten days and some "big job" every six months. Soon he had forty-four different projects under way and was taking out as many as four hundred patents a year. The Edison Laboratory was notable not only for the great diversity of its products, but also for thoroughness of research and testing. Contrary to the once-prevalent notion about Edison's dislike of theoretical scientists, he employed several distinguished mathematical physicists and university-trained engineers on his staff, as well as clockmakers and machinists. In short Edison "made a business out of invention itself," as Werner Sombart wrote. He delivered inventions to order, though the time of delivery was somewhat unpredictable. In developing practical new products Edison worked closely with big industrialists, and also with such leading financiers as the Vanderbilts and Morgans; yet he did not work primarily for money, but "to invent more"—and he repeatedly lost whole fortunes doing it.

At the little Edison Laboratory, the first strangled cries of the infant phonograph were heard; the brilliant light of the Edison lamp shone forth; America's earliest full-scale electric locomotive rumbled over a small track outside; and the mysterious two-electrode vacuum bulb also put in its appearance, hinting at the future of electronics and radio. One of the Edison Laboratory's most famous employees, A. E. Kennelly, paid tribute to it as "the meeting ground of practical inventive experience and scientific discovery.

Menlo Park was abandoned after a decade, as Edison moved on to a larger stage. Henry Ford, who attributed much of his success in the mass production of automobiles to Edison's ideas, built an exact reproduction of the old laboratory for the Ford Institute at Dearborn, signalizing it as the birthplace of modern American technology.

A man of "pure act," Edison did not stop to write down his original ideas about the first laboratory. But these are well defined in a letter he wrote in 1887 when he had completed its replica (but tenfold enlarged) at West Orange, New Jersey, the second Edison Laboratory—now in the custody of the National Park Service as a National Monument. Edison's let-

*ter was addressed to J. Hood Wright of New York, a friendly
financier who was one of the backers of the old Edison Electric Light Company; it was drafted by Edison in the pages of
his laboratory notebook in 1887, and is written with his characteristic imagination and in his own outrageous orthography.*

MY LABORATORY will soon be completed. The dimen-
sions are one building 250 ft long 50 wide & 3 stories
[high] 4 other bldgs. 25 x 100 ft one story high all of brick. I
will have the best equipped and largest Laboratory extant, and
the facilities incomparably superior to any other for rapid &
cheap development of an invention, & working it up into
Commercial shape with models, patterns & special machinery.
In fact there is no similar institution in Existence. We do our
own castings forgings. Can build anything from a ladys watch
to a Locomotive.

The Machine shop is sufficiently large to employ 50 men &
30 men can be worked in other parts of the works. Inventions
that formerly took months & cost a large sum can now be
done 2 or 3 days with very small expense, as I shall carry a
stock of almost every conceivable material of every size and
with the latest machinery a man will produce 10 times as
much as in a laboratory which has but little material, not of a
size, delays of days waiting for castings and machinery not
universal or modern. . . .

You are aware from your long acquaintance with me that I
do not fly any financial Kites, or speculate, and that the works
which I control are well managed. In the early days of the
shops it was necessary that I should largely manage them
[alone], first because the art had to be created. 2nd. because I
could get no men who were competent in such a new business.
But as soon as it was possible I put other persons in charge. I
am perfectly well aware of the fact that my place is in the
Laboratory; but I think you will admit that I know how a
shop should be managed & also know how to select men to
manage them.

With this prelude I will come to business.

My ambition is to build up a great Industrial Works in the
Orange Valley starting in a small way & gradually working up.
The Laboratory supplying the perfected inventions, models,

The letter, dated November 14, 1887, is taken from Edison's notebooks, which are preserved at the Edison Laboratory, West Orange,
New Jersey.

patterns & fitting up necessary special machinery in the factory for each invention.

My plan contemplates to working of only that class of inventions which requires but small investments. . . . Such a work in time could be running on 30 to 40 special things of so diversified nature that the average profit could scarcely be [varied] by competitors. Now Mr. Wright, do you think this is practicable. If so can you help me along with it.

It was with a sure instinct that the American people, after 1877, made Thomas Alva Edison one of the greatest of their folk heroes. He appealed to them as one of the old-fashioned, self-taught, individualistic Yankee inventors who epitomized the practical genius acclaimed as our national trait. During the era after the Civil War when America was dominated by great acquisitors, he was above all creative: new industries, untold new wealth flowed from his many innovations. Finally, the rise of the former train-boy and tramp telegrapher from rags to riches was an enactment of the American Dream.

Renewed study of Edison's career has led historians to revise sharply the traditional concept of him as an "antiscientific" mechanical inventor. Today he appears rather as a transitional figure in nineteenth-century science who introduced important changes into the very method of invention. With Edison the crude, single-handed methods of earlier contrivers gave way to the more complex ones of skilled and specialized men, working no longer alone, but as groups or teams engaged in systematic research. The individualistic inventors had pursued their experiments at a workbench in a factory, or in an attic or barn equipped with few scientific tools. Edison, at an early stage of his career, saw that it required an amplitude of good instruments, a group of expert helpers, and a proper establishment in order to pursue scientific investigations for prospective inventions in organized fashion.

Gradually, in the 1890's, a few large industrial concerns in America followed Edison's lead and established laboratories where scientific workers were employed in research, usually subordinated to the corporation's needs. Among the first and most important of the corporate laboratories were those of the Bell System, Eastman Kodak, and General Electric. During World War I the number of such research centers was rapidly multiplied—Germany's industrial corporations were far ahead of us then—and the scope of their activities was greatly expanded, to include basic scientific research as an ad-

junct to practical inventive work. In 1927, in advanced old age, Edison visited the gigantic laboratory of the General Electric Company at Schenectady, New York. By then this was staffed with hundreds of technicians, among them some of the nation's leading theoretical scientists, such as Charles Steinmetz, Irving Langmuir, and W. D. Coolidge. Edison beheld scientific instruments and devices of a power and complexity that even he had scarcely imagined: "lightning bolts" discharging all of 120,000 volts; lamps of 100,000 candlepower; and vacuum tubes for long-distance radio transmission.

Since that time a deluge of technological invention has transformed the world we live in; whole armies of scientific workers pursue their investigations in thousands of elaborate research institutions located throughout the United States, which are operated at a cost of billions of dollars each year. Inventions, nuclear, industrial, or military, are "made to order" by technical organizations or teams, though time of development and perfection are still no more certain than they were in Edison's day. All this multifarious activity in industrial research derives its essential form and character from the little "invention factory" pioneered by Edison in 1876.

Andrew Carnegie
Wealth
1889

EDITED BY ROBERT H. BREMNER

"Wealth" first appeared in the North American Review *for June, 1889. That year Andrew Carnegie celebrated his fifty-fourth birthday and the forty-first anniversary of his arrival in the United States. In 1889 Carnegie's fortune was approximately $30,000,000, his annual income about $1,850,000. He had been rich for twenty-five years and had every prospect of growing still richer.*

Carnegie once admitted that if he had been free to choose he would hardly have selected a business career. But in 1848, in Allegheny City, Pennsylvania, a poor immigrant boy from Dunfermline, Scotland, could not choose his occupation. "What I could get to do," Carnegie recalled, "not what I desired, was the question." Characteristically he made the best of the situation. He came from artisan stock and, like his ancestors, went to work while still a boy. His forebears, in their apprenticeships, learned to weave cloth or cobble shoes. Carnegie, in his youthful employments, learned how to get along with people and how to make money work. Before turning thirty he had learned and earned enough to become his own master.

A great capitalist, with unusual talents for salesmanship and public relations, Carnegie had the outlook of a master craftsman. Except in youth he was not a hard worker. He made it a practice to employ skilled assistants and to keep himself free from routine. He lived well, took long vacations, and spent part of every day in reading and recreation. Like his grandfathers—one was nicknamed "Professor," the other called himself a "thinking cobbler"—Carnegie took it for granted that a man could practice a trade, such as steel-making, and still lead a vigorous intellectual life.

The years just before Carnegie wrote "Wealth" were among the most eventful in his career. In the 1880's Carnegie strengthened his position in the steel industry, began making large-scale benefactions, published three books, started contributing to periodicals, attempted to convert England to republicanism, became interested in the peace movement, and cultivated friendships with John Morley, Herbert Spencer, Matthew Arnold, and William Gladstone. In 1886 a near-fatal illness and the deaths of his beloved brother and strong-willed mother brought one phase of his life to a close. Another began in 1887 when, after a courtship of seven years, he married Louise Whitfield.

For twenty-five years before 1889 Carnegie had been making private resolutions about the disposition of his fortune. In 1868 he had proposed to limit his income to $50,000 a year, spend his surplus on benevolence, and, as soon as possible, "Cast business aside forever except for others." Mrs. Carnegie shared her husband's philanthropic interests and, in a marriage settlement, formally approved his intention to devote the bulk of his estate to charitable and educational purposes.

Carnegie wrote "Wealth" in the library of his house at 5 West 51 Street, New York City. He sent it to the North American Review in May, 1889. The editor, Allen Thorndyke Rice, on receiving the manuscript, called on Carnegie and asked him to read it aloud. Rice recommended only one change: Carnegie had estimated that $900 of each $1,000 spent on charities was wasted; he revised this figure at Rice's suggestion to $950.

THE PROBLEM of our age is the proper administration of wealth, so that the ties of brotherhood may still bind together the rich and poor in harmonious relationship. The conditions of human life have not only been changed, but revolutionized, within the past few hundred years. In former days there was little difference between the dwelling, dress, food, and environment of the chief and those of his retainers. The Indians are to-day where civilized man then was. When visiting the Sioux, I was led to the wigwam of the chief. It was just like the others in external appearance, and even within the difference was trifling between it and those of the poorest of his braves. The contrast between the palace of the millionaire and the cottage of the laborer with us to-day measures the change which has come with civilization.

This change, however, is not to be deplored, but welcomed as highly beneficial. It is well, nay, essential for the progress of the race, that the houses of some should be homes for all that is highest and best in literature and the arts, and for all the refinements of civilization, rather than that none should be so. Much better this great irregularity than universal squalor. Without wealth there can be no Maecenas. The "good old times" were not good old times. Neither master nor servant was as well situated then as to-day. A relapse to old conditions would be disastrous to both—not the least so to him who serves—and would sweep away civilization with it. But whether the change be for good or ill, it is upon us, beyond our power to alter, and therefore to be accepted and made the best of. It is a waste of time to criticise the inevitable.

It is easy to see how the change has come. One illustration will serve for almost every phase of the cause. In the manufacture of products we have the whole story. It applies to all combinations of human industry, as stimulated and enlarged by the inventions of this scientific age. Formerly articles were manufactured at the domestic hearth or in small shops which formed part of the household. The master and his apprentices worked side by side, the latter living with the master, and therefore subject to the same conditions. When these apprentices rose to be masters, there was little or no change in their mode of life, and they, in turn, educated in the same routine succeeding apprentices. There was, substantially, social equality, and even political equality, for those engaged in industrial pursuits had then little or no political voice in the State.

But the inevitable result of such a mode of manufacture was crude articles at high prices. To-day the world obtains commodities of excellent quality at prices which even the generation preceding this would have deemed incredible. In the commercial world similar causes have produced similar results, and the race is benefited thereby. The poor enjoy what

The essay is reprinted as it originally appeared in the *North American Review*, CXLVIII (1889), 653–64.

the rich could not before afford. What were the luxuries have become the necessaries of life. The laborer has now more comforts than the farmer had a few generations ago. The farmer has more luxuries than the landlord had, and is more richly clad and better housed. The landlord has books and pictures rarer, and appointments more artistic, than the King could then obtain.

The price we pay for this salutary change is, no doubt, great. We assemble thousands of operatives in the factory, in the mine, and in the counting-house, of whom the employer can know little or nothing, and to whom the employer is little better than a myth. All intercourse between them is at an end. Rigid Castes are formed, and, as usual, mutual ignorance breeds mutual distrust. Each Caste is without sympathy for the other, and ready to credit anything disparaging in regard to it. Under the law of competition, the employer of thousands is forced into the strictest economies, among which the rates paid to labor figure prominently, and often there is friction between the employer and the employed, between capital and labor, between rich and poor. Human society loses homogeneity.

The price which society pays for the law of competition, like the price it pays for cheap comforts and luxuries, is also great; but the advantages of this law are also greater still, for it is to this law that we owe our wonderful material development, which brings improved conditions in its train. But, whether the law be benign or not, we must say of it, as we say of the change in the conditions of men to which we have referred: It is here; we cannot evade it; no substitutes for it have been found; and while the law may be sometimes hard for the individual, it is best for the race, because it insures the survival of the fittest in every department. We accept and welcome, therefore, as conditions to which we must accommodate ourselves, great inequality of environment, the concentration of business, industrial and commercial, in the hands of a few, and the law of competition between these, as being not only beneficial, but essential for the future progress of the race. Having accepted these, it follows that there must be great scope for the exercise of special ability in the merchant and in the manufacturer who has to conduct affairs upon a great scale. That this talent for organization and management is rare among men is proved by the fact that it invariably secures for its possessor enormous rewards, no matter where or under what laws or conditions. The experienced in affairs always rate the MAN whose services can be obtained as a partner as not only the first consideration, but such as to render the question of his capital scarcely worth considering, for such men soon create capital; while, without the special talent required, capital soon takes wings. Such men become interested in firms or corporations using millions; and estimating only simple interest to be made upon the capital invested, it is inevitable that their income must exceed their expenditures, and that they must accumulate wealth. Nor is there any middle ground which such men can occupy, because the great manufacturing or commercial concern which does not earn at least interest upon its capital soon becomes bankrupt. It must either go forward or fall behind: to stand still is impossible. It is a condition essential for its successful operation that it should be thus far profitable, and even that, in addition to interest on capital, it should make profit. It is a law, as certain as any of the others named, that men possessed of this peculiar talent for affairs, under the free play of economic forces, must, of necessity, soon be in receipt of more revenue than can be judiciously expended upon themselves; and this law is as beneficial for the race as the others.

Objections to the foundations upon which society is based are not in order, because the condition of the race is better with these than it has been with any others which have been tried. Of the effect of any new substitutes proposed we cannot be sure. The Socialist or Anarchist who seeks to overturn present conditions is to be regarded as attacking the foundation upon which civilization itself rests, for civilization took its start from the day that the capable, industrious workman said to his incompetent and lazy fellow, "If thou dost not sow, thou shalt not reap," and thus ended primitive Communism by separating the drones from the bees. One who studies this subject will soon be brought face to face with the conclusion that upon the sacredness of property civilization itself depends—the right of the laborer to his hundred dollars in the savings bank, and equally the legal right of the millionaire to his millions. To those who propose to substitute Communism for this intense Individualism the answer, therefore, is: The race has tried that. All progress from that barbarous day to the present time has resulted from its displacement. Not evil, but good, has come to the race from the accumulation of wealth by those who have the ability and energy that produce it. But even if we admit for a moment that it might be better for the race to discard its present foundation, Individualism,—that it is a nobler ideal that man should labor, not for himself alone, but in and for a brotherhood of his fellows, and share with them all in common, realizing Swedenborg's idea of Heaven, where, as he says, the angels derive their happiness, not from the laboring for self, but for each other,—even admit all this, and a sufficient answer is, This is not evolution, but revolution. It necessitates the changing of human nature itself—a work of eons, even if it were good to change it, which we cannot know. It is not practicable in our day or in our age. Even if desirable theoretically, it belongs to another and long-succeeding sociological stratum. Our duty is with what is practicable now; with the next step possible in our day and generation. It is criminal to waste our energies in endeavoring to uproot, when all we can profitably or possibly accomplish is to bend the universal tree of humanity a little in the direction most favorable to the production of good fruit under existing circumstances. We might as well urge the destruction of the highest existing type of man because he failed to reach our ideal as to favor the destruction of Individualism, Private Property, the Law of Accumulation of Wealth, the Law of Competition; for these are the highest results of human experience, the soil in which society so far has produced the best fruit. Unequally or unjustly, as these laws sometimes operate, and imperfect as they appear to the Idealist, they are, nevertheless, like the highest type of man, the best and most valuable of all that humanity has yet accomplished.

We start, then, with a condition of affairs under which the best interests of the race are promoted, but which inevitably gives wealth to the few. Thus far, accepting conditions as they exist, the situation can be surveyed and pronounced good. The question then arises,—and, if the foregoing be correct, it is the only question with which we have to deal,— What is the proper mode of administering wealth after the laws upon which civilization is founded have thrown it into the hands of the few? And it is of this great question that I believe I offer the true solution. It will be understood that *fortunes* are here spoken of, not moderate sums saved by many years of effort, the returns from which are required for the comfortable maintenance and education of families. This is not *wealth*, but only *competence*, which it should be the aim of all to acquire.

There are but three modes in which surplus wealth can be disposed of. It can be left to the families of the decedent; or it can be bequeathed for public purposes; or, finally, it can be administered during their lives by its possessors. Under the first and second modes most of the wealth of the world that has reached the few has hitherto been applied. Let us in turn consider each of these modes. The first is the most injudicious. In monarchical countries, the estates and the greatest portion of the wealth are left to the first son, that the vanity of the parent may be gratified by the thought that his name and title are to descend to succeeding generations unimpaired. The condition of this class in Europe today teaches the futility of such hopes or ambitions. The successors have become impoverished through their follies or from the fall in the value of land. Even in Great Britain the strict law of entail has been found inadequate to maintain the status of an hereditary class. Its soil is rapidly passing into the hands of the stranger. Under republican institutions the division of property among the children is much fairer, but the question which forces itself upon thoughtful men in all lands is: Why should men leave great fortunes to their children? If this is done from affection, is it not misguided affection? Observation teaches that, generally speaking, it is not well for the children that they should be so burdened. Neither is it well for the state. Beyond providing for the wife and daughters moderate sources of income, and very moderate allowances indeed, if any, for the sons, men may well hesitate, for it is no longer questionable that great sums bequeathed oftener work more for the injury than for the good of the recipients. Wise men will soon conclude that, for the best interests of the members of their families and of the state, such bequests are an improper use of their means.

It is not suggested that men who have failed to educate their sons to earn a livelihood shall cast them adrift in poverty. If any man has seen fit to rear his sons with a view to their living idle lives, or, what is highly commendable, has instilled in them the sentiment that they are in a position to labor for public ends without reference to pecuniary considerations, then of course, the duty of the parent is to see that such are provided for *in moderation*. There are instances of millionaires' sons unspoiled by wealth, who, being rich, still perform great services in the community. Such are the very salt of the earth, as valuable as, unfortunately, they are rare; still it is not the exception, but the rule, that men must regard, and, looking at the usual result of enormous sums conferred upon legatees, the thoughtful man must shortly say, "I would as soon leave to my son a curse as the almighty dollar," and admit to himself that it is not the welfare of the children, but family pride, which inspires these enormous legacies.

As to the second mode, that of leaving wealth at death for public uses, it may be said that this is only a means for the disposal of wealth, provided a man is content to wait until he is dead before it becomes of much good in the world. Knowledge of the results of legacies bequeathed is not calculated to inspire the brightest hopes of much posthumous good being accomplished. The cases are not few in which the real object sought by the testator is not attained, nor are they few in which his real wishes are thwarted. In many cases the bequests are so used as to become only monuments of his folly. It is well to remember that it requires the exercise of not less ability than that which acquired the wealth to use it so as to be really beneficial to the community. Besides this, it may fairly be said that no man is to be extolled for doing what he cannot help doing, nor is he to be thanked by the community to which he only leaves wealth at death. Men who leave vast sums in this way may fairly be thought men who would not have left it at all, had they been able to take it with them. The memories of such cannot be held in grateful remembrance, for there is no grace in their gifts. It is not to be wondered at that such bequests seem so generally to lack the blessing.

The growing disposition to tax more and more heavily large estates left at death is a cheering indication of the growth of a salutary change in public opinion. The State of Pennsylvania now takes—subject to some exceptions—onetenth of the property left by its citizens. The budget presented in the British Parliament the other day proposes to increase the death-duties; and, most significant of all, the new tax is to be a graduated one. Of all forms of taxation, this seems the wisest. Men who continue hoarding great sums all their lives, the proper use of which for public ends would work good to the community, should be made to feel that the community, in the form of the state, cannot thus be deprived of its proper share. By taxing estates heavily at death the state marks its condemnation of the selfish millionaire's unworthy life.

It is desirable that nations should go much further in this direction. Indeed, it is difficult to set bounds to the share of a rich man's estate which should go at his death to the public through the agency of the state, and by all means such taxes should be graduated, beginning at nothing upon moderate sums to dependents, and increasing rapidly as the amounts swell, until of the millionaire's hoard, as of Shylock's, at least

> "—— The other half
> Comes to the privy coffer of the state."

This policy would work powerfully to induce the rich man to attend to the administration of wealth during his life, which is the end that society should always have in view, as being that by far most fruitful for the people. Nor need it be feared that this policy would sap the root of enterprise and render men less anxious to accumulate, for to the class whose ambition it is to leave great fortunes and be talked about after their death, it will attract even more attention, and, indeed, be a somewhat nobler ambition to have enormous sums paid over to the state from their fortunes.

There remains, then, only one mode of using great fortunes; but in this we have the true antidote for the temporary unequal distribution of wealth, the reconciliation of the rich and the poor—a reign of harmony—another ideal, differing, indeed, from that of the Communist in requiring only the further evolution of existing conditions, not the total overthrow of our civilization. It is founded upon the present most intense individualism, and the race is prepared to put it in practice by degrees whenever it pleases. Under its sway we shall have an ideal state, in which the surplus wealth of the few will become, in the best sense, the property of the many, because administered for the common good, and this wealth, passing through the hands of the few, can be made a much more potent force for the elevation of our race than if it had been distributed in small sums to the people themselves. Even the poorest can be made to see this, and to agree that great sums gathered by some of their fellow-citizens and spent for public purposes, from which the masses reap the principal benefit, are more valuable to them than if scattered among them through the course of many years in trifling amounts.

If we consider what results flow from the Cooper Institute, for instance, to the best portion of the race in New York not possessed of means, and compare these with those which would have arisen for the good of the masses from an equal sum distributed by Mr. Cooper in his lifetime in the form of wages, which is the highest form of distribution, being for work done and not for charity, we can form some estimate of the possibilities for the improvement of the race which lie embedded in the present law of the accumulation of wealth. Much of this sum, if distributed in small quantities among the people, would have been wasted in the indulgence of appetite, some of it in excess, and it may be doubted whether even the part put to the best use, that of adding to the comforts of the home, would have yielded results for the race, as a race, at all comparable to those which are flowing and are to flow from the Cooper Institute from generation to generation. Let the advocate of violent or radical change ponder well this thought.

We might even go so far as to take another instance, that of Mr. Tilden's bequest of five millions of dollars for a free library in the city of New York, but in referring to this one cannot help saying involuntarily, How much better if Mr. Tilden had devoted the last years of his own life to the proper administration of this immense sum; in which case neither legal contest nor any other cause of delay could have interfered with his aims. But let us assume that Mr. Tilden's millions finally become the means of giving to this city a noble public library, where the treasures of the world contained in books will be open to all forever, without money and without price. Considering the good of that part of the race which congregates in and around Manhattan Island, would its permanent benefit have been better promoted had these millions been allowed to circulate in small sums through the hands of the masses? Even the most strenuous advocate of Communism must entertain a doubt upon this subject. Most of those who think will probably entertain no doubt whatever.

Poor and restricted are our opportunities in this life; narrow our horizon; our best work most imperfect; but rich men should be thankful for one inestimable boon. They have it in their power during their lives to busy themselves in organizing benefactions from which the masses of their fellows will derive lasting advantage, and thus dignify their own lives. The highest life is probably to be reached, not by such imitation of the life of Christ as Count Tolstoï gives us, but, while animated by Christ's spirit, by recognizing the changed conditions of this age, and adopting modes of expressing this spirit suitable to the changed conditions under which we live; still laboring for the good of our fellows, which was the essence of his life and teaching, but laboring in a different manner.

This, then, is held to be the duty of the man of Wealth: First, to set an example of modest, unostentatious living, shunning display or extravagance; to provide moderately for the legitimate wants of those dependent upon him; and after doing so to consider all surplus revenues which come to him simply as trust funds, which he is called upon to administer, and strictly bound as a matter of duty to administer in the manner which, in his judgment, is best calculated to produce the most beneficial results for the community—the man of wealth thus becoming the mere agent and trustee for his poorer brethren, bringing to their service his superior wisdom, experience, and ability to administer, doing for them better than they would or could do for themselves.

We are met here with the difficulty of determining what are moderate sums to leave to members of the family; what is modest, unostentatious living; what is the test of extravagance. There must be different standards for different condi-

tions. The answer is that it is as impossible to name exact
amounts of actions as it is to define good manners, good
taste, or the rules of propriety; but, nevertheless, these are
verities, well known although undefinable. Public sentiment is
quick to know and to feel what offends these. So in the case
of wealth. The rule in regard to good taste in the dress of
men or women applies here. Whatever makes one conspicuous offends the canon. If any family be chiefly known for display, for extravagance in home, table, equipage, for enormous sums ostentatiously spent in any form upon itself,—if
these be its chief distinctions, we have no difficulty in estimating its nature or culture. So likewise in regard to the use or
abuse of its surplus wealth, or to generous, freehanded cooperation in good public uses, or to unabated efforts to accumulate and hoard to the last, whether they administer or be-
queath. The verdict rests with best and most enlightened
public sentiment. The community will surely judge, and its
judgments will not often be wrong.

The best uses to which surplus wealth can be put have already been indicated. Those who would administer wisely
must, indeed, be wise, for one of the serious obstacles to the
improvement of our race is indiscriminate charity. It were
better for mankind that the millions of the rich was thrown
into the sea than so spent as to encourage the slothful, the
drunken, the unworthy. Of every thousand dollars spent in so
called charity to-day, it is probable that $950 is unwisely
spent; so spent, indeed, as to produce the very evils which it
proposes to mitigate or cure. A well known writer of
philosophic books admitted the other day that he had given a
quarter of a dollar to a man who approached him as he was
coming to visit the house of his friend. He knew nothing of
the habits of this beggar; knew not the use that would be
made of this money, although he had every reason to suspect
that it would be spent improperly. This man professed to be a
disciple of Herbert Spencer; yet the quarter-dollar given that
night will probably work more injury than all the money
which its thoughtless donor will ever be able to give in true
charity will do good. He only gratified his own feelings, saved
himself from annoyance,—and this was probably one of the
most selfish and very worst actions of his life, for in all respects he is most worthy.

In bestowing charity, the main consideration should be to
help those who will help themselves; to provide part of the
means by which those who desire to improve may do so; to
give those who desire to rise the aids by which they may rise;
to assist, but rarely or never to do all. Neither the individual

nor the race is improved by alms-giving. Those worthy of assistance, except in rare cases, seldom require assistance. The really valuable men of the race never do, except in cases of accident or sudden change. Every one has, of course, cases of individuals brought to his own knowledge where temporary assistance can do genuine good, and these he will not overlook. But the amount which can be wisely given by the individual for individuals is necessarily limited by his lack of knowledge of the circumstances connected with each. He is the only true reformer who is as careful and as anxious not to aid the unworthy as he is to aid the worthy, and, perhaps, even more so, for in alms-giving more injury is probably done by rewarding vice than by relieving virtue.

The rich man is thus almost restricted to following the examples of Peter Cooper, Enoch Pratt of Baltimore, Mr. Pratt of Brooklyn, Senator Stanford, and others, who know that the best means of benefiting the community is to place within its reach the ladders upon which the aspiring can rise—parks, and means of recreation, by which men are helped in body and mind; works of art, certain to give pleasure and improve the public taste, and public institutions of various kinds, which will improve the general condition of the people;—in this manner returning their surplus wealth to the mass of their fellows in the forms best calculated to do them lasting good.

Thus is the problem of Rich and Poor to be solved. The laws of accumulation will be left free; the laws of distribution free. Individualism will continue, but the millionaire will be but a trustee for the poor; intrusted for a season with a great part of the increased wealth of the community, but administering it for the community far better than it could or would have done for itself. The best minds will thus have reached a stage in the development of the race in which it is clearly seen that there is no mode of disposing of surplus wealth creditable to thoughtful and earnest men into whose hands it flows save by using it year by year for the general good. This day already dawns. But a little while, and although, without incurring the pity of their fellows, men may die sharers in great business enterprises from which their capital cannot be or has not been withdrawn, and is left chiefly at death for public uses, yet the man who dies leaving behind him millions of available wealth, which was his to administer during life, will pass away "unwept, unhonored, and unsung," no matter to what uses he leaves the dross which he cannot take with him. Of such as these the public verdict will then be: "The man who dies thus rich dies disgraced."

Such, in my opinion, is the true Gospel concerning Wealth, obedience to which is destined some day to solve the problem of the Rich and the Poor, and to bring "Peace on earth, among men Good-Will."

In June, 1889, Mrs. Carnegie sent a copy of "Wealth" to Gladstone, with a note saying, "We think we have found the true path—it is the one we mean to tread—if it commends itself to you we shall be so happy." At Gladstone's request W. T. Stead reprinted the article in the Pall Mall Gazette, *bestowing on it the name by which it has since been known, "The Gospel of Wealth." Subsequently published in England as a penny pamphlet, often reprinted, and widely commented on in newspapers and periodicals on both sides of the Atlantic, "The Gospel" won Carnegie greater fame than he had ever before enjoyed.*

Carnegie continued his discussion of the creation and employment of wealth in "The Best Fields for Philanthropy" published in the North American Review *in December, 1889. Again asserting that "great wealth must inevitably flow into the hands of the few exceptional managers of men," he offered more specific suggestions for putting private wealth to public use. Parks, concert halls, organs, baths, and church buildings struck him as suitable philanthropic projects. To large givers he particularly recommended the establishment or endowment of universities, technical institutes, museums, libraries, observatories, hospitals, medical school and laboratories, "and other institutions connected with the alleviation of human suffering, and expecially with the prevention rather than the cure of human ills."*

Contemporary critics found little to object to in Carnegie's advice to philanthropists. Both American and British commentators, however, disputed Carnegie's view on the origin of wealth. "Our great American fortunes," declared Albert Shaw in 1893, "are the products of social opportunities rather than the mere creative power of their holders." An English clergyman, Hugh Price Hughes, writing in 1890, denied that millionaires were the natural results of industrial enterprise. Free trade, free land, and a progressive income tax, Hughes said, would prevent the accumulation of absurdly large and potentially dangerous private fortunes. Carnegie, as was his way, genially adopted many of his critics' arguments. In his later writings, while still praising the judgment and ability of "great administrators," he paid more attention to the social bases of wealth and in 1908 forthrightly stated: "The community created the millionaire's wealth."

After the Homestead strike of 1892, Carnegie's principles and practice of philanthropy, although still widely endorsed, were sometimes derided. In Socialism for Millionaires *(1896) George Bernard Shaw observed, "We often give to public objects money that we should devote to raising wages . . . or substituting three eight-hour shifts for two twelve-hour ones." Carnegie's most persistent critic, Finley Peter Dunne's Mr. Dooley, mimicked the* Gospel: *"Him that giveth to th' poor, they say, lindeth to th' Lord; but in these days we look f'r quick returns on our invistmints." Confessing admiration and affection for his adversary, Mr. Dooley remarked in 1906 that Carnegie was giving in the way everyone would like to. "Ivry time he dhrops a dollar it makes a noise like a waither fallin' down stairs with a tray iv dishes."*

The gospel of wealth, as Carnegie formulated it in 1889, required possessors of surplus wealth to dispose of their bounty during their own lives. In the 1890's Carnegie continued to emphasize, in word and deed, the donor's personal responsibility for selecting and supervising suitable objects of philanthropy. After 1901, when he retired from business with a capital of $250,000,000 and an annual income of $12,500,000, the letter of the gospel no longer sufficed. Conventional giving, even on the scale he had long practiced, failed to answer his problem. His wealth was too great for any one man to administer in a normal human lifetime. Carnegie's solution was the creation of a series of perpetual trusts for the support of education, scientific research, international peace, and other causes in which he was interested. To the largest of his foundations, the Carnegie Corporation of New York, he gave $125,000,000 and the undistributed portion of his estate, so that it could do in perpetuity what he had attempted in life: give wisely and productively for fostering cultural amenities, advancing knowledge, and promoting human welfare.

"Wealth" is a nineteenth-century document; the foundations which bear Carnegie's name and which have served as models for so many later ones are products of the twentieth century. As avid for success in philanthropy as in business, Carnegie was receptive to new ideas and, with the help of the distinguished guests he frequently entertained, he kept abreast of expert opinion in a variety of fields. The course he ultimately followed in philanthropy departed in important respects from the path he charted in 1889. By his later practice he amended and dignified the gospel proclaimed in "Wealth."

*Laboring, as he would have said, in the spirit of 1889, but
laboring in a different manner, Carnegie devised and utilized
methods of giving that were suited to his means, to the
changed conditions of the age, and to the needs of the future.*

People's Party Platform
1892

EDITED BY JOHN D. HICKS

The People's Party platform of 1892 was the culmination of a quarter-century of agrarian protest against the growing pre-eminence of industry over agriculture in the United States. The blessings of civilization, many farmers believed, had not been distributed equally between cities and country, but had fallen disporportionately to the cities. "Towns and cities flourish and 'boom,' and grow and 'boom,' and yet agriculture languishes." Since the Civil War, the farmers had stated their case through four successive organizations—the Grangers, the Greenbackers, the Farmers' Alliance, and finally the People's (or Populist) Party. Probably their troubles were due less to the evil machinations of railroads, bankers, middlemen, and manufacturers, whom they tended to blame, than to unforeseen forces set loose by the revolutionary use of new machines and new transportation facilities. But the farmers, particularly those who suffered most, in the South and West, would not believe it. Governmental betrayals, they insisted, had funneled their rightful profits into the coffers of the "plutocrats." Only if the people themselves took control of their government, and wrote and administered new laws, could these evils be corrected.

The ideas expressed in the platform of 1892 did not stem,

533

therefore, from on-the-spot thinking by a single platform committee. These ideas had grown with the years, and the task of the committee was primarily one of lucid and orderly restatement. Probably the claim of Ignatius Donnelly that he had written nine-tenths of the platform was an exaggeration, but that he was its principal draftsman can hardly be doubted. Two preceding conventions, one held at Cincinnati, May 20, 1891, and another at St. Louis, February 22, 1892, had adopted platforms from which the Omaha version was drawn, and Donnelly had played a major part in the writing of each. His famous Preamble, which was actually longer than the platform proper, he had read to the St. Louis convention in only a slightly different form. On that occasion the St. Paul Pioneer Press had promptly branded his words as a "stereotyped Donnellian wail of woe."

Donnelly was an orator and an agitator, an outstanding demagogue in an age of demagogues. He earnestly favored third-party action; he knew that the Populist conventions needed a stirring, emotional appeal to inspire them; and he provided exactly what in his judgment the situation required. In contrast to the actions of delegates at most nominating conventions, the Omaha delegates, at a session held by previous planning on the Fourth of July, went wild about their platform rather than about their candidates. According to one reporter, "When that furious and hysterical arraignment of the present times, that incoherent intermingling of Jeremiah and Bellamy, the platform, was adopted, the cheers and yells which rose like a tornado from four thousand throats and raged without cessation for thirty-four minutes, during which women shrieked and wept, men embraced and kissed their neighbors, locked arms, marched back and forth, and leaped upon tables and chairs in the ecstasy of their delirium, —this dramatic and historical scene must have told every quiet, thoughtful witness that there was something at the back of all this turmoil more than the failure of crops or the scarcity of ready cash."

ASSEMBLED upon the one hundred and sixteenth anniversary of the Declaration of Independence, the People's Party of America in their first National Convention, invoking upon their action the blessing of Almighty God, puts forth, in the name and on behalf of the people of this country, the following preamble and declaration of principles:

[PREAMBLE]

The conditions which surround us best justify our co-operation. We meet in the midst of a nation brought to the verge of moral, political and material ruin. Corruption dominates the ballot box, the Legislatures, the Congress, and touches even the ermine of the Bench. The people are demoralized; most of the States have been compelled to isolate the voters at the polling places to prevent universal intimidation or bribery. The newspapers are largely subsidized or muzzled, public opinion silenced, business prostrated, our homes covered with mortgages, labor impoverished, and the land concentrating in the hands of the capitalists. The urban workmen are denied the right of organization for self-protection; imported pauperized labor beats down their wages; a hireling standing army, unrecognized by our laws, is established to shoot them down, and they are rapidly degenerating into European conditions. The fruits of the toil of millions are boldly stolen to build up colossal fortunes for a few, unprecedented in the history of mankind, and the possessors of these in turn despise the Republic and endanger liberty. From the same prolific womb of governmental injustice we breed the two great classes—tramps and millionaires.

The national power to create money is appropriated to enrich bond holders; a vast public debt, payable in legal tender currency, has been funded into gold-bearing bonds, thereby adding millions to the burdens of the people.

Silver, which has been accepted as coin since the dawn of history, has been demonetized to add to the purchasing power of gold by decreasing the value of all forms of property as well as human labor, and the supply of currency is purposely abridged to fatten usurers, bankrupt enterprise and enslave industry.

A vast conspiracy against mankind has been organized on

The original of the People's Party platform of 1892 seems not to exist; nor are the official proceedings of the Omaha convention available either in published or in unpublished form. *The People's Party Campaign Book* (Washington: National Watchman Publishing Company, 1892) appeared prior to the convention, and is therefore of no help. The platform was published at once, however, in the various party journals, including the *National Economist*, VII (July 9, 1892), 257–58. It appears also in the *Tribune Almanac* for 1892, pp. 38–40, and in Edward McPherson, *A Handbook of Politics for 1892* (Washington: James J. Chapman, 1892). Since the McPherson version contains sections omitted in some of the others, and is relatively free from the typographical errors that disfigure the *National Economist* text, it is the one reproduced here.

two continents, and it is rapidly taking possession of the world. If not met and overthrown at once, it forebodes terrible social convulsions, the destruction of civilization, or the establishment of an absolute despotism.

We have witnessed, for more than a quarter of a century, the struggles of the two great political parties for power and plunder, while grievous wrongs have been inflicted upon the suffering people. We charge that the controlling influences dominating both these parties have permitted the existing dreadful conditions to develop without serious effort to prevent or restrain them.

OLD PARTIES TREATED AS ONE.

Neither do they now promise us any substantial reform. They have agreed together to ignore, in the coming campaign, every issue but one. They propose to drown the outcries of a plundered people with the uproar of a sham battle over the tariff, so that capitalists, corporations, national banks, rings, trusts, watered stock, the demonetization of silver and the oppressions of the usurers may all be lost sight of. They propose to sacrifice our homes, lives and children, on the altar of mammon; to destroy the multitude in order to secure corruption funds from the millionaires.

Assembled on the anniversary of the birthday of the nation, and filled with the spirit of the grand general and chieftain who established our independence, we seek to restore the Government of the Republic to the hands of the "plain people" with whose class it originated. We assert our purposes to be identical with the purposes of the National Constitution, to form a more perfect Union and establish justice, insure domestic tranquility, provide for the common defense, promote the general welfare and secure the blessings of liberty for ourselves and our posterity.

We declare that this Republic can only endure as a free government while built upon the love of the whole people for each other and for the nation; that it cannot be pinned together by bayonets; that the civil war is over and that every passion and resentment which grew out of it must die with it, and that we must be in fact, as we are in name, one united brotherhood of freedom.

FARMERS' DEMANDS.

Our country finds itself confronted by conditions for which there is no precedent in the history of the world; our annual agricultural productions amount to billions of dollars in value, which must within a few weeks or months be exchanged for billions of dollars' worth of commodities consumed in their production; the existing currency supply is wholly inadeqaute to make this exchange; the results are falling prices, the formation of combines and rings, the impoverishment of the producing class. We pledge ourselves that, if given power, we will labor to correct these evils by wise and reasonable legislation, in accordance with the terms of our platform.

We believe that the powers of government—in other words, of the people—should be expanded (as in the case of the postal service) as rapidly and as far as the good sense of an intelligent people and the teachings of experience shall justify, to the end that oppression, injustice and poverty, shall eventually cease in the land.

While our sympathies as a party of reform are naturally upon the side of every proposition which will tend to make men intelligent, virtuous and temperate, we nevertheless regard these questions—important as they are—as secondary to the great issues now pressing for solution, and upon which not only our individual prosperity, but the very existence of free institutions depend; and we ask all men to first help us to determine whether we are to have a Republic to administer, before we differ as to the conditions upon which it is to be administered; believing that the forces of reform this day organized will never cease to move forward, until every wrong is righted, and equal rights and equal privileges securely established for all the men and women of this country.

[PLATFORM]

We declare, therefore,

PERPETUAL LABOR UNION.

First—That the union of the labor forces of the United States this day consummated shall be permanent and perpetual; may its spirit enter into all hearts for the salvation of the Republic, and the uplifting of mankind.

WEALTH FOR WORKERS.

Second—Wealth belongs to him who creates it, and every dollar taken from industry without an equivalent is robbery. "If any will not work, neither shall he eat." The interests of rural and civic labor are the same; their enemies are identical.

OWNERSHIP OF RAILWAYS.

Third—We believe that the time has come when the railroad corporations will either own the people or the people must own the railroads; and should the Government enter upon the work of owning and managing all railroads, we should favor an amendment to the Constitution by which all persons engaged in the Government service shall be placed under a civil service regulation of the most rigid character, so as to prevent the increase of the power of the national administration by the use of such additional Government employes.

FINANCE.

1st. We demand a national currency, safe, sound and flexible, issued by the General Government only, a full legal tender for all debts public and private, and that without the use of banking corporations; a just, equitable and efficient means of distribution direct to the people at a tax not to exceed 2 per cent. per annum, to be provided as set forth in the Sub-Treasury plan of the Farmers' Alliance, or a better system; also by payments in discharge of its obligations for public improvements.

(A) We demand free and unlimited coinage of silver and gold at the present legal ratio of 16 to 1.

(B) We demand that the amount of circulating medium be speedily increased to not less than $50 per capita.

(C) We demand a graduated income tax.

(D) We believe that the money of the country should be kept as much as possible in the hands of the people, and hence we demand that all State and National revenues shall be limited to the necessary expenses of the Government, economically and honestly administered.

(E) We demand that Postal Savings Banks be established by the Government for the safe deposit of the earnings of the people and to facilitate exchange.

TRANSPORTATION.

D. Transportation being a means of exchange and a public necessity, the government should own and operate the railroads in the interest of the people.

The telegraph and telephone, like the post office system, being a necessity for the transmission of news, should be owned and operated by the Government in the interest of the people.

LAND.

3d. The land, including all the natural sources of wealth, is the heritage of the people and should not be monopolized for speculative purposes, and alien ownership of land should be prohibited. All land now held by railroads and other corporations in excess of their actual needs, and all lands now owned by aliens, should be reclaimed by the Government and held for actual settlers only.

The following supplementary resolutions, not to be incorporated in the platform, came from the Committee on Resolutions and were adopted as follows:

THE SUPPLEMENTARY PLATFORM.

Whereas, Other questions having been presented for our consideration, we hereby submit the following, not as a part of the platform of the People's Party, but as resolutions expressive of the sentiment of this Convention:

1. *Resolved,* That we demand a free ballot and a fair count in all elections, and pledge ourselves to secure it to every legal voter without Federal intervention, through the adoption by the States of the unperverted Australian or secret ballot system.

2. That the revenue derived from a graduated income tax should be applied to the reduction of the burden of taxation now resting upon the domestic industries of this country.

3. That we pledge our support to fair and liberal pensions to ex-Union soldiers and sailors.

4. That we condemn the fallacy of protecting American labor under the present system, which opens our ports to the pauper and criminal classes of the world, and crowds out our wage-earners; and we denounce the present ineffective laws against contract labor, and demand the further restriction of undesirable immigration.

5. That we cordially sympathize with the efforts of organized workingmen to shorten the hours of labor, and demand a rigid enforcement of the existing eight-hour law on Government work, and ask that a penalty clause be added to the said law.

6. That we regard the maintenance of a large standing army of mercenaries, known as the Pinkerton system, as a menace to our liberties, and we demand its abolition; and we condemn the recent invasion of the Territory of Wyoming by the hired assassins of plutocracy, assisted by Federal officials.

7. That we commend to the favorable consideration of the

people and to the reform press the legislative system known as the initiative and referendum.

8. That we favor a constitutional provision limiting the office of President and Vice-President to one term, and providing for the election of Senators of the United States by a direct vote of the people.

9. That we oppose any subsidy or national aid to any private corporation for any purpose.

10. That this convention sympathizes with the Knights of Labor, and their righteous contest with the tyrannical combine of clothing manufacturers of Rochester, and declare[s] it to be the duty of all who hate tyranny and oppression, to refuse to purchase the goods made by the said manufacturers, or to patronize any merchants who sell such goods.

Donnelly's Preamble set forth in lurid language the evils that he and other Populists believed American society had suffered from plutocratic domination. His indictment was new only in its phraseology; the ills he recounted were the ills of which reformers had long complained. Donnelly's vigorous denunciations set the pattern for many other protests that were to come later. Bryan's "cross of gold," Theodore Roosevelt's "malefactors of great wealth," and Franklin D. Roosevelt's "economic royalists" were in the same tradition. To this day anyone who speaks out firmly against monopolistic excesses is likely to be classified as a "neo-Populist"; indeed, if he does not take care, he is in danger of repeating some of Donnelly's well-worn phrases. And "new conservatives" who deplore departures from the old American tradition, however they choose to define it, reserve their greatest scorn for whatever they deem "populist," or "populistic."

The Populists sought, unsuccessfully as it turned out, to unite the forces of rural and urban labor in a great crusade to wrest control of the government from the hands of special interests. They were individualists, however, not socialists, and the rural element, which in the end had to go it alone without the aid of urban labor, consisted primarily of farmers who were, or who aspired to be, landowners, and therefore small capitalists. As such, they hoped for a better chance to get on in the world. The only truly socialistic reform that the Populists demanded was government ownership and operation of the railroads and of the means of communication. But they could not hide their fear of big government, and, partly as a means of restraining it, they earnestly favored rigid civil service regulations for all governmental employees.

Many Populist proposals achieved a great measure of success after the People's Party itself had disappeared. For this result twentieth-century progressives, of whatever party, were primarily responsible. The post-Populist reformers were mainly urban and middle-class, but the unimportant status they occupied in society was due, they came to believe, to the unsavory behavior of the same overprivileged classes against whom the Populists had railed. Populist proposals often needed to be revamped for the purposes of later reformers, but the Populists were sometimes held to be right on diagnosis even when they erred on prescription. There was something wrong with banking and currency in the United States, as the Populists maintained, but a better answer than free silver or fiat money came with the Federal Reserve System. Grievances against the railroads might not best be remedied by public ownership, but the Progressives worked for and obtained a far greater degree of regulation than the nineteenth century had known. The reservation of government land for actual settlers only was hardly practicable, but the systematic conservation of natural resources certainly was. The subtreasury plan to establish federal depositories for imperishable farm products might not be immediately feasible, but a federal program of rural credits was presently adopted. Also, it can be argued that the Warehouse Act of 1916 constituted in effect the "better plan" for which the Populists were willing to settle as an alternative to the subtreasury, while Wallace's "ever normal granary" went far beyond their wildest dreams.

Other Populist proposals eventually were adopted, almost intact. Chief among these were the graduated income tax, the Australian ballot, certain restrictions on immigration, the eight-hour day, postal-savings facilities, the initiative and referendum, and the election of United States senators by direct vote of the people. The Populists did not originate all these reforms, but their platforms and orators took them up, popularized them, and passed them along to a later generation for enactment into law. Few platforms of any American political party have obtained a greater degree of affirmative legal response than the one the People's Party adopted in 1892.

Frederick Jackson Turner

The Significance of the Frontier in
American History

1893

EDITED BY RAY ALLEN BILLINGTON

The American mood during the 1890's was one of restlessness, of vaguely sensed uncertainty. Farmers met in revival-like political conventions to demand financial heresies that sent chills of alarm through Wall Street; workers banded into newfangled labor unions to slow the wheels of industry with calamitous strikes; social critics such as Henry George, Edward Bellamy, Jacob A. Riis, and Henry Demarest Lloyd boldly revealed society's ills and proposed sweeping reform; thousands of the dispossessed marched to the polls under banners of socialism raised by Daniel De Leon and Eugene V. Debs; New England Brahmins joined the Immigration Restriction League to press for laws that would forever close America's gates to European immigrants. These were all manifestations of the deep-seated unrest that marked the closing of one chapter in the nation's history. The era of cheap lands and westward expansion was drawing to an end. The United States would no longer be the land of limitless opportunity for the downtrodden which it had been in the past.

542

One who sought to analyze the causes of this unrest was a young historian at the University of Wisconsin named Frederick Jackson Turner. Taking his cue from a pronouncement of the Director of the Census of 1890 that for the first time an unbroken frontier line no longer existed in the West, Turner asked himself: "How have three centuries of constant expansion altered the thought, the character, and the institutions of the American people?" Could the unique features of the nation's civilization result partly from the repeated "beginning over again" as society moved ever westward? And so, what would be its fate in the dawning era of closed-space existence?

To answer these questions, Turner drew upon his own background and on the intellectual stimulation he had received while a student at the University of Wisconsin and at the Johns Hopkins University. As a boy in the backwoods town of Portage, Wisconsin, he had seen men subduing the wilderness and had observed the mingling of peoples from many backgrounds which is natural in such communities. As a young man he had visited settlements of newly arrived Germans and had been fascinated by watching their adjustments to primitive conditions of life. As an undergraduate he had been taught by his able mentor, Professor William Francis Allen, that society was a constantly evolving organism, adjusting to environmental changes as did the plants and animals described by Charles Darwin. As a graduate student he had been introduced to the works of such European economists as Achille Loria and Walter Bagehot, who stressed social evolution and the influence of the land-quest on peoples.

Merging these memories and concepts, Turner fashioned a remarkable essay, "Problems in American History," which set forth in a few paragraphs the "frontier hypothesis" in germinal form. When this was published locally in 1892, his old Johns Hopkins professor, Herbert Baxter Adams, recognized its importance and encouraged him to expand his brief references into a full-blown discussion. This Turner did during the autumn of 1892; he read a rough draft of the paper to his friend Woodrow Wilson when Wilson visited Madison that December. The president of the University of Wisconsin, Charles Kendall Adams, himself a famous historian, suggested that the essay be read when the American Historical Association gathered in Chicago that summer to help commemorate the World's Columbian Exposition. There, on July 12, 1893, Frederick Jackson Turner presented his views to a wider audience for the first time.

IN A RECENT bulletin of the superintendent of the census for 1890 appear these significant words: "Up to and including 1880 the country had a frontier of settlement, but at present the unsettled area has been so broken into by isolated bodies of settlement that there can hardly be said to be a frontier line. In the discussion of its extent, its westward movement, etc., it cannot, therefore, any longer have a place in the census reports." This brief official statement marks the closing of a great historic movement. Up to our own day American history has been in a large degree the history of the colonization of the Great West. The existence of an area of free land, its continuous recession, and the advance of American settlement westward explain American development.

Behind institutions, behind constitutional forms and modifications, lie the vital forces that call these organs into life and shape them to meet changing conditions. The peculiarity of American institutions is the fact that they have been compelled to adapt themselves to the changes of an expanding people—to the changes involved in crossing a continent, in winning a wilderness, and in developing at each area of this progress, out of the primitive economic and political conditions of the frontier, the complexity of city life. Said Calhoun in 1817, "We are great, and rapidly—I was about to say fearfully—growing!" So saying, he touched the distinguishing feature of American life. All peoples show development: the germ theory of politics has been sufficiently emphasized. In the case of most nations, however, the development has occurred in a limited area; and if the nation has expanded, it has met other growing peoples whom it has conquered. But in the case of the United States we have a different phenomenon. Limiting our attention to the Atlantic coast, we have the familiar phenomenon of the evolution of institutions in a limited area, such as the rise of representative government; the differentiation of simple colonial governments into complex organs; the progress from primitive industrial society, without division of labor, up to manufacturing civilization. But we have in addition to this *a recurrence of the process of evolution in each Western area reached in the process of expansion.* Thus American development has exhibited not merely

The document is here printed as it first appeared in the *Proceedings of the Forty-first Annual Meeting of the State Historical Society of Wisconsin* (Madison, 1894), pp. 79–112.

advance along a single line but a return to primitive conditions on a continually advancing frontier line, and a new development for that area. American social development has been continually beginning over again on the frontier. This perennial rebirth, this fluidity of American life, this expansion westward with its new opportunities, its continuous touch with the simplicity of primitive society, furnish the forces dominating American character. The true point of view in the history of this nation is not the Atlantic coast, it is the Great West. Even the slavery struggle, which is made so exclusive an object of attention by writers like Professor von Holst, occupies its important place in American history because of its relation to westward expansion.

In this advance the frontier is the outer edge of the wave —the meeting point between savagery and civilization. Much has been written about the frontier from the point of view of border warfare and the chase, but as a field for the serious study of the economist and the historian it has been neglected.

What is the [American] frontier? It is not the European frontier—a fortified boundary line running through dense populations. The most significant thing about it is that it lies at the hither edge of free land. In the census reports it is treated as the margin of that settlement which has a density of two or more to the square mile. The term is an elastic one, and for our purpose does not need sharp definition. We shall consider the whole frontier belt, including the Indian country and the outer margin of the "settled area" of the census reports. This paper will make no attempt to treat the subject exhaustively; its aim is simply to call attention to the frontier as a fertile field for investigation, and to suggest some of the problems which arise in connection with it.

In the settlement of America we have to observe how European life entered the continent, and how America modified and developed that life, and reacted on Europe. Our early history is the study of European germs developing in an American environment. Too exclusive attention has been paid by institutional students to the Germanic origins, too little to the American factors. The frontier is the line of most rapid and effective Americanization. The wilderness masters the colonist. It finds him a European in dress, industries, tools, modes of travel, and thought. It takes him from the railroad car and puts him in the birch canoe. It strips off the garments of civilization, and arrays him in the hunting shirt and the moccasin. It puts him in the log cabin of the Cherokee and the Iroquois, and runs an Indian palisade around him. Before

long he has gone to planting Indian corn and plowing with a
sharp stick; he shouts the war cry and takes the scalp in orthodox Indian fashion. In short, at the frontier the environment is at first too strong for the man. He must accept the
conditions which it furnishes, or perish, and so he fits himself
into the Indian clearings and follows the Indian trails. Little
by little he transforms the wilderness, but the outcome is not
the old Europe, not simply the development of Germanic
germs, any more than the first phenomenon was a case of
reversion to the Germanic mark. The fact is that here is a
new product that is American. At first the frontier was the
Atlantic coast. It was the frontier of Europe in a very real
sense. Moving westward, the frontier became more and more
American. *As successive terminal moraines result from successive glaciations, so each frontier leaves its traces behind it,
and when it becomes a settled area the region still partakes of
the frontier characteristics.* Thus the advance of the frontier
has meant a steady movement away from the influence of
Europe, a steady growth of independence on American lines.
And to study this advance, the men who grew up under these
conditions, and the political, economic, and social results of
it, is to study the really American part of our history.

THE STAGES OF FRONTIER ADVANCE

In the course of the seventeenth century the frontier was
advanced up the Atlantic river courses, just beyond the fall
line, and the tidewater region became the settled area. In the
first half of the eighteenth century another advance occurred.
Traders followed the Delaware and Shawnese Indians to the
Ohio as early as the end of the first quarter of the century.
Governor Spotswood of Virginia made an expedition in 1714
across the Blue Ridge. The end of the first quarter of the century saw the advance of the Scotch-Irish and the Palatine
Germans up the Shenandoah Valley into the western part of
Virginia, and along the Piedmont region of the Carolinas.
The Germans in New York pushed the frontier of settlement
up the Mohawk to German Flats. In Pennsylvania the town
of Bedford indicates the line of settlement. Settlements had
begun on New River, a branch of the Kanawha, and on the
sources of the Yadkin and French Broad. The king attempted
to arrest the advance by his proclamation of 1763 forbidding
settlements beyond the sources of the rivers flowing into the
Atlantic; but in vain. In the period of the Revolution the
frontier crossed the Alleghenies into Kentucky and Tennessee, and the upper waters of the Ohio were settled. When the
first census was taken in 1790, the continuous settled area

was bounded by a line which ran near the coast of Maine, and included New England except a portion of Vermont and New Hampshire, New York along the Hudson and up the Mohawk about Schenectady, eastern and southern Pennsylvania, Virginia well across the Shenandoah Valley, and the Carolinas and eastern Georgia. Beyond this region of continuous settlement were the small settled areas of Kentucky and Tennessee and the Ohio, with the mountains intervening between them and the Atlantic area, thus giving a new and important character to the frontier. The isolation of the region increased its peculiarly American tendencies, and the need for transportation facilities to connect it with the East called out important schemes of internal improvement, which will be noted farther on. The "West," as a self-conscious section, began to evolve.

From decade to decade distinct advances of the frontier occurred. By the census of 1820 the settled area included Ohio, southern Indiana and Illinois, southeastern Missouri, and about one-half of Louisiana. This settled area had surrounded Indian areas, and the management of these tribes became an object of political concern. The frontier region of the time lay along the Great Lakes, where Astor's American Fur Company operated in the Indian trade, and beyond the Mississippi, where Indian traders extended their activity even to the Rocky Mountains; Florida also furnished frontier conditions. The Mississippi River region was the scene of typical frontier settlements.

The rising steam navigation on Western waters, the opening of the Erie Canal, and the westward extension of cotton culture added five frontier states to the Union in this period. Grund, writing in 1836, declares: "It appears, then, that the universal disposition of Americans to emigrate to the western wilderness, in order to enlarge their dominion over inanimate nature, is the actual result of an expansive power, which is inherent in them, and which, by continually agitating all classes of society, is constantly throwing a large portion of the whole population on the extreme confines of the state, in order to gain space for its development. Hardly is a new state or territory formed before the same principle manifests itself again, and gives rise to a further emigration; and so it is destined to go until a physical barrier must finally obstruct its progress."

In the middle of this century the line indicated by the present eastern boundary of Indian Territory, Nebraska, and Kansas marked the frontier of the Indian country. Minnesota and Wisconsin still exhibited frontier conditions, but the distinctive frontier of the period is found in California, where the gold discoveries had sent a sudden tide of adventurous miners, and in Oregon and the settlements in Utah. As the frontier had leaped over the Alleghenies, so now it skipped the Great Plains and the Rocky Mountains; and in the same way that the advance of the frontiersmen beyond the Alleghenies had caused the rise of important questions of transportation and internal improvement, so now the settlers beyond the Rocky Mountains needed means of communication with the East, and in the furnishing of these arose the settlement of the Great Plains and the development of still another kind of frontier life. Railroads, fostered by land grants, sent an increasing tide of immigrants into the far West. The United States Army fought a series of Indian wars in Minnesota, Dakota, and the Indian Territory.

By 1880 the settled area had been pushed into northern Michigan, Wisconsin, and Minnesota, along Dakota rivers, and into the Black Hills region, and was ascending the rivers of Kansas and Nebraska. The development of mines in Colorado had drawn isolated frontier settlements into that region, and Montana and Idaho were receiving settlers. The frontier was found in these mining camps and the ranches of the Great Plains. The superintendent of the census for 1890 reports, as previously stated, that the settlements of the West lie so scattered over the region that there can no longer be said to be a frontier line.

In these successive frontiers we find natural boundary lines which have served to mark and to affect the characteristics of the frontiers, namely: the "fall line"; the Allegheny Mountains; the Mississippi; the Missouri where its direction approximates north and south; the line of the arid lands, approximately the ninety-ninth meridian; and the Rocky Mountains. The fall line marked the frontier of the seventeenth century; the Alleghenies that of the eighteenth; the Mississippi that of the first quarter of the nineteenth; the Missouri that of the middle of this century (omitting the California movement); and the belt of the Rocky Mountains and the arid tract, the present frontier. Each was won by a series of Indian wars.

THE FRONTIER FURNISHES A FIELD FOR COMPARATIVE

STUDY OF SOCIAL DEVELOPMENT

At the Atlantic frontier one can study the germs of processes repeated at each successive frontier. We have the complex European life, sharply precipitated by the wilderness into the simplicity of primitive conditions. The first frontier had to meet its Indian question, its question of the disposition of the public domain, of the means of intercourse with the older settlements, of the extension of political organization, of religious and educational activity. And the settlement of these and similar questions for one frontier served as a guide for the next. The American student need not go to the "prim little townships of Sleswick" for illustrations of the law of continuity and development. For example, he may study the origin of our land policies in the colonial land policy; he may see how the system grew by adapting the statutes to the customs of the successive frontiers. He may see how the mining experience in the lead regions of Wisconsin, Illinois, and Iowa was applied to the mining laws of the Sierras, and how our Indian policy has been a series of experimentations on successive frontiers. Each tier of new states has found, in the older ones, material for its constitutions. Each frontier has made similar contributions to American character, as will be discussed farther on.

But with all these similarities there are essential differences, due to the place element and the time element. It is evident that the farming frontier of the Mississippi Valley presents different conditions from the mining frontier of the Rocky Mountains. The frontier reached by the Pacific Railroad, surveyed into rectangles, guarded by the United States Army, and recruited by the daily immigrant ship, moves forward at a swifter pace and in a different way than the frontier reached by the birch canoe or the pack horse. The geologist traces patiently the shores of ancient seas, maps their areas, and compares the older and the newer. It would be a work worth the historian's labors to mark these various frontiers and in detail compare one with another. Not only would there result a more adequate conception of American development and characteristics, but invaluable additions would be made to the history of society.

Loria, the Italian economist, has urged the study of colonial life as an aid in understanding the stages of European development, affirming that colonial settlement is for economic science what the mountain is for geology, bringing to light primitive stratifications. "America," he says, "has the key to the historical enigma which Europe has sought for centuries in vain, and the land which has no history reveals luminously the course of universal history." He is right. The United States lies like a huge page in the history of society. Line by line as we read from west to east we find the record of social evolution. It begins with the Indian and the hunter; it goes on to tell of the disintegration of savagery by the entrance of the trader, the pathfinder of civilization; we read the annals of the pastoral stage in ranch life; the exploitation of the soil by the raising of unrotated crops of corn and wheat in sparsely settled farming communities; the intensive culture of the denser farm settlement; and finally the manufacturing organization with city and factory system. This page is familiar to the student of census statistics, but how little of it has been used by our historians.

Each of these areas has had an influence in our economic and political history; the evolution of each into a higher stage has worked political transformations. But what constitutional historian has made any adequate attempt to interpret political facts by the light of these social areas and changes?

The Atlantic frontier was compounded of fisherman, fur-trader, miner, cattle-raiser, and farmer. Excepting the fisherman, each type of industry was on the march toward the West, impelled by an irresistible attraction. Each passed in successive waves across the continent. Stand at Cumberland Gap and watch the procession of civilization, marching single file—the buffalo, following the trail to the salt springs, the Indian, the fur-trader and hunter, the cattle-raiser, the pioneer farmer—and the frontier has passed by. Stand at South Pass in the Rockies a century later and see the same procession with wider intervals between. The unequal rate of advance compels us to distinguish the frontier into the trader's frontier, the rancher's frontier or the miner's frontier, and the farmer's frontier. When the mines and the cowpens were still near the fall line, the traders' pack trains were tinkling across the Alleghenies, and the French on the Great Lakes were fortifying their posts, alarmed by the British trader's birch canoe. When the trappers scaled the Rockies, the farmer was still near the mouth of the Missouri.

THE INDIAN TRADER'S FRONTIER

Why was it that the Indian trader passed so rapidly across the continent? What effects followed from the trader's frontier? The trade was coeval with American discovery. The Norsemen, Vespucius, Verrazano, Hudson, John Smith, all trafficked for furs. The Plymouth pilgrims settled in Indian cornfields, and their first return cargo was of beaver and lumber. The records of the various New England colonies show how steadily exploration was carried into the wilderness by this trade. What is true for New England is, as would be expected, even plainer for the rest of the colonies. All along the coast from Maine to Georgia the Indian trade opened up the river courses. Steadily the trader passed westward, utilizing the older lines of French trade. The Ohio, the Great Lakes, the Mississippi, the Missouri, and the Platte, the lines of westward advance, were ascended by traders. They found the passes in the Rocky Mountains and guided Lewis and Clark, Frémont, and Bidwell.

The explanation of the rapidity of this advance is bound up with the effects of the trader on the Indian. The trading post left the unarmed tribes at the mercy of those that had purchased firearms—a truth which the Iroquois Indians wrote in blood, and so the remote and unvisited tribes gave eager welcome to the trader. "The savages," wrote La Salle, "take better care of us French than of their own children; from us only can they get guns and goods." This accounts for the trader's power and the rapidity of his advance. Thus the disintegrating forces of civilization entered the wilderness. Every river valley and Indian trail became a fissure in Indian society, and so that society became honeycombed. Long before the pioneer farmer appeared on the scene, primitive Indian life had passed away. The farmers met Indians armed with guns. The trading frontier, while steadily undermining Indian power by making the tribes ultimately dependent on the whites, yet through its sale of guns gave to the Indian increased power of resistance to the farming frontier. French colonization was dominated by its trading frontier, English colonization by its farming frontier. There was an antagonism between the two frontiers as between the two nations. Said Duquesne to the Iroquois, "Are you ignorant of the difference between the King of England and the king of France? Go see the forts that our king has established and you will see that you can still hunt under their very walls. They have been placed for your advantage in places which you frequent. The English, on the contrary, are no sooner in possession of a place than the game is driven away. The forest falls before them as they advance, and the soil is laid bare so that you can scarce find the wherewithal to erect a shelter for the night."

And yet, in spite of this opposition of the interests of the trader and the farmer, the Indian trade pioneered the way for civilization. The buffalo trail became the Indian trail, and this became the trader's "trade;" the trails widened into roads, and the roads into turnpikes, and these in turn were transformed into railroads. The same origin can be shown for the railroads of the South, the far West, and the Dominion of Canada. The trading posts reached by these trails were on the sites of Indian villages which had been placed in positions suggested by nature; and these trading posts, situated so as to command the water systems of the country, have grown into such cities as Albany, Pittsburg, Detroit, Chicago, St. Louis, Council Bluffs, and Kansas City. Thus civilization in America has followed the arteries made by geology, pouring an ever richer tide through them, until at last the slender paths of aboriginal intercourse have been broadened and interwoven into the complex mazes of modern commercial lines; the wilderness has been interpenetrated by lines of civilization, growing ever more numerous. It is like the steady growth of a complex nervous system for the originally simple, inert continent. If one would understand why we are today one nation rather than a collection of isolated states, he must study this economic and social consolidation of the country. In this progress from savage conditions lie topics for the evolutionist.

The effect of the Indian frontier as a consolidating agent in our history is important. From the close of the seventeenth century various intercolonial congresses have been called to treat with the Indians and establish common measures of defense. Particularism was strongest in colonies with no Indian frontier. This frontier stretched along the western border like a cord of union. The Indian was a common danger, demanding united action. Most celebrated of these conferences was the Albany Congress of 1754, called to treat with the Six Nations, and to consider plans of union. Even a cursory reading of the plan proposed by the Congress reveals the importance of the frontier. The powers of the general council and the officers were, chiefly, the determination of peace and war with the Indians, the regulation of Indian trade, the purchase of Indian lands, and the creation and government of new settlements as a security against the Indians. It is evident that the unifying tendencies of the Revolutionary period were facilitated by the previous co-operation in the regulation of the frontier. In this connection may be mentioned the importance of the frontier, from that day to this, as a military training school, keeping alive the power of resistance to aggression, and developing the stalwart and rugged qualities of the frontiersman.

THE RANCHER'S FRONTIER

It would not be possible in the limits of this paper to trace the other frontiers across the continent. Travelers of the eighteenth century found the "cowpens" among the cane-brakes and peavine pastures of the South, and the "cow drivers" took their droves to Charleston, Philadelphia, and New York. Travelers at the close of the War of 1812 met droves of more than a thousand cattle and swine from the interior of Ohio going to Pennsylvania to fatten for the Philadelphia market. The ranges of the Great Plains, with ranch and cowboy and nomadic life, are things of yesterday and of today. The experience of the Carolina cowpens guided the ranchers of Texas. One element favoring the rapid extension of the rancher's frontier is the fact that in a remote country lacking transportation facilities the product must be in small bulk, or must be able to transport itself, and the cattle-raiser could easily drive his product to market. The effect of these great ranches on the subsequent agrarian history of the localities in which they existed should be studied.

THE FARMER'S FRONTIER

The maps of the census reports show an uneven advance of the farmer's frontier, with tongues of settlement pushed forward and with indentations of wilderness. In part this is due to Indian resistance, in part to the location of river valleys and passes, in part to the unequal force of the centers of frontier attraction. Among the important centers of attraction may be mentioned the following: fertile and favorably situated soils, salt springs, mines, and army posts.

ARMY POSTS

The frontier army post, serving to protect the settlers from the Indians, has also acted as a wedge to open the Indian country, and has been a nucleus for settlement. In this connection mention should also be made of the government military and exploring expeditions in determining the lines of settlement. But all the more important expeditions were greatly indebted to the earliest pathmakers, the Indian guides, the traders and trappers, and the French voyageurs, who were inevitable parts of governmental expeditions from the days of Lewis and Clark. Each expedition was an epitome of the previous factors in western advance.

SALT SPRINGS

In an interesting monograph Victor Hehn has traced the effect of salt upon early European development and has pointed out how it affected the lines of settlement and the form of administration. A similar study might be made for the salt springs of the United States. The early settlers were tied to the coast by the need of salt, without which they could not preserve their meats or live in comfort. Writing in 1752, Bishop Spangenburg says of a colony for which he was seeking lands in North Carolina, "They will require salt & other necessaries which they can neither manufacture nor raise. Either they must go to Charleston, which is 300 miles distant . . . Or else they must go to Boling's Point in Va on a branch of the James, & is also 300 miles from here . . . or else they must go down to Roanoke—I know not how many miles— where salt is brought up from the Cape Fear." This may serve as a typical illustration. An annual pilgrimage to the coast for salt thus became essential. Taking flocks of furs and ginseng root, the early settlers sent their pack trains after seeding time each year to the coast. This proved to be an important educational influence, since it was almost the only way in which the pioneer learned what was going on in the East. But when discovery was made of the salt springs of the Kanawha, and the Holston, and Kentucky, and central New York, the West began to be freed from dependence on the coast. It was in part the effect of finding these salt springs that enabled settlement to cross the mountains.

From the time the mountains rose between the pioneer and the seaboard, a new order of Americanism arose. The West and the East began to get out of touch with each other. The settlements from the sea to the mountains kept connection with the rear and had a certain solidarity. But the overmountain men grew more and more independent. The East took a narrow view of American advance, and nearly lost these men. Kentucky and Tennessee history bears abundant witness to the truth of this statement. The East began to try to hedge and limited westward expansion. Though Webster could declare that there were no Alleghenies in his politics, yet in politics in general they were a very solid factor.

LAND

The exploitation of the beasts took hunter and trader to the West, the exploitation of the grasses took the rancher West, the exploitation of the virgin soil of the river valleys and prairies attracted the farmer. Good soils have been the most continuous attraction to the farmer's frontier. The land hunger of the Virginians drew them down the rivers into Carolina, in early colonial days; the search for soils took the Massachusetts men to Pennsylvania and to New York. As the Eastern lands were taken up, migration flowed across them to the West. Daniel Boone, the great backwoodsman, who combined the occupations of hunter, trader, cattle-raiser, farmer, and surveyor—learning, probably from the traders, of the fertility of the lands on the upper Yadkin, where the traders were wont to rest as they took their way to the Indians—left his Pennsylvania home with his father, and passed down the Great Valley road to that stream. Learning from a trader of its game and the rich pastures of Kentucky, he pioneered the way for the farmers to that region. Thence he passed to the frontier of Missouri, where his settlement was long a landmark on the frontier. Here again he helped to open the way for civilization, finding salt licks, and trails, and land. His son was among the earliest trappers ·in the passes of the Rocky Mountains, and his party are said to have been the first to camp on the present site of Denver. His grandson, Colonel A. J. Boone of Colorado, was a power among the Indians of the Rocky Mountains, and was appointed an agent by the government. Kit Carson's mother was a Boone. Thus this family epitomizes the backwoodsman's advance across the continent.

The farmer's advance came in a distinct series of waves. In Peck's *New Guide to the West,* published in Cincinnati in 1837, occurs this suggestive passage:

Generally, in all the western settlements, three classes, like the waves of the ocean, have rolled one after the other. First, comes the pioneer, who depends for the subsistence of his family chiefly upon the natural growth of vegetation, called the "range," and the proceeds of hunting. His implements of agriculture are rude, chiefly of his own make, and his efforts directed mainly to a crop of corn and a "truck patch." The last is a rude garden for growing cabbage, beans, corn for roasting ears, cucumbers and potatoes. A log cabin and, occasionally, a stable and corn-crib, and a field of a dozen acres, the timber girdled or "deadened," and fenced, are enough for his occupancy. It is quite immaterial whether he ever becomes the owner of the soil. He is the occupant for the time being, pays no rent, and feels as independent as the "lord of the manor." With a horse, cow, and one or two breeders of swine, he strikes into the woods with his family, and becomes the founder of a new county, or perhaps state. He builds his cabin, gathers around him a few other families of similar tastes and habits, and occupies till the range is somewhat subdued, and hunting a little precarious, or, which is more frequently the case, till neighbors crowd around, roads, bridges, and fields annoy him, and he lacks elbow room. The pre-emption law enables him to dispose of his cabin and corn-field to the next class of emigrants, and, to employ his own figures, he "breaks for the high timber," "clears out for the New Purchase," or migrates to Arkansas, or Texas, to work the same process over.

The new class of emigrants purchase the lands, add field to field, clear out the roads, throw rough bridges over the streams, put up hewn log houses, with glass windows, and brick or stone chimneys, occasionally plant orchards, build mills, school-houses, court-houses, etc., and exhibit the picture and forms of plain, frugal, civilized life.

Another wave rolls on. The men of capital and enterprise come. The "settler" is ready to sell out, and take the advantage of the rise of property—push farther into the interior, and become, himself, a man of capital and enterprise in turn. The small village rises to a spacious town or city; substantial edifices of brick, extensive fields, orchards, gardens, colleges and churches are seen. Broadcloths, silks, leghorns, crapes, and all the refinements, luxuries, elegancies, frivolities and fashions are in vogue. Thus wave after wave is rolling westward:—the real *Eldorado* is still farther on.

A portion of the two first classes remain stationary amidst the general movement, improve their habits and condition and rise in the scale of society.

The writer has traveled much amongst the first class—the real pioneers. He has lived many years in connection with the second grade; and now the third wave is sweeping over large districts of Indiana, Illinois and Missouri. Migration has become almost a habit in the West. Hundreds of men can be found, not over fifty years of age, who have settled for the fourth, fifth or sixth time on a new spot. To sell out, and remove only a few hundred miles, makes up a portion of the variety of backwoods life and manners.

Omitting those of the pioneer farmers who move from the love of adventure, the advance of the more steady farmer is easy to understand. Obviously the immigrant was attracted by the cheap lands of the frontier, and even the native farmer felt their influence strongly. Year by year the farmers who lived on soil, whose returns were diminished by unrotated crops, were offered the virgin soil of the frontier at nominal prices. Their growing families demanded more lands, and these were dear. The competition of the unexhausted, cheap, and easily tilled prairie lands compelled the farmer either to go West and continue the exhaustion of the soil on a new frontier or to adopt intensive culture. Thus the census of 1890 shows, in the Northwest, many counties in which there is an absolute, or a relative, decrease of population. These states have been sending farmers to advance the frontier on the plains, and have themselves begun to turn to intensive farming and to manufacture. A decade before this, Ohio had shown the same transition stage. Thus the demand for land and the love of wilderness freedom drew the frontier ever onward.

Having now roughly outlined the various kinds of frontiers, and their modes of advance, chiefly from the point of view of the frontier itself, we may next inquire what were the influences on the East and on the Old World. A rapid enumeration of some of the more noteworthy effects is all that I have time for.

COMPOSITE NATIONALITY

First, we note that the frontier promoted the formation of a composite nationality for the American people. The coast was preponderantly English, but the later tides of continental immigration flowed across to the free lands. This was the case from the early colonial days. The Scotch-Irish and the Palatine Germans, or "Pennsylvania Dutch," furnished dominant elements in the stock of the colonial frontier. With these peoples were also the freed indented servants, or redemptioners, who at the expiration of their time of service passed to the frontier. Governor Alexander Spotswood of Virginia writes in 1717, "The Inhabitants of our frontiers are composed generally of such as have been transported hither as Servants, and being out of their time, and settle themselves where Land is to be taken up and that will produce the necessarys of Life with little Labour." Very generally these redemptioners were of non-English stock. In the crucible of the frontier the immigrants were Americanized, liberated, and fused into a mixed race, English in neither nationality nor characteristics. The process has gone on from the early days to our own. Burke and other writers in the middle of the eighteenth century believed that Pennsylvania was threatened with the "danger of being wholly foreign in language, manners, and perhaps even inclinations." The German and Scotch-Irish elements in the frontier of the South were only less great. In the middle of the present century the German element in Wisconsin was already so considerable that leading publicists looked to the creation of a German state out of the commonwealth by concentrating their colonization. Such examples teach us to beware of misinterpreting the fact that there is a common English speech in America into a belief that the stock is also English.

INDUSTRIAL INDEPENDENCE

In another way the advance of the frontier decreased our dependence on England. The coast, particularly of the South, lacked diversified industries and was dependent on England for the bulk of its supplies. In the South there was even a dependence on the Northern colonies for articles of food. Governor James Glen of South Carolina writes in the middle of the eighteenth century: "Our trade with New York and Philadelphia was of this sort, draining us of all the little money and bills that we could gather from other places, for their bread, flowr, beer, hams, bacon, and other things of their produce, all which except beer, our new townships begin to supply us with, which are settled with very industrious and consequently thriving Germans. This no doubt diminishes the number of shipping, and the appearance of our trade, but is far from being a detriment to us."

Before long the frontier created a demand for merchants. As it retreated from the coast it became less and less possible for England to bring her supplies directly to the consumer's wharfs, and carry away staple crops; and staple crops began to give way to diversified agriculture for a time. The effect of this phase of the frontier action upon the northern section is perceived when we realize how the advance of the frontier aroused seaboard cities like Boston, New York, and Baltimore to engage in rivalry for what Washington called "the extensive and valuable trade of a rising empire."

EFFECTS ON NATIONAL LEGISLATION

The legislation which most developed the powers of the national government, and played the largest part in its activity, was conditioned on the frontier. Writers have discussed the subjects of tariff, land, and internal improvement as pendants to the slavery question. But when American history comes to be rightly viewed it will be seen that the slavery question is an incident. In the period from the end of the first half of the present century to the close of the Civil War, slavery rose to primary but far from exclusive importance. But this does not justify Professor von Holst, to take an example, in treating our constitutional history in its formative period down to 1828 in a single volume, giving six volumes chiefly to the history of slavery from 1828 to 1861, under the title of a *Constitutional History of the United States.* The growth of nationalism and the evolution of American political institutions were dependent on the advance of the frontier. Even so recent a writer as Rhodes, in his *History of the United States since the Compromise of 1850,* has treated the legislation called out by the western advance as incidental to the slavery struggle.

This is a wrong perspective. The pioneer needed the goods of the coast, and so the grand series of internal improvements and railroad legislation began, with potent nationalizing effects. But the West was not content with bringing the farm to the factory. Under the lead of Clay—"Harry of the West" —protective tariffs were passed, with the cry of bringing the factory to the farm.

THE PUBLIC DOMAIN

The public domain has been a force of profound importance in the nationalization and development of the government. The effects of the struggle of the landed and the landless states, and of the Ordinance of 1787, need no discussion. Administratively the frontier called out some of the highest and most vitalizing activities of the general government. The purchase of Louisiana was perhaps the constitutional turning point in the history of the republic, inasmuch as it afforded both a new area for national legislation, and the occasion of the downfall of the policy of strict construction. But the purchase of Louisiana was called out by frontier needs and demands. As frontier states accrued to the Union, the national power grew. In a speech on the dedication of the Calhoun monument, Mr. Lamar explained: "In 1789 the states were the creators of the federal government; in 1861 the federal government was the creator of a large majority of the states."

When we consider the public domain from the point of view of the sale and disposal of the public lands, we are again brought face to face with the frontier. The policy of the United States in dealing with its lands is in sharp contrast with the European system of scientific administration. Efforts to make this domain a source of revenue, and to withhold it from emigrants in order that settlement might be compact, were in vain. The jealousy and the fears of the East were powerless in the face of the demands of the frontiersmen. John Quincy Adams was obliged to confess: "My own system of administration, which was to make the national domain the inexhaustible fund for progressive and unceasing internal improvement, has failed." The reason is obvious; systems of administration were not what the West demanded; it wanted land. Adams states the situation as follows:

"The slave-holders of the South have bought the co-operation of the Western country by the bribe of the Western lands, abandoning to the new Western States their own proportion of this public property, and aiding them in the design of grasping all the lands into their own hands. Thomas H. Benton was the author of this system, which he brought forward as a substitute for the American system of Mr. Clay, and to supplant him as the leading statesman of the West. Mr. Clay, by his tariff compromise with Mr. Calhoun, abandoned his own American system. At the same time he brought forward a plan for distributing among all the States of the Union the proceeds of the sales of the public lands. His bill for that purpose passed both houses of Congress, but was vetoed by President

Jackson, who, in his annual message of December, 1832, formally recommended that all the public lands should be gratuitously given away to individual adventurers and to the States in which the lands are situated."

"No subject," said Henry Clay, "which has presented itself to the present, or perhaps any preceding, congress, is of greater magnitude than that of the public lands." When we consider the far-reaching effects of the government's land policy upon political, economic, and social aspects of American life, we are disposed to agree with him. But this legislation was framed under frontier influences, and under the lead of Western statesmen like Benton and Jackson. Said Senator Scott of Indiana in 1841: "I consider the pre-emption law merely declaratory of the custom or common law of the settlers."

NATIONAL TENDENCIES OF THE FRONTIER

It is safe to say that the legislation with regard to land, tariff, and internal improvements—the American system of the nationalizing Whig Party—was conditioned on frontier ideas and needs. But it was not merely in legislative action that the frontier worked against the sectionalism of the coast. The economic and social characteristics of the frontier worked against sectionalism. The men of the frontier had closer resemblances to the Middle region than to either of the other sections. Pennsylvania had been the seed plot of frontier emigration, and, although she passed on her settlers along the Great Valley into the west of Virginia and the Carolinas, yet the industrial society of these Southern frontiersmen was always more like that of the Middle region than like that of the tidewater portion of the South, which later came to spread its industrial type throughout the South.

The Middle region, entered by New York harbor, was an open door to all Europe. The tidewater part of the South represented typical Englishmen, modified by a warm climate and servile labor, and living in baronial fashion on great plantations; New England stood for a special English movement—Puritanism. The Middle region was less English than the other sections. It had a wide mixture of nationalities, a varied society, the mixed town and county system of local government, a varied economic life, many religious sects. In short, it was a region mediating between New England and the South, and the East and the West. It represented that composite nationality which the contemporary United States exhibits, that juxtaposition of non-English groups, occupying a valley or a little settlement, and presenting reflections of the map of Europe in their variety. It was democratic and nonsectional, if not national; "easy, tolerant, and contented;" rooted strongly in material prosperity. It was typical of the modern United States. It was least sectional not only because it lay between North and South but also because with no barriers to shut out its frontiers from its settled region, and with a system of connecting waterways, the Middle region mediated between East and West as well as between North and South. Thus it became the typically American region. Even the New Englander, who was shut out from the frontier by the Middle region, tarrying in New York or Pennsylvania on his westward march, lost the acuteness of his sectionalism on the way.

Until the spread of cotton culture into the interior gave homogeneity to the South, the western part .of it showed tendencies to fall away from the faith of the fathers into internal improvement legislation and nationalism. In the Virginia convention of 1829–30, called to revise the constitution, Mr. Leigh, of Chesterfield, one of the tidewater counties, declared:

> "One of the main causes of discontent which led to this convention, that which had the strongest influence in overcoming our veneration for the work of our fathers, which taught us to contemn the sentiments of Henry and Mason and Pendleton, which weaned us from our reverence for the constituted authorities of the state, was an overweening passion for internal improvement. I say this with perfect knowledge; for it has been avowed to me by gentlemen from the West over and over again. And let me tell the gentleman from Albemarle (Mr. Gordon) that it has been another principal object of those who set this ball of revolution in motion, to overturn the doctrine of state rights, of which Virginia has been the very pillar, and to remove the barrier she has interposed to the interference of the federal government in that same work of internal improvement, by so reorganizing the legislature that Virginia, too, may be hitched to the federal car."

It was this nationalizing tendency of the West that transformed the democracy of Jefferson into the national republicanism of Monroe and the democracy of Andrew Jackson. The West of the War of 1812, the West of Clay, and Benton, and Harrison, and Andrew Jackson, shut off by the Middle states and the mountains from the coast sections, had a solidarity of its own with national tendencies. On the tide of the Father of Waters, North and South met and mingled into a nation. Interstate migration went steadily on—a process of cross-fertilization of ideas and institutions. The fierce struggle of the sections over slavery on the western frontier does not diminish the truth of this statement; it proves the truth of it. Slavery was a sectional trait that would not down, but in the West it could not remain sectional. It was the greatest of frontiersmen who declared: "I believe this government cannot endure permanently half slave and half free. It will become all of one thing, or all of the other." Nothing works for nationalism like intercourse within the nation. Mobility of population is death to localism, and the Western frontier worked irresistibly in unsettling population. The effects reached back from the frontier and affected profoundly the Atlantic Coast, and even the Old World.

GROWTH OF DEMOCRACY

But the most important effect of the frontier has been in the promotion of democracy here and in Europe. As has been pointed out, the frontier is productive of individualism. Complex society is precipitated by the wilderness into a kind of primitive organization based on the family. The tendency is anti-social. It produces antipathy to control, and particularly to any direct control. The tax-gatherer is viewed as a representative of oppression. Professor Osgood, in an able article, has pointed out that the frontier conditions prevalent in the colonies are important factors in the explanation of the American Revolution, where individual liberty was sometimes confused with absence of all effective government. The same conditions aid in explaining the difficulty of instituting a strong government in the period of the confederacy. The frontier individualism has from the beginning promoted democracy.

The frontier states that came into the Union in the first quarter of a century of its existence came in with democratic suffrage provisions, and had reactive effects of the highest importance upon the older states whose peoples were being attracted there. It was *western* New York that forced an extension of suffrage in the constitutional convention of that state in 1821; and it was *western* Virginia that compelled the tidewater region to put a more liberal suffrage provision in the constitution framed in 1830, and to give to the frontier region a more nearly proportionate representation with the tidewater aristocracy. The rise of democracy as an effective force in the nation came in with Western preponderance under Jackson and William Henry Harrison, and it meant the triumph of the frontier—with all of its good and with all of its evil elements.

An interesting illustration of the tone of frontier democracy in 1830 comes from the debates in the Virginia convention already referred to. A representative from western Virginia declared: "But, sir, it is not the increase of population in the West which this gentleman ought to fear. It is the energy which the mountain breeze and western habits impart to those emigrants. They are regenerated, politically I mean, sir. They soon become *working politicians;* and the difference, sir, between a *talking* and a *working* politician is immense. The Old Dominion has long been celebrated for producing great orators; the ablest metaphysicians in policy; men that can split hairs in all abstruse questions of political economy. But at home, or when they return from congress, they have negroes to fan them asleep. But a Pennsylvania, a New York, an Ohio, or a western Virginia statesman, though far inferior in logic, metaphysics and rhetoric to an old Virginia statesman, has this advantage, that when he returns home he takes off his coat and takes hold of the plough. This gives him bone and muscle, sir, and preserves his republican principles pure and uncontaminated."

So long as free land exists, the opportunity for a competency exists, and economic power secures political power. But the democracy born of free land, strong in selfishness and individualism, intolerant of administrative experience and education, and pressing individual liberty beyond its proper bounds, has its dangers as well as its benefits. Individualism in America has allowed a laxity in regard to governmental affairs which has rendered possible the spoils system, and all the manifest evils that follow from the lack of a highly developed civic spirit. In this connection may be noted also the influence of frontier conditions in permitting lax business honor, inflated paper currency, and wildcat banking. The colonial and Revolutionary frontier was the region whence emanated many of the worst forms of an evil currency. The West in the War of 1812 repeated the phenomenon on the frontier of that day, while the speculation and wildcat banking of the period of the crisis of 1837 occurred on the new frontier belt of the next tier of states. Thus each one of the periods of lax financial integrity coincides with periods when a new set of frontier communities had arisen, and coincides in area with these successive frontiers, for the most part. The recent Populist agitation is a case in point. Many a state that now declines any connection with the tenets of the Populists itself adhered to such ideas in an earlier stage of the development of the state. A primitive society can hardly be expected to show the intelligent appreciation of the complexity of business interests in a developed society. The continual recurrence of these areas of paper-money agitation is another evidence that the frontier can be isolated and studied as a factor in American history of the highest importance.

ATTEMPTS TO CHECK AND REGULATE THE FRONTIER

The East has always feared the result of an unregulated advance of the frontier, and has tried to check and guide it. The English authorities would have checked settlement at the headwaters of the Atlantic tributaries and allowed the savages to enjoy their deserts in quiet lest the peltry trade should decrease. This called out Burke's splendid protest:

"[If] you stopped your grants, what would be the consequence? The people would occupy without grants. They have already so occupied in many places. You cannot station garrisons in every part of these deserts. If you drive the people from one place, they will carry on their annual tillage, and remove with their flocks and herds to another. Many of the people in the back settlements are already little attached to particular situations. Already they have topped the Appalachian mountains. From thence they behold before them an immense plain, one vast, rich, level meadow; a square of five hundred miles. Over this they would wander without a possibility of restraint; they would change their manners with their habits of life; would soon forget a government by which they were disowned; would become hordes of English Tartars; and, pouring down upon your unfortified frontiers a fierce and irresistible cavalry, become masters of your governors and your counselors, your collectors and comptrollers, and of all the slaves that adhered to them. Such would, and in no long time must, be the effect of attempting to forbid as a crime, and to suppress as an evil, the command and blessing of Providence, 'Increase and multiply.' Such would be the happy result of an endeavor to keep as a lair of wild beasts that earth which God by an express charter has given to the children of men."

But the English government was not alone in its desire to limit the advance of the frontier, and guide its destinies. Tidewater Virginia and South Carolina gerrymandered those colonies to ensure the dominance of the coast in their legislatures. Washington desired to settle a state at a time in the Northwest; Jefferson would have reserved from settlement the territory of his Louisiana purchase north of the thirty-second parallel, in order to offer it to the Indians in exchange for their settlements east of the Mississippi. "When we shall be full on this side," he writes, "we may lay off a range of states on the western bank from the head to the mouth, and so range after range, advancing compactly as we multiply."

Madison went so far as to argue to the French minister that the United States had no interest in seeing population extend itself on the right bank of the Mississippi, but should rather fear it. When the Oregon question was under debate, in 1824, Smyth of Virginia would have drawn an unchangeable line for the limits of the United States at the outer limit of two tiers of states beyond the Mississippi, complaining that the seaboard states were being drained of the flower of their population by the bringing of too much land into market. Even Thomas Benton, the man of widest views of the destiny of the West, at this stage of his career declared that along the ridge of the Rocky Mountains "the western limits of the republic should be drawn, and the statue of the fabled god Terminus should be raised upon its highest peak, never to be thrown down." But the attempts to limit our boundaries, to restrict land sales and settlement, and to deprive the West of its share of political power were all in vain. Steadily that frontier of settlement advanced and carried with it individualism, democracy, and nationalism, and powerfully affected the East and the Old World.

MISSIONARY ACTIVITY

The most effective efforts of the East to regulate the frontier came through its educational and religious activity, exerted by interstate migration and by organized societies. Speaking in 1835, Dr. Lyman Beecher declared: "It is equally plain that the religious and political destiny of our nation is to be decided in the West," and he pointed out that the population of the West "is assembled from all the states of the Union, and from all the nations of Europe, and is rushing in like the waters of the flood, demanding for its moral preservation the immediate and universal action of those institutions which discipline the mind, and arm the conscience and the heart. And so various are the opinions and habits, and so recent and imperfect is the acquaintance, and so sparse are the settlements of the West, that no homogeneous public sentiment can be formed to legislate immediately into being the requisite institutions. And yet they all needed immediately, in their utmost perfection and power. A nation is being 'born in a day'. . . . But what will become of the West, if her prosperity rushes up to such a majesty of power, while those great institutions linger which are necessary to form the mind, and the conscience, and the heart of that vast world. It must not be permitted. . . . let no man at the East quiet himself, and dream of liberty, whatever may become of the West. . . . Her destiny is our destiny."

With this appeal to the conscience of New England, he adds appeals to her fears lest other religious sects anticipate her own. The New England preacher and schoolteacher left their mark on the West. The dread of Western emancipation from New England's political and economic control was paralleled by fears lest the West cut loose from her religion. Commenting in 1850 on reports that settlement was rapidly extending northward in Wisconsin, the editor of the *Home Missionary* writes: "We scarcely know whether to rejoice or to mourn over this extension of our settlements. While we sympathize in whatever tends to increase the physical resources and prosperity of our country, we cannot forget that with all these dispersions into remote and still remoter corners of the land, the supply of the means of grace is becoming relatively less and less." Acting in accordance with such ideas, home missions were established and Western colleges were erected. As seaboard cities like Philadelphia, New York, and Baltimore strove for the mastery of Western trade, so the various denominations strove for the possession of the West. Thus an intellectual stream from New England sources fertilized the West. On the other hand, the contest for power and the expansive of a moving frontier must have had important results on the character of religious organization in the United States. The religious aspects of the frontier make a chapter in our history which needs study.

INTELLECTUAL TRAITS

From the conditions of frontier life came intellectual traits of profound importance. The works of travelers along each frontier from colonial days onward describe for each certain traits, and these traits have, while softening down, still persisted as survivals in the place of their origin, even when a higher social organization succeeded. The result is that to the frontier the American intellect owes its striking characteristics. That coarseness and strength combined with acuteness and inquisitiveness, that practical, inventive turn of mind, quick to find expedients, that masterful grasp of material things, lacking in the artistic but powerful to effect great ends, that restless, nervous energy, that dominant individualism, working for good and for evil, and withal that buoyancy and exuberance which comes with freedom, these are traits of the frontier, or traits called out elsewhere because of the existence of the frontier. Since the days when the fleet of Columbus sailed into the waters of the New World, America has been another name for opportunity, and the people of the United States have taken their tone from the incessant expansion which has not only been open but has even been forced upon them. He would be a rash prophet who should assert that the expansive character of American life has now entirely ceased. Movement has been its dominant fact, and, unless this training has no effect upon a people, the American intellect will continually demand a wider field for its exercise. But never again will such gifts of free land offer themselves. For a moment at the frontier the bonds of custom are broken, and unrestraint is triumphant. There is not *tabula rasa*. The stubborn American environment is there with its imperious summons to accept its conditions; the inherited ways of doing things are also there; and yet, in spite of environment, and in spite of custom, each frontier did indeed furnish a new field of opportunity, a gate of escape from the bondage of the past; and freshness, and confidence, and scorn of older society, impatience of its restraints and its ideas, and indifference to its lessons, have accompanied the frontier. What the Mediterranean Sea was to the Greeks, breaking the bond of custom, offering new experiences, calling out new institutions and activities, that, and more, the ever retreating frontier has been to the United States directly, and to the nations of Europe more remotely. And now, four centuries from the discovery of America, at the end of a hundred years of life under the Constitution, the frontier has gone, and with its going has closed the first period of American history.

No single interpretation of America's past has been more enthusiastically received at the time—or more violently rejected later—than Frederick Jackson Turner's "frontier hypothesis." For more than a generation after its initial statement in 1893 it remained the creed of nearly every American historian. There was a reason for this; Turner's explanation of the nation's uniqueness admirably fitted the popular mood during the first quarter of the twentieth century. The frontier thesis was a flattering formula; it assured the people that the mighty nation of which they were so proud was their own creation, and not a mere importation from Europe. It was a nationalistic formula; Americans could learn that the institutions responsible for this greatness—democracy, individualism, freedom—were uniquely their own. It was a democratic formula; citizens in that day of political Progressivism could glory in the fact that the humble as well as the mighty had shaped the destiny of the United States. It was an optimistic formula; America's greatness had been achieved by individual effort

which would continue to inspire progress in the future. So the nation embraced the frontier thesis as the gospel, and rewrote its textbooks to glorify the pioneer above the industrialist or the immigrant.

This was dangerous, as Turner recognized, for he was a better historian than some of his disciples and realized that no single force was responsible for such a complex social organism as the United States. The tide of reaction set in shortly after his death in 1932. Again the time was ripe for such a change. Scholars, readjusting their concepts to the terrible new world created by the Great Depression, began to wonder whether the United States had ever been the land of limitless opportunity pictured by frontier historians, just as they questioned the role of pioneer individualism in a land where cooperative effort seemed essential for economic rehabilitation. Others bridled against Turner's agrarian emphasis in a day when factories, cities, and class conflicts shaped the course of events.

So critics leaped to the attack during the 1930's and 1940's. Some quarreled with Turner's loose terminology and exact definitions, insisting that his very vagueness invalidated his hypothesis. Others singled out special areas for criticism, denying that the frontier had ever served as a safety valve for discontented easterners, or that it had fostered democracy. Still others damned the Turnerites for focusing undue attention on a single causal force, maintaining that industrialization, urbanization, and social unrest had always been more important than westward expansion in shaping the national character. Even more devastating was the charge that the frontier hypothesis had helped plunge the United States into its state of chaos. By stressing the uniqueness of the national experience, critics insisted, Turner's thesis had engendered an isolationist spirit that hindered the international cooperation needed to lift the country from depression and foster the one-world ideal of the twentieth century.

In the end these critics went too far, and once more in the 1950's and 1960's the pendulum began to swing in the other direction. A new generation of scholars, sensibly paying less attention to Turner's statement of the frontier hypothesis than to the hypothesis itself, launched investigations that have restored this challenging thesis to its rightful place in American historiography. Some, using the techniques of sociologists, political scientists, and statisticians, have concluded that the pioneering experience did stimulate the growth of democratic institutions differing from those of Europe. Others, drawing on findings of economists, have agreed that a fron-

tier safety valve had operated to influence the pattern of labor organization during the nineteenth century. Still others have demonstrated that comparative studies of frontier and nonfrontier countries suggested that expansion did stimulate innovation, mobility, and the blurring of class lines, just as Turner had postulated.

Whatever the results of the scholarly in-fighting, Turner's theories have become part of the nation's folklore and have altered the diplomatic and political behavior of the United States. Expansionist-minded diplomats, fastening on the Turnerian doctrine that the perennial rebirth of society on new frontiers has rekindled the democratic spirit, have argued for half a century that new territories must be acquired or the national heritage surrendered. Imperialists used this argument in demanding territorial acquisitions after the Spanish-American War; men of such differing beliefs as J. P. Morgan and Woodrow Wilson agreed that the extension of American authority abroad would foster both economic growth and democracy; Franklin D. Roosevelt insisted that the export of the nation's democratic institutions was a necessary prelude to the better world that would emerge from World War II; his successor advanced the "Truman Doctrine" as a device to expand and defend the frontiers of democracy throughout the world. Belief in the superiority of American democratic institutions was older than Turner, but his insistence that these institutions owed their greatness to the frontier experience was a significant force in their acceptance and propagation.

Domestic policy in the United States has similarly been altered by popular belief in the Turnerian doctrine. Progressive statesmen, agreeing that the end of the frontier closed the door on those who sought to rehabilitate themselves by exploiting nature's virgin resources, have through the twentieth century acted on the belief that the federal government must supply Americans with the opportunity and security formerly provided by free land. This was the philosophy that underlay the New Nationalism of Theodore Roosevelt, the New Freedom of Woodrow Wilson, the New Deal of Franklin D. Roosevelt, and the Fair Deal of Harry Truman. "Our last frontier has long since been reached," declared Franklin Roosevelt. "Equality of opportunity as we have known it no longer exists. Our task now is not the discovery or exploitation of natural resources or necessarily producing more goods. It is the sober, less dramatic business . . . of distributing wealth and products more equitably, of adapting existing economic organizations to the service of the people. The day *of enlightened administration has come." A still later president, John F. Kennedy, signaled his approval of these beliefs by adopting "the New Frontier" as a slogan for his Administration. And President Lyndon B. Johnson has proclaimed his predecessor's "frontier" as only the borderland of the "Great Society." In such programs Frederick Jackson Turner's essay endures today, as part of the public consciousness of the United States.*

Richard Warren Sears

Cheapest Supply House on Earth

1894

EDITED BY JOHN E. JEUCK

Mail-order selling and the money-back guaranty are widely identified with Richard Warren Sears, not because the founder of Sears, Roebuck and Company originated either, but because he exploited them most successfully by his compelling advertising copy and his success in achieving enormous catalogue circulations. Motivated initially by a search for profits and prosperity, Sears exhausted himself in a continuing search for the "right proposition," which he defined in terms of a merchandise offering, price, advertising copy, and circulation plan that would generate sales.

Sears sketched out his copy for the cover and the pages of the 1894 mail-order catalogue in the closing days of the Columbian Exposition Year, 1893. Whether he planned and wrote the copy in his sparely furnished office in Minneapolis' Globe Building, or in a Van Buren Street loft in Chicago, is not clear, since his mail-order company was then operating from both cities—moving finally to Chicago only in January, 1895. Indeed, Sears may have planned his "Book of Bargains" while en route between the two cities—or in the midnight hours at home or in his hotel. His mail-order business had become (and long remained) the absorbing interest of his life, second only to his devotion to his family, whose demands appear to have been modest compared to the excitement and the profit of the avalanche of orders which the mails brought in the wake of Sears's advertising efforts.

Separated by great distances from the market he sought to serve, Richard Sears was conscious of the need to promise "satisfaction or your money back," both to overcome the understandable reluctance of customers to buy without comparing merchandise, and to counter the campaigns waged against mail order by local merchants throughout the land. "YOU TAKE NO RISK," Sears spelled out his general guaranty, ". . . whether you send part or full amounts of cash with your order, as we ALWAYS REFUND MONEY where goods are not found perfectly satisfactory." Lest the distant farmers fail to be satisfied with even that promise, Sears tried further to reassure them by referring his unseen prospects to their neighbors, the express companies, and the Union National Bank of Minneapolis.

The catalogue of 1894 was significant in several respects. It was the largest (322 pages) yet issued; it was the first to make any pretense toward offering a "complete" line of goods; it was only the second catalogue using the new title "Sears, Roebuck and Company," and the earliest to list the new Chicago location. Also the cover of the 1894 catalogue appears to have been the first to be printed in color. Although catalogues were to vary in price to the customer, the company advertised the 1894 catalogue as free for the writing, a practice that Sears later was to adopt as policy. The catalogue was also one of the last to reflect the unfettered personality of Richard Sears. From 1895, catalogues increasingly reflected the expanding size and dignity of the growing corporation and the trend toward "truth in advertising" with more accurate and detailed descriptions of merchandise.

[Cover]

CHEAPEST SUPPLY HOUSE ON EARTH
OUR TRADE REACHES AROUND THE WORLD

SEARS, ROEBUCK AND CO.

Globe Building   149 W. Van Buren
Minneapolis, Minn.   Chicago, Ill.

CONSUMER'S GUIDE
FOR
1894.

[page 3]

OUR COMBINED CATALOGUE.

PRESERVE THIS BOOK.   IT'S A MONEY SAVER.

TO OUR PATRONS:

Again we come to you, and we honestly believe, with the grandest collection of Bargains ever printed in one volume. *This is a Book of Bargains; a Money Saver for Everyone.* It is not our aim to include in this book and confuse you with a great variety of goods on which we can save you no money, but it has been our aim to include goods on which you can make a great saving. By a comparison of our prices with those of any thoroughly reliable house, you will see at once *you can save money* on everything you buy from us. It would be useless for us to include in this book a lot of goods at prices which with transportation charges added would cost you as much as you could buy the same article for in your local market. *We have studied to avoid this* by offering you only such goods are we are in a position to buy from the manufacturers direct and in such quantities as enables us to deliver them to you for as little or less money than they would cost your local dealer.

OUR OLD FRIENDS AND PATRONS

Will remember us as originally an *Exclusive Watch House, and later, Watches, Diamonds, Jewelry and Silverware,* and we believe we can modestly claim what is universally conceded that we honestly earned and have since maintained the reputation of being *The* LARGEST WATCH *and* JEWELRY HOUSE *in the* WORLD selling goods direct to the consumer. *Our daily average sales of Watches have been over 400, Jewelry and*

The advertising copy reprinted here—cover and pages 3 and 4—comes from the Sears, Roebuck and Company catalogue of 1894.

Silverware in proportion, while in the *Diamond* business our sales have almost from the very start *exceeded that of any firm in America* selling direct to the consumer.

WE HAVE ADDED MANY NEW LINES

And we shall hope for the same support in our new departure that has been so liberally accorded us in the past. *We have studied* to carefully and honestly represent every article so that when it reaches you, its appearance will almost universally be *better* than the description we give.

ABOUT OUR RELIABILITY.

We are authorized and incorporated under the laws of the State of Minnesota, with a cash capital paid in full of $75,000.00. We refer you to The Union National Bank of Minneapolis, and you are at liberty, if you choose, to send your money to them with instructions not to turn it over to us unless they know us to be perfectly reliable. We refer to any Express Company doing business in Minneapolis or Chicago—Adams, American, United States, Great Northern or Northern Pacific, or you can very likely find people in your own locality who know of us. *Ask your nearest Express Agent* about us; most any Express Agent can tell you about us. *Every Express Agent* in the United States knows of our reputation, as they have delivered our goods, and must, in most cases, know what our customers think of us.

WHERE WE SELL GOODS.

Almost Everywhere! There isn't a town in the Union where we haven't sold goods, our goods go into every city, town and hamlet in every state, as well as most every country on the globe. *Don't think* you live too far away. Our biggest trade is in Pennsylvania; 2d, New York; 3d, Illinois; 4th, Ohio, and so on, according to the population of the several states. *Distance cuts no figure. We can serve you anywhere, anytime. Freight rates are low. Express rates are low.* We have *Special facilities for Shipping* and in many cases *Special rates.*

WE AIM TO MAKE CUSTOMERS

Of Everyone by treating every customer in such a manner as to insure their always remaining a customer. WE CAN'T

AFFORD TO LOSE A CUSTOMER, and by instructing our employes to treat every customer at a distance exactly as they would like to be treated were they in a customer's place, and rigidly enforcing this rule, we have grown into one of the first institutions of the country and our patrons far and near are talking in our favor and thus adding new customers daily.

WHO WE SELL.

We sell the consumer, by that we mean we deal direct with the party who buys for his own use, thus saving you the middle man's profit. Anyone can buy from us; there is no restriction. Our terms and conditions are the most liberal ever offered. We make it very easy to buy of us.

Read our Terms, Conditions, etc., on next page.

Very truly,

SEARS, ROEBUCK & CO.

Globe Building, Minneapolis, Minn. 149 West Van Buren Street, Chicago, Ill.

ADDRESS US AT EITHER PLACE.

[page 4]

TERMS, CONDITIONS OF SHIPMENT, ETC.

The terms and conditions of Shipment will usually be found under each description, but in all cases, unless otherwise specified, CASH IN FULL MUST ACCOMPANY YOUR ORDER. We have tried in all cases to make our terms as liberal as possible, and by comparison you will find we offer terms not given by any other house in existence. On account of weight and bulk some goods can not be sent by express or C.O.D., but so far as we can, we send C.O.D., subject to examination to anyone.

OUR WATCHES, DIAMONDS AND JEWELRY we continue sending C.O.D. to any one anywhere, subject to examination. NO MONEY IN ADVANCE. *Prepay all Express Charges on Watches,* excepting a few special cheap watches on which we require cash in full and do not pay charges as explained under each description. UNDERSTAND, *Diamonds, Watches and Jewelry* will be sent to anyone, NO MONEY IN ADVANCE. *No other*

House on Earth handling the fine line we do give such liberal terms.

PIANOS AND ORGANS we will send to anyone and allow TEN DAYS TRIAL FREE, subject to the conditions fully explained in Catalogue pages.

GUNS AND REVOLVERS we will send to anyone anywhere C.O.D., subject to examination, on receipt of 50c to $3.00 as a guarantee of good faith. For full particulars read GUN PAGES.

HARNESS. We send Harness C.O.D., subject to examination to any one, on receipt of $1.00 as a Guarantee. For particulars read HARNESS PAGES.

SILVERWARE. Some Silverware we send C.O.D., subject to examination, *No Money in Advance.* For particulars see SILVERWARE PAGES.

CLOTHING. We send Clothing C.O.D., subject to examination on VERY LIBERAL TERMS. For particulars see CLOTHING DEPARTMENT.

BICYCLES. C.O.D.; subject to examination on receipt of ONE DOLLAR.

BABY CARRIAGES. C.O.D., subject to examination on receipt of TWO DOLLARS.

FULL PARTICULARS as to TERMS OF SALE, CONDITION OF SHIPMENT, *Etc.*, will be found under the *General Descriptions throughout this Book,* and in most cases will be found *more liberal* than is offered by any other concern.

YOU TAKE NO RISK in ordering of us whether you send part or full amount of cash with your order, as we ALWAYS REFUND MONEY where goods are not found perfectly satisfactory.

HOW TO ORDER.

ALWAYS WRITE YOUR ORDERS PLAINLY: Order Everything by Number; Always sign your Name plainly and in full; Always give the Name of your nearest Express Office or Railroad Station to which you wish goods shipped. If goods are to be sent by Express, give Name of Express company, or Name of Railroad company if to be sent by freight. GOODS CAN NOT BE SENT BY MAIL C.O.D. Anything to be sent by mail must be paid for in Advance.

IF YOU DON'T FIND WHAT YOU WANT in this Book, write us. We may have the very thing in stock; if we haven't we can no doubt get it for you at a great saving. *Don't hesitate to write us* at any time. *We are always at your service.*

Your obedient servants,

SEARS, ROEBUCK & CO.,

Globe Building, Minneapolis, Minn. 149 West Van Buren St., Chicago, Ill.

ADDRESS US AT EITHER PLACE.

By the turn of the century, Sears, Roebuck and Company had out-stripped Montgomery Ward in sales, and Richard Sears was a rich man. His living standards were modest and his interest in added wealth, though real, had become secondary. The excitement of generating orders sustained his consuming interest in the catalogue until he resigned from the company in 1908. By then it was the largest mail-order business in the world, with sales in 1907 of more th·n *$50 million. Since that time, when the enterprise was still ·imited almost entirely to the rural market, Sears, Roebuck and Company has become the world's largest general merchandise house, with sales of some $5 billion in 1963 made through the catalogue and more than 700 retail stores located in the United States, Canada, Venezuela, Brazil, Colombia, Mexico, Peru, Costa Rica, Puerto Rico, El Salvador, and Panama.*

Excepting the Bible, the Sears catalogue has probably the widest circulation of any book in the world. Currently, the various editions of the big "wish book" number more than 50 million copies annually. It is found not only in households, but in libraries, schools, offices, army camps, and embassies throughout the world—on both sides of the "iron" and "bamboo curtains." The catalogue is one of the best-read titles in USIA libraries throughout the world.

The overriding purpose of the catalogue is—and always has been—to sell merchandise. But its side effects have been impressive. Company president Robert E. Wood observed in the company's 1937 catalogue: "We conceive of this company not only as a great retail organization but as a great public institution as well." General Wood's statement is not extravagant. The catalogue is not only a source book for theater costumes and set designers, but a sharer with Henry Ford's "tin lizzie" in the distinction of forming the substance of much American humor. On the larger stage of international politics, it is reported that President Franklin Roosevelt once remarked that Soviet propaganda might profitably be countered by bombing the Russians with Sears, Roebuck catalogues (Life Magazine, Nov. 11, 1957). And the one-time chief of the Associated Press Moscow Bureau, Eddy Gilmore is authority on the assertion that "Two innocent enough articles of American life—the Sears Roebuck catalogue and the phonograph record—are the most powerful pieces of foreign propaganda in Russia. The catalogue comes first" (Liberty Magazine, Jan. 18, 1947).

At home, the mail-order catalogue changed the face of retail trade in rural America—and, at a later date, contributed greatly to the establishment of more efficient distribution in the cities as well. Initially, the catalogue served to break down the monopoly of local retailers throughout the land. The extent to which it furnished a standard of prices and values on farms and in villages and hamlets is evident in the enormous editorial attack it received from small-town newspapers during their crusades to defend local merchants against the mail-order business. Perhaps the largest "book burnings" in the United States were the fires made by irate merchants who burned the catalogues in the public square. (A recent echo of the use of the catalogue as an instrument of protest was the 1962 campaign of the National Farmers Organization to persuade midwestern farmers to pile Sears catalogues up in front of Sears stores to protest against the Committee for Economic Development's published report on agricultural policy.)

Launched on the final quarter of its first centennial, the Sears catalogue continues as a standard of value. Catalogue prices are used to construct a "cost of living" index by professional economists. Writing in the fall of 1957, a journalist noted: "Only recently has the catalogue been intentionally used as a weapon in the cold war. This spring Radio Free Europe started beaming a series of broadcasts from Munich to Poland, Hungary, Czechoslovakia, Rumania and Bulgaria, describing in detail what the American worker is able to buy with his wages. The price of every item in the

Sears catalogue from 'A' (abdominal bands) to 'Z' (zircon rings) is now being beamed behind the Iron Curtain" (Life Magazine, Nov. 11, 1957). *Having survived numerous attacks by competing merchants, the catalogue has remained an object of study by its competitors.*

Louis H. Sullivan

The Tall Office Building
Artistically Considered

1896

EDITED BY CARL W. CONDIT

---

*When the first multistory office buildings began to rise in
New York after the Civil War, the architects were clearly
baffled by the formal and functional problems that they presented. The architects sought solutions either in irrelevant
aesthetic concepts or in historical or even pseudomystical
principles that had no architectural reference. Most of the results strike us today as ludicrous. It was not simply that the
architects fell back on styles derived from the past, for in the
hands of imaginative designers eclecticism could and did lead
to distinguished works of architecture. The trouble, rather,
was that the architects fled from the essential utilitarian,
structural, and geometric facts of the high office building.
Again and again they sought to deny its height, its iron and
steel structure, and its repetitive internal character by overloading the exterior of the building with lavish ornamental
detail that bore no relation to the internal divisions and structure. In extreme cases a single building could be made to
look like as many as six different buildings piled one above*

580

*the other, each badly done in itself and each unrelated to the
rest.*

*Sullivan's essay is directed precisely against this architectur-
al refusal to face the facts. His paper is a document of prime
importance in architectural aesthetics, and because of the unprecedented problem to which he addressed himself, it is revolutionary for the development of building form in our
mechanized industrial society. The positive program which he
offers has many of the features of an urgent manifesto (a
characteristic intensified by his overblown and rather turgid
rhetoric), but it is equally a description of the new architectural practice that had arisen in Chicago in the 1880's. William
Le Baron Jenny and John Welborn Root had already understood the problem of the multistory building and by 1890 had
produced solutions which are among the first masterpieces of
modern architecture. Yet Sullivan was the logical spokesman
for the new style emerging in Chicago. He had received international attention for his Transportation Building at the Columbian Exposition of 1893, had given the leading paper at
the annual meeting of the American Institute of Architects in
1894, and had been elected to the Institute's Board of Directors in 1895. The exact circumstances under which he wrote
the essay are unknown, but it seems reasonable to conclude
that the editors of* Lippincott's *first suggested the paper. It was
to be his only article in a magazine of general interest.*

*In the five years preceding the publication of the paper in
1896, Sullivan and his engineering partner Dankmar Adler
enjoyed a number of major commissions, three of which
offered the architect opportunities to realize the principles he
had already formulated in his mind. All three were epoch-
making buildings, and two still stand today among the best
we have produced—the Wainwright in St. Louis (1890–91),
the Garrick Theater in Chicago (1891–92; demolished
in 1961), and the Guaranty in Buffalo (1894–95).
Sullivan's designs for these buildings reveal the two essential
aspects of the program developed in his essay. The first is the
highly empirical approach, presented in the clear and exact
description of the demands posed by the tall office building
and the planning elements necessary to satisfy them. The assumption underlying this description is summed up in Sullivan's assertion that "every problem contains and suggests its
own solution." The second aspect seems antithetical to the
first and offers the most difficult problem in understanding
Sullivan's work. It is subjective and emotional, imbued with a
romantic naturalism and a sense of wonder before the new
technical possibilities. Sullivan wanted to do more than pre-*

sent the facts of a building. He was compelled to celebrate his powerful feelings for the new technology of steel construction and to search for a form that would seem at once organic in the naturalistic sense and expressive of his own inner, nonrational response to techniques. Thus his celebrated idea that form follows function must be understood in the context of highly charged feeling that expresses itself in descriptions of the tall building as "a proud and soaring thing," or as offering "the most stupendous" and "magnificent" opportunity "to the proud spirit of man." Sullivan's search for the union of emotional expressiveness and scientific reason is the dominant one that occupies the creative architect in the mid-twentieth century.

THE ARCHITECTS of this land and generation are now brought face to face with something new under the sun —namely, that evolution and integration of social conditions, that special grouping of them, that results in a demand for the erection of tall office buildings.

It is not my purpose to discuss the social conditions; I accept them as the fact, and say at once that the design of the tall office building must be recognized and confronted at the outset as a problem to be solved—a vital problem, pressing for a true solution.

Let us state the conditions in the plainest manner. Briefly, they are these: offices are necessary for the transaction of business; the invention and perfection of the high-speed elevators make vertical travel, that was once tedious and painful, now easy and comfortable; development of steel manufacture has shown the way to safe, rigid, economical constructions rising to a great height; continued growth of population in the great cities, consequent congestion of centers and rise in value of ground, stimulate an increase in number of stories; these successfully piled one upon another, react on ground values —and so on, by action and reaction, interaction and interreaction. Thus has come about that form of lofty construction called the "modern office building." It has come in answer to a call, for in it a new grouping of social conditions has found a habitation and a name.

Up to this point all in evidence is materialistic, an exhibition of force, of resolution, of brains in the keen sense of the

The essay is reprinted as it originally appeared in *Lippincott's Magazine*, LVII (March, 1896); 403–9.

word. It is the joint product of the speculator, the engineer, the builder.

Problem: How shall we impart to this sterile pile, this crude, harsh, brutal agglomeration, this stark, staring exclamation of eternal strife, the graciousness of those higher forms of sensibility and culture that rest on the lower and fiercer passions? How shall we proclaim from the dizzy height of this strange, weird, modern housetop the peaceful evangel of sentiment, of beauty, the cult of a higher life?

This is the problem; and we must seek the solution of it in a process analogous to its own evolution—indeed, a continuation of it—namely, by proceeding step by step from general to special aspects, from coarser to finer considerations.

It is my belief that it is of the very essence of every problem that it contains and suggests its own solution. This I believe to be natural law. Let us examine, then, carefully the elements, let us search out this contained suggestion, this essence of the problem.

The practical conditions are, broadly speaking, these:

Wanted—1st, a story below-ground, containing boilers, engines of various sorts, etc.—in short, the plant for power, heating, lighting, etc. 2nd, a ground floor, so called, devoted to stores, banks, or other establishments requiring large area, ample spacing, ample light, and great freedom of access. 3rd, a second story readily accessible by stairways—this space usually in large subdivisions, with corresponding liberality in structural spacing and expanse of glass and breadth of external openings. 4th, above this an indefinite number of stories of offices piled tier upon tier, one tier just like another tier, one office just like all the other offices—an office being similar to a cell in a honeycomb, merely a compartment, nothing more. 5th, and last, at the top of this pile is placed a space or story that, as related to the life and usefulness of the structure, is purely physiological in its nature—namely, the attic. In this the circulatory system completes itself and makes its grand turn, ascending and descending. The space is filled with tanks, pipes, valves, sheaves, and mechanical etcetera that supplement and complement the force-originating plant hidden below-ground in the cellar. Finally, or at the beginning rather, there must be on the ground floor a main aperture or entrance common to all the occupants or patrons of the building.

This tabulation is, in the main, characteristic of every tall office building in the country. As to the necessary arrangements for light courts, these are not germane to the problem, and as will become soon evident, I trust need not be considered here. These things, and such others as the arrangement of elevators, for example, have to do strictly with the economics of the building, and I assume them to have been fully considered and disposed of to the satisfaction of purely utilitarian and pecuniary demands. Only in rare instances does the plan or floor arrangement of the tall office building take on an aesthetic value, and this usually when the lighting court is external or becomes an internal feature of great importance.

As I am here seeking not for an individual or special solution, but for a true normal type, the attention must be confined to those conditions that, in the main, are constant in all tall office buildings, and every mere incidental and accidental variation eliminated from the consideration, as harmful to the clearness of the main inquiry.

The practical horizontal and vertical division or office unit is naturally based on a room of comfortable area and height, and the size of this standard office room as naturally predetermines the standard structural unit, and, approximately, the size of window openings. In turn, these purely arbitrary units of structure form in an equally natural way the true basis of the artistic development of the exterior. Of course the structural spacings and openings in the first or mercantile story are required to be the largest of all; those in the second or quasi-mercantile story are of a somewhat similar nature. The spacings and openings in the attic are of no importance whatsoever (the windows have no actual value), for light may be taken from the top, and no recognition of a cellular division is necessary in the structural spacing.

Hence it follows inevitably, and in the simplest possible way, that if we follow our natural instincts without thought of books, rules, precedents, or any such educational impedimenta to a spontaneous and "sensible" result, we will in the following manner design the exterior of our tall office building—to wit:

Beginning with the first story, we give this a main entrance that attracts the eye to its location, and the remainder of the story we treat in a more or less liberal, expansive, sumptuous way—a way based exactly on the practical necessities, but expressed with a sentiment of largeness and freedom. The second story we treat in a similar way, but usually with milder pretension. Above this, throughout the indefinite number of typical office tiers, we take our cue from the individual cell, which requires a window with its separating pier, its sill and lintel, and we, without more ado, make them look all alike because they are all alike. This brings us to the attic, which, having no division into office-cells, and no special requirement for lighting, gives us the power to show by means of its broad expanse of wall, and its dominating weight and character, that which is the fact—namely, that the series of office tiers has come definitely to an end.

This may perhaps seem a bald result and a heartless, pessimistic way of stating it, but even so we certainly have advanced a most characteristic stage beyond the imagined sinister building of the speculator-engineer-builder combination. For the hand of the architect is now definitely felt in the decisive position at once taken, and the suggestion of a thoroughly sound, logical, coherent expression of the conditions is becoming apparent.

When I say the hand of the architect, I do not mean necessarily the accomplished and trained architect. I mean only a man with a strong, natural liking for buildings, and a disposition to shape them in what seems to his unaffected nature a direct and simple way. He will probably tread an innocent path from his problem to its solution, and therein he will show an enviable gift of logic. If he have some gift for form in detail, some feeling for form purely and simply as form, some love for that, his result in addition to its simple straightforward naturalness and completeness in general statement, will have something of the charm of sentiment.

However, thus far the results are only partial and tentative at best; relatively true, they are but superficial. We are doubtless right in our instinct but we must seek a fuller justification, a finer sanction, for it.

I assume now that in the study of our problem we have passed through the various stages of inquiry, as follows: 1st, the social basis of the demand for tall office buildings; 2nd, its literal material satisfaction; 3rd, the elevation of the question from considerations of literal planning, construction, and equipment, to the plane of elementary architecture as a direct outgrowth of sound, sensible building; 4th, the question again elevated from an elementary architecture to the beginnings of true architectural expression, through the addition of a certain quality and quantity of sentiment.

But our building may have all these in a considerable degree and yet be far from that adequate solution of the problem I am attempting to define. We must now heed the imperative voice of emotion.

It demands of us, what is the chief characteristic of the tall office building? And at once we answer, it is lofty. This loftiness is to the artist-nature its thrilling aspect. It is the very open organ-tone in its appeal. It must be in turn the dominant chord in his expression of it, the true excitant of his imagination. It must be tall, every inch of it tall. The force and power of altitude must be in it, the glory and pride of exaltation must be in it. It must be every inch a proud and soaring thing, rising in sheer exultation that from bottom to top it is a unit without a single dissenting line—that it is the new, the unexpected, the eloquent peroration of most bald, most sinister, most forbidding conditions.

The man who designs in this spirit and with the sense of responsibility to the generation he lives in must be no coward, no denier, no bookworm, no dilettante. He must live of his life and for his life in the fullest, most consummate sense. He must realize at once and with the grasp of inspiration that the problem of the tall office building is one of the most stupendous, one of the most magnificent opportunities that the Lord of Nature in His beneficence has ever offered to the proud spirit of man.

That this has not been perceived—indeed, has been flatly denied—is an exhibition of human perversity that must give us pause.

One more consideration. Let us now lift this question into the region of calm, philosophic observation. Let us seek a comprehensive, a final solution: let the problem indeed dissolve.

Certain critics, and very thoughtful ones, have advanced the theory that the true prototype of the tall office building is the classical column, consisting of base, shaft and capital—the moulded base of the column typical of the lower stories of our building, the plain or fluted shaft suggesting the monotonous, uninterrupted series of office-tiers, and the capital the completing power and luxuriance of the attic.

Other theorizers, assuming a mystical symbolism as a guide, quote the many trinities in nature and art, and the beauty and conclusiveness of such trinity in unity. They aver the beauty of prime numbers, the mysticism of the number three, the beauty of all things that are in three parts—to wit, the day, subdividing into morning, noon, and night; the limbs, the thorax, and the head, constituting the body. So they say, should the building be in three parts vertically, substantially as before, but for different motives.

Others, of purely intellectual temperament, hold that such a design should be in the nature of a logical statement; it should have a beginning, a middle, and an ending, each clearly defined—therefore again a building, as above, in three parts vertically.

Others, seeking their examples and justification in the vegetable kingdom, urge that such a design shall above all things be organic. They quote the suitable flower with its bunch of leaves at the earth, its long graceful stem, carrying the gorgeous single flower. They point to the pine-tree, its massy roots, its lithe, uninterrupted trunk, its tuft of green high in the air. Thus, they say, should be the design of the tall office building: again in three parts vertically.

Others still, more susceptible to the power of a unit than to the grace of a trinity, say that such a design should be struck out at a blow, as though by a blacksmith or by mighty Jove, or should be thought-born, as was Minerva, full grown. They accept the notion of a triple division as permissible and welcome, but non-essential. With them it is a subdivision of their unit: the unit does not come from the alliance of the three; they accept it without murmur, provided the subdivision does not disturb the sense of singleness and repose.

All of these critics and theorists agree, however, positively, unequivocally, in this, that the tall office building should not, must not, be made a field for the display of architectural knowledge in the encyclopaedic sense; that too much learning in this instance is fully as dangerous, as obnoxious, as too little learning; that miscellany is abhorrent to their sense; that the sixteen-story building must not consist of sixteen separate, distinct and unrelated buildings piled one upon the other until the top of the pile is reached.

To this latter folly I would not refer were it not the fact that nine out of every ten tall office buildings are designed in precisely this way in effect, not by the ignorant, but by the educated. It would seem indeed, as though the "trained" architect, when facing this problem, were beset at every story, or at most, every third or fourth story, by the hysterical dread lest he be in "bad form"; lest he be not bedecking his building with sufficiency of quotation from this, that, or the other "correct" building in some other land and some other time; lest he be not copious enough in the display of his wares; lest he betray, in short, a lack of resource. To loosen up the touch of this cramped and fidgety hand, to allow the nerves to calm, the brain to cool, to reflect equally, to reason naturally, seems beyond him; he lives, as it were, in a waking nightmare filled with the disjecta membra of architecture. The spectacle is not inspiriting.

As to the former and serious views held by discerning and thoughtful critics, I shall, with however much of regret, dissent from them for the purpose of this demonstration, for I regard them as secondary only, non-essential, and as touching not at all upon the vital spot, upon the quick of the entire matter, upon the true, the immovable philosophy of the architectural art.

This view let me now state, for it brings to the solution of the problem a final, comprehensive formula.

All things in nature have a shape, that is to say, a form, an outward semblance, that tells us what they are, that distinguishes them from ourselves and from each other.

Unfailingly in nature these shapes express the inner life, the native quality, of the animal, tree, bird, fish, that they present to us; they are so characteristic, so recognizable, that we say, simply, it is "natural" it should be so. Yet the moment we peer beneath this surface of things, the moment we look through the tranquil reflection of ourselves and the clouds above us, down into the clear, fluent, unfathomable depth of nature, how startling is the silence of it, how amazing the flow of life, how absorbing the mystery. Unceasingly the essence of things is taking shape in the matter of things, and this unspeakable process we call birth and growth. Awhile the spirit and the matter fade away together, and it is this that we call decadence, death. These two happenings seem jointed and interdependent, blended into one like a bubble and its iridescence, and they seem borne along upon a slowly moving air. This air is wonderful past all understanding.

Yet to the steadfast eye of one standing upon the shore of things, looking chiefly and most lovingly upon that side on which the sun shines and that we feel joyously to be life, the heart is ever gladdened by the beauty, the exquisite spontaneity, with which life seeks and takes on its forms in an accord perfectly responsive to its needs. It seems ever as though the life and the form were absolutely one and inseparable, so adequate is the sense of fulfillment.

Whether it be the sweeping eagle in his flight or the open apple-blossom, the toiling work-horse, the blithe swan, the branching oak, the winding stream at its base, the drifting clouds, over all the coursing sun, form ever follows function, and this is the law. Where function does not change form does not change. The granite rocks, the ever-brooding hills, remain for ages; the lightning lives, comes into shape, and dies in a twinkling.

It is the pervading law of all things organic, and inorganic, of all things physical and metaphysical, of all things human and all things superhuman, of all true manifestations of the head, of the heart, of the soul, that the life is recognizable in its expression, that form ever follows function. This is the law.

Shall we, then, daily violate this law in our art? Are we so decadent, so imbecile, so utterly weak of eyesight, that we cannot perceive this truth so simple, so very simple? Is it indeed a truth so transparent that we see through it but do not see it? Is it really then, a very marvelous thing, or is it rather so commonplace, so everyday, so near a thing to us, that we cannot perceive that the shape, form, outward expression, design or whatever we may choose, of the tall office building should in the very nature of things follow the functions of the building, and that where the function does not change, the form is not to change?

Does this not readily, clearly, and conclusively show that the lower one or two stories will take on a special character suited to the special needs, that the tiers of typical offices, having the same unchanging function, shall continue in the same unchanging form, and that as to the attic, specific and conclusive as it is in its very nature, its function shall equally be so in force, in significance, in continuity, in conclusiveness of outward expression? From this results, naturally, spontaneously, unwittingly, a three-part division, not from any theory, symbol, or fancied logic.

And thus the design of the tall office building takes its place with all other architectural types made when architecture, as has happened once in many years, was a living art. Witness the Greek temple, the Gothic cathedral, the medieval fortress.

And thus, when native instinct and sensibility shall govern the exercise of our beloved art; when the known law, the respected law, shall be that form ever follows function; when architects shall cease struggling and prattling handcuffed and vainglorious in the asylum of a foreign school; when it is truly felt, cheerfully accepted, that this law opens up the airy sunshine of green fields, and gives to us a freedom that the very beauty and sumptuousness of the outworking of the law itself as exhibited in nature will deter any sane, any sensitive man from changing into license, when it becomes evident that we are merely speaking a foreign language with a noticeable American accent, whereas each and every architect in the land might, under the benign influence of this law, express in the simplest, most modest, most natural way that which it is in him to say; that he might really and would surely develop his own characteristic individuality, and that the architectural art with him would certainly become a living form of speech, a natural form of utterance, giving surcease to him and adding treasures small and great to the growing art of his land; when we know and feel that Nature is our friend, not our implacable enemy—that an afternoon in the country, an hour by the sea, a full open view of one single day, through dawn, high noon, and twilight, will suggest to us so much that is rhythmical, deep, and eternal in the vast art of architecture, something so deep, so true, that all the narrow formalities, hard-and-fast rules, and strangling bonds of the schools cannot stifle it in us—then it may be proclaimed that we are on the high-road to a natural and satisfying art, an architecture that will soon become a fine art in the true, the best sense of the word, an art that will live because it will be of the people, for the people, and by the people.

Sullivan's essay was widely read during the decade following its publication in Lippincott's Magazine. *We may assume this not only from the circulation which* Lippincott's *enjoyed among readers of serious periodical literature, but also from the fact that the paper was twice reprinted within ten years. Before the end of the century the architect's reputation had grown to national proportions. The great majority of his commissions came from Chicago, but in the decade of the 1890's he was designing buildings to be erected in New York, New Orleans, and Seattle, as well as in the cities of the Great Lakes and midwestern regions. He was acknowledged as the leading architect and philosopher of the Chicago movement; elsewhere, he was at least listened to with considerable respect. Yet the subsequent history of his brave and original document provides a clue to the fate of Sullivan's work and ideas. The two reprintings that followed within a few years of the original publication indicate that its ideas met an early acclaim. The reprinting of 1922, however, can only be regarded as a belated and ironic memorial to its author, now nearing death, poverty-stricken, forgotten by everyone save a few friends in the city he had made architecturally famous.*

The influence of "The Tall Office Building" has been as ambiguous as the architect's interpretation was bound to be. The three-part vertical division that Sullivan proposed for the skyscraper was perfectly rational and quickly accepted by many architects of the new office towers. This much was simple logic and provided an obviously sensible answer to the main utilitarian questions. But the ambiguity arose over the rival claims of functionalism and soaring height. The skyscraper architects of New York, who set the national pace, were unwilling to follow the organic principles of the Chicago school, preferring instead the eclectic approach of the nineteenth century. Within these limits, however, they were enthusiastic about exploring the possibilities of great height and found many ways to adapt the historical systems of ornament to an emphatic verticalism. The eclectic phase reached its culmination in Cass Gilbert's vivid design for the Woolworth Tower in New York (1911–13). In the skyscraper boom of the 1920's the derivative elements were gradually refined away until the architects reached the pure verticalism of Raymond Hood's Daily News Building in New York (1930), or Graham, Anderson, Probst and White's Field Building in Chicago (1934). But in these extreme forms we can see the confusion between creating true organic design and an obsession with stretching out height itself.

On the functional side Sullivan's ideas were brilliantly illustrated in a body of industrial and warehouse architecture that reached levels of remarkable power in the hands of the gifted Chicago architects. This strictly empirical approach spread from Chicago to other industrial centers. A highly refined factory architecture arose from the demands of the automotive industry in Detroit, where Albert Kahn transformed industrial requirements into the elegant and simple geometry of the modern curtain-wall factory. The high point of this development came with the power houses and other subsidiary buildings of the Tennessee Valley Authority, especially those erected during the hydroelectric phase of construction (1933-45). But even at the best this is technical and empirical form, and clearly does not possess the emotional expressiveness that Sullivan thought indispensable.

The question, then, of the precise influence of Sullivan's essay is not one that can be answered in clear-cut terms. If we consider in their entirety the norms that he laid down, we are forced to conclude that at least for the first third of the twentieth century American architecture was unprepared to explore fully the path he had opened. In the 1930's the new European ideas of Gropius and Le Corbusier began to gain headway in the United States. When large-scale building was resumed after the long hiatus of the Depression and World War II, the imported forms and associated technical innovations were in the ascendant. The revival of Sullivan's principles in commercial and public building did not come until the mid-century decade, and even now they appear in the work of only a small group of architects. The essential problem, again, is to avoid the two extremes of a mechanistic functionalism and a capricious self-expression—to find, in short, an organic union of technological necessities and emotional power. The most striking revival of Sullivan's program has come in Chicago itself, chiefly under the leadership of Mies van der Rohe and the Chicago office of Skidmore, Owings and Merrill. This work combines the clear statement of physical laws as they are embodied in scientific building technology with great dignity and power derived from the spatial and geometric possibilities of steel framing. In the delicate vertical tracery of Mies van der Rohe's high buildings, especially, one finds the proud and soaring quality that so excited Sullivan's imagination. In the East, Louis I. Kahn has designed buildings which reveal a greater measure of the uninhibited emotionalism that Sullivan loved. Kahn possesses a remarkable faculty for combining a rational plan with a plastic self-expression of a highly personal but disciplined nature.

The contemporary Chicago work is close in actual appearance to that of the original Chicago school, while Kahn's designs seem remote from it in visual impact. Each offers us examples of varying degrees of emphasis in the prescription that Sullivan set forth, one tending toward the public and anonymous, the other toward the subjective and nonrational. But it is impossible to argue that the ideas presented in "The Tall Office Building" form the immediate basis for this body of work, or for any other comparable to it. Men as different in background, training, and talent as the German Mies van der Rohe and the Philadelphian Kahn are not likely to have found in a Sullivan paper of 1896 the exclusive source of their inspiration. This underlying identity of thought and performance, surviving precariously for seventy years, tells us something more profound about the building arts of our time. Stripped of their rhetorical decoration and their peculiar emotional bias, Sullivan's key ideas are permanently valid and long ago entered into the mainstream of contemporary culture, where they eventually gained wide currency among the creative spirits of modern building.

William Jennings Bryan

"Cross of Gold" Speech

1896

EDITED BY RICHARD HOFSTADTER

---

*William Jennings Bryan's "Cross of Gold" speech, delivered
at the Democratic National Convention in Chicago on July 9,
1896, was probably the most effective speech in the history of
American party politics. Bryan, then only thirty-six, had
come to Chicago as a leader of the Nebraska delegation, but
with the avowed intention of vaulting from this relatively obscure role into the presidential nomination. He was, to be
sure, widely known in the party and had for some time been
soliciting the support of delegates. He was also known in
Congress as an eloquent speaker. But his hopes for the nomination seemed laughable to those to whom he confided
them. He went to the convention with hardly any assets other
than his fine voice and the outlines of this speech glimmering
in his head, and he swept the convention by storm.*

*The great issue before the convention was whether the
party should take its place behind President Cleveland and
the conservative Democrats in a continued defense of the
gold standard or yield to the fervent demand of the South
and West for free coinage of silver at 16 to 1 as the remedy
for depressed prices, unemployment, and the blight of depres-*

sion. *The question of the monetary standard, an important issue for twenty years, had come to a head with the panic and depression of 1893; it had been subjected to a continuous and heated debate since the summer of that year, when Cleveland, in a hard-fought defense of the Treasury's gold reserve, had pushed through Congress the repeal of the Sherman Silver Purchase Act of 1890.*

The circumstances under which the debate took place put Bryan in a favorable position. It is true that his first efforts at the convention were not auspicious. He had hardly arrived before he was engaged in a hard struggle, finally successful, to seat his Nebraska delegation against the opposition of gold delegates. He was unable to win serious consideration for the position of temporary chairman, which he had hoped to gain as a means of putting himself in a prominent spot, and a growing general awareness of his candidacy made him unthinkable as permanent chairman. Bryan hoped that he might still become chairman of the Committee on Resolutions, but this post he wisely yielded to the claims of the veteran silver Senator James K. Jones of Arkansas. Bryan himself, as a member of this committee, drafted the silver plank that touched off the great debate. His first stroke of good fortune came when Senator Jones asked him to conduct the defense of the platform. His second came when Senator "Pitchfork Ben" Tillman of South Carolina, who was eager to have time for a long speech, asked to be the first speaker among the silver advocates, thus leaving Bryan as the last, and possibly climactic, orator. His third came from the character of Tillman's speech itself, a rancorous performance so ill-conceived that its sectional aspersions had to be repudiated from the floor by other silver spokesmen. When Bryan rose to speak, therefore, he was left as the only effective spokesman of the silver cause. Three gold advocates had spoken with some persuasiveness, but they had poor voices, and at times were almost inaudible. The crowd leaned back in relief when Bryan began. He spoke in a splendidly calm and conciliatory manner, and his large, melodious voice could be heard without effort throughout the hall.

The speech itself was hardly an improvisation. In three years of debating and lecturing on the silver issue, Bryan had had ample opportunity to polish his arguments, to pick up and experiment with key phrases. Only a few days before, he had given a speech at Crete, Nebraska, which was a kind of dress rehearsal of some portions of the speech. In his Memoirs (still the best account of the occasion) he noted that his speech was extemporaneous only "in so far as the arrange-

*ment was concerned. No new arguments had been advanced
and therefore no new answers were required."*

*No one dares quarrel with the simple strategy of Bryan's
speech. Perceiving that the money question, faced head-on,
was a thicket of technicalities already all too familiar and
well-argued, and that the members of his audience were not
open to further persuasion on the merits of the issue, Bryan
offered a speech designed to set the right tone—first, to
soften the worst asperities of the family quarrel, but then
firmly to assert the justice of the silver case and rally its adherents not around a sectional interest but on the common
grounds of humanity.*

MR. CHAIRMAN AND GENTLEMEN OF THE CONVENTION:

I WOULD be presumptuous, indeed, to present myself against
the distinguished gentlemen to whom you have listened if
this were a mere measuring of abilities; but this is not a contest between persons. The humblest citizen in all the land,
when clad in the armor of a righteous cause, is stronger than
all the hosts of error. I come to speak to you in defense of a
cause as holy as the cause of liberty—the cause of humanity.

When this debate is concluded, a motion will be made to
lay upon the table the resolution offered in commendation of
the administration, and also the resolution offered in condemnation of the administration. We object to bringing this question down to the level of persons. The individual is but an
atom; he is born, he acts, he dies; but principles are eternal;
and this has been a contest over a principle.

Never before in the history of this country has there been
witnessed such a contest as that through which we have just
passed. Never before in the history of American politics has
a great issue been fought out as this issue has been, by the
voters of a great party. On the fourth of March, 1895, a few
Democrats, most of them members of Congress, issued an address to the Democrats of the nation, asserting that the
money question was the paramount issue of the hour; declaring that a majority of the Democratic party had the right to
control the action of the party on this paramount issue; and
concluding with the request that the believers in the free

The speech is taken from Bryan's book *The First Battle* (Chicago:
W. B. Conkey Company, 1896), pp. 199–206. Brackets appear in the
original.

coinage of silver in the Democratic party should organize, take charge of, and control the policy of the Democratic party. Three months later, at Memphis, an organization was perfected, and the silver Democrats went forth openly and courageously proclaiming their belief, and declaring that, if successful, they would crystallize into a platform the declaration which they had made. They began the conflict. With a zeal approaching the zeal which inspired the crusaders who followed Peter the Hermit, our silver Democrats went forth from victory unto victory until they are now assembled, not to discuss, not to debate, but to enter up the judgment already rendered by the plain people of this country. In this contest brother has been arrayed against brother, father against son. The warmest ties of love, acquaintance and association have been disregarded; old leaders have been cast aside when they have refused to give expression to the sentiments of those whom they would lead, and new leaders have sprung up to give direction to this cause of truth. Thus has the contest been waged, and we have assembled here under as binding and solemn instructions as were ever imposed upon representatives of the people.

We do not come as individuals. As individuals we might have been glad to compliment the gentleman from New York [Senator Hill] but we know that the people for whom we speak would never be willing to put him in a position where he could thwart the will of the Democratic party. I say it was not a question of persons; it was a question of principle, and it is not with gladness, my friends, that we find ourselves brought into conflict with those who are now arrayed on the other side.

The gentleman who preceded me [ex-Governor Russell] spoke of the State of Massachusetts; let me assure him that not one present in all this convention entertains the least hostility to the people of the State of Massachusetts, but we stand here representing people who are the equals, before the law, of the greatest citizens in the State of Massachusetts. When you [turning to the gold delegates] come before us and tell us that we are about to disturb your business interests, we reply that you have disturbed our business interests by your course.

We say to you that you have made the definition of a business man too limited in its application. The man who is employed for wages is as much a business man as his employer; the attorney in a country town is as much a business man as the corporation counsel in a great metropolis; the merchant at the cross-roads store is as much a business man as the mer-

chant of New York; the farmer who goes forth in the morning and toils all day—who begins in the spring and toils all
summer—and who by the application of brain and muscle to
the natural resources of the country creates wealth, is as
much a business man as the man who goes upon the board of
trade and bets upon the price of grain; the miners who go
down a thousand feet into the earth, or climb two thousand
feet upon the cliffs, and bring forth from their hiding places
the precious metals to be poured into the channels of trade
are as much business men as the few financial magnates who,
in a back room, corner the money of the world. We come to
speak for this broader class of business men.

Ah, my friends, we say not one word against those who
live upon the Atlantic coast, but the hardy pioneers who have
braved all the dangers of the wilderness, who have made the
desert to blossom as the rose—the pioneers away out there
[pointing to the West], who rear their children near to Nature's heart, where they can mingle their voices with the
voices of the birds—out there where they have erected
schoolhouses for the education of their young, churches
where they praise their Creator, and cemeteries where rest
the ashes of their dead—these people, we say, are as deserv-
ing of the consideration of our party as any people in this
country. It is for these that we speak. We do not come as
aggressors. Our war is not a war of conquest; we are fighting
in the defense of our homes, our families, and posterity. We
have petitioned, and our petitions have been scorned; we
have entreated, and our entreaties have been disregarded; we
have begged, and they have mocked when our calamity came.
We beg no longer; we entreat no more; we petition no more.
We defy them.

The gentleman from Wisconsin has said that he fears a
Robespierre. My friends, in this land of the free you need not
fear that a tyrant will spring up from among the people.
What we need is an Andrew Jackson to stand, as Jackson
stood, against the encroachments of organized wealth.

They tell us that this platform was made to catch votes.
We reply to them that changing conditions make new issues;
that the principles upon which Democracy rests are as everlasting as the hills, but that they must be applied to new conditions as they arise. Conditions have arisen, and we are here
to meet those conditions. They tell us that the income tax
ought not to be brought in here; that it is a new idea. They
criticize us for our criticism of the Supreme Court of the
United States. My friends, we have not criticized; we have
simply called attention to what you already know. If you

want criticisms, read the dissenting opinions of the court. There you will find criticisms. They say that we passed an unconstitutional law; we deny it. The income tax law was not unconstitutional when it was passed; it was not unconstitutional when it went before the Supreme Court for the first time; it did not become unconstitutional until one of the judges changed his mind, and we cannot be expected to know when a judge will change his mind. The income tax is just. It simply intends to put the burdens of government justly upon the backs of the people. I am in favor of an income tax. When I find a man who is not willing to bear his share of the burdens of the government which protects him, I find a man who is unworthy to enjoy the blessings of a government like ours.

They say that we are opposing national bank currency; it is true. If you will read what Thomas Benton said, you will find he said that, in searching history, he could find but one parallel to Andrew Jackson; that was Cicero, who destroyed the conspiracy of Cataline and saved Rome. Benton said that Cicero only did for Rome what Jackson did for us when he destroyed the bank conspiracy and saved America. We say in our platform that we believe that the right to coin and issue money is a function of government. We believe it. We believe that it is a part of sovereignty, and can no more with safety be delegated to private individuals than we could afford to delegate to private individuals the power to make penal statutes or levy taxes. Mr. Jefferson, who was once regarded as good Democratic authority, seems to have differed in opinion from the gentleman who has addressed us on the part of the minority. Those who are opposed to this proposition tell us that the issue of paper money is a function of the bank, and that the Government ought to go out of the banking business. I stand with Jefferson rather than with them, and tell them, as he did, that the issue of money is a function of government, and that the banks ought to go out of the governing business.

They complain about the plank which declares against life tenure in office. They have tried to strain it to mean that which it does not mean. What we oppose by that plank is the life tenure which is being built up in Washington, and which excludes from participation in official benefits the humbler members of society.

Let me call your attention to two or three important things. The gentleman from New York says that he will propose an amendment to the platform providing that the proposed change in our monetary system shall not affect contracts already made. Let me remind you that there is no intention of affecting those contracts which according to present laws are made payable in gold; but if he means to say that we cannot change our monetary system without protecting those who have loaned money before the change was made, I desire to ask him where, in law or in morals, he can find justification for not protecting the debtors when the act of 1873 was passed, if he now insists that we must protect the creditors.

He says he will also propose an amendment which will provide for the suspension of free coinage if we fail to maintain the party within a year. We reply that when we advocate a policy which we believe will be successful, we are not compelled to raise a doubt as to our own sincerity by suggesting what we shall do if we fail. I ask him, if he would apply his logic to us, why he does not apply it to himself. He says he wants this country to try to secure an international agreement. Why does he not tell us what he is going to do if he fails to secure an international agreement? There is more reason for him to do that than there is for us to provide against the failure to maintain the parity. Our opponents have tried for twenty years to secure an international agreement, and those are waiting for it most patiently who do not want it at all.

And now, my friends, let me come to the paramount issue. If they ask us why it is that we say more on the money question than we say upon the tariff question, I reply that, if protection has slain its thousands, the gold standard has slain its tens of thousands. If they ask us why we do not embody in our platform all the things that we believe in, we reply that when we have restored the money of the Constitution all other necessary reforms will be possible; but that until this is done there is no other reform that can be accomplished.

Why is it that within three months such a change has come over the country? Three months ago, when it was confidently asserted that those who believe in the gold standard would frame our platform and nominate our candidates, even the advocates of the gold standard did not think that we could elect a president. And they had good reason for their doubt, because there is scarcely a State here today asking for the gold standard which is not in the absolute control of the Republican party. But note the change. Mr. McKinley was nominated at St. Louis upon a platform which declared for the maintenance of the gold standard until it can be changed into bimetallism by international agreement. Mr. McKinley was the most popular man among the Republicans, and three months ago everybody in the Republican party prophesied his election. How is it today? Why, the man who was once pleased to think that he looked like Napoleon—that man shudders today when he remembers that he was nominated on the anniversary of the battle of Waterloo. Not only that, but as he listens he can hear with ever-increasing distinctness the sound of the waves as they beat upon the lonely shores of St. Helena.

Why this change? Ah, my friends, is not the reason for the change evident to any one who will look at the matter? No private character, however pure, no personal popularity, however great, can protect from the avenging wrath of an indignant people a man who will declare that he is in favor of fastening the gold standard upon this country, or who is willing to surrender the right of self-government and place the legislative control of our affairs in the hands of foreign potentates and powers.

We go forth confident that we shall win. Why? Because upon the paramount issue of this campaign there is not a spot of ground upon which the enemy will dare to challenge battle. If they tell us that the gold standard is a good thing, we shall point to their platform and tell them that their platform pledges the party to get rid of the gold standard and substitute bimetallism. If the gold standard is a good thing, why try to get rid of it? I call your attention to the fact that some of the very people who are in this convention today and who tell us that we ought to declare in favor of international bimetallism—thereby declaring that the gold standard is wrong and that the principle of bimetallism is better—these very people four months ago were open and avowed advocates of the gold standard, and were then telling us that we could not legislate two metals together, even with the aid of all the world. If the gold standard is a good thing, we ought to declare in favor of its retention and not in favor of abandoning it; and if the gold standard is a bad thing why should we wait until other nations are willing to help us to let go? Here is the line of battle, and we care not upon which issue they force the fight; we are prepared to meet them on either issue or on both. If they tell us that the gold standard is the standard of civilization, we reply to them that this, the most enlightened of all the nations of the earth, has never declared for a gold standard and that both the great parties this year are declaring against it. If the gold standard is the standard of civilization, why, my friends, should we not have it? If they come to meet us on that issue we can present the history of our nation. More than that; we can tell them that they will search the pages of history in vain to find a single instance where the common people of any land have ever declared themselves in favor of the gold standard. They can find where the holders of the fixed investments have declared for a gold standard, but not where the masses have.

Mr. Carlisle said in 1878 that this was a struggle between "the idle holders of idle capital" and "the struggling masses, who produce the wealth and pay the taxes of the country;" and, my friends, the question we are to decide is: Upon which side will the Democratic party fight; upon the side of "the idle holders of idle capital" or upon the side of "the struggling masses?" That is the question which the party must answer first, and then it must be answered by each individual hereafter. The sympathies of the Democratic party, as shown by the platform, are on the side of the struggling masses who have ever been the foundation of the Democratic party. There are two ideas of government. There are those who believe that, if you will only legislate to make the well-to-do prosperous, their prosperity will leak through on those below. The Democratic idea, however, has been that if you legislate to make the masses prosperous, their prosperity will find its way up through every class which rests upon them.

You come to us and tell us that the great cities are in favor of the gold standard; we reply that the great cities rest upon our broad and fertile prairies. Burn down your cities and leave our farms, and your cities will spring up again as if by magic; but destroy our farms and the grass will grow in the streets of every city in the country.

My friends, we declare that this nation is able to legislate for its own people on every question, without waiting for the aid or consent of any other nation on earth; and upon that issue we expect to carry every State in the Union. I shall not slander the inhabitants of the fair State of Massachusetts nor the inhabitants of the State of New York by saying that, when they are confronted with the proposition, they will declare that this nation is not able to attend to its own business. It is the issue of 1776 over again. Our ancestors, when but three millions in number, had the courage to declare their political independence of every other nation; shall we, their descendants, when we have grown to seventy millions, declare that we are less independent than our forefathers? No, my friends, that will never be the verdict of our people. Therefore, we care not upon what lines the battle is fought. If they say bimetallism is good, but that we cannot have it until other nations help us, we reply that, instead of having a gold standard because England has, we will restore bimetallism, and then let England have bimetallism because the United States has it. If they dare to come out in the open field and defend the gold standard as a good thing, we will fight them to the uttermost. Having behind us the producing masses of this nation and the world, supported by the commercial interests, the laboring interests, and the toilers everywhere, we will answer their demand for a gold standard by saying to them: You shall not press down upon the brow of labor this crown of thorns, you shall not crucify mankind upon a cross of gold.

"The audience," Bryan recalled of the immediate response to his address, "acted like a trained choir—in fact, I thought of a choir as I noticed how instantaneously and in unison they responded to each point made." He remembered, also, that they "seemed to rise and sit down as one man." When his last words had echoed through the hall, the convention dissolved in an uproar that went on for an hour. Although many of the eastern gold men sat immobile, there were some, even among them, who rose to bellow their appreciation of Bryan's performance. The next day he was nominated on the fifth ballot. Without influential backers or large funds, with the aid only of his golden tongue, his political shrewdness, and a few strokes of luck, he had won his objective. He had come to Chicago with $100, and when he and Mrs. Bryan checked out of their modest quarters in the Clifton House, he held the presidential nomination of his party and still had $40 in his pocket.

Immediate reactions to Bryan were mixed. Mark Hanna, Republican campaign manager, gleefully noted that "He's talking Silver all the time, and that's where we've got him." Hanna realized, as Bryan and his followers apparently did not, that "Free Silver" meant little to urban workingmen. Republican orators campaigned on the theme that America needed not an increase of coin, but an increase of confidence; not more money in circulation, but more jobs for the workers. Many Populist reformers saw in Bryan's nomination the wreckage of the farmer-labor alliance for which they had hoped. "Free silver is the cow-bird of the reform movement," claimed Henry Demarest Lloyd. "It waited till the nest had been built by the sacrifices and labor of others, and then it laids its eggs in it, pushing out the others which it smashed on the ground." When the Populist Party dutifully echoed the Democratic nomination, many urban radicals deserted. Lloyd proved correct. Although Bryan waged a vigorous campaign, every state east of the Mississippi and north of the Ohio went to McKinley. Within four years the issue of "Free Cuba" replaced "Free Silver" in national politics. Bryan had unconsciously prophesied the political crucifixion of agrarian Populism in his "Cross of Gold" speech.

If the issues of the speech soon died out as meaningful propaganda, the attitudes of mind which it represented lived on. Agrarian rhetoric championed the prohibition movement of later years, fought the battles of fundamentalist religion versus the forces of evolution in the famous Scopes trial (1925), and eventually lobbied successfully in New Deal days to establish the principle of parity price levels for agriculture. Commercial farmers eventually were subsidized by the products of the industrial America that Bryan once had denounced. Populism, as portrayed in the "Cross of Gold" speech, was only another episode in the well-established tradition of American entrepreneurial radicalism. Bryan's address marked the first tentative step in the direction of effective agrarian organization.

The speech has become a standard point of reference in the history of the American political mind, the one document to which historians of the silver controversy have been sure to refer, and a set piece of American oratory. Also, it remains significant in reconstructing the emotional content of agrarian complaints against the new American industrial order. On another occasion, Bryan argued that "the great political questions are in their final analysis great moral questions." Bryanism and Populism were cries of moral outrage against both the real and the imagined evils of urban America. A major issue of the "Cross of Gold" speech was who should control the government, the urban or the rural, the financial or the agrarian interests? In today's terms, the controversy is the "one man, one vote" problem. Does the city rule, or do "upstate" and "downstate" areas dominate our political life? The early sentiments voiced by Bryan remain active. Many people today share in the spirit of Vachel Lindsay's bombastic rhetoric:

Prairie avenger, mountain lion,
Bryan, Bryan, Bryan, Bryan,
Gigantic troubadour, speaking like a siege gun,
Smashing Plymouth Rock with his boulders from the West.

In the short run, Bryan and the Populists were defeated. But in the long run, the crusade given impetus by the "Cross of Gold" speech marches on.

William Allen White

What's the Matter with Kansas?

1896

EDITED BY WALTER JOHNSON

It was hot—hot as only Kansas can be under the unrelenting August sun. Politics were boiling as well in Emporia, Kansas. The nomination of thirty-six-year-old William Jennings Bryan as the Democratic-Populist candidate for the Presidency was being assailed by the twenty-eight-year-old editor of the Emporia Gazette as a threat to true "Americanism."

Bryan voiced the protests of an older rural America against the increasing dominance of a new industrial-urban society. Until the closing decade of the nineteenth century, a fairly democratic society had been able to maintain itself largely as a result of the unlimited resources of a land of plenty. All that had been needed was freedom for the individual to exploit these rich resources. But by the stormy nineties, pioneer America had disappeared. And unlimited freedom for the individual in this changed situation now often meant the exploitation of others, an exploitation that was to be seen in its starkest form in the slums, the poverty, and the unemployment of the heartbreaking years from 1893 to 1896.

The silver-tongued orator of the Platte contended that, if democracy were to survive, the federal government must reg-

ulate the menace to freedom by a minority in order to guarantee that all would still have equality of opportunity. To
William Allen White—imbued with the beliefs of the Gospel
of Wealth that governments existed only to protect property
and that unemployment, poverty, and slums were individual
responsibilities—the Democratic-Populist ticket of Bryan
meant the destruction of the American way of life. "In this
American government," he wrote in an editorial, "paternalism plays no part. It is every man for himself. It is a free for
all, and in the end the keenest, most frugal, and most industrious win."

All that summer of '96 White argued with Vernon L. Par-
rington, then teaching at the College of Emporia, who tried
to explain that urban-industrialism had altered the American
scene and that new ideas were necessary to cope with the
new situations. White was adamant. As he denounced the
Democrats and the Populists in his daily editorials, they retaliated by parading through Emporia's dusty streets carrying
signs picturing William Allen White as a jackass.

Then, one day in mid-August, as White was returning from
the Post Office, a group of Populists began to argue
with him. The thermometer stood at 107 that morning. The
red-faced editor was in no mood to debate the campaign in
the stifling heat, but the Populists were incensed over the Gazette's editorials. Finally he broke away, with his brain—and
his emotions—sizzling. When he reached the Gazette office,
the editorial page needed more copy. He sat down at his old
roll-top desk and, with his big pen scratching across the
paper, he ridiculed Bryan, the Democrats, and the Populists
in slashing, picturesque language.

TODAY the Kansas department of agriculture sent out a
statement which indicates that Kansas has gained less
than two thousand people in the past year. There are about
125,000 families in the state, and there were about 10,000
babies born in Kansas, and yet so many people have left the
state the natural increase is cut down to less than 2,000
net.

This has been going on for eight years.

If there had been a high brick wall around the state eight
years ago, and not a soul had been admitted or permitted to
leave, Kansas would be a half million souls better off than

The text is taken from the *Emporia Gazette*, August 16, 1896.

she is today. And yet the nation has increased in population. In five years ten million people have been added to the national population, yet instead of gaining a share of this—say, half a million—Kansas has apparently been a plague spot and, in the very garden of the world, has lost population by the ten thousands every year.

Not only has she lost population, but she has lost wealth. Every moneyed man in the state who could get out without great loss has gone. Every month in every community sees someone who has a little money pick up and leave the state. This has been going on for eight years. Money is being drained out all the time. In towns where ten years ago there were three or four or half a dozen money-lending concerns, stimulating industry by furnishing capital, there is now none, or one or two that are looking after the interests and principal already outstanding.

No one brings any money into Kansas any more. What community knows over one or two men who have moved in with more than $5,000 in the past three years. And what community cannot count half a score of men in that time who have left, taking all the money they could scrape together.

Yet the nation has grown rich. Other states have increased in population and wealth—other neighboring states. Missouri has gained nearly two million, while Kansas has been losing half a million. Nebraska has gained in wealth and in population while Kansas has gone downhill. Colorado has gained in every way, while Kansas has lost in every way since 1888.

What is the matter with Kansas?

There is no substantial city in the state. Every big town save one has lost in population. Yet Kansas City, Omaha, Lincoln, St. Louis, Denver, Colorado Springs, Sedalia, Des Moines, the cities of the Dakotas, St. Paul and Minneapolis —all cities and towns in the West, have steadily grown.

Take up the Government Blue Book and you will see that Kansas is virtually off the map. Two or three little scabby consular places in yellow fever stricken communities that do not aggregate ten thousand dollars a year is all the recognition Kansas has. Nebraska draws about one hundred thousand dollars; little old North Dakota draws fifty thousand dollars; Oklahoma doubles Kansas; Missouri leaves her a thousand miles behind; Colorado is almost seven times greater than Kansas—the whole west is ahead of Kansas.

Take it by any standard you please, Kansas is not in it.

Go east and you hear them laugh at Kansas; go west and they sneer at her; go south and they "cuss" her; go north and they have forgotten her. Go into any crowd of intelligent people gathered anywhere on the globe, and you will find the Kansas man on the defensive. The newspaper columns and magazines once devoted to praise of the state, to boastful facts and startling figures concerning her resources, are now filled with cartoons, jibes and Pefferian speeches. Kansas just naturally isn't in the civilized world. She has traded places with Arkansas and Timbuctoo.

What's the matter with Kansas?

We all know; yet here we are at it again. We have an old mossback Jacksonian who snorts and howls because there is a bathtub in the State house; we are running that old jay for governor. We have another shabby, wild-eyed, rattle-brained fanatic who has said openly in a dozen speeches that "the rights of the user are paramount to the rights of the owner"; we are running him for chief justice, so that capital will come tumbling over itself to get into the state. We have raked the ash heap of human failure in the state and found an old hoop skirt of a man who has failed as a businessman, who has failed as an editor, who has failed as a preacher, and we are going to run him for congressman-at-large. He will help the looks of the Kansas delegation in Washington. Then we have discovered a kid without a law practice and have decided to vote for him as attorney general. Then, for fear some hint that the state had become respectable might percolate through the civilized portions of the nation, we have decided to send three or four harpies out lecturing, telling the people that Kansas is raising hell and letting the corn go to weeds.

Oh, this is a state to be proud of! We are a people who can hold up our heads! What we need here is less money, less capital, fewer white shirts and brains, fewer men with business judgment, and more of these fellows who boast that they are "just ordinary old clodhoppers, but that they know more in a minute about finance than John Sherman"; we need more men who are "posted," who can bellow about the crime of '73, who hate prosperity, and who think that because a man believes in national honor, that he is a tool of Wall street. We have had a few of them—some hundred fifty thousand—but we want more.

We need several thousand gibbering idiots to scream about the "Great Red Dragon" of Lombard street. We don't need population, we don't need wealth, we don't need well-dressed men on the streets; we don't need standing in the nation; we don't need cities on these fertile prairies; you bet we don't! What we are after is the money power. Because we have become poorer and ornerier and meaner than a spavined, distempered mule, we, the people of Kansas, propose to kick; we don't care to build up, we wish to tear down.

"There are two ideas of government," said our noble Bryan at Chicago. "There are those who believe that if you just legislate to make the well-to-do prosperous, their prosperity will leak through on those below. The Democratic idea has been that if you legislate to make the masses prosperous their prosperity will find its way up and through every class and rest upon us."

That's the stuff! Give the prosperous man the dickens! Legislate the thriftless into ease, whack the stuffing out of the creditors and tell the debtor who borrowed money five years ago when money in circulation was more general than it is now, that the contraction of currency gives him a right to repudiate.

Whoop it up for the ragged trousers; put the lazy, greasy fizzle, who can't pay his debts on an altar and bow down and worship him. Let the state ideal be high. What we need is not the respect of our fellow men, but a chance to get something for nothing.

Oh, yes, Kansas is a great state. Here are people fleeing from it by the score every day, capital going out of the state by the hundreds of dollars; and every industry except farming paralyzed, and that crippled, because its products have to go across the ocean before they can find a laboring man at work who can afford to buy them. Let's don't stop this year. Let's drive all the decent, self-respecting men out of the state. Let's keep the old clodhoppers who know it all. Let's encourage the man who is "posted". He can talk, and what we need is not mill hands to eat our meat, nor factory hands to eat our wheat, nor cities to oppress the farmer by consuming his butter and eggs and chickens and produce; what Kansas needs is men who can talk, who have large leisure to argue the currency question while their wives wait at home for that nickel's worth of bluing.

What's the matter with Kansas?

Nothing under the shining sun. She is losing wealth, population and standing. She has got her statesmen, and the money power is afraid of her. Kansas is all right. She has started in to raise hell, as Mrs. Lease advised, and she seems to have an over-production. But that doesn't matter. Kansas never did believe in diversified crops. Kansas is all right. There is absolutely nothing wrong with Kansas. "Every prospect pleases and only man is vile."

☆

White's biting, sarcastic language in "What's the Matter with Kansas?" expressed views held by millions of his fellow citizens. H. H. Kohlsaat, publisher of the Chicago Times-Herald *and* Evening Post, *reprinted the editorial, explaining to his readers: "This is one of the most bitterly ironical arraignments of the shiftless spirit that has handicapped that rich state." The* New York Sun *followed suit and then Mark Hanna, chairman of the Republican National Committee, had it distributed across the nation as a campaign document. And White was deeply flattered when his political idol, B. Reed, speaking in the House of Representatives, wrote him on September 17, 1896: "Would you have the goodness to present to the author of 'The Matter With Kansas' my personal thanks. I have not seen as much sense in one column in a dozen years."*

Yet in just a few years the young conservative editor of the Emporia Gazette *was to become a loyal supporter and publicist of Theodore Roosevelt's attack on the "malefactors of great wealth." And he would join T. R. in 1912 to do battle for the Lord and the Bull Moose party. Roosevelt's New Nationalism—profoundly influenced by Herbert Croly's book,* The Promise of American Life—*was a far more comprehensive demand for enlarging the power of the federal government to regulate the economy than that of Bryan and the Populists. As White himself said many years later: "All we Progressives did was catch the Populists in swimming and steal all their clothing except the frayed underdrawers of Free Silver."*

The Progressive Era from 1901 to World War I was a period of rapid readjustment in American attitudes. Under the leadership of Theodore Roosevelt, Woodrow Wilson, Senator Robert M. La Follette, Governor Hiram Johnson, and a host of others, and influenced by the "muckrake" writings of Lincoln Steffens, Ida Tarbell, and Ray Stannard Baker, and by the novels of Winston Churchill, Upton Sinclair, and William Allen White, millions of middle-class citizens became convinced that unlimited freedom for the individual to amass great wealth and wield immense political power had become a threat to the continuation of American democracy. To counteract private power on a scale unheard of before in the United States, these progressive-minded citizens supported the expansion of governmental power to curb the misuse of private power.

Although the now-famous editor of the Emporia Gazette

no longer believed in the ideas of the Gospel of Wealth as he had expressed them in "What's the Matter with Kansas?" many of these ideas survived the Progressive Era and occupied a prominent place in the decade of the 1920's. Certainly Calvin Coolidge, who epitomized the political thinking of the prosperous twenties, found the Gospel of Wealth most congenial, as did the large majority of citizens who supported him.

But another economic depression—even more serious than that of the 1890's—shook the faith of the majority in the doctrine of strictly limited governmental power. Nevertheless, despite the social and political changes of the era of the New Deal, some Americans have continued to have a deep, abiding faith in many of the ideas of the Gospel of Wealth and a contempt for social legislation. Such legislation, in their opinion, transports "the thirties into ease," it "whacks the stuffings out of the creditors," and offers a "chance to get something for nothing." It is significant that, until his death in 1944, William Allen White received thousands of requests yearly for copies of his famed editorial—requests which were invariably met from the large stack of reprints in the Gazette office.

During the 1950's a number of writers—both of a conservative and a liberal bent—charged the Populists with being, among other things, irrational, anti-intellectual, antiforeign, and anti-Semitic demagogues. William Allen White never accused the Populists of being anti-Jewish or antiforeign, but such phrases as "old mossback Jacksonian who snorts and howls," "shabby, wild-eyed, rattle-brained fanatic," and "gibbering idiots" helped shape a mythology about the Populists which some later writers have embellished.

Contempt for the unsuccessful, so blatantly expressed in "What's the Matter with Kansas?" has been a deep current in American thinking. The followers of Theodore Roosevelt, Woodrow Wilson, Franklin D. Roosevelt, Harry S Truman, and John F. Kennedy have been willing through governmental legislation and regulation to help protect people from exploitation and to aid the victims of unforeseen economic disasters to regain the opportunity to forge ahead. But they have not been inclined, any more than their conservative opponents, to put "the lazy, greasy fizzle who can't pay his debts on an altar and bow down and worship him."

Although William Allen White's scathing editorial is an

overdrawn picture of the Populists, it reflects much of the thinking of the 1890's. And its belief in the value of hard work, in the necessity of individual initiative, and in the importance of being successful are still deeply ingrained in the American conscience.

Oliver Wendell Holmes, Jr.

The Path of the Law

1897

EDITED BY LON L. FULLER

"The Path of the Law" was originally an oration in the sense that term bore when it could be used without irony or hint of disparagement. It was indeed, in the language of the time, an elegant oration. The date was January 8, 1897; the occasion was the dedication of a new building of the Boston University School of Law. Holmes was then fifty-five and had been a member of the Supreme Judicial Court of Massachusetts for fourteen years. Some five years later President Theodore Roosevelt appointed him to the Supreme Court of the United States, where he served for thirty years. It has truly been said of him that he is the only American jurist who competes with John Marshall for the superlative. There can be no doubt that the most familiar summing up of his thought is to be found in "The Path of the Law."

The course of Holmes's intellectual development prior to "The Path of the Law" makes it plain that "The Path" is best understood as a reaction against two strains of legal thought current in Holmes's time which he found thoroughly uncongenial.

The first of these reveals its influence quite plainly in the animadversions against "logic" with which Part II of "The Path" is sprinkled. During the period from about 1870 to 1920, it was quite common to encounter in legal discussions statements like these: An offer is by its very nature revocable. It would be a violation of logic to permit a person who is not a party to a contract to sue on it. The legal nature of a claim to damages does not permit an assignment of it. Holmes himself once described this method by saying that the schools "take their premises on inspiration and then use logic as the only tool to develop the results."

The other object of Holmes's intellectual aversion lay in the "will theory," a theory that tended to rest legal responsibility not on what a defendant did, but on what he "willed." Thus, a contractual promisor was held to his promise because he "willed" to be held, or a criminal was punished because he "willed" an evil act. Holmes saw in this kind of reasoning a confusion of morality and law, and he set about in Part I to remove that confusion.

A remarkable amalgam of abstract logic and the will theory can be found in the writings of Christopher Columbus Langdell, Dean of the Harvard Law School from 1870 to 1895. In Langdell's day it had been pretty well established, for sound commercial reasons, that the posted acceptance of an offer to enter a contract is effective at the moment of posting, and before it reaches the mind, or even the mail slot, of the offeror. Since this rule imposed a contract on the parties before their wills had been brought together by a completed circuit, Langdell condemned the rule as a violation of proper legal reasoning. In response to an argument that the rule in question best served "the purposes of substantial justice, and the interests of contracting parties as understood by themselves," Langdell replied, "The true answer to this argument is, that it is irrelevant," though, to be sure, he continued with a half-hearted and highly abstract attempt to demonstrate that the rule in question did in fact serve badly the needs of commerce.

To the mental torment that such an argument was certain to inflict on Holmes, there was added another dimension. Having taught himself German, Holmes became exposed to the Teutonic version of Langdellian logic. In this version, what might in an American have been dismissed as an innocent naiveté, appeared now clothed with a cosmic profundity that made it doubly offensive to one of Holmes's skeptical temper.

One influence that probably shaped Holmes's thought affirmatively was the positivistic philosophy of science asso-

ciated with the names of Bacon, Comte, Mach, Poincaré, and Pearson. There is certainly a close affinity between Holmes's predictive theory of law and a view that asks of the scientist not that he understand nature, but that he simply set about observing and charting her regularities. Holmes himself, after reading Pearson's Grammar of Science, *wrote to Pollock that it "hits my way of thinking better than books of philosophy." But this acquaintance with Pearson came some nine years after "The Path of the Law." Since there is no evidence that Holmes was ever a close student of the philosophy of science, it seems likely that we are dealing not with anything like a direct influence, but with independent expressions of a generally prevailing intellectual mood.*

It was no accident that Holmes seized the occasion he did for presenting the thoughts of "The Path of the Law." A friend, Melville M. Bigelow, had been a leading figure in the creation of the Boston University School of Law. With Holmes he shared a tough, Darwinian approach to social phenomena. Bigelow's general conception of law was expressed in 1906 in a book with a curious but significant title, Centralization of the Law. *This book urged a "scientific method in law and education." It declared:*

> *The conception of law which the Faculty of the Boston University Law School stands for is that the law is the expression, more or less deflected by opposition, of the dominant force in society. . . . It follows from the view that law is the resultant of actual, conflicting forces in society, that the notion of abstract, eternal principles as a governing power, with their author the external sovereign, must go.*

The transition from this passage to Holmes's own words is an easy one.

I

WHEN we study law we are not studying a mystery but a well known profession. We are studying what we shall want in order to appear before judges, or to advise people in

---

"The Path of the Law" first appeared in print as an article in the *Harvard Law Review*, X (1897), 457 ff. As it appears here it has been abridged by about one half. Commentators have remarked that the article is really divided into two distinct parts; Roman numerals have been inserted to make this division plain. In Holmes's own words, the first part deals with "the limits of the law," the second with "the forces which determine its content and its growth."

such a way as to keep them out of court. The reason why it is a profession, why people will pay lawyers to argue for them or to advise them, is that in societies like ours the command of the public force is intrusted to the judges in certain cases, and the whole power of the state will be put forth, if necessary, to carry out their judgments and decrees. People want to know under what circumstances and how far they will run the risk of coming against what is so much stronger than themselves, and hence it becomes a business to find out when this danger is to be feared. The object of our study, then, is prediction, the prediction of the incidence of the public force through the instrumentality of the courts.

The means of the study are a body of reports, of treatises, and of statutes, in this country and in England, extending back for six hundred years, and now increasing annually by hundreds. In these sibylline leaves are gathered the scattered prophecies of the past upon the cases in which the axe will fall. These are what properly have been called the oracles of the law. Far the most important and pretty nearly the whole meaning of every new effort of legal thought is to make these prophecies more precise, and to generalize them into a thoroughly connected system. The process is one, from a lawyer's statement of a case, eliminating as it does all the dramatic elements with which his client's story has clothed it, and retaining only the facts of legal import, up to the final analyses and abstract universals of theoretic jurisprudence. The reason why a lawyer does not mention that his client wore a white hat when he made a contract, while Mrs. Quickly would be sure to dwell upon it along with the parcel gilt goblet and the sea-coal fire, is that he foresees that the public force will act in the same way whatever his client had upon his head. It is to make the prophecies easier to be remembered and to be understood that the teachings of the decisions of the past are put into general propositions and gathered into text-books, or that statutes are passed in a general form. The primary rights and duties with which jurisprudence busies itself again are nothing but prophecies. One of the many evil effects of the confusion between legal and moral ideas, about which I shall have something to say in a moment, is that theory is apt to get the cart before the horse, and to consider the right or the duty as something existing apart from and independent of the consequences of its breach, to which certain sanctions are added afterward. But, as I shall try to show, a legal duty so called is nothing but a prediction that if a man does or omits certain things he will be made to suffer in this or that way by judgment of the court;—and so of a legal right. . . .

I wish, if I can, to lay down some first principles for the study of this body of dogma or systematized prediction which we call the law, for men who want to use it as the instrument of their business to enable them to prophesy in their turn, and, as bearing upon the study, I wish to point out an ideal which as yet our law has not attained.

The first thing for a business-like understanding of the matter is to understand its limits, and therefore I think it desirable at once to point out and dispel a confusion between morality and law, which sometimes rises to the height of conscious theory, and more often and indeed constantly is making trouble in detail without reaching the point of consciousness. You can see very plainly that a bad man has as much reason as a good one for wishing to avoid an encounter with the public force, and therefore you can see the practical importance of the distinction between morality and law. A man who cares nothing for an ethical rule which is believed and practised by his neighbors is likely nevertheless to care a good deal to avoid being made to pay money, and will want to keep out of jail if he can.

I take it for granted that no hearer of mine will misinterpret what I have to say as the language of cynicism. The law is the witness and external deposit of our moral life. Its history is the history of the moral development of the race. The practice of it, in spite of popular jests, tends to make good citizens and good men. When I emphasize the difference between law and morals I do so with reference to a single end, that of learning and understanding the law. For that purpose you must definitely master its specific marks, and it is for that that I ask you for the moment to imagine yourselves indifferent to other and greater things.

I do not say that there is not a wider point of view from which the distinction between law and morals becomes of secondary or no importance, as all mathematical distinctions vanish in presence of the infinite. But I do say that that distinction is of the first importance for the object which we are here to consider,—a right study and mastery of the law as a business with well understood limits, a body of dogma enclosed within definite lines. I have just shown the practical reason for saying so. If you want to know the law and nothing else, you must look at it as a bad man, who cares only for the material consequences which such knowledge enables him to predict, not as a good one, who finds his reasons for conduct, whether inside the law or outside of it, in the vaguer sanctions of conscience. The theoretical importance of the distinction is no less, if you would reason on your subject aright. The law is full of phraseology drawn from morals, and by the mere force of language continually invites us to pass from one domain to the other without perceiving it, as we are sure to do unless we have the boundary constantly before our minds. The law talks about rights, and duties, and malice, and intent, and negligence, and so forth, and nothing is easier, or, I may say, more common in legal reasoning, than to take these words in their moral sense, at some stage of the argument, and so to drop into fallacy. For instance, when we speak of the rights of man in a moral sense, we mean to mark the limits of interference with individual freedom which we think are prescribed by conscience, or by our ideal, however reached. Yet it is certain that many laws have been enforced in the past, and it is likely that some are enforced now, which are condemned by the most enlightened opinion of the time, or which at all events pass the limit of interference as many consciences would draw it. Manifestly, therefore, nothing but confusion of thought can result from assuming that the rights of man in a moral sense are equally rights in the sense of the Constitution and the law. No doubt simple and extreme cases can be put of imaginable laws which the statute-making power would not dare to enact, even in the absence of written constitutional prohibitions, because the community would rise in rebellion and fight; and this gives some plausibility to the proposition that the law, if not a part of morality, is limited by it. But this limit of power is not coextensive with any system of morals. For the most part it falls far within the lines of any such system, and in some cases may extend beyond them, for reasons drawn from the habits of a particular people at a particular time. I once heard the late Professor Agassiz say that a German population would rise if you added two cents to the price of a glass of beer. A statute in such a case would be empty words, not because it was wrong, but because it could not be enforced. No one will deny that wrong statutes can be and are enforced, and we should not all agree as to which were the wrong ones.

The confusion with which I am dealing besets confessedly legal conceptions. Take the fundamental question, What constitutes the law? You will find some text writers telling you that it is something different from what is decided by the courts of Massachusetts or England, that it is a system of reason, that it is a deduction from principles of ethics or admitted axioms or what not, which may or may not coincide with the decisions. But if we take the view of our friend the bad man we shall find that he does not care two straws for the axioms or deductions, but that he does want to know what the Massachusetts or English courts are likely to do in fact. I am much of his mind. The prophecies of what the courts will do in fact, and nothing more pretentious, are what I mean by the law.

Take again a notion which as popularly understood is the widest conception which the law contains;—the notion of legal duty, to which already I have referred. We fill the word with all the content which we draw from morals. But what does it mean to a bad man? Mainly, and in the first place, a prophecy that if he does certain things he will be subjected to disagreeable consequences by way of imprisonment or compulsory payment of money. But from his point of view, what is the difference between being fined and being taxed a certain sum for doing a certain thing? That his point of view is the test of legal principles is shown by the many discussions which have arisen in the courts on the very question whether a given statutory liability is a penalty or a tax. On the answer to this question depends the decision whether conduct is legally wrong or right, and also whether a man is under compulsion or free. Leaving the criminal law on one side, what is the difference between the liability under the mill acts or statutes authorizing a taking by eminent domain and the liability for what we call a wrongful conversion of property where restoration is out of the question? In both cases the party taking another man's property has to pay its fair value as assessed by a jury, and no more. What significance is there in calling one taking right and another wrong from the point of view of the law? It does not matter, so far as the given consequence, the compulsory payment, is concerned, whether the act to which it is attached is described in terms of praise or in terms of blame, or whether the law purports to prohibit it or to allow it. . . .

Nowhere is the confusion between legal and moral ideas more manifest than in the law of contract. Among other things, here again the so called primary rights and duties are invested with a mystic significance beyond what can be assigned and explained. The duty to keep a contract at common law means a prediction that you must pay damages if you do not keep it,—and nothing else. If you commit a tort, you are liable to pay a compensatory sum. If you commit a contract, you are liable to pay a compensatory sum unless the promised event comes to pass, and that is all the difference. . . .

I have spoken only of the common law, because there are some cases in which a logical justification can be found for speaking of civil liabilities as imposing duties in an intelligible sense. These are the relatively few in which equity will grant an injunction, and will enforce it by putting the defendant in prison or otherwise punishing him unless he complies with the order of the court. But I hardly think it advisable to shape general theory from the exception, and I think it would be better to cease troubling ourselves about primary rights and sanctions altogether, than to describe our prophecies concerning the liabilities commonly imposed by the law in those inappropriate terms. . . .

. . . Morals deal with the actual internal state of the individual's mind, what he actually intends. From the time of the Romans down to now, this mode of dealing has affected the language of the law as to contract, and the language used has reacted upon the thought. We talk about a contract as a meeting of the minds of the parties, and thence it is inferred in various cases that there is no contract because their minds have not met; that is, because they have intended different things or because one party has not known of the assent of the other. Yet nothing is more certain than that parties may be bound by a contract to things which neither of them intended, and when one does not know of the other's assent. Suppose a contract is executed in due form and in writing to deliver a lecture, mentioning no time. One of the parties thinks that the promise will be construed to mean at once, within a week. The other thinks that it means when he is ready. The court says that it means within a reasonable time. The parties are bound by the contract as it is interpreted by the court, yet neither of them meant what the court declares that they have said. In my opinion no one will understand the true theory of contract or be able even to discuss some fundamental questions intelligently until he has understood that all contracts are formal, that the making of a contract depends not on the agreement of two minds in one intention, but on the agreement of two sets of external signs,—not on the parties' having *meant* the same thing but on their having *said* the same thing. . . .

II

So much for the limits of the law. The next thing which I wish to consider is what are the forces which determine its content and its growth. You may assume, with Hobbes and Bentham and Austin, that all law emanates from the sovereign, even when the first human beings to enunciate it are the judges, or you may think that law is the voice of the Zeitgeist, or what you like. It is all one to my present purpose.

Even if every decision required the sanction of an emperor with despotic power and a whimsical turn of mind, we should be interested none the less, still with a view to prediction, in discovering some order, some rational explanation, and some principle of growth for the rules which he laid down. In every system there are such explanations and principles to be found. It is with regard to them that a second fallacy comes in, which I think it important to expose.

The fallacy to which I refer is the notion that the only force at work in the development of the law is logic. In the broadest sense, indeed, that notion would be true. The postulate on which we think about the universe is that there is a fixed quantitative relation between every phenomenon and its antecedents and consequents. If there is such a thing as a phenomenon without these fixed quantitative relations, it is a miracle. It is outside the law of cause and effect, and as such transcends our power of thought, or at least is something to or from which we cannot reason. The condition of our thinking about the universe is that it is capable of being thought about rationally, or, in other words, that every part of it is effect and cause in the same sense in which those parts are with which we are most familiar. So in the broadest sense it is true that the law is a logical development, like everything else. The danger of which I speak is not the admission that the principles governing other phenomena also govern the law, but the notion that a given system, ours, for instance, can be worked out like mathematics from some general axioms of conduct. . . .

This mode of thinking is entirely natural. The training of lawyers is a training in logic. The processes of analogy, discrimination, and deduction are those in which they are most at home. The language of judicial decision is mainly the language of logic. And the logical method and form flatter that longing for certainty and for repose which is in every human mind. But certainty generally is illusion, and repose is not the destiny of man. Behind the logical form lies a judgment as to the relative worth and importance of competing legislative grounds, often an inarticulate and unconscious judgment, it is true, and yet the very root and nerve of the whole proceeding. . . . We do not realize how large a part of our law is open to reconsideration upon a slight change in the habit of the public mind. No concrete proposition is self-evident, no matter how ready we may be to accept it, not even Mr. Herbert Spencer's. Every man has a right to do what he wills, provided he interferes not with a like right on the part of his neighbors.

Why is a false and injurious statement privileged, if it is made honestly in giving information about a servant? It is because it has been thought more important that information should be given freely, than that a man should be protected from what under other circumstances would be an actionable wrong. Why is a man at liberty to set up a business which he knows will ruin his neighbor? It is because the public good is supposed to be best subserved by free competition. Obviously such judgments of relative importance may vary in different times and places. . . .

I think that the judges themselves have failed adequately to recognize their duty of weighing considerations of social advantage. The duty is inevitable, and the result of the often proclaimed judicial aversion to deal with such considerations is simply to leave the very ground and foundation of judgments inarticulate, and often unconscious, as I have said. When socialism first began to be talked about, the comfortable classes of the community were a good deal frightened. I suspect that this fear has influenced judicial action both here and in England, yet it is certain that it is not a conscious factor in the decisions to which I refer. I think that something similar has led people who no longer hope to control the legislatures to look to the courts as expounders of the Constitutions, and that in some courts new principles have been discovered outside the bodies of those instruments, which may be generalized into acceptance of the economic doctrines which prevailed about fifty years ago, and a wholesale prohibition of what a tribunal of lawyers does not think about right. I cannot but believe that if the training of lawyers led them habitually to consider more definitely and explicitly the social advantage on which the rule they lay down must be justified, they sometimes would hesitate where now they are confident, and see that really they were taking sides upon debatable and often burning questions.

So much for the fallacy of logical form. Now let us consider the present condition of the law as a subject for study, and the ideal toward which it tends. We still are far from the point of view which I desire to see reached. No one has reached it or can reach it as yet. We are only at the beginning of a philosophical reaction, and of a reconsideration of the worth of doctrines which for the most part still are taken for granted without any deliberate, conscious, and systematic questioning of their grounds. The development of our law has gone on for nearly a thousand years, like the development of a plant, each generation taking the inevitable next step, mind, like matter, simply obeying a law of spontaneous growth. It is perfectly natural and right that it should have been so. Imitation is a necessity of human nature, as has been illustrated by a remarkable French writer, M. Tarde, in an admirable book, "Les Lois de l'Imitation." Most of the things we do, we do for no better reason than that our fathers have done them or that our neighbors do them, and the same is true of a larger part than we suspect of what we think. The reason is a good one, because our short life gives us no time for a better, but it is not the best. It does not follow, because we all are compelled to take on faith at second hand most of the rules on which we base our action and our thought, that each of us may not try to set some corner of his world in the order of reason, or that all of us collectively should not aspire to carry reason as far as it will go throughout the whole domain. In regard to the law, it is true, no doubt, that an evolutionist will hesitate to affirm universal validity for his social ideals, or for the principles which he thinks should be embodied in legislation. He is content if he can prove them best for here and now. He may be ready to admit that he knows nothing about an absolute best in the cosmos, and even that he knows next to nothing about a permanent best for men. Still it is true that a body of law is more rational and more civilized when every rule it contains is referred articulately and definitely to an end which it subserves, and when the grounds for desiring that end are stated or are ready to be stated in words. . . .

. . . The rational study of law is still to a large extent a study of history. History must be a part of the study, because without it we cannot know the precise scope of rules which it is our business to know. It is a part of the rational study, because it is the first step toward an enlightened scepticism, that is, toward a deliberate reconsideration of the worth of those rules. When you get the dragon out of his cave on to the plain and in the daylight, you can count his teeth and claws, and see just what is his strength. But to get him out is only the first step. The next is either to kill him, or to tame him and make him a useful animal. For the rational study of the law the black-letter man may be the man of the present, but the man of the future is the man of statistics and the master of economics. It is revolting to have no better reason for a rule of law than that so it was laid down in the time of Henry IV. It is still more revolting if the grounds upon which it was laid down have vanished long since, and the rule simply persists from blind imitation of the past. I am thinking of the technical rule as to trespass *ab initio*, as it is called, which I attempted to explain in a recent Massachusetts case. . . .

Far more fundamental questions still await a better answer than that we do as our fathers have done. What have we better than a blind guess to show that the criminal law in its present form does more good than harm? I do not stop to refer to the effect which it has had in degrading prisoners and in plunging them further into crime, or to the question whether fine and imprisonment do not fall more heavily on a criminal's wife and children than on himself. I have in mind more far-reaching questions. Does punishment deter? Do we deal with criminals on proper principles? A modern school of Continental criminalists plumes itself on the formula, first suggested, it is said, by Gall, that we must consider the criminal rather than the crime. The formula does not carry us very far, but the inquiries which have been started look toward an answer of my questions based on science for the first time. If the typical criminal is a degenerate, bound to swindle or to murder by as deep seated an organic necessity as that which makes the rattlesnake bite, it is idle to talk of deterring him by the classical method of imprisonment. He must be got rid of; he cannot be improved, or frightened out of his structural reaction. If, on the other hand, crime, like normal human conduct, is mainly a matter of imitation, punishment fairly may be expected to help to keep it out of fashion. The study of criminals has been thought by some well known men of science to sustain the former hypothesis. The statistics of the relative increase of crime in crowded places like large cities, where example has the greatest chance to work, and in less populated parts, where the contagion spreads more slowly, have been used with great force in favor of the latter view. But there is weighty authority for the belief that, however this may be, "not the nature of the crime, but the dangerousness of the criminal, constitutes the only reasonable legal criterion to guide the inevitable social reaction against the criminal." . . .

I trust that no one will understand me to be speaking with disrespect of the law, because I criticise it so freely. I venerate the law, and especially our system of law, as one of the vastest products of the human mind. No one knows better than I do the countless number of great intellects that have spent themselves in making some addition or improvement, the greatest of which is trifling when compared with the mighty whole. It has the final title to respect that it exists, that it is not a Hegelian dream, but a part of the lives of men. But one may criticise even what one reveres. Law is the business to which my life is devoted, and I should show less than devotion if I did not do what in me lies to improve it, and, when I perceive what seems to me the ideal of its future, if I hesitated to point it out and to press toward it with all my heart. . . .

. . . I look forward to a time when the part played by history in the explanation of dogma shall be very small, and instead of ingenious research we shall spend our energy on a study of the ends sought to be attained and the reasons for desiring them. As a step toward that ideal it seems to me that every lawyer ought to seek an understanding of economics. The present divorce between the schools of political economy and law seems to me an evidence of how much progress in philosophical study still remains to be made. In the present state of political economy, indeed, we come again upon history on a larger scale, but there we are called on to consider and weigh the ends of legislation, the means of attaining them, and the cost. We learn that for everything we have to give up something else, and we are taught to set the advantage we gain against the other advantage we lose, and to know what we are doing when we elect.

There is another study which sometimes is undervalued by the practical minded, for which I wish to say a good word, although I think a good deal of pretty poor stuff goes under that name. I mean the study of what is called jurisprudence. Jurisprudence, as I look at it, is simply law in its most generalized part. Every effort to reduce a case to a rule is an effort of jurisprudence, although the name as used in English is confined to the broadest rules and most fundamental conceptions. One mark of a great lawyer is that he sees the application of the broadest rules. There is a story of a Vermont justice of the peace before whom a suit was brought by one farmer against another for breaking a churn. The justice took time to consider, and then said that he had looked through the statutes and could find nothing about churns, and gave judgment for the defendant. The same state of mind is shown in all our common digests and text-books. Applications of rudimentary rules of contract or tort are tucked away under the head of Railroads or Telegraphs or go to swell treatises on historical subdivisions, such as Shipping or Equity, or are gathered under an arbitrary title which is thought likely to appeal to the practical mind, such as Mercantile Law. If a man goes into law it pays to be a master of it, and to be a master of it means to look straight through all the dramatic incidents and to discern the true basis for prophecy. Therefore, it is well to have an accurate notion of what you mean by law, by a right, by a duty, by malice, intent, and negligence, by ownership, by possession, and so forth. . . .

I have been speaking about the study of the law, and I have said next to nothing of what commonly is talked about in that connection,—text-books and the case system, and all the machinery with which a student comes most immediately in contact. Nor shall I say anything about them. Theory is my subject, not practical details. The modes of teaching have been improved since my time, no doubt, but ability and industry will master the raw material with any mode. Theory is the most important part of the dogma of the law, as the architect is the most important man who takes part in the building of a house. The most important improvements of the last twenty-five years are improvements in theory. It is not to be feared as unpractical, for, to the competent, it simply means going to the bottom of the subject. For the incompetent, it sometimes is true, as has been said, that an interest in general ideas means an absence of particular knowledge. I remember in army days reading of a youth who, being examined for the lowest grade and being asked a question about squadron drill, answered that he never had considered the evolutions of less than ten thousand men. But the weak and foolish must be left to their folly. The danger is that the able and practical minded should look with indifference or distrust upon ideas the connection of which with their business is remote. I heard a story, the other day, of a man who had a valet to whom he paid high wages, subject to deduction for faults. One of his deductions was, "For lack of imagination, five dollars." The lack is not confined to valets. The object of ambition, power, generally presents itself nowadays in the form of money alone. Money is the most immediate form, and is a proper object of desire. "The fortune," said Rachel, "is the measure of the intelligence." That is a good text to waken people out of a fool's paradise. But, as Hegel says, "It is in the end not the appetite, but the opinion, which has to be satisfied." To an imagination of any scope the most far-reaching form of power is not money, it is the command of ideas. If you want great examples read Mr. Leslie Stephen's "History of English Thought in the Eighteenth Century," and see how a hundred years after his death the abstract speculation of Descartes had become a practical force controlling the conduct of men. Read the works of the great German jurists, and see how much more the world is governed to-day by Kant than by Bonaparte. We cannot all be Descartes or Kant, but we all want happiness. And happiness, I am sure from having known many successful men, cannot be won simply by being counsel for great corporations and having an income of fifty thousand dollars. An intellect great enough to win the prize needs other food beside success. The remoter and more general aspects of the law are those which give it universal interest. It is through them that you not only become a great master in your calling, but connect your subject with the universe and catch an echo of the infinite, a glimpse of its unfathomable process, a hint of the universal law.

The abuses of reason attacked by Holmes in "The Path" certainly did not disappear the next day. Indeed one of Holmes's concerns, how to keep logic on a suitably taut leash without incapacitating it for proper uses, remains a perennial problem for legal philosophy. What is clear, however, is that a remarkable change in the temper of legal reasoning took place during the first half of this century. No doubt Holmes had his share in bringing this change about. But it is equally certain that it would to some extent have occurred without him. During the same period in Germany and France, for example, a similar reaction was taking place against methods of legal thinking characteristic of the last half of the nineteenth century—methods that on the Continent as well as in this country had become abstract, dogmatic, and Lebensfremd.

Aside from its contribution to a general change in the atmosphere of legal scholarship, Holmes's thought had a quite traceable and significant influence on a movement during the 1920's and '30's that came to be known as American Legal Realism. The participants in this movement, it need hardly be said, were not realists in the Platonic sense; their self-image was that of tough-minded empiricists with little use for abstractions and universals. Holmes took no personal part in this movement and in fact tended to view it with a considerable detachment. No doubt he did not find to his liking what might be called its style. One can hardly imagine his subscribing to the Realist definition of law as "the behavior patterns of judges and other state officials," though this definition merely converted into the clichés of the day his own conception of law as a prophecy of what courts will do in fact.

Perhaps the most infelicitous turn of thought in "The Path" is to be found in Holmes's discussion of legal rights and duties. He accused legal theorists of putting the cart before the horse when they regarded rights and duties as giving rise to consequences—when they said, for example, that the defendant in a particular case had violated a duty and therefore ought to pay damages. According to Holmes, "a legal duty so called is nothing but a prediction that if a man does or omits certain things he will be made to suffer in this or that way by judgment of the court;—and so of a legal right."

Now it is quite true that a bad man—or at least the rather special kind of bad man postulated by Holmes—is not interested in being told about his duties. He simply wants to know how likely he is to be hit by the ax of state power if he follows a particular course of action. On the other hand, he is interested in predicting judicial decisions; this is, indeed, the whole point of his appearance in Holmes's analysis. But if the concept of duty plays no part in the reasoning of judges, it is hard to see how it can serve as a tool of prediction. If the man who enters a contract merely subjects himself to the alternative of performing or of paying damages, it is hard to see why the word "duty" is more appropriate for one branch of this alternative than for the other, or, from the bad man's point of view, why there is any reason to use it at all. In other words, instead of startling his audience with a novel and paradoxical definition of the word "duty," Holmes would have done better simply to have said that from a certain point of view toward the law the term becomes irrelevant.

Unfortunately the confusion Holmes introduced proved contagious. For example, Arthur L. Corbin and Walter Wheeler Cook, following the lead of Wesley Newcomb Hohfeld, became interested in clarifying the meaning of such terms as "duty," "right," "privilege," and "power." They criticized the courts for using these terms in confused and improper ways. In doing so they plainly violated Holmes's injunction not to put the cart before the horse; they were treating duties as giving rise to consequences, as playing a significant role in legal reasoning. On the other hand, they found the predictive theory too attractive to be abandoned; so we find Corbin writing (in the Yale Law Journal, *XXIX*, 163-64:

> When we state that some particular legal relation [such as a duty] exists we are impliedly asserting the existence of certain facts, and we are expressing our present mental concept of the societal consequences that will normally follow in the future. A statement that a legal relation exists between A and B is a prediction as to what society, acting through its courts or executive agents, will do or not do for one and against the other.

Yet if the term "duty" merely expresses a prediction of the probable future course of judicial decisions, whether they are well reasoned or not, it is hard to see how Corbin can criticize courts for using the term improperly, for he certainly doesn't mean that they are incorrectly predicting today what *they are going to do tomorrow. With a proper harness you can put the horse either behind or in front of the cart; the one thing certain is that you can't put him in both places at once. Yet this is precisely what Corbin and Cook—no doubt out of their reverence for Holmes—tried to do.*

Curiously, this confusion could have been avoided if heed had been given to words written by Holmes himself in 1872, a quarter of a century before "The Path." These words plainly refute his whole argument that duty expresses merely vulnerability to a sanction, rather than a reason for imposing a sanction:

> *The notion of duty involves something more than a tax on a certain line of conduct. A protective tariff on iron does not create a duty not to bring it into the country. The word imports the existence of an absolute wish on the part of the power imposing it to bring about a certain course of conduct, and to prevent the contrary. A legal duty cannot be said to exist if the law intends to allow the person supposed to be subject to it an option at a certain price.*

What impulse it was that led Holmes to desert the unexciting wisdom of this passage for the sparkling paradoxes of "The Path" must remain a mystery, though in seeking some clue to it we may recall William James's remark about the friend of his youth: "Wendell amuses me by being composed of at least two and a half different people rolled into one, and the way he keeps them together in one tight skin, without quarrelling any more than they do, is remarkable."

Surveying "The Path" from the perspective of the present, we can safely conclude that the Holmesian influence on American Legal Realism and the Hohfeldian analysis has now run its full course and made its final contribution, whether negative or affirmative.

John Dewey
My Pedagogic Creed
1897

EDITED BY LAWRENCE A. CREMIN

---

*It was in the spring of 1896 that Ossian H. Lang, editor of
the* School Journal, *first conceived the idea of running a series of "pedagogic creeds" by eminent American educators.
Lang, a serious student of the theory and history of education, had long been concerned with what struck him as a pervasive aimlessness among American teachers. "There is something radically and fatally wrong with a teacher who has no
educational creed," he once observed. "Education is a responsible and complicated work, which must be carefully planned
from beginning to end. There must be a definite aim and a
clear understanding of the ways and means of reaching it. In
other words, the educator must have in his mind some fixed
principles of action."*

*How might teachers come by such fixed principles? Lang
thought the writings of the ancients were certainly a prime
source, as were the insights of contemporary Europeans, such
as Pestalozzi, Herbart, and Froebel. Yet something more was
needed. Americans had committed themselves to universal
public education, one of the most novel and radical experiments in history. If the commitment was to mean anything,*

*American teachers would need to work out a whole new set
of principles, thoroughly consistent with the values and demands of their own civilization. And in working out such
principles, there was no better place to begin than the wisdom of their own leaders.*

*Lang's series of "pedagogic creeds" was explicitly designed
to make that wisdom readily available, and his list of invited
authors was appropriately star-studded. It included William
T. Harris, the universally esteemed United States Commissioner of Education; Francis W. Parker, the redoubtable principal
of the Cook County (Illinois) Normal School; Burke A. Hins-
dale, the eminent professor of pedagogy at the University of
Michigan; and a young psychologist named John Dewey, who
had been brought to the University of Chicago in 1894 to
head the combined departments of philosophy, psychology,
and education.*

*We know that Lang's letters of invitation went out during
the spring of 1896; and we know that Dewey's particular
contribution appeared in the* School Journal *for January 16,
1897, as the ninth in the series. Since the various "creeds"
seem to have appeared in order of receipt, Dewey probably
prepared his statement sometime during the autumn of 1896.
That, incidentally, would place the writing squarely within
the formative period of the Laboratory School of the University of Chicago, which Dr. and Mrs. Dewey founded in 1896
for the express purpose of testing in practice the very sort of
proposition Dewey enunciated in the "creed."*

ARTICLE I. WHAT EDUCATION IS.

I BELIEVE that all education proceeds by the participation of
the individual in the social consciousness of the race. This
process begins unconsciously almost at birth, and is continually shaping the individual's powers, saturating his consciousness,
forming his habits, training his ideas, and arousing his feelings and emotions. Through this unconscious education the
individual gradually comes to share in the intellectual and
moral resources which humanity has succeeded in getting together. He becomes an inheritor of the funded capital of civilization. The most formal and technical education in the
world cannot safely depart from this general process. It can
only organize it; or differentiate it in some particular direction.

The text is reprinted as it originally appeared in the *School Journal,*
LIV (January 16, 1897), 77–80.

I believe that the only true education comes through the stimulation of the child's powers by the demands of the social situations in which he finds himself. Through these demands he is stimulated to act as a member of a unity, to emerge from his original narrowness of action and feeling and to conceive of himself from the standpoint of the welfare of the group to which he belongs. Through the responses which others make to his own activities he comes to know what these mean in social terms. The value which they have is reflected back into them. For instance, through the response which is made to the child's instinctive babblings the child comes to know what those babblings mean; they are transformed into articulate language and thus the child is introduced into the consolidated wealth of ideas and emotions which are now summed up in language.

I believe that this educational process has two sides—one psychological and one sociological; and that neither can be subordinated to the other or neglected without evil results following. Of these two sides, the psychological is the basis. The child's own instincts and powers furnish the material and give the starting point for all education. Save as the efforts of the educator connect with some activity which the child is carrying on his own initiative independent of the educator, education becomes reduced to a pressure from without. It may, indeed, give certain external results but cannot truly be called educative. Without insight into the psychological structure and activities of the individual, the educative process will, therefore, be haphazard and arbitrary. If it chances to coincide with the child's activity it will get a leverage; if it does not, it will result in friction, or disintegration, or arrest of the child nature.

I believe that knowledge of social conditions, of the present state of civilization, is necessary in order properly to interpret the child's powers. The child has his own instincts and tendencies, but we do not know what these mean until we can translate them into their social equivalents. We must be able to carry them back into a social past and see them as the inheritance of previous race activities. We must also be able to project them into the future to see what their outcome and end will be. In the illustration just used, it is the ability to see in the child's babblings the promise and potency of a future social intercourse and conversation which enables one to deal in the proper way with that instinct.

I believe that the psychological and social sides are organically related and that education cannot be regarded as a compromise between the two, or a superimposition of one upon the other. We are told that the psychological definition of education is barren and formal—that it gives us only the idea of a development of all the mental powers without giving us any idea of the use to which these powers are put. On the other hand, it is urged that the social definition of education, as getting adjusted to civilization, makes of it a forced and external process, and results in subordinating the freedom of the individual to a preconceived social and political status.

I believe each of these objections is true when urged against one side isolated from the other. In order to know what a power really is we must know what its end, use, or function is; and this we cannot know save as we conceive of the individual as active in social relationships. But, on the other hand, the only possible adjustment which we can give to the child under existing conditions, is that which arises through putting him in complete possession of all his powers. With the advent of democracy and modern industrial conditions, it is impossible to foretell definitely just what civilization will be twenty years from now. Hence it is impossible to prepare the child for any precise set of conditions. To prepare him for the future life means to give him command of himself; it means so to train him that he will have the full and ready use of all his capacities; that his eye and ear and hand may be tools ready to command, that his judgment may be capable of grasping the conditions under which it has to work, and the executive forces be trained to act economically and efficiently. It is impossible to reach this sort of adjustment save as constant regard is had to the individual's own powers, tastes, and interests—say, that is, as education is continually converted into psychological terms.

In sum, I believe that the individual who is to be educated is a social individual and that society is an organic union of individuals. If we eliminate the social factor from the child we are left only with an abstraction; if we eliminate the individual factor from society, we are left only with an inert and lifeless mass. Education, therefore, must begin with a psychological insight into the child's capacities, interests, and habits. It must be controlled at every point by reference to these same considerations. These powers, interests, and habits must be continually interpreted—we must know what they mean. They must be translated into terms of their social equivalents —into terms of what they are capable of in the way of social service.

ARTICLE II. WHAT THE SCHOOL IS.

I believe that the school is primarily a social institution. Education being a social process, the school is simply that form of community life in which all those agencies are concentrated that will be most effective in bringing the child to share in the inherited resources of the race, and to use his own powers for social ends.

I believe that education, therefore, is a process of living and not a preparation for future living.

I believe that the school must represent present life—life as real and vital to the child as that which he carries on in the home, in the neighborhood, or on the play-ground.

I believe that education which does not occur through forms of life, or that are worth living for their own sake, is always a poor substitute for the genuine reality and tends to cramp and to deaden.

I believe that the school, as an institution, should simplify existing social life; should reduce it, as it were, to an embryonic form. Existing life is so complex that the child cannot be brought into contact with it without either confusion or distraction; he is either overwhelmed by the multiplicity of activities which are going on, so that he loses his own power of orderly reaction, or he is so stimulated by these various activities that his powers are prematurely called into play and he becomes either unduly specialized or else disintegrated.

I believe that, as such simplified social life, the school life should grow gradually out of the home life; that it should take up and continue the activities with which the child is already familiar in the home.

I believe that it should exhibit these activities to the child, and reproduce them in such ways that the child will gradually learn the meaning of them, and be capable of playing his own part in relation to them.

I believe that this is a psychological necessity, because it is the only way of securing continuity in the child's growth, the only way of giving a back-ground of past experience to the new ideas given in school.

I believe it is also a social necessity because the home is the form of social life in which the child has been nurtured and in connection with which he has had his moral training. It is the business of the school to deepen and extend his sense of the values bound up in his home life.

I believe that much of present education fails because it neglects this fundamental principle of the school as a form of community life. It conceives the school as a place where certain information is to be given, where certain lessons are to be learned, or where certain habits are to be formed. The value of these is conceived as lying largely in the remote future; the child must do these things for the sake of something else he is to do; they are mere preparation. As a result they do not become a part of the life experience of the child and so are not truly educative.

I believe that the moral education centers about this conception of the school as a mode of social life, that the best and deepest moral training is precisely that which one gets through having to enter into proper relations with others in a unity of work and thought. The present educational systems, so far as they destroy or neglect this unity, render it difficult or impossible to get any genuine, regular moral training.

I believe that the child should be stimulated and controlled in his work through the life of the community.

I believe that under existing conditions far too much of the stimulus and control proceeds from the teacher, because of neglect of the idea of the school as a form of social life.

I believe that the teacher's place and work in the school is to be interpreted from this same basis. The teacher is not in the school to impose certain ideas or to form certain habits in the child, but is there as a member of the community to select the influences which shall affect the child and to assist him in properly responding to these influences.

I believe that the discipline of the school should proceed from the life of the school as a whole and not directly from the teacher.

I believe that the teacher's business is simply to determine on the basis of larger experience and riper wisdom, how the discipline of life shall come to the child.

I believe that all questions of the grading of the child and his promotion should be determined by reference to the same standard. Examinations are of use only so far as they test the child's fitness for social life and reveal the place in which he can be of the most service and where he can receive the most help.

ARTICLE III. THE SUBJECT-MATTER OF EDUCATION.

I believe that the social life of the child is the basis of concentration or correlation, in all his training or growth. The social life gives the unconscious unity and the background of all his efforts and of all his attainments.

I believe that the subject-matter of the school curriculum

should mark a gradual differentiation out of the primitive unconscious unity of social life.

I believe that we violate the child's nature and render difficult the best ethical results, by introducing the child too abruptly to a number of special studies, of reading, writing, geography, etc., out of relation to this social life.

I believe, therefore, that the true center of correlation on the school subjects is not science, nor literature, nor history, nor geography, but the child's own social activities.

I believe that education cannot be unified in the study of science, or so called nature study, because apart from human activity, nature itself is not a unity; nature in itself is a number of diverse objects in space and time, and to attempt to make it the center of work by itself, is to introduce a principle of radiation rather than one of concentration.

I believe that literature is the reflex expression and interpretation of social experience; that hence it must follow upon and not precede such experience. It, therefore, cannot be made the basis, although it may be made the summary of unification.

I believe once more that history is of educative value in so far as it presents phases of social life and growth. It must be controlled by reference to social life. When taken simply as history it is thrown into the distant past and becomes dead and inert. Taken as the record of man's social life and progress it becomes full of meaning. I believe, however, that it cannot be so taken excepting as the child is also introduced directly into social life.

I believe accordingly that the primary basis of education is in the child's powers at work along the same general constructive lines as those which had brought civilization into being.

I believe that the only way to make the child conscious of his social heritage is to enable him to perform those fundamental types of activity which make civilization what it is.

I believe, therefore, in the so-called expressive or constructive activities as the center of correlation.

I believe that this gives the standard for the place of cooking, sewing, manual training, etc., in the school.

I believe that they are not special studies which are to be introduced over and above a lot of others in the way of relaxation or relief, or as additional accomplishments. I believe rather that they represent, as types, fundamental forms of social activity; and that it is possible and desirable that the child's introduction into the more formal subjects of the curriculum be through the medium of these activities.

I believe that the study of science is educational in so far as it brings out the materials and processes which make social life what it is.

I believe that one of the greatest difficulties in the present teaching of science is that the material is presented in purely objective form, or is treated as a new peculiar kind of experience which the child can add to that which he has already had. In reality, science is of value because it gives the ability to interpret and control the experience already had. It should be introduced, not as so much new subject-matter, but as showing the factors already involved in previous experience and as furnishing tools by which that experience can be more easily and effectively regulated.

I believe that at present we lose much of the value of literature and language studies because of our elimination of the social element. Language is almost always treated in the books of pedagogy simply as the expression of thought. It is true that language is a logical instrument, but it is fundamentally and primarily a social instrument. Language is the device for communication; it is the tool through which one individual comes to share the ideas and feelings of others. When treated simply as a way of getting individual information, or as a means of showing off what one has learned, it loses its social motive and end.

I believe that there is, therefore, no succession of studies in the ideal school curriculum. If education is life, all life has, from the outset, a scientific aspect; an aspect of art and culture and an aspect of communication. It cannot, therefore, be true that the proper studies for one grade are mere reading and writing, and that at a later grade, reading, or literature, or science, may be introduced. The progress is not in the succession of studies but in the development of new attitudes towards, and new interests in, experience.

I believe finally, that education must be conceived as a continuing reconstruction of experience; that the process and the goal of education are one and the same thing.

I believe that to set up any end outside of education, as furnishing its goal and standard, is to deprive the educational process of much of its meaning and tends to make us rely upon false and external stimuli in dealing with the child.

ARTICLE IV. THE NATURE OF METHOD.

I believe that the question of method is ultimately reducible to the question of the order of development of the child's powers and interests. The law for presenting and treating material is the law implicit within the child's own nature. Because this is so I believe the following statements are of supreme importance as determining the spirit in which education is carried on:

1. I believe that the active side precedes the passive in the development of the child nature; that expression comes before conscious impression; that the muscular development precedes the sensory; that movements come before conscious sensations; I believe that consciousness is essentially motor or impulsive; that conscious states tend to project themselves in action.

I believe that the neglect of this principle is the cause of a large part of the waste of time and strength in school work. The child is thrown into a passive, receptive or absorbing attitude. The conditions are such that he is not permitted to follow the law of his nature; the result is friction and waste.

I believe that ideas (intellectual and rational processes) also result from action and devolve for the sake of the better control of action. What we term reason is primarily the law of orderly or effective action. To attempt to develop the reasoning powers, the powers of judgment, without reference to the selection and arrangement of means in action, is the fundamental fallacy in our present methods of dealing with this matter. As a result we present the child with arbitrary symbols. Symbols are a necessity in mental development, but they have their place as tools for economizing effort; presented by themselves they are a mass of meaningless and arbitrary ideas imposed from without.

2. I believe that the image is the great instrument of instruction. What a child gets out of any subject presented to him is simply the images which he himself forms with regard to it.

I believe that if nine tenths of the energy at present directed towards making the child learn certain things, were spent in seeing to it that the child was forming proper images, the work of instruction would be indefinitely facilitated.

I believe that much of the time and attention now given to the preparation and presentation of lessons might be more wisely and profitably expended in training the child's power of imagery and in seeing to it that he was continually forming definite, vivid, and growing images of the various subjects with which he comes in contact in his experience.

3. I believe that interests are the signs and symptoms of growing power. I believe that they represent dawning capacities. Accordingly the constant and careful observation of interests is of the utmost importance for the educator.

I believe that these interests are to be observed as showing the state of development which the child has reached.

I believe that they prophesy the stage upon which he is about to enter.

I believe that only through the continual and sympathetic observation of childhood's interests can the adult enter into the child's life and see what it is ready for, and upon what material it could work most readily and fruitfully.

I believe that these interests are neither to be humored nor repressed. To repress interest is to substitute the adult for the child, and so to weaken intellectual curiosity and alertness, to suppress initiative, and to deaden interest. To humor the interests is to substitute the transient for the permanent. The interest is always the sign of some power below; the important thing is to discover this power. To humor the interest is to fail to penetrate below the surface and its sure result is to substitute caprice and whim for genuine interest.

4. I believe that the emotions are the reflex of actions.

I believe that to endeavor to stimulate or arouse the emotions apart from their corresponding activities, is to introduce an unhealthy and morbid state of mind.

I believe that if we can only secure right habits of action and thought, with reference to the good, the true, and the beautiful, the emotions will for the most part take care of themselves.

I believe that next to deadness and dullness, formalism and routine, our education is threatened with no greater evil than sentimentalism.

I believe that this sentimentalism is the necessary result of the attempt to divorce feeling from action.

ARTICLE V. THE SCHOOL AND SOCIAL PROGRESS.

I believe that education is the fundamental method of social progress and reform.

I believe that all reforms which rest simply upon the enactment of law, or the threatening of certain penalties, or upon changes in mechanical or outward arrangements, are transitory and futile.

I believe that education is a regulation of the process of coming to share in the social consciousness; and that the adjustment of individual activity on the basis of this social consciousness is the only sure method of social reconstruction.

I believe that this conception has due regard for both the individualistic and socialistic ideals. It is duly individual because it recognizes the formation of a certain character as the only genuine basis of right living. It is socialistic because it recognizes that this right character is not to be formed by merely individual precept, example, or exhortation, but rather by the influence of a certain form of institutional or community life upon the individual, and that the social organism through the school, as its organ, may determine ethical results.

I believe that in the ideal school we have the reconciliation of the individualistic and the institutional ideals.

I believe that the community's duty to education is, therefore, its paramount moral duty. By law and punishment, by social agitation and discussion, society can regulate and form itself in a more or less haphazard and chance way. But through education society can formulate its own purposes, can organize its own means and resources, and thus shape itself with definiteness and economy in the direction in which it wishes to move.

I believe that when society once recognizes the possibilities in this direction, and the obligations which these possibilities impose, it is impossible to conceive of the resources of time, attention, and money which will be put at the disposal of the educator.

I believe it is the business of every one interested in education to insist upon the school as the primary and most effective interest of social progress and reform in order that society may be awakened to realize what the school stands for, and aroused to the necessity of endowing the educator with sufficient equipment properly to perform his task.

I believe that education thus conceived marks the most perfect and intimate union of science and art conceivable in human experience.

I believe that the art of thus giving shape to human powers and adapting them to social service, is the supreme art; one calling into its service the best of artists; that no insight, sympathy, tact, executive power is too great for such service.

I believe that with the growth of psychological service, giving added insight into individual structure and laws of growth; and with growth of social science, adding to our knowledge of the right organization of individuals, all scientific resources can be utilized for the purposes of education.

I believe that when science and art thus join hands the most commanding motive for human action will be reached; the most genuine springs of human conduct aroused and the best service that human nature is capable of guaranteed.

I believe, finally, that the teacher is engaged, not simply in the training of individuals, but in the formation of the proper social life.

I believe that every teacher should realize the dignity of his calling; that he is a social servant set apart for the maintenance of proper social order and the securing of the right social growth.

I believe that in this way the teacher always is the prophet of the true God and the usherer in of the true kingdom of God.

University   of   Chicago.   JOHN   DEWEY

There is a story that soon after Dewey had drafted his "pedagogic creed," he read it to the faculty of the Cook County Normal School, which had been a leading center of educational reform ever since Colonel Francis W. Parker had assumed the principalship in 1883. Parker, whom Dewey once referred to as the "father of progressive education," was one of those artist-teachers whose zeal for educational improvement is always better expressed in practice than in theory. The story goes that when Dewey finished his reading, Parker jumped to his feet and exclaimed: "This educational theory I have never been able to state satisfactorily. This is what I have been struggling all my life to put into action."

Apparently, Dewey served a whole generation of reformist educators in similar fashion. He was truly one of Emerson's "representative men," those rare individuals who can articulate clearly and fully what their contemporaries feel only vaguely and partially. In brief, Dewey was able to synthesize the many and varied impulses that went to make up the progressive-education movement into a single comprehensive view of education. This view appeared for the first time in the "pedagogic creed." It was elaborated substantially in Dewey's 1899 lecture series, The School and Society. *And it received its fullest—and now classic—statement in what Dewey himself believed to be the most comprehensive philosophical work,* Democracy and Education *(1916). That Dewey's "creed" would somehow stand apart from the others in Lang's series was early apparent. In the* School Journal *for March 20, 1897, John S. Clark, Director of Prang Normal Art Classes in Boston, wrote his contribution to the series simply as a commentary on Dewey's statement, contending that it was the most sound, sensible, and suggestive contribution to the literature of education since Herbert Spencer's essays. In 1898, when Lang republished the whole series in book form, Dewey's "creed" was no longer ninth in order, as it had been originally, but first, and it was followed by Clark's. Moreover, Lang's recognition was only the beginning. The "creed" was translated into Italian in 1913, into German in 1925, into French and Spanish in 1931, and into Polish in 1933. Next to* The School and Society, *it has probably given Dewey his largest audience abroad.*

In the United States, the document was first republished in pamphlet form in 1897 (along with an essay by Dewey's colleague, Albion W. Small), and then again in 1910. In 1929 the Progressive Education Association reissued it in recognition of Dewey's seventieth birthday. More significant, perhaps, the National Education Association also republished the "creed" that year in its Journal, *observing that Dewey's text now belonged in the "professional Bible" of every teacher. The comments accompanying the "creed" on that occasion tell us much about the place it had come to occupy in the liturgy of American pedagogy. The editor of the NEA* Journal *called it "the emancipation proclamation of childhood." The school superintendent of Sioux City, Iowa, referred to it as "the genesis of public school education." And his counterpart in Ithaca, New York, was moved to rank Dewey as one of the world's four greatest educational reformers, noting that he "strove successfully to free children from formalism in education." By 1929 the fervor of Dewey's propositions, and their effectiveness in synthesizing the education-reform currents of the Progressive era, had made his "creed" a document of general inspiration, in which teachers of virtually every persuasion could find something of value.*

Reform movements have a way of running their course, and the years after 1945 saw a rapid decline in the vitality and influence of progressive education. Throughout the United States, there were charges that progressive theory had hardened into clichés, that progressive practice had ossified into a new traditionalism. Dewey himself, in a 1952 essay that was destined to be one of his last, expressed dismay over what had become of the progressive cause. And yet even in these circumstances his "creed" remained pertinent, as relevant for the critics of progressive education as it had once been for the partisans. In 1961, when Jerome Bruner of Harvard, one of the leading theorists of the post-progressive era, sought to clarify his own pedagogical position vis-à-vis that of the progressives, he titled his essay "After John Dewey, What?"

*and he began with the ringing phrases of the 1897 "creed,"
still the most succinct and powerful statement of the revolution through which American education had so recently
passed.*

Albert J. Beveridge
The March of the Flag
1898

EDITED BY ERNEST R. MAY

"The March of the Flag" was a speech delivered in Tomlinson's Hall, Indianapolis, on September 16, 1898, by Albert Jeremiah Beveridge. Then twenty days short of his thirty-sixth birthday, Beveridge was a lawyer, an active campaigner for the Republican Party, and an orator already famed outside his own state of Indiana. In April, 1898, shortly after the United States declared war on Spain, he had spoken at a banquet of the Middlesex Club in Boston. Although Admiral Dewey had not yet won his victory at Manila Bay and most Americans did not even know that Spain had a colony in the Far East, Beveridge called at that time for conquest of the Philippine Islands. By the date of his Tomlinson's Hall address, the war with Spain was over and an American army occupied Manila. It was not clear whether or not the McKinley Administration intended to keep the Islands. The armistice terms left the question to be decided during negotiations for a peace treaty, and those negotiations were in progress in Paris. Leading Democrats, including former President Cleveland and William Jennings Bryan, had come out in opposition to holding the Philippines as a colony. Beveridge wanted the Republican Ad-

644

ministration to annex the islands and the Republican Party to adopt a frankly imperialist policy. His speech was designed to prod McKinley, to provide his party with battlecries for the approaching state and congressional campaigns, and, not incidentally, to further his own prospects for election to the United States Senate if the Republicans should win the Indiana legislature. Short, slim, handsome, immaculately dressed, looking even younger than his years, Beveridge spoke from a memorized text, making few gestures but using the full range of a practiced and penetrating voice.

It is a noble land that God has given us; a land that can feed and clothe the world; a land whose coastlines would inclose half the countries of Europe; a land set like a sentinel between the two imperial oceans of the globe, a greater England with a nobler destiny.

It is a mighty people that He has planted on this soil; a people sprung from the most masterful blood of history; a people perpetually revitalized by the virile, man-producing working-folk of all the earth; a people imperial by virtue of their power, by right of their institutions, by authority of their Heaven-directed purposes—the propagandists and not the misers of liberty.

It is a glorious history our God has bestowed upon His chosen people; a history heroic with faith in our mission and our future; a history of statesmen who flung the boundaries of the Republic out into unexplored lands and savage wilderness; a history of soldiers who carried the flag across blazing deserts and through the ranks of hostile mountains, even to the gates of sunset; a history of a multiplying people who overran a continent in half a century; a history of prophets who saw the consequences of evils inherited from the past and of martyrs who died to save us from them; a history divinely logical, in the process of whose tremendous reasoning we find ourselves to-day.

Therefore, in this campaign, the question is larger than a party question. It is an American question. It is a world ques-

The speech was first published in the *Indianapolis Journal* for September 17, 1898. With minor revisions it appeared in pamphlet form immediately afterward. This text, following exactly that of the pamphlet, was incorporated by Beveridge in a collection of essays and orations, *The Meaning of the Times* (Indianpolis: The Bobbs-Merrill Company, 1908), pp. 47–57.

tion. Shall the American people continue their march toward the commercial supremacy of the world? Shall free institutions broaden their blessed reign as the children of liberty wax in strength, until the empire of our principles is established over the hearts of all mankind?

Have we no mission to perform, no duty to discharge to our fellowman? Has God endowed us with gifts beyond our deserts and marked us as the people of His peculiar favor, merely to rot in our own selfishness, as men and nations must, who take cowardice for their companion and self for their deity— as China has, as India has, as Egypt has?

Shall we be as the man who had one talent and hid it, or as he who had ten talents and used them until they grew to riches? And shall we reap the reward that waits on our discharge of our high duty; shall we occupy new markets for what our farmers raise, our factories make, our merchants sell —aye, and, please God, new markets for what our ships shall carry?

Hawaii is ours; Porto Rico is to be ours; at the prayer of her people Cuba finally will be ours; in the islands of the East, even to the gates of Asia, coaling stations are to be ours at the very least; the flag of a liberal government is to float over the Philippines, and may it be the banner that Taylor unfurled in Texas and Fremont carried to the coast.

The Opposition tells us that we ought not to govern a people without their consent. I answer, The rule of liberty that all just government derives its authority from the consent of the governed, applies only to those who are capable of self-government. We govern the Indians without their consent, we govern our territories without their consent, we govern our children without their consent. How do they know that our government would be without their consent? Would not the people of the Philippines prefer the just, humane, civilizing government of this Republic to the savage, bloody rule of pillage and extortion from which we have rescued them?

And, regardless of this formula of words made only for enlightened, self-governing people, do we owe no duty to the world? Shall we turn these peoples back to the reeking hands from which we have taken them? Shall we abandon them, with Germany, England, Japan, hungering for them? Shall we save them from those nations, to give them a self-rule of tragedy?

They ask us how we shall govern these new possessions. I answer: Out of local conditions and the necessities of the case methods of government will grow. If England can govern foreign lands, so can America. If Germany can govern foreign lands, so can America. If they can supervise protectorates, so can America. Why is it more difficult to administer Hawaii than New Mexico or California? Both had a savage and an alien population; both were more remote from the seat of government when they came under our dominion that the Philippines are to-day.

Will you say by your vote that American ability to govern has decayed; that a century's experience in self-rule has failed of a result? Will you affirm by your vote that you are an infidel to American power and practical sense? Or will you say that ours is the blood of government; ours the heart of dominion; ours the brain and genius of administration? Will you remember that we do but what our fathers did—we but pitch the tents of liberty farther westward, farther southward—we only continue the march of the flag?

The march of the flag! In 1789 the flag of the Republic waved over 4,000,000 souls in thirteen states, and their savage territory which stretched to the Mississippi, to Canada, to the Floridas. The timid minds of that day said that no new territory was needed, and, for the hour, they were right. But Jefferson, through whose intellect the centuries marched; Jefferson, who dreamed of Cuba as an American state; Jefferson, the first Imperialist of the Republic—Jefferson acquired that imperial territory which swept from the Mississippi to the mountains, from Texas to the British possessions, and the march of the flag began!

The infidels to the gospel of liberty raved, but the flag swept on! The title to that noble land out of which Oregon, Washington, Idaho and Montana have been carved was uncertain; Jefferson, strict constructionist of constitutional power though he was, obeyed the Anglo-Saxon impulse within him, whose watchword then and whose watchword throughout the world to-day is, "Forward!": another empire was added to the Republic, and the march of the flag went on!

Those who deny the power of free institutions to expand urged every argument, and more, that we hear, to-day; but the people's judgment approved the command of their blood, and the march of the flag went on!

A screen of land from New Orleans to Florida shut us from the Gulf, and over this and the Everglade Peninsula waved the saffron flag of Spain; Andrew Jackson seized both, the American people stood at his back, and, under Monroe, the Floridas came under the dominion of the Republic, and the march of the flag went on! The Cassandras prophesied every prophecy of despair we hear, to-day, but the march of the flag went on!

Then Texas responded to the bugle calls of liberty, and the march of the flag went on! And, at last, we waged war with Mexico, and the flag swept over the southwest, over peerless California, past the Gate of Gold to Oregon on the north, and from ocean to ocean its folds of glory blazed.

And, now, obeying the same voice that Jefferson heard and obeyed, that Jackson heard and obeyed, that Monroe heard and obeyed, that Seward heard and obeyed, that Grant heard and obeyed, that Harrison heard and obeyed, our President to-day plants the flag over the islands of the seas, outposts of commerce, citadels of national security, and the march of the flag goes on!

Distance and oceans are no arguments. The fact that all the territory our fathers bought and seized is contiguous, is no argument. In 1819 Florida was farther from New York than Porto Rico is from Chicago today; Texas, farther from Washington in 1845 than Hawaii is from Boston in 1898; California, more inaccessible in 1847 than the Philippines are now. Gibraltar is farther from London than Havana is from Washington; Melbourne is farther from Liverpool than Manila is from San Francisco.

The ocean does not separate us from lands of our duty and desire—the oceans join us, rivers never to be dredged, canals never to be repaired. Steam joins us; electricity joins us—the very elements are in league with our destiny. Cuba not contiguous! Porto Rico not contiguous! Hawaii and the Philippines not contiguous! The oceans make them contiguous. And our navy will make them contiguous.

But the Opposition is right—there is a difference. We did not need the western Mississippi Valley when we acquired it, nor Florida, nor Texas, nor California, nor the royal provinces of the far northwest. We had no emigrants to people this imperial wilderness, no money to develop it, even no highways to cover it. No trade awaited us in its savage fastnesses. Our productions were not greater than our trade. There was not one reason for the land-lust of our statesmen from Jefferson to Grant, other than the prophet and the Saxon within them. But, to-day, we are raising more than we can consume, making more than we can use. Therefore we must find new markets for our produce.

And so, while we did not need the territory taken during the past century at the time it was acquired, we do need what we have taken in 1898, and we need it now. The resources and the commerce of these immensely rich dominions will be increased as much as American energy is greater than Spanish sloth. In Cuba, alone, there are 15,000,000 acres of forest unacquainted with the ax, exhaustless mines of iron, priceless deposits of manganese, millions of dollars' worth of which we must buy, to-day, from the Black Sea districts. There are millions of acres yet unexplored.

The resources of Porto Rico have only been trifled with. The riches of the Philippines have hardly been touched by the finger-tips of modern methods. And they produce what we consume, and consume what we produce—the very predestination of reciprocity—a reciprocity "not made with hands, eternal in the heavens." They sell hemp, sugar, cocoanuts, fruits of the tropics, timber of price like mahogany; they buy flour, clothing, tools, implements, machinery and all that we can raise and make. Their trade will be ours in time. Do you indorse that policy with your vote?

Cuba is as large as Pennsylvania, and is the richest spot on the globe. Hawaii is as large as New Jersey; Porto Rico half as large as Hawaii; the Philippines larger than all New England, New York, New Jersey and Delaware combined. Together they are larger than the British Isles, larger than France, larger than Germany, larger than Japan.

If any man tells you that trade depends on cheapness and not on government influence, ask him why England does not abandon South Africa, Egypt, India. Why does France seize South China, Germany the vast region whose port is Kaouchou?

Our trade with Porto Rico, Hawaii and the Philippines must be as free as between the states of the Union, because they are American territory, while every other nation on earth must pay our tariff before they can compete with us. Until Cuba shall ask for annexation, our trade with her will, at the very least, be like the preferential trade of Canada with England. That, and the excellence of our goods and products; that, and the convenience of traffic; that, and the kinship of interests and destiny, will give the monopoly of these markets to the American people.

The commercial supremacy of the Republic means that this Nation is to be the sovereign factor in the peace of the world. For the conflicts of the future are to be conflicts of trade—struggles for markets—commercial wars for existence. And the golden rule of peace is impregnability of position and invincibility of preparedness. So, we see England, the greatest strategist of history, plant her flag and her cannon on Gibraltar, at Quebec, in the Bermudas, at Vancouver, everywhere.

So Hawaii furnished us a naval base in the heart of the Pacific; the Ladrones another, a voyage further on; Manila another, at the gates of Asia—Asia, to the trade of whose hundreds of millions American merchants, manufacturers, farmers, have as good right as those of Germany or France or Russia or England; Asia, whose commerce with the United Kingdom alone amounts to hundreds of millions of dollars every year; Asia, to whom Germany looks to take her surplus products; Asia, whose doors must not be shut against American trade. Within five decades the bulk of Oriental commerce will be ours.

No wonder that, in the shadows of coming events so great, free-silver is already a memory. The current of history has swept past that episode. Men understand, to-day, that the greatest commerce of the world must be conducted with the steadiest standard of value and most convenient medium of exchange human ingenuity can devise. Time, that unerring reasoner, has settled the silver question. The American people are tired of talking about money—they want to make it. Why should the farmer get a half-measure dollar of money any more than he should give a half-measure bushel of grain?

Why should not the proposition for the free coinage of silver be as dead as the proposition of irredeemable paper money? It is the same proposition in a different form. If the Government stamp can make a piece of silver, which you can buy for 45 cents, pass for 100 cents, the Government stamp can make a piece of pewter, worth one cent, pass for 100 cents, and a piece of paper, worth a fraction of a cent, pass for 100 cents. Free-silver is the principle of fiat money applied to metal. If you favor fiat silver, you necessarily favor fiat paper.

If the Government can make money with a stamp, why does the Government borrow money? If the Government can create value out of nothing, why not abolish all taxation?

And if it is not the stamp of the Government that raises the value, but the demand which free coinage creates, why has the value of silver gone down at a time when more silver was bought and coined by the Government than ever before? Again, if the people want more silver, why do they refuse what we already have? And if free silver makes money more plentiful, how will *you* get any of it? Will the silver-mine owner give it to you? Will he loan it to you? Will the Government give or loan it to you? Where do you or I come in on this free-silver proposition?

The American people want this money question settled for ever. They want a uniform currency, a convenient currency, a currency that grows as business grows, a currency based on science and not on chance.

And now, on the threshold of our new and great career, is the time permanently to adjust our system of finance. The American people have the mightiest commerce of the world to conduct. They can not halt to unsettle their money system every time some ardent imagination sees a vision and dreams a dream. Think of Great Britain becoming the commercial monarch of the world with her financial system periodically assailed! Think of Holland or Germany or France bearing their burdens, and, yet, sending their flag to every sea, with their money at the mercy of politicians-out-of-an-issue. Let us settle the whole financial system on principles so sound that no agitation can shake it. And then, like men and not like children, let us on to our tasks, our mission and our destiny.

There are so many real things to be done—canals to be dug, railways to be laid, forests to be felled, cities to be builded, fields to be tilled, markets to be won, ships to be launched, peoples to be saved, civilization to be proclaimed and the flag of liberty flung to the eager air of every sea. Is this an hour to waste upon triflers with nature's laws? Is this a season to give our destiny over to word-mongers and prosperity-wreckers? No! It is an hour to remember our duty to our homes. It is a moment to realize the opportunities fate has opened to us. And so it is an hour for us to stand by the Government.

Wonderfully has God guided us. Yonder at Bunker Hill and Yorktown His providence was above us. At New Orleans and on ensanguined seas His hand sustained us. Abraham Lincoln was His minister and His was the altar of freedom the Nation's soldiers set up on a hundred battle-fields. His power directed Dewey in the East and delivered the Spanish fleet into our hands, as He delivered the elder Armada into the hands of our English sires two centuries ago. The American people can not use a dishonest medium of exchange; it is ours to set the world its example of right and honor. We can not fly from our world duties; it is ours to execute the purpose of a fate that has driven us to be greater than our small intentions. We can not retreat from any soil where Providence has unfurled our banner; it is ours to save that soil for liberty and civilization.

Beveridge's speech had immediate impact. Some 300,000 copies of it were distributed in pamphlet form during the campaigns then in progress for seats in Congress and the

state legislature. Since McKinley reached his decision in favor of Philippine annexation at about the time when the speech was delivered, it seems unlikely that Beveridge's words affected the President. But there were many Republican triumphs in areas where Beveridge's speech had circulated. Beveridge's personal ambition was fulfilled, for in January, 1899, the Indiana legislature elected him to the United States Senate. Although he did not take his seat until after the Senate debate on the peace treaty, his voice was heard in Indiana and other states repeating the themes of the "March of the Flag" address. His election and his oratory may have had some effect on the close vote by which the Senate approved the treaty and the annexation of the Philippines.

But, whatever its immediate consequences, the "March of the Flag" address was to have more importance later. Imperialism drew the attention of powerful theoretical minds. In 1902 the English economist J. A. Hobson published Imperialism: A Study. *In 1916 Lenin brought out in Zürich* Imperialism: The Highest Stage of Capitalism, *a commentary on Hobson. Although neither Hobson nor Lenin mentioned Beveridge, their disciples in America soon saw how his words could be used to support Hobson's thesis that imperialism flowed from industrial overproduction or to buttress Lenin's subtler, more complex argument that imperialism came at "the monopoly stage of capitalism." Taken together, the "March of the Flag" speech and Beveridge's earlier Middlesex Club oration urging conquest of the Philippines became key texts in the interpretation of American imperialism. In* The Idea of National Interest *(1934),* The Open Door at Home *(1935), and other works, Charles A. Beard relied heavily on Beveridge's words in advancing an economic interpretation of the expansionism of the 1890's. The two speeches were also to be cited in Soviet and Chinese works on the United States written during the Cold War (among them, the books of A. A. Fursenko, S. B. Gorelik, and Sun Ho-gan). Writers contesting the Sino-Soviet point of view also went to Beveridge, making different exegeses of his language. Julius W. Pratt in* Expansionists of 1898 *(1936) emphasized Beveridge's predestinarianism. Returning again and again to "The March of the Flag" and the Middlesex Club speech, Albert K. Weinberg in* Manifest Destiny *(1935), pointed out in them a variety of strands of rationalization for expansionism—the ideas of geographical predestination, God-given title, divine mission, duty, para-*

mount interest, political affinity, and self-defense. Beveridge's words, meant to affect a single partisan campaign, lived on to be read, even in remote parts of the world, as keys to the explanation of his country's motives, behavior, and character.

John Wanamaker

On the Department Store

1900

EDITED BY MALCOLM P. MC NAIR

The application of large sums of capital to the business of retailing came relatively late in the Industrial Revolution. Indeed, most of this development in the United States occurred after the Civil War, lasting into the twentieth century. At first this retail manifestation of capitalism took predominantly the form of the department store, offering a wide range of consumer merchandise under one roof. It is true that even before the Civil War Alexander Stewart in New York City had shown that it was practical to conduct a retail dry-goods business on a large scale, but he limited himself to dry goods and did not organize departmentally. Furthermore, like many other retail merchants of the time, he was also engaged in the wholesale business.

No single person can be said to have invented the department store. The idea, both in Europe and in the United States, developed independently, as merchants, principally with backgrounds in dry goods or men's clothing, sometimes as wholesalers, sometimes as retailers, sought ways of bringing very large numbers of customers to their stores. Nevertheless, one man, John Wanamaker, was mainly responsible for developing and promoting the idea of the department store; and in the last two decades of the nineteenth century his establishment in Philadelphia became the largest department store in the United States and probably in the world.

John Wanamaker was a man with a great flair for publicity and a gift for writing distinctive advertising. He was also a strongly religious person, active in Presbyterian church and Sunday school work, a crusader who exemplified the best of the Protestant ethic. Referring to John Wanamaker, the late Professor N.S.B. Gras of the Harvard Business School often remarked to his business history class that Calvinism was a religion of enthusiasm, fervor, and hustling, and that anyone with a Presbyterian training was likely to have a religious background favorable to capitalism. Wanamaker had established a men's clothing store, Oak Hall, before he was twenty-five years old, following this a few years later with another store, Chestnut Street, for the carriage trade. In his mid-thirties he began revolving in his mind the idea of a "new kind of store" by means of which he might make his business one of the nation's largest retailing enterprises. In late 1874 or early 1875, he had the opportunity to buy from the Pennsylvania Railroad its old freight depot at Thirteenth and Market Streets; the building had become obsolete because of the plan to build a new city hall immediately to the west. Although the structure was much larger than required for his immediate needs, and although it was a considerable distance west of what was then the retailing hub of the city, John Wanamaker could not resist buying the old freight depot.

The first new use of this building was to house a series of revival meetings held by Dwight L. Moody and Ira D. Sankey, who had sought to rent the premises only to find that John Wanamaker held the option. Wanamaker's reaction on hearing of their wishes was characteristic. "The new store can wait a few months for its opening; the Lord's business first." And he promptly came home from Europe to help organize the revival meetings.

At this time Wanamaker was also playing a major part in promoting the Centennial Exposition of 1876, and he saw the opportunity to tie in his new acquisition with this important celebration. After the end of the Moody and Sankey meetings he remodeled the old freight depot; and, still sticking to the men's and boys' clothing business, he opened a huge store there May 6, 1876—essentially an expanded version of his existing retail businesses, Oak Hall and Chestnut Street. During the Centennial Exposition large crowds visited this store;

and as the celebration drew to a close, Wanamaker began to cast about for some concept of a retail business with inherent attractions of its own that would continue to bring in crowds. He drew on the ideas that had been accumulating in his mind for several years, particularly those suggested by his study of the large dry-goods stores of Paris during his European trip in 1875. In early 1877, after extensive remodeling, the new store was ready to open. For a week a double-column advertisement in all the Philadelphia papers announced "The Inauguration of the Dry Goods Business at the Grand Depot will take place March 12, from 9 to 6 o'clock." Then on the Saturday preceding the opening the announcement read in part:

NEXT MONDAY THE GRAND INAUGURATION OF THE DRY GOODS BUSINESS AT THE GRAND DEPOT, JOHN WANAMAKER, THIRTEENTH STREET AND NEW CITY HALL

TO THE LADIES.   **TO THE LADIES.**
In introducing the Dry Goods business as the principle feature at the Grand Depot for merchandise (Thirteenth Street and new City Hall), it seems proper to say that the growth of the city and the accommodation of the public seemed to call for such a central and extensive point for shopping.

John Wanamaker in his advertising repeatedly emphasized the basic policies of the new business. It was not, however, until a number of years later, after the enterprise had overcome early vicissitudes which called forth all the courage and resourcefulness of the founder, that Wanamaker, at the annual meeting of the American Academy of Political and Social Science in Philadelphia in 1900, comprehensively summed up the guiding policies of his "new kind of storekeeping" in an address entitled "The Evolution of Mercantile Business."

MY TOPIC is one car of the long train made up by the general subject of the afternoon—"Combination of Capital as a Factor of Industrial Progress." This annual congress forms a kind of sounding-board for live questions for the entire country, and because of this I wish to contribute what I can to the general stock of information.

Evolution is that series of steps through which anything has passed in acquiring its present characteristics. The term "mercantile" covers everything relating to trade and commerce. . . .

As late as forty years ago, or before the war, the transaction of business in producing and distributing merchandise required many agencies: The manufacturer, importer, commission men, bankers, jobbers, commercial travelers, and retailers.

Until twenty years ago trade rules limited the sales of manufacturers to commission men, and those of commission houses to jobbers, so that the only market door open to retailers were the jobbers, whose goods were loaded, when they reached the retailer, with three or four unavoidable profits incident to passing the various fixed stages toward the consumer.

The conditions governing the placing of goods in the retailer's hands were not only heavily weighted with expense, but, in the main, the retail merchant was badly handicapped as a rule by

(a) Small capital, commonly borrowed by long credit for merchandise.
(b) Necessity of selling upon credit.
(c) Necessity for larger percentage of profit.
(d) Impossibility of utilizing to advantage store and people all seasons of the year.
(e) Non-accumulation of capital.

The consequence was, according to accepted statistics, that but four out of every hundred merchants succeeded in business. Getting a mere living forty years ago was generally secured in part by the occupancy of a part of the store premises as a residence. Naturally, an undercurrent of discontent with these conditions manifested itself, protesting against two or more prices for the same article, meagre assortments of goods, high prices and the custom that probably grew out of one rate to cash buyers and a different rate to buyers upon credit.

The Centennial Exposition of 1876 was, in my judgment,

About half of Wanamaker's speech on "The Evolution of Mercantile Business" is given here. It is quoted as it originally appeared in *Corporations and Public Welfare: Addresses at the Fourth Annual Meeting of the American Academy of Political and Social Science, April 19–20, 1900. Supplement to the Annals of the American Academy of Political and Social Science* (Philadelphia: American Academy of Political and Social Science, May, 1900), pp. 123–34.

the moving cause of a departure toward general business by single ownership. The rising tide of popular desire to assemble under one roof articles used in every home and with freedom to purchase was a constant suggestion in 1876, not alone because of its convenience, but because to some degree it would form a permanent and useful exhibition. This idea culminated in the formation of a Permanent Exhibition Company, which succeeded the Centennial. Being located in Fairmount Park and not in a business centre, and without skilled management, the scheme was abandoned in a short time.

Up to 1877, so far as now known, no extensive, well-systemized mercantile retail establishment upon a large scale existed in the United States. The nearest approach was the A. T. Stewart store in New York, which limited itself to dry goods of the higher class, until the death of Mr. A. T. Stewart, when it took on lower classes of goods, and a wider, but still limited scope.

That Centennial Exhibition in 1876 at Philadelphia, the principal manufacturing centre of the country, the first great exhibition in America, opened a new vision to the people of the United States. It was the cornerstone upon which manufacturers everywhere rebuilt their businesses to new fabrics, new fashions and more courageous undertakings by reason of the lessons taught them from the exhibits of the nations of the world. The continuing outgrowth of that exhibition has revolutionized the methods of almost every class of mercantile business in the United States.

The tendency of the age toward simplification of business systems and to remove unnecessary duplication of expenses, awakened throughout the United States a keen study of means to bring about a closer alliance with the producer and consumer. Almost simultaneously in a number of cities, long-established stores gradually enlarged and new stores sprang up to group at one point masses of merchandise in more or less variety. The movement everywhere arrested attention and provoked discussion because of the approval and practical support of the people at large. . . .

Though there probably was never a time in any city that there were not bankruptcies of merchants and vacant stores, yet after the opening of the large stores, it everywhere became common with storekeepers and renters to charge all the causes of disaster to the large stores, then and now commonly called department stores, and an unsuccessful effort was made to decry them as monopolies. . . .

I respectfully submit that the evolution in mercantile business during the last quarter of a century has been wrought not by combinations of capital, corporations or trusts, but by the natural growth of individual mercantile enterprises born of new conditions out of the experience, mistakes and losses of old-time trading; that the underlying basis of the new order of business and its principal claim for favor is that it distributes to the consumer in substance or cash compounded earnings hitherto wasted unnecessarily on middlemen; that thus far the enlarged retailing has practically superseded agents, commission houses, importers and large and small jobbers, thereby saving rentals, salaries and various expenses of handling; that the establishing of direct relations with mills and makers proves to be not only desirable for the saving of such costs as are dispensed with, but because less risks are incurred in preparing products and finding quick markets, thereby favoring lower prices; that the people must be taken into the equation when considering the right of certain businesses to a title of life, as they are responsible for the new conditions, highly value and heartily support them.

It is an old axiom that the water of a stream cannot rise beyond its level. Neither can any business rise or thrive except at the will of the people who are served by it.

I contend that the department store development would not be here but for its service to society; that it has done a public service in retiring middlemen; that its organization neither denies rights to others nor claims privileges of state franchises, or favoritism of national tariff laws; that if there is any suffering from it it is by the pressure of competition, and not from the pressure of monopoly; that so long as competition is not suppressed by law, monopolies cannot exist in storekeeping, and that the one quarter of the globe that cannot be captured by trusts is most assuredly that of the mercantile trading world.

I hold that the evolution in trade was inevitable, because it was waterlogged by old customs that overtaxed purchasers; that there was at work for a long time a resistless force moving towards the highest good of humanity; that the profit therefrom to individuals who have risked their own capital, as any man may still do if he chooses, has been insignificant, compared to the people benefited both by the cheapening of the comforts of life and by the improved condition of persons employed. . . .

I believe the new American system of storekeeping is the most powerful factor yet discovered to compel minimum prices. Perhaps some one will ask what relation reduced prices of merchandise have upon labor. It is a noticeable fact that lowered prices stimulate consumption and require additional labor in producing, transporting and distributing. The care of such large stocks, amounting in one single store upon an average at all times to between four and five millions of dollars, and the preparation of and handling from reserves to forward stocks, require large corps of men. Under old conditions of storekeeping a man and his wife or daughter did all the work between daylight and midnight. The new systems make shorter hours of duty and thus the number of employes is increased, while many entirely new avenues of employment for women are opened, as typewriters, stenographers, cashiers, check-clerks, inspectors, wrappers, mailing clerks and the like. The division of labor creates many places for talented and high-priced men, whose salaries range alongside of presidents of banks and trust companies and similar important positions. It is universally admitted that the sanitary conditions that surround the employes of the large stores are better than in the old-time smaller stores and that employes are considerably better paid. . . .

Public service is the sole basic condition of retail business growth. To give the best merchandise at the least cost is the modern retailer's ambition. He cannot control costs of production, but he can modify costs of distribution and his own profits. His principle is the minimum of profit for the creation of the maximum of business. The keen rivalry of retail trading is inimical to a combination between different and competing firms and companies. . . .

The evolution in business which I have endeavored to discuss has not sought nor has it the power to limit production or stifle competition or raise prices. On the contrary, its chief objectors are those who claim that it makes prices too low. It affects articles of supply of every home and of so many thousands of kinds and ever changing character that no other restriction can obtain than the natural demand. The fact that it deals with distribution and affords intelligent and economic treatment of merchandise increases employment.

It has demonstrated advantages to the public hitherto not common, if at all possible, to former systems. In increasing values of real estate, wherever large businesses are located, smaller stores crowd around them, in some instances changing the values of an entire neighborhood. Statistics prove that it does not anywhere crowd out competent and useful merchants. It saves a multiplication of agencies to the benefit of the consumer in reduced prices. . . .

☆

In after years John Wanamaker, describing the inception of his "new kind of store," said, "The fact was that business in Philadelphia had gone along in the same ancient way so long that innovation was almost a duty." The innovation by which he reinvigorated retail competition was based on a combination of policies:

> *A large variety of merchandise offered to the shopper under one roof through a departmental form of organization.*
> *Low competitive prices made possible by large volume and direct dealing with manufacturing suppliers.*
> *Assumption of full responsibility to the consumer for quality and values, with one price to all comers and a guarantee of "money back if not satisfied."*
> *Vigorous and distinctive large-scale advertising.*

Not all these concepts were original, but the combination and publicizing of them and their widespread imitation created a greater impact on retailing than perhaps any previous development in American business. As always, innovation was stoutly opposed. John Wanamaker was ridiculed, abused, threatened, and plotted against; and the new business narrowly escaped failure on more than one occasion. But, as always in the history of American marketing, when the customers embraced the innovation its long-run success was assured. Merchants in other cities who had been thinking along the same lines were encouraged, and imitators rapidly appeared. By the turn of the century the acceptance of the department store was unquestioned, and institutions such as Macy's, Gimbel's, Marshall Field, and Jordan Marsh were well established. At that time Wanamaker had the largest retail business in Philadelphia, and also in New York, where he had acquired the former A. T. Stewart store.

With his searching mind and lively imagination, John Wanamaker continued to pioneer throughout his life; and over the years his business has been credited, perhaps not always accurately, with a long series of "firsts," comprising such diverse innovations as customer restaurants, store lighting by electricity, a continuing educational program for store employees, August and February furniture sales events, summer vacations with pay, use of pneumatic tubes as cash carriers, Christmas bonuses, and the installation of Marconi wireless stations. That age did not lessen John Wanamaker's capacity for imaginative leadership is shown by his inauguration, in May, 1920 (only a little more than two years before his

*death), of the famous 20-per-cent store-wide price reduction
in both the Philadelphia and New York stores which signalized the end of the great price inflation following World War I.*

*Wanamaker's vigorous assertion that large-scale operations
in retailing would enhance the social effectiveness of competition and in no way conduce to monopoly has been amply verified. So long as retail distribution remained predominantly in
the hands of small neighborhood shopkeepers, competition at
the retail level was ineffective. Small specialty shops enjoyed
their neighborhood monopolies, and competition existed only
at the manufacturing level. The advent of large-scale retail
operations, first the department store and later mail-order,
chain-store, and other types, changed all this. These innovations broke down small-scale monopolies by drawing trade
from much wider areas; they competed vigorously not only
with the older trade channels but also among themselves; and
eventually they added a whole new dimension to competition
by raising retail enterprise to such stature and economic importance that it could exercise countervailing power in bargaining with manufacturers, and even in assuming such functions as brand ownership and merchandise development. It
was a significant and exciting chapter in American business
that John Wanamaker started to write in 1877, and the chapter is not yet closed.*

*In the eastern seaboard cities in the 1870's the time was
undoubtedly ripe for mercantile innovation. For roughly the
next fifty years the conditions of urban growth continued to
be highly favorable to large downtown department stores.
Public transportation systems—street cars, elevated lines, sub-
ways, and commuter rail service—all radiated from the
downtown centers, where the department stores were located,
like the spokes of a wheel; and as they extended their radius
and increased their speed they brought larger and larger consumer markets into the retail trading areas of the department
stores. At the same time, the growth of newspaper circulation
went hand in hand with the increase in department-store advertising, each reinforcing the other and carrying the merchandise message to a larger and larger community. Thus the
period of wide acceptance and great growth of the original
department-store type of business in the United States extended well into the 1920's, almost coinciding, in fact, with John
Wanamaker's business lifetime. Subsequently, far-reaching social, economic, and technological changes were to create
greatly different patterns of living and transportation, setting
the stage for fresh developments in department-store retailing.*

The first major challenge to the department store in its mature phase began to appear just before World War II and grew rapidly in the immediate postwar years. This development stemmed from the "suburban revolution," with its substantially changed patterns of living and transportation. As consumers moved farther away from central business districts and found it increasingly difficult to use their preferred form of transportation (the private automobile) to reach downtown locations in large and medium-size cities, stores had to go where their customers were. And department stores, with their heavy investment in downtown structures housing enormous varieties and quantities of merchandise under one roof, found themselves dangerously inflexible. They were handicapped for making the transition to suburbia, in comparison with the multistore organizations, such as the variety chains and the general merchandise chains (Sears had perceived the trend long before anyone else). Nevertheless, the department stores rallied their forces and met this challenge. They opened suburban branches, drawing in many instances half their volume from these stores. In fact, the department stores themselves played a large part in one of the most important new retail developments of the mid-century—the planned regional shopping center. The full transition is not yet completed. The obverse side of the coin is the problem that has arisen of renovating downtown, and here department stores are still seeking to find a solution that is right for them as well as for the other business and civic interests of the metropolitan complex. But by transforming themselves successfully into multistore organizations, the department stores have clearly met the major challenge growing out of the suburban revolution.

Following closely on the suburban revolution, indeed in some ways a part of it, has come another marked innovation in retailing, the discount department store, utilizing supermarket self-service methods for non-food lines (and frequently offering food as well on a low-price basis). This kind of store, by its rapid growth in the late 1950's and early 1960's, has posed a challenge alike to department stores, to general merchandise and variety chains, and to conventional food supermarket chains. How the department store is meeting this challenge cannot yet be fully appraised. But evidence points to such policies as greater flexibility in serving a more sharply segmented market, with increased emphasis on the service image for some segments and on cost-reducing innovations for other segments. In the meantime all the important retail marketing institutions are beginning to think about the poten-

tial challenges from the innovations that are growing out of the current new retailing revolution, namely, the technological revolution in data processing, inventory logistics, and materials handling. Thus as of the mid-1960's the department store is still a retail marketing institution of great vitality.

It is pleasant to note that the Wanamaker business itself continues to exemplify this vitality of the department store as an institution. Although a substantial number of other department-store organizations, many of them operating on a national basis, have surpassed it in total sales volume, John Wanamaker Philadelphia with its five area branches, built or being built, is still the largest department store in that city; and it is managed wholly for the Wanamaker family interest by a Board of Trustees headed by John R. Wanamaker, the great-grandson of the founder. Not without effect has been the injunction inscribed in the capstone of the new store building in 1910:

LET THOSE WHO FOLLOW ME
CONTINUE TO BUILD
WITH THE PLUMB OF HONOR
THE LEVEL OF TRUTH
AND THE SQUARE OF INTEGRITY
EDUCATION, COURTESY
AND MUTUALITY

Jacob A. Riis

Introduction to "The Battle with the Slum"

1902

EDITED BY RICHARD C. WADE

Jacob A. Riis's How the Other Half Lives *appeared in 1890. The book not only added a familiar phrase to American speech, but also introduced a new issue and a new author to a national audience. If the phrase "the other half" quickly became a synonym for the poor, so too the problem of the slum soon insinuated itself into every discussion of social questions, and Jacob Riis emerged as a popular spokesman for the conscience of the community on housing reform. It was "a curiously popular book," Riis could write with surprise more than a decade after its publication.*

There was nothing contrived about the issue Riis raised. Residential congestion in American cities at the end of the nineteenth century was greater than anywhere else in the world. New York presented the problem in its starkest form. In the Tenth Ward the population density reached 1,000 per acre and over 300,000 people per square mile. No other city matched these figures, but everywhere American metropolises were faced with unparalleled housing pressures. Old commercial buildings were transformed into dwelling space; single-family homes were converted into crowded apartments; new

665

tenements were designed to accommodate the flood of new-comers. With the resultant congestion came disease, crime, want, and deprivation as well as a large harvest of stunted opportunity for youth and abandoned hope for adults.

And Riis knew these conditions well. Coming to New York City as a young immigrant from Denmark, he had difficulty in finding his footing in America. Unemployed for weeks at a time, he had gone hungry and even resorted to police lodging houses for shelter and sleep. In 1877, however, he became a newspaper reporter and began a career which would give him a national reputation. For twenty-two years his beat included the "foul core of New York's slums," where such notorious spots as Bandit's Roost, Bottle Alley, Kerosene Row, and Thieves' Alley became as much a part of his life as his own comfortable neighborhood in Richmond Hills.

Riis was not the first person to discover the slums; by 1890 others had already marshaled the grim statistics and pointed to the mounting danger. Riis's contribution lay in the human dimension he gave to the problem. "I had but a vague idea of these horrors," James Russell Lowell wrote, "before you brought them so feelingly home to me." Riis rejected the more scientific and "sociological" approach because it would "reduce men and women and children to mere items" and "classify and sub-classify" them until they were dry. "One throb of the human heart," he concluded, "is worth a whole book" of theory.

Riis disliked the label of "reformer," yet he found himself an increasingly important part of a campaign to improve the dreadful conditions he had described. Civic organizations, political groups, and even some public agencies mounted a determined attack on the slum. It was an uneven war, with as many failures as victories. In 1902 he wrote The Battle with the Slum as a report on the first ten years of the struggle. It should be viewed, in Riis's words, as a "sequel" to How the Other Half Lives, because it "tells how far we have come and how." The volume contained detailed accounts of particular engagements, especially the replacement of some of the most infected buildings with Mulberry Bend Park. But in the Introduction, Riis put the problem of the slum in its broadest context and viewed it less as a mere matter of housing and more as a measure of the standard of civilization.

☆

THE SLUM is as old as civilization. Civilization implies a race to get ahead. In a race there are usually some who for one cause or another cannot keep up, or are thrust out from among their fellows. They fall behind, and when they have been left far in the rear they lose hope and ambition, and give up. Thenceforward, if left to their own resources, they are the victims, not the masters, of their environment; and it is a bad master. They drag one another always farther down. The bad environment becomes the heredity of the next generation. Then, given the crowd, you have the slum ready-made. The battle with the slum began the day civilization recognized in it her enemy. It was a losing fight until conscience joined forces with fear and self-interest against it. When common sense and the golden rule obtain among men as a rule of practice, it will be over. The two have not always been classed together, but here they are plainly seen to belong together. Justice to the individual is accepted in theory as the only safe groundwork of the commonwealth. When it is practised in dealing with the slum, there will shortly be no slum. We need not wait for the millennium, to get rid of it. We can do it now. All that is required is that it shall not be left to itself. That is justice to it and to us, since its grievous ailment is that it cannot help itself. When a man is drowning, the thing to do is to pull him out of the water; afterward there will be time for talking it over. We got at it the other way in dealing with our social problems. The wise men had their day, and they decided to let bad enough alone; that it was unsafe to interfere with "causes that operate sociologically," as one survivor of these unfittest put it to me. It was a piece of scientific humbug that cost the age which listened to it dear. "Causes that operate sociologically" are the opportunity of the political and every other kind of scamp who trades upon the depravity and helplessness of the slum, and the refuge of the pessimist who is useless in the fight against them. We have not done yet paying the bills he ran up for us. Some time since we turned to, to pull the drowning man out, and it was time. A little while longer, and we should hardly have escaped being dragged down with him.

The slum complaint had been chronic in all ages, but the great changes which the nineteenth century saw, the new industry, political freedom, brought on an acute attack which put that very freedom in jeopardy. Too many of us had supposed that, built as our commonwealth was on universal suf-

Riis's Introduction, entitled "What the Fight Is About," is taken from *The Battle with the Slum* (New York: The Macmillan Company, 1902), pp. 1–8.

frage, it would be proof against the complaints that harassed older states; but in fact it turned out that there was extra hazard in that. Having solemnly resolved that all men are created equal and have certain inalienable rights, among them life, liberty, and the pursuit of happiness, we shut our eyes and waited for the formula to work. It was as if a man with a cold should take the doctor's prescription to bed with him, expecting it to cure him. The formula was all right, but merely repeating it worked no cure. When, after a hundred years, we opened our eyes, it was upon sixty cents a day as the living wage of the working-woman in our cities; upon "knee pants" at forty cents a dozen for the making; upon the Potter's Field taking tithe of our city life, ten per cent each year for the trench, truly the Lost Tenth of the slum. Our country had grown great and rich; through our ports was poured food for the millions of Europe. But in the back streets multitudes huddled in ignorance and want. The foreign oppressor had been vanquished, the fetters stricken from the black man at home; but his white brother, in his bitter plight, sent up a cry of distress that had in it a distinct note of menace. Political freedom we had won; but the problem of helpless poverty, grown vast with the added offscourings of the Old World, mocked us, unsolved. Liberty at sixty cents a day set presently its stamp upon the government of our cities, and it became the scandal and the peril of our political system.

So the battle began. Three times since the war that absorbed the nation's energies and attention had the slum confronted us in New York with its challenge. In the darkest days of the great struggle it was the treacherous mob;[1] later on, the threat of the cholera, which found swine foraging in the streets as the only scavengers, and a swarming host, but little above the hog in its appetites and in the quality of the shelter afforded it, peopling the back alleys. Still later, the mob, caught looting the city's treasury with its idol, the thief Tweed, at its head, drunk with power and plunder, had insolently defied the outraged community to do its worst. There were meetings and protests. The rascals were turned out for a season; the arch-chief died in jail. I see him now, going through the gloomy portals of the Tombs, whither, as a newspaper reporter, I had gone with him, his stubborn head held high as ever. I asked myself more than once, at the time when the vile prison was torn down, whether the comic clamor to have the ugly old gates preserved and set up in Central Park had anything to do with the memory of the

[1] The draft riots of 1863.

"martyred" thief, or whether it was in joyful celebration of the fact that others had escaped. His name is even now one to conjure with in the Sixth Ward. He never "squealed," and he was "so good to the poor"—evidence that the slum is not laid by the heels by merely destroying Five Points and the Mulberry Bend. There are other fights to be fought in that war, other victories to be won, and it is slow work. It was nearly ten years after the Great Robbery before decency got a good upper grip. That was when the civic conscience awoke in 1879.

And after all that, the Lexow disclosures of inconceivable rottenness of a Tammany police; the woe unto you! of Christian priests calling vainly upon the chief of the city "to save its children from a living hell," and the contemptuous reply on the witness-stand of the head of the party of organized robbery, at the door of which it was all laid, that he was "in politics, working for his own pocket all the time, same as you and everybody else!"

Slow work, yes! but be it ever so slow, the battle has got to be fought, and fought out. For it is one thing or the other: either wipe out the slum, or it wipes out us. Let there be no mistake about this. It cannot be shirked. Shirking means surrender, and surrender means the end of government by the people.

If any one believes this to be needless alarm, let him think a moment. Government by the people must ever rest upon the people's ability to govern themselves, upon their intelligence and public spirit. The slum stands for ignorance, want, unfitness, for mob-rule in the day of wrath. This at one end. At the other, hard-heartedness, indifference, self-seeking, greed. It is human nature. We are brothers whether we own it or not, and when the brotherhood is denied in Mulberry Street we shall look vainly for the virtue of good citizenship on Fifth Avenue. When the slum flourishes unchallenged in the cities, their wharves may, indeed, be busy, their treasure-houses filled—wealth and want go so together,—but patriotism among their people is dead.

As long ago as the very beginning of our republic, its founders saw that the cities were danger-spots in their plan. In them was the peril of democratic government. At that time, scarce one in twenty-five of the people in the United States lived in a city. Now it is one in three. And to the selfishness of the trader has been added the threat of the slum. Ask yourself then how long before it would make an end of us, if let alone.

Put it this way: you cannot let men live like pigs when you

need their votes as freemen; it is not safe.[1] You cannot rob a child of its childhood, of its home, its play, its freedom from toil and care, and expect to appeal to the grown-up voter's manhood. The children are our to-morrow, and as we mould them to-day so will they deal with us then. Therefore that is not safe. Unsafest of all is any thing or deed that strikes at the home, for from the people's home proceeds citizen virtue, and nowhere else does it live. The slum is the enemy of the home. Because of it the chief city of our land came long ago to be called "The Homeless City." When this people comes to be truly called a nation without homes there will no longer be any nation.

Hence, I say, in the battle with the slum we win or we perish. There is no middle way. We shall win, for we are not letting things be the way our fathers did. But it will be a running fight, and it is not going to be won in two years, or in ten, or in twenty. For all that, we must keep on fighting, content if in our time we avert the punishment that waits upon the third and the fourth generation of those who forget the brotherhood. As a man does in dealing with his brother so it is the way of God that his children shall reap, that through toil and tears we may make out the lesson which sums up all the commandments and alone can make the earth fit for the kingdom that is to come.

In his Introduction, Riis transformed housing reform into a general attack on the broad range of problems which increasingly afflict an urban society. Practical experience had convinced him that the slum was merely a symptom of a deeper environmental malaise. Moreover, the nation's future was irretrievably cast with the city; every year the exodus from the farms indicated that the twentieth century would be shaped by the metropolis. If the slums were permitted to enlarge and fester, the new age would produce a sorry climax to the historic hopes and ideals of the Republic.

The clue to a better future was to be found in the young generation. Children were the special victims of the slums. "The boy who flings mud and stones," he wrote, "is entering

---

[1] "The experiment has been long tried on a large scale, with a dreadful success, affording the demonstration that if, from early infancy, you allow human beings to *live* like brutes, you can degrade them down to their level, leaving them scarcely more intellect, and no feelings and affections proper to human hearts."—*Report on the Health of British Towns.*

his protest in his own way against the purblind policy that gave him jails for schools and the gutter for a playground; that gave him dummies for laws and the tenement for a home." Better housing thus became the major instrument in breaking the vicious cycle of poverty, inadequate education, and limited opportunity. *"The home, the family are the rallying points of civilization,"* he contended. *"The greatness of a city is to be measured, not by its balance sheets of exports and imports, not by its fleet of merchantmen, or by its miles of paved streets, nor even by its colleges, its art museums, its schools of learning, but by its homes."*

The method of civic improvement was political action. From the free ballot, wisely used, would flow new tenement legislation, better schools, new playgrounds, and attractive neighborhoods. This faith led Riis, as well as later urban reformers, into continual conflict with local city bosses and political machines. To the reformer the central battleground for civic improvement was the political arena, and the great object was the control of City Hall. Riis could conveniently use Tammany as a symbol of the evil forces which prevented needed changes, but it was simply a New York expression of the enemy which frustrated decent people in every city.

Despite the apparent odds in this contest against the slums and its allies—entrenched economic interests and exasperating public apathy—Riis was optimistic about the future. He never doubted that men of good will would eventually conquer the tenement, eliminate substandard housing, and create a better metropolis. The more sophisticated might consider this faith naive, and the Annals of the American Academy of Political and Social Science might observe slightingly that *"with his usual hopefulness,"* Riis *"is still looking forward to better things in the future,"* yet later events were to vindicate his uncomplicated optimism.

The slums, of course, endured, but not to the extent or with the virulence of fifty or seventy-five years ago. In the 1960's the air would be filled with complaints about spreading blight, the decay of old neighborhoods, and the sickness of the ghetto. In historical perspective, however, the situation has vastly changed. Each year since World War II the proportion of substandard housing had declined. Federal, state, and local programs had wiped out many of the worst buildings, and a general prosperity made it possible for the children of former slum dwellers to move into better neighborhoods. The "other half" had been reduced to less than a fifth. To be sure, too many, especially Negroes, still languished in congestion and deprivation, but the mayors of cities like New

York, Chicago, and Atlanta were for the first time predicting the elimination of slums in the foreseeable future. When this generation declared war on poverty, it owed more than it knew to those like Jacob Riis who had established a beachhead against the enemy more than half a century before.

Lincoln Steffens

The Shame of the Cities

1902-1904

EDITED BY ARTHUR MANN

The Shame of the Cities, *published as a book in 1904 after first appearing as a series of articles in* McClure's Magazine *from October, 1902, to November, 1903, is a muckraking classic directed against municipal corruption during the Progressive Era. Yet its genesis was wholly unrelated to muckraking, urban politics, or progressivism. Lincoln Steffens stumbled into his subject by wandering, and he arrived at his purpose through afterthought.*

The wandering resulted from a conversation at McClure's on a December day in 1901. Steffens had been the managing editor of that popular monthly for three months, and his publisher, S. S. McClure, was telling him that he did not know how to manage a magazine. When Steffens asked how he was to learn, McClure advised him to get out of the office, board a train, and travel. "Meet people, find out what's on, and write yourself." The thirty-five-year-old journalist left for the Midwest, visiting a dozen cities or so by May 18, 1902, when he wrote to his father from Detroit: "My business is to find subjects and writers, to educate myself in the way the world is wagging, so as to bring the magazine up to date."

This odyssey of an editor in search of his craft led by chance to St. Louis, the subject of the first article of the series that grew into The Shame of the Cities, *yet the future dean of muckraking failed, at first, to recognize he had happened on his vocation. When the circuit (district) attorney of that corrupt river town revealed to Steffens a tale of bribery, Steffens commissioned a St. Louis reporter, Claude H. Wetmore, to write the article for McClure's, and then returned to his New York City desk. "I was not yet a muckraker," he later wrote.*

Then came the afterthought. Steffens compared what he had just learned about the Butler machine with what he already knew about Tammany Hall. Were "the extraordinary conditions of St. Louis and New York," he asked himself, "the ordinary conditions of city government in the United States?" Not yet certain that bribery was "a revolutionary process . . . going on in all cities," he inserted the idea as a hypothesis in Wetmore's manuscript, which he entitled "Tweed Days in St. Louis" and co-signed in order to take responsibility for adding lurid details the Missouri newsman had been afraid to include.

By the time the public read the article in the October, 1902, issue of McClure's, Steffens was back on the road, seeking proof for his hypothesis from bosses, reformers, crooks, cops, and businessmen; and installment followed installment, without the collaboration of local Wetmores, on the shame or near-shame or shamelessness of Minneapolis, again of St. Louis, of Pittsburgh, Philadelphia, Chicago, and New York. But Steffens was more than a reporter of graft; his exposés were aimed toward igniting a civic revival that would redeem democracy from dishonest politicians before corruption destroyed the American experiment in representative government. The series' last article, which follows immediately, expressed his purpose with particular force.

JUST about the time this article will appear, Greater New York will be holding a local election on what has come to be a national question—good government. . . . We can grasp firmly the essential issues involved and then watch with

The article, entitled "New York: Good Government to the Test," appeared first in *McClure's Magazine,* XXII (November, 1903), 84–92. It is reprinted here from *The Shame of the Cities* (New York: McClure, Phillips and Company, 1904), pp. 279–94, 302–3. The one footnote was part of the original text.

equanimity the returns for the answer, plain yes or no, which New York will give to the only questions that concern us all:*

Do we Americans really want good government? Do we know it when we see it? Are we capable of that sustained good citizenship which alone can make democracy a success? Or, to save our pride, one other: Is the New York way the right road to permanent reform?

For New York has good government, or, to be more precise, it has a good administration. It is not a question there of turning the rascals out and putting the honest men into their places. The honest men are in, and this election is to decide whether they are to be kept in, which is a very different matter. Any people is capable of rising in wrath to overthrow bad rulers. Philadelphia has done that in its day. New York has done it several times. With fresh and present outrages to avenge, particular villains to punish, and the mob sense of common anger to excite, it is an emotional gratification to go out with the crowd and "smash something." This is nothing but revolt, and even monarchies have uprisings to the credit of their subjects. But revolt is not reform, and one revolutionary administration is not good government. That we free Americans are capable of such assertions of our sovereign power, we have proven; our lynchers are demonstrating it every day. That we can go forth singly also, and, without passion, with nothing but mild approval and dull duty to impel us, vote intelligently to sustain a fairly good municipal government, remains to be shown. And that is what New York has the chance to show; New York, the leading exponent of the great American anti-bad government movement for good government.

According to this, the standard course of municipal reform, the politicians are permitted to organize a party on national lines, take over the government, corrupt and deceive the people, and run things for the private profit of the boss and his ring, till the corruption becomes rampant and a scandal. Then the reformers combine the opposition: the corrupt and unsatisfied minority, the disgruntled groups of the majority, the reform organizations; they nominate a mixed ticket, headed by a "good business man" for mayor, make a "hot campaign" against the government with "Stop, thief!" for the cry, and make a "clean sweep." Usually, this effects only the disciplining of the reckless grafters and the improvement of the graft system of corrupt government. The good mayor

* Tammany tried to introduce national issues, but failed, and "good government" was practically the only question raised.

turns out to be weak or foolish or "not so good." The politicians "come it over him," as they did over the business mayors who followed the "Gas Ring" revolt in Philadelphia, or the people become disgusted as they did with Mayor Strong, who was carried into office by the anti-Tammany rebellion in New York after the Lexow exposures. Philadelphia gave up after its disappointment, and that is what most cities do. The repeated failures of revolutionary reform to accomplish more than the strengthening of the machine have so discredited this method that wide-awake reformers in several cities—Pittsburg, Cincinnati, Cleveland, Detroit, Minneapolis, and others —are following the lead of Chicago.

The Chicago plan does not depend for success upon any one man or any one year's work, nor upon excitement or any sort of bad government. The reformers there have no ward organizations, no machine at all; their appeal is solely to the intelligence of the voter and their power rests upon that. This is democratic and political, not bourgeois and business reform, and it is interesting to note that whereas reformers elsewhere are forever seeking to concentrate all the powers in the mayor, those of Chicago talk of stripping the mayor to a figurehead and giving his powers to the aldermen who directly represent the people, and who change year by year.

The Chicago way is but one way, however, and a new one, and it must be remembered that this plan has not yet produced a good administration. New York has that. Chicago, after seven years' steady work, has a body of aldermen honest enough and competent to defend the city's interests against boodle capital, but that is about all; it has a wretched administration. New York has stuck to the old way. Provincial and self-centered, it hardly knows there is any other. Chicago laughs and other cities wonder, but never mind, New York, by persistence, has at last achieved a good administration. Will the New Yorkers continue it? That is the question. What Chicago has, it has secure. Its independent citizenship is trained to vote every time and to vote for uninteresting, good aldermen. New York has an independent vote of 100,-000, a decisive minority, but the voters have been taught to vote only once in a long while, only when excited by picturesque leadership and sensational exposures, only *against*. New York has been so far an anti-bad government, anti-Tammany, not a good-government town. Can it vote, without Tammany in to incite it, for a good mayor? I think this election, which will answer this question, should decide other cities how to go about reform.

The administration of Mayor Seth Low may not have been

perfect, not in the best European sense: not expert, not co-ordinated, certainly not wise. Nevertheless, for an American city, it has been not only honest, but able, undeniably one of the best in the whole country. Some of the departments have been dishonest; others have been so inefficient that they made the whole administration ridiculous. But what of that? Corruption also is clumsy and makes absurd mistakes when it is new and untrained. The "oaths" and ceremonies and much of the boodling of the St. Louis ring seemed laughable to my corrupt friends in Philadelphia and Tammany Hall, and New York's own Tweed régime was "no joke," only because it was so general, and so expensive—to New York. It took time to perfect the "Philadelphia plan" of misgovernment, and it took time to educate Croker and develop his Tammany Hall. It will take time to evolve masters of the (in America) unstudied art of municipal government—time and demand. So far there has been no market for municipal experts in this country. All we are clamoring for to-day in our meek, weak-hearted way, is that mean, rudimentary virtue miscalled "common honesty." Do we really want it? Certainly Mayor Low is pecuniarily honest. He is more; he is conscientious and experienced and personally efficient. Bred to business, he rose above it, adding to the training he acquired in the conduct of an international commercial house, two terms as mayor of Brooklyn, and to that again a very effective administration, as president, of the business of Columbia University. He began his mayoralty with a study of the affairs of New York; he has said himself that he devoted eight months to its finances: and he mastered this department and is admitted to be the maser in detail of every department which has engaged his attention. In other words, Mr. Low has learned the business of New York; he is just about competent now to become the mayor of a great city. Is there a demand for Mr. Low?

No. When I made my inquiries—before the lying had begun—the Fusion leaders of the anti-Tammany forces, who nominated Mr. Low, said they might renominate him. "Who else was there?" they asked. And they thought he "might" be re-elected. The alternative was Richard Croker or Charles F. Murphy, his man, for no matter who Tammany's candidate for mayor was, if Tammany won, Tammany's boss would rule. The personal issue was plain enough. Yet was there no assurance for Mr. Low.

Why? There are many forms of the answer given, but they nearly all reduce themselves to one—the man's personality. It is not very engaging. Mr. Low has many respectable qualities, but these never are amiable. "Did you ever see his smile?" said a politician who was trying to account for his instinctive dislike for the mayor. I had; there is no laughter back of it, no humor, and no sense thereof. The appealing human element is lacking all through. His good abilities are self-sufficient; his dignity is smug; his courtesy seems not kind; his self-reliance is called obstinacy because, though he listens, he seems not to care; though he understands, he shows no sympathy, and when he decides, his reasoning is private. His most useful virtues—probity, intelligence, and conscientiousness—in action are often an irritation; they are so contented. Mr. Low is the bourgeois reformer type. Even where he compromises he gets no credit, his concessions make the impression of surrenders. A politician can say "no" and make a friend, where Mr. Low will lose one by saying "yes." Cold and impersonal, he cools even his heads of departments. Loyal public service they give, because his taste is for men who would do their duty for their own sake, not for his, and that excellent service the city has had. But members of Mr. Low's administration helped me to characterize him; they could not help it. Mr. Low's is not a lovable character.

But what of that? Why should his colleagues love him? Why should anybody like him? Why should he seek to charm, win affection, and make friends? He was elected to attend to the business of his office and to appoint subordinates who should attend to the business of their offices, not to make "political strength" and win elections. William Travers Jerome, the picturesque District Attorney, whose sincerity and intellectual honesty made sure the election of Mr. Low two years ago, detests him as a bourgeois, but the mayoralty is held in New York to be a bourgeois office. Mr. Low is the ideal product of the New York theory that municipal government is business, not politics, and that a business man who would manage the city as he would a business corporation, would solve for us all our troubles. Chicago reformers think we have got to solve our own problems; that government is political business; that men brought up in politics and experienced in public office will make the best administrators. They have refused to turn from their politician mayor, Carter H. Harrison, for the most ideal business candidate, and I have heard them say that when Chicago was ripe for a better mayor they would prefer a candidate chosen from among their well-tried aldermen. Again, I say, however, that this is only one way, and New York has another, and this other is the standard American way.

But again I say, also, that the New York way is on trial,

for New York has what the whole country has been looking for in all municipal crises—the non-political ruler. Mr. Low's very faults, which I have emphasized for the purpose, emphasize the point. They make it impossible for him to be a politician even if he should wish to be. As for his selfishness, his lack of tact, his coldness—these are of no consequence. He has done his duty all the better for them. Admit that he is uninteresting; what does that matter? He has served the city. Will the city not vote for him because it does not like the way he smiles? Absurd as it sounds, that is what all I have heard against Low amounts to. But to reduce the situation to a further absurdity, let us eliminate altogether the personality of Mr. Low. Let us suppose he has no smile, no courtesy, no dignity, no efficiency, no personality at all; suppose he were an It and had not given New York a good administration, but had only honestly tried. What then?

Tammany Hall? That is the alternative. The Tammany politicians see it just as clear as that, and they are not in the habit of deceiving themselves. They say "it is a Tammany year," "Tammany's turn." They say it and they believe it. They study the people, and they know it is all a matter of citizenship; they admit that they cannot win unless a goodly part of the independent vote goes to them; and still they say they can beat Mr. Low or any other man the anti-Tammany forces may nominate. So we are safe in eliminating Mr. Low and reducing the issue to plain Tammany.

Tammany is bad government; not inefficient, but dishonest; not a party, not a delusion and a snare, hardly known by its party name—Democracy; having little standing in the national councils of the party and caring little for influence outside of the city. Tammany is Tammany, the embodiment of corruption. All the world knows and all the world may know what it is and what it is after. For hypocrisy is not a Tammany vice. Tammany is for Tammany, and the Tammany men say so. Other rings proclaim lies and make pretensions; other rogues talk about the tariff and imperialism. Tammany is honestly dishonest. Time and time again, in private and in public, the leaders, big and little, have said they are out for themselves and for their own; not for the public, but for "me and my friends"; not for New York, but for Tammany. Richard Croker said under oath once that he worked for his own pockets all the time, and Tom Grady, the Tammany orator, has brought his crowds to their feet cheering sentiments as primitive, stated with candor as brutal.

The man from Mars would say that such an organization, so self-confessed, could not be very dangerous to an intelligent people. Foreigners marvel at it and at us, and even Americans—Pennsylvanians, for example—cannot understand why we New Yorkers regard Tammany as so formidable. I think I can explain it. Tammany is corruption with consent; it is bad government founded on the suffrages of the people. The Philadelphia machine is more powerful. It rules Philadelphia by fraud and force and does not require the votes of the people. The Philadelphians do not vote for their machine; their machine votes for them. Tammany used to stuff the ballot boxes and intimidate voters; to-day there is practically none of that. Tammany rules, when it rules, by right of the votes of the people of New York.

Tammany corruption is democratic corruption. That of the Philadelphia ring is rooted in special interests. Tammany, too, is allied with "vested interests"—but Tammany labors under disadvantages not known in Philadelphia. The Philadelphia ring is of the same party that rules the State and the nation, and the local ring forms a living chain with the State and national rings. Tammany is a purely local concern. With a majority only in old New York, it has not only to buy what it wants from the Republican majority in the State, but must trade to get the whole city. Big business everywhere is the chief source of political corruption, and it is one source in New York; but most of the big businesses represented in New York have no plants there. Offices there are, and head offices, of many trusts and railways, for example, but that is all. There are but two railway terminals in the city, and but three railways use them. These have to do more with Albany than New York. So with Wall Street. Philadelphia's stock exchange deals largely in Pennsylvania securities, New York's in those of the whole United States. There is a small Wall Street group that specializes in local corporations, and they are active and give Tammany a Wall Street connection, but the biggest and the majority of our financial leaders, bribers though they may be in other cities and even in New York State, are independent of Tammany Hall, and can be honest citizens at home. From this class, indeed, New York can, and often does, draw some of its reformers. Not so Philadelphia. That bourgeois opposition which has persisted for thirty years in the fight against Tammany corruption was squelched in Philadelphia after its first great uprising. Matt Quay, through the banks, railways, and other business interests, was able to reach it. A large part of his power is negative; there is no opposition. Tammany's power is positive. Tammany cannot reach all the largest interests and its hold is upon the people.

Tammany's democratic corruption rests upon the corruption of the people, the plain people, and there lies its great significance; its grafting system is one in which more individuals snare than any I have studied. The people themselves get very little; they come cheap, but they are interested. Divided into districts, the organization subdivides them into precincts or neighborhoods, and their sovereign power, in the form of votes, is bought up by kindness and petty privileges. They are forced to a surrender, when necessary, by intimidation, but the leader and his captains have their hold because they take care of their own. They speak pleasant words, smile friendly smiles, notice the baby, give picnics up the River or the Sound, or a slap on the back; find jobs, most of them at the city's expense, but they have also news-stands, peddling privileges, railroad and other business places to dispense; they permit violations of the law, and, if a man has broken the law without permission, see him through the court. Though a blow in the face is as readily given as a shake of the hand, Tammany kindness is real kindness, and will go far, remember long, and take infinite trouble for a friend.

The power that is gathered up thus cheaply, like garbage, in the districts is concentrated in the district leader, who in turn passes it on through a general committee to the boss. This is a form of living government, extra-legal, but very actual, and, though the beginnings of it are purely democratic, it develops at each stage into an autocracy. In Philadelphia the boss appoints a district leader and gives him power. Tammany has done that in two or three notable instances, but never without causing a bitter fight which lasts often for years. In Philadelphia the State boss designates the city boss. In New York, Croker has failed signally to maintain vice-bosses whom he appointed. The boss of Tammany Hall is a growth, and just as Croker grew, so has Charles F. Murphy grown up to Croker's place. Again, whereas in Philadelphia the boss and his ring handle and keep almost all of the graft, leaving little to the district leaders, in New York the district leaders share handsomely in the spoils. . . .

Tammany leaders are usually the natural leaders of the people in these districts, and they are originally good-natured, kindly men. No one has a more sincere liking than I for some of those common but generous fellows; their charity is real, at first. But they sell out their own people. They do give them coal and help them in their private troubles, but, as they grow rich and powerful, the kindness goes out of the charity and they not only collect at their saloons or in rents —cash for their "goodness"; they not only ruin fathers and sons and cause the troubles they relieve; they sacrifice the children in the schools; let the Health Department neglect the tenements, and, worst of all, plant vice in the neighborhood and in the homes of the poor.

This is not only bad; it is bad politics; it has defeated Tammany. Woe to New York when Tammany learns better. Honest fools talk of the reform of Tammany Hall. It is an old hope, this, and twice it has been disappointed, but it is not vain. That is the real danger ahead. The reform of a corrupt ring means, as I have said before, the reform of its system of grafting and a wise consideration of certain features of good government. Croker turned his "best chief of police," William S. Devery, out of Tammany Hall, and, slow and old as he was, Croker learned what clean streets were from Colonel Waring, and gave them. Now there is a new boss, a young man, Charles F. Murphy, and unknown to New Yorkers. He looks dense, but he acts with force, decision, and skill. The new mayor will be his man. He may divide with Croker and leave to the "old man" all his accustomed graft, but Charlie Murphy will rule Tammany and, if Tammany is elected, New York also. . . .

As a New Yorker, I fear Murphy will prove sagacious enough to do just that: stop the scandal, put all the graft in the hands of a few tried and true men, and give the city what it would call good government. Murphy says he will nominate for mayor a man so "good" that his goodness will astonish New York. I don't fear a bad Tammany mayor; I dread the election of a good one. For I have been to Philadelphia.

The Shame of the Cities was an immediate success and helped to prepare the ground for a new era in popular journalism. Steffens' second installment, on Minneapolis, appeared in the same issue that carried Ida Tarbell's "History of the Standard Oil" and Ray Stannard Baker's "The Right to Work." S. S. McClure explained: "We did not plan it so; it is a coincidence that this number contains three arraignments of American character such as should make every one of us stop and think." The coincidence was so well received that arraignments became McClure's trademark, and Steffens was soon writing to his father that circulation had increased by 55 per cent. Other magazines followed suit; by 1904 muckraking was a movement.

Previously a successful enough young reporter (on the Evening Post) and newspaper editor (of the Commercial Advertiser) whose audience had been limited to New York City,

Steffens became a braintruster to reformers—from E. A. Filene's Boston to Rudolph Spreckels' San Francisco. In 1906 he turned down an offer from William Randolph Hearst, the most flamboyant muckraker of the age, to edit a new journal at a salary of $20,000 a year, plus a half share in the net profits. Steffens started his own American Magazine that year. His first book (four others were to follow by 1913) had made his reputation. Deriving immense personal satisfaction from his triumph, he confided to his father: "Why not the praise? I won it without a sacrifice, without one single compromise."

That self-estimate was fair. The Shame of the Cities was carefully researched, honestly indignant, and relatively free of the sentimental claptrap that Steffens would later compose about the paradox of good bad bosses. And if he was wrong to suppose that bribery was the norm for "all" American cities, he was right to think that it was a national problem. No other writer before, not even the celebrated Lord Bryce, made the American people so conscious of that fact.

Yet the movements that stemmed from that consciousness were only temporarily successful. Corrupt rulers were thrown out of office, but they came back, and the cycle of exposé and reform had to begin again. Why, after the public was alerted, did crooked government return? In a letter to President Theodore Roosevelt in 1908, Steffens located the cause of corruption in the need of businesses for special privileges from government, but not until his Autobiography, published in 1931, did he carry this idea to what he then thought was its inevitable conclusion about the uselessness of American liberalism.

And it is here that we touch on the Marxist misuse of The Shame of the Cities, for which Steffens himself was to blame. Writing under the influence of the Russian Revolution and convinced that the Depression had doomed American capitalism, the former muckraker retold his experiences as a municipal reformer during the Progressive Era and concluded that it had been futile to try to patch up the System. The only solution was to take away the means of production and exchange from private ownership. Just how many readers agreed with this message is unknown, but for "those of us who were well on our way to Communism when the Autobiography appeared," Granville Hicks has written, "the book . . . showed that there was a strictly American path to Communist conclusions. . . ." Although Steffens did not join the Communist Party, he openly blessed it and, what is equally important, used his immense prestige to denounce liberal reform. Had he not tried it, led it, sustained it, and failed at it?

According to Hicks, Steffens had always been an absolutist, his pragmatic stance notwithstanding. The Autobiography strongly supports this interpretation, but the Letters, published in 1938, suggest the presence of an open, inquiring, flexible mind to about the time of World War I. Yet, whatever the final verdict will be about Steffens' quest for certitude, it is clear that the Autobiography read uses into The Shame of the Cities that were not there in 1904.

The Steffens who acclaimed Lenin as "the greatest of liberals" was not the same Steffens who had expressed qualified admiration for Mayor Seth Low. Where the later ideologue insisted that all roads must lead to Moscow, the earlier reporter had perceived that what worked in Chicago was not necessarily the way to improve New York. Every city has its own history, its own causes for graft, its own resources for progressive change. Before he succumbed to the metaphysics of inevitability and the mysticism of utopianism, Steffens' high moral purpose had assumed a respect for evidence, an appreciation for diversity, and an understanding that freedom means choice. The Shame of the Cities belongs to our usable past because it reminds us, in plain yet passionate language, that the struggle for good government is varied and unending. And that one must be prepared for disappointments.

Oliver Wendell Holmes, Jr.

Two Dissenting Opinions

1904, 1919

EDITED BY PAUL A. FREUND

LOCHNER v. NEW YORK

As part of a comprehensive law regulating the conditions of labor in bakeries, the New York legislature in 1897 made it a misdemeanor to allow any bakery employee to work more than ten hours a day or sixty hours a week. Lochner, a proprietor of a bakery in Utica, was convicted under the law for permitting an employee to work in excess of the weekly limit. The highest court of the state upheld the conviction by a four-to-three decision, and an appeal was taken to the Supreme Court of the United States. On April 17, 1905, that Court reversed the conviction, dividing five to four.

The central issue was whether the law violated the due-process clause of the Fourteenth Amendment of the United States Constitution: "nor shall any state deprive any person of life, liberty or property without due process of law." For the majority of the Supreme Court, Mr. Justice Peckham asserted that a legal limitation on hours of labor of able-bodied men in industries not peculiarly unhealthful was an arbitrary deprivation of the employer's and the employees' liberty of

685

contract. Such restrictions, he said, were "mere meddlesome interferences with the rights of the individual." A dissenting opinion of Mr. Justice Harlan, joined by two associates, drew upon studies showing the actual conditions confronting workers in bakeshops, and the bearing of excessive hours upon the health of workers. The dissenting opinion of Mr. Justice Holmes, here printed, spoke for himself alone. Eschewing alike the abstractions of the majority regarding liberty of contract, and the empirical data garnered by the other dissenters, he pitched his position characteristically on philosophic ground: the responsibility of the judge called on to apply the vague terms of an enduring constitution to novel social legislation with which as a private individual he may have no sympathy.

I REGRET sincerely that I am unable to agree with the judgment in this case, and that I think it my duty to express my dissent.

This case is decided upon an economic theory which a large part of the country does not entertain. If it were a question whether I agreed with that theory, I should desire to study it further and long before making up my mind. But I do not conceive that to be my duty, because I strongly believe that my agreement or disagreement has nothing to do with the right of a majority to embody their opinions in law. It is settled by various decisions of this court that state constitutions and state laws may regulate life in many ways which we as legislators might think as injudicious or if you like as tyrannical as this, and which equally with this interfere with the liberty to contract. Sunday laws and usury laws are ancient examples. A more modern one is the prohibition of lotteries. The liberty of the citizen to do as he likes so long as he does not interfere with the liberty of others to do the same, which has been a shibboleth for some well-known writers, is interfered with by school laws, by the Post Office, by every state or municipal institution which takes his money for purposes thought desirable, whether he likes it or not. The Fourteenth Amendment does not enact Mr. Herbert Spencer's Social Statics. The other day we sustained the Massachusetts vaccination law. *Jacobson v. Massachusetts,* 197 U.S. 11. United States and state statutes and decisions cutting down the liberty to contract by way of combi-

The opinion is reprinted here from 198 U.S. 74 (1904).

nation are familiar to this court. *Northern Securities Co. v. United States,* 193 U.S. 197. Two years ago we upheld the prohibition of sales of stock on margins or for future delivery in the constitution of California. *Otis v. Parker,* 187 U.S. 606. The decision sustaining an eight hour law for miners is still recent. *Holden v. Hardy,* 169 U.S. 366. Some of these laws embody convictions or prejudices which judges are likely to share. Some may not. But a constitution is not intended to embody a particular economic theory, whether of paternalism and the organic relation of the citizen to the State or of laissez faire. It is made for people of fundamentally differing views, and the accident of our finding certain opinions natural and familiar or novel and even shocking ought not to conclude our judgment upon the question whether statutes embodying them conflict with the Constitution of the United States.

General propositions do not decide concrete cases. The decision will depend on a judgment or intuition more subtle than any articulate major premise. But I think that the proposition just stated, if it is accepted, will carry us far toward the end. Every opinion tends to become a law. I think that the word liberty in the Fourteenth Amendment is perverted when it is held to prevent the natural outcome of a dominant opinion, unless it can be said that a rational and fair man necessarily would admit that the statute proposed would infringe fundamental principles as they have been understood by the traditions of our people and our law. It does not need research to show that no such sweeping condemnation can be passed upon the statute before us. A reasonable man might think it a proper measure on the score of health. Men whom I certainly could not pronounce unreasonable would uphold it as a first instalment of a general regulation of the hours of work. Whether in the latter aspect it would be open to the charge of inequality I think it unnecessary to discuss.

In an address delivered in 1913, nine years after the Lochner *dissent, Justice Holmes described the issue with a candor reserved for extrajudicial utterances: "When twenty years ago a vague terror went over the earth and the word socialism began to be heard, I thought and still think that fear was translated into doctrines that had no proper place in the Constitution or the common law. . . . We too need education in the obvious—to learn to transcend our own convictions and*

*to leave room for much that we hold dear to be done away
with short of revolution by the orderly change of law."*

But the tide was beginning to recede. The Lochner *decision
itself was probably the high-water mark of judicial vetoes of
social legislation by judges indoctrinated with a laissez faire
philosophy. In the precise field of that decision, the setting of
maximum hours of labor, the Court in 1917 sustained an
Oregon ten-hour law as a valid health measure. The* Lochner
*case was not even mentioned in the Court's opinion; as
Holmes was to say later, it was given a deserved repose. Indeed the Oregon law was more sweeping than the earlier
New York act, since it applied to all forms of manufacturing
establishments. Thus, as Holmes had foreseen in his dissenting opinion, the ten-hour day for bakers was the "first instalment of a general regulation of the hours of work."*

As legislative controls came to permeate more and more
deeply the American economic structure, the special quality
of Holmes's opinion became increasingly significant. The
older view of the so-called constitutional police powers of the
state—that they were to be exercised for the public health,
safety, or morals—was hardly adequate for the more pervasive and sophisticated forms of modern social legislation.
Hours-of-labor laws themselves moved a long way from the
ten-hour day at which the Court had balked. A thirty-hour
week, with provision for overtime rates of pay, can scarcely
find its justification as a protection against fatigue; it must be
dealt with as a measure to spread employment or increase actual wages. And so, by taking broad constitutional ground, by
calling on judges to transcend the limitations of their private
outlook, Holmes laid the basis for judicial toleration of economic legislation more novel and sophisticated than that
which, primitive as it was, a majority of his own colleagues in
1904 had frustrated.

Holmes's constitutional philosophy was carried on and
strengthened by his later colleagues Hughes, Brandeis, and
Stone, and his successor, Cardozo. Not until after his death
was a majority of the Court mustered, in 1937, to sustain a
minimum-wage law. But thereafter Herbert Spencer's social
statics ceased to place constitutional obstacles in the Supreme
Court to economic regulation, whether of hours, wages,
prices, competitive practices, or even the aesthetics of zoning.
The debate over state intervention centers, as Holmes insisted
it should, on issues of public policy rather than constitutional
law. Indeed the question is sometimes raised whether the
Court has gone too far in its abstention; whether, that is,
some kinds of economic regulation, like restrictions on access

to certain occupations, touch so centrally the development of human personality that they should be reviewed more critically by the Court under the rubric of liberty in the Fourteenth Amendment.

ABRAMS v. UNITED STATES

The wartime Espionage Act of 1917, as amended in 1918, made it a felony punishable by imprisonment up to twenty years to urge the curtailment of production of any things necessary to the prosecution of the war, with intent to hinder its prosecution. Abrams and four associates were indicted for conspiracy to violate this Act; they were accused of having printed and disseminated leaflets assailing in vehement terms the dispatch of American forces to Russia in 1918, and of having urged workers to strike rather than produce arms to be used against the Soviet people. The defendants were young Russian immigrants employed in a hat factory in New York City. Their trial was presided over by Judge Clayton of Alabama, sitting by special assignment in New York. Upon a finding of guilty by the jury, they were sentenced to the maximum term of twenty years. Their case was appealed to the United States Supreme Court and was decided there on November 10, 1919. By a vote of seven to two the convictions were affirmed. Mr. Justice Holmes was joined in his dissenting opinion by Mr. Justice Brandeis.

The opening part (not printed here) of Holmes's dissenting opinion is concerned with the question whether the leaflets could in fact be said to violate the terms of the statute in view of the equivocal intention of the defendants. They were heartily opposed to Germany and German militarism; their animus was directed at a military expedition which in their view (and in the view of some competent military critics and historians) did not contribute to the successful prosecution of the war against Germany, but instead was a threat to the revolutionary struggle going on within Russia. From his analysis of the issue of specific intent required by law, Holmes proceeded to the larger question of the constitutional guarantee of freedom of speech. Here he advances the test of "clear and present danger" in order to mark the line between permissible speech and criminal incitement; in this case, he argued, the circumstances were short of any clear and imminent danger of actual obstruction of the conduct of the war, and hence the defendants were constitutionally immune from liability for their words. In correspondence with Holmes following the decision, Sir Frederick Pollock remarked that the defendants' conduct, if punished at all in England, would have met with a sentence of perhaps three months' imprisonment. The severity of the sentence, however, was not a matter over which the Supreme Court of the United States could exercise a reviewing authority. In fact, the sentences of the defendants were commuted by the President late in 1921, on condition that they be deported to Russia.

I T SEEMS to me that this statute must be taken to use its words in a strict and accurate sense. They would be absurd in any other. A patriot might think that we were wasting money on aeroplanes, or making more cannon of a certain kind than we needed, and might advocate curtailment with success, yet even if it turned out that the curtailment hindered and was thought by other minds to have been obviously likely to hinder the United States in the prosecution of the war, no one would hold such conduct a crime. I admit that my illustration does not answer all that might be said but it is enough to show what I think and to let me pass to a more important aspect of the case. I refer to the First Amendment to the Constitution that Congress shall make no law abridging the freedom of speech.

I never have seen any reason to doubt that the questions of law that alone were before this Court in the cases of *Schenck, Frohwerk* and *Debs,* 249 U.S. 47, 204, 211, were rightly decided. I do not doubt for a moment that by the same reasoning that would justify punishing persuasion to murder, the United States constitutionally may punish speech that produces or is intended to produce a clear and imminent danger that it will bring about forthwith certain substantive evils that the United States constitutionally may seek to prevent. The power undoubtedly is greater in time of war than in time of peace because war opens dangers that do not exist at other times.

But as against dangers peculiar to war, as against others, the principle of the right to free speech is always the same. It is only the present danger of immediate evil or an intent to bring it about that warrants Congress in setting a limit to the expression of opinion where private rights are not concerned. Congress certainly cannot forbid all effort to change the mind of the country. Now nobody can suppose that the surrepti-

The opinion is reprinted here from 250 U.S. 627 (1919).

tious publishing of a silly leaflet by an unknown man, without more, would present any immediate danger that its opinions would hinder the success of the government arms or have any appreciable tendency to do so. Publishing those opinions for the very purpose of obstructing however, might indicate a greater danger and at any rate would have the quality of an attempt. So I assume that the second leaflet if published for the purposes alleged in the fourth count might be punishable. But it seems pretty clear to me that nothing less than that would bring these papers within the scope of this law. An actual intent in the sense that I have explained is necessary to constitute an attempt where a further act of the same individual is required to complete the substantive crime, for reasons given in *Swift & Co. v. United States,* 196 U.S. 375, 396. It is necessary where the success of the attempt depends upon others because if that intent is not present the actor's aim may be accomplished without bringing about the evils sought to be checked. An intent to prevent interference with the revolution in Russia might have been satisfied without any hindrance to carrying on the war in which we were engaged.

I do not see how anyone can find the intent required by the statute in any of the defendants' words. The second leaflet is the only one that affords even a foundation for the charge, and there, without invoking the hatred of German militarism expressed in the former one, it is evident from the beginning to the end that the only object of the paper is to help Russia and stop American intervention there against the popular government—not to impede the United States in the war that it was carrying on. To say that two phrases taken literally might import a suggestion of conduct that would have interference with the war as an indirect and probably undesired effort seems to me by no means enough to show an attempt to produce that effect.

I return for a moment to the third count. That charges an intent to provoke resistance to the United States in its war with Germany. Taking the clause in the statute that deals with that in connection with the other elaborate provisions of the act, I think that resistance to the United States means some forcible act of opposition to some proceeding of the United States in pursuance of the war. I think the intent must be the specific intent that I have described and for the reasons that I have given I think that no such intent was proved or existed in fact. I also think that there is no hint at resistance to the United States as I construe the phrase.

In this case sentences of twenty years imprisonment have

been imposed for the publishing of two leaflets that I believe the defendants had as much right to publish as the Government has to publish the Constitution of the United States now vainly invoked by them. Even if I am technically wrong and enough can be squeezed from these poor and puny anonymities to turn the color of legal litmus paper; I will add, even if what I think the necessary intent were shown; the most nominal punishment seems to me all that possibly could be inflicted, unless the defendants are to be made to suffer not for what the indictment alleges but for the creed that they avow—a creed that I believe to be the creed of ignorance and immaturity when honestly held, as I see no reason to doubt that it was held here, but which, although made the subject of examination at the trial, no one has a right even to consider in dealing with the charges before the Court.

Persecution for the expression of opinions seems to me perfectly logical. If you have no doubt of your premises or your power and want a certain result with all your heart you naturally express your wishes in law and sweep away all opposition. To allow opposition by speech seems to indicate that you think the speech impotent, as when a man says that he has squared the circle, or that you do not care whole-heartedly for the result, or that you doubt either your power or your premises. But when men have realized that time has upset many fighting faiths, they may come to believe even more than they believe the very foundations of their own conduct that the ultimate good desired is better reached by free trade in ideas—that the best test of truth is the power of the thought to get itself accepted in the competition of the market, and that truth is the only ground upon which their wishes safely can be carried out. That at any rate is the theory of our Constitution. It is an experiment, as all life is an experiment. Every year if not every day we have to wager our salvation upon some prophecy based upon imperfect knowledge. While that experiment is part of our system I think that we should be eternally vigilant against attempts to check the expression of opinions that we loathe and believe to be fraught with death, unless they so imminently threaten immediate interference with the lawful and pressing purposes of the law that an immediate check is required to save the country. I wholly disagree with the argument of the Government that the First Amendment left the common law as to seditious libel in force. History seems to me against the notion. I had conceived that the United States through many years had shown its repentance for the Sedition Act of 1798, by repaying fines that it imposed. Only the emergency that makes it immediately dangerous to leave the correction of evil counsels to time warrants making any exception to the sweeping command, "Congress shall make no law . . . abridging the freedom of speech." Of course I am speaking only of expressions of opinion and exhortations, which were all that were uttered here, but I regret that I cannot put into more impressive words my belief that in their conviction upon his indictment the defendants were deprived of their rights under the Constitution of the United States.

The problem which Justice Holmes faced in the Abrams *case is near the center of the theory of democracy: when, if ever, is a state justified in suppressing the speech of nonconformity; in Milton's words, what are the utterances that "no law can possibly permit, that intends not to unlaw itself"? As a student of the common law Holmes drew on an analogy from the law of crimes: the line between mere preparation to commit an offense, which is left unpunished by the law, and an attempt to do so which is sufficiently close to fruition to constitute a social danger recognized by the law.*

As a criterion in constitutional law for marking the bounds of speech that must be immune under the First Amendment, the doctrine of "clear and present danger" has had a significant role, though it has been subjected to some refinements and qualifications. In the field of seditious speech, where it had its origin, it proved most decisive in the case of Herndon v. Lowry, *decided in 1937, where the Supreme Court reversed the conviction of a Negro Communist in Georgia who was in possession of a booklet urging a Negro insurrection and Negro rule in an interstate domain in the South. In other cases the ambiguities of the doctrine produced certain modifications. Must the evil which is threatened in consequence of the speech be that which the speaker has meant to produce? It has been reasonably clear that no such identity is required; speech intended to produce a revolution may lose its immunity if it presents a clear and present danger of inciting a riot. But suppose the unlawful consequence which is imminent is relatively trivial, like trespass to land, and the speech itself is on a great public theme. In such a balance, Mr. Justice Brandeis suggested that, despite the clear and present danger of unlawful acts, the speech would retain its immunity, for the evil to be avoided must be relatively serious in relation to the significance of the speech. Thus the test, in the hands of a sensitive judge, is far from a mechanical one.*

In the contemporary world the converse problem has proved still more troublesome—a danger to the state of utmost seriousness, but not an imminent one. The prosecution of officers of the Communist Party under the Smith Act of 1940 elicited a qualification of the doctrine moving in the opposite direction from Justice Brandeis. Judge Learned Hand in the Federal Court of Appeals, and Chief Justice Vinson for a majority of the Supreme Court, formulated the doctrine as permitting punishment where the gravity of the danger, discounted by its improbability, represented, in the judgment of the legislature and of the Court, a threat calling for intervention by the law. More recent decisions have placed limits on the law not so much through the application of a modified "clear and present danger" test as through an interpretation of the statutory term "advocacy" to require something like a call to action and not simply an abstract or philosophic effort at persuasion.

The question remains open how far the "clear and present danger" test is appropriate for speech not in the area of sedition. If the rationale of the doctrine is that the free play of ideas must be permitted so long as there is time to meet them with counter-speech, the doctrine has limited relevance to speech which by its nature is not part of the forum of ideas. Thus problems of obscenity and of newspaper comment on pending trials can be distinguished in that the evils apprehended are not of a kind which can be counteracted by offsetting speech. In these kinds of cases the Supreme Court has divided on the pertinence of the "clear and present danger" doctrine.

A further aspect of Holmes's dissenting opinion deserves to be noticed. In this case he formulated a standard of judicial review of legislation quite different from that in his dissenting opinion in the Lochner *case. There the legislative judgment was to prevail unless patently arbitrary; here the legislative judgment must satisfy a stricter standard. Taken together, the two opinions pose implicitly the problem of what has been called a double standard in judicial review of legislation; or, as it has sometimes been put, whether the basic freedoms of speech, press, and assembly have a "preferred position" among constitutionally protected interests. While explanations have differed, there has been general agreement on the Supreme Court that the two approaches to judicial review are not rationally inconsistent. Perhaps the most articulate reconciliation holds that, while the legislative judgment is normally to be given every presumptive support, a law which by interfering with speech or press or assembly fetters the political*

*process itself should be viewed more critically just because
the respect normally owing to the legislative product presupposes a properly functioning political process.*

*The final theme of Holmes's opinion is a pervasive skepti-
cism (tempered for him by a puritanic sense of duty and a
romantic faith in action—the soldier's faith, he called it).
How far does his argument for freedom of speech depend on
his skeptical view of truth? That view has brought condemnation of Holmes by a number of natural-law philosophers. But
other orthodox theologians have in effect come to Holmes's
position by another path: absolute truth can be apprehended
by man in only a fragmentary, historically distorted form,
and hence it behooves us not to suppress, in our historical
predicament, even the most radical questionings.*

William L. Riordon

Plunkitt of Tammany Hall

1905

EDITED BY JOHN P. ROCHE

---

*George Washington Plunkitt was at the turn of this century
what students of American politics sometimes call a "second-
level political entrepreneur," an erudite term for a ward boss
and inside man at City Hall. It was Plunkitt's good fortune to
meet William L. Riordon, a political reporter for the* New
York Evening Post *who was impressed by the old rascal and
began taking notes of their conversations. At regular intervals
Riordon would call on Plunkitt at his "office"—Graziano's
shoeshine parlor in the New York County Court House—and
stimulate the Tammany sage to deliver his thoughts on events
of the day. The result was a "Series of Very Plain Talks on
Very Practical Politics" which Riordon published in the* Post
*and later the same year, 1905, published as a book under the
title* Plunkitt of Tammany Hall.

*In his introduction, Riordon gave the following summary
of Plunkitt's career:*

> He was born, as he proudly tells, in Central Park—that is,
> in the territory now included in the park. He began life as a
> driver of a cart, then became a butcher's boy, and later went

*into the butcher business for himself. . . . He was in the
[New York State] Assembly soon after he cast his first vote
and has held office most of the time for forty years. [At one
point in his career he] drew three salaries at once—a record
unexampled in New York politics.*

Needless to say, Plunkitt was an Irish-American stalwart and
an important cog in the Irish political machine which dominated Manhattan, with occasional intervals of Anglo-Saxon
Protestant reform, for almost a century. Elsewhere in his discourses Plunkitt expresses his frank view of the reformers. In
a curious anticipation of Max Weber's thesis on the inter-
connection between Protestantism and capitalism, Plunkitt
argued that the reformers were miserly thieves who had no
sense of community obligation and puritanically refused to
share the loot.

There have been suggestions that Riordon may have improved a little on his original, but Plunkitt never complained.
Like a Boston politician who was quoted by a newspaperman
in most felicitous fashion to the suspicious astonishment of
his intimates, Plunkitt could well have observed, "If I didn't
say it, by God I should have." And Socrates, of course, owes
his good press to Plato. Yet even if Plunkitt of Tammany
Hall was a triumph of art over life, the views expressed were
in substance clearly authentic—as was the "Tribute" penned
by Tammany's austere boss, "Mister" Murphy, at the beginning of the book:

> Senator Plunkitt is a straight organization man. He believes
> in party government; he does not indulge in cant and hypoc-
> risy and he is never afraid to say exactly what he thinks. He is
> a believer in thorough political organization and all-the-year-
> around work, and he holds to the doctrine that, in making ap-
> pointments to office, party workers should be preferred if they
> are fitted to perform the duties of the office. Plunkitt is one of
> the veteran leaders of the organization; he has always been
> faithful and reliable, and he has performed valuable services
> for Tammany Hall.

CHARLES F. MURPHY

HONEST GRAFT AND DISHONEST GRAFT

EVERYBODY is talkin' these days about Tammany men grow-
in' rich on graft, but nobody thinks of drawin' the distinction between honest graft and dishonest graft. There's all the
difference in the world between the two. Yes, many of our

men have grown rich in politics. I have myself. I've made a big fortune out of the game, and I'm getting richer every day, but I've not gone in for dishonest graft—blackmailin' gamblers, saloonkeepers, disorderly people, etc.—and neither has any of the men who have made big fortunes in politics.

There's an honest graft, and I'm an example of how it works. I might sum up the whole thing by sayin': "I seen my opportunities and I took 'em."

Just let me explain by examples. My party's in power in the city, and it's goin' to undertake a lot of public improvements. Well, I'm tipped off, say, that they're going to lay out a new park at a certain place.

I see my opportunity and I take it. I go to that place and I buy up all the land I can in the neighborhood. Then the board of this or that makes its plan public, and there is a rush to get my land, which nobody cared particular for before.

Ain't it perfectly honest to charge a good price and make a profit on my investment and foresight? Of course, it is. Well, that's honest graft.

Or supposin' it's a new bridge they're goin' to build. I get tipped off and I buy as much property as I can that has to be taken for approaches. I sell at my own price later on and drop some more money in the bank.

Wouldn't you? It's just like lookin' ahead in Wall Street or in the coffee or cotton market. It's honest graft, and I'm lookin' for it every day in the year. I will tell you frankly that I've got a good lot of it, too.

I'll tell you of one case. They were goin' to fix up a big park, no matter where. I got on to it, and went lookin' about for land in that neighborhood.

I could get nothin' at a bargain but a big piece of swamp, but I took it fast enough and held on to it. What turned out was just what I counted on. They couldn't make the park complete without Plunkitt's swamp, and they had to pay a good price for it. Anything dishonest in that?

Up in the watershed I made some money, too. I bought up several bits of land there some years ago and made a pretty good guess that they would be bought up for water purposes later by the city.

Somehow, I always guessed about right, and shouldn't I enjoy the profit of my foresight? It was rather amusin' when the condemnation commissioners came along and found piece

The first three chapters of the book are reprinted from *Plunkitt of Tammany Hall*, edited by William L. Riordon (New York: McClure, Phillips and Company, 1905).

after piece of the land in the name of George Plunkitt of the Fifteenth Assembly District, New York City. They wondered how I knew just what to buy. The answer is—I seen my opportunity and I took it. I haven't confined myself to land; anything that pays is in my line.

For instance, the city is repavin' a street and has several hundred thousand old granite blocks to sell. I am on hand to buy, and I know just what they are worth.

How? Never mind that. I had a sort of monopoly of this business for a while, but once a newspaper tried to do me. It got some outside men to come over from Brooklyn and New Jersey to bid against me.

Was I done? Not much. I went to each of the men and said: "How many of these 250,000 stones do you want?" One said 20,000, and another wanted 15,000, and other wanted 10,000. I said: "All right, let me bid for the lot, and I'll give each of you all you want for nothin'."

They agreed, of course. Then the auctioneer yelled: "How much am I bid for these 250,000 fine pavin' stones?"

"Two dollars and fifty cents," says I.

"Two dollars and fifty cents!" screamed the auctioneer. "Oh, that's a joke! Give me a real bid."

He found the bid was real enough. My rivals stood silent. I got the lot for $2.50 and gave them their share. That's how the attempt to do Plunkitt ended, and that's how all such attempts end.

I've told you how I got rich by honest graft. Now, let me tell you that most politicians who are accused of robbin' the city get rich the same way.

They didn't steal a dollar from the city treasury. They just seen their opportunities and took them. That is why, when a reform administration comes in and spends a half million dollars in tryin' to find the public robberies they talked about in the campaign, they don't find them.

The books are always all right. The money in the city treasury is all right. Everything is all right. All they can show is that the Tammany heads of departments looked after their friends, within the law, and gave them what opportunities they could to make honest graft. Now, let me tell you that's never goin' to hurt Tammany with the people. Every good man looks after his friends, and any man who doesn't isn't likely to be popular. If I have a good thing to hand out in private life, I give it to a friend. Why shouldn't I do the same in public life?

Another kind of honest graft. Tammany has raised a good many salaries. There was an awful howl by the reformers, but don't you know that Tammany gains ten votes for every one it lost by salary raisin'?

The Wall Street banker thinks it shameful to raise a department clerk's salary from $1500 to $1800 a year, but every man who draws a salary himself says: "That's all right. I wish it was me." And he feels very much like votin' the Tammany ticket on election day, just out of sympathy.

Tammany was beat in 1901 because the people were deceived into believin' that it worked dishonest graft. They didn't draw a distinction between dishonest and honest graft, but they saw that some Tammany men grew rich, and supposed they had been robbin' the city treasury or levyin' blackmail on disorderly houses, or workin' in with the gamblers and lawbreakers.

As a matter of policy, if nothing else, why should the Tammany leaders go into such dirty business, when there is so much honest graft lyin' around when they are in power? Did you ever consider that?

Now, in conclusion, I want to say that I don't own a dishonest dollar. If my worst enemy was given the job of writin' my epitaph when I'm gone, he couldn't do more than write:

"George W. Plunkitt. He Seen His Opportunities, and He Took 'Em."

HOW TO BECOME A STATESMAN

There's thousands of young men in this city who will go to the polls for the first time next November. Among them will be many who have watched the careers of successful men in politics, and who are longin' to make names and fortunes for themselves at the same game. It is to these youths that I want to give advice. First, let me say that I am in a position to give what the courts call expert testimony on the subject. I don't think you can easily find a better example than I am of success in politics. After forty years' experience at the game I am—well, I'm George Washington Plunkitt. Everybody knows what figure I cut in the greatest organization on earth, and if you hear people say that I've laid away a million or so since I was a butcher's boy in Washington Market, don't come to me for an indignant denial. I'm pretty comfortable, thank you.

Now, havin' qualified as an expert, as the lawyers say, I am goin' to give advice free to the young men who are goin' to cast their first votes, and who are lookin' forward to political glory and lots of cash. Some young men think they can learn how to be successful in politics from books, and they cram their heads with all sorts of college rot. They couldn't

make a bigger mistake. Now, understand me, I ain't sayin'
nothin' against colleges. I guess they'll have to exist as long as
there's bookworms, and I suppose they do some good in a
certain way, but they don't count in politics. In fact, a young
man who has gone through the college course is handicapped
at the outset. He may succeed in politics, but the chances are
100 to 1 against him.

Another mistake: some young men think that the best way
to prepare for the political game is to practice speakin' and
becomin' orators. That's all wrong. We've got some orators in
Tammany Hall, but they're chiefly ornamental. You never
heard of Charlie Murphy delivering a speech, did you? Or
Richard Croker, or John Kelly, or any other man who has
been a real power in the organization? Look at the thirty-six
district leaders of Tammany Hall today. How many of them
travel on their tongues? Maybe one or two, and they don't
count when business is doin' at Tammany Hall. The men who
rule have practiced keepin' their tongues still, not exercisin'
them. So you want to drop the orator idea unless you mean
to go into politics just to perform the skyrocket act.

Now, I've told you what not to do; I guess I can explain
best what to do to succeed in politics by tellin' you what I
did. After goin' through the apprenticeship of the business
while I was a boy by workin' around the district headquarters
and hustlin' about the polls on election day, I set out when I
cast my first vote to win fame and money in New York City
politics. Did I offer my services to the district leader as a
stump-speaker? Not much. The woods are always full of
speakers. Did I get up a book on municipal government and
show it to the leader? I wasn't such a fool. What I did was to
get some marketable goods before goin' to the leaders. What
do I mean by marketable goods? Let me tell you: I had a
cousin, a young man who didn't take any particular interest
in politics. I went to him and said: "Tommy, I'm goin' to be
a politician, and I want to get a followin'; can I count on
you?" He said: "Sure, George." That's how I started in business. I got a marketable commodity—one vote. Then I went
to the district leader and told him I could command two
votes on election day, Tommy's and my own. He smiled on
me and told me to go ahead. If I had offered him a speech or
a bookful of learnin', he would have said, "Oh, forget it!"

That was beginnin' business in a small way, wasn't it? But
that is the only way to become a real lastin' statesman. I soon
branched out. Two young men in the flat next to mine were
school friends. I went to them, just as I went to Tommy, and
they agreed to stand by me. Then I had a followin' of three

voters and I began to get a bit chesty. Whenever I dropped into district headquarters, everybody shook hands with me, and the leader one day honored me by lightin' a match for my cigar. And so it went on like a snowball rollin' down a hill. I worked the flat-house that I lived in from the basement to the top floor, and I got about a dozen young men to follow me. Then I tackled the next house and so on down the block and around the corner. Before long I had sixty men back of me, and formed the George Washington Plunkitt Association.

What did the district leader say then when I called at headquarters? I didn't have to call at headquarters. He came after me and said: "George, what do you want? If you don't see what you want, ask for it. Wouldn't you like to have a job or two in the departments for your friends?" I said: "I'll think it over; I haven't yet decided what the George Washington Plunkitt Association will do in the next campaign." You ought to have seen how I was courted and petted then by the leaders of the rival organizations. I had marketable goods and there was bids for them from all sides, and I was a risin' man in politics. As time went on, and my association grew, I thought I would like to go to the Assembly. I just had to hint at what I wanted, and three different organizations offered me the nomination. Afterwards, I went to the Board of Aldermen, then to the State Senate, then became leader of the district, and so on up and up till I became a statesman.

That is the way and the only way to make a lastin' success in politics. If you are goin' to cast your first vote next November and want to go into politics, do as I did. Get a followin', if it's only one man, and then go to the district leader and say: "I want to join the organization. I've got one man who'll follow me through thick and thin." The leader won't laugh at your one-man followin'. He'll shake your hand warmly, offer to propose you for membership in his club, take you down to the corner for a drink and ask you to call again. But go to him and say: "I took first prize at college in Aristotle; I can recite all Shakespeare forwards and backwards; there ain't nothin' in science that ain't as familiar to me as blockades on the elevated roads and I'm the real thing in the way of silver-tongued orators." What will he answer? He'll probably say: "I guess you are not to blame for your misfortunes, but we have no use for you here."

THE CURSE OF CIVIL SERVICE REFORM

The civil service law is the biggest fraud of the age. It is the curse of the nation. There can't be no real patriotism while it lasts. How are you goin' to interest our young men in their country if you have no offices to give them when they work for their party? Just look at things in this city today. There are ten thousand good offices, but we can't get at more than a few hundred of them. How are we goin' to provide for the thousands of men who worked for the Tammany ticket? It can't be done. These men were full of patriotism a short time ago. They expected to be servin' their city, but when we tell them that we can't place them, do you think their patriotism is goin' to last? Not much. They say: "What's the use of workin' for your country anyhow? There's nothin' in the game." And what can they do? I don't know, but I'll tell you what I do know. I know more than one young man in past years who worked for the ticket and was just overflowin' with patriotism, but when he was knocked out by the civil service humbug he got to hate his country and became an Anarchist.

This ain't no exaggeration. I have good reason for sayin' that most of the Anarchists in this city today are men who ran up against civil service examinations. Isn't it enough to make a man sour on his country when he wants to serve it and won't be allowed unless he answers a lot of fool questions about the number of cubic inches of water in the Atlantic and the quality of sand in the Sahara desert? There was once a bright young man in my district who tackled one of these examinations. The next I heard of him he had settled down in Herr Most's saloon smokin' and drinkin' beer and talkin' socialism all day. Before that time he had never drank anything but whisky. I knew what was comin' when a young Irishman drops whisky and takes to beer and long pipes in a German saloon. That young man is today one of the wildest Anarchists in town. And just to think! He might be a patriot but for the cussed civil service.

Say, did you hear about that Civil Service Reform Association kickin' because the tax commissioners want to put their fifty-five deputies on the exempt list, and fire the outfit left to them by Low? That's civil service for you. Just think! Fifty-five Republican and mugwumps holdin' $3000 and $4000 and $5000 jobs in the tax department when 1555 good Tammany men are ready and willin' to take their places! It's an outrage! What did the people mean when they voted for Tammany? What is representative government, anyhow? Is it all a fake that this is a government of the people, by the people and for the people? If it isn't a fake, then why isn't the people's voice obeyed and Tammany men put in all the offices?

When the people elected Tammany, they knew just what they were doin'. We didn't put up any false pretenses. We didn't go in for humbug civil service and all that rot. We stood as we have always stood, for rewardin' the men that won the victory. They call that the spoils system. All right; Tammany is for the spoils system, and when we go in we fire every anti-Tammany man from office that can be fired under the law. It's an elastic sort of law and you can bet it will be stretched to the limit. Of course the Republican State Civil Service Board will stand in the way of our local Civil Service Commission all it can; but say!—suppose we carry the State sometime, won't we fire the upstate Board all right? Or we'll make it work in harmony with the local board, and that means that Tammany will get everything in sight. I know that the civil service humbug is stuck into the constitution, too, but, as Tim Campbell said: "What's the constitution among friends?"

Say, the people's voice is smothered by the cursed civil service law; it is the root of all evil in our government. You hear of this thing or that thing goin' wrong in the nation, the State or the city. Look down beneath the surface and you can trace everything wrong to civil service. I have studied the subject and I know. The civil service humbug is underminin' our institutions and if a halt ain't called soon this great republic will tumble down like a Park Avenue house when they were buildin' the subway, and on its ruins will rise another Russian government.

This is an awful serious proposition. Free silver and the tariff and imperialism and the Panama Canal are triflin' issues when compared to it. We could worry along without any of these things, but civil service is sappin' the foundation of the whole shootin' match. Let me argue it out for you. I ain't up on sillygisms, but I can give you some arguments that nobody can answer.

First, this great and glorious country was built up by political parties; second, parties can't hold together if their workers don't get the offices when they win; third, if the parties go to pieces, the government they built up must go to pieces, too; fourth, then there'll be h − − − to pay.

Could anything be clearer than that? Say, honest now; can you answer that argument? Of course you won't deny that the government was built up by the great parties. That's history, and you can't go back of the returns. As to my second proposition, you can't deny that either. When parties can't get offices, they'll bust. They ain't far from the bustin' point now, with all this civil service business keepin' most of the good things from them. How are you goin' to keep up patriotism if this thing goes on? You can't do it. Let me tell you that patriotism has been dying out fast for the last twenty years. Before then when a party won, its workers got everything in sight. That was somethin' to make a man patriotic. Now, when a party wins and its men come forward and ask for their rewards, the reply is, "Nothin' doin', unless you can answer a list of questions about Egyptian mummies and how many years it will take for a bird to wear out a mass of iron as big as the earth by steppin' on it once in a century?"

I have studied politics and men for forty-five years, and I see how things are driftin'. Sad indeed is the change that has come over the young men, even in my district, where I try to keep up the fire of patriotism by gettin' a lot of jobs for my constituents, whether Tammany is in or out. The boys and men don't get excited any more when they see a United States flag or hear "The Star-Spangled Banner." They don't care no more for firecrackers on the Fourth of July. And why should they? What is there in it for them? They know that no matter how hard they work for their country in a campaign, the jobs will go to fellows who can tell about the mummies and the bird steppin' on the iron. Are you surprised then that the young men of the country are beginnin' to look coldly on the flag and don't care to put up a nickel for firecrackers?

Say, let me tell of one case. After the battle of San Juan Hill, the Americans found a dead man with a light complexion, red hair and blue eyes. They could see he wasn't a Spaniard, although he had on a Spanish uniform. Several officers looked him over, and then a private of the Seventy-first Regiment saw him and yelled, "Good Lord, that's Flaherty." That man grew up in my district, and he was once the most patriotic American boy on the West Side. He couldn't see a flag without yellin' himself hoarse.

Now, how did he come to be lying dead with a Spanish uniform on? I found out all about it, and I'll vouch for the story. Well, in the municipal campaign of 1897, that young man, chockful of patriotism, worked day and night for the Tammany ticket. Tammany won, and the young man determined to devote his life to the service of the city. He picked out a place that would suit him, and sent in his application to the head of department. He got a reply that he must take a civil service examination to get the place. He didn't know what these examinations were, so he went, all lighthearted, to the Civil Service Board. He read the questions about the mummies, the bird on the iron, and all the other fool questions—and he left that office an enemy of the country that he had loved so well. The mummies and the bird blasted his patriotism. He went to Cuba, enlisted in the Spanish army at the breakin' out of the war, and died fightin' his country.

That is but one victim of the infamous civil service. If that young man had not run up against the civil examination, but had been allowed to serve his country as he wished, he would be in a good office today, drawin' a good salary. Ah, how many young men have had their patriotism blasted in the same way!

Now, what is goin' to happen when civil service crushes out patriotism? Only one thing can happen: the republic will go to pieces. Then a czar or a sultan will turn up, which brings me to the fourthly of my argument—that is, there will be h --- to pay. And that ain't no lie.

These selections may seem quaint, and, of course, they do have an archaic flavor at a time when an Irish-American Harvard graduate has recently occupied the White House and the old Irish ghettos have long since vanished from the big cities. However, a serious student of the history of American politics can learn a good deal from Plunkitt's random, and seemingly immoral, observations.

In New York, or Boston, or Chicago, or any other big immigrant center a century, or even a half-century, ago, the choice was not between Good Government and Bad Government, but rather between two varieties of corruption. The upstate, Protestant farmers in New York (or the downstate rurals in Illinois) were no less corrupt in their political machinations than the city organizations. Indeed, in our day authorities are generally agreed that the greatest source of political corruption in the United States is county government. But city corruption was highly visible; it was in a sense philanthropic corruption: while some got more than others, nobody was left to starve. A corrupt rural machine controlling the State House would operate in a different fashion. Factory safety laws, health laws, franchises would be manipulated for the benefit of a few, but starvation among the slum dwellers could be viewed with equanimity: if those immigrants don't like it here, let them go back where they came from. A contemporary manifestation of this philosophy occurred in 1963 when the Illinois state legislature, dominated by downstate Republicans, cut off relief for the unemployed (overwhelmingly Negroes) in Chicago. In Massachusetts, dominated by lineal descendants of Plunkitt, this would be inconceivable; a Boston politician who would engage in a "sweetheart deal," or put three generations of his family on the public payroll, without blinking an eye would be horrified by the immorality of letting voters starve. Even, as Plunkitt emphasizes, if they are Republicans.

From the 1880's, when urbanization began to accelerate at a fantastic rate to the 1930's (and later in some states, notably Pennsylvania) the big cities lived in a state of political siege. Gerrymandering cut down their representation in the state legislatures and in Congress, and often state constitutions made it impossible for the cities ever to achieve real self-government. Alfred E. Smith once observed that the New York state legislature was Republican by constitutional enactment: no more than 40 per cent of the state senate could come from any two adjoining counties, a provision whose purpose becomes clear when one looks at a map of New York City and its five counties. Other states had their own gimmicks; it is symbolic that in only a few instances are state capitols located in major population centers.

In political terms, the warfare between the states and the cities was a battle between the so-called reform movements and the city machines. The city reform movements were, in other words, the urban task-forces of the rural armies. Characteristically these reform movements were led by upper-class urban Protestants, and, while they contained a large number of genuinely dedicated reformers, their major objective was to restore the urban areas to the feudal jurisdiction of the state organizations. The reformers were especially interested in civil service. Theoretically they hoped to improve the public service by eliminating political appointments—and dismissals—and by establishing instead a tradition of "merit." In fact, as opposed to theory, civil service has been used as a weapon by groups in power to protect their appointees from the opposition. Let us take the national case: in 1895 there were 54,222 officials of the national government holding "protected" jobs; that is, under the Pendleton Act of 1884 these positions were exempted from patronage and their occupants could not be dismissed on political grounds by a new administration. In 1896, the figure suddenly jumped to 87,034, and the innocent observer may conclude that the spirit of reform was carrying all before it. Nothing could be further from the truth. What happened was that the Democrats lost the election of 1896 and hastily blanketed in their faithful officeholders; i.e., Congress enacted a statute which widened civil service coverage and protected those currently holding the jobs. In fact, in 1896 only 5,086 individuals were appointed to office under the competitive merit system.

The Hatch Acts of 1939 and 1940 must be understood in this same framework. In essence, this legislation prohibited federal officeholders, and state officeholders whose salaries were drawn from federal funds, from engaging in partisan political activities. It was hailed by what Plunkitt would have called the "goo-goos" (the good government militants) as a noble act of disinterested public policy; in reality it was designed by shrewd congressmen to frustrate any attempts by President Franklin D. Roosevelt to build a national political party with government workers as his cadres. Southern Democratic legislators were particularly concerned lest Roosevelt use the W.P.A. and other work-relief programs as the basis for political machines that might compete with their own "court-house rings"; their solution was to sterilize politically all federal employees while, of course, maintaining the patronage system at full throttle on the state and local level where their strength was rooted.

In the context Plunkitt was examining, civil service was the weapon of the rural, educated Protestants against the urban, badly educated Catholic immigrants. In the common-sense view of the Irish, Italian, or Polish proletarian there was no legitimate connection between ability to answer questions on an examination and ability to dig up streets, run street cars, or serve in the police or fire department. James Michael Curley, Boston's engaging addition to the line-up of Irish-American bosses, first became beloved among his constituents for his willingness to take civil service examinations in their behalf, and in their name. He was jailed for it, but that did little to tarnish his reputation; since time immemorial, it has been no crime among the oppressed to swindle the oppressors.

In short, George Washington Plunkitt provides sharp insights into a real "class struggle" which, though it did not proceed in Marxist terms, had all the elements of confrontation between an old élite and a new, including a fair amount of violence. Immigrant America confronted Jeffersonian America across an abyss which reached the proportions of a chasm in the 1920's, particularly in the presidential election of 1928. In that contest Al Smith, a Tammany product, a Catholic, and "sopping wet" (not a big drinker—he was not—but a militant opponent of Prohibition), went down in defeat before a wave of scurrility and bigotry. Then, almost before anyone realized it, the real crisis was over: a new gener-

ation, faced by a different set of problems such as Depression and War, simply abandoned the old battlefield. In certain ways, then, Plunkitt of Tammany Hall *must be understood as a battle monument.*

William James

Pragmatism

1907

EDITED BY SIDNEY HOOK

William James's Pragmatism *is indisputably the most important book in American philosophy. It is important not so much because of its profundity as because of its popular influence. At home and especially abroad it is accepted as representative of a distinctively American philosophy, and is considered a work that articulates with candor and dash those elements and attitudes in the American experience which transformed the pioneers of a trackless waste into the masters of a supremely powerful technological civilization.*

Pragmatism *was published in May, 1907. It contains the substance of James's popular lectures delivered in 1906 at the Lowell Institute in Boston and in 1907 at Columbia University. Long before the publication of the book, James had begun developing its central ideas in other lectures and articles. He expressed the pragmatic theory of meaning as early as 1878 and the pragmatic theory of truth a few years later. But in* Pragmatism *James sought to bring together and to give systematic expression to some of the central notions of his philosophic thought. His pragmatic theory of meaning held that the meaning of an idea is clarified by ex-*

plicating its consequences in experience; according to his pragmatic theory of truth, the truth of an idea depends upon whether its consequences lead to useful results or work satisfactorily in helping to solve the problem at issue. In addition, James also briefly discussed, with a vivid imagery unsurpassed in the writings of any other philosopher, his conceptions of God, man, and experience. There is no doubt that James in writing Pragmatism felt at the top of his form. Of the delivery and reception of the lectures at Columbia University, he wrote that they were "certainly the high tide of my existence, so far as energizing and being 'recognized' were concerned."

Nonetheless, despite, or because of, James's ability to command attention—he was incapable of writing a dull line even on abstruse themes—he spent the rest of the few years left him after the publication of Pragmatism in amplifying his positions, replying to critics, repudiating misconceptions, and pleading that his words not be read with near-sighted literalness. But the price of imprecision on matters of moment is excited misunderstanding. Even those who sympathized with James's philosophic intent had difficulty in accepting his formulations as an adequate analysis of meaning and truth.

James dedicated his Pragmatism to John Stuart Mill. Because of this dedication, as well as the subtitle of the work— "A New Name for Some Old Ways of Thinking"—and the brilliant drumfire James kept up against intellectualism and traditional rationalism, many critics failed to grasp the extent to which he had abandoned the positions of British empiricism from Locke to Mill. In his Principles of Psychology, James had already given the coup de grâce to the theory of association and to the belief that the mind is passive in knowing. Pragmatism eloquently reinforces James's central conception that the mind is active in knowing and that the truth is not a matter of origins or agreement with an antecedently existing reality but depends upon the future outcome of the changes we set up in acting upon our ideas. James's empiricism was nothing short of a revolutionary reconstruction of the entire tradition of previous empiricism. By emphasizing the active, prospective character of attention and interest in human thinking, James brought the theory of knowledge into line with the deliverances of biology and psychology. Although James inveighed against vicious intellectualism and otiose rationalism, he did so on the ground that they had a false conception of the actual role of reason and intelligence in human experience and not on the ground that they had no value. On the contrary. Intelligence for him had a creative function *even though it could not create its own conditions. To believe that the world is rational through and through or in and of itself is as absurd, according to James, as the belief that intelligence is an ineffectual spectator limited to idle commentary on events. The function of thought is to make human decisions, actions, and institutions as reasonable as possible. James was not an existentialist.*

This strand of James's thought is apparent in his attempt to assimilate pragmatism to the methods and logic of modern science, with its recognition of the indispensability of hypotheses, which are conceived not as summaries of past experience but as plans or experiments for acting on the world in order to win new insights into, and power over, the future. James pointed to Dewey as the heir and continuator of pragmatism so conceived, whose origins go back to the early writings of Charles Peirce—to whom James made overgenerous acknowledgment.

There was another interest in behalf of which James sought to use pragmatism—religion. Like Faust, James could have said, "Ach! zwei Seelen wohnen in meinem Brust." He was not only a tough-minded scientist seeking clarity and new truth, but a tender-minded literary and religious man in quest of salvation. He sought to vindicate on rational ground the right to believe in what, with a reasonable interpretation of the logic and ethics of scientific inquiry, one could not legitimately believe in save on faith. This dichotomy is the basic source of the difficulties in his work and must be recognized even by those who are sympathetic to one or another of his specific philosophical doctrines.

THE PRAGMATIC method is primarily a method of settling metaphysical disputes that otherwise might be interminable. Is the world one or many?—fated or free?—material or spiritual?—here are notions either of which may or may not hold good of the world; and disputes over such notions are unending. The pragmatic method in such cases is to try to interpret each notion by tracing its respective practical consequences. What difference would it practically make to any one if this notion rather than that notion were true? If no practical difference whatever can be traced, then the alterna-

The passages given here come from the original edition of *Pragmatism* (New York: Longmans, Green and Company, 1907). They comprise about one-sixth of the whole and are taken from Lectures II, VI, and VIII.

tives mean practically the same thing, and all dispute is idle. Whenever a dispute is serious, we ought to be able to show some practical difference that must follow from one side or the other's being right.

A glance at the history of the idea will show you still better what pragmatism means. The term is derived from the same Greek word πρᾶγμα, meaning action, from which our words 'practice' and 'practical' come. It was first introduced into philosophy by Mr. Charles Peirce in 1878. In an article entitled 'How to Make Our Ideas Clear', in the 'Popular Science Monthly' for January of that year, Mr. Peirce, after pointing out that our beliefs are really rules for action, said that, to develop a thought's meaning, we need only determine what conduct it is fitted to produce: that conduct is for us its sole significance. And the tangible fact at the root of all our thought-distinctions, however subtle, is that there is no one of them so fine as to consist in anything but a possible difference of practice. To attain perfect clearness in our thoughts of an object, then, we need only consider what conceivable effects of a practical kind the object may involve—what sensations we are to expect from it, and what reactions we must prepare. Our conception of these effects, whether immediate or remote, is then for us the whole of our conception of the object, so far as that conception has positive significance at all. ...

To take in the importance of Peirce's principle, one must get accustomed to applying it to concrete cases. I found a few years ago that Ostwald, the illustrious Leipzig chemist, had been making perfectly distinct use of the principle of pragmatism in his lectures on the philosophy of science, though he had not called it by that name.

"All realities influence our practice," he wrote me, "and the influence is their meaning for us. I am accustomed to put questions to my classes in this way: In what respects would the world be different if this alternative or that were true? If I can find nothing that would become different, then the alternative has no sense."

That is, the rival views mean practically the same thing, and meaning, other than practical, there is for us none. Ostwald in a published lecture gives this example of what he means. Chemists have long wrangled over the inner constitution of certain bodies called 'tautomerous'. Their properties seemed equally consistent with the notion that an instable hydrogen atom oscillates inside of them, or that they are instable mixtures of two bodies. Controversy raged, but was never decided. "It would never have begun," says Ostwald, "if the combatants had asked themselves what particular experimental fact could have been made different by one or the other view being correct. For it would then have appeared that no difference of fact could possibly ensue; and the quarrel was as unreal as if, theorizing in primitive times about the raising of dough by yeast, one party should have invoked a 'brownie,' while another insisted on an 'elf' as the true cause of the phenomonon."

It is astonishing to see how many philosophical disputes collapse into insignificance the moment you subject them to this simple test of tracing a concrete consequence. There can *be* no difference anywhere that doesn't *make* a difference elsewhere—no difference in abstract truth that doesn't express itself in a difference in concrete fact and in conduct consequent upon that fact, imposed on somebody, somehow, somewhere, and somewhen. The whole function of philosophy ought to be to find out what definite difference it will make to you and me, at definite instants of our life, if this world-formula or that world-formula be the true one. . . .

Pragmatism represents a perfectly familiar attitude in philosophy, the empiricist attitude, but it represents it, as it seems to me, both in a more radical and in a less objectionable form than it has ever yet assumed. A pragmatist turns his back resolutely and once for all upon a lot of inveterate habits dear to professional philosophers. He turns away from abstraction and insufficiency, from verbal solutions, from bad *a priori* reasons, from fixed principles, closed systems, and pretended absolutes and origins. He turns towards concreteness and adequacy, towards facts, towards action and towards power. That means the empiricist temper regnant and the rationalist temper sincerely given up. It means the open air and possibilities of nature, as against dogma, artificiality, and the pretence of finality in truth.

At the same time it does not stand for any special results. It is a method only. But the general triumph of that method would mean an enormous change in what I called in my last lecture the 'temperament' of philosophy. Teachers of the ultra-rationalistic type would be frozen out, much as the courtier type is frozen out in republics, as the ultramontane type of priest is frozen out in protestant lands. Science and metaphysics would come much nearer together, would in fact work absolutely hand in hand.

Metaphysics has usually followed a very primitive kind of quest. You know how men have always hankered after unlawful magic, and you know what a great part in magic *words* have always played. If you have his name, or the formula of incantation that binds him, you can control the spirit, genie, afrite, or whatever the power may be. Solomon knew the names of all the spirits and having their names, he held them subject to his will. So the universe has always appeared to the natural mind as a kind of enigma, of which the key must be sought in the shape of some illuminating or power-bringing word or name. That word names the universe's *principle,* and to possess it is after a fashion to possess the universe itself. 'God,' 'Matter,' 'Reason,' 'the Absolute,' 'Energy,' are so many solving names. You can rest when you have them. You are at the end of your metaphysical quest.

But if you follow the pragmatic method, you cannot look on any such word as closing your quest. You must bring out of each word its practical cash-value, set it at work within the stream of your experience. It appears less as a solution, then, than as a program for more work, and more particularly as an indication of the ways in which existing realities may be *changed.*

Theories thus become instruments, not answers to enigmas, in which we can rest. We don't lie back upon them, we move forward, and, on occasion, make nature over again by their aid. Pragmatism unstiffens all our theories, limbers them up and sets each one at work. Being nothing essentially new, it harmonizes with many ancient philosophic tendencies. It agrees with nominalism for instance, in always appealing to particulars; with utilitarianism in emphasizing practical aspects; with positivism in its disdain for verbal solutions, useless questions and metaphysical abstractions. . . .

No particular results then, so far, but only an attitude of orientation, is what the pragmatic method means. *The attitude of looking away from first things, principles, 'categories,' supposed necessities; and of looking towards last things, fruits, consequences, facts. . . .*

. . . The word pragmatism has come to be used in a still wider sense, as meaning also a certain *theory of truth.* . . .

One of the most successfully cultivated branches of philosophy in our time is what is called inductive logic, the study of the conditions under which our sciences have evolved. Writers on this subject have begun to show a singular unanimity as to what the laws of nature and elements of fact mean, when formulated by mathematicians, physicists and chemists. When the first mathematical, logical and natural uniformities, the first *laws,* were discovered, men were so carried away by the clearness, beauty and simplification that resulted, that they believed themselves to have deciphered authentically the eternal thoughts of the Almighty. His mind also thundered and reverberated in syllogisms. He also thought in conic sections, squares and roots and ratios, and geometrized like Euclid. He made Kepler's laws for the planets to follow; he made velocity increase proportionally to the time in falling bodies; he made the law of sines for light to obey when refracted; he established the classes, orders, families and genera of the plants and animals, and fixed the distances between them. He thought the archetypes of all things, and devised their variations; and when we rediscover any one of these his wondrous institutions, we seize his mind in its very literal intention.

But as the sciences have developed farther, the notion has gained ground that most, perhaps all, of our laws are only approximations. The laws themselves, moreover, have grown so numerous that there is no counting them; and so many rival formulations are proposed in all the branches of science that investigators have become accustomed to the notion that no theory is absolutely a transcript of reality, but that any one of them may from some point of view be useful. Their great use is to summarize old facts and to lead to new ones. They are only a man-made language, a conceptual short-hand as some one calls them, in which we write our reports of nature; and languages, as is well known, tolerate much choice of expression and many dialects.

Thus human arbitrariness has driven divine necessity from scientific logic. If I mention the names of Sigwart, Mach, Ostwald, Pearson, Milhaud, Poincaré, Tuhem, Ruyssen, those of you who are students will easily identify the tendency I speak of, and will think of additional names.

Riding now on the front of this wave of scientific logic Messrs. Schiller and Dewey appear with their pragmatic account of what truth everywhere signifies. Everywhere, these teachers say, 'truth' in our ideas and beliefs means the same thing that it means in science. It means, they say, nothing but this, *that ideas (which themselves are but parts of our experience) become true just in so far as they help us to get into satisfactory relation with other parts of our experience*, to summarize them and get about among them by conceptual short-cuts instead of following the interminable succession of particular phenomena. Any idea upon which we can ride, so to speak; any idea that will carry us prosperously from any one part of our experience to any other part, linking things satisfactorily, working securely, simplifying saving labor; is true for just so much, true in so far forth, true *instrumentally*. This is the 'instrumental' view of truth taught so successfully at Chicago, the view that truth in our ideas means their power to 'work,' promulgated so brilliantly at Oxford. . . .

The observable process which Schiller and Dewey particularly singled out for generalization is the familiar one by which any individual settles into *new opinions*. The process here is always the same. The individual has a stock of old opinions already, but he meets a new experience that puts them to a strain. Somebody contradicts them; or in a reflective moment he discovers that they contradict each other; or he hears of facts with which they are incompatible; or desires arise in him which they cease to satisfy. The result is an inward trouble to which his mind till then had been a stranger, and from which he seeks to escape by modifying his previous mass of opinions. He saves as much of it as he can, for in this matter of belief we are all extreme conservatives. So he tries to change first this opinion, and then that (for they resist change very variously), until at last some new idea comes up which he can graft upon the ancient stock with a minimum of disturbance of the latter, some idea that mediates between the stock and the new experience and runs them into one another most felicitously and expediently. . . .

. . . A new opinion counts as 'true' just in proportion as it gratifies the individual's desire to assimilate the novel in his experience to his beliefs in stock. It must both lean on old truth and grasp new fact; and its success (as I said a moment ago) in doing this, is a matter for the individual's appreciation. When old truth grows, then, by new truth's addition, it is for subjective reasons. We are in the process and obey the reasons. That new idea is truest which performs most felicitously its function of satisfying our double urgency. It makes itself true, gets itself classed as true, by the way it works; grafting itself then upon the ancient body of truth, which thus grows much as a tree grows by the activity of a new layer of cambium. . . .

The trail of the human serpent is thus over everything. Truth independent; truth that we *find* merely; truth no longer malleable to human need; truth incorrigible, in a word; such truth exists indeed superabundantly—or is supposed to exist by rationalistically minded thinkers; but then it means only the dead heart of the living tree, and its being there means only that truth also has its paleontology, and its 'prescription,' and may grow stiff with years of veteran service and petrified in men's regard by sheer antiquity. But how plastic even the oldest truths nevertheless really are has been vividly shown in our day by the transformation of logical and mathematical ideas, a transformation which seems even to be invading physics. The ancient formulas are reinterpreted as special expressions of much wider principles, principles that our ancestors never got a glimpse of in their present shape and formulation. . . .

. . . Pragmatism is uncomfortable away from facts. Rationalism is comfortable only in the presence of abstractions. This pragmatist talk about truths in the plural, about their utility and satisfactoriness, about the success with which they 'work,' etc., suggests to the typical intellectualist mind a sort of coarse lame second-rate makeshift article of truth. Such truths are not real truths. Such tests are merely subjective. As against this, objective truth must be something non-utilitarian, haughty, refined, remote, august, exalted. It must be an absolute correspondence of our thoughts with an equally absolute reality. It must be what we *ought* to think unconditionally. The conditioned ways in which we *do* think are so much irrelevance and matter for psychology. Down with psychology, up with logic, in all this question!

See the exquisite contrast of the types of mind! The pragmatist clings to facts and concreteness, observes truth at its work in particular cases, and generalizes. Truth, for him, becomes a class-name for all sorts of definite working-values in experience. For the rationalist it remains a pure abstraction, to the bare name of which we must defer. When the pragmatist undertakes to show in detail just *why* we must defer, the rationalist is unable to recognize the concretes from which his own abstraction is taken. He accuses us of denying truth; whereas we have only sought to trace exactly why people follow it and always ought to follow it. Your typically ultra-abstractionist fairly shudders at concreteness; other things equal, he positively prefers the pale and spectral. If the two universes were offered, he would always choose the skinny outline rather than the rich thicket of reality. It is so much purer, clearer, nobler. . . .

Men who are strongly of the fact-loving temperament, you may remember me to have said, are liable to be kept at a distance by the small sympathy with facts which that philosophy from the present-day fashion of idealism offers them. It is far too intellectualistic. Old fashioned theism was bad enough, with its notion of God as an exalted monarch, made up of a lot of unintelligible or preposterous 'attributes'; but, so long as it held strongly by the argument from design, it kept some touch with concrete realities. Since, however, darwinism has once for all displaced design from the minds of the 'scientific,' theism has lost that foothold; and some kind of an immanent or pantheistic deity working *in* things rather than above them is, if any, the kind recommended to our contemporary imagination. Aspirants to a philosophic religion turn, as a rule, more hopefully nowadays towards idealistic pantheism than towards the older dualistic theism, in spite of the fact that the latter still counts able defenders. . . .

. . . The brand of pantheism offered is hard for them to assimilate if they are lovers of facts, or empirically minded. . . .

Now pragmatism, devoted though she be to facts, has no such materialistic bias as ordinary empiricism labors under. Moreover, she has no objection whatever to the realizing of abstractions, so long as you get about among particulars with their aid and they actually carry you somewhere. Interested in no conclusions but those which our minds and our experiences work out together, she has no *a priori* prejudices against theology. *If theological ideas prove to have a value for concrete life, they will be true, for pragmatism, in the sense of being good for so much. For how much more they are true, will depend entirely on their relations to the other truths that also have to be acknowledged.* . . .

I am well aware how odd it must seem to some of you to hear me say that an idea is 'true' so long as to believe it is profitable to our lives. That it is *good,* for as much as it profits, you will gladly admit. If what we do by its aid is good, you will allow the idea itself to be good in so far forth, for we are the better for possessing it. But is it not a strange misuse of the word 'truth,' you will say, to call ideas also 'true' for this reason? . . .

. . . Let me now say only this, that truth is one *species of good,* and not, as is usually supposed, a category distinct from good, and co-ordinate with it. *The true is the name of whatever proves itself to be good in the way of belief, and good, too, for definite, assignable reasons.* Surely you must admit this, that if there were *no* good for life in true ideas, or if the knowledge of them were positively disadvantageous and false ideas the only useful ones, then the current notion that truth is divine and precious, and its pursuit a duty, could never have grown up or become a dogma. In a world like that, our duty would be to *shun* truth, rather. But in this world, just as certain foods are not only agreeable to our taste, but good for our teeth, our stomach, and our tissues; so certain ideas are not only agreeable to think about, or agreeable as supporting other ideas that we are fond of, but they are also helpful in life's practical struggles. If there be any life that it is really better we should lead, and if there be any idea which, if believed in, would help us to lead that life, then it would be really *better for us* to believe in that idea, *unless, indeed, belief in it incidentally clashed with other greater vital benefits.*

'What would be better for us to believe'! This sounds very like a definition of truth. It comes very near to saying 'what we *ought* to believe': and in *that* definition none of you would find any oddity. Ought we ever not to believe what it is *better for us* to believe? And can we then keep the notion of what is better for us, and what is true for us, permanently apart?

Pragmatism says no, and I fully agree with her. Probably you also agree, so far as the abstract statement goes, but with a suspicion that if we practically did believe everything that made for good in our own personal lives, we should be found indulging all kinds of fancies about this world's affairs, and all kinds of sentimental superstitions about a world hereafter. Your suspicion here is undoubtedly well founded, and it is evident that something happens when you pass from the abstract to the concrete that complicates the situation.

I said just now that what is better for us to believe is true *unless the belief incidentally clashes with some other vital benefit.* Now in real life what vital benefits is any particular belief of ours most liable to clash with? What indeed except the vital benefits yielded by other beliefs when these prove incompatible with the first ones? In other words, the greatest enemy of any one of our truths may be the rest of our truths. Truths have once for all this desperate instinct of self-preservation and of desire to extinguish whatever contradicts them. My belief in the Absolute, based on the good it does me, must run the gauntlet of all my other beliefs. Grant that it may be true in giving me a moral holiday. Nevertheless, as I conceive it,—and let me speak now confidentially, as it were, and merely in my own private person,—it clashes with other truths of mine whose benefits I hate to give up on its account. It happens to be associated with a kind of logic of which I am the enemy, I find that it entangles me in metaphysical paradoxes that are inacceptable, etc. But as I have enough trouble in life already without adding the trouble of carrying these intellectual inconsistencies, I personally just give up the Absolute. I just *take* my moral holidays; or else as a professional philosopher, I try to justify them by some other principle. . . .

. . . Rationalism sticks to logic and the empyrean. Empiricism sticks to the external senses. Pragmatism is willing to take anything, to follow either logic or the senses and to count the humblest and most personal experiences. She will count mystical experiences if they have practical consequences. She will take a God who lives in the very dirt of private fact—if that should seem a likely place to find him.

Her only test of probable truth is what works best in the way of leading us, what fits every part of life best and combines with the collectivity of experience's demands, nothing being omitted. If theological ideas should do this, if the notion of God, in particular, should prove to do it, how could pragmatism possibly deny God's existence? She could see no meaning in treating as 'not true' a notion that was pragmatically so successful. What other kind of truth could there be, for her, than all this agreement with concrete reality? . . .

I fully expect to see the pragmatist view of truth run through the classic stages of a theory's career. First, you know, a new theory is attacked as absurd; then it is admitted to be true, but obvious and insignificant; finally it is seen to be so important that its adversaries claim that they themselves discovered it. Our doctrine of truth is at present in the first of these three stages, with symptoms of the second stage having begun in certain quarters. I wish that this lecture might help it beyond the first stage in the eyes of many of you.

Truth, as any dictionary will tell you, is a property of certain of our ideas. It means their 'agreement,' as falsity means their disagreement, with 'reality.' Pragmatists and intellectuals both accept this definition as a matter of course. They begin to quarrel only after the question is raised as to what may precisely be meant by the term 'agreement,' and what by the term 'reality,' when reality is taken as something for our ideas to agree with.

In answering these questions the pragmatists are more analytic and painstaking, the intellectualists more offhand and irreflective. The popular notion is that a true idea must copy its reality. Like other popular views, this one follows the analogy of the most usual experience. Our true ideas of sensible things do indeed copy them. Shut your eyes and think of yonder clock on the wall, and you get just such a true picture or copy of its dial. But your idea of its 'works' (unless you are a clockmaker) is much less of a copy, yet it passes muster, for it in no way clashes with the reality. Even though it should shrink to the mere word 'works,' that word still serves you truly; and when you speak of the 'time-keeping function' of the clock, or of its spring's 'elasticity,' it is hard to see exactly what your ideas can copy.

You perceive that there is a problem here. Where our ideas cannot copy definitely their object, what does agreement with that object mean? Some idealists seem to say that they are true whenever they are what God meant that we ought to think about that object. Others hold the copy-view all through, and speak as if our ideas possessed truth just in proportion as they approach to being copies of the Absolute's eternal way of thinking. . . .

These views, you see, invite pragmatistic discussion. But the great assumption of the intellectualists is that truth means essentially an inert static relation. When you've got your true idea of anything, there's an end of the matter. You're in possession; you *know*; you have fulfilled your thinking destiny. You are where you ought to be mentally; you have obeyed your categorical imperative; and nothing more need follow on that climax of your rational destiny. Epistemologically you are in stable equilibrium.

Pragmatism, on the other hand, asks its usual question. "Grant an idea or belief to be true," it says, "what concrete difference will its being true make in any one's actual life? How will the truth be realized? What experiences will be different from those which would obtain if the belief were false? What, in short, is the truth's cash-value in experiential terms?"

The moment pragmatism asks this question, it sees the answer: *True ideas are those that we can assimilate, validate, corroborate and verify.* That is the practical difference it makes to us to have true ideas; that, therefore, is the meaning of truth, for it is all that truth is known-as.

This thesis is what I have to defend. The truth of an idea is not a stagnant property inherent in it. Truth *happens* to an idea. It *becomes* true, is *made* true by events. Its verity *is* in fact an event, a process: the process namely of its verifying itself, its veri-*fication*. Its validity is the process of its valid-*ation*.

But what do the words verification and validation themselves pragmatically mean? They again signify certain practical consequences of the verified and validated idea. It is hard to find any one phrase that characterizes these consequences better than the ordinary agreement-formula—just such consequences being what we have in mind whenever we say that our ideas 'agree' with reality. They lead us, namely, through the acts and other ideas which they instigate, into or up to, or towards, other parts of experience with which we fell all the while—such feeling being among our potentialities—that the original ideas remain in agreement. The connexions and transitions come to us from point to point as being progressive, harmonious, satisfactory. This function of agreeable leading is what we mean by an idea's verification. . . .

Let me begin by reminding you of the fact that the possession of true thought means everywhere the possession of invaluable instruments of action; and that our duty to gain truth, so far from being a blank command from out of the blue, or a 'stunt' self-imposed by our intellect, can account for itself by excellent practical reasons. The importance to human life of having true beliefs about matters of fact is a thing too notorious. We live in a world of realities that can be infinitely useful or infinitely harmful. Ideas that tell us which of them to expect count as the true ideas in all this primary sphere of verification, and the pursuit of such ideas is a primary human duty. The possession of truth, so far from being here an end in itself, is only a preliminary means towards other vital satisfactions. If I am lost in the woods and starved, and find what looks like a cow-path, it is of the utmost importance that I should think of a human habitation at the end of it, for if I do so and follow it, I save myself. The true thought is useful here because the house which is its object is useful. The practical value of true ideas is thus primarily derived from the practical importance of their objects to us. Their objects are, indeed, not important at all times. I may on another occasion have no use for the house; and then my idea of it, however verifiable, will be practically irrelevant, and had better remain latent. Yet since almost any object may some day become temporarily important, the advantage of having a general stock of *extra* truths, of ideas that shall be true of merely possible situations, is obvious. We store such extra truths away in our memories, and with the overflow we fill our books of reference. Whenever such an extra truth becomes practically relevant to one of our emergencies, it passes from cold-storage to do work in the world and our belief in it grows active. You can say of it then either that 'it is useful because it is true' or that 'it is true because it is useful.' Both these phrases mean exactly the same thing, namely that here is an idea that gets fulfilled and can be verified. True is the name for whatever idea starts the verification-process, useful is the name for its completed function in experience. True ideas would never have been singled out as such, would never have acquired a class-name, least of all a name suggesting value, unless they had been useful from the outset in this way.

From this simple cue pragmatism gets her general notion of truth as something essentially bound up with the way in which one moment in our experience may lead us towards other moments which it will be worth while to have been led to. Primarily, and on the common-sense level, the truth of a state of mind means this function of *a leading that is worth while*. When a moment in our experience, of any kind whatever, inspires us with a thought that is true, that means that sooner or later we dip by that thought's guidance into the particulars of experience again and make advantageous connexion with them. This is a vague enough statement, but I beg you to retain it, for it is essential. . . .

Realities mean, then, either concrete facts, or abstract kinds of things and relations perceived intuitively between them. They furthermore and thirdly mean, as things that new ideas of ours must no less take account of, the whole body of other truths already in our possession. But what now does 'agreement' with such threefold realities mean?—to use again the definition that is current.

Here it is that pragmatism and intellectualism begin to part company. Primarily, no doubt, to agree means to copy, but we say that the mere word 'clock' would do instead of a mental picture of its works, and that of many realities our ideas can only be symbols and not copies. 'Past times,' 'power,' 'spontaneity,'—how can our mind copy such realities?

To 'agree' in the widest sense with a reality *can only mean to be guided either straight up to it or into its surroundings, or to be put into such working touch with it as to handle either it or something connected with it better than if we disagreed*. Better either intellectually or practically! And often agreement will only mean the negative fact that nothing contradictory from the quarter of that reality comes to interfere with the way in which our ideas guide us elsewhere. To copy a reality is, indeed, one very important way of agreeing with it, but it is far from being essential. The essential thing is the process of being guided. Any idea that helps us to *deal*, whether practically or intellectually, with either the reality or its belongings, that doesn't entangle our progress in frustrations, that *fits*, in fact and adapts our life to the reality's whole setting, will agree sufficiently to meet the requirement. It will hold true of that reality.

Thus, *names* are just as 'true' or 'false' as definite mental pictures are. They set up similar verification-processes, and lead to fully equivalent practical results.

All human thinking gets discursified; we exchange ideas; we lend and borrow verifications, get them from one another by means of social intercourse. All truth thus gets verbally built out, stored up, and made available for every one. Hence, we must talk consistently just as we must *think* consistently: for both in talk and thought we deal with kinds. Names are arbitrary, but once understood they must be kept to. We mustn't now call Abel 'Cain' or Cain 'Abel.' If we do, we ungear ourselves from the whole book of Genesis, and from all its connexions with the universe of speech and fact down to the present time. We throw ourselves out of whatever truth that entire system of speech and fact may embody.

The overwhelming majority of our true ideas admit of no direct or face-to-face verification—those of past history, for example, as of Cain and Abel. The stream of time can be remounted only verbally, or verified indirectly by the present prolongations or effects of what the past harbored. Yet if they agree with these verbalities and effects, we can know that our ideas of the past are true. *As true as past time itself was*, so true was Julius Caesar, so true were antediluvian monsters, all in their proper dates and settings. That past time itself was, is guaranteed by its coherence with everything that's present. True as the present *is*, the past *was* also.

Agreement thus turns out to be essentially an affair of leading—leading that is useful because it is into quarters that contain objects that are important. True ideas lead us into useful verbal and conceptual quarters as well as directly up to useful sensible termini. They lead to consistence, stability and flowing human intercourse. They lead away from eccentricity and isolation, from foiled and barren thinking. The untrammelled flowing of the leading-process, its general freedom from clash and contraction, passes for its indirect verification; but all roads lead to Rome, and in the end and eventually, all true processes must lead to the face of directly verifying sensible experiences *somewhere*, which somebody's ideas have copied.

Such is the large loose way in which the pragmatist interprets the word agreement. He treats it altogether practically. He lets it cover any process of conduction from a present idea to a future terminus, provided only it run prosperously. It is only thus that 'scientific' ideas, flying as they do beyond common sense, can be said to agree with their realities. It is, as I have already said, *as if* reality were made of ether, atoms or electrons, but we mustn't think so literally. The term 'energy' doesn't even pretend to stand for anything 'objective.' It is only a way of measuring the surface of phenomena so as to string their changes on a simple formula.

Yet in the choice of these man-made formulas we can not be capricious with impunity any more than we can be capricious on the common-sense practical level. We must find a theory that will *work;* and that means something extremely difficult; for our theory must mediate between all previous truths and certain new experiences. It must derange common sense and previous belief as little as possible, and it must lead to some sensible terminus or other that can be verified exactly. To 'work' means both these things; and the squeeze is so tight that there is little loose play for any hypothesis. Our theories are wedged and controlled as nothing else is. Yet sometimes alternative theoretic formulas are equally compatible with all the truths we know, and then we choose between them for subjective reasons. We choose the kind of theory to which we are already partial; we follow 'elegance' or 'economy.' Clerk-Maxwell somewhere says it would be 'poor scientific taste' to choose the more complicated of two equally well-evidenced conceptions and you will all agree with him. Truth in science is what gives us the maximum possible sum of satisfactions, taste included, but consistency both with previous truth and with novel fact is always the most imperious claimant. . . .

. . . 'The true,' to put it very briefly, is only the expedient in the way of our thinking, just as 'the right' is only the expedient in the way of our behaving.' Expedient in almost any fashion and expedient in the long run and on the whole of course for what meets expediently all the experience in sight won't necessarily meet all farther experiences equally satisfactorily. Experience, as we know, has ways of *boiling over,* and making us correct our present formulas.

The 'absolutely' true, meaning what no farther experience will ever alter, is that ideal vanishing-point towards which we imagine that all our temporary truths will some day converge. It runs on all fours with the perfectly wise man, and with the absolutely complete experience; and, if these ideals are ever realized, they will all be realized together. Meanwhile we have to live to-day by what truth we can get to-day, and be ready to-morrow to call it falsehood. Ptolemaic astronomy, euclidean space, aristotelian logic, scholastic metaphysics, were expedient for centuries, but human experience has boiled over those limits, and we now call these things only relatively true, or true within those borders of experience. 'Absolutely' they are false for we know that those limits were casual, and might have been transcended by past theorists just as they are by present thinkers.

When new experiences lead to retrospective judgments, using the past tense, what these judgments utter *was* true, even tho no past thinker had been led there. We live forwards, a Danish thinker has said, but we understand backwards. The present sheds a backward light on the world's previous processes. They may have been truth-processes for the actors in them. They are not so for one who knows the later revelations of the story.

This regulative notion of a potential better truth to be established later, possibly to be established some day absolutely, and having powers of retroactive legislation, turns its face, like all pragmatist notions, towards concreteness of fact, and towards the future. Like the half-truths, the absolute truth will have to be *made,* made as a relation incidental to the growth of a mass of verification-experience, to which the half-true ideas are all along contributing their quota.

I have already insisted on the fact that truth is made largely out of previous truths. Men's beliefs at any time are so much experience *funded.* But the beliefs are themselves parts of the sum total of the world's experience, and become matter, therefore, for the next day's funding operations. So far as reality means experienceable reality, both it and the truths men gain about it are everlastingly in process of mutation—mutation towards a definite goal, it may be—but still mutation.

Mathematicians can solve problems with two variables. On the Newtonian theory, for instance, acceleration varies with distance, but distance also varies with acceleration. In the realm of truth-processes facts come independently and determine our beliefs provisionally. But these beliefs make us act, and as fast as they do so, they bring into sight or into existence new facts which re-determine the beliefs accordingly. So the whole coil and ball of truth, as it rolls up, is the product of a double influence. Truths emerge from facts but they dip forward into facts again and add to them which facts again create or reveal new truth (the word is indifferent) and so on indefinitely. The 'facts' themselves meanwhile are not *true.* They simply *are.* Truth is the function of the beliefs that start and terminate among them.

The case is like a snowball's growth, due as it is to the distribution of the snow on the one hand, and to the successive pushes of the boys on the other, with these factors co-determining each other incessantly. . . .

I fear that my previous lectures, confined as they have been to human and humanistic aspects, may have left the impression on many of you that pragmatism means methodically to leave the superhuman out. I have shown small respect indeed for the Absolute, and I have until this moment spoken of no other superhuman hypothesis but that. But I trust that you see sufficiently that the Absolute has nothing but its superhumanness in common with the theistic God. On pragmatistic principles, if the hypothesis of God works satisfactorily in the widest sense of the word, it is true. Now whatever its residual difficulties may be, experience shows that it certainly does work, and that the problem is to build it out and determine it so that it will combine satisfactorily with all the other working truths. I can not start upon a whole theology at the end of this last lecture, but when I tell you that I have written a book on men's religious experience, which on the whole has been regarded as making for the reality of God, you will perhaps exempt my own pragmatism from the charge of being an atheistic system. I firmly disbelieve, myself, that our human experience is the highest form of experience extant in the universe. I believe rather that we stand in much the same relation to the whole of the universe as our canine and feline pets do to the whole of human life. They inhabit our drawing-rooms and libraries. They take part in scenes of whose significance they have no inkling. They are merely tangent to curves of history the beginning and ends and forms of which pass wholly beyond their ken. So we are tangent to the wider life of things. But, just as many of the dog's and cat's ideals coincide with our ideals, and the dogs and cats have daily living proof of the fact, so we may well believe, on the proofs that religious experience affords, that higher powers exist and are at work to save the world on ideal lines similar to our own.

You see that pragmatism can be called religious, if you allow that religion can be pluralistic or merely melioristic in type. But whether you will finally put up with that type of religion or not is a question that only you yourself can decide. Pragmatism has to postpone dogmatic answer, for we do not yet know certainly which type of religion is going to work best in the long run. The various overbeliefs of men, their several faith-ventures, are in fact what are needed to bring the evidence in. You will probably make your own ventures severally. If radically tough, the hurly-burly of the sensible facts of nature will be enough for you, and you will need no religion at all. If radically tender, you will take up with the more monistic form of religion: the pluralistic form, with its reliance on possibilities that are not necessities, will not seem to afford you security enough.

If success be measured by the interest aroused in the general public, the intensity of the intellectual excitement generated, and the number of criticisms and refutations published, then no book in the history of American philosophy, possibly in

the history of American thought, has been as successful as William James's Pragmatism. *It seemed as if the author's jubilant anticipation in a letter to his brother, Henry James, that his book would be "rated 'epoch-making' . . . something quite like the protestant reformation" was about to be realized. But if success be measured by the influence the book had on professional philosophers on both sides of the Atlantic, by its fruitfulness in clarifying philosophical issues and establishing a consensus of agreement among philosophers, it was a profound failure. With few exceptions, the American and European philosophers rejected its central contentions. Even John Dewey, in reviewing the book, felt that some of James's formulations contributed to further misunderstanding of what pragmatism meant by "practical." Whatever intellectual influence James's pragmatism had in law, religion, and psychology,—and its indirect effects were considerable—in philosophy James established no school and won no following. To this day he remains a towering figure, still more alive than most living philosophers, appealing to readers in virtue of his insights, his personality, and his attitude of open-mindedness. He remains influential insofar as some of the specific doctrines he espoused are concerned—his pluralism, temporalism, and radical empiricism—but unconvincing with respect to the particular pragmatic doctrines he treasured most.*

Two generic reasons account for James's failure to make of pragmatism a plausible philosophical doctrine. The first is the impression his colorful rhetoric gives that he denies the possibility of objective truth, "that by saying whatever you find it pleasant to say and calling it truth you fulfil every pragmatistic requirement." These are the words which James puts in the mouths of his prospective critics and he denounces in advance such an interpretation of pragmatism as "an impudent slander." Nonetheless, the expressions James uses to describe his theory of truth are a perennial source of this misunderstanding. His statement, "On pragmatistic principles, if the hypothesis of God works satisfactorily in the widest sense of the word, it is true," has often been read as justifying the attribution of "truth" to beliefs which are useful, pleasant, convenient, or expedient, despite the fact that it is perfectly comprehensible to speak of a useful or pleasant, a convenient or expedient—indeed, of a satisfactory—falsehood.

The second reason is more technical and more important. The pragmatic theory of meaning is an oversimplification of highly complex linguistic phenomena. Although James's pragmatic theory contributed substantially to further exploration of the meaning of meaning, it did not make the necessary ex-

plicit distinctions among various senses or types of meaning recognized in human discourse, even when we restrict ourselves, as James did, to meanings of statements of which truth or falsity can be predicated.

There are at least three senses of meaning involved in James's pragmatic theory of meaning. The first sense is derived from the fact that expressions are used for purposes of communication on the basis of a certain familiarity long before we seek to specify their consequences in experience. For example, "Diamonds are harder than lead" and "Women are more merciful than men" have an intelligible sense in the funded traditions of ordinary discourse independent of the experimental or practical consequences which their assertion implies. Otherwise we would be unable to indicate which set of experimental consequences follows from which assertion.

The second sense of meaning is the one which James is most interested in. It is closest to the verifiability theory of meaning subsequently developed by logical empiricists and operationalists. This is the sense in which James maintains that every intelligible statement which purports to give knowledge about human affairs must in principle lead to some possible set of concrete observations, that every cognitive distinction must make some experimental or practical difference, and that if the sets of consequences implied by the assertion of two different expressions are indistinguishable from each other, then their intellectual meaning is the same. A great many technical difficulties arise in the quest for a precise formulation of the criteria of meaningfulness, but it would not be unjust to say that, according to James, unless we can indicate the kind of evidence which would tend to confirm or disconfirm an assertion about any state of affairs, the assertion would not have cognitive significance.

There is a third sense of meaning in James which he himself does not distinguish from the second. A statement is meaningful if belief in it has some bearing on human conduct. Here the consequences are not the actual or possible observations following from an experimental or controlled procedure that tests the statement, but are consequences of the psychological act of belief in the statement. This introduces an altogether different order of considerations. A statement may be false or even self-contradictory in the second sense above, but belief in it may have consequences which, even if confirmed, have no relevance whatsoever to the truth, falsity, or meaningfulness of the statement. For example, "Santa Claus exists" is a false statement which no set of consequences of belief in his existence, regardless of their beneficial or useful or convenient character, can in any way affect. This confusion between the second and third senses of meaning contributed to the interpretation of James's theory of pragmatism as a method by which the emotional demands of our nature received gratification at the sacrifice of intellectual responsibility. The statement "Santa Claus exists" may be false, and the statement "Belief in the existence of Santa Claus is beneficial to children" may be true. The truth of this latter statement does not itself depend upon the consequences of belief in it.

When pruned of inconsistencies and dissociated from the needs of religious apologetics, the pragmatic theory of meaning and truth has left a permanent bequest to schools of philosophical thought which take science and scientific methods as paradigms of human knowledge and of the most reliable ways of winning new truths. The pragmatic theory of meaning seeks to clarify expressions of discourse by examining carefully the contexts in which they are used, and the range of their applications, positive and negative. The pragmatic theory of truth tends to identify the meaning of truth with the criteria of evidence which warrants assertion. It denies that ideas are images and that true ideas are maps of an antecedent reality. If the truth of a statement is defined independently of the criteria of evidence, it would follow that we could never be warranted in asserting the truth of any statement of fact. The very growth of scientific knowledge justified the pragmatic conception of truth in its refusal to define truth about matters of fact in absolute terms.

Theodore Roosevelt

The New Nationalism

1910

EDITED BY ELTING E. MORISON

Theodore Roosevelt, on his way home from all the exciting times in Africa, arrived in London in May, 1910, to represent his country at the funeral of Edward VII. Elihu Root, setting out for a vacation on the Continent, broke the trip to visit his old friend, who was staying at Dorchester House. There on May 30 the two discussed at length the fortunes of the Republican Party as they had developed since the close of Roosevelt's second term as President, and while he had been off on his long safari. At the end Roosevelt, as his visitor recalled, gave his word to stay out of "things political" on his return to the United States. Such indeed seems to have been his intention for, a few days earlier, he had written to President Taft that he was taking pains to keep his mind open and his mouth shut.

The intention expressed, it soon appeared, was easier to keep on the far side of the water than on home ground. Roosevelt arrived in New York on June 18, 1910, to an ecstatic welcome from his fascinated countrymen. In the days that followed, men concerned with the developing fortunes of the Republican Party made their way out to Sagamore Hill to

732

talk with the great man. One of the matters they talked about most often was Governor Charles Evans Hughes's decision to call a special session of the New York legislature to consider a measure whereby candidates for certain state offices would be nominated by direct primaries. The governor's action pleased progressive members of the party, but roused the antagonism of the new party boss in the state, William Barnes, Jr. This difference between governor and boss had produced a cleavage within the Republican Party in the state at the moment Roosevelt arrived home. He was put under pressure by both sides to make a public declaration of his position. For a few days he resisted these importunities, mindful perhaps of his words with Root. Then he went off to the Harvard Commencement exercises on June 29, where he met both Henry Cabot Lodge and Governor Hughes. While the former whispered words of caution, the latter spoke convincingly for action. Persuaded by the appeal for his help, Roosevelt at noon announced his support of the direct-primary legislation.

Thus Theodore Roosevelt became mixed up again in "things political." There have been various explanations. He was ambitious and his ambitions were played upon by schemers like the Pinchots, who saw in him a source of further power for themselves. He was annoyed by the ineptitudes of his successor, William Howard Taft, and therefore annoyed with himself for picking Taft to succeed him. He was at fifty-two a healthy, high-spirited man seeking once again a legitimate outlet for his frustrated energies in the only task in the country that fitted his ample powers. He was moved by his sense of loyalty to certain public officials who had supported him—Bass of New Hampshire, Garfield of Ohio, Osborn of Missouri, Hadley of Michigan, Stimson of New York, and to all those others less renowned who had shared the burden and the heat of an earlier day with him.

Doubtless he was moved in subtle ways by all these influences—mean and noble, conscious and unconscious—as most men have been. But he was moved too by another concern. Once, near the turn of the century, he had said to a friend that there was in a society that rested upon industry the constant danger of barbarism. Unhappily prominent in American life, he went on, was "the spirit of the Birmingham School, the spirit of the banker, the broker, the mere manufacturer, the mere merchant." Such a spirit, he came early in his Presidency to believe, if left ungoverned would in time destroy even the society that held out the last best hopes of earth. Therefore, he had said, "It behooves us to look ahead and plan out the right kind of civilization as that which we *intend to develop from these wonderful new conditions of vast industrial growth."*

In the years from 1901 to 1909 Roosevelt as President had given life to these sentiments. From a hundred platforms, at a thousand whistle stops, he had given the society an objective by defining in striking words the nature of what he believed was the right kind of civilization, and by a score of bold and skillful actions he had demonstrated it was possible to create out of an industrial society a satisfying environment. He had used his authority to set safe limits on the power of the corporation, to conserve the natural resources of the country, to produce a more equitable distribution of goods, services, and opportunities among the citizens. Upon leaving office in 1909 he looked to the Republican Party as the instrument to continue his efforts.

And so when he returned to this country in 1910, an election year, it was in the nature of things political for him, as he told Henry Cabot Lodge, "to try to help the Republican Party at the polls this fall." By so doing he would perform "the greatest service I can render to Taft, the service which beyond all others will tend to secure his renomination and to make that renomination of use" by ensuring Taft's re-election in 1912.

Here was the problem confronted by Roosevelt in 1910. The conflict that had brought Roosevelt back into politics, the struggle between the enlightened Governor Hughes and the party boss Barnes in New York, was a conflict that extended in fact within the Republican Party throughout the country. Broadly speaking, what divided the members was a difference of opinion about the proper role of the central government. The liberal spirits—the insurgents or progressives as they were called—believed that the state should play a large part in the ordering of affairs within the economy; the conservative spirits—the Old Guard—were inclined to leave well enough alone. Roosevelt was one of the liberal spirits—a man with a specific program that added up to what he called doing good to the nation and a man who believed the central government was under obligation to take action to do this good. So in 1910 he wanted to help the party win and he wanted to make it take what he thought of as "the proper position." On July 23, 1910, he started out on a speaking tour that began in New York and wound through the Middle West to Colorado. In many states and places he gave specifically his support to Republican candidates simply because they were Republicans. Then in other places, where the nature of the occasion seemed to take matters beyond the mere

*search for votes, he cut loose with his own ideas. By this
means he hoped both to elect Republicans and to define advanced positions from which, after election, the party could
not retreat.*

*The best opportunity to speak his full mind occurred on
August 31 at Osawatomie, Kansas. Roosevelt there took part
in a celebration dedicating the ancient field where John
Brown in 1856 entered our history. The place was appropriate for a striking statement. It was here that Roosevelt first
fully defined what he called "The New Nationalism," a
phrase which became one of the great passwords of American politics.*

WE COME here to-day to commemorate one of the epoch-making events of the long struggle for the rights
of man—the long struggle for the uplift of humanity. Our
country—this great Republic—means nothing unless it means
the triumph of a real democracy, the triumph of popular government, and, in the long run, of an economic system under
which each man shall be guaranteed the opportunity to show
the best that there is in him. That is why the history of
America is now the central feature of the history of the
world for the world has set its face hopefully toward our democracy; and, O my fellow citizens, each one of you carries
on your shoulders not only the burden of doing well for the
sake of your own country, but the burden of doing well and
of seeing that this nation does well for the sake of mankind.

There have been two great crises in our country's history:
first, when it was formed, and then, again, when it was perpetuated; and, in the second of these great crises—in the time
of stress and strain which culminated in the Civil War, on the
outcome of which depended the justification of what had
been done earlier, you men of the Grand Army, you men
who fought through the Civil War, not only did you justify
your generation, not only did you render life worth living for
our generation, but you justified the wisdom of Washington
and Washington's colleagues. If this Republic had been founded by them only to be split asunder into fragments when the
strain came, then the judgment of the world would have been
that Washington's work was not worth doing. It was you who

The speech is reprinted here from the National Edition of *The
Works of Theodore Roosevelt*, edited by Hermann Hagedorn (20 vols.;
New York: Charles Scribner's Sons, 1926), XVII, 5–22.

crowned Washington's work, as you carried to achievement the high purpose of Abraham Lincoln.

Now, with this second period of our history the name of John Brown will be forever associated and Kansas was the theatre upon which the first act of the second of our great national life dramas was played. It was the result of the struggle in Kansas which determined that our country should be in deed as well as in name devoted to both union and freedom that the great experiment of democratic government on a national scale should succeed and not fail. In name we had the Declaration of Independence in 1776, but we gave the lie by our acts to the words of the Declaration of Independence until 1865 and words count for nothing except in so far as they represent acts. This is true everywhere but, O my friends, it should be truest of all in political life. A broken promise is bad enough in private life. It is worse in the field of politics. No man is worth his salt in public life who makes on the stump a pledge which he does not keep after election; and, if he makes such a pledge and does not keep it, hunt him out of public life. I care for the great deeds of the past chiefly as spurs to drive us onward in the present. I speak of the men of the past partly that they may be honored by our praise of them, but more that they may serve as examples for the future.

It was a heroic struggle; and, as is inevitable with all such struggles, it had also a dark and terrible side. Very much was done of good, and much also of evil and, as was inevitable in such a period of revolution, often the same man did both good and evil. For our great good fortune as a nation, we, the people of the United States as a whole, can now afford to forget the evil, or, at least, to remember it without bitterness, and to fix our eyes with pride only on the good that was accomplished. Even in ordinary times there are very few of us who do not see the problems of life as through a glass, darkly and when the glass is clouded by the murk of furious popular passion, the vision of the best and the bravest is dimmed. Looking back, we are all of us now able to do justice to the valor and the disinterestedness and the love of the right, as to each it was given to see the right, shown both by the men of the North and the men of the South in that contest which was finally decided by the attitude of the West. We can admire the heroic valor, the sincerity, the self-devotion shown alike by the men who wore the blue and the men who wore the gray, and our sadness that such men should have had to fight one another is tempered by the glad knowledge that ever hereafter their descendants shall be found fighting side by side, struggling in peace as well as in war for the uplift of their common country, all alike resolute to raise to the highest pitch of honor and usefulness the nation to which they all belong. As for the veterans of the Grand Army of the Republic, they deserve honor and recognition such as is paid to no other citizens of the Republic, for to them the republic owes its all; for to them it owes its very existence. It is because of what you and your comrades did in the dark years that we of to-day walk, each of us, head erect, and proud that we belong, not to one of a dozen little squabbling contemptible commonwealths, but to the mightiest nation upon which the sun shines.

I do not speak of this struggle of the past merely from the historic standpoint. Our interest is primarily in the application to-day of the lessons taught by the contest of half a century ago. It is of little use for us to pay lip-loyalty to the mighty men of the past unless we sincerely endeavor to apply to the problems of the present precisely the qualities which in other crises enabled the men of that day to meet those crises. It is half melancholy and half amusing to see the way in which well-meaning people gather to do honor to the men who, in company with John Brown, and under the lead of Abraham Lincoln, faced and solved the great problems of the nineteenth century, while, at the same time, these same good people nervously shrink from, or frantically denounce, those who are trying to meet the problems of the twentieth century in the spirit which was accountable for the successful solution of the problems of Lincoln's time.

Of that generation of men to whom we owe so much, the man to whom we owe most is, of course, Lincoln. Part of our debt to him is because he forecast our present struggle and saw the way out. He said:

"I hold that while man exists it is his duty to improve not only his own condition, but to assist in ameliorating mankind."

And again:

"Labor is prior to, and independent of, capital. Capital is only the fruit of labor, and could never have existed if labor had not first existed. Labor is the superior of capital, and deserves much the higher consideration."

If that remark was original with me, I should be even more strongly denounced as a Communist agitator than I shall be anyhow. It is Lincoln's. I am only quoting it; and that is one side; that is the side the capitalist should hear. Now, let the working man hear his side.

"Capital has its rights, which are as worthy of protection as any other rights. . . . Nor should this lead to a war upon the owners of property. Property is the fruit of labor; . . . property is desirable; is a positive good in the world."

And then comes a thoroughly Lincolnlike sentence:

"Let not him who is houseless pull down the house of another, but let him work diligently and build one for himself, thus by example assuring that his own shall be safe from violence when built."

It seems to me that, in these words, Lincoln took substantially the attitude that we ought to take; he showed the proper sense of proportion in his relative estimates of capital and labor, of human rights and property rights. Above all, in this speech, as in many others, he taught a lesson in wise kindliness and charity; an indispensable lesson to us of to-day. But this wise kindliness and charity never weakened his arm or numbed his heart. We cannot afford weakly to blind ourselves to the actual conflict which faces us to-day. The issue is joined, and we must fight or fail.

In every wise struggle for human betterment one of the main objects, and often the only object, has been to achieve in large measure equality of opportunity. In the struggle for this great end, nations rise from barbarism to civilization, and through it people press forward from one stage of enlightenment to the next. One of the chief factors in progress is the destruction of special privilege. The essence of any struggle for healthy liberty has always been, and must always be, to take from some one man or class of men the right to enjoy power, or wealth, or position, or immunity, which has not been earned by service to his or their fellows. That is what you fought for in the Civil War, and that is what we strive for now.

At many stages in the advance of humanity, this conflict between the men who possess more than they have earned and the men who have earned more than they possess is the central condition of progress. In our day it appears as the struggle of freemen to gain and hold the right of self-government as against the special interests, who twist the methods of free government into machinery for defeating the popular will. At every stage, and under all circumstances, the essence of the struggle is to equalize opportunity, destroy privilege, and give to the life and citizenship of every individual the highest possible value both to himself and to the commonwealth. That is nothing new. All I ask in civil life is what you fought for in the Civil War. I ask that civil life be carried on according to the spirit in which the army was carried on. You never get perfect justice, but the effort in handling the army was to bring to the front the men who could do the job. Nobody grudged promotion to Grant, or Sherman, or Thomas, or Sheridan, because they earned it. The only complaint was when a man got promotion which he did not earn.

Practical equality of opportunity for all citizens, when we achieve it, will have two great results. First, every man will have a fair chance to make of himself all that in him lies; to reach the highest point to which his capacities, unassisted by special privilege of his own and unhampered by the special privilege of others, can carry him, and to get for himself and his family substantially what he has earned. Second, equality of opportunity means that the commonwealth will get from every citizen the highest service of which he is capable. No man who carries the burden of the special privileges of another can give to the commonwealth that service to which it is fairly entitled.

I stand for the square deal. But when I say that I am for the square deal, I mean not merely that I stand for fair play under the present rules of the game, but that I stand for having those rules change so as to work for a more substantial equality of opportunity and of reward for equally good service. One word of warning, which, I think, is hardly necessary in Kansas. When I say I want a square deal for the poor man, I do not mean that I want a square deal for the man who remains poor because he has not got the energy to work for himself. If a man who has had a chance will not make good, then he has got to quit. And you men of the Grand Army, you want justice for the brave man who fought, and punishment for the coward who shirked his work. Is not that so?

Now, this means that our government, National and State, must be freed from the sinister influence or control of special interests. Exactly as the special interests of cotton and slavery threatened our political integrity before the Civil War, so now the great special business interests too often control and corrupt the men and methods of government for their own profit. We must drive the special interests out of politics. That is one of our tasks to-day. Every special interest is entitled to justice —full, fair, and complete—and, now, mind you, if there were any attempt by mob-violence to plunder and work harm to the special interest, whatever it may be, that I most dislike, and the wealthy man, whomsoever he may be, for whom I have the greatest contempt, I would fight for him, and you would if you were worth your salt. He should have justice. For every special interest is entitled to justice, but not one is entitled to a vote in Congress, to a voice on the bench, or to representation in any public office. The Constitution guarantees protection to property, and we must make that promise good. But it does not give the right of suffrage to any corporation.

The true friend of property, the true conservative, is he who insists that property shall be the servant and not the master of the commonwealth; who insists that the creature of man's making shall be the servant and not the master of the man who made it. The citizens of the United States must effectively control the mighty commercial forces which they have themselves called into being. There can be no effective control of corporations while their political activity remains. To put an end to it will be neither a short nor an easy task, but it can be done.

We must have complete and effective publicity of corporate affairs, so that the people may know beyond peradventure whether the corporations obey the law and whether their management entitles them to the confidence of the public. It is necessary that laws should be passed to prohibit the use of corporate funds directly or indirectly for political purposes; it is still more necessary that such laws should be thoroughly enforced. Corporate expenditures for political purposes, and especially such expenditures by public service corporations, have supplied one of the principal sources of corruption in our political affairs.

It has become entirely clear that we must have government supervision of the capitalization, not only of public-service corporations, including, particularly, railways, but of all corporations doing an interstate business. I do not wish to see the nation forced into the ownership of the railways if it can possibly be avoided, and the only alternative is thoroughgoing and effective regulation, which shall be based on a full knowledge of all the facts, including a physical valuation of property. This physical valuation is not needed, or, at least, is very rarely needed, for fixing rates; but it is needed as the basis of honest capitalization.

We have come to recognize that franchises should never be granted except for a limited time, and never without proper provision for compensation to the public. It is my personal belief that the same kind and degree of control and supervision which should be exercised over public-service corporations should be extended also to combinations which control necessaries of life, such as meat, oil, and coal, or which deal in them on an important scale. I have no doubt that the ordinary man who has control of them is much like ourselves. I have no doubt he would like to do well, but I want to have enough supervision to help him realize that desire to do well.

I believe that the officers, and, especially, the directors, of corporations should be held personally responsible when any corporation breaks the law.

Combinations in industry are the result of an imperative economic law which cannot be repealed by political legislation. The effort at prohibitng all combination has substantially failed. The way out lies, not in attempting to prevent such combinations, but in completely controlling them in the interest of the public welfare. For that purpose the Federal Bureau of Corporations is an agency of first importance. Its powers, and, therefore, its efficiency, as well as that of the Interstate Commerce Commission, should be largely increased. We have a right to expect from the Bureau of Corporations and from the Interstate Commerce Commission a very high grade of public service. We should be as sure of the proper conduct of the interstate railways and the proper management of interstate business as we are now sure of the conduct and management of the national banks, and we should have as effective supervision in one case as in the other. The Hepburn Act, and the amendment to the act in the shape in which it finally passed Congress at the last session, represent a long step in advance, and we must go yet further.

There is a wide-spread belief among our people that, under the methods of making tariffs which have hitherto obtained, the special interests are too influential. Probably this is true of both the big special interests and the little special interests. These methods have put a premium on selfishness, and, naturally, the selfish big interests have gotten more than their smaller, though equally selfish, brothers. The duty of Congress is to provide a method by which the interest of the whole people shall be all that receives consideration. To this end there must be an expert tariff commission, wholly removed from the possibility of political pressure or of improper business influence. Such a commission can find the real difference between cost of production, which is mainly the difference of labor cost here and abroad. As fast as its recommendations are made, I believe in revising one schedule at a time. A general revision of the tariff almost inevitably leads to logrolling and the subordination of the general public interest to local and special interests.

The absence of effective State, and, especially, national, restraint upon unfair money-getting has tended to create a small class of enormously wealthy and economically powerful men, whose chief object is to hold and increase their power. The prime need is to change the conditions which enable these men to accumulate power which it is not for the general welfare that they should hold or exercise. We grudge no man a fortune which represents his own power and sagacity, when exercised with entire regard to the welfare of his fellows. Again, comrades over there, take the lesson from your own experience. Not only did you not grudge, but you gloried in the promotion of the great generals who gained their promotion by leading the army to victory. So it is with us. We grudge no man a fortune in civil life if it is honorably obtained and well used. It is not even enough that it should have been gained without doing damage to the community. We should permit it to be gained only so long as the gaining represents benefit to the community. This, I know, implies a policy of a far more active governmental interference with social and economic conditions in this country than we have yet had, but I think we have got to face the fact that such an increase in governmental control is now necessary.

No man should receive a dollar unless that dollar has been fairly earned. Every dollar received should represent a dollar's worth of service rendered—not gambling in stocks, but service rendered. The really big fortune, the swollen fortune, by the mere fact of its size acquires qualities which differentiate it in kind as well as in degree from what is possessed by men of relatively small means. Therefore, I believe in a graduated income tax on big fortunes, and in another tax which is far more easily collected and far more effective—a graduated inheritance tax on big fortunes, properly safeguarded against evasion and increasing rapidly in amount with the size of the estate.

The people of the United States suffer from periodical financial panics to a degree substantially unknown among the other nations which approach us in financial strength. There is no reason why we should suffer what they escape. It is of profound importance that our financial system should be promptly investigated, and so thoroughly and effectively revised as to make it certain that hereafter our currency will no longer fail at critical times to meet our needs.

It is hardly necessary for me to repeat that I believe in an efficient army and a navy large enough to secure for us abroad that respect which is the surest guaranty of peace. A word of special warning to my fellow citizens who are as progressive as I hope I am. I want them to keep up their interest in our internal affairs; and I want them also continually to remember Uncle Sam's interests abroad. Justice and fair dealing among nations rest upon principles identical with those which control justice and fair dealing among the individuals of which nations are composed, with the vital exception that each nation must do its own part in international police work. If you get into trouble here, you can call for the police; but if Uncle Sam gets into trouble, he has got to be his own policeman, and I want to see him strong enough to encourage the peaceful aspirations of other peoples in connection with us. I believe in national friendships and heartiest good-will to all nations; but national friendships, like those between men, must be founded on respect as well as on liking, on forbearance as well as upon trust. I should be heartily ashamed of any American who did not try to make the American Government act as justly toward the other nations in international relations as he himself would act toward any individual in private relations. I should be heartily ashamed to see us wrong a weaker power, and I should hang my head forever if we tamely suffered wrong from a stronger power.

Of conservation I shall speak more at length elsewhere. Conservation means development as much as it does protection. I recognize the right and duty of this generation to develop and use the natural resources of our land; but I do not recognize the right to waste them, or to rob, by wasteful use, the generations that come after us. I ask nothing of the nation except that it so behave as each farmer here behaves with reference to his own children. That farmer is a poor creature who skins the land and leaves it worthless to his children. The farmer is a good farmer who, having enabled the land to support himself and to provide for the education of his children, leaves it to them a little better than he found it himself. I believe the same thing of a nation.

Moreover, I believe that the natural resources must be used for the benefit of all our people, and not monopolized for the benefit of the few, and here again is another case in which I am accused of taking a revolutionary attitude. People forget now that one hundred years ago there were public men of good character who advocated the nation selling its public lands in great quantities, so that the nation could get the most money out of it, and giving it to the men who could cultivate it for their own uses. We took the proper democratic ground that the land should be granted in small sections to the men who were actually to till it and live on it. Now, with the water-power, with the forests, with the mines, we are brought face to face with the fact that there are many people who will go with us in conserving the resources only if they are to be allowed to exploit them for their benefit. That is one of the fundamental reasons why the special interests should be driven out of politics. Of all the questions which can come before this nation, short of the actual preservation of its existence in a great war, there is none which compares in importance with the great central task of leaving this land even a better land for our descendants than it is for us, and training them into a better race to inhabit the land and pass it on. Conservation is a great moral issue, for it involves the patriotic duty of insuring the safety and continuance of the nation. Let me add that the health and vitality of our people are at least as well worth conserving as their forests, waters, lands, and minerals, and in this great work the national government must bear a most important part.

I have spoken elsewhere also of the great task which lies before the farmers of the country to get for themselves and their wives and children not only the benefits of better farming, but also those of better business methods and better conditions of life on the farm. The burden of this great task will fall, as it should, mainly upon the great organizations of the farmers themselves. I am glad it will, for I believe they are all well able to handle it. In particular, there are strong reasons why the Departments of Agriculture of the various States, the United States Department of Agriculture, and the agricultural colleges and experiment stations should extend their work to cover all phases of farm life, instead of limiting themselves, as they have far too often limited themselves in the past, solely to the question of the production of crops. And now a special word to the farmer. I want to see him make the farm as fine a farm as it can be made; and let him remember to see that the improvement goes on indoors as well as out; let him remember that the farmer's wife should have her share of thought and attention just as much as the farmer himself.

Nothing is more true than that excess of every kind is followed by reaction; a fact which should be pondered by reformer and reactionary alike. We are face to face with new conceptions of the relations of property to human welfare, chiefly because certain advocates of the rights of property as against the rights of men have been pushing their claims too far. The man who wrongly holds that every human right is secondary to his profit must now give way to the advocate of human welfare, who rightly maintains that every man holds his property subject to the general right of the community to regulate its use to whatever degree the public welfare may require it.

But I think we may go still further. The right to regulate the use of wealth in the public interest is universally admitted. Let us admit also the right to regulate the terms and conditions of labor, which is the chief element of wealth, directly in the interest of the common good. The fundamental thing to do for every man is to give him a chance to reach a place in which he will make the greatest possible contribution to the public welfare. Understand what I say there. Give him a chance, not push him up if he will not be pushed. Help any man who stumbles; if he lies down, it is a poor job to try to carry him; but if he is a worthy man, try your best to see that he gets a chance to show the worth that is in him. No man can be a good citizen unless he has a wage more than sufficient to cover the bare cost of living, and hours of labor short enough so that after his day's work is done he will have time and energy to bear his share in the management of the community, to help in carrying the general load. We keep countless men from being good citizens by the conditions of life with which we surround them. We need comprehensive workmen's compensation acts, both State and national laws to regulate child labor and work for women, and, especially we need in our common schools not merely education in booklearning, but also practical training for daily life and work. We need to enforce better sanitary conditions for our workers and to extend the use of safety appliances for our workers in industry and commerce, both within and between the States. Also, friends, in the interest of the working man himself we need to set our faces like flint against mob-violence just as against corporate greed; against violence and injustice and lawlessness by wage-workers just as much as against lawless cunning and greed and selfish arrogance of employers. If I could ask but one thing of my fellow countrymen, my request would be that, whenever they go in for reform, they remember the two sides, and that they always exact justice from one side as much as from the other. I have small use for the public servant who can always see and denounce the corruption of the capitalist, but who cannot persuade himself, especially before election, to say a word about lawless mob-violence. And I have equally small use for the man, be he a judge on the bench, or editor of a great paper, or wealthy and influential private citizen, who can see clearly enough and denounce the lawlessness of mob-violence, but whose eyes are closed so that he is blind when the question is one of corruption in business on a gigantic scale. Also remember what I said about excess in reformer and reactionary alike. If the reactionary man, who thinks of nothing but the rights of property, could have his way, he would bring about a revolution; and one of my chief fears in connection with progress comes because I do not want to see our people, for lack of proper leadership, compelled to follow men whose intentions are excellent, but whose eyes are a little too wild to make it really safe to trust them. Here in Kansas there is one paper which habitually denounces me as the tool of Wall Street, and at the same time frantically repudiates the statement that I am a Socialist on the ground that that is an unwarranted slander of the Socialists.

National efficiency has many factors. It is a necessary result of the principle of conservation widely applied. In the end it will determine our failure or success as a nation. National efficiency has to do, not only with natural resources and with men, but it is equally concerned with institutions. The State must be made efficient for the work which concerns only the people of the State; and the nation for that which concerns all the people. There must remain no neutral ground to serve as a refuge for lawbreakers, and especially for lawbreakers of great wealth, who can hire the vulpine legal cunning which will teach them how to avoid both jurisdictions. It is a misfortune when the national legislature fails to do its duty in providing a national remedy, so that the only national activity is the purely negative activity of the judiciary in forbidding the State to exercise power in the premises.

I do not ask for overcentralization; but I do ask that we work in a spirit of broad and far-reaching nationalism when we work for what concerns our people as a whole. We are all Americans. Our common interests are as broad as the continent. I speak to you here in Kansas exactly as I would speak in New York or Georgia, for the most vital problems are those which affect us all alike. The National Government belongs to the whole American people, and where the whole American people are interested, that interest can be guarded effectively only by the National Government. The betterment which we seek must be accomplished, I believe, mainly through the National Government.

The American people are right in demanding that New Nationalism, without which we cannot hope to deal with new problems. The New Nationalism puts the national need before sectional or personal advantage. It is impatient of the utter confusion that results from local legislatures attempting to treat national issues as local issues. It is still more impatient of the impotence which springs from overdivision of governmental powers, the impotence which makes it possible for local selfishness or for legal cunning, hired by wealthy special interests, to bring national activities to a deadlock. This New Nationalism regards the executive power as the steward of the public welfare. It demands of the judiciary that it shall be interested primarily in human welfare rather than in property, just as it demands that the representative body shall represent all the people rather than any one class or section of the people.

I believe in shaping the ends of government to protect property as well as human welfare. Normally, and in the long run, the ends are the same; but whenever the alternative must be faced, I am for men and not for property, as you were in the Civil War. I am far from underestimating the importance of dividends; but I rank dividends below human character. Again, I do not have any sympathy with the reformer who says he does not care for dividends. Of course, economic welfare is necessary, for a man must pull his own weight and be able to support his family. I know well that the reformers must not bring upon the people economic ruin, or the reforms themselves will go down in the ruin. But we must be ready to face temporary disaster, whether or not brought on by those who will war against us to the knife. Those who oppose all reform will do well to remember that ruin in its worst form is inevitable if our national life brings us nothing better than swollen fortunes for the few and the triumph in both politics and business of a sordid and selfish materialism.

If our political institutions were perfect, they would absolutely prevent the political domination of money in any part of our affairs. We need to make our political representatives more quickly and sensitively responsive to the people whose servants they are. More direct action by the people in their own affairs under proper safeguards is vitally necessary. The direct primary is a step in this direction, if it is associated with a corrupt-practices act effective to prevent the advantage of the man willing recklessly and unscrupulously to spend money over his more honest competitor. It is particularly important that all moneys received or expended for campaign purposes should be publicly accounted for, not only after election, but before election as well. Political action must be made simpler, easier, and freer from confusion for every citizen. I believe that the prompt removal of unfaithful or incompetent public servants should be made easy and sure in whatever way experience shall show to be most expedient in any given class of cases.

One of the fundamental necessities in a representative government such as ours is to make certain that the men to whom the people delegate their power shall serve the people by whom they are elected, and not the special interests. I believe that every national officer, elected or appointed, should be forbidden to perform any service or receive any compensation, directly or indirectly, from interstate corporations;

and a similar provision could not fail to be useful within the States.

The object of government is the welfare of the people. The material progress and prosperity of a nation are desirable chiefly so far as they lead to the moral and material welfare of all good citizens. Just in proportion as the average man and woman are honest, capable of sound judgment and high ideals, active in public affairs—but, first of all, sound in their home life, and the father and mother of healthy children whom they bring up well—just so far, and no farther, we may count our civilization a success. We must have—I believe we have already—a genuine and permanent moral awakening, without which no wisdom of legislation or administration really means anything; and, on the other hand, we must try to secure the social and economic legislation without which any improvement due to purely moral agitation is necessarily evanescent. Let me again illustrate by a reference to the Grand Army. You could not have won simply as a disorderly and disorganized mob. You needed generals; you needed careful administration of the most advanced type; and a good commissary—the cracker line. You well remember that success was necessary in many different lines in order to bring about general success. You had to have the administration at Washington good, just as you had to have the administration in the field; and you had to have the work of the generals good. You could not have triumphed without that administration and leadership; but it would all have been worthless if the average soldier had not had the right stuff in him. He had to have the right stuff in him, or you could not get it out of him. In the last analysis, therefore, vitally necessary though it was to have the right kind of organization and the right kind of generalship, it was even more vitally necessary that the average soldier should have the fighting edge, the right character. So it is in our civil life. No matter how honest and decent we are in our private lives, if we do not have the right kind of law and the right kind of administration of the law, we cannot go forward as a nation. That is imperative; but it must be an addition to, and not a substitution for, the qualities that make us good citizens. In the last analysis, the most important elements in any man's career must be the sum of those qualities which, in the aggregate, we speak of as character. If he had not got it, then no law that the wit of man can devise, no administration of the law by the boldest and strongest executive, will avail to help him. We must have the right kind of character—character that makes a man, first of all, a good man in the home, a good father, a good husband

—that makes a man a good neighbor. You must have that, and, then, in addition, you must have the kind of law and the kind of administration of the law which will give to those qualities in the private citizen the best possible chance for development. The prime problem of our nation is to get the right type of good citizenship, and, to get it, we must have progress, and our public men must be genuinely progressive.

Much that Roosevelt said of "the new nationalism" he had said—one way and another, in one place or another—before. Indeed Elihu Root remarked that "the only real objection I see to it is calling it 'new.'" Still, the speaker did succeed in defining his political philosophy in such a way that he seemed to many citizens not only in advance of his party but also in advance of his time. Especially, he suggested that the rights of human beings were on the whole superior to property rights. He tried to make this suggestion more palatable to the more laggard members in his following by supporting it with a quotation from Lincoln, but this device simply mortified one group in his party even more. In fact, the ideas presented throughout the speech disturbed the Old Guard as much as they excited the progressives in the party. In a sense, from Roosevelt's speech, it can be made to appear, flowed great consequences to the Republican Party. In 1910 in New York an election was lost and a division was created between the good man who was President of the United States and the man who had been his great predecessor in office. In 1911 confusion and disorder mounted in the Grand Old Party. Finally, in 1912, came the decisive defeat of all the forces of the divided party.

On September 2, 1920, Elihu Root was again in the city of London. Walking along Park Lane that afternoon, he came to Dorchester House. Before that impressive old structure he paused, looked up, and said to his companion, "It is there that I had an interesting interview with Roosevelt. And if he had done as he promised me—kept out of things political— we would have been spared much of our past trouble." It is possible, indeed it is probable, that in the somber mood of his own personal recollections, Root overstated the case. The troubles visited upon his party could not all have been produced simply because Theodore Roosevelt changed his mind. But still, Root was an acute observer, and no doubt some of the troubles were the product of Theodore Roosevelt's decision to return to things political.

For this reason the speech is important in our history. But there are other reasons for reading it. For instance, those who search for irony as the primary substance in history will be pleased to know that Warren Gamaliel Harding took the "Osawatomie speech [as] the platform on which he stood" in 1920. And those who search for continuity as the source of meaning in history will be reassured to note in this speech many if not most of the ideas and attitudes that Theodore Roosevelt's cousin, Franklin, thought up as novelties a quarter of a century later.

Walter Rauschenbusch
Prayers of the Social Awakening
1910

EDITED BY WINTHROP S. HUDSON

---

*Walter Rauschenbusch has been called "the real founder of
social Christianity" in the United States and "its most brilliant and generally satisfying exponent." He gained his social
passion as a young man when he was pastor of a small Baptist church near the tough "Hell's Kitchen" section of New
York City. There at first hand he became acquainted with the
ills suffered by the families of immigrant workingmen. Later
he became professor of church history in the Rochester
Theological Seminary, and in 1907 the publication of his*
Christianity and the Social Crisis, *won him national fame and
centered attention upon him as a major voice of the Christian
church. Other books by him dealing with the same theme followed—*Christianizing the Social Order *(1912),* Dare We
Be Christians? *(1914),* The Social Principles of Jesus *(1916),
and* A Theology for the Social Gospel *(1917). His "favorite
book," however, was a small volume published in 1910 under
the title* For God and the People: Prayers of the Social
Awakening.*

Rauschenbusch had become convinced that the new social
movement within the churches would never be deeply rooted*

until it found expression in the prayers of the people. The traditional prayers of the church lacked social feeling. They were too individualistic in concern, too general in scope, too antique in language; and they seldom voiced either the needs or the aspirations of modern man. In the seminary chapel and at conferences and other public gatherings, Rauschenbusch sought to rectify this deficiency by fashioning "models" which would be suggestive to others. He also composed prayers for specific vocational groups. One of these prayers was published as the frontispiece in each issue of the American Magazine *in 1910. The publication of these created something of a sensation, and before the year was out the little volume known in subsequent editions as* Prayers of the Social Awakening *had been rushed through the press in order to satisfy a widespread popular demand. In addition to an introductory exposition of the social meaning of the Lord's Prayer, there were prayers for morning, noon, and night; prayers for specific groups and classes (workingmen and employers, doctors and nurses, newspapermen and teachers, artists and musicians, lawyers and judges, legislators and public officials, immigrants and the unemployed); prayers of wrath; and prayers for the progress of humanity. Later editions of the book contained seven additional prayers and "A Social Litany."*

PREFACE

THE NEW social purpose, which has laid its masterful grasp on modern life and thought, is enlarging and transforming our whole conception of the meaning of Christianity. The Bible and all past history speak a new and living language. The life of men about us stands out with an open-air color and vividness which it never had in the dusky solemnity of the older theological views about humanity. All the older tasks of church life have taken on a new significance, and vastly larger tasks are emerging as from the mists of a new morning.

Many ideas that used to seem fundamental and satisfying seem strangely narrow and trivial in this greater world of God. Some of the old religious appeals have utterly lost their power over us. But there are others, unknown to our fathers,

The prayers reprinted here comprise about one-fifth of the total which appeared in *For God and the People: Prayers of the Social Awakening* (Boston: The Pilgrim Press, 1910).

which kindle religious passions of wonderful intensity and purity. The wrongs and sufferings of the people and the vision of a righteous and brotherly social life awaken an almost painful compassion and longing, and these feelings are more essentially Christian than most of the fears and desires of religion in the past. Social Christianity is adding to the variety of religious experience, and is creating a new type of Christian man who bears a striking family likeness to Jesus of Galilee.

The new religious emotions ought to find conscious and social expression. But the Church, which has brought down so rich an equipment from the past for the culture of individual religion, is poverty-stricken in the face of this new need. The ordinary church hymnal rarely contains more than two or three hymns in which the triumphant chords of the social hope are struck. Our liturgies and devotional manuals offer very little that is fit to enrich and purify the social thoughts and feelings.

Even men who have absorbed the social ideals are apt to move within the traditional round in public prayer. The language of prayer always clings to the antique for the sake of dignity, and plain reference to modern facts and contrivances jars the ear. So we are inclined to follow the broad avenues beaten by the feet of many generations when we approach God. We need to blaze new paths to God for the feet of modern men.

I offer this little book as an attempt in that direction. . . . I realize keenly the limitations which are inevitable when one mind is to furnish a vehicle for the most intimate spiritual thoughts of others. But whenever a great movement stirs the deeper passions of men, a common soul is born, and all who feel the throb of the new age have such unity of thought and aim and feeling, that the utterance of one man may in a measure be the voice of all. . . .

WALTER RAUSCHENBUSCH

Rochester, N.Y.

INTRODUCTORY: THE SOCIAL MEANING OF THE LORD'S PRAYER

The Lord's Prayer is recognized as the purest expression of the mind of Jesus. It crystallizes his thoughts. It conveys the atmosphere of his childlike trust in the Father. It gives proof of the transparent clearness and peace of his soul.

It first took shape against the wordy flattery with which men tried to wheedle their gods. He demanded simplicity and sincerity in all expressions of religion, and offered this as an example of the straightforwardness with which men might deal with their Father. . . .

The Lord's Prayer is so familiar to us that few have stopped to understand it. The general tragedy of misunderstanding which has followed Jesus throughout the centuries has frustrated the purpose of his model prayer also. He gave it to stop vain repetitions, and it has been turned into a contrivance for incessant repetition. . . .

The Lord's Prayer is part of the heritage of social Christianity which has been appropriated by men who have had little sympathy with its social spirit. It belongs to the equipment of the soldiers of the kingdom of God. I wish to claim it here as the great charter of all social prayers.

When he bade us say, "Our Father," Jesus spoke from that consciousness of human solidarity which was a matter of course in all his thinking. He compels us to clasp hands in spirit with all our brothers and thus to approach the Father together. This rules out all selfish isolation in religion. Before God no man stands alone. Before the All-seeing he is surrounded by the spiritual throng of all to whom he stands related near and far, all whom he loves or hates, whom he serves or oppresses, whom he wrongs or saves. We are one with our fellow-men in all our needs. We are one in our sin and our salvation. To recognize that oneness is the first step toward praying the Lord's Prayer aright. That recognition is also the foundation of social Christianity.

The three petitions with which the prayer begins express the great desire which was fundamental in the heart and mind of Jesus: "Hallowed be thy name. Thy kingdom come. Thy will be done, as in heaven, so on earth." Together they express his yearning faith in the possibility of a reign of God on earth in which his name shall be hallowed and his will be done. They look forward to the ultimate perfection of the common life of humanity on this earth, and pray for the divine revolution which is to bring that about. . . .

With that understanding we can say that the remaining petitions deal with personal needs.

Among these the prayer for the daily bread takes first place. Jesus was never as "spiritual" as some of his later followers. He never forgot or belittled the elemental need of men for bread. The fundamental place which he gives to this petition is a recognition of the economic basis of life.

But he lets us pray only for the bread that is needful, and for that only when it becomes needful. The conception of what is needful will expand as human life develops. But this prayer can never be used to cover luxuries that debilitate, nor accumulations of property that can never be used but are sure to curse the soul of the holder with the diverse diseases of mammonism.

In this petition, too, Jesus compels us to stand together. We have to ask in common for our daily bread. We sit at the common table in God's great house, and the supply of each depends on the security of all. The more society is socialized, the clearer does that fact become, and the more just and humane its organization becomes, the more will that recognition be at the bottom of all our institutions. As we stand thus in common, looking up to God for our bread, every one of us ought to feel the sin and shame of it if he habitually takes more than his fair share and leaves others hungry that he may surfeit. It is inhuman, irreligious, and indecent.

The remaining petitions deal with the spiritual needs. Looking backward, we see that our lives have been full of sin and failure, and we realize the need of forgiveness. Looking forward, we tremble at the temptations that await us and pray for deliverance from evil.

In these prayers for the inner life, where the soul seems to confront God alone, we should expect to find only individualistic religion. But even here the social note sounds clearly.

This prayer will not permit us to ask for God's forgiveness without making us affirm that we have forgiven our brothers and are on a basis of brotherly love with all men: "Forgive us our debts, as we also have forgiven our debtors." We shall have to be socially right if we want to be religiously right. Jesus will not suffer us to be pious toward God and merciless toward men.

In the prayer, "Lead us not into temptation," we feel the human trembling of fear. Experience has taught us our frailty. Every man can see certain contingencies just a step ahead of him and knows that his moral capacity for resistance would collapse hopelessly if he were placed in these situations. Therefore Jesus gives voice to our inarticulate plea to God not to bring us into such situations. . . . No church can interpret this petition intelligently which closes its mind to the debasing or invigorating influence of the spiritual environment furnished by society. No man can utter this petition without conscious or unconscious hypocrisy who is helping to create the temptations in which others are sure to fall.

The words "Deliver us from the evil one" have in them the ring of battle. They bring to mind the incessant grapple between God and the permanent and malignant powers of evil in humanity. To the men of the first century that meant Satan and his host of evil spirits who ruled in the oppressive, extortionate, and idolatrous powers of Rome. Today the original spirit of that prayer will probably be best understood by those who are pitted against the terrible powers of organized covetousness and institutionalized oppression.

Thus the Lord's Prayer is the great prayer of social Christianity. It is charged with what we call "social consciousness." It assumes the social solidarity of men as a matter of course. It recognizes the social basis of all moral and religious life even in the most intimate personal relations to God. . . . Its dominating thought is the moral and religious transformation of mankind in all his social relations. It was left us by Jesus, the great initiator of the Christian revolution; and it is the rightful property of those who follow his banner in the conquest of the world.

. . .

PRAYERS FOR THE PROGRESS OF HUMANITY

FOR THE KINGDOM OF GOD

O Christ, thou has bidden us to pray for the coming of thy Father's kingdom, in which his righteousness shall be done on earth. We have treasured thy words, but we have forgotten their meaning, and thy great hope has grown dim in thy Church. We bless thee for the inspired souls of all ages who saw afar the shining city of God, and by faith left the profit of the present to follow their vision. We rejoice that today the hope of these lonely hearts is becoming the clear faith of millions. Help us, O Lord, in the courage of faith to seize what has now come so near, that the glad day of God may dawn at last. As we have mastered Nature that we might gain wealth, help us now to master the social relations of mankind that we may gain justice and a world of brothers. For what shall it profit our nation if it gain numbers and riches, and lose the sense of the living God and the joy of human brotherhood?

Make us determined to live by truth and not by lies, to found our common life on the eternal foundations of righteousness and love, and no longer to prop the tottering house of wrong by legalized cruelty and force. Help us to make the welfare of all the supreme law of our land, that so our commonwealth may be built strong and secure on the love of all its citizens. Cast down the throne of Mammon who ever grinds the life of men, and set up thy throne, O Christ, for thou didst die that men might live. Show thy erring children at last the way from the City of Destruction to the City of

Love, and fulfil the longings of the prophets of humanity. Our Master, once more we make thy faith our prayer: "Thy kingdom come! Thy will be done on earth!"

FOR THOSE WHO COME AFTER US

O God, we pray thee for those who come after us, for our children, and the children of our friends, and for all the young lives that are marching up from the gates of birth, pure and eager, with the morning sunshine on their faces. We remember with a pang that these will live in the world we are making for them. We are wasting the resources of the earth in our headlong greed, and they will suffer want. We are building sunless houses and joyless cities for our profit, and they must dwell therein. We are making the burden heavy and the pace of work pitiless, and they will fall wan and sobbing by the wayside. We are poisoning the air of our land by our lies and our uncleanness, and they will breathe it.

O God, thou knowest how we have cried out in agony when the sins of our fathers have been visited upon us, and how we have struggled vainly against the inexorable fate that coursed in our blood or bound us in a prison-house of life. Save us from maiming the innocent ones who come after us by the added cruelty of our sins. Help us to break the ancient force of evil by a holy and steadfast will and to endow our children with a purer blood and nobler thoughts. Grant us grace to leave the earth fairer than we found it; to build upon it cities of God in which the cry of needless pain shall cease; and to put the yoke of Christ upon our business life that it may serve and not destroy. Lift the veil of the future and show us the generation to come as it will be if blighted by our guilt, that our lust may be cooled and we may walk in the fear of the Eternal. Grant us a vision of the far-off years as they may be if redeemed by the sons of God, that we may take heart and do battle for thy children and ours.

ON THE HARM WE HAVE DONE

Our Father, we look back on the years that are gone and shame and sorrow come upon us, for the harm we have done to others rises up in our memory to accuse us. Some we have seared with the fire of our lust, and some we have scorched by the heat of our anger. In some we helped to quench the glow of young ideals by our selfish pride and craft, and in some we have nipped the opening bloom of faith by the frost of our unbelief.

We might have followed thy blessed footsteps, O Christ,

binding up the bruised hearts of our brothers and guiding the wayward passions of the young to firmer manhood. Instead, there are poor hearts now broken and darkened because they encountered us on the way, and some perhaps remember us only as the beginning of their misery or sin.

O God, we know that all our prayers can never bring back the past, and no tears can wash out the red marks with which we have scarred some life that stands before our memory with accusing eyes. Grant that at least a humble and pure life may grow out of our late contrition, that in the brief days still left to us we may comfort and heal where we have scorned and crushed. Change us by the power of thy saving grace from sources of evil into forces for good, that with all our strength we may fight the wrongs we have aided, and aid the right we have clogged. Grant us this boon, that for every harm we have done, we may do some brave act of salvation, and that for every soul that has stumbled or fallen through us, we may bring to thee some other weak or despairing one, whose strength has been renewed by our love, that so the face of thy Christ may smile upon us and the light within us may shine undimmed.

• • •

FOR A SHARE IN THE WORK OF REDEMPTION

O God, thou great Redeemer of mankind, our hearts are tender in the thought of thee, for in all the afflictions of our race thou has been afflicted, and in the sufferings of thy people it was thy body that was crucified. Thou hast been wounded by our transgressions and bruised by our iniquities, and all our sins are laid at last on thee. Amid the groaning of creation we behold thy spirit in travail till the sons of God shall be born in freedom and holiness.

We pray thee, O Lord, for the graces of a pure and holy life that we may no longer add to the dark weight of the world's sin that is laid upon thee, but may share with thee in thy redemptive work. As we have thirsted with evil passions to the destruction of men, do thou fill us now with hunger and thirst for justice that we may bear glad tidings to the poor and set at liberty all who are in the prison-house of want and sin. Lay thy Spirit upon us and inspire us with a passion of Christlike love that we may join our lives to the weak and oppressed and may strengthen their cause by bearing their sorrows. And if the evil that is threatened turns to smite us and if we must learn the dark malignity of sinful power, comfort us by the thought that thus we are bearing in our body the marks of Jesus, and that only those who share in his free sacrifice shall feel the plenitude of thy life. Help us in patience to carry forward the eternal cross of Christ, counting it joy if we, too, are sown as grains of wheat in the furrows of the world, for only by the agony of the righteous comes redemption.

FOR THE CHURCH

O God, we pray for thy Church, which is set today amid the perplexities of a changing order, and face to face with a great new task. We remember with love the nurture she gave to our spiritual life in its infancy, the tasks she set for our growing strength, the influence of the devoted hearts she gathers, the steadfast power for good she has exerted. When we compare her with all other human institutions, we rejoice, for there is none like her. But when we judge her by the mind of her Master, we bow in pity and contrition. Oh, baptize her afresh in the life-giving spirit of Jesus! Grant her a new birth, though it be with the travail of repentance and humiliation. Bestow upon her a more imperious responsiveness to duty, a swifter compassion with suffering, and an utter loyalty to the will of God. Put upon her lips the ancient gospel of her Lord. Help her to proclaim boldly the coming of the kingdom of God and the doom of all that resist it. Fill her with the prophets' scorn of tyranny, and with a Christlike tenderness for the heavy-laden and down-trodden. Give her faith to espouse the cause of the people, and in their hands that grope after freedom and light to recognize the bleeding hands of the Christ. Bid her cease from seeking her own life, lest she lose it. Make her valiant to give up her life to humanity, that like her crucified Lord she may mount by the path of the cross to a higher glory.

FOR OUR CITY

O God, we pray thee for this, the city of our love and pride. We rejoice in her spacious beauty and her busy ways of commerce, in her stores and factories where hand joins hand in toil, and in her blessed homes where heart joins heart for rest and love.

Help us to make our city the mighty common workshop of our people, where every one will find his place and task, in daily achievement building up his own life to resolute manhood, keen to do his best with hand and mind. Help us to make our city the greater home of our people, where all may live their lives in comfort, unafraid, loving their loves in peace and rounding out their years in strength.

Bind our citizens, not by the bond of money and of profit alone, but by the glow of neighborly good will, by the thrill of common joys, and the pride of common possessions. As we set the greater aims for the future of our city, may we ever remember that her true wealth and greatness consist, not in the abundance of the things we possess, but in the justice of her institutions and the brotherhood of her children. Make her rich in her sons and daughters and famous through the lofty passions that inspire them.

We thank thee for the patriot men and women of the past whose generous devotion to the common good has been the making of our city. Grant that our own generation may build worthily on the foundation they have laid. If in the past there have been some who have sold the city's good for private gain, staining her honor by their cunning and greed, fill us, we beseech thee, with the righteous anger of true sons that we may purge out the shame lest it taint the future years.

Grant us a vision of our city, fair as she might be: a city of justice, where none shall prey on others; a city of plenty, where vice and poverty shall cease to fester; a city of brotherhood, where all success shall be founded on service, and honor shall be given to nobleness alone; a city of peace, where order shall not rest on force, but on the love of all for the city, the great mother of the common life and weal. Hear thou, O Lord, the silent prayer of all our hearts as we each pledge our time and strength and thought to speed the day of her coming beauty and righteousness.

The immediate response to Rauschenbusch's little manual of devotion was astonishing. Letters flooded in from everywhere. The prayers were reprinted in the Baltimore Sun *and other newspapers. Individual prayers were printed on wall cards to be hung in offices and homes. The Child Labor Commission printed 13,000 copies of the prayer "For Children Who Work." The labor press featured the prayers "For Workingmen" and "For Women Who Toil." The prayer "For All True Lovers" was incorporated into marriage services. Other prayers were printed in books of public worship, in hymnals as aids to worship, and in manuals for private devotion. And the book itself continued to live—a French translation being published in 1914, an English edition in 1927, a German translation in 1928, and a Japanese translation in 1932.*

A curious reversal, however, has taken place in the years since 1910. Rauschenbusch sought to fashion prayers that were pointed and specific, and those that were most pointed and specific won the greatest immediate response and were most widely used at the time the book was published. With changing social conditions many of these became dated and "antique." It is the more general prayers that have endured and have found their place in the living liturgy of the American churches, where they continue to provide luminous language for the expression of the needs and aspirations of worshippers.

Frederick W. Taylor

On Scientific Management

1912

EDITED BY DANIEL BELL

Frederick W. Taylor was born in Germantown, Pennsylvania, on March 20, 1856, of parents who on both sides traced descent from English colonial families. His father, a lawyer, was a Quaker. His mother, a fervent abolitionist, was a Puritan. It was the mother's character and will that prevailed in Taylor's upbringing and personality. He received his early education at home from her. Then, at his father's insistence, he spent two years in school in France and Germany, and another year and a half traveling on the Continent, an experience of which he remarked later, characteristically, "all of which I disapprove for a young boy." At sixteen, Fred Taylor entered Philips Exeter Academy to prepare for Harvard Law School, but he broke down from overwork, his eyesight impaired, and though he graduated two years later, he abandoned the idea of a career in law. Since his doctor had prescribed manual labor, Taylor went into a machine shop, owned by a friend of the family, to learn the trade of pattern-maker and machinist. In 1878, after four years of apprenticeship, he took a job as a common laborer at the Midvale Steel Company, where he soon became a foreman. He obtained a degree in mechanical engineering from the Stevens Institute of Technology by studying at night, and at age twenty-eight, six years after he had begun work at the Midvale plant, he was made chief engineer there. In engineering he found his métier.

In Frederick W. Taylor, character and work were fused in one. He always looked back, with admiration, to the "very severe Exeter discipline" as "perhaps the very best experience of my early life." He did not drink or smoke, or use such stimulants as tea or coffee—not on moral grounds, but as the result, his biographer Frank Copley remarks, "of a truly scientific analysis of ways to conserve one's forces." He split his world into its minutest parts. When he walked, he counted his steps to learn the most efficient stride. Playing croquet, he plotted carefully the angles of his strokes. Sports, which he loved (in 1881, with C. M. Clark, he won the U.S. doubles championship in tennis), took possession of him with the same terribly earnest spirit of his work, and became equally exhausting. Nervous, high-strung, he was a victim all his life of insomnia and nightmares, and, fearing somehow to lie on his back, he could sleep in peace only when bolstered upright in a bed or in a chair for the night. He never loafed, and he hated to see anyone else do so. It was this compulsive character that Taylor stamped onto a civilization.

Taylor proved himself, among other things, a talented inventor. He designed the largest successful steam hammer ever built in the United States. Later, with a colleague, he devised a process of tempering tool steel which allowed for high-speed methods of cutting metals, a process that was eventually used in machine shops all over the world. Altogether, he secured over a hundred patents in his lifetime.

But his fame came from the career, which he began in 1903, as a consulting engineer. His business card read: "Systematizing Shop Management and Manufacturing Costs a Specialty." Taylor was a consulting engineer in the vocational sense for only a brief period, however. For him, "scientific management," as he called the new system he had begun to develop, became an evangelical creed. Gathering a number of disciples about him, he began to spread the gospel, first through publishing (in 1903) his book Shop Management, then by training younger men to install his system into industry. Other men, such as Frank Gilbreth, took up the cause by systematizing motion study. Harrington Emerson popularized the title "efficiency engineer," with a plan of bonuses and incentives in work. By 1910, the movement had become almost a fad and hundreds of persons proclaimed themselves efficiency engineers, promising to install the Taylor system in half the two to four years' time Taylor said was necessary for the scientific study of a job, and for the "mental revolution" management and workers would have to undergo before they could accept his principles.

The rapid spread of "Taylorism" resulted, in part, from the eagerness of many firms to "speed up" work and to "sweat" labor. A strong reaction against scientific management developed within the labor movement. In 1912, Congress voted to set up a special House Committee, under Congressman William B. Wilson, former official of the Miners Union (soon to become the first Secretary of Labor), "to investigate the Taylor and other systems of shop management." Before this Committee, Taylor made a cogent and eloquent defense of his ideas and methods.

THE CHAIRMAN. In developing and collating the different parts of this system and in introducing it in different establishments, by what name have you designated it?

MR. TAYLOR. The first general designation was a "piece-rate system," because the prominent feature—the feature which at that time interested me most—was a new and radically different type of piecework than anything introduced before. I afterwards pointed out, however, that piecework was really one of the comparatively unimportant elements of our system of management. The next paper written by me on the subject was called "Shop Management," and in that paper the task idea—the idea of setting a measured standard of work for each man to do each day—was the most prominent feature, and for some time after this, the system was called the "task system." The word "task," however, had a severe sound and did not at all adequately represent the sentiment of the system; it sounded as though you were treating men severely, whereas the whole idea underlying our system is justice and not severity. So it was recognized that this designation was not the proper one, but at the time no better name appeared. Finally, the name was agreed upon which I think is correct and which does represent the system better than any

The selections reprinted here first appeared, with one brief exception, in *Hearings Before the Special Committee of the House of Representatives to Investigate the Taylor and Other Systems of Shop Management Under the Authority of House Resolution 90* (1912), III, 1377–1508. The exception is the seventh paragraph of the present text, beginning "At the works of the Bethlehem Steel Company"; this originally appeared in Taylor's Book *The Principles of Scientific Management* (New York: Harper and Brothers, 1911), p. 39.

other name yet suggested, namely, "scientific management." . . .

I ordinarily begin with a description of the pig-iron handler. For some reason, I don't know exactly why, this illustration has been talked about a great deal, so much, in fact, that some people seem to think that the whole of scientific management consists in handling pig iron. The only reason that I ever gave this illustration, however, was that pig-iron handling is the simplest kind of human effort; I know of nothing that is quite so simple as handling pig-iron. A man simply stoops down and with his hands picks up a piece of iron, and then walks a short distance and drops it on the ground. Now, it doesn't look as if there was very much room for the development of a science; it doesn't seem as if there was much room here for the scientific selection of the man nor for his progressive training, nor for cooperation between the two sides; but, I can say, without the slightest hesitation, that the science of handling pig-iron is so great that the man who is fit to handle pig-iron as his daily work cannot possibly understand that science; the man who is physically able to handle pig-iron and is sufficiently phlegmatic and stupid to choose this for his occupation is rarely able to comprehend the science of handling pig-iron; and this inability of the man who is fit to do the work to understand the science of doing his work becomes more and more evident as the work becomes more complicated, all the way up the scale. I assert, without the slightest hesitation, that the high class mechanic has a far smaller chance of ever thoroughly understanding the science of his work than the pig-iron handler has of understanding the science of his work, and I am going to try and prove to your satisfaction, gentlemen, that the law is almost universal —not entirely so, but nearly so—that the man who is fit to work at any particular trade is unable to understand the science of that trade without the kindly help and cooperation of men of a totally different type of education, men whose education is not necessarily higher but a different type from his own. . . .

Under the old system you would call in a first-rate shoveler and say, "See here, Pat, how much ought you to take on at one shovel load?" And if a couple of fellows agreed, you would say that's about the right load and let it go at that. But under scientific management absolutely every element in the work of every man in your establishment, sooner or later, becomes the subject of exact, precise, scientific investigation and knowledge to replace the old, "I believe so," and "I guess so." Every motion, every small fact becomes the subject of careful, scientific investigation. . . .

Now, gentlemen, I know you will laugh when I talk again about the science of shoveling. I dare say some of you have done some shoveling. Whether you have or not, I am going to try to show you something about the science of shoveling, and if any of you have done much shoveling, you will understand that there is a good deal of science about it. . . .

There is a good deal of refractory stuff to shovel around a steel works; take ore, or ordinary bituminous coal, for instance. It takes a good deal of effort to force the shovel down into either of these materials from the top of the pile, as you have to when you are unloading a car. There is one right way of forcing the shovel into materials of this sort, and many wrong ways. Now, the way to shovel refractory stuff is to press the forearm hard against the upper part of the right leg just below the thigh, like this (indicating), take the end of the shovel in your right hand and when you push the shovel into the pile, instead of using the muscular effort of your arms, which is tiresome, throw the weight of your body on the shovel like this (indicating); that pushes your shovel in the pile with hardly any exertion and without tiring the arms in the least. Nine out of ten workmen who try to push a shovel in a pile of that sort will use the strength of their arms, which involves more than twice the necessary exertion. Any of you men who don't know this fact just try it. This is one illustration of what I mean when I speak of the science of shoveling, and there are many similar elements of this science. . . .

[At the works of the Bethlehem Steel Company, for example . . . Instead of allowing each shoveler to select and own his own shovel, it became necessary to provide some 8 to 10 different kinds of shovels, etc., each one appropriate to handling a given type of material; not only so as to enable the men to handle an average load of 21 pounds, [i.e., the ideal weight for least fatigue and greatest productivity] but also to adapt the shovel to several other requirements which became perfectly evident when this work is studied as a science. A large shovel tool room was built, in which were stored not only shovels but carefully designed and standardized labor implements of all kinds such as picks, crowbars, etc. This made it possible to issue to each workman a shovel which would hold a load of 21 pounds of whatever class of material they were to handle: a small shovel for ore, say, or a large one for ashes. Iron ore is one of the heavy materials which are handled in a works of this kind, and rice coal, owing to the fact that it is so slippery on the shovel, is one of the lightest materials. And it was found on studying the rule-of-thumb plan at the Bethlehem Steel Company, where each shoveler owned his own shovel, that he would frequently go from shoveling ore, with a load of about 30 pounds per shovel, to handling rice coal, with a load on the same shovel of less than 4 pounds. In one case he was so overloaded that it was impossible for him to do a full day's work, and in the other case he was so ridiculously underloaded that it was manifestly impossible to even approximate a day's work. . . .]

. . . Under the old method the work of 50 or 60 men was weighed up together; the work done by a whole gang was measured together. But under scientific management we are dealing with individual man and not with gangs of men. And in order to study and develop each man you must measure accurately each man's work. At first we were told that this would be impossible. The former managers of this work told me, "You cannot possibly measure up the work of each individual laborer in this yard; you might be able to do it in a small yard, but our work is of such an intricate nature that it is impossible to do it here. . . .

At the end of some three and a half years we had the opportunity of proving whether or not scientific management did pay in its application to yard labor. When we went to the Bethlehem Steel Co. we found from 400 to 600 men at work in that yard, and when we got through, 140 men were doing the work of the 400 to 600, and these men handled several million tons of material a year.

. . . Under the old system the cost of handling a ton of materials had been running between 7 and 8 cents. . . . Now, after paying all the clerical work which was necessary under the new system for the time study and the teachers, for building and running the labor office and the implement room, for constructing a telephone system for moving men about the yard, for a great variety of duties not performed under the old system, after paying for all these things incident to the development of the science of shoveling and managing the men the new way, and including the wages of the workmen, the cost of handling a ton of material was brought down from between 7 and 8 cents to between 3 and 4 cents. . . . That is what the company got out of it; while the men who were on the labor gang received an average of sixty per cent more wages than their brothers got or could get anywhere around that part of the country. And none of them were overworked, for it is no part of scientific management ever to overwork any man . . . because it is one of the first requirements of scientific management that no man shall ever be given a job which he cannot do and thrive under through a long term of years. . . .

The illustration of shoveling . . . which I have given you has thus far been purposely confined to the more elementary types of work, so that a very strong doubt must still remain as to whether this kind of cooperation is desirable in the case of more intelligent mechanics, that is, in the case of men who are more capable of generalization, and who would therefore be more likely, of their own volition, to choose the more scientific and better methods. The following illustration will be given for the purpose of demonstrating the fact that in the higher classes of work the scientific laws which are developed are so intricate that the high-priced mechanic needs—even more than the cheap laborer—the cooperation of men better educated than himself in finding the laws, and then in selecting, developing, and training him to work in accordance with these laws. This illustration should make perfectly clear my original proposition that in practically all of the mechanic arts the science which underlies each workman's act is so great and amounts to so much that the workman who is best suited to actually doing the work is incapable, either through lack of education or through insufficient mental capacity, of understanding this science. . . .

A number of years ago, a company employing in one of their departments about 300 men, which had been manufacturing the same machine for 10 to 15 years, sent for my friend Mr. Barth to report as to whether any gain could be made in their work through the introduction of scientific management. . . .

The machine selected by the superintendent fairly represented the work of the shop. It had been run for 10 or 12 years by a first-class mechanic, who was more than equal in his ability to the average workmen in the establishment. . . . A careful record was therefore made, in the presence of both parties, of the time actually taken in finishing each of the parts which this man worked upon. The total time required by the old-fashioned skilled lathe hand to finish each piece, as well as the exact speeds and feeds which he took, were noted, and a record was kept of the time which he took in setting the work in the machine and in removing it. . . .

By means of . . . four quite elaborate slide rules which have been made especially for the purpose of determining the all-round capacity of metal cutting machines, Mr. Barth made a careful analysis of every element of this machine in its relation to the work in hand. Its pulling power at various speeds, its feeding capacity, and its proper speeds were determined by means of the slide rules, and changes were then made in the countershaft and driving pulleys so as to run the lathe at its proper speed. Tools made of high-speed steel and of the proper shapes were properly dressed, treated, and ground. . . . Mr. Barth then made a large special slide rule, by means of which the exact speeds and feeds were indicated at which each kind of work could be done in the shortest possible time in this particular lathe. . . .

. . . the scientifically equipped man, Mr. Barth, who had never before seen these particular jobs, and who had never worked on this machine, [was able] to do work from two and one-half to nine times as fast as it had been done before by a good mechanic who had spent his whole time for some 10 to 12 years in doing this very work upon this particular machine. In a word, this was possible because the art of cutting metals involves a true science of no small magnitude, a science, in fact, so intricate that it is impossible for any machinist who is suited to running a lathe year in and year out either to understand it or to work according to its laws without the help of men who have made this their specialty. . . .

. . . In the early eighties, about the time that I started to make the investigations above referred to to determine the proper movements to be made by machinists in putting their work into and removing it from machines and time required to do this work, I also obtained permission of Mr. William Sellers, the president of the Midvale Steel Co., to make a series of experiments to determine what angles and shapes of tools were the best for cutting steel, and also to try to determine the proper cutting speed for steel. At the time that these experiments were started it was my belief that they would not last longer than six months. . . .

Experiments in this field were carried on, with occasional interruptions, through a period of about 26 years, in the course of which 10 different experimental machines were especially fitted up to do this work. Between 30,000 and 50,000 experiments were carefully recorded, and many other experiments were made of which no record was kept. In studying these laws more than 800,000 pounds of steel and iron was cut up into chips with the experimental tools. . . .

All of these experiments were made to enable us to answer correctly the two questions which face every machinist each time that he does a piece of work in a metal-cutting machine, such as a lathe, planer, drill press or milling machine. The two questions are:

In order to do the work in the quickest time, at what cutting speed shall I run my machine? and what feed shall I use?

These questions sound so simple that they would appear to call for merely the trained judgment of any good mechanic. In fact, however, after working 26 years, it has been found that the answer in every case involves the solution of an intricate mathematical problem, in which the effect of 12 independent variables must be determined. . . .

It may seem preposterous to many people that it should have required a period of 26 years to investigate the effect of these 12 variables upon the cutting speed of metals. To those, however, who have had personal experience as experimenters it will be appreciated that the great difficulty of the problem lies in the fact that it contains so many variable elements. And, in fact, the great length of time consumed in making each single experiment was caused by the difficulty of holding 11 variables constant and uniform throughout the experiment, while the effect of the twelfth variable was being investigated. Holding the 11 variables constant was far more difficult than the investigation of the twelfth element. . . .

I want to clear the deck, sweep away a good deal of rubbish first by pointing out what scientific management is not.

Scientific management is not any efficiency device, not a device of any kind for securing efficiency; nor is it any bunch or group of efficiency devices. It is not a new system of figuring costs; it is not a new scheme of paying men; it is not a piecework system; it is not a bonus system; it is not a premium system; it is no scheme for paying men; it is not holding a stop watch on a man and writing things down about him; it is not time study; it is not motion study nor an analysis of the movements of men; it is not the printing and ruling and unloading of a ton or two of blanks on a set of men and saying, "Here's your system; go use it." It is not divided foremanship or functional foremanship; it is not any of the devices which the average man calls to mind when scientific management is spoken of. The average man thinks of one or more of these things when he hears the words "scientific management" mentioned, but scientific management is not any of these devices. I am not sneering at cost-keeping systems, at time study, at functional foremanship, nor at any new and improved scheme of paying men, nor at any efficiency devices, if they are really devices that make for efficiency. I believe in them; but what I am emphasizing is that these devices in whole or in part are not scientific management;

they are useful adjuncts to scientific management, so are they also useful adjuncts of other systems of management.

In its essence, scientific management involves a complete mental revolution on the part of the workingman engaged in any particular establishment or industry—a complete mental revolution on the part of these men as to their duties toward their work, toward their employers. And it involves the equally complete mental revolution on the part of those on the management's side—the foreman, the superintendent, the owner of the business, the board of directors—a complete mental revolution on their part as to their duties toward their fellow workers in the management, toward their workmen, and toward all of their daily problems. And without this complete mental revolution on both sides scientific management does not exist. . . .

The great revolution that takes place in the mental attitudes of the two parties under scientific management is that both sides take their eyes off the division of the surplus as the all important matter, and together turn their attention toward increasing the size of the surplus until this surplus becomes so large that it is unnecessary to quarrel over how it shall be divided. . . .

. . . This, gentlemen, is the beginning of the great mental revolution which constitutes the first step toward scientific management. It is along this line of complete change in the mental attitude of both sides; of the substitution of peace for war; the substitution of hearty brotherly cooperation for contention and strife; of both pulling hard in the same direction instead of pulling apart; of replacing suspicious watchfulness with mutual confidence; of becoming friends instead of enemies; it is along this line, I say, that scientific management must be developed.

. . . There is, however, one more change in viewpoint which is absolutely essential to the existence of scientific management. Both sides must recognize as essential the substitution of exact scientific investigation and knowledge for the old individual judgment or opinion, either of the workingmen or the boss, in all matters relating to the work done in the establishment. And this applies both as to the methods to be employed in doing the work and the time in which each job should be done.

Scientific management cannot be said to exist, then, in any establishment until after this change has taken place in the mental attitude of both the management and the men, both as to their duty to cooperate in producing the largest possible surplus and as to the necessity for substituting exact scientific knowledge for opinions or the old rule-of-thumb or individual knowledge.

These are two absolutely essential elements of scientific management.

Taylor's genius consisted in the simple introduction of the idea of measurement in work. Traditional management, operating by rule of thumb, intuition, or experience, had little exact knowledge of the time a job should take, the tools best adapted to a task, or the pace at which a man should work. Taylor's innovations, based on painstaking study rather than on any new technique or technology, consisted of applying the experimental method to the analysis of work: of breaking down each job into its simplest components, varying each component systematically (in one instance, it took twenty-six years to work out a problem with twelve variables), and arriving at a mathematical formula which would specify the "one best way" in which the job should be done. Out of Taylor's work came time and motion study, the incentive and bonus system, differential rates of pay based on distinctive skill classification, the standardization of tools and equipment, and, most important, the removal of all planning and scheduling from the work floor into a new function, directed by a figure new in the history of work, the industrial engineer.

To many people today, Taylorism represents the dehumanization of work: the breakdown of tasks into their simplest components treats men as "objects," as appendages to machines; the primary emphasis on productivity ignores the question of the human satisfactions of the man on the job. Yet, in a way, this view is paradoxical, for when Taylorism first appeared, it was hailed as "progressive" and "advanced," and indeed, many of Taylor's disciples, such as Morris L. Cooke and Henry Gantt, played distinguished political roles as liberals. One has to appreciate the historical setting to understand the subtle change in the nature of these evaluations and the resolution of the paradox.

Scientific management had actually begun to emerge in the 1880's as a response to a fundamental alteration in the character of production, namely, the introduction of the mechanical engineer as the key figure in the new movement of mechanization. It was this development which led Thorstein Veblen some time later to talk of an inherent cleavage between "business" (represented by the financier looking only at the balance sheet) and "industry" (symbolized by the engineer who focused his attention on production). Veblen saw in the engineer, "the General Staff of the Industrial System," the agency of radical change in society. And he saw in the machine the basis of new rationalistic modes of thought. Could there be a metaphysical dispute, he asked, about the amount of stress a bridge could take? On the contrary, he felt, there had to be a factual answer.

The engineer, and his new methods, were indeed forcing a change in the old-fashioned practices of management. When Taylor, for example, on assuming office as president of the American Society of Mechanical Engineers in 1906, circulated a questionnaire asking companies how many of them sponsored research, the characteristic response was: "Why do I need research? Don't I know my own business?" The magic word for Taylor was "science." Science was for him inherently progressive. And to his disciples, scientific management was "the extension to industrial organization of the 'positive' movement in current thought." The positive movement, or positivism, the philosophical system elaborated by Auguste Comte, saw society as passing in a social evolution through defined stages in which the scientific had finally begun to replace the earlier—and inadequate—theological and metaphysical stages of the human mind.

For Taylor himself, rationality had become a religion, and his chief purpose in developing the system of scientific management, as his biographer, Frank Copley, puts it, was "to find a remedy for the labor problem that had grown up . . . in consequence of the development of large-scale production." As a rationalist, Taylor saw no inherent conflict of interest between management and worker (as, in effect, Comte had seen none fifty years before). In his social physics, once work was scientifically plotted, there could be no dispute about how hard a man should work or how much he should receive for his labor. All such matters could be settled by impersonal, impartial judgment. One man who appreciated Taylor was V. I. Lenin; in an article in Pravda in 1918, Lenin urged "the study and teaching of the Taylor system and its systematic trial and adoption."

In a personal sense, the source of Taylor's zeal and drive was the Puritan inheritance from his mother, which, despite a current tendency to read that thought as a narrowness of spirit, represented for Taylor an independence of judgment, a discipline of mind, and a search for rational proofs. But this drive, harnessed as it was to mechanics, became an abstract rationality, the rationality of things, of functional adjustments of means, and not the questioning of ends. And here one sees the resolution of the paradox. For what American industry took from Taylor—and his stamp is everywhere—was the techniques: the stop watch, the job classifications, the functional principle of organization; but in this drive for the rationalization of work, the spirit of inquiry and the moral dimension which had infused the original Puritanism had ebbed away.

Calvin Coolidge

Have Faith in Massachusetts

1914

EDITED BY WALTER MUIR WHITEHILL

Calvin Coolidge, son of a storekeeper in Plymouth Notch, Vermont, was born on Independence Day, 1872. After graduation from Amherst College in 1895, he settled in Northampton, Massachusetts, where he studied and practiced law. Almost immediately after admission to the bar, Coolidge began to climb the local and state political ladder as a member of the Republican Party. In 1898 he was elected to the Northampton city council; the following year he became city solicitor. In 1906 he was elected to the Massachusetts House of Representatives, where he served two terms. In 1910 and 1911 he was mayor of Northampton. For the next two years he was again in Boston as a state senator.

In February and March, 1912, during his first term, Coolidge was chairman of a conciliation committee of three senators and five representatives that succeeded in settling the Lawrence strike. Although party custom normally dictated retirement from the senate at the end of a second term, Coolidge again sought re-election in 1913 because of a possibility of succeeding to the presidency of the senate. In both attempts he was successful. This is the speech that he gave on

January 7, 1914, to the state senate of Massachusetts on being elected its president. It was, in William Allen White's words, "the crowning plea of scholarly conservatism in a day of reaction." Of the background of this laconic address, Coolidge wrote in his Autobiography in 1929:

It appeared to me in January, 1914, that a spirit of radicalism prevailed which unless checked was likely to prove very destructive. It had been encouraged by the opposition and by a large faction of my own party.

It consisted of the claim in general that in some way the government was to be blamed because everybody was not prosperous, because it was necessary to work for a living, and because our written constitution, the legislatures, and the courts protected the rights of private owners especially in relation to large aggregations of property.

The previous session had been overwhelmed with a record number of bills introduced, many of them in an attempt to help the employee by impairing the property of the employer. Though anxious to improve the condition of our wage earners, I believed this doctrine would soon destroy business and deprive them of a livelihood. What was needed was a restoration of confidence in our institutions and in each other, on which economic progress might rest.

In taking the chair as President of the Senate I therefore made a short address, which I had carefully prepared, appealing to the conservative spirit of the people. I argued that the government could not relieve us from toil, that large concerns are necessary for the progress in which capital and labor all have a common interest, and I defended representative government and the integrity of the courts. The address has since been known as "Have Faith in Massachusetts." Many people in the Commonwealth had been waiting for such a word, and the effect was beyond my expectation. Confusion of thought began to disappear, and unsound legislative proposals to diminish.

Or, as William Allen White described it: "Moses smote the water and the sea gave way."

I THANK you—with gratitude for the high honor given, with appreciation for the solemn obligations assumed—I thank you.

This Commonwealth is one. We are all members of one

The speech is reprinted from *Have Faith in Massachusetts: A Collection of Speeches and Messages*, by Calvin Coolidge (2d ed.; Boston: Houghton Mifflin Company, 1919), pp. 3–9.

WALTER MUIR WHITEHILL   **777**

body. The welfare of the weakest and the welfare of the most powerful are inseparably bound together. Industry cannot flourish if labor languish. Transportation cannot prosper if manufactures decline. The general welfare cannot be provided for in any one act, but it is well to remember that the benefit of one is the benefit of all, and the neglect of one is the neglect of all. The suspension of one man's dividends is the suspension of another man's pay envelope.

Men do not make laws. They do but discover them. Laws must be justified by something more than the will of the majority. They must rest on the eternal foundation of righteousness. That state is most fortunate in its form of government which has the aptest instruments for the discovery of laws. The latest, most modern, and nearest perfect system that statesmanship has devised is representative government. Its weakness is the weakness of us imperfect human beings who administer it. Its strength is that even such administration secures to the people more blessings than any other system ever produced. No nation has discarded it and retained liberty. Representative government must be preserved.

Courts are established, not to determine the popularity of a cause, but to adjudicate and enforce rights. No litigant should be required to submit his case to the hazard and expense of a political campaign. No judge should be required to seek or receive political rewards. The courts of Massachusetts are known and honored wherever men love justice. Let their glory suffer no diminution at our hands. The electorate and judiciary cannot combine. A hearing means a hearing. When the trial of causes goes outside the court-room, Anglo-Saxon constitutional government ends.

The people cannot look to legislation generally for success. Industry, thrift, character, are not conferred by act or resolve. Government cannot relieve from toil. It can provide no substitute for the rewards of service. It can, of course, care for the defective and recognize distinguished merit. The normal must care for themselves. Self-government means self-support.

Man is born into the universe with a personality that is his own. He has a right that is founded upon the constitution of the universe to have property that is his own. Ultimately, property rights and personal rights are the same thing. The one cannot be preserved if the other be violated. Each man is entitled to his rights and the rewards of his service be they never so large or never so small.

History reveals no civilized people among whom there were not a highly educated class, and large aggregations of wealth, represented usually by the clergy and the nobility. Inspiration has always come from above. Diffusion of learning has come down from the university to the common school—the kindergarten is last. No one would now expect to aid the common school by abolishing higher education.

It may be that the diffusion of wealth works in an analogous way. As the little red schoolhouse is builded in the college, it may be that the fostering and protection of large aggregations of wealth are the only foundation on which to build the prosperity of the whole people. Large profits mean large pay rolls. But profits must be the result of service performed. In no land are there so many and such large aggregations of wealth as here; in no land do they perform larger service; in no land will the work of a day bring so large a reward in material and spiritual welfare.

Have faith in Massachusetts. In some unimportant detail some other States may surpass her, but in the general results, there is no place on earth where the people secure, in a larger measure, the blessings of organized government, and nowhere can those functions more properly be termed self-government.

Do the day's work. If it be to protect the rights of the weak, whoever objects, do it. If it be to help a powerful corporation better to serve the people, whatever the opposition, do that. Expect to be called a stand-patter, but don't be a stand-patter. Expect to be called a demagogue, but don't be a demagogue. Don't hesitate to be as revolutionary as science. Don't hesitate to be as reactionary as the multiplication table. Don't expect to build up the weak by pulling down the strong. Don't hurry to legislate. Give administration a chance to catch up with legislation.

We need a broader, firmer, deeper faith in the people—a faith that men desire to do right, that the Commonwealth is founded upon a righteousness which will endure, a reconstructed faith that the final approval of the people is given not to demagogues, slavishly pandering to their selfishness, merchandising with the clamor of the hour, but to statesmen, ministering to their welfare, representing their deep, silent, abiding convictions.

Statutes must appeal to more than material welfare. Wages won't satisfy, be they never so large. Nor houses; nor lands; nor coupons, though they fall thick as the leaves of autumn. Man has a spiritual nature. Touch it, and it must respond as the magnet responds to the pole. To that, not to selfishness, let the laws of the Commonwealth appeal. Recognize the immortal worth and dignity of man. Let the laws of Massachusetts proclaim to her humblest citizen, performing the most menial task, the recognition of his manhood, the recognition that all men are peers, the humblest with the most exalted, the recognition that all work is glorified. Such is the path to equality before the law. Such is the foundation of liberty under the law. Such is the sublime revelation of man's relation to man—Democracy.

The speech was like the man, a simple Vermont performance —"hard granite," as Mark Sullivan characterized all of Coolidge's public remarks. Coolidge clearly wrote it. It exemplifies the "adequate brevity" that President Meiklejohn praised in conferring an Amherst LL.D. upon him in 1919. This speech so enchanted conservatives who wished to preserve the existing order that it brought Coolidge support from unexpected quarters. Early in 1915 Coolidge's Amherst classmate, Dwight W. Morrow, called him to the attention of Frank Waterman Stearns, Amherst '78, a Boston dry-goods merchant. A few weeks later Stearns arranged a complimentary dinner for Coolidge with representative Amherst graduates to be present; as a preliminary for this he distributed a hundred reprints of the speech. Stearns soon became convinced that Coolidge was, politically, destined for a limitless future, and backed his conviction with warm friendship and generous support.

With the blessing of the Republican Party and with Stearns's steady assistance, Coolidge was elected lieutenant governor in 1915 and governor of Massachusetts three years later. In 1919, during Coolidge's second term as governor, with the thought of letting him speak for himself, Stearns instigated the publication by Houghton Mifflin Company of a volume of selections from Coolidge's addresses, originally to be called Bay State Orations. *The final title,* Have Faith in Massachusetts, *was taken from the present 1914 address to the state senate by Roger L. Scaife, then an editor for Houghton Mifflin. While the galley proof was being read, the Boston Police Strike occurred, and several of Coolidge's messages concerning it were hastily added, among them the telegram of September 14, 1919, to Samuel Gompers containing the sentence, "There is no right to strike against the public safety by anybody, anywhere, any time." Although less than 8,000 copies of the book sold during the next twenty years,* by Mr. Stearns's indefatigable efforts more than 65,000 were distributed to libraries, newspapers, and any individuals any-where who might be helpful to Coolidge within the Republi-can Party. Stearns was unsuccessful in obtaining the Republi-can presidential nomination for Coolidge at Chicago in 1920, but the second place on the ticket became Coolidge's in con-siderable part through the image created by Have Faith in Massachusetts. William Allen White noted that, as delegates and alternates to the Republican National Convention were chosen in all parts of the country, they were each sent a copy of Have Faith in Massachusetts, accompanied by a pleasant note from Frank Stearns calling their attention to the author, "who might possibly interest them later on." On the death of Harding in 1923, Coolidge became the thirtieth President of the United States. His six years in the White House might never have occurred without the 1914 address to the Massa-chusetts senate.

Opinions of the speech, as of its author, differ markedly. As early as 1916, Stearns reported that Theodore N. Vail, president of the American Telephone and Telegraph Com-pany, had read it four or five times and had stated, "That is the greatest speech ever made by an American." Harold J. Laski, who regarded Coolidge as "dull, illiterate, stupid, and obstinate," "a third-rate, ungenerous person with a low mean cunning that is contemptible," wrote Mr. Justice Holmes on August 7, 1923, in support of this view: "Look at his volume of speeches and you will have no further illusions." But Holmes, just after the 1924 election that returned Coolidge to the White House in his own right, countered to Laski: "If I had had a vote I should have voted for Coolidge. . . . I think your judgment of Coolidge is prejudiced—and while I don't expect anything very astonishing from him I don't want any-thing very astonishing." Neither did a majority of the Ameri-can voters in that year. The conservative sentiments and laconic Vermont phrases of this speech so moved thousands and thousands of his fellow men that, in Walter Lippmann's words of 1926, "At a time when Puritanism as a way of life is at its lowest ebb among the people, the people are de-lighted with a Puritan as their national symbol." To all except his devout admirers, who were many, Coolidge seemed color-less, passive, inactive, and somnolent. On his death in 1933 H. L. Mencken concluded an obituary entitled "The Darling of the Gods" with the sentence: "He had no ideas, and he was not a nuisance." The second phrase is incontrovertible; the first is not strictly true, for the ideas that he had were *succinctly expressed in this speech. But to Laski they were the ideas of "a natural churchwarden in a rural parish who has by accident strayed into great affairs." Is not this speech one of the major causes of the accident?*

Louis D. Brandeis

The Curse of Bigness

1915

EDITED BY ALPHEUS THOMAS MASON

*The McNamara brothers were on trial. Despairing of helping
the workingman by peaceful means, these desperate union
officials had dynamited the antilabor* Los Angeles Times, *killing twenty people. Shortly after two o'clock on December 1,
1911, Clarence Darrow, attorney for the defendants, nodded
to a colleague who rose to announce: "May it please the
Court, our clients wish to change their plea from not guilty
to guilty." It was a dark day for organized labor; the use of
violence shocked America's sensibilities. The long-run benefits, however, redounded to the good of all, leading to the
creation of the United States Commission on Industrial Relations.*

*What is wrong in our society, Lincoln Steffens asked, when
men feel that the only way to improve working conditions is
to destroy lives and property? Paul U. Kellogg, editor of the*
Survey, *set out to find the answer, addressing Steffens' query
to prominent persons in various fields, including the Boston
lawyer Louis D. Brandeis. The replies were published in the
magazine's issue of December 30, 1911, along with a petition
to President William Howard Taft, urging the creation of a*

Federal Commission on Industrial Relations. Brandeis' name was among the signatories. On February 2, 1912, the President sent a message to Congress, calling for a "searching inquiry into the subject of industrial relations." The Commission was authorized August 23, but Taft's nominations for membership were never confirmed. Appointments to the Commission fell to his successor, Woodrow Wilson.

Brandeis, who had been seriously considered for Cabinet posts in the new administration, was Wilson's first choice for the chairmanship of the Commission. "There is no one in the United States," the President wrote in making the offer, "who could preside over and direct such an inquiry so well as you could." After conferring with the President, Brandeis declined. But he was still available as a willing and eloquent witness.

A stickler for facts with a rare gift for forging them into effective instruments of social action, Brandeis had already explored the roots of industrial unrest. "Is there not a causal connection," he asked in his letter to the Survey, *"between the development of these huge, indomitable trusts and the horrible crimes now under investigation? . . . Is it not irony to speak of equality of opportunity in a country cursed with bigness?" Broad experience had developed in Brandeis a profound sense of urgency. He had fought corporate waste and aggrandizement in New England transportation and in Boston's public utilities. He had waged a bitter war against the abuses of wage earners' insurance. For New York's strife-torn garment industry, he had invented the preferential union shop. Drawing on this vast experience, he prepared for* Harper's Weekly *a series of ten articles, a massive arsenal of facts and figures indicting "Our Financial Oligarchy"; the articles were later published as a book under the title* Other People's Money. *The eighth essay of the series bore the searing title with which Brandeis' name is closely linked—"The Curse of Bigness."*

The ill effects of bigness weighed heavily on both men and things. "By their by-products," he had told the Senate Committee on Interstate Commerce in 1911, "shall ye know the trusts." Study them "through the spectacles of peoples' rights and peoples' interests. . . . When you do that you will realize the extraordinary perils to our institutions which attend the trusts. . . ." Aside from whether a corporation has exceeded the power of "greatest economic efficiency or not, it may be too large to be tolerated among the people who desire to be free."

Brandeis' habit of mind was, as he said, "to move from

*one problem to another giving to each, while it is before me,
my undivided study." "I have my opinions," he told an inter-
viewer, "but I am not doctrinaire." Since Brandeis was a man
of action, his method did not lend itself to abstraction or to
the isolated utterance of a single document. His views on "the
curse of bigness"—the dominant theme in his social philosophy—are effectively voiced in the statements made before the
United States Commission on Industrial Relations. No stranger to committee hearing rooms, Brandeis appeared on April 16,
1914. Recalled on January 23, 1915, he gave the testimony
that appears here.*

CHAIRMAN FRANK P. WALSH. Do . . . financial directors,
in your opinion, Mr. Brandeis, have sufficient knowledge of
industrial conditions and social conditions to qualify them to
direct labor policies involving hundreds of thousands of men?

MR. BRANDEIS. I should think most of them did not; but
what is perhaps more important or fully as important is the
fact that neither these same men nor anybody else can properly deal with these problems without a far more intimate
knowledge of the facts than it is possible for men to get who
undertake to have a voice in so many different businesses.
They are prevented from obtaining an understanding not so
much because of their point of view or motive, but because
of human limitations. These men have endeavored to cover
far more ground than it is possible for men to cover properly
and without an intimate knowledge of the facts they can not
possibly deal with the problems involved.

CHAIRMAN WALSH. Does the fact that many large corporations with thousands of stockholders, among whom are large
numbers of employees, in anyway whatever affect the policy
of large corporations?

MR. BRANDEIS. I do not believe that the holding of stock
by employees—what is practically almost an insignificant participation, considering their percentage to the whole body of
stockholders in large corporations—improves the condition of
labor in those corporations. I think its effect is rather the
opposite. . . .

My observation leads me to believe that while there are
many contributing causes to unrest, that there is one cause

The text is excerpted from "Testimony before the U.S. Commission
on Industrial Relations, January 23, 1915," *Senate Documents*, 64th
Cong. 1st sess., 1915–1916, XXVI, *Commission on Industrial Relations
Report and Testimony*, VIII, 7658–76, *passim*.

which is fundamental. That is the necessary conflict—the contrast between our political liberty and our industrial absolutism. We are as free politically, perhaps, as free as it is possible for us to be. Every male has his voice and vote; and the law has endeavored to enable, and has succeeded practically, in enabling him to exercise his political franchise without fear. He therefore has his part; and certainly can secure an adequate part in the Government of the country in all of its political relations; that is, in all relations which are determined directly by legislation or governmental administration.

On the other hand, in dealing with industrial problems the position of the ordinary worker is exactly the reverse. The individual employee has no effective voice or vote. And the main objection, as I see it, to the very large corporation is, that it makes possible—and in many cases makes inevitable —the exercise of industrial absolutism. It is not merely the case of the individual worker against employer which, even if he is a reasonably sized employer, presents a serious situation calling for the interposition of a union to protect the individual. But we have the situation of an employer so potent, so well-organized, with such concentrated forces and with such extraordinary powers of reserve and the ability to endure against strikes and other efforts of a union, that the relatively loosely organized masses of even strong unions are unable to cope with the situation. We are dealing here with a question, not of motive, but of condition. Now, the large corporation and the managers of the powerful corporation are probably in large part actuated by motives just the same as an employer of a tenth of their size. Neither of them, as a rule, wishes to have his liberty abridged; but the smaller concern usually comes to the conclusion that it is necessary that it should be, where an important union must be dealt with. But when a great financial power has developed—when there exists these powerful organizations, which can successfully summon forces from all parts of the country, which can afford to use tremendous amounts of money in any conflict to carry out what they deem to be their business principle, and can also afford to suffer large losses—you have necessarily a condition of inequality between the two contending forces. Such contests, though undertaken with the best motives and with strong conviction on the part of the corporate managers that they are seeking what is for the best interests not only of the company but of the community, lead to absolutism. The result, in the cases of these large corporations, may be to develop a benevolent absolutism, but it is an absolutism all the same; and it is that which makes the great corporation so dangerous. There develops within the State a state so powerful that the ordinary social and industrial forces existing are insufficient to cope with it.

I noted, Mr. Chairman, that the question you put to me concerning the employees of these large corporations related to their physical condition. Their mental condition is certainly equally important. Unrest, to my mind, never can be removed—and fortunately never can be removed—by mere improvement of the physical and material condition of the workingman. If it were possible we should run great risk of improving their material condition and reducing their manhood. We must bear in mind all the time that however much we may desire material improvement and must desire it for the comfort of the individual, that the United States is a democracy, and that we must have, above all things, men. It is the development of manhood to which any industrial and social system should be directed. We Americans are committed not only to social justice in the sense of avoiding things which bring suffering and harm, like unjust distribution of wealth; but we are committed primarily to democracy. The social justice for which we are striving is an incident of our democracy, not the main end. It is rather the result of democracy—perhaps its finest expression—but it rests upon democracy, which implies the rule by the people. And therefore the end for which we must strive is the attainment of rule by the people, and that involves industrial democracy as well as political democracy. That means that the problem of a trade should be no longer the problems of the employer alone. The problems of his business, and it is not the employer's business alone, are the problems of all in it. The union can not shift upon the employer the responsibility for conditions, nor can the employer insist upon determining, according to his will, the conditions which shall exist. The problems which exist are the problems of the trade; they are the problems of employer and employee. Profit sharing, however liberal, can not meet the situation. That would mean merely dividing the profits of business. Such a division may do harm or it might do good, dependent on how it is applied.

There must be a division not only of profits, but a division also of responsibilities. The employees must have the opportunity of participating in the decisions as to what shall be their condition and how the business shall be run. They must learn also in sharing that responsibility that they must bear the suffering arising from grave mistakes, just as the employer must. But the right to assist in making the decisions, the right of making their own mistakes, if mistakes there must be, is a privilege which should not be denied to labor. We must insist upon labor sharing the responsibilities for the result of the business.

Now, to a certain extent we are gradually getting it—in smaller businesses. The grave objection to the large business is that, almost inevitably, the form of organization, the absentee stockholdings, and its remote directorship prevent participation, ordinarily, of the employees in such management. The executive officials become stewards in charge of the details of the operation of the business, they alone coming into direct relation with labor. Thus we lose that necessary cooperation which naturally flows from contact between employers and employees—and which the American aspirations for democracy demand. It is in the resultant absolutism that you will find the fundamental cause of prevailing unrest; no matter what is done with the superstructure, no matter how it may be improved in one way or the other, unless we eradicate that fundamental difficulty, unrest will not only continue, but, in my opinion, will grow worse.

CHAIRMAN WALSH. From your observation, Mr. Brandeis, what would you say is the responsibility of these so-called absentee owners of industries for conditions, wages, and other conditions existing in the corporations in which they are financially interested? . . .

MR. BRANDEIS. . . . The obligation of a director must be held to be absolute. Of course, I said a little while ago that one of the grave objections to this situation with large corporations was the directors did not know what was going on, and they could not therefore pass an intelligent judgment on these questions of the relations between employer and employee, because they did not have the facts.

Nobody can form a judgment that is worth having without a fairly detailed and intimate knowledge of the facts, and the circumstances of these gentlemen, largely bankers of importance, with a multitude of different associations and occupations—the fact that these men can not know the facts is conclusive to my mind against a system by which the same men are directors in many different companies. I doubt whether anybody who is himself engaged in any important business has time to be a director in more than one large corporation. If he seeks to know about the affairs of that one corporation as much as he should know, not only in the interest of the stockholders, but in the interest of the community, he will have a field for study that will certainly occupy all the time that he has.

CHAIRMAN WALSH. Have you observed, Mr. Brandeis, in

the development of these large corporations, the percentage of stock which might give control, or in practical everyday life does give control. . . .

MR. BRANDEIS. . . . These corporations are not controlled through a majority of the stock; they are controlled very largely by position. And that is an almost inevitable result of the wide distribution of stock.

From the standpoint of the community, the welfare of the community and the welfare of the workers in the company, what is called a democratization in the ownership through the distribution of stock is positively harmful. Such a wide distribution of the stock dissipates altogether the responsibility of stockholders, particularly of those with 5 shares, 10 shares, 15 shares, or 50 shares. They recognize that they have no influence in a corporation of hundreds of millions of dollars capital. Consequently they consider it immaterial whatever they do, or omit to do, the net result is that it becomes almost impossible to dislodge the men who are in control, unless there should be such a scandal in the corporation as to make it clearly necessary for the people on the outside to combine for self-protection. Probably even that necessity would not be sufficient to ensure a new management. That comes rarely except when those in control withdraw because they have been found guilty of reprehensible practices resulting in financial failure.

The wide distribution of stock, instead of being a blessing, constitutes, to my mind, one of the gravest dangers to the community. It is absentee landlordism of the worst kind. It is more dangerous, far more dangerous than the absentee landlordism from which Ireland suffered. There, at all events, control was centered in a few individuals. By the distribution of nominal control among ten thousand or a hundred thousand stockholders, there is developed a sense of absolute irresponsibility on the part of the person who holds that stock. The few men that are in position continue absolute control without any responsibility except to their stockholders of continuing and possibly increasing the dividends.

Now, that responsibility, while proper enough in a way, may lead to action directly contrary to the public interest.

CHAIRMAN WALSH. For the purpose of illustration, take a corporation such as the Steel Corporation and explain what you mean by the democratization of industry. . . .

MR. BRANDEIS. I think the difficulty of applying it to that corporation, I mean a corporation as large as that and as powerful as that, is this: The unit is so large that it is almost inconceivable that the men in control can be made to realize the necessity of yielding a part of their power to the employee.

Now, when they resist a particular labor policy, for instance, the unionization of shops, and they do resist it violently, most of the officials do so in absolute good faith, convinced that they are doing what they ought to do. They have in mind the excesses of labor unions and their obligations to stockholders to protect the property; and having those things in mind and exaggerating, no doubt, the dangers of the situation, they conclude that they can not properly submit to so-called union demands. They are apt to believe that it is "un-American" to do so—and declare it to be contrary to our conceptions of liberty and the rest. And they believe they are generally sincere in their statements.

The possession of almost absolute power makes them believe this. It is exactly the same condition that presents itself often in the political world.

No doubt the Emperor of Russia means just as well toward each of his subjects as most rulers of a constitutional government or the executives of a Republic. But he is subject to a state of mind that he cannot overcome. The fact that he possesses the power and that he is the final judge of what is right or wrong prevents his seeing clearly and doing that which is necessary to give real liberty and freedom.

It is almost inconceivable to my mind that a corporation with powers so concentrated as the Steel Corporation could get to a point where it would be willing to treat with the employees on equal terms. And unless they treat on equal terms then there is no such thing as democratization. The treatment on equal terms with them involves not merely the making of a contract; it must develop into a continuing relation. The making of a contract with a union is a long step. It is collective bargaining—a great advance. But it is only the first step. In order that collective bargaining should result in industrial democracy it must go further and create practically an industrial government—a relation between employer and employee where the problems as they arise from day to day, or from month to month, or from year to year, may come up for consideration and solution as they come up in our political government.

In that way conditions are created best adapted to securing proper consideration of any question arising. The representative of each party is heard—and strives to advance the interest he represents. It is the conflict of these opposing forces which produces the contract ultimately. But to adequately solve the trade problems there must be some machinery which will deal with these problems as they arise from day to day. You must create something akin to a government of the trade before you reach a real approach to democratization. . . .

CHAIRMAN WALSH. Past experience indicates that large corporations can be trusted to bring about these reforms themselves?

MR. BRANDEIS. I think all of our human experience shows that no one with absolute power can be trusted to give it up even in part. That has been the experience with political absolutism; it must prove the same with industrial absolutism. Industrial democracy will not come by gift. It has got to be won by those who desire it. And if the situation is such that a voluntary organization like a labor union is powerless to bring about the democratization of a business, I think we have in this fact some proof that the employing organization is larger than is consistent with the public interest. I mean by larger, is more powerful, has a financial influence too great to be useful to the State; and the State must in some way come to the aid of the workingmen if democratization is to be secured.

CHAIRMAN WALSH. Are the workmen employed by large corporations in a position to work out their own salvation by trade-union organization to-day?

MR. BRANDEIS. I think our experience, taking the steel trade as an example, has certainly shown that they are not. And this is true also of many other lines of business. Even in case of corporations very much smaller than the Steel Corporation, the unions have found it impossible to maintain their position against the highly centralized, well-managed, highly financed company. Such corporations as a means of overcoming union influence and democratization frequently grant their employees more in wages and comforts than the union standard demands. But "man can not live by bread alone." Men must have industrial liberty as well as good wages.

CHAIRMAN WALSH. Do you believe that the existing State and Federal legislation is adequately and properly drawn to provide against abuses in industry, so far as the employees are concerned?

MR. BRANDEIS. I have grave doubt as to how much can be accomplished by legislation, unless it be to set a limit upon the size of corporate units. I believe in dealing with this labor problem, as in dealing with the problem of credit, we must meet this question.

CHAIRMAN WALSH. Of what?

MR. BRANDEIS. Size. And in dealing with the problem of

industrial democracy there underlies all of the difficulties the question of the concentration of power. This factor so important in connection with the subject of credit and in connection with the subject of trusts and monopolies is no less important in treating the labor problem. As long as there is such concentration of power no effort of the workingmen to secure democratization will be effective. The statement that size is not a crime is entirely correct when you speak of it from the point of motive. But size may become such a danger in its results to the community that the community may have to set limits. A large part of our protective legislation consists of prohibiting things which we find are dangerous, according to common experience. Concentration of power has been shown to be dangerous in a democracy, even though that power may be used beneficently. For instance, on our public highways we put a limit on the size of an autotruck, no matter how well it is run. It may have the most skillful and considerate driver, but its mere size may make it something which the community can not tolerate, in view of the other uses of the highway and the danger inherent in its occupation to so large an extent by a single vehicle. . . .

COMMISSIONER JOHN B. LENNON. Now, to apply it to the work that the unions have done for physical betterment, increase of wages and limitation of the hours and the elimination of children like in the coal industry.

MR. BRANDEIS. Oh, I think those are all positive gains, unqualified gains.

COMMISSIONER LENNON. Gains for manhood?

MR. BRANDEIS. They are all gains for manhood; and we recognize that manhood is what we are striving for in America. We are striving for democracy; we are striving for the development of men. It is absolutely essential in order that men may develop that they be properly fed and properly housed, and that they have proper opportunities of education and recreation. We can not reach our goal without those things. But we may have all those things and have a nation of slaves. . . .

COMMISSIONER HARRIS WEINSTOCK. . . . Now, as an economic student do you believe there is such a thing as overproduction, or is it because of underconsumption?

MR. BRANDEIS. I think it is underconsumption, or maladjustment in distribution. I think it is entirely true that at a given time you may have produced an amount that the market can not take. You may disarrange conditions or produce an article which the market does not want. But we have not the power to produce more than there is a potential desire to consume.

Commissioner Weinstock. In other words, so long as there are hungry mouths and naked bodies in the world there can not be overproduction?

Mr. Brandeis. Not only hungry mouths and naked bodies, but there are many other things that people want.

Commissioner Weinstock. Well, then, if we are laboring under a condition of underconsumption rather than of overproduction, is it or is it not wise to minimize production?

Mr. Brandeis. I believe it is one of the greatest economic errors to put any limitation upon production. If we took all the property there is in the country to-day and distributed it equally among the people of the country, we should not improve conditions materially. The only way in which we can bring that improvement in the condition of the workers . . . is to make not only the worker but all the people produce more so that there will be more to divide. . . .

And I have felt in connection with scientific management, with the introduction of that method of producing more, that we ought to make up for the opportunity we lost when we changed from hand labor to machine labor. I think it is perfectly clear that when that change was made the employer got more than he ought to have got; and labor did not get its share, because labor was not organized. Now, when labor is to a very considerable extent organized, labor ought to insist upon scientific management. It has a just cause of complaint if a business is not well managed. Then, when the proceeds of good management are secured, labor ought to insist upon getting its share; and, as I have said, I think its share ought to be large, because of the reason that when machines were introduced labor did not get its share.

Commissioner Weinstock. . . . will you be good enough to point out, Mr. Brandeis, what you have observed to be the mistakes of employers in dealing with labor. . . .

Mr. Brandeis. I think the main mistake that the employers have made has been a failure to acquire understanding of the conditions and facts concerning labor. There has been ignorance in this respect on the part of employers—ignorance due in large part to lack of imagination. Employers have not been able to think themselves into the labor position. They do not understand labor and many successful business men have never recognized that labor presents the most important problem in the business. . . .

The other cause of employers' difficulties is a failure to think clearly. The employers' refusal to deal with a union is ordinarily due to erroneous reasoning or false sentiment. The man who refuses to deal with the union acts ordinarily from a good motive. He is impressed with "union dictation." He is apt to think "this is my business and the American has the right of liberty of contract." He honestly believes that he is standing up for a high principle and is willing often to run the risk of having his business ruined rather than abandon that principle. They have not thought out clearly enough that liberty means exercising one's rights consistently with a like exercise of rights by other people; that liberty is distinguished from license in that it is subject to certain restrictions, and that no one can expect to secure liberty in the sense in which we recognize it in America without having his rights curtailed in those respects in which it is necessary to limit them in the general public interest. The failure of many employers to recognize these simple truths is a potent reason why employers have not been willing to deal with unions. . . .

COMMISSIONER WEINSTOCK. On the other hand, Mr. Brandeis, what are the mistakes of organized labor, as you see them? . . .

MR. BRANDEIS. . . . Now, what the employer needs most is to have proper representatives of labor understand the problems of his business; how serious they are, how great is the chance of losing money, how relatively small is the chance of making large profits, and how great is the percentage of failures. Put a competent representative of labor on your board of directors; make him grapple with the problems whether to do or not to do a specific thing, and undertake to balance the advantages and disadvantages presented, and he will get a realizing sense of how difficult it is to operate a business successfully and what the dangers are of the destruction of the capital in the business. . . .

COMMISSIONER JAMES O'CONNELL. You believe that all things, except possibly the question of wages, . . . should be regulated by law?

MR. BRANDEIS. No; I think the question of what we should regulate by law is purely a question to be determined by experience. We should not regulate anything by law except where an evil exists which the existing forces of unionism or otherwise, labor, are unable to deal with it. You can not lay down any better rule than this, that it is desirable that people should be left with the powers of free contract between one another except so far as experience shows that the existing forces will prevent contracts fair in their results. The provisions made for the protection of women and children or for sanitary conditions and safety of all wage earners are justified, so far and only so far as experience shows that without them we shall suffer evils. We ought to go as far as, from time to time, it may be necessary to protect the community from those evils, but no further. . . .

COMMISSIONER O'CONNELL. Has the single individual as a wage worker or wealth producer in our town any opportunity or chance, as an individual, to protect and take care of himself and get right and justice as a wage worker? . . .

MR. BRANDEIS. . . . As an industry develops into a larger unit, the chances of the individual being able to protect himself diminishes. Self-protection is possible only where real freedom of contract exists. The only freedom the individual worker has is to leave and go to another employer. But if that is the only alternative and the other employer is equally as large, then the worker passes from pillar to post, and he has no protection at all. But where the situation is that the workman has some other alternative or where the employer needs the workman as much as the workman needs the employer, he may get protection, even without being a member of a union. But such cases are growing constantly less. . . .

COMMISSIONER AUSTIN B. GARRETSON. . . . It has been testified to before this commission that control—financial control—of industrial and transportation interests can be traced to certain well-defined banking groups. . . . If you feel free to tell us from your experience and information I would be glad to know whether you think such control can be traced?

MR. BRANDEIS. I believe it perfectly clear that it can be traced. . . . Those who deny control are using that word "control" in a very restricted sense. They mean that these particular individuals have not definitely said, "This thing shall be done and that thing shall not be done." But, as a matter of fact, control is exercised and exercised to an extraordinary degree by the existence of a great power whom people believe and usually have reason to believe, would be pleased or displeased with the adoption or rejection of a given course. Great power controls without issuing orders.

No specific legislation came out of the Commission's hearings and reports, yet Brandeis' contributions have endured. His dissenting opinion of 1932 in Liggett v. Lee *reads like a page from his testimony before the Commission on Industrial Relations. By that time "able and discerning scholars" were*

aware of the economic and social results of removing all limitations on the size of business corporations. The evil consequences were then recognized as "so fundamental and far-reaching as to lead these scholars to compare the evolving corporate system with the feudal system; and to lead other men of insight and experience to assert that this master institution of civilized life is converting us to the rule of a plutocracy."

Certain of Brandeis' ideas were translated into Franklin D. Roosevelt's New Deal. Others have been challenged as obsolete; still others seem radical fifty years later. The combiners continued to combine; interlocking directorates flourished. Congressional investigations during the early 1930's revealed Samuel Insull serving on more than eighty boards, Richard B. Mellon on nearly fifty, and Percy A. Rockefeller on sixty-eight. The collapse of 1929 confirmed Brandeis' forecast. Gains came largely through government action. The war Brandeis declared on the "money trust" in 1913 was finally won with the passage of the Banking Act of 1933, requiring national and member banks to divest themselves of their securities affiliates. A year later, legislation struck at such "combiners" as the House of Morgan, against which Brandeis had battled two decades earlier. The Securities Act of 1933 fulfilled his demand for publicity. "The mere substitution of knowledge for ignorance," he had said, "of publicity for secrecy will go far toward preventing monopoly." The Public Utility Holding Company Act of 1935 was a direct assault on bigness, requiring the elimination of the upper layers in the holding-company structures, and conferring extensive regulatory power upon the Securities Exchange Commission. All this was a source of gratification. "There is evidence that the difficulties of bigness are being realized in government matters," the Justice wrote Norman Hapgood, October 31, 1934. The curb had set in on a wide front. He noted "decentralization of plants by big concerns as a step—; and federal legislation going a little way is imminent."

Though certain of the measures enacted were welcome, no frontal attack was made on the major curse—industrial and financial bigness. Aggravating his concern was the evidence he saw on all sides of the dreaded curse spreading to government itself. Repelled by the encouragement of bigness implicit in the National Industrial Recovery Act (1933), Brandeis singled out the Court's unanimous decision outlawing the Blue Eagle—Black Monday, New Dealers called it—as "the most important day in the history of the Court and the most beneficent." "Tell the President we're not going to let this government centralize everything," he warned Tommy Corcoran. Big government was no solution. "Many men are all wool," he said, "but none is more than a yard wide."

Echoes of Brandeis' forebodings are still heard. Joined in 1948 by three colleagues, Justice William O. Douglas deplored "the power of a handful of men over our economy." "Industrial power," Douglas pleaded, "should be decentralized. It should be scattered into many hands so that the fortunes of the people will not be dependent on the whim or caprice, the political prejudices, the emotional stability of a few self-appointed men." That same year, Theodore K. Quinn, formerly vice president of General Electric, sounded a familiar, humanistic note. "Monster organizations," Quinn declared, were "creating an increasingly dependent society where only masses count, genuine individual freedom languished and individual opportunity and expression are strangled."

In certain quarters, bigness is now considered inevitable. "Bigness is with us and the technicians tell us it is necessary," Adolf A. Berle, Jr., comments. Contending that in big business "we have a social institution that promotes the human freedom and individualism," David Lilienthal cautions against the "curse of smallness." But the continuing vitality of Brandeis' thought does not depend on whether or not bigness is efficient or predestined. Material gains may obscure the prime consideration—man himself. "We must have, above all things, men. It is the development of manhood to which every industrial system should be directed."

Though Brandeis' ideas on industrial self-government are still far from realized, certain recent developments, here and abroad, incorporate his basic thought—that division of responsibility for management must go hand in hand with the division of profits. Some contracts now provide for joint company-union committees to deal with the troublesome issues growing out of automation, including distribution of its benefits; others offer continuous negotiation as a safeguard against breakdowns at contract time. In Germany and Yugoslavia, workers participate in the actual management of business. Unconscionable tie-ups in basic industries underscore the growing need for a fresh approach.

Over fifty years have elapsed since Brandeis appeared before the U.S. Commission on Industrial Relations. The ideas he then expressed transcend time and circumstance.

Woodrow Wilson

"Fourteen Points" Address

1918

EDITED BY ARTHUR S. LINK

Colonel Edward M. House, intimate adviser of President Woodrow Wilson, arrived at the White House at nine o'clock on the evening of Friday, January 4, 1918. House ate dinner hurriedly; then he and Wilson went to the President's study to discuss a matter that seemed too important to permit further delay. It was the preparation of a statement of American objectives in the war against Germany. Wilson had been tempted several times during 1917 to make a definitive avowal, particularly after the moderate Socialist government of Russia and the German Reichstag had issued calls for a peace based on the principles of no annexations and no indemnities. Wilson had been deterred from speaking out only by warnings from advisers at home and Allied governments abroad that dissensions among the Allies would ensue and that the strategic situation did not augur well, from the Allied point of view, for peace discussions.

Wilson believed by the beginning of 1918 that he did not dare to wait any longer. The Bolsheviks (radical Socialists) had seized control of the Russian government on November 7, 1917, and appealed to the Allies to seek an armistice with

Germany upon the basis of no annexations and no indemnities. When the Allies refused, the Bolsheviks concluded an armistice with Germany on December 5 and then appealed to the workers of the Western belligerents to overthrow their capitalistic and allegedly imperialistic governments. At the same time they published Russia's secret treaties with the Western Allies to prove their claim that both sides were fighting for spoils and plunder. This move stirred much discussion in labor and liberal circles in the United States and western Europe; and Wilson concluded that some definitive answer to the Bolsheviks had to be made.

Wilson and House discussed the proposed statement in general terms during the late evening of January 4. Their guide was a long report on the general diplomatic situation and war objectives prepared by the "inquiry," a group of experts assembled by House at Wilson's request in September, 1917. The two men met again in the President's study on the following morning, January 5, and discussed the various points that Wilson should make in his address. Wilson typed them on three sheets of note paper on his own portable Hammond typewriter, and House numbered them, grouping the general points first, the specific points next. Wilson accepted House's arrangement, except to place the general point concerning the League of Nations last for emphasis.

Wilson began to draft his speech in shorthand and then to transcribe it on his typewriter soon after House left his study on Saturday afternoon. He had finished a first draft by late Sunday afternoon, January 6, and read it to House then. The colonel returned to the White House for a final conference on Monday afternoon. Wilson made only one important change at this meeting. It was to say that Alsace-Lorraine "should" be returned to France. He also went over the points again, deciding when to use "must" and when to use "should" in defining their urgency. Then he read the text to Secretary of State Robert Lansing, making a few verbal changes at Lansing's suggestion. Wilson gave the text of his typewritten copy, by now much altered, to Charles L. Swem, his private secretary, for copying. Since there was not time for the Government Printing Office to print a reading copy, Wilson may have used the typewritten copy when he delivered the address to a joint session of Congress on the morning of January 8, 1918.

☆

ONCE MORE, as repeatedly before, the spokesmen of the Central Empires have indicated their desires to discuss the objects of the war and the possible bases of a general peace. Parleys have been in progress at Brest-Litovsk between representatives of the Central Powers to which the attention of all the belligerents has been invited for the purpose of ascertaining whether it may be possible to extend these parleys into a general conference with regard to terms of peace and settlement. The Russian representatives presented not only a perfectly definite statement of the principles upon which they would be willing to conclude peace but also an equally definite programme of the concrete application of these principles. The representatives of the Central Powers, on their part, presented an outline of settlement which, if much less definite, seemed susceptible of liberal interpretation until their specific programme of practical terms was added. That programme proposed no concessions at all either to the sovereignty of Russia or to the preferences of the populations with whose fortunes it dealt, but meant, in a word, that the Central Empires were to keep every foot of territory their armed forces had occupied,—every province, every city, every point of vantage,—as a permanent addition to their territories and their power. It is a reasonable conjecture that the general principles of settlement which they at first suggested originated with the more liberal statesmen of Germany and Austria, the men who have begun to feel the force of their own peoples' thought and purpose, while the concrete terms of actual settlement came from the military leaders who have no thought but to keep what they have got. The negotiations have been broken off. The Russian representatives were sincere and in earnest. They cannot entertain such proposals of conquest and domination.

The whole incident is full of significance. It is also full of perplexity. With whom are the Russian representatives dealing? For whom are the representatives of the Central Empires speaking? Are they speaking for the majorities of their respective parliaments or for the minority parties, that military and imperialistic minority which has so far dominated their whole policy and controlled the affairs of Turkey and of the Balkan states which have felt obliged to become their associates in this war? The Russian representatives have in-

The text of Wilson's address given here is that of the original typewritten copy. The President handed this copy to his daughter, Mrs. Francis B. Sayre, as they were walking out of the chamber of the House of Representatives after he had delivered the speech; the copy is now in the Woodrow Wilson papers at the Library of Congress.

sisted, very justly, very wisely, and in the true spirit of modern democracy, that the conferences they have been holding with the Teutonic and Turkish statesmen should be held within open, not closed, doors, and all the world has been audience, as was desired. To whom have we been listening, then? To those who speak the spirit and intention of the Resolutions of the German Reichstag of the ninth of July last, the spirit and intention of the liberal leaders and parties of Germany, or to those who resist and defy that spirit and intention and insist upon conquest and subjugation? Or are we listening, in fact, to both, unreconciled and in open and hopeless contradiction? These are very serious and pregnant questions. Upon the answer to them depends the peace of the world.

But, whatever the results of the parleys at Brest-Litovsk, whatever the confusions of counsel and of purpose in the utterances of the spokesmen of the Central Empires, they have again attempted to acquaint the world with their objects in the war and have again challenged their adversaries to say what their objects are and what sort of settlement they would deem just and satisfactory. There is no good reason why that challenge should not be responded to, and responded to with the utmost candor. We did not wait for it. Not once, but again and again, we have laid our whole thought and purpose before the world, not in general terms only, but each time with sufficient definition to make it clear what sort of definitive terms of settlement must necessarily spring out of them. Within the last week Mr. Lloyd George has spoken with admirable candor and in admirable spirit for the people and Government of Great Britain. There is no confusion of counsel among the adversaries of the Central Powers, no uncertainty of principle, no vagueness of detail. The only secrecy of counsel, the only lack of fearless frankness, the only failure to make definite statement of the objects of the war, lies with Germany and her Allies. The issues of life and death hang upon these definitions. No statesman who has the least conception of his responsibility ought for a moment to permit himself to continue this tragical and appalling outpouring of blood and treasure unless he is sure beyond a peradventure that the objects of the vital sacrifice are part and parcel of the very life of Society and that the people for whom he speaks think them right and imperative as he does.

There is, moreover, a voice calling for these definitions of principle and of purpose which is, it seems to me, more thrilling and more compelling than any of the many moving voices with which the troubled air of the world is filled. It is the voice of the Russian people. They are prostrate and all but helpless, it would seem, before the grim power of Germany, which has hitherto known no relenting and no pity. Their power, apparently, is shattered. And yet their soul is not subservient. They will not yield either in principle or in action. Their conception of what is right, of what it is humane and honorable for them to accept, has been stated with a frankness, a largeness of view, a generosity of spirit, and a universal human sympathy which must challenge the admiration of every friend of mankind; and they have refused to compound their ideals or desert others that they themselves may be safe. They call to us to say what it is that we desire, in what, if in anything, our purpose and our spirit differ from theirs; and I believe that the people of the United States would wish me to respond, with utter simplicity and frankness. Whether their present leaders believe it or not, it is our heartfelt desire and hope that some way may be opened whereby we may be privileged to assist the people of Russia to attain their utmost hope of liberty and ordered peace.

It will be our wish and purpose that the processes of peace, when they are begun, shall be absolutely open and that they shall involve and permit henceforth no secret understandings of any kind. The day of conquest and aggrandizement is gone by; so is also the day of secret covenants entered into in the interest of particular governments and likely at some unlooked-for moment to upset the peace of the world. It is this happy fact, now clear to the view of every public man whose thoughts do not still linger in an age that is dead and gone, which makes it possible for every nation whose purposes are consistent with justice and the peace of the world to avow now or at any other time the objects it has in view.

We entered this war because violations of right had occurred which touched us to the quick and made the life of our own people impossible unless they were corrected and the world secured once for all against their recurrence. What we demand in this war, therefore, is nothing peculiar to ourselves. It is that the world be made fit and safe to live in; and particularly that it be made safe for every peace-loving nation which, like our own, wishes to live its own life, determine its own institutions, be assured of justice and fair dealing by the other peoples of the world as against force and selfish aggression. All the peoples of the world are in effect partners in this interest, and for our own part we see very clearly that unless justice be done to others it will not be done to us. The programme of the world's peace, therefore, is our programme;

and that programme, the only possible programme, as we see it, is this:

I. Open covenants of peace, openly arrived at, after which there shall be no private international understandings of any kind but diplomacy shall proceed always frankly and in the public view.

II. Absolute freedom of navigation upon the seas, outside territorial waters, alike in peace and in war, except as the seas may be closed in whole or in part by international action for the enforcement of international covenants.

III. The removal, so far as possible, of all economic barriers and the establishment of an equality of trade conditions among all the nations consenting to the peace and associating themselves for its maintenance.

IV. Adequate guarantees given and taken that national armaments will be reduced to the lowest point consistent with domestic safety.

V. A free, open-minded, and absolutely impartial adjustment of all colonial claims, based upon a strict observance of the principle that in determining all such questions of sovereignty the interests of the populations concerned must have equal weight with the equitable claims of the government whose title is to be determined.

VI. The evacuation of all Russian territory and such a settlement of all questions affecting Russia as will secure the best and freest cooperation of the other nations of the world in obtaining for her an unhampered and unembarrassed opportunity for the independent determination of her own political development and national policy and assure her of a sincere welcome into the society of free nations under institutions of her own choosing; and, more than a welcome, assistance also of every kind that she may need and may herself desire. The treatment accorded Russia by her sister nations in the months to come will be the acid test of their good will, of their comprehension of her needs as distinguished from their own interests, and of their intelligent and unselfish sympathy.

VII. Belgium, the whole world will agree, must be evacuated and restored, without any attempt to limit the sovereignty which she enjoys in common with all other free nations. No other single act will serve as this will serve to restore confidence among the nations in the laws which they have themselves set and determined for the government of their relations with one another. Without this healing act the whole structure and validity of international law is forever impaired.

VIII. All French territory should be freed and the invaded

portions restored, and the wrong done to France by Prussia in 1871 in the matter of Alsace-Lorraine, which has unsettled the peace of the world for nearly fifty years, should be righted, in order that peace may once more be made secure in the interest of all.

IX. A readjustment of the frontiers of Italy should be effected along clearly recognizable lines of nationality.

X. The peoples of Austria-Hungary, whose place among the nations we wish to see safeguarded and assured, should be accorded the freest opportunity of autonomous development.

XI. Rumania, Serbia, and Montenegro should be evacuated; occupied territories restored; Serbia accorded free and secure access to the sea; and the relations of the several Balkan states to one another determined by friendly counsel along historically established lines of allegiance and nationality; and international guarantees of the political and economic independence and territorial integrity of the several Balkan states should be entered into.

XII. The Turkish portions of the present Ottoman Empire should be assured a secure sovereignty, but the other nationalities which are now under Turkish rule should be assured an undoubted security of life and an absolutely unmolested opportunity of autonomous development, and the Dardanelles should be permanently opened as a free passage to the ships and commerce of all nations under international guarantees.

XIII. An independent Polish state should be erected which should include the territories inhabited by indisputably Polish populations, which should be assured a free and secure access to the sea, and whose political and economic independence and territorial integrity should be guaranteed by international covenant.

XIV. A general association of nations must be formed under specific covenants for the purpose of affording mutual guarantees of political independence and territorial integrity to great and small states alike.

In regard to these essential rectifications of wrong and assertions of right we feel ourselves to be intimate partners of all the governments and peoples associated together against the Imperialists. We cannot be separated in interest or divided in purpose. We stand together until the end.

For such arrangements and covenants we are willing to fight and to continue to fight until they are achieved; but only because we wish the right to prevail and desire a just and stable peace such as can be secured only by removing the chief provocations to war, which this programme does remove. We have no jealousy of German greatness, and there is nothing in this program that impairs it. We grudge her no achievement or distinction of learning or of pacific enterprise such as have made her record very bright and very enviable. We do not wish to injure her or to block in any way her legitimate influence or power. We do not wish to fight her either with arms or with hostile arrangements of trade if she is willing to associate herself with us and the other peace-loving nations of the world in covenants of justice and law and fair dealing. We wish her only to accept a place of equality among the peoples of the world,—the new world in which we now live, —instead of a place of mastery.

Neither do we presume to suggest to her any alteration or modification of her institutions. But it is necessary, we must frankly say, and necessary as a preliminary to any intelligent dealings with her on our part, that we should know whom her spokesmen speak for when they speak to us, whether for the Reichstag majority or for the military party and the men whose creed is imperial domination.

We have spoken now, surely, in terms too concrete to admit of any further doubt or question. An evident principle runs through the whole programme I have outlined. It is the principle of justice to all peoples and nationalities, and their right to live on equal terms of liberty and safety with one another, whether they be strong or weak. Unless this principle be made its foundation no part of the structure of international justice can stand. The people of the United States could act upon no other principle; and to the vindication of this principle they are ready to devote their lives, their honor, and everything that they possess. The moral climax of this the culminating and final war for human liberty has come, and they are ready to put their own strength, their own highest purpose, their own integrity and devotion to the test.

The "Fourteen Points" Address at once became the single great manifesto of World War I. It was Western democracy's answer in its first full-dress debate with international communism. It raised a standard to which men of good will in all nations, Germany included, could rally. This was true, first, because of Wilson's striking success in synthesizing what might be called the liberal peace program. Not a single one of the Fourteen Points was original. All of them had been proposed and discussed by various groups of idealists and pacifists in all leading belligerent countries. But Wilson did

more than recapitulate the liberal peace program. He also succeeded in assimilating many of the announced German peace objectives. Restoration of Belgium, freedom of the seas, destruction of barriers to trade, and establishment of an independent Poland were all as much German objectives as they were Allied objectives.

Wilson, in fact, hoped that the Fourteen Points Address would lead to conversations with the German and Austrian governments concerning the conclusion of peace. The Austrian Foreign Minister replied responsively on January 24, but the German Chancellor was evasive in a speech delivered on the same day. Then the Germans gave their answer by imposing a Carthaginian peace on Russia on March 3 and by beginning a great offensive to win the war on the western front two weeks later. There was but one response the American people could make, Wilson said on April 6: "Force, Force to the utmost, Force without stint or limit, the righteous and triumphant Force which shall make Right the law of the world, and cast every selfish dominion down in the dust."

The Fourteen Points Address did not sink out of sight even while the fighting in France reached a crescendo. It became the single most important weapon in the American and Allied propaganda campaign to undermine German morale. Hundreds of thousands of copies were dropped by airplanes over German cities and lines. Opinions differ only as to the degree of its effectiveness; no authority doubts that it helped to shorten the war.

The Fourteen Points Address enjoys the unique distinction of being the only speech that served as the documentary basis for the ending of a great war and conclusion of a general settlement. The German government, frightened by an Allied and American counteroffensive that seemed destined to thrust into Germany, appealed on October 3, 1918, for an armistice looking toward a peace treaty based on the Fourteen Points and Wilson's subsequent elaborations of war aims. The Pre-Armistice Agreement of November 11, which ended World War I, specifically recognized the Fourteen Points and other Wilsonian pronouncements as the standard for peacemaking, subject to reservations on freedom of the seas, reparations, and Czech independence.

The Fourteen Points Address was Wilson's shield and standard all during the Paris Peace Conference that met from January 18 through June 28, 1919, to hammer out a treaty for Germany. Forces beyond his control prevented complete vindication of the points, notably those concerning the colo-

nial settlement, reparations, and disarmament. But the Versailles Treaty honored the Fourteen Points more in the observance than in the breach, and Wilson was certain that the new League of Nations, to which was entrusted enforcement of the Treaty, would go far toward redeeming broken pledges to Germany, as, indeed, it did.

The Fourteen Points Address has shown enduring vitality and power in changing historical circumstances since 1919. It was not only Wilson's greatest speech, but one of the few really notable pronouncements of the twentieth century. Idealists, antiwar groups, and Germans appealed under the Fourteen Points' authority for revision of the Versailles Treaty. The ideals and general objectives enunciated in the address fell out of sight or into obloquy in the United States in the wake of an isolationist upsurge in the 1930's. So-called realists in the 1940's and 1950's condemned its alleged romanticism about the possibilities of a world order based on justice and good will. But Wilson's address remains today, as it has been since it was first uttered, a goad and challenge to its critics and a charter of world liberty to men who treasure its hope of a new world organized for peace and the advancement of mankind.

Henry Cabot Lodge

Speech on the League of Nations

1919

EDITED BY JOHN A. GARRATY

When Henry Cabot Lodge rose to address the Senate on August 12, 1919, the United States was in the midst of a "Great Debate" over its future foreign policy. Should it join the new League of Nations that President Wilson had hammered into shape at the Versailles Peace Conference, or should the nation retain its traditional aloofness from the kind of "permanent alliances" that George Washington had warned against in his hallowed Farewell Address? Ardent internationalists, of course, favored joining the League. If the bloody battles of the World War were not to be repeated, some international organization would have to be created to settle disputes and preserve the peace, they argued. But certain "irreconcilables" were dead set against any involvement in European affairs. Between these extremes stood the majority of the people, willing to see the country assume its responsibilities as a world power, but uneasy about committing themselves irrevocably to a supranational organization.

Senator Lodge belonged in this middle group. However, his position was unusual. He was a Republican (an extremely partisan one) and also Senate Majority Leader and chairman of the Foreign Relations Committee. His political instincts, highly refined by years of experience, told him that Wilson must not be allowed to monopolize the credit for having devised a scheme for preserving world peace. He had also the task of shaping a strategy that all Republicans, isolationists as well as internationalists, could accept. His position was further complicated on the one hand by his personal dislike of Wilson, and on the other by his belief that America should play an important role in world affairs. He therefore took the position that the League should be accepted with "reservations" which, by limiting American obligations, would make it impossible for the League or any of its members to involve the nation in important international commitments without the consent of Congress.

This speech was Lodge's first full-dress statement of his position in the Senate. He prepared for it with extreme care, writing out every word and delivering it, as one observer noted, in a manner "studiously, if not painfully devoid of accentuation or emphasis." Seldom did he even raise his eyes from his manuscript.

Nonetheless, his carefully measured phrases, appealing to the mood of the audience, unleashed a storm of applause from the packed galleries. A group of Marines, just returned from France, pounded their helmets enthusiastically against the gallery railing; men and women cheered, whistled, waved handkerchiefs and hats. It was minutes before order could be restored, and when a Democratic Senator attempted to reply to Lodge's arguments, his remarks were greeted with boos and hisses.

I OBJECT in the strongest possible way to having the United States agree, directly or indirectly, to be controlled by a league which may at any time, and perfectly lawfully and in accordance with the terms of the covenant, be drawn in to deal with internal conflicts in other countries, no matter what those conflicts may be. We should never permit the United States to be involved in any internal conflict in another country, except by the will of her people expressed through the Congress which represents them.

The address is reprinted here from the *Congressional Record, Proceedings and Debates of the First Session of the Sixty-sixth Congress of the United States of America,* Vol. LVIII, Part 4 (Washington, D.C.: Government Printing Office, 1919), August 12, 1919, pp. 3778–84. One line of type inadvertently omitted there has been restored in brackets.

With regard to wars of external aggression on a member of the league, the case is perfectly clear. There can be no genuine dispute whatever about the meaning of the first clause of article 10. In the first place, it differs from every other obligation in being individual and placed upon each nation without the intervention of the league. Each nation for itself promises to respect and preserve as against external aggression the boundaries and the political independence of every member of the league. . . .

It is, I repeat, an individual obligation. It requires no action on the part of the league, except that in the second sentence the authorities of the league are to have the power to advise as to the means to be employed in order to fulfill the purpose of the first sentence. But that is a detail of execution, and I consider that we are morally and in honor bound to accept and act upon that advice. The broad fact remains that if any member of the league suffering from external aggression should appeal directly to the United States for support the United States would be bound to give that support in its own capacity and without reference to the action of other powers, because the United States itself is bound, and I hope the day will never come when the United States will not carry out its promises. If that day should come, and the United States or any other great country should refuse, no matter how specious the reasons, to fulfill both in letter and spirit every obligation in this covenant, the United States would be dishonored and the league would crumble into dust, leaving behind it a legacy of wars. If China should rise up and attack Japan in an effort to undo the great wrong of the cession of the control of Shantung to that power, we should be bound under the terms of article 10 to sustain Japan against China, and a guaranty of that sort is never involved except when the question has passed beyond the stage of negotiation and has become a question for the application of force. I do not like the prospect. It shall not come into existence by any vote of mine. . . .

Any analysis of the provisions of this league covenant, however, brings out in startling relief one great fact. Whatever may be said, it is not a league of peace; it is an alliance, dominated at the present moment by five great powers, really by three, and it has all the marks of an alliance. The development of international law is neglected. The court which is to decide disputes brought before it fills but a small place. The conditions for which this league really provides with the utmost care are political conditions, not judicial questions, to be reached by the executive council and the assembly, purely political bodies without any trace of a judicial character about them. Such being its machinery, the control being in the hands of political appointees whose votes will be controlled by interest and expedience it exhibits that most marked characteristic of an alliance—that its decisions are to be carried out by force. Those articles upon which the whole structure rests are articles which provide for the use of force; that is, for war. This league to enforce peace does a great deal for enforcement and very little for peace. It makes more essential provisions looking to war than to peace for the settlement of disputes. . . .

Taken altogether, these provisions for war present what to my mind is the gravest objection to this league in its present form. We are told that of course nothing will be done in the way of warlike acts without the assent of Congress. If that is true let us say so in the covenant. But as it stands there is no doubt whatever in my mind that American troops and American ships may be ordered to any part of the world by nations other than the United States, and that is a proposition to which I for one can never assent. It must be made perfectly clear that no American soldiers, not even a corporal's guard, that no American sailors, not even the crew of a submarine, can ever be engaged in war or ordered anywhere except by the constitutional authorities of the United States. To Congress is granted by the Constitution the right to declare war, and nothing that would take the troops out of the country at the bidding or demand of other nations should ever be permitted except through congressional action. The lives of Americans must never be sacrificed except by the will of the American people expressed through their chosen Representatives in Congress. This is a point upon which no doubt can be permitted. American soldiers and American sailors have never failed the country when the country called upon them. They went in their hundreds of thousands into the war just closed. They went to die for the great cause of freedom and of civilization. They went [at their country's bidding and because their country summoned them] to service. We were late in entering the war. We made no preparation, as we ought to have done, for the ordeal which was clearly coming upon us; but we went and we turned the wavering scale. It was done by the American soldier, the American sailor, and the spirit and energy of the American people. They overrode all obstacles and all shortcomings on the part of the administration or of Congress and gave to their country a great place in the great victory. It was the first time we had been called upon to rescue the civilized world. Did we fail? On the contrary, we succeeded, succeeded largely and nobly, and we did it without any command from any league of nations. When the emergency came, we met it and we were able to meet it because we had built up on this continent the greatest and most powerful Nation in the world, built it up under our own policies, in our own way, and one great element of our strength was the fact that we had held aloof and had not thrust ourselves into European quarrels; that we had no selfish interest to serve. We made great sacrifices. We have done splendid work. I believe that we do not require to be told by foreign nations when we shall do work which freedom and civilization require. I think we can move to victory much better under our own command than under the command of others. Let us unite with the world to promote the peaceable settlement of all international disputes. Let us try to develop international law. Let us associate ourselves with the other nations for these purposes. But let us retain in our own hands and in our own control the lives of the youth of the land. Let no American be sent into battle except by the constituted authorities of his own country and by the will of the people of the United States.

Those of us, Mr. President, who are either wholly opposed to the league, or who are trying to preserve the independence and the safety of the United States by changing the terms of the league, and who are endeavoring to make the league, if we are to be a member of it, less certain to promote war instead of peace have been reproached with selfishness in our outlook and with a desire to keep our country in a state of isolation. So far as the question of isolation goes, it is impossible to isolate the United States. I well remember the time, 20 years ago, when eminent Senators and other distinguished gentlemen who were opposing the Philippines and shrieking about imperialism sneered at the statement made by some of us, that the United States had become a world power. I think no one now would question that the Spanish war marked the entrance of the United States into world affairs to a degree which had never obtained before. It was both an inevitable and an irrevocable step, and our entrance into the war with Germany certainly showed once and for all that the United States was not unmindful of its world responsibilities. We may set aside all this empty talk about isolation. Nobody expects to isolate the United States or to make it a hermit Nation, which is a sheer absurdity. But there is a wide difference beween taking a suitable part and bearing a due responsibility in world affairs and plunging the United States into every controversy and conflict on the face of the globe. By meddling in all the differences which may arise among any portion or fragment of humankind we simply fritter away our influence and injure ourselves to no good purpose. We shall be of far more value to the world and its peace by occupying, so far as possible, the situation which we have occupied for the last 20 years and by adhering to the policy of Washington and Hamilton, of Jefferson and Monroe, under which we have risen to our present greatness and prosperity. The fact that we have been separated by our geographical situation and by our consistent policy from the broils of Europe has made us more than any one thing capable of performing the great work which we performed in the war against Germany and our disinterestedness is of far more value to the world than our eternal meddling in every possible dispute could ever be.

Now, as to our selfishness, I have no desire to boast that we are better than our neighbors, but the fact remains that this Nation in making peace with Germany had not a single selfish or individual interest to serve. All we asked was that Germany should be rendered incapable of again breaking forth, with all the horrors, incident to German warfare, upon an unoffending world, and that demand was shared by every free nation and indeed by humanity itself. For ourselves we asked absolutely nothing. We have not asked any government or governments to guarantee our boundaries or our political independence. We have no fear in regard to either. We have sought no territory, no privileges, no advantages, for ourselves. That is the fact. It is apparent on the face of the treaty. I do not mean to reflect upon a single one of the powers with which we have been associated in the war against Germany, but there is not one of them which has not sought individual advantages for their own national benefit. I do not criticize their desires at all. The services and sacrifices of England and France and Belgium and Italy are beyond estimate and beyond praise. I am glad they should have what they desire for their own welfare and safety. But they all receive under the peace territorial and commercial benefits. We are asked to give, and we in no way seek to take. Surely it is not too much to insist that when we are offered nothing but the opportunity to give and to aid others we should have the right to say what sacrifices we shall make and what the magnitude of our gifts shall be. In the prosecution of the war we gave unstintedly American lives and American treasure. When the war closed we had 3,000,000 men under arms. We were turning the country into a vast workshop for war. We advanced ten billions to our allies. We refused no assistance that we could possibly render. All the great energy and power of the Republic were put at the service of the good cause. We have not been ungenerous. We have been devoted to the cause of freedom, humanity, and civilization everywhere. Now we are asked, in the making of peace, to sacrifice our sovereignty in important respects, to involve ourselves almost without limit in the affairs of other nations and to yield up policies and rights which we have maintained throughout our history. We are asked to incur liabilities to an unlimited extent and furnish assets at the same time which no man can measure. I think it is not only our right but our duty to determine how far we shall go. Not only must we look carefully to see where we are being led into endless disputes and entanglements, but we must not forget that we have in this country millions of people of foreign birth and parentage.

Our one great object is to make all these people Americans so that we may call on them to place America first and serve America as they have done in the war just closed. We cannot Americanize them if we are continually thrusting them back into the quarrels and difficulties of the countries from which they came to us. We shall fill this land with political disputes about the troubles and quarrels of other countries. We shall have a large portion of our people voting not on American questions and not on what concerns the United States but dividing on issues which concern foreign countries alone. That is an unwholesome and perilous condition to force upon this country. We must avoid it. We ought to reduce to the lowest possible point the foreign questions in which we involve ourselves. Never forget that this league is primarily—I might say overwhelmingly—a political organization, and I object strongly to having the politics of the United States turn upon disputes where deep feeling is aroused but in which we have no direct interest. It will all tend to delay the Americanization of our great population, and it is more important not only to the United States but to the peace of the world to make all these people good Americans than it is to determine that some piece of territory should belong to one European country rather than to another. For this reason I wish to limit strictly our interference in the affairs of Europe and of Africa. We have interests of our own in Asia and in the Pacific which we must guard upon our own account, but the less we undertake to play the part of umpire and thrust ourselves into European conflicts the better for the United States and for the world.

It has been reiterated here on this floor, and reiterated to the point of weariness, that in every treaty there is some sacrifice of sovereignty. That is not a universal truth by any means, but it is true of some treaties and it is a platitude which does not require reiteration. The question and the only question before us here is how much of our sovereignty we are justified in sacrificing. In what I have already said about other nations putting us into war I have covered one point of sovereignty which ought never to be yielded—the power to send American soldiers and sailors everywhere, which ought never to be taken from the American people or impaired in the slightest degree. Let us beware how we palter with our independence. We have not reached the great position from which we were able to come down into the field of battle and help to save the world from tyranny by being guided by others. Our vast power has all been built up and gathered together by ourselves alone. We forced our way upward from the days of the Revolution, through a world often hostile and always indifferent. We owe no debt to anyone except to France in that Revolution, and those policies and those rights on which our power has been founded should never be lessened or weakened. It will be no service to the world to do so and it will be of intolerable injury to the United States. We will do our share. We are ready and anxious to help in all ways to preserve the world's peace. But we can do it best by not crippling ourselves.

I am as anxious as any human being can be to have the United States render every possible service to the civilization and the peace of mankind, but I am certain we can do it best by not putting ourselves in leading strings or subjecting our policies and our sovereignty to other nations. The independence of the United States is not only more precious to ourselves but to the world than any single possession. Look at the United States to-day. We have made mistakes in the past. We have had shortcomings. We shall make mistakes in the future and fall short of our own best hopes. But none the less is there any country to-day on the face of the earth which can compare with this in ordered liberty, in peace, and in the largest freedom? I feel that I can say this without being accused of undue boastfulness, for it is the simple fact, and in making this treaty and taking on these obligations all that we do is in a spirit of unselfishness and in a desire for the good of mankind. But it is well to remember that we are dealing with nations every one of which has a direct individual interest to serve, and there is grave danger in an unshared idealism. Contrast the United States with any country on the face of the earth to-day and ask yourself whether the situation of the United States is not the best to be found. I will go as far as anyone in world service, but the first step to world service is the maintenance of the United States. You may call me selfish if you will, conservative or reactionary, or use any other harsh adjective you see fit to apply, but an American I was born, an American I have remained all my life. I can never be anything else but an American, and I must think of the United States first, and when I think of the United States first in an arrangement like this I am thinking of what is best for the world, for if the United States fails the best hopes of mankind fail with it. I have never had but one allegiance—I cannot divide it now. I have loved but one flag and I cannot share that devotion and give affection to the mongrel banner invented for a league. Internationalism, illustrated by the Bolshevik and by the men to whom all countries are alike provided they can make money out of them, is to me repulsive. National I must remain, and in that way I like all other Americans can render the amplest service to the world. The United States is the world's best hope, but if you fetter her in the interests and quarrels of other nations, if you tangle her in the intrigues of Europe, you will destroy her power for good and endanger her very existence. Leave her to march freely through the centuries to come as in the years that have gone. Strong, generous, and confident, she has nobly served mankind. Beware how you trifle with your marvelous inheritance, this great land of ordered liberty, for if we stumble and fall freedom and civilization everywhere will go down in ruin.

We are told that we shall "break the heart of the world" if we do not take this league just as it stands. I fear that the hearts of the vast majority of mankind would beat on strongly and steadily and without any quickening if the league were to perish altogether. If it should be effectively and beneficiently changed the people who would lie awake in sorrow for a single night could be easily gathered in one not very large room but those who would draw a long breath of relief would reach to millions.

We hear much of visions and I trust we shall continue to have visions and dream dreams of a fairer future for the race. But visions are one thing and visionaries are another, and the mechanical appliances of the rhetorician designed to give a picture of a present which does not exist and of a future which no man can predict are as unreal and shortlived as the steam or canvas clouds, the angels suspended on wires and the artificial lights of the stage. They pass with the moment of effect and are shabby and tawdry in the daylight. Let us at least be real. Washington's entire honesty of mind and his fearless look into the face of all facts are qualities which can never go out of fashion and which we should all do well to imitate.

Ideals have been thrust upon us as an argument for the league until the healthy mind which rejects cant revolts from them. Are ideals confined to this deformed experiment upon a noble purpose, tainted, as it is, with bargains and tied to a peace treaty which might have been disposed of long ago to the great benefit of the world if it had not been compelled to carry this rider on its back? "Post equitem sedet atra cura," Horace tells us, but no blacker care ever sat behind any rider than we shall find in this covenant of doubtful and disputed interpretation as it now perches upon the treaty of peace.

No doubt many excellent and patriotic people see a coming fulfillment of noble ideals in the words "league for peace." We all respect and share these aspirations and desires, but some of us see no hope, but rather defeat, for them in this murky covenant. For we, too, have our ideals, even if we differ from those who have tried to establish a monopoly of idealism. Our first ideal is our country, and we see her in the future, as in the past, giving service to all her people and to the world. Our ideal of the future is that she should continue to render that service of her own free will. She has great problems of her own to solve, very grim and perilous problems, and a right solution, if we can attain to it, would largely benefit mankind. We would have our country strong to resist a peril from the West, as she has flung back the German menace from the East. We would not have our politics distracted and embittered by the dissensions of other lands. We would not have our country's vigor exhausted or her moral force abated, by everlasting meddling and muddling in every quarrel, great and small, which afflicts the world. Our ideal is to make her ever stronger and better and finer, because in that way alone, as we believe, can she be of the greatest service to the world's peace and to the welfare of mankind.

Of course, Lodge's speech alone did not account for the rejection of the League of Nations by the Senate or for the fact that the American people as a whole, in the years between World Wars I and II, firmly opposed the idea of surrendering any part of their sovereignty to an international organization. But his basic point, so clearly and forcefully expressed in the speech, was the controlling consideration in American for-

eign-policy discussions at all levels during the twenties and thirties. This fact does not mean that the United States isolated itself from the rest of the world. The nation participated actively in international affairs and in doing so accepted obligations and made commitments of various sorts to other nations. Lodge himself, for example, was a delegate to the Washington Disarmament Conference, and put his name freely to treaties restricting the size of the Navy and accepting other limits on American freedom of action. However, these treaties were separately considered and ratified by the Senate in the traditional manner. But even so imaginary a surrender of sovereignty as would have been involved in American membership in the World Court was rejected. And as, in critical situations, the members of the League repeatedly proved unwilling to employ forceful means of preventing aggression by the dictators, Americans were further strengthened in the conviction that the position outlined by Lodge was sound.

Then, when World War II erupted with all its horrors, people began once again to consider employing some form of international organization as a means of preventing war. The result was the Charter of the United Nations. In the drafting of that Charter much consideration was given to Lodge's arguments against the League. Time had shown that these arguments reflected a widespread feeling in many nations besides the United States that national sovereignty ought not to be surrendered, no matter how desirable the objective. The influence of Lodge's thinking can be seen in many aspects of the organization of the United Nations, but especially in the veto granted to each of the great powers in the Security Council. The veto is the very antithesis of the principle behind Article 10 of the League, which Wilson called "the heart of the Covenant" and which Lodge, in his speech, so strongly opposed. It is important to remember that, while the Soviet Union has frequently abused the veto, the United States is as much against abolishing it as are the Russians.

Henry Cabot Lodge, Jr., grandson of the Senator and for many years United States Ambassador to the United Nations, summarized his grandfather's influence on the United Nations Charter in these words, written in 1953:

All the principal steps which have been taken since the end of World War II which relate to issues of peace and war specifically and categorically reserve the principle of national sovereignty and the principle of constitutional process. . . . [The Lodge Reservation to Article 10] simply preserved the power of Congress—a power which is jealously guarded today, which

> is completely safeguarded both in the United Nations Charter
> and in the Atlantic Pact, and which President Wilson was un-
> willing categorically to express at that time.

Speaking more generally, the historian Richard W. Leopold
writes: "The obligations of the United States under the Charter resemble closely those it would have assumed under the
Lodge reservations. Wilson intended the League to be a coer-
cive type of body. . . . Lodge sought to transform the League
into a noncoercive organization."

At the time of the League fight, and ever since, many
high-minded believers in international cooperation have condemned Lodge bitterly, blaming him for the smashing of Wilson's bright hopes, and even for World War II. Partly Lodge
deserved their opprobrium, because his personal hatred of the
President and his partisan ambitions certainly added to his
prejudice against the League. Yet in the long run Lodge
taught his critics (and the lesson was clear in his great Senate
speech) that no drafter of foreign policy can go beyond the
limits of what the public will support and still remain successful. The idea of a world government is as attractive today as
it was in 1919 and a good deal closer to reality, but it is not
yet within our grasp. The United Nations, built to conform to
the limitations of public support in each of the member nations, is a functioning and useful institution precisely because
it recognizes the fact that men all over the world still place
their own country first in their hearts, as Lodge did, and as
he knew his countrymen did.

H. L. Mencken

Preface to "The American Language"

1919

EDITED BY THOMAS PYLES

By 1919, when The American Language *was first published, Henry Louis Mencken was a well-known man. It is not surprising, if only from the sheer bulk of his production—and it usually had quality as well—that Mencken should have acquired a considerable reputation and influence as a literary critic, later enhanced by his brilliant editorship from 1924 to 1933 of the* American Mercury, *which with George Jean Nathan he founded. In the course of his zestful career he poleaxed many a sacred cow and deftly needled many a windbag, but the Preface to the first edition of* The American Language *reflects primarily his concern with the speech of what he liked to refer to as "this Great Republic."*

Well before 1919, Mencken had written in the Baltimore Evening Sun *and in* The Smart Set, *a magazine whose literary critic he was, on what he refers to in the Preface reprinted here as the "salient differences between the English of England and the English of America." His interest in the subject had been aroused in youth in the course of his work as a police reporter in his native Baltimore. As he himself testifies in the Preface to* The American Language: Supplement One*

(1945), this interest was kindled specifically around 1905, by his discovery in Baltimore's Enoch Pratt Free Library of the riches to be unearthed in Dialect Notes, *a journal which had been published since 1890 by the American Dialect Society. Thereafter, he tells us, "I was a steady customer of Dialect* Notes," *which in time sent him scurrying to earlier works on American English. These, as he points out in the Preface of 1919, were few in number and poor in scholarship. He set out to do something better, and his success can be gauged, not alone by the four editions and the many printings of* The American Language, *which with its two supplements grew from 374 into more than 2,500 pages, but also and perhaps best by the universal respect in which it is held and by the influence which it has had upon the study of American English.*

H. L. Mencken was not a trained linguist and never claimed to be one. Indeed, his formal education ended with his graduation from the Baltimore Polytechnic Institute, a public high school of high repute. Wisely fearing "the odium which attaches justly to those amateurs who 'because they speak, fancy they can speak about speech,'" he declared in the Preface to the fourth edition of The American Language *(1936) that, until trained scholars appear, "I can only go on accumulating materials and arranging them as plausibly as possible"—a task which he performed superbly. He was, however, mistaken in his belief that his "inquiries and surmises will probably be of small value" to future scholars.*

T HE AIM of this book is best exhibited by describing its origin. I am, and have been since early manhood, an editor of newspapers, magazines and books, and a critic of the last named. These occupations have forced me into a pretty wide familiarity with current literature, both periodical and within covers, and in particular into a familiarity with the current literature of England and America. It was part of my daily work, for a good many years, to read the principal English

The Preface is reprinted here from the first edition of *The American Language*, by H. L. Mencken, by permission of Alfred A. Knopf, Inc. Copyright 1919 by Alfred A. Knopf, Inc. Renewed 1947 by H. L. Mencken. The typescript of the Preface, in the collection of the Enoch Pratt Free Library of Baltimore, shows that Mencken made no significant revision in his manuscript save for the insertion of *spoken and* before *written* in the fifth sentence of the opening paragraph. The change indicates that he had become quite aware of the priority of speech over writing, a rather sophisticated concept in those days.

newspapers and reviews; it has been part of my work, all the time, to read the more important English novels, essays, poetry and criticism. An American born and bred, I early noted, as everyone else in like case must note, certain salient differences between the English of England and the English of America as practically spoken and written—differences in vocabulary, in syntax, in the shades and habits of idiom, and even, coming to the common speech, in grammar. And I noted too, of course, partly during visits to England but more largely by a somewhat wide and intimate intercourse with English people in the United States, the obvious differences between English and American pronunciation and intonation.

Greatly interested in these differences—some of them so great that they led me to seek exchanges of light with Englishmen—I looked for some work that would describe and account for them with a show of completeness, and perhaps depict the process of their origin. I soon found that no such work existed, either in England or in America—that the whole literature of the subject was astonishingly meagre and unsatisfactory. There were several dictionaries of Americanisms, true enough, but only one of them made any pretension to scientific method, and even that one was woefully narrow and incomplete. The one more general treatise, the work of a man foreign to both England and America in race and education, was more than 40 years old, and full of palpable errors. For the rest, there was only a fugitive and inconsequential literature—an almost useless mass of notes and essays, chiefly by the minor sort of pedagogues, seldom illuminating, save in small details, and often incredibly ignorant and inaccurate. On the large and important subject of American pronunciation, for example, I could find nothing save a few casual essays. On American spelling, with its wide and constantly visible divergencies from English usages, there was little more. On American grammar there was nothing whatever. Worse, an important part of the poor literature that I unearthed was devoted to absurd efforts to prove that no such thing as an American variety of English existed—that the differences I constantly encountered in English and that my English friends encountered in American were chiefly imaginary, and to be explained away by denying them.

Still intrigued by the subject, and in despair of getting any illumination from such theoretical masters of it, I began a collection of materials for my own information, and gradually it took on a rather formidable bulk. My interest in it being made known by various articles in the newspapers and magazines, I began also to receive contributions from other persons of the same fancy, both English and American, and gradually my collection fell into a certain order, and I saw the workings of general laws in what, at first, had appeared to be mere chaos. The present book then began to take form —its preparation a sort of recreation from other and far different labor. It is anything but an exhaustive treatise upon the subject; it is not even an exhaustive examination of the materials. All it pretends to do is to articulate some of those materials—to get some approach to order and coherence into them, and so pave the way for a better work by some more competent man. That work calls for the equipment of a first-rate philologist, which I am surely not. All I have done here is to stake out the field, sometimes borrowing suggestions from other inquirers and sometimes, as in the case of American grammar, attempting to run the lines myself.

That it should be regarded as an anti-social act to examine and exhibit the constantly growing differences between English and American, as certain American pedants argue sharply—this doctrine is quite beyond my understanding. All it indicates, stripped of sophistry, is a somewhat childish effort to gain the approval of Englishmen—a belated efflorescence of the colonial spirit, often commingled with fashionable aspiration. The plain fact is that the English themselves are not deceived, nor do they grant the approval so ardently sought for. On the contrary, they are keenly aware of the differences between the two dialects, and often discuss them, as the following pages show. Perhaps one dialect, in the long run, will defeat and absorb the other; if the two nations continue to be partners in great adventures it may very well happen. But even in that case, something may be accomplished by examining the differences which exist today. In some ways, as in intonation, English usage is plainly better than American. In others, as in spelling, American usage is as plainly better than English. But in order to develop usages that the people of both nations will accept it is obviously necessary to study the differences now visible. This study thus shows a certain utility. But its chief excuse is its human interest, for it prods deeply into national idiosyncrasies and ways of mind, and that sort of prodding is always entertaining.

I am thus neither teacher, nor prophet, nor reformer, but merely inquirer. The exigencies of my vocation make me almost completely bilingual; I can write English, as in this clause, quite as readily as American, as in this here one. Moreover, I have a hand for a compromise dialect which embodies the common materials of both, and is thus free from offense on both sides of the water—as befits the editor of a magazine published in both countries. But that compromise dialect is the living speech of neither. What I have tried to do here is to make a first sketch of the living speech of These States. The work is confessedly incomplete, and in places very painfully so, but in such enterprises a man must put an arbitrary term to his labors, lest some mischance, after years of diligence, take him from them too suddenly for them to be closed, and his laborious accumulations, as Ernest Walker says in his book on English surnames, be "doomed to the waste-basket by harassed executors."

If the opportunity offers in future I shall undoubtedly return to the subject. For one thing, I am eager to attempt a more scientific examination of the grammar of the American vulgar speech, here discussed briefly in Chapter VI. For another thing, I hope to make further inquiries into the subject of American surnames of non-English origin. Various other fields invite. No historical study of American pronunciation exists; the influence of German, Irish-English, Yiddish and other such immigrant dialects upon American has never been investigated; there is no adequate treatise on American geographical names. Contributions of materials and suggestions for a possible revised edition of the present book will reach me if addressed to me in care of the publisher at 220 West Forty-second Street, New York. I shall also be very grateful for the correction of errors, some perhaps typographical but others due to faulty information or mistaken judgment.

In conclusion I borrow a plea in confession and avoidance from Ben Jonson's pioneer grammar of English, published in incomplete form after his death. "We have set down," he said, "that that in our judgment agreeth best with reason and good order. Which notwithstanding, if it seem to any to be too rough hewed, let him plane it out more smoothly, and I shall not only not envy it, but in the behalf of my country most heartily thank him for so great a benefit; hoping that I shall be thought sufficiently to have done my part if in tolling this bell I may draw others to a deeper consideration of the matter; for, touching myself, I must needs confess that after much painful churning this only would come which here we have devised."

Baltimore, January 1, 1919.   MENCKEN.

☆

Mencken's opinions on language, like those he expressed on other subjects, have given rise to much comment and controversy. One wonders what he had in mind when he referred in the fourth paragraph of his Preface to British intonation as "plainly better" than American, or, for that matter, why he thought American spelling better than English, inasmuch as the differences affect comparatively few words. And one wonders also at an obtuseness not customary with him when in his fifth paragraph he contrasts the supposedly American "this here" with the supposedly British "this." What he is actually setting up for comparison in these examples is American folk usage with Standard English wherever spoken, which for no particularly good reason has always avoided "this here" used adjectivally. The fact is that "this here" is about as frequent in the nonstandard speech of England as in that of America, and the locution is condemned with equal vigor by schoolmasters and "marms" on both sides of the Atlantic. But Mencken's comparisons of humble American speech with Standard British English have been sufficiently stressed by other writers, to such an extent that he omitted from the fourth edition of his book "The Declaration of Independence in American" (beginning "When things get so balled up that the people of a country have got to cut loose from some other country, and go it on their own hook . . ."), even though he had plainly labeled this as a specimen of the American Vulgate.

Mencken was also to recant his faith, expressed in his first three editions, that "the American form of the English language was plainly departing from the parent stem"; instead, he had by 1936 come to the conclusion that British English was yielding to American example and that some of the differences which he had made so much of were beginning to disappear: British English would "on some not too remote tomorrow," he predicted, become "a kind of dialect of American"—which is, of course, about as fantastic as his earlier notion. (He doubtless had in mind only vocabulary items, like OK, blizzard, caucus, and a good many other terms of American origin which have indeed been naturalized in British English.) But these are venial errors to some extent forced upon Mencken by his title; later, when he would have preferred to change this title, it was too late. His faulty prognostications in no way lessened the influence of what was to all intents the earliest full-scale study of American English, ap-

pearing at a time when, as he implies in his Preface, there was little or no professional interest in the subject.

Since the publication of Mencken's work, the study of American English has gone on at a very lively rate, though Professor George Philip Krapp could say as late as 1925, in his English Language in America, *that "one may question whether even now the time is ripe for writing a history of the English language in America." There have nevertheless been a number of such attempts, with varying degrees of success. In addition, succeeding years have seen the publication of the first part of the monumental* Linguistic Atlas of the United States and Canada, A Dictionary of American English, *and* A Dictionary of Americanisms, *all works of the utmost importance in the study of American English.* American Speech, *the raciest of learned journals, was founded by Mencken, Kemp Malone, Louise Pound, and A. G. Kennedy in 1925. According to Professor Malone, "the idea was Mencken's." It has published scores of articles of the highest importance. The American Dialect Society, of which Mencken ultimately became a faithful member though he never contributed anything to its journal, continues to include the most distinguished linguistic scholars in the country.* Dialect Notes *is no longer published; its successor has since 1944 been called simply* Publication of the American Dialect Society.

In its investigations of its own speech America has in recent years been far more active than the Mother Country has been in studying its vernacular. Much, if not all, of this activity can be attributed to what was in effect Mencken's linguistic declaration of independence—his recognition that the English of America is not a corruption, but a development, of British English as it was brought to this country by the early settlers. In view of Mencken's frequent jibes at professors and institutions of higher learning—though some of his best friends were professors—it is not without irony that his own work helped make the study of American English academically respectable.

It is true that Noah Webster had long before asserted the independence of what he also miscalled "the American language." But Webster's motives were not untainted by a rather unpleasant form of jingoism and a desire to promote the sales of his own books. Moreover, his humorless, heavily magisterial manner terrorized the linguistically insecure and antagonized the secure. Though Webster did little that inspired investigation by others, he was able to bulldoze a good many people into believing that he had spoken the final word on the English language. His greatest achievement has turned

*out to be the indoctrination of a rigorously authoritarian atti-
tude toward language envincing itself in the phrase "according to Webster," which would have pleased self-righteous
old Noah no end.*

*Mencken, as we have seen, never thought that he knew all
the answers. He was never too proud to admit and correct his
mistakes. Furthermore, he was the master of as lively and
readable a style as this country has ever known, even though
its special brand of humor may have antagonized a great
many sour and serious people. Best of all, he was, despite his
satirical bent, a kindly and generous-hearted man, always interested in the encouragement of promising young people,
who in their turn found him enormously attractive. He reserved his thunder for charlatans and frauds, mainly for
those who played at being God.*

*The ideological drift since his day makes one hesitant to
predict any renascence of interest in H. L. Mencken as a writer, critic, and commentator on nonlinguistic American life.
But, even if he should be forgotten for everything else he
wrote, his* American Language *is sure to live on as a monument of American linguistic scholarship.*

Herbert Hoover

On American Individualism

1928

EDITED BY IRVIN G. WYLLIE

Carrying the fight to his opponent's home ground in the last days of the 1928 election campaign, Herbert Hoover invaded New York, the political stronghold of Alfred E. Smith. Hoover's task was to rally the New York business community through a review of Republican economic policy, and to discredit Smith by representing that his proposals in regard to public power and agriculture were dangerously socialistic. Persuaded that the United States was "being infected from the revolutionary caldrons of Europe," Hoover decided that the Republican Party should "draw the issue of the American system, as opposed to all forms of collectivism." Perhaps because they recalled that he had already developed this theme at some length in his book American Individualism *(1922), his campaign managers advised him that the subject was not of great public interest and that harping on it might carry liabilities. But Hoover, sincerely believing that the Democrats represented a threat from the left and that the voters were entitled to a statement of his views on the principles and ideals underlying the conduct of government, refused to be diverted. "I felt that this infection was around and I dealt with it definitely in an address in New York on October 22, 1928."*

Because radio always exposed him to the same national audience, Hoover felt that he needed ten days or two weeks between addresses in order to prepare something original. Altogether he invested two weeks in composing his Madison Square Garden address. He followed his usual custom of soliciting advice, suggestion, and criticism from colleagues, but from beginning to end the speech was his, written out "with my own hand." Hoover boasted that he had "never delivered a ghost-written public statement of importance," and that he had handwritten drafts of every major speech to prove it.

He could have used a ghost speaker at Madison Square Garden, where an enthusiastic crowd of 22,000, including 3,000 standees, assembled to hear him. Their enthusiasm barely survived his arrival. An eyewitness reported that an enlarged picture of the candidate, dominating the sports arena, conveyed an image "much more cheerful and jolly than that which sat upon his countenance when he appeared." Grim and unresponsive, he waited through four minutes of a tumultuous greeting before raising a hand and forcing a smile. At 9:08 P.M. he began reading in a low, rapid voice, blurring many words. He made no gestures, rarely looked up from his text, even on the few occasions when he was interrupted by applause. Having responded with hand and voice, the audience now responded with feet. Within half an hour after Hoover began, the standees had vanished and empty benches could be seen in the top gallery. Hoover, aware of the shuffling feet, increased his reading speed. When he finished at 10:03 P.M., at least 5,000 of his original audience had slipped away. Though he felt deeply about the principles he had expounded, he had been unable to stir his listeners, owing to his personal remoteness and tedious forensic style. A reporter for the Christian Science Monitor, sensing the significance of his central theme, put the best face on Hoover's performance when he described his language and delivery as those of "a learned teacher expounding to a gathering of other learned men and women the tenets of a great theme, a mighty project."

THIS CAMPAIGN now draws near a close. The platforms of the two parties defining principles and offering solutions of various national problems have been presented and are being earnestly considered by our people.

After four months' debate it is not the Republican Party which finds reason for abandonment of any of the principles it has laid down or of the views it has expressed for solution of the problems before the country. The principles to which it adheres are rooted deeply in the foundations of our national life. The solutions which it proposes are based on experience with government and on a consciousness that it may have the responsibility for placing those solutions in action.

In my acceptance speech I endeavored to outline the spirit and ideals by which I would be guided in carrying that platform into administration. Tonight, I will not deal with the multitude of issues which have been already well canvassed. I intend rather to discuss some of those more fundamental principles and ideals upon which I believe the government of the United States should be conducted.

RECENT PROGRESS AS THE EFFECT OF REPUBLICAN POLICIES

The Republican Party has ever been a party of progress. I do not need to review its seventy years of constructive history. It has always reflected the spirit of the American people. Never has it done more for the advancement of fundamental progress than during the past seven and one-half years since we took over the government amidst the ruin left by war.

It detracts nothing from the character and energy of the American people, it minimizes in no degree the quality of their accomplishments to say that the policies of the Republican Party have played a large part in recuperation from the war and the building of the magnificent progress which shows upon every hand today. I say with emphasis that without the wise policies which the Republican Party has brought into action during this period, no such progress would have been possible.

CONFIDENCE RESTORED

The first responsibility of the Republican administration was to renew the march of progress from its collapse by the war. That task involved the restoration of confidence in the future and the liberation and stimulation of the constructive energies of our people. It discharged that task. There is not a person within the sound of my voice who does not know the

Hoover entitled his speech "New York City." The text as reprinted here appeared in *The New Day: Campaign Speeches of Herbert Hoover, 1928* (Stanford University, Calif.: Stanford University Press, 1928), pp. 149–76.

profound progress which our country has made in this period. Every man and woman knows that American comfort, hope, and confidence for the future are immeasurably higher this day than they were seven and one-half years ago.

CONSTRUCTIVE MEASURES ADOPTED

It is not my purpose to enter upon a detailed recital of the great constructive measures of the past seven and one-half years by which this has been brought about. It is sufficient to remind you of the restoration of employment to the millions who walked your streets in idleness; to remind you of the creation of the budget system; the reduction of six billions of national debt which gave the powerful impulse of that vast sum returned to industry and commerce; the four sequent reductions of taxes and thereby the lift to the living of every family; the enactment of adequate protective tariff and immigration laws which have safeguarded our workers and farmers from floods of goods and labor from foreign countries; the creation of credit facilities and many other aids to agriculture; the building up of foreign trade; the care of veterans; the development of aviation, of radio, of our inland waterways, of our highways; the expansion of scientific research, of welfare activities; the making of safer highways, safer mines, better homes; the spread of outdoor recreation; the improvement in public health and the care of children; and a score of other progressive actions.

DELICACY OF THE TASK

Nor do I need to remind you that government today deals with an economic and social system vastly more intricate and delicately adjusted than ever before. That system now must be kept in perfect tune if we would maintain uninterrupted employment and the high standards of living of our people. The government has come to touch this delicate web at a thousand points. Yearly the relations of government to national prosperity become more and more intimate. Only through keen vision and helpful co-operation by the government has stability in business and stability in employment been maintained during this past seven and one-half years. There always are some localities, some industries, and some individuals who do not share the prevailing prosperity. The task of government is to lessen these inequalities.

Never has there been a period when the Federal Government has given such aid and impulse to the progress of our people, not alone to economic progress but to the development of those agencies which make for moral and spiritual progress.

THE AMERICAN SYSTEM

But in addition to this great record of contributions of the Republican Party to progress, there has been a further fundamental contribution—a contribution underlying and sustaining all the others—and that is the resistance of the Republican Party to every attempt to inject the government into business in competition with its citizens.

After the war, when the Republican Party assumed administration of the country, we were faced with the problem of determination of the very nature of our national life. During one hundred and fifty years we have builded up a form of self-government and a social system which is peculiarly our own. It differs essentially from all others in the world. It is the American system. It is just as definite and positive a political and social system as has ever been developed on earth. It is founded upon a particular conception of self-government in which decentralized local responsibility is the very base. Further than this, it is founded upon the conception that only through ordered liberty, freedom, and equal opportunity to the individual will his initiative and enterprise spur on the march of progress. And in our insistence upon equality of opportunity has our system advanced beyond all the world.

SUSPENDED BY THE WAR

During the war we necessarily turned to the government to solve every difficult economic problem. The government having absorbed every energy of our people for war, there was no other solution. For the preservation of the state the Federal Government became a centralized despotism which undertook unprecedented responsibilities, assumed autocratic powers, and took over the business of citizens. To a large degree we regimented our whole people temporarily into a socialistic state. However justified in time of war, if continued in peacetime it would destroy not only our American system but with it our progress and freedom as well.

When the war closed, the most vital of all issues both in our own country and throughout the world was whether governments should continue their war-time ownership and operation of many instrumentalities of production and distribution. We were challenged with a peace-time choice between the American system of rugged individualism and a European philosophy of diametrically opposed doctrines—doctrines of paternalism and state socialism. The acceptance of these ideas would have meant the destruction of self-government through centralization of government. It would have meant the undermining of the individual initiative and enterprise through which our people have grown to unparalleled greatness.

RESTORED UNDER REPUBLICAN DIRECTION

The Republican Party from the beginning resolutely turned its face away from these ideas and these war practices. A Republican Congress co-operated with the Democratic administration to demobilize many of our war activities. At that time the two parties were in accord upon that point. When the Republican Party came into full power it went at once resolutely back to our fundamental conception of the state and the rights and responsibilities of the individual. Thereby it restored confidence and hope in the American people, it freed and stimulated enterprise, it restored the government to its position as an umpire instead of a player in the economic game. For these reasons the American people have gone forward in progress while the rest of the world has halted, and some countries have even gone backward. If anyone will study the causes of retarded recuperation in Europe, he will find much of it due to stifling of private initiative on one hand, and overloading of the government with business on the other.

PROPOSALS NOW MENACING THIS SYSTEM

There has been revived in this campaign, however, a series of proposals which, if adopted, would be a long step toward the abandonment of our American system and a surrender to the destructive operation of governmental conduct of commercial business. Because the country is faced with difficulty and doubt over certain national problems—that is, prohibition, farm relief, and electrical power—our opponents propose that we must thrust government a long way into the businesses which give rise to these problems. In effect, they abandon the tenets of their own party and turn to state socialism as a solution for the difficulties presented by all three. It is proposed that we shall change from prohibition to the state purchase and sale of liquor. If their agricultural relief program means anything, it means that the government shall directly or indirectly buy and sell and fix prices of agricultural products. And we are to go into the hydro-electric power business. In other words, we are confronted with a huge program of government in business.

There is, therefore, submitted to the American people a question of fundamental principle. That is: shall we depart from the principles of our American political and economic system, upon which we have advanced beyond all the rest of the world, in order to adopt methods based on principles destructive of its very foundations? And I wish to emphasize the seriousness of these proposals. I wish to make my position clear; for this goes to the very roots of American life and progress.

CENTRALIZATION FATAL TO SELF-GOVERNMENT

I should like to state to you the effect that this projection of government in business would have upon our system of self-government and our economic system. That effect would reach to the daily life of every man and woman. It would impair the very basis of liberty and freedom not only for those left outside the fold of expanded bureaucracy but for those embraced within it.

Let us first see the effect upon self-government. When the Federal Government undertakes to go into commercial business it must at once set up the organization and administration of that business, and it immediately finds itself in a labyrinth, every alley of which leads to the destruction of self-government.

Commercial business requires a concentration of responsibility. Self-government requires decentralization and many checks and balances to safeguard liberty. Our government to succeed in business would need become in effect a despotism. There at once begins the destruction of self-government.

UNWISDOM OF GOVERNMENT IN BUSINESS

The first problem of the government about to adventure in commercial business is to determine a method of administration. It must secure leadership and direction. Shall this leadership be chosen by political agencies or shall we make it elective? The hard practical fact is that leadership in business must come through the sheer rise in ability and character. That rise can only take place in the free atmosphere of competition. Competition is closed by bureaucracy. Political agencies are feeble channels through which to select able leaders to conduct commercial business.

Government, in order to avoid the possible incompetence, corruption, and tyranny of too great authority in individuals entrusted with commercial business, inevitably turns to boards and commissions. To make sure that there are checks and balances, each member of such boards and commissions must have equal authority. Each has his separate responsibility to the public, and at once we have the conflict of ideas and the lack of decision which would ruin any commercial business. It has contributed greatly to the demoralization of our shipping business. Moreover, these commissions must be representative of different sections and different political parties, so that at once we have an entire blight upon co-ordinated action within their ranks which destroys any possibility of effective administration.

Moreover, our legislative bodies cannot in fact delegate their full authority to commissions or to individuals for the conduct of matters vital to the American people; for if we would preserve government by the people we must preserve the authority of our legislators in the activities of our government.

Thus every time the Federal Government goes into a commercial business, five hundred and thirty-one Senators and Congressmen become the actual board of directors of that business. Every time a state government goes into business one or two hundred state senators and legislators become the actual directors of that business. Even if they were supermen and if there were no politics in the United States, no body of such numbers could competently direct commercial activities; for that requires initiative, instant decision, and action. It took Congress six years of constant discussion to even decide what the method of administration of Muscle Shoals should be.

When the Federal Government undertakes to go into business, the state governments are at once deprived of control and taxation of that business; when a state government undertakes to go into business, it at once deprives the municipalities of taxation and control of that business. Municipalities, being local and close to the people, can, at times, succeed in business where federal and state governments must fail. We have trouble enough with log-rolling in legislative bodies today. It originates naturally from desires of citizens to advance their particular section or to secure some necessary service. It would be multiplied a thousandfold were the federal and state governments in these businesses.

The effect upon our economic progress would be even worse. Business progressiveness is dependent on competition. New methods and new ideas are the outgrowth of the spirit of adventure, of individual initiative, and of individual enterprise. Without adventure there is no progress. No government administration can rightly take chances with taxpayers' money.

There is no better example of the practical incompetence of government to conduct business than the history of our railways. During the war the government found it necessary to operate the railways. That operation continued until after the war. In the year before being freed from government operation they were not able to meet the demands for transportation. Eight years later we find them under private enterprise transporting fifteen per cent more goods and meeting every demand for service. Rates have been reduced by fifteen per cent and net earnings increased from less than one per cent on their valuation to about five per cent. Wages of employees have improved by thirteen per cent. The wages of railway employees are today one hundred and twenty-one per cent above pre-war, while the wages of government employees are today only sixty-five per cent above pre-war. That should be a sufficient commentary upon the efficiency of government operation.

DANGERS OF BUREAUCRACY

Let us now examine this question from the point of view of the person who may get a government job and is admitted into the new bureaucracy. Upon that subject let me quote from a speech of that great leader of labor, Samuel Gompers, delivered in Montreal in 1920, a few years before his death. He said:

> I believe there is no man to whom I would take second position in my loyalty to the Republic of the United States, and yet I would not give it more power over the individual citizenship of our country. . . .
> It is a question of whether it shall be government ownership or private ownership under control. . . . If I were in the minority of one in this convention, I would want to cast my vote so that the men of labor shall not willingly enslave themselves to government authority in their industrial effort for freedom. . . .
> Let the future tell the story of who is right or who is wrong; who has stood for freedom and who has been willing to submit their fate industrially to the government.

I would amplify Mr. Gompers' statement. The great body of government employees which would be created by the proposals of our opponents would either comprise a political machine at the disposal of the party in power, or, alternatively, to prevent this, the government by stringent civil-service rules must debar its employees from their full political rights as free men. It must limit them in the liberty to bargain for their own wages, for no government employee can strike against his government and thus against the whole people. It makes a legislative body with all its political currents their final employer and master. Their bargaining does not rest upon economic need or economic strength but on political potence.

But what of those who are outside the bureaucracy? What is the effect upon their lives?

The area of enterprise and opportunity for them to strive and rise is at once limited.

The government in commercial business does not tolerate amongst its customers the freedom of competitive reprisals to which private business is subject. Bureaucracy does not tolerate the spirit of independence; it spreads the spirit of submission into our daily life and penetrates the temper of our people not with the habit of powerful resistance to wrong but with the habit of timid acceptance of irresistible might.

FATAL TO TRUE LIBERALISM

Bureaucracy is ever desirous of spreading its influence and its power. You cannot extend the mastery of the government over the daily working life of a people without at the same time making it the master of the people's souls and thoughts. Every expansion of government in business means that government in order to protect itself from the political consequences of its errors and wrongs is driven irresistibly without peace to greater and greater control of the nation's press and platform. Free speech does not live many hours after free industry and free commerce die.

It is a false liberalism that interprets itself into the government operation of commercial business. Every step of bureaucratizing of the business of our country poisons the very roots of liberalism—that is, political equality, free speech, free assembly, free press, and equality of opportunity. It is the road not to more liberty, but to less liberty. Liberalism should be found not striving to spread bureaucracy but striving to set bounds to it. True liberalism seeks all legitimate freedom first in the confident belief that without such freedom the pursuit of all other blessings and benefits is vain. That belief is the foundation of all American progress, political as well as economic.

Liberalism is a force truly of the spirit, a force proceeding from the deep realization that economic freedom cannot be sacrificed if political freedom is to be preserved. Even if governmental conduct of business could give us more efficiency instead of less efficiency, the fundamental objection to it would remain unaltered and unabated. It would destroy political equality. It would increase rather than decrease abuse and corruption. It would stifle initiative and invention. It would undermine the development of leadership. It would cramp and cripple the mental and spiritual energies of our people. It would extinguish equality and opportunity. It would dry up the spirit of liberty and progress. For these reasons primarily it must be resisted. For a hundred and fifty years liberalism has found its true spirit in the American system, not in the European systems.

FLEXIBILITY OF THE AMERICAN SYSTEM

I do not wish to be misunderstood in this statement. I am defining a general policy. It does not mean that our government is to part with one iota of its national resources without complete protection to the public interest. I have already stated that where the government is engaged in public works for purposes of flood control, of navigation, of irrigation, of scientific research or national defense, or in pioneering a new art, it will at times necessarily produce power or commodities as a by-product. But they must be a by-product of the major purpose, not the major purpose itself.

Nor do I wish to be misinterpreted as believing that the United States is free-for-all and devil-take-the-hindmost. The very essence of equality of opportunity and of American individualism is that there shall be no domination by any group or combination in this republic, whether it be business or political. On the contrary, it demands economic justice as well as political and social justice. It is no system of laissez faire.

I feel deeply on this subject because during the war I had some practical experience with governmental operation and control. I have witnessed not only at home but abroad the many failures of government in business. I have seen its tyrannies, its injustices, its destructions of self-government, its undermining of the very instincts which carry our people forward to progress. I have witnessed the lack of advance, the lowered standards of living, the depressed spirits of people working under such a system. My objection is based not upon theory or upon a failure to recognize wrong or abuse, but I know the adoption of such methods would strike at the very roots of American life and would destroy the very basis of American progress.

Our people have the right to know whether we can continue to solve our great problems without abandonment of our American system. I know we can. We have demonstrated that our system is responsive enough to meet any new and intricate development in our economic and business life. We have demonstrated that we can meet any economic problem and still maintain our democracy as master in its own house, and that we can at the same time preserve equality of opportunity and individual freedom.

PRACTICABILITY OF REGULATION

In the last fifty years we have discovered that mass production will produce articles for us at half the cost they required previously. We have seen the resultant growth of large units of production and distribution. This is big business. Many businesses must be bigger, for our tools are bigger, our country is bigger. We now build a single dynamo of a hundred thousand horsepower. Even fifteen years ago that would have been a big business all by itself. Yet today advance in production requires that we set ten of these units together in a row.

The American people from bitter experience have a rightful fear that great business units might be used to dominate our industrial life and by illegal and unethical practices destroy equality of opportunity.

Years ago the Republican administration established the principle that such evils could be corrected by regulation. It developed methods by which abuses could be prevented while the full value of industrial progress could be retained for the public. It insisted upon the principle that when great public utilities were clothed with the security of partial monopoly, whether it be railways, power plants, telephones, or what not, then there must be the fullest and most complete control of rates, services, and finances by government or local agencies. It declared that these businesses must be conducted with glass pockets.

As to our great manufacturing and distributing industries, the Republican Party insisted upon the enactment of laws that not only would maintain competition but would destroy conspiracies to destroy the smaller units or dominate and limit the equality of opportunity amongst our people.

One of the great problems of government is to determine to what extent the government shall regulate and control commerce and industry and how much it shall leave it alone. No system is perfect. We have had many abuses in the private conduct of business. That every good citizen resents. It is just as important that business keep out of government as that government keep out of business.

Nor am I setting up the contention that our institutions are perfect. No human ideal is ever perfectly attained, since humanity itself is not perfect.

The wisdom of our forefathers in their conception that progress can only be attained as the sum of the accomplishment of free individuals has been reinforced by all of the great leaders of the country since that day. Jackson, Lincoln, Cleveland, McKinley, Roosevelt, Wilson, and Coolidge have stood unalterably for these principles.

EFFECTIVENESS OF THE AMERICAN SYSTEM

And what have been the results of our American system? Our country has become the land of opportunity to those born without inheritance, not merely because of the wealth of its resources and industry but because of this freedom of initiative and enterprise. Russia has natural resources equal to ours. Her people are equally industrious, but she has not had the blessings of one hundred and fifty years of our form of government and of our social system.

By adherence to the principles of decentralized self-government, ordered liberty, equal opportunity, and freedom to the individual, our American experiment in human welfare has yielded a degree of well-being unparalleled in the world. It has come nearer to the abolition of poverty, to the abolition of fear of want, than humanity has ever reached before. Progress of the past seven years is the proof of it. This alone furnishes the answer to our opponents, who ask us to introduce destructive elements into the system by which this has been accomplished.

Let us see what this system has done for us in our recent years of difficult and trying reconstruction and then solemnly ask ourselves if we now wish to abandon it.

POST-WAR RECOVERY

As a nation we came out of the war with great losses. We made no profits from it. The apparent increases in wages were at that time fictitious. We were poorer as a nation when we emerged from the war. Yet during these last eight years we have recovered from these losses and increased our national income by over one-third, even if we discount the inflation of the dollar. That there has been a wide diffusion of our gain in wealth and income is marked by a hundred proofs. I know of no better test of the improved conditions of the average family than the combined increase in assets of life and industrial insurance, building and loan associations, and savings deposits. These are the savings banks of the average man. These agencies alone have in seven years increased by nearly one hundred per cent to the gigantic sum of over fifty billions of dollars, or nearly one-sixth of our whole national wealth. We have increased in home ownership, we have expanded the investments of the average man.

HIGHER STANDARDS OF LIVING

In addition to these evidences of larger savings, our people are steadily increasing their spending for higher standards of living. Today there are almost nine automobiles for each ten families, where seven and one-half years ago only enough automobiles were running to average less than four for each ten families. The slogan of progress is changing from the full dinner pail to the full garage. Our people have more to eat, better things to wear, and better homes. We have even gained in elbow room, for the increase of residential floor space is over twenty-five per cent, with less than ten per cent increase in our number of people. Wages have increased, the cost of living has decreased. The job of every man and woman has been made more secure. We have in this short period decreased the fear of poverty, the fear of unemployment, the fear of old age; and these are fears that are the greatest calamities of humankind.

All this progress means far more than increased creature comforts. It finds a thousand interpretations into a greater and fuller life. A score of new helps save the drudgery of the home. In seven years we have added seventy per cent to the electric power at the elbows of our workers and further promoted them from carriers of burdens to directors of machines. We have steadily reduced the sweat in human labor. Our hours of labor are lessened; our leisure has increased. We have expanded our parks and playgrounds. We have nearly doubled our attendance at games. We pour into outdoor recreation in every direction. The visitors at our national parks have trebled and we have so increased the number of sportsmen fishing in our streams and lakes that the longer time between bites is becoming a political issue. In these seven and one-half years the radio has brought music and laughter, education and political discussion to almost every fireside.

Springing from our prosperity with its greater freedom, its vast endowment of scientific research, and the greater resources with which to care for public health, we have according to our insurance actuaries during this short period since the war lengthened the average span of life by nearly eight years. We have reduced infant mortality, we have vastly decreased the days of illness and suffering in the life of every man and woman. We have improved the facilities for the care of the crippled and helpless and deranged.

EDUCATIONAL PROGRESS

From our increasing resources we have expanded our educational system in eight years from an outlay of twelve hundred millions to twenty-seven hundred millions of dollars. The education of our youth has become almost our largest and certainly our most important activity. From our greater income and thus our ability to free youth from toil we have increased the attendance in our grade schools by fourteen per cent, in our high schools by eighty per cent, and in our institutions of higher learning by ninety-five per cent. Today we have more youth in these institutions of higher learning twice over than all the rest of the world put together. We have made notable progress in literature, in art, and in public taste.

We have made progress in the leadership of every branch of American life. Never in our history was the leadership in our economic life more distinguished in its abilities than today, and it has grown greatly in its consciousness of public responsibility. Leadership in our professions and in moral and spiritual affairs of our country was never of a higher order. And our magnificent educational system is bringing forward a host of recruits for the succession to this leadership.

I do not need to recite more figures and more evidence. I cannot believe that the American people wish to abandon or in any way to weaken the principles of economic freedom and self-government which have been maintained by the Republican Party and which have produced results so amazing and so stimulating to the spiritual as well as to the material advance of the nation.

SIGNIFICANCE TO NEW YORK CITY

Your city has been an outstanding beneficiary of this great progress and of these safeguarded principles. With its suburbs it has, during the last seven and one-half years, grown by over a million and a half of people until it has become the largest metropolitan district of all the world. Here you have made abundant opportunity not only for the youth of the land but for the immigrant from foreign shores. This city is the commercial center of the United States. It is the commercial agent of the American people. It is a great organism of specialized skill and leadership in finance, industry, and commerce which reaches every spot in our country. Its progress and its beauty are the pride of the whole American people. It leads our nation in its benevolences to charity, to education, and to scientific research. It is the center of art, music, literature, and drama. It has come to have a more potent voice than any other city in the United States.

But when all is said and done, the very life, progress, and prosperity of this city is wholly dependent on the prosperity of the 115,000,000 people who dwell in our mountains and valleys across the three thousand miles to the Pacific Ocean. Every activity of this city is sensitive to every evil and every favorable tide that sweeps this great nation of ours. Be there a slackening of industry in any place, it affects New York far more than any other part of the country. In a time of depression one-quarter of all the unemployed in the United States can be numbered in this city. In a time of prosperity the citizens of the great interior of our country pour into your city for business and entertainment at the rate of one hundred and fifty thousand a day. In fact, so much is this city the reflex of the varied interests of our country that the concern of every one of your citizens for national stability, for national prosperity, for national progress, for preservation of our American system is far greater than that of any other single part of our country.

UNFINISHED TASKS

We still have great problems if we would achieve the full economic advancement of our country. In these past few years some groups in our country have lagged behind others in the march of progress. I refer more particularly to those engaged in the textile, coal, and agricultural industries. We can assist in solving these problems by co-operation of our government. To the agricultural industry we shall need to advance initial capital to assist them to stabilize their industry. But this proposal implies that they shall conduct it themselves, and not the government. It is in the interest of our cities that we shall bring agriculture and all industries into full stability and prosperity. I know you will gladly co-operate in the faith that in the common prosperity of our country lies its future.

In bringing this address to a conclusion I should like to restate to you some of the fundamental things I have endeavored to bring out.

THE COMING DECISION FUNDAMENTAL

The foundations of progress and prosperity are dependent as never before upon the wise policies of government, for government now touches at a thousand points the intricate web of economic and social life.

Under administration by the Republican Party in the last seven and one-half years our country as a whole has made unparalleled progress and this has been in generous part reflected to this great city. Prosperity is no idle expression. It is a job for every worker; it is the safety and the safeguard of every business and every home. A continuation of the policies of the Republican Party is fundamentally necessary to the further advancement of this progress and to the further building up of this prosperity.

I have dwelt at some length on the principles of relationship between the government and business. I make no apologies for dealing with this subject. The first necessity of any nation is the smooth functioning of the vast business machinery for employment, feeding, clothing, housing, and providing luxuries and comforts to a people. Unless these basic elements are properly organized and function, there can be no progress in business, in education, literature, music, or art. There can be no advance in the fundamental ideals of a people. A people cannot make progress in poverty.

I have endeavored to present to you that the greatness of America has grown out of a political and social system and a method of control of economic forces distinctly its own—our American system—which has carried this great experiment in human welfare farther than ever before in all history. We are nearer today to the ideal of the abolition of poverty and fear from the lives of men and women than ever before in any land. And I again repeat that the departure from our American system by injecting principles destructive to it which our opponents propose will jeopardize the very liberty and freedom of our people, will destroy equality of opportunity not alone to ourselves but to our children.

THE NEW DAY

To me the foundation of American life rests upon the home and the family. I read into these great economic forces, these intricate and delicate relations of the government with business and with our political and social life, but one supreme end—that we reinforce the ties that bind together the millions of our families, that we strengthen the security, the happiness, and the independence of every home.

My conception of America is a land where men and women may walk in ordered freedom in the independent conduct of their occupations; where they may enjoy the advantages of wealth, not concentrated in the hands of the few but spread through the lives of all; where they build and safeguard their homes, and give to their children the fullest advantages and opportunities of American life; where every man shall be respected in the faith that his conscience and his heart direct him to follow; where a contented and happy people, secure in their liberties, free from poverty and fear, shall have the leisure and impulse to seek a fuller life.

Some may ask where all this may lead beyond mere material progress. It leads to a release of the energies of men and women from the dull drudgery of life to a wider vision and a higher hope. It leads to the opportunity for greater and greater service, not alone from man to man in our own land, but from our country to the whole world. It leads to an America, healthy in body, healthy in spirit, unfettered, youthful, eager—with a vision searching beyond the farthest horizons, with an open mind, sympathetic and generous. It is to these higher ideals and for these purposes that I pledge myself and the Republican Party.

The immediate effect of Hoover's delineation of American and un-American social principles was to harden partisan political sentiment. Senator George Norris of Nebraska, a Republican liberal and an advocate of public power, was so deeply offended that he declared immediately for Al Smith. "How any progressive in the United States can support him now, after his Madison Square Garden address . . . my God, I cannot conceive it," Norris asserted. Al Smith, stung by the socialism charge, answered two days later in Boston, declaring that Hoover had confused democratic social action with socialism. For a quarter of a century Republicans had opposed every measure for human betterment with the cry of socialism, with the result that "the people of the state of New York are sick and tired of listening to it." Franklin D. Roosevelt, campaigning to succeed Smith as governor, declared that if Smith was a socialist under Hoover's definition, he would declare himself to be one too. Democratic newspapers generally saw nothing but low partisanship in Hoover's highsounding statement of principles. The Nashville Tennessean

assailed him for knocking over a straw man, while the Birmingham Age-Herald *dismissed the speech as "a diffuse dissertation on the horrors of state socialism," deriving from "warmed-over recollections of Leland Stanford courses in economics of the year '95." The* Atlanta Constitution *accused Hoover of trying to "out Hamilton Hamilton," and of naively claiming that the Republican Party was responsible for all progress, even in the arts and sciences, since March 4, 1921.*

Republicans received Hoover's message as divine revelation, a reliable catechism of political faith. The Chicago Daily Tribune *hailed it as one of the most important utterances by any public man in a generation. The* Camden Courier Post *praised the address for exposing the antidemocratic character of Democratic liberalism: "Herbert Hoover is the true liberal candidate in this campaign." Many other Republican newspapers also proclaimed their enthusiasm for Hoover's creed, calling it progressive but not radical, conservative but not reactionary. The* New York Herald Tribune *said the speech was profoundly constructive—an aid to progress, prosperity, and the cause of human liberty. The same newspaper also hailed the shift in betting odds following the speech; though less elevating than Hoover's sentiments, the bookmakers' reports were very gratifying. Wall Street betting brokers, who had previously quoted 6 to 5 odds on Smith to carry New York, kept the same odds, but now put Hoover on top.*

After he became President, Hoover did much to guarantee that his Madison Square Garden address would have a partisan afterlife. He used it as a test for legislation, as in the case of the Muscle Shoals Bill of 1931, "to which piece of socialism I would not agree." He also used it to justify his limited response to mass unemployment, agricultural overproduction, bank failure, industrial collapse, and other problems of the depression years. It served as a ready defense for his unchanging view that the federal government's proper role was that of "umpire instead of a player in the economic game." After accepting the Republican presidential nomination in 1932, Hoover refurbished the old theme that the election was more than a contest between parties and men. "It is a contest between two philosophies of government." Returning to Madison Square Garden on October 31, 1932, he got additional mileage out of many of the arguments, ideas, and phrases that he had uttered there four years before. Later he attacked the economic planning of the New Deal which, in his view, involved "the pouring of a mixture of socialism and fascism into the American system." Whenever he returned to the po-

litical wars in the 1930's, he warned the people that the economic interventions of the New Dealers were "more dangerous to free men than the depression itself." In his Memoirs, published in 1951–52, he quoted extensively from his 1928 address, for the instruction and benefit of posterity. "While campaign statements are of no great romantic interest," he declared, "the historian gleans something of economics, ideologies, and politics from them."

As Hoover and other partisans of his generation have passed from the political scene in recent years, it has been possible to view his first Madison Square Garden address as a serious and responsible analysis of the difficulty of preserving human liberty, guaranteeing equality of opportunity, and providing incentives to progress in societies in which government assumes the dominant role. The follies, failures, and crimes of modern totalitarian states have undermined blind faith in state action as the cure for every social ill, and underscored the propriety of concern for the welfare of the individual man, as against collective mankind. Only recently have Americans begun to acquire the comparative knowledge of the world that Hoover already possessed when he phrased his 1928 statement of faith. As an international businessman and American public servant, he had observed at first hand the operations of the managed economy. "I have seen its tyrannies, its injustices, its destructions of self-government, its undermining of the very instincts which carry our people forward to progress." Convinced by his experience abroad that America owed its distinctive character to individualism as a principle of social action, he became an unashamed individualist. His faith in American individualism was "confirmed and deepened by the searching experiences of seven years of service in the backwash and misery of war." Changing times have invested Hoover's utterances with a wisdom and credibility that they appeared to lack in 1928. The troubles of the contemporary world have helped to transform his originally partisan formulation into an appealing testimony to the American faith.

Sinclair Lewis

The American Fear of Literature

1930

EDITED BY MARK SCHORER

On November 5, 1930, Sinclair Lewis learned that he was the first American to win the Nobel Prize in Literature. The announcement brought on a storm of criticism from many of Lewis' American colleagues, none of it so bitter as that of the more conservative members of the American Academy of Arts and Letters, especially of that renowned protector of cultural gentility, the Reverend Henry Van Dyke. It is, in fact, a public utterance by Van Dyke that helps us date and place the composition of the address that Lewis was presently to deliver in Stockholm.

On the back of a telegram that he received on November 26, Lewis jotted down some random notes for that address, notes which indicate that up to this point he had prepared no text. On November 28, in a luncheon address delivered before a group of businessmen in Germantown, Pennsylvania, Van Dyke took occasion to remark that the award to Sinclair Lewis was an insult to the United States. "It shows," he declared, "the Swedish Academy knows nothing of the English language. They handed Lewis a bouquet, but they have given America a very backhanded compliment." Once, he continued,

Americans were taught to honor traditions; today they only scoffed at them. Sinclair Lewis was among the great scoffers, and novels like Main Street *and* Elmer Gantry *bore no relation to the best in American writing.*

On the next day, November 29, Lewis was to sail for Sweden on the Drottningholm. *When he was interviewed on shipboard and asked to comment on Van Dyke's remarks, his face clouded, he hesitated, and then, almost as if his speech were at that moment taking shape in his mind, he said, "What can I say? Nothing. If I were to say what I think it would burn up the paper. . . . I am honored no less that American colleagues have attacked my work, and I am particularly honored that the attack came from where it did." The academicians might have been warned by the very restraint of those remarks.*

The address was written during the long winter passage to Sweden on the Drottningholm. *Arriving in Stockholm on the afternoon of December 9, Lewis cabled his publisher, Alfred Harcourt, on December 10 as follows:*

HAVE YOU ARRANGED FOR PUBLICATION FULL TEXT MY ADDRESS NOBEL COMMITTEE NEXT FRIDAY. IF SO WHERE WHEN. OTHERWISE PLEASE TRY GET SUNDAY SECTIONS TIMES OR HERALD TRIBUNE. SPEECH AS IT WILL BE REPORTED PRESS CERTAIN CAUSE REPERCUSSIONS AND VERY IMPORTANT EXACT TEXT APPEARS SOMEWHERE AMERICA.

On that afternoon Lewis received his award. On the afternoon of December 12 he delivered his address and took his revenge: the American Academy and Henry Van Dyke had provided him not only with his theme but with his motive.

The entire address was cabled to the United States and, following what he presumed to be his author's wishes, Alfred Harcourt rushed the newspaper text into print, together with the ceremonial presentation remarks of Erik Axel Karfeldt, the permanent secretary of the Swedish Academy; the two speeches were bound into a small pamphlet with the title Why Sinclair Lewis Got the Nobel Prize. *But unfortunately the cablese was full of errors, a few of them rather appalling. Of the edition of 3,000 copies, it was possible to destroy 2,000, but 1,000 had been distributed and copies can still be come across today.*

In London now, Lewis corrected his own text in two copies and appended a footnote to Dr. Karlfeldt's, thus correcting that gentleman's notions about sewage disposal in the United States, and on February 18, 1931, he sent one of these cor-

rected copies to Donald Brace, Harcourt's partner, and explained that if he had added remarks, he had added them
when he delivered the address as well. The corrected pamphlet was published by Harcourt, Brace and Company in an
edition of 2,000 copies on April 2, 1931.

Six years later—two years after he had been inducted into
the National Institute of Arts and Letters—Lewis moved
into the parent body, the once-offensive American Academy
of Arts and Letters.

MEMBERS OF THE SWEDISH ACADEMY; LADIES AND GENTLEMEN

WERE I to express my feeling of honor and pleasure of
having been awarded the Nobel Prize in Literature, I
should be fulsome and perhaps tedious, and I present my
gratitude with a plain "Thank you."

I wish, in this address, to consider certain trends, certain
dangers, and certain high and exciting promises in present-
day American literature. To discuss this with complete and
unguarded frankness—and I should not insult you by being
otherwise than completely honest, however indiscreet—it will
be necessary for me to be a little impolite regarding certain
institutions and persons of my own greatly beloved land.

But I beg of you to believe that I am in no case gratifying
a grudge. Fortune has dealt with me rather too well. I have
known little struggle, not much poverty, many generosities.
Now and then I have, for my books or myself, been somewhat warmly denounced—there was one good pastor in California who upon reading my *Elmer Gantry* desired to lead a
mob and lynch me, while another holy man in the State of
Maine wondered if there was no respectable and righteous
way of putting me in jail. And, much harder to endure than
any raging condemnation, a certain number of old acquaintances among journalists, what in the galloping American

Lewis' corrected text is reproduced here from the revised pamphlet,
Why Sinclair Lewis Got the Nobel Prize (New York: Harcourt, Brace
and Company, 1931), except that one addition by Lewis, in the final
paragraph, is not included here: "there are Michael Gold, who reveals
the new frontier of the Jewish East Side, and William Faulkner, who
has freed the South from hoop-skirts." This addition Lewis must have
written into his galley proof, and it is also written into the second corrected copy of the original pamphlet, which Lewis later gave to his
Hollywood friends, Mr. and Mrs. Jean Hersholt, who in turn gave it,
with all the papers of Jean Hersholt, to the Library of Congress.

slang we call the "I Knew Him When Club," have scribbled that since they know me personally, therefore I must be a rather low sort of fellow and certainly no writer. But if I have now and then received such cheering brickbats, still I, who have heaved a good many bricks myself, would be fatuous not to expect a fair number in return.

No, I have for myself no conceivable complaint to make, and yet for American literature in general, and its standing in a country where industrialism and finance and science flourish and the only arts that are vital and respected are architecture and the film, I have a considerable complaint.

I can illustrate by an incident which chances to concern the Swedish Academy and myself and which happened a few days ago, just before I took ship at New York for Sweden. There is in America a learned and most amiable old gentleman who has been a pastor, a university professor, and a diplomat. He is a member of the American Academy of Arts and Letters and no few universities have honored him with degrees. As a writer he is chiefly known for his pleasant little essays on the joy of fishing. I do not suppose that professional fishermen, whose lives depend on the run of cod or herring, find it altogether an amusing occupation, but from these essays I learned, as a boy, that there is something very important and spiritual about catching fish, if you have no need of doing so.

This scholar stated, and publicly, that in awarding the Nobel Prize to a person who has scoffed at American institutions as much as I have, the Nobel Committee and the Swedish Academy had insulted America. I don't know whether, as an ex-diplomat, he intends to have an international incident made of it, and perhaps demand of the American Government that they land Marines in Stockholm to protect American literary rights, but I hope not.

I should have supposed that to a man so learned as to have been made a Doctor of Divinity, a Doctor of Letters, and I do not know how many other imposing magnificences, the matter would have seemed different; I should have supposed that he would have reasoned, "Although personally I dislike this man's books, nevertheless the Swedish Academy has in choosing him honored America by assuming that the Americans are no longer a puerile backwoods clan, so inferior that they are afraid of criticism, but instead a nation come of age and able to consider calmly and maturely any dissection of their land, however scoffing."

I should even have supposed that so international a scholar would have believed that Scandinavia, accustomed to the works of Strindberg, Ibsen, and Pontoppidan, would not have been peculiarly shocked by a writer whose most anarchistic assertion has been that America, with all her wealth and power, has not yet produced a civilization good enough to satisfy the deepest wants of human creatures.

I believe that Strindberg rarely sang the "Star-Spangled Banner" or addressed Rotary Clubs, yet Sweden seems to have survived him.

I have at such length discussed this criticism of the learned fisherman not because it has any conceivable importance in itself, but because it does illustrate the fact that in America most of us—not readers alone but even writers—are still afraid of any literature which is not a glorification of everything American, a glorification of our faults as well as our virtues. To be not only a best-seller in America but to be really beloved, a novelist must assert that all American men are tall, handsome, rich, honest, and powerful at golf; that all country towns are filled with neighbors who do nothing from day to day save go about being kind to one another; that although American girls may be wild, they change always into perfect wives and mothers; and that, geographically, America is composed solely of New York, which is inhabited entirely by millionaires; of the West, which keeps unchanged all the boisterous heroism of 1870; and of the South, where every one lives on a plantation perpetually glossy with moonlight and scented with magnolias.

It is not today vastly more true than it was twenty years ago that such novelists of ours as you have read in Sweden, novelists like Dreiser and Willa Cather, are authentically popular and influential in America. As it was revealed by the venerable fishing Academician whom I have quoted, we still most revere the writers for the popular magazines who in a hearty and edifying chorus chant that the America of a hundred and twenty million population is still as simple, as pastoral, as it was when it had but forty million; that in an industrial plant with ten thousand employees, the relationship between the worker and the manager is still as neighborly and uncomplex as in a factory of 1840, with five employees; that the relationships between father and son, between husband and wife, are precisely the same in an apartment in a thirty-story palace today, with three motor cars awaiting the family below and five books on the library shelves and a divorce imminent in the family next week, as were those relationships in a rose-veiled five-room cottage in 1880; that, in fine, America has gone through the revolutionary change from rustic colony to world-empire without having in the least altered the bucolic and Puritanic simplicity of Uncle Sam.

I am, actually, extremely grateful to the fishing Academician for having somewhat condemned me. For since he is a leading member of the American Academy of Arts and Letters, he has released me, has given me the right to speak as frankly of that Academy as he has spoken of me. And in any honest study of American intellectualism today, that curious institution must be considered.

Before I consider the Academy, however, let me sketch a fantasy which has pleased me the last few days in the unavoidable idleness of a rough trip on the Atlantic. I am sure that you know, by now, that the award to me of the Nobel Prize has by no means been altogether popular in America. Doubtless the experience is not new to you. I fancy that when you gave the award even to Thomas Mann, whose *Zauberberg* seems to me to contain the whole of intellectual Europe, even when you gave it to Kipling, whose social significance is so profound that it has been rather authoritatively said that he created the British Empire, even when you gave it to Bernard Shaw, there were countrymen of those authors who complained because you did not choose another.

And I imagined what would have been said had you chosen some American other than myself. Suppose you had taken Theodore Dreiser.

Now to me, as to many other American writers, Dreiser more than any other man, marching alone, usually unappreciated, often hated, has cleared the trail from Victorian and Howellsian timidity and gentility in American fiction to honesty and boldness and passion of life. Without his pioneering, I doubt if any of us could, unless we liked to be sent to jail, seek to express life and beauty and terror.

My great colleague Sherwood Anderson has proclaimed this leadership of Dreiser. I am delighted to join him. Dreiser's great first novel, *Sister Carrie*, which he dared to publish thirty long years ago and which I read twenty-five years ago, came to housebound and airless America like a great free Western wind, and to our stuffy domesticity gave us the first fresh air since Mark Twain and Whitman.

Yet had you given the Prize to Mr. Dreiser, you would have heard groans from America; you would have heard that his style—I am not exactly sure what this mystic quality "style" may be, but I find the word so often in the writings of minor critics that I suppose it must exist—you would have heard that his style is cumbersome, that his choice of words is insensitive, that his books are interminable. And certainly respectable scholars would complain that in Mr. Dreiser's world, men and women are often sinful and tragic and despairing, instead of being forever sunny and full of song and virtue, as befits authentic Americans.

And had you chosen Mr. Eugene O'Neill, who has done nothing much in American drama save to transform it utterly, in ten or twelve years, from a false world of neat and competent trickery to a world of splendor and fear and greatness, you would have been reminded that he has done something far worse than scoffing—he has seen life as not to be neatly arranged in the study of a scholar but as a terrifying, magnificent and often quite horrible thing akin to the tornado, the earthquake, the devastating fire.

And had you given Mr. James Branch Cabell the Prize, you would have been told that he is too fantastically malicious. So would you have been told that Miss Willa Cather, for all the homely virtue of her novels concerning the peasants of Nebraska, has in her novel, *The Lost Lady*, been so untrue to America's patent and perpetual and possibly tedious virtuousness as to picture an abandoned woman who remains, nevertheless, uncannily charming even to the virtuous, in a story without any moral; that Mr. Henry Mencken is the worst of all scoffers; that Mr. Sherwood Anderson viciously errs in considering sex as important a force in life as fishing; that Mr. Upton Sinclair, being a Socialist, sins against the perfectness of American capitalistic mass-production; that Mr. Joseph Hergesheimer is un-American in regarding graciousness of manner and beauty of surface as of some importance in the endurance of daily life; and that Mr. Ernest Hemingway is not only too young but, far worse, uses language which should be unknown to gentlemen; that he acknowledges drunkenness as one of man's eternal ways to happiness, and asserts that a soldier may find love more significant than the hearty slaughter of men in battle.

Yes, they are wicked, these colleagues of mine; you would have done almost as evilly to have chosen them as to have chosen me; and as a chauvinistic American—only, mind you, as an American of 1930 and not of 1880—I rejoice that they are my countrymen and countrywomen, and that I may speak of them with pride even in the Europe of Thomas Mann, H. G. Wells, Galsworthy, Knut Hamsun, Arnold Bennett, Feuchtwanger, Selma Lagerlöf, Sigrid Undset, Werner von Heidenstam, D'Annunzio, Romain Rolland.

It is my fate in this paper to swing constantly from optimism to pessimism and back, but so is it the fate of any one who writes or speaks of anything in America—the most contradictory, the most depressing, the most stirring, of any land in the world today.

Thus, having with no muted pride called the roll of what seem to me to be great men and women in American literary life today, and having indeed omitted a dozen other names of which I should like to boast were there time, I must turn again and assert that in our contemporary American literature, indeed in all American arts save architecture and the film, we—yes, we who have such pregnant and vigorous standards in commerce and science—have no standards, no healing communication, no heroes to be followed nor villains to be condemned, no certain ways to be pursued and no dangerous paths to be avoided.

The American novelist or poet or dramatist or sculptor or painter must work alone, in confusion, unassisted save by his own integrity.

That, of course, has always been the lot of the artist. The vagabond and criminal François Villon had certainly no smug and comfortable refuge in which elegant ladies would hold his hand and comfort his starveling soul and more starved body. He, veritably a great man, destined to outlive in history all the dukes and puissant cardinals whose robes he was esteemed unworthy to touch, had for his lot the gutter and the hardened crust.

Such poverty is not for the artist in America. They pay us, indeed, only too well; that writer is a failure who cannot have his butler and motor and his villa at Palm Beach, where he is permitted to mingle almost in equality with the barons of banking. But he is oppressed ever by something worse than poverty—by the feeling that what he creates does not matter, that he is expected by his readers to be only a decorator or a clown, or that he is good-naturedly accepted as a scoffer whose bark probably is worse than his bite and who probably is a good fellow at heart, who in any case certainly does not count in a land that produces eighty-story buildings, motors by the million, and wheat by the billions of bushels. And he has no institution, no group, to which he can turn for inspiration, whose criticism he can accept and whose praise will be precious to him.

What institutions have we?

The American Academy of Arts and Letters does contain along with several excellent painters and architects and statesmen, such a really distinguished university-president as Nicholas Murray Butler, so admirable and courageous a scholar as Wilbur Cross, and several first-rate writers: the poets Edwin Arlington Robinson and Robert Frost, the free-minded publicist James Truslow Adams, and the novelists Edith Wharton, Hamlin Garland, Owen Wister, Brand Whitlock and Booth Tarkington.

But it does not include Theodore Dreiser, Henry Mencken, our most vivid critic, George Jean Nathan who, though still young, is certainly the dean of our dramatic critics, Eugene O'Neill, incomparably our best dramatist, the really original and vital poets, Edna St. Vincent Millay and Carl Sandburg, Robinson Jeffers and Vachel Lindsay and Edgar Lee Masters, whose *Spoon River Anthology* was so utterly different from any other poetry ever published, so fresh, so authoritative, so free from any gropings and timidities that it came like a revelation, and created a new school of native American poetry. It does not include the novelists and short-story writers, Willa Cather, Joseph Hergesheimer, Sherwood Anderson, Ring Lardner, Ernest Hemingway, Louis Bromfield, Wilbur Daniel Steele, Fannie Hurst, Mary Austin, James Branch Cabell, Edna Ferber, nor Upton Sinclair, of whom you must say, whether you admire or detest his aggressive Socialism, that he is internationally better known than any other American artist whosoever, be he novelist, poet, painter, sculptor, musician, architect.

I should not expect any Academy to be so fortunate as to contain all these writers, but one which fails to contain any of them, which thus cuts itself off from so much of what is living and vigorous and original in American letters, can have no relationship whatever to our life and aspirations. It does not represent literary America of today—it represents only Henry Wadsworth Longfellow.

It might be answered that, after all, the Academy is limited to fifty members; that, naturally, it cannot include every one of merit. But the fact is that while most of our few giants are excluded, the Academy does have room to include three extraordinarily bad poets, two very melodramatic and insignificant playwrights, two gentlemen who are known only because they are university presidents, a man who was thirty years ago known as a rather clever humorous draughtsman, and several gentlemen of whom—I sadly confess my ignorance—I have never heard.

Let me again emphasize the fact—for it is a fact—that I am not attacking the American Academy. It is a hospitable and generous and decidedly dignified institution. And it is not altogether the Academy's fault that it does not contain many of the men who have significance in our letters. Sometimes it is the fault of those writers themselves. I cannot imagine that grizzly-bear Theodore Dreiser being comfortable at the serenely Athenian dinners of the Academy, and were they to invite Mencken, he would infuriate them with his boisterous jeering. No, I am not attacking—I am reluctantly considering the Academy because it is so perfect an example of the divorce in America of intellectual life from all authentic standards of importance and reality.

Our universities and colleges, or gymnasia, most of them, exhibit the same unfortunate divorce. I can think of four of them, Rollins College in Florida, Middlebury College in Vermont, the University of Michigan, and the University of Chicago—which has had on its roll so excellent a novelist as Robert Herrick, so courageous a critic as Robert Morss Lovett—which have shown an authentic interest in contemporary creative literature. Four of them. But universities and colleges and musical emporiums and schools for the teaching of theology and plumbing and signpainting are as thick in America as the motor traffic. Whenever you see a public building with Gothic fenestration on a sturdy backing of Indiana concrete, you may be certain that it is another university, with anywhere from two hundred to twenty thousand students equally ardent about avoiding the disadvantage of becoming learned and about gaining the social prestige contained in the possession of a B.A. degree.

Oh, socially our universities are close to the mass of our citizens, and so are they in the matter of athletics. A great college football game is passionately witnessed by eighty thousand people, who have paid five dollars apiece and motored anywhere from ten to a thousand miles for the ecstasy of watching twenty-two men chase one another up and down a curiously marked field. During the football season, a capable player ranks very nearly with our greatest and most admired heroes—even with Henry Ford, President Hoover, and Colonel Lindbergh.

And in one branch of learning, the sciences, the lords of business who rule us are willing to do homage to the devotees of learning. However bleakly one of our trader aristocrats may frown upon poetry or the visions of a painter, he is graciously pleased to endure a Millikan, a Michelson, a Banting, a Theobald Smith.

But the paradox is that in the arts our universities are as cloistered, as far from reality and living creation, as socially and athletically and scientifically they are close to us. To a true-blue professor of literature in an American university, literature is not something that a plain human being, living today, painfully sits down to produce. No; it is something dead; it is something magically produced by superhuman beings who must, if they are to be regarded as artists at all, have died at least one hundred years before the diabolical invention of the typewriter. To any authentic don, there is something slightly repulsive in the thought that literature could be created by any ordinary human being, still to be seen walking the streets, wearing quite commonplace trousers and coat and looking not so unlike a chauffeur or a farmer. Our American professors like their literature clear and cold and pure and very dead.

I do not suppose that American universities are alone in this. I am aware that to the dons of Oxford and Cambridge, it would seem rather indecent to suggest that Wells and Bennett and Galsworthy and George Moore may, while they commit the impropriety of continuing to live, be compared to any one so beautifully and safely dead as Samuel Johnson. I suppose that in the universities of Sweden and France and Germany there exist plenty of professors who prefer dissection to understanding. But in the new and vital and experimental land of America, one would expect the teachers of literature to be less monastic, more human, than in the traditional shadows of old Europe.

They are not.

There has recently appeared in America, out of the universities, an astonishing circus called "the New Humanism." Now of course "humanism" means so many things that it means nothing. It may infer anything from a belief that Greek and Latin are more inspiring than the dialect of contemporary peasants to a belief that any living peasant is more interesting than a dead Greek. But it is a delicate bit of justice that this nebulous word should have been chosen to label this nebulous cult.

Insofar as I have been able to comprehend them—for naturally in a world so exciting and promising as this today, a life brilliant with Zeppelins and Chinese revolutions and the Bolshevik industrialization of farming and ships and the Grand Canyon and young children and terrifying hunger and the lonely quest of scientists after God, no creative writer would have time to follow all the chilly enthusiasms of the New Humanists—this newest of sects reasserts the dualism of man's nature. It would confine literature to the fight between man's soul and God, or man's soul and evil.

But, curiously, neither God nor the devil may wear modern dress, but must retain Grecian vestments. Oedipus is a tragic figure for the New Humanists; man, trying to maintain himself as the image of God under the menace of dynamos, in a world of high-pressure salesmanship, is not. And the poor comfort which they offer is that the object of life is to develop self-discipline—whether or not one ever accomplishes anything with this self-discipline. So this whole movement results in the not particularly novel doctrine that both art and life must be resigned and negative. It is a doctrine of the blackest reaction introduced into a stirringly revolutionary world.

Strangely enough, this doctrine of death, this escape from the complexities and danger of living into the secure blankness of the monastery, has become widely popular among professors in a land where one would have expected only boldness and intellectual adventure, and it has more than ever shut creative writers off from any benign influence which might conceivably have come from the universities.

But it has always been so. America has never had a Brandes, a Taine, a Goethe, a Croce.

With a wealth of creative talent in America, our criticism has most of it been a chill and insignificant activity pursued by jealous spinsters, ex-baseball-reporters, and acid professors. Our Erasmuses have been village schoolmistresses. How should there be any standards when there has been no one capable of setting them up?

The great Cambridge-Concord circle of the middle of the Nineteenth Century—Emerson, Longfellow, Lowell, Holmes, the Alcotts—were sentimental reflections of Europe, and they left no school, no influence. Whitman and Thoreau and Poe and, in some degree, Hawthorne, were outcasts, men alone and despised, berated by the New Humanists of their generation. It was with the emergence of William Dean Howells that we first began to have something like a standard, and a very bad standard it was.

Mr. Howells was one of the gentlest, sweetest, and most honest of men, but he had the code of a pious old maid whose greatest delight was to have tea at the vicarage. He abhorred not only profanity and obscenity but all of what H. G. Wells has called "the jolly coarseness of life." In his fantastic vision of life, which he innocently conceived to be realistic, farmers and seamen and factory-hands might exist, but the farmer must never be covered with muck, the seaman must never roll out bawdy chanteys, the factory-hand must be thankful to his good employer, and all of them must long for the opportunity to visit Florence and smile gently at the quaintness of the beggars.

So strongly did Howells feel this genteel, this New Humanistic philosophy that he was able vastly to influence his contemporaries, down even to 1914 and the turmoil of the Great War.

He was actually able to tame Mark Twain, perhaps the greatest of our writers, and to put that fiery old savage into an intellectual frock coat and top hat. His influence is not altogether gone today. He is still worshipped by Hamlin Garland, an author who should in every way have been greater than Howells but who under Howells' influence was changed from a harsh and magnificent realist into a genial and insignificant lecturer. Mr. Garland is, so far as we have one, the dean of American letters today, and as our dean, he is alarmed by all of the younger writers who are so lacking in taste as to suggest that men and women do not always love in accordance with the prayer-book, and that common people sometimes use language which would be inappropriate at a women's literary club on Main Street. Yet this same Hamlin Garland, as a young man, before he had gone to Boston and become cultured and Howellized, wrote two most valiant and revelatory works of realism, *Main-Travelled Roads* and *Rose of Dutcher's Coolly*.

I read them as a boy in a prairie village in Minnesota—just such an environment as was described in Mr. Garland's tales. They were vastly exciting to me. I had realized in reading Balzac and Dickens that it was possible to describe French and English common people as one actually saw them. But it had never occurred to me that one might without indecency write of the people of Sauk Centre, Minnesota, as one felt about them. Our fictional tradition, you see, was that all of us in Midwestern villages were altogether noble and happy; that not one of us would exchange the neighborly bliss of living on Main Street for the heathen gaudiness of New York or Paris or Stockholm. But in Mr. Garland's *Main-Travelled Roads* I discovered that there was one man who believed that Midwestern peasants were sometimes bewildered and hungry and vile—and heroic. And, given this vision, I was released; I could write of life as living life.

I am afraid that Mr. Garland would not be pleased but acutely annoyed to know that he made it possible for me to write of America as I see it, and not as Mr. William Dean Howells so sunnily saw it. And it is his tragedy, it is a completely revelatory American tragedy, that in our land of freedom, men like Garland, who first blast the roads to freedom, become themselves the most bound.

But, all this time, while men like Howells were so effusively seeking to guide America into becoming a pale edition of an English cathedral town, there were surly and authentic fellows—Whitman and Melville, then Dreiser and James Huneker and Mencken—who insisted that our land had something more than tea-table gentility.

And so, without standards, we have survived. And for the strong young men, it has perhaps been well that we should have no standards. For, after seeming to be pessimistic about my own and much beloved land, I want to close this dirge with a very lively sound of optimism.

I have, for the future of American literature, every hope and every eager belief. We are coming out, I believe, of the stuffiness of safe, sane, and incredibly dull provincialism. There are young Americans today who are doing such passionate and authentic work that it makes me sick to see that I am a little too old to be one of them.

There is Ernest Hemingway, a bitter youth, educated by the most intense experience, disciplined by his own high standards, an authentic artist whose home is in the whole of life; there is Thomas Wolfe, a child of, I believe, thirty or younger, whose one and only novel, *Look Homeward, Angel,* is worthy to be compared with the best in our literary production, a Gargantuan creature with great gusto of life; there is Thornton Wilder, who in an age of realism dreams the old and lovely dreams of the eternal romantics; there is John Dos Passos, with his hatred of the safe and sane standards of Babbitt and his splendor of revolution; there is Stephen Benét who, to American drabness, has restored the epic poem with his glorious memory of old John Brown; and there are a dozen other young poets and fictioneers, most of them living now in Paris, most of them a little insane in the tradition of James Joyce, who, however insane they may be, have refused to be genteel and traditional and dull.

I salute them, with a joy in being not yet too far removed from their determination to give to the America that has mountains and endless prairies, enormous cities and lost farm cabins, billions of money and tons of faith, to an America that is as strange as Russia and as complex as China, a literature worthy of her vastness.

The immediate historic importance of Lewis' address in 1930 was the international recognition that the literature of the United States had, in spite of certain named obstacles, arrived at a state of maturity that made it the peer of any literature in Europe or of any other continent, and, more important,

that America itself was a major power in the world as, twenty years before, Europe would have denied, and as, until Lewis stood up in Stockholm, she had been reluctant to concede.

Of those obstacles to literary maturity in the United States that Lewis named—academicism and gentility—one can only insist that, in 1930, he made too much. The extraordinary success of his own novels since the publication of Main Street *ten years before would seem to demonstrate that for at least a decade American readers were as ready for self-criticism as the best American writers were prepared to give it. All through the decade of the twenties, the very writers whom Lewis named in his address as the déclassé were the most favorably received by any audience of critical consequence: Dreiser, Cather, Anderson, O'Neill, Mencken, Sinclair, Hemingway. Even those oddities, as they appear to us now, Cabell and Hergesheimer, were thought of indeed as among the liberators. It was a decade of liberation that climaxed a sporadic movement going back at least as far as 1900 and the suppression of the first publication of Dreiser's* Sister Carrie. *The remnants of academicism and gentility were, by the time that Sinclair Lewis made his address in Stockholm, remnants only.*

Those remnants Lewis' address was probably instrumental in dispelling. The American Academy rapidly changed its character and was presently inviting all manner of experimental artists into its once stodgy fold. In the universities, the New Humanism was routed; the study not only of American literature but of the most contemporary American literature became, for better or worse, a major academic concern, and the close examination of American culture generally was presently a commonplace in most university curricula. How much of this may be attributed directly to Lewis's Nobel speech it is hard to say, and it is possible that once more, as he had done so often in his novels, Sinclair Lewis had anticipated by the smallest fraction of time a national mood that was ready for articulation.

Certainly the decade of the 1920's has freed American literature once and for all from timidity and chauvinism. A spokesman was still required to announce to the world that the event had taken place, and December 10, 1930, was an effectively round date for the world of international letters to have given the invitation to an American to make that declaration. "The American Fear of Literature" stands as probably our chief reminder that American literature is without fear.

Franklin D. Roosevelt

First Inaugural Address

1933

EDITED BY FRANK FREIDEL

In February, 1933, as the cruelest depression winter in American history began to draw toward a close, people looked forward expectantly to the event they hoped would bring an upturn in their own and the nation's fortunes. They awaited the inauguration on March 4 of the new Democratic President, Franklin D. Roosevelt. As the President-elect planned his Inaugural Address, economic machinery seemed to be slowing to a standstill. One-quarter of the wage-earners were unable to find work to support themselves or their families, and only one-quarter of these unemployed were receiving even paltry relief funds. A fourth of the farmers were losing or had lost their farms. For most of the remainder of the populace, whether located in the country or in the cities, incomes were appallingly inadequate. Every economic indicator pointed to disaster. Grain prices were the lowest since the reign of the first Queen Elizabeth; steel production, the bellwether of industry, slid to less than one-fifth of capacity. Already five thousand banks had succumbed to the long strain of the depression, and in February the banks had begun to close at such an alarming rate that, first in Michigan and then in al-

most every other state, the various governors proclaimed banking holidays or placed drastic restrictions on banking activities. Still people waited, and with incredibly little disorder. "Did you ever dream of anything like the docility of the American people under the crushing burden of these times?" William Allen White had inquired in Janaury, 1933. "Why don't they smash windows? Why don't they go and get it?" The answer to White's query was that they were waiting to see what the Roosevelt Administration could bring to them. If it had little to offer, then the docility might give way to violence. One seasoned old senator remarked privately, "We may be closer to revolution than we have ever been in our lives."

Against this ominous backdrop Roosevelt worked upon his Inaugural Address. On the surface all the portents were grim, but beneath the surface the nation continued to possess economic resources and an industrial and agricultural capacity so huge that, if properly employed, they could provide for everyone a high standard of living. What the economic system needed, Roosevelt and his advisers felt, was not scrapping, but relatively minor reforms and a mild stimulus. The first task was to restore public confidence. With a confident public and some economic adjustments, prosperity could be attained.

It was in this spirit that Roosevelt outlined to his chief brain truster, Professor Raymond Moley of Columbia University, the topics to be covered in the Inaugural Address. Moley prepared a first draft on February 12 and 13, then on February 26 and 27, while conferring with Roosevelt at Hyde Park, he drafted a revision. At about nine o'clock on Monday evening, February 27, Roosevelt seated himself at a card table in the living room of his home at Hyde Park. Writing in a flowing hand on lined yellow legal paper, Roosevelt, following Moley's draft, prepared his own first version. By one-thirty in the morning Roosevelt had completed his draft, almost as he would deliver it: one of the very few addresses for which he prepared a complete draft in his own hand. When he had finished with Moley's draft, Moley took it and threw it into the fire.

The ideas and phrasing in Roosevelt's address, as in most speeches, came from many sources. The often quoted attack upon fear (inserted after Roosevelt reached Washington) is at least as old as Francis Bacon. Moley was responsible for the statement of the Good Neighbor Policy. The biblically phrased indictment of bankers occurred to Roosevelt as he sat in St. James Church, Hyde Park, on Sunday, February

26. Finally, as Roosevelt sat in the Capitol waiting to take the oath of office, he added a new first sentence to his reading copy, "This is a day of consecration." When he delivered the address, he interpolated the word "national" into his opening sentence. Whatever the origin of the concepts or the method of their assemblage, the completed speech represented what Roosevelt wanted to convey to the American people as he stood under the chilly gray skies in front of the Capitol on March 4 and assumed his responsibilities as President. He wished to share with them his own vigor and optimism—and he succeeded in doing so.

THIS IS a day of national consecration.

I am certain that my fellow Americans expect that on my induction into the Presidency I will address them with a candor and a decision which the present situation of our Nation impels. This is pre-eminently the time to speak the truth, the whole truth, frankly and boldly. Nor need we shrink from honestly facing conditions in our country today. This great Nation will endure as it has endured, will revive and will prosper. So, first of all, let me assert my firm belief that the only thing we have to fear is fear itself—nameless, unreasoning, unjustified terror which paralyzes needed efforts to convert retreat into advance. In every dark hour of our national life a leadership of frankness and vigor has met with that understanding and support of the people themselves which is essential to victory. I am convinced that you will again give that support to leadership in these critical days.

In such a spirit on my part and on yours we face our common difficulties. They concern, thank God, only material things. Values have shrunken to fantastic levels; taxes have risen; our ability to pay has fallen; government of all kinds is faced by serious curtailment of income; the means of exchange are frozen in the currents of trade; the withered leaves of industrial enterprise lie on every side; farmers find no markets for their produce; the savings of many years in thousands of families are gone.

More important, a host of unemployed citizens face the grim problem of existence, and an equally great number toil

The text comes from Franklin D. Roosevelt, *The Public Papers and Addresses* (New York: Random House, 1937), 1933 vol., pp. 11–16. The first sentence has been added from the reading copy of the address now at the Franklin D. Roosevelt Library, Hyde Park, New York.

with little return. Only a foolish optimist can deny the dark realities of the moment.

Yet our distress comes from no failure of substance. We are stricken by no plague of locusts. Compared with the perils which our forefathers conquered because they believed and were not afraid, we have still much to be thankful for. Nature still offers her bounty and human efforts have multiplied it. Plenty is at our doorstep, but a generous use of it languishes in the very sight of the supply. Primarily this is because rulers of the exchange of mankind's goods have failed through their own stubbornness and their own incompetence, have admitted their failure, and have abdicated. Practices of the unscrupulous money changers stand indicted in the court of public opinion, rejected by the hearts and minds of men.

True they have tried, but their efforts have been cast in the pattern of an outworn tradition. Faced by failure of credit they have proposed only the lending of more money. Stripped of the lure of profit by which to induce our people to follow their false leadership, they have resorted to exhortations, pleading tearfully for restored confidence. They know only the rules of a generation of self-seekers. They have no vision, and when there is no vision the people perish.

The money changers have fled from their high seats in the temple of our civilization. We may now restore that temple to the ancient truths. The measure of the restoration lies in the extent to which we apply social values more noble than mere monetary profit.

Happiness lies not in the mere possession of money; it lies in the joy of achievement, in the thrill of creative effort. The joy and moral stimulation of work no longer must be forgotten in the mad chase of evanescent profits. These dark days will be worth all they cost us if they teach us that our true destiny is not to be ministered unto but to minister to ourselves and to our fellow men.

Recognition of the falsity of material wealth as the standard of success goes hand in hand with the abandonment of the false belief that public office and high political position are to be valued only by the standards or pride of place and personal profit; and there must be an end to a conduct in banking and in business which too often has given to a sacred trust the likeness of callous and selfish wrongdoing. Small wonder that confidence languishes, for it thrives only on honesty, on honor, on the sacredness of obligations, on faithful protection, on unselfish performance; without them it cannot live.

Restoration calls, however, not for changes in ethics alone. This Nation asks for action, and action now.

Our greatest primary task is to put people to work. This is no unsolvable problem if we face it wisely and courageously. It can be accomplished in part by direct recruiting by the Government itself, treating the task as we would treat the emergency of a war, but at the same time, through this employment, accomplishing greatly needed projects to stimulate and reorganize the use of our natural resources.

Hand in hand with this we must frankly recognize the overbalance of population in our industrial centers and, by engaging on a national scale in a redistribution, endeavor to provide a better use of the land for those best fitted for the land. The task can be helped by definite efforts to raise the values of agricultural products and with this the power to purchase the output of our cities. It can be helped by preventing realistically the tragedy of the growing loss through foreclosure of our small homes and our farms. It can be helped by insistence that the Federal, State, and local governments act forthwith on the demand that their cost be drastically reduced. It can be helped by the unifying of relief activities which today are often scattered, uneconomical, and unequal. It can be helped by national planning for and supervision of all forms of transportation and of communications and other utilities which have a definitely public character. There are many ways in which it can be helped, but it can never be helped merely by talking about it. We must act and act quickly.

Finally, in our progress toward a resumption of work we require two safeguards against a return of the evils of the old order: there must be a strict supervision of all banking and credits and investments, so that there will be an end to speculation with other people's money; and there must be provision for an adequate but sound currency.

These are the lines of attack. I shall presently urge upon a new Congress, in special session, detailed measures for their fulfillment, and I shall seek the immediate assistance of the several States.

Through this program of action we address ourselves to putting our own national house in order and making income balance outgo. Our international trade relations, though vastly important, are in point of time and necessity secondary to the establishment of a sound national economy. I favor as a practical policy the putting of first things first. I shall spare no effort to restore world trade by international economic readjustment, but the emergency at home cannot wait on that accomplishment.

The basic thought that guides these specific means of national recovery is not narrowly nationalistic. It is the insistence, as a first consideration, upon the interdependence of the various elements in and parts of the United States—a recognition of the old and permanently important manifestation of the American spirit of the pioneer. It is the way to recovery. It is the immediate way. It is the strongest assurance that the recovery will endure.

In the field of world policy I would dedicate this Nation to the policy of the good neighbor—the neighbor who resolutely respects himself and, because he does so, respects the rights of others—the neighbor who respects his obligations and respects the sanctity of his agreements in and with a world of neighbors.

If I read the temper of our people correctly, we now realize as we have never realized before our interdependence on each other; that we cannot merely take but we must give as well; that if we are to go forward, we must move as a trained and loyal army willing to sacrifice for the good of a common discipline, because without such discipline no progress is made, no leadership becomes effective. We are, I know, ready and willing to submit our lives and property to such discipline, because it makes possible a leadership which aims at a larger good. This I propose to offer, pledging that the larger purposes will bind upon us all as a sacred obligation with a unity of duty hitherto evoked only in time of armed strife.

With this pledge taken, I assume unhesitatingly the leadership of this great army of our people dedicated to a disciplined attack upon our common problems.

Action in this image and to this end is feasible under the form of government which we have inherited from our ancestors. Our Constitution is so simple and practical that it is possible always to meet extraordinary needs by changes in emphasis and arrangement without loss of essential form. That is why our constitutional system has proved itself the most superbly enduring political mechanism the modern world has produced. It has met every stress of vast expansion of territory, of foreign wars, of bitter internal strife, of world relations.

It is to be hoped that the normal balance of Executive and legislative authority may be wholly adequate to meet the unprecedented task before us. But it may be that an unprecedented demand and need for undelayed action may call for temporary departure from that normal balance of public procedure.

I am prepared under my constitutional duty to recommend the measures that a stricken Nation in the midst of a stricken world may require. These measures, or such other measures as the Congress may build out of its experience and wisdom, I shall seek, within my constitutional authority, to bring to speedy adoption.

But in the event that the Congress shall fail to take one of these two courses, and in the event that the national emergency is still critical, I shall not evade the clear course of duty that will then confront me. I shall ask the Congress for the one remaining instrument to meet the crisis—broad Executive power to wage a war against the emergency, as great as the power that would be given to me if we were in fact invaded by a foreign foe.

For the trust reposed in me I will return the courage and the devotion that befit the time. I can do no less.

We face the arduous days that lie before us in the warm courage of national unity; with the clear consciousness of seeking old and precious moral values; with the clean satisfaction that comes from the stern performance of duty by old and young alike. We aim at the assurance of a rounded and permanent national life.

We do not distrust the future of essential democracy. The people of the United States have not failed. In their need they have registered a mandate that they want direct, vigorous action. They have asked for discipline and direction under leadership. They have made me the present instrument of their wishes. In the spirit of the gift I take it.

In this dedication of a Nation we humbly ask the blessing of God. May He protect each and every one of us. May He guide me in the days to come.

To a weary nation and world, President Roosevelt's Inaugural Address delivered on that raw March day in 1933 seemed the first tentative ray of sunlight to break through the clouds of the depression. It brought promise of action, of a reversal of the slow, sickening drift into economic chaos. Instantly it enlisted the support of Congress. With few exceptions, senators and congressmen of both parties declared their approval. Senator Hiram Johnson of California, a Republican progressive who had long harassed President Hoover, like many others hailed Roosevelt's "real courage." "We have the new era," as-

serted Johnson, "and if we can judge from today, we have the new man." The American people were even more enthusiastic: nearly a half-million of them wrote to the White House in the next few days to express directly to Roosevelt himself their appreciation. One person wrote, "It seemed to give the people, as well as myself, a new hold upon life." Republican and Democratic newspapers alike acclaimed the address in superlatives. The Chicago Tribune declared that it "strikes the dominant note of courageous confidence." To the Nashville Banner it was proof "that, as every great epoch has called for a great leader, so never has the nation lacked the citizen to measure to the demands." Some newspapers such as these, which were subsequently to revise their estimates of Roosevelt, were for the moment eager to see Congress grant the President whatever authority he might desire.

In the crisis of the times, Roosevelt's firm assumption of leadership seemed to Americans the most encouraging aspect of his first Inaugural Address. In the perspective of the years that followed it came to assume another and even greater significance, the pronouncement of a decisive shift in the direction of national government and, indeed, of the national purpose. But even at the time, some newspapers, such as the Republican Deseret News of Salt Lake City and the Democratic News of Dayton, focused their approval upon Roosevelt's castigation of the "money-changers." The Dayton News declared, "This means the abandonment of the pivot on which American power has turned for twelve years past. Those were years of dependence upon a hierarchy of favorite interest. We gave them power; they were to return us prosperity. What we see now is the prosperity we got. Now for the laying of a broader base. Thus Roosevelt in the spirit of Lincoln calls the country to a right about face."

To a few critics like Edmund Wilson, Roosevelt's generalities were no more than flat-sounding empty verbiage, phrases which were no more than "the echoes of Woodrow Wilson's eloquence without Wilson's glow of life behind them." To the more optimistic observers these familiar phrases carried promise of a vital change. While the New Republic printed Edmund Wilson's pessimistic indictment, the Nation proclaimed, "Never in our national history has there been so dramatic a coincidence as this simultaneous transfer of power and the complete collapse of a system and of a philosophy. At that zero hour Roosevelt's words had something of the challenge, the symbolism, and the simplicity of a trumpet blast." In the light of the events that followed, the Inaugural Address was not so much what Edmund Wilson had seen in it and in the parade that followed—the weary symbol of the passing of an old order—as it was what the Nation had considered it to be—the exhilarating portent of a redirection of America "toward a goal such as Jefferson envisaged—a democracy based on full economic, as well as political, equality." For America this was the importance of the address.

For the world as well, Roosevelt's Inaugural Address was of serious purport. Radio carried it to Europe and even to Australia; it was widely read in Latin America. It came at a time when the German people in crisis had allowed Adolf Hitler and the Nazis to come to power, when democracies elsewhere seemed helpless to cope with the depression. Was the new American President joining the drive toward totalitarianism? Sitting by her husband, Mrs. Roosevelt was dismayed when the crowd broke into its most vociferous applause when the President warned that if Congress failed to act he would be forced to ask for wartime power. The press in Mussolini's Italy diagnosed the address as presaging a resort of Fascist techniques in the United States. Il Giornale d'Italia commented: "President Roosevelt's words are clear and need no comment to make even the deaf hear that not only Europe but the whole world feels the need of executive authority capable of acting with full powers of cutting short the purposeless chatter of legislative assemblies. This method of government may well be defined as Fascist."

The events that unfolded as the President and Congress fabricated the New Deal proved Mussolini's press wrong. To the world as a whole the address, far from being an endorsement of totalitarianism, was a proclamation that a democratic alternative could and would work—that the United States under the Presidency of Roosevelt could fight the depression and institute sweeping reforms without abandoning the traditional machinery of democracy. In the months and years that followed, the President and the nation demonstrated dramatically to all people everywhere that the crisis could be met with courage, humanitarianism, and vigor through a strengthening, rather than the destruction, of democracy. These were the factors which in the decades since its pronouncement have given a transcendent significance to Roosevelt's First Inaugural Address.

Franklin D. Roosevelt

"Quarantine" Address

1937

EDITED BY WILLIAM E. LEUCHTENBURG

In the late summer of 1937, Franklin Roosevelt decided to embark on a tour of the country to repair his political fortunes. Re-elected in November, 1936, by the greatest electoral margin of any President since James Monroe, he had seen his political strength dissipated only a short time later by his ill-starred attempt to reform the Supreme Court. The President was certain that Congress had misinterpreted the popular will, and he hoped that his forthcoming journey would demonstrate that the nation was still behind him. Moreover, after the fretful irritations of the abortive 168-day struggle over the Court bill, he sought to regain his good temper. He later told a crowd in Boise that he felt like Antaeus: "I regain strength by just meeting the American people."

Most of the President's attention was centered on domestic politics. Yet he could not ignore what was happening in the rest of the world. In a year's time, civil war had erupted in Spain, Hitler's legions had entered the Rhineland, and the governments of Germany, Italy, and Japan had moved closer to the creation of a common front against democracies. In July, 1937, the very month the Court measure went down to defeat, Chinese and Japanese troops clashed at night at the Marco Polo Bridge just west of Peiping. As the Japanese drove into northern China and inflicted severe losses on civilians in Shanghai, the "China Incident" developed into full-scale undeclared war.

Both Secretary of State Cordell Hull and America's roving ambassador, Norman Davis, were deeply troubled by the rising danger of a new world war. They were even more disturbed by the growth of isolationist sentiment in America. Consequently, they called on the President to urge him to make an address on international cooperation during his transcontinental trip, "particularly in a large city where isolation was entrenched." Roosevelt consented, and asked his callers to prepare a draft.

Before the President departed for the West, Norman Davis sent him four memoranda. The first two, probably drafted with Hull, Roosevelt used almost in their entirety. These paragraphs discussed the chaos that Germany, Italy, and Japan were creating; stressed the fact that discord anywhere in the world jeopardized the security of the rest of the world; and urged peace-loving nations to concert their efforts to avert war.

The other two memoranda were drafted by Davis in New York and cleared with James Dunn in the State Department before being forwarded to the President. Roosevelt discarded passages in these two memoranda and improvised instead the striking "quarantine" section. (The metaphor may well have been suggested by a sentence in Davis' draft: "War is a contagion.") The President made one other significant revision. In place of Davis' ending, Roosevelt wrote four concluding sentences which stressed America's quest for peace. In its final form, the President's address did not differ substantially from the spirit of the four memoranda. Yet the President's revisions had momentous consequences. In the last four sentences, Roosevelt set down what he believed to be the theme of his speech: the need for positive endeavors to search for peace. It was the President's other improvisation, however— his vivid use of the "quarantine" analogy—which was to capture the attention of the world.

On the afternoon of October 5, 1937, before a crowd of 50,000 at the dedication of the Public Works Administration's Outer Drive Bridge in Chicago, President Roosevelt delivered the "Quarantine" Address.

☆

I AM GLAD to come once again to Chicago and especially to have the opportunity of taking part in the dedication of this important project of civil betterment.

On my trip across the continent and back I have been shown many evidences of the result of common sense cooperation between municipalities and the Federal Government, and I have been greeted by tens of thousands of Americans who have told me in every look and word that their material and spiritual well-being has made great strides forward in the past few years.

And yet, as I have seen with my own eyes, the prosperous farms, the thriving factories and the busy railroads, as I have seen the happiness and security and peace which covers our wide land, almost inevitably I have been compelled to contrast our peace with very different scenes being enacted in other parts of the world.

It is because the people of the United States under modern conditions must, for the sake of their own future, give thought to the rest of the world, that I, as the responsible executive head of the Nation, have chosen this great inland city and this gala occasion to speak to you on a subject of definite national importance.

The political situation in the world, which of late has been growing progressively worse, is such as to cause grave concern and anxiety to all the peoples and nations who wish to live in peace and amity with their neighbors.

Some fifteen years ago the hopes of mankind for a continuing era of international peace were raised to great heights when more than sixty nations solemnly pledged themselves not to resort to arms in furtherance of their national aims and policies. The high aspirations expressed in the Briand-Kellogg Peace Pact and the hopes for peace thus raised have of late given way to a haunting fear of calamity. The present reign of terror and international lawlessness began a few years ago.

It began through unjustified interference in the internal affairs of other nations or the invasion of alien territory in violation of treaties; and has now reached a stage where the very foundations of civilization are seriously threatened. The landmarks and traditions which have marked the progress of civilization toward a condition of law, order and justice are being wiped away.

The address is printed here from Franklin D. Roosevelt, *The Public Papers and Addresses*, edited by S. I. Rosenman, 13 vols. (New York: The Macmillan Company, 1938–50), VI, 406–11.

Without a declaration of war and without warning or justification of any kind, civilians, including vast numbers of women and children, are being ruthlessly murdered with bombs from the air. In times of so-called peace, ships are being attacked and sunk by submarines without cause or notice. Nations are fomenting and taking sides in civil warfare in nations that have never done them any harm. Nations claiming freedom for themselves deny it to others.

Innocent peoples, innocent nations, are being cruelly sacrificed to a greed for power and supremacy which is devoid of all sense of justice and humane considerations.

To paraphrase a recent author [James Hilton in *Lost Horizon*] "perhaps we foresee a time when men, exultant in the technique of homicide, will rage so hotly over the world that every precious thing will be in danger, every book and picture and harmony, every treasure garnered through two millenniums, the small, the delicate, the defenseless—all will be lost or wrecked or utterly destroyed."

If those things come to pass in other parts of the world, let no one imagine that America will escape, that America may expect mercy, that this Western Hemisphere will not be attacked and that it will continue tranquilly and peacefully to carry on the ethics and the arts of civilization.

If those days come "there will be no safety in arms, no help from authority, no answer in science. The storm will rage till every flower of culture is trampled and all human beings are leveled in a vast chaos."

If those days are not to come to pass—if we are to have a world in which we can breathe freely and live in amity without fear—the peace-loving nations must make a concerted effort to uphold laws and principles on which alone peace can rest secure.

The peace-loving nations must make a concerted effort in opposition to those violations of treaties and those ignorings of humane instincts which today are creating a state of international anarchy and instability from which there is no escape through mere isolation or neutrality.

Those who cherish their freedom and recognize and respect the equal right of their neighbors to be free and live in peace, must work together for the triumph of law and moral principles in order that peace, justice and confidence may prevail in the world. There must be a return to a belief in the pledged word, in the value of a signed treaty. There must be recognition of the fact that national morality is as vital as private morality.

A bishop [Bishop Frank W. Sterett] wrote me the other

day: "It seems to me that something greatly needs to be said in behalf of ordinary humanity against the present practice of carrying the horrors of war to helpless civilians, especially women and children. It may be that such a protest might be regarded by many, who claim to be realists, as futile, but may it not be that the heart of mankind is so filled with horror at the present needless suffering that that force could be mobilized in sufficient volume to lessen such cruelty in the days ahead. Even though it may take twenty years, which God forbid, for civilization to make effective its corporate protest against this barbarism, surely strong voices may hasten the day."

There is a solidarity and interdependence about the modern world, both technically and morally, which makes it impossible for any nation completely to isolate itself from economic and political upheavals in the rest of the world, especially when such upheavals appear to be spreading and not declining. There can be no stability or peace either within nations or between nations except under laws and moral standards adhered to by all. International anarchy destroys every foundation for peace. It jeopardizes either the immediate or the future security of every nation, large or small. It is, therefore, a matter of vital interest and concern to the people of the Untied States that the sanctity of international treaties and the maintenance of international morality be restored.

The overwhelming majority of the peoples and nations of the world today want to live in peace. They seek the removal of barriers against trade. They want to exert themselves in industry, in agriculture and in business, that they may increase their wealth through the production of wealth-producing goods rather than striving to produce military planes and bombs and machine guns and cannon for the destruction of human lives and useful property.

In those nations of the world which seem to be piling armament on armament for purposes of aggression, and those other nations which fear acts of aggression against them and their security, a very high proportion of their national income is being spent directly for armaments. It runs from thirty to as high as fifty percent. We are fortunate. The proportion that we in the United States spend is far less—eleven or twelve percent.

How happy we are that the circumstances of the moment permit us to put our money into bridges and boulevards, dams and reforestation, the conservation of our soil and many other kinds of useful works rather than into huge standing armies and vast supplies of implements of war.

I am compelled and you are compelled, nevertheless, to look ahead. The peace, the freedom and the security of ninety percent of the population of the world is being jeopardized by the remaining ten percent who are threatening a breakdown of all international order and law. Surely the ninety percent who want to live in peace under law and in accordance with moral standards that have received almost universal acceptance through the centuries, can and must find some way to make their will prevail.

The situation is definitely of universal concern. The questions involved relate not merely to violations of specific provisions of particular treaties; they are questions of war and peace, of international law and especially of principles of humanity. It is true that they involve definite violations of agreements, and especially of the Covenant of the League of Nations, the Briand-Kellogg Pact and the Nine Power Treaty. But they also involve problems of world economy, world security and world humanity.

It is true that the moral consciousness of the world must recognize the importance of removing injustices and well-founded grievances; but at the same time it must be aroused to the cardinal necessity of honoring sanctity of treaties, of respecting the rights and liberties of others and of putting an end to acts of international aggression.

It seems to be unfortunately true that the epidemic of world lawlessness is spreading.

When an epidemic of physical disease starts to spread, the community approves and joins in a quarantine of the patients in order to protect the health of the community against the spread of the disease.

It is my determination to pursue a policy of peace. It is my determination to adopt every practicable measure to avoid involvement in war. It ought to be inconceivable that in this modern era, and in the face of experience, any nation could be so foolish and ruthless as to run the risk of plunging the whole world into war by invading and violating, in contravention of solemn treaties, the territory of other nations that have done them no real harm and are too weak to protect themselves adequately. Yet the peace of the world and the welfare and security of every nation, including our own, is today being threatened by that very thing.

No nation which refuses to exercise forbearance and to respect the freedom and rights of others can long remain strong and retain the confidence and respect of other nations. No nation ever loses its dignity or its good standing by conciliating its differences, and by exercising great patience with, and consideration for, the rights of other nations.

War is a contagion, whether it be declared or undeclared. It can engulf states and peoples remote from the original scene of hostilities. We are determined to keep out of war, yet we cannot insure ourselves against the disastrous effects of war and the dangers of involvement. We are adopting such measures as will minimize our risk of involvement, but we cannot have complete protection in a world of disorder in which confidence and security have broken down.

If civilization is to survive the principles of the Prince of Peace must be restored. Trust between nations must be revived.

Most important of all, the will for peace on the part of peace-loving nations must express itself to the end that nations that may be tempted to violate their agreements and the rights of others will desist from such a course. There must be positive endeavors to preserve peace.

America hates war. America hopes for peace. Therefore, America actively engages in the search for peace.

President Roosevelt's Quarantine Address has a special place in the folklore of the 1930's. In this speech, it has been claimed, Roosevelt proposed nothing less than the abandonment of the isolationism of the past two decades in favor of American participation in a system of collective security. Unhappily, it has been noted, the President's appeal to "quarantine the aggressors" raised such a storm of protest that Roosevelt was compelled to retreat. Shackled by public opinion, which lacked the President's awareness of the threat posed by the Axis, Roosevelt thereafter found himself powerless to use the influence of the United States either to curb Fascist aggression or to avert a second world war. Such is the traditional view of the Quarantine Address.

Writers who have advanced this interpretation have been compelled to explain why, on the very day after the President's Chicago oration, Roosevelt "retreated." When reporters pressed him on what he meant by "quarantine," Roosevelt expostulated: "Look, 'sanctions' is a terrible word to use. They are out of the window." Newspapermen were bewildered by what seemed to be an abrupt volte-face. When they persisted in trying to discern the meaning of the speech, Roosevelt admonished them to look at the final sentence of his address: "Therefore, America actively engages in the search for peace."

Both memoirists and historians have explained the President's "retreat" as a response to the intensely unfavorable reaction to his speech. "This bold effort to awaken public opinion overshot the mark, for its rash phrases frightened people who feared the country might be dragged into a new cauldron of battle," Allan Nevins has written. "It had a bad press." Cordell Hull recalled: "The reaction against the quarantine idea was quick and violent. As I saw it, this had the effect of setting back for at least six months our constant educational campaign intended to create and strengthen public opinion toward international cooperation." Roosevelt's speech writer, Samuel Rosenman, has observed: "The President was attacked by a vast majority of the press. . . . Telegrams of denunciation came in at once. . . . 'It's a terrible thing,' he once said to me, having in mind I'm sure, this occasion, 'to look over your shoulder when you are trying to lead—and to find no one there.'"

It is true that both the isolationist press and isolationist leaders in Congress denounced the President's speech. Hearst's San Francisco Examiner pleaded: "Don't Stick Out Your Neck, Uncle!" When the Philadelphia Inquirer conducted a telegraphic poll of Congress, it found better than 2-to-1 opposition to cooperation with the League of Nations in sanctions against Japan. Representative Hamilton Fish of New York assailed the speech as the "most provocative, inflammatory and dangerous ever delivered by any President," and Senator Gerald Nye of North Dakota cried: "Once again we are baited to thrill to a call to save the world." Roosevelt received little public support from his own lieutenants, and some of his diplomats were dismayed. After seeing "Gone with the Wind," Ambassador to Japan Joseph Grew noted that this was "precisely the way I felt" in response to Roosevelt's address.

But is this unfavorable public reaction an adequate explanation for Roosevelt's retreat? His statements at the press conference were made before much of the response, especially letters to the White House, could have been assessed. He could hardly have expected a favorable reception from the Hearst press or from senators like Nye. The Inquirer's poll diminishes in importance when it is noted that only forty-nine congressmen commented. If senators like Nye disliked the address, the chairman of the Senate Foreign Relations Committee, Key Pittman, who often opposed the Administration's proposals for international cooperation, announced that he favored the "ostracism" of Japan by economic action. The President had, too, the backing of Republican Henry Stimson, who had been Hoover's Secretary of State. Moreover, an *entry in a contemporary diary suggests that Hull's recollection that he was disconcerted by the "quarantine" reference is in error. J. Pierrepont Moffat, chief of the State Department's Division of European Affairs, was in Hull's office when the ticker reported Roosevelt's address; "The Secretary," he noted, "was delighted at the speech."*

There is an even more compelling reason for doubting the familiar version. Historians have remarked on the popular indignation expressed in the torrent of hostile letters and wires directed to the White House. Yet an examination of the White House files (now at the Franklin D. Roosevelt Library at Hyde Park) reveals that the letters and telegrams the President received were overwhelmingly favorable.

Moreover, again contrary to the traditional exegesis, most of the press response to the Quarantine Address was favoraable. The New York Times *of October 6 printed excerpts from editorials under the headline "Roosevelt Speech Widely Approved." The anti-Administration* New York Herald Tribune *ran a survey of newspaper opinion under the banner "Press Accepts Roosevelt Talk As Vital Step."* Time *observed that the press had "produced more words of approval, some enthusiastic and some tempered, than have greeted any Roosevelt step in many a month." Even the* Chicago Tribune *commented that the response to the address must have been "gratifying" to the internationalists. The very newspapers the President was most likely to read supported him warmly: journals such as the* New York Times, *the* Baltimore Sun, *the* Washington Post, *and the* Washington Evening Star. *The* Star, *often critical of Roosevelt, wrote: "Not since Woodrow Wilson's message to Congress in April, 1917, have more prescient words fallen from the lips of the President of the United States."*

The anti-Roosevelt writer David Lawrence thought Roosevelt's address "penetrating and incisive," and Westbrook Pegler commented, "Roosevelt May Have Said Just What Was Needed to Avert New World War." The President received the anticipated support in the southern press. More striking is the endorsement he received from Pacific Coast newspapers like the San Francisco Chronicle *and the* Portland Oregonian, *which had opposed him in 1936, and, in the "isolationist" Middle West, from such journals as the* Indianapolis Star, *the* Cleveland Plain Dealer, *and the* Cincinnati Enquirer. *Roosevelt himself confided to Colonel House: "I thought, frankly, that there would be more criticism."*

If the response to the speech was largely affirmative, why, then, did Roosevelt "retreat" so quickly? This is much more debatable. The answer would appear to be that the President did not "retreat," because he had never really advanced, or at least not very far. The crux of the problem is what Roosevelt meant by "quarantine." It has always been supposed that he meant the use of some kind of sanctions, and there is impressive evidence to support this belief. Harold Ickes noted in his diary that Roosevelt in September, 1937, contemplated proposing joint action of the "peace-loving nations" to cut off all trade with future aggressors. Sumner Welles has written that Roosevelt used the word "quarantine" to connote an embargo on Japan enforced by the American and British fleets. In December, 1937, the President argued at a Cabinet meeting that economic sanctions could be effective. "We don't call them economic sanctions; we call them quarantines," he observed. Joseph Alsop and Robert Kintner, who had access to restricted documents, concluded that Roosevelt intended by "quarantine" to suggest a strong form of sanctions: total nonintercourse with an aggressor.

Yet there is persuasive reason for doubting that Roosevelt intended his Quarantine Address to mark a new departure in foreign policy that would embrace collective action to impose sanctions. His letters and memoranda in 1937 indicate that his thinking was not that sharply defined. He was disturbed by the drift toward war, and felt called on to do something to prevent it, but he was not sure what specific action to recommend. He toyed with different ideas at different times—a new world peace conference, an economic embargo, perhaps even a naval blockade.

But he had not yet reached the conviction that the aggressors could be deterred only by military or economic coercion. He seems still to have hoped that the dictators could be swayed by the threat of disapproval. In many respects a nineteenth-century moralist, Roosevelt had a gentleman's dismay at the violation of treaties and a gentleman's faith that fear of ostracism might deter men from violating the code. His first step would be to alert the American people to the peril they faced, and to point out to them that isolation and neutrality were inadequate responses. Beyond this, he would impress on the world the distinction between the peace-loving and the aggressor states, and the need for the peace-loving states to take joint action. By joint action, he seems to have meant a warning to future war-makers that they would be ostracized if they broke the peace. Ostracism would take the form of breaking off diplomatic relations and of joint expressions of condemnation; if these did not suffice, economic measures might be considered. But it was not any specific program so much as the need to take common counsel in search of peace that Roosevelt stressed. After his speech, Roosevelt went directly to the house of Cardinal Mundelein. Subsequently, Mundelein gave a lucid report to the Apostolic Delegate to the United States on the President's thinking: "His plan does not contemplate either military or naval action against the unjust aggressor nation, nor does it involve 'sanctions' as generally understood but rather a policy of isolation, severance of ordinary communications in a united manner by all the governments of the pact."

Roosevelt's intentions were obscured by his unfortunate choice of the word "quarantine." It seemed natural for the President to use a medical metaphor; he often conceived of himself as Dr. Roosevelt attending to the ills of a sick society. But, in employing the term "quarantine," he appeared to be serving notice on Japan of an imminent embargo. When, on the very next day, the League of Nations censured Japan, Roosevelt's address seemed to be an episode in a concert of powers against Tokyo, although the President had, in fact, made no commitment to Geneva. After his speech, the President was nonplussed by the attention focused on the word "quarantine." He confided to Norman Davis that he regarded "quarantine" as a much milder term than "ostracism" or similar synonyms.

Neither friend nor foe comprehended the intent of Roosevelt's address. His critics were certain he sought to achieve "peace through war," his friends wondered why the President did not follow up his Chicago speech with specific recommendations. By the time the President spoke, thought had become polarized between isolationists, who believed that any questioning of their assumptions implied a commitment to collective security, and internationalists, who assumed that any departure from isolation carried with it an acceptance of sanctions. Each found in the President's speech what he expected to find.

Roosevelt himself believed, or professed to believe, that the speech had achieved its main purpose: the education of the nation. He wrote Nicholas Murray Butler: "Much can be accomplished by the iteration of moralities even though the tangible results seem terrifically slow." He had no doubt that the meaning of the speech lay not in the interpretation that was given to his "quarantine" image, but rather in the modest conclusion he had interpolated: "There must be positive endeavors to preserve peace. America hates war. America hopes for peace. Therefore, America actively engages in the search for peace."

Albert Einstein
Letter to Franklin D. Roosevelt
1939

EDITED BY DONALD FLEMING

On August 2, 1939, Albert Einstein wrote a letter to President Roosevelt; this letter drafted the atom for war. Less than a year before, nuclear physics was still the standing illustration of intellectual curiosity for its own sake. The situation began to be transformed when the Germans Otto Hahn and Fritz Strassmann announced in January, 1939, that bombardment of uranium by neutrons appeared to produce the much lighter element barium. This conclusion, as they said, played such havoc with accepted notions in physics that they hesitated to believe it themselves. From her exile in Sweden, Hahn's former associate Lise Meitner, driven from Germany in 1938 as a Jew, promptly concluded that Hahn had indeed split uranium into two lighter elements—a process which she and her physicist-nephew Otto Frisch compared with "fission" in bacteria. Meitner and Frisch surmised, and Frisch speedily demonstrated, that fission ought to be accompanied by a tremendous release of energy according to Einstein's formula $E = mc^2$. Frédéric Joliot-Curie in Paris and, almost simultaneously, Enrico Fermi and Leo Szilard in the United States made the further demonstration that fission of uranium liberated additional neutrons. That discovery was a lever for moving the world. If neutrons on splitting uranium kept breeding

882

more neutrons to split more uranium, a chain reaction would result. Two possibilities loomed, later succinctly described as the "bomb" and the "boiler"—explosive chain reactions for war, or controlled reactions for industry.

Yet Hahn and those who repeated his experiments did not get a chain reaction. The question became why not. This was one of the points that Fermi discussed with Niels Bohr when the latter attended a conference in the United States in January, 1939, and told the Americans what Meitner and Frisch had deduced. Bohr's solution to the puzzle turned upon the existence of two principal isotopes of uranium—238, overwhelmingly predominant, and 235, of which an ordinary sample would yield only 0.7 per cent. Bohr argued on theoretical grounds that ordinary "slow" neutrons would split 235 but merely be absorbed by 238. The chain reaction would be choked off by the scarcity of appropriate targets. The situation was further complicated by the fact that the neutrons liberated on fission of 235 were "fast" and therefore less adapted to keep the reaction going. Fermi and others, however, had shown in 1935 that fast neutrons could be "moderated," i.e., slowed down, by passing through hydrogenous substances like water and paraffin; and carbon was another moderator. The inference was that by interspersing even ordinary uranium with a moderating substance, fast neutrons could be slowed down and the chain reaction maintained. The line of reasoning was tenuous. If, alternatively, that separation of pure 235 from 238 was contemplated, that was an almost inconceivable feat in 1939.

Even if all the links of the argument held and all the strategies proved workable in the laboratory, to turn these academic triumphs into actual bombs or power plants would be the greatest achievement in the history of technology. There was no assurance that the problems could be solved, either in theory or in practice; they could not even be tackled without diverting men and resources from other more immediately promising research, as on radar; and at best the anticipated war might be over before the scientists had anything tangible to show for their labors—even before any politicians would blindly stake them out of the public funds.

When the doubts inside the scientific community and the general incomprehension without are added together, the wonder becomes that the bomb did materialize in time to play a part in the war. This was undoubtedly the doing of the refugee scientists from the continent of Europe—men who had seen their own countries succumb to Hitler and who now turned to make a last stand by the side of the decent but ap-

pallingly innocent Anglo-Saxons who had never known utter defeat and did not really believe it could happen to them. The refugees knew better. They were desperately afraid that Hitler, with the still considerable resources of German science and German industry, would get the atomic bomb and gain the final victory.

Somehow the refugees must shake the democracies awake to this terrible new menace before it was too late. The Italian refugee Fermi talked with people in the Navy Department in March, 1939, but they were not impressed by his presentation. His English was halting and the legend has it that some of his interrogators dismissed him as a "crazy wop." By summer Fermi and the Hungarian refugee Szilard, with the latter's compatriots Edward Teller and Eugene Wigner, were in despair as they tried to think how to attract the notice of somebody in authority. Szilard knew the most famous refugee of all, Albert Einstein, and he knew the Dowager Queen of the Belgians. The least Szilard could do was to get Einstein to warn the Queen to keep the uranium of the Belgian Congo out of German hands. Einstein was willing, but before he could send a letter to the Queen, Szilard met an economist with Lehman Brothers named Alexander Sachs. Sachs told him to forget about the Queen. Einstein was the one man whose name was a big trumpet to catch the ear of Franklin D. Roosevelt. Sachs had an entree to the White House and undertook to deliver a letter from Einstein to the President personally. Though dated August 2, the letter was not in fact delivered till October 11. In the meantime the war had come.

Albert Einstein
Old Grove Road
Nassau Point
Peconic, Long Island
August 2, 1939

F. D. Roosevelt
President of the United States
White House
Washington, D. C.

SIR:

Some recent work by E. Fermi and L. Szilard, which has been communicated to me in manuscript, leads me to expect that the element uranium may be turned into a new and important source of energy in the immediate future. Certain aspects of the situation seem to call for watchfulness and, if necessary, quick action on the part of the Administration. I believe, therefore, that it is my duty to bring to your attention the following facts and recommendations.

In the course of the last four months, it has been made probable—through the work of Joliot in France as well as Fermi and Szilard in America—that it may become possible to set up nuclear chain reactions in a large mass of uranium, by which vast amounts of power and large quantities of new radium-like elements would be generated. Now it appears almost certain that this could be achieved in the immediate future.

This new phenomenon would also lead to the construction of bombs, and it is conceivable—though much less certain—that extremely powerful bombs of a new type may thus be constructed. A single bomb of this type, carried by boat or exploded in a port, might very well destroy the whole port together with some of the surrounding territory. However, such bombs might very well prove to be too heavy for transportation by air.

The United States has only very poor ores of uranium in moderate quantities. There is some good ore in Canada and the former Czechoslovakia, while the most important source of uranium is the Belgian Congo.

In view of this situation you may think it desirable to have some permanent contact maintained between the Administration and the group of physicists working on chain reactions in America. One possible way of achieving this might be for you to entrust with this task a person who has your confidence and who could perhaps serve in an unofficial capacity. His task might comprise the following:

a) To approach Government Departments, keep them informed of the further developments, and put forward recommendations for Government action, giving particular attention to the problem of securing a supply of uranium ore for the United States.

b) To speed up the experimental work which is at present being carried on within the limits of the budgets of University laboratories, by providing funds, if such funds be required, through his contacts with private persons who are willing to make contributions for this cause, and perhaps also

The letter as reprinted here appeared in Otto Nathan and Heinz Norden, eds., *Einstein on Peace* (New York: Simon and Schuster, 1960), pp. 294–96.

by obtaining the cooperation of industrial laboratories which have the necessary equipment.

I understand that Germany has actually stopped the sale of uranium from the Czechoslovakian mines which she has taken over. That she should have taken such early action might perhaps be understood on the ground that the son of the German Under-Secretary of State, von Weizsäcker, is attached to the Kaiser Wilhelm Institute in Berlin, where some of the American work on uranium is now being repeated.

Yours very truly,

A. EINSTEIN

Some time after Einstein wrote the letter to Roosevelt, he said in exculpation that he had merely been used as a mailbox by Szilard. At the time neither Einstein nor any of the other refugee scientists had any hesitation in setting in motion the wheels in motion. They were not, after all, proposing to use the bomb, but merely to have the means of calling Hitler's bluff if he got it and tried atomic blackmail, and they thought the odds were in his favor. They were sure that scientists on the other side had already set the same wheels in motion under worse auspices.

For a long time, the only thing Szilard and Fermi worried about was their failure to get the wheels moving fast enough on their side. Roosevelt did set up a committee on uranium immediately after his interview with Sachs, and a year's contract for research was actually let on November 1, 1939—for $6,000. Though other research was financed by universities and foundations, really sizable government contracts did not come till autumn, 1940. At mid-summer, 1941, there was still no crash program to build an atomic bomb. The refugee scientists had failed to convey their own sense of urgency to the Americans. Technically, the United States was still at peace. The situation might well have been transformed in the wake of Pearl Harbor. But if the decisive commitment had been delayed even a few months beyond December 7, 1941, the war might have been over before the bomb was ready.

In fact, the great decision to go all out on the bomb was taken on December 6. The refugees who got to America had failed to communicate their urgency; but Hitler had seeded England with his enemies too. They included some of the most brilliant nuclear scientists—above all, Otto Frisch, Rudolf Peierls, and two leading members of Joliot-Curie's team, Hans Halban and Lew Kowarski. All of these men were rigor-

ously excluded by British security regulations for participating in the sensitive military research already in progress. Conversely, they were almost alone in having the leisure to speculate on other matters. Radar they could not touch; the only thing they were free to occupy themselves with was working out the atomic bomb. They were severely confined in the name of security to the most explosive security issue of the war. They demonstrated, in collaboration with the great English nuclear physicists Sir James Chadwick (the discoverer of the neutron) and G. P. Thomson, that the bomb could probably be built in time to affect the war. Their optimistic report of July, 1941, and the detailed case they made to American scientists who visited England in the fall, played a major, perhaps critical, part in the American decision to make a big push on the eve of Pearl Harbor rather than later. It does not follow that Einstein's letter of August, 1939, served no purpose. The decision of December 6, 1941, would have been comparatively empty if the Americans had had no base to build upon.

In the spring of 1945, when the bomb was almost ready for testing, the grim ironies began to pile up. The refugees' target, Hitler, was already beaten without the bomb; the Germans, incredibly, had made no real progress toward building one; and the only possible target was a country—Japan—that had never been in the running, and still less in the minds of the European refugees. Leo Szilard began frantically distributing petitions to stave off consequences of his own initiative, but it was too late. Einstein, for his part, on learning of Hiroshima cried out, "Oh, weh!" He, the great enemy of war, had brought flaming death upon hundreds of thousands of Japanese to whom neither he nor his counselors had given a moment's thought when they were drafting the letter to Roosevelt. The Japanese took Hitler's medicine.

Wendell L. Willkie

One World

1943

EDITED BY MAX LERNER

One World *was Wendell Willkie's prime contribution to World War II, its fighting aims, its coalition strategy, and its postwar settlements. The 1940 Republican candidate for the Presidency, who had seemed to waver during the campaign on the issue of interventionism or isolationism, was actually a strong interventionist despite his German ancestry and his Indiana-Ohio Midwest roots. After his defeat in the election he remained a figure with considerable personal and political following and with hopes for success in the next presidential contest, as well as with a deep commitment to the struggle against a fascism which threatened what he held dear—personal and economic freedom. While the bombs were still falling, he paid a sympathetic visit to London early in 1941 and was enthusiastically received. He was a leader in the successful battle at home for Lend-Lease aid to Britain.*

After the entrance of both Russia and America into the war, Willkie was restless about what role he could play. When he received a cable in July, 1942, from three American war reporters in Russia's wartime capital at Kuibishev—Maurice Hindus, Eddie Gilmore, and Ben Robertson—urging him

*to make a good-will visit to beleaguered Russia, he eagerly
agreed. After securing some broad commissions from President Roosevelt, he set off on August 26 in a converted
bomber for a round-the-world trip, accompanied by Joseph
Barnes and Gardner Cowles, Jr., both of them his friends,
both from the Office of War Information. The trip took fifty
days and covered 31,000 miles on five continents, with stops
at the Middle Eastern, Russian, and Chinese war fronts.
Aside from showing that the Allies still dominated the
world's airways even at the low ebb of their fortunes in the
war, the aim was to carry the tidings of America's massive
war-production effort around the world, and to dramatize to
America's allies the unity of the two major parties in their
determination to win the war. But Willkie was not content to
stop there. Speaking for himself, in a statement at Moscow,
he called for a second front, and added that American military leaders "will need some public prodding." At Chungking
he called for "an end to the empire of nations over other nations," and a timetable to give the colonial peoples a chance
to "work out and train governments of their own choosing."
Both statements stirred worldwide controversy.*

*After a striking popular response to a radio broadcast he
delivered after his return to America, Willkie decided to put
into book form what he had seen on his trip and learned
from it. Working from notes and outlines submitted by
Barnes and Cowles as well as from his own recollections,
Willkie spent every morning from nine to noon for six weeks
on the book, at the apartment of Irita Van Doren, a close
friend and his literary adviser. His publishers, Simon and
Schuster, had suggested as a title* One War, One Peace, One
World; *in the end Willkie cut it down, at the suggestion of
one of the editors, Tom Bevans, to* One World. *The book was
published April 8, 1943, and was an immediate and resounding success, reaching the figure of a million copies in print in
seven weeks, and going into many editions later. With his
basic themes of Allied unity in war and peacemaking, and the
recognition of new forces everywhere demanding freedom,
Willkie struck a strong and deep contemporary chord.*

M Y SECOND memory of Alexandria is of a dinner that
night at the home of Admiral Harwood, hero of the
epic fight of the *Exeter* against the *Graf Spee* in South American waters, and now commander of the British Navy in the
eastern Mediterranean. He invited to dine with us ten of his

compatriots in the naval, diplomatic, or consular service in Alexandria. We discussed the war in the detached, almost impersonal way in which the war is discussed all over the world by officers engaged in fighting it, and then the conversation turned to politics. I tried to draw out these men, all of them experienced and able administrators of the British Empire, on what they saw in the future, and especially in the future of the colonial system and of our joint relations with the many peoples of the East.

What I got was Rudyard Kipling, untainted even with the liberalism of Cecil Rhodes. I knew that informed Englishmen in London and all over the British Commonwealth were working hard on these problems, that many of them, for example, were trying to find a formula which will go farther toward self-government than the older concept of "trusteeship." But these men, executing the policies made in London, had no idea that the world was changing. The British colonial system was not perfect in their eyes; it seemed to me simply that no one of them had ever thought of it as anything that might possibly be changed or modified in any way. The Atlantic Charter most of them had read about. That it might affect their careers or their thinking had never occurred to any of them. That evening started in my mind a conviction which was to grow strong in the days that followed it in the Middle East: that brilliant victories in the field will not win for us this war now going on in the far reaches of the world, that only new men and new ideas in the machinery of our relations with the peoples of the East can win the victory without which any peace will be only another armistice. . . .

. . . One senses a ferment in these lands, a groping of the long-inert masses, a growing disregard of restrictive religious rites and practices. In every city I found a group—usually a small group—of restless, energetic, intellectual young people who knew the techniques of the mass movement that had brought about the revolution in Russia and talked about them. They knew also the history of our own democratic development. In their talk with me they seemed to be weighing

---

These excerpts from *One World* have been reprinted from the original edition (New York: Simon and Schuster, 1943). They comprise roughly one-eighth of the total book. The sequence of chapters follows the stages of the flight, with emphasis on the Middle Eastern, Russian, and Chinese fronts, and on the subsurface revolutionary changes that Willkie felt at work in each. The present excerpts, omitting some preliminary pages on the first leg of the trip, plunge into what Willkie found at El Alamein, in Egypt. The excerpts end with the crucial passages of two concluding chapters on "What We Are Fighting For" and "One World."

in their minds the course through which their own intense, almost fanatical, aspirations should be achieved. Likewise I found in this part of the world, as I found in Russia, in China, everywhere, a growing spirit of fervid nationalism, a disturbing thing to one who believes that the only hope of the world lies in the opposite trend. . . .

I shall . . . never forget my visit with General de Gaulle. I was met at the airport at Beirut, received by an elaborately uniformed color guard and band, and whisked several miles to the house where the general was living—a great white structure, surrounded by elaborate and formal gardens, where guards saluted at every turn. We talked for hours in the general's private room, where every corner, every wall, held busts, statues, and pictures of Napoleon. The conversation continued through an elaborate dinner and went on late into the night, as we sat out on a beautiful starlit lawn.

Frequently the general, in describing his struggle of the moment with the British as to whether he or they should dominate Syria and the Lebanon, would declare dramatically, "I cannot sacrifice or compromise my principles." "Like Joan of Arc," his aide added. When I referred to my great interest in the Fighting French movement, he corrected me sharply. "The Fighting French are not a movement. The Fighting French are France itself. We are the residuary legatees of all of France and its possessions." When I reminded him that Syria was but a mandated area under the League of Nations, he said, "Yes, I know. But I hold it in trust. I cannot close out that mandate or let anyone else do so. That can be done only when there is a government again in France. In no place in this world can I yield a single French right, though I am perfectly willing to sit with Winston Churchill and Franklin Roosevelt and consider ways and means by which French rights and French territories can be momentarily and temporarily used in order to help drive the Germans and the collaborators from the control of France.

"Mr. Willkie," he continued, "some people forget that I and my associates represent France. They apparently do not have in mind France's glorious history. They are thinking in terms of its momentary eclipse." . . .

After a few formal speeches, the dinner [given by the Syrian Prime Minister, Nuri el-Said, at his Bagdad home] became a concert, and the concert became an exhibition of Arab dancing girls, and this in turn became a Western ball with English nurses and American soldiers up from Basra on the Persian Gulf and Iraqi officers dancing under an Arabian sky. No man could have sat through that evening and preserved any notion that the East and the West will never meet, or that Allah is determined to keep the Arabs a desert folk, ruled by foreigners from across the seas.

The next day, flying from Bagdad to Teheran, I was thinking over the events of the night before. And I became aware of certain sober undercurrents that had been beneath the gaiety, the same undercurrents I had noticed before in talking with students, newspapermen, and soldiers throughout the Middle East. It all added up to the conviction that these newly awakened people will be followers of some extremist leader in this generation if their new hunger for education and opportunity for a release from old restrictive religious and governmental practice is not met by their own rulers and their foreign overlords. The veil, the fez, the sickness, the filth, the lack of education and modern industrial development, the arbitrariness of government, all commingled in their minds to represent a past imposed upon them by a combination of forces within their own society and the self-interest of foreign domination. Again and again I was asked: does America intend to support a system by which our politics are controlled by foreigners, however politely, our lives dominated by foreigners, however indirectly, because we happen to be strategic points on the military roads and trade routes of the world? Or, they would say, to put it your way: because we are strategic points which must be held to prevent Axis or some other non-democratic domination of the key military roads and trade routes of the world? Because our canals, our seas, and our countries are necessary to the control of the eastern Mediterranean and constitute the road to Asia?

I know this problem can be oversimplified in its statement and is not susceptible of easy answers. I know that the retention of points such as Suez, the eastern Mediterranean, and the roads through Asia Minor to the East obviously, if our Western democracy is not to be threatened by hostile forces, must be kept in both friendly and stabilized hands. Likewise, I know there is much historical and even present-day justification for the current "protective" colonial system. Pragmatically, however, in view of the ferment which is going on, it is a question whether that system can be maintained. Idealistically, we must face the fact that the system is completely antipathetic to all the principles for which we claim we fight. Furthermore, the more we preach those principles, the more we stimulate the ferment that endangers the system.

I know all this. But I am here reporting what is in the minds of Prime Ministers, Foreign Ministers, awakened intellectual groups to be found in every city of the Middle East, and even vaguely in the minds of uneducated masses. Somehow, with a new approach and a patient wisdom, the question must be answered or a new leader will arise with a fierce fanaticism who will coalesce these discontents. And the result will be of necessity either the complete withdrawal of outside powers with a complete loss of democratic influence or complete military occupation and control of the countries by those outside powers.

If we believe in the ends we proclaim and if we want the stirring new forces within the Middle East to work with us toward those ends, we must cease trying to perpetuate control by manipulation of native forces, by playing off one against the other for our own ends. . . .

. . . I had not sufficiently taken into account, in appraising modern Russia, that it is ruled by and composed almost entirely of people whose parents had no property, no education, and only a folk heritage. That there is hardly a resident of Russia today whose lot is not as good as or better than his parents' lot was prior to the revolution. The Russian individual, like all individuals, naturally finds some good in a system that has improved his own lot, and has a tendency to forget the ruthless means by which it has been brought about. This may be difficult for an American to believe or like. But it was plainly the explanation among all sorts of people, everywhere, and it was clearly expressed during a stimulating evening I spent in Moscow when I was trying to put a group of intelligent modern Russians on the spot to defend their system.

But I had not gone to Russia to remember the past. Besides my concrete assignments for the President, I had gone determined to find an answer for myself to the actual problems posed for our generation of Americans by the simple fact that the Soviet Union, whether we like it or not, exists.

Some of these answers I believe I found, at least to my own satisfaction. I can sum up the three most important in a few sentences.

First, Russia is an effective society. It works. It has survival value. The record of Soviet resistance to Hitler has been proof enough of this to most of us, but I must admit in all frankness that I was not prepared to believe before I went to Russia what I now know about its strength as a going organization of men and women.

Second, Russia is our ally in this war. The Russians, more sorely tested by Hitler's might even than the British, have met the test magnificently. Their hatred of Fascism and the Nazi system is real and deep and bitter. And this hatred makes them determined to eliminate Hitler and exterminate the Nazi blight from Europe and the world.

Third, we must work with Russia after the war. At least it seems to me that there can be no continued peace unless we learn to do so.

Those conclusions were reinforced by what I saw and heard in various parts of the Soviet Union. I saw one portion of the Russian front, close enough to know something at first hand of what the Red Army has done. I saw a good many of the factories behind the front, where the Soviet workers have fooled too many of our experts by keeping up a steady flow of supplies to the fighting men. And I saw collective farms. Behind the factories and the farms, I saw and talked with the Soviet newspapermen and writers who have given all Russians the strangely exalted feeling of being in a crusade. Behind the journalists, I saw the Kremlin, having talked twice at great length with Mr. Stalin, and observed something of how power is really exercised under the dictatorship of the proletariat. Finally, behind all these, I saw the Russian people from one end of Russia to the other, and if my sampling of the 200,000,000 was absurdly small, it had the advantage of being chosen entirely by chance. . . .

In Moscow I had two long talks with Joseph Stalin. Much of what was said I am not at liberty to report. But about the man himself there is no reason to be cautious. He is one of the significant men of this generation.

At his invitation I called on him one evening at 7:30. He apparently has most of his conferences at night. His office was a fair-sized room about eighteen by thirty-five feet. On its walls hung pictures of Marx and Engels and Lenin, and profiles of Lenin and Stalin together, the same pictures that you see in practically every schoolhouse, public building, factory, hotel, hospital, and home in Russia. Often you find in addition the picture of Molotov. In an anteroom visible from the office was a huge globe some ten feet in diameter.

Stalin and Molotov were standing to welcome me at the far end of a long oak conference table. They greeted me simply and we talked for some three hours—about the war, about what would come after, about Stalingrad and the front, about America's position, the relationship of Great Britain, the United States, and Russia, and about many other important and unimportant subjects.

A few days later I spent some five hours sitting next to Stalin, through the numerous courses of a state dinner which he gave for me; later while we all drank coffee at little tables in another room, and finally through a private showing of a motion picture of the siege and defense of Moscow.

It was at this dinner, incidentally, that we toasted the interpreters. We had toasted our respective countries and leaders; we had toasted the Russian people and the American people and our hopes for future collaboration; we had toasted each other. Finally it occurred to me that the only people really working at that dinner were the interpreters who were kept bobbing up and down to translate. So I proposed a toast to them. Later, I said to Mr. Stalin, "I hope I didn't step out of line in suggesting that we toast the interpreters." And he replied, "Not at all, Mr. Willkie, we are a democratic country."

Stalin, I should judge, is about five feet four or five, and gives the appearance of slight stockiness. I was surprised to find how short he is; but his head, his mustache, and his eyes are big. His face, in repose, is a hard face, and he looked tired in September—not sick, as is so often reported, but desperately tired. He had a right to be. He talks quietly, readily, and at times with a simple, moving eloquence. When he described to me Russia's desperate situation as to fuel, transportation, military equipment, and man power, he was genuinely dramatic.

He has, I would say, a hard, tenacious, driving mind. He asked searching questions, each of them loaded like a revolver, each of them designed to cut through to what he believed to be the heart of the matter that interested him. He pushes aside pleasantries and compliments and is impatient of generalities.

When he asked me about my trips through various factories, he wanted detailed reports, department by department, not general judgments as to their operating methods and efficiency. When I asked him about Stalingrad, he developed for me logically not alone its geographical and military importance, but the moral effect on Russia, Germany, and particularly the Middle East, of the successful or unsuccessful defense. He made no predictions as to Russia's ability to hold it and he was quite definite in his assertion that neither love of homeland nor pure bravery could save it. Battles were won or lost primarily by numbers, skill, and matériel.

He told me again and again that his propaganda was deliberately designed to make his people hate the Nazis, but it was obvious that he himself had a certain bitter admiration for the efficiency by which Hitler had transplanted to Germany as much as ninety-four per cent of the working population from some of the conquered Russian territory, and he respected the completely professional training of the German

Army, particularly its officers. He discounted, just as Winston Churchill did to me two years before in England, the notion that Hitler was but a tool in the hands of abler men. He did not think we should count upon an early internal collapse in Germany. He said that the way to defeat Germany was to destroy its army. And he believed that one of the most effective methods of destroying faith in Hitler's invincibility throughout Europe was in continuous air-raid bombings of German cities and of German-held docks and factories in the conquered countries.

When we talked of the causes of the war and the economic and political conditions that would face the world after it was over, his comprehension was broad, his detailed information exact, and the cold reality of his thinking apparent. Stalin is a hard man, perhaps even a cruel man, but a very able one. He has few illusions.

His admiration for the effectiveness of American production methods would more than satisfy the National Association of Manufacturers. But he does not understand the indirections and some of the restraints of the democratic methods of waging war. He wondered, for instance, why the democracies should not insist upon using certain bases for war purposes that would be of great value to them, particularly if the nations that owned them were unco-operative and not able to defend them.

Quite contrary to general report, Stalin has great respect for Winston Churchill; he almost said it to me—the respect of one great realist for another.

On the personal side Stalin is a simple man, with no affectations or poses. He does not seek to impress by any artificial mannerisms. His sense of humor is a robust one, and he laughs readily at unsubtle jokes and repartee. Once I was telling him of the Soviet schools and libraries I had seen—how good they seemed to me. And I added, "But if you continue to educate the Russian people, Mr. Stalin, the first thing you know you'll educate yourself out of a job."

He threw his head back and laughed and laughed. Nothing I said to him, or heard anyone else say to him, through two long evenings, seemed to amuse him as much.

Strange as it may seem, Stalin dresses in light pastel shades. His well-known tunic is of finely woven material and is apt to be a soft green or a delicate pink; his trousers a light-tannish yellow or blue. His boots are black and highly polished. Ordinary social pleasantries bother him a little. As I was leaving him after my first talk, I expressed appreciation of the time he had given me, the honor he conferred in talking so candidly. A little embarrassed, he said:

"Mr. Willkie, you know I grew up a Georgian peasant. I am unschooled in pretty talk. All I can say is I like you very much."

Inevitably, Stalin's simple ways have set a fashion of a kind for other Soviet leaders. Especially in Moscow and in Kuibishev, there is an absence of flamboyance about Russian leaders that is remarkable. They all dress simply. They talk little and listen well. A surprising number of them are young, in their thirties. It would be my guess, which I could not prove or document, that Stalin likes a pretty heavy turnover of young people in his immediate entourage in the Kremlin. It is his way, I think, of keeping his ear to the ground.

Among the other leaders I met and talked to at any great length were Viacheslav Molotov, the Foreign Minister, Andrei Vishinsky and Solomon Lozovsky, his assistants, Marshal Voroshilov, the former Commissar of Defense, Anastasia Mikoyan, Commissar of Supply and head of the Soviet foreign-trade apparatus. Each of these is an educated man, interested in the foreign world, completely unlike in manner, appearance, and speech the uncouth, wild Bolshevik of our cartoons.

In Kuibishev, at a dinner given for me by Mr. Vishinsky, who was the chief state prosecutor in all the grim treason trials of four and five years ago, I caught myself studying his white hair, his professor's face, and his quiet, almost studious manner, and wondering if this could possibly be the same man who had purged some of the oldest heroes of the Russian Revolution on charges of murder and betrayal of their country.

Whenever the talk of these men ran to the peace, to what the world must be prepared to do after the war is over, they talked with statesmanship and real understanding.

Since I have returned to the United States, Mr. Stalin has defined the program, as he sees it, of the Anglo-American-Soviet coalition in the European war. These are the goals he calls for:

"Abolition of racial exclusiveness, equality of nations and integrity of their territories, liberation of enslaved nations and restoration of their sovereign rights, the right of every nation to arrange its affairs as it wishes, economic aid to nations that have suffered and assistance to them in attaining their material welfare, restoration of democratic liberties, the destruction of the Hitlerite regime."

We may ask: does Stalin mean what he says? Some will

point out that only two years ago Russia was in an alliance of expediency with Germany. I make no defense of expediency, military, political, temporary, or otherwise. For I believe the moral losses of expediency always far outweigh the temporary gains. And I believe that every drop of blood saved through expediency will be paid for by twenty drawn by the sword. But a Russian, feeling that by the German alliance his country was buying time, might well remind the democracies of Munich, and of the seven million tons of the best grade of scrap iron the United States shipped to Japan between 1937 and 1940.

Perhaps we can better measure the good faith of Stalin's statement in the light of the millions of Russians who have already died defending their fatherland and of the sixty million who have become slaves of the Nazis; in those other millions of Russian men and women who are working feverishly sixty-six hours a week in factories and mines to forge and produce instruments of war for the fighters at the front; and in the effort that went into the almost miraculous movement of great factories, hundreds of miles, that they might operate, uninterrupted, beyond Nazi reach. For it is in the attitude of the people that we may find the best interpretation of Stalin's purpose.

Many among the democracies fear and mistrust Soviet Russia. They dread the inroads of an economic order that would be destructive of their own. Such fear is weakness. Russia is neither going to eat us nor seduce us. That is—and this is something for us to think about—that is, unless our democratic institutions and our free economy become so frail through abuse and failure in practice as to make us soft and vulnerable. The best answer to Communism is a living, vibrant, fearless democracy—economic, social, and political. All we need to do is to stand up and perform according to our professed ideals. Then those ideals will be safe.

No, we do not need to fear Russia. We need to learn to work with her against our common enemy, Hitler. We need to learn to work with her in the world after the war. For Russia is a dynamic country, a vital new society, a force that cannot be bypassed in any future world. . . .

I arrived in Chungking late in the afternoon, at an airport some miles from the city. Long before our automobiles had reached the city, the road on either side was lined with people. Before we reached the middle of the city, the crowds stood packed from curb to store front. Men, women, young boys and girls, bearded old gentlemen, Chinese with fedora hats, others with skullcaps, coolies, porters, students, mothers nursing their children, well dressed and poorly dressed—they packed eleven miles of road over which our cars slowly moved on our way to the guesthouse in which we were to stay. On the other side of the Yangtze River, they stood and waited. On all the hills of Chungking, which must be the world's hilliest city, they stood and smiled and cheered and waved little paper American and Chinese flags.

Any man who has run for President of the United States is used to crowds. But not to this one. I could discount it in my mind as much as I wished, but to no avail. The paper flags waved by the people were all of the same size, suggesting that the hospitable and imaginative Mayor of Chungking, Dr. K. C. Wu, had had a hand in planning this demonstration. It was perfectly clear that not all these people, many of whom were barefoot or dressed in rags, had any clear idea of who I was or why I was there. The firecrackers which were exploding on every street corner, I told myself, are an old Chinese passion, anyway.

But in spite of all my efforts to discount it, this scene moved me profoundly. There was nothing synthetic or fake about the faces I looked at. They were seeing, in me, a representative of America and a tangible hope of friendship and help that might be forthcoming. It was a mass demonstration of good will. And it was an impressive show of the simple strength, in people and in emotions, which is China's greatest national resource.

I had seen a crowd like this one, but a little smaller, on my arrival in Lanchow, far into the northwest. I was later to see another, as impressive as any, which waited for hours in the rain on the streets of Sian, capital of Shensi province, because our plane was late. They never failed to move me deeply. It is impossible in a short trip through a country as big as China to make as many close and personal friendships as one would like, those relationships through which one generally comes to know the spirit and the ideas of a foreign people. But these crowds of Chinese people gave me a sure and lasting feeling that my surface impressions of China were backed by something no one could misread in those thousands of faces.

The Chinese I came to know well were, inevitably, leaders in one field or another. Some of them I will describe later in this account, and in high terms. But I know no praise high enough for the anonymous people of China. . . .

Possibly no other country on our side in this war is so dominated by the personality of one man as China. His name is Chiang Kai-shek, although he is universally referred to in China as "The Generalissimo," sometimes affectionately shortened to "Gissimo."

I had a number of long talks with the Generalissimo, as well as family breakfasts and other meals alone with him and Mme Chiang.

One late afternoon we drove to the Chiangs' country place, high on the steep bank of the Yangtze River. . . . Across the front of the simple frame house was a large porch where we sat looking out to the hills of Chungking. In the river below, a number of small boats moved in the swift current, carrying the Chinese farmer and his produce downstream to market. It had been a hot day in Chungking but here a pleasant breeze was blowing, and as Mme Chiang served us tea, the Generalissimo and I began to talk. . . .

We discussed the past and his administration's aim to change China from an almost exclusively agricultural society into a modern industrial one. He hoped in the change to retain the best of the old traditions and to avoid the social dislocations of large-scale Western industrial development by the establishment of a great number of widely distributed small plants. He was sure that in the teachings of Dr. Sun, the father of the republic, concerning a combined agricultural and industrial society he would find the way. But he was eager to discuss the question with someone from the West and he asked me many questions. I explained to him that the social problems created by mass production in America and the large industrial combinations which he wanted to avoid had not arisen, as he seemed to think, solely because of desire for power and the building of individual fortunes, though these elements undoubtedly contributed. In part, at least, they arose because of economic requirements: mass production greatly lowers costs.

I gave him the illustration of the automobile, which he hoped to see manufactured at low cost in China to fill Chinese roads. I pointed out to him that an automobile manufactured in a small plant would cost five times as much as an automobile manufactured on an assembly line under scientific management in a large plant. That it is impossible to have some of the products that make for a high standard of living at prices within the reach of the great masses of the people, if they must be produced exclusively in small plants. That every thoughtful American knew that in many instances we have created large industrial combinations unnecessarily. That for our social and economic good we should give the utmost encouragement and preference to the small industries.

But that in certain industries, in order to maintain our stand-ard of living, it was necessary to have large-scale production. I told him that we recognized the social, economic, and al-most non-democratic maladjustments created by the collec-tion of thousands of workers under single factory roofs, with the consequent possibility of unemployment of whole com-munities at one time. That we regretted the stratification of large groups of our population into a permanent employee class which this system produced, and the reduction of the opportunity for individual men to become owners of their own businesses. I also told the Generalissimo that we had not as yet found all the answers. But we did know that the solu-tion did not consist in breaking up necessary large units into inefficient small ones.

I reminded him that there was an experiment going on much closer to him than any in the Western world, the Com-munist one in Russia, and that part of its success was due to the mass-production technique of using large groups for the accomplishment of a particular purpose.

He suggested that perhaps he could find the solution in having necessary large units partly owned by government and partly by private capital.

The discussion went on for hours. Then Mme Chiang, who had been acting as interpreter for us, with pleasant but firm feminine authority, said: "It's ten o'clock and you men haven't had anything to eat. Come on now; we must drive into town and get at least a bite. You can finish this some other time."

At other times we did talk more of this, and of many other things. We talked of India, of the whole East, of its aspira-tions, of its purposes, of how it should fit into a world-wide order, of military strategy, of Japan and its resources, of Pearl Harbor and the fall of Singapore and their profound psychological effect on the attitude of the East toward the West. We talked of the growing spirit of intense, almost fa-natical nationalism which I had found developing in the countries of the Middle East, in Russia and now in China, of how such a spirit might upset the possibility of world co-op-eration. We talked of Russia and of Chiang's relationship to the Communists within China, of Great Britain and her poli-cy in the East, of Franklin Roosevelt and Winston Churchill and Joseph Stalin.

In fact, the six days I was with the Generalissimo were filled with talk. . . .

Millions have already died in this war and many thousands

more will go before it is over. Unless Britons and Canadians and Russians and Chinese and Americans and all our fighting allies, in the common cooperation of war, find the instrumentalities and the methods of cooperative effort after the war, we, the people, have failed our time and our generation. . . .

The statement of Mr. Stalin [a statement of Russian war aims on November 6, 1942, emphasizing "the liberation of enslaved nations and the restoration of their sovereign rights" and "the right of every nation to arrange its affairs as it wishes"] and the Atlantic Charter seem to me to have a common fallacy. They forecast the re-creation of western Europe in its old divisions of small nations, each with its own individual political, economic, and military sovereignty. It was this outmoded system that caused millions in Europe to be captivated by Hitler's proposed new order. For even with Hitler tyranny they at least saw the hope of the creation of an area large enough so that the economics of the modern world could successfully function. They had come to realize through bitter experience that the restricted areas of trade imposed by the high walls of a multitude of individual nationalisms, with the consequent manipulations of power politics, made impoverishment and war inevitable.

The re-creation of the small countries of Europe as political units, *yes;* their re-creation as economic and military units, *no,* if we really hope to bring stabilization to western Europe both for its own benefit and for the peace and economic security of the world. . . .

If our withdrawal from world affairs after the last war was a contributing factor to the present war and to the economic instability of the past twenty years—and it seems plain that it was—a withdrawal from the problems and responsibilities of the world after this war would be sheer disaster. Even our relative geographical isolation no longer exists.

At the end of the last war, not a single plane had flown across the Atlantic. Today that ocean is a mere ribbon, with airplanes making regular scheduled flights. The Pacific is only a slightly wider ribbon in the ocean of the air, and Europe and Asia are at our very doorstep.

America must choose one of three courses after this war: narrow nationalism, which inevitably means the ultimate loss of our own liberty; international imperialism, which means the sacrifice of some other nation's liberty; or the creation of a world in which there shall be an equality of opportunity for every race and every nation. I am convinced the American people will choose, by overwhelming majority, the last of these courses. To make this choice effective, we must win not only the war, but also the peace, and we must start winning it now.

To win this peace three things seem to me necessary—first, we must plan now for peace on a world basis; second, the world must be free, politically and economically, for nations and for men, that peace may exist in it; third, America must play an active, constructive part in freeing it and keeping its peace.

When I say that peace must be planned on a world basis, I mean quite literally that it must embrace the earth. Continents and oceans are plainly only parts of a whole, seen, as I have seen them, from the air. England and America are parts. Russia and China, Egypt, Syria and Turkey, Iraq and Iran are also parts. And it is inescapable that there can be no peace for any part of the world unless the foundations of peace are made secure throughout all parts of the world.

This cannot be accomplished by mere declarations of our leaders, as in an Atlantic Charter. Its accomplishment depends primarily upon acceptance by the peoples of the world. For if the failure to reach international understanding after the last war taught us anything it taught us this: even if war leaders apparently agree upon generalized principles and slogans while the war is being fought, when they come to the peace table they make their own interpretations of their previous declarations. So unless today, while the war is being fought, the people of the United States and of Great Britain, of Russia and of China, and of all the other United Nations, fundamentally agree on their purposes, fine and idealistic expressions of hope such as those of the Atlantic Charter will live merely to mock us as have Mr. Wilson's Fourteen Points. The Four Freedoms will not be accomplished by the declarations of those momentarily in power. They will become real only if the people of the world forge them into actuality.

When I say that in order to have peace this world must be free, I am only reporting that a great process has started which no man—certainly not Hitler—can stop. Men and women all over the world are on the march, physically, intellectually, and spiritually. After centuries of ignorant and dull compliance, hundreds of millions of people in eastern Europe and Asia have opened the books. Old fears no longer frighten them. They are no longer willing to be Eastern slaves for Western profits. They are beginning to know that men's welfare throughout the world is interdependent. They are resolved, as we must be, that there is no more place for imperialism within their own society than in the society of nations.

The big house on the hill surrounded by mud huts has lost its awesome charm.

Our Western world and our presumed supremacy are now on trial. Our boasting and our big talk leave Asia cold. Men and women in Russia and China and in the Middle East are conscious now of their own potential strength. They are coming to know that many of the decisions about the future of the world lie in their hands. And they intend that these decisions shall leave the peoples of each nation free from foreign domination, free for economic, social, and spiritual growth.

Economic freedom is as important as political freedom. Not only must people have access to what other peoples produce, but their own products must in turn have some chance of reaching men all over the world. There will be no peace, there will be no real development, there will be no economic stability, unless we find the method by which we can begin to break down the unnecessary trade barriers hampering the flow of goods. Obviously, the sudden and uncompromising abolition of tariffs after the war could only result in disaster. But obviously, also, one of the freedoms we are fighting for is freedom to trade. I know there are many men, particularly in America, where our standard of living exceeds the standard of living in the rest of the world, who are genuinely alarmed at such a prospect, who believe that any such process will only lessen our own standard of living. The reverse of this is true.

Many reasons may be assigned for the amazing economic development of the United States. The abundance of our national resources, the freedom of our political institutions, and the character of our population have all undoubtedly contributed. But in my judgment the greatest factor has been the fact that by the happenstance of good fortune there was created here in America the largest area in the world in which there were no barriers to the exchange of goods and ideas.

And I should like to point out to those who are fearful one inescapable fact. In view of the astronomical figures our national debt will assume by the end of this war, and in a world reduced in size by industrial and transportation developments, even our present standard of living in America cannot be maintained unless the exchange of goods flows more freely over the whole world. It is also inescapably true that to raise the standard of living of any man anywhere in the world is to raise the standard of living by some slight degree of every man everywhere in the world.

Finally, when I say that this world demands the full participation of a self-confident America, I am only passing on an invitation which the peoples of the East have given us. They would like the United States and the other United Nations to be partners with them in this grand adventure. They want us to join them in creating a new society of independent nations, free alike of the economic injustices of the West and the political malpractices of the East. But as partners in that great new combination they want us neither hesitant, incompetent, nor afraid. They want partners who will not hesitate to speak out for the correction of injustice anywhere in the world.

Our allies in the East know that we intend to pour out our resources in this war. But they expect us now—not after the war—to use the enormous power of our giving to promote liberty and justice. Other peoples, not yet fighting, are waiting no less eagerly for us to accept the most challenging opportunity of all history—the chance to help create a new society in which men and women the world around can live and grow invigorated by independence and freedom.

Long after Wendell Willkie's sturggle with the TVA and the details of his campaign for the Presidency have become footnotes to a history of the New Deal era, his "one world" will remain as his most enduring achievement. As a phrase it has become part of the language, and part also of the current hopes of people who have never heard of Willkie.

One World appeared just when the Allied fortunes of war were changing, and to some extent it helped change them by reassuring the Allies about American war and postwar aims. It also helped to overcome the distrust of Russian aims in a reading public which included the intellectuals of both major parties. It thus had considerable impact (questionable from the vantage point of the present) in winning public acceptance for later American military and diplomatic decisions which had far-reaching political consequences: the holding back of American armies from Berlin, the Yalta decision on Poland, the willingness to allow the Soviet armies to occupy the East European capitals, the premature withdrawal of American troops from Europe.

It is true that Stalin attacked some of Willkie's own speeches and positions, and that Willkie ruefully asked the British ambassador to Russia, Sir Archibald Clark Kerr, to find out from Stalin what was troubling him. Willkie, like Roosevelt, thought of himself as a realist toward the Russians. He would have been horrified, had he lived, to see the ruthlessness of Russian expansionism in the last months of the war and the years immediately following it. Yet the book had its autonomous existence. What counted was not Willkie's intention but his theme that the world was stirring out of feudalism and nationalism, and that there were overriding postwar purposes that went beyond differences in political institutions and viewpoints. This seemed to give sanction to the new antifeudal postwar "people's democracies" in Eastern Europe and later to the success of the Communist revolution in China. Willkie's "one world" was thus a prelude to the more naïve formulation by Henry Wallace of the "century of the common man."

Although Roosevelt, Stalin, and Churchill had not yet agreed on their idea of a United Nations in 1943, Willkie's book anticipated them. There was in it a strong strain of Wilsonian idealist internationalism, not surprising when one remembers that Willkie was one of the "Newton Baker Boys" at the 1924 Democratic Convention, when Baker fought for a stronger position on the League of Nations. In fact it was *One World*, even more than the Atlantic Charter, that was the real analogue to Wilson's Fourteen Points, except that it did not have official sanction. Roosevelt was caught, during and after the war, between a distrust of British imperialism and a distrust of Wilsonian idealism. The Four Freedoms plus the Concert of Powers (which was how he saw the United Nations) was as far as he was willing to go in his postwar formulation. Not only was Willkie against British imperialism, but he hit at the nationalism and militarism which he saw as the root of the decay of the Old Order. Curiously he saw both de Gaulle and Chiang Kai-shek as new rather than as old figures, despite their nationalism and militarism. To the extent that the book crystallized British opinion it may have added to the British feeling in 1945 that Churchill was a great war captain but not a peace leader, which led to his electoral defeat. In the age of nuclear weapons, which started two years after the book was published (the Manhattan Project was already under way), Willkie's conviction that national sovereignty could not organize world order was to prove a crucial insight. The idea of "one world" needed only another step to become the basis of the movement for a policing force against aggression, and for the development of a body of world law.

The book, more than any other of its day, foreshadowed the "revolution of rising expectations" which, along with nuclear technology, has dominated the postwar world. Willkie was not a sharp thinker. He did not see the contradiction between his harshness about nationalism and militarism in the old Europe and his acceptance of both in the new Middle East, Russia, and China. He looked for the new enemies in people as diverse as de Gaulle, Stalin, Chiang Kai-shek, Chou En-lai, Nuri el-Said. All he knew was that people were stirring everywhere, and that something was coming to birth in them very different from what had dominated the old order of things. Whatever his blurrings there were perceptive insights in the book which expressed—and evoked—the inner spirit of the new national-identity revolutions of our time. His hopes for a reformed Chinese social system under Chiang never materialized, but in its place came a stern new Communist empire which spoke in the name of anticolonialism. In Asia and Africa the Bandung anticolonialist movement was the first of a series which used for their own anti-Western purposes Willkie's idea of a surge of popular aspirations cutting across national boundaries. The French, Dutch, and Portuguese, as well as the British, were to discover the truth of Willkie's warning that unless the West recognized the validity of the new revolutions they would come under less welcome direction. The timetable that Willkie asked for, in the withdrawal of colonialist power, was foreshortened by the event, and in some places—like the Congo and Kenya—the retreat came before authentic self-governing forces could be shaped for a multiracial society. Governments based on the rule of force rather than law, and in many cases on inverse racism, would have shocked Willkie. Yet it can be said of few of his contemporaries as it can of him, that so much of history has marched to the rhythm of his words.

George C. Marshall
The Marshall Plan
1947

EDITED BY HANS J. MORGENTHAU

The Marshall Plan, as formulated in the Commencement Address which Secretary of State George C. Marshall delivered at Harvard University on June 5, 1947, owes its existence to the Truman Doctrine. The Marshall Plan and the Truman Doctrine are, in the words of President Truman, "two halves of the same walnut." On March 12, 1947, President Truman declared before a joint session of Congress, "It must be the policy of the United States to support free peoples who are resisting attempted subjugation by armed minorities or by outside pressure. . . . I believe that our help should be primarily through economic and financial aid which is essential to economic stability and orderly political processes." Two developments appeared to make an authoritative elaboration of the Truman Doctrine necessary: the widespread interpretation of the Truman Doctrine primarily in terms of ideological warfare and military defense, and the rapidly deteriorating economic and political situation in Europe. This elaboration was to take the form of a proposal for the economic reconstruction of all of Europe, east and west alike.

This proposal was made in considerable detail in the ad-

dress which Under Secretary of State Dean G. Acheson gave on May 8, 1947, before the Delta Council in Cleveland, Mississippi. Acheson's address was intended as preparation for an authoritative statement of policy by Marshall. On May 29, 1947, Marshall decided to make this statement in the form of a Commencement Address at Harvard; he had tentatively accepted an invitation to be present. He asked Charles E. Bohlen, his special assistant, to draft the speech. Bohlen drew primarily upon two documents supplied respectively by George F. Kennan, head of the Policy Planning Staff of the Department of State, and William L. Clayton, Under Secretary of State for Economic Affairs. Marshall had asked Kennan on April 28 to develop within two weeks recommendations for an American foreign aid policy for Europe. Kennan submitted the recommendations on May 23. Clayton had returned on May 19 to Washington after a stay of six weeks in Europe. He brought with him a memorandum stressing the economic devastation of Europe and outlining a policy of American aid, and gave it on May 27 to Acheson, who in turn sent it the same day to Marshall.

Bohlen's draft, incorporating verbatim passages from both documents, was checked by Acheson and Clayton before it was submitted to Marshall. Twice—once in his office and again on the plane that took him to Cambridge on June 4—Marshall rewrote the next-to-last paragraph, stressing the need for European initiative. After reading the text of the address as printed here, which is the official version, Marshall added extemporaneously three sentences emphasizing "the vast importance to our people to reach some general understanding rather than to react to the passions and prejudices of the moment."

I NEED not tell you gentlemen that the world situation is very serious. That must be apparent to all intelligent people. I think one difficulty is that the problem is one of such enormous complexity that the very mass of facts presented to the public by press and radio make it exceedingly difficult for the man in the street to reach a clear appraisement of the situation. Furthermore, the people of this country are distant from the troubled areas of the earth and it is hard for them

The text is reprinted from U.S. Department of State *Bulletin*, Vol. XVI, No. 415 (June 15, 1947), pp. 1159–60.

to comprehend the plight and consequent reactions of the long-suffering peoples, and the effect of those reactions on their governments in connection with our efforts to promote peace in the world.

In considering the requirements for the rehabilitation of Europe, the physical loss of life, the visible destruction of cities, factories, mines, and railroads was correctly estimated, but it has become obvious during recent months that this visible destruction was probably less serious than the dislocation of the entire fabric of European economy. For the past 10 years conditions have been highly abnormal. The feverish preparation for war and the more feverish maintenance of the war effort engulfed all aspects of national economies. Machinery has fallen into disrepair or is entirely obsolete. Under the arbitrary and destructive Nazi rule, virtually every possible enterprise was geared into the German war machine. Long-standing commercial ties, private institutions, banks, insurance companies, and shipping companies disappeared, through loss of capital, absorption through nationalization, or by simple destruction. In many countries, confidence in the local currency has been severely shaken. The breakdown of the business structure of Europe during the war was complete. Recovery has been seriously retarded by the fact that two years after the close of hostilities a peace settlement with Germany and Austria has not been agreed upon. But even given a more prompt solution of these difficult problems, the rehabilitation of the economic structure of Europe quite evidently will require a much longer time and greater effort than had been foreseen.

There is a phase of this matter which is both interesting and serious. The farmer has always produced the foodstuffs to exchange with the city dweller for the other necessities of life. This division of labor is the basis of modern civilization. At the present time it is threatened with breakdown. The town and city industries are not producing adequate goods to exchange with the food-producing farmer. Raw materials and fuel are in short supply. Machinery is lacking or worn out. The farmer or the peasant cannot find the goods for sale which he desires to purchase. So the sale of his farm produce for money which he cannot use seems to him an unprofitable transaction. He, therefore, has withdrawn many fields from crop cultivation and is using them for grazing. He feeds more grain to stock and finds for himself and his family an ample supply of food, however short he may be on clothing and the other ordinary gadgets of civilization. Meanwhile people in the cities are short of food and fuel. So the governments are forced to use their foreign money and credits to procure these necessities abroad. This process exhausts funds which are urgently needed for reconstruction. Thus a very serious situation is rapidly developing which bodes no good for the world. The modern system of the division of labor upon which the exchange of products is based is in danger of breaking down.

The truth of the matter is that Europe's requirements for the next three or four years of foreign food and other essential products—principally from America—are so much greater than her present ability to pay that she must have substantial additional help or face economic, social, and political deterioration of a very grave character.

The remedy lies in breaking the vicious circle and restoring the confidence of the European people in the economic future of their own countries and of Europe as a whole. The manufacturer and the farmer throughout wide areas must be able and willing to exchange their products for currencies the continuing value of which is not open to question.

Aside from the demoralizing effect on the world at large and the possibilities of disturbances arising as a result of the desperation of the people concerned, the consequences to the economy of the United States should be apparent to all. It is logical that the United States should do whatever it is able to do to assist in the return of normal economic health in the world, without which there can be no political stability and no assured peace. Our policy is directed not against any country or doctrine but against hunger, poverty, desperation, and chaos. Its purpose should be the revival of a working economy in the world so as to permit the emergence of political and social conditions in which free institutions can exist. Such assistance, I am convinced, must not be on a piecemeal basis as various crises develop. Any assistance that this Government may render in the future should provide a cure rather than a mere palliative. Any government that is willing to assist in the task of recovery will find full cooperation, I am sure, on the part of the United States Government. Any government which maneuvers to block the recovery of other countries cannot expect help from us. Furthermore, governments, political parties, or groups which seek to perpetuate human misery in order to profit therefrom politically or otherwise will encounter the opposition of the United States.

It is already evident that, before the United States Government can proceed much further in its efforts to alleviate the situation and help start the European world on its way to recovery, there must be some agreement among the countries of Europe as to the requirements of the situation and the part those countries themselves will take in order to give proper effect to whatever action might be undertaken by this Government. It would be neither fitting nor efficacious for this Government to undertake to draw up unilaterally a program designed to place Europe on its feet economically. This is the business of the Europeans. The initiative, I think, must come from Europe. The role of this country should consist of friendly aid in the drafting of a European program and of later support of such a program so far as it may be practical for us to do so. The program should be a joint one, agreed to by a number, if not all, European nations.

An essential part of any successful action on the part of the United States is an understanding on the part of the people of America of the character of the problem and the remedies to be applied. Political passion and prejudice should have no part. With foresight, and a willingness on the part of our people to face up to the vast responsibility which history has clearly placed upon our country, the difficulties I have outlined can and will be overcome.

Marshall's speech, outlining a course of action which then became official policy as the European Recovery Program, had an immediate galvanizing effect in Europe. The effect was comparable to that of American intervention in the two world wars. America had put its enormous resources in the scale of Western Europe, and victory was certain. The economic and political recovery of Europe can well be said to have begun the day after that speech.

The speech also laid the foundation for the division of Europe at the line of military demarcation of 1945 and for the economic unification of Western Europe. It was the distinct novelty of Marshall's proposal that it offered aid to Europe as a whole rather than to individual nations. The rejection of that aid by the members of the Soviet bloc made inevitable their economic dependence on the Soviet Union, their separate and slow economic development, and, hence, the division of Europe on economic as well as military and political lines. On the other hand, the collective approach to economic recovery on the part of the United States required a corresponding approach on the part of nations of Western Europe. A few weeks after Marshall's speech the Committee for European Economic Cooperation was formed, and in quick succession other European organizations, seeking economic, political, and military unification, came into being.

The speech thus stands as a symbol of American generosity, foresight, and wisdom in action. However, it is exactly by dint of the soundness of its philosophy, proved in action, that the speech came to be regarded as a prescription universally applicable. What the Marshall Plan had achieved in Europe, it was widely believed, could be accomplished elsewhere by similar means. The Marshall Plan became the inspiration and the model for the foreign aid policies of the United States in the 1950's and the early 1960's.

Yet not only was the philosophy of the Marshall Plan less applicable to conditions elsewhere, but that philosophy itself, in the process of being made universal, changed. The collective approach to a group of nations in similar conditions of economic distress was transformed into piecemeal aid to individual nations. The emphasis of the Marshall Plan on economic reconstruction rather than on ideological warfare and military defense was reversed. Finally, the requirements of effective cooperation among the recipient nations, and of their initiative rather than unilateral action by the United States, were largely lost sight of. It is only in the Alliance for Progress of 1961, a kind of Marshall Plan for Latin America, that these three elements of the Marshall Plan have been—at least in theory—restored.

Perhaps the highest tribute to the practical wisdom of the Marshall Plan is that it proved to be a mere temporary emergency program. It made itself superfluous through its success.

Harry S Truman
The Point IV Program
1949

EDITED BY HERBERT FEIS

The imposition of Communist control over Czechoslovakia in early 1948, by conspiracy and threat, jolted Americans toward the conclusion that the international Communist movement would not restrain itself. This opinion was confirmed by the Russian attempt to force the democracies to submit to its terms by blockading Berlin. The Communist parties in Western Europe were concurrently grasping for power. The main formal Western European allies were impelled by these events to conclude a military pact which was the forerunner of the North Atlantic Treaty.

The American government and people by this time had also begun to display their resistant will and strength. Greece and Turkey were being protected from an imminent threat of civil war provoked by the Communists. A good start had been made in uplifting the economies and spirits of the countries of Western Europe by the Marshall Plan. The purpose of the Soviet blockade of Berlin was being defeated by our air lift. These were some of the encouraging signs of what could be achieved by courageous and assertive leadership.

American attention turned to the dangers besetting Latin

America and the more distant areas of the world—the Far East, the Middle East, and Africa. The Communists in China were on their way to victory and control of the whole vast mainland of that country. Korea and the Philippines were being given emergency economic assistance. India and Pakistan, angrily arguing over Kashmir, were both in trouble. Indonesia was in the last stages of its struggle for independence from the Netherlands. In Africa, independence movements were increasingly successful, and the new nations that were coming into existence had little experience, capital, or technical knowledge.

Meanwhile, the economic efforts of many countries were restricted by what was called the "dollar gap." Almost all countries sought to procure more American products than they could pay for in dollars. This condition, it was thought at the time, was going to last indefinitely. It was hoped that by transmitting some of our technical knowledge to them their plight would be eased.

Such were the circumstances behind the "Point IV" proposal which was enunciated by President Harry S Truman in his Inaugural Address of January 20, 1949.

The proffer that was made in Point IV had been looking for influential sponsors in the State Department and the White House. But the memoranda of its first active advocate, Benjamin Hardy, a member of the Office of Public Affairs of the State Department, had not gained effective attention. When the Policy Planning staff, then under the direction of Paul Nitze, proposed modest extension of the kinds of technical assistance then being given Latin America be extended to all countries, the Bureau of the Budget turned down the suggestion.

Hardy turned to friends in the White House for support. Clark Clifford, eager to have new ideas to give the Inaugural Address life and appeal, took up the idea at once. He and the members of his staff—particularly David Lloyd and George Elsey—shaped the form and language of the proposal for inclusion in the Inaugural Address. Nitze and Charles Bohlen, then counselor of the State Department, believed that what had been favored as a modest practical effort, to be expanded with experience, was being blown up too dramatically for political effect. They feared that the expectations aroused could not be satisfied, since Congress would not provide for the purpose the large sums implicitly promised. But the President was enthusiastically for the bold version of Clifford and his staff. He approved its inclusion in the Inaugural Address.

IN THE coming years, our program for peace and freedom will emphasize four major courses of action: . . .

Fourth—we must embark on a bold new program for making the benefits of our scientific advances and industrial progress available for the improvement and growth of under-developed areas. More than half the people of the world are living in conditions approaching misery. Their food is inadequate. They are victims of disease. Their economic life is primitive and stagnant. Their poverty is a handicap and a threat both to them and to more prosperous areas.

For the first time in history, humanity possesses the knowledge and the skill to relieve the suffering of these people.

The United States is preeminent among nations in the development of industrial and scientific techniques. The material resources which we can afford to use for the assistance of other peoples are limited. But our imponderable resources in technical knowledge are constantly growing and are inexhaustible.

I believe that we should make available to peace-loving peoples the benefits of our store of technical knowledge in order to help them realize their aspirations for a better life. And, in cooperation with other nations, we should foster capital investment in areas needing development.

Our aim should be to help the free peoples of the world, through their own efforts, to produce more food, more clothing and more materials for housing, more mechanical power to lighten their burdens.

We invite other countries to pool their technological resources in this undertaking. Their contributions will be warmly welcomed. This should be a cooperative enterprise in which all nations work together through the United Nations and its specialized agencies wherever practicable. It must be a world-wide effort for the achievement of peace, plenty, and freedom.

The Point IV Program is reprinted here from President Truman's Inaugural Address, January 20, 1949. Following the outline of the program are excerpts from the "Message of the President to the Congress Recommending the Enactment of Legislation to Authorize an Expanded Program of Technical Assistance for the Underdeveloped Areas of the World," which President Truman delivered on June 24, 1949. Both the address and the message appeared in the *Congressional Record, Proceedings and Debates of the 81st Congress First Session*, Vol. 95—Parts 1 & 6 (Washington, D.C.: Government Printing Office, 1949), January 20, and June 24, 1949, pp. 477–78, and 8397–99.

With the cooperation of business, private capital, agriculture, and labor in this country, this program can greatly increase the industrial activity in other nations and can raise substantially their standards of living.

Such new economic developments must be devised and controlled to benefit the peoples of the areas in which they are established. Guaranties to the investor must be balanced by guaranties in the interest of the people whose resources and whose labor go into these developments.

The old imperialism—exploitation for foreign profit—has no place in our plans. What we envisage is a program of development based on the concepts of democratic fair-dealing. . . .

Only by helping the least fortunate of its members to help themselves can the human family achieve the decent, satisfying life that is the right of all people.

Democracy alone can supply the vitalizing force to stir the peoples of the world into triumphant action, not only against their human oppressors, but also against their ancient enemies—hunger, misery, and despair. . . .

[From President Truman's message to Congress, June 24, 1949:]

In order to enable the United States, in cooperation with other countries, to assist the peoples of economically underdeveloped areas to raise their standards of living, I recommend the enactment of legislation to authorize an expanded program of technical assistance for such areas, and an experimental program for encouraging the outflow of private investment beneficial to their economic development. These measures are the essential first steps in an undertaking which will call upon private enterprise and voluntary organizations in the United States, as well as the Government, to take part in a constantly growing effort to improve economic conditions in the less-developed regions of the world.

The grinding poverty and the lack of economic opportunity for many millions of people in the economically underdeveloped parts of Africa, the Near and Far East, and certain regions of Central and South America, constitute one of the greatest challenges of the world today. In spite of their age-old economic and social handicaps, the peoples in these areas have in recent decades been stirred and awakened. The spread of industrial civilization, the growing understanding of modern concepts of government, and the impact of two World Wars have changed their lives and their outlook. They are eager to play a greater part in the community of nations.

All these areas have a common problem. They must create a firm economic base for the democratic aspirations of their citizens. Without such an economic base, they will be unable to meet the expectations which the modern world has aroused in their peoples. If they are frustrated and disappointed, they may turn to false doctrines which hold that the way of progress lies through tyranny. . . .

The major effort in such a program must be local in character; it must be made by the people of the underdeveloped areas themselves. It is essential, however, to the success of their effort that there be help from abroad. In some cases the peoples of these areas will be unable to begin their part of this great enterprise without initial aid from other countries.

The aid that is needed falls roughly into two categories. The first is the technical, scientific, and managerial knowledge necessary to economic development. This category includes not only medical and educational knowledge, and assistance and advice in such basic fields as sanitation, communications, road building and governmental services, but also, and perhaps most important, assistance in the survey of resources and in planning for long-range economic development.

The second category is production goods—machinery and equipment—and financial assistance in the creation of productive enterprises. The under-developed areas need capital for port and harbor development, roads and communications, irrigation and drainage projects, as well as for public utilities and the whole range of extractive, processing, and manufacturing industries. Much of the capital required can be provided by these areas themselves, in spite of their low standards of living. But much must come from abroad.

The two categories of aid are closely related. Technical assistance is necessary to lay the groundwork for productive investment. Investment, in turn, brings with it technical assistance. In general, however, technical surveys of resources and of the possibilities of economic development must precede substantial capital investment. Furthermore, in many of the areas concerned, technical assistance in improving sanitation, communications, or education is required to create conditions in which capital investment can be fruitful.

This country, in recent years, has conducted relatively modest programs of technical cooperation with other countries. . . . Through these various activities we have gained considerable experience in rendering technical assistance to other countries. What is needed now is to expand and integrate these activities and to concentrate them particularly on the economic development of underdeveloped areas.

Much of the aid that is needed can be provided most effectively through the United Nations. . . . In addition to our participation in this work of the United Nations, much of the technical assistance required can be provided directly by the United States to countries needing it. A careful examination of the existing information concerning the under-developed countries shows particular need for technicians and experts with United States training in plant and animal diseases, malaria and typhus control, water supply and sewer systems, metallurgy and mining, and nearly all phases of industry.

It has already been shown that experts in these fields can bring about tremendous improvements. For example, the health of the people of many foreign communities has been greatly improved by the work of United States sanitary engineers in setting up modern water-supply systems. The food supply of many areas has been increased as the result of the advice of United States agricultural experts in the control of animal diseases and the improvement of crops. These are only examples of the wide range of benefits resulting from the careful application of modern techniques to local problems. The benefits which a comprehensive program of expert assistance will make possible can only be revealed by studies and surveys undertaken as a part of the program itself. . . .

All countries concerned with the program should work together to bring about conditions favorable to the flow of private capital. To this end we are negotiating agreements with other countries to protect the American investor from unwarranted or discriminatory treatment under the laws of the country in which he makes his investment. . . .

Many of these conditions of instability in under-developed areas which deter foreign investment are themselves a consequence of the lack of economic development which only foreign investment can cure. Therefore, to wait until stable conditions are assured before encouraging the outflow of capital to under-developed areas would defer the attainment of our objectives indefinitely. It is necessary to take vigorous action now to break out of this vicious circle.

Since the development of underdeveloped economic areas is of major importance in our foreign policy, it is appropriate to use the resources of the Government to accelerate private efforts toward that end. . . .

The enactment of these two legislative proposals, the first pertaining to technical assistance and the second to the encouragement of foreign investment, will constitute a national endorsement of a program of major importance in our efforts for world peace and economic stability. Nevertheless, these measures are only the first steps. We are here embarking on a venture that extends far into the future. We are at the beginning of a rising curve of activity—private, governmental, and international—this will continue for many years to come. It is all the more important, therefore, that we start promptly. . . .

Before the peoples of these areas we hold out the promise of a better future through the democratic way of life. It is vital that we move quickly to bring the meaning of that promise home to them in their daily lives.

Congress settled down to long hearings on the proposed legislation to give effect to Point IV. The atomic bomb set off by the Soviet government in the summer of 1949 undoubtedly helped overcome resistance to the program. At last, in June, 1950, the Act for International Development was passed, with a small allocation of funds to finance the first year of the program. Concurrently, the American government in 1950 made its first substantial pledge of funds for the expanded Technical Assistance Program of the United Nations. It set about at the same time to increase the lending and insurance capacity of the Export-Import Bank. During the same year the countries of the British Commonwealth, led by Great Britain, inaugurated a greatly expanded "Colombo Plan" for Cooperative Economic Development in South and Southeast Asia, including India and Pakistan. In sum, the Western democratic world, led by the United States and the British Commonwealth, during these two years (1949–50) definitely committed themselves to make an effort to assist poor peoples everywhere to better their living conditions, prolong their life, and ease the burden of their work.

During the next decade the United States demonstrated its willingness to open almost the whole lexicon of technical knowledge to the rest of the world. It and other leading industiral countries no longer waited for seekers of information about methods and processes of production to come to them. They began to purvey it on an ever-larger scale through books and articles. They displayed and demonstrated their new devices at fairs. They sought our purchasers of licenses and patent rights, and when the needy countries could not afford to pay, the aiding countries handed these over free or as a charge against the future. They established missions in the industrial and political capitals of the poorer countries to study local needs and wants and the best possible uses of technical knowledge. They responded willingly to requests for experts to give instruction in the new methods. The subsequent experience contains many significant achievements— dimmed by failure of results to match anticipations and realize potentialities. It has also brought a clearer and graver appreciation of the obstacles to the diffusion of technology among the poorer peoples.

When Point IV was first announced, the American government did not intend to provide large sums of capital out of the public treasury—sums comparable to those being given to our associates in Europe under the Marshall Plan. It was conceived that if the technical innovations were of evident value, private capital would be available from both local and foreign sources.

But only sparse amounts of private capital have thus far been ventured in the poorer countries; the only really substantial investments have been in the development of natural resources—especially oil and minerals, for which there was a reliable foreign market. Capital was not attracted into those fields of activity which were prerequisites for increasing industrial productivity. For the prospects of profit have been poor, and government controls and impositions severe, and involvement in local political issues inevitable. Even had private capital been more venturesomely disposed, many poorer countries would have wanted to retain government ownership or control of enterprise in these fields. They did not want foreign private capitalists to have as important a part in their national life as they almost inevitably would have had if engaged in basic branches of production. This reservation has caused them to seek the capital from various national governments and from the multinational agencies such as the International Bank for Reconstruction and Development, the Inter-American Bank, and the United Nations, which, however, has little capital to lend or give. The American government has been impelled to make up for the lack of private capital, domestic and foreign, by making large loans and grants, mounting in recent years to almost $2 billion—for technical aid, economic development, social progress, financial stability. But now American legislation and appropriations are again being reshaped with the intention of inducing or compelling the poorer countries to court private capital more and public treasuries less.

These are some of the sobering lessons that have been learned since the ideal of Point IV was propounded. Probably the wish for the benefits of technology is so strong and commanding that it will prevail more often than not over human and natural deficiencies. The American people and their associates in world affairs will continue to make a great effort to see that they do prevail. Point IV may well be elevated again to its original conception.

William Faulkner

Speech on Acceptance of the Nobel Prize

1950

EDITED BY RICHARD ELLMANN

The award to William Faulkner of the Nobel Prize for Literature in November, 1950, aroused more approval than has been accorded many of these awards. By that year Faulkner had published twenty books, which were widely known in Europe and Asia as well as in the United States. Americans noted that he was the first writer from the South to win the prize and praised his intimate knowledge of his own region.

This famous localism was in danger of being misunderstood. Some of his readers interpreted him too narrowly as a portrayer of a dying culture who recognized only with reluctance and disappointment the encroachments of a new century upon a feudal past. Others took his subject matter, in which lynching, rape, and murder figure prominently, for a rustic variation, in a Mississippi accent, of the conditions which Theodore Dreiser and other naturalists had berated in northern cities.

While Faulkner usually made no complaint when he was described as a southern naturalist or anything else, he did remark on one occasion with a little impatience, "I try to tell the truth of man. The area is incidental. That's just all I know." The other criticism, that he was stiffened in a backward look, devoted to reviewing what was dead, was equally far from the truth, though he waited a long time to say so explicitly.

All his life Faulkner had avoided speeches, and insisted that he not be taken as a man of letters. "I'm just a farmer who likes to tell stories," he once said. Because of his known aversion to making formal pronouncements, there was much interest, when he traveled to Stockholm to receive the prize on December 10, 1950, in what he would say in the speech that custom obliged him to deliver. Faulkner evidently wanted to set right the misinterpretation of his own work as pessimistic. But beyond that, he recognized that, as the first American novelist to receive the prize since the end of World War II, he had a special obligation to take the changed situation of the writer, and of man, into account.

I FEEL that this award was not made to me as a man but to my work—a life's work in the agony and sweat of the human spirit, not for glory [and least of all for profit,] but to make out of the material of the human spirit something which was not there before; so this award is only mine in trust. It will not be hard to find a dedication for the money part of it to commemorate with the purpose and the significance of its origin but I would like to do the same with the acclaim too by using this fine moment as a pinnacle from which I might be listened to by the young man or young woman, already dedicated to the same anguish and sweat, who will some day stand here where I am standing.

Our tragedy today is a general and universal physical fear so long sustained by now that we can even bear it. There are no longer problems of the spirit. There is only the question: When will I be blown up? Because of this, the young man or woman writing today has forgotten the problems of the

The speech is reprinted here from the official record of the Nobel Prize ceremonies, *Les Prix Nobel en 1950* (Stockholm: Imprimerie Royale, P. A. Norstedt & Söner, 1951), pp. 71–72. Bracketed words, added by the editor, are the significant variations made by Faulkner from the original text. Most of the versions which have appeared in this country include Faulkner's changes made in the manuscript which he supplied his publishers after delivering the address. *The Nobel Prize Speech* (New York: The Spiral Press, 1951) was the first impression inscribed by Faulkner for his editor. An amended version also appeared in *The Faulkner Reader: Selections from the Works of William Faulkner* (New York: Random House, 1954). For reference to other versions see, James B. Meriwether, *The Literary Career of William Faulkner: A Bibliographical Study* (Princeton: Princeton University Library, 1961), p. 49.

human heart in conflict with itself which alone can make good writing because only that is worth writing about, worth the agony and the sweat.

He must learn them again, he must teach himself that the basest of all things is to be afraid, and teaching himself that, forget it forever leaving no room in his workshop for anything but the old verities and truths of the heart, the old universal truths lacking which any story is ephemeral and doomed— love and honor and pity and pride and compassion and sacrifice. Until he does so, he labors under a curse. He writes not of love but of lust, of defeats in which nobody loses anything of value, of victories without hope and, worst of all, without pity or compassion. His griefs grieve on no universal bones, leaving no scars. He writes not of the heart but of the gland.

Until he relearns these things, he will write as though he stood among and watched the end of man. I do not believe in the end of man. It is easy enough to say that man is immortal simply because he will endure: then when the last ding-dong of doom has clanged and faded from the last worthless rock hanging tideless in the last red and dying evening, that even then there will still be one more sound: that of his puny inexhaustible voice still talking. I believe more than this. I believe man will not merely endure, he will prevail. He is immortal, not because he, alone among creatures, has an inexhaustible voice but because he has a soul, a spirit, capable of compassion and sacrifice and endurance. The poet's, the writer's duty is to write about these things. It is his privilege to help man endure by lifting his heart, by reminding him of courage and honor and hope and pride and compassion and pity [and sacrifice which have been the glory of his past]. The poet's voice need not merely be the record of man, it can be one of the props to help him endure and prevail.

This speech, after having been printed by the Nobel Prize authorities in 1950, went into a succession of reprintings in newspapers, magazines, and pamphlets. Its special strength comes from the fact that a great writer uttered it in response to the threat, then only five years old, of atomic destruction. Faulkner might have argued on rational grounds that the extinction of man was unlikely, but he preferred to assert his position as a creative artist, at once undeceived and unvanquished.

Faulkner derives his authority from the fact that the business of the writer is to bring into being what has never ex-

isted before. In so defining his own occupation and character, he gives the lie to the notion that the writer is either a grave-yard ghost enthralled by time past, on the one hand, or on the other, a photographer of disrupted living conditions of the present. Although he never says so directly, he regards the writer as a kind of rebel against the inhibiting forces of the external world, who denies the mechanical denier and affirms continued human experience by prolonging its crea-tion in his own fiction. The special quality which Faulkner celebrates in the creative process is compassion, and this quality, which all men share in their degree, will help to bring them to something better.

In his earlier work Faulkner had stressed the importance of simply enduring. He liked to use that verb intransitively, to embody patient persistence, as in the case of the Negroes in The Sound and the Fury. That "they endured" is his high-est praise. But in his novel A Fable, published in the year of his Nobel Prize speech and closely related to it in thought, Faulkner said that "man and his folly" will do more than en-dure; "they will prevail." In Stockholm he reaffirmed, in the characteristic rhythms of his prose, that man's voice was in-exhaustible, and added that the creative writer had the specif-ic task of disburdening man of the curse of fear which now seems to immobilize him.

Faulkner's proud assertion, "I do not believe in the end of man," is one of those statements which assume their moral force because the speaker has encompassed all the agony which might have prompted an opposite view. It is this sense of the moral depths out of which the words have been wrung that gives Faulkner's speech its defiant grandeur and capacity of its own for enduring.

The United States Supreme Court

Brown v. Board of Education of Topeka

1954

EDITED BY HARRY W. JONES

The United States Supreme Court decision in the case of Brown v. Board of Education of Topeka was a long time on the way. "All men are created equal," the framers of the Declaration had proclaimed as self-evident truth in 1776, and Lincoln at Gettysburg had reaffirmed this as the distinctive proposition of American national dedication. In 1868, the Fourteenth Amendment had written the proposition plainly into the Constitution of the United States: "nor shall any State . . . deny to any person within its jurisdiction the equal protection of the laws."

On what theory, then, was it maintained until 1954 that racial segregation in the public schools is consistent with the Fourteenth Amendment? The argument in defense of the constitutionality of school segregation proceeded from an 1896 decision, Plessy v. Ferguson (163 U.S. 537), in which the Supreme Court held that a Louisiana statute requiring separate accommodations for white and colored railway passengers was not a denial of the equal protection of the laws. Distinctions based on color are constitutionally permissible, the Court ruled over the passionate dissent of the first Justice Harlan, if the separate accommodations provided for "white" persons and "colored" persons are, in other respects, equal in quality. Over

*the years, this "separate but equal" doctrine became an accept-
ed gloss on the Fourteenth Amendment and was extended by
analogy from railroad accommodations to other facilities and,
most importantly, to the public schools.*

*The erosion away of "separate but equal" began in 1938,
when the Supreme Court held, in* Missouri ex rel. Gaines v.
Canada *(305 U.S. 337), that the equal protection of the laws
had been denied to a qualified Negro applicant who had been
refused admission to the University of Missouri Law School
and had been offered, instead, a money grant sufficient to pay
his law-school tuition at some state university outside Missouri. In the fifteen years between the* Gaines *decision and
the argument in* Brown V. Board of Education, *three other
cases, all involving public higher education, were decided by
the Supreme Court in favor of the respective Negro appli-
cants. In each instance, however, the stated theory of the decision was that the separate educational facilities provided for
Negroes in the State concerned were not genuinely "equal"
in dignity and educational quality. The central question
remained: is "separate but equal" a contradiction in terms?
Can segregated schools and colleges be "equal" in a constitutional sense?*

*During its 1952–53 term, the Supreme Court heard argu-
ment in five separate cases challenging the constitutionality of
racial segregation in public schools of Kansas, South Carolina,
Virginia, Delaware, and the District of Columbia. The five
cases remained undecided throughout the term, and, on June
8, 1953, they were ordered restored to the Court's docket and
assigned for reargument together during the 1953–54 term.
The Court's order invited the Attorney General of the United
States to take part in the argument and stated five questions
that counsel in the cases were requested "to discuss particularly." From the stated questions, it was clear that the Court
was now ready to face the issue squarely: Does segregation in
the public schools violate the Fourteenth Amendment?*

*The long-awaited argument began on December 7, 1953,
and continued for three days. The constitutional points at
issue were argued eloquently and in depth by gifted advocates
including, for the South, John W. Davis, acknowledged
leader of the Supreme Court bar, and, for the desegregation
forces, Thurgood Marshall, then chief counsel of the
NAACP (later a judge of the Court of Appeals of the United
States and then Solicitor General). Assistant Attorney General J. Lee Rankin appeared for the United States and spoke in
general support of the desegregation position. The Attorneys
General of southern states defended the constitutionality of*

the school laws of their states. No case in Supreme Court history was ever presented more exhaustively by the advocates for both sides, or weighed more carefully by the members of the Court.

The three-day argument was concluded on December 9. Tension grew as five months passed without a decision, and the Court approached the end of the 1953–54 term. On Monday, May 17, 1954, the decision at last came down. It was unanimous. For once, there was no dissent, not even a separate concurring opinion. Chief Justice Earl Warren's Brown *opinion is precisely what the report declares it to be, "the opinion of the Court." Warren of California, Black of Alabama, Reed of Kentucky, Frankfurter of Massachusetts, Douglas of Connecticut, Jackson of New York, Burton of Ohio, Clark of Texas, and Minton of Indiana—Democrats and Republicans, "liberals" and "conservatives"—agreed that "in the field of public education, the doctrine of 'separate but equal' has no place."*

THESE cases come to us from the States of Kansas, South Carolina, Virginia, and Delaware. They are premised on different facts and different local conditions, but a common legal question justifies their consideration together in this consolidated opinion.

In each of the cases, minors of the Negro race, through their legal representatives, seek the aid of the courts in obtaining admission to the public schools of their community on a nonsegregated basis. In each instance, they had been denied admission to schools attended by white children under laws requiring or permitting segregation according to race. This segregation was alleged to deprive the plaintiffs of the equal protection of the laws under the Fourteenth Amendment. In each of the cases other than the Delaware case, a three-judge federal district court denied relief to the plaintiffs on the so-called "separate but equal" doctrine announced by this Court in *Plessy* v. *Ferguson,* 163 U.S. 537. Under that doctrine, equality of treatment is accorded when the races are provided substantially equal facilities, even though these facilities be separate. In the Delaware case, the Supreme Court of Delaware adhered to that doctrine, but ordered that the plaintiffs be admitted to the white schools because of their superiority to the Negro schools.

The decision is reprinted from 347 U.S. 483.

The plaintiffs contend that segregated public schools are not "equal" and cannot be made "equal," and that hence they are deprived of the equal protection of the laws. Because of the obvious importance of the question presented, the Court took jurisdiction. Argument was heard in the 1952 Term, and reargument was heard this Term on certain questions propounded by the Court.

Reargument was largely devoted to the circumstances surrounding the adoption of the Fourteenth Amendment in 1868. It covered exhaustively consideration of the Amendment in Congress, ratification by the states, then existing practices in racial segregation, and the views of proponents and opponents of the Amendment. This discussion and our own investigation convince us that, although these sources cast some light, it is not enough to resolve the problem with which we are faced. At best, they are inconclusive. The most avid proponents of the post-War Amendments undoubtedly intended them to remove all legal distinctions among "all persons born or naturalized in the United States." Their opponents, just as certainly, were antagonistic to both the letter and the spirit of the Amendments and wished them to have the most limited effect. What others in Congress and the state legislatures had in mind cannot be determined with any degree of certainty.

An additional reason for the inconclusive nature of the Amendment's history, with respect to segregated schools, is the status of public education at that time. In the South, the movement toward free common schools, supported by general taxation, had not yet taken hold. Education of white children was largely in the hands of private groups. Education of Negroes was almost non-existent, and practically all of the race were illiterate. In fact, any education of Negroes was forbidden by law in some states. Today, in contrast, many Negroes have achieved outstanding success in the arts and sciences as well as in the business and professional world. It is true that public school education at the time of the Amendment had advanced further in the North, but the effect of the Amendment on Northern States was generally ignored in the congressional debates. Even in the North, the conditions of public education did not approximate those existing today. The curriculum was usually rudimentary; ungraded schools were common in rural areas; the school term was but three months a year in many states; and compulsory school attendance was virtually unknown. As a consequence, it is not surprising that there should be so little in the history of the Fourteenth Amendment relating to its intended effect on public education.

In the first cases in this Court construing the Fourteenth Amendment, decided shortly after its adoption, the Court interpreted it as proscribing all state-imposed discriminations against the Negro race. The doctrine of "separate but equal" did not make its appearance in this Court until 1896 in the case of *Plessy* v. *Ferguson supra*, involving not education but transportation. American courts have since labored with the doctrine for over half a century. In this Court, there have been six cases involving the "separate but equal" doctrine in the field of public education. In *Cumming* v. *Board of Education of Richmond County*, 175 U.S. 528, and *Gong Lum* v. *Rice*, 275 U.S. 78, the validity of the doctrine itself was not challenged. In more recent cases, all on the graduate school level, inequality was found in that specific benefits enjoyed by white students were denied to Negro students of the same educational qualifications. *Missouri ex rel. Gaines* v. *Canada*, 305 U.S. 337; *Sipuel* v. *Board of Regents of University of Oklahoma*, 332 U.S. 631; *Sweatt* v. *Painter*, 339 U.S. 629; *McLaurin* v. *Oklahoma State Regents*, 339 U.S. 637. In none of these cases was it necessary to re-examine the doctrine to grant relief to the Negro plaintiff. And in *Sweatt* v. *Painter, supra*, the Court expressly reserved decision on the question whether *Plessy* v. *Ferguson* should be held inapplicable to public education.

In the instant cases, that question is directly presented. Here, unlike *Sweatt* v. *Painter*, there are findings below that the Negro and white schools involved have been equalized, or are being equalized, with respect to buildings, curricula, qualifications and salaries of teachers, and other "tangible" factors. Our decision, therefore, cannot turn on merely a comparison of these tangible factors in the Negro and white schools involved in each of the cases. We must look instead to the effect of segregation itself on public education.

In approaching this problem, we cannot turn the clock back to 1868 when the Amendment was adopted, or even to 1896 when *Plessy* v. *Ferguson* was written. We must consider public education in the light of its full development and its present place in American life throughout the Nation. Only in this way can it be determined if segregation in public schools deprives these plaintiffs of the equal protection of the laws.

Today, education is perhaps the most important function of state and local governments. Compulsory school attendance laws and the great expenditures for education both demonstrate our recognition of the importance of education to our democratic society. It is required in the performance of our most basic public responsibilities, even service in the armed forces. It is the very foundation of good citizenship. Today it is a principal instrument in awakening the child to cultural values, in preparing him for later professional training, and in helping him to adjust normally to his environment. In these days, it is doubtful that any child may reasonably be expected to succeed in life if he is denied the opportunity of an education. Such an opportunity, where the state has undertaken to provide it, is a right which must be made available to all on equal terms.

We come then to the question presented: Does segregation of children in public schools solely on the basis of race, even though the physical facilities and other "tangible" factors may be equal, deprive the children of the minority group of equal educational opportunities? We believe that it does.

In *Sweatt* v. *Painter, supra,* in finding that a segregated law school for Negroes could not provide them equal educational opportunities, this Court relied in large part on "those qualities which are incapable of objective measurement but which make for greatness in a law school." In *McLaurin* v. *Oklahoma State Regents, supra,* the Court, in requiring that a Negro admitted to a white graduate school be treated like all other students, again resorted to intangible considerations: ". . . his ability to study, to engage in discussions and exchange views with other students, and, in general, to learn his profession." Such considerations apply with added force to children in grade and high schools. To separate them from others of similar age and qualifications solely because of their race generates a feeling of inferiority as to their status in the community that may affect their hearts and minds in a way unlikely ever to be undone. The effect of this separation on their educational opportunities was well stated by a finding in the Kansas case by a court which nevertheless felt compelled to rule against the Negro plaintiffs:

> Segregation of white and colored children in public schools has a detrimental effect upon the colored children. The impact is greater when it has the sanction of the law; for the policy of separating the races is usually interpreted as denoting the inferiority of the negro group. A sense of inferiority affects the motivation of a child to learn. Segregation with the sanction of law, therefore, has a tendency to [retard] the educational and mental development of negro children and to deprive them of some of the benefits they would receive in a racial[ly] integrated school system.

Whatever may have been the extent of psychological knowledge at the time of *Plessy* v. *Ferguson*, this finding is amply supported by modern authority. Any language in *Plessy* v. *Ferguson* contrary to this finding is rejected.

We conclude that in the field of public education the doctrine of "separate but equal" has no place. Separate educational facilities are inherently unequal. Therefore, we hold that the plaintiffs and others similarly situated for whom the actions have been brought are, by reason of the segregation complained of, deprived of the equal protection of the laws guaranteed by the Fourteenth Amendment. This disposition makes unnecessary any discussion whether such segregation also violates the Due Process Clause of the Fourteenth Amendment.

Because these are class actions, because of the wide applicability of this decision, and because of the great variety of local conditions, the formulation of decrees in these cases presents problems of considerable complexity. On reargument, the consideration of appropriate relief was necessarily subordinated to the primary question—the constitutionality of segregation in public education. We have now announced that such segregation is a denial of the equal protection of the laws. In order that we may have the full assistance of the parties in formulating decrees, the cases will be restored to the docket, and the parties are requested to present further argument on Questions 4 and 5 previously propounded by the Court for the reargument this Term. The Attorney General of the United States is again invited to participate. The Attorneys General of the states requiring or permitting segregation in public education will also be permitted to appear as *amici curiae* upon request to do so by September 5, 1954, and submission of briefs by October 1, 1954.

On May 17, 1954, seventeen southern and border states maintained segregated elementary and secondary schools. In four other states, as in Kansas, school segregation was permitted to school districts on a local-option basis. How were the offending states to be brought into compliance with the constitutional principle established in Brown v. Board of Education?

Questions 4 and 5, referred to in the last paragraph of the Brown *opinion, concerned the ways and means by which the Court's substantive decision might be implemented. On May 31, 1955, a year after its original* Brown *ruling, the Supreme*

Court announced a second unanimous decision, this one directed to the manner in which "relief is to be afforded" to the plaintiffs in the several cases. The Court took approving notice of the progress that had already occurred in Kansas, Delaware, and several other states, and in the District of Columbia, where steps to end school segregation were taken on the day immediately following the decision in the Brown *case and its District of Columbia counterpart,* Bolling v. Sharpe *(347 U.S. 497 [1954]). No such progress had taken place in Virginia and South Carolina, however, and the cases from these two states were remanded to the District Courts, with instructions to enter such decrees as might be required to assure that the plaintiff Negro children would be admitted to schools, on a racially nondiscriminatory basis, "with all deliberate speed."*

Has school desegregation gone forward "with all deliberate speed" in the southern and border states where racially separate public schools were required by local law at the time of the Brown *decisions? By 1965, ten years after the Supreme Court's implementing decision in the* Brown *cases, approximately one out of nine of the three million Negro children who live in these seventeen states were attending school with white children. This was measurable progress, although hardly "speed" even by the most deliberate of standards, but almost all of the gain had been registered in the border states. Whereas, by 1965, 60 per cent of border-state Negro children were in biracial schools, only 2 per cent of the Negro children were attending biracial schools in the nine southern (once Confederate) states. It was evident, however, that the next decade would see a stepping-up of progress toward school desegregation, partly because of changed social attitudes, partly in response to federal court orders requiring desegregation of specific school districts, and partly under the influence of federal legislation providing for the withholding of grants in aid of education from state educational systems that continued to maintain segregation in their schools.*

Racial segregation in the schools is not, of course, a phenomenon unique to the South; it exists, factually if not formally, in the North, Midwest, and West as well. Since children are normally assigned to schools nearest their homes, racial discrimination in housing, particularly in urban areas, is inevitably accompanied by racial segregation in the schools. Private elementary and secondary schools, which have increased greatly since World War II, contribute to school segregation in the North, although some of these schools, most notably the Roman Catholic parochial schools, have made determined efforts to achieve substantial integration. Brown v. Board of Education was but the first step toward the desegregation of American education. Difficult problems of racial discrimination in housing and employment will have to be solved before genuinely integrated schools become a fact of American life.

Brown v. Board of Education was a school case, and conceivably its holding might have been limited by later Supreme Court rulings to situations involving racial segregation in schools and colleges. The decision, however, became a landmark case in American constitutional law, and its influence as a judicial precedent was extended far beyond the area of segregation in the schools. In successive decisions since 1955, the Supreme Court and other federal courts have drawn on the analogy of the Brown decision to invalidate many other forms of state-enforced racial segregation, at public beaches and bathhouses, on municipal golf courses, on local buses, and in public parks and theaters. It is clear enough from the consistent trend of the Court's decisions that the "separate but equal" doctrine retains no vitality in any area of regulation of public service.

One limitation should be noted on the future reach of the Brown precedent. The "equal protection" clause of the Fourteenth Amendment applies, in terms, only to "State" action. Racially discriminatory conduct of individual private citizens is not within the ban of the Fourteenth Amendment unless sponsored or in some way supported by state or local public authority. But such individual discriminatory conduct can be made unlawful by specific act of Congress, and this is the great significance of the Civil Rights Act of 1964. In the long-range strategy of the civil rights movement, legislation and political action are fully as important as constitutional litigation. The Supreme Court, very promptly and by unanimous vote, upheld the validity of the challenged "public accommodations" provisions of the Civil Rights Act of 1964, and there appears to be no serious question concerning the constitutionality of the Voting Rights Act, passed by Congress in 1965. Both in its direct effect and in its indirect influence as the first great breakthrough in the campaign for racial equality, Brown v. Board of Education has become one of the three or four leading cases in American constitutional history.

However far-reaching the influence of Brown v. Board of Education may be for constitutional jurisprudence generally, the crucial problem remains that of securing effective desegregation of the public schools. The intransigent refusal of southern political leaders to give even grudging assent to the principle of equality declared in the school cases created a grave crisis in American constitutional morality. Compulsory school-attendance laws were suspended in several southern states, provisions requiring the maintenance of free public schools were deleted from state constitutions, and state legislatures enacted a variety of schemes designed to evade the constitutional requirement that their schools be desegregated. Such legalistic evasions as these were only part of the pattern of resistance. Segregationist spokesmen characterized the Brown decision as "usurpation" and "mere fiat" and flatly denied the Supreme Court's constitutional authority to decide the case as it did. Notions of "nullification" and "interposition" were withdrawn from the museum of ancient constitutional curiosities and heard again. Outright defiance of specific federal court decrees occurred, as at Little Rock in 1958 and at Oxford, Mississippi, in 1962, and two successive Presidents of the United States had to make the painful decision to use troops to enforce the orders of the federal courts.

Will enforced desegregation be worth its heavy cost in strife and disaffection? The issue must be seen in historical perspective. For the historic American injustice to the Negro, the United States has already suffered the penance of an appalling civil war. The account is far from settled. The nation is paying still in racial estrangement, in the flight of the Negro from the South to northern industrial cities, and in the increasing but understandable bitterness with which Negro intellectuals of the younger generation tend to appraise the declared aspirations of American society. Conceivably it is too late, even now, to achieve a genuine fellowship of reconciliation among Americans of various shades of pigmentation. But, at least, Justice Harlan's protest in Plessy v. Ferguson has become a principle of the American legal order: "Our constitution is color-blind and neither knows nor tolerates classes among citizens." In a free and responsible society, the maintenance of just law can exert a powerful force for public education. If our Constitution is color-blind, perhaps there is reason to hope that, some day, American culture and American society will be color-blind, too.

John F. Kennedy

Inaugural Address

1961

EDITED BY JAMES MAC GREGOR BURNS

President-elect John F. Kennedy wrote most of his Inaugural Address early in January, 1961, at his father's home in Palm Beach, Florida. He wrote it in the open air, under a warm sun, on yellow legal-sized paper, with draft material spread out on a low glass coffee table beside him. The speech was the product of long and extensive labors by a large number of public men. Assembling of materials had begun the previous November under the direction of Kennedy's aide, Theodore Sorensen. Ideas, paragraphs, even whole drafts came from Adlai Stevenson, Walter Lippmann, Kenneth Galbraith, Chester Bowles, Billy Graham, and others. Kennedy had asked Sorensen to study all past inaugural addresses, especially Lincoln's, to see what could be learned from them. Kennedy told his aide that he wanted a short, eloquent, nonpartisan, optimistic speech that would focus on foreign policy and would shun cold-war stereotypes on the one hand and, on the other, "weasel words" that could be mistaken for weakness by the Communists. Many of the most evocative phrases, such as the passing of the torch to a new generation of Americans, came from earlier campaign talks. The most quoted sentence—"ask not what you can do . . ."—had a much earlier origin: in a passage from Rousseau that Kenne-

937

dy had jotted down in 1945, and in his nomination acceptance speech in Los Angeles in 1960. Concerned that people would expect of him a Rooseveltian "Hundred Days" of miracles, he instructed Sorensen: "Let's put in that this won't all be finished in a hundred days or a thousand." The concept of the "thousand days" had been contributed early in the presidential campaign by a political scientist who knew of Kennedy's distaste for the F.D.R. parallel and who computed that in four years there would be about one thousand working days. Kennedy continued to work on his address on his flight to Washington three days before the Inaugural, and at his house in Georgetown, where he kept a copy by his side at odd moments so that he could continue to rework it. He was changing words as late as the morning of Inaugural Day.

VICE PRESIDENT JOHNSON, MR. SPEAKER, MR. CHIEF JUSTICE, PRESIDENT EISENHOWER, VICE PRESIDENT NIXON, PRESIDENT TRUMAN, REVEREND CLERGY, FELLOW CITIZENS:

WE OBSERVE today not a victory of a party but a celebration of freedom—symbolizing an end as well as a beginning—signifying renewal as well as change. For I have sworn before you and Almighty God the same solemn oath our forebears prescribed nearly a century and three quarters ago.

The world is very different now. For man holds in his mortal hands the power to abolish all forms of human poverty and all forms of human life. And yet the same revolutionary beliefs for which our forebears fought are still at issue around the globe—the belief that the rights of man come not from the generosity of the state but from the hand of God.

We dare not forget today that we are the heirs of that first revolution. Let the word go forth from this time and place, to friend and foe alike, that the torch has been passed to a new generation of Americans—born in this century, tempered by war, disciplined by a hard and bitter peace, proud of our ancient heritage—and unwilling to witness or permit the slow undoing of those human rights to which this Nation has al-

The address is reprinted here as it appeared in the *Congressional Record, Proceedings and Debates of the 87th Congress, 1st Session*, Vol. 107, Part 1 (Washington, D.C.: Government Printing Office, 1961), January 20, 1961, pp. 1012–13.

ways been committed, and to which we are committed today at home and around the world.

Let every nation know, whether it wishes us well or ill, that we shall pay any price, bear any burden, meet any hardship, support any friend, oppose any foe to assure the survival and success of liberty.

This much we pledge—and more.

To those old allies whose cultural and spiritual origins we share, we pledge the loyalty of faithful friends. United, there is little we cannot do in a host of cooperative ventures. Divided, there is little we can do—for we dare not meet a powerful challenge at odds and split asunder.

To those new states whom we welcome to the ranks of the free, we pledge our word that one form of colonial control shall not have passed away merely to be replaced by a far more iron tyranny. We shall not always expect to find them supporting our view. But we shall always hope to find them strongly supporting their own freedom—and to remember that, in the past, those who foolishly sought power by riding the back of the tiger ended up inside.

To those peoples in the huts and villages of half the globe struggling to break the bonds of mass misery, we pledge our best efforts to help them help themselves, for whatever period is required—not because the Communists may be doing it, not because we seek their votes, but because it is right. If a free society cannot help the many who are poor, it cannot save the few who are rich.

To our sister republics south of our border, we offer a special pledge—to convert our good words into good deeds—in a new alliance for progress—to assist free men and free governments in casting off the chains of poverty. But this peaceful revolution of hope cannot become the prey of hostile powers. Let all our neighbors know that we shall join with them to oppose aggression or subversion anywhere in the Americas. And let every other power know that this hemisphere intends to remain the master of its own house.

To that world assembly of sovereign states, the United Nations, our last best hope in an age where the instruments of war have far outpaced the instruments of peace, we renew our pledge of support—to prevent it from becoming merely a forum for invective—to strengthen its shield of the new and the weak—and to enlarge the area in which its writ may run.

Finally, to those nations who would make themselves our adversary, we offer not a pledge but a request: that both sides begin anew the quest for peace, before the dark powers of destruction unleashed by science engulf all humanity in planned or accidental self-destruction.

We dare not tempt them with weakness. For only when our arms are sufficient beyond doubt can we be certain beyond doubt that they will never be employed.

But neither can two great and powerful groups of nations take comfort from our present course—both sides overburdened by the cost of modern weapons, both rightly alarmed by the steady spread of the deadly atom, yet both racing to alter that uncertain balance of terror that stays the hand of mankind's final war.

So let us begin anew—remembering on both sides that civility is not a sign of weakness, and sincerity is always subject to proof. Let us never negotiate out of fear. But let us never fear to negotiate.

Let both sides explore what problems unite us instead of belaboring those problems which divide us. Let both sides, for the first time, formulate serious and precise proposals for the inspection and control of arms—and bring the absolute power to destroy other nations under the absolute control of all nations.

Let both sides seek to invoke the wonders of science instead of its terrors. Together let us explore the stars, conquer the deserts, eradicate disease, tap the ocean depths and encourage the arts and commerce.

Let both sides unite to heed in all corners of the earth the command of Isaiah—to "undo the heavy burdens and to let the oppressed go free."

And if a beach-head of cooperation may push back the jungle of suspicion, let both sides join in a new endeavor; not a new balance of power, but a new world of law, where the strong are just and the weak secure and the peace preserved.

All this will not be finished in the first one hundred days. Nor will it be finished in the first one thousand days, nor in the life of this Administration, nor even perhaps in our lifetime on this planet. But let us begin.

In your hands, my fellow citizens, more than mine, will rest the final success or failure of our course. Since this country was founded, each generation of Americans has been summoned to give testimony to its national loyalty. The graves of young Americans who answered the call to service surround the globe.

Now the trumpet summons us again—not as a call to bear arms, though arms we need—not as a call to battle, though embattled we are—but a call to bear the burden of a long twilight struggle, year in and year out, "rejoicing in hope, patient in tribulation"—a struggle against the common enemies of man: tyranny, poverty, disease and war itself.

Can we forge against these enemies a grand and global alliance, North and South, East and West, that can assure a more fruitful life for all mankind? Will you join in that historic effort?

In the long history of the world, only a few generations have been granted the role of defending freedom in its hour of maximum danger. I do not shrink from this responsibility —I welcome it. I do not believe that any of us would exchange places with any other people or any other generation. The energy, the faith, the devotion which we bring to this endeavor will light our country and all who serve it—and the glow from that fire can truly light the world.

And so, my fellow Americans: Ask not what your country can do for you—ask what you can do for your country.

My fellow citizens of the world: Ask not what America will do for you, but what together we can do for the freedom of man.

Finally, whether you are citizens of America or citizens of the world, ask of us here the same high standards of strength and sacrifice which we ask of you. With a good conscience our only sure reward, with history the final judge of our deeds, let us go forth to lead the land we love, asking His blessing and His help, but knowing that here on earth God's work must truly be our own.

Kennedy's Inaugural Address kindled a tremendous immediate response, set the tone and style of the whole Administration to come, and presaged both the triumph and the tragedy of the thirty-four months ahead. The speech immensely moved the throng shivering in the cold of the Capitol Plaza, the millions watching television, and countless Americans and foreigners huddled around radios overseas. The President's summons to new beginnings, to sustained effort, to higher standards of strength and sacrifice, to a long twilight struggle was cited again and again in the conduct of affairs in Washington. And in the end his Administration was just a beginning; he was given only a thousand days to do his work, if we count—as we must—every day as a working day.

The address reflected Kennedy's main concern with foreign affairs and forecast some of his memorable foreign policies. He urged a host of cooperative ventures with our older allies

—and later he issued a new "Declaration of Interdependence" and gained passage of a major trade-expansion bill. He spoke to the new states and to the people in the huts and villages—and followed up with expanded political and economic efforts in Asia and Africa and with a Peace Corps. He made a special pledge to our sister republics to the South— and soon proclaimed the Alliance for Progress. He called the United Nations our last best hope in an age of unrest—and gave to it the most beloved leader of his party. He warned of the dangers of arms escalation in itself—and took the potential momentous "first step" in proposing the partial nuclear test ban treaty and gaining its approval by the Senate.

Kennedy indicated almost nothing about domestic policy in his Inaugural, and this too was prophetic. The exception was his reference to "those human rights to which this nation has always been committed, and to which we are committed today at home and around the world." Nothing in his speech forecast his efforts to obtain expanded social welfare, medicare, general federal aid to education, and the other natural extensions of the New Deal and Fair Deal. Was this an early hint that while he was long and deeply committed in campaign speeches and party promises to a New Frontier at home as well as abroad, he would give priority to his foreign-policy goals when he felt he had to make a choice? Later he deferred even civil-rights commitments until he won passage of the Trade Expansion Act.

What will be the "afterlife" of John Kennedy's Inaugural Address? One can speculate that its main importance in the long run may be much like that of the Kennedy Administration as a whole—more a matter of tone and style than of substance. This is not to underestimate the concrete achievements of the Kennedy Administration, which were considerable, especially in light of the roadblocks to action in Congress and in some of the agencies. But Kennedy's "radical rhetoric," as compared to his moderately liberal domestic proposals and fairly conservative fiscal policies, had in itself a profound influence in focusing men's hopes and in raising—perhaps inflating—their expectations. In the long run the most significant sentence might be his appeal to explore the stars, conquer the deserts, eradicate disease, tap the ocean depths and encourage the arts and commerce. In short, the speech, like Franklin Roosevelt's Inaugural, was in itself a decisive political act that had immense possibilities for influencing later politicians and publics. Especially in the more comfortable days of the future, when people will seem torpid and their affairs seem to be drifting, Presidents will evoke memories of the vibrant young leader who summoned his country and his world to a long twilight struggle against the common enemies of man.

Lyndon B. Johnson
Address on Voting Rights
1965

EDITED BY OSCAR HANDLIN

Six years of inaction after the school desegregation decision of 1954 touched off the Negro revolution. The awareness that normal political procedures would not, in the South, secure an early redress of ancient grievances drew the disadvantaged colored people into direct action—sit-ins, boycotts, and demonstrations—that challenged the legitimacy of government itself. The movement gained rapid momentum after 1960 and brought measurable results in some parts of the nation. Above all, these dramatic incidents were eloquent appeals to the conscience of Americans, committed to the ideal of equality, even if only in the abstract.

Nevertheless, the hard-core resistance in the southern states remained intransigent. By the end of 1964 there were few signs that either Alabama or Mississippi was about to alter its attitudes toward race. There were ominous indications that this defiance might actually take more overt, forceful forms. The 87 per cent of the vote that Barry Goldwater gained in Mississippi was a measure of the distance that separated that state from the rest of the nation.

In the 1950's, neither John F. Kennedy nor Lyndon B. Johnson had stood in the forefront of the civil rights struggle. By 1963, both were aware of the issues at stake. When Presi-

dent Kennedy that year gave official recognition to the March on Washington, he clearly affirmed the commitment of the federal government to the cause of Negro equality. President Johnson, for whom principle and necessity blended, assumed the burden with the office. Altogether apart from his need to earn the loyalty of Negro voters in the northern cities, he viewed equality as a goal that conformed to his emerging concept of the Great Society.

By 1964, the right to the ballot had become central. That year only about 7½ per cent of the southerners registered as voters were Negro, although Negroes constituted 20 per cent of the voting-age population. Disenfranchisement perpetuated demagoguery in the politics of the Deep South and left control of the rural counties to local court-house groups callous toward the welfare of minorities and willing to tolerate violence, even murder, directed against dissidents. The refusal of juries to convict whites guilty of crimes against Negroes outraged Americans everywhere.

In these circumstances, Negroes unwilling to acquiesce in the loss of their rights had to turn to nonpolitical, extralegal means. The hard line of the Mississippi Freedom Democratic Party in the Democratic Convention of 1964 showed the danger of further drifting. Only if the Negroes were assured the full rights of citizenship could they be persuaded to act as citizens. Lyndon Johnson proposed to provide such assurance, in part, by means of a voting-rights bill which he presented to a joint session of Congress in a speech delivered on March 15, 1965. The concept of federal intervention to protect civil rights was not novel; it had roots in the Fifteenth Amendment. President Johnson's address was fresh not in its ideas, but in its ringing determination to make those ideas effective.

MR. SPEAKER, MR. PRESIDENT, MEMBERS OF THE CONGRESS:

I SPEAK tonight for the dignity of man and the destiny of democracy. I urge every member of both parties, Americans of all religions and of all colors, from every section of this country, to join me in that cause.

The address is reprinted here as it appeared in the *Congressional Record, Proceedings and Debates of the 89th Congress, 1st Session,* Vol. 111, No. 47 (Washington, D.C.: Government Printing Office, 1965), March 15, 1965, pp. 4924–26.

At times history and fate meet at a single time in a single place to shape a turning point in man's unending search for freedom. So it was at Lexington and Concord. So it was a century ago at Appomattox. So it was last week in Selma, Alabama.

There, long-suffering men and women peacefully protested the denial of their rights as Americans. Many were brutally assaulted. One good man, a man of God, was killed.

There is no cause for pride in what has happened in Selma. There is no cause for self-satisfaction in the long denial of equal rights of millions of Americans.

But there is cause for hope and for faith in our democracy in what is happening here tonight.

For the cries of pain and the hymns and protests of oppressed people, have summoned into convocation all the majesty of this great government of the greatest nation on earth.

Our mission is at once the oldest and the most basic of this country: to right wrong, to do justice, to serve man.

In our time we have come to live with the moments of great crisis. Our lives have been marked with debate about great issues, issues of war and peace, issues of prosperity and depression. But rarely in any time does an issue lay bare the secret heart of America itself. Rarely are we met with a challenge, not to our growth or abundance, or our welfare of our security, but rather to the values and the purposes and the meaning of our beloved nation.

The issue of equal rights for American Negroes is such an issue. And should we defeat every enemy, and should we double our wealth and conquer the stars and still be unequal to this issue, then we will have failed as a people and as a nation.

For with a country as with a person, "What is a man profited, if he shall gain the whole world, and lose his own soul?"

There is no Negro problem. There is no Southern problem. There is no Northern problem. There is only an American problem. And we are met here tonight as Americans, not as Democrats or Republicans, we are met here as Americans to solve that problem.

This was the first nation in the history of the world to be founded with a purpose. The great phrases of that purpose still sound in every American heart, North and South: "All men are created equal"—"government by consent of the governed"—"give me liberty or give me death." Those are not just clever words. Those are not just empty theories. In their name Americans have fought and died for two centuries, and tonight around the world they stand there as guardians of our liberty, risking their lives.

Those words are a promise to every citizen that he shall share in the dignity of man. This dignity cannot be found in a man's possessions. It cannot be found in his power or in his position. It really rests on his right to be treated as a man equal in opportunity to all others. It says that he shall share in freedom, he shall choose his leaders, educate his children, provide for his family according to his ability and his merits as a human being.

To apply any other test—to deny a man his hopes because of his color or race, or his religion, or the place of his birth —is not only to do injustice, it is to deny America and to dishonor the dead who gave their lives for American freedom.

Our fathers believed that if this noble view of the rights of man was to flourish, it must be rooted in democracy. The most basic right of all was the right to choose your own leaders. The history of this country in large measure is the history of expansion of that right to all of our people.

Many of the issues of civil rights are very complex and most difficult. But about this there can and should be no argument. Every American citizen must have an equal right to vote. There is no reason which can excuse the denial of that right. There is no duty which weighs more heavily on us than the duty we have to ensure that right.

Yet the harsh fact is that in many places in this country men and women are kept from voting simply because they are Negroes.

Every device of which human ingenuity is capable has been used to deny this right. The Negro citizen may go to register only to be told that the day is wrong, or the hour is late, or the official in charge is absent. And if he persists and if he manages to present himself to the registrar, he may be disqualified because he did not spell out his middle name or because he abbreviated a word on the application. And if he manages to fill out an application he is given a test. The registrar is the sole judge of whether he passes this test. He may be asked to recite the entire constitution, or explain the most complex provisions of state laws. And even a college degree cannot be used to prove that he can read and write.

For the fact is that the only way to pass these barriers is to show a white skin.

Experience has clearly shown that the existnig process of law cannot overcome systematic and ingenious discrimination. No law that we now have on the books—and I have helped to put three of them there—can ensure the right to vote when local officials are determined to deny it.

In such a case our duty must be clear to all of us. The Constitution says that no person shall be kept from voting because of his race or his color. We have all sworn an oath before God to support and to defend that Constitution. We must now act in obedience to that oath.

Wednesday I will send to Congress a law designed to eliminate illegal barriers to the right to vote.

The broad principle of that bill will be in the hands of the Democratic and Republican leaders tomorrow. After they have reviewed it, it will come here formally as a bill. I am grateful for this opportunity to come here tonight at the invitation of the leadership to reason with my friends, to give them my views and to visit with my former colleagues.

I have had prepared a more comprehensive analysis of the legislation which I have intended to transmit to the clerks tomorrow, but which I will submit to the clerks tonight; but I want to really discuss with you now briefly the main proposals of this legislation.

This bill will strike down restrictions to voting in all elections—Federal, State, and local—which have been used to deny Negroes the right to vote.

This bill will establish a simple, uniform standard which cannot be used however ingenious the effort to flout our Constitution.

It will provide for citizens to be registered by officials of the United States government, if the state officials refuse to register them.

It will eliminate tedious, unnecessary lawsuits which delay the right to vote.

Finally, this legislation will ensure that properly registered individuals are not prohibited from voting.

I will welcome the suggestions from all of the members of Congress. I have no doubt that I will get some on ways and means to strengthen this law and to make it effective. But experience has plainly shown that this is the only path to carry out the command of the Constitution.

To those who seek to avoid action by their national government in their own communities, who want to and who seek to maintain purely local control over elections, the answer is simple.

Open your polling places to all your people.

Allow men and women to register and vote whatever the color of their skin.

Extend the rights of citizenship to every citizen of this land.

There is no constitutional issue here. The command of the Constitution is plain.

There is no moral issue. It is wrong to deny any of your fellow Americans the right to vote in this country.

There is no issue of states rights or national rights. There is only the struggle for human rights.

I have not the slightest doubt what will be your answer.

But the last time a President sent a civil rights bill to the Congress it contained a provision to protect voting rights in Federal elections. That civil rights bill was passed after eight long months of debate. And when that bill came to my desk from the Congress for my signature, the heart of the voting provision had been eliminated.

This time, on this issue, there must be no delay, or no hesitation or no compromise with our purpose.

We cannot, we must not refuse to protect the right of every American to vote in every election that he may desire to participate in. And we ought not, we must not wait another eight months before we get a bill. We have already waited a hundred years and more and the time for waiting is gone.

So I ask you to join me in working long hours, nights, and weekends if necessary, to pass this bill. And I don't make that request lightly. Far from the window where I sit with the problems of our country, I recognize that from outside this chamber is the outraged conscience of a nation, the grave concern of many nations and the harsh judgment of history on our acts.

But even if we pass this bill, the battle will not be over. What happened in Selma is part of a far larger movement which reaches into every section and state of America. It is the effort of American Negroes to secure for themselves the full blessings of American life.

Their cause must be our cause too. Because it is not just Negroes, but really it is all of us, who must overcome the crippling legacy of bigotry and injustice. And we shall overcome.

As a man whose roots go deeply into Southern soil I know how agonizing racial feelings are. I know how difficult it is to reshape the attitudes and the structure of our society.

But a century has passed, more than a hundred years, since the Negro was freed. And he is not fully free tonight.

It was more than a hundred years ago that Abraham Lincoln, the great President of the Northern party, signed the

Emancipation Proclamation, but emancipation is a proclamation and not a fact.

A century has passed, more than a hundred years since equality was promised. And yet the Negro is not equal.

A century has passed since the day of promise. And the promise is unkept.

The time of justice has now come. I tell you that I believe sincerely that no force can hold it back. It is right in the eyes of man and God that it should come. And when it does, I think that day will brighten the lives of every American.

For Negroes are not the only victims. How many white children have gone uneducated, how many white families have lived in stark poverty, how many white lives have been scarred by fear because we wasted our energy and our substance to maintain the barrier of hatred and terror.

So I say to all of you here and to all in the nation tonight, that those who appeal to you to hold on to the past do so at the cost of denying you your future.

This great, rich, restless country can offer opportunity and education and hope to all—all black and white, all North and South, sharecropper, and city dweller. These are the enemies —poverty, ignorance, disease. They are enemies, not our fellow man, not our neighbor, and these enemies too, poverty, disease and ignorance, we shall overcome.

Now let none of us in any section look with prideful righteousness on the troubles in another section or the problems of our neighbors. There is really no part of America where the promise of equality has been fully kept. In Buffalo as well as in Birmingham, in Philadelphia as well as in Selma, Americans are struggling for the fruits of freedom.

This is one nation. What happens in Selma or in Cincinnati is a matter of legitimate concern to every American. But let each of us look within our own hearts and our own communities, and let each of us put our shoulder to the wheel to root out injustice wherever it exists.

As we meet here in this peaceful historic chamber tonight, men from the South, some of whom were at Iwo Jima, men from the North who have carried Old Glory to far corners of the world and brought it back without a stain on it, men from the East and West are all fighting together without regard to religion, or color, or region, in Vietnam, men from every region fought for us across the world twenty years ago. And now in these common dangers and these common sacrifices the South made its contribution of honor and gallantry no less than any other region of the great Republic. In some instances, a great many of them more. And I have not the slightest doubt that good men from everywhere in this country, from the Great Lakes to the Gulf of Mexico, from the Golden Gate to the harbors along the Atlantic, will rally now together in this cause to vindicate the freedom of all Americans. For all of us owe this duty; and I believe all of us will respond to it.

Your President makes that request of every American.

The real hero of this struggle is the American Negro. His actions and protests, his courage to risk safety and even to risk his life, have awakened the conscience of this nation. His demonstrations have been designed to call attention to injustice, designed to provoke change, designed to stir reform. He has called upon us to make good the promise of America. And who among us can say that we would have made the same progress were it not for his persistent bravery, and his faith in American democracy.

For at the real heart of battle for equality is a deep seated belief in the democratic process. Equality depends not on the force of arms or tear gas but depends upon the force of moral right—not on recourse to violence but on respect for law and order.

There have been many pressures upon your President and there will be others as the days come and go, but I pledge you tonight that we intend to fight this battle where it should be fought, in the courts, and in the Congress, and in the hearts of men.

We must preserve the right of free speech and the right of free assembly. But the right of free speech does not carry with it as has been said, the right to holler fire in a crowded theater. We must preserve the right to free assembly but free assembly does not carry with it the right to block public thoroughfares to traffic.

We do have a right to protest, and a right to march under conditions that do not infringe the Constitutional rights of our neighbors. I intend to protect all those rights as long as I am permitted to serve in this Office.

We will guard against violence, knowing it strikes from our hands the very weapons with which we seek progress—obedience to law, and belief in American values.

In Selma as elsewhere we seek and pray for peace. We seek order. We seek unity. But we will not accept the peace of stifled rights, or the order imposed by fear, or the unity that stifles protest. For peace cannot be purchased at the cost of liberty.

In Selma tonight—and we had a good day there—as in every city, we are working for just and peaceful settlement.

We must all remember that after this speech I am making to-night, after the police and the FBI and the marshals have all gone, and after you have promptly passed this bill, the people of Selma and the other cities of the nation must still live and work together. And when the attention of the nation has gone elsewhere they must try to heal the wounds and to build a new community. This cannot be easily done on a battle-ground of violence as the history of the South itself shows. It is in recognition of this that men of both races have shown such an outstandingly impressive responsibility in recent days, last Tuesday, again today.

The bill that I am presenting to you will be known as a civil rights bill. But, in a larger sense, most of the program I am recommending is a civil right. Its object is to open the city of hope to all people of all races, because all Americans just must have the right to vote. And we are going to give them that right.

All Americans must have the privileges of citizenship regardless of race. And they are going to have those privileges of citizenship regardless of race.

But I would like to caution you and remind you that to exercise these privileges takes much more than just legal right. It requires a trained mind and a healthy body. It requires a decent home, and the chance to find a job, and the opportunity to escape from the clutches of poverty.

Of course people cannot contribute to the nation if they are never taught to read or write, if their bodies are stunted from hunger, if their sickness goes untended, if their life is spent in hopeless poverty just drawing a welfare check.

So we want to open the gates to opportunity. But we are also going to give all our people, black and white, the help that they need to walk through those gates.

My first job after college was as a teacher in Cotulla, Texas, in a small Mexican-American school. Few of them could speak English and I couldn't speak much Spanish. My students were poor and they often came to class without breakfast, hungry, and they knew even in their youth that pain of prejudice. They never seemed to know why people disliked them. But they knew it was so. Because I saw it in their eyes. I often walked home late in the afternoon after the classes were finished, wishing there was more that I could do. But all I knew was to teach them the little that I knew, hoping that it might help them against the hardships that lay ahead.

Somehow you never forget what poverty and hatred can

do when you see its scars on the hopeful face of a young child.

I never thought then in 1928 that I would be standing here in 1965. It never even occurred to me in my fondest dreams that I might have the chance to help the sons and daughters of those students and to help people like them all over this country. But now I do have that chance and I let you in on a secret, I mean to use it. And I hope that you will use it with me.

This is the richest and most powerful country which ever occupied this globe. The might of past empires is little compared to ours.

But I do not want to be the President who built empires, or sought grandeur, or extended dominion. I want to be the President who educated young children to the wonders of their world. I want to be the President who helped to feed the hungry and to prepare them to be taxpayers instead of taxeaters. I want to be the President who helped the poor to find their own way and who protected the right of every citizen to vote in every election. I want to be the President who helped to end hatred among his fellow men and who prompted love among the people of all races and all regions and all parties. I want to be the President who helped to end war among the brothers of this earth.

And so at the request of your beloved Speaker and Senator from Montana, the Majority Leader, the Senator from Illinois, the Minority Leader, Mr. McCulloch and other leaders of both parties, I came here tonight not as President Roosevelt came down one time in person to veto a bonus bill, not as President Truman came down one time to urge the passage of a railroad bill, but I came down here to ask you to share this task with me and to share it with the people that we both work for. I want this to be the Congress, Republicans and Democrats alike, which did all those things for all these people.

Beyond this great chamber, out yonder, the fifty states are the people we serve. Who can tell what deep and unspoken hopes are in their hearts tonight as they sit there and listen. We all can guess, from our own lives, how difficult they often find their own pursuit of happiness. How many problems each little family has. They look most of all to themselves for their futures. But I think that they also look to each of us.

Above the pyramid on the great seal of the United States it says—in Latin—"God has favored our undertaking."

God will not favor everything that we do. It is rather our

duty to divine His will. But I cannot help believing that He truly understands and that He really favors the undertaking that we begin here tonight.

President Johnson's call for action to "overcome the crippling legacy of bigotry and injustice" mobilized the means for enacting the most drastic voting-rights legislation since Reconstruction. Events outside Washington emphasized the urgency of his appeal. A week after he spoke, the Selma march drew together representatives of every sector of American opinion; and a few days later, the murder of one of the marchers showed the danger of the Alabama situation. The prominence of the clergy in the Selma demonstration exerted a particularly powerful impact on opinion. Vigorous expressions of support from throughout the country sustained the pressure for passage of the law in the months of debate that followed.

Senators Mansfield and Dirksen, the majority and minority leaders of the Senate, together with sixty-six bipartisan cosponsors, introduced the bill which embodied the President's views and on which the Justice Department had worked for some time. An impressive demonstration of unity, however, was not in itself enough to carry the day. The defenders of the southern status quo had often before shown the capacity for blocking action by parliamentary maneuver and the filibuster when the odds were against them. But this time it was clear at the outset that evasive tactics would not be effective. The Senate imposed a fifteen-day limit on the Judiciary Committee's hearings and proceeded to act with unaccustomed speed. Indeed, while some amendments were offered in the committee and from the floor, the most controversial were those in which supporters of the bill attempted to extend its provisions by banning the poll tax.

The debate opened on April 22 and continued for about a month. Pressure from the President and from the Senate leaders averted the threat of a filibuster. On May 25, the Senate imposed closure of further debate by a vote of 70 to 30. The fate of the measure was then clear. The Senate passed the Act by a vote of 77 to 19; and on July 9, the House passed its own version by a vote of 333 to 85. A conference committee ironed out the differences between the two houses and the President's signature made the voting-rights bill law on August 6, 1965.

The long-term consequences were not immediately appar-

ent. Some states—notably Alabama, Arkansas, and Mississippi—relaxed their restrictions on voting rights even before passage of the law. The specter of federal intervention was enough to persuade them to ease access to the registration rolls. A variety of civil-rights groups labored through the summer and fall to help Negroes, long deprived of the ballot, prepare to exercise the rights of citizenship. The number of Negro voters registered rose steadily.

The number of such candidates for office also increased. By the spring of 1966, for instance, Negroes were running in the Democratic primaries of every Alabama county, evidence of their potential political strength. Furthermore, white aspirants even in the Deep South were taking a much more moderate position on race issues than formerly.

The new law was far from a cure-all, however. Much depended upon the quality of leadership and the total political situation in the localities in which the law was applied. It was not enough to register the Negroes; it was also necessary to get them to vote and to help them understand the issues on which they cast their ballots. In communities like Atlanta, Georgia, where a basis for collaboration and effective action existed, Negroes were able to make their weight felt at once. Elsewhere, the election of 1965 still found the Negro vote a negligible factor. The voting-rights law put the instruments of democratic political action within reach of the Negro; how they would be used remained to be seen.

Acknowledgments

The preparation of this volume within five years would have been impossible without the friendly collaboration not only of the eighty-three chapter-editors who have been generous, scrupulous, and patient in their efforts to distil much learning into a few words, but of many others too numerous to list by name.

The general editor has been lucky to have as his right hand Mrs. Ann B. Congdon of Cleveland Heights, Ohio, who has handled much of the correspondence with authors, and whose editorial skill, discriminating judgment, eye for detail, and passion for precision have added immensely to the life and style of this volume. Her help has been invaluable.

In preparing the manuscript for the press and in settling countless questions of fact, the general editor has greatly benefited from the resourcefulness and historical imagination of Mr. Stanley K. Schultz, a postgraduate student in the Department of History at the University of Chicago.

Thanks are due to Miss Isabel Garvey of Yarmouth Port, Massachusetts, for the copious and detailed subject index. The phrase index, which has required a special feeling for the classic or the familiar (or should-be familiar) phrase and an understanding of the context of the documents and their promise of new meanings, is the work of Mrs. Lila Weinberg of Chicago.

The general editor wishes to thank his wife, Ruth F.

Boorstin, who, as usual, had been unstinting in her editorial and other assistance.

The following chapter-editors wish to give special thanks to these individuals and institutions: Lawrence W. Towner, to the Massachusetts Historical Society; Edmund S. Morgan, to Philip A. Hennessey, Clerk of the Courts, Salem, Massachusetts; Ralph L. Ketcham, to the Cornell University Library; L. H. Butterfield, to Harold R. Manakee, Director, the Maryland Historical Society; Robert E. Spiller, to the Harvard College Library; Barbara M. Solomon, to Miss Alma Lutz, Boston, Massachusetts, and the Women's Archives, Radcliffe College; William G. McLoughlin, to Roger E. Stoddard, Assistant Curator, the Harris Collection, Brown University Library; Matthew Josephson, to the United States Park Service, Edison Laboratory, West Orange, New Jersey; Lon L. Fuller, to Mark De Wolfe Howe; Thomas Pyles, to the Enoch Pratt Free Library, Baltimore, Maryland; William E. Leuchtenburg, to the Franklin D. Roosevelt Library, Hyde Park, New York. The general editor wishes to give to Dr. L. H. Butterfield special acknowledgment for his generosity in sharing with the general editor his unpublished researches in connection with his editing of the letter from John Adams to Hezekiah Niles.

The University of Chicago Press wishes to thank the following for permission to reprint their versions of the material indicated: The Princeton University Press: The Declaration of Independence; The Rutgers University Press: Abraham Lincoln's Second Annual Message to Congress, and his Second Inaugural Address; The University of North Carolina Press: The Ballad of John Henry; Trustees Under the Will of Mary Baker Eddy: Excerpts from *Science and Health;* The Catholic University of America Press: "The Question of the Knights of Labor"; Time, Inc.: Quotation from *Life* Magazine, November 11, 1957, reprinted in the Introduction to "Cheapest Supply House on Earth"; The Macmillan Company: Excerpt from Vachel Lindsay's poem "Bryan, Bryan, Bryan, Bryan"; Charles Scribner's Sons: Theodore Roosevelt's Speech on "The New Nationalism"; The Pilgrim Press: Excerpts from *For God and the People: Prayers of the Social Awakening;* Harper & Row, Publishers: The paragraph from Frederick W. Taylor's *The Principles of Scientific Management* beginning "At the works of the Bethlehem Steel Company"; the Estate of Calvin Coolidge and Houghton Mifflin Company: "Have Faith in Massachusetts"; Alfred A. Knopf, Inc.: The Preface to *The American Language;* The Estate of Herbert Hoover: The speech entitled here "On American In-

dividualism"; The Estate of Sinclair Lewis: The speech enti-
tled here "The American Fear of Literature"; Random
House, Inc.: Franklin D. Roosevelt's First Inaugural Address;
The Macmillan Company: Franklin D. Roosevelt's "Quaran-
tine" Address; The Estate of Albert Einstein: Einstein's Let-
ter to Franklin D. Roosevelt; The Wendell L. Willkie Fund:
Excerpts from *One World;* Elsevier Publishing Company,
Amsterdam: William Faulkner's speech on acceptance of the
Nobel Prize.

Index of Authors, Titles, and Editors

The authors of documents are in Roman type (with birth and death dates in parentheses); editors' names are in small capital letters; and titles are italicized.

General Index

American Academy of Arts and Letters, and Nobel Prize address of Sinclair Lewis, 847–61

American character: arraignments of, 682; Bill of Rights and, 179; contempt for the unsuccessful, 606–12; economic abundance and, 64–65; frontier in formation of, 566–67, 568, 569; idealism of, expressed by Lincoln, 443–44, 445; practical genius in, 516; surrender terms at Appomattox as symbol of, 450; Washington's First Inaugural Address as expression of, 195

American Dream, Edison's career as enactment of, 516

American Federation of Labor, 510

American language, H. L. Mencken on, 819–26

American Legal Realism, 627, 628

American Mercury, 819

American mission (*see also* Destiny, American), 257; "Battle Hymn of the Republic" as expression of, 402, 403; imperialist view of, 646–51, 652; Jackson on, 288; Johnson on, 946; Lincoln's expressions of, 195, 413, 425–26, 436–37, 439–40; Lodge on, 815; Puritan concept of, 27, 39–41, 43, 402; as refuge, 478, 479–82, 883–84; Roosevelt, Theodore, on, 735

American Revolution, 231; frontier conditions as factors in, 562; meaning of, John Adams on, 246–57

American Speech, 825

Americanism, 605; sectional, 554

Americanization, 480; frontier in, 545–46, 557; League of Nations vs., 813

Ames, Fisher, 191

Anarchists: Carnegie on, 522; in labor movement, 503, 505; Plunkitt of Tammany Hall on, 703

Anderson, Sherwood, 852, 853, 855, 861

Andrew, John, 399

Angell, James Burrill, 438

Anthony, Susan B., 386, 396

Antifederalists, 99, 169, 452

Antitrust Act of 1890, used against labor unions, 334

Appomattox Court House, Va., surrender at, 446–50, 492, 493

Architecture, 850, 854; Louis H. Sullivan and the tall office building, 580–92

Aristocracy: distinguished from people's government, 141–42, 146; President seen as instrument of elite, 127–28; primogeniture and entail, 92, 523–24; titles of nobility banned by Constitution, 114

Aristotle, 84

Armament race, 940, 942

Armies: American, frontier in development of, 552, 553; British in America, 87–88; Constitution on, 113; mercenary, vs. labor, 535, 539; quartering of soldiers, 88, 174

Arms, right to bear, 172, 174

Arms control, 940, 942

Armstrong, John, 99

Arnold, Isaac N., on Gettysburg Address, 439

Arnold, Matthew, 519

Articles of Confederation, 101, 102, 160, 168; Congress under, 106–07, 157–58; federal-state relations under, 157–58; judicial power under, 131, 132, 157–58; on states, 140

Arts, 850, 854, 856–57; freedom in, 178; government promotion of, suggested by Hamil-

Index of Words and Phrases